Arnol'd Lakhovsky. A Russian Provincial Town in Winter. *Oil on canvas. Signed in latin letters. 61 x 50 cm.*
Reproduced by kind permission of Sotheby's London, sale 16.6.1992, lot 66.

A DICTIONARY OF
RUSSIAN AND SOVIET ARTISTS

1420-1970

John Milner

Antique Collectors' Club

© 1993 John Milner
World copyright reserved
First published 1993

ISBN 1 85149 182 1

British Library Cataloguing in Publication Data:
A catalogue record for this book is available from the British Library

Printed on Consort Royal Satin from Donside Mills, Aberdeen

Licence is given to reproduce copyright works by the following artists:

Title page illustration: **Kuz'ma Petrov-Vodkin.** The Virgin of Tenderness Moving Evil Hearts, *1914-15. Oil on canvas
mounted on board. Signed with initials lower right. 100.2 x 100 cm.
State Russian Museum, St. Petersburg.*

Printed in England by the Antique Collectors' Club Ltd, Woodbridge, Suffolk

For Snegurochka, a lover of winter

Contents

Acknowledgements

A book of this kind depends upon many sources that cannot all be acknowledged. Some debts are personal and some are academic. On the personal side my first debt is to my wife, the medievalist art historian Lesley Milner F.S.A. She first came with me to Russia and she has with insistent regularity provoked my thoughts with contrary views. To her I am most grateful of all. Secondly I want to record the vitality, generosity and sheer enthusiastic practical help of Nikita and Nina Lobanov-Rostovsky whose collection of Russian theatre design is the result of irrepressible excitement at the art that it contains. Their collection is of world renown and is recorded in many references in this book. I feel honoured by their involvement which I have greatly enjoyed. A particular gratitude is also due to Alan Bird for the extraordinary and impressive generosity of his assistance in the realisation of this book.

In addition I have found collectors and galleries immediately helpful, particularly Annely Juda at Annely Juda Fine Art and Roy Miles at the Roy Miles Gallery in London both of whom have generously provided photographs.

Beyond this there are innumerable academic debts. John Bowlt, for example, has always been the model of an open-handed scholar who by his example and his outstanding contribution to the subject of the history of Russian art has had a profound influence upon all who study this field. He is both accurate and prolific. He too is an irrepressible enthusiast whose scholarship has made this vast subject accessible to many including myself.

Finally I should mention Dr. Anthony Parton of the University of Newcastle-upon-Tyne whose pursuit of Larionov and Russian Futurism has clarified much of my own understanding of the period, as well as the creative and scholarly encouragement of Dr. Avril Pyman and her husband the painter Kirill Sokolov in Durham.

I have endeavoured to recognise debts to the publications of other scholars in the individual bibliographic entries listed under artists' names. Similarly I have made every effort to acknowledge the source of photographs although this has not been possible in every case.

The University of Newcastle-upon-Tyne and its Department of Fine Art have also provided financial support for the completion of this work.

Preface

Many features of Russian art are unique. Its centuries old traditions of ikon painting maintained techniques and themes long overshadowed by the Gothic and Renaissance revolutions of Western art. In addition there was folk art of extraordinary vigour and decorative flair and the tradition of the *lubok* or popular print. It is not surprising that these traditions have remained alive and respected by Russian artists: they have fed directly into the development of the art of the late 19th and 20th centuries in Russia. Yet between the ikon and the art of today there lies a vast gulf. Russia under the early Tsars is now all but unimaginable. Across its vast tracts of land lived many cultures which only slowly accommodated one to another. Russia's Asian expanse was invaded by Mongols, Tartars and others. Each invasion added its contribution to the rich mixture of Russian culture, from the Islamic cultures of the South to the Baltic cultures of the North. Artists only slowly found their place in this milieu. At first they depended wholly upon the demands and protection of the Church. Gradually a court art evolved and only then was artistic contact with Western traditions and conventions an urgent necessity.

Peter the Great (1682-1725) changed Russian art permanently. He established Western art as a model for Russian art. His founding of the city of St. Petersburg sums up his achievement. With one superhuman effort of building and learning he wrenched the arts of Russia from their almost changeless traditions into a mirror of the West. This was extraordinary not least because the forces which had evolved West European art were missing from Russian history. This new art had scarcely any Russian roots at all. Yet its transplantation to Russia succeeded. By bringing Western artists to teach Russians he enabled Russian artists to compete in ambition, range and purpose with their Western counterparts. They travelled to Holland, France and above all to Italy. As St. Petersburg rose on the northern swamps at Russia's Western edge there began a dialogue between East and West that transformed the arts of Russia. As communications grew throughout succeeding centuries Russian artists reflected Western developments. In the 19th century there were Russian neo-classicists, Russian Romantics, Russian Realists, Russian Impressionists and Russian Post-Impressionists. As artists worked for the new art periodicals, designed posters and above all worked for the theatre just as they did in France or Germany, it is tempting to assume that the societies which produced comparable art were closely similar, but this was far from the case. The arts of exhibitions, periodicals and the theatre were urban arts dependent upon St. Petersburg, Moscow and other major cities. Sometimes they were more aware of developments in Rome, Munich or Paris than the endless expanses of provincial rural Russia. Only in the 19th century, when the Wanderers made social criticism a feature of their paintings, did the peasantry escape from a decorative, sentimental or idealised role in art to become a force and a problem that could no longer be ignored. This followed the abolition of serfdom. It is astonishing to learn of artists called back to their *owners'* estates from studies at the Academy. Facts like these provide a glimpse of a different Russia where a serf could first of all attend the Academy, and secondly where a man was still the property of another. In this context landscape painting was transformed from decorative views of the estate to an image of Russia itself. In a sense landscapes took on a national and public significance that far exceeded the requirements of the individual patron.

The vigour and splendour of Russian art has then its own resources, characteristics and dynamic. With the growth of museums, beginning with the great collections of the Hermitage in St. Petersburg, with the growth of travel and publishing, the awareness of Western European art was paralleled by a growing awareness of Russian traditions and Russian roots. In the late 19th century there were moves to preserve and revive folk art traditions, ikons were recognised as great art, particularly by the Tretyakov brothers, and artists who had once looked with an insatiable appetite to the art of Munich and Paris began to turn their attention to their own roots, reversing the gaze of Peter the Great to seek inspiration from the peasantry, from folk stories and folk decorations, looking to Caucasia, to the Black Sea and to Central Asia, to Islamic Samarkand. The synthesis of East and West which resulted combined Cubist art with folklore and introduced the culture of Matisse and Picasso to that of the Siberian shaman. Almost all Russian artists faced the dilemma of identity. It was the heritage of Peter the Great and the result of Russia's geographical position, part European part Asian, on the edge of Europe but extending away far beyond the boundaries of Europe to the distant Pacific Ocean.

Revolution in 1917 in some ways confirmed the isolation of Russia from Western Europe. The demands of art became once more overtly politicised by the communist regime that called for an art of the streets which focused its attention deliberately upon the worker and the peasant for its own ideological reasons. Noble patronage vanished and with it the language of taste and great private collectors. Artists responded in a multitude of ways to the opportunities and vicissitudes of the Revolution, but they could not ever ignore it. It affected every aspect of artistic life and only emigration provided an escape from its requirements, a course taken by many Russian artists who contributed greatly to the arts in the West. The arts flourished however in Russia. There a great number of women artists were able to develop fully their considerable talents. The graphic arts in literature, periodicals and posters were politically useful as were theatre, film and monumental sculpture, all of which were emphatically public and therefore communal art forms responsive to ideological requirements. But even painters moved into public works decorating streets and trains, designing ceramics and clothing. The Revolution demanded the creation of a whole new culture and it provided unprecedented problems and opportunities to which many artists responded with vigour and inventiveness.

When all artistic groups were disbanded in 1932 artists were made dependent upon a single artists' union. The great proliferation of experimental groups ceased overnight. Old academic techniques were revived in painting as they were intelligible to the majority of the population. They told their stories clearly and provided an efficient vehicle for the dissemination of political views and ideals. The role of the artist was severely circumscribed by the demands of the State. There were remarkable achievements in this period but artists' work, however impressive it might be, was inevitably informed by political criteria. Only after the death of Stalin did independent initiatives again begin to flourish. Unofficial art, often once more reflecting both Russian roots and Western inspiration, began to be exhibited independently in the 1960s. Its problematic aspects were at first resolved by the bulldozing of an open air exhibition, but slowly it grew as communications with the West developed. Since the advent of Gorbachev Russian artists have again become independent, a process only completed by the collapse of communism and the dissolution of the Soviet Union.

Russian art throughout all of this remained extraordinarily vigorous and assertive. Its vitality is unparalleled. This Dictionary provides an outline of an extraordinary story in which history plays an inescapable role in almost every drawing, painting or sculpture. This is part of the fascination of Russian art. Its richness, complexity and sheer beauty are part of the reward.

Introduction

Russian art reflects the vast diversity of its landscape, cultures and history. Stretching from Europe to the Pacific and from Siberia to Central Asia, even until relatively recent times including Alaska, Russian culture has embraced an enormously wide span of influences. In religious terms alone it has celebrated ancient Slav deities, Orthodox Christianity, the Muslim beliefs of Kazakhs and Uzbeks, Buddhism, Shamanism and atheism, as well as a myriad diversity of other beliefs and folklore. Indeed Folk Art itself has exerted the powerful influence of its abiding presence and anonymous richness well into the 20th century. Invasions from those of the Vikings and Mongols to the Napoleonic and World Wars have all deflected the development of Russian art and have left a mark. Russia, a country of ice and of desert, part Asia and part Europe, has for centuries balanced these strong influences and made of them a distinct and rich culture of its own.

A recurrent concern in recent centuries has been Russia's relationship with the West and this has profoundly affected its art. In earlier times its relationship with Byzantium in the South was of equal importance. The identity of Russia has itself changed and evolved, alternating periods of isolation with periods of intensive communication and of learning from foreign sources. Within this shifting framework the artist has responded to available opportunities and it is perhaps those responses to opportunities which most clearly reveal the range, development and extraordinary achievements of Russian art.

Only in the 20th century did the systematic study of Russian art become a major intellectual discipline. The ikon, the *lubok* or popular print, and folk art were

suddenly recognised as features of a unique and rich culture. It is ironic that this surge of interest coincided with a period of intense intellectual exchange with West European countries, particularly France and Germany, as if the distinct qualities of Russian traditions needed to be asserted in the face of the intense and powerful influx of new ideas from the West. The study of Russian art has had another extraordinary feature in this century, for it has effectively had two histories. The narrative described by soviet historians has differed substantially from that recorded by Western scholars, collectors and exhibitions. Soviet historians emphasised different criteria and works. They devised methods of analysis utterly different from those arising from conditions prevailing in France, Germany, Britain or America. The Russian avant-garde has been much discussed, interpreted and exhibited in the West. In Russia it was certainly in severe difficulties by 1932 and after that time was consigned to a degree of oblivion which, until recently, only works of scholarship published outside of Russia have been able to retrieve or alleviate. The practice of Socialist Realism affected writers on art just as surely as it affected painters, sculptors or printmakers. Russia, which established some of the first museums of contemporary art, was among the first to close them down or to restrict what could be shown to their publics. Only since the demise of communist government in

Russia has the scholarship of Western historians really been able to join with the scholarship of Russian historians without ideological difficulties intervening. Increasing contact has revealed the extent to which works of the Russian avant-garde were preserved with an impartial professionalism in the enormous collections and archives of Russia. It is inevitable that the history of Russian art will continue to change in the face of this new access to a great wealth of information.

To the Western eye the most startling feature to emerge from a survey of Russian art is the simple fact that in Russia there was neither a medieval Gothic period nor any equivalent to the Renaissance which spread from Italy to such spectacular effect in all of the arts in Western Europe. Russia in this was utterly different. When Russian artists embraced the Baroque, for example, this had no precedent for them. References to the art of ancient Greece or Rome were not historical revivals in any sense there. They were almost entirely alien and new.

As this makes clear Russian art had distinct origins and its own strong traditions. Folk art and the ikon both existed in the West but in Russia they played a vital role through many centuries and are frequently referred to in art even now. Both are substantially anonymous traditions with strict social purposes and meanings. They have provided a firm backbone for Russian art which is inexplicable without them.

Ikon painting had an extraordinary history in Russia and continued to flourish in the face of many other influences well into the 18th century and beyond. But by the early 20th century the tail end of a great tradition which had endured for a thousand years, had overlapped its conscious revival. Even soviet artists from time to time adopted and adapted its images and iconography to their own ends. In terms of opportunities for painters, the ikon painting tradition, for all its anonymity, supplied a vast demand penetrating not only into churches but into the homes of peasants as well as aristocracy. Repetitive, mysterious and even supernatural in the beliefs which it could inspire, the Russian ikon left an indelible mark. Ikon painting workshops provided, for example, the historical origin of the Russian art school. Art and religion, and therefore art and the church, were for centuries interwoven inextricably and even exclusively in a way that scarcely survived the Renaissance in Europe. For much of its development Russian art was sacred and anonymous. Originality was not a virtue.

This fact illustrates the degree to which opportunities controlled the work a painter produced. If opportunity provided a means to work, gain recognition and further commissions, it equally made demands. It restricted and refined the aims of art, fixing individual artists within a framework of ideas and concerns that were not under their control and were not of their making.

Art and the Origins of Russia

Long before the country of Russia existed the warm lands of the Black Sea attracted settlers. Herodotus noted the existence of the Scythians there in the 7th to 3rd centuries B.C. Greeks too were there from the 6th century and in 329-327 B.C. Alexander the Great conquered Central Asia.

In the early Christian era the Byzantine Empire extended into the Caucasus. Greater Armenia was divided between Byzantium and Persia in 387 A.D. In addition the Huns had invaded the Black Sea steppes in 375 and Arab forces dominated Central Asia by the mid-8th century. Elements were already in place which still cause friction and warfare in the area today. It was already an area of intense cultural clashes and conflicts of belief and tradition.

Russia grew from an area of conflicting forces in a shifting balance. The country takes its name from ancient *Rus'* formed in Kiev, now the capital of the Ukraine, in the later 9th century. The connections between Kiev Rus' and Byzantium established the single most substantial foundation for Russian culture. Prince Oleg, ruler in Kiev in 882-912, made a treaty with Byzantium in 911. Under Vladimir, who was enthroned in 980, Christianity was adopted in Rus'. As monasteries, church building and education followed in Rus', it was Byzantine Constantinople that provided the model. In terms of painting this meant the ikon and mosaics in particular. For a thousand years that influence could still be detected within Russian art. Even in the early 20th century it was not rare for painters to work in ikon painting studios. Tenth century St. Sophia Cathedral in Kiev formed the focus of this initial response to Byzantium. Its mosaics overtly reflected those of Constantinople in their form, content, purpose and appearance.

If Kiev was of cardinal importance, it was also relatively close to Byzantium. Other cities further away from this source inevitably evolved their distinct characters dependent upon trade, leadership, and geography. Novgorod in the North was far from Byzantium and established trading connections with the Baltic, Germany and Scandinavia. Vladimir-Suzdal' had contacts to the East as well as South. Only gradually was political cohesion established and a degree of independence was inevitably reflected in the art of different centres. The first references to Moscow, for example, do not occur until 1147. One of the most important ikons in Russia, the *Virgin of Vladimir*, was painted in the early 12th century and was Greek. For centuries Byzantine art provided the model, iconography and format for a severely controlled and formulaic religious art. Opportunities for painters were accessible through training in workshops; they responded to the church's demand for ikons, murals and mosaics.

All of this was abruptly challenged in the 13th century when Mongol-Tartar hordes attacked. They conquered Central Asia in 1219-21, Transcaucasia in 1231-4, and in 1237 they invaded the territories of Rus' itself, finally overrunning Kiev in 1237. The direct line of influence from the South was cut. Independence from the cultural traditions of Western Europe deepened the isolation. The splendours of Gothic art and architecture scarcely penetrated at all into the territories of Rus'.

Art and the Rise of Moscow
Prince Aleksandr Yaroslavich routed Swedish forces on the River Neva in the North in 1240. He is still remembered as Aleksandr Nevsky after the river which runs through what is now St. Petersburg. Two years later he defeated the Livonian Knights and Danish Crusaders in the Battle on the Ice at Lake Chudskoe, an event depicted in the 20th century for patriotic purposes by the director Sergei Eisenstein in his film *Alexander Nevsky*. It was Moscow which grew as the city with links to the North and to the South over the next century and a half to become the centre and axis of Russia.

The Metropolitan seat, and therefore the centre of the church, moved to Moscow in 1326. Over fifty years later Dmitry Donskoy began to push back the Mongol-Tartar invaders at the Battle of Vozha River in 1378 and at Kulikovo in 1380, 140 years since the fall of Kiev and long enough for the invaders to leave their mark upon Russian culture. In Central Asia Tamerlane, who ruled his empire from Samarkand from 1370 to 1405, routed the Golden Horde in 1395. Almost a century more was to pass before the Mongol-Tartars were finally expelled from Rus' in 1480. This was 240 years after the fall of Kiev. It is not surprising that Russian art has periodically sought its roots in a past that was Asian as well as Byzantine and only later European.

It was during this period that the rise of Moscow became irresistible. Simultaneously a school of ikon painting arose which perhaps for the first time was distinctly Russian. Since the conversion of Vladimir in 980 painting had been anonymous. Named individuals now began to emerge whose paintings established a uniquely Russian art. For this reason historians have placed great emphasis upon the achievements and importance of Andrei Rublev who was working in Moscow with Theophanes the Greek (Feofan Grek) and Prokhor of Gorodets in 1405. His grave and harmonious ikon of the Old Testament *The Holy Trinity*, now in the Tretyakov Gallery in Moscow, has been dated 1410-20. More than any other single painting it

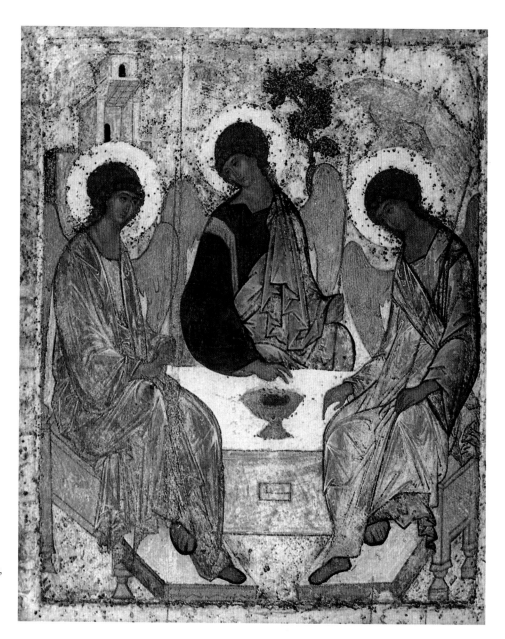

Andrei Rublev. The Holy Trinity, *c.1410-20. Panel. 142 x 114 cm. The single most celebrated ikon by an identified Russian artist. State Tretyakov Gallery, Moscow.*

has been taken as evidence of the emergence of a distinct Russian art. Its debt to the long Byzantine tradition is evident. The removal of the Greek ikon of the *Virgin of Vladimir* to Moscow in 1395 and the presence there of Theophanes the Greek are other signs of the vigour of this tradition continuing through Greece. This provides a stark contrast with the demise of Byzantine models in Italy. Giotto had died in 1337 — almost a century before Rublev's *The Holy Trinity* was painted — and Rublev's refined elegance should be contrasted with the achievements of Italian art in the 15th century to appreciate the gulf which separated Russian culture from that of the West. Masaccio and Rublev inhabited utterly different cultures. The Renaissance, like the Gothic art which preceded it, was passing Russia by. On the other hand Moscow grew rapidly in strength and influence. The Moscow principality encompassed Suzdal'-Nizhny Novgorod in 1392, Yaroslav in 1463, Perm in 1472, Rostov in 1474, Novgorod in 1478, Tver' in 1485 and Vyatka in 1489. By that time there were many foreign craftsmen in Moscow. The emergence of known individual artists occurred during the rise of Moscow.

It was during the reign of Grand Prince Ivan IV Vasil'evich, known as Ivan the Terrible, that a significant disaster occurred which was to have a profound effect

Leon Bakst. Costume for a
Jewish Dancer with a
Tambourine, *1909-10. Gouache,
pencil, gold paint. 34 x 24 cm.
A design for the ballet 'Cleopatra' to
music by A.S.Arensky, with musical
excerpts from N.N.Cherepnin,
Glazunov, Glinka, Rimsky-Korsakov
and Taneev. Performed by
Diaghilev's company at the Théâtre
du Chatelet, Paris.
Collection Mr. and Mrs. Nikita
D. Lobanov-Rostovsky, London.*

on Russian painting. Moscow was largely built in wood and in 1547 much of the city
was destroyed by a great fire. This destruction affected art immediately by creating
an urgent demand for ikons to replace those lost. On the one hand this created an
urgent demand which greatly encouraged the practice of ikon painting; on the other
hand it caused Tsar Ivan the Terrible to transfer whole schools of ikon painters to
Moscow, including the important Novgorod School. This in turn brought ikon
painting much more firmly under the control of the Tsar and compromised the
power of the church as sole patron and producer of ikons. In addition contacts to the

East and West were growing. The first printed book appeared, for example, in 1564. The artist now had a relationship with the court of the Tsar as well as the church, although its nature was utterly distinct from that in Italy where, for example, Michelangelo had begun his *Last Judgement* in the Sistine Chapel in 1536, a vast contrast with the ikon painting traditions of Russia. Patronage was of a very different kind in Russia. Only with the emergence of merchant wealth did ikon painting respond to the changing taste of new patrons. Prokopi Chirin, for example, was active in Moscow in 1620-c.1642 developing a precious and decorative style in the manner of the Stroganov School so named in recognition of the patronage of the Stroganov family. Commercial incentives of this kind brought innovations visible in the work of Simon Ushakov and others who began finally to respond to Western example. This effectively ushered in the complex subject of Russia's relations with the West in matters of art. It became a clash and fusion of cultures with vastly different circumstances and traditions. It was also in effect a clash of centuries and a conflict of purpose. Specific contacts which reveal Russian attitudes to the West began effectively in the 17th century with the Romanov dynasty whose first Tsar was Mikhail Romanov who ruled from 1613 to 1645. It was during his reign that the Stroganov School arose. In the mid-17th century the painter Hans Detterson was employed in Russia and engaged to teach Russian artists. In 1671 Tsar Aleksis sat for his portrait and the window on the West began to open. Seven hundred years of Byzantine tradition had at last eased its grip before this could happen. Western influence and practice was to flood into Russia irresistibly and to permanent effect. The man who encouraged and controlled this great influx was Tsar Peter I.

Art under Peter the Great

Tsar Peter I transformed Russian art and architecture during his reign from 1682 to 1725. He travelled to Western Europe in 1697-8 and assumed Western dress. In 1700 he adopted the Julian calendar and in 1702 he invited Western artists to work in Russia. Most significant of all he founded the new city of St. Petersburg in 1703 on barren marshland at the western extremity of Russia. This city, since named Petrograd, then Leningrad and now once again St. Petersburg, was the single most astonishing, unforeseeable and blatant sign of his commitment to making Russia a great European country. It opened up opportunities for artists that were colossal in every sense. Architects were employed on projects of the grandest scale to construct an entire city that would challenge any in Europe. The Italian Tressini (Andrei Petrovich Trezin), the German Schlüter and the French Jean-Baptiste Le Blond envisaged projects scarcely imaginable in their native countries. Le Blond brought painters too, including Louis Caravacque, to organise teaching for Russian artists. Baroque architecture arrived in Russia fully formed. Only nine years after its foundation Peter was able to move the capital from Moscow to St. Petersburg with all that this implied concerning a radical break with the past and a shift to the West.

By 1716 he was sending Russian artists West. Nikitin went to Italy and Matveev to Holland. However this new situation, which produced an art and architecture indebted to the West and seeking to rival the splendours of Italy, Germany and France, was the product of unique aims which themselves had no Western parallel. It was a great synthesis of foreign styles for a royal court demanding great civic works in profusion in order to establish its confidence, status and radical direction. In this respect the new city of St. Petersburg was symbolic in concept and execution; it had no history and it had a foreign face. It was an assertion that Russia was part of the West, a message broadcast to Russians and Westerners alike. It did not therefore arise from Russian traditions. In art this meant that the church would no longer play its former dominant role. Indeed Peter I abolished the patriarch in 1721 and instituted a synod. The same year he was proclaimed Emperor Peter the Great.

What followed in art was in response to this single great patron and his court. Peter's immense vision could not instantly create the vast and intricate network of patronage that had arisen historically in Italy or France. What he needed urgently was a propagandist art that was tendentious, splendid and confident. These classical forms and energetic Baroque buildings, as well as formal court portraits, were alien in Russia. In the West they had grown from a constant revision of the classical past, but Russia had little classical past and no Renaissance. Yet Russian artists assimilated the lessons of French, Italian and German art with a rapacious hunger and enthusiasm which perhaps in itself suggests something of the restriction felt by painters who for so long had been unable to extend their range beyond the conventions of ikon painting. Peter's reforms elicited an astonishing virtuosity from painters who responded to the new opportunities that he had created.

The Heritage of Peter the Great
Court art founded upon the influx of foreign talents and pursued on an immense scale flourished vigorously after Peter's death. The Empress Anna Ioanovna introduced her German tastes, whilst the Empress Elizaveta was dedicated to French tastes during her reign from 1741 to 1761. During this whole period the construction and beautification of St. Petersburg continued relentlessly. The output, for example, of the Italian architect Rastrelli was immense. He had come to Russia with Le Blond in 1715. He worked on some of the greatest Russian palaces including Peterhof and the Winter Palace in St. Petersburg in 1754-62. The German artists Georg and Johann Groot came to Russia and the Italian Pietro Rotari arrived there in 1756. The following year the Academy of Arts in St. Petersburg was founded to rival its Western counterparts and to train Russian artists so that they too might equal their foreign tutors and contemporaries.

Aleksei Antropov. Empress Catherine II of Russia. *Oil on canvas. 88 x 66 cm.*

The Academy of Arts nurtured the first state art school in Russia. Like its foreign models it was at once the centre of learning and also the source of authority which articulated opportunities, commissions, recognition and status. Initially directed by the French painter Louis Joseph, the Academy found its formative and first long-term director in the French sculptor Nicolas Gillet (Zhille). The pre-eminence of drawing, the study of the art of ancient Greece and Rome, the predominance of figure composition leading to history painting were all systematised in the French way. The portraitists Antropov, Argunov and Rokotov emerged to fulfil roles first defined in the West.

During the long reign of the Empress Catherine II, from 1762 to 1796, construction proceeded and began to contribute less imitatively to Western fashions in art and architecture. Catherine was born in Germany. She superseded Peter's Baroque with an imported Rococo style that gave way in time to a distinctive Russian neo-classicism. Foreign artists were still instrumental in this however. The Scottish architect Cameron worked at St. Petersburg, Tsarskoe Selo, Pavlovsk and elsewhere, and the Italians Torelli and Quarenghi undertook major commissions, but, alongside this, Russian neo-classical architects were also contributing, among them Blazhenov and Starov who had attended the Academy in 1758.

As if to complete her own splendour and the education of Russian artists at the same time, Catherine began to acquire major works of Western art for the Hermitage Museum in St. Petersburg. Like the Louvre in Paris, this was to fill the role of an archive that provided an example and inspiration to Russian artists. All the mechanisms of a European powerhouse of culture were now in place. Russian artists emerged from the Academy schools well able to hold their position internationally. Levitsky gained overnight fame after exhibiting paintings at the Academy in 1770.

Aleksei Venetsianov. Cleaning the Sugar Beet, *1820s. Pastel. State Russian Museum, St. Petersburg.*

Russian history painting emerged with Levitsky and Ugryumov and genre painting was perfected by Venetsianov.

As the period of immense change was consolidated court art filtered down to become that of the aristocracy who required portraits and records of their estates. Russian neo-classicism was distinctive and no longer an imitation of the contemporary neo-classicism of Germany, Italy or France. Merchants too became more numerous as patrons. The celebration of ownership through paintings of great estates gave way gradually to paintings of the Russian landscape and a celebration of its people. Increasingly Russian artists were able to travel and learn new techniques in Italy and France. The Academy awarded valuable bursaries and exhibition opportunities that permitted recognition and private commissions. As exhibitions and exhibition societies were established new kinds of opportunities emerged for the advancement of reputations and sales. The market steadily grew for the work of painters, sculptors, medalists, decorators and printmakers. Ultimately this made a wide range of the public into potential patrons and art became a public matter in a new sense.

Art and the War with Napoleon

The Emperor Alexander I continued to embellish St. Petersburg during his reign from 1801 to 1825. The Kazan Cathedral and the Admiralty there were erected in this period but his reign was also marked by war with France culminating in the Napoleonic invasion of 1812. French art had played a formative role in the early years of the Academy. Stylistically this even survived the Napoleonic invasion. It is curious to see portraits of dashing military men painted in the manner of Gros at such a time. Napoleon's troops burnt Moscow but Russian troops pursued the French retreat all the way to Paris in 1814. This completed the assertion of Russia as a European power.

Under Nicholas I stricter censorship was accompanied by the development of genre painting into an instrument of social commentary and even criticism. The opening of railways began to make travel and communications in Russia easier. The Napoleonic War left a legacy of patriotism that encouraged the concept of landscape painting as a celebration of the national identity. This was in itself an artistic legacy which has frequently been reintroduced at times of national danger and crisis. St. Petersburg in all its splendour was after all the capital of a vast agrarian country populated by a peasantry with few legal rights. Until the abolition of serfdom in 1861 landowners also owned their serfs. Several serf artists however were able to study at the Academy as long as their owners tolerated this. Sometimes they were called back to work on their owners' estates where one at least committed suicide rather than face flogging. When Russian artists looked at French Realist paintings of peasants in the 1850s, they did so from a very different cultural context.

Art after the Abolition of Serfdom

Under Alexander II, who ruled from 1855 until his assassination in 1881, the arts proliferated under a more tolerant regime. Many Russian painters worked in Rome, some for almost the whole of their career. The extraordinary case of the painter Aleksandr Ivanov illustrates this. He spent most of his life in Rome where he knew the German Nazarene painters. He was working primarily on a single painting, the enormous *Christ Appearing to the People*, which occupied him for many years. The painting was finally exhibited in Russia in 1858. It was almost a manifesto of its time as awareness of the desperate plight of many of the people of Russia was rapidly growing. The poor peasant and impoverished city dweller appeared more and more frequently in paintings and graphic arts often contrasted with corrupt officials or cynical churchmen. The abolition of serfdom reinforced this theme. The peasantry became a major preoccupation for Russian artists as well as for intellectuals, writers and political activists.

In 1863 students at the Academy rebelled against the obscurity of the historicist themes that they were obliged to depict. When their demand for a subject of contemporary relevance was rejected they resigned as a group from the Academy, first forming an artists' co-operative and then establishing an exhibition society of influence and importance which they called the Wanderers or Itinerants (*Peredvizhniki*) because they intended to organise travelling exhibitions of their works of Realist social commentary. By elevating landscape painting to an image of national identity and by elevating genre painting to a level of fiercely astute observation and social criticism they achieved a new forcefulness and directness in Russian art. Their portraits, for example, described peasant and intellectual with the same impressive immediacy and monumentality. It was pointless to present the legends of ancient Greece and Rome to viewers who lacked the education to understand them. The immediacy and the use of narrative in their paintings had a new ideological purpose that was contemporary with the Zemstvo reforms in Russia and the intellectuals' movement towards the people.

In terms of artists' opportunities, the Academy students' revolt of 1863 proved to be a turning point. Unable to accommodate to the Academy's requirements they had to devise their own means of exhibition and advancement. The collector Pavel Tretyakov assisted them in their early attempts at independence and ultimately they succeeded to become important figures with a powerful influence on the development of Russian art. Their paintings demanded attention from a wide range of people and they were popularly appreciated and understood. Their opportunities were largely of their own making and this made them independent. Their works were addressed to the public and widely exhibited. In a sense the public had become the patron for whom they worked. The Tretyakov brothers were important among those who bought their works and their paintings can now be seen in the Tretyakov Gallery in Moscow.

This growing awareness of an art which dealt with contemporary Russian themes encouraged an interest in the roots of Russian art. The Tretyakov brothers were again important collectors in this and amassed a significant collection of Russian ikons. These were now being viewed as artworks not solely as objects of religious

Mstislav Dobuzhinsky.
St. Petersburg, c.1902. 11.5 x 17 cm.
Signed 'M.D.' lower left.
A vignette designed for the 'World of
Art' periodical.

veneration. In the decades which separated the founding of the Wanderers from the outbreak of war in 1914 Russian artists developed insatiable interests in a frenetic cosmopolitanism manifest in frequent international travel, and also an equal fascination with the origins of Russian art.

Cosmopolitanism was a feature of the activities of the World of Art (*Mir Iskusstva*) group which included the exhibition organiser and impresario Diaghilev as well as many painters among whom some of the best known were Bakst, Benois, Serov, Korovin and Somov. Diaghilev organised exhibitions surveying Russian art and in 1906 he took an exhibition of Russian art to Paris where it was displayed in an elegant *fin de siècle* setting by Bakst at the Salon d'Automne. The World of Art was in many ways aristocratic in its tastes. It promoted a belief in beauty that was heir to the Symbolist movement. Its publications were lavish, expensive and full of urbane art and commentary and it sought to promote Russian art in an international context. As a result Russian and Western art were both contrasted and blended together. Not surprisingly perhaps this was essentially a phenomenon arising in St. Petersburg, the city which itself became a wistful evocation of past glories when depicted by Benois, Dobuzhinsky, Somov or Ostroumova-Lebedeva. A converse trend within the World of Art evoked a more distant Russian past of Vikings and traders in a mythical past of rosy Kremlin walls around gilded citadels. This made some World of Art painters sympathetic to craft revivals established in workshops at Abramtsevo and Talashkino. Among the World of Art painters Serov and Dobuzhinsky were artists of great originality well able to sustain an international reputation. Perhaps the only artists to bridge the gulf between the Wanderers and the World of Art were the landscape painter Isaak Levitan and the robust Ilya Repin, a man of wide-ranging talents and versatility who dominated Russian art in the last years of the century. This was a period in which individual talent was most valued in Russia as in France, Germany and elsewhere. One such painter was Mikhail Vrubel' whose dramatic and dynamic demons inhabited a spangled wealth of colour that was a suggestive, rich and impressive Russian contribution to the international Symbolist movement that seized the imagination of his generation in the dying years of the century. In these same years a Russian-French political alliance was formed which can only have encouraged travel by artists between the two countries. The alliance was formalised in 1893 by the state visit of the Russian Emperor to Paris where the new Art Nouveau bridge across the Seine, the Pont Alexandre III, was named in his honour. Russian art had already been visible at the 1889 International Exhibition in Paris but now a new period of cultural exchange was initiated. Russian art again appeared at the International Exhibition of 1900 in Paris and contacts flourished as

Valentin Serov. Landscape in Finland, *before 1911. Oil on paper. 95.4 x 74 cm.*
Malmö Konstmuseum.

never before. Remarkable Russian merchants, particularly Shchukin and Morozov began to buy recent French painting for their collections in Moscow. They progressed rapidly from Impressionist works by Monet to paintings by Gauguin, Denis, Vuillard and Bonnard and then they acquired major paintings by Matisse and Picasso. Both Denis and Matisse visited Russia. These collections were made available for Russian artists to see and their impact on Russian art was enormous. The latest Parisian painting had become accessible in Moscow.

In 1904-5 the confidence of Russia was shaken by defeat in the Russo-Japanese War and by revolution at home. Liberal cosmopolitan values were shocked by the bloody suppression of the revolution. Painters responded at once. Serov, Dobuzhinsky and many others made drawings and bitterly satirical paintings directly critical of the government and responsible authorities including the military and politicians. Satirical magazines proliferated which pulled no punches and revolutionary activity continued in secret and earnest determination.

Diaghilev meanwhile was bringing Russian art to Paris at the 1906 Salon d'Automne and, within a few years, he was introducing the spectacular displays of his Russian Ballet. Right up to the First World War in 1914 Russian artists were present in Paris in such abundance that they began to make a real contribution to Parisian art. Diaghilev's ballets not only revealed composer, choreographer, dancers, musicians and artists working in a new synthesis of the arts, they also brought the sheer vigour and imagination of Russian culture home to the budding international focus of world art. After the dominance of otherworldly decorations by Bakst and Benois came the fierce neo-primitive energy of Roerich, Larionov and Goncharova. By 1912 Russian artists were central contributors to Cubism in Paris. It could not have evolved as it did without Archipenko, Chagall, Sonia Delaunay, Zadkine or many others. Marie Wassilieff even opened a Russian academy in Paris where Léger among others lectured. The Russian painters Popova and Udaltsova studied Cubism first hand under Gleizes, Metzinger and Le Fauconnier. There was a great multitude of other contacts in the pre-war period. In Munich, Russian artists were making a major contribution to German art. Kandinsky in particular formed a cultural link that was to prove of vital importance in both Russia and Germany when he formed the *Blaue Reiter* (Blue Rider) together with the Russian painters Jawlensky and Werefkin, the Germans Marc and Macke and the Swiss Paul Klee in 1912, the same year that his enormously influential book *Concerning the Spiritual in Art* was first published.

In Russia these developments found a sympathetic reception in the artists' organisations the Golden Fleece (*Zolotoe runo*), the Union of Youth (*Soyuz molodezhi*) and Knave of Diamonds (*Bubnovy valet*) which consistently kept abreast of developments in Paris, Munich and Berlin. When this tide of influence and involvement was at its height, some Russian artists, including figures most closely aware of the example of the West, determined that Russian art should seek its own indigenous roots by turning to the ikon, the popular Russian print and to folk art for inspiration. Larionov and Goncharova were central figures in this before they fled the war to join Diaghilev in Switzerland. In this period Russian Futurism was also at its most vigorous, vociferous and anarchic height in Russia. During the war years the importance of Russian Futurism grew until it became a major feature of revolutionary art in Russia after 1917.

The war had cut off the great wealth of foreign influences from France and Germany. Artists were again thrown together in shared isolation. But their experience of Western art had been rich and immediate. The isolation lasted beyond the Revolution of 1917, effectively until the First Russian Art Exhibition in Berlin in 1922. During this time the most radical innovations had been revealed and Revolution had again transformed the Russian art world.

In December 1915 at 0.10. The Last Futurist Exhibition of Paintings held in Petrograd, Tatlin had displayed constructed corner-reliefs and Malevich had shown paintings in which all trace of recognisable subject matter had vanished into

Nicolas Roerich. The Forefathers,
1911. Tempera on canvas.
69.3 x 89.8 cm.
Ashmolean Museum, Oxford.

assemblages of coloured geometric forms which appeared to glide through an infinite white space, a mode of painting which he named Suprematism. Both appeared to reject representation and both were called 'non-objective' which in Russian simply means 'without subject'. They rapidly gained many followers who established positions between these two innovators and non-objective art flourished in the work of Exter, Popova, Klyun, Rodchenko and very many others who attempted after the Revolution to assert that their new art was appropriate as the outward sign of the new communist culture. In origin however it was pre-revolutionary.

With the installation of Bolshevik communist power under Lenin in 1917 this dynamic and radical art gained new significance and potential.

Art under Communism

In 1917, with the abdication of Tsar Nicholas II, the Romanov dynasty ended after 304 years. Bolshevik rule began in October 1917. The effect of this upon the arts was fundamental and immediate. The whole support system for artists was changed by the new circumstances. Private ownership was undermined so that commercial galleries as an outlet for artists' sales were compromised. Similarly the private wealthy collector was no longer able to operate as patron. The merchant Shchukin, for example, had his collection 'nationalised'. The whole structure of patronage from aristocrat to merchant vanished. The whole ideology of art changed.

It was soon made evident that art under communism would be communal in production, public in expression and political in content. The first manifestation of this came with the street decorations of 1918 marking May Day and also the first anniversary of the Revolution. Many Futurists, Cubists and Suprematists, as well as rather more conventional artists, contributed to these initial expressions of communal, public and political art. Art schools were made into Free Art Studios and Lenin instituted a programme calling for Monumental Propaganda to commemorate heroes and forerunners of the Revolution. Tatlin played an important role in this. New arts organisations were established under Lunacharsky to reassess the role, practice and effectiveness of art. Artists including Shterenberg, Kandinsky, Tatlin and Chagall became commissars of art charged with the clarification and implementation of a whole new communist culture. Some theorists, artists and writers argued that communist art must be classless, but others argued that it should be proletarian. In the first case recent artistic experiments appeared to have great

Kazimir Malevich. Suprematist Composition, *c.1915. Charcoal on paper. 16.5 x 11.5 cm. In Suprematism, launched by Malevich in 1915, geometric forms float through space forming 'constellations' in a dynamic relationship. Private collection, courtesy Annely Juda Fine Art, London.*

potential, but they could scarcely be called a proletarian art as long as their canvases and sculptures appeared to be unintelligible to the masses. Debates on many related issues followed throughout the 1920s among a plethora of art groups and publications. Ideological issues had entered art in Russia as an active and urgent consideration. Art was no longer to be a more or less passive reflection of the world but a new constructive force within communist social organisation. Furthermore the aesthetic conception of art was frequently attacked as mystificatory, self-indulgent and unnecessary within a materialist view of the world. When Kandinsky was made director of the new Institute of Artistic Culture (INKhUK) in Moscow he sought to investigate the psychological effects of colours and forms, but he soon resigned under pressure from Constructivists whose attitude relied upon an insistence that material factors were more important in the formation of a Constructive attitude to communist culture. Rodchenko and the Moscow Constructivists working with him were themselves attacking non-objective art by 1921 even though they had been among its significant exponents.

At the exhibition 5 x 5 = 25 held in Moscow in 1921 Rodchenko exhibited a triptych of monochrome red, yellow and blue canvases which he called the *Last Painting* and the call went up from theorists of his circle that 'Art is Dead!' In this way non-objective painters renounced non-objective art and turned their attention to Constructive communal work in design, theatre, film, clothing and in many other fields. Non-objective art was attacked from within and found to be unnecessary. Big

State Exhibitions surveyed the whole range of art available in major cities. It was clearly the State which acted ultimately as arbiter, exhibitor and patron in art. Ideologists were necessary to clarify this for artists and public alike. Much of what emerged was brilliant and innovative. Tatlin's great double-spiral *Monument to the Third International*, for example, was a utopian vision of the centre of a future world government, a cockpit for a unified planet Earth gliding harmoniously through the heavens with its decision-making committees revolving in gigantic glass halls in time to the relative movements of the sun, moon and stars. Such innovations were unseen in the West until the establishment of diplomatic relations with the Soviet government in the early post-war years. The new art was revealed to great effect at the First Russian Art Exhibition at the Van Diemen Gallery in Berlin in 1922, at the Venice Biennale in 1924, and at the Soviet Pavilion of the Paris International Exhibition of 1925.

During this period of renewed openness numerous Russian artists emigrated to France and Germany and a new Russian presence was felt in the artistic circles of Berlin and Paris. The majority stayed in Russia to evolve within the ideology of communism. By 1927 when large exhibitions surveyed the achievements of artists during the first ten years of communism, the reaction to avant-garde experimentation was consolidating. Groups such as the 4 Arts society, NOZh (New Society of Painters), OST (Society of Easel Painters), and, most effectively, AKhRR (Association of Artists of Revolutionary Russia), argued with increasing urgency for a return to easel painting and a return also to subject matter that was intelligible and an effective vehicle therefore for propagating communist ideology. Opinion steadily hardened in favour of traditional techniques and a return to the lessons of the Wanderers.

In 1932 all artistic groups were abolished by decree. State control became explicit

Mikhail Larionov. Design for the First Scene of the Ballet 'Chout', *1921. Gouache.*
50 x 69 cm.
Prokofiev's ballet 'Chout' was staged by Larionov and T.Slavinsky for Diaghilev at the Théâtre Gaiété-Lyrique, Paris, in 1921.
Collection Mr. and Mrs. Nikita D Lobanov-Rostovsky, London.

through the institution of a single, monolithic Union of Artists which monitored ideological effectiveness in form, method and content, which provided (and denied) opportunities, status and recognition and which organised the entire artistic life of the Soviet Union. What prevailed from the 1930s to the 1950s was the politicised academic art known as Socialist Realism. Every 19th century device and technique from landscape to genre, history painting and portraiture, was harnessed to create an authoritative, optimistic, heroic and always successful image of Russian Soviet Communism. A few artists achieved a synthesis of earlier innovation with Socialist Realism. Deineka was one such painter. Other innovators were at work in design where their non-objective principles were hidden beneath an ulterior purpose of exhibition, theatre, film or book design. This was the case with Lissitzky and Rodchenko. The majority conformed to make an art that was political and readily intelligible. Some of these artists too were undoubtedly figures of remarkable talent, flair and ability. The sculptor Vera Mukhina would have been impressive in any

Aleksandr Rodchenko. Construction, *1921.*
Crayon on paper.
This is one of a series of drawings entitled 'Construction' to distinguish them from compositions. Construction was considered a more fundamental approach common, for example, to engineering and art.
State Tretyakov Gallery, Moscow.

context. It was her colossal *Worker and Collective Farm Worker* that rose to a dynamic
pinnacle above the Soviet Pavilion at the 1937 Paris International Exhibition. Only
twelve years had elapsed since the previous occasion of this kind. In that time Soviet
culture had changed enormously.

By 1937 the avant-garde had effectively vanished from sight. They even vanished
from Soviet histories of the period. It was in Western Europe that their story was
revived from the 1960s onwards whilst in Russia they remained figures of great
obscurity. In Russia it was an academic and monumental art of propaganda that
flourished at least until the 1960s. During the war years when Russia was subject to
determined and ruthless German invasion, the machinery of State art was thrown
into top gear to produce patriotic and anti-fascist art at its most fierce. The Battle of
Stalingrad, the Siege of Leningrad, the conquest of Berlin and Hitler's death in his
bunker were all events depicted with a stern and stirring patriotism by painters
whilst sculptors in the immediate post-war years found many opportunities to design
monuments to the dead, their heroes and their leaders. The best of these colossal
monuments have a grandiloquent rhetoric restrained by solemnity in which human

Vladimir Tatlin. Untitled,
c.1916-17. Tempera on wood.
75.5 x 41.5 cm.
Private collection, courtesy Annely
Juda Fine Art, London.

sympathy can survive in the sculptor's ability to fulfil the commission with conviction. Mukhina, once again, was able to achieve this.

From the death of Stalin in 1953 Soviet art entered a curious twilight phase, less confident of its means but still sure of its message. Much art was made celebrating a broad and vigorous Soviet Union of many constituent republics typified in the healthy faces of it heroes and citizens of Kazakhstan, Uzbekistan and elsewhere as well as those of Russia itself. As Russian artists became steadily more aware of contemporary Western art, they began slowly to respond to its innovations once again. The sculptor Ernst Neizvestny, for example, attained a considerable reputation both in Russia and in the West, and the group *Dvizhenie* (Movement) constructed kinetic sculptures that attracted a degree of official recognition within Russia in the 1960s even though they operated independently, exhibited in the West and drew their inspiration from the vanished Constructivists' work of the 1920s. The window upon the West was steadily prised open despite the Cold War. American art was discussed in Soviet periodicals and slowly museum displays and exhibitions began to broaden their range a little. When bulldozers were used to break up a street exhibition of unofficial art it was clear that such art existed in some strength. In the last years of communism in Russia a greater tolerance was growing which was superseded by the commercialism which replaced communism.

It is only now becoming evident that throughout all the ideological changes of the Soviet period and despite devastating warfare, museums in Russia preserved their collections and archives of works which might easily have been lost or destroyed. Collections long unseen are re-emerging into the light of day as the history of Russian art as it is written in Russia once again comes into line with the history of Russian art as it has been written in the West. Much new information will come to light which will serve to increase the range and detail of the present book in subsequent editions.

Russia is again looking to the West in the post-communist period. It is an ancient and shifting balance that has to be established. In the past such shifts of balance have been equally radical and they have led to enormous achievements in the realm of art.

John Milner
June 1993

Conventions

Abbreviations
a. active
Coll collections which feature works by the artist
Costakis Collection see Bibliography under Rudenstine
Lit literature about the artist, listed in chronological order of publication
Moscow College Moscow College of Painting, Sculpture and Architecture
RM State Russian Museum, St. Petersburg
RSFSR Russian Socialist Federation of Soviet Republics
TG State Tretyakov Gallery, Moscow

* (Asterisk)
The Dictionary's entries frequently describe particular works of art to help identify artists' styles and characteristics. These passages are marked by * followed by the italicised title of the example discussed

Acronyms
These are names for organisations abbreviated to their initial letters or syllables. An example is **Zhivskul'ptarkh**, formed from **zhiv**opis' (painting), **skul'pt**ura (sculpture) and **arkh**itektura (architecture). Many acronyms are given individual entries in this dictionary.

AKhR	Association of Artists of the Revolution
AKhRR	Association of Artists of Revolutionary Russia
ARMU	Association of Ukrainian Revolutionary Art
ASNOVA	Association of New Architects
FOSKh	Federation of Unions of Soviet Artists
GAKhN	State Academy of Artistic Sciences, Moscow
GINKhUK	State Institute of Artistic Culture, Petrograd-Leningrad/Moscow
GITIS	The A.V.Lunacharsky State Institute of Theatre Art, Moscow
GRM	State Russian Museum, Leningrad
GSKhM	State Free Art Studios, Moscow
GTG	State Tretyakov Gallery, Moscow
GTsKhRM	Central State Art Restoration Studios
INKhUK	Institute of Artistic Culture, Moscow
INPII	Institute of Proletarian Plastic Arts, Leningrad
IZhSA	Institute of Painting, Sculpture and Architecture, Leningrad
IZO	Department of Fine Arts of the People's Commissariat of the Enlightenment
LEF	Left Front of the Arts
LGIII	Leningrad State Institute of Art History
LINZhAS	Leningrad Institute of Painting, Architecture and Sculpture
MAKhD	Moscow Association of Artist Decorators
MGKhI	V.I.Surikov State Art Institute, Moscow
MGU	M.V.Lomonosov State University, Moscow
MIII	Moscow Fine Art Institute
MIPIDI	Institute of Applied and Decorative Art, Moscow

MOSKh	Moscow Section of Soviet Artists
MPI	Moscow Polygraphic Institute
MTI	Moscow Textile Institute
MUZhVZ	Moscow College of Painting, Sculpture and Architecture
MVKhPU	Moscow Higher College of Art and Design (former Stroganov College)
Narkompros	People's Commissariat of the Enlightenment
NOKh	New Society of Artists
NOZh	New Society of Painters
Obmokhu	Society of Young Artists
OKhK	Society of Book Artists
OKhR	Society of Artist-Realists
OKhU	Odessa Art College
OMKh	Society of Moscow Artists
OPKh	Society for the Encouragement of the Arts
ORP	Society of Revolutionary Poster Designers
ORRP	Society of Revolutionary Poster Workers
ORS	Society of Russian Sculptors
OSA	Society of Contemporary Architects
OSMU	Society of Contemporary Artists of the Ukraine
OST	Society of Easel Painters
PGSKhUM	Petrograd State Free Art Studios
Proletkul't	The Proletarian Culture Movement
RAKhN	Russian Academy of Artistic Sciences
RAPKh	Russian Association of Proletarian Artists
SARMA	Association of Revolutionary Artists of Georgia
SKhUM	Free Art Teaching Studios, Petrograd
SRKh	Union of Russian Artists
STsKhPU	Stroganov Central College of Art and Design, Moscow
SVOMAS	Free Art Studios
TPKhV	The Wanderers (Fellowship of Travelling Art Exhibitions)
TsUTR	A.L.Shtiglits (Stieglitz) Central College of Technical Drawing, Moscow
TYuRKh	Fellowship of South Russian Artists
UNOVIS	Affirmers of New Art
VGIK	All-Union State Institute of Cinematography
VIFF	All-Union Institute of Photography and Photographic Technology
VKhPI	Vitebsk Art and Practical Institute
VKhTI	Higher Artistic and Technical Institute, Saratov
VKhU	Higher Art College, St. Petersburg
VKhUTEIN	Higher Artistic and Technical Institute, Moscow/Leningrad
VKhUTEMAS	Higher Artistic and Technical Studios, Moscow/Leningrad
VSKhV	All-Union Agricultural Exhibition, Moscow

Names of People

In Russian the first name is followed by the patronymic, derived from the father's first name normally by adding **-ovich** for a male or **-ovna** for a female, and concluding with the family name. As readers of Tolstoy's *War and Peace* will realise, it is common in speech, letters and reminiscences to employ the first two names only. **Yuri Alekseevich Vasnetsov** is Yuri Vasnetsov son of Aleksei Vasnetsov. Family names are also given feminine endings, hence **Elena Mikhailovna Bebutova** is Elena Bebutova daughter of Mikhail Bebutov, and **Sofia Lyudvigovna**

Zaklikovskaya is Sofia Zaklikovskaya daughter of Lyudvig Zaklikovsky.

Established Westernised spelling of names has been retained with the Russian spelling cross-referenced. Hence **Shagal'=Chagall** leads to the main entry. As **Ivan Puni** became **Jean Pougny** on moving to France both spellings are listed. Other variations are not listed however: **Chichkine** (French spelling), **Schischkin** (German spelling) and **Sziszkin** (Polish spelling) are all the same painter **Shishkin**.

Foreign artists with significant careers in Russia or the Soviet Union are listed under the native spelling of their name with the Russian spelling cross-referenced: hence **Karavakk=Caravacque** leads to the entry **Caravacque, Louis.**

Where variation in a name occurs, the main entry is cross-referenced, hence **Nefedov = Er'zya** leads to the main entry.

Names of Countries and Cities

It is normal in Russian to use the name of a city as it was in the time referred to. It is possible therefore to have been born in St. Petersburg, to have studied in Petrograd, to have flourished in Leningrad and to have died in St. Petersburg without ever leaving the city which has known all of these name changes within a single century. As the Soviet Union changed numerous city names which since its dissolution have recently been renamed, some inconsistency is inevitable but this has been clarified in individual entries wherever possible with the alternative name in brackets: Tiflis (Tblisi).

Caveat

Whilst every effort has been made to verify information, a book of this kind inevitably draws upon a multitude of sources some of which cannot be cross-checked fully. In the interests of accuracy readers are invited to indicate any error so that it may be corrected in subsequent editions.

A.D. see **DEINEKA, A.A.**
A.D. (latin) see **DREVIN, A.D.**
A.E. see **EGOROV, A.E.; EXTER, A.**
A.G. (cyrillic or latin) see **GONCHAROV, A.D.**
A.G. see **GRISHCHENKO, A.V.**
A.K. see **KRAVCHENKO, A.I.; KULIKOV, A.E.**
A.M. see **MATVEEV, A.T.**
A.O. (in a monogram), see **OSTROUMOVA-LEBEDEVA, A.**
A.P. (in a monogram), see **PAKHOMOV, A.F.**
A.P. see **PLASTOV, A.A.**
A.R. (in a monogram), see **RODCHENKO, A.M.**
A.R.B. see **BOGOMOLOV-ROMANOVICH, A.S.**
A.S. see **SAMOKHVALOV, A.N.**
A.Z. see **ZELENTSOV, K.A.**

ABAKELIYA, Tamara Grigor'evna   **1905-1953**
Georgian sculptor and graphic artist who also worked in theatre
and film. She studied under V.F.Il'yushin at Batum in 1920 and
at the Tblisi Academy under the sculptor Ya.A.Nikoladze and
studied drawing under E.E.Lansere and I.A.Sharleman 1923-9.
She exhibited from 1927 and was a member of SARMA from
1930. Her sculptures include friezes in cement at the Institute of
Marxism-Leninism at Tblisi, 1936-7. She worked for the theatre
in Georgia from 1930. She died at Tblisi.
Theatre design Sh.M.Taktakishvili's ballet *Mltakva* at the
Z.P.Paliashvili Opera and Ballet Theatre at Tblisi. The pastel
and pencil designs show a gloomy evocation of a stormy
countryside with basic huts erected beneath overhanging trees
and with a glowing distant skyline.
Lit G.Kikodze *T.Abakeliya*, Tblisi, 1941. O.Piralishvili
T.Abakeliya, Tblisi, 1956. R.D.Dzhaparidze *T.Abakeliya*,
Moscow, 1957.
Coll Bakhrushin Theatre Museum, Moscow.

ABDULLAEV, Abdulkhak Aksakalovich   **b.1918**
Portrait painter. Born in Turkestan. He was the brother of the
painter Lutfulla Aksakalovich Abdullaev. He studied under
P.P.Ben'kov, L.A.Bure and Z.M.Kovalevskoy at Samarkand
1930-2 and under V.P.Efanov and A.A.Osmerkin 1938-41. He
exhibited from 1934 including exhibitions in Hungary in
1949, Finland in 1950 and India in 1954. He taught at
Tashkent in 1950-5.
Coll TG.

ABDURAKHMANOV, Faud Gasan Ogli   **1915-1971**
Azerbaijani sculptor of patriotic figures. He studied under
M.G.Manizer in Leningrad 1935-9. He exhibited from 1934.
He taught at the Azerbaijan Art School 1942-8. He executed a
monument at Kirovabad in 1946, Ulan Bator in 1954 and
monuments to Lenin in Omsk and Alma-Ata in 1957. He
exhibited in India in 1954, Japan in 1954, Bulgaria in 1956 and
in Yugoslavia in 1959.
Lit M.Nadzhafov *Abdurakhmanov*, Moscow, 1955.
Coll Azerbaijan Museum of Art.

ABEGYAN, Mger (Meger) Manukovich   **1909-1962+**
Painter, graphic artist. Born in Armenia. Studied in Armenia
under S.M.Agadzhanyan and S.A.Arakelyan 1922-7 and at the
Moscow Vkhutemas under S.V.Gerasimov 1927-30. He then
studied in Leningrad 1930-1 under A.A.Osmerkin. He
exhibited in Erevan in 1932. He illustrated Armenian epics
and legends and taught in Erevan 1937-44 and 1954-9. He
exhibited in London in 1938, Budapest in 1949, Delhi in 1952,
Bucharest in 1961, Montevideo in 1962 and New York in 1962.
Coll TG; RM.

ABRAMOV, A. I.   **a.1913**
Painter. He contributed to Larionov's exhibition The Target
in Moscow in 1913.

ABUGOV, Semen L'vovich (Shimon Leybovich) 1877-1950
Painter of portraits and landscapes, graphic artist. Born at
Minsk. He graduated from the School of Drawing in Odessa
in 1900 and then studied under D.N.Kardovsky and
V.E.Makovsky at the St. Petersburg Academy 1900-8. He
exhibited from 1903.
After the Revolution he was engaged in Agitprop decorations at
Vasilieostrovsky Sovdep, Petrograd, in 1918. He was included in
the enormous survey Exhibition of Paintings by Petrograd
Artists of All Tendencies 1919-1923 held in Petrograd in 1923.
He taught at the Repin Institute, Leningrad, from 1932 to 1950.
He died at Leningrad.

ADAMOVICH, Mikhail Mikhailovich   **1884-1947**
Painter, exponent of monumental decorative art and applied arts
including ceramics. Born in Moscow. He studied at the
Stroganov School during 1894-1907, then studied decorative art
in Italy from 1907 to 1909. He was working on architectural
decorations in St. Petersburg 1909-13, and he also visited
Greece. In 1914 he made mosaic decorations for the tomb of
George V for the Greek Government. Military service followed
1914-17.
After the Revolution he was engaged in Agitprop decorations
at Pokrovsky Square, Petrograd, in 1918. He also worked for
the State Porcelain Factory during 1918-19. Here in 1919 he
produced a series of plates illustrating old St. Petersburg but
he also produced propaganda porcelain including *Workers of
the World Unite*, 1918, and *Red Star*, 1919. He served in the
Red Army 1919-21. He was again with the State Porcelain
Factory 1921-4 where his works included a porcelain plate
decorated with a portrait of Lenin and the words 'Who Does
Not Work Shall Not Eat'. He was represented at the Paris
International Exhibition in 1925 and awarded a gold medal.
He subsequently worked at the Volkov Factory near
Novgorod 1924-7 and as a painter at the Dulevo Factory to
1937. He was represented at the jubilee exhibition Artists of
the RSFSR over 15 Years held at the Russian Museum,
Leningrad, in 1932.
He worked on decorative paintings for architectural interiors
1934-7. He died in Moscow.
Lit N.Lobanov-Rostovsky *Revolutionary Ceramics*, London,
1990.
Coll RM; Ceramics Museum, Moscow; Museum of the
Lomonosov Porcelain Factory, Leningrad.

**ADAMSON, Amandus Genrikh (Heinrich) (ADAMSON,
Amand Ivanovich)**   **1855-1929**
Estonian sculptor, painter. His work encompassed genre

sculptures and monumental projects. He studied at the Academy of Art under A.F.Bok and taught at the Drawing School of the Society for the Encouragement of the Arts in St. Petersburg 1886-7. He had an exhibition of his work in St. Petersburg in 1887. He worked in Paris 1887-91 where he exhibited at the International Exhibition in 1889. He subsequently worked in St. Petersburg-Petrograd until 1918. He made sculptures of the *The Liberation of Genius* and *The Triumph of Truth* for the All-Russian Exhibition at Nizhny-Novgorod in 1896.

After the Revolution he returned to Estonia where he lived at Paldiski. He executed monumental and decorative sculptures including allegorical works. He died at Paldiski, Estonia. An exhibition of his work was held at Tallin in 1955.

Monument to the Ship 'Rusalka', 1902, erected at Tallin, is an elegant winged angel upon an outcrop of artificial rocks.

Coll TG; RM; Estonian Art Museum, Tallin.

ADLIVANKIN, Samuil Yakovlevich　　　　**1897-1966**
Painter, graphic artist, cinema artist. Born at Tatarsk. He studied at the School of Art in Odessa under K.K.Kostandi 1912-17. He exhibited from 1916.

After the Revolution he studied at the Free Art Studios in Moscow under Tatlin 1918-19. He worked on the organisation of the Free State Studios at Samara 1919-21. He briefly adopted a non-objective approach close to the examples of Rodchenko, Popova and others c.1918-20. He was a founder member of the New Society of Painters (NOZh) formed in 1922. He produced some neo-primitive paintings in the early 1920s. He worked for the journal *Molodaya Gvardiya* (Young Guard) 1923-8 and produced illustrations for numerous periodicals including *Voenniy krokodil* (War Crocodile), *Krasnaya zvezda* (Red Star) and *Bezbozhnik* (Godless). He designed political posters in collaboration with Mayakovsky. He was represented at the jubilee exhibition Artists of the RSFSR over 15 Years held at the Russian Museum, Leningrad, in 1932. By this time his primitivism was less evident although his painting still retained a directness and even a crudeness of handling.

He was given a one-man exhibition in Moscow in 1961. He died in Moscow.

Tram B, 1922, RM, is a consciously primitive work with his signature along the side of the tram. There is a hint of children's art or of Pirosmanashvili about the painting.

Film design His work for films at the studios of Sovkino included *Chashka chaya* (Cup of Tea) in 1927 and *Troe s odnoy ulitsy* (Three From One Street) in 1936.

Lit A.M.Muratov, V.Manin et al. *Zhivopis' 20-30kh godov*, Sankt-Peterburg, 1991. *L'Avant-garde russe 1905-1925*, exh. cat., Musée des Beaux-Arts, Nantes, 1993.

Coll TG; RM; Astrakhan Regional Museum of Art; Krasnodar Art Museum; Yaroslav Art Museum.

AFANAS'EV, Aleksei Fedorovich　　　　**1850-1920**
Painter of genre, graphic artist. An authority on folklore and an illustrator of stories. He studied as an external student at the Academy in St. Petersburg. His work included portraits of the painters *K.K.Kostandi* in 1884 and *A.M.Vasnetsov* in 1886. He taught in St. Petersburg 1887-1905. He was a member of the Wanderers with whom he exhibited from 1889. His illustrations to stories included I.P.Ershov's *Konek-Gorbunok*, and Pushkin's *Tale of Tsar Saltan* and *Of Fishermen and Fishes*. He was the director of the Penza Art School 1905-9 where he taught Tatlin and Lentulov. From 1909 he was again teaching in St. Petersburg. From 1912 he illustrated journals including

Shut, *Oskolki*, and *Lukomor'e*.

He participated in the First State Free Exhibition of Artworks in Petrograd in 1919 and was represented at the enormous First State Exhibition of Art and Science, which included ethnographic material, held in Kazan in 1920. Sometimes he signed his work 'Athonasev'. He died in Petrograd.

Coll TG; Ulyanov Art Museum; Omsk Art Museum; Gorky Art Museum.

AGABABOV, S. I.　　　　**a.1923**
He was included in the enormous survey Exhibition of Paintings by Petrograd Artists of All Tendencies 1919-1923 held in Petrograd in 1923.

AGABABYAN, Vartkes Karapetovich　　　　**b.1906**
Painter, sculptor. Born in Turkey. He studied under S.M.Agadzhanyan and S.A.Arakelyan at the Erevan Art School 1921-7.

Coll Armenian Picture Gallery; Moldavian Art Museum.

AGADZHANYAN, Stepan Meliksetovich　　　　**1863-1940**
Armenian painter of landscapes, still-lifes, and portraits. Born in the Elizavetpol region. He studied in France in 1885 and at the Académie Julian in Paris 1897-1900 under J.P.Laurens and Benjamin-Constant. After 1900 he worked in Baku and Rostov-on-Don where he taught 1903-22. He then moved to Erevan where he taught at the Erevan Art School until 1927. He was given one-man exhibitions in Erevan in 1938, 1952 and 1963 and in Moscow in 1951. He died in Erevan.

Lit A.Eremyan, G.Gyurdzhan *Zhizn' i tvorchestvo S.Agadzhanyana*, Erevan, 1927. E.A.Martikyan *Tvorchestvo khudozhnika S.Agadzhanyana*, Erevan, 1953. V.A.Agadzhanyan *Moi vospominaniya ob S.Agadzhanyana*, Erevan, 1953.

Coll Armenian Picture Gallery; State Museum of Eastern Art, Moscow.

AGAFONOV, Vasily Semenovich　　　　**a.1893-1917**
Silversmith and cloisonné designer active in Moscow.

Lit *Twilight of the Tsars*, London, 1991.

Coll State Historical Museum, Moscow.

AGAFONOVA, Zinaida Dmitrievna　　　　**1870-1904+**
Painter. Born at Kazan. She studied at the Kazan Art School and exhibited from 1890. She also studied at the Academy in St. Petersburg under Kuindzhi and Repin 1902-4.

AGAP'EVA (-ZAKHAROVA), Natalya Nikolaevna 1883-1956
Graphic artist. Born at Tblisi. She studied under O.I.Shmerling at the Tiflis (Tblisi) Art School 1904-6, in the Moscow studio of K.Yuon and I.Mashkov, and at the Moscow College under A.E.Arkhipov and N.A.Kasatkin 1907-11. She exhibited with the Moscow Salon 1910-17.

After the Revolution she was engaged on Agitprop projects in 1918 including costumes for street parades and decorative panels, one of which showed a sheaf of corn with flowers and a sickle. She was represented at the First Exhibition of Works of the Professional Union of Artists in Moscow in 1918 and at the First Exhibition of the Moscow Contemporary Art Store in January 1919. An exhibition of her work was held in Moscow in 1922. She also exhibited with the group *Zhar-tsvet* (Fire-Colour) 1925-6. She worked with her husband I.Zakharov. She died in Moscow.

Coll TG; Tolstoy Museum, Moscow; N.G.Chernyshevsky Museum, Saratov.

Ivan Aivazovsky. The Bay of Naples by Moonlight, *1892. Oil on canvas. 107,7 x 178,2 cm.*

AGARYKH = STEPANOVA, V.F.

AGIBALOV, Vasili Ivanovich   **1913-1963+**
Monumental and portrait sculptor. Born in the Voronezh region. He studied at the Kharkov Institute of Art 1934-42 under L.A.Blokh and exhibited from 1942. Together with Vera Mukhina and V.Kh.Fedchenko he executed a bronze monument to *Lenin* in 1944. He taught at the Lugansk Art School 1944-9 and at the Art Institute in Kharkov 1949-54. Other monuments were erected at Lugansk in 1947 and at Krasnodon in 1954. He exhibited in Peking in 1954, Bucharest 1956 and Sofia in 1956. Late portrait works include *Lenin*, granite, 1961, and *T.G.Shevchenko*, stone, 1963.
Coll Ukrainian Museum of Fine Art, Kiev.

AGIN, Aleksandr Alekseevich   **1817-1875**
Draughtsman and illustrator. Born Pskov region. He studied at the Academy in St. Petersburg from 1834 and under K.P.Bryullov from 1836. His illustrations included M.Yu.Lermontov's *Demon*, RM, and works by Pushkin. He worked in collaboration with the printmaker E.E.Bernadsky. Other works illustrated by him included Gogol's *Dead Souls*, RM, finally published whole in 1924. He lived in Kiev from 1853. He died in the Chernygovsk region.
*Illustration to Gogol's Dead Souls, c.1846, is comparable with French lithographic illustrations by Gavarni, but it is here less concerned with the contemporary way of life and is directly related to Gogol's text. Grotesque figures of men gather round a table frantically reading through papers. There is an atmosphere of underworld mischief and industrious malevolence.
Lit K.Kuzmin'sky *Khudozhnik-illyustrator A.A.Agin. Ego zhizn' i tvorchestvo*, Moscow, 1913. M.G.Fleer *Neizdanniy risunok Agina*, Petrograd, 1922. I.Lazarevsky *A.A.Agin*, Moscow,

1946. G.Sternin *A.A.Agin*, Moscow, 1955.
Coll TG; RM; Pushkin Museum, Moscow; Saratov Art Museum.

AGNIT-SLEDZEVSKY, Kazimir Genrikhovich (Frantsevich)   **1898-1963+**
Graphic artist. Born in St. Petersburg. He studied in Kiev under A.A.Murashko from 1913 and at the Polytechnic Institute under I.F.Seleznev 1916-22. He exhibited from 1922 in Kiev. He submitted caricatures to Ukrainian reviews in the 1920s,1930s and 1940s. He designed and illustrated books for publishing houses in Kiev in the 1950s. An exhibition of his work was held in Kiev in 1958.
Coll Odessa Art Museum; Ukrainian Fine Art Museum, Kiev.

AIVAZOVSKY (AYVAZOVSKY), Ivan Konstantinovich
1817-1900
Major marine painter. Born at Fedosia. He studied under an architect in Feodosia and then from 1833 under M.N.Vorob'ev and F.Tanner at the Academy in St. Petersburg. He exhibited from 1835. He travelled on a scholarship to Italy, Germany, France, Spain and Holland 1840-4. His *Isle of Capri* won a gold medal in Paris in 1843. He was made an Academician in 1844. He travelled on an expedition to Turkey, Asia Minor and Greece in 1845. He settled in Feodosia but he was in Paris 1857-8 where he painted a series of *The Four Seasons*. He also painted in the Ukraine and Caucasus in the period 1850-70. The poet Pushkin inspired a number of his works. He was a member of the Academies of Rome, Florence, Stuttgart and Amsterdam. He produced over 6,000 works. He died at Feodosia.
*The Ninth Wave, 1850, RM: A few survivors of a shipwreck float on a mast, about to succumb to a vast translucent breaking wave, its crest catching the yellow light of the declining sun. It

was painted with consummate and beguiling illusionism.
Lit N.I.Kuzmin *Vospominaniya ob I.K.Aivazovskom*, St. Petersburg, 1901. N.Nikolaeva *I.K.Aivazovsky*, Moscow, 1914. N.S.Barsanov *I.K.Aivazovsky*, Feodosia, 1930. A.Savinov *I.K.Aivazovsky*, Leningrad, 1950. N.Novpuspensky *A Aivazovsky*, Leningrad, 1980.
Coll Significant holdings at TG; RM; Feodosia Art Gallery; Erevan Art Museum; Yaroslavl' Art Museum; Sebastopol Art Museum; Odessa Art Museum and many others.

AIZENBERG (AYZENBERG), Nina Evseevna 1902-1974
Theatre designer. Born in Moscow. She studied at the Moscow Free State Studios/Vkhutemas 1918-24 under Mashkov, Osmerkin and others. Her design for the theatre began in 1924. She worked for the Blue Blouse Theatre in Moscow in the period 1926-9. Stylistically indebted to constructivism, she designed Blue Blouse posters with Evgeniya Korbut at this time. She exhibited at Moscow Theatres during Ten Years of the October Revolution in Moscow in 1928 and was a member of the Moscow Association of Stage Designers 1928-30. She also designed a cycle of performances based on the life of Spichkin, a member of the Communist Youth Organisation, in 1929. She was a member of the group October 1930-2. She worked on street decorations and parades 1930-5 and was still working on parades and displays 1938-41. She was given a one-woman exhibition in Moscow in 1964. She died in Moscow. She signed her designs with a monogram of Russian 'NA' run together.
Theatre design 1926 the revue *Pianka Durman* (Drunken Stupor), including a stylised costume for a Café Girl, for the Blue Blouse Theatre, Moscow.
1927 V.Mayakovsky's and O.Brik's *Radio Operator* for the Blue Blouse Theatre.
1927 M.D.Volpin's *The Queen's Mistake* for the Blue Blouse Theatre.
1929 *Le Bourgeois Gentilhomme* at the Maly Theatre, Moscow.
Lit T.Strizhenova *Iz istorii sovetskogo kostyuma*, Moscow, 1972 (English edition: Tatiana Strizhenova, *Soviet Costume and Textiles 1917-1945*, Paris, 1991). J.E.Bowlt *Russian Stage Design. Scenic Innovation. From the Collection of Mr. and Mrs. Nikita D.Lobanov-Rostovsky*, Jackson, MS, exh. cat.,1982. Nancy Van Norman Baer *Theatre in Revolution, Russian Avant-Garde Stage Design 1913-1935*, San Francisco and London, 1991. Dzhon Boult (John Bowlt) *Khudozhniki russkogo teatra. Sobranie Nikity i Niny Lobanovykh-Rostovskikh*, Moscow, 1991.
Coll Bakhrushin Theatre Museum, Moscow.

AKHANOV, N. G. a.1919
He participated in the First State Free Exhibition of Artworks in Petrograd in 1919.

AKHMET'EV, Vladimir Petrovich 1892-1959
Theatre designer, decorative artist. Born in Moscow. He studied under F.Rerberg in Moscow 1911-18. He contributed to the exhibition Art of Moscow Theatre 1918-1923 held in Moscow in 1923. He was chief artist of the All Union Agricultural Exhibition in Moscow in 1939. With V.Mukhina he executed bas-relief decorations for the Semenovskaya Station of the Moscow Metro in 1944. He died in Moscow.

AKHREMCHIK, Ivan Osipovich 1903-1971
Painter, decorative artist. Born at Minsk. He studied under

K.N.Istomin and A.V.Shevchenko at the Moscow Vkhutemas. He was included in the 1928 exhibition of Acquisitions by the State Art Collections Fund held in Moscow. His work included military themes and portraits as well as decorative works in Minsk in Belorussia. He taught in Minsk from 1931. He was executing rather calligraphic watercolours in 1937. He was still actively teaching at Minsk in 1963.
Coll Belorussian Art Museum, Minsk.

AKhR
The abbreviated name of the Association of Artists of the Revolution (*Assotsiatsiya khudozhnikov revolyutsii*) operative 1928-32.

AKhRR
The abbreviated name for the Association of Artists of Revolutionary Russia (*Assotsiatsiya khudozhnikov revolyutsionoi Rossii*) operative 1922-8.
Lit A.V.Grigorev et al *4 goda AkhRR. 1922-26. Sbornik*, Moscow, 1926. I.M.Gronsky, V.N.Perlman, eds., *Assosiatsiya khudozhnikov revolyutsionnoi Rossii. Sbornik vospominanii, statei, dokumentov*, Moscow, 1973.

AKIMOV, Ivan Akimovich 1754-1814
A leading academic history painter who featured scenes of Russian history. Born at St. Petersburg. He was a pupil of A.P.Losenko at the Academy in St. Petersburg from 1764. Awarded a gold medal in 1773, he travelled on a scholarship to Italy, visiting Bologna, Venice and Rome. He taught at the Academy from 1779 and became a professor there in 1785. His pupils included A.E.Egorov, G.I.Ugryumov and V.K.Shebuev. He was made an Academician in 1782. He sometimes signed his work 'I.A'. He died at St. Petersburg.
Coll TG; RM; Ryazan Art Museum.

AKIMOV, Nikolai Pavlovich 1901-1968
Designer for theatre and film, also director and graphic artist. Born at Kharkov. In 1914 he was studying at the School for the Encouragement of the Arts, and worked in the studio of S.M.Zeidenberg 1915-16, moving to the New Studio of Dobuzhinsky and B.Shukaev 1915-18.
After the Revolution he worked in the poster studios of Proletkult in Petrograd in 1918. He lived and taught in Kharkov 1920-2 where he began exhibiting in 1921 and where he also took up theatre design including the décor and playbills for his own productions. Between 1922 and 1924 he was at the Leningrad Vkhutemas. He designed for numerous theatres including the Contemporary Theatre in 1924 and the Academic Drama Theatre in 1926, 1927 and 1931. In Moscow he designed for the Vakhtangov Theatre in 1927, 1929 and 1932 as well as the Moscow Art Theatre in 1936. From 1935 he worked for the Leningrad Comedy Theatre and was its chief director 1945-9. He was the director of the Lensovet Theatre in Leningrad 1951-5.
He designed for films from 1928. He produced witty, lively and energetic posters in the 1930s. Amongst his portraits were *Dmitri Shostakovich* 1931 and *S.I.Yutkevich* 1934. He exhibited in New York in 1934 and Paris in 1937. He taught at the Leningrad Institute of Theatre, Music and Cinema 1954-68. He was artistic director, director and designer at the Leningrad Comedy Theatre 1955-68. He won a silver medal at the World Fair in Brussels in 1958. He died in Moscow.
Theatre design 1923 I.Kal'man's *Bayaderka*, Leningrad.

1926 *Evgraf the Adventurer*.
1936 December K.A.Trenev's *Lyubov' yarovaya* (Summer Love) at the Moscow Art Theatre.
1940 December Sheridan's *School for Scandal* at the Moscow Art Theatre.
1945 May A.A.Kron's *Ofitser flota* (Officer of the Fleet) at the Moscow Art Theatre.
Film design 1928 *Tret'ya Molodost'*, Sovkino. 1945 *Kashchey bessmertnyi*, Soyuzdetfil'm. 1947 *Zolushka*, Lenfil'm.
Writings N.P.Akimov *O Teatre*, Leningrad, 1962. N.P.Akimov *Ne Tol'ko o Teatre*, Leningrad, 1966.
Lit. A. Bartashevich *Akimov*, Leningrad, 1933. M.G.Etkind *N.P.Akimov — khudozhnik*, Leningrad, 1960. T.Strizhenova *Iz istorii sovetskogo kostyuma*, Moscow, 1972 (English edition: Tatiana Strizhenova, *Soviet Costume and Textiles 1917-1945*, Paris, 1991).

AKIMOV, Vasili Petrovich 1894-1959+
Monumental and portrait sculptor. Born in the Samara region. He studied art education under F.K.Petrov in Samara 1918-19. He was active as a teacher in schools from 1918 to 1930. He was a member of AKhRR from 1926. He worked at Kuybishev where he executed a frieze for the Palace of Culture 1937-8. He executed numerous portraits of the writers *Gorky* and *Mayakovsky* between 1939 and 1957. Other portraits include an equestrian sculpture of *M.V.Frunze* in Kuybishev in 1947, *Lenin* in 1950 and *Tolstoy* in 1953.
Coll Kuybishev Art Museum.

AKININOV, Aleksei 1849-1877
Painter. Born in the Ryazan region. He studied at the Academy in St. Petersburg under B.P.Villevalde 1872-3.
Coll TG; Kursk Art Gallery.

AKISHIN, Leonid Ilich 1893-1966
Painter.
Coll RM.

AKSEL'ROD, Meer (Mark) Moiseevich 1902-1970
Painter, graphic artist, theatre designer. Born at Molodechno, Belorussia. He studied graphics under P.Ya.Pavlinov and V.A.Favorsky at the Moscow Vkhutein 1921-7. He exhibited in Minsk from 1921. He was a member of the 4 Arts society which was founded in 1924, was included in the major exhibition in Moscow in 1927 marking the tenth anniversary of the Revolution and in the All-Union Polygraphic Exhibition in Moscow in 1927. He contributed to the exhibition of graphic art Liberation Movements: The Sixteenth to the Twentieth Century held in Moscow in 1928 and was included in the 1928 exhibition of Acquisitions by the State Art Collections Fund held in Moscow. He was represented in the exhibition of Russian Graphic Art at Riga and in the First Touring Exhibition of Paintings and Graphics which opened in Moscow in 1929. He taught at the Moscow Vkhutein 1929-30 and in the art faculty of the Moscow Textile Institute 1931-2.
He was represented at the jubilee exhibition Artists of the RSFSR over 15 Years held at the Russian Museum, Leningrad, in 1932. Personal exhibitions were held at Alma-Ata in 1943 and Moscow in 1966. He died in Moscow.
Theatre design He designed for the First Belorussian Jewish Theatre at Minsk 1932-44, and for the Mossovet Theatre, Moscow, in 1936.
Coll Belorussian Art Museum, Minsk; Odessa Art Museum.

ALADZHALOV, Manuil (Emmanuil, Manuk) Khristoforovich 1862-1934
Painter who specialised in landscapes of central Russia. Born at Rostov-on-Don. He studied at the Moscow College under Levitan, V.E.Makovsky and A.K.Savrasov. He exhibited with the Moscow Society of Art Lovers 1892-9, the Wanderers 1900-2, the World of Art in 1903 and the Union of Russian Artists 1908-17. He taught at the Stroganov School from 1902.
After the Revolution his work was included in the First Exhibition of the Moscow Contemporary Art Store in January 1919. He exhibited with the Society of Artist-Realists (OKhR) 1927-8. He died in Moscow.
Coll TG; Museum of History, Architecture and Art of Yaroslav-Rostov; Irkutsk Art Museum; Astrakhan Art Gallery; Perm Art Gallery.

AL'BREKHT, Leonid Pavlovich d.1942
Painter and art restorer. Born at St. Petersburg. He studied under Repin first at Tenisheva's art school and then at the Academy from 1899. He exhibited from 1903. He worked as a restorer for the Hermitage Museum from 1914 until the 1940s.
After the Revolution he participated in the First State Free Exhibition of Artworks in Petrograd in 1919. He died in Leningrad.

ALEKSANDROV, Grigoriy Grigorevich 1897-1959+
Designer. Born in Moscow. He studied at the Stroganov College 1909-17.
After the Revolution he studied under A.V.Lentulov and F.F.Fedorovsky at the Moscow Vkhutemas 1917-24. He exhibited with the First Working Organisaton of Artists in 1924 at the First Discussional Exhibition of Active Revolutionary Art alongside Petruzhkov, A.Vanetsian, M.Sapegin, I.Korolev, K.Loginov, N.Men'shutin, I.Yakovlev and N.Prusakov. He participated in the design of the pavilions at the Exhibitions in Cologne in 1928 and Königsberg 1930-1. He designed the wine industry pavilion at the All-Union Agricultural Exhibition in 1953.

ALEKSANDROV, Yuri Vladimirovich b.1930-1964+
Late Socialist Realist sculptor of monuments and portraits. Born in Moscow. He studied at the Moscow Higher Art Industrial School 1945-54 and exhibited from 1956.
The Geologist N.Doynikov, 1959-60, TG: A three-quarter length portrait of an intellectual hero, rough but sensitive, the twist of the head still employing the conventions of early ikonic images of Lenin.
Coll TG.

ALEKSANDROVA, Tatiana Borisovna 1907-1987
Painter, graphic artist, theatre designer. She studied in the Proletkult studios under L.F.Zhegin from 1921 and at the Moscow Vkhutemas from 1924. She exhibited at the third and last exhibition of the *Makovets* group in Moscow 1925-6.
She exhibited work in Paris in 1928. She was a member of the group *Put' zhivopisi* (Path of Painting) formed by Lev Zhegin in 1927. She was represented at the jubilee exhibition Artists of the RSFSR over 15 Years held at the Russian Museum,

Leningrad, in 1932. She designed for the Central Puppet Theatre in Moscow in the 1930s and also illustrated children's books. From 1957 she worked in industrial graphics producing trade marks.
Coll RM.

ALEKSANDROVICHUS, Pyatras Pavlovich   1906-1950+
Academic genre sculptor.

ALEKSANDROVSKY, Stepan Fedorovich   1842-1906
Portrait painter. Born in Riga. He studied at the Academy in St. Petersburg. He was a founder member of the Society of Russian Watercolourists in 1880 and executed numerous portraits in watercolour including *N.L.Benois* in 1890. He also executed portraits in oils. He died in St. Petersburg.
Coll TG; Kursk Art Gallery; Far East Art Museum, Khabarovsk; Kazakh Art Gallery.

ALEKSEEV, Alcksandr Alekseevich   1811-1878
Portrait painter. He studied under the ikon painter N.S.Krylov and then from 1826 he became the first pupil of Venetsianov. He painted *The Studio of the Artist Venetsianov*, RM, in 1827. He executed a number of copies of works in the Hermitage Museum. He taught at Pskov from 1835.
Coll TG, RM.

ALEKSEEV, Aleksandr Ipat'evich   1842-1911+
Painter. Born in Moscow. He studied at the Moscow College and from 1872 at the Academy in St. Petersburg. He exhibited from 1873 at the Academy, with the Moscow Society of Art Lovers, the St. Petersburg Society of Artists and the Society of Russian Watercolourists. His work included portraits and landscapes, amongst which were views of Italy and of the Crimea.
Coll Saratov Art Museum.

ALEKSEEV, Fedor Yakovlevich   1753/5-1824
Painter of poetic landscapes and an initator of the metier of panoramic views of St. Petersburg, for example *View of the Palace Embankment from the Peter and Paul Fortress*, 1794. He studied at the Academy in St. Petersburg and visited Venice on a scholarship to study theatre design and perspective under D.Moretti and then under P.Gaspari. He employed figures in a manner reminiscent of Canaletto from whose work he made a number of copies (TG, RM). On returning to St. Petersburg he designed for the Imperial Theatres. His first views of St. Petersburg date from the 1780s. He travelled to the Crimea in 1795, producing views of Kherson, Nikolaev (TG, RM) and Bakhchisarai (RM). He also executed views of Moscow which predate the destruction of 1812. These include *Red Square in Moscow* 1801 and *Parade in the Moscow Kremlin* early 1800s. He taught perspective from 1803. M.N.Vorob'iev was amongst his pupils. He died in St. Petersburg. His two hundredth anniversary was marked by exhibitions in Moscow and Leningrad in 1953.
*View of the Palace Embankment from the Peter Paul Fortress, 1794, TG, is somewhat in the tradition ultimately derived from Canaletto. The architecture is meticulously depicted beneath an exquisite sky which bathes the city in a golden light. Figures enliven the foreground and boats float by including a raft with a small shed on it.
Lit A.M.Skvortsov *F.Ya.Alekseev*, Leningrad, 1945. A.A.Fedorov-Davydov *F.Ya.Alekseev*, Moscow, 1955.
Coll Major holdings at TG; RM; History Museum, Moscow.

ALEKSEEV, Georgiy Dmitrievich   1881-1951
Sculptor, graphic artist. Born in the Moscow region. He worked as a graphic artist in a textile factory in Moscow from 1896. He studied under S.A.Korovin, N.A.Kasatkin and V.A.Serov at the Moscow College 1900-7 as a painter. He exhibited with the Wanderers from 1905. He travelled to Western Europe in 1909. He studied sculpture under S.M.Volnukhin and P.P.Trubetskoy at the Moscow College until 1914.
After the Revolution he made a lithographic poster in 1917 of *The First Days of the Revolution* depicting the street fighting with the army attacking the people in a mounted charge whilst the bodies of children and their dolls lay in the snow. He produced drawings of Lenin taken from life in 1918 and he produced a number of portrait busts and full-length figures of Lenin in the period 1919-24. He also designed graphic work for the Rosta poster agency 1921-2. He was a member of AKhR from 1926. He was included in the major exhibition in Moscow in 1927 marking the tenth anniversary of the Revolution. He died in Moscow.
*Karl Marx, RM, a plaster head toned and deeply modelled to give a rough-hewn look.
Coll RM; Central Lenin Museum, Moscow; M.I.Kalinin Museum, Moscow.

ALEKSEEV, Ivan Viktorovich   1894-1964
Painter, ceramics artist, theatre designer. Born in Moscow. He was the brother of the artist O.V.Alekseeva. He studied at the Moscow College from 1911 to 1914 under K.Korovin, S.Korovin, S.Malyutin and Leonid Pasternak. He made designs for the Moscow Chamber Theatre from 1914. He exhibited with the World of Art 1915-16.
After the Revolution he exhibited with the World of Art in December 1917 in Moscow. He exhibited with the Association of Artists of Free Creation in 1918 and his name appeared on the April 1919 list of artists for acquisitions by the proposed Museum of Painterly Culture. He exhibited at the juryless Eighth State Exhibition in Moscow in 1919. At that time he was also engaged in Agitprop decorations with O.V.Alekseeva including the painting of market sheds on Okhotny Row, Moscow (TG). A painting from this time shows the zigzag of huts covered in dazzling Futurist decorations, but the painting itself is reportage and not Futurist at all. From 1920 he made studies for porcelain and glass at the Leningrad and Gusevsky works. Numerous theatre designs followed throughout his career. He taught at Omsk Art School 1939-41 and at Lugansk Art School 1944-52. He was given one-man exhibitions in 1960 and 1962. He died in Moscow.
Theatre design 1914-15 Tairov's production of *Sakuntala* at the Moscow Kamerny (Chamber) Theatre in which Alekseev worked from designs by P.V.Kuznetsov. Numerous later productions were designed for theatres in Moscow (Ermolaeva Theatre 1920-4), in Nikolaev from 1937, Omsk 1939-42 and from 1943 in Lugansk.
Coll Bakhrushin Theatre Museum, Moscow; TG; RM; Pushkin Museum, Moscow; Leningrad Theatre Museum.

ALEKSEEV, Nikolai Mikhailovich   1813-1880
Portrait painter and mosaics artist. Born in the Penza region. He studied at the A.V.Stupin Arzamasskoy School 1820-8 and became its director in the 1830s after a period of study at the Academy. He exhibited from 1830. He was active in mosaics at

the Academy from 1853 and executed mosaics for the Isaak Cathedral. He also painted subjects from the writings of Pushkin and Krylov in the 1860s as well as ikons for churches at Nizhny-Novgorod, Penza and Ural'sk. After 1873 he lived in the Tver region and then at Yaroslavl. He died at Yaroslavl.
Coll TG; Gorky Art Museum.

ALEKSEEV, Nikolai Vasil'evich   **1894-1934**
Graphic artist. Stylistically he was indebted to the techniques evolved by Favorsky. His wood engravings included illustrations to K.A.Fedin's story *Starik* (The Old Man) in 1930.

ALEKSEEV, Ya.   **1753-1824**
Coll TG.

ALEKSEEVA, K. K.   **a.1918-1919**
She was represented at the First Exhibition of Works of the Professional Union of Artists in Moscow in 1918, at the Artists of the Leftist Federation of the Professional Union in 1918 along with Popova, Rodchenko, Tatlin and others and in the Fifth State Exhibition in Moscow 1918-19.

ALEKSEEVA, N.V.   **a.1919**
She exhibited at the juryless Eighth State Exhibition in Moscow in 1919.

ALEKSEEVA, Olga Viktorovna   **b.1895-1954+**
Theatre designer and applied artist. Born Moscow. She was the sister of the artist I.V.Alekseev. She was studying under Konstantin Yuon and Ivan Dudin in 1916.
After the Revolution she studied at the Moscow Vkhutemas 1917-22 under P.V.Kuznetsov and I.I.Nivinsky. Agitprop decorations were executed by her in Moscow in 1918 (see I.V.Alekseev). She exhibited from 1919 when she contributed to the juryless Eighth State Exhibition in Moscow. Theatre designs included A.N.Ostrovsky's *Groza* (The Storm) 1937-8 and A.S.Griboedov's *Gore ot Uma* in 1940. From 1939 to 1953 she made designs for fabrics in Moscow and continued to design for the theatre.

ALEKSEEVA, P.V.   **a.1919**
She exhibited at the juryless Eighth State Exhibition in Moscow in 1919.

ALESHIN, Sergei Semenovich   **1886-1963**
Monumental and portrait sculptor. Born Kaluga region. Studied under N.Andreev at the Stroganov Institute between 1901 and 1911 when he began to exhibit. He taught at the Stroganov Institute from 1911 to 1918. In 1913 he moved to Paris where he studied under Bourdelle. He executed figures for the Bryansk Railway Station, now the Kiev Station, in Moscow.
After the Revolution he taught at the Moscow Institute of Civil Engineering from 1917 to 1924. He also made Agitprop decorations and the *S.Khalturin Monument* in Miuskaya Square, Moscow, in 1918. He won first prize in 1919 for a monument to the Paris Commune submitting a head of Karl Marx (Marx and Engels Museum, Moscow). He was a member of the group Relief in 1922. He taught at the N.E.Bauman Higher Technical School in Moscow from 1924 to 1932. In 1925 he evolved the *Karl Marx Monument* for Sverdlov Square, Moscow, in collaboration with S.Koltsov, S.Mezentsev and G.Kepinov, which surmounted a complex

base by the brothers Aleksandr and Viktor Vesnin. He was included in the major exhibition in Moscow in 1927 marking the tenth anniversary of the Revolution.
He executed a monument to the *February Revolution* in 1929 (RM) and a *Red Army Soldier and Worker* for the Arbatskaya Station of the Moscow Metro in 1935. He executed various monuments to *Marx* in 1923 (variant erected at Penza in 1958) and 1947, and to *Lenin* in 1934, 1952, 1954. From 1932 to 1937 he taught at the V.V.Kuybishev Military Engineering Academy, from 1939 to 1952 at the Moscow Institute of Applied and Decorative Arts, and from 1953 at the M.I.Kalinin Art and Industrial College. He died in Moscow.

AL'MEDINGEN, Boris Alekseevich   **1887-1960**
Theatre designer, painter, architect. Born in St. Petersburg. He studied at the Academy in St. Petersburg under L.N.Benois 1906-15. He worked for the Mariinsky Theatre from 1906 where he assisted A.Ya.Golovin.
After the Revolution he was active as a theatre designer and also, 1926-7, as a designer in films.
Theatre design 1917 January Meyerhold's production of A.Sukhovo-Kobylin's *Marriage of Krechinsky* at the Aleksandrinsky Theatre, Petrograd.
1917 August Meyerhold's production of A.Sukhovo-Kobylin's *Affair* at the Aleksandrinsky Theatre, Petrograd.
1917 October Meyerhold's production of A.Sukhovo-Kobylin's *Tarelkin's Death* at the Aleksandrinsky Theatre, Petrograd. This was essentially a Realist set with striations applied to the walls in a painterly way.
1917 L.N.Andreev's *Milye prizraki* (Dear Spectres) at the Aleksandrinsky Theatre.
Many other theatre designs followed well into the 1950s including work for the Opera and Drama Theatre at Kharkov in 1926 and at the Belorussian Theatre of Youth Workers at Minsk in 1934.
Coll Leningrad Theatre Museum; Bakhrushin Theatre Museum, Moscow.

AL'TMAN, Natan Isaevich   **1889-1970**
Painter, designer for the theatre, ceramics and graphics. Born at Vinnitsa. He studied at the Odessa School of Art under K.Kostandi, L.Ladyzhensky and the sculptor L.Yorina in 1901 or 1902 until 1907. He exhibited with the First Izdebsky International Salon 1909-10 and with the Society of South Russian Artists in 1910. He was a member of the group Apartment No.5 with Tatlin, Bruni and others in the 1910s. He also studied in Paris at the Free Russian Academy of Marie Wassilieff 1910-12 and exhibited at the Salon in 1911.
On his return to Russia he exhibited with the World of Art in 1913 and 1915-16 and at several avant-garde exhibitions including the Union of Youth 1913-14, 0.10. The Last Futurist Exhibition of Paintings in 1915 and the Knave of Diamonds in 1916. He attended meetings at the apartment of Lev Bruni in St. Petersburg 1914-16 along with V.Lebedev, Annenkov, Miturich and others. He taught at the Bernshtein School in Petrograd 1915-17.
In March 1917 he was a founder of the Freedom of Art Association in Petrograd with the artists Isakov and Zdanevich as well as Mayakovsky, Meyerhold, Punin and Prokofiev. He exhibited with the Knave of Diamonds in Moscow in 1917. He executed Agitprop decorations in Palace (*Uritsky*) Square, Petrograd, in 1918 marking the first anniversary of the

Natan Al'tman. Untitled, *1916. Wood relief. 47 x 37 cm.*
Courtesy Annely Juda Fine Art, London.

Revolution. He taught at the Free Art Studios (SVOMAS) in Petrograd 1918-21, and was a member of IZO, the art section of Narkompros.

In January 1919 he became a founder member of *Komfut* (Communist Futurism) in Petrograd. This included the theorists Boris Kushner (chairman) and Osip Brik as well as the poet-painter Mayakovsky and the painter David Shterenberg. Its *Programme Declaration* was published in the periodical *Iskusstvo Kommuny* (Art of the Commune), No.8, 26 January, 1919.

Al'tman was responsible for the revolutionary decoration of Petrograd to mark May Day 1919, heading a committee which included Baranoff-Rossiné, Karev, Matveev, Rudnev and Shkolnik. His name appeared on the April 1919 list of artists for acquisitions by the proposed Museum of Painterly Culture. He was represented at the First State Free Exhibition of Artworks in Petrograd in 1919 and exhibited along with Kandinsky, Chagall and others at the First State Exhibition of Paintings by Local and Moscow Artists held in Vitebsk in December 1919.

He made a series of drawings of Lenin, so called *Leniniana*, from life in the early revolutionary period. His work as a book illustrator included Natan Vengrov *Zverushki* (Little Beasts) published in 1921. He participated in the activities of the Institute of Artistic Culture (INKhUK) in Moscow in 1922. He also collaborated with Chagall and Shterenberg on the exhibition The Three in 1922, was represented at the exhibition of Studies for Theatre Decoration and Works from the Studios of the Decorative Institute held in Petrograd in 1922 and also at the First Russian Art Exhibition in Berlin in 1922. Further exhibitions abroad followed at Venice in 1924,

at the Paris International Exhibition in 1925 and at Dresden in 1926. He participated in the seventh exhibition of the group *L'Araignée* (The Spider) at the Galerie Devambe in Paris in 1925. He was working in Moscow from 1921 to 1928 and was given an exhibition in Leningrad in 1926. He was represented at the Second Exhibition of Cinema Posters held at the Kamerny (Chamber) Theatre, Moscow, in 1926. His work was included in the exhibition of Soviet art held at Harbin in 1926 and in Japan in 1927 and in the major exhibition in Moscow in 1927 marking the tenth anniversary of the Revolution. He was also included in the 1928 exhibition of Acquisitions by the State Art Collections Fund held in Moscow.

In 1928 he emigrated to Paris until 1935 but he also exhibited at New York in 1929 and Stockholm in 1930. He was represented at the jubilee exhibition Artists of the RSFSR over 15 Years held at the Russian Museum, Leningrad, in 1932.

He returned to Leningrad in 1936 and exhibited at Moscow and Leningrad in 1938. He designed many theatrical productions and was engaged in illustrating and designing books. He was awarded a gold medal at the World Fair in Paris in 1937 and was exhibited in Leningrad in 1940, 1941 and 1961. He died in Leningrad.

*Self-portrait, 1916, bronze, TG: A sculpture which manages to be slightly Rodinesque in surface whilst simultaneously echoing Cubo-Futurist devices. This striking self-portrait has a theatrical assertiveness. Al'tman appears in a wide-brimmed hat, a piece of some architectural device or furniture protrudes from the neck, as, following the precedent of Boccioni, Al'tman endeavoured to incorporate the figure's surroundings into the sculpture. Compositionally this counterbalances the vertical thrust of the head and the undulating surface of the hat brim.

*Agitprop Decorations, 1918, Palace Square, Petrograd: Still Al'tman's most celebrated work. He surrounded the Alexander Column outside the Winter Palace with red and orange diagonal motifs that transformed the geometric forms of Suprematist paintings into Futurist flags. In this way he was amongst the first to realise how efficiently the pictorial dynamics of Suprematist painting could be adapted to the purposes of a politicised rhetoric. Elsewhere in the square gigantic drapes depicted heroic images of the peasant and worker amidst large-scale geometric banners.

*Agitprop Porcelain, 1919: A plate by Al'tman illustrates a Futurist factory embraced in heraldic fashion by a sickle and an ear of corn, the whole set within a rhomboid and executed in red-orange against a green background. Around this is the legend 'The World to the Workers'.

*Material Assemblage, 1920, RM: Al'tman was an able synthesiser of current tendencies and this work reveals his sensitivity to several trends. As a relief construction of diverse materials it recalls Tatlin, yet it is also highly pictorial and is perhaps more closely related to the reliefs of those who developed Suprematism three-dimensionally. Klyun and Puni both did this, for example. It is an assemblage of Cubist and Suprematist devices presented with elegance and economy. Its open frontality recalls David Shterenberg's paintings, whilst its compositional scheme appears as systematic as the Purism of Le Corbusier and Ozenfant which had begun to attract Klyun.

Theatre design 1921 *Mystery-Bouffe* by Mayakovsky at the Moscow Circus, designed in part by Al'tman.
1922 *Uriel Acosta* by K.Gutzkow, directed by Aleksei

Natan Al'tman. *Agitprop Decorations in Palace Square, Petrograd, 1918. Documentary photograph.*
Red and orange canvas constructions of Suprematist forms assembled around the Aleksandr Column. The forms are derived from Suprematist painting evolved before the Revolution but here they are adapted to suggest red flags in movement which obscure the extant monument and assert a dynamic and rhetorical style for the public and politicised art of the new regime.

Natan Al'tman. *Agitprop Decorations in Palace Square, Petrograd, 1918. Documentary photograph.*
A gathering of the Petrograd Children's Commune in front of Al'tman's decorations. Some are in historical dress.

Granovsky at the State Jewish Theatre, Moscow, for which Al'tman's set comprised a severely edited and sparse construction of low steps, a platform and background flats at centre, all of which was dominated by an incomplete arch from left, a stark and dramatic setting which left the actors unencumbered.

1922 *The Dybbuk* by S.An-sky (Solomon Rappoport) directed by Evgeni Vakhtangov at the Habimah Theatre, Moscow.

After his return to Russia Al'tman designed for the theatre in Leningrad, Kiev and elsewhere including, for example, 1954 Shakespeare's *Hamlet* at the Pushkin-Leningrad Drama Theatre.

Film design He designed a poster for Aleksei Granovsky's film *Evreiskoe Schastie* (Jewish Luck) in 1925.

1955-56 *Don Quixote*, Lenfil'm.

Illustration Cover for Marcel Aymé *Les Contes du chat perché*, Paris, 1934.

Lit A.Efros *Portret Al'tmana*, Moscow, 1922. M.Osborn *Evreyskaya grafika N.Al'tmana*, Berlin, 1923. B.Arvatov *N.Al'tman*, Petrograd-Berlin, 1924. W.George, I.Ehrenburg *Nathan Altman*, Paris, 1933. A retrospective exhibition was held in Leningrad in 1968, exh. cat. M.Etkind *N.A.*, Moscow, 1971. C.Lodder *Russian Constructivism*, New Haven and London, 1983. Nancy Van Norman Baer *Theatre in Revolution, Russian Avant-Garde Stage Design 1913-1935*, San Francisco and London, 1991. D.Elliott, V.Dudakov *100 Years of Russian Painting*, London, 1991.

Coll TG; RM; Bakhrushin Theatre Museum, Moscow; Lenin Museum, Moscow; Perm Museum; Sammlung Ludwig, Cologne.

ALTUKHOV, Iov Kornilovich   b.1884-1960+
Sculptor. Born at Koleno in the Voronezh region. He was fellow student with Tatlin at the Moscow College c.1911. He graduated in 1915.

His work included bas-reliefs for the theatre at Leninakan in 1927 and an obelisk *Sever* (The North) 1929-30.

He taught at the Abramtsevo Art and Industrial College 1942-60. He was working at the village of Khot'kovo, Moscow region, in the 1960s.

AL'VANG, V. A.   a.1918
Architect, artist. 1918 Agitprop decorations at Sampsonievsky Bridge, Petrograd.

ALYAKRINSKY, Petr Aleksandrovich   1892-1961
Painter, theatre designer, graphic artist. He studied at the Moscow College under S.V.Ivanov 1909-10. He exhibited from 1910. He worked as a theatre designer in Ryazan and Kozlov in 1917.

After the Revolution he became a member of the Art Section of the People's Commissariat of the Enlightenment (IZO Narkompros) in 1917 in Moscow. He taught in the Free State Studios in Yaroslavl 1918-21, headed the local Rosta poster section and was engaged in the restoration of architectural monuments. He returned to Moscow in 1922 where he provided illustrations to many books and periodicals. He exhibited at Leipzig in 1927 and at Amsterdam in 1929. He produced propaganda posters in the Second World War.

Theatre design *Spring* 1930s.

Coll Lenin Museum, Moscow; Gorky Museum, Moscow; Irkutsk Art Museum; Kursk Art Gallery.

AMMON (AMMONT), Vladimir Fedorovich   1826-1879
Painter of views and landscapes. He studied at the Stroganov School and in the 1840s at the Moscow College under K.I.Rabus. He was a participant of the first Wanderers Exhibition. He died in Moscow.

Coll RM.

AMMOSOV (AMOSOV), Sergei Nikolaevich   1837-1886
Landscape painter. He studied at the Stroganov School and at the Moscow College under A.K.Savrasov 1860-4. He worked in Moscow. He was a founder member of the Wanderers and a participant in its first exhibition. He was painting at Orenburg 1874-5. He also painted portraits. He died in Moscow.

Coll TG; Uzbek Art Museum.

AMOSOVA (-BUNAK), Olga Fedorovna   b.1892-1952+
Graphic artist, painter, theatre and film designer. Born at St. Petersburg. She studied under Ya.S.Gol'dblat in St. Petersburg 1903-5 and then in Rome from 1911 to 1914. She exhibited from 1912. She was given an exhibition at Tsarskoe Tselo in 1915.

After the Revolution she participated in the First State Free Exhibition of Artworks in Petrograd in 1919. She designed for the theatre in Moscow from 1918 to 1923 and also worked on films. She contributed to the exhibition Art of Moscow Theatre 1918-1923 held in Moscow in 1923.

She worked in graphic design for Goznak, designing stamps for example, 1928-31. Later she illustrated books and executed landscapes and portraits.

Theatre design B.Bromme's *Maskotta* at the Operetta Theatre. M.Martine's *Night* at the Theatre of the Revolution.

Film design 1918-19 A.A.Khanzhonkov's *Krotkaya*. 1918-19 *Timbuts - groza Parizha*.

Coll Bakhrushin Theatre Museum, Moscow.

ANDERSON, A. P.   a.1919
He participated in the First State Free Exhibition of Artworks in Petrograd in 1919.

ANDREENKO (-NECHITAYLO), Mikhail Fedorovich 1894-1982
Theatre designer, painter, writer. Born at Kherson, Ukraine. He studied law at St. Petersburg University whilst also, from 1912, attending the Society for the Encouragement of the Arts under Bilibin and Roerich and Rylov. He exhibited from 1914 at the Dobychina Bureau, the Union of Art Workers and Contemporary Trends in Petrograd as well as at the 1914 International Exhibition of Book Design and Graphics at Leipzig. He also designed for the Savurin Theatre, Petrograd.

After the Revolution he returned to Kherson in 1917 before moving to Odessa 1918-19 where he designed for Konstantin Miklashevsky's Odessa Chamber Theatre 1918-19 and theatre design became his primary activity.

He moved to Bucharest in 1920 then worked in Prague in 1921. In 1923 he settled in Paris but ceased to work for the theatre in 1928 turning instead to painting and writing. His designs were in a lively, rather geometric style derived from Constructivist example. A one-man exhibition was held at the Galerie Houston-Brown, Paris, in 1964.

Theatre design 1918-19 Plautus' *Menaechmi* at the Odessa Chamber Theatre.

1919 March *The Four Lady-Killers* at the Odessa Chamber Theatre.

1921 *Harlequin's Millions* (*Les Millions d'Arlequin*), opera-ballet

Boris Anisfel'd. Costume Study for an Arab Dancer in the Ballet 'Islamey', *1912. Gouache, pencil, silver and gold. 44.2 x 30.6 cm. The ballet to music by M.A.Balakirev was devised by M.M.Fokine for the Mariinsky Theatre, St. Petersburg. Collection Mr. and Mrs. Nikita D.Lobanov-Rostovsky, London.*

Le Carnaval and Schéhérazade in Paris.
1910-12 M.A.Balakirev's ballet Islamey produced by M.Fokine at the Mariinsky Theatre, St. Petersburg. A design in purple and orange for the costume of a female dancer shows a stylisation and decorative richness reminiscent of Bakst but with a less firm line.
1911 June Rimsky-Korsakov's opera-ballet Sadko - au royaume sous-marin produced by Diaghilev with choreography by M.Fokine at the Théâtre du Châtelet, Paris. Redesigned by

Goncharova in 1916.
1911 executed Benois' designs for Diaghilev's production of Petrushka in Paris.
1912 Ballet Islamey to music by M.A.Balakirev, choreographed by Fokine at the Mariinsky Theatre, St. Petersburg.
1913 Ballet to Liszt's Preludes, choreographed by Fokine for Anna Pavlova.
1913 An Egyptian Night (Une Nuit d'Egypte), ballet based on a text by T.Gautier set to music by A.S.Arensky, choreographed

Yuri Annenkov. Construction, *1919. 71 x 52 cm. Signed lower right.*
This work incorporates Suprematist forms in card, paper, drawing and wood as well as wire and a photograph of Notre Dame in Paris. Several kinds of depiction are assembled together. The elliptical lines of the wire suggest a reference to diagrams of atomic structure current by 1919. Within the composition they balance the rose window of Notre Dame as if to suggest a new image of the world equivalent but replacing the older view. The geometric forms then suggest the elements of a new architecture.
Thyssen Collection, courtesy Annely Juda Fine Art, London.

by Fokine and performed by the Fokine Ballet Company at the Royal Opera, Stockholm.
1913 *Les Préludes* for Anna Pavlova at the Manhattan Opera House.
1914 Vaslav Nijinsky's production of *Les Sylphides* in London.
1919 Xavier Laroux's *La Reine Fiammette* at the Metropolitan Opera, New York.
1919 December Maurice Maeterlinck's *L'Oiseau Bleu*, opera with music by Albert Wolff, at the Metropolitan Opera, New York.
1921 S.Prokofiev's *Love of Three Oranges* at the Chicago Opera.
1922 *The Snow Maiden*, libretto by A.Ostrovsky, music by Rimsky-Korsakov, Metropolitan Opera Company, New York.
1926 Puccini's *Turandot* (unrealised).
Lit *Boris Anisfeldt: 20 Years of Design for the Theater*, exh. cat., Smithsonian Institution, Washington, D.C., 1971. *Diaghilev and Russian Stage Designers, a Loan Exhibition from the Collection of Mr. and Mrs. N.Lobanov-Rostovsky*, International Exhibitions Foundation, Washington, 1972-4. *Boris Anisfeldt*, exh. cat., William Benton Museum of Art, University of Connecticut, Storrs, 1979. *Paintings by Boris Anisfeld*, exh. cat., Adler Fine Arts, New York, 1979-80. *Boris Anisfeld*, exh. cat., Gilman Galleries, Chicago, 1981-2. J.E.Bowlt *Russian Stage Design.*

Scenic Innovation. From the Collection of Mr. and Mrs. Nikita D.Lobanov-Rostovsky, Jackson, MS, exh. cat.,1982. E.Kashey *Boris Anisfeld in St. Petersburg*, exh. cat., Shepherd Gallery, New York, 1984. Dzhon Boult (John Bowlt) *Khudozhniki russkogo teatra. Sobranie Nikity i Niny Lobanovykh-Rostovskikh*, Moscow, 1991.
Coll TG; RM; Brodsky Museum, Leningrad; Bakhrushin Theatre Museum, Moscow; Lobanov-Rostovsky Collection, London.

ANISIMOV, V. K.   **a.1912**
He was a member of the *Oslinyy Khvost* (Donkey's Tail) group with Larionov, Goncharova and others in 1912.

ANISIMOV, Yu. I.   **a.1913**
Painter. He contributed to Larionov's exhibition The Target in Moscow in 1913.

ANNENKOV, Yuri (Georges) Pavlovich   **1889-1974**
Graphic artist, painter and designer for the theatre and film. He was an able and elegant synthesiser of styles. Born at Petropavlovsk on Kamchatka. He was already producing political caricatures by 1905-6. He studied privately in St. Petersburg under Savelii M.Zeidenberg 1908-9 and under Yan Tsionglinsky 1909-10.
He travelled to Paris where he studied under Maurice Denis

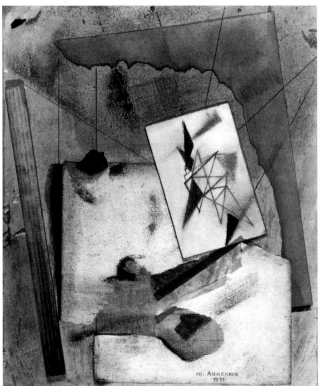

Yuri Annenkov. Abstract Collage of Materials, *1920. Collage on card. 31 x 26 cm. Signed lower right.*
Ripped paper implies old plans abandoned. The complete drawing made of straight lines emerges as a priority. Its angular rhythms are contained also in the overall composition of the collage.
Courtesy Annely Juda Fine Art, London.

Yuri Annenkov. The Storming of the Winter Palace. *Drawing.*
Futurist images of the city were constructed against the actual buildings of
Palace Square for the politicised rewriting of Revolutionary events staged in
situ as a mass pageant. The black areas indicate a dense mass of participants.

Yuri Annenkov. The Writer Zamyatin, *1921. Signed lower right.*
The style, which combines transparent geometric planes with recognisable
portraiture, is characteristic of Annenkov's energetic but light touch.

and Félix Vallotton 1911-12. In 1913 he was in Switzerland.
On his return to St. Petersburg he was associated with the
Union of Youth. He developed his great facility and
immediacy as a draughtsman and illustrator by contributing to
the periodicals *Satirikon*, *Lukomor'e* and *Solntse Rossii* in the
period 1913-17. He also developed as a theatre designer in St.
Petersburg and Moscow in the period 1913-15. He attended
meetings at the appartment of Lev Bruni in St. Petersburg
1914-16 along with V.Lebedev, Al'tman, Miturich and others.
After the Revolution his name appeared on the April 1919 list
of artists for acquisitions by the proposed Museum of
Painterly Culture and he contributed to the exhibition of
Paintings by Russian Artists held at Pskov in Spring 1920.
Amongst the continuous stream of portrait drawings executed
in a stylised Cubo-Futurist idiom was a portrait of H.G.Wells
at the House of Arts in Petrograd in 1920.
In 1918 he had illustrated the poem *The Twelve* by Aleksandr
Blok. In 1923 a French edition, *Les Douze*, was issued by the
publisher Au Sans Pareil in Paris in a translation by Y.Sidersky.
Annenkov's dramatic designs employed loosely Cubist
techniques, elegantly transformed into precise black and white
illustrations, all pervaded by expressive details which
occasionally but unmistakably recalled the drawings of George
Grosz who was receiving recognition as an honorary
Constructivist in Russia at that time. He made portraits of many
celebrated figures of the early revolutionary years including
Lenin, Lunacharsky, Akhmatova, Evreinov, Sologub, Chukovsky,
Al'tman and *Efros.* In 1920 he designed the pageant *The Hymn to*
Liberated Labour in collaboration with M.V.Dobuzhinsky and
V.A.Shchuko in front of the old stock exchange in Petrograd.
His most celebrated revolutionary work was his involvement on
7 November 1920 in the mass pageant of the re-enactment of
The Storming of the Winter Palace directed by Nikolai Evreinov
in Palace Square (formerly Uritsky Square), Petrograd. This
involved 6,000 actors and 500 musicians.
He was represented at the First Russian Art Exhibition in
Berlin in 1922 and also at the exhibition of Studies for

Theatre Decoration and Works from the Studios of the
Decorative Institute held in Petrograd in 1922. He executed a
lithographic portrait of the theatre director Meyerhold in
1922.
He illustrated and designed numerous books. His work was
represented in Venice in 1924.
From 1924 he lived in France and Germany working as a theatre
and cinema artist. He was represented in the international
exhibitions in Paris in 1925 and Leipzig in 1927. He was a
founder member of the Society of Easel Painters in 1925.
He contributed to the exhibition of Contemporary Russian
Art held at Philadelphia in 1932. He died in Paris.
Theatre design c.1913 Nikolai Evreinov's *Homo Sapiens* at
the Krivoe Zerkalo (Crooked Mirror) Cabaret in St.
Petersburg.
1914 Dickens' *A Christmas Carol* at the Vera Komissarzhevskaya
Theatre.
1915 Fedor Sologub's *Night Dancers* at the Vera
Komissarzhevskaya Theatre.
1919 Lev Tolstoy's *The First Distiller* produced by Annenkov
and Meyerhold at the Hermitage Theatre, Petrograd.
1921 N.Evreinov's *The Chief Thing* at the Theatre of Free
Comedy, Petrograd.
1922 Georg Kaiser's *Gas.*
1924 A.Tolstoy's *Mutiny of the Machines.*
Illustrations numerous including: N.Evreinov *Teatr dlya sebya*
(Theatre For Itself), with N.Kul'bin, Petrograd, 1915-16.
Writings Yu.Annenkov *Portrety*, Petropolis, 1922.
Yu.Annenkov *Dnevnik moikh vstrech*, New York, 1966.
Annenkov *La révolution derrière la porte*, Paris, 1988.
Lit P.Courthion *Georges Annenkov*, Paris, 1930. *Russian*
Painters and the Stage 1884-1965, a loan exhibition of stage and
costume designs from the Collection of Mr. and Mrs. Nikita D.
Lobanov-Rostovsky, exh. cat., University of Texas at Austin,

Aleksei Antropov. Tsar Peter III, *1762. Oil on canvas. 58.3 x 46.8 cm.*

1978-9. *Paris-Moscou*, 1979. J.E.Bowlt *Russian Stage Design. Scenic Innovation. From the Collection of Mr. and Mrs. Nikita D.Lobanov-Rostovsky*, Jackson, MS, exh. cat.,1982. *Twilight of the Tsars*, London, 1991. Nancy Van Norman Baer *Theatre in Revolution, Russian Avant-Garde Stage Design 1913-1935*, San Francisco and London, 1991. Dzhon Boult (John Bowlt) *Khudozhniki russkogo teatra. Sobranie Nikity i Niny Lobanovykh-Rostovskikh*, Moscow, 1991.
Coll Bakhrushin Theatre Museum, Moscow; Ivanovo Art Museum.
Colour plate p.55.

ANREP, Boris Vaslievich 1883-1969
Poet, critic and mosaic artist. He lived in London and Paris after 1917.

ANTOKOLSKY, Mark Matveevich 1843-1902
Major history and figure sculptor who designed numerous busts, monuments and made many terracotta maquettes some of which recall the handling of Carpeaux. He was born at Vilno. In the late 1850s he assisted in the construction of the iconostasis for churches. From 1862 he worked with N.S.Pimenov and 1863-8 with I.I.Reymers. He exhibited from 1862 and in 1868 he was associated with the Academy in Berlin. He became a very able academic sculptor.
He lived abroad in Rome and Paris after 1871 but continued to exhibit in Russia. He contributed to the first exhibition of the Wanderers 1870-1. Exhibitions of his work were held in St. Petersburg in 1872, 1880 and 1893.
His work included a series of *trompe-l'oeil* high reliefs of figures in windows in 1865, RM, also *Socrates*, 1875, RM, and *Spinoza*, 1882, RM, He was a member of the Academies of Paris, Berlin and Urbino. He died in Germany. Exhibitions were held in Moscow and Leningrad in 1937 and 1952.

Ivan the Terrible, 1871, bronze, RM, for which he was made an Academician. A piece of impressive costume drama in which the seated Tsar appears authoritative and fierce.
Mephistopheles, 1883, marble, RM, inscribed 'Antokolsky Paris 1883'. This is an angular male model of a certain age posed impishly upon a boulder, his elbows on his knees and his chin upon his hands.
Lit V.V.Stasov (ed.) *M.M.Antokol'sky. Ego zhizn', tvoreniya, pis'ma i stat'i*, St. Petersburg, 1905. A.D.Alferov *M.M.Antokol'sky*, Moscow, 1905. L.Varshavsky *M.M.Antokol'sky*, Moscow, 1944. A.K.Lebedev, G.Burova *Tvorchestvoe sodruzhestvo. M.M.Antokol'sky i V.V.Stasov*, Leningrad, 1968.
Coll Well represented at RM; TG; Irkutsk Art Museum; Kiev Museum of Russian Art; Perm Art Gallery; Victoria and Albert Museum, London.

ANTONOV, F. V. b.1904-1937+
Theatre designer. He was represented at the jubilee exhibition *Artists of the RSFSR over 15 Years* held at the Russian Museum, Leningrad, in 1932.
Theatre design 1937 April Meyerhold's unperformed production of L.Seifulina's *Natasha* for the Meyerhold Theatre.

ANTONOV, Mikhail Ivanovich 1771-1829+
Landscape and portrait painter. He worked with Venetsianov at Safonkov from 1837 to the early 1840s. In 1845 he made views of Korsun' in the Kiev region and in the South of Russia. He also executed views of St. Petersburg.
Coll TG.

ANTONOVSKY, Boris Ivanovich 1891-1934
Caricaturist, graphic artist and film artist. He studied at the Odessa Institute until 1914 and drew caricatures for Odessa journals from 1909.
After the Revolution his work was published in the journal *Krasnyy Voron* (Red Raven) 1922-3. Many other publications followed of his satirical work. He participated in the seventh exhibition of the group *L'Araignée* (The Spider) at the Galerie Devambe in Paris in 1925. He taught at the Leningrad Vkhutein 1928-9. He designed for films in the early 1930s. He died in Leningrad.
Lit *B.Antonovsky*, Moscow, 1930. *B.Antonovsky. Izbrannye risunki*, Moscow, 1961.

ANTROPOV, Aleksei Petrovich 1716-1795
Portraitist to the Imperial Court. Born at St. Petersburg. He studied under A.M.Matveev from 1732, M.A.Zakharov in 1734 and Louis Caravacque from 1739. He worked in St. Petersburg and Moscow. During the 1740s and 1750s he worked in the Painting Detachment of the Building Office executing palace murals including ceiling paintings at the Winter Palace, the Summer Palace and at Tsarskoe Selo under D.Valeriani and A.Perezinotti in the period 1744-9. He was working in Kiev in 1752 and in Moscow in 1755. He also painted ikons. He became President of the Academy of Arts which opened in 1758. His Imperial portraits included the *Empress Elizabeth*, 1751, TG, and the *Tsar Peter III*, 1762, TG. He died in St. Petersburg. An exhibition of his work was held in Moscow in 1966.
Portrait of A.M.Izmailova, 1759, is an intense court portrait with a solidity to it which is distinct from its French or English equivalents. It is grand portraiture in finest clothes

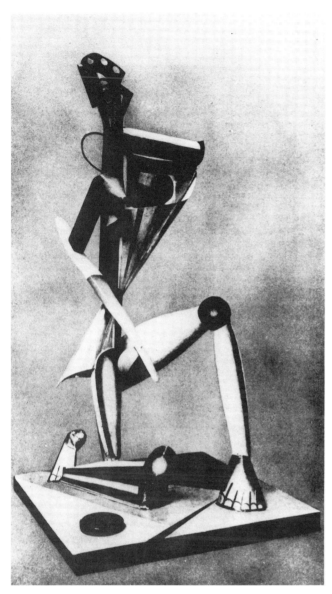

Alexandre Archipenko. Médrano I, *1912. Painted wood, glass, sheet metal, wire, found objects. 96.5 cm. high. Destroyed. Documentary photograph.*

and with medals in place.
Lit A.Savinov *A.P.Antropov*, Moscow-Leningrad, 1947.
Coll TG; RM.
See p.17.

ANTROPOV, Anatoli Petrovich   b.1906-1960+
Sculptor. Born in Moscow. He studied under A.T.Matveev at the Institute of Proletarian Art in Leningrad until 1931 and exhibited from 1932. His work included portraits of *Romain Rolland* 1936, a monument to *Gorky* 1939 and various sculptures for industrial exhibitions. See S.M.Orlov.

ANUFRIEV = ANDREEV, N.A.

**APOSTOLI (TRIONDAFILOS), Vladimir Aleksandrovich
1890-1942**
Painter. Born at Saratov. He studied at Kazan School of Art and at the Academy under D.N.Kardovsky 1912-18.
After the Revolution he was engaged in Agitprop projects at

Saratov in the early revolutionary years. He worked at Astrakhan, Saratov and Leningrad. He was included in the enormous survey Exhibition of Paintings by Petrograd Artists of All Tendencies 1919-1923 held in Petrograd in 1923. He illustrated a number of books. He died in Leningrad.

APSIT (APSITIS), Aleksandr Petrovich   1880-1944
Latvian graphic artist. He was a major soviet poster designer. Born at Riga. He studied under L.E.Dmitriev-Kavkazsky in St. Petersburg 1898-9. Between 1902 and 1906 he produced illustrations for periodicals including *Rodina* (Native Land), *Zvezda* (Star) and *Niva* (Field) as well as illustrations to works

Alexandre Archipenko. Seated Nude, *1911. Bronze. 60 x 32 x 34 cm. Musée National d'Art Moderne, Paris.*

by Gorky, Leskov and Chekhov and others.
After the Revolution he became one of the most active designers of political posters from 1918 onwards using various pseudonyms including A-t, Aspid, A.Petrov, Osiyanin and Skif. He also illustrated works by D.Bedny, I.S.Nikritin and M.E.Saltykov-Shchedrin.
He lived in Latvia from 1921. He died in Germany.
*A Year of the Dictatorship of the Proletariat depicts a distant blaze of sun behind the city factories before which throngs a procession of workers carrying banners and flags through the fields. Framing this a worker and a peasant tread underfoot the symbols of tsardom and their chains.
Lit *Apsit*, Riga, 1959.
Coll Perm Art Gallery; Art Museum of Latvia.

APTER, Yakov Natanovich   1899-1941
Graphic artist. Born at Shpola in the Kiev region. He studied at the Odessa Art school 1915-18 and then under V.A Favorsky in Moscow 1924-9. He was represented at the jubilee exhibition Artists of the RSFSR over 15 Years held at the Russian Museum, Leningrad, in 1932. He was killed at the front during the Second World War.
Coll Pushkin Museum, Moscow.

APUSHKIN, A.V.   a.1919
He exhibited at the juryless Eighth State Exhibition in Moscow in 1919.

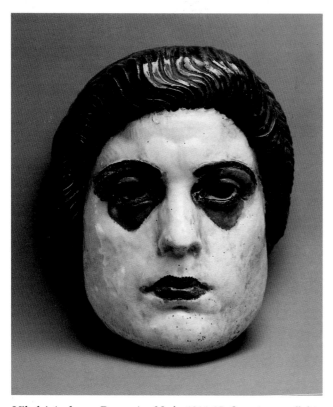

Nikolai Andreev. Decorative Mask. *1914-15. Ceramic enamelled in colours. 38.5 x 31 x 18.5 cm.*
State Tretyakov Gallery, Moscow.

ARAKELYAN, Sedrak Arakelovich   1884-1942
Painter. Born in Armenia. He studied at Tiflis Art School under E.M.Tatevosyan and B.A.Fogel' 1904-8 and at the Moscow College under A.Arkhipov, A.M.Vasnetsov and K.A.Korovin 1908-17. He taught at the Erevan Technical School 1921-35. His work was included in international exhibitions at Venice in 1924, New York in 1929 and Stockholm in 1930. He produced panoramic Socialist Realist works. He died at Erevan. Exhibitions of his work were held at Erevan in 1942 and at Erevan and Moscow in 1957.
Baking Bread, 1914, Armenian Art Gallery, Erevan, colourful interior with work going on.
Gathering in the Cotton, 1930, TG, has a large number of women workers in local dress picking cotton and dotted across the landscape as far as the eye can see to where the distant mountains rise. In the foreground it is packed into bags to be loaded on to camels. The colour is light to support this celebration of communal agricultural labour.
Coll TG; Armenian Art Gallery, Erevan.

ARAPOV, Anatoli Afanas'evich   1876-1949
Painter, theatre and film designer. Born at St. Petersburg. He studied at the Moscow College 1897-1906. His first theatre designs date from 1905 and he designed for several theatres including the Moscow Art Theatre and the V.F. Komissarzhevsky Theatre. He was influenced by the Blue Rose group with whom he exhibited in 1907 and he exhibited in Diaghilev's display of Russian art at the Salon d'Automne, Paris, in 1906. He contributed to the *Stefanos* exhibition 1907-8. He exhibited with the Union of Russian Artists in 1910 and with the World of Art 1911-13 and 1917.
After the Revolution he exhibited with the World of Art in December 1917 in Moscow. He showed work in the Fifth State Exhibition in Moscow 1918-19 and was involved in numerous theatrical productions including Rimsky-Korsakov's *Pskovityanka* at the Bolshoi Theatre in Moscow in 1919. He also designed productions at the Moscow Art Theatre and the Maly Theatre as well as theatres in Vitebsk and Saratov. He worked on film design from 1926. Exhibitions of his work were held in Moscow in 1941 and 1946 and posthumously in 1954. He died in Moscow.
Theatre design 1916 October: Tairov's production of the pantomime *Pokryvalo P'eretty* (Pierrette's Veil) to music by Dohnany.
1918 A.K.Tolstoy's *Posadnik* (The Mayor) at the Maly Theatre in Moscow, a vigorous design dominated by a domed Moscow Kremlin Cathedral.
Lit E.Rakitina *A.A.Arapov*, Moscow, 1965. *Twilight of the Tsars*, London, 1991.
Coll Saratov Art Museum; Bakhrushin Theatre Museum, Moscow; Museum of the Maly Theatre, Moscow.

ARAPOVA, Yulia   a.1925
Painter. She was a member of Filonov's school, the Collective of Masters of Analytical Art, established in Leningrad in 1925.

ARCHIPENKO, Alexandre (ARKHIPENKO, Aleksandr Porfir'evich)   1887-1964
Sculptor and painter. A major figure in the development of Cubist sculpture in Paris. Born at Kiev, Ukraine. His grandfather was an ikon painter and his father an engineer. He studied at Kiev School of Art 1902-5. He exhibited in the Ukraine in 1906 before moving to Moscow where he began to

Nikolai Andreev. Bacchante on a Goat. *1905. Terracotta group painted in polychrome. 46.5 x 55 x 21 cm.*
State Tretyakov Gallery, Moscow.

contribute to group exhibitions.

He then settled in Paris in 1908 and associated with the artists of La Ruche in Montparnasse. His contacts with Modigliani and other Parisian artists led him into a central role in Cubist sculpture and made him an important figure for Russian artists visiting Paris in the Cubist years. He opened his own art school in Paris in 1912. He began to develop sculpto-paintings in 1912 as a synthesis of painting and sculpture. He exhibited at the Salon des Indépendants 1910-14, including the Cubist room there in 1911, at the Salon d'Automne 1911-13 and at the Section d'Or exhibition of 1912.

His development of mixed-media high relief works led to wholly free-standing constructions, notably *Médrano I* (p.49) of 1912, a figure half kneeling made of wood, glass, sheet metal, metal wire, found objects and paint. He held an exhibition at the Folkwang Museum at Hagen in Germany in 1912, exhibited 57 works with the gallery *Der Sturm* in Berlin in 1913, and was represented at the Armory Show in New York in 1913. Popova visited him in Paris in 1913 and in 1914 he exhibited with Olga Rozanova and Aleksandra Exter at the Sprovieri Gallery in Rome.

He was in Nice 1914-18. After the war he exhibited widely. He travelled in Europe 1919-21 and directed an art school in Germany during the period 1921-3. He was represented at the First Russian Art Exhibition in Berlin in 1922. He executed

mobile paintings which he called *Archipentura* in 1924.

He settled in the United States in 1923 where he opened an art school in New York, and he obtained U.S. citizenship in 1928. He held an exhibition in Japan in 1927. He contributed to the exhibition of Contemporary Russian Art held at Philadelphia in 1932.

He taught at the University of Washington 1935-6 and later at Kansas City. In 1938 he was teaching at Moholy-Nagy's New Bauhaus. During 1939 his work was confiscated from German museums. He opened a sculpture studio in New York in 1939 and taught there, as well as lecturing at numerous other institutions, until his last years. He died in New York.

*Médrano II, 1913, Guggenheim Museum, New York: A polychrome standing figure in very high relief, constructed from diverse materials and partly painted. Close in kind to experiments by Klyun and Baranoff-Rossiné, this work is one of the origins of constructed sculpture along with *Médrano I* which is now lost.

Lit I.Goll, T.Däubler, B.Cendrars *Archipenko Album*, Potsdam, 1921. N.Golubetz *Archipenko*, Lwow, 1922. H.Hildebrandt *Alexander Archipenko*, Berlin, 1923 (4 language edition). L.Mitzitch *Archipenko. Plastique nouvelle*, Belgrade, 1923. D.H.Karshan *Archipenko: International Visionary*, Washington, 1969. D.H.Karshan *Archipenko: the Sculpture and*

Ivan Argunov. Peasant Woman in Russian Costume, *1784. Oil on canvas. 67 x 53.6 cm.*
State Tretyakov Gallery, Moscow.

Ivan Argunov. Sir Samuel Treit of Inverkeithing, Grand Admiral of Russia under Empress Catherine the Great. *Oil on canvas.153.9 x 123.1 cm.*

Graphic Work, Tübingen, 1974.
Coll His work is in numerous collections including MNAM, Paris; The Guggenheim Museum, New York and the Philadelphia Museum of Art.
See page 49.

ARGUNOV (ORGUNOV), Ivan Petrovich   1727-1803
Court portrait painter. He had been a serf to the family of Counts Sheremetev. An ikon by him dates from 1749 but he painted a *Dying Cleopatra* in 1750, TG. He was an organiser of the Academy of Arts in 1758. He painted the *Empress Catherine II* in 1762, RM, and many other portraits. He sometimes signed his work *Orgunov* or *Argunoff*. He died in Moscow.
Peasant Woman in Russian Costume, 1784, TG, has qualities comparable with the work of Venetsianov. It is a superbly finished portrait with a tall headdress and calm rounded forms.
Portrait of P.I.Kovaleva-Zhemchugova, 1803, reveals some technical difficulties with perspective but a sophisticated use of a striped costume to describe the contours of the figure.
Coll TG; RM; Ostankino Palace Museum; Museum of Russian Art, Kiev.

ARGUNOV, Nikolai Ivanovich   1771-1829+
Portrait painter. He was the son of the painter I.P.Argunov. In 1797 he was given permission to make copies in the Hermitage and these included works by Rembrandt, Angelica Kaufman and others. He was primarily a portrait painter however. He sometimes signed his work 'Argounoff'. An exhibition of his work was held at the Ostankino Palace Museum im 1951.
Coll TG; RM; Ostankino Palace Museum.

ARIONESKO-BALLER, Lidiya   a.1909-1910
She exhibited with Nikolai Kul'bin's Impressionists 1909-10. Her husband was the artist A.I.Ball'er.

ARKHANGEL'SKY, Dmitriy Ivanovich   1885-1940+
Graphic artist, painter. Born at Simbirsk where he studied under P.I.Puzyrevsky but without receiving formal academic training. In 1908 he won a silver medal at an exhibition in Simbirsk for his views of Simbirsk and the Volga. He was a school teacher in Simbirsk 1908-16.
After the Revolution he was included in the 1928 exhibition of Acquisitions by the State Art Collections Fund held in Moscow. He lived in Moscow from 1934. Exhibitions were held in Kazan in 1926 and 1953 as well as Moscow in 1955 and 1956.
Coll Central State Lenin Museum, Moscow.

ARKHIPENKO, A. P. = ARCHIPENKO, A.

ARKHIPOV, Abram Efimovich   1862-1930
Painter of peasant themes reminiscent of the dynamic loose style of Malyavin. He also painted landscapes and portraits. He was one of the so-called Young Wanderers. Born of a peasant family in the Ryazan region. He studied at the Moscow College 1877-83 and 1886-7, first under Perov, Pryanishnikov and A.K.Savrasov, and then under V.E.Makovsky and V.D.Polenov

Nikolai Argunov. Unknown Man. *Oil on canvas. Inscribed 'N.Argunoff'. 100 x 71 cm.*
National Museum, Warsaw.

from 1882. In between these periods he studied at the Academy in St. Petersburg under Chistyakov 1884-5. He travelled extensively to Central Russia and to the White Sea. He produced illustrations for periodicals and books in the 1880s. He exhibited with the Wanderers from 1889 and became a member in 1891. He was made an Academician in 1898. He taught at the Moscow College from 1894 to 1918. He exhibited at the International Exhibition in Paris in 1900, with the group 36 Artists from 1901 and he joined the Union of Russian Artists in 1903. He exhibited with the World of Art in 1903. He travelled abroad in 1896, exhibited in Rome in 1911 and again visited France, Germany and Italy in 1912. He designed a poster for the Red Cross in 1914 depicting two nurses against the background of a smoking landscape.

After the Revolution he produced a sequence of portraits of peasants from different regions. His name appears on the April 1919 list of artists for acquisitions by the proposed Museum of Painterly Culture and he was represented at the Nineteenth Exhibition of the All-Russian Exhibitions Bureau in Moscow in 1920.

He was represented at the First Russian Art Exhibition in Berlin in 1922 and he joined the Association of Artists of Revolutionary Russia (AKhRR) the same year. He taught at the Moscow Vkhutemas from 1922 to 1924 and exhibited in Venice in 1924. By this time his paintings of peasants and labour had taken on a new significance. His work was included in the exhibition of Soviet art held at Harbin in 1926 and in Japan in 1927 and in the major exhibition in Moscow in 1927 marking the tenth anniversary of the Revolution. He was included in the 1928 exhibition of Acquisitions by the State Art Collections Fund held in Moscow and also represented at exhibitions in New York in 1929 and Stockholm in 1930.

He contributed to the exhibition of Contemporary Russian Art held at Philadelphia in 1932. He died in Moscow.

Posthumous exhibitions were held in Moscow in 1949 and 1962 in Moscow, Leningrad and elsewhere.

Laundresses, 1889-1901, RM: Sweating figures are depicted hard at work in a dark interior with light streaming from a high, open central window. Loose slashed brushwork establishes broad planes and resolves into an energetic image of the figures. Other works include *On the Volga*, 1889, and *Women Day-labourers at a Cast Iron Foundry*, 1895.

Lit V.Lobanov *Tvorcheskiy put' A.E.Arkhipova*, Moscow, 1927. N.Rozhdestvenskaya *Narodnyy khudozhnik A.E.Arkhipov*, Moscow, 1930. *A.E.Arkhipov*, album, Moscow, 1959. O.Zhivova *Arkhipov*, Moscow, 1958. *A.E.Arkhipov*, exh. cat., Moscow, 1963.

Coll Well represented in TG and RM; Ryazan Art Museum; Brodsky Museum, Leningrad.

ARMU

The abbreviated name of the Association of Ukrainian Revolutionary Art (*Assotsiatsia revolyutsionogo mistetstva Ukrainy*) operative 1925-32.

ARNSHTAM, Aleksandr Martynovich   **1881-1969**
Painter, theatre designer, graphic artist. Born in Moscow. He studied under K.Yuon in Moscow and worked in Paris. He settled in St. Petersburg in 1908. He designed illustrations for periodicals including *Zolotoe Runo* (Golden Fleece) and book covers. He designed for Konstantin Nezlobin's theatre in Petrograd in 1914 and he exhibited with the World of Art in 1915-17. He designed an elegant filigree cover for the journal

Iskusstvo (Art), issue No.1-2 Petrograd 1917, framing a photographic portrait of the painter Repin.

After the Revolution he edited and designed the *Khudozhestvennyy zhurnal* (Art Journal) and also executed Agitprop decorations for the Baltisky Shipyards, Petrograd, in 1918. He was a member of the Art Collegium for Literary Publishing in 1919 with responsibility for illustrations to the works of Pushkin. He moved to Moscow in 1920. In the early 1920s he illustrated books and periodicals. He was represented at the First Russian Art Exhibition in Berlin in 1922. He exhibited with AKhRR.

In 1922 he emigrated and lived in Berlin until 1940. He subsequently settled in Paris in 1940. He died in Paris.

Lit *Russian Painters and the Stage 1884-1965, a loan exhibition of stage and costume designs from the Collection of Mr. and Mrs. Nikita D. Lobanov-Rostovsky*, exh. cat., University of Texas at Austin, 1978-9. J.E.Bowlt *Russian Stage Design. Scenic Innovation. From the Collection of Mr. and Mrs. Nikita D.Lobanov-Rostovsky*, Jackson, MS, exh. cat., 1982.

ARONSON, Boris Solomonovich   **1900-1980**
Theatre designer. He trained under Exter in Kiev.

Lit F.Rich, L.Aronson *The Theater Art of Boris Aronson*, New York, 1987. Dzhon Boult (John Bowlt) *Khudozhniki russkogo teatra. Sobranie Nikity i Niny Lobanovykh-Rostovskikh*, Moscow, 1991.

ARONSON, M.   **a.1922-25**
He was represented at the First Russian Art Exhibition in Berlin in 1922. He was a member of the Union of Moscow Artists formed in 1925.

ARONSON, Naum L'vovich   **1872-1943**
Sculptor. Born in the Vitebsk region. He studied under I.P.Trutnev 1889-91. He went to Paris in 1891 where he studied at the Académie Colarossi and at the Ecole des Arts Décoratifs and where he exhibited at the Salon in 1897. He first exhibited in Russia in 1902. He executed numerous historical portraits of poets and musicians including Dante, Wagner, Turgenev, Chopin and Tolstoy.

He returned to the Soviet Union 1934-5 where his work included sculptures of Lenin and sculptures for the Metro. He died in New York.

Young Boy, before 1902, RM: A bust executed with a slightly Rodin-like informality and somewhat soapy surface texture.

Coll RM; Kirov Art Museum; Leningrad Theatre Museum.

ARTSEULOV, Konstantin Konstantinovich b.1891-1951+
Pilot, graphic artist. Born at Yalta. He was the grandson of the painter Aivazovsky. He studied under P.Ya.Pavlinov at Sevastopol and under K.Yuon in Moscow 1908-11. He was a pilot from 1911. He became interested in gliding in the 1920s and 1930s and became involved with Tatlin's researches into the *Letatlin* glider project c.1930-2. He became an artist again in 1934. He later illustrated several books and periodicals including *Tekhnika molodezhi* (Young Technician). He executed decorative panels for the Central House of Aviation in Moscow 1950-1. An exhibition of his work was held in Moscow in 1962.

ARTSYBUSHEV, Yuri Konstantinovich   **1877-1952**
Draughtsman. He studied at the Academy in St. Petersburg 1898-1900. He produced illustrations for periodicals including, *Zritel'* in 1905, and later other periodicals including *Ogonek*.

Yury Annenkov. Jester. *1915. Watercolour, bronze paint and lead pencil on paper. Signed with cyrillic initials 'Yu.A' and inscribed in Russian 'Shut' (The Fool). 29.4 x 16.4 cm.*
Costume design for Sologub's play 'Night Dances'.

ARZHENIKOV, S. V. a.1919
Printmaker. He was represented in the Sixth State Exhibition: The Print (*VI Gosudarstvennaya vystavka gravyur*) in Moscow in 1919.

ARZHENNIKOV, Aleksei Nikolaevich 1891-1952
Printmaker, painter. Born in Moscow. He studied under Arkhipov, A.M.Vasnetsov and K.A.Korovin at the Moscow College until 1916.
After the Revolution he exhibited with the Moscow School Society of Artists active 1917-25. He was represented at the First Exhibition of Works of the Professional Union of Artists in Moscow in 1918 and at the Sixth State Exhibition: The Print (*VI Gosudarstvennaya vystavka gravyur*) in Moscow in 1919. He joined AKhRR in 1926. An exhibition of his work was held in Moscow in 1938. He died in Moscow.

ASKAR-SARYDZHA, Khaz-Bulat Nukhbekovich
b.1900-1950+
Sculptor. Born in Dagestan. He studied under Ya.I.Nikoladze in Tblisi from 1922 and at the Vkhutein in Leningrad 1923-6 under V.V.Lishev and A.T.Matveev. He exhibited from 1925. He travelled to Italy in 1926 and then returned to Dagestan. He settled in Moscow in 1937. His works include the equestrian monument to *A.Imanov*, bronze, 1950, at Alma-Ata as well as various monumental works at Makhachkala.
Female Collective Farm Worker, 1939, destroyed, is a plaster figure for the Azerbaijani pavilion at the All-Russian Agricultural Exhibition. With her basket of grapes, her vine and with fruit at her feet she is an archetypal image of Plenty here applied to the theme of Soviet agriculture.

ASKNAZI, Isaak L'vovich 1856-1902
Painter of biblical themes, portraits and genre. Born at Drisse. He studied at the Academy in St. Petersburg. He worked abroad 1880-3 including Berlin and a period under Hans Makart in Rome. He exhibited from 1881. He died in Moscow. His work was exhibited in St. Petersburg in 1903.
Coll Museum of the Academy of the USSR, Leningrad; Odessa Art Museum; Rostov Museum of Art; Kursk Art Gallery.

ASKRANOV
Aleksei Gan, Aleksandr Drevin, Aleksandr Rodchenko and Varvara Stepanova formed the group *Askranov* (Association of Extreme Innovators) in January 1919 in Moscow.

ASNOVA
The abbreviated name for the Association of New Architects (*Assotsiatsiya novykh arkhitektorov*).

ASTRAKHOV, Vasili Egorovich (Georgievich) d.1867?
Painter of Moscow views. He studied at the Moscow College. His work was exhibited in Moscow in 1852 and 1853.
Coll TG.

AVETOV, Mikhail Nikitich (Mikael Mkrtichevich)
1894/5-1949+
Painter. Born in Turkmenia. He studied at the Society for the Encouragement of the Arts in Petrograd 1915-16 under Roerich and A.A. Rylov.

After the Revolution he studied at the Academy under D.N.Kardovsky 1917-18. He travelled to the Far East and to China 1918-20. He was a member of the *Bytie* (Existence) Society of Artists formed in Moscow in 1921 and he also exhibited with the Society of Moscow Painters founded in 1925. He taught at the Communist University of the Workers of the East in Moscow 1922-5. Exhibitions of his work were held at Vladivostok and Chita 1918-20, Moscow in 1936 and at Samarkand in 1943.

AVILOV, Mikhail Ivanovich 1882-1954
Painter. Born at St. Petersburg. He studied at in St. Petersburg under L.E.Dmitriev-Kavkazsky 1903-4 and at the Academy under F.A.Rubo from 1904 and N.S.Samokish from 1910. He exhibited from 1908.
After the Revolution he worked in Siberia designing posters, illustrations and theatrical productions 1918-21. He returned to Petrograd and designed books and a series of *lubki* on the theme of the Red Army. He was included in the enormous survey Exhibition of Paintings by Petrograd Artists of All Tendencies 1919-1923 held in Petrograd in 1923. He contributed to numerous periodicals including *Niva*, *Sol'ntse Rossii*, *Ogonek*, *Tvorchestvo* and *Iskusstvo*. He was a member of the Kuindzhi Society of Artists in Leningrad in 1929. Exhibitions of his work were held in Leningrad in 1935 and 1940 and in Moscow in 1947. He died in Leningrad.
Kolchak Soldiers Handing in their Weapons near Krasnodar, 1929, shows prisoners making piles of rifles and other weapons which are loaded on to sledges. In the background trains wait. This is Socialist Realist history competently illustrated.
Lit V.Ya.Brodsky *M.I.Avilov*, Moscow, 1956.
Coll TG, RM.

AZBE, Anton 1862-1905
Painter and tutor whose numerous celebrated pupils at his Munich academy included Bilibin, David Burlyuk, Dobuzhinsky, Grabar', Jawlensky, Kandinsky and Petrov-Vodkin.

AZGUR, Zair Isaakovich b.1908-1960+
Belorussian sculptor of heroic portrait busts. Born in Vitebsk region. He studied in Vitebsk 1922-5 and at the Leningrad Vkhutein 1925-8. He exhibited from 1923. He was largely active at Minsk where he executed reliefs for the Opera and Ballet Theatre. In the 1940s he made a series of portrait busts of war heroes and military leaders. He won a silver medal at the World Fair in Brussels in 1958. He designed monuments erected at Lugansk in 1947, Minsk in 1947, Borodino in 1949, Suzdal in 1950, and a monument to *Lenin* in Leninogorsk in Kazakhstan in 1957. He exhibited in Bucharest in 1959 and Paris in 1961.
Portrait of the Hero of the Soviet Union Partisan M.F.Sel'nitsky is a straightforward Socialist Realist half-length of a healthy and discerning figure.
Lit N.Vorkunova *Z.I.Azgur*, Moscow, 1953. F.S.Roginskaya *Z.I.Azgur*, Moscow, 1961.
Coll Belorussian Art Museum; Astrakhan Art Gallery; Altai Art Museum.

B

BAAR, V. G. a.1925

Baar exhibited with the Society of Moscow Painters at its inaugural exhibition in Moscow in 1925.

BABICHENKO, Dmitri Naumovich b.1901-1964+

Graphic artist, cinema designer. Born at Zhitomir. He studied at the Art Institute in Kiev under F.G.Krichenko and V.G.Meller 1920-3. He published caricatures for journals 1925-30 including *Pravda* and *Krokodil*. He also designed cinema posters and from 1932 he worked on animated films at the Soyuzmul'tfilm Studios becoming a director in the 1940s. He was still engaged on animation in the 1960s. He also illustrated children's books for the publisher Detgiz.

Writings D.N.Babichenko *Iskusstvo mul'tiplikatatsiy*, Moscow, 1964.

BABICHEV, Aleksei Vasilevich 1887-1963

Sculptor, graphic artist, painter. Born in Moscow. He studied art privately under I.Dudin and K.Yuon whilst also studying mathematics at Moscow University during 1905-6. He then studied at the Moscow College 1907-12, first as a painter under K.Korovin and then as a sculptor and under S.M.Volnukhin. He exhibited with the World of Art in 1913 and then visited Vienna, Berlin and Paris where he studied briefly under Bourdelle at the Académie de la Grande Chaumière where he encountered Vera Mukhina and possibly Boris Ternovets. In 1914 he visited Greece and Italy. By 1915 he had a studio in Moscow.

After the Revolution he exhibited with the World of Art in December 1917 in Moscow. He was engaged in Revolutionary decorations in Moscow and he taught sculpture at the Free Art Studios (SVOMAS) there 1918-20 along with Bromirsky, Er'zya, Konen'kov and Vatagin. He submitted a projected *Monument to Ibsen* in 1918. In 1919 he was listed as leader of a course for art teachers along with Tatlin and others.

During 1919-20 he was a founder of the *Monolit* (Monolith) group of sculptors, which included Mukhina, Konen'kov, Krandevskaya, Korolev, Strakhovskaya, Zlatovratsky, Ternovets, V.Popova, Blazhevich and Kudinov. They worked on monumental propaganda and entered the competitive exhibition for a Monument to Liberated Labour held in Moscow in May 1920. Babichev executed a sculpture of *Vrubel'* in 1920. He was represented at the enormous First State Exhibition of Art and Science, which included ethnographic material, held in Kazan in 1920. Projects included a *Monument to V.M.Zagorsky*, 1921, and *Samson*, 1921-2.

He taught at the Vkhutemas 1920-5, contributing to the Foundation department and the Workers' Faculty *Rabfak*. At this point, 1920-3, he became closely involved with the theoretical debates and laboratory experiments of the Institute of Artistic Culture (INKhUK), contributing in particular to the analysis of composition and construction which comprised a vital debate in the emergence of Constructivist theory and practice emerging from the General Working Group of Objective Analysis within INKhUK.

He increased his activity as a painter after 1924. From 1925 until 1930 he was head of art at *Rabfak*, the Workers' Faculty, at the Vkhutemas. His projected *Monument to Y.M.Sverdlov*, 1924, consisted essentially of two interlocked metal arches and was designed for a site at the Bolshoi Theatre, Moscow. It was a characteristic synthesis of sculpture, architecture and engineering. His project for a mobile cinema, designed in 1926 was similarly unaesthetic, being simply a screen mounted upon the backs of two lorries.

He exhibited with AKhRR 1926-9. His later work reverted to more traditional conventions recalling Bourdelle, Maillol and Despiau.

He executed a head of *Lenin* in 1933, TG, and portrait sculptures. He taught at the Moscow Polygraphic Institute during the war and at the Architectural Institute 1944-63. He died in Moscow. An exhibition of his work was held in Moscow in 1965.

Lit A.Abramova *A.V.Babichev*, exh. cat., Moscow, 1965. A.Babichev *O konstruktsii i kompozitsii* (On Construction and Composition) in *Dekorativnoe Iskusstvo*, no.3, 1967. D.Sarabyanov *A.V.Babichev, khudozhnik, teoretik, pedagog*,

Aleksei Babichev. Study in Monumental Form, *1920-1. Clay. Documentary photograph.*

Léon Bakst. Costume design for the ballet 'La Peri', *1911. Gouache, pencil, gold. 68 x 48.5 cm. Designed for an unrealised production by Diaghilev.*
Collection Mr. and Mrs. Nikita D. Lobanov-Rostovsky, London.

Konstantin Bogaevsky. Ships. Evening Sun, *1912. Oil on canvas. 133 x 155 cm. State Russian Museum, St. Petersburg.*

Moscow, 1974. A.Z.Rudenstine *Costakis Collection*, London, 1981. C.Lodder *Russian Constructivism*, New Haven and London, 1983.
Coll TG; RM; Museum of the Revolution, Moscow.

BABICHEV, Petr P. a.1925-1927
Graphic artist. He participated in the seventh exhibition of the group *L'Araignée* (The Spider) at the Galerie Devambe in Paris in 1925 and in the third and last exhibition of the *Makovets* group in Moscow 1925-6. He was a member of the group *Put' zhivopisi* (Path of Painting) formed by Lev Zhegin in 1927.

BACHINDJAGHIAN = BASHINDZHAGYAN, G.

BACHMANN = BAKHMAN, A.

BAEV a.1917
Painter. He exhibited with the World of Art in Petrograd in 1917.

BAIKOVA, Z. A. a.1908-1910
Painter. She exhibited with the Golden Fleece in Moscow in 1908, 1909 and 1910.

BAKAL, Ippolit Ivanovich 1871-1896+
Painter. Born in Bessarabia. He studied at the Kiev Drawing School 1889-94. He was painting Parisian scenes in 1896.
Coll TG.

BAKALOVICH, Stepan Vladislavovich 1857-1947
Classicising painter. Born in Warsaw. He studied in Warsaw and at the Academy in St. Petersburg from 1876. He lived in Paris for a time. He worked on classical themes and produced images of Rome in 1885 and 1890. He sometimes signed works 'Bakalowicz'.
Coll TG; RM; Saratov Art Museum; Museum of Russian Art, Kiev; Gorky Art Museum.

BAKALOWICZ = BAKALOVICH, S.

BAKANOV, N. a.1925
He was represented at the Paris International Exhibition in 1925.

BAKHMAN, Aleksandr a.1806-1812+
Landscape painter. He studied at the Academy in St.

Léon Bakst. Vision of Antiquity *1906. Pen and ink on paper. 16.1 x 17.9 cm. Russian Museum, St. Petersburg.*

Petersburg in 1806-12. He sometimes signed works 'Bachmann'.
Coll TG.

BAKHTIN, K. **a.1927**
He was a member of the Society of Artist-Realists founded in 1927.

BAKSHEEV, Vasili Nikolaevich **1862-1958**
Painter of birch tree landscapes and genre. Born in Moscow. He studied under Makovsky, Savrasov and Polenov at the Moscow College 1878-88. He exhibited with the Wanderers from 1891 and became a member in 1896. From 1894 to 1918 he taught at the Moscow College. He exhibited with the World of Art in 1901. Together with the painter and architect Sergei Malyutin he designed the interior of his house in Moscow in 1909 in a style that was heavily inspired by the revival of folk art and craft pursued at the Abramtsevo and Talashkino workshops. Wooden architectural features were shaped and carved with high relief designs that were unapologetically crude or at least rural in appearance, although the total effect was of a kind of sophistication that reflected tendencies within the Arts and Craft movement internationally.

After the Revolution, 1917-19, he was a member of the committee for the the preservation of monuments of art and he took part in the organisation of Moscow museums. His name appears on the April 1919 list of artists for acquisitions by the proposed Museum of Painterly Culture. He participated in the First State Free Exhibition of Artworks in Petrograd in 1919 and in the Third Exhibition of Paintings held at Ryazan in 1919.

He joined AKhRR in 1922. He was amongst the organisers of the Society of Artist-Realists (OKhR) in Moscow in 1927. He executed numerous paintings on the theme of the Revolution and also landscapes of the Soviet Union. He was represented in the First Touring Exhibition of Paintings and Graphics which opened in Moscow in 1929.

He later taught at several educational institutions in Moscow between 1933 and 1958. He held one-man exhibitions in Moscow in 1937, 1944, 1947 and 1953. He was awarded numerous honours including State Prize Laureate and the Order of the Red Banner of Labour in 1943, full membership of the Academy of Arts in 1947, People's Artist of the U.S.S.R. in 1956 and the Order of Lenin in 1953 and 1958.

Blue Spring 1930, TG, shows the azure blue of a spring sky and a blistering brilliance of light striking the tall thin birch trees.

Lit M.Sokol'nikov *V.N.Baksheev*, Moscow, 1949. A.Tikhomirov *V.N.Baksheev*, Moscow, 1950. G.G.Sheyn *V.N.Baksheev. Zhizn' i tvorchestvo*, Moscow, 1952. A.M.Muratov, V.Manin et al. *Zhivopis' 20-30kh godov*, Sankt-Peterburg, 1991.

Coll TG; RM; Central Lenin Museum, Moscow; Saratov Art Museum; Kursk Art Gallery; Gorky Art Museum; Perm Art Gallery; Irkutsk Art Museum.

BAKST, Léon (ROZENBERG, Lev Samoilovich) 1866-1924

Painter, graphic artist, and an artist of major significance as a designer for the theatre and ballet. A prime mover within the World of Art, he became a prolific designer for the ballet in particular and an important contributor to the first phase of Diaghilev's Russian Ballet. Whilst he was indebted stylistically to Art Nouveau, he was able to combine great elegance and refinement with a rough vigour and overt eroticism. In his designs spectacularly patterned and colourful costumes adorn dancers who are often heavy, more or less naked to a degree and even hairy. He was an enormously inventive and prolific designer. His overwhelming sense of pattern expressed his love of the exotic, for which he drew upon many sources. His backdrops were evocative and lavish. He was amongst the first and most significant of Diaghilev's designers who proved by their vigour and exuberance the equal role that the painter was able to assume in theatrical and musical productions. He sometimes signed his work 'L.B'.

Born the son of a merchant in a Jewish family at Grodno. He attended school in St. Petersburg, the family having moved there in the 1870s. He studied art from 1883 as an external student at the Academy in St. Petersburg under Isaak Asknazi, Pavel Chistyakov, and Karl Venig, but was required to leave his studies prematurely in 1887. After this he worked as an illustrator. He changed his name to Bakst in 1889. He met Alexandre Benois whose portrait he executed in 1892, RM, and 1898, RM, and through Benois he met the artists K.Somov, D.Filosofov and also the future impresario Diaghilev.

In 1891 he travelled widely, visiting Germany, France, Spain and Italy. He took lessons in watercolour painting from Alexandre Benois' brother Albert Benois, and 1891-7 exhibited with the Society of Watercolourists in St. Petersburg.

Between 1893 and 1896 he was studying under Jean-Léon Gérome and at the Académie Julian in Paris. All of this helped to make him a highly informed and sophisticated figure. He travelled to Spain in 1896 and to Tunisia in 1897.

He suggested to Diaghilev an Exhibition of Russian and Finnish Artists to which he contributed in 1898 and he became a co-founder, organiser and participant of the activities of the World of Art. He exhibited with the World of Art 1899-1910 and in 1913. In 1903 he designed vases for the Imperial Porcelain Factory. He also designed covers and vignettes for numerous periodicals including *Mir Iskusstva* (World of Art), *Vesy* (Libra) and *Apollon*. He produced satirical illustrations for the journals *Zhupel'*, *Adskaya Pochta* and *Satirikon*. He also designed the World of Art insignia and made regular contributions to its publications as a graphic artist of luxurious elegance. These were evident qualities of his painting *The Supper* which caused a scandal when it was exhibited in 1902.

He developed a designer's interest in display, exhibiting a delicately sparse boudoir interior design 1902-3. He collected Japonaiserie and in 1903 he assisted in an exhibition of Japanese prints in St. Petersburg.

He exhibited with the Union of Russian Artists 1903-10. In 1906 he was invited to teach at the Zvantseva Academy in St. Petersburg along with Dobuzhinsky. The same year he designed Diaghilev's display of Russian art at the Salon d'Automne in Paris. He also provided illustrations for the periodical *The Golden Fleece* in 1906 and was elected a full Academician that year. With the painter Valentin Serov he visited Greece and Crete in 1907. He designed a poster for the Vienna Secession in 1903 and exhibited with the First Izdebsky International Salon 1909-10. Although he had become a Lutheran in 1903 he reverted to Judaism in 1910, the year of his divorce.

He settled in Paris where his large painting *Terror Antiquus* had been received with acclaim at the Salon d'Automne in 1908, and he became a life member of the Salon d'Automne in 1910. He exhibited in Brussels in 1910 and in Rome in 1911. He was exiled from Russia in 1912 but was elected an Academician in 1914 and regained the right to return. He visited Switzerland in 1916. He became friendly with Picasso in 1917. The final break with Diaghilev concerned costume designs for Stravinsky's *Mavra* which were not used in 1922.

Bakst remained vigorously active as a theatre designer, painter and graphic artist of great refinement and decorative brilliance. He was represented at the enormous First State Exhibition of Art and Science, which also included ethnographic material, held in Kazan in 1920. He died in Paris.

Cover for the World of Art periodical, 1901-2, overtly evokes the 18th century with a garden folly lightly drawn within an oval cartouche in either side of which sit a rake of some age and a young woman of elegance. The effect is feminine, elegant and provocatively witty.

The Supper, 1902, RM, is a crudely worked painting with harsh edges to the paint areas. It depicts a young woman clad in black evening gown, enormous black hat and an extremely low-cut neckline, seated at the table of a restaurant. Both the sexual innuendo and the daring brushwork were capable of scandalising Bakst's audience.

Andrey Bely, 1906, drawing in coloured crayons. An example among many of the immaculately executed academic portrait drawing which was a speciality of certain members of the World of Art. Somov could do it too with strikingly similar results.

Portrait of Sergei Diaghilev with his Nurse, 1906, RM, is an alert psychological study with the elegant Diaghilev standing

Viktor Borisov-Musatov. Zubrilovka, *1901. Watercolour, white, brush, pen and pencil on cardboard. Signed and dated lower right. 46.2 x 36.9 cm.*
State Tretyakov Gallery, Moscow.

in the foreground of a domestic interior with paintings visible in the background. The aged nurse sits sadly by the window watching the portrait emerge. It is a dark-toned study of a relationship well characterised without any hint of caricature.
Terror Antiquus, 1908, RM, is a *tour de force* of drama and dizzy perspective in which an immensely high viewpoint reveals the Greek city struck by lightning, or the thunderbolt of Zeus, with the ocean rushing in to swallow up its civilisation. In the foreground, and executed in a different spacial system, an archaic Greek sculpture confronts the viewer, calm and fatal. As a decorative panel it is unsurpassed in its sheer destructive spectacle and drama.

Early theatre designs
1901 designed costumes with Serov and a set for Scene 2 of an unrealised production of the ballet *Sylvia* to music by Delibes. Benois designed Scenes 1 and 2, Lansere Scene 4, Serov and Korovin Scene 3.
1902 costumes for the one act ballet-pantomime *Serdtsa Markisi (Le Coeur de la Marquise)*, music by G.Guiraud, at the Hermitage Theatre, St. Petersburg.
1902 and 1904 Euripedes' tragedy *Hippolytus* at the Aleksandrinsky Theatre, St. Petersburg.
1903 Bayer's ballet *Feya Kukol (Die Puppenfee)* at the Hermitage Theatre, St. Petersburg.

Aleksandr Bogomazov. Spring, *1914. Oil on canvas.*
Collection Mr. and Mrs. Nikita D. Lobanov-Rostovsky, London.

1904 Sophocles' tragedy *Oedipus Rex* (Oedipus at Colonus) at the Aleksandrinsky Theatre, St. Petersburg, which had costume designs in which the Greek decorative motifs of the clothes were coloured by Bakst with sumptuous effect to provide a lavish impression in indigo, Indian red, a rich gold and washed out blues. The figures were drawn in attitudes derived from vase paintings to emphasise the stylised actions and ancient appearance (Bakhrushin Theatre Museum).

1904 Sophocles' *Antigone* at the New Theatre, St. Petersburg.

1906 *Elysium*, curtain for the Vera Komissarzhevskaya Theatre, had a decorative panel (TG) executed almost entirely in greens in which, from a high viewpoint, the viewer looks down through a mass of trees upon the Elysian scene, scarcely noticing the Sphinx which flies through the air above these evocative pastoral pleasures.

For the Mariinsky Theatre, St. Petersburg:

1907 Saint-Saën's *Dying Swan*, Anton Arensky's *Torch Dance*, *Chopiniana* and A.Shcherbatov's *Eunice*.

1908 Meyerhold's production of Oscar Wilde's *Salome* (banned and therefore unrealised) with music by A.K.Glazunov for the Mikhailovsky Theatre, St. Petersburg.

Designs for Diaghilev's Russian Ballet

1909 costumes for Diaghilev's production of *Le Festin* at the Théâtre du Châtelet, Paris, in collaboration with Bilibin and

Benois. Décor by K.Korovin.

1909 June *Cléopâtre* at the Théâtre du Châtelet, Paris. Performed to music by A.S.Arensky and various other composers, choreographed by Fokine and based upon Arensky's *An Egyptian Night*.

1909 Costumes for Act 3 of Aleksandr Serov's opera *Judith* at the Théâtre du Châtelet, Paris.

1909 Costumes for part of Chaikovsky's *Sleeping Beauty* at the Théâtre du Châtelet, Paris.

1910 *Le Carnaval* , a pantomime ballet in one act to a libretto by Bakst and Fokine to music by Schumann. This had costumes designs with the exaggerated elegance of fashion plates (Theatre Museum, Leningrad), scarcely shaking off the line of Beardsley yet more actively substantial and less wan and sinister. Performed at Pavlova Hall, St. Petersburg and revived at the Theater des Westens, Berlin, and at the Mariinsky Theatre, St. Petersburg (1911).

1910 Bakst's one act drama *Schéhérazade* to music by Rimsky-Korsakov and choreography by Fokine, performed at the Théâtre de l'Opéra, Paris. Lavishly colourful costumes were emphatically part of the fantasy Orient of the 1001 Nights.

1910 Stravinsky's *Firebird*, the costume designs for which are lightly spangled with colour. 1910 décor and costumes with K.Korovin for *Les Orientales* to music by Glazunov, Grieg, Christian Sinding, Arensky and Borodin at the Théâtre de l'Opéra, Paris.

1911 *Le Spectre de la Rose*, a choreographic tableau from a poem by Théophile Gautier and employing music by Weber. Produced at the Théâtre de Monte Carlo and Paris.

1911 *Narcisse*, a mythological poem by Bakst to music by Nikolai Cherepnin at the Théâtre de Monte Carlo, for which the costume designs (Theatre Museum, St. Petersburg) show Bakst at his most muscular and dynamic, cladding heavy-limbed figures in patterned robes of overwhelming decorative excess, filling the page with their swift and vigorous choreography. Here the originality of his combinations of colour makes him a decorative painter of great originality, and the designs themselves go far to describe the dance and sense of event and movement: they are a synthesis of different requirements which also constitute paintings that reveal how much Bakst understood and contributed to the synthesis of the arts that Diaghilev sought in his productions.

1911 Théophile Gautier's *La Péri* to music by Paul Dukas and choreography by Fokine (original production unrealised). Exotic costumes on a Persian theme. The scenario was by Bakst. Performed in 1912 with designs by René Piot.

1912 May Jean Cocteau and Federigo de Madrazo's adaptation of Hindu legend, *Le Dieu Bleu*, to music by Reynaldo Hahn and choreography by Fokine, performed at the Théâtre du Châtelet, Paris. This had costume designs (Bakhrushin Theatre Museum, Moscow) that splintered the page with patterned colour, each area of clothing isolated by its own pattern and colour that conflicted with its neighbours. Areas were in this way distinguished by their patterns, much as Kandinsky used pattern in certain early works not directly associated with the theatre.

1912 *Thamar* at the Théâtre du Châtelet, Paris, to a libretto by Bakst and music by Balakirev; Bakst's décor executed by Sudeikin.

1912 Debussy's *L'Après-midi d'un Faune*, after the poem by Mallarmé, at the Théâtre du Châtelet, Paris. Choreography by Nijinsky.

1912 Ravel's *Daphnis et Chloë*, after the pastorale by Longus, at the Théâtre du Châtelet, Paris.

1913 Debussy's ballet *Jeux* at the Théâtre des Champs-Elysées, Paris. Choreography by Nijinsky.

1914 *Papillons*, ballet in one act to music by Schumann. Scenery by M.Dobuzhinsky, costumes by Bakst. First performed in Monte Carlo.

1914 costumes for *Le Légende de Joseph* (sets by José Maria Sert) to music by Richard Strauss at the Théâtre de l'Opéra, Paris: costume designs (RM) in which saturated colour and pattern fill the page and employ such close colour combinations as reds, oranges and browns. Bonnard designed a poster for this. The libretto was by Count Harry von Kessler and Hugo von Hofmannsthal.

1914 *Midas*, a mythological comedy by Bakst. First performed to music by M.Steinberg at the Paris Opera with décor by M.Dobuzhinsky and not Bakst.

1915 Chaikovsky's *Sleeping Beauty* (revised production). Rimsky-Korsakov's *Schéhérazade* (revised production).

1917 *Les Femmes de Bonne Humeur*, after Carlo Goldoni with music by Scarlatti at the Teatro Costanzi, Rome, and at the Théâtre du Châtelet, Paris.

1917 Rimsky-Korsakov's opera *Sadko* (unrealised). The design for a sea urchin shows a fiercely grotesque creature folded up on itself to form zigzag shapes in the drawing.

1918 *La Boutique Fantasque* at the Alhambra Theatre, London, to music by G.Rossini. This production caused disagreement; the designs used were by André Derain.

1921 *La Belle au Bois Dormant* (Sleeping Beauty; The Sleeping Princess), ballet with music by Chaikovsky, fragments orchestrated by Stravinsky, choreography by M.Petipa, produced at the Alhambra Theatre, London. Décor and whole production by Bakst. The set for The Awakening in Scene 4 depicts a colossal bed surmounted by an enormous eagle which looks more alive than heraldic. The princess is barely visible in the depths of the bed. The set for the final scene is a Piranesian maze of twisted columns forming a vast arcade.

1922 Stravinsky's *Mavra*. Bakst's designs were not used.

Other theatre designs

1909 Curtain for the Komissarzhevskaya Theatre, assisted by Boris Anisfeld.

1910 Glazunov's *La Bacchanale*, costumes, at the Nobility Assembly, a charity performance, St. Petersburg.

1910 A costume for Massenet's opera *Thaïs* at the St. Petersburg Conservatoire.

1911 May D'Annunzio's *Le Martyre de St. Sebastien* for the Ida Rubinstein Company at the Théâtre du Châtelet, Paris, with music by Debussy and choreography by Fokine. Revived without Act 2 in 1922. The curtain for the start of Act 1 of the revived production is in blue and yellow and depicts a low archway beyond which a spiralling tower, archways and stairs appear.

1911 sets for R.Ginsburg's *Ivan the Terrible* at the Théâtre du Gaîté-Lyrique, Paris.

1911 Arigo Boïto's *Mefistofeles* (unrealised) for the Royal Opera House, London.

1912 Oscar Wilde's *Salomé*, music by Glazunov, for the Ida Rubinstein Company at the Théâtre du Châtelet, Paris.

1912 Emile Verhaeren's four act tragedy *Hélène de Sparte* for Ida Rubinstein's Company at the Théâtre du Châtelet, Paris.

1913 Maeterlinck's *Mary Magdalen* at the Casino municipal and at the Théâtre du Châtelet, Paris.

1913 June Gabriele d'Annunzio's *La Pisanella (La Pisanelle ou La Mort Parfumée)* for Ida Rubinstein's Company at the Théâtre du Châtelet, Paris, directed by Vsevolod Meyerhold. Choreography by M.Fokine. Music by I.da Parma.

1916 Chaikovsky's *Sleeping Beauty* at the Hippodrome, New York.

1919 costumes for *Aladin ou La Lampe Merveilleuse* at the Théâtre Marigny, Paris.

1922 costumes with Sudeikin for *Spectacle de l'Art Russe* at the Théâtre Fémina, Paris.

1922 April *Artemis Troublée*, ballet by Bakst, music by Paul Paray, for the Ida Rubinstein Company at the Paris Opera. Choreography by Nicola Guerra.

1922 Costumes for Henry Bernstein's dramatic comedy *Judith* at the Théâtre du Gymnase, Paris. The set was by Sergei Sudeikin.

1922 costumes with George Barbier for the *Bal du Grand Prix* at the Paris Opera.

1923 D'Annunzio's *Phèdre* and *La Nuit Magique*, music by Chopin, at the Paris Opera.

1923 Racine's *Phèdre* at the Théâtre de l'Opéra, Paris, for the Ida Rubinstein Company. Colourful designs featuring Cretan decorations based upon the palace at Knossos.

1923 *La Nuit Ensorcelée*, to music by Chopin, at the Paris Opera.

1923 decorations for the Evergreen Theatre, Baltimore.

1924 the ballet *Istar*, music by Vincent d'Indy, for the Ida Rubinstein Company at the Paris Opera.

Lit P.Barchan *L.Bakst*, Berlin, 1913. A.Alexandre *The Decorative Art of Leon Bakst*, London, 1913. A.Levinson *Bakst*, London, 1923. C.Einstein *L.Bakst*, Berlin, 1927. R.Lister *The Muscovite Peacock*, Cambridge, 1954. C.Spencer *L.Bakst*, London, 1973. I.Pruzhan *Bakst*, Moscow, 1975. N.Borisovskaya *Bakst*, Moscow, 1979. S.Golynets *Bakst*, Moscow, 1981. J.E.Bowlt *Russian Stage Design. Scenic Innovation. From the Collection of Mr. and Mrs. Nikita D.Lobanov-Rostovsky*, Jackson, MS, exh. cat., 1982. I.Pruzhan *L.Bakst*, Leningrad, 1986. A.Schouvaloff *The Thyssen-Bornemisza Collection: Set and Costume Designs for Ballet and Theatre*, New York-London, 1987. A.Kamensky *The World of Art Movement*, Leningrad, 1991. Dzhon Boult (John Bowlt) *Khudozhniki russkogo teatra. Sobranie Nikity i Niny Lobanovykh-Rostovskikh*, Moscow, 1991.

Coll TG; RM; Bakhrushin Theatre Museum, Moscow; Theatre Museum, St. Petersburg; Lenin Library, Moscow; Kazakh Art Gallery; Krasnodar Art Museum; Sverdlovsk Art Gallery; National Gallery of Armenia; Odessa Art Museum; Theatre Museum, Victoria and Albert Museum, London; Ashmolean Museum, Oxford; Fitzwilliam Museum, Cambridge; Lobanov-Rostovsky Collection, London; Baron

Thyssen-Bornemisza Collection, England; The Fine Art Society, London; Musée des Arts Décoratifs, Paris; Musée des Beaux-Arts, Strasbourg; Australian National Gallery, Canberra; Museum of Fine Arts, Boston; Fine Arts Museums, San Francisco; Wadsworth Atheneum, Hartford, Connecticut. Colour plates pp.15 and 18.

BAKULINA, L.   a.1932
She was represented at the jubilee exhibition Artists of the RSFSR over 15 Years held at the Russian Museum, Leningrad in 1932.

BAKUSHINSKY   a.1926
Sculptor. He was a member of the Society of Russian Sculptors from 1926.

BALL'ER (BAL'ER, BALLER), Avgust Ivanovich
1879-1962
Painter, graphic artist. Born at Budaki, Bessarabia. He first exhibited in the *Blanc et Noir* exhibition in St. Petersburg in 1903. In the early years of the century he lived with his wife Lidiya Arionesko-Ball'er in The Netherlands, graduating from the Amsterdam Academy in 1911. He exhibited with Kul'bin's Impressionists in 1909-10 and with the Union of Youth 1911-12. He then lived largely in St. Petersburg until 1919 and subsequently at Kishinev where he taught at the Art Institute until 1941. He moved to Bucharest in 1943. He died at Bucharest.
Lit J.Howard *The Union of Youth — An Artists' Society of the Russian Avant-Garde*, Manchester and New York, 1992.
Coll Moldavian Art Museum.

BANDYSHEV, M.S.   a.1919
He participated in the First State Free Exhibition of Artworks in Petrograd in 1919.

BARANOFF-ROSSINE, Vladimir Davidovich
(ROSSINE, Daniel)   **1888-1944**
Painter and sculptor. Born at Kherson. He studied at Odessa Art School under K.Kostandi and G.Ladyzhensky and then at the St. Petersburg Academy 1903-7. He contributed to the *Stefanos* exhibition 1907-8 and the exhibition *Zveno* (The Link) in Kiev in 1908. He exhibited in *Venok* (The Wreath) in St. Petersburg in 1909.

He lived in Paris between 1910 and 1914 where he met the poets and painters of Apollinaire's circle and exhibited at the Salon des Indépendants in 1910 and 1912-14. His sculptural innovations at this time were highly experimental and may have influenced Archipenko and other Cubist sculptors to assemble sculpture from the most diverse and surprising materials including, for example, such untraditional materials as eggshells. In addition he executed mobile sculptures. He also experimented with colour-sound relationships and devised an optophonic piano in 1914. This range of experiment also suggests an awareness of Russian Futurist innovation. During the years 1915-17 he lived in Christiania.

He returned to Russia at the time of the Revolution and worked under Al'tman on the committee responsible for the Revolutionary decorations marking 1 May in Petrograd in 1919. He executed Agitprop decorations for Znamenskaya

Square and Vosstanie Square, Petrograd, in 1918, and taught at the Vkhutemas. He participated in the First State Free Exhibition of Artworks in Petrograd in 1919. He was represented at the First Russian Art Exhibition in Berlin in 1922.

In 1925 he emigrated to Paris, again exhibiting at the Salon des Indépendants between 1925 and 1942. In 1943 he was arrested by the Gestapo and deported. He died in a concentration camp.

Lit *V.Baranoff-Rossiné*, exh. cat., Galerie Jean Chauvelin, Paris, 1970. *V.Baranoff-Rossiné*, exh. cat., MNAM, Paris, 1973. *Paris-Moscou*, exh. cat., Paris, 1979.

Coll RM; MNAM Paris.

BARANOVSKY, A. Ya.   a.1921
He contributed to the First State Exhibition in Orenburg in 1921.

BARI, O.   a.1913-1919
Painter. Bari exhibited with the World of Art in 1913.

After the Revolution Bari was represented in the Fourth State Exhibition of Paintings (*IV Gosudarstvennaya vystavka kartin*) in Moscow in 1919.

BART, Viktor Sergeevich   1887-1954
Painter, graphic artist. Born Velichaevo. He studied at the Moscow College 1906-11 and at the Academy in St. Petersburg from 1911. In 1912 he was working in the studio complex The Tower with Grishchenko, Popova, Tatlin and Zdanevich. He exhibited with the Knave of Diamonds 1910-11 and with the Donkey's Tail in 1912 in Moscow where he showed over twenty works some of which were illustrations to Montaigne, Pushkin and Sologub. He contributed to Larionov's exhibition The Target in Moscow in 1913.

After the Revolution his work was included in the First Exhibition of the Moscow Contemporary Art Store in January 1919 and his name appeared on the April 1919 list of artists for acquisitions by the proposed Museum of Painterly Culture. He worked for the journal *Udar* 1922-4 and was engaged in the design of the Soviet Pavilion at the International Exhibition in Paris in 1925. He worked for the journal *Nash soyuz* (Our Union) 1926-36. He moved to Moscow in 1936 and illustrated numerous books there. He died Moscow.

Some of his drawings used the inconsistent light source and rhythmically repeated shapes of Cubo-Futurism to construct his figures. The effect was not unlike Exter's stage designs and was highly appropriate to illustration.

BARTO, Rostislav Nikolaevich   1902-1974
Graphic artist, painter. Born in Moscow. He studied under N.N.Kupreyanov, I.I.Nivinsky and A.V.Shevchenko at the Moscow Vkhutein 1922-30. A member of the *Bytie* (Existence) Society of Artists formed in Moscow in 1926. He was included in the 1928 exhibition of Acquisitions by the State Art Collections Fund held in Moscow. He exhibited at the 1932 Venice Biennale. He was represented at the jubilee exhibition Artists of the RSFSR over 15 Years held at the Russian Museum, Leningrad, in 1932. His work was exhibited in London in 1935. Exhibitions were held in Moscow in 1933 and 1956.

Derbent, 1932, RM, is a decisively painted and colourful village scene in the hot south with sharp contrasts of light and dark and figures moving through the shade.

Coll TG; RM; Perm Art Gallery.

BARUZDINA, Varvara Matveevna   1862-1941
Painter. Born in the Tver region. She studied under Chistyakov and at the St. Petersburg Academy between 1880 and 1885. She died at the town of Pushkin in the Leningrad region.

Coll TG; RM.

BARYSHNIKOV, A. A.   a.1914-1917
He contributed to the exhibition No.4 in Moscow in 1914.

After the Revolution he exhibited with the Knave of Diamonds in Moscow in November 1917.

BASHILOV, Mikhail Sergeevich   1821-1870
Painter, draughtsman. He studied at the University of Kharkov. He lived in Kiev from the late 1850s and was illustrating books in the 1860s. He sometimes signed his work 'M.B'.

Coll TG.

BASHILOV, Yakov Stepanovich   1839-1896
Genre painter. He studied at the Moscow College and was awarded a silver medal in 1871.

Coll TG.

BASHINZHAGYAN, Georgiy (Gevorg) Zakharovich 1857-1925
Landscape painter. Born in Georgia. He studied at the Drawing School in Tiflis and under M.K.Klodt at the Academy in St. Petersburg from 1879. In 1884 he visited Italy and Switzerland. He worked in Paris from 1899 to 1902 and exhibited there in 1900. Thereafter he worked mainly in Tiflis where he had numerous exhibitions between 1883 and 1916. He also exhibited in Baku, Pyatigorsk, Novocherkassk and Nakhichevan.

After the Revolution he became involved in the artistic life of Tiflis/Tblisi in Georgia and also Erevan in Armenia. Sometimes he signed his work 'Bachindjaghian'. He died at Tiflis.

Sevan. Cloudy Day, 1897, Armenian Art Gallery, Erevan, depicts the church on an island rising into the light. Two still boats in the foreground are dwarfed by the enormous, mistily clouded sky.

Coll TG; Armenian Art Gallery, Erevan.

BASHKIROV, G. A.   a.1919-1927
He exhibited at the Twelfth State Exhibition: Colourdynamo and Tectonic Primitivism (*XII Gosudarstvennaya vystavka. Tsvetodinamos i tektonichesky primitivizm*) in Moscow in 1919 along with Grishchenko, Shevchenko and others. He was included in the 1928 exhibition of Acquisitions by the State Art Collections Fund held in Moscow.

BASHKIRTSEFF, Marie (BASHKIRTSEVA, Mariya Konstantinova)   1860-1884
Painter, sculptor. She lived in Paris from 1870. She was much inspired by Bastien-Lepage whose work she knew whilst studying at the Académie Julian where she enrolled in 1877. She was awarded a gold medal in 1879. She exhibited at the

Vladimir Baranoff-Rossiné. Symphony No.1, *1913. Polychrome wood, cardboard, and crushed eggshells.*
161.1 x 72.2 x 63.4 cm.
The title points to Baranoff-Rossiné's interest in the synthesis of music and art. The construction is a little like the
assembled sculptures of Archipenko and Klyun.
Collection the Museum of Modern Art, New York.

Salon in 1880, 1881, 1883, 1884 and posthumously in 1885. She died very young but left a copious journal. The *Union des Femmes Peintres et Sculpteurs* organised a retrospective exhibition in 1885, including paintings, pastels, drawings and sculpture. She is buried at Père Lachaise Cemetery in Paris.

Lit *The Journal of Marie Bashkirtseff* (first published in France in 1887, English edition London, 1890), republished with an introduction by Rozsika Parker and Griselda Pollock, London, 1985. G.H.Perris *Further Memoirs of Marie Bashkirtseff*, London, 1907. Pierre Borel *Le Visage inconnu de Marie Bashkirtseff*, Paris, 1925. Alberic Cahuet *Moussia, ou la vie et mort de Marie Bashkirtseff*, Paris, 1926. Dormer Creston *The Life of Marie Bashkirtseff*, London, 1943. Doris Langley Moore *Marie and the Duke of H.; The Daydream Love Affair of Marie Bashkirtseff* London, 1966. Colette Cosnier *Marie Bashkirtseff: un portrait sans retouche*, Paris, 1985.

Coll Hermitage, St. Petersburg; TG; RM; Kharkov Art Museum; Musée d'Orsay, Paris; Musée des Beaux Arts Jules Chéret, Nice.

BASIN, Petr Vasilevich   **1793-1877**
Portrait and landscape painter. He studied at the Academy in St. Petersburg from 1811 and was later made an Academician. He worked in Italy 1819-30, made studies after paintings in the Vatican and was painting in Rome in 1822. He was painting at the Winter Palace in St. Petersburg in the 1830s and taught at the Academy from 1831. He also executed lithographs. Sometimes signed works 'P.B'.

Coll TG has substantial holdings; RM; Astrakhan Art Gallery.

BASMANOV, Pavel Ivanovich   **b.1906**
Painter. His work included watercolours loosely brushed in to depict figures in an open landscape, poised and atmospheric but lacking in detail.

Coll RM.

BATURIN, Viktor Pavlovich   **1863-1938**
Landscape and still-life painter. He studied at the Moscow College and exhibited from 1884. He exhibited with the Wanderers and with the Moscow Society of Art Lovers.
After the Revolution he worked at Pavlodar 1920-30. He died in Moscow.

Coll TG; Tolstoy Museum, Moscow; Irkutsk Art Museum; Tula Art Museum.

BAUMANIS = ZEMDEGA, K. Ya.

BAUMER, Georgiy Albertovich   **1833-1881**
Painter.

Coll TG.

BAYBARISHEV, Petr Mikhailovich   **1894-1942?**
Applied artist. He studied at the Art School in Kazan under N.I.Feshin until 1917.
After the Revolution he was included in the Third Touring Exhibition of the Sovetsk Regional subdepartment of the Museums Bureau along with Kandinsky, Rodchenko and others in 1921.
He studied at the Vkhutemas in Moscow in 1923. He designed materials and book covers. He died on military service.

BAZHENOV, Aleksandr Vladimirovich   **b.1904-1960+**
Graphic artist. Born at Tula. He studied at the Vkhutemas in Moscow 1925-8 and exhibited from 1932. He produced caricatures in the 1920s and was an active illustrator of books in the 1950s and 1960s.

BAZHENOV, Pavel Dmitrievich   **1904-1941**
Miniaturist, puppet theatre designer, film animation artist. He studied in the Palekh school of ikon painting. He exhibited works decorating papier mâché utensils with Soviet themes from 1929 in Leningrad. He designed for productions at the Leningrad Puppet Theatre in 1937. He contributed to animated films 1935-6.

BEBUTOVA (-KUZNETSOVA), Elena Mikhailovna (BEBOUTOFF, Helene)   **1892-1970**
Theatre designer, painter. Born at St. Petersburg. She studied under Roerich, Rylov and Tsionglinsky at the Society for the Encouragement of the Arts at St. Petersburg 1907-14. She began exhibiting in 1913.
After the Revolution she designed for theatres in Moscow from 1917. She exhibited in the 1921 exhibition of the World of Art in Moscow. An exhibition of her work was held in Moscow in 1923. She was in Paris in 1923-4. She was a member of the 4 Arts society which was founded in 1924. Her work was included in the exhibition of Soviet art held at Harbin in 1926 and in Japan in 1927 and in the 1928 exhibition of Acquisitions by the State Art Collections Fund held in Moscow. She was represented in the First Touring Exhibition of Paintings and Graphics which opened in Moscow in 1929.
She exhibited in Venice in 1928, Berlin in 1930 and New York in 1935. She was represented at the jubilee exhibition Artists of the RSFSR over 15 Years held at the Russian Museum, Leningrad, in 1932. She died in Moscow.

Theatre design 1921 Meyerhold's second production of Mayakovsky's *Mystery-Bouffe*, in collaboration with V.Kiselev, A.Lavinsky and V.Khrakhovsky.
1921 Meyerhold's production of *Nora* by Ibsen.
1922 plays by Dumas père.
1926 designed for the musical theatre including Mozart's *Don Giovanni*.
1935 worked for the Lensovet Theatre designing plays by Ostrovsky, and for Schiller's *Mary Stuart* in 1940.
1946 designed a production of *Hamlet* at the Belorussian Drama Theatre.

Lit A.M.Muratov, V.Manin et al. *Zhivopis' 20-30kh godov*, Sankt-Peterburg, 1991.

Coll Kostroma Art Museum; Perm Art Gallery.

BEGGROV, Aleksandr Karlovich   **1841-1914**
Painter of cityscapes. Born in St. Petersburg. He was the son of K.P.Beggrov. He studied under L.Bonnat and A.P.Bogolyubov in Paris 1871-4. He exhibited with the Wanderers from 1874 and became a member in 1876. He exhibited at the International Exhibition in Paris in 1878. His work included views of Venice and Normandy. He was a member of the Society of Russian Watercolourists from 1885.

Coll TG; RM; Perm Art Gallery.

BEGGROV, Ivan Petrovich (Johann-Friedrich)   **1793-1877**
Lithographer. Born at Riga. He was the brother of K.P.Beggrov. He taught drawing in Moscow and then in St. Petersburg. He began to work as a lithographer in 1817 and opened a shop to sell work. He made lithographs of paintings by D.Skotti and others.He died in St. Petersburg.

Coll Far East Art Museum, Khabarovsk.

BEGGROV, Karl Petrovich (Karl-Joachim)   **1799-1875**
Lithographer, watercolourist, painter of cityscapes of St.
Petersburg. Born in Riga. He was the brother of the
lithographer I.P.Beggrov and father of the painter
A.K.Beggrov. He studied under M.N.Vorob'ev at the
Academy in St. Petersburg 1818-21. In 1828 he was executing
paintings at the Winter Palace. He made series of lithographs
of in 1820, 1822, and views of St. Petersburg 1821-6.
Sometimes he signed his work 'C.B'. He died in St.
Petersburg.
Coll TG; RM; Hermitage Museum, St. Petersburg; History
Museum, Moscow; Far East Art Museum, Khabarovsk.

BEKHTEEV, Vladimir Georgievich   **1878-1971**
Graphic artist, painter. Born in Moscow. He attended military
school in Moscow before studying under Knirr in Munich in
1902-5 and under Cormon in Paris in 1906. He joined the
Neue Künstlervereinigung in Munich in 1909 and exhibited
with the First Izdebsky International Salon in 1909-10. He
exhibited a *Battle of the Amazons* with the Knave of Diamonds
in Moscow in 1910-11 and became a member of the *Blaue
Reiter* group in Munich in 1911.
After the Revolution he served in the Red Army in 1917. He
showed work in the Fifth State Exhibition in Moscow 1918-19.
He produced designs for the circus from 1921 after his
appointment as artistic director of the First State Circus in
Moscow. He was represented at the Paris International
Exhibition in 1925. He exhibited with the 4 Arts society in
Leningrad including the exhibition of 1928 at the Russian
Museum. He was included in the 1928 exhibition of
Acquisitions by the State Art Collections Fund held in Moscow.
He also produced graphic work for books, designing for
publishing houses including Detgiz and Goslitizdat. He was
still illustrating books in 1957. Exhibitions of his work were
held in Moscow in 1955 and 1961. He died in Moscow. He
sometimes signed his work in latin script: 'W.B.'.
Lit *Bekhteev*, exh. cat., Moscow, 1970. D.Kogan *Vladimir
Bekhteev*, Moscow, 1977. J.E.Bowlt *Russian Stage Design. Scenic
Innovation. From the Collection of Mr. and Mrs. Nikita
D.Lobanov-Rostovsky*, Jackson, MS, exh. cat.,1982.
Coll TG; Gorky Literary Museum, Moscow; Pushkin
Museum, Moscow.

BEKLEMISHEV, Vladimir Aleksandrovich   **1861-1920**
Sculptor. Born in the Ekaterinoslav region. He studied under
N.A.Laveretsky at the Academy in St. Petersburg 1878-9. He
was a friend of the painter Malyavin. He taught at the Society
for the Encouragement of the Arts in St. Petersburg in 1887
and at the Academy from 1888. He lived in Paris and Rome
1888-92. His *Boy*, 1890, RM, is a classicising bust employing
fine cutting and smooth simplified surfaces. He was Professor
of Sculpture at the St. Petersburg Academy 1894-1918.
In 1897 he made the marble sculpture of Chaikovsky now
installed in the St. Petersburg Conservatory. He was awarded
a gold medal at the International Exhibition in Paris in
1900.He executed monuments at Novocherkassk and St.
Petersburg and in 1914 collaborated on the monument to the
painter Kuindzhi installed at the Aleksandr Nevsky Cemetery
in Leningrad. He also produced numerous small sculptures
and his work sometimes revealed traces of Art Nouveau.
He participated in the First State Free Exhibition of Artworks

in Petrograd in 1919.
Peter I, 1909, RM, is a study for the monument erected at
Revel (Tallin) in 1909.
Coll Well represented at RM; TG; T.G.Shevchenko
Museum, Kiev.

BEKTEEVA, Nina Petrovna   **b.1897-1965+**
Theatre designer. Born in in the Orenburg region. She
studied under Lentulov and Fedorovsky at the Moscow
Vkhutemas 1921-5. She contributed to the exhibition Art of
Moscow Theatre 1918-1923 held in Moscow in 1923. She was
active also as an exhibition designer from 1925.
She worked as chief artistic designer at the Music and Drama
Theatre at Ulan Bator, Mongolia, 1934-6. Exhibitions of her
work were held in Ulan Bator and Moscow in 1939.
She executed panels for the All-Union Agricultural Exhibition
in Moscow 1952-5 and for the Park of Culture 1961-5.

BELASHOVA-ALEKSEEVA, Ekaterina Fedorovna
b.1906-1966+
Academic sculptor of figures and genre. Born at St.
Petersburg. She studied at the Industrial Art Technicum in
Leningrad 1923-4 and at the Vkhutein 1926-30. She exhibited
from 1930. She worked in Moscow. Her works include a
bronze of *Pushkin*, 1957, Pushkin Museum, Moscow, group
compositions, figures for fountains and monumental works at
Volgograd 1939-40 and Simferopol 1950. She taught at the
Moscow Institute of Applied and Decorative Art 1947-52 and
at the Higher Art and Industrial College (former Stroganov
College) in Moscow where she became a professor in 1952.
Exhibitions of her work were held in Moscow in 1947, 1956
and 1966. She was awarded the Order of Lenin in 1966.
Coll RM; Pushkin Museum, Moscow; Simferopol Art
Museum.

BELKIN, Veniamin Pavlovich   **1884-1951**
Painter and graphic artist. Born in the Ekaterinburg region.
He studied under Shesterkin in Moscow and privately at the
A.P.Bolshakov School under Borisov-Musatov 1904-5. He
studied in Paris under Guérin and Cottet 1907-9 and
exhibited in Paris in 1908. He provided illustrations for the
periodicals *Apollon* and *Satirikon* 1909-11 and exhibited with
the Union of Youth. He exhibited with the World of Art
1913-16.
After the Revolution he executed Agitprop decorations in
Pushkin Square, Petrograd, in 1918, and made designs for the
decoration of ceramic plates during 1919-24. He participated
in the First State Free Exhibition of Artworks in Petrograd in
1919 and was included in the enormous survey Exhibition of
Paintings by Petrograd Artists of All Tendencies 1919-1923
held in Petrograd in 1923. He also taught at the
Vkhutemas/Vkhutein 1921-3 and in 1928. He exhibited in
New York and Boston in 1924. He taught at the Leningrad
Architectural School 1924-7 and made illustrations for the
periodical *Krasnaya Panorama* (Red Panorama) in 1928-29. He
also designed books for publishers in Leningrad.
He was represented at the jubilee exhibition Artists of the
RSFSR over 15 Years held at the Russian Museum, Leningrad,
in 1932. Exhibitions of his work were held in Leningrad in
1941 and 1955. He died in Leningrad.
Coll RM; Kazakh Art Gallery.

BELOBORODOV, Andrei Yakovlevich   1886 -1965
Theatre designer inspired by Italian Baroque design.
Lit Dzhon Boult (John Bowlt) *Khudozhniki russkogo teatra. Sobranie Nikity i Niny Lobanovykh-Rostovskikh*, Moscow, 1991.

BELOGRUD, Andrei Evgenevich   a.1918
He was engaged on Agitprop decorations at Ligovka, corner of Obvodnogo, Petrograd, in 1918.

BELOSTOTSKY, Anatoli Efimovich   b.1921-1960+
Sculptor of Socialist Realist genre. Born at Odessa. He was the son of E.I.Belostotsky. He studied under M.G.Lysenko at the Art Institute in Kiev 1946-52. He worked in Kiev.
Coll Ukrainian Fine Art Museum, Kiev; Sebastopol Art Museum.

BELOSTOTSKY, Efim (Yukhim) Isaevich   1893-1961
Ukrainian scuptor. Born Elizavetgrad. He studied under K.K.Kostandi and B.V.Eduards at the Odessa School of Art 1913-18.
After the Revolution he continued to study in Odessa 1919-22. He began to exhibit in 1933 in Kiev. He executed numerous monuments. He died at Kiev.
Coll TG; Kharkov Art Museum; Ukrainian Fine Art Museum, Kiev.

BELOUSOV, Fedor Vasilevich   1885-1939
Painter. Born at Saratov. He studied at the School of Painting in Saratov 1897-1903 and at the Drawing School of the Society for the Encouragement of the Arts in St. Petersburg 1903-4 before enrolling at the Moscow College where he studied from 1904 to 1914. He began to exhibit in 1913.
After the Revolution he executed Agitprop decorations at Saratov and then taught at the Saratov Art College 1923-36.
Coll Saratov Art Museum.

BELOV, I. V.   a.1919
He exhibited at the Twelfth State Exhibition: Colourdynamo and Tectonic Primitivism (*XII Gosudarstvennaya vystavka. Tsvetodinamos i tektonichesky primitivizm*) in Moscow in 1919 along with Grishchenko, Shevchenko and others.

BELOV, M. S.   a.1919
He exhibited at the Twelfth State Exhibition: Colourdynamo and Tectonic Primitivism (*XII Gosudarstvennaya vystavka. Tsvetodinamos i tektonichesky primitivizm*) in Moscow in 1919 along with Grishchenko, Shevchenko and others.

BELOV, Petr Aleksandrovich   1929-1988
Theatre designer, painter. He studied at the Central Art School in Moscow 1944-9 and studied stage design at the Nemirovich-Danchenko Theatre Faculty, the Moscow Art Theatre 1949-53 and at the Surikov Art Institute 1950-8. He worked for several theatres including the Moscow Region Youth Theatre and the Soviet Army Central Theatre.
Lit D.Elliott, V.Dudakov *100 Years of Russian Painting*, London, 1991.

BEL'SKY, Aleksei Ivanovich   1726-1796
Painter of city views. His birthdate is sometimes given as 1730. He studied under I.Ya.Vishnyakov. From 1747 he worked under I.Valeriani, A.Perezinotti and P.Gradizzi. He executed decorations for palaces, churches and theatres including work at Tsarskoe Selo and the Winter Palace in the early 1770s.
Coll TG; RM.

BEL'SKY, Anatoli Pavlovich   1896-1971
Graphic artist, theatre designer. Born in Moscow. He studied under V.E.Egorov at the Stroganov College 1908-17.
After the revolution he studied under Konchalovsky and F.F.Fedorovsky at the Moscow Vkhutemas 1917-21 and exhibited at the juryless Eighth State Exhibition in Moscow in 1919. He was engaged on propaganda decorations including work on the Agit-train *Lenin (October Revolution)*, c.1920. He executed designs for Mayakovsky's *Mystery-Bouffe* in 1921 as well as other theatrical productions. In 1928 he was involved in the installation of the Soviet Pavilion at the International Exhibition in Philadelphia. He designed cinema posters from the 1920s to the 1950s including *Aleksandr Nevsky* 1936.

BEL'SKY, Ivan Ivanovich   1719-1799
Painter of biblical themes. He studied under I.Ya.Vishnyakov and was engaged on paintings at the New Summer Palace in 1748, in churches in 1749, at Tsarskoe Selo in 1755 and at the Winter Palace in 1760. He was appointed overseer of painting in the palaces and churches of St. Petersburg and district in 1786. He sometimes signed his work 'Bel'skoy'.
Coll TG.

BEL'SKY, Mikhail Ivanovich   1753-1794
Portrait painter. He was the son of I.I.Bel'sky. He travelled on a scholarship from the Academy in St. Petersburg from 1773, visiting England, France and Italy. In 1780 he was in contact with Greuze in France.
Coll TG; Museum of Russian Art, Kiev.

BELY, Aleksandr Fedorovich   1874-1934
Landscape painter. Born in the Kherson region. He studied at the Odessa School of Drawing and from 1894 to 1900 under A.A.Kiselev at the Academy in St. Petersburg. He taught at the Society for the Encouragement of the Arts in St. Petersburg from 1902.
After the Revolution he participated in the First State Free Exhibition of Artworks in Petrograd in 1919. He was included in the enormous survey Exhibition of Paintings by Petrograd Artists of All Tendencies 1919-1923 held in Petrograd in 1923. His work included posters in the period 1920-30 as well as paintings some of which were propagandist in theme. He was included in the 1928 exhibition of Acquisitions by the State Art Collections Fund held in Moscow. He was represented at the jubilee exhibition Artists of the RSFSR over 15 Years held at the Russian Museum, Leningrad, in 1932.
He exhibited with the Kuindzhi Society and the Association of Artists. He died in Leningrad.
Coll Kalinin Art Gallery.

BELYAEV, Aleksandr   a.1913
He contributed to Larionov's exhibition The Target in Moscow in 1913.

BELYAEV, Aleksandr Nikolaevich   1816-1863
Sculptor. Born at Moscow. He studied at the Stroganov College in 1833 and at the Academy under P.K.Klodt from 1840. He executed a marble portrait of *Aivazovsky* in 1843. His work might be described as late neo-classical in style. He worked as a restorer at the Hermitage Museum from 1857. He died at St. Petersburg.
Young David, Victor over Goliath, 1849, plaster, RM, is an

Alexandre Benois.
The Exchange of Favourites,
1902. 11 x 17 cm.
Vignette for the 'World of Art'
periodical, No.12, 1902.

academic piece derived ultimately from the Apollo Belvedere plus the head of Goliath and the sword.
Coll Ryazan Art Museum.

BELYAEVA, N. a.1923
Theatre designer. She contributed to the exhibition Art of Moscow Theatre 1918-1923 held in Moscow in 1923.

BELYAKOVA, Ekaterina Mikhailovna 1892-1980
Decorative artist, painter. Born in Moscow. She studied at the Stroganov College 1909-13 and at the Moscow Vkhutemas until 1924. She exhibited at the third and last exhibition of the *Makovets* group in Moscow 1925-6.
She decorated a series of Moscow buildings in the 1930s including the Rodina Cinema in 1934 as well as cinemas in Astrakhan, Makhachkala and elsewhere in the period 1934-40. She died in Moscow.

BELYANIN, Nikolai Yakovlevich 1888-1962
Landscape painter. Born at Nizhny-Novgorod. He studied at Kazan School of Art under G.A.Medvedev and N.I.Feshin 1906-12 and at the Academy in St. Petersburg under P.E.Myasoedov and N.N.Dubovsky 1912-16.
After the Revolution he was included in the Third Touring Exhibition of the Sovetsk Regional subdepartment of the Museums Bureau along with Kandinsky, Rodchenko and others in 1921.
He moved to Moscow in 1923 and became a member of AKhRR. His work was included in the exhibition of Soviet art held at Harbin in 1926 and in Japan in 1927.
He was represented at the jubilee exhibition Artists of the RSFSR over 15 Years held at the Russian Museum, Leningrad, in 1932. He taught at the Moscow Institute of Applied and Decorative Art 1949-51. He died in Moscow. An exhibition of his work was held in Moscow in 1962.
Coll Odessa Art Museum; Astrakhan Art Gallery; Perm Art Gallery.

BEMBEL', Andrei Onufrevich b.1905-1953+
Belorussian monumental and portrait sculptor. Born in Vitebsk region. He studied at the local art school 1919-22, at the Vitebsk Art Technicum 1924-7 and at the Institute of Proletarian Art in Leningrad 1927-31.

He was represented at the jubilee exhibition Artists of the RSFSR over 15 Years held at the Russian Museum, Leningrad, in 1932. He executed reliefs of workers 1933-4. In 1943 he produced a fragmentary and theatrical bust of *Captain N.F.Gastello*.
He taught at the Minsk Art College 1948-50. His sculpture *Belorussia*, 1950, essentially an image of plenteous fecundity, was installed at the All-Russian Agricultural and Industrial Exhibition in Moscow. He taught at the Belorussian Institute of Theatre Art from 1953. An exhibition of his work was held in Minsk in 1955.
Coll Belorussian Art Museum; Romanian National Gallery, Bucharest.

BEN'KOV, Pavel Petrovich 1879-1949
Painter, theatre designer. Born at Kazan. He studied at Kazan Art School in 1896-1901 and then under D.N.Kardovsky, A.A.Kiselev and Ilya Repin at the Academy in St. Petersburg. He exhibited with the Wanderers. He taught at Kazan School of Art 1909-29. He exhibited in Rome in 1912.
After the Revolution he was represented at the enormous First State Exhibition of Art and Science, which included ethnographic material, held in Kazan in 1920. He was also included in the Third Touring Exhibition of the Sovetsk Regional subdepartment of the Museums Bureau along with Kandinsky, Rodchenko and others in 1921.
He became a member of AKhRR in 1922. He designed the operas *Ivan Susanin* by Glinka and *Carmen* by Bizet for productions at Kazan. In 1923 he designed for the Drama Theatre including Mayakovsky's *Mystery-Bouffe* in 1923 as well as productions in Irkutsk and Omsk. He lived in Samarkand from 1930 and painted landscapes and figures in Bukhara, Samarkand and Khiva including the spinning *Girl of Khiva*, 1931, TG. He taught at the Samarkand Art College 1930-49. He died at Samarkand.
*Friends, 1940, is an idyllic work faintly reminiscent of Sargent in its technique and theme. Eight young girls and an old man laugh, peep and collect grapes beneath the vine's dappled shade and sunlight. This was a form of escapism in 1940.
Coll Uzbek Art Museum; Kuibyshev Art Museum.

BENOIS, Albert Nikolaevich (BENUA, A.N.) 1852-1936
Landscape painter in watercolours. He was the brother of

Alexandre Benois. He studied art and architecture at the Academy in St. Petersburg and exhibited with the Society of Russian Watercolourists which he helped to organise from 1876. He travelled on a scholarship to Italy, France and Spain 1883-5. His watercolours featured the district of St. Petersburg, Western Europe, Asia and North Africa. In 1891 he gave lessons in watercolour painting to Léon Bakst. He exhibited in St. Petersburg in 1903 and 1909, Kiev in 1904 and Petrograd in 1915.

After the Revolution he participated in the First State Free Exhibition of Artworks in Petrograd in 1919. He took part in a geological expedition to the Far North of Russia in 1920 producing landscapes of the Barents Sea and Novaya Zemlya. He also exhibited in Petrograd in 1920 and was included in the enormous survey Exhibition of Paintings by Petrograd Artists of All Tendencies 1919-1923 held in Petrograd in 1923.

He lived in Paris from 1924 exhibiting there in 1928, 1929 and 1930. He died in Paris.

Coll TG; Astrakhan Art Gallery; Far East Art Museum, Khabarovsk; Irkutsk Art Museum; Perm Art Gallery; Volgograd Museum of Fine Art.

BENOIS, Alexandre (BENUA, Aleksandr Nikolaevich) 1870-1960

Painter, theatre and ballet designer, book illustrator and art

Alexandre Benois. Frontispiece for 'Theatre. A Book about the New Theatre', *St. Petersburg, 1907.*

historian. He was a central figure of the World of Art movement as a theorist, organiser and practising artist. His paintings are richly historicist in that elegant and even witty way which was only ever achieved within the World of Art movement. There is no trace of dustiness in his erudite work. His themes, frequently derived from the lost age of Louis XIV or of Elizabeth, Peter and Catherine the Great in Russia, were treated with intelligence and a lightness of touch. Examples include *The Bath of the Marquise* 1906, *Catherine the Great Making Her Entry into the Palace at Tsarskoe Selo* 1909, and *Peter the Great Walking in the Summer Garden* 1910. They were in a sense theatrical works and directly related sometimes to his theatre designs proper.

He was born, the youngest of nine children, into a cultured family of French and Italian extraction living in St. Petersburg. His father, Nikolai Leontevich Benua, was an Academician and an architect. Between 1885 and 1890 he attended high school in St. Petersburg along with Filosofov and Somov both of whom were later to become colleagues within the World of Art movement. He studied art under his brother Albert. In 1889 he was much impressed by a performance of Wagner's Ring cycle of operas. He travelled to Germany the following year where in Munich he saw works by Böcklin, Lenbach and Menzel. He studied briefly as an external student at the Academy of Arts in St. Petersburg 1887-8 but he also attended the University in St. Petersburg from 1890 to study law, graduating in 1894. In 1890 he visited Germany.

He began exhibiting in 1891 with the Society for the Encouragement of the Arts and then with the Society of Russian Watercolourists 1893-6. In addition he began to write as an art-historian, an activity which was to become a significant part of his diverse achievements. His chapter on Russian Art for Richard Muther's *Geschichte der Malerei im XIX Jahrhundert* was published in 1893. He visited Germany, Switzerland and Italy in 1894.

Two other significant activities soon followed. He began to design for the theatre and he began to work as a curator of art. By 1896 the full range of his artistic abilities was engaged. In 1895 he had designed an unrealised production of Glück's opera *Orpheus and Eurydice*, and in 1896 he was invited to organise a Russian art section at the Munich Secession Exhibition at the Glaspalast. He was also engaged as curator of Princess Tenisheva's collection 1895-8. He travelled to Paris with Bakst and Somov in 1896 remaining there until autumn 1899, having produced a series of paintings in 1897 based on the theme of the court of Louis XIV. He attended Whistler's teaching studio in Paris. He published art criticism regularly in the press and produced numerous illustrations including those in 1901 for Nikolai Kutepov's *The Tsarist and Imperial Hunt in Russia. Late Seventeenth and Eighteenth Centuries.*

He was an organiser of the World of Art in the late 1890s. He was represented at the Exhibition of Russian and Finnish Artists in St. Petersburg in 1898, exhibited assiduously with the World of Art from 1899 to 1915 and contributed to its periodical *Mir Iskusstva* 1899-1904. He was a vigorous contributor to many World of Art activities. He also exhibited with the Union of Russian Artists 1903-10. In 1901 he founded the journal *Art Treasures of Russia* and remained its editor until 1903. He designed a dining room in collaboration with Evgeni Lansere displayed at the Contemporary Art Store and Exhibition in St. Petersburg 1902-3. The *World of Art*

Alexandre Benois. November's Breath of Autumn Cold. *Ink on paper. 13.9 x 18.9 cm.*
This design was an illustration to 'The Bronze Horseman' by Pushkin.
State Russian Museum, St. Petersburg.

journal published his illustrations to *The Bronze Horseman* by Pushkin in its first issue in 1904 and Benois effectively became its chief editor. He settled in Paris 1905-7 and saw his work included in Diaghilev's exhibition of Russian art at the 1906 Salon d'Automne. He contributed to the journal *Zolotoe Runo* (Golden Fleece) 1906-8.

He was co-editor of the journal *Starie Gody* (Bygone Years) from 1907 and became Vice-President of the St. Petersburg Society for the Protection and Preservation of Russian Monuments of Art and Antiquity. From 1909 to 1914 he was artistic director of the Moscow Arts Theatre. He executed decorative paintings representing *Asia* and *Europe* for the Kazan Railway Station in Moscow 1914-17.

After the Revolution he was an editor of the children's book publishing house *Parus* (Sail) 1917-18. He was teaching art history at the Free Art Studios in Moscow c.1918 and became Keeper of French and English paintings at the Hermitage Museum from 1918 to 1926. His name appeared on the April 1919 list of artists for acquisitions by the proposed Museum of Painterly Culture and he participated in the First State Free Exhibition of Artworks in Petrograd in 1919. He was represented at the First Russian Art Exhibition in Berlin in 1922. He contributed to the Third Exhibition of Paintings by Artists from Kaluga and Moscow held in Kaluga in 1925.

He emigrated to Paris in 1926 and worked primarily for the stage. He died in Paris.

*Anteroom of the Grand Palace in Pavlovsk, 1902, TG, is characteristic of the ambiguous atmosphere of so much of his work. Ostensibly a recording of the architectural detail of the interior, it in fact becomes an elegy to a lost age of great splendour. Benois could achieve this without the use of costumed characters to fill out a narrative, as he, Serov and Lanceray often employed.

**Frontispiece for Pushkin's *The Bronze Horseman*, 1905, depicts with intense drama the moment when Falconet's celebrated sculpture takes on a terrifying life, casting a long shadow in the moonlight, so that the diminutive figure flies headlong before it.

*Fantasy on a Theme of Versailles, 1906, TG, is a costume piece full of wit and credibly depicted so that the figures dwarfed by the most grandiose of surroundings, hasten windblown between vast hedges and ornamental sculptures like intimate and vigorous ghosts evoked by the painter in his vision of a lost age.

*Parade in the Reign of Paul I, 1907, RM, takes place in a snowstorm; it illustrates how Benois in an imaginative historical evocation could construct a narrative which brought his paintings close to stage design.

Early theatre designs

1901 set for Delibes' ballet *Sylvia*, Act 1 (unrealised). Costumes by Bakst and Serov, Acts 2 and 3 by Korovin, Act 4 by Lansere.

1902 Aleksandr Taneev's opera *Cupid's Vengeance* at the Hermitage Theatre, St. Petersburg (designed 1900): a set design shows a garden of bygone years, grand and formal, with elegant pavilions and immense hedges, peopled by aristocratic 18th century figures wanly drawn in watercolour.

1903 Wagner's *Gotterdämmerung* (Twilight of the Gods) at the Mariinsky Theatre, St. Petersburg, designed in collaboration with K.Korovin.

1907 assisted in the establishment of Nikolai Evreinov's Antique Theatre in St. Petersburg and designed its curtain.

1907 N.Evrienov's *Yarmarka na indikt sv. Denisa* (Fair on St. Denis' Day) at the Starinniy Teatr (Antique Theatre), St. Petersburg.

1907 November *Le Pavillon d'Armide*, ballet pantomime with scenario by Benois based upon T.Gautier's *Omphale*, performed with music by Nikolai N.Cherepnin and choreography by Fokine, at the Mariinsky Theatre, St. Petersburg. It had a set design (RM) which was overwhelmingly dominated by an architectural fantasy worthy of the decorative device of some old architectural book of engravings.

1908 set for Act 4 of *Boris Godunov*, music by Mussorgsky and Rimsky-Korsakov, at the Paris Opera.

1908 Clementi's ballet *The Cheated Buyer* at the Russian Merchant's Club, St. Petersburg.

1908 Franz Grillparzer's *Die Ahnfrau* (The Ancestress) at the V.Komissarzhevskaya Theatre, St. Petersburg.

Designs for Diaghilev's Russian Ballet

1909 *Le Pavillon d'Armide* at the Théâtre du Châtelet, Paris. See 1907 above. Libretto also by Benois.

1909 *Les Sylphides* (Chopiniana), Chopin's music orchestrated by Stravinsky and others, choreography for this one-act ballet by Fokine, at the Théâtre du Châtelet, Paris.

1909 costumes for Diaghilev's production of *Le Festin* at the Théâtre du Châtelet, Paris, in collaboration with Bilibin and Bakst. Décor by K.Korovin.

1910 *Giselle* to music by Adolphe Adam at the Théâtre de l'Opéra, Paris.

1911 June: Benois and Stravinsky's burlesque *Petrushka*, music by Stravinsky and choreography by Fokine, at the Théâtre du Châtelet, Paris: costume designs are loosely handled, full of action and they stress decorative materials as part of the characterisation (Bakhrushin Theatre Museum). The set designs, however, are of decorative and theatrical brilliance with interiors of puppet-like exaggeration and the heaviest, most imaginative form, so that, for example, one interior is decorated with preposterous palm trees against a vermilion background (Thyssen-Bornemisza Collection) and another is filled with the stars of a night sky (Bolshoi Theatre Museum, Moscow).

1914 May: three-act opera *Le Rossignol*, after the story by Hans Andersen, performed at the Théâtre de l'Opéra, Paris. *Mise-en-scène* by Benois and A.Sanin. Music by Stravinsky, choreography by Boris Romanov. The set for the seashore (RM) was closely modelled on Chinese painting and executed substantially in blue to resemble blue and white china. The set for Act 2 was a spacious, deep blue and gold palace interior with a golden throne set among standing vases. The costume designs (RM) are practical and adventurous but have none of the spectacular graphic flare of Bakst.

1922 Chaikovsky's *Marriage of Aurora*, also known as *Le Mariage de la Belle au Bois Dormant*, a one-act ballet. Benois décor in collaboration with Goncharova at the Paris Opera.

1924 January: *Le Medecin malgré lui*, comic opera by Jules Barbier and Michel Carre based upon Molière's text, produced at the Théâtre de Monte Carlo to music by Gounod and Satie and choreography by Bronislava Nijinska. The set for Act 4 depicts the French city seen through two great symmetrical arches in terms close to the historicist architectural fantasias that characterised some of his earlier stage work.

1924 Gounod's *Philémon et Baucis* at the Théâtre de Monte Carlo.

Other designs

1912 Molière's *Tartuffe* (unrealised) and *Le Malade imaginaire* at the Moscow Art Theatre.

1913 Molière's *Le Mariage forcé* and Goldoni's *La Locandiera* at the Moscow Art Theatre.

1914 Pushkin's *Pir vo vremya chumi* (The Feast during the Plague), *Kammenniy Gost* (The Stone Guest) and *Mozart i Salieri* (Mozart and Salieri) at the Moscow Art Theatre.

1916 Chopin's *Les Sylphides* and Stravinsky's *Petrushka* at the Royal Theatre in Madrid.

1917 *Petrushka* at the Mariinsky Theatre, Petrograd (produced 1920, recreated at the Maly Theatre, Leningrad, in 1962).

1919 Cherepnin's *Le Pavillon d'Armide* (revised) at the Mariinsky Theatre, Petrograd.

1920 Stravinsky's *Petrushka* at the Bolshoi Theatre, Moscow (recreated 1964).

1920 Merezhkovsky's *Tsarevich Aleksis*, Shakespeare's *Merchant of Venice* and Goldoni's *Servant of Two Masters* (produced 1921) at the Bolshoi Drama Theatre, Petrograd.

1921 Chaikovsky's opera *Pikovaya Dama* (Queen of Spades) at the Opera and Ballet (Mariinsky) Theatre, Petrograd.

1921 Molière's *Précieuses ridicules* and *Le Médecin malgré lui* at the Bolshoi Drama Theatre, Petrograd.

1922 Shakespeare's *Julius Caesar* at the Bolshoi Drama Theatre, Petrograd, in collaboration with Nicolas Benois.

1923 Henri Meilhac and L.Halévy's *La Boule* (Grelka/The Warming Pan) at the Bolshoi Drama Theatre, Petrograd.

1923 Shakespeare's *A Midsummer Night's Dream* at the People's House Theatre, Petrograd.

1923 Molière's *Le Bourgeois Gentilhomme* at the Academic Theatre, Petrograd.

1923 Verdi's version of Dumas' *La Dame aux camélias* for the Ida Rubinstein Company at the Théâtre Sarah Bernhardt, Paris.

1924 Goldoni's *Fan* (unrealised).

1924 Edouard Pailleron's *Le Monde où l'on s'ennuie* (Act 3) at the Academic Theatre, Petrograd.

1925 Dostoevsky's *The Idiot* adapted for the Ida Rubinstein Company at the Théâtre du Vaudeville, Paris.

1925 the ballet *The Happy Deception* at the London Coliseum.

1926 Beaumarchais' *Marriage of Figaro* at the Moscow Art Theatre/Bolshoi Drama Theatre, Leningrad.

1927 Victor Hugo's *Ruy Blas* at the Comédie Française, Paris.

1927 Honneger's *L'Impératrice des Rochers*, and *Les Noces de Psyché et de l'Amour* at the Paris Opera.

1927 *The Sleeping Beauty* at the Casino, Paris.

1927 Rimsky-Korsakov's *Le Coq d'Or* at the Paris Opera.

1928 Borodin's *Nocturne*, *La Bien-aimée* to music by Schubert and Liszt, Stravinsky's *Le Baiser de la Fée*, Ravel's *Boléro* and Rimsky-Korsakov's ballet *La Cygne Princesse* (The Swan Princess) with choreography by Bronislava Nijinska for the Ida Rubinstein Company at the Théâtre de l'Opéra, Paris.

1929 Georges Auric's *Les Enchantements d'Alcine* for the Ida Rubinstein Company at the Paris Opera.

1930 Rimsky-Korsakov's *Sadko* and Stravinsky's *Petrushka* at the Théâtre des Champs-Elysées, Paris.

1930 Paul Valéry's *Amphion*, music by Honneger, at the Paris Opera.

1932 Bizet's *Carmen* at the Paris Opera.

1934 Honneger's *Sémiramide*, Ravel's *Boléro* and *Diane de Poitiers* at the Paris Opera.

Alexandre Benois. Set Design for 'Petrushka', *1948.*
Watercolour. Signed lower left 'Alexandre Benois' and inscribed lower right 'Petrouchka. II Tableau. 1948'. 23.5 x 35.5 cm.
Collection Mr. and Mrs. Nikita D.Lobanov-Rostovsky, London.

1935 Franck's ballet *Psyché* at the Opéra-Comique, Paris.
1938 Chaikovsky's *Nutcracker* and Massenet's *Le Jongleur de Notre-Dame* at La Scala, Milan.
1940 H.C.Andersen's *Les deux tisserands* at the Théâtre Marigny, Paris. Scene 1 featured a scarlet throne room with white twisted columns.
1941 Chaikovsky's *Eugène Onegin* at the Théâtre Gaîté-Lyrique, Paris.
1942 K.Konstantinov's *Don Philippe* at the Théâtre Pigalle, Paris.
1946 Puccini's *La Bohème* at the Cambridge Theatre, London.
1947 Stravinsky's *Petrushka* at La Scala, Milan.
1948 designs for La Scala, Milan, and for the Paris Opera.
1949 Donizetti's *Lucia di Lamamuir* and other designs for La Scala, Milan, as well as designs for the Paris Opera and for Sadlers Wells Opera, London.
1950-9 Numerous designs for La Scala, Milan.
Film design 1924 *Napoléon.* 1929 *La Capitaine Fracasse* with Eric Aés. 1930 *Mikhail Strogov.* 1936 *Don Quixote.* 1945 *The Idiot* after Dostoevsky.
Art history *Istoriya russkoi zivopisi v XIX veke* (History of Russian Painting in the 19th Century), St. Petersburg, 1901-2. Monograph on *Levitsky*, 1902. Monograph on *Goya*, 1908. *History of Art of All Nations and All Times*, published in twenty-two volumes between 1912 and 1917.
Lit S.Ernst *A.Benua*, Petrograd, 1921. A.Vetrov *A.Benua*, Petrograd, 1921. A.Benois *Reminiscences of the Russian Ballet*, London, 1941. A.Benois *Memoirs*, London, vol.1 1960, vol.2 1964. M.Etkind *A.Benua*, Leningrad-Moscow, 1965. I.S.Zilbershtein and A.N.Savinov *Aleksandr Benua Razmyshlyaet*, Moscow, 1968. G.Bernardt *Aleksandr Benua i muzyka*, Moscow, 1969. *Aleksandr Benua*, exh. cat., Tretyakov Gallery, Moscow, 1972. *Diaghilev and Russian Stage Designers, a Loan Exhibition from the Collection of Mr. and Mrs. N.Lobanov-Rostovsky*, International Exhibitions Foundation, Washington, 1972-4. A.N.Benua *Moi vospominaniya*, Moscow, 1980. J.E.Bowlt *Russian Stage Design. Scenic Innovation. From the Collection of Mr. and Mrs. Nikita D.Lobanov-Rostovsky*, Jackson, MS, exh. cat., 1982. A.Schouvaloff *The Thyssen-Bornemisza Collection: Set and Costume Designs for Ballet and Theatre*, New York-London, 1987. *Twilight of the Tsars*, London, 1991. A.Kamensky *The World of Art Movement*, Leningrad, 1991. Dzhon Boult (John Bowlt) *Khudozhniki russkogo teatra. Sobranie Nikity i Niny Lobanovykh-Rostovskikh*, Moscow, 1991.
Coll TG; RM; Bakhrushin Theatre Museum, Moscow; Pushkin Museum, St. Petersburg; Bolshoi Theatre Museum, Moscow; Odessa Art Museum; Ashmolean Museum, Oxford; Baron Thyssen-Bornemisza Collection, England; Lobanov-Rostovsky Collection, London; Victoria and Albert Museum, London; La Scala Museum, Milan; Bibliothèque Nationale, Paris.

BENOIS, Nicolas (Nikolai Aleksandrovich)   1901-1988
Theatre designer. Born at Oranienbaum, the son of the painter, theatre designer and art historian Alexandre Benois under whom he studied. In collaboration with his father he designed Shakespeare's *Julius Caesar* for the Bolshoi Theatre, Moscow, in 1922.
He emigrated in 1924 and was designing for Nikita Balieff's Chauve-Souris company in Paris 1924-5. He worked as resident designer at La Scala, Milan, from 1936. He became a celebrated and prolific theatre designer working mostly on productions for La Scala in Milan and for the Opera in Rome from the 1920s until the 1960s. He also designed productions for the Teatro Colón in Buenos Aires (1927, 1947), for the Metropolitan Opera House in New York (1975), the National Opera in Sofia (1975) and elsewhere. He settled in Milan.
Theatre design 1924 *Amour et Hiérarchie. Une Bouffonerie du*

Nikolas Benois. Costume Study for an Admiral, *1924. Watercolour. 48 x 32 cm. Signed.*
This design was for the musical review 'Cupid and the Hierarchy, a Buffoonery of Times Past' by A.A.Arkhangelsky performed by the Balieff's Chauve-Souris theatre company at the Théâtre Femina, Paris, in 1924. Collection Mr. and Mrs. Nikita D. Lobanov-Rostovsky, London.

Temps Passé, revue with music by A.Arkhangelsky and libretto by P.Potemkin for the Balieff Chauve-Souris company at the Théâtre Femina, Paris.
1926 Rimsky-Korsakov's opera *The Tale of Tsar Saltan*, based on the poem by Pushkin, libretto by Vladimir Belsky, at the Teatro Colón, Buenos Aires.
Lit *Diaghilev and Russian Stage Designers, a Loan Exhibition from the Collection of Mr. and Mrs. N.Lobanov-Rostovsky*, International Exhibitions Foundation, Washington, 1972-4. *Russian Painters and the Stage 1884-1965, a loan exhibition of stage and costume designs from the Collection of Mr. and Mrs. Nikita D. Lobanov-Rostovsky*, exh. cat., University of Texas at Austin, 1978-9. J.E.Bowlt *Russian Stage Design. Scenic Innovation. From the Collection of Mr. and Mrs. Nikita D.Lobanov-Rostovsky*, Jackson, MS, exh. cat., 1982. A.Schouvaloff *The Thyssen-Bornemisza Collection: Set and Costume Designs for Ballet and Theatre*, New York-London, 1987. Dzhon Boult (John Bowlt) *Khudozhniki russkogo teatra. Sobranie Nikity i Niny Lobanovykh-Rostovskikh*, Moscow, 1991.

BENUA = BENOIS

BERENDGOF, Georgiy Sergeevich 1903-1946
Graphic artist. He studied at the V.N.Meshkov Art School in Moscow in 1916.
After the Revolution he studied at the Proletcult School in 1918 under Falileev and at the Vkhutemas under Pavlinov and Favorsky. He was a member of the Society of Easel Painters which was founded in 1925. He exhibited from 1926 and contributed drawings to numerous periodicals in the 1920s, including *Sinyaya Bluza* (Blue Blouse) and *Smekh* (Laughter).
He contributed to the All-Union Polygraphic Exhibition in Moscow in 1927 and the jubilee exhibition Artists of the RSFSR over 15 Years held at the Russian Museum, Leningrad, in 1932. An exhibition of his work was held in Moscow in 1939.
Coll Perm Art Gallery.

BEREZIN, Ivan Koz'min (Kuz'mich) 1721-1784
Formal portrait painter.
Coll TG.

BERGGOL'TS, Richard Aleksandrovich 1865-1920
Painter. Born in St. Petersburg. He studied in Naples, Paris and Düsseldorf before attending the Academy in St. Petersburg 1888-9. He exhibited with the Society of Russian Watercolourists and became its president. He was painting Italian landscapes in 1898. Sometimes he signed his work 'Bergholz'. He died in Petrograd.
Coll TG; Kursk Art Gallery; Omsk Museum of Fine Art; Tallin Art Museum .

BERINGOV, Mitrofan Mikhailovich 1889-1937
Painter. Born in the Penza region. He initially studied painting at a seminary in Penza under N.K.Grandkovsky 1903-5. He was involved in the 1905 Revolution. He studied at the Drawing School for the Society for the Encouragement of the Arts in Petrograd 1913-15 under Nikolai Roerich and A.A.Rylov.
He was involved in the Revolution of 1917 and made a portrait of Lenin from life in 1917. He became a member of the Commission for the Preservation of Art Treasures and one of the organisers of the art museum during his time in Tomsk 1919-21. He moved to Moscow in 1922 and the same year became a member of AKhR. He specialised in Revolutionary history painting during the 1920s. From 1925 he travelled in the far north and executed paintings of the Soviet Arctic. He was represented at the jubilee exhibition Artists of the RSFSR over 15 Years held at the Russian Museum, Leningrad, in 1932. He died in Moscow.
Coll TG; RM; Perm Art Museum; Saratov Art Museum; Astrakhan Regional Picture Gallery.

BERKHOL'TS = BERGGOL'TS, R.A.

BERKHOVSKY, G.E. a.1911
He exhibited with the Union of Youth in 1911.

BERMAN, Evgeni (Eugène) Gustavovich 1899-1972
Painter, theatre designer. Born in St. Petersburg. In 1908 he travelled to Germany, Switzerland and France. He studied painting under Pavel Naumov from 1914.
He settled in Paris in 1918 where he studied at the Académie Ranson under Vuillard and Denis in 1919. He visited Italy in 1922 and exhibited with a group which included Tchelitchew at the Galerie Druet in Paris in 1924. He exhibited at the Julien Levy Gallery, New York, in 1930. He turned to theatre design

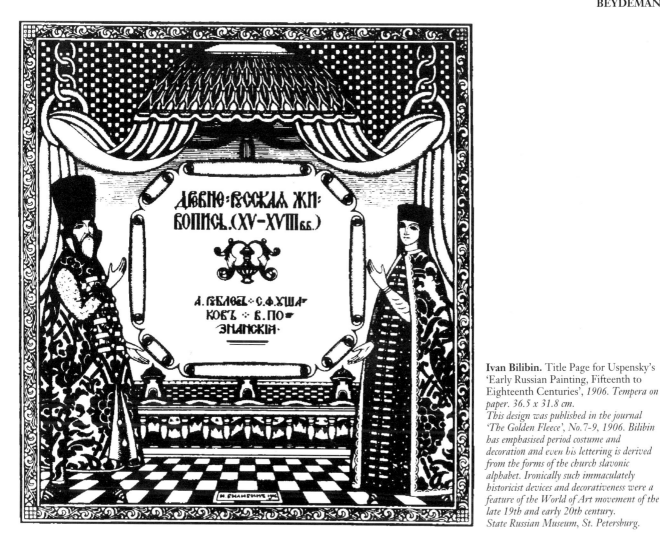

Ivan Bilibin. Title Page for Uspensky's 'Early Russian Painting, Fifteenth to Eighteenth Centuries', *1906. Tempera on paper. 36.5 x 31.8 cm.*
This design was published in the journal 'The Golden Fleece', No.7-9, 1906. Bilibin has emphasised period costume and decoration and even his lettering is derived from the forms of the church slavonic alphabet. Ironically such immaculately historicist devices and decorativeness were a feature of the World of Art movement of the late 19th and early 20th century.
State Russian Museum, St. Petersburg.

in 1936. He took U.S. citizenship in 1937. He died in Rome.
Theatre design 1939 October *The Devil's Holiday* (Le diable s'amuse), comic ballet, libretto by V.Tommasini on themes from Paganini, for the sadlers Wells Ballet, London.
Lit *Eugene Berman*, exh. cat. Instituto de Arte moderno, Buenos Aires, 1950. *Eugene Berman in Perspective*, exh. cat., University of Texas, Austin, 1975. J.E.Bowlt *Russian Stage Design. Scenic Innovation. From the Collection of Mr. and Mrs. Nikita D.Lobanov-Rostovsky*, Jackson, MS, exh. cat.,1982.

BERNGOF, M. Yu.   **a.1919**
Painter. He was represented in the Fourth State Exhibition of Paintings (*IV Gosudarstvennaya vystavka kartin*) in Moscow in 1919.

BERNSHTEIN, Mikhail Davidovich   1875-1960
Painter, graphic artist. Born at Rostov-on-Don. He studied in London 1894-9 and then Munich and Paris until 1901 before attending the Academy in St. Petersburg under Ilya Repin until 1903. He organised and directed an art school in St. Petersburg 1907-16 where wrestling was part of the study of the figure. His pupils included Sarra Lebedeva from 1910 and Vladimir Lebedev in 1912.
After the Revolution directed the art school at Zhitomir until 1924. He subsequently taught at the Art Institute at Kiev 1924-32 and the Repin Academy in Leningrad 1932-48. He died at Leningrad.

BERSHADSKY, Grigori Solomonovich   1895-1963
Painter and graphic artist. Born Kiev region. He studied under P.A.Vlasov in Astrakhan 1908-13 and at the Odessa School of Art 1913-15. He exhibited from 1915.
After the Revolution he designed posters and illustrated numerous books. He worked in Kharkov 1920-3 and then in Moscow. He concentrated on typography and book design in the 1940s and 1950s. An exhibition of his work was held in Moscow in 1956. He died in Moscow.
*Nizhny-Novgorod Exhibition, poster, 1928, featured camels by the river, whilst a poster advertising *Export USSR* of the late 1920s was assembled in such a way as to fill the lettering with export goods.
Lit *G.S.Bershadsky*, exh. cat., MOSKh (Moscow Section of Soviet Artists), Moscow, 1956.
Coll Astrakhan Art Gallery.

BESPALOVA, T.   **a.1932**
She was represented at the jubilee exhibition Artists of the RSFSR over 15 Years held at the Russian Museum, Leningrad, in 1932.

BEYDEMAN, Aleksandr Egorovich   1826-1869
Painter of biblical themes and genre as well as ikons, etcher. Born in St. Petersburg. He studied at the Academy in St. Petersburg under K.P.Bryullov and A.T.Markov in the 1850s. He lived abroad 1857-60 visiting Munich in 1857 and also

travelling to France and Italy. On his return he taught at the Academy. He died in St. Petersburg.
Coll TG.

BEYGUL', A.N.   a.1919
He exhibited at the juryless Eighth State Exhibition in Moscow in 1919.

BEYGUN   a.1919
He was represented along with Kandinsky, Chagall and others at the First State Exhibition of Paintings by Local and Moscow Artists held in Vitebsk in December 1919.

BIBIKOV, Georgiy Nikolaevich   **1903-1976**
Painter of industrial themes, theatre designer. He studied at the Omsk Art and Industrial School 1920-5 and at the Institute for Proletarian Art in Leningrad until 1930. He specialised in Socialist Realist themes, including *Osoaviakhim-1*, 1935, RM, which depicts Red Army soldiers restraining a stratospheric balloon prior to its ascent whilst the occupants of its metal sphere are saluted by the military man in charge. He was represented at the jubilee exhibition Artists of the RSFSR over 15 Years held at the Russian Museum, Leningrad, in 1932.
Theatre design 1936 V.M.Gusev's *Slava* (Glory) designed in collaboration with A.N.Samokhvalov at the Leningrad Bolshoi Drama Theatre.
1944 K.A.Korchmarev's *Aldar Kose* at the Kazakh Music Theatre.
Lit A.M.Muratov, V.Manin et al. *Zhivopis' 20-30kh godov*, Sankt-Peterburg, 1991.
Coll RM.

BIGOS, Sergei Dem'yanovich   **1895-1937**
Graphic artist. He studied at the Moscow Vkhutein 1924-30. He was active as an illustrator of periodicals, including *Krasnie*

Ivan Bilibin. Tailpiece for Alexandre Benois' 'Russian School of Painting', *1906. Tempera on paper mounted on card. 21.9 x 26.5 cm. Medieval boats are glimpsed sailing past the open portal of a castle wall. A stylised and decorative sun, worthy of a lubok print, dominates the symmetrical composition. Bilibin creates an atmosphere of a fictional Russian past. State Russian Museum, St. Petersburg.*

zori (Red Dawn) at Irkutsk in 1923, and of books in the later 1920s and 1930s. He was represented at the jubilee exhibition Artists of the RSFSR over 15 Years held at the Russian Museum, Leningrad, in 1932.
Coll TG.

BIKSHE, Karl Karlovich (PIKSHE, Zhanno) b.1887-1918+
Architect and artist. Studied at the St. Petersburg Academy 1909-15. He executed Agitprop decorations for Pantelemonovsky Bridge and Summer Garden, Petrograd, in 1918.

BILIBIN, Alexander (BILIBINE, Aleksandr Ivanovich) 1903-1972
Theatre designer. Born at St. Petersburg. The eldest son of Ivan Bilibin and Maria Chembers-Bilibina. He left Russia with his mother in 1914 and from 1917 he lived in Egypt. He studied in London at the Central School of Art and at the Royal Academy Schools under Sickert and McEvoy. He died at Harting in England.
Theatre design 1941 *The Mask of Death*, ballet based upon E.A.Poe and choreographed by Fokine (unrealised).
Lit J.E.Bowlt *Russian Stage Design. Scenic Innovation. From the Collection of Mr. and Mrs. Nikita D.Lobanov-Rostovsky*, Jackson, MS, exh. cat., 1982.

BILIBIN, Ivan Yakovlevich   **1876-1942**
Painter, theatre designer and illustrator. Born St. Petersburg region into the family of a naval doctor. From 1895 to 1898 he attended the School for the Encouragement of the Arts but also enrolled in 1896 as a student of law at St. Petersburg University. In 1898 he briefly attended the Azbé School in Munich and then Princess Tenisheva's art school under Repin 1898-1900. Bakst introduced him to the World of Art which he joined in 1899. He subsequently became an external student under Repin at the Academy in St. Petersburg 1900-4. He exhibited with the World of Art 1900-17 and with the Union of Russian Artists.
A recurrent fascination with folk art formed a major theme of his early work. He produced lavish illustrations to folk stories early in his career 1901-10. He exhibited with the Union of Russian Artists from 1903 to 1910. He travelled on ethnographic expeditions to the north of Russia in the period 1902-4 and his article *Popular Art of the Russian North* appeared in the *World of Art* journal in 1904. Diaghilev included his work in his exhibition of Russian art at the 1906 Salon d'Automne in Paris. Early illustrative work included his richly colourful and lavish decorations to Pushkin's *Golden Cockerel* which were created 1906-7, also contributions to the satirical journal *Zhupel'*, in which he published *An Ass (Equus Asinus) 1/20th. Natural Size* in 1906, as well as the journals *Zolotoe Runo* (Golden Fleece) in 1907 and *Satirikon* 1908-13.
He taught at the Society for the Encouragement of the Arts in St. Petersburg from 1907 until the Revolution. At the same time he became an active theatre designer. He exhibited with the First Izdebsky International Salon 1909-10 and the same year was a co-founder of a revival of the World of Art with Benois, Dobuzhinsky, Roerich, Somov and others, becoming its President in 1916. He made illustrations for the periodical *New Satirikon* 1914-18. He executed murals for a bank in Nizhny-Novgorod in 1913 and for the Kazan Station in Moscow in 1915.
After the Revolution he left Petrograd to live in the Crimea

from 1917 until 1920 but he participated in the First State Free Exhibition of Artworks in Petrograd in 1919.

He then emigrated, first to Cairo in 1920 and then to Alexandria. He subsequently moved to Paris where he lived from 1925.

He returned to the Soviet Union in 1936. He illustrated books for Goslitizdat, including works by A.N.Tolstoy in 1937 and Lermontov in 1941, and was Professor in the Graphic Art Studio of the Leningrad Academy 1936-42. He died of hunger in the siege of Leningrad.

An exhibition of his work was held in Leningrad in 1952.

Theatre design 1904 Rimsky-Korsakov's *Snegurochka* in Prague.

1907 décors for Rutebeuf's *The Miracle of Theophilus* at Evreinov's Antique Theatre: a monumental and decoratively stylised backdrop inspired directly by Last Judgement ikons, featuring a monstrous hell mouth at the bottom, a fairy tale citadel on liquid-looking rocks and a vacant apse raised in the heavens (Bakhrusin Theatre Museum).

1908 May: costumes and accessories for Mussorgsky's opera *Boris Godunov* produced by Diaghilev at the Paris Opera with sets by Benois and Golovin.

1908 Meyerhold's production of P.Potemkin's *Petrushka* designed in collaboration with Dobuzhinsky.

1908 December Meyerhold's production of F.L.Sologub's *Honour and Vengeance* at the Lukomor'e Theatre Club in St. Petersburg.

1909 costumes for Diaghilev's production of *Le Festin* at the Théâtre du Châtelet, Paris, in collaboration with Bakst, Benois. Décor by K.Korovin.

1909 sets and costumes for Rimsky-Korsakov's *Golden Cockerel* at S.I.Zimin's Opera Theatre in Moscow show the graphic precision and love of decoration that characterised his illustrations to folk stories. The costume designs are overtly fantastic, amusing and decorative (Bakhrushin Theatre Museum). The set design for Act 1 could be a book illustration: it is executed in minute and precise detail depicting Dadon's Palace without a single lie loose, soft or out of place. This is the precision of the graphic artist who, fascinated by his scholarship, seeks to recreate in fairy-tale terms an enjoyable illusion rather than an elegant or mysterious design.

1911 décors for Rutebeuf's *The Miracle of Theophilus*. See 1907 above.

1911 Lope de Vega's *Fuente ovejuna* and Calderon's *Purgatory of St.Patrick* at the Antique Theatre, St. Petersburg.

1911-12 Aleksei Verstovsky's *Tomb of Askold* at S.I.Zimin's Opera Company, Moscow.

1913-14 Glinka's *Ruslan and Ludmila* at the People's House Theatre, St. Petersburg: Chernomor's Gardens in Scene 1 (Theatre Museum, Leningrad) reveal his ability with scale as immense rocks viewed from a cave form a grim gorge through which a tall slot of space reveals a crescent moon in the night sky.

1914 Rimsky-Korsakov's *Sadko* at the People's House Theatre, St. Petersburg: a set design for the Chambers of the Novgorod Fraternity (Theatre Museum, Leningrad) evokes in detail the low arched vaults of a medieval monastic interior every wall surface of which is decorated with colourful stylised paintings.

Later theatre design

1929 Rimsky-Korsakov's *The Tale of the Invisible City of Kitezh*

Ivan Bilibin. Study of a costume for the Billy Goat in the Entourage of Kashcha in the ballet 'The Firebird', *1910. Watercolour, gouache, pencil. Signed 'I.B.1910' in Russian and 'I.Bilibine' lower right. 38 x 27 cm. Designed for Stravinsky's 'Firebird' (Zhar-ptitsa) staged by M.M.Fokine at the Teatro Colón, Buenos Aires, in 1931, originally produced by Diaghilev in 1910.*
Collection Mr. and Mrs. Nikita D. Lobanov-Rostovsky, London.

and the Maid Fevronia, produced by the M.N.Kuznetsova (Marie Kousnetsoff) Opéra Privé de Paris at the Théâtre des Champs-Elysées, Paris. Libretto by V.Belsky and finally staged with designs by A.Korovin.

1929 Rimsky-Korsakov's opera *The Tale of Tsar Saltan*, produced by the M.N.Kuznetsova Opéra Privé de Paris at the Théâtre des Champs-Elysées, Paris.

1931 costumes for Stravinsky's *Firebird* ballet.

1934 sets and costumes for *The Tale of the Invisible City of Kitezh and the Maid Fevronia* at Brno.

Book design 1899 *Mariya Morevna*; 1902 *The White Duckling*; 1904-1906, published1907, *The Tale of Tsar Saltan*; 1906-1907, published 1910, *The Tale of the Golden Cockerel*; 1919 Pushkin's *Ruslan and Ludmila*; 1939 Lermontov's *The Song of the Merchant Kalashnikov*; 1941 *Diuk Stepanovich*.

Lit I.N.Lipovich *I.Ya.Bilibin*, Leningrad, 1966. G.V. and S.V.Golynets *I.Ya.Bilibin*, Leningrad, 1972. *Diaghilev and Russian Stage Designers, a Loan Exhibition from the Collection of Mr. and Mrs. N.Lobanov-Rostovsky*, International Exhibitions Foundation, Washington, 1972-4. J.E.Bowlt *Russian Stage Design. Scenic Innovation. From the Collection of Mr. and Mrs. Nikita D.Lobanov-Rostovsky*, Jackson, MS, exh. cat.,1982.

A.Kamensky *The World of Art Movement*, Leningrad, 1991.
Dzhon Boult (John Bowlt) *Khudozhniki russkogo teatra. Sobranie Nikity i Niny Lobanovykh-Rostovskikh*, Moscow, 1991.
Coll TG; RM; Goznak Museum, Moscow; Pushkin Museum, St. Petersburg; Kalinin Art Gallery; Bakhrushin Theatre Museum, Moscow; Ashmolean Museum, Oxford.

BILINSKY, Boris Konstantinovich   1910-1948
Painter, theatre and film designer associated with the style of the World of Art. Born at Bendery near Odessa. He grew up in the Ukraine.
After the Revolution he moved to Berlin in 1920 working for cabarets including the Blaue Vogel. He settled in Paris in 1922. He turned to stage design in the later 1920s in Western Europe. He moved to Sicily in 1939. He died at Catania, Sicily.
Theatre design 1930 June: Glinka's opera *Ruslan and Ludmila*, produced by N.Evreinov for the Opéra Russe de Paris, Théâtre des Champs-Elysées, Paris.
1932 *La Princesse Cygne*, ballet based on Pushkin's *Tale of Tsar Saltan* with music from Rimsky-Korsakov's opera with choreography by Bronislava Nijinska. Performed by the Ballets Nijinska at the Théâtre de l'Opéra Comique, Paris.
1933 *Symphonie Fastastique*, ballet.
Film design 1927 *Casanova*; 1928 A.Volkoff's *Schéhérazade*, Universum Film Aktien Gesellschaft (UFA-Film), Berlin. 1929 *Monte Cristo*.
Lit *Diaghilev and Russian Stage Designers, a Loan Exhibition from the Collection of Mr. and Mrs. N.Lobanov-Rostovsky*, International Exhibitions Foundation, Washington, 1972-4. *Russian Painters and the Stage 1884-1965, a loan exhibition of stage and costume designs from the Collection of Mr. and Mrs. Nikita D. Lobanov-Rostovsky*, exh. cat., University of Texas at Austin, 1978-9. J.E.Bowlt *Russian Stage Design. Scenic Innovation. From the Collection of Mr. and Mrs. Nikita D.Lobanov-Rostovsky*, Jackson, MS, exh. cat.,1982.

BIRULYA = BYALYNITSKY-BIRULYA, V.K.

BLAK, Lyubov' Karlovna   b.1908-1964+
Artist, ceramics artist. Born in Moscow. She studied at the Leningrad Art and Industry Technikum under N.I.Dormidontov 1927-31. She executed designs for the Leningrad Lomonosov Porcelain Factory from 1931. She was represented at the jubilee exhibition Artists of the RSFSR over 15 Years held at the Russian Museum, Leningrad, in 1932 and at the Paris International Exhibition of 1937. She was still decorating ceramic ware in the 1960s.
Coll RM; Museum of the Leningrad Lomonosov Porcelain Factory.

BLAZHEVICH, A. N.   a.1919-1920
Sculptor. His work was included in the First Exhibition of the Moscow Contemporary Art Store in January 1919 and he entered the competion for a *Monument to Karl Marx* that year. From 1919 to 1920 he was a founder of the *Monolit* (Monolith) group of sculptors, which included Babichev, Mukhina, Konen'kov, Krandevskaya, Korolev, Strakhovskaya, Zlatovratsky, Ternovets, V.Popova, Blazhevich and Kudinov. They worked on monumental propaganda and entered the competitive exhibition for a Monument to Liberated Labour held in Moscow in May 1920.

BLOKH, Leonora (Eleonora) Abramovna   1881-1943
Sculptor of figures and portraits in plaster, granite and bronze. She studied at the school of the Society for the Encouragement

Boris Bilinsky. Costume for the Priest in the 'Swan Princess'. *Watercolour. Signed lower right and inscribed in Italian. 49.5 x 31 cm. Collection Mr. and Mrs. Nikita D. Lobanov-Rostovsky, London.*

of the Arts in St. Petersburg in 1898 under R.R.Bakh and then under Rodin in Paris from 1898 to 1905. She exhibited from 1910 and lived in St. Petersburg from 1912 to 1917. She exhibited with the World of Art in 1917.
After the Revolution she lived at Kharkov where she taught at the Art Tekhnikum from 1922 and at the Art Institute. Her portrait sculptures included a bust of Rodin. She made busts of Marx and Engels 1933-4 as well as T.G.Shevchenko 1932, Gorky 1933, and V.G.Korolenko 1944. She died at Talgor, Kazakhstan.
Coll Kharkov Art Museum.

BLUMENFELD, G.   a.1916-1917
Painter. Exhibited with the World of Art 1916-17.

BLUMENFELD, N.   a.1916-1917
Painter. Exhibited with the World of Art 1916-17.

BLUVSHTEIN, Ya.Z. = BUVSHTEIN, Ya.Z.

BOBKOV, Ivan   a.1914
Painter. He contributed twenty-four works to the exhibition No.4 in Moscow in 1914.

BOBOKHOVA   a.1916
Painter. She exhibited with the World of Art in Moscow in 1916.

BOBROV, Aleksei Alekseevich   **1849-1899**
Painter whose subjects included interiors. He was an external student at the Academy in St. Petersburg from 1866. Mostly an engraver of other artists' paintings after 1875.
Coll TG; RM.

BOBROV, Sergei Pavlovich   **1899-1971**
Writer, graphic artist. He was a member of the group *Oslinyy Khvost* (Donkey's Tail) along with Larionov and Goncharova in 1912. After the Revolution he executed book designs for the Tsentrifuga publishing house in a loose calligraphic style over collage elements. Popova designed the cover of his *Vosstanie mizantropov* (Revolt of the Misanthropes) in 1922.
Book design Cover for *Lira lir* (Lyre of Lyres), Moscow, 1917.
Lit S.Compton *Russian Avant-Garde Books 1917-34*, London, 1992.

BOBROV, Vasili Dmitrievich   **a.1920-1921**
He studied under Kandinsky and worked as his secretary until 1921. Untitled watercolours of 1921 strongly resemble those of Kandinsky.
Lit A.Z.Rudenstine *Costakis Collection*, 1981.

BOBROV, Viktor Alekseevich   **1842-1918**
Portrait painter, engraver. Born in the St. Petersburg region. He was the brother of A.A.Bobrov. He studied at the Academy in St. Petersburg 1860-7. He worked in oils but also in water-colour and was active as an etcher and engraver from the 1870s. He died in Petrograd.
Coll TG; RM; Pavlovsk Palace Museum; Perm Art Gallery.

BOBROVSKY, Grigori Mikhailovich   **1873-1942**
Portrait and landscape painter. Born at Vitebsk. He studied at the Academy in St. Petersburg under Repin 1893-1900. He taught at the Drawing School of the Society for the Encouragement of the Arts in St. Petersburg 1905-17. He became a member of the Union of Russian Artists and exhibited with the World of Art in 1911. He exhibited in Munich in 1911 and 1913, and painted Neapolitan scenes 1915-16.
After the Revolution he was in charge of the Agitprop decorations for Blagoveshchensky Square, Petrograd, in 1918. He continued to work as a landscape and portrait painter and taught in Leningrad from 1921. He exhibited work in New York in 1924. He died at Leningrad where an exhibition of his work was held in 1947.
Lit *Twilight of the Tsars*, London, 1991.
Coll RM; Astakhan Art Gallery; Krasnodar Art Museum.

BOCHAROV, Mikhail Ilych   **1831-1895**
Painter of Italian views, theatre designer. He designed sets for Shakespeare's *Hamlet* in the 1890s and also for Glinka's opera *Ruslan and Lyudmila*.
After the Revolution he held an exhibition in Kazan in 1925.
Coll TG.

BODAREVSKY, Nikolai Kornilievich   **1850-1921**
Portrait painter. Born at Odessa. He studied at the Academy in St. Petersburg from 1869 and exhibited with the Wanderers from 1880. He worked in the Ukraine. An exhibition of his work was held in St. Petersburg in 1913.
Coll TG; RM; Odessa Art Museum.

BODNEK, Yu. Yu.   **a.1922**
He exhibited with the Union of New Tendencies in Art in Petrograd in June 1922 and was included in the enormous survey Exhibition of Paintings by Petrograd Artists of All Tendencies 1919-1923 held in Petrograd in 1923.

BODRI, Karl-Fridrikh Petrovich   **1812-1894**
Landscape painter. He studied at the Moscow College 1833-9 and at the Academy in St. Petersburg from 1843.
Coll TG; RM.

BOEV, Petr Nikolaevich   **1868-1919**
Painter. He taught at the Art School in Saratov in the 1900s. After the Revolution he was engaged in Agitprop decorations at Saratov in 1918.

BOGAEVSKY, I.S. = BUGAEVSKY, I.S.

BOGAEVSKY, Konstantin Fedorovich   **1872-1943**
Landscape painter, graphic artist associated with the World of Art. Born at Feodosia. He studied there under A.Fessler and Ivan Aivazovsky in the 1880s and subsequently at the Academy in St. Petersburg from 1891 to 1897 under Kuindzhi. He visited France, Germany and Austria in 1897. He exhibited in Munich and Venice in 1903. He exhibited with the New Society of Artists 1904-7, was included in Diaghilev's display of Russian art at the 1906 Salon d'Automne in Paris, and in 1907 he again exhibited in Munich. He exhibited with the Union of Russian Artists from 1907 to 1910. He exhibited with the World of Art 1907-9 and 1911-13. He travelled to Italy and Greece 1907-8. He also exhibited with the Union of Russian Artists from 1908 to 1916, with the Society of South Russian Artists and he exhibited with the First Izdebsky International Salon 1909-10. He showed work in Paris in 1910, Venice in 1911, London in 1912, Venice again in 1913 and Leipzig in 1914.
After the Revolution he was represented at the enormous First State Exhibition of Art and Science, which included ethnographic material, held in Kazan in 1920. He produced works celebrating Soviet construction achievements at the Dneprostroy Dam, Baku and in the Donbass. He exhibited with the *Zhar-tsvet* (Fire-colour) group between 1924 and 1928 when he was given a special exhibition by the group. He sent work to Venice in 1924. He was included in the 1928 exhibition of Acquisitions by the State Art Collections Fund held in Moscow. He was represented in the exhibition of Russian Graphics at Riga and in the First Touring Exhibition of Paintings and Graphics which opened in Moscow in 1929. Exhibitions of his work were held in Kazan in 1927, Moscow 1928 and Feodosia in 1932.
He was represented at the jubilee exhibition Artists of the RSFSR over 15 Years held at the Russian Museum, Leningrad, in 1932. He died at Feodosia. Exhibitions were held in Moscow in 1961 and Feodosia in 1964.
Kaffa (Old Feodosia), 1927, TG, is a deliberately historicising coastal landscape meticulously painted and somewhat classical, lying in style somewhere between Claude and Roerich.
Lit *K.F.Bogaevsky*, Kazan, 1927. R.D.Bashchenko *K.F.Bogaevsky*, Simferopol, 1963. *Twilight of the Tsars*, London, 1991. A.M.Muratov, V.Manin et al. *Zhivopis' 20-30kh godov*, Sankt-Peterburg, 1991.
Coll TG; RM; Feodosia Art Gallery; Perm Art Gallery; Simferopol Art Museum.
Colour plate p.59.

BOGATOV, Nikolai Alekseevich   1854-1935
Painter of horses, graphic artist, theatre designer. Born in
Moscow. He studied at the Moscow College until 1875. He
exhibited with the Wanderers and was active as an illustrator
of books in the 1880s.
After the Revolution in 1918 he painted *The Liberation of the
Political Prisoners from Butyrsky Prison on 2 March 1917*.
Coll TG; Kalinin Art Gallery; Omsk Fine Art Museum.

BOGATOV, V. V.   a.1919
He exhibited at the Twelfth State Exhibition: Colourdynamo
and Tectonic Primitivism (*XII Gosudarstvennaya vystavka.
Tsvetodinamos i tektonichesky primitivizm*) in Moscow in 1919
along with Grishchenko, Shevchenko and others.

BOGATYREV, Vasili Semenovich   1871-1941
Sculptor. Born in the Tver region. He studied at the Academy
in St. Petersburg 1893-9 and later exhibited with the
Wanderers. With M.Ya.Kharlamov he executed a frieze for
the Ethnographic Museum in St. Petersburg in 1902-8. He
worked in Kazan from 1908, teaching at the Art School there
until 1925.
After the Revolution he continued to sculpt portraits including
Lenin and *Chaikovsky*. He was represented at the enormous
First State Exhibition of Art and Science, which included
ethnographic material, held in Kazan in 1920, and he was also
included in the Third Touring Exhibition of the Sovetsk
Regional subdepartment of the Museums Bureau along with
Kandinsky, Rodchenko and others in 1921. He taught at the
Leningrad Academy 1934-41. He died at Leningrad.

BOGDANOV, Ivan Petrovich   1855-1932
Genre and history painter. Born in Moscow. He studied at the
Moscow College from 1878 to 1889 under Makovsky and
Pryanishnikov. From 1891 he exhibited with the Wanderers,
becoming a member in 1895.
After the Revolution he taught in several art schools in the
1920s and in 1929 he became a member of the Moscow Union
of Realist Artists. He died in Moscow.
Coll TG; Volgograd Art Gallery.

BOGDANOV, N.T.   a.1919
Painter. He exhibited at the Ninth State Exhibition of Paintings:
Naturalism and Realism in Moscow in 1919.

BOGDANOV, Sergei Aleksandrovich   b.1888-1940+
Painter. Born at Tambov. He studied under Arkhipov and
Korovin at the Moscow College 1914-17.
After the Revolution he contributed to the First State
Exhibition in Orenburg in 1921. He became a member of
AKhRR. He was represented in the First Touring Exhibition
of Paintings and Graphics which opened in Moscow in 1929.

BOGDANOV-BEL'SKY, Nikolai Petrovich   1868-1945
Painter of rural life and portraits. He was born of a peasant
family in the Smolensk region. After studying as an ikon
painter, from 1884 to 1889 he studied at the Moscow College
under Polenov, Makovsky and Pryanishnikov. He then studied
at the Academy in St. Petersburg under Repin and at the
Académie Colarossi in Paris. He exhibited with the
Wanderers from 1890, becoming a member in 1895, and he
exhibited in Paris in 1900. He was an Academician from 1903.

His portraits include the singer *Chaliapine*, 1916.
After the Revolution he participated in the First State Free
Exhibition of Artworks in Petrograd in 1919. He lived in
Latvia from 1921. He exhibited work in New York in 1924.
His portrait of the writer *Maxim Gorky*, 1940, is in Gorky
Museum, Moscow.
Coll TG; RM; Perm Art Gallery; Smolensk Museum.

BOGDANOVICH, Vladimir Evgen'evich   a.1907-d.1918
Printmaker, painter. He was active as an etcher in Moscow in
the early 1900s. He exhibited at the Lemers'e (Lemercier)
Gallery, Moscow, in 1915 and at the Eighth Exhibition of
Russian and Foreign Graphic Artists in Moscow in 1917.
After the Revolution he was represented at the Exhibition of
Pictures by the Professional Union of Artists in Moscow in
1918 and posthumously at the Sixth State Exhibition: The
Print (*VI Gosudarstvennaya vystavka gravyur*) in Moscow in
1919. He died in Moscow.

BOGOLYUBOV, Aleksei Petrovich   1824-1896
Academic landscape and marine painter, lithographic artist,
theatre designer. Born in the Novgorod region. He attended
Naval Academy before becoming an external student under
V.P.Villevalde and M.N.Vorob'ev at the Academy in St.
Petersburg from 1850 to 1853. He then worked abroad from
1854 to 1860 in Geneva, Paris under Isabey, and Düsseldorf
under Achenbach whilst also visiting Italy, Switzerland and
Turkey. He undertook painting expeditions along the Volga
in 1861, 1862 and 1869.
He was one of the organisers of the Wanderers and he
exhibited in the first Wanderers exhibition. He again worked
abroad after 1873 and taught Russian artists at his studio in
Paris where he founded the Circle of Russian Artists in Paris
in 1878. He also painted in Venice. He exhibited with the
Society of Russian Watercolourists from 1882.
He taught in Saratov where he founded the Saratov Museum
of Russian Art (now the Radishev Art Museum), to which he
bequeathed his possessions, and its associated art school which
opened in 1897. Sometimes he signed his work 'Bogoluboff'.
He died in Paris.
Baku. Street at Midday, 1861, RM, is a glimpse of a backstreet
with sun, shade and shops among the minarets. Some goods
are laid out for sale. There are two figures in tall hats.
Lit G.Kozhevnikov *A.P.Bogolyubov*, Moscow, 1949.
M.I.Andronikova *Bogolyubov*, Moscow, 1962.
Coll Substantial holdings in TG; RM; Saratov Art Museum;
Irkutsk Art Museum.

BOGOLYUBOV, Veniamin Yakovlevich   1895-1954
Sculptor. Born at Tsarskoe Selo. He served on the Baltic Fleet
until 1927. He then studied under R.R.Bakh, V.V.Lishev and
A.T.Matveev at the Leningrad Vkhutemas 1926-30. He
collaborated on the mosaic decorations of the *Lenin
Mausoleum* in 1930. He executed a monument to *Rimsky-
Korsakov*, 1944-8, erected in Leningrad in 1952, and a *Lenin*
for Riga in 1950. He executed numerous portraits of
academics, artistic personalities and military figures. An
exhibition of his work was held in Leningrad in 1951. He died
at Leningrad.
Monument to S.Ordzhonikidze, 1935 and version 1937, TG

and RM, executed in collaboration with B.I.Ingal and V.I.Ingal, with whom he worked on several monuments, is an imposing full-length with a clenched fist.
Coll TG; RM; Sverdlovsk Art Gallery.

BOGOMAZOV, Aleksandr Konstantinovich   1880-1930
Painter, graphic artist. Born at Yampol' in the Kharkov region of the Ukraine. He studied under V.K.Menk, A.A.Murashko and I.F.Seleznev at the Kiev Art Institute 1902-11, but he also attended the studios of F.I.Rerberg and K.Yuon in Moscow 1907-8. He worked in Kiev and contributed to the exhibition *Zveno* (The Link) in Kiev in 1908. He visited Finland in 1911.He contributed to the All-Russian Exhibition in Kiev in 1913. He probably also received tuition from Aleksandra Exter with whom he exhibited at the The Ring which he organised at the Polytechnic Institute in Kiev in 1914. He wrote an unpublished book *Elementy zhivopisi* (Elements of Painting) in 1914. He worked at Heriusi in the northern Caucasus 1914-17. After the Revolution he returned to Kiev in 1917 and in 1919 he taught at the First State Painting and Decorative Studio there. He was engaged on Agitprop decorations 1919-20. He taught at the Kiev School of Printmaking 1918-22 and at the Art Institute there 1922-30. He became a founder member of ARMU in the 1927. He died at Kiev. An exhibition of his work was held in Kiev in 1966.
Lit J.E.Bowlt *Russian Stage Design. Scenic Innovation. From the Collection of Mr. and Mrs. Nikita D.Lobanov-Rostovsky*, Jackson, MS, exh. cat.,1982. D.Elliott, V.Dudakov *100 Years of Russian Painting*, London, 1991. Dzhon Boult (John Bowlt) *Khudozhniki russkogo teatra. Sobranie Nikity i Niny Lobanovykh-Rostovskikh*, Moscow, 1991.
Coll Ukrainian Fine Art Museum, Kiev; Sammlung Ludwig, Cologne.
Colour plate p.63.

BOGOMAZOV, Timotei I.   a.1913-14
Painter. He contributed to Larionov's exhibition The Target in Moscow in 1913 and to the exhibition No.4 in Moscow in 1914.

BOGOMOLOV-ROMANOVICH, Aleksandr Safonovich 1830-1867
Painter of views and portraits. He studied at the Academy in St. Petersburg under S.M.Vorob'ev. He painted a landscape in Switzerland in 1858. He died in St. Petersburg.
Coll TG.

BOGORAD, I. D.   a.1925-1926
Graphic artist. He contributed to the First Exhibition of Cinema Posters held in Moscow in 1925 and to the Second Exhibition of Cinema Posters held at the Kamerny (Chamber) Theatre, Moscow, in 1926.

BOGORODSKY, Fedor Semenovich   1895-1959
Painter of contemporary life, naval and war themes as well as landscapes. Born at Nizny-Novgorod. He studied in the studio of Leblond in 1914 and at the Moscow Institute 1914-16.
After the Revolution he was active at Nizhny-Novgorod where he collaborated with the painter Aleksandr Kuprin on the staging of V.Kamensky's *Stepan Razin* c.1921. He also studied at the Faculty of Law in Moscow before attending the

Vkhutemas there under Arkhipov 1922-4.
He was a member of the *Bytie* (Existence) society of artists formed in Moscow in 1921 and a member of AKhRR from 1924. He was included in the major exhibition in Moscow in 1927 marking the tenth anniversary of the Revolution. His work was included in the exhibition of Soviet art held at Harbin in 1926 and in Japan in 1927. He exhibited in Venice in 1928 and was included in the 1928 exhibition of Acquisitions by the State Art Collections Fund held in Moscow. He was represented in the First Touring Exhibition of Paintings and Graphics which opened in Moscow in 1929. During the period 1928 to 1930 he worked in Italy, Germany and Austria. He showed work in New York in 1929. An exhibition of his work was held in Rome in 1929 and he lived with Gorky at Sorrento 1929-30.
He returned to Moscow in 1930 where exhibitions of his work were held in 1931 and 1934. He was represented at the jubilee exhibition Artists of the RSFSR over 15 Years held at the Russian Museum, Leningrad, in 1932. In 1932 he again exhibited in Venice. His painting *At the Photographers* of 1932 is in the Russian Museum. He exhibited work in Venice and London in 1934 and in Turkey in 1935. He taught at the Institute for Cinematography 1938-59.
He made drawings at the front in the Second World War in Volgograd and Leningrad. He died in Moscow.
*Sailors in an Ambush illustrates its theme with a measure of dramatic success as the sailors creep anxiously and alert along a wall with their weapons ready.
Writings F.Bogorodsky *Avtobiografiya*, Moscow, 1938.
Lit S.Vasiliev *F.S.Bogorodsky* , Moscow, 1948. K.S.Kravchenko *F.S.Bogorodsky* , Moscow, 1952. V.Polevoy *F.Bogorodsky*, Moscow, 1956. D.Elliott, V.Dudakov *100 Years of Russian Painting*, London, 1991. A.M.Muratov, V.Manin et al. *Zhivopis' 20-30kh godov*, Sankt-Peterburg, 1991.
Coll TG; RM; A.M.Gorky Museum, Moscow; Central Lenin Museum, Moscow; Gorky Art Museum; Kalinin Art Gallery; Kiev Museum of Russian Art; L'vov Art Gallery.

BOGOSLOVSKY, A. V.   a.1918
He was involved in the decorations at the Café Pittoresque in Moscow in 1918 along with Tatlin, Rodchenko, Yakulov and others.

BOGUSLAVSKAYA (-PUNI), Ksenia Leonidova 1892-1972
Painter. She exhibited with the World of Art 1916-17.
After the Revolution she exhibited with the Knave of Diamonds in Moscow in 1917. She married the painter Ivan Puni. She was represented at the First Russian Art Exhibition in Berlin in 1922. With Puni she illustrated his children's book *Tsveten* (Pollen), Berlin, 1922; black and white illustrations in a lightly Cubo-Futurist style reminiscent of both Chagall and Annenkov.
*Design for a Decoration for Okhtensky Bridge, 1918-20, RM, is in the style of V.Lebedev A worker with shovel against a simplified background of buildings and telegraph wires, painted in watercolour but like a cut-out in the simplicity of its shapes.
Coll RM.

Boguslavskaya, Puni, Tatlin and Others, *1915.*
A newspaper cartoon depicting artists at 0.10. The Last Futurist Exhibition of Paintings in Petrograd.

BOIKOV, I. M.   **late 19th century**
Painter. Worked at Saratov.

BOITCHUK, M. L. = BOYCHUK, M.L.

BOIM, Solomon Samsonovich   **1899-1978**
Graphic artist. Represented at the jubilee exhibition Artists of the RSFSR over 15 Years held at the Russian Museum, Leningrad, in 1932. He died in Moscow.

BOK, Aleksandr Romanovich von   **1829-1895**
Sculptor. He studied under P.K.Klodt at the Academy of Art in St. Petersburg from 1850. He travelled abroad on a scholarship to Germany, France and Italy 1858-64 executing classical themes. He then taught at the Academy of Art from 1865 to 1895. His work includes fountains at Peterhof 1876-7 and a monumént to *Glinka* for Smolensk in 1885. He died at St. Petersburg.
Cupid Releasing a Butterfly, 1862, marble, RM, is a precise, slightly sweet but in fact highly disciplined carving of the late neo-classical nude.
Coll RM; Museum of the Academy of Art, St. Petersburg.

BOKLEVSKY, Petr Mikhailovich   **1816-1897**
Graphic artist, lithographer, painter. Born at Ryazan. He studied law at Moscow University until 1840 and painting under A.E.Egorov in St. Petersburg. He then studied under K.P.Bryullov at the Academy in 1845. In the early 1850s he visited Switzerland, Italy, Spain, Germany and France. In 1855 he published a series of lithographs critical of the Crimean Campaign. He produced an album of lithographs of the characters in Gogol's *Revizor* (The Government Inspector) in Moscow in 1858 and an album of illustrations to Gogol's *Dead Souls* in 1881. Other illustrations included Turgenev's *Fathers and Sons* in 1869 and Dostoevsky's *Crime and Punishment* in 1881. He also made pastel portraits in the period 1850s-80s which included Gogol and Glinka. He died in Moscow.

Lit K.Kuz'minsky *P.M.Boklevsky*, Moscow, 1910.
Coll TG; RM; Ryazan Museum.

BOM-GRIGOR'EVA, Nadezhda Sergeevna   **b.1884-1929+**
Graphic artist, painter. Born at Serpukhov. She exhibited from 1916.
After the Revolution she studied under M.A.Dobrov in Moscow. Her work was presented at the First Exhibition of Works of the Professional Union of Artists in Moscow in 1918 and at the First Exhibition of the Moscow Contemporary Art Store in January 1919. Her name appeared on the April 1919 list of artists for acquisitions by the proposed Museum of Painterly Culture. She was a member of the Society of Artist-Realists founded in 1927. She was represented in the First Touring Exhibition of Paintings and Graphics which opened in Moscow in 1929. Among her graphic works was a series of ex-libris prints.
Lit S.A.Sil'vansky *Knizhnie-znaki N.S.Bom-Grigor'evoy*, Moscow, 1932.

BONDI, Yu. M.   **a.1912-1914**
Theatre designer. He made designs for Meyerhold's productions at the Artists' Co-operative at Terioki in the summer of 1912, including P. de Calderón de la Barca's *Adoration of the Cross* in K.Balmont's translation in June, A.Strindberg's *Crimes* in June, and G.B.Shaw's *You Wouldn't Have Said That For Anything* in July. He also designed and co-directed Meyerhold's production of A.Blok's *Unknown Lady*, with music by M.A.Kuzmin, at the Tenishevsky Auditorium in April 1914.

BORISOV, Aleksandr Alekseevich   **1866-1934**
Landscape painter specialising in scenes of the Far North. Born in the Vologda region. He worked in the ikon-painting studios of the Solovetsky Monastery 1884-6 and then studied at the Drawing School of the Society for the Encouragement of the Arts at St. Petersburg 1888-97 under Kuindzhi and Shishkin. He organised expeditions to the Far North

including Novaya Zemlya 1897-9 and 1900-1. In 1899 the Tretyakov Gallery in Moscow acquired sixty-five studies by him. He was represented at the International Exhibition in Paris in 1900. He worked in St. Petersburg until 1909 and exhibited there between 1903 and 1914. After 1909 he lived at Krasnoborsk in the Archangel region.

After the Revolution he exhibited at Petrograd in 1919, Vologda in 1920, Archangel in 1926 and Moscow in 1930. He was also included in the 1928 exhibition of Acquisitions by the State Art Collections Fund held in Moscow. He died in the Archangel region.

His work was exhibited in Archangel in 1955, 1956, 1959 and 1966.

Lit A.I.Yatsimirsky *Khudozhnik Kraynego Severa* (Artist of the Far North), St. Petersburg, 1903. A.Munin *A.Borisov*, Vologda, 1967.

Coll Major holdings at TG; Penza Art Gallery; Krasnodar Art Museum; Omsk Art Museum; Archangel Museum of Fine Art; Vologda Art Museum.

BORISOV, Boris Ivanovich   1902-1968

Painter, designer. He studied at the Moscow Vkhutemas under N.M.Grigor'ev and A.A.Osmerkin 1919-25. He exhibited with the Society of Moscow Painters at its inaugural exhibition in Moscow in 1925. He was represented in the First Touring Exhibition of Paintings and Graphics which opened in Moscow in 1929. He exhibited with the *Bytie* (Existence) group. He was mostly active as a designer from the 1940s. He died in Moscow.

BORISOV, Grigori Ilych   a.1921-1926

Graphic artist. He exhibited with the 1921 exhibition of the World of Art in Moscow and with the Obmokhu group exhibition in 1921. He received his diploma from the Vkhutemas in 1924. He designed cinema posters using geometric pattern and photographically derived images particularly after 1924, often working with Prusakov, Naumov and Zhukov. He was represented at the Second Exhibition of Cinema Posters held at the Kamerny (Chamber) Theatre, Moscow, in 1926. He collaborated with Petr Zhukov on the poster for F.Otsep's film *Living Corpse* in 1929. The poster was in the style of the Stenberg Brothers with a striking image of a figure interwoven with lettering.

BORISOV, N.   a.1923

Theatre designer. He contributed to the exhibition Art of Moscow Theatre 1918-1923 held in Moscow in 1923.

BORISOV-MUSATOV, Viktor Elpidiforovich   1870-1905

Fin de siècle painter of evocative and wistful landscapes and garden scenes with elegantly dressed figures. Born at Saratov, where from the age of eleven he studied at the Society of Lovers of the Fine Arts under V.V.Konovalov. Subsequently he studied at the Moscow College under Polenov 1890-1 and 1893-5, as well as the Academy in St. Petersburg under Chistyakov 1891-3. He then visited Paris 1895-8 where he studied in Cormon's studio. He exhibited from 1893. He was impressed by the monumental art of both Puvis de Chavannes and Gauguin. In 1897 and 1898 he went to Munich. He was a leading member of the Moscow Society of Artists 1899-1905. He planned mural decorations, unexecuted, for the house of A.I.Derozhinskaya which the architect Shekhtel' had designed. He exhibited with the World of Art in 1906. He returned to Saratov until 1903 and was a member of the Union of Russian Artists 1904-5. Paul Cassirer arranged an exhibition of his work

Viktor Borisov-Musatov.
Spring, *1898.*
Oil on canvas. Signed and dated lower left. 71 x 98 cm. State Russian Museum, St. Petersburg.

Vladimir Borovikovsky. Mutaza-Kuli-Khan, *1796. Oil on canvas. 74 x 53.5 cm. State Russian Museum, St. Petersburg.*

Vladimir Borovikovsky. Catherine the Great in the Park at Tsarskoe Selo, *1794. Oil on canvas. 94.5 x 66 cm.*
State Tretyakov Gallery, Moscow.

Vladimir Borovikovsky. Madam Skobeeva, *c.1797. Oil on canvas. 68.5 x 54 cm.*
State Russian Museum, St. Petersburg.

in Munich in 1904 and the following year he exhibited at the Salon d'Automne in Paris. He was represented in Diaghilev's display of Russian art at the 1906 Salon d'Automne in Paris. He moved to Podolsk in the Moscow region and then settled at Tarusa in the Kaluga region where he died in 1905. Sometimes he signed his work simply 'Musatov'.
Exhibitions of his work were held in Moscow in 1907 and 1917.
Lit V.Stanyukovich *V.E.Borisov-Musatov*, St. Petersburg, 1906. N.N.Vrangel' *V.E.Borisov-Musatov*, St. Petersburg, 1910. I.Evdokimov *Borisov-Musatov*, Moscow, 1924. A.Rusakova *V.E.Borisov-Musatov*, Moscow-Leningrad, 1966 and 1975 (also English edition). I.Mochalov *Borisov-Musatov*, Leningrad, 1976.
Coll TG; RM; Erevan Art Museum; Kharkov Art Museum; Perm Art Museum; Saratov Art Museum and many others.
Colour plate p.62.

BORKIN, Vasili Vasilevich   **a.1930**
Sculptor. He studied under Tatlin at the Ceramics Faculty of the Vkhutein, Moscow, where his works included a shaving kit and a pepper shaker dated 1930.

BORODAY, Vasili (Vasil') Zakharovich   **b.1917**
Monumental sculptor. Born at Ekaterinoslav. He was active in Kiev. His work included portraits in marble and in granite. His monumental works included those dedicated to *N.A.Shors*, 1953-4, with Lysenko, bronze and granite, and *To the Revolution in Kiev*, 1966, with V.I.Znoba and I.S.Znoba.
Exhibitions of his work were held in Moscow and Kiev in 1964, and in Odessa in 1968.
See Lysenko, M.G.

Lit Z.Fogel' *V.Z.Boroday*, Moscow, 1968.
Coll Museum of Ukrainian Art, Kiev.

BOROVIKOVSKY, Vladimir Lukich   **1757-1825**
Major 18th century portrait painter. His portraits stress elegance of dress, gently asserting the status of his sitters. He was born at Mirgorod in the Ukraine of Cossack descent and was taught initially by his father. He was engaged on military service from 1774. He studied painting from 1783 under D.G.Levitsky. He executed a number of miniatures and ikons for the Troitsa Church at Mirgorod in 1784. In 1787 he decorated a temporary palace for the Empress Catherine at Kremchug on the Dneiper.
He settled in St. Petersburg in 1788, gained recognition during the 1790s, and in 1797 was admitted to the Academy. His portrait of *Catherine the Great in the Park at Tsarskoe Selo* (p.87), TG, contains hints of the great full-length portraits of both France and England. His portraits include the painter *D.G.Levitsky*, 1802-3, RM. He died in St. Petersburg. His pupils included A.G.Venetsianov.
*Portrait of Maria I. Lopukhova, 1797, TG, is an extremely sensitive painting with minute attention to textures of clothing and flesh. The effect is soft with carefully modulated shadows describing the fall of light across flesh. The pose too is alert and intelligent. For a formal portrait this is revealing beyond the call of duty, and clearly a painting of a person rather than a statement of rank or importance. He was a little like David or Ingres in his ability to produce portraits with a distinctly contemporary appearance.
Lit A.M.Skvortsov *V.L.Borovikovsky*, Moscow, 1944. N.G.Mashkovtsev *V.L.Borovikovsky*, Moscow, 1950. T.V.Alekseeva *Borovikovsky*, Moscow, 1956. K.V.Mikhailova *V.L.Borovikovsky*, Leningrad, 1968.
Coll Substantially represented in TG; RM; Dnepropetrovsk Art Museum; Museum of Ukrainian Art, Kiev; Kalinin Art Gallery; Kazan Art Gallery.

BORZOV, V. F.   **a.1919**
He exhibited at the Twelfth State Exhibition: Colourdynamo and Tectonic Primitivism (*XII Gosudarstvennaya vystavka. Tsvetodinamos i tektonichesky primitivizm*) in Moscow in 1919 along with Grishchenko, Shevchenko and others.

BOTKIN, Fedor Vladimirovich   **1861-1905**
Portrait painter. Born in Moscow. After studying law at Moscow University, he moved to Italy where he studied art at the Academy in Milan and Florence, and to Paris where he studied under Philippe Roll. In 1897 he introduced the great collector Sergei Shchukin to the French art dealer Durand-Ruel, a liaison which was to have a profound impact on Russian art. He exhibited with the Vienna Secession, with the Salon des Indépendants and the Salon National in Paris and also with the World of Art in Russia 1899-1900 and 1902. He was stricken with a nervous desease which confined him to a clinic near Paris from 1901. Sometimes he signed his work 'Th.Botkine'.
Lit S.Glagol' *F.V.Botkin*, Moscow, 1907. *Twilight of the Tsars*, London, 1991.
Coll TG; Perm Art Gallery; Omsk Museum of Fine Art; Irkutsk Art Museum.

BOTKIN, Mikhail Petrovich   **1839-1914**
Painter, etcher. Born in Moscow. He studied at the Academy under F.A.Bruni and F.S.Zav'yalov 1856-8. He lived abroad 1859-69 and was a member of the German Archaeological Institute in Rome in 1869. He exhibited at the Academy and

with the Wanderers. His religious paintings included *The Women of Golgotha*, 1867. He published a book on the painter A.A.Ivanov in St. Petersburg in 1880 and he joined the Russian Archaeological Society in the same year. He died in St. Petersburg.
Coll TG; Omsk Museum of Fine Art; Novosibirsk Art Gallery.

BOUCHENE, D. = BUSHEN, D.

BOYCHUK, Mikhail (Mikhaylo) Lvovich   1882-1939
Ukrainian painter. He studied in L'vov from 1898 and then at the Cracow Academy attaining his diploma in 1905. He attended the Munich and Vienna Academies, and worked in L'vov after 1907 where he restored ikons. He worked in Paris 1908-11 and visited Italy 1910-11. After the Revolution he settled in Kiev in 1917 and taught at Kiev Art School in 1917-19. He was engaged on Agitprop decorations including decorating the agitboat *The Bolshevik* and others. He taught at the Ukrainian Academy 1919-22 and at the Kiev Art Institute 1924-36.
He gathered around him a group, known as the Boychukists, who sought to revive monumental painting inspired by Ukrainian ikons and Giotto. He produced work for the Ukrainian Pavilion at the All-Russian Agricultural Exhibition in Moscow in 1923. He was a member of ARMU from 1925. He was included in the 1928 exhibition of Acquisitions by the State Art Collections Fund held in Moscow.
Lit *Paris-Moscou*, 1979.

BRAZ, Osip (Iosif) Emmanuilovich   1873-1936
Painter, lithographer. His work included portraits, still-lifes and landscapes. He was born at Odessa where he studied at the Drawing School under Kostandi until 1890 before attending the Academy at St. Petersburg in 1895-6 under Repin. He exhibited from 1893. Subsequently he studied at the Simon Hollosy School in Munich and privately in Paris. His portraits included *Chekhov* in 1898. He taught at the Drawing School of the Society for the Encouragement of the Arts in St. Petersburg 1902-3. He exhibited with the World of Art 1900-5, the Union of Russian Artists 1903-6, and the World of Art again 1911-15 and 1917. He was painting in Brittany in 1911. He was a member of the organising committee of the 1912 World of Art exhibition under the presidency of Roerich. He painted in Finland 1915-17.
After the Revolution he participated in the First State Free Exhibition of Artworks in Petrograd in 1919 and in the Third Exhibition of Paintings held at Ryazan in 1919. He was represented at the First Russian Art Exhibition in Berlin in 1922. He taught at the Vkhutein in Leningrad 1920-4 and 1927-8. He emigrated in 1928 and died in Paris.
**Mstislav Dobuzhinsky*, 1922, is a half-length seated portrait reminiscent of Somov in its delicacy and precision. The face and hands are depicted with minute attention to likeness and drawing. The sitter is portrayed as a man of urban correctness and taste, with book in hand and porcelain still-life objects in the foreground.There is no indication that the sitter is a celebrated painter.
Lit *Twilight of the Tsars*, London, 1991.
Coll TG; Odessa Art Gallery; Perm Art Gallery.

BRAZER, Abram Markovich   1892-1942
Sculptor, painter. Born at Kishinev. After studying at Kishinev Art School until 1910, he travelled to Paris to study 1912-14 and remained in Paris until 1916. A Brazer exhibited with the

Osip Braz. Landscape, *1912. Oil on canvas. Signed 'O.Braz' in Russian. 92.5 x 72 cm.*
Malmö Konstmuseum.

World of Art in Petrograd in 1917.
After the Revolution he taught at the Vitebsk Art Institute 1918-23 and was represented along with Kandinsky, Chagall and others at the First State Exhibition of Paintings by Local and Moscow Artists held in Vitebsk in December 1919. At Vitebsk he executed a bust of *I.G.Pestalozzi* 1919-20 and at portrait of the painter *Yuri Pen* in 1921. From 1924 he lived at Minsk.
An exhibition of his work was held at Minsk in 1941. He was killed in a prison camp in the Second World War.
Coll Belorussian Art Museum, Minsk.

BRIEDIS, Aleksandra Yanovna (BRIEDE, née KALNINA) b.1901-1956+
Latvian sculptor of genre figures. She studied at the Latvian Academy under K.I.Ronchevsky 1923-31. She sculpted in terracotta, plaster, granite, marble and produced bronzes. She exhibited in Paris in 1948 and Helsinki in 1950. In 1956 she was awarded the Order of Lenin. Her works included *The Young Sculptor* of 1947. She worked at Riga.
Coll Latvian Art Museum, Riga.

BRIMMER, Nikolai Leonidovich   1898-1929
Graphic artist. He studied V.M.Konashevich, D.Mitrokhin and P.A.Shillingovsky at the Leningrad Vkhutein 1923-7. He exhibited from 1927. Stylistically inspired by the achievements of Favorsky, his wood engravings were witty and historicist. His illustrations included Gogol's *Kolyaska* (The Carriage) in 1928 as well as trademarks and ex-libris. He died in Leningrad. He drew for the journal *Krasnaya Niva* 1927-9 and he was one of the founders of the journal *Gravyura na derevne*

(Wood Engraving) of which he became the editor.

He was represented at the jubilee exhibition Artists of the RSFSR over 15 Years held at the Russian Museum, Leningrad, in 1932.

Coll TG.

BRITANISHSKY, Lev Romanovich (Ruvimovich) 1897-1971

Painter, graphic artist, lithographer. Born at Kronstadt. His subjects included landscapes. He studied at St. Petersburg in 1910.

After the Revolution he studied at Petrograd in 1918-23. He was a member of the *Krug khudozhnikov* (Circle of Artists) formed in 1926 and exhibited from 1928. He was represented at the jubilee exhibition Artists of the RSFSR over 15 Years held at the Russian Museum, Leningrad, in 1932. He taught art in the Leningrad region 1930-41 and at Sverdlovsk 1943-4. He died at Leningrad.

BRIULLOV = BRYULLOV

BRODATY, Lev Grigor'evich   1889-1954

Painter, political caricaturist. He was born in Warsaw and from 1904 he lived in Vienna. He studied under D.Kon in 1905, and in due course at the Vienna Academy 1909-10. He drew for periodicals in Vienna, Berlin, Cracow and Warsaw before moving to Russia in 1915. He lived in Petrograd-Leningrad from 1916.

After the Revolution he executed numerous satirical drawings for *Pravda* from 1917 to 1954, perhaps the first published Soviet satirical graphic work. He was a founder and designer of the satirical review *Krasny Dyavol* (Red Devil) 1917-18, and was working on Agitprop window posters for the Rosta agency 1919-21. Editor of the periodical *Mukhomor* 1922-3, he also contributed to the reviews *Behemot*, 1924-8, and *Smekhach*, 1924-8, and made book illustrations. He participated in the seventh exhibition of the group *L'Araignée* (The Spider) at the Galerie Devambe in Paris in 1925. He taught at the Leningrad Vkhutemas 1928-30. He lived in Moscow from 1930 and contributed to the satirical journal *Krokodil* from 1931. He died in Moscow.

*Germany, watercolour, 1935, TG, is intensely theatrical and executed wholly in blue. Two figures, gothic in themselves, head for the immense mass of a gothic cathedral beneath a stormy and moonlit sky.

Lit L.L.Ioffe *L.G.Brodaty*, Moscow, 1959. *Paris-Moscou*, 1979.

Coll TG; RM; Perm Art Gallery.

BRODIN, A.   a.1925

Painter. He contributed to the Third Exhibition of Paintings by Artists from Kaluga and Moscow held in Kaluga in 1925.

BRODSKY, Isaak Izrailovich   1883/4-1939

Major painter of revolutionary themes, portraits and landscapes, graphic artist. Born in the Zaporozhe region. He studied at Odessa Art College under K.Kostandi and G.Ladyzhensky 1896-1902 before attending the Academy at St. Petersburg where he studied under Masoedov and Tsionglinsky from 1902 and Repin 1902-8.

He took part in the student protests at the Academy in 1905 and painted *Red Funerals* in that year. He also drew for the satirical journals *Pulemet*, *Adskaya Pochta* and *Plamya*. He exhibited with the Wanderers, the World of Art and, 1907-18, with the Union of Russian Artists. He also exhibited with the First Izdebsky International Salon 1909-10. He travelled

widely on a scholarship 1909-11 visiting Germany, France, Italy, Greece, Spain and Austria. During this tour he painted the writer Gorky at Capri in 1910. He won a gold medal at the Munich International Exhibition in 1913.

After the Revolution he executed Agitprop decorations for Bolshoi Prospekt and Kamennostrovsky Street in Petrograd in 1918. He participated in the First State Free Exhibition of Artworks in Petrograd in 1919 and he contributed to the Exhibition of Paintings by Russian Artists held at Pskov in Spring 1920. He was included in the enormous survey Exhibition of Paintings by Petrograd Artists of All Tendencies 1919-1923 held in Petrograd in 1923. He joined the Association of Artists of Revolutionary Russia, AKhRR, in 1924. He contributed to the Third Exhibition of Paintings by Artists from Kaluga and Moscow held in Kaluga in 1925. He was included in the major exhibition in Moscow in 1927 marking the tenth anniversary of the Revolution.

Lenin became a prime theme of his work. *Lenin at the Rostrum*, 1927, RM, is painted with a documentary precision. He became President of the Kuindzhi Society in 1930, the year that he painted his most celebrated portrait, *Lenin at Smolny* (Brodsky Museum, Leningrad).

He exhibited at the 1932 Venice Biennale. He was represented at the jubilee exhibition Artists of the RSFSR over 15 Years held at the Russian Museum, Leningrad, in 1932.

He became Director of the Russian Academy of Arts in Leningrad from 1934 to 1939 and won a Grand Prix at the Paris International Exhibition of 1937. In 1937 he painted a Socialist Realist full-length portrait of *Voroshilov Skiing*. He died in Leningrad.

*The Shooting of the 26 Baku Commissars, study, 1925, TG, is a dramatic and partisan painting in which the commissars hurl defiance as they are shot.

*Lenin at Smolny, 1930-2, Lenin Museum, Moscow (versions in TG and Brodsky Museum, Leningrad); despite its date this is in many ways perhaps the last great 19th century realist-academic portrait technically speaking, although in other ways it is very much of the 1930s. Lenin makes a note, seated on one of several chairs covered in dust sheets. He is presented as the still centre of the revolutionary storm, an urban and ordinary looking figure. Only newspapers on the table indicate the historical events to which he is the key. Every detail is meticulously painted and made credible. Brodsky has achieved a kind of rhetoric that abandons the dramatic gesture, a monumental painting that is disturbing by virtue of its curiously atmospheric and almost intimate ordinariness. It is also a *tour de force* in a long outdated technique, eschewing every trace of avant-garde experiment. In this respect it is also of its day, heralding the emergence of Socialist Realism and the dissolution of all independent groups in 1932.

Lit I.I.Brodsky *Sbornik Statei*, Leningrad, 1929. *Pamyati I.I.Brodskogo*, Leningrad, 1959. I.I.Brodsky *Moi Tvorchesky Put'*, Leningrad, 1965. I.A.Brodsky *I.I.Brodsky*, Moscow, 1973. *Twilight of the Tsars*, London, 1991.

Coll TG; RM; Brodsky Appartment Museum, St. Petersburg; Gorky Art Museum.

BROMIRSKY, Petr Ignat'evich   1886-1919

Sculptor, painter. He studied at the Moscow College. He worked at Abramtsevo and was influenced by the Blue Rose group. He exhibited with the Blue Rose group in 1907, the *Stefanos* exhibition 1907-8 and the exhibition *Zveno* (The Link) in Kiev in 1908.

After the Revolution he made a project for a *Monument to*

Fedor Bruni. The Death of Camilla, Sister of Horatio, *1824. Oil on canvas. 350 x 526.5 cm.*
State Russian Museum, St. Petersburg.

Surikov. He showed work in the Fifth State Exhibition: From Impressionism to Non-Objective Art in Moscow 1918-19 and his name appeared on the April 1919 list of artists for acquisitions by the proposed Museum of Painterly Culture. He was teaching sculpture at the Free State Studios in Moscow c.1918-19 along with Babichev, Er'zya, Konen'kov and Vatagin. In 1919 he was listed as leader of a course for art teachers along with Tatlin and others.
Coll RM; Abramtsevo Museum.

BRONNIKOV, Fedor Andreevich   **1827-1902**
Genre and portrait painter. His subjects included themes of ancient life. Born in the Perm region. He studied ikon painting under his father and printmaking under E.E.Bershadsky from 1843 in St. Petersburg. He then studied at the Academy under A.T.Markov from 1845. He won a travel scholarship for five years from 1854. He was active in Rome in 1858, 1869, 1874 and 1878. Sometimes he signed his work 'Bronnicoff'. He died in Rome.
Coll Good holdings at TG; RM; Perm Art Gallry; Saratov Art Museum; Irkutsk Art Museum.

BRULLOFF = BRYULLOV

BRUNI, Fedor (Fidelio) Antonovich   **1799-1875**
Painter of Romantic themes stylistically academic and indebted to David. He also made portraits. Born in Milan. He came to Russia with his father, A.O.Bruni, in 1807. He studied under A.E.Egorov, A.I.Ivanov and V.K.Shebuev at the Academy in St. Petersburg and worked in Italy 1818-35. He became Professor and then Rector of the Academy in St. Petersburg, and an honorary member of the Academies of

Rome, Florence, Milan and Bologna. His *The Death of Camilla, Sister of Horatio*, 1824, RM, was painted in Rome and gained him acceptance into the Academy of St. Luke in Rome. The painting is severe, controlled and like a relief in its composition which is dominated by dramatic and even theatrical gestures. He made copies after Raphael in Rome in 1827.
He taught at the Academy 1836-8 and 1846-71. He painted 1837-41 the colossal *Bronze Serpent*, RM, which measures over forty square metres. His academic and Italianate *Bacchante* is in the TG. He returned to Rome until 1845. He was a conservator at the Hermitage from 1849 to 1864. From 1866 he led the mosaics studio at the Academy. He died in St. Petersburg.
Lit A.V.Polovtsev *F.A.Bruni*, 1907, St. Petersburg. A.Savinov *F.A.Bruni*, Moscow, 1949.
Coll Good holdings at TG; RM.

BRUNI, Lev Aleksandrovich   **1894-1948**
Painter, graphic artist, theatre designer, sculptor whose work was for a time inspired by Tatlin's constructions of diverse materials.
Born at Malaya Vishera in the Novgorod region, the son of the architect A.A.Bruni. After studying at Princess Tenisheva's School in St. Petersburg in 1904-9, he attended the Academy there under Rubo, Samokish and Tsionglinsky from 1909 to 1912. He began to exhibit in 1910.
In 1912 he was in Paris studying under J.P.Laurens at the Académie Julian but also becoming aware of the Cubism of Braque, Picasso, Léger and Delaunay.
On his return to Russia he was associated with the Union of Youth. He held meetings at his apartment in St. Petersburg 1914-16 which Al'tman, Annenkov, Miturich, V.Lebedev and others attended. He drew for the journals *Golos Zhizni*,

Verishchiny and *30 Dney* in 1915. In 1915-16 he was exhibiting with the World of Art where he showed a *Portrait of A. Lure* (the composer Artur Lourié) and the painting *Rainbow*. On the other hand he contributed two constructions of metal, glass, wood and paint to the exhibition *Magazin* with Tatlin and others in 1916. For a period he made material constructions inspired by Tatlin's examples which had been evolving since 1914 and which had most recently been displayed in the exhibition 0.10. The Last Futurist Exhibition of Paintings in December 1915 in Petrograd. He was a founder of the society Apartment No. 5 in Petrograd along with Tyrsa, Isakov, Lebedev, Miturich, Punin and Tatlin in 1915. He was called up for military service in 1916.
After the Revolution with Tatlin, Yakulov and others he was involved in the decoration of the Café Pittoresque in Moscow 1917-18. He exhibited with the Artists of the Leftist

Lev Bruni. Construction, *c.1920. Mixed media.*
Bruni was primarily a painter but he executed a number of constructions at the time when he was close to Tatlin.

Federation of the Professional Union in 1918 along with Popova, Rodchenko, Tatlin and others.
From 1920 to 1921 he taught at the Steiglitz Institute in Petrograd. He was represented at the First Russian Art Exhibition in Berlin in 1922 and he was included in the enormous survey Exhibition of Paintings by Petrograd Artists of All Tendencies 1919-1923 held in Petrograd in 1923.
He moved to Moscow in 1923 where he taught in the graphics studio at the Vkhutemas until 1930. He exhibited at Venice in 1924. He was a member of the 4 Arts society which was founded in 1924 and a member of the Union of Moscow Artists formed in 1925. He was represented at the Paris International Exhibition in 1925. He exhibited at the third and last exhibition of the *Makovets* group in Moscow 1925-6 and with the 4 Arts society in Moscow in 1925. He contributed to the Third Exhibition of Paintings by Artists from Kaluga and Moscow held in Kaluga in 1925, to the seventh exhibition of the group *L'Araignée* (The Spider) at the Galerie Devambe in Paris in 1925 and the All-Union Polygraphic Exhibition in Moscow in 1927. He exhibited in Tokyo in 1927. He was included in the 1928 exhibition of Acquisitions by the State Art Collections Fund held in Moscow, in the fourth exhibition of *Iskusstvo dvizheniya* (The Art of Movement) that year in Moscow, Russian Graphic Art at Riga and in the First Touring Exhibition of Paintings and Graphics which opened in Moscow in 1929.
He taught at the Moscow Textile Institute 1930-3. He was represented at the jubilee exhibition Artists of the RSFSR over 15 Years held at the Russian Museum, Leningrad, in 1932. He directed the Studio of Monumental Painting at the Academy of Architecture of the USSR 1935-48. During this period he made frescoes for the façade of the Textile Combine in Tashkent. He painted series of works devoted to different regions: *Caucasus* 1931, *Tadzhikistan* 1934, *Crimea* 1937-8, and *Kazakhstan* 1943. He died in Moscow.
*Twilight, Goldfish, 1926, RM, is a fine fresh watercolour in red, blue and black depicting the furniture and window of a country interior in which each mark is calligraphic in its immediacy.
Illustration Firdousi's *Shakhname*, 1915. Cervantes' *Don Quixote*, 1924. A.M.Gorky's *Detstvo* (Childhood), 1927.
Theatre design 1926-7 appears to have been involved in designs for a production of Khlebnikov's *Zangezi* at the Vkhutemas (see also Tatlin).
1931 Unrealised designs for B.Nord's production of Bizet's opera *Carmen* at the Moscow Music Hall.
Lit *L.A.Bruni*, exh. cat., Moscow, 1956. V.I.Rakitin *L.A.Bruni*, Moscow, 1970. *Twilight of the Tsars*, London, 1991. C.Lodder *Russian Constructivism*, New Haven and London, 1983.
Coll RM; Gorky Art Museum; Ivanovo Art Museum.

BRUNI, Tat'yana Georgievna　　　　　**b.1902-1979+**
Graphic artist, theatre designer. Born at St. Petersburg where she studied at the School of the Association for the Encouragement of the Arts 1918-20. She then studied at the Vkhutein, Leningrad, under O.Braz and N.Radlov 1920-6. She worked on theatre design and also exhibited from 1923. She was still designing for the theatre in the 1970s. She also designed for the puppet theatre.
Theatre design 1931 *Bolt*, a ballet with music by D.Shostakovich, choreography by F.Lopukhov and libretto by V.Smirnov at the State Academic Theatre for Opera and Ballet, Leningrad, designed in collaboration with Georgiy N.Korshikov. She supervised a reconstruction of the ballet in Leningrad in

Karl Bryullov. The Last Days of Pompeii, *1830-3. Oil on canvas. 456 x 651 cm. State Russian Museum, St. Petersburg.*

1979. Designs for this show a highly geometricised factory interior with mechanistic figures of factory workers among the girders, ladders and machinery. The costume for a Bureaucrat is a parody involving legs made of piles of paper.
1942 Chaikovsky's *Swan Lake*.
1944 *Giselle*.
1946 sets for Verdi's *La Traviata*.
1964 Prokofiev's *Zolushka*.
Lit Nancy Van Norman Baer *Theatre in Revolution, Russian Avant-Garde Stage Design 1913-1935*, San Francisco and London, 1991. Dzhon Boult (John Bowlt) *Khudozhniki russkogo teatra. Sobranie Nikity i Niny Lobanovykh-Rostovskikh*, Moscow, 1991.
Coll Bakhrushin Theatre Museum, Moscow.

BRUSKETTI-MITROKHINA, Alisa Yakovlevna 1872-1942
Sculptor, ceramics artist. She graduated from the Moscow College in 1904 having studied under Volnukhin, Levitan and Serov, and subsequently worked as a sculptor at the Abramtsevo ceramics studio.She taught design at Tver 1905-9, at St. Petersburg 1909-14 and at Pskov 1915-19.
After the Revolution she produced ceramic sculptures of Petrograd types in 1918 designed for the State Porcelain Factory in Petrograd between 1918 and 1920. She was represented at the jubilee exhibition Artists of the RSFSR over 15 Years held at the Russian Museum, Leningrad, in 1932. She died in Leningrad.
Lit N.Lobanov-Rostovsky *Revolutionary Ceramics*.

BRYANTSEVA, Maria Aleksandrovna   1885-1942
Ceramics artist. Born at St. Petersburg. She graduated from the Deaf and Dumb School, St. Petersburg, in 1904. She then studied textile design at the Baron A.Stieglitz School from 1904 to 1913. She was employed at the Imperial Porcelain Factory and its successors until 1941. She died in Leningrad.
Coll RM.

BRYULLOV (BRYULLO), Aleksandr Pavlovich 1798-1877
Architect, portrait painter, watercolourist. Born at St. Petersburg. He studied under his father P.I.Briullo, an Italian sculptor who brought his sons to Russia, and from 1810 he studied at the Academy. His brother was the celebrated painter Karl Bryullov. In 1822 he travelled to Germany, Italy and France on a scholarship, returning to St. Petersburg in 1829. His buildings there included the Mikhailovsky Theatre 1831-3, the Lutheran Church 1833-8 and the Pulkovsky Observatory 1834-9. He became a professor at the Academy in 1832. He was also a member of the academies of Paris and Milan. He was also involved in the remodelling of the interior of the Winter Palace. He died in St. Petersburg.
Lit G.A.Ol' *Arkhitektor Bryullov*, Leningrad, 1955.
Coll TG; RM.

BRYULLOV, Karl Pavlovich   1799-1852
Major Romantic mythological painter, portraitist and landscape painter. Born in Italy. He was the son of an academic ornamental sculptor, whom he accompanied to

Karl Bryullov. Portrait of a
Woman. *Watercolour and body colour.*
43.1 x 29.5 cm.
The sitter was Maria Isabella, Queen
of Naples, who died in 1848.
Ashmolean Museum, Oxford.

Russia as a child, and the brother of A.P.Bryullov. His family
name was Briullo which was later russified to Bryullov. From
1809 he was studying at the Academy in St. Petersburg under
Andrei Ivanov, V.K.Shebuev and A.E.Egorov. He attained a
major gold medal from the Academy and in 1821 travelled
abroad with his brother on a scholarship in 1822, visiting
Munich and Dresden, and living in Rome 1823-4. His subjects
included mythological, biblical and Italian themes and he
made copies after Raphael 1823-7. *The Last Days of Pompeii*,
for which there are studies in TG, was painted 1830-3 in Italy
and exhibited there to great acclaim. Sir Walter Scott was
among its admirers. Bryullov was active in Rome between
1827 and 1835 when he visited Greece and Turkey.
He returned to Russia where he undertook a sequel history
painting *The Seige of Pskov by Stepan Batory in 1581*, 1836-43,
which he never finished. He lived in Moscow and came to
know Pushkin. He gained increasing recognition and became
an important portraitist. Pushkin and Gogol both admired his
work and he attained an international reputation. He executed
paintings for the Isaak Cathedral 1843-7 and for other

Karl Bryullov. Countess Samoilova. *Oil on canvas.*
Smithsonian Institution, Washington D.C.

churches. He returned to Italy via Madeira in 1849. He sometimes signed his work 'Brulloff' or 'C.B.'.

The Last Days of Pompeii, 1830-3, RM, was inspired by visiting the ruins of Pompeii and by Pacini's opera *L'ultimo giorno di Pompei* of 1825. It is an immesely dramatic painting filled with figures in surprisingly casual flight from the fiery disaster which is causing sculptures to fall and horses to rear in terror. Light illuminates the central area in which groups of carefully arranged figures respond to the encroaching fury, expressing their emotion by their gestures. The painting's finish is polished and immaculate. Nowhere does the handling of the paint have to carry the viewer's response into a sympathetic mood as everything is depicted with a clarity and academic professionalism which defies emotional involvement. The effect is that of a grandiose piece of theatre filled with gestures and pattern book expressions of emotion. The painting is immensely detailed with every tiny pebble casting its own clear shadow (p.93).

Lit I.Ramazanov *Vospominaniya o K.P.Bryullov*, Moscow, 1852. N.P.Stepanov *Biografiya K.P.Bryullova*, St. Petersburg, 1858. N.N.Derzhavin *Bryullov*, St. Petersburg, 1900. O.Lyaskovskaya *K.Bryullov*, Moscow, 1940. N.G.Mashkovtsev *Karl Bryullov v pis'makh*, 1961. E.Smirnova *Bryullov - puteshestvennik*, 1969.

Coll Major holdings in TG; RM; Kharkov Art Museum; San Diego Museum, California.

BRYULLOV, Pavel Aleksandrovich　　　　**1840-1914**

Landscape painter. Born at Pavlovsk, the son of A.P.Bryullov. In 1874 he studied architecture at the Academy under his grandfather.

He moved to Paris 1865-6 where he studied painting under Léon Bonnat. He exhibited with the Wanderers 1872-7 and became a member in 1873. He worked in Algeria 1882-3. He died at Pavlovsk.

Coll TG; Irkutsk Art Museum.

BUBELO = GERMANSHEV

BUBNOV, Aleksandr Pavlovich　　　　**1908-1964**

Painter and graphic artist. Born at Tiflis. He studied art in Atkarsk. His subjects included landscapes, battle paintings and Socialist Realist themes.

After the Revolution he studied under N.Ya.Fedorov in the early 1920s and under K.N.Istomin, P.V.Kuznetsov and N.M.Chernyshev at the Moscow Vkhutein 1926-30. He worked in Moscow and exhibited from 1929. He became a member of AKhR. He died at Moscow.

Morning on the Kulikovo Field, 1943-7, TG, is a colourful and historicist battle painting depicting an ancient theme with methods derived from Repin. Medieval warriors with lances, gigantic banner and the image of Christ prepare for battle. Despite the storytelling this depiction of patriotic war retained a relevance to the time in which it was painted.

Lit Yu.Neyman *A.Bubnov*, Leningrad, 1938. K.Stepanova *A.Bubnov*, Moscow, 1950. I.G.Akimova *A.Bubnov*, Moscow, 1956.

Coll TG, RM; Ulyanovsk Art Museum.

BUBNOVA, Varvara Dmitrievna　　　　**1886-1983**

Painter, graphic artist, illustrator. Born at St. Petersburg. From 1903 she studied at the Society for the Encouragement of the Arts at St. Petersburg and then at the Academy in St. Petersburg 1907-14 under Nikolai Dubovskoy. She exhibited with the Union of Youth in 1910. She moved to Moscow in 1917.

After the Revolution she showed work in 1919 at the Sixth,

Eighth and Ninth State Exhibitions and became involved in the activities of IZO Narkompros, the art section of the People's Commissariat of the Enlightenment, in Moscow c.1920, and she contributed to the work of the Institute of Artistic Culture (INKhUK) there. She was represented in the Sixth State Exhibition: The Print (*VI Gosudarstvennaya vystavka gravyur*) in Moscow in 1919. She was included in the Third Touring Exhibition of the Sovetsk Regional subdepartment of the Museums Bureau along with Kandinsky, Rodchenko and others in 1921. She was included in the First Russian Art Exhibition at the Van Diemen Gallery in Berlin in 1922. She was a member of the Institute of Artistic Culture (INKhUK) in Moscow.

She then moved to Japan for most of her career, 1922-58, where she painted and also translated and illustrated Russian books. She lived at Sukhumi from 1958 and was given an exhibition in Moscow in 1961. She returned to Leningrad in 1979.

Lit A.Z.Rudenstine *Costakis Collection*, London, 1981. J.Howard *The Union of Youth — An Artists' Society of the Russian Avant-Garde*, Manchester and New York, 1992.

Coll RM.

BUCHKIN, Petr Dmitrievich　　　　**1886-1965**

Painter, graphic artist, etcher, poster designer. Born Tver region. He studied ikon painting and from 1904 attended the Academy under V.V.Maté and V.E.Savinsky. He made drawings for journals from 1905 and exhibited from 1907. In 1912 he visited Italy, France, Germany and Spain on a travel scholarship.

After the Revolution he was a member of the Art Collegium for Literary Publishing in 1919 with responsibility for illustrations of Russian life. In the 1930s he produced work on the theme of Lenin. He died at Leningrad.

Writings P.D.Buchkin *O tom, chto v pamyati. Zapiski khudozhnika* (On What is in my Memory. Notes of an Artist), Leningrad, 1962.

BUCHKURI, Aleksandr Alekseevich　　　　**1870-1941**

Painter of portraits and landscapes. Born at Taganrog. His family moved to Voronezh in 1893 where he studied at the School of Drawing and Painting. He lived in St. Petersburg 1898-1907 where he studied under Repin both before and after entering the Academy. He returned to Voronezh in 1907.

After the Revolution he taught at the Technical College of Art in Voronezh 1919-23. He became a member of AKhRR there and was instrumental in organising the local branch of the Union of Artists in 1933. He and his wife were killed fleeing the advancing German armies in 1941. His work appears to have developed fairly seamlessly from a Repin-like style appropriate to the Wanderers to its equivalent Socialist Realist counterpart in the 1930s. Much of his work was destroyed during the Second World War.

Lit M.V.Iliinsky *A.A.Buchkuri*, Voronezh, 1958.

Coll Voronezh Art Gallery.

BUDKOVSKAYA-KIBAL'CHICH, Nadezhda Turvetovna 1874-1918+

Painter. She studied at the Moscow College 1906-11. She worked in Moscow.

After the Revolution she was represented at the *First Exhibition of Works of the Professional Union of Artists in Moscow* in 1918.

BUDOGOSSKY, Eduard Anatol'evich　　　　**1903-1954+**

Graphic artist. He studied under V.V.Lebedev and

P.A.Shillingovsky at the Leningrad Vkhutein 1922-7 and exhibited from 1927. He was represented at the jubilee exhibition Artists of the RSFSR over 15 Years held at the Russian Museum, Leningrad, in 1932. He illustrated and designed books for the publishers Detgiz and Lenizdat, produced trade marks and ex-libris. He drew the siege of Leningrad 1941-2 and lived in Leningrad until 1954.
Coll TG; RM.

BUGAEVSKY(-BLAGODARNYY), Ivan Semenovich 1773-1859
Portrait painter. His name is sometimes given as Ivan Vasilievich Bugaevsky or Bogaevsky and his dates as 1777-1860. He studied under S.S.Shchukin at the Academy from 1779. He painted heroes of the Napoleonic War. He also made satirical drawings in the 1820s. He worked in the Ukraine.
Portrait of the Professor of the Academy of Arts A.I.Ivanov, 1824, is an elegant, Ingresque portrait of the sitter surrounded by the implements of his work and status.
Coll TG; Museum of the Academy of Arts, St. Petersburg.

BUKHGOL'TS, Fedor Fedorovich 1857-1942
Painter, graphic artist. Born in the Warsaw region. He studied under Chistyakov and Yakobi at the Academy from 1878 and exhibited from 1888. He taught at the School of the Society for the Encouragement of the Arts at St. Petersburg 1893-1910. His paintings included *I.E.Repin among Friends*, 1900, RM. He was represented in exhibitions at Munich in 1901, in the United States in 1904, and in Rome in 1911.
After the Revolution he executed agitational decorations on Bolshoi Prospekt, Vasiliev Island, Petrograd, in 1918 and he participated in the First State Free Exhibition of Artworks in Petrograd in 1919. He contributed to the Exhibition of Paintings by Russian Artists held at Pskov in Spring 1920 and he was included in the enormous survey Exhibition of Paintings by Petrograd Artists of All Tendencies 1919-1923 held in Petrograd in 1923. He taught at schools in Leningrad until 1932. He died at Leningrad.

BUKOVETSKY, Evgeniy Iosipovich 1866-1948
Painter. A painting of 1895, *In Court*, Museum of Ukrainian Art, Kiev, remotely recalls Leibl in the precision of its figure painting. All of the figures are dressed in black and sit waiting for the process to begin or for judgement to be given. The central figure and her mother are fine portraits which are so resolved that they almost distract from the full coherence of the narrative.
Coll TG; Museum of Ukrainian Art, Kiev.

BULAKOVSKY, Sergei Fedorovich 1880-1937
Sculptor, graphic artist. Born at Odessa where he worked under B.V.Edwards 1893-1902, and then in other marble work studios in Odessa until 1906 when, being an active revolutionary, he emigrated.
His studies continued under E.Pellini in Milan and at the Academy there 1906-9. He then moved to Paris where he adopted the name Alexandre Soukhov and studied with A.Mercié. He was a founder of the Académie Russe de Peinture et de Sculpture in 1912 and director of its sculpture studio. He also exhibited at the Salon des Indépendants and the Salon d'Automne. In 1917 he returned to Russia, working on Agitprop window posters for the Rosta agency in the Ukraine and the Caucasus. He worked in Moscow from 1922 where he taught at the Vhutemas-Vkhutein until 1930. He exhibited with AKhRR and with the Society of Russian Sculptors after 1924. He was included in the 1928 exhibition of Acquisitions by the State Art Collections Fund held in Moscow. He died in the Moscow region.
Lit *Paris-Moscou*, 1979.

BULANOV, Dmitri A. a.1919-1930
Poster designer. He participated in the First State Free Exhibition of Artworks in Petrograd in 1919. He worked for the National Publicity Agency, Leningrad, 1920-30. In posters promoting radio in 1927 he employed symmetrical horns with fishes listening in. A similar symmetry was used for a tram poster in 1927. Posters of the early 1930s employed freehand drawing, collage effects and photomontage.
Lit *Paris-Moscou*, 1979.

BUNAKOV, Ivan Mikhailovich a.1857-1859
Painter of portraits and ikons. He taught Repin at Chuguev in the Kharkov region in 1857-59.
Coll Kharkov Museum of Art.

BUNAT'YAN, L. a.1921-1922
Painter. He was a founder member of the group *Bytie* (Existence) formed in 1921 partly in protest at 'the narrowness of leftist art' and he contributed to its first exhibition in 1922.

BURLYUK (BURLIUK), David Davidovich 1882-1967
Painter, poet and a central figure of the Russian Futurist movement. He was born in the Khar'kov region, the son of a successful merchant and landowner. He was the brother of Nikolai and Vladimir Burlyuk. His initial studies were divided between Kazan School of Art 1898-9 and 1901, and the art school at Odessa 1899-1900 and 1909 or 1910 to 1911. He attended the Munich Academy 1902-3 and the Atelier Cormon in Paris in 1904 where his brother Vladimir also studied. This gave him every opportunity to develop a wide awareness of art as an international phenomenon. He was an

David Burlyuk. Illustration to Vladimir Mayakovsky's Poem 'A Most Extraordinary Adventure', *1920-1*.
Here the poet greets the blazing sun and invites him into his garden for a talk.

ambitious, imaginative and active organiser of groups and exhibitions which were increasingly avant-garde in their programmes, particularly as he became more and more involved in the iconoclastic and provocative innovations of Russian Futurist literary and artistic experiment. He was a creator of the group *Venok* (Wreath) 1907-8, and with Georgiy Yakulov he organised the exhibition *Stefanos* (Stephanos) in Moscow 1907-8. This was followed by the exhibition *Zveno* (The Link) in Kiev in 1908 and *Venok* (The Wreath) in St. Petersburg in 1909. He exhibited with the Golden Fleece salon in St. Petersburg in 1909. He was a founder of the South Russian Association of Artists in 1910 and exhibited with the Union of Youth and The Triangle in 1910. He exhibited twenty-six works with the Izdebsky Salon of 1910-11 in Odessa. He enrolled at the Moscow College in 1911 and exhibited with the Knave of Diamonds in Moscow 1912-13. He exhibited with the Union of Youth 1911-14.

He travelled to Germany, where he exhibited with the *Blaue Reiter* (Blue Rider) at Munich in 1912, to France, Switzerland and Italy in the summer of 1912 and on 20 November 1912 he lectured on *What is Cubism?* at an evening event of the Union of Youth. He had also recently performed with Mayakovsky at the Stray Dog cabaret in St. Petersburg in mid-November. In December 1912 he returned to Moscow with Mayakovsky for the publication of the Futurist book *A Slap in the Face of Public Taste*. In 1913 he lectured on contemporary art at the Polytechnic Museum together with Kamensky and he contributed to the film *Drama in Cabaret No.13* together with Mayakovsky and Kamensky.

He consolidated his German connections by contributing to the exhibitions of the *Blaue Reiter* in Munich and *Der Sturm* in Berlin. With Mayakovsky and Kamensky he departed on a Russian Futurist Tour of Russia and the south in December 1913 to March 1914, travelling as far as Tiflis (Tblisi) and Baku. He lived in the Urals 1915-17. He exhibited with the World of Art, Petrograd, in 1915, with the exhibition Modern Russian Painting in Petrograd and with the Knave of Diamonds in Moscow in 1916.

After the Revolution together with Mayakovsky and Kamensky he signed the *Decree No.1 for the Democratisation of Art* in 1917. He exhibited with the Knave of Diamonds in Moscow in November 1917. He held a one-man exhibition at Samara in 1917. He contributed to the decoration of the Poets' Café in Moscow along with Lentulov, Mayakovsky, Khodasevich and Yakulov 1917-18. He collaborated on a film with Mayakovsky in 1918 (see below).

His name appeared on the April 1919 list of artists for acquisitions by the proposed Museum of Painterly Culture. He was represented along with Kandinsky, Chagall and others at the First State Exhibition of Paintings by Local and Moscow Artists held in Vitebsk in December 1919 and at the First Russian Art Exhibition in Berlin in 1922.

He moved East to Vladivostok in 1918 where he collaborated with future members of *Lef*, Left Front of the Arts, on the periodical *Tvorchestvo* (Creativity). In 1920 fighting in Siberia caused Burlyuk to flee to Japan where he remained active as a Futurist.

He settled in New York in 1922. He continued to paint and collaborated with Mayakovsky on his visit to New York in the 1920s. He contributed to the exhibition of Contemporary Russian Art held at Philadelphia in 1932. He visited Russia in 1956 and 1965 and in America edited the periodical *Color and Rhyme*. He died at Long Island, New York.

*Portrait of the Futurist Poet Vasili Kamensky, 1917, RM, is a full frontal head in the format of Christ in an ikon with rays emanating from the head which is encircled by a halo of text and flanked by fragments of manuscripts. Whilst this is not overtly Christian except in the ikonic composition, Kamensky with prominent brow and staring eyes, appears as a kind of superhuman visionary, the emissary of the new age of Futurism.

Futurist books V.Kamensky, D.,V. and N.Burlyuk, Guro, Khlebnikov et al. *Sadok sudey* (Trap for Judges), St. Petersburg, 1910. This included nineteen poems by David Burlyuk.

D.Burlyuk, N.Burlyuk et al. *Poshchechina obshchestvennomu vkusu* (A Slap in the Face of Public Taste), 1912-13.

V.Khlebnikov, V.Mayakovsky, D. and N.Burlyuk *Trebnik troikh* (The Service Book of the Three), 1913, illustrated by D., N. and V.Burlyuk, V.Mayakovsky and Tatlin.

V.Khlebnikov, D., V. and N.Burlyuk *Zatychka* (The Bung), 1913, illustrated by V.Burlyuk.

A.Kruchenykh *Chort i rechetvortsy* (The Devil and the Wordmakers), with illustrations by Rozanova, St. Petersburg, 1913.

A.Kruchenykh, music by M.Matyushin, *Pobeda nad Solntsem* (Victory Over the Sun), with illustrations by K.Malevich and D.Burlyuk, St. Petersburg, 1913.

D., V. and N.Burlyuk et al. *Dokhlaya luna* (Croaked Moon), with illustrations by V. and D.Burlyuk, Moscow, 1913.

V.Khlebnikov *Ryav'! Perchatki!* (Roar! Gauntlets!), with illustrations by D.Burlyuk and K.Malevich, St. Petersburg, 1914.

D.Burlyuk et al. *Futuristy: Rykayushchiy Parnas* (Futurists: Roaring Parnassus), with illustrations by D.Burlyuk and others, St. Petersburg, 1914.

V.Khlebnikov et al. *Moloko kobylits* (Mares' Milk), with illustrations by A.Exter and D. and V.Burlyuk, Moscow, 1914.

V.Mayakovsky *Vladimir Mayakovsky, tragediya* (Vladimir Mayakovsky, a Tragedy), with illustrations by V. and D.Burlyuk, Moscow, 1914.

V.Kamensky *Futuristy: Pervyy zhurnal russkykh futuristov* (Futurists: First Journal of the Russian Futurists), with illustrations by D. and V.Burlyuk and A.Exter, Moscow, 1914.

V.Kamensky *Tango s korovami* (Tango with Cows), with illustrations by V. and D.Burlyuk, Moscow, 1914.

D.Burlyuk, S.Vermel' *Vesennee kontragentsvo muz* (The Vernal Forwarding Agency of the Muses), with illustrations by V. and D.Burlyuk and A.Lentulov, Moscow, 1915.

V.Mayakovsky et al. *Vzyal: baraban futuristov* (Took: The Futurists' Drum), with illustrations by D.Burlyuk, Petrograd, 1915.

D.Burlyuk, G.Zolotukhin, V.Kamensky, V.Khlebnikov *Chetyre ptitsi* (Four Birds), with illustrations by A.Lentulov and G.Zolotukhin, Moscow, 1916.

V.V.Mayakovsky *Otkrytye Ameriki* (Open Americas), with illustrations by D.Burlyuk, New York, 1925.

Other writings D.D.Burlyuk *Stikhi, kartiny, avtobiografiya* (Verses, Paintings, Autobiography), New York, 1924. D.Burlyuk *Manifesto. Radio-Style*, City of USA (New York), 1926. D.Burlyuk *Radio-Futurist, Artist, Poet. Second Manifesto*, New York, 1927. D.D.Burlyuk *Fifty-Five Years of Painting*, New York, 1962. D.Burlyuk *Entelekhizm — Iskusstvo kak* *organicheskyy protses*, New York, 1930. D.D.Burlyuk, M.N.Burlyuk *Vospominaniya*, New York, 1932. D.Burliuk (ed.) *Color and Rhyme* (periodical), New York, 1930-66.

Futurist films 1918 *Ne dlya deneg rodivshiysya* (Not Born for Money, known also as Creation Can't Be Bought). Mayakovsky played the leading role as the poet Ivanov. The scenario, based upon Jack London's *Martin Eden* was devised by David Burlyuk and Mayakovsky together and the design was by David Burlyuk and Vladimir Egorov. The cast included V.Kamensky.

Lit E.F.Gollerbakh *Iskusstvo D.D.Burlyuka*, New York, 1930. K.Dreier *Burliuk*, New York, 1944. *David Burlyuk*, exh. cat., Galerie Gmurzynska, Cologne, 1966. S.P.Compton *The World Backwards, Russian Futurist Books 1912-16*, London, 1978. *David Burliuk: Years of Transition, 1910-1931*, exh. cat., Parrish Art Museum, Southampton, New York, 1978. *L'Avant-garde russe 1905-1925*, exh. cat., Musée des Beaux-Arts, Nantes, 1993.

Coll TG; RM; Irkutsk Art Museum; Erevan Art Museum; Kazan Art Museum; Kuibyshev Art Museum; Perm Art Gallery; Samara Art Museum; Tashkent Art Museum; Ufa Art Museum.

BURLYUK (- KUZNETSOVA), Lyudmila Davidovna a.1907-1908

She contributed to the *Stefanos* exhibition 1907-8 and to the exhibition *Zveno* (The Link) in Kiev in 1908.

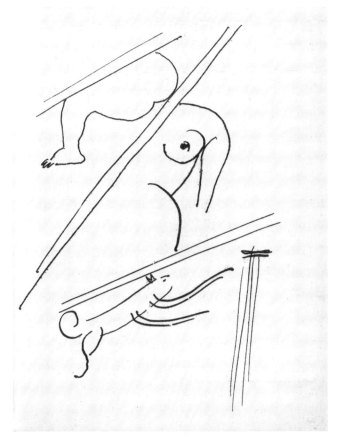

David Burlyuk. Drawing of a Nude and a Dog. *Lithograph illustration to 'Trebnik troikh' (The Service Book of the Three), Moscow, 1913.*

BURLYUK, Nikolai Davidovich   1890-1920

Russian Futurist painter. The brother of David and Vladimir Burlyuk.

Futurist books V.Kamensky, D.,V. and N.Burlyuk, Guro, Khlebnikov et al. *Sadok sudey* (Trap for Judges), St. Petersburg, 1910. This included three poems by Nikolai Burlyuk.
D.Burlyuk, N.Burlyuk et al. *Poshchechina obshchestvennomu vkusu* (A Slap in the Face of Public Taste), 1912-13.
V.Khlebnikov, V.Mayakovsky, D.and N.Burlyuk *Trebnik troikh* (The Service Book of the Three), 1913, illustrated by D., N. and V.Burlyuk, V.Mayakovsky and Tatlin.
V.Khlebnikov, D., V. and N.Burlyuk *Zatychka* (The Bung), 1913, illustrated by V.Burlyuk.
D., V. and N.Burlyuk et al. *Dokhlaya luna* (Croaked Moon), with illustrations by V. and D.Burlyuk, Moscow, 1913.
V.Khlebnikov *Izbornik stikhov* (Selection of Poems), with illustrations by N.Burlyuk, K.Malevich and P.Filonov, St. Petersburg, 1914.

Lit S.P.Compton *The World Backwards, Russian Futurist Books 1912-16*, London, 1978.

BURLYUK, Vladimir Davidovich   1886/7-1917

Russian Futurist painter and graphic artist. Brother of David and Nikolai Burlyuk. Born in the Ukraine. He studied periodically at the art school in Odessa and, and in 1903 at the Azbé School in Munich. The following year he was with his brother David in Cormon's studio in Paris. He contributed to numerous avant-garde exhibitions including that of the Blue Rose group in Moscow in 1907, *Stefanos* (Stephanos) in Moscow 1907-198, *Zveno* (The Link) in Kiev in 1908, and the Moscow Association of Artists exhibition in 1908. He exhibited at *Venok* (The Wreath) in St. Petersburg in 1909. He was a member of both the Knave of Diamonds, with whom he exhibited in Moscow 1910-11, and of the Union of Youth with whom he exhibited in 1910. In 1909 he had married the sister of the painter Lentulov. In 1910 he showed work at Kul'bin's exhibition The Triangle in St. Petersburg and at the Izdebsky Salon in Odessa 1910-11where his works included portraits of Larionov, Izdebsky and Lentulov. His best known work is the *Portrait of Benedikt Livshits* painted in 1911. He exhibited with the Union of Youth 1911-12 and 1913-14 and also with the Knave of Diamonds in 1912.

His close association with Russian Futurist artists and poets led to the illustration of Futurist books in Moscow in 1913-15, including *Dokhlaya Luna* (Croaked Moon) 1913-14 and *Moloko Kobylits* (Mares' Milk) 1914. Like his brother David he sustained connections in Germany and was a member of both the *Neue Künstler Vereinigung* (New Artists' Federation) and the *Blaue Reiter* in Munich. He also exhibited at the First German Autumn Salon in Berlin in 1913 as well as the Salon des Indépendants in Paris in 1914 and the Italian Futurist exhibition *Parole in Libertà* in Rome that year.

In Moscow he was included in the Exhibition of Paintings: The Year 1915. During the war he was engaged in active service in the Balkans and was killed near Salonika in Greece.

After the Revolution he exhibited with the Knave of Diamonds in Moscow in 1917. His name appeared on the April 1919 list of artists for acquisitions by the proposed Museum of Painterly Culture.

Flowers, RM, is as flat as a mosaic and similar also in its subdivision of the painting into blocks of colour bound by delineating bands. This is a deliberately primitive painting which has evolved from the milieu of Russian Futurism.

Futurist books V.Kamensky, D.,V. and N.Burlyuk, Guro, Khlebnikov et al. *Sadok sudey* (Trap for Judges), St. Petersburg, 1910.

V.Khlebnikov, V.Mayakovsky, D. and N.Burlyuk *Trebnik troikh* (The Service Book of the Three), 1913, illustrated by D., N. and V.Burlyuk, V.Mayakovsky and Tatlin.

V.Khlebnikov, D., V. and N.Burlyuk *Zatychka* (The Bung), 1913, illustrated by V.Burlyuk.

D., V. and N.Burlyuk et al. *Dokhlaya luna* (Croaked Moon), with illustrations by V. and D.Burlyuk, Moscow, 1913.

V.Khlebnikov et al. *Moloko kobylits* (Mares' Milk), with illustrations by A.Exter and D. and V.Burlyuk, Moscow, 1914.

V.Mayakovsky *Vladimir Mayakovsky, tragediya* (Vladimir Mayakovsky, a Tragedy), with illustrations by V. and D.Burlyuk, Moscow, 1914.

V.Kamensky *Futuristy: Pervyy zhurnal russkykh futuristov* (Futurists: First Journal of the Russian Futurists), with illustrations by D. and V.Burlyuk and A.Exter, Moscow, 1914.

V.Kamensky *Tango s korovami* (Tango with Cows), with illustrations by V. and D.Burlyuk, Moscow, 1914.

D.Burlyuk, S.Vermel' *Vesennee kontragentsvo muz* (The Vernal Forwarding Agency of the Muses), with illustrations by V. and D.Burlyuk and A.Lentulov, Moscow, 1915.

Lit A.Z.Rudenstine *Costakis Collection*, 1981; S.P.Compton *The World Backwards, Russian Futurist Books 1912-16*, London, 1978. *Paris-Moscou*, 1979.

Coll TG; RM; Sammlung Ludwig, Cologne.

BURMEISTER, Iza   a.1912-1914
Sculptor. With Ternovets she was studying under Antoine Bourdelle at the Académie de la Grande Chaumière in Paris c.1912. From Paris she travelled to Italy with the painter Lyubov' Popova and the sculptor Vera Mukhina in 1914.

BUROV, Nikolai Gerasimovich   1899-1959+
Painter, sculptor. Born at Ivanovo-Voznesensk. He studied under Golubkina and Osmerkin at the Moscow Vkutemas 1920-6 and exhibited with the Society of Moscow Painters at its inaugural exhibition in Moscow in 1925. He was a member of AKhR 1926-32. His work included portraits and revolutionary themes. His sculptural portraits included *Pushkin*, 1954, and *M.V.Frunze*, 1959.

BUROVA = VERSILOVA-NERCHINSKAYA, M. N.

BURYSHKIN, David Petrovich   1889-1959
He executed Agitprop decorations commemorating the victims of the October Revolution, Petrograd, in 1918.

BURZHE
This name appears on the April 1919 list of artists for acquisitions by the proposed Museum of Painterly Culture.

BUSHEN, Dmitri Dmitrievich (BOUCHENE, Dimitri) b.1893.
Graphic artist, theatre designer. Born at St.Tropez. He grew up in St. Petersburg where he attended the School of the Society for the Encouragement of the Arts.

After the Revolution he contributed to the exhibitions of the revived World of Art society in 1918, 1922 and 1924, and was employed as Assistant Curator of Paintings at the Hermitage Museum from 1918 to 1925.

He moved to France in 1925 and attended the Académie Ranson in Paris, turning to theatre design in 1926 and illustrating numerous books.

Theatre design 1934 Jean Giraudoux's *Tessa*.
1937 Jean Giraudoux's *Electra*.
1937 Michel Fokine's *Eléments* at the London Coliseum.
1951 Maurice Yvain's *Blanche Neige*.
1969 May: Stravinsky's *Firebird* at the Tivoli Theatre, Lisbon.

Lit J.E.Bowlt *Russian Stage Design. Scenic Innovation. From the Collection of Mr. and Mrs. Nikita D.Lobanov-Rostovsky*, Jackson, MS, exh. cat., 1982.

BUTKOVSKY, Artemi   a.1768
Painter. Born in Kiev.
Coll TG.

BUTURIN, S. S.   a.1919
He exhibited at the juryless Eighth State Exhibition in Moscow in 1919.

BUVSHTEIN (BLUVSHTEIN), Yakov Zeilikovich 1878-1933
Architect and artist. He studied at the Academy in St. Petersburg 1900-8 and became involved in Agitprop projects in the early years after the Revolution.

BYALYNITSKY-BIRULYA, Vitol'd Kaetanovich 1872-1957
Graphic artist and painter of lyrical landscapes. He studied

Vladimir Burlyuk. Velimir Khlebnikov, *1913. Lithograph.*

Vladimir Burlyuk. Profile of Nikolai Burlyuk, *1911. Ink drawing.*

under N.I.Murashko at the Kiev Art School and then under S.A.Korovin, V.D.Polenov and I.M.Pryanishnikov at the Moscow College 1889-97. He exhibited from 1891. He exhibited with the Wanderers from 1899 and became a member in 1904. He won gold medals at the International Exhibitions in Munich in 1911 and Barcelona in 1912.

After the Revolution he participated in the First State Free Exhibition of Artworks in Petrograd in 1919 and the Third Exhibition of Paintings held at Ryazan in 1919. He joined AKhR in 1922 and was represented at the international exhibition in New York in 1924. He was a member of the Society of Artist-Realists founded in 1927 and was included in the major exhibition in Moscow in 1927 marking the tenth anniversary of the Revolution.

He made landscape paintings of Belorussia. He was given exhibitions in 1936 and 1937 and was represented at the International Exhibition in Paris in 1937. Sometimes he signed his work 'Birulya'. He died in Moscow.

*Spring is Coming, 1911, TG, is a landscape of snow, birches and fir trees featuring the liquid reflection of a stream flowing, free of ice, between snowy banks.
Lit L.M.Tarasov *V.K.Byalinitsky-Birulya*, Moscow, 1949. G.V.Zhidkov *V.K.Byalinitsky-Birulya*, Moscow, 1953.
Coll TG; Omsk Art Gallery; Perm Art Gallery; Sverdlovsk Art Gallery.

BYCHKOV, Vyacheslav Pavlovich   1877-1954
Painter. Born at Yaroslavl. He exhibited from 1896. He studied under Arkhipov, Kasatkin and Serov at the Moscow College from 1896 and under K.A.Korovin from 1903.

After the Revolution he painted a *Demonstration. May Day. Moscow* in 1920. He was a member of AKhR 1926-30. His work was included in the exhibition of Soviet art held at Harbin in 1926 and in Japan in 1927. He was represented in the First Touring Exhibition of Paintings and Graphics which opened in Moscow in 1929. He was given an exhibition in Moscow in 1950.
Coll TG; Astrakhan Art Galery; Krasnodar Art Museum.

BYKHOVSKY, Aleksandr Yakovlevich   1888-1978
Belorussian graphic artist, sculptor. He had no professional training. His posters included *Krasnyy nabat* (Red Alert), 1920, and *Smert' za smert'* (Death for Death), 1942. He held an exhibition in Moscow in 1923. He was included in the major exhibition in Moscow in 1927 marking the tenth anniversary of the Revolution.

He worked on the Soviet pavilion at the International Exhibition in Tokyo in 1933. He also designed ex-libris. He died in Moscow.
Lit L.S.Vygotsky *Grafika A.Bykhovskogo*, Moscow, 1926.

BYKOV, G. N.   a.1919
He exhibited at the Twelfth State Exhibition: Colourdynamo and Tectonic Primitivism (*XII Gosudarstvennaya vystavka. Tsvetodinamos i tektonichesky primitivizm*) in Moscow in 1919 along with Grishchenko, Shevchenko and others.

BYKOV, Zakhar   1898-1925+
Sculptor, designer. Born in the Ryazan region. He studied at the Stroganov College under Noakovsky and Shekhtel' 1910-17.

After the Revolution he studied at the Vkhutemas-Vkhutein under Rodchenko and Vesnin 1922-9.
Lit E.Weiss *Russische Avant-Garde, 1910-1930, Sammlung Ludwig, Köln*, Munich, 1986.
Coll Sammlung Ludwig, Cologne.

BYKOVSKY, Nikolai Mikhailovich   1834-1917
Painter. Son of the architect M.D.Bykovsky. He studied under M.I.Skotti at the Moscow College in the 1850s. He executed paintings on the theme of Goethe's *Faust*. He lived abroad after 1857.
Coll TG; Abramtsevo Museum.

BYSTRENIN, Valentin Ivanovich   1872-1944
Printmaker, sculptor, theatre designer. He studied under N.I.Murashko at the Kiev School of Drawing and, from 1892-1902, at the Academy in St. Petersburg under Tvorozhnikov and Maté. He first exhibited at the Third Exhibition of the Society of Russian Watercolourists in St. Petersburg in 1895. He made designs for Gogol's *Dead Souls* in 1897 (published 1901) and made a series of etchings of *Samarkand* in 1902. He drew for the journals *Shut* in 1897 and 1903 and *Fonar'* in 1906. He was a founder member of the Union of Youth with whom he exhibited in 1910. He produced stage designs for the Troitsky Theatre 1911-12 and for the Liteiny Theatre, St. Petersburg, 1912-13.

He was head of the Bogorodskoe School of Artistic Wood Carving in the Moscow region for twenty-two years from 1915 to 1937. He did series of etchings of *Paris* in 1917 and 1922.

He taught at the art faculty of the Moscow Textile Institute from 1935 to 1941.
Lit J.Howard *The Union of Youth — An Artists' Society of the Russian Avant-Garde*, Manchester and New York, 1992.

C

C.B. see **BEGGROV, K.P.; BRYULLOV, K.P.**

CARAVACQUE, Louis (KARAVAKK, L.) pre-1700-1754
Imperial portrait painter. He probably originated from Marseilles. He studied in Paris. He settled in Russia in 1716 to work with a group of French painters under the architect Le Blond. This arrangement resulted from the visit of Peter the Great to Paris. His imperial portraits included *Peter I, Empress Elizabeth Petrovna* and *Empress Anna Ioannovna*, 1730, TG. He was popular with the Empress Anna for whom he executed portraits and also ceiling paintings at her Winter Palace. He also executed tapestry and theatre designs, led a studio of painters and suggested the founding of an Academy. He taught at the Academy of Sciences.
Coll TG; RM.

CHACHBA = SHERVASHIDZE, A.K.

CHAGALL, Marc (SHAGAL', Mark Zakharovich) 1887-1985
Born at Liozno in the Vitebsk region. He studied under Yuri Pen in Vitebsk before enrolling at the Society for the Encouragement of the Arts in St. Petersburg in 1907. He also studied 1908-9 at the private art schools of Zeidenberg and Zvantseva under Bakst and Dobuzhinsky.

In 1910 he moved to Paris where he first rented an apartment from the writer Ehrenburg and then settled in the winter of 1911-12 in a studio on the top floor of the cheap studio complex in Montparnasse known as La Ruche. In Paris he was to meet artists and poets associated with Cubism, in particular the poets Cendrars, Jacob and Apollinaire and the painters Léger, Modigliani and Lhote. In 1912 he exhibited at the Salon des Indépendants and at the Salon d'Automne, but he also exhibited in Russia with the World of Art in St. Petersburg, the *Oslinyy Khvost* (Donkey's Tail) in Moscow and the exhibition Target in Moscow in 1913, the year that he met Apollinaire in Paris. This network of contacts made Chagall a sophisticated painter despite the apparently ingenuous nature of his paintings. He formed a link between the conscious primitivism of Russian Futurist artists and the maelstrom of innovative developments that was Parisian Cubism. The resulting synthesis was unique. Chagall was almost alone amongst the Cubists in his fantastic subjects which frequently featured themes derived from memories of Vitebsk, even when they were painted in Paris. He used the divergent and inconsistent perspectives of Cubism to assemble images in an unrealistic and strange manner that prefigured Surrealist art. The poet and critic Apollinaire noted this and considered Chagall as an Orphic Cubist quite distinct from his Parisian contemporaries except in so far as he shared certain features of Robert Delaunay's work. Delaunay had certainly impressed Chagall but perhaps more in his evocations of an otherworldly harmony than in terms of superficial and specific painterly borrowings, although there were a few of these too. In 1914 Chagall extended his contacts further with a one-man exhibition at the gallery *Der Sturm* in Berlin.

With the coming of war he returned to Russia, the most prolific formative experience behind him. He settled in Vitebsk once more and in 1915 he married Bela Rozenberg who was to feature in many of his canvases, lending them an air of rapturous and autobiographical celebration. In this period at Vitebsk the fantastic and the mundane collided in Chagall's paintings: the painter and his wife flew through the air of his townscapes. It was also a period when the Jewish themes, which had always played an important part in his imagery, became overtly and enigmatically clear. He exhibited at the Exhibition of Painting: The Year 1915 at the Mikhailova Art Salon in Moscow and with the Knave of Diamonds in Moscow in 1916. He began to diversify his activities: he produced theatre designs for the director Evreinov and made illustrations to Jewish books.

Although he exhibited with the Knave of Diamonds in Moscow in 1917, the Revolution found Chagall in Vitebsk where he became Commissar of Art and head of the Vitebsk art school. He worked briefly on Agitprop decorations and taught there. Sometimes he reworked themes in a way that underplayed religious imagery and in a few works the new ideological purpose of art found expression in his paintings. However the driving force of his art was more indelibly personal than politicised art readily permitted and he produced very little that was overtly communist in its imagery or aims. What interested him more was the revival of Jewish culture in the early revolutionary years. He designed for the

Marc Chagall. The Artist at the Easel, *1918-20. Drawing.*

State Jewish Theatre in 1919 and devised murals for the Jewish Chamber Theatre in 1920, for example, as well as designing for the Theatre of Revolutionary Satire. In the art school at Vitebsk in 1919 there arose a conflict of aims between Malevich, who was appointed to teach there in that year, and Chagall. Malevich, the inventor of Suprematism, was antagonistic to the personal and representational paintings of Chagall. El Lissitzky, who had learnt much from Chagall, also became a convert to Malevich's Suprematism, indeed Vitebsk was to become for a while the centre of Suprematist innovation. Chagall was represented along with Kandinsky and others at the First State Exhibition of Paintings by Local and Moscow Artists held in Vitebsk in December 1919 and he contributed to the Exhibition of Paintings by Russian Artists held at Pskov in Spring 1920.

He collaborated on the exhibiton The Three with Natan Al'tman and David Shterenberg in 1922 but he also left his post at Vitebsk. He emigrated to Berlin. He was included in the First Russian Art Exhibition at the Van Diemen Gallery in Berlin but by 1923 he had settled in Paris where he held a retrospective at the Galerie Brabazanges in 1924. France was his home for the majority of his career and he remained little recognised in Russia throughout most of this time, although he was included in the Exhibition of French Art in Moscow in 1928. He visited Palestine in 1931. He contributed to the exhibition of Contemporary Russian Art held at Philadelphia in 1932.

He lived in the United States 1941 6. His recognition in Western Europe and America grew enormously so that his work is now represented in most major collections in the West. An exhibition drawn from private collections was held in Novosibirsk in 1968 and Chagall travelled to Moscow for an exhibition of his work there in 1973.

Theatre design 1942 *Aleko*, a ballet based on Pushkin's poem *The Gypsies*, with music by Chaikovsky, performed at the Ballet Theatre at the Palacio de Bellas Artes, Mexico City, and at the Metropolitan Opera House, New York.

Lit Extensive including: A.Efros, Ya.Tugendkhol'd *Iskusstvo M.Shagalya*, Moscow, 1918, with a cover design by Chagall. B.Aronson *M.Shagal'*, Petrograd, 1923. M.Chagall *Ma Vie*, Paris, 1931. J.J.Sweeney *Marc Chagall*, New York, 1946. F.Meyer *Marc Chagall: Life and Work*, London, 1962, 1964. S.Alexander *Marc Chagall: a Biography*, 1978. J.E.Bowlt *Russian Stage Design. Scenic Innovation. From the Collection of Mr. and Mrs. Nikita D.Lobanov-Rostovsky*, Jackson, MS, exh. cat.,1982. S.Compton *Chagall*, exh. cat., Royal Academy of Arts, London, 1985. A.Kamensky *Chagall: Russian and Soviet Period 1907-1922*, London, 1989. I.Antonova *Chagall*, Moscow, 1989. Dzhon Boult (John Bowlt) *Khudozhniki russkogo teatra. Sobranie Nikity i Niny Lobanovykh-Rostovskikh*, Moscow, 1991. S.Compton *Russian Avant-Garde Books 1917-34*, London, 1992.

Coll Represented in many museums worldwide including TG; RM; Brodsky Museum, Leningrad; Bakhrushin Theatre Museum, Moscow; The Tate Gallery, London; MOMA, New York; MNAM, Paris, etc.

CHAIKOV (TCHAIKOV, CHAYKOV), Iosif Moisevich 1888-1939+

Sculptor. Born in Kiev. He studied in Paris at the Ecole des Arts Décoratifs under Aronson 1910-12 and at the Ecole des Beaux

Marc Chagall. Revolution and the Palace, *1918. Watercolour.*
This design is squred up for transfer on to a larger scale. It probably relates to a project for revolutionary street decorations in Vitebsk where Chagall worked immediately after the Revolution. The image of the giant peasant or worker was common to a number of artists' street decorations and revolutionary paintings. Here Chagall depicts the peasantry literally overthrowing the landowners.

Arts 1912-13. He exhibited at the Salon d'Automne in 1913.

After the Revolution he contributed to the First Jewish Art Exhibition of Sculpture, Graphics and Drawing held in Kiev in 1920. He taught on the foundation course at the Moscow Vkhutemas with the sculptors A.Babichev, R.Iodko, B.Korolev and N.Niss-Gol'dman c.1920.

In 1922 he was in Berlin where he was represented at the First Russian Art Exhibition in 1922. Back in Moscow in 1923, he was appointed to teach at the Vkhutein where he worked from 1924 to 1931.

He was represented at the First Discussional Exhibition of Active Revolutionary Art in Moscow in 1924 and he exhibited with the 4 Arts society in Moscow in 1925. He was a member of the Society of Russian Sculptors in 1926. He exhibited at the International Exhibition in Paris in 1925, at Milan in 1927 and Venice 1928-30. He was a member of the 4 Arts society which was founded in 1924 and he joined the Association of Russian Sculptors (ORS) in 1926 becoming its President in 1929. He exhibited with Sarra Lebedeva, A.E.Zelensky, Vera Mukhina, Ilya Slonim, Vladimir Favorsky and I.G.Frikh-Khar

Iosif Chaikov. Footballers, *1928-9. Bronze. 290 x 170 x 200 cm.*
Sport became an heroic theme in Soviet art as it suggested a dynamic energy and strength in a cultural field to which anyone could contribute. It also stressed communal endeavour and encouraged enthusiastic popular support. Chaikov learned his control of dynamic composition from his experience of experimental sculpture in the early 1920s but here applies it to a more academic modelling. This sculpture was installed beside the State Tretyakov Gallery, Moscow.

in Moscow in 1935.
Karl Marx, 1922, erected as a monument in Kiev, the figure is a half-length surmounting a vaguely Suprematist plinth of cubic blocks placed off-centre, one above another and intersecting.
Footballers, 1928-9, erected in front of the Tretyakov Gallery in Moscow, executed in bronze, is a spiralling, dynamic and gravity-defying composition of two players complete with bronze boots, socks and football.

Girl with Medal, marble, 1939, shows him reverting to the traditional academic female nude.
Lit I.Shmidt *Chaikov*, Moscow, 1977. *I.M.Chaikov*, exh. cat., Moscow, 1979. *Paris-Moscou*, 1979.

CHARCHOUNE (SHARSHUN), Serge   **1888-1975**
Painter. Born at Samara, Russia. In 1910 he studied under Ilya Mashkov and met Larionov and Goncharova. He was also impressed by the works of Picasso and Braque which he saw in

Moscow. In 1912 he moved to Paris, studying at the Académie Russe and the Académie de la Palette. He met Le Fauconnier, Metzinger and Dunoyer de Segonzac. In 1913 he exhibited at the Salon des Indépendants in Paris. He lived in Barcelona during the war period 1914-17, still experimenting with an ornamental form of Cubism. He exhibited at the Galerie Dalmau. By 1919 he was back in Paris and aware of Dadaist activities as they developed there, collaborating in particular with Picabia and with Philippe Soupault who was instrumental in publishing Charchoune's poem *Foule immobile* in 1921. His contacts were increasingly international: he exhibited at *Der Sturm* and at the First Russian Art Exhibition in Berlin in 1922 and met Lissitzky and Puni. In 1923 he returned to Paris and two years later he became an anthroposophist. In 1927 he met the painter Ozenfant and developed an interest in Purism. He contributed to the exhibition of Contemporary Russian Art held at Philadelphia in 1932.

Lit *Charchoune*, exh. cat., CNAC, Paris, 1971. R.Creuze *Serge Charchoune*, Paris, 1975. *Paris-Moscou*, 1979. E.Weiss *Russische Avant-Garde, 1910-1930, Sammlung Ludwig, Köln*, Munich, 1986.

CHASHNIK, Ilya Grigorevich   1902-1929

Suprematist painter, graphic artist and designer. Born at Vitebsk. He studied there under Yuri Pen 1917-19. He studied also with Chagall and then with Malevich, graduating from the art school at Vitebsk in 1922. Contact with Malevich was decisive in his development: it made him a thorough convert to the principles and practice of Suprematism. He contributed to the Suprematist collective *Posnovis*, susequently renamed *Unovis*, for which Lissitzky also worked. In November 1920 he wrote the editorial of the *Unovis Almanac* and published the article *The Architectural Faculty* in *Unovis* No.2, Vitebsk, 1921. With Lazar Khidekel' he published the journal *Aero* under the *Unovis* imprint. He contributed to all of the Unovis exhibitions. When Malevich left Vitebsk for Petrograd in 1922 to work at INKhUK there, Chashnik followed him together with Suetin, Ermolaeva and Yudin.

With Suetin he produced Suprematist designs for ceramics at the State Porcelain Factory in Leningrad 1923-4. These usually applied Suprematist geometric designs to the already established ceramic shapes of plates and other vessels. He was included in the Exhibition of Paintings by Petrograd Artists of All Tendencies in 1919-1923. With Malevich he worked from 1924 at the renamed GINKhUK (State Institute of Artistic Culture) on the development of three-dimensional Suprematist models which were in effect prototype architectural projects. This architectural extension of his activities continued 1925-6 when he collaborated with Suetin and the architect Aleksandr Nikolsky. He taught at the Institute of Art History, Leningrad 1926-9. He was represented at the jubilee exhibition Artists of the RSFSR over 15 Years held at the Russian Museum, Leningrad, in 1932.

Lit *Tschaschnik*, exh. cat., Kunstmuseum, Düsseldorf, 1978. *Chashnik*, Leonard Hutton Galleries, New York, 1980. *Ilya Chashnik and the Russian Avant-Garde*, exh. cat., University of Texas at Austin, 1981. A.Z.Rudenstine *Costakis Collection*, New York, 1981. N.Lobanov-Rostovsky *Revolutionary Ceramics*, London, 1990. E.Weiss *Russische Avant-Garde, 1910-1930, Sammlung Ludwig, Köln*, Munich, 1986.

Coll TG; RM; Costakis Collection; Sammlung Ludwig,

Serge Charchoune. 15F, *1944. Oil on canvas. 48.2 x 63.5 cm. Signed lower right.*
Courtesy Annely Juda Fine Art, London

Cologne.
Colour plates p.114.

CHASHNIKOV, D.   a.1927-1932

Painter. He was included in the major exhibition in Moscow in 1927 marking the tenth anniversary of the Revolution and in the First Touring Exhibition of Paintings and Graphics which opened in Moscow in 1929. He was also represented at the jubilee exhibition Artists of the RSFSR over 15 Years held at the Russian Museum, Leningrad, in 1932.

CHAYKOV = CHAIKOV, I.O.

CHEBOTAREV, Konstantin Konstantinovich 1892-1974

Painter. He studied under N.I.Feshin at Kazan Art School 1910-17.

After the Revolution he studied at the Kazan Artistic-Technical Institute 1918-22 and taught there 1921-6 as well as the Kazan Theatrical Technicum 1923-6. He was included in the Third Touring Exhibition of the Sovetsk Regional subdepartment of the Museums Bureau along with Kandinsky, Rodchenko and others in 1921. He also participated in the Second IZO Exhibition of Laboratory-Production Works under the auspices of *Lef* which was held in Kazan in 1925.

He worked on Tass propaganda windows in the 1940s.

Coll Fine Art Museum of the Tatar Republic, Kazan.

Lit V.Manin et al. *Zhivopis' 20-30kh godov*, Sankt-Peterburg, 1991.

CHEDRIN, S. = SHCHEDRIN, S. F.

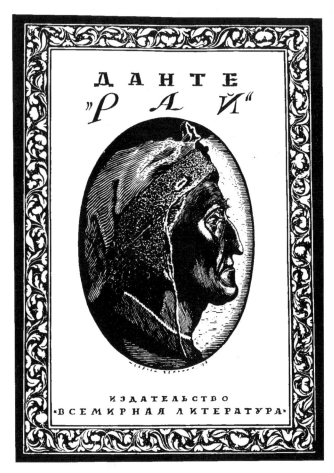

Sergei Chekhonin. Cover for Dante's 'Paradise', *1918.*
Published by 'Vsemirnaya Literatura' (World Literature) in Petrograd in 1918.

CHEKHONIN (TCHEKHONINE), Sergei Vasil'evich
1878-1936

Draughtsman, illustrator, watercolourist and major decorator of ceramics combining the sophisticated artistry and techniques of the Imperial Porcelain Factory with the new dynamics of Agitprop art. He also designed for the theatre.

Born at the village of Lykoshino in the Tver region. He studied at the school of the Society for the Encouragement of the Arts at St. Petersburg 1896-7 and at Princess Tenisheva's Studio under Repin until 1904. He also attended the Free Studios in St. Petersburg and worked at the Abramtsevo ceramics studio in Moscow 1904-7. His drawing *The Tale of a Certain Mother and her Dirty Little Boy*, 1905, was a satirical criticism of the Tsar and revealed his revolutionary aspect. He was in Paris in 1906-7. Ceramic decoration and design became his speciality in which he was able to combine the refinement of his drawing abilities with great technical expertise. He worked with the ceramics artist Petr Vaulin at Kikerino near St. Petersburg and in 1907 executed maijolica panels for buildings in St. Petersburg. He exhibited with the Golden Fleece in Moscow 1909-10. He joined the revived World of Art group in 1910 and exhibited with them from 1911. From 1913 he was director of the school of decorative enamel work at Rostov-Yaroslavsky. He exhibited with the World of Art in St. Petersburg in 1913, Moscow 1913-14, Petrograd and Moscow 1915-16 and Petrograd in 1917.

After the Revolution he assisted Lunacharsky in the reorganisation of the arts under the auspices of the People's Commissariat of Enlightenment. In 1918 he worked on Agitprop decorations at the Aleksandr Nevsky Cemetery, Petrograd, and his name appeared on the April 1919 list of artists for acquisitions by the proposed Museum of Painterly Culture. He contributed to the Exhibition of Paintings by Russian Artists held at Pskov in Spring 1920. He was represented at the First Russian Art Exhibition in Berlin in 1922 and at the exhibition of Studies for Theatre Decoration and Works from the Studios of the Decorative Institute held in Petrograd in 1922.

He was also appointed to the art section of State Porcelain Factory in 1918 where he held posts until 1927, except for the period 1923-4 when he was director of the Volkhov Factory near Novgorod. He attained a gold medal at the Paris Exhibition in 1925. He was included in the major exhibition in Moscow in 1927 marking the tenth anniversary of the Revolution. He was active mainly as a book illustrator and

Sergei Chekhonin. 'Russkoe Iskusstvo' (Russian Art), *1918. Ink. 25 x 32 cm.*
A design for the Periodical 'Russian Art' in which Chekhonin adapts the geometry of Suprematism with decorative flair. Here the geometric shapes surround a suggested opening recalling a canvas or the proscenium arch of a theatre.
Collection Pierre Ino, Paris.

Sergei Chekhonin. The Russian Letters 'A' and 'B', *1920. Ink. 18 x 29 cm.*
Designs of animated lettering, perhaps for a children's alphabet. 'A' is a clown; 'B' is a fawn.
Collection Pierre Ino, Paris.

Sergei Chekhonin. Abstract Composition, *1922. 10.5 x 19 cm. Signed lower left.*
This is a characteristically precise and elegant translation of Suprematist and Constructivist forms by Chekhonin in which every mark is considered with exactness. The result is a dynamic and rhythmic commentary upon contemporary trends.
Collection Pierre Ino, Paris.

decorator of porcelain in the period 1925-8.

In 1928 he emigrated to Paris and had a one-man exhibition at the Salon de la rue de la Paix. He subsequently worked on graphic design and theatre design including work for the Chauve-Souris cabaret and the Ballets Russes Vera Nemtchinova. In addition he produced designs for jewellery and for *Vogue* magazine.

He was represented at the jubilee exhibition Artists of the RSFSR over 15 Years held at the Russian Museum, Leningrad, in 1932. He died at Lörrach near Basel whilst travelling to Paris.

Illustration M.Moravskaya *Apelsinnie korki* (Orange Peels), Berlin, c.1923, a book of children's nonsense verse, featuring elegant cartouche designs.

Ceramics The plate inscribed 'Who is not for us is against us', 1918, is an example of agitational propaganda applied to a luxury object, typical of the ironical setting of such slogans on artefacts of the factory which had formerly produced the finest imperial porcelain. The expertise was retained but adapted to ends that were political. An emblematic design of 1919 shows a refined and elegantly slender hammer and sickle with the arc of a cogwheel and Suprematist geometry around the rim in red, blue, yellow and black. Similarly elegant works followed. A large oval agitational dish was dedicated to the Red Army Fleet in 1920, and in the same year Chekhonin executed a dish inscribed 'The Workers' Kingdom will have No End', around the rim of which runs a stylised red banner. Within the floriated lettering RSFSR is a sun disk and the recumbent hammer and sickle are laid to rest amongst ears of corn suggesting an era of plenty.

Theatre design 1929 *The Story-tellers of Novgorod* at the New York Miniatures Theatre.

1929 *The Blind Street Musician* for Nikita Balieff's Chauve-Souris Theater, New York.

1930 *Segurochka*, Glazunov's opera based on A.Ostrovsky's play for the Ballets Russes Vera Nemtchinova, Paris (unrealised).

Lit A.Efros, N.Punin *S.Chekhonin*, Moscow-Petrograd, 1923. J.E.Bowlt *Russian Stage Design. Scenic Innovation. From the*

Collection of Mr. and Mrs. Nikita D.Lobanov-Rostovsky, Jackson, MS, exh. cat.,1982. N.Lobanov-Rostovsky *Revolutionary Ceramics*, London, 1990. *Twilight of the Tsars*, London, 1991. D.Elliott, V.Dudakov *100 Years of Russian Painting*, London, 1991. Dzhon Boult (John Bowlt) *Khudozhniki russkogo teatra. Sobranie Nikity i Niny Lobanovykh-Rostovskikh*, Moscow, 1991.

Coll RM; Ashmolean Museum, Oxford.

Colour plate p.115.

CHEKMAZOV, Ivan Ivanovich   a.1901-1961

Painter. He exhibited at the inaugural exhibition of the Society of Moscow Painters in 1925. He was represented at the jubilee exhibition Artists of the RSFSR over 15 Years held at the Russian Museum, Leningrad, in 1932. He died at Tarusa.

CHEKRYGIN, Vasili Nikolaevich   1897-1922

Painter, theatre designer, graphic artist. Born at Zhizdra in the Kaluga region. He studied ikon painting at the Kiev-Pechersky Monastery 1906-10 and then entered the Moscow College until 1914. He became involved in Russian Futurist activities after meeting Larionov in 1913 through his friends Vladimir Mayakovsky and Lev Zhegin with whom he illustrated Mayakovsky's *Ya! (Me!)* in 1913. He contributed eighteen works to Larionov's exhibition No.4 in 1914 in Moscow including one piece of sculpture. He also travelled with Zhegin visiting Germany, France and London in 1914. War service followed 1915-17.

After the Revolution he exhibited with the World of Art in December 1917 in Moscow and at the First Exhibition of Works of the Professional Union of Artists in Moscow in 1918. He was engaged by the Commission for the Protection of Art Treasures in Moscow 1917-18 and in 1918 he taught at the Sokolniki House of the Arts in Moscow. He was engaged on Agitprop decorations in Kiev as well as theatre design and city planning work 1918-20. He exhibited at the Fifth State Exhibition: From Impressionism to Non-Objective Art in Moscow 1918-19. He was included in the Third Touring Exhibition of the Sovetsk Regional subdepartment of the Museums Bureau along with Kandinsky, Rodchenko and others in 1921.

He subsequently developed a mystical aspect and became a founder member of the *Makovets* group in 1922 but was killed in a railway accident that year. A memorial exhibition was held in Moscow in 1923. His work was also included in the First Russian Art Exhibition in Berlin in 1922 as well as the seventh exhibition of the group *L'Araignée* (The Spider) at the Galerie Devambe in Paris in 1925.

Theatre design 1920 Gozzi's *Princess Turandot*.

Lit *V.N.Chekrygin*, exh. cat., Moscow, 1923. A.Z.Rudenstine *Costakis Collection*. D.Elliott, V.Dudakov *100 Years of Russian Painting*, London, 1991.

Coll TG; Samara Art Museum; Costakis Collection.

CHELISHCHEV = TCHELITCHEW, P.V.

CHEMBERS-BILIBINA, Mariya Yakovlevna   1874-1962

Graphic artist. She contributed to the exhibition *Zveno* (The Link) in Kiev in 1908 and was associated with the World of Art in 1911. She exhibited watercolours of flowers at the First Izdebsky International Salon in Odessa 1909-10. She exhibited with the Union of Russian Artists in St. Petersburg and Kiev in 1910, and with the World of Art in Moscow 1911-12, St. Petersburg 1912-13 and Kiev in 1913.

Vasili Chekrygin. Illustration to Vladimir Mayakovsky's book 'Ya!' (Me!), *1913*.
The image recalls Kandinsky's contemporary paintings of St. George and the dragon.

Sergei Chekhonin. 'Russkoe Iskusstvo' (Russian Art), *1930. Ink. 21 x 29.5 cm. Signed 'Serge Tchekhonine' Paris.*
A design for the periodical 'Russian Art' evoking the stylisations of folk art and ikon painting.
Collection Pierre Ino, Paris.

CHEPIK, Sergei   b.1953

Painter, graphic artist, ceramic artist. Born in Kiev into a family of artists, the son of a sculptor mother Lyudmila Sabaneeva and a painter father Mikhail Chepik. He studied at the Shevchenko Art Institute in Kiev 1971-3 and then moved to Leningrad after the death of his father. There he studied under Andrei Mylnikov at the Repin Art Institute from 1973 to 1978. He became a member of the Young Artists' Union in 1978 and continued to study under Mylnikov until 1981. He contributed to group exhibitions in Leningrad, Moscow and elsewhere including Prague, Tokyo and Tashkent in 1981, Leningrad and Tokyo in 1982, Moscow in 1983, Leningrad and Tokyo in 1984 and Cologne in 1985. He became a member of the Artists' Union of the USSR in 1981 and held a one-man exhibition of landscapes with the Artists' Union in 1985 in Leningrad. A retrospective exhibition was held at the Palace of Youth, Leningrad, in 1986.

In 1988 he moved to Paris and exhibited at the Salon d'Automne. He also began to exhibit at the Roy Miles Gallery in London where he has received considerable recognition through several exhibitions to the present day including retrospectives there in 1990 and 1993. He also exhibited at Monte-Carlo in 1989 and at the Salon d'Automne in Paris in 1992.

His work is intensely dramatic. It shares with earlier Russian

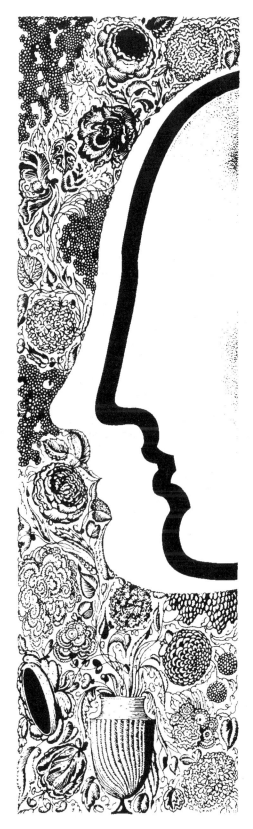

Sergei Chekhonin. Composition for the periodical 'Vogue', *1930. Ink. 12 x 25 cm.*
This is an evocation of the sense of smell responding to the profusion of flowers that issue from the vase at the base of the drawing
Collection Pierre Ino, Paris.

art of this century a dynamic synthesis of theatre and painting in which tumultuous compositions employ a variety of styles ranging from a colourful and modified Russian Futurism to a stark and grotesque technique used to dramatise allegorical themes. He exhibits a remarkable academic facility which adds to the conviction of his frequently panoramic scenes of figures, as in *The First Circle* of 1990-2, or of cityscapes such as his recent views of Paris, including *The Gargoyles* of 1992.

Lit Marie-Aude Albert *Sergei Chepik*, exh. cat., The Roy Miles Gallery, London, 1993.

Coll The Roy Miles Gallery, London.

CHEPTSOV, Efim Mikhailovich   **1874-1950**

Painter of revolutionary genre. He studied at the Tenisheva School and at the Academy 1905-11. He visited Germany, Austria-Hungary, France and Italy on a scholarship 1911-13. After the Revolution he executed Agitprop designs for the Moscow Gates at Petrograd in 1918, and he participated in the First State Free Exhibition of Artworks in Petrograd in 1919. He was included in the enormous survey Exhibition of Paintings by Petrograd Artists of All Tendencies 1919-1923 held in Petrograd in 1923. He became a member of AKhRR. He was represented at the jubilee exhibition Artists of the RSFSR over 15 Years held at the Russian Museum, Leningrad, in 1932.

Meeting of the Rural Communist Cell, 1925, translates essentially 19th century traditions of genre painting into revolutionary terms to produce a work that is effective in promoting the regime because it is endearing, easily enjoyed and readily comprehensible to a wide audience. At several removes it echoes the dramatic skill of Repin. The meeting takes place in the village hall with its speakers appearing as performers. The orator speaks within a crude stage set of a domestic interior decorated in flowery wallpaper. The meeting itself looks ambiguously like theatre performed beneath a bust of Lenin. One man sits at a table, another holds a briefcase. The painting's viewer assumes the role of audience encouraged to succumb to the wry and forlorn humour of the piece.

Lit A.M.Muratov, V.Manin et al. *Zhivopis' 20-30kh godov*, Sankt-Peterburg, 1991.

Coll TG; Kursk Art Museum.

CHEREMNYKH, Mikhail Mikhailovich   **1890-1962**

Graphic artist, painter, theatre designer, academician of the USSR. Born at Tomsk. From 1911 to 1917 he was a student at the Moscow College under Korovin and Malyutin. He was the inventor of the window poster, a device used by Rosta, the Russian Telegraph Agency, whereby empty shop windows were decorated with propaganda posters in the early years of

Sergei Chepik. The First Circle
(or The Bath), *1990-2. Oil on
canvas. 177 x 190 cm.
Roy Miles Gallery, London.*

Yuri Cherkesov. Stage Design for Russian Village Scene, *1925. Watercolour. Signed 'G. Tcherkessoff' and dated lower right. 34 x 45 cm. Designed for the Cricket on the Hearth cabaret, Leningrad 1925.* Collection Mr. and Mrs. Nikita D. Lobanov-Rostovsky, London.

the Revolution. Mayakovsky, Radakov and I.Malyutin also executed many Rosta posters. Cheremnykh's window posters, which first appeared in late August or early September 1919, used fresh imagery in a format arranged like a strip cartoon and printed in three or four colours. Close in style to Mayakovsky, they were a little more elegant and a little less original. He was active as a poster designer in 1919. He exhibited at the Ninth State Exhibition of Paintings: Naturalism and Realism in Moscow in 1919.

From 1922 he organised numerous review publications including *Krokodil*, and collaborated on others including *Bednota, Smekhach, Krasnyy Perets, Bezbozhnik* and *Stanka*. He participated in the seventh exhibition of the group *L'Araignée* (The Spider) at the Galerie Devambe in Paris in 1925 and he was included in the major exhibition in Moscow in 1927 marking the tenth anniversary of the Revolution. He produced many political and commercial posters. He was represented in the First Touring Exhibition of Paintings and Graphics which opened in Moscow in 1929. He was still a strong poster artist 1938-9. He died in Moscow.

*No Need for Heavenly Rewards, poster, c.1918, features a round-faced priest pointing to Heaven with a worker who smiles to indicate that he no longer needs clerical or spiritual approval.

*War, poster, 1938-9, has two firm hands grasping a sinister arm which bears the swastika and holds a knife marked 'War'.

Lit *M.M.Cheremnykh* , exh. cat., Moscow, 1950. O.Savostyuk, B.Uspensky *M.Cheremnykh*, Moscow, 1970. *Paris-Moscou*, 1979. D.Elliott, V.Dudakov *100 Years of Russian Painting*, London, 1991.

CHERKESOV (TCHERKESSOV), Yuri Yur'evich 1900-1943
Theatre designer. He executed a decorative panel for the Cricket on the Hearth cabaret in Leningrad in 1925.

CHERNETSOV, Grigori Grigor'evich   1801-1865
Portrait and landscape painter. Pupil of M.Vorobiev. He was the brother of Nikanor Chernetsov. In 1838 Nikanor and Grigori Chernetsov were travelling on the Volga. Both brothers journeyed through Russia to the East and also to Italy where Grigori painted views of Rome 1840-1. Signed 'G.Ch'. He died in St. Petersburg.
Coll TG.

CHERNETSOV, Nikanor Grigor'evich   1805-1879
Landscape painter, lithographer. His birthdate is sometimes given as 1804. He was the brother of Grigori Chernetsov and a fellow pupil of M.Vorobiev. He was in the Caucasus 1830-1 and the Crimea 1834-5. In 1838 Nikanor and Grigori Chernetsov were travelling on the Volga. His landscapes include work in the Crimea in 1840, Florence, Rome and Naples in 1841, Venice 1846 and Jerusalem 1854. He died in St. Petersburg.
Coll TG.

CHERNOV, Ivan Potapovich   1768-1817
Painter of biblical themes.
Coll TG.

CHERNOV, V.   a.1918
He designed Agitprop decorations at the Putilovsky Factory, Petrograd, in 1918, with F.Tikhonov.

CHERNY, Daniil   a.1408
Ikon painter. He was probably working with the great ikon painter Andrei Rublev at the Cathedral of the Assumption at Vladimir in 1408.

CHERNYSHEV, Aleksei Filippovich   1824-1863
Genre painter.
Coll TG.

CHERNYSHEV, Nikolai Mikhailovich   1885-1973
Painter. Born in the Tambov region. He studied at the Moscow College under Arkhipov, Serov and Korovin between 1901 and 1911 but attended the Académie Julian in Paris in 1910. Next

he studied at the Academy in St. Petersburg 1911-4 under D.Kiplik and V.Maté. He was also teaching in St. Petersburg in the period 1911-15.

After the Revolution he was represented at the First Exhibition of Works of the Professional Union of Artists in Moscow in 1918. His name appeared on the April 1919 list of artists for acquisitions by the proposed Museum of Painterly Culture. He taught in the Monumental Art studios of the Leningrad Vkhutemas/Vkhutein between 1920 and 1930. He exhibited in the 1921 exhibition of the World of Art in Moscow, with the *Makovets* group of which he was a member from 1922 to 1926 and with the Society of Moscow Artists (OMKh) 1928-9. He was included in the major exhibition in Moscow in 1927 marking the tenth anniversary of the Revolution and in the First Touring Exhibition of Paintings and Graphics which opened in Moscow in 1929. He was represented at the jubilee exhibition Artists of the RSFSR over 15 Years held at the Russian Museum, Leningrad, in 1932. He died in Moscow.
Lit L.Bubnova *Chernyshev*, Moscow, 1960. *N.M.Chernyshev*, exh. cat., Moscow, 1963. *Paris-Moscou*, 1979. A.M.Muratov, V.Manin et al. *Zhivopis' 20-30kh godov*, Sankt-Peterburg, 1991.
Coll TG; RM; Sartov Art Museum.

CHERNYSHEV, Sergei   **1881-1963**
He studied at the Academy in St. Petersburg, graduating in 1907. He taught in Moscow at the Free Art Studios (SVOMAS), at the Vkhutemas/Vkhutein and at the Architectural Institute.

CHERNYSHEV, Tikhon Pavlovich   **1882-1942**
Painter. He graduated from Penza School of Art in 1903 and then studied at the Academy in St. Petersburg from 1904 to 1914. He was engaged on Agitprop decorations at Blagoveshchensky Square, Petrograd, in 1918. He participated in the First State Free Exhibition of Artworks in Petrograd in 1919 and was included in the enormous survey Exhibition of Paintings by Petrograd Artists of All Tendencies 1919-1923 held in Petrograd in 1923. He also exhibited with the Society of Russian Watercolourists and AKhRR. He was represented at the jubilee exhibition Artists of the RSFSR over 15 Years held at the Russian Museum, Leningrad, in 1932.

CHICHAKOVA, Galina Dmitrievna   **1891-1967**
Graphic artist and designer impressed by Constructivism. She was the sister of Olga Chichakova. She studied graphics at the Vkhutemas in Moscow until 1920. She exhibited with the First Working Group of Constructivsts in 1924 at the First Discussional Exhibition of Active Revolutionary Art alongside L.Sanina, A.Gan, G.Miller, Olga Chichagova, N.G.Smirnov and A.Mirolyubova. She designed numerous children's books. She contributed to the International Press Exhibition in Cologne in 1928.
Lit. C.Lodder *Russian Constructivism*, New Haven and London, 1983.

CHICHAKOVA, Olga Dmitrievna   **1892-1956**
Graphic artist and designer impressed by Constructivism. She was the sister of Galina Chichakova. She studied graphics at the Vkhutemas in Moscow until 1920. She exhibited with the First Working Group of Constructivsts in 1924 at the First Discussional Exhibition of Active Revolutionary Art alongside L.Sanina, A.Gan, G.Miller, Galina Chichagova, N.G.Smirnov and A.Mirolyubova. She designed numerous children's books.

She contributed to the International Press Exhibition in Cologne in 1928.
Lit. C.Lodder *Russian Constructivism*, New Haven and London, 1983.

CHIRIN, Prokopi   **a.1593-1621**
He was a major ikon painter of the Stroganov School. His work was elegant and had certain qualities of the miniature. His *Warrior Nikita* of 1593 is preserved in the Tretyakov Gallery in Moscow. He died in the mid-17th century.
Coll TG;RM.

CHIRKOV, Aleksandr Inokent'evich   **1865/76-1913**
Landscape painter.
Coll TG.

CHISTYAKOV, Pavel Petrovich   **1832-1919**
Academic painter of classical allegories and portraits. He worked in Italy in the period 1867-70. He taught at the Academy in St. Petersburg and taught Vrubel' amongst his many pupils.
Lit P.P.Chistyakov, V.E.Savinsky *Perepiska 1883-1888g*, 1939.
Coll TG.

CHITOV, M. A.   **a.1908**
He exhibited with the Golden Fleece in Moscow in 1908.

CHIZHOV, Matvei Afanas'evich   **1838-1916**
Genre and portrait sculptor. His subjects were often charming figure compositions which sometimes broached themes of social criticism without much persuasive effect. He also executed portrait busts of several artists including *A.P.Bogolyubov* and *Aivazovsky*.
Children Playing with a Blindfold, 1869, marble, RM, is inventive in its composition of a girl on a chair hiding from a blindfolded boy who is trying to find her.
Peasant in Misfortune, 1873, TG, adapts basically neo-classical forms to a genre theme. The bearded peasant sits wearily on a rock. A child leans against him, anxious at his dismay. Both are barefoot.
Coll Well represented at RM; TG.

CHIZHOVA, M. I.   **a.1918-1919**
Painter. She was represented at the First Exhibition of Works of the Professional Union of Artists in Moscow in 1918 and at the Ninth State Exhibition of Paintings: Naturalism and Realism in Moscow in 1919.

CHLEBOWSKI = KHLEBOVSKY, S.

CHORCHO, A. G.   **a.1909-1910**
Chorcho exhibited with the Golden Fleece in Moscow in 1909-10.

CHRISTENECK, C. L. = KHRISTENEK, K. L.

CHUBARYAN, Gukas Grigorevich   **b.1923**
Sculptor of dramatic and heroic heads.

CHUGUNOV, Sergei   **a.c.1926**
He was a member of the *Krug khudozhnikov* (Circle of Artists) formed in 1926.

CHUKAEV, B.   **a.1916-1918**
During the period 1916-1918 he was teaching at the New Art Studio with Dobuzhinsky in Petrograd. Nikolai Akimov was amongst his pupils there.

Mikolajus Ciurlionis. The History of the Castle, *1908. Tempera. 49.6 x 67 cm.*
M.K.Ciurlionis Art Museum, Kaunas, Lithuania.

CHUMAKOV, Arkady Afanasevich   **1868-1948**
Painter. He visited Venice.
Coll TG.

CHUPYATOV, Leonid Terentevich   **1890-1941**
Painter, graphic artist, theatre designer. He was studying at
the school of the Society for the Encouragement of the Arts in
St. Petersburg 1909-12. In 1912 he was studying under
Tsionglinsky and in 1916 under M.Bernshtein.
After the Revolution, between 1918 and 1921, he worked
under Petrov-Vodkin at the Petrograd Free Studios and he
participated in the First State Free Exhibition of Artworks in
Petrograd in 1919. He also taught at the Art School of the
Baltic Fleet 1918-20. He was included in the enormous survey
Exhibition of Paintings by Petrograd Artists of All Tendencies
1919-1923 held in Petrograd in 1923. He taught at the Kiev
Art Institute 1926-8. He was included in the major exhibition
in Moscow in 1927 marking the tenth anniversary of the
Revolution. He taught at the Academy in 1929 and was
included in the jubilee exhibition Artists of the RSFSR over 15
Years held at the Russian Museum, Leningrad, in 1932. He
taught at GINKhUK (State Art Institute of Artistic Cultures)
from 1933. He died in Leningrad.
Still-life in Black, 1922, RM, is in fact largely in black and
white. It recalls a tabletop with paper, book, picture mount
and sphere scattered across it. Its loose composition is
reminiscent of certain works by Petrov-Vodkin or David
Shterenberg but the objects depicted verge upon independent
geometric forms.
Still-life in White, 1936, RM, is like Petrov-Vodkin in its high
viewpoint and meticulous delineation of tablecloth, napkin,
plate, mug and eggs.
Theatre design 1927 *Sadie* at the Ivan Franko Ukrainian

Drama Theatre, Kiev. A costume design is highly stylised in a
geometric way.
1935 January Meyerhold's production of Chaikovsky's
Pikovaya dama (The Queen of Spades) at the Maly Opera,
Leningrad. He also designed a cover for the programme.
Lit *Paris-Moscou*, 1979. D.Elliott, V.Dudakov *100 Years of
Russian Painting*, London, 1991. A.M.Muratov, V.Manin et al.
Zhivopis' 20-30kh godov, Sankt-Peterburg, 1991. S.Compton
Russian Avant-Garde Books 1917-34, London, 1992.
Coll RM.

CHUYKOV, Semen Afanasevich   **1902-1980**
Kirghiz Socialist Realist painter. He was represented in the
First Touring Exhibition of Paintings and Graphics which
opened in Moscow in 1929 and in the exhibition of Russian
Graphic Art in Riga in 1929.
Hunter with a Golden Eagle, 1938, Kirghiz Fine Art Museum,
Frunze, features a firm-jawed Asian hero against a low skyline
of distant mountains and a landscape flooded with light.
Daughter of Soviet Kirghizia, 1948, TG, has as its setting a low
skyline of fields and distant mountains, and shows the young
paragon clasping her books purposefully. She is seen proud,
resolute and ikonic against a cloudless sky.
Coll TG.

CIURLIONIS, Mikolajus Konstantinas   **1875-1911**
Lithuanian symbolist painter and composer. He moved to St.
Petersburg in 1909 where he was well received by Russian
Symbolists. In November 1911 a large memorial exhibition
was held within the World of Art exhibition. The zodiac series
were among the 158 works exhibited here.
Lit V.Ciurlionyte-Karuzenie *M.K.Cirlionis*, Vilnius, 1961.

COROVIN = KOROVIN, K. A.

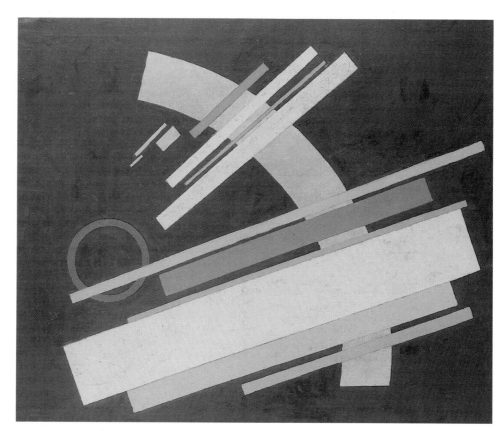

Ilya Chashnik. Composition, *1923-5. Oil on canvas. 70 x 85 cm.*
Private collection, courtesy Annely Juda Fine Art, London

Ilya Chashnik. Composition, *1923-4. Oil on canvas. 30.5 x 38.5 cm.*
Private collection, courtesy Annely Juda Fine Art, London

Sergei Chekhonin. Programme Cover for the Ballets Russes Vera Nemtchinova, *1930. Watercolour. Signed lower left 'Serge Tchekonine'. 32 x 24.5 cm. Collection Mr. and Mrs. Nikita D.Lobanov-Rostovsky, London.*

D

DAN'KO, Elena Yakovlevna **1898-1942**
Ceramics decorator, writer. She studied at the Aleksandr Murashko School, Kiev, in 1915, and then in Moscow under Mashkov and Rerberg 1915-18. She worked for the State Porcelain Factory from 1918 to 1941, studied the history of ceramics and wrote a history of the Lomonosov Porcelain Factory. Her literary activities included puppet plays 1919-20, acting as secretary of the Leningrad poet's society in 1925, and writing children's books. She was represented at the Paris International Exhibition of 1925 and at the jubilee exhibition Artists of the RSFSR over 15 Years held at the Russian Museum, Leningrad, in 1932.
Lit N.Lobanov-Rostovsky *Revolutionary Ceramics*, London, 1990.

DAN'KO (-ALEKSEENKO), Nataliya Yakovlevna 1892-1942
Ceramics artist, sculptor. Born at Tiflis. She studied at the Stroganov School in Moscow 1900-2. She also studied at Vilnius and under the sculptor Leonid Shervud 1908-9. From 1909 she worked in the studio of the sculptor Vasili Kuznetsov. Architectural reliefs followed in 1910-11 and her work was exhibited at Turin and Milan. She became Vasili Kuznetsov's assistant at the Imperial Porcelain Factory in 1914. After the Revolution she became director of the sculpture workshops at the State Porcelain Factory from 1919 to1941. She continued to exhibit abroad, including Königsberg and Milan in 1920, Helsinki and London in 1922, Stockholm in 1923, the Paris International Exhibition in 1925 (gold medal) and 1928, Lyon in 1926, and Milan in 1927 (gold medal). She produced figurines, portraits and satirical statuettes as well as decorative sculpture for numerous buildings including the Sverdlov Square Station and River Station (Khimki) of the Moscow Metro 1936-7. She had personal exhibitions in Leningrad in 1929 and posthumously in 1946. She was represented at the jubilee exhibition Artists of the RSFSR over 15 Years held at the Russian Museum, Leningrad, in 1932. The Russian Museum has her plaster bust *Portrait of a Girl*. She died at Irbit, Sverdlovsk.
Lit I.Grabar' *Dan'ko-Alekseenko*, Moscow, 1934. Yu. Ovsyannikov *N.Ya.Dan'ko*, 1965. N.Lobanov-Rostovsky *Revolutionary Ceramics* , London, 1990. D.Elliott, V.Dudakov *100 Years of Russian Painting*, London, 1991.
Coll RM.

DARAN (RAYKHMAN), Daniil Borisovich **1894-1964**
Painter. He was born in Voronezh. He was engaged on Agitprop decorations at Saratov c.1918. He exhibited with the group The Thirteen in 1929 and 1931. He died in Moscow.

DARMOLATOVA, S. = LEBEDEVA, S.D.

DAVYDOV, Ivan Grigorievich **1826-1856**
Landscape painter. Themes include Rome in 1856.
Coll TG.

DAVYDOV, Mikhail Fedorovich **early 19th century**
Painter. His themes included interiors signed 'M. Davidoff'.
Coll TG.

DAVYDOV, Petr Prokhorovich **1895-1943**
Painter. Born Simbirsk region. Executed mural decorations at the Vkhutein Club, Moscow, c.1928.

DAVYDOVA, A. P. **a.1918**
She was represented at the First Exhibition of Works of the Professional Union of Artists in Moscow in 1918.

DAVYDOVA, N. M. **a.1917-1919**
Textile designer. She exhibited with the Knave of Diamonds in Moscow in November 1917. She was teaching textiles along with Malyutina, Exter and Rozanova at the Free Art Studios in Moscow c.1918. She was one of the nine exhibitors at the Tenth State Exhibition: Non-Objective Creativity and Suprematism in Moscow in 1919. Her name appeared on the April 1919 list of artists for acquisitions by the envisaged Museum of Painterly Culture. She was instrumental in the Verbovka handicraft workshops in the Ukraine.

DAVYDOVA, Natalya Yakovlevna **1873-1926**
Painter, applied artist. She studied at the Moscow College and subsequently became instrumental in the revival of handicrafts at the workshops at Solomenko of which she became the director. Together with Maria Fedorovna Yakunchikova she directed the Abramtsevo Workshops from 1908.

DEINEKA (DEYNEKA), Aleksandr Aleksandrovich 1899-1969
Painter, draughtsman, sculptor. Born at Kursk. He studied at Kharkov School of Art under M.Pestrikov and Lyubimov 1914-18 and then at the Moscow Vkhutemas under V.Favorsky and I.Nivinsky 1921-5. He was a member of the Group of Three with A.Deineka and Yu.Pimenov, who exhibited together as a group at the First Discussional Exhibition of Active Revolutionary Art in 1924, and he was a founder member of OST from 1925. He participated in the seventh exhibition of the group *L'Araignée* (The Spider) at the Galerie Devambe in Paris in 1925. He contributed to the International Exhibition in Dresden in 1926 and was included in the major exhibition in Moscow in 1927 marking the tenth anniversary of the Revolution.
Deineka brought much of the spatial and pictorial experiment of the previous generation to bear upon painting that was figurative, monumental and politically committed. Before the advent of Socialist Realism Deineka had evolved an approach that was heroic, readily intelligible, dramatic and public without reverting to 19th century academic formulas of composition and technique. He taught at the Vkhutein 1928-30 and was a founder member of the group October in 1928. He was included in the 1928 exhibition of Acquisitions by the State Art Collections Fund held in Moscow. He was also represented in the exhibition of Russian Graphics at Riga in 1929.
He became a member of the Academy of Arts of the USSR. He exhibited at the 1932 Venice Biennale. He was represented

Aleksandr Deineka. Workmen Loading Coal. *Indian ink, wash and body colour. 23.5 x 35.5 cm. Reproduced by kind permission of Sotheby's London, sale 23.2.1983, lot 224.*

at the jubilee exhibition Artists of the RSFSR over 15 Years held at the Russian Museum, Leningrad, in 1932. In 1935 he visited Italy, France and the USA. He painted panels for the Soviet Pavilion at the 1937 Paris International Exhibition and for an exhibition in Minsk in 1938. He exhibited in Moscow together with Sarra Lebedeva, Sergei Gerasimov, P.P.Konchalovsky, Vera Mukhina and D.A.Shmarinov in 1943. He was Vice-President of the Academy of Arts 1962-6. He died in Moscow.

Before Descending the Mine, 1925, Pushkin Museum, Moscow, shows Deineka employing many devices ultimately derived from Cubism, including broken perspectives and an element of construction in the composition. But this is used to build dramatic, narrative works depicting the interplay of machinery and the workers who attend and manipulate it. The effect is to evoke a superhuman construction peopled with clean cut figures who adopt an active and even gymnastic role. Deineka, here and elsewhere, reconciles the discoveries of the previous generation with a didactic and rhetorical purpose. The means are essentially graphic. They rely upon simplified drawing and aspire to the direct impact of posters but retain the authority of figure composition in painting. Something of this achievement was sometimes managed also by Pimenov.

On the Building of the New Factory, 1926. This monumental painting presents the image of two women workers seen against the metal girders of the new factory shed. A dislocation of scale ensures their monumental and heroic effect by enlarging them to emphasise their importance, a little in the manner employed for saints in ikon paintings. It is a dynamic, original and collage-like composition celebrating their athletic prowess in heroic terms.

The Defence of Petrograd, 1928, RM, is an unprecedented composition. Citizens with rifles march across the lower part of the painting. Behind them and above them citizens and wounded soldiers cross a bridge.

The Defence of Sebastopol, 1942, RM. Painted in the war years when propaganda played a role of immediate significance once again, this is a grandiloquently heroic canvas with the crisp directness of a poster. It is theatrical and declamatory in the manner of a film poster. In a spiralling gesture almost worthy of the discus thrower of ancient Greece, a white-clad marine hurls explosives at the invaders who are represented by opposing horizontal bayonets.

Theatre design Mayakovsky's play *Banya* (The Bathhouse) designed in collaboration with S.Vakhtangov.

Writings A.Deineka *Zhizn', iskusstvo, vremya* (Life, Art, Time), Leningrad, 1974.

Lit B.M.Nikiforov *A.Deineka*, Moscow, 1937. A.D.Chegodaev *A.A.Deineka*, Moscow, 1959. M.N.Yablonskaya *A.A.Deineka*, Leningrad, 1964. D.Elliott, V.Dudakov *100 Years of Russian Painting*, London, 1991.

Coll TG; RM; Pushkin Museum, Moscow.

DEINEKO, Olga Konstantinovna   1897-1970

Painter, graphic artist. Born in the Chernigov region. She studied at the Stieglitz School in St. Petersburg 1916-18. After the Revolution she assisted N.N.Kupreyanov and V.Favorsky at the Vkhutemas between 1919 and 1923. At this time her work responded directly to the example set by the Suprematism of Malevich and his followers. She illustrated children's books in the 1920s. She belonged to a group

designing revolutionary posters 1931-2. She was given a personal exhibition in Moscow in 1946. She died in Moscow.
Lit *L'Avant-garde russe 1905-1925*, exh. cat., Musée des Beaux-Arts, Nantes, 1993.
Coll Tula Art Museum.

DELAUNAY (-TERK), Sonia Elievna   1885-1979

Painter, graphic artist, theatre designer, fashion designer. Born at Gradiesk in the Ukraine. She studied at Karlsruhe in Germany under Schmidt-Reutter in 1903 and went to Paris in 1905. Four years later she married the critic Wilhelm Uhde who knew Cubism first hand and sat for a Cubist portrait by Picasso. She divorced Uhde almost at once in 1910, and married the French painter Robert Delaunay. She studied in Paris at the Académie de la Palette and met many Cubist painters. She also provided a valuable link with Parisian Cubists for Russian artists travelling to Paris. She met Yakulov, for example, in 1912. She was closely involved with Robert Delaunay on the evolution of Simultanéisme. She met the traveller and poet Blaise Cendrars in 1913 and illustrated his poem the *Prose du trassibérien et de la petite Jehanne de France* as a decorated scroll. This was shown at the Stray Dog cabaret in St. Petersburg on 22 December 1913 where A.A.Smirnov, who had recently returned from Paris, lectured on Simultanéisme, Apollinaire and Blaise Cendrars. Among those present were Pavel Filonov, Nikolai Burlyuk and Nikolai Kul'bin. The scroll was also among her exhibits at the First German Autumn Salon held at the *Der Sturm* gallery, Berlin, in 1913.

From 1914 to 1920 the Delaunays lived in Portugal and Spain. During this time she was employed by Diaghilev to make designs for his Russian Ballet's 1918 production of *Cléopâtre*. As a result of her work for the stage she met Stravinsky and Massine.

After returning to Paris in 1920 she designed her first materials for fashion, bringing to this work all the colourful force of her paintings and adding a new crispness and immediacy which arose from her involvement in the necessarily decisive procedures of printing. *Simultanéisme* had been extended into a style of living. Robert Delaunay pursued this too, but Sonia Delaunay brought to it the refinement and daring of *haute couture* in which field she was a unique example of the painter-fashion designer willing to employ loose painterly marks and to explore colour as freely in a fashion print as on a canvas. To a degree her involvement with theatre design encouraged this development. She designed costumes for Tristan Tzara's *Coeur à Gaz* which was performed on 6 July 1923 in Paris, to which Ilya Zdanevich also contributed.

She opened a fashion house with Jacques Heim in 1924. She exhibited at the Paris Exhibition in 1925. She published two albums in 1929-30, *Tissus et tapis* and *Compositions, couleurs, idées*. Her involvement with painters did not diminish. In 1932 she exhibited with the group *Abstraction-Création* and worked with Robert Delaunay on murals 1935-7 for the Paris International Exhibition of 1937, at which she was awarded a gold medal. She contributed to the first exhibition of the group Réalités Nouvelles in 1939.

After the death of Delaunay she moved to Grasse in 1941. She was made a member of the Légion d'Honneur in 1964. A retrospective was held at the Musée national d'art moderne, Paris, in 1967. She died in Paris.

Theatre design 1918 worked on Diaghilev's production of *Cleopatra* in London.

1923 *Soirée du Coeur à Barbe* by Ilya Zdanevich and Serge Romoff for the Cherez group in Paris.

1924 Tristan Tzara's *Coeur à Gaz* in Paris.

Lit A.Lhote *Sonia Delaunay, ses peintures, ses objets, ses tissus simultanés, ses modes*, Paris, 1925. J.Damase *Sonia Delaunay — Rhythmes et couleurs*, Paris, 1971. A.Cohen *Sonia Delaunay*, New York, 1975. J.Damase *Homage à Sonia Delaunay*, Paris-Bruxelles, 1976. J.E.Bowlt *Russian Stage Design. Scenic Innovation. From the Collection of Mr. and Mrs. Nikita D.Lobanov-Rostovsky*, Jackson, MS, exh. cat.,1982. Dzhon Boult (John Bowlt) *Khudozhniki russkogo teatra. Sobranie Nikity i Niny Lobanovykh-Rostovskikh*, Moscow, 1991.

DELLA-VOS-KARDOVSKAYA, Olga Lyudvigovna 1875-1952

Portrait painter and graphic artist. She studied at the Schreider School in Kharkov 1891-4 and at the Academy in St. Petersburg from 1894 to1899. She then attended the Azbé School in Munich 1899-1900. She exhibited with the New Society of Artists between 1903 and 1917 and with the Union of Russian Artists 1911-16.

She exhibited with the *Zhar-tsvet* (Fire-colour) group between 1924 and 1928. She was included in the major exhibition in Moscow in 1927 marking the tenth anniversary of the Revolution. Sometimes she signed her work 'O.Della-Vos'.
Lit *Twilight of the Tsars*, London, 1991.
Coll TG.
Colour plate opposite.

DELOV, Mikhail Alekseevich   b.1918

Sculptor. Born at Kursk.
Coll TG, RM.
See Levitskaya.

DEMIDOV, Mikhail Afanasevich   1885-1929

Born at Vyatka. He was included in the Third Touring Exhibition of the Sovetsk Regional subdepartment of the Museums Bureau along with Kandinsky, Rodchenko and others in 1921.
He died at Vyatka.

DEMIDOV, Vasili Kuz'mich (Koz'mich) early 19th century

History painter.
Coll TG.

DEMINA, Klavdiya Petrovna   1900-1932+

She was represented at the jubilee exhibition Artists of the RSFSR over 15 Years held at the Russian Museum, Leningrad, in 1932.

DEMUT-MALINOVSKY, Vasili Ivanovich   1779-1846

Major neo-classical sculptor who worked with architects. He became rector of sculpture at the Academy in St. Petersburg.
Russian Scaevola, 1813, plaster, RM, is a full-length of considerable power and strength, based perhaps on an antique sculpture of an athlete. The muscular figure exhudes confidence, assurance and physical bravery as he prepares to chop off his own hand which he has positioned upon a tree stump. The intense drama of this is handled with cool restraint and meticulously controlled technique.
Coll Well represented at RM.

DENI (DENISOV), Viktor Nikolaevich   1893-1946

Poster designer, graphic artist. Born in Moscow. He studied

Olga Della-Vos-Kardovskaya. The Poet Anna Akhmatova, *1914. Oil on canvas. Signed lower right. 85 x 82 cm.*
State Tretyakov Gallery, Moscow.

under N.Ulyanov in Moscow and from 1906 exhibited with the Association of Independent Artists of which he was a member from 1910 to 1917. He made illustrations for the journal *Budilnik* in 1910. Between 1913 and 1917 he lived in St. Petersburg/Petrograd and contributed to the journals *Solntse Rossii* (Sun of Russia), *Rampa i Zhizn'* and *Satirikon*.
After the Revolution he became one of the most celebrated Soviet poster designers (p.120) and also continued to produce illustrations for the press, including *Pravda*, *Izvestiya* and *Krokodil* (pp.120, 121). He died in Moscow.

**Constituent Assembly*, 1921, poster, shows France at sea in a shoe, carrying a bag of gold beneath shredded sails and accompanied by representatives of the military and finance. The style borrows its absurdity from children's books to apply it as political caricature.

Lit Zh.M.Zabrodina *V.N.Deni*, Leningrad, 1970. I.A.Sviridova *V.N.Deni*, Moscow, 1978. *Paris-Moscou*, 1979. D.Elliott, V.Dudakov *100 Years of Russian Painting*, London, 1991.

DENISOV, Aleksandr Gavrilovich 1811-1834
Painter. He studied under Venetsianov in the late 1820s, but his career was cut short by his early death. His paintings are consequently scarce.
Sailors at a Cobblers, 1832, RM, which is a study in lighting. Three sailors, one standing, two seated, examine a boot. Each is an individual portrait caught in a moment of stillness before a window the light of which throws their features into relief. This is portrait painting masquerading as genre painting. In fact nothing appears to move and the effect is staged; it does not suggest figures unaware of the painter or caught up in their daily activities.
Coll RM.

DENISOV, Ivan Andreevich 1867-1928
Born at Kazan. He was represented at the enormous First State Exhibition of Art and Science, which included ethnographic material, held in Kazan in 1920 and he was included in the Third Touring Exhibition of the Sovetsk Regional subdepartment of the Museums Bureau along with Kandinsky, Rodchenko and others in 1921. He died at Kazan.

DENISOV, M. a.1927
Sculptor. He was included in the major exhibition in Moscow in 1927 marking the tenth anniversary of the Revolution.

DENISOV, M. P. a.1908
Painter. He contributed to the exhibition *Zveno* (The Link) in Kiev in 1908.

Viktor Deni. Caricature of Demyan Bedny, *c.1922. Satirical drawing.*

Viktor Deni. Lenin Speaks, *1924. Poster design. Signed lower right. The leader is given gigantic stature rising above a citadel of factory chimneys.*

DENISOV, Vasili Ivanovich 1862-1921
Painter, illustrator, theatre designer. Born in Poland. He studied as a musician at the Warsaw Music Institute but in 1895 he began to paint. He studied painting under Korovin in Moscow and was included in Diaghilev's display of Russian art at the 1906 Salon d'Automne in Paris. He exhibited as a neo-primitive at the Moscow Society of Art in 1907. He visited Greece with the sculptor Konenkov in 1912. He exhibited with the Izdebsky Salon of 1910-11 in Odessa. He died in Moscow.
Theatre design 1905 S.Przybyszewski's *Sneg* (Snow) produced by Meyerhold at the Theatre Studio, Moscow.
1906 S.Przybyszewski's *Vechnaya skazka* (The Eternal Story) produced by Meyerhold.
1906 December H.Ibsen's *The Doll's House* produced by Meyerhold at the Komissarzhevskaya Theatre in St. Petersburg.
1907 January H.Ibsen's *Love's Comedy* produced by Meyerhold at the Komissarzhevskaya Theatre in St. Petersburg.
1907 September F.Wedekind's *Awakening of Spring* produced by Meyerhold at the Komissarzhevskaya Theatre in St. Petersburg.
1907 October M.Maeterlinck's *Pelléas et Mélisande*, translated by V.Bryusov, produced by Meyerhold at the Komissarzhevskaya Theatre in St. Petersburg.
1907 Mussorgsky's *Boris Godunov* at the Opera Theatre.
1907 Rimsky-Korsakov's *Sadko* at the Opera Theatre.
Lit *Twilight of the Tsars*, London, 1991.
Coll TG; RM; Bakhrushin Theatre Museum, Moscow.

DENISOV, Vladimir   a.c.1926
He was a member of the group *Krug khudozhnikov* (Circle of Artists) founded in 1926.

DENISOVA (-SHCHADENKO), Maria Aleksandrovna 1894-1944
She exhibited at the 1932 Venice Biennale.

DENISOVSKY, Nikolai Fedorovich   1901-1932+
Painter, graphic artist. Born in Moscow. He studied at the Stroganov College.
After the Revolution he studied under Yakulov at the Free Art Studios (SVOMAS) in Moscow. He was engaged in Agitprop art c.1921 and he designed posters for the Rosta Agency. He was a member of the Society of Young Artists, Obmokhu, 1919-23, along with the Stenberg brothers, Medunetsky and others. He exhibited in the first Obmokhu exhibition in May 1919 in Moscow. He was represented at the First Russian Art Exhibition in Berlin in 1922. He was a founder member of the Society of Easel Painters (OST) in 1925 and participated in the seventh exhibition of the group *L'Araignée* (The Spider) at the Galerie Devambe in Paris in 1925. He was included in the major exhibition in Moscow in 1927 marking the tenth anniversary of the Revolution and in the 1928 exhibition of Acquisitions by the State Art Collections Fund held in Moscow. He was represented in the First Touring Exhibition of Paintings and Graphics which opened in Moscow in 1929 and at the jubilee exhibition Artists of the RSFSR over 15 Years held at the Russian Museum, Leningrad, in 1932.

Lit. C.Lodder *Russian Constructivism*, New Haven and London, 1983.

DEN'SHIN, Aleksei Ivanovich   1893-1948
He was included in the Third Touring Exhibition of the Sovetsk Regional subdepartment of the Museums Bureau along with Kandinsky, Rodchenko and others in 1921.

DERFAK
The abbreviated name for the Woodwork Faculty at the Moscow Vkhutemas (*Derevoobrabatyvayushchii falul'tet*).

DERGACH, M.   a.1909
Dergach exhibited with the Golden Fleece in Moscow in 1909-10.

DERMETFAK
The abbreviated name for the Wood and Metalwork Faculty at the Moscow Vkhutemas (*Derevo i metalloobrabatyvayushchii fakul'tet*).

DERUNOV, Vladimir Ivanovich   1908-1979
Sculptor. He enrolled at the Vkhutein in 1930 where he studied under Tatlin briefly before working at the Dulevo Ceramics Factory. He studied at the Faculty of Sculpture of the Academy 1930-6.

DERVIZ, Vladimir Dmitrievich   1859-1937
A contemporary of Serov.

DESYATOV, Pavel Alekseevich   1820-1888
Portrait painter.
Coll TG.

Viktor Deni. Lenin with the Angel of Peace, *before 1926. Political satirical drawing.*

DEYKIN, Boris Nikolaevich   1890-1945
Painter. He exhibited at the juryless Eighth State Exhibition in Moscow in 1919. He was represented at the jubilee exhibition Artists of the RSFSR over 15 Years held at the Russian Museum, Leningrad, in 1932.

DEYNEKA = DEINEKA, A. A.

DIDCHENKO, G.   a.1906-1912
Taught at Kiev Art School c.1906-12 where his pupils included Radakov.

DIDERIKHS, Andrei Romanovich   1884-1942
Painter, graphic artist. Born in St. Petersburg. He studied in Munich, first at the Academy 1905-8 and then at the Azbé School 1908-9. He also studied in Paris under Kees Van Dongen. He returned to St. Petersburg in 1909. He showed work at Kul'bin's Triangle exhibition there in 1912 and at the Moscow Exhibition of Painting: The Year 1915. In 1918 he collaborated with V.A. Al'vang on Agitprop decorations at Sampsonievsky Bridge, Petrograd. He was the husband of Valentina Khodasevich. He died at Tashkent.
Lit *Paris-Moscou*, 1979.

DIONYSIUS (DIONISIY)   c.1440-1503+
Ikon painter. The Tretyakov Gallery, Moscow, has ikons executed by Dionysius for the Moscow Kremlin in 1482 and for the Obnorsky Monastery in 1500. With his sons Theodosi and Vladimir he painted frescoes at the Cathedral of the Dormition of the Virgin in the Ferapontov (Therapont) Monastery at Vologda 1500-1.
Coll TG; RM.

DITRIKH, Leopold Yakovlevich (Avgustovich) 1877-1954
Monumental sculptor. Born at Warsaw. He participated in the First State Free Exhibition of Artworks in Petrograd in 1919 and was included in the enormous survey Exhibition of Paintings by Petrograd Artists of All Tendencies 1919-1923 held in Petrograd in 1923. His works include the monument to *A.Navoi* at Tashkent. He died at Leningrad.

DLUGACH, Mikhail Oskarovich   1893-1989
Graphic designer. He studied at Kiev Art School 1905-17.
After the Revolution he concentrated on cinema posters but also produced political and circus posters. He contributed to the First Exhibition of Cinema Posters held in Moscow in 1925 and to the Second Exhibition of Cinema Posters held at the Kamerny (Chamber) Theatre, Moscow, in 1926. He designed a poster for V.Vilner's film *Cement* in 1929.

DMITRIEV, Andrei Ivanovich   1893-1921
Painter, theatre designer. An A.Dmitriev was represented at the First Exhibition of Works of the Professional Union of Artists in Moscow in 1918. He died in Moscow.

DMITRIEV, Pavel Dmitrievich   1878-1907
Portrait painter.
Coll TG.

DMITRIEV, Pavel Sergeevich   1841-1900
Theatre designer.
Lit Dzhon Boult (John Bowlt) *Khudozhniki russkogo teatra. Sobranie Nikity i Niny Lobanovykh-Rostovskikh*, Moscow, 1991.

DMITRIEV, Vladimir Vladimirovich   1900-1948
Theatre designer. Born in Moscow. He studied at the Zvantseva School, Petrograd, 1916-17.
After the Revolution he studied at the Free Art Studios (SVOMAS), Petrograd, under Petrov-Vodkin 1918-22. In addition he studied stage design with Meyerhold at the Borodinskaya Street studios. His own theatre designs began in 1917. He contributed to the Exhibition of Paintings by Russian Artists held at Pskov in Spring 1920. He was a member of the group *Put' zhivopisi* (Path of Painting) formed by Lev Zhegin in 1927. He died in Moscow.
Theatre design 1918 June Meyerhold's production of H.Ibsen's *The Doll's House* at the Theatre of the Worker's Club, Petrograd.
1920 November Meyerhold's production of Emile Verhaeren's *Les Aubes* (Zori, Dawn) at the No.1 Theatre of the RSFSR, Moscow. Dmitriev revealed an awareness of contemporary Constructivist experiment by Tatlin and his circle in his designs. The set was conceived as an adjustable construction of diverse materials assembled like a great relief and accompanied by Futurist costumes and large cubes on stage painted with Futurist motifs in the manner of Miturich. It was an adventurous, pioneering and unwieldy essay in the synthesis of the arts and in the prevention of the suspension of disbelief, a concept that was to become essential in much of Meyerhold's theatrical work. It exemplified Meyerhold's demand for the juxtaposition of the surfaces and shapes of tangible materials. A public discussion of the production was held on 17 January 1921 which the director Tairov attended.
1926 Meyerhold's production of *Revizor* (The Government Inspector).
1930 January L.N.Tolstoy's *Resurrection* at the Moscow Art Theatre.
1935 October M.Gorky's *Vragi* (Enemies) at the Moscow Art Theatre.
1937 May Tolstoy's *Anna Karenina* at the Moscow Art Theatre.
1938 May L.M.Leonov's *Polovchanskie sady* at the Moscow Art Theatre.
1938 October A.S.Griboedov's *Gore ot Uma* at the Moscow Art Theatre.
1940 April Chekhov's *Tri Sestry* (The Three Sisters) at the Moscow Art Theatre.
1941 Dostoevsky's *Dyadyushkin son* at the Moscow Art Theatre.
1942 January A.E.Korneychuk's *Front* (The Front) at the Moscow Art Theatre.
1943 September K.M.Semenov's *Russkie lyudi* (Russian People) at the Moscow Art Theatre.
1944 July A.N.Ostrovsky's *Poslednyaya zhertva* (The Last Sacrifice) at the Moscow Art Theatre.
1947 June Chekhov's *Dyadya Vanya* (Uncle Vanya) at the Moscow Art Theatre.
1948 May A.N.Ostrovsky's *Les* (The Forest) at the Moscow Art Theatre.
1948 June N.E.Virta's *Khleb nash nasushchniy* (Our Daily Bread) at the Moscow Art Theatre.
1956 February N.F.Pogodin's *Kremlevskie kuranty* (Kremlin Chimes) at the Moscow Art Theatre.
Lit E.Kostina *V.Dmitriev*, Moscow, 1957. Nancy Van Norman Baer *Theatre in Revolution, Russian Avant-Garde Stage Design 1913-1935*, San Francisco and London, 1991. Dzhon Boult (John Bowlt) *Khudozhniki russkogo teatra. Sobranie Nikity i Niny Lobanovykh-Rostovskikh*, Moscow, 1991.
Coll Bakhrushin Theatre Museum, Moscow.

Vladimir Dmitriev. Stage Construction for Meyerhold's Production of Emile Verhaeren's Play 'Les Aubes', *Moscow, 1920.*
Documentary photograph.
The tower-like constructions recall the material assemblages of Tatlin or Puni carried out on a grand scale for Meyerhold's theatre but the painted cubic forms appear to derive from the graphic constructions of Miturich.

DMITRIEV-KAVKAZSKY, Lev Evgrafovich   1849-1916
Painter of landscapes and portraits, draughtsman, illustrator and teacher. Born in the Caucasus. He depicted battles and near eastern themes. He studied in Stavropol and then in St. Petersburg. He was an Academician who also taught privately. Amongst his numerous pupils were Apsit, Dobuzhinsky, Filonov, Kakabadze and Kuprin.

DMITRIEV-ORENBURGSKY, Nikolai Dmitrievich 1837-1898
A founder of the Artel which led to the Wanderers. Signed 'N.D.Or'.
Coll TG

DMITRIEVSKY, Nikolai Pavlovich   1890-1938
Graphic artist. He was impressed by the technical and stylistic innovations of Vladimir Favorsky, producing historicising wood engravings of which *Portrait of P.A.Vyazemsky*, 1932, is an example.

DOBROKOVSKY, Mechislav Vasil'evich   1895-1937
Painter. He was represented at the Paris International Exhibition of 1925, at the first exhibition of the Society of Easel Painters (OST) in Moscow in 1925 and at the seventh exhibition of the group *L'Araignée* (The Spider) at the Galerie

Devambe in Paris in 1925. A Dobrokovsky was listed as a founder member of the group October in 1928. He was included in the 1928 exhibition of Acquisitions by the State Art Collections Fund held in Moscow.

DOBROMYSLOVA   a.1925
Painter. She contributed to the Third Exhibition of Paintings by Artists from Kaluga and Moscow held in Kaluga in 1925.

DOBROV, Matvei Alekseevich   1877-1958
Graphic artist. Born in Moscow. He was represented at the First Exhibition of Works of the Professional Union of Artists in Moscow in 1918 and at the First Exhibition of the Moscow Contemporary Art Store in January 1919. His name appeared on the April 1919 list of artists for acquisitions by the envisaged Museum of Painterly Culture. He was represented in the Sixth State Exhibition: The Print (*VI Gosudarstvennaya vystavka gravyur*) in Moscow in 1919. He worked on Agitprop train decorations including work on the train *Lenin (October Revolution)* in 1920. He exhibited with the *Zhar-tsvet* (Firecolour) group between 1924 and 1928. He was included in the 1928 exhibition of Acquisitions by the State Art Collections Fund held in Moscow and in the fourth exhibition of *Iskusstvo dvizheniya* (The Art of Movement) that year in Moscow. He was represented in the First Touring Exhibition of Paintings

Mstislav Dobuzhinsky. Cossacks in Paris. *Watercolour. Signed with a monogram lower left. Costume designs for two cossacks flirting with two girls, for a production of the Théâtre de la Chauve-Souris, Paris 1926. 31.8 x 24.3 cm.*
Collection Mr. and Mrs. Nikita D. Lobanov-Rostovsky, London.

and Graphics which opened in Moscow in 1929 and at the jubilee exhibition Artists of the RSFSR over 15 Years held at the Russian Museum, Leningrad, in 1932. He died in Moscow.

DOBROVOL'SKY, I. N.   a.1921
He contributed to the First State Exhibition in Orenburg in 1921.

DOBROVOL'SKY, Vasili Stepanovich   1789-1855
Painter. His self-portrait is in the Tretyakov Gallery, Moscow.
Coll TG.

DOBUZHINSKY, Mstislav Valerianovich   1875-1957
Painter, graphic artist and theatre designer. Born at Novgorod. He studied at the Society for the Encouragement of the Arts in St. Petersburg 1885-7 and then under Lev Dmitriev-Kavkazsky, but also took a law degree at the University of St. Petersburg 1895-9. His first illustrations were in the satirical journal *Shut* (Buffoon) in 1898. He then returned to art studies, 1899-1901, at the Azbé School and the Simon Hollósy School in Munich were he became aware of the activities of the artists associated with the periodicals *Jugend* and *Simplicissimus*. After failing to gain entry to the Academy on his return to St. Petersburg in 1901, he joined the World of Art. He studied etching under Vasili Maté and like several other members of the World of Art he used his graphic skills to make fiercely satirical comments at the time of the 1905 revolutionary events. *October Idyll*,1905, published in

Zhupel' (Bugbear) is an example of this depicting a bloodstained wall and an abandoned doll, a shoe and spectacles on the cobblestones of a street corner, and *Pacification*, also 1905, which showed the Kremlin surrounded by a sea of blood. He exhibited with the Union of Russian Artists 1904-10 and was included in Diaghilev's display of Russian art at the Salon d'Automne in Paris in 1906. He exhibited assiduously with the World of Art 1911-19. He was a member of the organising committee of the 1912 World of Art exhibition under the presidency of Roerich.

He also responded to the current interest in folk art, achieving a blend of simplicity and elegance that was unique, applying it to illustration and theatre design. He was an active teacher for much of his career and was co-director of the Zvantseva art school with Leon Bakst from 1906. In 1907 he produced costumes and sets for Adam de la Halle's *Robin and Marion*. Many other theatre designs and illustrations followed. He began to exhibit internationally, including Paris in 1908, Brussels in 1910 and Rome in 1911. He also travelled annually in the pre-war years, visiting Switzerland, Italy (1908, 1911), Germany, France, Denmark, Sweden, Norway and England. He executed studies of Amsterdam and Haarlem in 1910. He exhibited in Venice in 1913.

During the 1914-18 war he served as a medical orderly and recorded his observations of life on the Polish and Galician fronts. He exhibited studies of the war at the Art Bureau of Nadezhda Dobychina in Petrograd in 1915. He was in Finland in 1916 but he also designed murals that year for the Kazan Railway Station in Moscow.

After the Revolution he exhibited with the World of Art in December 1917 in Moscow. In 1918 he worked on revolutionary Agitprop decorations of flags, banners, swags and drapes with sailing ship sails erected at the Admiralty in Petrograd. He also taught at the reorganised Academy there. In addition he became active in the theatre department of the People's Commissariat of the Enlightenment (Narkompros) and his name appeared on the April 1919 list of artists for acquisitions by the proposed Museum of Painterly Culture. In 1918 he taught briefly under Chagall at the art school in Vitebsk. He became vice-president of the House of Arts in Petrograd in 1919 and participated in the First State Free Exhibition of Artworks in Petrograd in 1919. He worked on mass pageants with Yuri Annenkov in 1920 and was represented at the enormous First State Exhibition of Art and Science, which included ethnographic material, held in Kazan in 1920. He produced an album illustrating the *Second Congress of the Communist International* in 1920. He was also represented at the First Russian Art Exhibition in Berlin in 1922 and the exhibition Art of Moscow Theatre 1918-1923 held in Moscow in 1923. He was included in the survey Exhibition of Paintings by Petrograd Artists of All Tendencies 1919-1923 held in Petrograd in 1923.

He travelled West to Kaunas and France in 1923 and in 1924 he exhibited in Dresden. He then emigrated to Lithuania. He was however represented at the Paris International Exhibition of 1925 and at the Third Exhibition of Paintings by Artists from Kaluga and Moscow held in Kaluga in 1925.

He also exhibited in Copenhagen and Amsterdam in 1928. He later settled in the United States where he remained active as a painter, illustrator and theatre designer and where he compiled a bibliography on Russian art for the Library of

Mstislav Dobuzhinsky. Illustration for Dostoevsky's 'White Nights', *1922.*

Congress. He travelled widely and visited London in 1939. He became an American citizen in 1947 and died in New York.

Man with Spectacles (the Art Critic and Poet K.Sunnerberg), 1905-6, charcoal and watercolour on card, TG, is a very original portrait in which the sitter is placed centrally before a window so that he is seen against the light, fixed in place by the precise dark blue vertical window bars. Beyond is a mundane view of the tenements of the city as experienced by the workers with a factory visible at left. This image of the proletarian suburbs is common to a number of works of 1904-6 and forms a strong contrast to the exotic lyricism of much of the decorative work of the painters of the World of Art.

Peter the Great in Holland. Amsterdam, the Wharf of the East India Company, 1910, TG, is a historicising scene of

shipbuilding with the skeletons of ships rising up against the towering sky. It could serve as a stage design and shares with theatre the convincing narrative evocation of other times. This has however a theme relevant to the history of St. Petersburg and is in line with the imagery of past times employed by other members of the World of Art, particularly Benois, Serov and Lanceray.

City Types (City Grimaces), 1908, TG, illustrates his love of the grotesque and potentially fantastic aspects of everyday life which was to have a profound effect on Chagall's early work. The city street, lashed with wet sleet, goes doggedly about its business. In the foreground the railings of a canal support a street performer with his dressed up monkey holding a feathered cap and at right is a cluster of umbrellas beneath which pedestrians stare at the procession of white clad horses preceded by men with lanterns. The event lacks grandeur and is potentially absurd, a point driven home by the advertisement of a leering female head, large indicator hand and lettering which dwarfs the figures. This use of fragments of lettering precedes its use by Cubists and Futurists. *Barbershop Window*, 1906, TG, is a comparable homage to the

Mstislav Dobuzhinsky. Decoration for the Letter Paper of the Community of St. Eugenia of the Red Cross, *1908. Silhouette drawing. 8 x 6.6 cm.*
Entitled 'Madrigal', this design shows the poet or composer devising a song of love to the woman whose profile hangs on the wall. A dog waits patiently. The traditions of silhouette drawings and shadow puppets remained popular in Russia. Here Dobuzhinsky is evoking the time of Pushkin by the style and costume of his figures.

Vladimir Domogatsky. Alexander Pushkin, *1926. Toned plaster. 64 x 59 x 38 cm.*

demonic life of the advertising image within the city street.

Illustrations Designs for the periodicals *Zhupel'*, *Shut* (Buffoon), *Zolotoe Runo* (Golden Fleece), *Apollon* and *Zhar-Ptitsa* (Fire Bird).
1906 A.Pushkin *The Station Inspector*.
1909 N.Gogol *The Nose* and Sergei Auslender *The Night Prince*.
1910 cover for collected works of Sologub.
1910-11 two *ABC* books for children.
1911 S.Rafaelovich *Seculum Animae*.
1912 H.C.Andersen *The Little Match Girl*.
1914 Lermontov *Kaznacheisha* (The Paymaster's Wife), Petrograd.
1917 H.C.Andersen *The Swineherd*.
1918 *The Wonderful Life of Joseph Bolsano, Count Cagliostro*, and H.C.Andersen *The Princess and the Pea*.
1921 Karamzin *Bednaya Liza* (Poor Liza).
1922 Nikolai Leskov *The Toupée Artist*, Alexander Pushkin *The Miserly Knight* and Fedor Dostoevsky *White Nights*, brilliantly evocative and melancholy images of St. Petersburg executed in solid black and white.
1922 H.C.Andersen's children's story *Svinopas* (The Swineherd), Berlin.
1925 Nadezhda Pavlovich *Smeshnaya Azbuka* (Funny ABC).
Theatre design 1907 A.Remizov's *A Devilish Act on a Certain Husband, and also Life's Disputes with Death*, produced by Meyerhold at the Komisarzhevskaya Theatre, St. Petersburg, featured a towering citadel with Hell installed in vaults beneath the town square so that demons can ascend to the raised level of the mortal protagonists. The design for the

Prologue (Bakhrushin Theatre Museum) also featured the Hell-basement above which fairy-tale knights, horse and a skeleton cavort in front of a midnight sky in which shines Ursa Major beneath a dramatic and stylised shooting star.
1908 Adam de la Halle's *Jeu de Robin et Marion*, *Pastorale* produced by Evreinov at the Antique Theatre, St. Petersburg: a historicist West-European medieval set design (Bakhrushin Theatre Museum) inspired by manuscript illuminations, with tiled floor, hanging drapes, stylised trees and a horse on wheels like an enormous toy.
1908 December P.Potemkin's *Petrushka* produced by Vsevolod Meyerhold at his Lukomor'e Theatre Club in St. Petersburg with music by V.F.Nuvel. Boldly *faux-naif* set of a city street of lamp-posts and cobbles dominated by upside down shop signs of the kind that Chagall was later to employ.
1908 December Meyerhold's production of E.A.Poe's *The Fall of the House of Usher*, adapted by V.Trakhtenberg, at the Lukomor'e Theatre Club in St. Petersburg. Designed in collaboration with V.Ya.Chembers.
1908 D'Annunzio's *Francesca di Rimini* at the Komisarzhevskaya Theatre, St. Petersburg.
1909 Turgenev's *A Month in the Country* produced by Stanislavsky at the Moscow Arts Theatre featured a most elegant interior drawing room of the early 19th century, oval, broad and displaying a chandelier. At the centre an arched window opened into an expansive garden. This was a wholly convincing, but lightly achieved, period reconstruction. Another scene,TG, projected a corner of a room with richly comfortable upholstery and deep grey-blue wallpaper.
1910 Turgenev's *Lunch with the Marshall of Nobility* (unrealised).
1911 Shakespeare's *Hamlet* at the Moscow Art Theatre. Turgenev's *Evening in Sorrento* (unrealised).
1912 Turgenev's *Where It's Thin, It Breaks, The Provincial Lady* and *The Parasite* at the Moscow Art Theatre.
1913 Chekhov's *The Seagull* (unrealised). Schiller's *Kabale und Liebe* (unrealised).
1914 *Papillons*, a ballet in one act produced by Diaghilev at Monte Carlo to music by Schumann: scenery by Dobuzhinsky and costumes by Bakst.
1914 *Midas* produced by Diaghilev at the Paris Opera to music by M.Steinberg. The libretto was by Bakst but the décors by Dobuzhinsky.
1914 J.Bayer's *Die Puppenfee*.
1915 Hertel's *La Fille mal gardée* at the Mariinsky Theatre, Petrograd.
1917 Aleksandr Blok's *The Rose and the Cross* produced by Nemirovich-Danchenko at the Moscow Arts Theatre, which featured a medievalising architectural setting.
1917 designs for Kuzmin's *The Supper* at the Comedian's Halt night club in Petrograd.
1917 Dostoevsky's *The Village of Stepanchikovo* at the Moscow Art Theatre.
1918 Sophocles' *Oedipus Rex* at the Petrograd Theatre of Tragedies.
1918 Tirso de Molina's *Seducer from Seville* at the Petrograd Art Drama Theatre.
1919 H.C.Andersen's *Fairy Tales* at the Comedians' Halt night-club.
1919 Gounod's *Faust* at the Bolshoi Opera Theatre and other productions including Gutskov's *Uriel Akosta* at the Jewish Theatre, Petrograd.

1920 Shakespeare's *King Lear* at the Bolshoi Drama Theatre.

1921 Lunacharsky's *Oliver Cromwell* at the Maly Theatre, Moscow: a curtain design (Maly Theatre Museum, Moscow) features an heraldic cartouche of Cromwell flanked by dragons beheaded and dominating an upturned royal crown. Designs for an interior evoke an historicist reconstruction of English interiors of the period of the English revolution.

1924 Chaikovsky's *Eugène Onegin* at the Dresden Opera.

1934 Chaikovsky's ballet *Sleeping Beauty*, based on Charles Perrault's story, choreography by N.M.Zverev after Petipa, for the Lithuanian State Ballet, Kaunas.

1935 L.Delibes' *Coppelia* for De Basil Ballets at Monte Carlo, choreography by M.Lambert, revived by the Ballet Rambert, Mercury Theatre, London, in 1956.

1935 *Harlequinade*, music by R.Drigo, choreography N.M.Zverev, for the Lithuanian State Ballet, Kaunas.

1943 October: *Mam'zelle Angot*, ballet, music by Charles Lecoq, choreography by L.Massine, Metropolitan Opera House, New York.

1956 May: *Coppélia* ballet to music by Delibes for the Ballet Rambert at the Cambridge Arts Theatre, Cambridge, England.

Writings M. Dobuzhinsky *Vospominaniya*, New York, 1976.

Lit E.Gollerbakh *Risunki M.Dobuzhinskogo*, Moscow-Petrograd, 1923. *Diaghilev and Russian Stage Designers, a Loan Exhibition from the Collection of Mr. and Mrs. N.Lobanov-Rostovsky*, International Exhibitions Foundation, Washington, 1972-4. R.Dobujinsky and V.Dobujinsky *Mstislav V. Dobujinsky*, New York-Paris, 1973. *M.V.Dobujinsky* , exh. cat., Ashmolean Museum, Oxford, 1975. *M.V.Dobuzhinsky*, exh. cat., Tretyakov Gallery, Moscow, 1975. John E. Bowlt *The Silver Age*, Newtonville, Mass., 1979. A.Gusarova *Dobuzhinsky*, Moscow, 1982. J.E.Bowlt *Russian Stage Design. Scenic Innovation. From the Collection of Mr. and Mrs. Nikita D.Lobanov-Rostovsky*, Jackson, MS, exh. cat.,1982. G.Chugunov *Dobuzhinsky*, Leningrad, 1984. A.Kamensky *The World of Art Movement*, Leningrad, 1991. Dzhon Boult (John Bowlt) *Khudozhniki russkogo teatra. Sobranie Nikity i Niny Lobanovykh-Rostovskikh*, Moscow, 1991.

Coll TG; RM; Bakhrushin Theatre Museum, Moscow; Gorky Art Museum, Kirov; Armenian Art Museum, Yerevan; Pushkin Museum, Moscow; Maly Theatre Museum, Moscow; Brodsky Museum, St. Petersburg; Ashmolean Museum, Oxford.

See pp.20, 124, 125

DOLIN, V. K. a.1912

Painter. He exhibited with the Knave of Diamonds in 1912.

DOMASHNIKOV, Boris Fedorovich b.1924

Landscape painter. Born in the Vladimir region.
Coll TG, RM.

DOMAZHIROV a.1925

Graphic artist. He contributed to the First Exhibition of Cinema Posters held in Moscow in 1925.

DOMOGATSKY, Vladimir Nikolaevich 1876-1939

Portrait sculptor. Born at Odessa. He studied under Volnukhin 1895-1902 and Sergei Ivanov 1903-4, but also took a law degree at the University of Moscow 1897-1902. He made four visits to Paris in the period 1896-1912 and was teaching by 1908.

After the Revolution he exhibited with the World of Art in December 1917 in Moscow. He taught at the State Academy of Artistic Sciences in the 1920s. His works include *Blyumental-Tamarina* (1918) and *Pushkin* (1926). He was a consultant to the committee organising the Soviet display at the Venice Biennale of 1924. He exhibited with the *Zhar-tsvet* (Fire-colour) group between 1924 and 1928. He was included in the major exhibition in Moscow in 1927 marking the tenth anniversary of the Revolution and in the 1928 exhibition of Acquisitions by the State Art Collections Fund held in Moscow. He was also represented at the jubilee exhibition Artists of the RSFSR over 15 Years held at the Russian Museum, Leningrad, in 1932. He died in Moscow.

Michelangelo, 1917, plaster, TG, is a square relief profile portrait of the sculptor working with hammer and chisel to evoke the theme of creativity through labour.

Coll TG.

DOMRACHEV, Makariy Fedorovich 1887-1958

He was represented at the Paris International Exhibition of 1925.

DORMIDONTOV, Nikolai Ivanovich 1897-1962

Painter, graphic artist. Born in St. Petersburg. He studied at the Society for the Encouragement of the Arts in Petrograd under A.Rylov and I.Bilibin 1914-18 and 1920-2 he studied under D.Kardovsky, Vladimir Tatlin, Kuzma Petrov-Vodkin and V.Shukhaev. He was one of the initiators of the Association of Artists of Revolutionary Russia (AKhRR) in 1922 in Leningrad. He taught at the Leningrad Technical Institute of Industrial Art in 1923-29. He was included in the major exhibition in Moscow in 1927 marking the tenth anniversary of the Revolution and in the 1928 exhibition of Acquisitions by the State Art Collections Fund held in Moscow. He exhibited abroad in New York, Athens (1927), and at the 1928 Venice Biennale. He was represented at the jubilee exhibition Artists of the RSFSR over 15 Years held at the Russian Museum, Leningrad, in 1932. He died in Leningrad.

Dneprostroi, 1931, TG, is a dramatic hymn to industrial technology caught between Piranesi and skyscrapers in its effect. It depicts the colossal dam rising like a vision of the future from a mass of wooden hoardings and cranes.

Skier, 1931, TG, is a reworking of Breughel's *Winter* dominated in the foreground by the large profile of the modern, athletic Soviet woman purposefully proceding on skis.

Lit V.Knyazeva *N.I.Dormidontov*, Moscow, 1955. *Paris-Moscou*, 1979. A.M.Muratov, V.Manin et al. *Zhivopis' 20-30kh godov*, Sankt-Peterburg, 1991.

Coll TG; RM.

DOSEIKIN, Nikolai Vasilevich 1863-1935

Landscape painter, sculptor, theatre designer. He studied under Shreyder in Kharkov, under Kiselev in Moscow and with Kruglikova in Paris. He exhibited from 1888 including the Salon in Paris in 1898 and the World of Art 1900-1 in St. Petersburg. He was a member of the Union of Russian Artists from 1903. He again exhibited in Paris in 1906.

After the Revolution he participated in the Third Exhibition of Paintings held at Ryazan in 1919. He also exhibited at the juryless Eighth State Exhibition in Moscow in 1919. He was a member of the Society of Artist-Realists founded in 1927. Sometimes he signed his work 'N.D'.

Lit D.Elliott, V.Dudakov *100 Years of Russian Painting*, London, 1991.

Coll TG; RM.

DREVIN, Aleksandr Davidovich (DREVINSH, Rudolf-Aleksandr)   **1889-1938**
Painter. Born in Latvia. He was married to the painter Nadezhda Udal'tsova. He was arrested for revolutionary activities in 1906. After graduating from the Maritime School at Riga in 1908, he studied under Wilhelm Purvit at the art school in Riga until 1913. He contributed to the Second and Third Exhibitions of Latvian Art at the Riga City Art Museum in 1912 and 1913. He was evacuated with his family to Moscow in 1914 where he came to know Petrov-Vodkin.
After the Revolution he worked in both representational and other modes of painting. He exhibited with Red Kremlin Riflemen Artists in 1918, with the Artists of the Leftist Federation of the Professional Union in 1918 along with Popova, Rodchenko and others, and at the Fifth State Exhibition: From Impressionism to Non-Objective Art in 1918-19. Together with Aleksei Gan, Aleksandr Rodchenko and Varvara Stepanova he formed the group *Askranov* (the Association of Extreme Innovators) in January 1919.
He worked under Tatlin for the People's Commissariat of the Enlightenment's Art Section (IZO Narkompros) in 1919 and his name appeared on the April 1919 list of artists for acquisitions by the envisaged Museum of Painterly Culture. He was active in the Institute of Artistic Culture (INKhUK) 1920-1 until the Constructivists dominated its activities after the departure of Kandinsky. He was included in the Third Touring Exhibition of the Sovetsk Regional subdepartment of the Museums Bureau along with Kandinsky, Rodchenko and others in 1921.
He taught painting at the Moscow Free Art Studios/ Vkhutemas/Vkhutein from 1920 until 1930. In 1921 he exhibited with the revived World of Art and was represented at the First Russian Art Exhibition in Berlin in 1922.
He returned to painting from observation in 1923. His work of the later 1920s was characterised by a liquid and calligraphic figurative style and pale earth colours. The handling is rough and decisive whilst the atmosphere evoked is sparse, crude and romantic. He exhibited with the Society of Moscow Painters at its inaugural exhibition in Moscow in 1925. In 1926 he was exhibiting with AKhRR. His work was included in the exhibition of Soviet art held at Harbin in 1926 and in Japan in 1927 and in the major exhibition in Moscow in 1927 marking the tenth anniversary of the Revolution. He was a member of the Society of Moscow Artists (OMKh) 1927-32.
He visited the Ural Mountains with his wife Udal'tsova in 1927 and had a two-person exhibition with her at the Russian Museum, Leningrad, in 1928. He was included in the 1928 exhibition of Acquisitions by the State Art Collections Fund held in Moscow. He visited the Altai region with Udal'tsova 1930-1. He exhibited with the group The Thirteen in 1931.
He exhibited at the 1932 Venice Biennale. He contributed to the exhibition Artists of the RSFSR over 15 Years 1932-3 and visited Armenia with Udal'tsova in 1933, exhibiting there with her at the State Cultural and Historical Museum at Erevan in 1934. Later paintings depicted nudes and landscapes in a loose and energetic calligraphic style not dissimilar from late Udal'tsova. Sometimes he signed his work 'A.D'. He died in exile in the Altai region.
Red Jug, 1915, TG, has a more austere composition than even the still-lifes of Shterenberg. The earth red jug is centrally placed against an ochre background which has a rudimentary indication of a shelf or architectural moulding.

There is an impression of the mural quality of fresco.
Free Composition of Coloured Masses, 1920, is essentially comparable to Rayist work with a stress upon angular intersections and material qualities and in this respect it is perhaps compatible with this theme in Popova's work.
Outskirts, 1931, TG, is a loosely handled and simple composition with considerable presence. It employs earthy browns and creams to present the house in a brutal perspective stopped by a steep hill or earthwork. There is perhaps a deliberate neo-primitive element in its immediacy of execution.
Lit E.Rakitina *Drevin*, exh. cat., Moscow Union of Artists, 1979. M.Markevich *Aleksandrs Drévins*. A.Z.Rudenstine *Costakis Collection*, London 1981. *Seven Moscow Artists 1910-30*, exh. cat., Galerie Gmurzynska, Cologne, 1984. E.Weiss *Russische Avant-Garde, 1910-1930, Sammlung Ludwig, Köln*, Munich, 1986. D.Elliott, V.Dudakov *100 Years of Russian Painting*, London, 1991.
Coll TG; RM; Costakis Collection; Société Anonyme, Yale University.

DRITTENPREIS, Vladimir Petrovich   **1878-1910+**
Painter of masquerades and puppets. He exhibited with the Blue Rose group in 1907 and contributed to the *Stefanos* exhibition 1907-8 and with the First Izdebsky International Salon 1909-10.

DROZDOV, Ivan Georgevich (Egorovich)   **1880-1939**
Painter, graphic artist. He graduated from the art school at Penza in 1902, and then studied at the Academy in St. Petersburg under Repin and V.E.Makovsky 1904-10.
He participated in the First State Free Exhibition of Artworks in Petrograd in 1919 and was included in the enormous survey Exhibition of Paintings by Petrograd Artists of All Tendencies 1919-1923 held in Petrograd in 1923. He exhibited with the Kuindzhi Society and AKhRR.

DROZDOVSKAYA, M. G.   **a.1919**
She exhibited at the Twelfth State Exhibition: Colourdynamo and Tectonic Primitivism (*XII Gosudarstvennaya vystavka. Tsvetodinamos i tektonichesky primitivizm*) in Moscow in 1919 along with Grishchenko, Shevchenko and others.

DROZHDIN (DROZHZHIN), Petr Semenovich **1745-1805**
Portrait painter.
Coll TG.

DRUTSKY = ERDMAN, B.R.

DRUZHINNIN, F. K.   **a.1919**
Painter. He exhibited at the juryless Eighth State Exhibition in Moscow in 1919.

DUBASOV, Ivan Ivanovich   **1897-1925+**
He was represented at the Paris International Exhibition of 1925.

DUBINOVSKY, Lazar Isaakevich   **b.1910**
Sculptor of socialist realist genre. Born in Bessarabia. Active in Kishinev. Works include *Grape Pickers*, a wood carving of 1949.

DUBOVSKOY, Nikolai Nikanorovich   **1859-1918**
Landscape painter. Born at Novocherkassk of a Don cossack family. He studied at the Academy under Klodt 1877-81. A

member of the Wanderers from 1886, he became Professor of Landscape Painting at the Academy in St. Petersburg.
Coll TG.

DUCKER, Eugen Gustav (DYUKKER, Evgeniy Eduardovich) **1841-1916**
Painter. Born at Arensburg, Germany. Dücker studied at the Academy in St. Petersburg. He executed decorative paintings in Moscow in 1873 and was painting coastal scenes in 1875. He also worked in Estonia and taught at the Düsseldorf Academy. Sometimes he signed his work 'E.Dücker' in latin script.
Coll TG; RM.

DUDIN, Ivan Osipovich (Iosipovich) **1867-1924**
Painter and teacher. He established his own teaching studios with Konstantin Yuon and had numerous students including Babichev 1905-6 and Popova 1908-9.
Coll TG.

DUDIN (-MARTSYNKEVICH), Samuil Martynovich 1863-1929
Painter and orientalist. He was engaged in Agitprop decorations for the Petrograd Sovdep in 1918. He participated in the First State Free Exhibition of Artworks in Petrograd in 1919 and was included in the enormous survey Exhibition of Paintings by Petrograd Artists of All Tendencies 1919-1923 held in Petrograd in 1923.

DUNDUK, Pavel Fedorovich **1890-1940**
Sculptor, painter. Born at Saratov. He executed Agitprop decorations there c.1918. He died at Yalta.

DUNKEL', Evgeniy (Eugene) Borisovich **1890-1972**
Theatre designer. Born at Vernyi, Alma-Ata, in Russian Turkestan. He studied at Vilnius under Ivan Trutnev and in Moscow under Yuon. He completed his studies at the Stieglitz school in Petrograd in 1916.
After the Revolution he went to Bulgaria in 1919 and to Greece in 1920 before travelling to Paris and to New York in 1923. He worked for several theatre companies including the Metropolitan Opera, the Ballet Theater and the Ballet Russe de Monte Carlo.
He died at Pelham, New York. He remained active as a theatre designer working internationally.
Lit J.E.Bowlt *Russian Stage Design. Scenic Innovation. From the Collection of Mr. and Mrs. Nikita D.Lobanov-Rostovsky*, Jackson, MS, exh. cat.,1982. Dzhon Boult (John Bowlt) *Khudozhniki russkogo teatra. Sobranie Nikity i Niny Lobanovykh-Rostovskikh*, Moscow, 1991.

DURNOV (DURUNOV), Grigori Nikitich **1825-1853**
Sculptor. He executed portrait herms of academicians including *N.I.Utkin*, 1848, RM.
Coll RM; Museum of the Academy of Art, St. Petersburg.

DURNOV, Modest Aleksandrovich **1867-1928**
Portrait painter. He was a member of the Union of Russian Artists in 1903. The name M.Durnov appeared on the April 1919 list of artists for acquisitions by the envisaged Museum of Painterly Culture.
Coll TG.

DVORNIKOV, Tit Yakovlevich (Yakovich) **1862-1922**
Landscape painter. He exhibited pastels with the First

Izdebsky International Salon 1909-10.
Coll TG.

D'YACHKOV, Vasili Vasil'evich **d.1920**
Theatre designer. He designed for Wilde's *Florentine Tragedy* in 1917. He was represented at the exhibition Art of Moscow Theatre 1918-1923 held in Moscow in 1923.

DYDYSHKO, Konstantin Vikent'evich **1876-1932**
Painter and theatre designer. Born near Kovno (Kaunas), Lithuania. He studied at the Tiflis (Tblisi) Art Institute, at Munich under Franz Von Stuck and Azbé in 1905, and at the St. Petersburg Academy 1905-12 under D.N.Kardovsky, A.A.Kiselev and Dubovskoy. He exhibited with the World of Art and in 1910 with the Union of Youth. He exhibited with the Izdebsky Salon of 1910-11 in Odessa. He travelled in Europe in the period 1906-13. He exhibited with the Union of Youth in St. Petersburg in 1912 and 1913-14.
After the Revolution he executed Agitprop designs for the Zabalkansky Square and Bridge, Petrograd, in 1918. He participated in the First State Free Exhibition of Artworks in Petrograd in 1919 and contributed to the Exhibition of Paintings by Russian Artists held at Pskov in Spring 1920.
In 1929 he moved to Copenhagen and later died there.
Lit J.Howard *The Union of Youth — An Artists' Society of the Russian Avant-Garde*, Manchester and New York, 1992.

DYMSHITS-TOLSTAYA (PESSATI), Sof'ya Isaakovna 1889-1963
Painter, graphic artist. Born at St. Petersburg. She studied under S.S.Egorov at St. Petersburg 1906-7, at the Zvantseva School under Bakst and Dobuzhinsky, and under Guérin in Paris 1910-11. She contributed reliefs in glass to Tatlin's exhibition *Magazin* in 1916.
After the Revolution she assisted in the decoration of the Café Pittoresque in 1918 and worked with Tatlin. She was associated with IZO in Moscow and she exhibited with the Artists of the Leftist Federation of the Professional Union in 1918 along with Popova, Rodchenko, Tatlin and others.
She became secretary of the Moscow Collegium of IZO Narkompros under Tatlin in 1919 and her name appeared on the April 1919 list of artists for acquisitions by the envisaged Museum of Painterly Culture. She worked with Tatlin and moved with him to Petrograd in 1919. She also collaborated on the construction of the model of Tatlin's *Monument to the Third International* in 1919. She exhibited with the Union of New Tendencies in Art in Petrograd in June 1922 and was included in the enormous survey Exhibition of Paintings by Petrograd Artists of All Tendencies 1919-1923 held in Petrograd in 1923. She exhibited in Venice in 1924. After 1925 she worked for periodicals including *Rabotnitsa* (Working Woman) and *Krestyanka* (Peasant Woman). She died at Leningrad.
Lit *L'Avant-garde russe 1905-1925*, exh. cat., Musée des Beaux-Arts, Nantes, 1993.
Coll RM; Samara Art Museum.

DYUKKER, Evgeniy Eduardovich = DUCKER, E. G.

DZHIN-DZHIKH-SHVIL' = TYSHLER, A.G.

DZHOGIN, Pavel Pavlovich **1834-1885**
Landscape painter.
Coll TG.

E

EBERLING, Alfred Rudolfovich 1871-1950
Painter, graphic artist, book designer. Born near Lodz, Poland. He studied under Lenbach in Munich, in Italy, and under Repin at the St. Petersburg Academy 1889-9 where he later taught. He painted fourteen scenes from the life of Jesus for the Russian Church at Constantinople.
After the Revolution he participated in the First State Free Exhibition of Artworks in Petrograd in 1919. He exhibited with the Kuindzhi Society, AKhRR and the Repin Society.
Coll Saratov Art Museum.

EBERLING, V. a.1916
Graphic artist. He executed a poster for War Bonds in 1916 featuring red Art Nouveau lettering and a dramatic close up image of a gunner standing upon an aeroplane in flight firing his gun among the clouds.

EBERMAN, Maks Vladimirovich a.1909-1920
Painter. He exhibited with the First Izdebsky International Salon 1909-10 in Odessa.
After the Revolution he was involved in Agitprop design including decorations on the propaganda train *Red Cossack* in 1920.

ECHEISTOV, Georgiy Aleksandrovich 1897-1946
Graphic artist and theatre designer. Born in Moscow. He studied at the Stroganov College 1912-19.
After the Revolution he studied at the Moscow Vkhutemas 1919-27 under Favorsky who influenced his wood engraving technique. He began to exhibit in 1927. He worked mainly in xylography. He illustrated books for numerous publishers including Akademiya, Goslitizdat and Detizdat.
He made theatre designs for several productions 1931-4. He executed a series of print portraits of artists past and present including Géricault, Delacroix, Menzel, Leonardo, Gauguin, Matisse and Picasso 1933-4. He made dramatic illustrations to Heine in 1936 one of which quotes Favorsky's portrait image of Shakespeare but here caught up in a headlong night ride on horseback. He also designed postage stamps. His work was included in the International Exhibitions in Paris in 1937 and New York in 1939. He died in Moscow. One-man exhibitions were held in Moscow in 1947 and 1965 and in Leningrad in 1966.
Coll TG; RM; Vologda Art Gallery.

EFIMENKO, Sergei Mitrofanovich 1896-1971
Theatre designer. He was working for the Meyerhold Theatre during 1925-6. Here he produced Constructivist designs on several levels for the ship-board scenes in Fedorov's production of *Rychi, Kitay!* (Roar, China!) which opened in January 1926.

EFIMOV, Aleksandr Alekseevich 1905-1964
Painter. Born St. Petersburg. He was engaged in Agitprop decorations on Novoderevenskaya Square and the Sovdep in Petrograd in 1918. He was included in the enormous survey Exhibition of Paintings by Petrograd Artists of All Tendencies 1919-1923 held in Petrograd in 1923. He died in Kishinev.

EFIMOV, Ivan Semenovich 1878-1959
Sculptor, painter, graphic artist, designer. Born in Moscow. In 1899 he studied in the Faculty of Science at Moscow University. He also studied at the Zvantseva School and learnt maijolica techniques at Abramtsevo. He married the painter and puppeteer Nina Simonovich (-Efimova) in 1906. In 1906-8 he was studying at the Moscow College under Serov, Korovin and Volnukhin, graduating in 1913. However he was often in Paris 1908-11, and he exhibited at the Salon des Indépendents and the Salon d'Automne. He also visited Italy, Germany, England and Spain.
After the Revolution together with Simonovich-Efimova he opened the Theatre of Marionettes, Petrushkas and Shadows in October 1918 in Moscow which attracted collaboration from Vladimir Favorsky, Pavel Florensky, Exter, Popova and others and which continued until 1940. He taught from 1918 to 1930 at the Vkhutemas/Vkhutein and was represented in the Sixth State Exhibition: The Print (*VI Gosudarstvennaya vystavka gravyur*) in Moscow in 1919.
He was represented at the Paris International Exhibition in 1925 and he contributed to the second exhibition of *Iskusstvo dvizheniya* (Art of Movement) held in Moscow in 1926. He was a member of the Society of Russian Sculptors from 1926 and was included in the major exhibition in Moscow in 1927 marking the tenth anniversary of the Revolution. He exhibited with the 4 Arts society in Leningrad including the exhibition of 1928 at the Russian Museum. He was included in the 1928 exhibition of Acquisitions by the State Art Collections Fund held in Moscow and the exhibition of Russian Graphics at Riga in 1929.
He exhibited at the 1932 Venice Biennale and was represented at the jubilee exhibition Artists of the RSFSR over 15 Years held at the Russian Museum, Leningrad, in 1932. He executed numerous reliefs for public buildings including the Yaroslavl and Leningrad Railway Stations in Moscow and the stations of the Moscow Metro. He died in Moscow.
Bison, 1913, TG, is almost kitsch but is saved by a monumental strength. This woodcarving is roughly worked, but smoothed in its ridges and hollows producing an oily finish. The bison relies upon its profile to contrast its massive head and shoulders against its slender hindquarters.
Writings I.Efimov *Ob iskusstve i khudozhnikakh* (On Art and Artists), Moscow, 1977.
Lit I.Khvoinik *Skul'ptor I.S.Efimov*, Moscow, 1934. A.Matveeva *I.S.Efimov*, Moscow, 1965. *Paris-Moscou*, 1971. *Twilight of the Tsars*, 1991.
Coll TG; RM; Efimov Museum, Moscow.

EFIMOV, Nikolai Efimovich 1838-1891
Painter of roman mythological themes.
Coll TG.

EGANBURY = ZDANEVICH, I.M.

EGOROV, A. Z. a.1919
Painter. He exhibited at the Ninth State Exhibition of Paintings: Naturalism and Realism in Moscow in 1919.

EGOROV, Aleksei Egorovich 1776-1851
Neo-classical history painter and portraitist inspired by

Raphael, Guercino and Guido Reni. Born in the steppes, he was taken prisoner by cossacks at the age of six. He was brought up in Moscow. He studied under Ugryumov and Akimov at the Academy in St. Petersburg. He travelled to Italy on a scholarship in 1803 where he met Canova in Rome. He executed works for several churches, for Peterhof and for Tsarskoe Selo. He was also active as a printmaker. He died in St. Petersburg.
Coll Well represented at TG; RM; Museum of the Academy, St. Petersburg.

EGOROV, Vladimir Evgenevich   **1878-1960**
Painter, theatre designer, graphic artist. He studied monumental painting and decorative applied art at the Stroganov Institute, Moscow, under S.Ivanov, K.Korovin, S.Noakovsky and F.Shekhtel' 1892-1900. He exhibited in the Russian Pavilion at the Glasgow International Exhibition in 1900. He worked on theatre design at the Moscow Art Theatre 1906-11. From 1911 to 1917 he taught at the Stroganov Institute. He was working in the cinema by 1915. He designed about a hundred films.
After the Revolution he collaborated with Mayakovsky on Futurist films in 1918 (see below). His cinema designs included the film *Stenka Razin*. He was represented at the Paris International Exhibition in 1925. He was recognised as a National Artist of the USSR in 1944. He taught at the Moscow Higher Art and Industrial School (Stroganov Institute) from 1945. He died in Moscow.
Theatre design 1907 Stanislavsky's production of L.N.Andreev's *Zhizn' cheloveka* (Life of Man) at the Moscow Art Theatre. The sets comprised Beardsley-like and distinctly graphic décor in black and yellow, stylised and patterned.These designs are preserved in the Bakhrushin Theatre Museum in Moscow. Another design entitled *Gosti* (Guests) shows a row of grotesquely fat women in bulging yellow evening wear whose gloved hands resemble crabs (Moscow Art Theatre Museum).
Other productions designed by him for the Moscow Art Theatre included Maeterlinck's *Oiseau bleu* and Scribe's *Bataille des dames*.
Film design 1915 *Portrait of Dorian Gray*, released December, scenario by V.Meyerhold from Oscar Wilde's book. This was his first realised film design.
1916 *Strong Man* by S.Przybyszewski, released December, directed by V.Meyerhold.
1916 *Zelenyy pauk* (The Green Spider).
1918 *Ne dlya deneg rodivshiysya* (Not Born for Money, known also as Creation Can't Be Bought). Scenario by Mayakovsky and David Burlyuk. Designed by David Burlyuk and Vladimir Egorov.
1918 *Barishnya i khuligan* (The Young Lady and the Hooligan) featuring Mayakovsky and A.Rebikova. Released by the Neptune film company.
1918 *Vosstanie* (Uprising) directed by Aleksandr Razumni and V.I.Karin.
Other film design in the 1920s included: 1920 A.Razumny's *Mat'* (Mother); 1921 *Andzhelo* (Angelo); 1921 *Domovoy agitator* (Goblin Agitator); 1923 *Prizrak brodit po Evrope* (The Phantom Wanders across Europe); 1924 *Slesar' i kantselar* (The Locksmith and the Chancellor); 1925 *Stepan Khalturin*, designed with A.Utkin; 1925 *Zakroyshchik iz Torzhka*; 1925 *Ego prizyv* (His Call); 1926 *Kryl'ya kholopa* (The Serf's Wings);

Sergei Eisenstein. Set design for a play by George Bernard Shaw, *1922. Drawing.*

1929 *Chiny i lyudi* (Ranks and People).
Many other designs followed at least up to 1953.
Lit E.Kumankova *V.Egorov*, Moscow, 1965. *Paris-Moscou*, 1979.
Coll Bakhrushin Theatre Museum, Moscow.

EGOSHIN, German Pavlovich   **b.1931**
Painter. Born at Leningrad. He exhibited in Madrid in 1972 and in Dresden in 1975.
Coll RM.

EISENSTEIN, Sergei Mikhailovich (EIZENSHTEIN)
1898-1948
Major film director who used drawing extensively to design his productions. He also produced and designed theatrical works. He was born in Riga. His theatre work began in 1920 with décors for the First Workers' Theatre of Proletkult in Moscow. His sets for Jack London's *The Mexican*, directed by V.Shmyshlyaev and Eisenstein at the Proletkult Theatre in 1921, evoke a mood of fantasy which still recalls Benois despite its hectic splintering of planes, suggesting that he saw Cubo-Futurism as simply a style that could be adopted for effect at this point. He began to design for film in 1921. He was studying under the innovative theatre director Vsevolod Meyerhold 1921-2 but soon became the most celebrated of Soviet cinema directors. He was a founder member of the group October in 1928. He travelled in Mexico 1930-2 working on the film *Long Live Mexico!* He taught at the State Cinema Institute, Moscow, from 1932.
He signed some designs with cursive 'S.E' in latin script joined at the top to form a monogram with the date underneath. He died in Moscow.
Theatre design 1921 *The Mexican* adapted by Boris Arvatov from the novel by Jack London, directed by Eisenstein and V.Shmyshlyaev, and designed by Eisenstein as a kind of Agitposter at the First Workers' Theatre of Proletkult in Moscow. A set design for Act 2 shows a fantastic evocation of

the office of an American boxing promoter whose desk is flanked by stage flats which form zig-zag intrusions at either side, decorated with aggressive images of boxers and headings declaring 'The Kelly Brothers, Boxing, New York'.

1921 Shakespeare's *Macbeth* directed by V.Tikhonovich at the V.Polenov Theatre, Moscow. The set was designed in collaboration with Sergei Yutkevich.

1921 L.Andreev's *King Hunger*, directed by V.Tikhonovich at the First Workers' Theatre of Proletkult. Moscow.

1922 G.B.Shaw's *Heartbreak House* for an unrealised production by Meyerhold. A collage set design is thoroughly Constructivist and seems to be closely modelled on Popova's design for *The Magnanimous Cuckold*, a contemporary project for the same director. Here a wheel effect dominates the set which includes platforms, trapeze, lifts, cables and signboards.

1922 V.Pletnev's *Precipice* produced at the Proletkult Theatre, Moscow.

1922 V.Mass' *Good Treatment for Horses* directed by Nikolai Foregger at the Foregger Studio, Moscow. Costume designs thoroughly geometric and stylised in a loosely Suprematist

way, employing arcs, straight lines, triangles and patterning. The female costumes remain provocatively erotic however with more than a hint of the cabaret.

1922-3 Ostrovsky's *Enough Simplicity for Every Wiseman* (*Na vsyakogo mudretsa - dovol'no prostoty*) produced at the Proletkult Theatre employing music hall effects and film.

1923 Sergei Tretyakov's agitational piece written for the Proletkult Theatre *Listen, Moscow!*.

1923 Sergei Tretyakov's *Gas Masks*, staged in a Moscow gas factory and directed by Eisenstein.

Films His major films include: 1925 *Sachka* (Strike), 1925 *Battleship Potemkin*, 1927-8 *October*, 1929-32 *The General Line*, 1931 *Que Viva Mexico*, 1938 *Alexander Nevsky*, and 1943-4 *Ivan the Terrible* (Part Two 1958).

Lit *Eisenstein* (facsimile reproductions of his drawings), four volumes, Moscow, 1967-71. *Russian Painters and the Stage 1884-1965, a loan exhibition of stage and costume designs from the Collection of Mr. and Mrs. Nikita D. Lobanov-Rostovsky*, exh. cat., University of Texas at Austin, 1978-9. Nancy Van Norman Baer *Theatre in Revolution, Russian Avant-Garde Stage Design 1913-1935*, San Francisco and London, 1991.

Coll Bakhrushin Theatre Museum, Moscow.

EKGORST, Vasili Efimovich   **1831-1901**
Painter. He studied under at the Academy in St. Petersburg and exhibited landscapes from 1867. Twenty-one landscapes were published in St. Petersburg in 1870 as an album of lithographs. He exhibited in Philadelphia in 1876.
Coll TG.

EKSTER, A. A.= EXTER, A.

ELLERT, Nikolai Lyudvigovich   **1845-1901**
Landscape painter, theatre designer. He studied in Moscow in 1880 and thereafter painted landscapes and animals. He was awarded a silver medal in 1883. Executed designs for the theatre in 1890 and was employed by the Imperial Opera in Moscow.
Coll TG.

ELLONEN, Viktor V.   **a.1923-1932**
Sculptor. Ellonen was included in the enormous survey Exhibition of Paintings by Petrograd Artists of All Tendencies 1919-1923 held in Petrograd in 1923 and at the Paris International Exhibition in 1925. He was a member of the 4 Arts society which was founded in 1925. A member of the Society of Russian Sculptors from 1926, he was included in the 1928 exhibition of Acquisitions by the State Art Collections Fund held in Moscow. He exhibited at the 1932 Venice Biennale and at the jubilee exhibition Artists of the RSFSR over 15 Years held at the Russian Museum, Leningrad, in 1932.

EMME, Vladimir Vladimirovich   **1875-1920**
Painter, theatre designer. He exhibited at the Academy of Arts in St. Petersburg. He exhibited studies of the Caucasus at the Izdebsky International Salons 1909-11 in Odessa.

After the Revolution he produced Agitprop decorations at the Morskoy Korpus, Petrograd, in 1918. He participated in the First State Free Exhibition of Artworks in Petrograd in 1919.

ENDER, Boris Vladimirovich   **1893-1960**
Painter. Born at St. Petersburg. He was the brother of Ksenia, Mariya and Yuri Ender. Between 1905 and 1907 he studied under Ivan Bilibin. From the time of the Revolution he became closely involved in the experimental art of the painter-composer

Sergei Eisenstein. Design for Prince Andrei Kurbsky on his Knees in front of Anastasia, the Wife of Ivan IV. *Pencil, signed with monogram. 30.8 x 22.2 cm.*
Collection Mr. and Mrs. Nikita D. Lobanov-Rostovsky, London.

Boris Erdman. Foxtrot Championship, *1923. Costume study in pencil, brush and ink on paper. 19.4 x 17.4 cm.*
Erdman's costume studies were often a witty amalgam of geometry and figures assembled in such a way as to give the rhythm of the dancers' movements.
Bakhrushin Theatre Museum, Moscow.

Mikhail Matyushin in whose studio he was studying in 1917. After the Revolution he entered the Petrograd Free Art Studios in 1918 to work under Petrov-Vodkin and Malevich. The relation of sound and colour was a key concern as it was for Matyushin, hence he became a member of Matyushin's Spatial Realism Studio 1919-21, and was in Matyushin's *Zorved* (See-Know) group in 1923. He was included in the Exhibition of Paintings by Petrograd Artists of All Tendencies 1919-1923 in 1923. He produced a colour/sound chart for A.Tufanov's book *K Zaumi* (On Zaum), Petrograd, 1924, and exhibited at the Venice Biennale that year. Subsequently he carried out research at the Department of Organic Culture at the Museum of Artistic Culture in Leningrad 1923-7. He was included in the exhibition of Soviet art in Tokyo in 1927. He moved to Moscow in 1928. He became active as a designer with an interest in colour and architecture and he designed interiors, exhibitions, clothes and books. Together with Mariya Ender he assisted Suetin on the Soviet displays at the International Exhibitions in Paris, 1937, and New York, 1939.
Lit E.C.Masetti and D.A.Perilli *Boris Ender*, Rome, 1977. A.Z.Rudenstine *Costakis Collection*, 1981. V.Manin et al. *Zhivopis' 20-30kh godov*, Sankt-Peterburg, 1991.
Coll RM.

ENDER, Ksenia (Xenia) Vladimirovna   **1894-1955**
Painter. Born in St. Petersburg. She was the sister of Boris, Mariya and Yuri Ender. After studying at the Petrograd Free Art Studios 1919-22, she joined the *Zorved* (See-Know) group around Matyushin, as did her brother Boris. She too became a researcher at the Museum of Artistic Culture in Leningrad working with Matyushin there, and she too was included in the Exhibition of Paintings by Petrograd Artists of All Tendencies 1919-1923 in 1923 and the Venice Biennale of 1924.
Lit A.Z.Rudenstine *Costakis Collection*, 1981; E.Weiss *Russische Avant-Garde, 1910-1930, Sammlung Ludwig, Köln*, Munich, 1986.
Coll Costakis Collection; Sammlung Ludwig, Cologne.

ENDER, Mariya Vladimirovna   **1897-1942**
Painter. Like her brother Boris and her sister Ksenia Ender, she studied under Matyushin at the Petrograd Free Studios in 1919, joined Matyushin at the Museum of Artistic Culture in 1923, and exhibited at the Venice Biennale in 1924. She was director of the laboratory for the study of the perception of colour and form at GINKhUK 1925-6. In 1927 she joined the Institute of Art History in Leningrad. She taught at the Academy in Leningrad 1929-32. Her involvement with Matyushin continued in 1932 when she assisted in the production of his *Colour Manual*. She was engaged with Boris Ender on the Soviet Pavilions at the International Exhibitions in Paris in 1937 and New York in 1939.
Lit A.Z.Rudenstine *Costakis Collection*, 1981.
Coll RM.

ENDER, Yuri Vladimirovich   **a.1923**
Painter of loosely handled watercolour studies derived from landscape. He was the brother of Boris, Ksenia and Mariya Ender.
Lit A.Z.Rudenstine *Costakis Collection*, 1981.

ENDOGUROV, Ivan Ivanovich   **1861-1898**
Landscape painter. Born at Kronstadt. He won a silver medal at the Paris International Exhibition in 1889.
Coll TG.

ENGEL'S, O. V.   **a.1919-1926**
Painter, graphic artist. He was represented in the Fourth State Exhibition of Paintings (*IV Gosudarstvennaya vystavka kartin*) in Moscow in 1919 and in the Sixth State Exhibition: The Print (*VI Gosudarstvennaya vystavka gravyur*) in Moscow in 1919. He participated in the Third Exhibition of Paintings held at Ryazan in 1919 and he contributed to the second exhibition of *Iskusstvo dvizheniya* (Art of Movement) held in Moscow in 1926.

EPIFANOV, Gennadiy Dmitrievich   **b.1900-1940+**
Graphic artist active in Leningrad. His technique showed the influence of Favorsky particularly in his details and in his depiction of 18th or early 19th century themes. However he also employed large areas of flat colour as in his illustrations to Dickens' *Great Expectations*, wood engraved in 1940.

ERASSI, Mikhail Spiridonovich   **1823-1898**
Landscape painter. He died in Berlin.
Coll TG; RM.

ERDMAN (DRUTSKY), Boris Robertovich   **1899-1960**
Theatre designer. Born in Moscow. He was the brother of the playwright and producer Nikolai Erdman. He worked with the theatre director Aleksandr Tairov as an actor 1916-18. After the Revolution he was associated with the painter

Yakulov and the Imagist poets at the cabaret *The Stable of Pegasus* in 1919. The same year he joined the Circus section of the Theatre Department of IZO. He worked with Meyerhold and other directors at the State Institute of Theatre Art in the 1920s. He was represented at the Paris International Exhibition in 1925 and he contributed to the second exhibition of *Iskusstvo dvizheniya* (Art of Movement) held in Moscow in 1926. He designed for several theatres including the Moscow Art Theatre and became a prolific and important theatre designer. He moved to Odessa c.1927.

He directed the Art Section of the State Circus in Moscow 1941-5 and the Art Section of the Stanislavsky Drama Theatre, Moscow 1950-60. He died in Moscow.

Theatre design 1916 I.Annensky's *Famira Kifared* (Thamyris Kitharados) directed by Tairov at the Kamerny (Chamber) Theatre, Moscow.

1922 Eugène Labiche's *Money Box* directed by Boris Ferdinandov at the Experimental-Heroic Theatre, Moscow.

1923 *Electric Dances* and *Machine Dances*, choreography by Nikolai Foregger, at the Foregger Workshop, Moscow. Designs in flat black and white, ideal for publication, are witty and intricate geometric assemblages of several figures together engaged in athletic dances which the viewer has to interpret as a bare minimum of information, but a lot of action, is represented.

1923 *Foxtrot Championship*, choreography by K.Goleizovsky, at the Crooked Jimmy Theatre, Moscow. Designs comparable with those for *Electric Dances*.

1923 *Eccentric Dances* and *Spanish Dances*, choreography by K.Goleizovsky, Moscow. Designs comparable with those above but with Spanish touches.

1925 *Joseph the Beautiful*, ballet with choreography by K.Goleizovsky and music by S.Vasilenko, at the Experimental-Heroic Theatre, Moscow. Costume designs in flat colours have the figure drawn in flat geometricised forms and filling the paper. They use only two or three colours and are substantially executed with compass and ruler.

1930 May: Yuri K.Olesha's *Tri tolstyaka* (Three Fat Men) at the Moscow Art Theatre.

1957 March: F.Schiller's *Mary Stuart* at the Moscow Art Theatre.

1958 October: G.Figreydo's *Lisa i vinograd* (The Fox and the Vine) at the Moscow Art Theatre.

1959 November: G.E.Nikolaeva's *Bitva v puti* (The Battle is Underway) at the Moscow Art Theatre.

1960 June: Ibsen's *The Doll's House* at the Moscow Art Theatre.

Book design Cover of two geometric figures of clowns in green, sienna and black for the sheet music of Yuri Milyutin's waltz *Tsirkachi* (Circus Performers), Moscow, 1924.

Lit J.E.Bowlt *Russian Stage Design. Scenic Innovation. From the Collection of Mr. and Mrs. Nikita D.Lobanov-Rostovsky*, Jackson, MS, exh. cat.,1982. Nancy Van Norman Baer *Theatre in Revolution, Russian Avant-Garde Stage Design 1913-1935*, San Francisco and London, 1991.

Coll Bakhrushin Theatre Museum, Moscow.

EREMICHEV, M. A. a.1918-1919
He exhibited at the Fifth State Exhibition: From Impressionism to Non-Objective Art in Moscow in 1918-19.

ERIKSON, L. R. a.1918-1925
He was represented at the First Exhibition of Works of the Professional Union of Artists in Moscow in 1918. This name appears without initials on the April 1919 list of artists for acquisitions by the proposed Museum of Painterly Culture and at the Third Exhibition of Paintings by Artists from Kaluga and Moscow held in Kaluga in 1925.

ERMAKOV, Ivan Dmitrievich 1875-1928+
He exhibited with the Knave of Diamonds in Moscow in 1917. This name appears on the April 1919 list of artists for acquisitions by the proposed Museum of Painterly Culture. He exhibited with the 4 Arts society in Moscow in 1925.

ERMICHEV a.1919
He exhibited in the first *Obmokhu* exhibition in May 1919 in Moscow.

ERMILOV, I. a.1913
He contributed to Larionov's exhibition The Target in Moscow in 1913.

ERMILOV, Vasili Dmitrievich 1894-1968
Ukrainian painter and designer of posters, tribunes, kiosks, murals, books and revues. Born at Kharkov. He studied at the Kharkov School of Drawing and Painting and in private studios 1910-11, before moving to the Moscow College in 1912 to study under Mashkov and Konchalovsky. In 1913 he contributed to the sixteenth exhibition of the Society of Kharkov Artists and in 1914 he was awarded the title of Master of Decorative Painting. He then became involved with Futurists in Kharkov. After the Revolution he became a member of the Group of Seven in 1918, and he worked for IZO Narkompros in 1919 including the decoration of street festivals in Kharkov. He was director of UKROST (Ukranian Telegraph Agency) in 1920 and decorated the Red Army Club in Kharkov that year. In 1921 he directed the Central Studio of Creativity and Art Propaganda and decorated the Agitprop train *Red Ukraine*. In 1922 he taught at the Kharkov Technical Art Institute and in 1927 he was a member of ARMU, the Association of Ukrainian Revolutionary Art. He died at Kharkov.

Lit B.Fogel *V.Ermilov*, Moscow, 1975; E.Weiss *Russische Avant-Garde, 1910-1930, Sammlung Ludwig, Köln*, Munich, 1986.

Coll Sammlung Ludwig, Cologne.

ERMILOVA-PLATOVA, Efrosin'ya Fedoseevna
1895-1974
Painter, graphic artist. She was represented at the jubilee exhibition Artists of the RSFSR over 15 Years held at the Russian Museum, Leningrad, in 1932. She died in Moscow.

ERMOLAEV, Boris Nikolaevich 1903-1982
Painter, graphic artist. He studied at the Petrograd art and technical college under V.N.Fedorovich and M.I.Avilov 1921-5. His work was distinctly primitive, stiff and frontal but explicit in its information which gave it both interest and a degree of monumentality. It encompassed portraits of naval groups and simple street and village scenes. He also executed illustrations for newspapers and for children's books. He was working in the South 1936-7. He worked on colour lithography from the 1940s.

Lit A.M.Muratov, V.Manin et al. *Zhivopis' 20-30kh godov*, Sankt-Peterburg, 1991.

Coll RM.

ERMOLAEVA, Vera Mikhailovna 1893-1938

Painter, illustrator. Born at Petrovsky in the Saratov region. She studied under Mikhail D.Bernshtein and L.V.Shervud between 1910 and 1914 in St. Petersburg but subsequently graduated from the Archaeological Institute, Petrograd, in 1917. She visited England, France and Switzerland.

After the Revolution she was closely involved in the development of Suprematism in the circle of Malevich. In 1918 she was a founder of the *Segodnya* (Today) workshop and was a member of the Visual Art Section of IZO. She worked at the City Museum, Petrograd, 1918-19 and her name appeared on the April 1919 list of artists for acquisitions by the proposed Museum of Painterly Culture. She became rector of the Vitebsk Art Institute and a member of the *Unovis* group at Vitebsk centred on Malevich. She followed Malevich to Petrograd from Vitebsk, along with Chashnik, Suetin and Yudin in 1923. She taught at the Leningrad INKhUK. She exhibited in Moscow in 1920 and was represented at the First Russian Art Exhibition in Berlin in 1922, as well as in Five Years of Leningrad Painters, Leningrad, 1925. She was represented at the jubilee exhibition Artists of the RSFSR over 15 Years held at the Russian Museum, Leningrad, in 1932. She later illustrated many children's books. She died in Siberia.

Theatre design 1920 February: *Victory Over the Sun*, prologue by V.Khlebnikov, libretto by A.Kruchenykh, music by M.Matyushin, designed by Ermolaeva with some costumes by Malevich.

Lit E.Г.Kovtun *Khudozhnik Detskoy Knigi Vera Ermolaeva* in *Detskaya Literatura*, No.2, Moscow, 1971. J.E.Bowlt *Russian Stage Design. Scenic Innovation. From the Collection of Mr. and Mrs. Nikita D.Lobanov-Rostovsky*, Jackson, MS, exh. cat.,1982. E.Weiss *Russische Avant-Garde, 1910-1930, Sammlung Ludwig, Köln*, Munich, 1986. Dzhon Boult (John Bowlt) *Khudozhniki russkogo teatra. Sobranie Nikity i Niny Lobanovykh-Rostovskikh*, Moscow, 1991.

Coll RM; Sammlung Ludwig, Cologne.

ERMOLIN, Vasili Dmitrievich d.c.1481-85

Sculptor, architect. Little is known about him, but he provides an early example of an identifiable stone carver in Russia. The Tretyakov Gallery has a fragmentary *St. George* dating from 1464 which is from the Frolovsky Gate of the Moscow Kremlin. Another gate had his *Miracle of Dmitri Solunsky*.

ERTE (TIRTOV, Roman; TIRTOFF, Romain de) b.1892

Fashion designer, theatre designer, graphic artist. The name Erté, formed from the Russian for his initials RT, was adopted as his professional name in 1913.

Born in St. Petersburg. He studied under Repin and his pupil Dmitri Lossevsky in St. Petersburg in 1910.

Erté settled in Paris in 1912 and attended the Académie Julian under Jean-Paul Laurens. He submitted drawings of French fashions to the Russian magazine *Damskiy Mir* (Woman's World). He became dedicated to both fashion and theatre. He submitted work to the *Gazette du Bon Ton* in 1913 and executed fashion drawings for Paul Poiret in 1913-14. Exquisitely decorative and exotic costume became his speciality and his drawings for them became works of decorative art in their own right. In this respect they perhaps recall aspects of the theatre costume designs of Leon Bakst. He produced theatre designs from 1912.

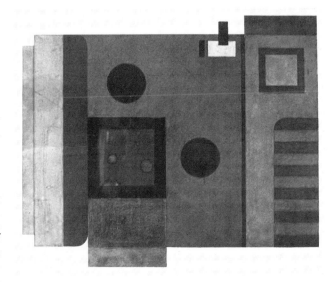

Vasili Ermilov. Composition, *1926. Gouache and collage. 31 x 33 cm. This is probably a design for the decoration of a tram. In formal terms it is partly comparable with certain earlier designs by members of the Unovis collective working with Malevich and Lissitzky in Vitebsk. Courtesy Annely Juda Fine Art, London.*

He lived in Monte Carlo 1914-23 but he contributed to the fashion periodical *Harper's Bazaar* from 1915 and *Vogue* in 1916. He designed for the Théâtre Fémina in Paris between 1917 and 1921. He designed costumes for many performances at the Folies Bergère in Paris 1919-36.

He had an exclusive contract with *Harper's Bazaar* from 1916 to 1936.

He was a prolific and spectacular theatre designer working internationally in the whole range of productions from opera to vaudeville and film. He worked for numerous theatres including the Théâtre du Châtelet, Théâtre Marigny and the Bal Tabarin in Paris. He designed sets and costumes for *Wonderworld* at the New York World Fair in 1964 and for *Flying Colors* at Expo '67 in Montreal. He was still working in the theatre in 1980, designing Richard Srauss' *Der Rosenkavalier* for the Glyndebourne Opera and for *The Last Days of Mrs. Cheyney* at the Cambridge Theatre, London.

Theatre design He was immensely prolific and ceaselessly active as a theatre designer. Productions include:

1920 costumes for various operas by the Chicago Opera Company.

1923-4 sets and costumes for the Ziegfeld Folies, New York.

1924 costumes for the *Bal du Grand Prix* at the Paris Opera.

1927 costumes for productions at the Metropolitan Opera House, New York.

1947 Poulenc's *Les Mammelles de Tirésias* at the Opéra-Comique, Paris.

Film design 1920 costumes for the Ball of the Gods in Robert Z.Leonard's *The Restless Sex*, released by Paramount. 1925 *Paris, The Mystic, Dance Madness, A Little Bit of Broadway, Time the Comedian, La Bohème* and some costumes for *Ben Hur*. 1952 *Maske in Blau* for Bavaria Films.

Lit Charles Spencer *Erté*, London, 1970. R.Barthes *Erté*, Parma, 1972. Erté *Erté Fashions*, London, 1972. Erté *Things I Remember*, London-New York, 1975. Stella Blum *Designs by Erté*, New York, 1976. T.Walters *Erté*, New York, 1978. Erté *Fashion Designs*, New York, 1981. L.Marshall *Erté at Ninety: the Complete Graphics*, London, 1982. A.Schouvaloff *The*

Thyssen-Bornemisza Collection: Set and Costume Designs for Ballet and Theatre, New York-London, 1987.
Coll Ashmolean Museum, Oxford; Baron Thyssen-Bornemisza Collection, England.

ER'ZYA, Stepan Dmitrievich (NEFEDOV, S.) 1876-1959
Sculptor. He was teaching sculpture at the Free Art Studios in Moscow c.1918-19 along with Babichev, Bromirsky, Konen'kov and Vatagin. He was a member of the Society of Russian Sculptors from 1926.
Female Portrait (Calm), 1919, marble, Saransk Art Gallery, has the figure emerging from the rough hewn block in the manner employed by Rodin although the portrait is distinctly that of a contemporary woman. The block reads effectively as her dress against which her smoothly carved hand is held gently.
Portrait of an Argentinian Woman, 1944, a curiously soft and original wood carving.

ESAKOV, Aleksei Ekimovich (Yakimovich) 1787-1815
Neo-classical sculptor and medallist. He graduated from the

Alexandra Exter. Illustration for Aleksandr Tairov's 'Notes of a Director'.
The design is inscribed with the chapter title 'Scenic Atmosphere'. Exter's image shows part of the stage cut across by a ladder-like construction, perhaps in use for the hanging of the geometric shapes which feature here and were devised by Exter for her set for Tairov's production of 'Phèdre'. Part of the auditorium is also visible here. Exter has revealed all of this as if through curtains drawn back in a theatre box.

Academy in St. Petersburg in 1793. The Russian Museum has a relief of 1808. He taught at the Academy 1813-15.
Coll TG; RM; Hermitage Museum, St. Petersburg; Museum of the Academy of Art, St. Petersburg.

ESAKOVA, M. S. a.1919
She exhibited at the Twelfth State Exhibition: Colourdynamo and Tectonic Primitivism (*XII Gosudarstvennaya vystavka. Tsvetodinamos i tektonichesky primitivizm*) in Moscow in 1919 along with Grishchenko, Shevchenko and others.

ESSEN, Benita Nikolaevna b.1893
Painter. Member of Proletkult. She contributed to the Exhibition of Paintings by Russian Artists held at Pskov in Spring 1920 and was included in the enormous survey Exhibition of Paintings by Petrograd Artists of All Tendencies 1919-1923 held in Petrograd in 1923. She exhibited with the *Zhar-tsvet* (Fire-colour) group between 1924 and 1928 and with the Anti-individualists. She exhibited mostly in Leningrad.

EVENBAKH, Evgeniya Konstantinovna 1889-1981
Painter. Faintly reminiscent of Petrov-Vodkin in her separation of colour areas in her painting of *Two Students*, 1923, RM. The town is stylised and painted wholly in shades of red divided by a blue river. One foreground portrait is in yellows, the other in pale mauves.
Coll RM.

EVGRAFOV, Nikolai Ivanovich 1904-1941
Painter. He studied at the Nizhy-Novgorod Free Art Studios 1921-3, in the Art-Industrial Technical College in Leningrad in 1923 and worked in the formal-technical section of INKhUK in 1923. He was a follower of Filonov. His *Carnival*, 1938-40, RM, is painterly in its handling, however, and built up from a mass of brushmarks difficult to decipher beyond a lively suggestion of hectic lights and activity suitable to its theme.
Coll RM.

EVSEEV, Konstantin Ivanovich 1879-1944
Painter, theatre designer. Studied in Munich and Paris. He exhibited with the Union of Russian Artists 1907. He was designing for the Kommissarzhevskaya Theatre in St. Petersburg in 1909.

EVSEEV, Sergei Aleksandrovich 1882-1955
Sculptor, theatre designer. Born in Moscow. A specialist in sculpting Lenin. His most celebrated work was the statue of *Lenin*, 1926, bronze, erected at the Finland Station in Leningrad in which Lenin appears in a long, open coat and with his arm raised, standing on top of a cylindrical form which rises from an asymmetrical base designed by Shchuko in a substantially Suprematist style with two curious propeller-like blades projecting from the assemblage of blocks. He died in Leningrad. The date of his death is sometimes given as 1959.

EVSTAF'EV, M. a.1926
Poster designer. He was represented at the Second Exhibition of Cinema Posters held at the Chamber (Kamerny) Theatre, Moscow, in 1926.

EXTER, Alexandra (EKSTER, Aleksandra Aleksandrovna, née GRIGOROVICH) 1882-1949
Major painter, theatre designer and graphic artist of Russian Cubist, Suprematist and Constructivist styles.
Born at Belestok, near Kiev. She studied at the Kiev School of

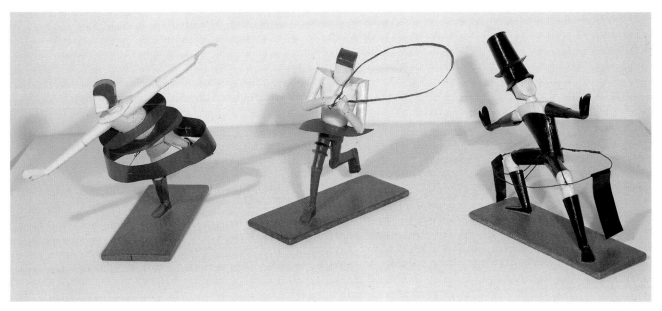

Alexandra Exter. Three Puppets, *1927. Papier maché and wire. Figure with top hat 26 cm high, figure in blue and white 30 cm high, figure in red and white 27 cm. high.*
Museum collection, courtesy Annely Juda Fine Art, London.

Art, graduating in 1907. In 1908 she married Nikolai Ekster (Exter) and also began to visit France regularly. She studied under Henri Caraux-Delvai at the Académie de la Grande Chaumière in Paris 1908-14 and soon came to know a wide range of arists and writers in Paris including Picasso, Braque, Delaunay, Léger, Max Jacob and Apollinaire. She was therefore well placed to learn about Cubism at first hand and became an important figure in the transmission of Parisian artistic developments to Russian artists. From 1909 her studio in Paris provided a base for contact with Cubists and also with the Italian Futurists Marinetti and Giovanni Papini.

Her involvement in Russian groups was also extensive. In 1908 she exhibited with Contemporary Trends in St. Petersburg and *Zveno* (The Link) in Kiev which she organised together with David Burlyuk, Larionov and Goncharova. In 1909 she exhibited with *Stefanos-Venok* (Stephanos-Wreath) and with Kul'bin's Triangle exhibition. Many other exhibitions followed, including the first and second Izdebsky Salons in Odessa 1909-11, all of the Knave of Diamonds exhibitions of 1910-16, the Union of Youth in 1910 at Riga and 1913-14 in St. Petersburg, *Kol'tso* (The Ring) in Kiev 1914, and Larionov's exhibition No.4 in Moscow in 1914.

Abroad she exhibited with the Salon des Indépendents and the *Section d'Or* in Paris in 1912 and was visited by Pestel', Popova and Udaltsova in Paris in 1913. She also exhibited at the Salon des Indépendants in 1914. Her Italian Futurist connections led her to visit Soffici, Papini and others in Italy in 1914 where she showed work at the First International Futurist Exhibition at the Galleria Sprovieri in Rome.

During the war she remained in Russia, exhibiting at *Tramvay V* (Tramway V) in 1915, and *Magazin* (The Store) in Moscow 1916. She also began to execute theatre designs for the Kamerny (Chamber) Theatre in Moscow from 1916.

After the Revolution she exhibited with the Knave of Diamonds in Moscow in November 1917. She exhibited with the Artists of the Leftist Federation of the Professional Union in 1918 along with Popova, Rodchenko, Tatlin and others. She was teaching textiles at the Free Art Studios in Moscow

c.1918. Her name appeared on the April 1919 list of artists for acquisitions by the proposed Museum of Painterly Culture. She was represented along with Kandinsky, Chagall and others at the First State Exhibition of Paintings by Local and Moscow Artists held in Vitebsk in December 1919.

She taught at her studio in Kiev 1918-20 where her students included I.Rabinovich, Pavel Tchelitchew, Aleksandr Tyshler, Nisson Shifrin and Anatoli G.Petritsky. She may have contributed to the decoration of propaganda trains together with her students. She then taught at the Moscow Vkhutemas 1920-2 and during this period became involved with the radical and materialist views of the Constructivists around Rodchenko at the Institute of Artistic Culture (INKhUK). She was one of the five participants of the exhibition 5 x 5=25 in Moscow in 1921 which preceded the formal denunciation of easel painting and the Constructivists' move into the production of utilitarian design. She was represented at the First Russian Art Exhibition in Berlin in 1922 and contributed to the exhibition Art of Moscow Theatre 1918-1923 held in Moscow in 1923.

Exter, who had designed textiles with Rozanova, began to design clothing and by 1923. During this period she also designed fashion costumes and work clothes for the Fashion Studio (*Atel'e mod*) along with Lamanova, Mukhina and others. Given her theatrical experience this was a natural extension of her abilities, but in 1923 she also executed constructions in an architectural framework for pavilions at the All-Russian Agricultural Exhibition in Moscow. A synthesis of these activities occurred in 1924 with the release of the film *Aelita* which was directed by Protozanov and depicted the Revolution spreading from earth to the planet Mars. She collaborated on the design for the film which was humorous but politically committed. Its fantastic aspect allowed her to use all of her theatrical experience, as well as her awareness of Constructivist principles.

In 1924 she exhibited at the Venice Biennale and in the same year emigrated to France which remained her home until she died. She was represented at the Paris International Exhibition in 1925. She was teaching at Léger's Academy of Contemporary

Art in Paris in 1925 and at her own studio. In 1926 she designed some forty marionettes with Nechama Szmuszkowicz in various materials for a film which was never realised. These were exhibited with theatre designs at the gallery *Der Sturm* in Berlin in 1927. Puppets by Exter are preserved at the Hirshhorn Museum and Sculpture Garden, Smithsonian Institution, Washington D.C.

Thereafter she continued to paint, illustrate books and design for the theatre. She settled at Fontenay-aux-Roses in 1928 and exhibited with the group Cercle et Carré in 1930. She had a personal exhibition in Prague in 1937. She died at Fontenay-aux-Roses near Paris.

She sometimes signed her work 'A.E' linked to form a monogram.

Theatre design 1914 Curtain for the Kamerny (Chamber) Theatre, Moscow.

1916 With Lentulov she decorated the interior of the Kamerny Theatre.

1916 November: I.F.Annensky's bacchic drama *Famira Kifared* (Thamyris Kitharados; Thamira of the Cythern) directed by A.Tairov at the Kamerny (Chamber) Theatre in Moscow. The plot concerns the blinding of a Thracian bard. The poster design has stylised Greek figures fighting in a square shape above geometricised lettering. A costume design for a Bacchante has dense colour almost worthy of Bakst but shows a drawing style indebted to Russian Futurist technique characterised by arcs in red cross-hatched inconsistently along one side of the line. She also emphasised the gestures of her figures to illustrate the relation of costume to its appearance in performance, which in its way is also reminiscent of Bakst but replaces his elegance with a cruder vigour. A frieze composition reveals how closely painting and design coalesced in her work even before her interest in Constructivism.

1917 costumes for *Etudes de Bach* for the Leonidov Ballet Company, Kiev.

1917 October: Oscar Wilde's *Salomé*, directed by A.Tairov at the Kamerny (Chamber) Theatre in Moscow, had costumes that were a far cry from Beardsley's original illustrations to Oscar Wilde's text. She employed a Cubo-Futurist stylisation, faceting the costumes into geometric, decorative and partly rigid forms. Spectacular colour was employed to identify particular characters. A loosely handled set design for the end of the play shows steps, a raised platform and hanging geometric drapes suspended from the top of the stage, as if to apply Suprematist forms to the relief space of the stage like a moving painting. This was also evident in the designs for earlier scenes where blue, white and black diagonal and triangular striations dominated part of the backdrop. Silver drapes were also used and some of the hangings were able to move to accompany the action. In some designs the geometric forms are slotted together in a way which recalls the Suprematist paintings of Rozanova.

1921 May: Shakespeare's *Romeo and Juliet* directed by A.Tairov at the Kamerny (Chamber) Theatre in Moscow. A design for the curtain is a translation of the dramatic potential of Suprematist painting on to the stage, in which a large white zig-zag leaps like lightning between swirling shapes of yellow against a background of slaty indigo that evokes the atmosphere of a stormy night sky. The set incorporated a spiral tower at right and the balcony at left with bridges between and a low platform with steps. This is more recognisably stage architecture and less

of a kind of painting on stage. Masked figures had swift movements in the designs and rich colour for their costumes, implying a menacing blend of glamorous anonymity and purposeful action. The effect is both stylised and dramatic.

1922 *Satanic Ballet* (unrealised), music by Skryabin: Constructivist designs, in red-brown, black and white, of figures performing among a mass of equipment including ladders, trapezes, cables, bridges and machinery but without a backdrop. The design is a painting in itself and conforms to a blend of Suprematist and Constructivist compositional principles.

1924 P.Calderón de la Barca's *La Dama Duende* (The Phantom Lady) produced by Mikhail Chekhov at the Second Studio of the Moscow Art Theatre with designs by Ignats Nivinsky.

1926 ballet designs for Elsa Krueger at the Romantique Theatre.

After 1924 she designed productions in Paris, London, Vienna and Cologne.

Film design 1923-24 *Aelita*, directed by Yakov Protozanov and based upon the novel by A.Tolstoy, designed by Exter in collaboration with Isaak Rabinovich, S.Kozlovsky and others. The costumes for the Martians in the palace where Revolution spreads from planet earth were asymmetrical with transparent plastic armour and headgear, a surviving record of the essentially Russian Futurist development of the stiff or constructed costume which had begun in the work of Malevich a decade earlier. One Martian palace attendant had hinged wooden lath pantaloons which flexed as she walked. The Martian Queen had three breasts.

Futurist books V.Khlebnikov et al. *Moloko kobylits* (Mares' Milk), with illustrations by A.Exter and D. and V.Burlyuk, Moscow, 1914.

V.Kamensky *Futuristy: Pervyy zhurnal russkykh futuristov* (Futurists: First Journal of the Russian Futurists), with illustrations by D. and V.Burlyuk and A.Exter, Moscow, 1914. I.Aksenov *Neuvazhitel'nye osnovanie* (Weak Foundations), with illustrations by A.Exter, Moscow, 1916.

Other book design Illustrations for Aleksandr Tairov *Zapiski Rezhissera* (Notes of a Director), Moscow, 1921. Cover for Yakov Tugendkhold *Iskusstvo Dega* (The Art of Degas), Moscow, 1922. Cover for Marie Colmon *Panorama du fleuve*, Paris, 1937. Cover for Marie Colmon *Panorama de la montagne*, Paris, 1938.

Lit Ya.Tugendkhold *Alexandra Exter*, Berlin, 1922. A.Exter *Alexandra Exter: Décors de Théâtre*, preface by Tairov, 1930. A.B.Nakov *Alexandra Exter*, exh. cat., Galerie Jean Chauvelin, Paris, 1972. T.Strizhenova *Iz istorii sovetskogo kostyuma*, Moscow, 1972 (English edition: Tatiana Strizhenova, *Soviet Costume and Textiles 1917-1945*, Paris, 1991). *Diaghilev and Russian Stage Designers, a Loan Exhibition from the Collection of Mr. and Mrs. N.Lobanov-Rostovsky*, International Exhibitions Foundation, Washington, 1972-4. *Artist of the Theater: Alexandra Exter*, exh. cat., Lincoln Center, New York, 1974. *Alexandra Exter Marionettes*, Leonard Hutton Galleries, New York, 1975. S.P.Compton *The World Backwards, Russian Futurist Books 1912-16*, London, 1978. J.E.Bowlt *Russian Stage Design. Scenic Innovation. From the Collection of Mr. and Mrs. Nikita D.Lobanov-Rostovsky*, Jackson, MS, exh. cat.,1982. C.Lodder *Russian Constructivism*, New Haven and London, 1983. E.Weiss *Russische Avant-Garde, 1910-1930, Sammlung Ludwig, Köln*, Munich, 1986. A.Schouvaloff *The Thyssen-*

Alexandra Exter. Design for Yakov Protozanov's film 'Aelita', *1924.*
The film concerns the theme of Revolution on the planet Mars. The woman is a servant of the Martian queen.
Her constructed clothes are comparable with Exter's later puppet designs. Her pantaloons are hinged at the
waist, knees and ankles so that they flex open and close as she walks.

Bornemisza Collection: Set and Costume Designs for Ballet and Theatre, New York-London, 1987. *Aleksandra Ekster. Eskizy dekoratsiy i kostyumov*, exh. cat., Moscow, 1988. M.N.Yablonskaya *Women Artists of Russia's New Age*, London, 1990. Nancy Van Norman Baer *Theatre in Revolution, Russian Avant-Garde Stage Design 1913-1935*, San Francisco and London, 1991. F.Ciofi degli Atti, M.M.Kolesnikov *Alexandra Exter e il Teatro da Camera*, Milan, 1991. Dzhon Boult (John Bowlt) *Khudozhniki russkogo teatra. Sobranie Nikity i Niny Lobanovykh-Rostovskikh*, Moscow, 1991. *L'Avant-garde russe 1905-1925*, exh. cat., Musée des Beaux-Arts, Nantes, 1993.
Coll TG; RM; Bakhrushin Theatre Museum, Moscow; St. Petersburg Theatre Museum; Museum of Ukrainian Art, Kiev; Dagestan Art Museum, Makhachkala; Krasnodar Art Museum; Radishchev Art Museum, Saratov; Serpukhov Art Historical Museum; Yaroslav Art Museum; Victoria and Albert Museum, London; Ashmolean Museum, Oxford; Lobanov-Rostovsky Collection, London; Baron Thyssen-Bornemisza Collection, England; Costakis Collection; Sammlung Ludwig, Cologne.
Colour plates frontispiece and p.137.

EYGES, V. R.   a.1910-1929
Exhibited with the Knave of Diamonds in Moscow 1910-11. After the Revolution he became a member of the *Bytie* (Existence) Society of Artists formed in Moscow in 1921, was represented at the First Russian Art Exhibition in Berlin in 1922 and was included in the 1928 exhibition of Acquisitions by the State Art Collections Fund held in Moscow. He was represented in the First Touring Exhibition of Paintings and Graphics which opened in Moscow in 1929.

EYSNER, Petr Ivanovich   1839-1872
Portrait painter.
Coll TG.

Robert Fal'k. Indian Boy. *Oil on canvas. 99 x 71 cm. Signed.*
Reproduced by kind permission of Sotheby's London, sale 6.4.1989, lot 580.

F

F. see **FAL'K, R.R.**

FABERGE, Peter Carl   1846-1920
Head of the firm of Fabergé from 1870, specialising in luxury
objects employing precious metals and jewels. The firm was
founded in 1842 and directed by Peter Carl Fabergé from
1870. He was born in St. Petersburg and studied in Germany.
His brother Agathon joined the firm in 1882 and in the same
year they exhibited with success at the Pan-Russian Exhibition
in Moscow. Fabergé were most celebrated for their elaborately
jewelled Easter eggs which they supplied to the Imperial
family from 1884. International recognition followed their
display of eggs at the 1900 Exposition Universelle in Paris.
Fabergé were also employed to decorate the gilded dome of
Princess Tenisheva's church at Talashkino c.1911-14. After
the death of Peter Carl Fabergé his sons opened Fabergé &
Cie in Paris in 1921.
Lit *Twilight of the Tsars*, London, 1991.
Coll State Historical Museum, Moscow.

FADEEV, A. V.   a.1925
Painter. He contributed to the Third Exhibition of Paintings
by Artists from Kaluga and Moscow held in Kaluga in 1925.

FALILEEV, Vadim Dmitrievich   1879-1948
Etcher, engraver, wood engraver. He contributed to the
exhibition *Zveno* (The Link) in Kiev in 1908 and to the First
Izdebsky International Salon 1909-10 in Odessa where he
showed coloured woodcuts and watercolours. He exhibited
with the World of Art in 1906. He exhibited with the Union
of Russian Artists in 1906, 1909 and 1910. He again exhibited
with the World of Art 1911-13 and 1916.
After the Revolution he again exhibited with the World of Art
in December 1917 in Moscow. He was teaching graphic art
along with Pavlov and Masyutin at the Free Art Studios in
Moscow c.1918. He was represented in the Sixth State
Exhibition: The Print (*VI Gosudarstvennaya vystavka gravyur*)
in Moscow in 1919. He was included in the Third Touring
Exhibition of the Sovetsk Regional subdepartment of the
Museums Bureau along with Kandinsky, Rodchenko and
others in 1921 and he exhibited in the 1921 exhibition of the
World of Art in Moscow. He was represented at the Paris
International Exhibition in 1925. He contributed to the
exhibition of graphic art Liberation Movements: The
Sixteenth to the Twentieth Century held in Moscow in 1928.
**The Wave*, 1918, coloured lino-cut, is substantially indebted
to Hokusai's famous wave but here the water swells up against
a rock in a clearly symbolic image of the Revolution.
**Revolutionary Uprising*, 1919, linocut, is an intense image of
flag waving figures against a stormy sky executed in solid areas
of black and white to maximise the dramatic effect.

FALILEEVA, E. N.   a.1917
She exhibited with the World of Art in December 1917 in
Moscow.

FAL'K, Robert Rafailovich   1886-1958
Painter, graphic artist. Born in Moscow. He studied privately
under Yuon and Dudin in Moscow 1904-5 and then at the
Moscow College under Arkhipov, A.M.Vasnetsov, Pasternak,
Serov and Korovin 1905-12. He was aware of Post-
Impressionist painting and with Konchalovsky and Mashkov
comprized the Cézannistes. He exhibited with the Golden
Fleece in Moscow 1909-10. He visited Italy 1910-11. He
exhibited with the Izdebsky Salon of 1910-11 in Odessa. He
was a co-founder of the Knave of Diamonds in 1910 and he
exhibited with the Knave of Diamonds in Moscow 1910-12.
He became a member of the World of Art in 1911.
After the Revolution he exhibited with the World of Art in
December 1917 in Moscow. He also exhibited at the Fifth
State Exhibition: From Impressionism to Non-Objective Art
in Moscow in 1918-19. He served under Tatlin on the
Moscow Collegium of IZO Narkompros in 1919. He was
represented along with Kandinsky, Chagall and others at the
First State Exhibition of Paintings by Local and Moscow
Artists held in Vitebsk in December 1919, the Third
Exhibition of Paintings held at Ryazan in 1919 and at the
enormous First State Exhibition of Art and Science, which
included ethnographic material, held in Kazan in 1920.
He taught at the Vkhutemas/Vkhutein between 1918 and
1928 and exhibited in the 1921 exhibition of the World of Art
in Moscow. He was represented at the First Russian Art
Exhibition in Berlin in 1922. He was given an exhibition at the
Tretyakov Gallery in Moscow in 1924. He was represented at
the Paris International Exhibition in 1925. He became a

Peter Carl Fabergé. Cactus, *c.1900. Hardstone, enamel and gold.
Wartski, London.*

member of the Society of Moscow Painters founded in 1925 and of AKhRR 1925-8. His work was included in the exhibition of Soviet art held at Harbin in 1926 and in Japan in 1927 and in the major exhibition in Moscow in 1927 marking the tenth anniversary of the Revolution. He was also included in the 1928 exhibition of Acquisitions by the State Art Collections Fund held in Moscow.

He then emigrated to Paris where he lived from 1928 to 1938, exhibiting at the Salon d'Automne in 1928 and also exhibiting that year with Al'tman, Vechegzhanin and Chekhonin at the Galerie Hirondelle in Paris. He returned from Paris to Samarkand until 1944 where he taught at the art school 1941-2. He sometimes signed his work in cyrillic script simply: 'F'. He died in Moscow.

Landscape with Sailing Boat, 1912, Radishev Art Museum, Saratov, shows Fal'k as the most austere of the Cézannistes, ordering his landscape with strict geometric discipline. Taut and angular trees amongst the tilting planes of a village scene act as the setting for block-like figures and animals entirely caught up in the rhythms of their earthy surroundings. Despite Fal'k's fondness for earth colours his painting remained clear and colourful. The composition engages boat-sail, quayside and hillside into a single firm arc. He resolved his paintings thoroughly, progressing beyond the borrowing of devices from Cézanne and Cubism to make a personal style of gravity and strength.

Theatre design *A Night in the Old Market* by Perez for the Jewish Chamber Theatre, Moscow.

Writings R.Fal'k *Besedy ob iskusstve. Pisma. Vospominaniya o khudozhnike* (Conversations about Art. Letters. Recollections of the Artist), Moscow, 1981.

Vladimir Favorsky. Novodeivichy Monastery, Moscow, *1919. Wood engraving. Signed 'VF' lower left.*
Favorsky was a master of wood engraving. He combined traditional techniques with a complex organisation of space that reflected his thorough awareness of new developments in Suprematism, Constructivism and other movements.

Lit D.Sarabjanow *Robert Falk*, Dresden, 1974. D.Elliott, V.Dudakov *100 Years of Russian Painting*, London, 1991. *L'Avant-garde russe 1905-1925*, exh. cat., Musée des Beaux-Arts, Nantes, 1993.
Coll TG; RM; Astrakhan Art Museum; Perm Art Museum; Radishev Art Museum, Saratov.
Colour plate p.140.

FANDERFLIT, Natalya Konstantinovna   **b.1901-1926+**
Graphic artist. Her technique reveals a debt to the examples of both Favorsky and Ostroumova-Lebedeva.
Still-Life, Chess, 1926, linocut, skilfully depicts a winter atmosphere through an image comprising scattered chessmen, a vase and flowers in front of a window through which is visible driving rain and the mirror-like surface of a wet road.

FATEEV, P. P.   **a.1918-1919**
Painter. He was represented at the First Exhibition of Works of the Professional Union of Artists in Moscow in 1918 and at the juryless Eighth State Exhibition in Moscow in 1919.

FAVORSKAYA, Maria Vladimirovna   **1887-1959**
Painter. She was represented at the First Exhibition of Works of the Professional Union of Artists in Moscow in 1918.

FAVORSKAYA, Vera Vasilevna   **1896-1977**
Painter, graphic artist. She exhibited at the inaugural exhibition of the Society of Moscow Painters in 1925. She died in Moscow.

FAVORSKY, Vladimir Andreevich   **1886-1964**
Graphic artist, theatre designer. A specialist in wood engraving, Favorsky became an important and influential figure in the post-revolutionary period, neglected outside Russia because of the traditional associations of his chosen medium.

Born in Moscow. He studied privately under Yuon and Dudin in Moscow 1903-4 and subsequently at the Simon Hollósy School in Munich 1906-7. He then studied in the Faculty of Philosophy and History at Moscow University 1907-13. He concentrated on wood engraving from 1907 and made of this old technique a vehicle of great sophistication which had immense influence on Russian graphic artists. These used black ink and were much employed for book illustrations. He visited Italy, Austria and Switzerland. He exhibited with the Association of Moscow Artists 1911-12. He exhibited with the World of Art in 1913.

After the Revolution he was represented at the First Exhibition of Works of the Professional Union of Artists in Moscow in 1918. He taught at the Second Free Art Studios from 1918 and at the Vkhutemas/Vkhutein in Moscow from 1920 to 1930. He exhibited at the Fifth State Exhibition: From Impressionism to Non-Objective Art in Moscow 1918-19 and was represented in the Sixth State Exhibition: The Print (*VI Gosudarstvennaya vystavka gravyur*) in Moscow in 1919.

He was made an academician in 1923 and rector of the Vkhutemas 1923-5. He was a member of the group 4 Arts 1924-8 and was represented at the 14th Venice Biennale (1924) and the Paris International Exhibition in 1925. He exhibited with the 4 Arts society in Moscow in 1925. He was included in the major exhibition in Moscow in 1927 marking the tenth anniversary of the Revolution and he contributed to the exhibition of graphic art Liberation Movements: The

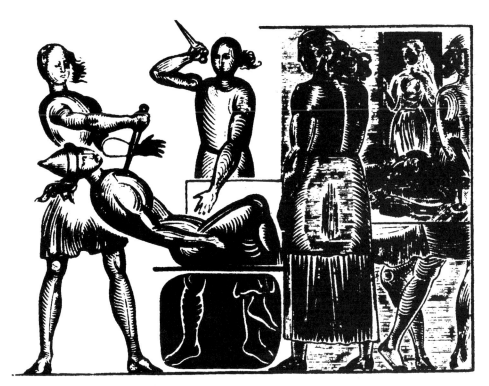

Vladimir Favorsky. Illustration to A.Globa's Tragedy 'Famar' (Tamar), *1932. Wood engraving.*
The print incorporates several kinds of interplay of light and dark, or of positive and negative space. This is a subtlety evident in much of Favorsky's work.

Sixteenth to the Twentieth Century held in Moscow in 1928. He was also included in the 1928 exhibition of Acquisitions by the State Art Collections Fund held in Moscow and in the First Touring Exhibition of Paintings and Graphics which opened in Moscow in 1929. He was also represented in the exhibition of Russian Graphic Art in Riga in 1929.

He became professor at the Graphics Institute in Moscow in 1930 until 1934. In addition to his great skilfulness as a wood engraver he was well aware of the wide range of creative tendencies around him. These, as well as his intellectual interest in scientific and philosophical theories, are reflected in his graphic works.

He was represented at the jubilee exhibition Artists of the RSFSR over 15 Years held at the Russian Museum, Leningrad, in 1932 and at the 1932 Venice Biennale. He taught at the Institute of Fine Art 1934-8. He exhibited with Sarra Lebedeva, A.E.Zelensky, G.I.Kepinov, Vera Mukhina, Ilya Slonim, I.G.Frikh-Khar and I.M.Chaykov in Moscow in 1935. He taught at the Institute of Applied and Decorative Arts 1942-8 and produced several series of prints including *Samarkand* 1942-4 and graphic portraits of *Great Russian Military Leaders* 1945-7.

He was awarded a Lenin Prize in 1962 for his *Shakespeare's Sonnets*, published in 1948, his illustrations to Marshak's translations from Robert Burns, published 1950, together with his illustrations to Pushkin's *Tale of Igor's Campaign*, 1954, *Boris Godunov*, 1955-6, and *Little Tragedies*, 1961.

Book design numerous including: 1918 A.France's *Les Opinions de M.Jérome Coignard*, published 1963.
A.Globa's *Famar* (Tamar), Moscow, 1923.
The Book of Ruth, published 1925.
Pushkin's *The Little House in Kolomna*, published 1929.
S.D.Spassky's *New Year's Eve*, published 1932.
Dante's *Vita Nuova* published 1934.   *(cont.)*

Vladimir Favorsky. The Sverdlov Hall in the Moscow Kremlin, *1921. Wood engraving. Signed 'WF' in monogram lower right.*
Favorsky has used the architectural framework to devise complex effects of space and lighting.

Pavel Filonov. The Three at Table, *1914-15. Oil on canvas. 100 x 102 cm.
State Russian Museum, St.Petersburg.*

G.Shtorm *The Life and Works of Mikhail Lermontov*, published 1934.
Cover, in black, for the sheet music of *L.Betkhoven: Pesni* (Beethoven: Songs), Moscow, 1927. This featured a diminutive figure of Beethoven seen in profile executed in a wood-engraved style amidst lettering of varied boldness.
Theatre design 1934 Shakespeare's *Twelfth Night* at the Second Moscow Art Theatre.
Writings V.Favorsky *O khudozhnike, o tvorchestve, o knige* (About the Artist, About Creativity, About Books), Moscow, 1966. V.Favorsky *Rasskazy khudozhnika-gravera* (Stories of an Artist-Engraver), Moscow, 1976.
Lit T.Gureva *V.A.Favorsky: Izbrannye proizvedeniya*, 1959. Yu.Khalaminsky *V.A.Favorsky*, Moscow, 1964. C.Lodder *Russian Constructivism*, New Haven and London, 1983. S.Compton *Russian Avant-Garde Books 1917-34*, London, 1992.
Coll TG; RM.

**FAYDYSH-KRANDIEVSKY, Andrei Petrovich
1920-1967**
Sculptor of socialist realist genre. Works include *Komsomol Member*, 1952, complete with cogwheels.

**FEDDERS , Julius (FEDDER, Yuliy Ivanovich)
1838-1909**
Latvian landscape painter. Born at Kokenhusen. After a period at the Düsseldorf Academy he moved to Russia where he studied under Vorob'ev at the Academy in St. Petersburg 1862-75. He won medals for landscape painting at the International

Exhibitions in London in 1875 and Paris in 1889.
He worked in Latvia and was painting panoramic landscapes in 1891.
The Cemetery, 1880s, Latvian Art Gallery, Riga, is a fine vertical landscape of a stream crossed by a bridge of planks. Behind this rises a steep hillock upon which the cemetery stands surrounded by trees. The creamy light is reminiscent of Corot.
Coll TG; Latvian Art Gallery, Riga.

FEDORENKO, V. P.   **a.1925**
He exhibited with the 4 Arts society in Moscow in 1925.

FEDORICHEVA, Maria A.   **a.1926-1932+**
She was a member of the group *Krug khudozhnikov* (Circle of Artists) founded in 1926 and was represented at the jubilee exhibition Artists of the RSFSR over 15 Years held at the Russian Museum, Leningrad, in 1932.

FEDOROV, German Vasil'evich   **1886-1976**
Painter. He studied at the Moscow College 1902-11. He exhibited landscapes with the Knave of Diamonds in 1911-17 in Moscow.
After the Revolution he exhibited with the Knave of Diamonds in Moscow in November 1917, with the World of Art in December 1917 in Moscow and at the First Exhibition of Works of the Professional Union of Artists in Moscow in 1918. He was also assisting Konchalovsky in 1918 and his work sometimes resembles that of Konchalovsky in style. His name appeared on the April 1919 list of artists for acquisitions by the envisaged Museum of Painterly Culture. He exhibited

in the 1921 exhibition of the World of Art in Moscow. He was represented at the First Russian Art Exhibition in Berlin in 1922. He was a member of the Society of Moscow Painters founded in 1925 and he exhibited with AKhRR 1924-8. His work was included in the exhibition of Soviet art held at Harbin in 1926 and in Japan in 1927 and in the major exhibition in Moscow in 1927 marking the tenth anniversary of the Revolution. He was also included in the 1928 exhibition of Acquisitions by the State Art Collections Fund held in Moscow and in the First Touring Exhibition of Paintings and Graphics which opened in Moscow in 1929. He was painting industrial scenes for Narkompros at Novorssisk in 1929. He was represented at the jubilee exhibition Artists of the RSFSR over 15 Years held at the Russian Museum, Leningrad, in 1932. He died in Moscow.

Lit A.M.Muratov, V.Manin et al. *Zhivopis' 20-30kh godov*, Sankt-Peterburg, 1991.

Coll Tula Art Museum.

FEDOROV, Vasili F.   **1891-1925+**

Theatre designer. Born in Moscow. He executed designs for Meyerhold's production of *Les* (The Forest) by A.Ostrovsky at the Meyerhold Theatre, Moscow, in January 1923. He was represented at the Paris International Exhibition in 1925. He died in Moscow.

Lit Nancy Van Norman Baer *Theatre in Revolution, Russian Avant-Garde Stage Design 1913-1935*, San Francisco and London, 1991.

Coll Bakhrushin Theatre Museum, Moscow.

FEDOROVA (IONOVA), Mariya Alekseeva   **1859-1916**

Painter.

Coll TG.

FEDOROVA-MASHKOVA, E.   **a.1917**

She exhibited with the World of Art in December 1917 in Moscow.

FEDOROVSKY, Fedor Fedorovich   **1883-1955**

Painter, theatre designer. Born at Chernigov. He studied under K.Korovin and Mikhail Vrubel' at the Stroganov Institute, graduating in 1907 and taught there until the Revolution. He exhibited with the Moscow Association of Artists in 1906 and became a resident artist in the Sergei Zimin Opera Company, Moscow, after 1907. He exhibited with the World of Art in Moscow in 1915.

After the Revolution he was engaged on Agitprop decorations for the Gymnasts' Parade in Red Square, Moscow, and taught naturalist painting and theatre design at the Free Art Studios/Vkhutemas 1918-23. From 1921 he was artist-decorator at the Bolshoi Theatre, Moscow. He was included in the Third Touring Exhibition of the Sovetsk Regional subdepartment of the Museums Bureau along with Kandinsky, Rodchenko and others in 1921 and he exhibited with the 1921 exhibition of the World of Art in Moscow. He was represented at the First Russian Art Exhibition in Berlin in 1922 and at the exhibition Art of Moscow Theatre 1918-1923 held in Moscow in 1923. In fact he became a colourful, prolific and highly professional theatre designer. He was represented at the Paris International Exhibition in 1925. He became a member of the Academy of Arts of the USSR and continued to design many operatic productions. He died in Moscow.

Theatre design 1910 *Snegurochka* for the Sergei Zimin Opera Company, Moscow.

1913 M.P.Mussorgsky's *Khovanshchina*, choreography by A.Bolm, produced at the Théâtre des Champs-Elysées in Paris by Diaghilev.

1913-14 Rimsky-Korsakov's *La Nuit de Mai* produced in London.

1922 Bizet's *Carmen* at the Bolshoi Theatre, Moscow.

1927 *Boris Godunov*.

1934 Rimsky-Korsakov's *Prince Igor*.

1935 Rimsky-Korsakov's *Sadko* at the Bolshoi Theatre, Moscow. Beneath a vast vault decorated with an image of the sun and Asiatic patterns sit countless heads at table for a grand banquet. Pinks, oranges, reds and purples coalesce in the

Vasili Fedorov. Stage set of Meyerhold's production of Ostrovsky's 'The Forest', *1924.*

dominant blue. A *tour de force* of exotic colour.
1946 Boris Godunov.
Lit E.Kostina *F.F.Fedorovsky*, Moscow, 1960. *Diaghilev and Russian Stage Designers, a Loan Exhibition from the Collection of Mr. and Mrs. N.Lobanov-Rostovsky*, International Exhibitions Foundation, Washington, 1972-4. J.E.Bowlt *Russian Stage Design. Scenic Innovation. From the Collection of Mr. and Mrs. Nikita D.Lobanov-Rostovsky*, Jackson, MS, exh. cat.,1982. Dzhon Boult (John Bowlt) *Khudozhniki russkogo teatra. Sobranie Nikity i Niny Lobanovykh-Rostovskikh*, Moscow, 1991.
Coll Bakhrushin Theatre Museum, Moscow.

FEDOTOV, Ivan Sergeevich   1881-1951
Theatre designer. Born in Moscow. He studied at the Stroganov Institute, Moscow, until 1901. He designed for the Moscow Private Opera from 1902 and for the Zimin Opera Company 1908-17.
After the Revolution he exhibited with the Knave of Diamonds in Moscow in 1917 and was decorator to the Theatre of the Workers' Council of Peasants and Deputies in Moscow 1917-19. He was teaching theatre design at the Free Art Studios in Moscow along with Tatlin, Fedorovsky and Yakulov c.1918.

Fedor Fedorovsky and O.Vinogradov. Costume for Wagner's 'Lohengrin', *before 1927. Documentary photograph of costume maquette. Stylistically inspired by the constructed costumes of Exter, Vesnin and others.*

He was represented at the enormous First State Exhibition of Art and Science, which included ethnographic material, held in Kazan in 1920, and at the exhibition Art of Moscow Theatre 1918-1923 held in Moscow in 1923. He worked for the Theatre of the RSFSR No.1 1920-1.
He was resident artist at the Central Theatre of the Soviet Army in Moscow 1934-51.
Theatre design 1915 December: Tairov's production of Tor Hedberg's *Dva mira* (Two Worlds) at the Kamerny (Chamber) Theatre, Moscow.
1916-17 December/January Tairov's production of Labiche's *Solomennaya Shlyapka* (An Italian Straw Hat) at the Kamerny (Chamber) Theatre, Moscow.
1918 *Die Lustigen Weiber von Windsor*, comic opera by Otto Nicolai based on Shakespeare's *Merry Wives of Windsor*, performed at the Theatre of the Soviets of Workers' Deputies, Petrograd.
1925-6 Volkonsky's production of *Zagmuk* at the Maly Theatre. This included a set comprising three plain screens with a stylised African gate flanked by palm trees.
1947 November N.A.Asanov's *Almazy* (Diamonds) at the Moscow Art Theatre.
1949 March A.N.Ostrovsky's *Pozdnyaya lyubov'* (Last Love) at the Moscow Art Theatre.
Lit J.E.Bowlt *Russian Stage Design. Scenic Innovation. From the Collection of Mr. and Mrs. Nikita D.Lobanov-Rostovsky*, Jackson, MS, exh. cat.,1982.

FEDOTOV, Pavel Andreevich   1815-1852
Painter of satirical genre, fine stuffs and small portraits.He was a prolific draughtsman and also executed woodcuts. He was born and raised in Moscow, the son of a lesser official. After attending a military school he remained in military service until 1844 as an officer of the Imperial Guard. He visited the Hermitage where he copied small Dutch genre paintings and he also visited the Academy in St. Petersburg attending evening classes there from 1834 where he impressed Bryullov. His precise and highly descriptive paintings were remarkable also for the drama with which he was able to infuse his subjects which may in part reflect his study of engravings after Wilkie and Hogarth. This rescued his paintings from sentimentality, permitted a shrewd observation of human behaviour and provided an element of social criticism. He exhibited three paintings, including *A Choosy Bride*, in 1849 and he was awarded an honorary title from the Academy. He died in a psychiatric hospital.
*A Choosy Bride, 1847, TG, is a costume piece in which an ageing, unattractive and presumably wealthy suitor begs on bended knee for the hand of the young woman. The interior where this action is set is comfortable without being at all splendid. Behind a curtain her parents listen with some interest and anxiety. This is a wry and novel-like situation designed to produce a knowing response from the viewer.
*The Widow, 1850s, is highly original and memorable for its minute description of the interior within which the widow adopts a grief stricken pose that is neither affected nor melodramatic.
*The Gamblers (study) 1851-2, pencil and crayon, RM, is not recognisably the same artist. Its soft shadowy interior is pervaded by an air of sinister confrontation and is drawn in an atmospheric cross-hatched technique that is appropriate for the gloomy stark room where the action occurs.
Coll TG; RM; Ashmolean Museum, Oxford.

Fedor Fedorovsky. Two costumes for Prince Ivan Khovansky for Mussorgsky's 'Khovanshchina', *1912-13. Gouache. Signed and dated lower right in Russian.*
86.5 x 101.5 cm.
Designs for Diaghilev's production of 'Khovanshchina' at the Théâtre des Champs-Elysées, Paris, in 1913. Collection Mr. and Mrs. Nikita D.Lobanov-Rostovsky, London.

FEINBERG (FEYNBERG), Leonid Evgenevich 1896-1979
Graphic artist. His work was included in the First Exhibition of the Moscow Contemporary Art Store in January 1919. He was engaged in the decoration of the Agitprop trains *Lenin (October Revolution)* and *Soviet Caucasus* in 1920. He died in Moscow.

FELDEN, K.   **a.1904**
Painter. Included in the Scarlet Rose exhibition in Saratov in 1904.

FEOFAN GREK = THEOPHANES THE GREEK

FEOFILAKTOV, Nikolai Petrovich   **1878-1941**
Painter and graphic artist associated with the World of Art. He became the principle designer for the *Skorpion* (Scorpio) publishing house, where his work included the firm's logo in the style of a late Beardsley drawing in 1904, and for its periodical *Vesy* (Libra) which had his covers from 1907. He participated in the exhibition the Scarlet Rose in Saratov in 1904 and in the same year his designs were published in the *World of Art* periodical. He designed the title page for the almanac *Severnye tsvety assiriiskie* (Northern Assyrian Flowers), St. Petersburg, 1905. He exhibited with the Union of Russian Artists 1906-9. He was included in Diaghilev's display of Russian art at the Salon d'Automne in Paris 1906-9. He exhibited with the Blue Rose group in 1907. A cover design for *Vesy* in 1908 shows him working with an elegance indebted to Beardsley, digested via Bakst, to depict intricate filigree lettering and swags held aloft by black nudes. He exhibited with the World of Art 1911-16.
His drawings sometimes recalled the bleak visions of Alfred

Pavel Fedotov. Preliminary study for a humorous drawing. *Pencil. 24.7 x 16.4 cm. Inscribed in Russian 'This is all very well, but how many serfs do you have?'*
Ashmolean Museum, Oxford.

School of Filonov. Illustration to L.P.Belsky's translation of the Finnish epic 'Kalevala', *1933*.

Kubin but with a stress upon fine etching-like lines building up to tentatively evoked areas of different and contrasting textures in moody landscapes raked by a harsh light. He exhibited with the 4 Arts society in Moscow in 1925.
Lit *Twilight of the Tsars*, London, 1991.

FERAT, Count Serge Jastrebzoff　　　**1881-1958**
Painter, graphic artist, theatre designer. Born in Moscow. He made journeys with his family to England, France, Italy and Germany as a child.
He moved to Paris to study under Bouguereau at the Académie Julian 1901-2. He exhibited regularly at the Salon des Indépendants from 1906. He met Picasso and Apollinaire and became involved in Cubist theatre design 1910-11. It was Apollinaire who coined his pseudonym 'Ferat'. He was co-director of the periodical *Les Soirées de Paris* with Apollinaire 1912-14. He volunteered for military service in 1914.
He designed Cubist sets and costumes for Apollinaire's *Les Mamelles de Tirésias* in 1917 and the same year he held an exhibition in Paris. He suffered financial disaster through the Russian Revolution. He exhibited with the revived Section d'Or group in Paris in 1920. He died in Paris.
Lit *Paris-Moscou*, 1979.

FERDINANDOV, Boris A.　　　**1889-1959**
Theatre designer. He directed as well as designed a production of A.Ostrovsky's *The Storm* at the Experimental-Heroic Theatre, Moscow, in 1922. He contributed to the exhibition Art of Moscow Theatre 1918-1923 held in Moscow in 1923.
Theatre design 1917 November: Tairov's production of the pantomime *Korol'-Arlekin* (King Harlequin) for the Kamerny (Chamber) Theatre, Moscow. The costumes combined Commedia dell'Arte effects with those of the circus. There were some Suprematist traits evident in costumes with geometrical devices on them and by, for example, a hat which comprised a flat square upon a cylinder.
1917 December: Tairov's production of Debussy's *Yashchik s igrushkami* (The Box of Toys) at the Kamerny (Chamber) Theatre in Moscow. The theme of childhood permitted some geometric stylisation inspired by toys. The actress Alice G.Koonen played the doll.
1919 November: Tairov's production of Scribe and Legouvé's *Adrienne Lecouvreur* at the Kamerny (Chamber) Theatre in Moscow. This contrasted 18th century costumes against a background of tall plinth-like structures from which sprouted flat curvilinear and kinetic shapes.
1922 A.Ostrovsky's *The Storm* at the Experimental-Heroic Theatre, Moscow.
Lit Nancy Van Norman Baer *Theatre in Revolution, Russian Avant-Garde Stage Design 1913-1935*, San Francisco and London, 1991.
Coll Bakhrushin Theatre Museum, Moscow.

FESHIN, Nikolai Ivanovich　　　**1881-1955**
He was teaching at the Kazan School of Art 1908-12 where his students included N.M.Nikonov. He was represented at the enormous First State Exhibition of Art and Science, which included ethnographic material, held in Kazan in 1920 and at the Third Touring Exhibition of the Sovetsk Regional subdepartment of the Museums Bureau along with Kandinsky, Rodchenko and others in 1921. He contributed to the exhibition of Contemporary Russian Art held at Philadelphia in 1932.
Coll TG.

FEYNBERG = FEINBERG, L.E.

FIDMAN, Vladimir Ivanovich　　　**1884-1949**
Graphic artist. He studied at the Academy and at the Art School in Odessa. After the Revolution his work included political posters, illustrations and design work for industry and architecture.
Lit D.Elliott, V.Dudakov *100 Years of Russian Painting*, London, 1991.

FILIPPOV, Konstantin Nikolaevich　　　**1830-1878**
Painter of war.
Coll TG.

FILKOVICH, K. I.　　　**1865-1908**
Painter. He entered the Academy at St. Petersburg in 1891 and Azbé's school in Munich in 1898. He returned to Russia in 1905. In 1908 he showed work at the exhibition Contemporary Trends.

FILONOV, Pavel Nikolaevich　　　**1883-1941**
A Russian Futurist painter and graphic artist of great originality. Born in Moscow. His parents died young and he worked as a dancer in fairground booths as a child and embroidered towels. In 1896 he was working as a painter and decorator in St. Petersburg. His art education began at the Society for the Encouragement of the Arts where he attended evening classes from 1898. He studied under Lev Dmitriev-Kavkazsky 1903-8 and 1908-10 attended evening classes at the

Academy. Contact with avant-garde groups followed. He exhibited with the Union of Youth in 1910, 1912 and 1913-14. He also visited France and Italy 1911-12. He exhibited with the Nonparty Society of Artists in St. Petersburg in 1913, and the same year collaborated with Iosif Shkolnik on the sets and costumes for Mayakovsky's Futurist drama *Vladimir Mayakovsky* which was performed at Luna Park, St. Petersburg, on two nights in December 1913 alternating with Matyushin's Futurist opera *Victory over the Sun* which was designed by Malevich. In 1914 he made illustrations for futurist books including *Roaring Parnassus* and V.Khlebnikov's *Izbornik stikhov* (Selected Verses) in which the individual letters of the text are drawn and decorated in a way that gives them an independent life. He also published his own *Sermon on Universal Flowering* in 1914. Active military service on the Romanian front followed 1916-18.

After the Revolution his name appeared on the April 1919 list of artists for acquisitions by the proposed Museum of Painterly Culture. He contributed to numerous exhibitions in Petrograd including the First State Free Exhibition of Works of Art in 1919, the exhibitions of the Community of Artists in 1921, 1922 and 1924, and the Exhibition of Paintings by Petrograd Artists of All Tendencies 1919-1923 in 1923. His work was also displayed at the First Russian Art Exhibition in Berlin in 1922. From 1923 he taught at the Petrograd Academy and he was a member of GINKhUK from 1924. Gathering followers around him he ran his own school the Collective of Masters of Analytical Art from 1925 to 1932. A retrospective exhibition planned for the Russian Museum in 1929 was aborted.

He was represented at the jubilee exhibition Artists of the RSFSR over 15 Years held at the Russian Museum, Leningrad, in 1932. With his students he illustrated the Finnish epic *Kalevala* in 1933. He died in the siege of Leningrad.

Mardi Gras, 1913-14, RM, reveals the extraordinary originality of Filonov's style. Like other major paintings this is grotesque and unrealistic in a particular way. It is stylised in that it draws upon the artificial, anonymous and exaggerated forms of toys, folk pictures and puppets. But the stiff and rhythmic figures which result appear archaic and timeless. Yet Filonov was highly sophisticated as a painter and every detail is intended. His consciously primitive style was supported by a knowledge of Cubism and Russian Futurism. This gave him the means to devise large compositions filled with incident and crowded with figures and events, sustaining a meticulous technique at every point. The result is both intricate and grandiose. His knowledge of Finnish and North Russian legend further encouraged his otherworldly tendency and enriched the narrative of his paintings. On the other hand his involvement with Russian Futurists encouraged complex theories of time and space. This permitted the juxtaposition of different incidents and differing scale of figures in his paintings. His *Carnival*, 1913, RM, is a comparable instance dominated in the foreground by a sleigh drawn by three horses which resemble toy horses with multiple legs describing their movement, yet the canvas is filled to an intricate, dense pattern with numerous figures and other horses. Traces of the handling employed by the Italian Futurist Boccioni coalesce in the tumult of images with motifs from folk art to suggest a myth or ancient legend.

Untitled (The First Symphony of D.Shostakovich), 1925-7, RM, presents a spangled chequerboard of blue and brown planes which reveals a continuum of huts and houses. From this large faces emerge, blue, hairless and wan, some inverted, some repeated. Filonov is remotely like Chagall in his fantastic cosmology but he is unique in the deliberate and meticulous intricacy of his paintings, in the cellular construction and in the archaism of their folk art stylisations.

The Formula of the Petrograd Proletariat, late 1920s, RM, is a painting constructed in bizarre crystalline facets formed by intersecting arcs of great precision. From the midst of this profusion there emerge figures, buildings, animals and vistas which range in scale from the minute to the enormous. These are painted throughout with a consistent palette of small red, blue and white planes which mark the clashing of arcs and lines. Out of this fecund mass emerge larger figures, limbs, fingers, feet and eyes as if crystallising into existence. This is the work of a spectacular, unnerving and extraordinary visionary.

Futurist books V.Khlebnikov *Izbornik stikhov* (Selection of Poems), with illustrations by N.Burlyuk, K.Malevich and P.Filonov, St. Petersburg, 1914.
P.Filonov *Propoven' o prorosli mirovoy* (A Sermon Chant about Universal Flowering), with illustrations by Filonov, Petrograd, 1915.
Lit J.Kriz *Filonov*, Prague, 1966. S.P.Compton *The World*

Pavel Filonov. Self-portrait, *c.1925. Pen and ink drawing. State Russian Museum, St. Petersburg.*

Backwards, Russian Futurist Books 1912-16, London, 1978. E.Kovtun *Pavel Filonov*, Leningrad, 1988. N.Misler and J.E.Bowlt *Pavel Filonov: A Hero and his Fate*, Austin, Texas, 1983. E.Weiss *Russische Avant-Garde, 1910-1930, Sammlung Ludwig, Köln*, Munich, 1986. *Filonov*, exh. cat., Centre Georges Pompidou, Paris, 1990. E.Kovtun *Filonov*, Leningrad, 1990. N.Misler, J.Bowlt *Pavel Filonov*, Moscow, 1990. *L'Avant-garde russe 1905-1925*, exh. cat., Musée des Beaux-Arts, Nantes, 1993.
Coll TG; RM; Erevan Art Museum; Costakis Collection; Sammlung Ludwig, Cologne.
See R.Leviton and A.Liandsberg.
Colour plate p.144.

FIRSOV, I. M.   a.1914
He contributed twenty-six works to the exhibition No.4 in Moscow in 1914 including a Primitivist work and five drawings which he described as portrait studies executed according to the theory of transparency which was of current interest to Larionov.

FIRSOV, Ivan I.   1733-1785+
Little is known of his career. *The Young Artist*, 1765, TG, is an overtly sweet genre painting rather reminiscent of the work of Greuze. In this painting the nanny has the little girl pose for her portrait by a young boy painter in an elegantly simple interior.
Coll TG

FISHER   a.1926
Sculptor. A member of the Society of Russian Sculptors from 1926.

FLAVITSKY, Konstantin Dmitievich   1830-1866
History painter. He studied at the Academy in St. Petersburg and later taught there. His painting of *The Last Moments of Princess Tarankova*, 1866, showed her trapped in her cell in the Peter-Paul Fortress as the tide began to flood it. He died in St. Petersburg.
Coll TG; RM; Saratov Art Museum.

FON-VIL'DEMAN = VIL'DE, R.F.

**FONVIZIN (FON-VIZEN), Artur Vladimirovich
1882-1973**
Painter, watercolourist, draughtsman. He studied at the Moscow College under K.N.Gorsky and V.N.Baksheev 1901-4 and then in Munich 1904-6. He exhibited with the Blue Rose group in 1907 and contributed to the *Stefanos* exhibition 1907-8 including illustrations to Hoffmann, Krylov and the Goncourt brothers as well as a *Portrait of Larionov*. He also contributed to the exhibition *Zveno* (The Link) in Kiev in 1908. He exhibited with the Golden Fleece in Moscow in 1908. He was associated with Russian Futurists of Larionov's circle. He exhibited with the Izdebsky Salon of 1910-11 in Odessa, with the Knave of Diamonds in Moscow 1910-11, with the Union of Youth 1911-12, and with the Donkey's Tail group. He exhibited with the World of Art in 1913.
After the Revolution he was associated with the *Makovets* group 1922-5 and taught at the Tambov Art Technical College 1926-7. He was included in the 1928 exhibition of Acquisitions by the State Art Collections Fund held in Moscow and in the First Touring Exhibition of Paintings and Graphics which opened in Moscow in 1929. He was also represented in the exhibition of Russian Graphic Art in Riga in 1929 and at the jubilee exhibition Artists of the RSFSR over 15 Years held at the Russian Museum, Leningrad, in 1932.
Motherhood, 1936, watercolour, TG, is painterly, soft and evocative in its technique.
Lit A.M.Muratov, V.Manin et al. *Zhivopis' 20-30kh godov*, Sankt-Peterburg, 1991.
Coll TG; RM.

**FOREGGER (VON GREIFENTURN), Nikolai
Mikhailovich**   1892-1939
Dance theorist and producer, theatre designer. Born in Moscow. He directed a studio theatre/cabaret, Mastfor, in Moscow in the 1920s, for which Boris Erdman, Eisenstein, Yutkevich and others made designs. His own designs included costumes in the early 1920s. Eisenstein trained at his studio. He sometimes signed his designs with a latin 'NF' joined into a monogram. He died at Kuibyshev.
Theatre design Tairov's production of S.Benelli's *Supper of Jokes* at the Kamerny (Chamber) Theatre in Moscow.
Lit Nancy Van Norman Baer *Theatre in Revolution, Russian Avant-Garde Stage Design 1913-1935*, San Francisco and London, 1991.
Coll Bakhrushin Theatre Museum, Moscow.

FRANKETTI, V. F.   a.1918-1927
This name appeared at the exhibition of the Artists of the Leftist Federation of the Professional Union in 1918 along with Popova, Rodchenko and others, on the April 1919 list of artists for acquisitions by the envisaged Museum of Painterly Culture and at the enormous First State Exhibition of Art and Science, which included ethnographic material, held in Kazan in 1920. Franketti exhibited with the 4 Arts society in Moscow in 1925. Franketti's work was included in the exhibition of Soviet art held at Harbin in 1926 and in Japan in 1927 and in the 1928 exhibition of Acquisitions by the State Art Collections Fund held in Moscow.

FRENKEL'-MANYUSSON, R. V.   a.1918-1929
Painter. An exhibitor at the First Exhibition of Works of the Professional Union of Artists in Moscow in 1918, at the Ninth State Exhibition of Paintings: Naturalism and Realism in Moscow in 1919 and at the exhibition of Russian Graphic Art in Riga in 1929.

FRENTS (FRENZ), Rudol'f Rudol'fovich   1888-1956
Painter of cityscapes, battle scenes and revolutionary themes. He studied at the Higher Institute of the Academy under Samokish and Savinsky 1909-18. He visited England, France and Italy in 1912.
Aftert he Revolution he directed the agitational poster studio of the Leningrad Decorative Institute of Narkompros 1919-25. He was a member of the 4 Arts society founded in 1925. His *Merry-Go-Round*, 1922, RM, has a mass of figures visiting the fair. The central merry-go-round and the general background are dominated by reds and browns. The figures recall the simplification and Primitivism of Shevchenko or the heritage of Larionov. He was a member of AKhRR 1929-32 and taught at the Leningrad Vkhutein 1929-56.
Lit A.M.Muratov, V.Manin et al. *Zhivopis' 20-30kh godov*, Sankt-Peterburg, 1991.
Coll RM.

FREZE, Varvara Petrovna 1883-1970
Ceramics artist, illustrator. After studying at the Society for the Encouragement of the Arts in St. Petersburg 1900-4, she became a specialist in ceramics. In the post-revolutionary years she worked periodically for the State Porcelain Factory up to 1939. She also painted porcelain for the Novgorod Porcelain Trust 1924-6. She illustrated scientific publications 1939-41 and later taught at the V.I.Mukhina Central School of Industrial Design in Leningrad.
Lit N.Lobanov-Rostovsky *Revolutionary Ceramics*, London, 1990.

FRIDBERG a.1919
Graphic artist. He was a member of the Art Collegium for Literary Publishing in 1919, responsible with Kurilko for illustrations to Tolstoy and Gogol.

FRIDLENDER a.1919
He was represented along with Kandinsky, Chagall and others at the First State Exhibition of Paintings by Local and Moscow Artists held in Vitebsk in December 1919.

FRIKH-KHAR, Isidor Grigor'evich 1894-1978
Sculptor. He was a member of the Society of Russian Sculptors from 1925 and of the Union of Moscow Artists formed in 1925. He was included in the major exhibition in Moscow in 1927 marking the tenth anniversary of the Revolution and in the 1928 exhibition of Acquisitions by the State Art Collections Fund held in Moscow. He worked in a variety of media including ceramics and wood.
He exhibited at the 1932 Venice Biennale. He exhibited with Sarra Lebedeva, A.E.Zelensky, Vera Mukhina, Ilya Slonim, Vladimir Favorsky and I.M.Chaykov in Moscow in 1935. He died in Moscow
Portrait of A.S.Griboedov, 1930, wood, TG, is an example of apparently crude carving to give a primitive effect but it is in fact executed with experience, ability and an alert wit. The historic writer is even provided with wooden spectacles in this head and shoulders portrait.

FRIKKE, Loggin Khristyanovich 1820-1893
Landscape painter.
Coll TG.

FROLOV, A. a.1920s
Graphic artist. He produced numerous covers for sheet music published in the 1920s including work for the composers M.Levin, V.Kruchinin, A.Polonsky, M.Nikolaevsky and others.

FROLOVA-BAGREEVA, Lidiya Fedorovna b.1907
Sculptor.

FUFAEV, A. S. a.1919
Painter. He exhibited at the juryless Eighth State Exhibition in Moscow in 1919.

Artur Fonvizin. Horseman. *Ink drawing. 20.5 x 29 cm.*
Collection the Reverend Sergei Hackel, Sussex.

G

GABO, Sir Naum (PEVZNER, Naum or Neemia Borisovich)   **1890-1977**

Sculptor. The brother of the sculptor Antoine Pevsner. One of the pioneers of constructed sculpture frequently working with such new materials as plastics, exploring complex symmetries through geometric forms and aware of the potential of his work in terms of architecture and design. His writings clearly indicate however that sculpture for Gabo was closely based upon a study of growth in nature.

Born at Bryansk. He travelled to Munich 1910-14 to study medicine, but studied scientific mathematics and engineering. Whilst there he attended lectures by the art historian Wölfflin 1911-12 and visited the exhibitions of the *Blaue Reiter*. He also travelled in Italy 1913 and 1913-14 went to Paris to visit his brother Anton Pevsner. There he met Archipenko.

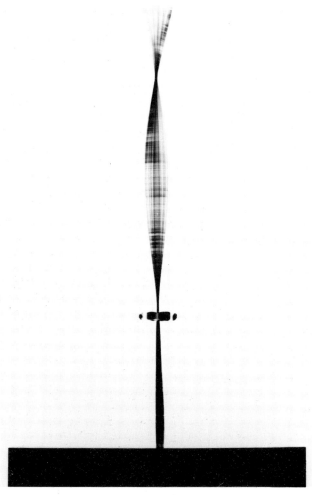

Naum Gabo. Kinetic Sculpture (Standing Wave), *1920. Wire and electric motor. 61.6 x 19.1 x 24.1 cm.*
Gabo's articulation of empty space by planar surfaces was taken to an extreme point in this experimental sculpture in which the form exists only when the sculpture vibrates. The synthesis of construction in engineering and in sculpture was a tenet of the early phases of Constructivism.
The Tate Gallery, London.

Naum Gabo. Torso, *1917. Sheet metal treated with sand. Documentary photograph.*

During the war years he was in Oslo and here he began to construct sculpture. Constructed sculpture had its origins in the work of Picasso, Braque, Laurens and Archipenko but for Gabo it became an essential method of investigation to which he could also bring his knowledge of engineering and mathematics. Not surprisingly his initial works were distinctly Cubist in appearance although the heads he constructed in Norway revealed in addition an interest in the anonymous geometric heads of certain kinds of African carving.

In 1917 he returned to Russia. By this time Tatlin had also exhibited constructed reliefs which bore no identifiable reference to recognisable imagery. Gabo's attitude rapidly emerged as distinct from that of Tatlin and was characterised by its preoccupation with mathematical structures, symmetries, new materials, transparency and architectural potential. In 1920 he exhibited on Tverskoy Boulevard in Moscow together with his brother Pevsner who was similarly exploring construction in sculpture. They published a statement of aims, *The Realistic Manifesto*, as a broadsheet to accompany the exhibition. By 1921

Andrei Gennadiev. Danger, *1978. Etching with watercolour. 29.5 x 29.5 cm.*
Roy Miles Gallery, London.

the emergence of Constructivism in Russia had become closely allied to communist ideological thinking, particularly at Moscow INKhUK. For Gabo this was not a priority. His sculpture was included in the First Russian Art Exhibition at the Van Diemen Gallery in Berlin in 1922 and Gabo emigrated at this time.

In 1923 Gabo exhibited with the *Novembergruppe* and in 1924 he exhibited with his brother Pevsner at the Galerie Percier in Paris. They also collaborated on designs for constructed sets and costumes for Diaghilev's production of Sauguet's ballet *La Chatte* 1926-7. To a degree his constructions allied the study of

Petr Galadzhev. Dancer, *c.1923. Signed.*
A lively Cubo-Futurist style gives the dancer's energetic movements. The style is typical of Galadzhev's theatrical and book illustrations.

Création, remaining a member of the group until 1935.

He settled in England in 1935 in the orbit of Ben Nicholson and the contributors to Circle. He visited the United States in 1938 but stayed in England during the war, mostly living in Cornwall.

He emigrated to the United States in 1946 and retained links in England in particular. With Pevsner he held an exhibition at the Museum of Modern Art, New York, in 1948. He became an American citizen in 1952. He was appointed Professor at Harvard University Graduate School of Architecture 1953-4. A number of monumental commissions were realised in the 1950s including the sculpture for the Bijenkorf Building, Rotterdam, in 1955.

His enormous post-war reputation as a Constructivist was challenged from the 1960s by the growing scholarship which recognised the work of Tatlin, Rodchenko, Klucis and others, but this has also revealed the uniqueness of Gabo's own achievements independent of the political aims or constraints of his Soviet contemporaries. Gabo's attitude was ultimately a philosophical one as his numerous writings have clearly and convincingly shown.

He was knighted in 1971.

Theatre design 1927 with Pevsner he designed the constructed costumes and sets for Diaghilev's production of Sobeka's *La Chatte*, a ballet based upon Aesop to music by Henri Sauguet at the Théâtre Sarah Bernhardt, Paris. First

materials with the strength of stereometric cubes, spheres and other mathematical shapes but his primary concern was the articulation of empty space by these means. Characteristically his sculptural arrangements grew outwards from a core element or focal point reaching into the space which their planes divided. This involved intricate symmetries and transformations as well as a most meticulous craftsmanship with new materials. Although much of his work was as scaleless in essence as a mathematical diagram it involved two aspects which carried the potential for architectural construction. The manipulation of materials which was not in itself a mathematical issue, and the strength of certain geometric structures that minimised solid closed masses of material in favour of a skeletal framework. He could observe this in the complex structures of natural forms and he could also apply it to constructions on a grand scale. This architectural potential was independent of stylistic influences from the architectural profession but it provided the confidence to work periodically on an architectural scale. In 1931 he submitted an ambitious project to the competition for designs for the Palace of the Soviets in Moscow. The project envisaged two enormous shell-like auditoria in which the example of natural structures played an evident role. In 1932 he settled in Paris and exhibited with the group *Abstraction-*

Petr Galadzhev. Harlequin, *1922. Signed.*
Poster for the ballet 'Arlekin' (Harlequin) performed by the State Choreographic Workshops. Stylistically this design recalls the dynamic effects of Exter and the elegance of Chekhonin's graphic work.

performed at Monte Carlo.
Lit Extensive including: N.Gabo *Of Divers Arts*, Washington, 1959. H.Read and L.Martin *Naum Gabo*, Neuchâtel, 1961. C.Lodder *Russian Constructivism*, New Haven and London, 1983.
Coll Gabo's work features in numerous major museums internationally including: MOMA, New York; MNAM, Paris; Musée de l'Opera, Paris; Tate Gallery, London.

GABRIKOV, Rodion Alekseevich   1887-1965
Painter. Born in Belorussia. In 1918 he collaborated with S.F.Simkhovich on Agitprop decorations for Tuchkov Bridge, Petrograd. He died at Kishinev.

GAGARIN   a.1911
A Gagarin exhibited with the World of Art 1911-12.

GAGARIN, Grigori Grigorevich   1810-1893
Battle painter and illustrator. Born at St. Petersburg. He was a remarkable portrait draughtsman as his *Portrait of Cholokaeva*, 1840s, pencil, RM, reveals with its Ingresque line depicting a young woman of South Russian appearance. The effect is both severely controlled and exotic. He also depicted scenes from Russian history. He died at Châtellerault.
Coll TG.

GAGEN, Dominik Ernestovich   1810s-1876
Portrait painter.
Coll TG.

GAKhN
The abbreviated name of the State Academy of Artistic Sciences (*Gosudarstvennaya akademiya khudozhestvennykh nauk*).

GALADZHEV, Petr Stepanovich   1900-1971
Theatre designer, graphic designer. Born at Staryy Krym. He designed *Fantasy*, choreographed by K.Goleizovsky to music by Skryabin, for the Chamber Ballet in Moscow in 1922, and produced designs for the Lukin Ballet Studio in Moscow in the period 1921-2. He designed the cover, in black, yellow and white, of the sheet music of Matvei Blantner's *Zolara*, Moscow, 1926. This design included a stylised vignette of an elegant couple set within the grid of a chequerboard motif. He died in Moscow.
Lit Nancy Van Norman Baer *Theatre in Revolution, Russian Avant-Garde Stage Design 1913-1935*, San Francisco and London, 1991.
Coll Central Cinema Museum, Moscow.

GALAKTIONOV, Stepan Filippovich   1779-1854
Painter.
Coll TG.

GAL'BERG, Samuil Ivanovich   1787-1839
Neo-classical sculptor of portrait busts and monumental works. He studied under I.P.Martos and executed a bronze bust of Martos in 1837, RM. He was in Rome on an Academy scholarship 1819-21 and was an admirer of the Danish neo-classical sculptor Thorwaldsen. His monumental figures include *G.R.Derzhavin* at Kazan and *N.M.Karamzin* at Simbirsk. Characteristically his portrait busts surmount a column in the ancient herm format. The result sometimes looks distinctly Roman and sometimes is obviously a carving of the contemporary city dweller.
Bust of A.N.Olenin, 1831, marble, recalls the sheer control of Canova but lacks his formal precision and appears softer in its

finish. It is however alert in expression and an example of academic professionalism of a high order.
Coll Well represented at RM; TG.

GAL'VICH, V. A.   a.1919-1920
He exhibited at the First Exhibition of Works of the Professional Union of Artists in Moscow in 1918 and at the juryless Eighth State Exhibition in Moscow in 1919. He appeared on the April 1919 list of artists for acquisitions by the envisaged Museum of Painterly Culture. He was represented at the enormous First State Exhibition of Art and Science, which included ethnographic material, held in Kazan in 1920.

GAMPEL'N, Karl Karlovich   1794-1880+
Painter.
Coll TG.

GAMREKELI, Irakliy Il'ich   1894-1943
Georgian theatre designer. Born at Gori. He was studying under B.Fogel and B.Shebuev at the Sklifasovsky School of Art in Tblisi (Tiflis) in 1908. In 1921 he was appointed designer to the Rustaveli Theatre in Tblisi. He was associated with Georgian Futurist activities in 1927. He died at Tblisi.
Theatre design 1928 S.I.Shanshiashvili's play *Anzor* at the Shota Rustaveli Theatre, Tblisi. This features an architectural assemblage of steps and platforms resembling a ziggurat.
Lit N.Gudiashvili *I.Gamrekeli*, Moscow, 1958. *Paris-Moscou*, 1979. Dzhon Boult (John Bowlt) *Khudozhniki russkogo teatra: Sobranie Nikity i Niny Lobanovykh-Rostovskikh*, Moscow, 1991.
Coll Bakhrushin Theatre Museum, Moscow.

GAN, Aleksei Mikhailovich   1893-1942
Theoretician, designer. A theorist of Constructivism who collaborated with Rodchenko and others, evolving the politicised extension of Constructivism into utilitarian design in the early 1920s. He worked in the Theatre Section of the People's Commissariat of the Enlightenment (TEO Narkompros) from 1918 to 1920. Together with Aleksandr Drevin, Aleksandr Rodchenko and Varvara Stepanova he formed the group

Petr Galadzhev. Set design of A.M.Fayko's play 'Lake Lyul', *1923. Drawing. Signed in cyrillic 'P.S.G.' lower right*

Aleksandr Golovin. Woman Sewing, *1914. Tempera and pastel on canvas. Signed in cyrillic 'A.Golovin'. 145.5 x 151.6 cm. Malmö Konstmuseum.*

Askranov (the Association of Extreme Innovators) in January 1919. He seems to have been dismissed from TEO Narkompros by Lunacharsky for his extreme ideological position.

He was a member of the Institute of Artistic Culture (INKhUK) in Moscow in 1921 where he was a founder member of the First Working Group of Constructivists. He executed a number of designs for Constructivist street kiosks. His assertive and declamatory book *Konstruktivizm* (Constructivism), published in Tver in 1922, was the result of his close involvement with the politicised Constructivist circle at the Moscow INKhUK and it loudly proclaimed the death of art. He was also associated with several periodicals editing *Kino-Fot* (Cinema-Photo) 1922-3, *Sovremennaya Arkhitektura*

(Contemporary Architecture) and *Lef* (Left). He exhibited with the First Working Group of Constructivsts in 1924 at the First Discussional Exhibition of Active Revolutionary Art alongside L.Sanina, G.Miller, Olga and Galina Chichagova, N.G.Smirnov and A.Mirolyubova. He contributed to the First Exhibition of Cinema Posters held in Moscow in 1925.

In 1927 he organised the First International Exhibition of Contemporary Architecture. He was a member of the October group 1928-32.

Book design Cover for the periodical *S.A.: Sovremmenaya Arkhitektura* (C.A.: Contemporary Architecture), No.2, 1926.

Writings include A.Gan *Konstruktivizm*, Tver, 1922. A.Gan *Fakty za nas* (The Facts are on Our Side) in *S.A.*, No.2, 1926.

Natalya Goncharova. Rabbi with Cat, *1912. Oil on canvas. 100 x 92 cm.*
Scottish National Gallery of Modern Art.

A.Gan *Shto takoe Konstruktivizm?* (What is Constructivism?) in
S.A., No.3, 1928.
Lit C.Lodder *Russian Constructivism*, New Haven and London,
1983. S.Compton *Russian Avant-Garde Books 1917-34*,
London, 1992.

GANF, Yuliy Abramovich   **1898-1927+**
Graphic artist. He participated in the seventh exhibition of the
group *L'Araignée* (The Spider) at the Galerie Devambe in Paris

in 1925 and was included in the major exhibition in Moscow in
1927 marking the tenth anniversary of the Revolution.

GAPONENKO, Taras Gur'evich   **1906-1935+**
Painter. Born Smolensk region. He was involved in decorating
the Vkhutein Club, Moscow, c.1928. He produced monumental
genre painting of a Socialist Realist tendentiousness.
*Feeding Time with the Mothers, 1935, TG, shows a cart of
sunlit, healthy babies arriving in a cornfield where their

Aleksandr Gaush. Gondolas, *c.1913. Oil on canvas. 102 x 134 cm. Malmö Konstmuseum.*

vigorous mothers break with delight from their agricultural labours to greet and feed their babies.
Coll TG.

GARSHIN, V. M. 1855-1888

GAUCHE = GAUSH, L. N.

GAUSH, Aleksandr Fedorovich 1873-1947
Landscape and still-life painter. Born at St. Petersburg. He studied under Chistyakov at the Academy in St. Petersburg 1893-9. A founder member of the New Society of Artists with whom he exhibited 1904-7. He also exhibited with the Blue Rose group and *Venok* (The Wreath) in St. Petersburg in 1909, with the Union of Youth in 1910 and with the Union of Russian Artists in 1910. He exhibited a decorative triptych with the Izdebsky Salon of 1910-11 in Odessa. He joined the World of Art in 1911. He became the Keeper of the Museum of Old St. Petersburg in 1912.
After the Revolution he participated in the First State Free Exhibition of Artworks in Petrograd in 1919 and his name appeared on the April 1919 list of artists for acquisitions by the envisaged Museum of Painterly Culture. He was represented at the First Russian Art Exhibition in Berlin in 1922 and also at the exhibition of Studies for Theatre Decoration and Works from the Studios of the Decorative Institute 1919-1923 held in Petrograd in 1922. He was included in the enormous survey Exhibition of Paintings by Petrograd Artists of All Tendencies 1919-1923 held in Petrograd in 1923. In 1924 he was a founder of the Petrushka Theatre in Leningrad but he moved that year to Odessa.
In 1935 he moved to the Crimea. He contributed to the exhibition of Contemporary Russian Art held at Philadelphia in 1932. He died at Simferopol.
Lit *Twilight of the Tsars*, London, 1991. J.Howard *The Union of Youth — An Artists' Society of the Russian Avant-Garde*, Manchester and New York, 1992.
Coll TG; RM.

GAUSH (GAUCHE), Lyubov' Nikolaevna 1877-1943
Ceramics artist, painter. She completed her studies at the Society for the Encouragement of the Arts in St. Petersburg in 1909 and later attended the Académie Julian in Paris. She exhibited from 1909 contributing to the World of Art, the K.Kostandi Association and she exhibited with the Union of Youth in 1910. She was employed at the State Porcelain Factory in 1919-22.
Lit N.Lobanov-Rostovsky *Revolutionary Ceramics*, London, 1990.

GAVRILOV, Vladimir Nikolaevich 1923-1970
Socialist Realist. Born in Moscow where he also died.

GAVRILOVICH, Sergei 1897-1967
Graduated from the Vkhutemas in 1924 and subsequently worked on Soviet Exhibition Pavilions at New York, Leipzig and elsewhere.

GAY, N. N. = GE, N. N.

GE (GUE, GAY), Nikolai Nikolaevich 1831-1894
Painter of biblical and historical themes and portraits. Born at Voronezh to a family of French descent. He grew up on the family estate in the Ukraine. He studied at the St. Petersburg Academy from 1850 to 1857 when he won the first gold medal and a travelling scholarship. His *Last Supper*, 1863, RM, which was exhibited at the Academy in 1863, employs a concealed light source reminiscent of Caravaggio or Rembrandt to heighten the dramatic tension. He became a painter of force and originality who used loose expressive brushwork to drive home the emotive and often religious message of his paintings. He painted a portrait of *Herzen* in 1867.
He was a founder member of the Wanderers but lived largely in Florence until 1869.
Major works painted after his return to St. Petersburg include *Peter the Great Interrogating the Tsarevich Aleksei Petrovich at Peterhof*, 1871, TG, which is a finely finished historicist genre painting. He taught at the Moscow College.
He subsequently withdrew from teaching, retired to his estate

in the Ukraine and from 1882 became a follower of Tolstoy whose portrait he executed in 1884. There is a sculpture by Ge in the Russian Museum which is a bronze bust of *Tolstoy* of 1890, frontal and stiff but still intense with long beard and peasant shirt. His later painting was intensely dramatic and emotional. *Golgotha*, 1892-3, is an example of his loose and fiercely expressive late technique.

What is Truth ?, 1890, TG, highlights the dramatic encounter of Christ and Pilate. Pilate wearing a toga stands with his back to the viewer in contrast to Christ, poorly dressed, long-haired and gaunt. There is no superfluous distraction in the painting. Christ, in the shadows, is intense and self-contained.

Golgotha, 1892-3, TG, is intensely and frighteningly dramatic. Very loose, expressive handling activates the entire canvas and is articulated so that the relative importance of specific figures is brought out by resolving the rougher paintwork into a higher degree of finish. Here the scumbled background is wholly vague but from it emerge the shadowy silhouettes of a group of soldiers. A further subsidiary figure of a priest is given more substance at one side, so that the handling of the paint itself leads the eye forward to focus upon the intense drama of the central trio of the figures of the two thieves, and absolutely in the centre, Jesus who holds up his hands to his head in suffering. All of this is lit as if by a raking spotlight: the upturned face of Christ is thrown into sharply focused relief, and the central group casts a deep shadow upon the ground. Finally at left the pointing arm of accusation and authority stands out with equal force in a decisive gesture

Nikolai Ge. Golgotha, *1892-3. Oil on canvas. 222.4 x 191.8 cm. State Tretyakov Gallery, Moscow.*

Natalya Goncharova. Costume Design for Saint Mark from 'Liturgie'. *Gouache au pochoir, unframed. Signed within the image, signed again in pencil on the margin and dated 'Lausanne 1915'. 64 x 39 cm.*
Reproduced by kind permission of Sotheby's London, sale 28.11.1991, lot 452.

Natalya Goncharova. Costume Design for an Apostle from 'Liturgie'. *Gouache au pochoir, unframed. Signed on the margin and dated '1915'. 64 x 39 cm.*
Reproduced by kind permission of Sotheby's London, sale 28.11.1991, lot 453.

worthy of the theatre. Everything in Ge's painting reinforces the intense emotion of the event. He was unique in this respect in his day, recalling perhaps only Max Liebermann amongst contemporaries, but even here the comparison is inexact: Ge's painterly approach is academic in his grasp of drawing and proportion, but utterly unacademic in the rough, unresolved finish of his works. His techniques found no real parallel in the 19th century.

Coll Major holdings at TG; RM; Russian Art Museum, Kiev.

GELLER, Petr Isaakovich   1862-1933
Academic history and military painter. He studied at the St. Petersburg Academy in 1878-87.

After the Revolution he participated in the First State Free Exhibition of Artworks in Petrograd in 1919 and was included in the enormous survey Exhibition of Paintings by Petrograd Artists of All Tendencies 1919-1923 held in Petrograd in 1923.

GEL'MAN, Maks Isaevich (Isayovich)   b.1892
Ukrainian sculptor. Born at Odessa.

GEL'TSER, Anatoliy Fedorovich   1852-1918
Theatre designer.

GENKE (-SHIFRINA), Margarita Genrikhovna 1889-1954
Theatre designer. She was still designing for the theatre in 1954.

GENNADIEV, Andrei   b.1947
Painter, graphic artist. He became a member of the Artists' Union in 1978. His paintings have concentrated upon depictions of the city of St. Petersburg and have reflected 18th century engravings of the city. He has illustrated Gogol's tale *The Nose*.

Coll. Metropolitan Museum, New York; Roy Miles Gallery, London.

Colour plate p.153.

GERASIMOV, Aleksandr Mikhailovich   1881-1963
Socialist Realist painter. His work was included in the exhibition of Soviet art held at Harbin in 1926 and in Japan in

Nikolai Ge. Christ and His Disciples Leaving Gethsemane after the Last Supper (preliminary study), *1888. Oil on canvas. 65.3 x 85 cm. State Tretyakov Gallery, Moscow.*

1927 and in the major exhibition in Moscow in 1927 marking the tenth anniversary of the Revolution. He was represented in the First Touring Exhibition of Paintings and Graphics which opened in Moscow in 1929 and at the jubilee exhibition Artists of the RSFSR over 15 Years held at the Russian Museum, Leningrad, in 1932.

*His patriotic propaganda piece *Lenin on the Tribune*, 1930, shows a monumental figure of Lenin crossed by diagonal red flags with the additional red flags of the masses glimpsed below.

Writings A.Gerasimov *Za sotsialisticheskii realizm*, Moscow, 1952. A.Gerasimov *Zhizn' khudozhnika*, Moscow, 1963.

Coll TG; RM.

GERASIMOV, Sergei Vasil'evich　　　　**1885-1964**
Painter. Born at Mozhaisk. He studied at the Stroganov Institute under K.Korovin and S.Ivanov 1901-7 and then at the Moscow College 1907-12. He was exhibiting by 1911. He taught at the typography department of the I.D.Sytin Society 1912-14 and 1917-23.

After the Revolution he was engaged on Agitprop decorations in Moscow. His decorations of the State Duma building, now the Lenin Museum, featured a gigantic peasant and banner, easily intelligible but executed in a loosely Futurist style, set against the sky and accompanied by corn and fruit.

His work was included in the First Exhibition of Works of the Professional Union of Artists in Moscow in 1918 and in the First Exhibition of the Moscow Contemporary Art Store in January 1919. His name appeared on the April 1919 list of artists for acquisitions by the envisaged Museum of Painterly Culture. He was represented along with Kandinsky, Chagall and others at the First State Exhibition of Paintings by Local and Moscow Artists held in Vitebsk in December 1919 and he participated in the Third Exhibition of Paintings held at Ryazan in 1919.

He taught at the Vkhutemas in 1920 and was engaged on the decoration of the Agitprop trains *Red Cossack*, Ukrainian *Lenin* and *Soviet Cossack*. In 1921 he exhibited with the revived World of Art. He was represented at the First Russian Art Exhibition in Berlin in 1922. He then joined the *Makovets* group, exhibiting with them 1922-5. He visited Italy, Greece and Turkey and participated in the seventh exhibition of the group *L'Araignée* (The Spider) at the Galerie Devambe in Paris in 1925. His work was included in the exhibition of Soviet art held at Harbin in 1926 and in Japan in 1927 and in the major exhibition in Moscow in 1927 marking the tenth anniversary of the Revolution. He exhibited with the Society of Moscow Artists 1927-9 and was included in the 1928 exhibition of Acquisitions by the State Art Collections Fund held in Moscow. He was represented in the exhibition of Russian Graphics at Riga and in the First Touring Exhibition of Paintings and Graphics which opened in Moscow in 1929. He was represented at the jubilee exhibition Artists of the RSFSR over 15 Years held at the Russian Museum, Leningrad, in 1932. He exhibited in Moscow together with Sarra Lebedeva, A.A.Deineka, P.P.Konchalovsky, Vera Mukhina and D.A.Shmarinov in 1943. He died in Moscow.

*ature*Peasant of the Earth*, 1918, watercolour, a study for revolutionary street decorations in which a rather Cubist peasant marches with his banner. The study is squared up ready for transfer on to a large-scale decoration.

The Oath of the Siberian Partisans, 1933, RM, a heavy, grim and monumental propaganda painting.

Collective Farm Holiday, 1936-7, TG, is a Socialist Realist idyll on the theme of the workers' holiday in which all is bathed in sunlight so that even the worker's bicycle glistens.

Lit S.Razumovskaya *S.V.Gerasimov*, Moscow, 1936. S.Razumovskaya *S.V.Gerasimov*, 1951. *S.V.Gerasimov*, exh. cat., Moscow, 1966. *Gerasimov Album*, Leningrad, 1975. *Paris-Moscou*, 1979.

Coll TG; RM.

GERASIMOVICH, Iosif Vasil'evich　　　**1894-1932+**
Graphic designer. His birthdate is sometimes given as 1893. He contributed to the First Exhibition of Cinema Posters held in Moscow in 1925 and to the Second Exhibition of Cinema Posters held at the Kamerny (Chamber) Theatre, Moscow, in 1926. He designed posters, rather in the style of the Stenberg Brothers, for the films *Prince Charming* in 1929 and *Glory of the World* in 1932.

GERMANSHEV (BUBELO), Mikhail Markianovich (Mikhailovich)　　　　**1868-1920**
Landscape painter. Born at Kharkov. He studied at the Moscow College. He exhibited at the juryless Eighth State Exhibition in Moscow in 1919. He emigrated to France.

Coll TG.

GERTS, Konstant Karlovich　　　　**1826?-1879**
Painter of views.

Coll TG.

GILLET, Nicolas-François, (ZHILLE, Nikola) 1709-1791
French sculptor. Born at Metz. He became the first long-standing Director of the Imperial Academy of Art in 1758. His sculpture included a marble bust of *Peter I* after the bronze by Rastrelli the Elder. He was teaching at the Academy in St. Petersburg in the 1760s where his pupils, including Feodosii Shchedrin and Mikhail Kozlovsky, showed strong neo-classical traits.

He returned to France in 1777. He died in Paris.

Painting, 1758-60, RM, is a personification of painting as a young woman weaving laurels.

Coll TG; RM; Museum of the Academy, St. Petersburg; Hermitage Museum; Louvre.

GINE, Aleksandr Vasil'evich　　　　**1830-1880**
Painter.

Coll TG.

GINKhUK
The abbreviated name of the State Institute of Artistic Culture (*Gosudarstvennyi institut khudozhestvennoi kul'tury*) in Petrograd.

GINTSBURG, Il'ya Yakovlevich　　　　**1859-1939**
Sculptor. Born at Grodno. He studied under M.M.Antokolsky in St. Petersburg 1871-8 and at the Academy from 1878. He executed monumental and smaller genre sculptures and was close to the Wanderers. He exhibited from 1884 and was represented at the Paris International Exhibitions of 1889 and 1900. His portrait busts included *Kramskoy*, 1886, TG, *Lev Tolstoy*, 1891, Perm Art Gallery, *Aivazovsky*, 1898, and *M.M.Antokolsky*, 1901, RM.

After the Revolution he taught at the Vkhutemas 1918-23. He joined AKhRR in 1923. He made a portrait sculpture of the painter *Repin* in 1925. He was a member of the Kuindzhi Society 1929-30. He died in Leningrad.

Tolstoy Writing at his Desk, 1891, bronze, RM, is a small scale

Natalya Goncharova. Costume for Shah Shariar, *1922. Gouache, gold, silver and pencil. Signed lower right 'N.Gontcharova'. 41.3 x 27.5 cm.*
A design for Diaghilev's production of 'Les Noces d'Aurore' or 'Le Mariage de la Belle au Bois Dormant', an extract from the ballet 'La Belle au Bois Dormant' (Sleeping Beauty) performed at the Paris Opera in May 1922.
Collection Mr. and Mrs. Nikita D.Lobanov-Rostovsky, London.

full-length complete with table and chair showing the writer at work.
*V.V.Vereshchagin, 1892, bronze, RM, similarly shows the painter about his business at the easel with a portfolio leaning against it.
Coll TG; RM; Museum of the Academy of Art, St. Petersburg; Museum of Russian Art, Kiev; Perm Art Gallery; Sevastopol Art Museum.

GINTSLING, Esfir' Mikhailovna　　　　**b.1904**
Ceramic artist. She studied under Tatlin in the Ceramics Faculty of the Moscow Vkhutein. She became an Honoured Art Worker of the USSR.

GIPPIUS (HIPPIUS), Natal'ya Nikolaevna　　　**1880-1941+**
Sculptor. She was the sister of the poet Zinaida Gippius. She studied under V.A.Beklemishev at the Academy in St. Petersburg between 1903 and 1912. In 1908 she contributed to the exhibitions Modern Trends and The Link in Kiev. She participated in the Spring exhibitions at the Academy 1913-17.

GIRSHFELD, Natal'ya A.　　　　**a.1919-1922**
Ceramics artist. She worked at the State Porcelain Factory in 1919-22.
Lit. N.Lobanov-Rostovsky *Revolutionary Ceramics*, London, 1990.

Boris Grigoriev. The Peasant Family, *1923. Oil on canvas laid down on board. 89 x 175 cm.*
Reproduced by kind permission of Christie's London, sale 27.11.1991, lot 209.

GLADYSHEV, Vladimir Petrovich   1898-1919+
He exhibited at the Twelfth State Exhibition: Colourdynamo
and Tectonic Primitivism (*XII Gosudarstvennaya vystavka.
Tsvetodinamos i tektonichesky primitivizm*) in Moscow in 1919
along with Grishchenko, Shevchenko and others.

GLAGOL' = SERGEEVICH, S. S.

GLAGOLEVA (-UL'YANOVA), Anna Semenovna
1873-c.1944
Painter. She contributed to the *Stefanos* exhibition 1907-8 in
Moscow.
After the Revolution she was represented in the Fourth State
Exhibition of Paintings (*IV Gosudarstvennaya vystavka kartin*)
in Moscow in 1919. She exhibited with the 4 Arts society in
Moscow from 1925.

GLAZUNOV, Aleksandr Aleksandrovich   1884-1952
He was active in Agitprop projects particularly the decoration
of propaganda trains including *The Red Cossack*, Ukrainian
Lenin and *Soviet Caucasus* c.1920. Designs on *The Red Cossack*
train showed a landowner bridled like a horse and whipped by
peasants. He was represented at the Paris International
Exhibition of 1925.
See Kostyanitsyn.

GLEBOV, Aleksei Konstantinovich   1908-1968
Belorussian monumental sculptor who also made Socialist
Realist genre pieces. Born Smolensk region. He produced
monumental sculptures including *The Liberation of Belorussia* of
1939. Other works included the two-piece figure composition
Gorky and Kupala, 1948. He died at Minsk.

GLEBOVA, Tat'yana Nikolaevna   1900-1932+
Painter. She was a member of Filonov's school, the Collective of
Masters of Analytical Art, established in Leningrad in 1925. She
was represented at the jubilee exhibition Artists of the RSFSR
over 15 Years held at the Russian Museum, Leningrad, in 1932.

GLEBOVA-SUDEYKINA, O. A.   a.1932
She was represented at the jubilee exhibition Artists of the
RSFSR over 15 Years held at the Russian Museum, Leningrad,
in 1932.

GLOVACHEVSKY = GOLOVACHEVSKY, K. I.

GLUSKIN, Aleksandr Mikhailovich   1899-1969
Painter. He was a founder member of the New Society of
Painters (NOZh) formed in 1922. He was represented at the
jubilee exhibition Artists of the RSFSR over 15 Years held at
the Russian Museum, Leningrad, in 1932.

GOGOLINSKY, Nil Alekseevich   1844-1895
Theatre designer. He produced designs for Gogol's *Revizor*
(The Government Inspector) in 1868.

GOL'DINA   a.1926
Sculptor and a member of the Society of Russian Sculptors
from 1926.

GOL'DINGER, Ekaterina Vasil'evna   1881-1973
Graphic artist, painter. She was represented in the Fourth
State Exhibition of Paintings (*IV Gosudarstvennaya vystavka
kartin*) in Moscow in 1919 and at the enormous First State
Exhibition of Art and Science, which included ethnographic
material, held in Kazan in 1920. She also showed work in the
major exhibition in Moscow in 1927 marking the tenth
anniversary of the Revolution and was represented at the
jubilee exhibition Artists of the RSFSR over 15 Years held at
the Russian Museum, Leningrad, in 1932.

GOLEIZOVSKY (GOLEYZOVSKY), Kasian   1892-1970
Choreographer, dance costume designer. Born in Moscow.
He was choreographer to the Chamber Ballet in Moscow and
he produced designs for the ballet *The Tragedy of the Masks*,
which he also choreographed, in 1922. A design for Harlequin
is dynamic, elegant and evidently balletic, faintly reminiscent
of the theatricality of Bakst or Erté. He contributed to the

Illarion Golitsyn. Portrait of Mansurova, *1970. Wood engraving. 57 x 41 cm.*
The print shows that Favorsky's impact upon printmaking in Russia was long lasting and open to considerable stylistic variety. Here the interplay of light and shade enlivens the whole composition and evokes the vitality of the sitter within the lamplit interior of the room.

second exhibition of *Iskusstvo dvizheniya* (Art of Movement) held in Moscow in 1926. He died in Moscow.
Lit Nancy Van Norman Baer *Theatre in Revolution, Russian Avant-Garde Stage Design 1913-1935*, San Francisco and London, 1991.
Coll Bakhrushin Theatre Museum, Moscow.

GOLENKINA, Alisa Rudolfovna　　　　**1884-1970**
Ceramics artist, illustrator. Born at St. Petersburg. Some sources give 1892 as her birthdate. She completed her studies at the Stieglitz School of Design in St. Petersburg in 1910 and worked at the State Porcelain Factory as a painter and designer from 1919 to 1924. A plate of 1922 depicts a red horseman above the flaming ruins of the past, with the inscription around the rim 'We shall set the world ablaze with the fire of the Third International'. She later worked as an illustrator to the All-Russian Institute of Botany.
Lit N.Lobanov-Rostovsky *Revolutionary Ceramics*, London, 1990. *Paris-Moscou*, 1979.

GOLIKE, Vasili (Wilhelm-August) Aleksandrovich 1802-1848
Portrait painter.
Coll TG.

GOLIKOVA, V M.　　　　　　　　　　　**a.1918**
She was represented at the First Exhibition of Works of the Professional Union of Artists in Moscow in 1918.

GOLITSYN, Illarion Vladimirovich　　　**1928-1965+**
Graphic artist and printmaker. Born in Moscow. Like G.F.Zakharov he was much impressed by the example of Favorsky. His *Morning at Favorsky's House*, 1965, TG, is a print which pays direct homage to Favorsky in both subject and technique.
Coll TG.

GOLOPOLOSOV, Boris Aleksandrovich　　**1900-1983**
Painter. He was included in the major exhibition in Moscow in 1927 marking the tenth anniversary of the Revolution and in the 1928 exhibition of Acquisitions by the State Art Collections Fund held in Moscow. He was represented in the First Touring Exhibition of Paintings and Graphics which opened in Moscow in 1929. He died in Moscow.

GOLOSHCHAPOV, Nikolai Nikolaevich　　**1889-1968**
Born in Moscow where he also died. He assisted in the decoration of the Café Pittoresque with Yakulov, Tatlin, Rodchenko and others 1917-18.

GOLOUSHEV, S. = SERGEEVICH, S. S.

GOLOVA, L. G.　　　　　　　　　　　　**a.1918**
She worked with Yakulov, Tatlin and others on decorations at the Café Pittoresque, Moscow, in 1918.

GOLOVACHEVSKY (GLOVACHEVSKY),
Kirill Ivanovich　　　　　　　　　　　**1735-1823**
Painter.
Coll TG.

GOLOVANOV, Aleksandr Sergeevich　　　**1901-1930**
He exhibited at the Twelfth State Exhibition: Colourdynamo and Tectonic Primitivism (*XII Gosudarstvennaya vystavka. Tsvetodinamos i tektonichesky primitivizm*) in Moscow in 1919 along with Grishchenko, Shevchenko and others.

GOLOVANOV (EFIMOV-GOLOVANOV),
Mikhail Efimovich　　　　　　　　　　　**d.1880**
Painter.
Coll TG.

GOLOVIN, Aleksandr Yakovlevich　　　　**1863-1930**
Painter, major theatre designer, graphic artist. Born in Moscow. He studied at the Moscow College, initially in architecture and subsequently in painting under Polenov, V.Makovsky and I.Pryanishnikov 1881-9. In 1889 he was studying under Jacques-Emile Blanche and Simone in Paris. He visited Italy, France and Spain in 1895. In 1897 he was at the Witte studio in Paris under R.Collain and O.Meerson. He began to produce theatre designs from 1897. He designed a Russian Dining Room for Yakunchikova in 1898. He exhibited with the World of Art 1899-1907. He settled in St. Petersburg in 1901. He produced decorations for the Abramtsevo colony workshops 1899-1900 and designed the Crafts Pavilion at the Paris International Exhibition of 1900 in collaboration with K.Korovin.
In 1901 he moved from Moscow to St. Petersburg and became a member of the World of Art in 1902 having exhibited with them from 1899 and having designed covers for the *World of Art* periodical. He acted as adviser to the Imperial Theatres between 1902 and 1917 and became principal designer in 1908. He was represented in Diaghilev's display of Russian art at the 1906 Salon d'Automne in Paris and he designed major

projects for Diaghilev from 1908. He executed a number of Spanish scenes and portraits in the period 1908-11. He exhibited with the World of Art in 1911 and was made an Academician in 1912.

After the Revolution he participated in the First State Free Exhibition of Artworks in Petrograd in 1919 and was represented at the enormous First State Exhibition of Art and Science, which included ethnographic material, held in Kazan in 1920. He was also represented at the exhibition of Studies for Theatre Decoration and Works from the Studios of the Decorative Institute held in Petrograd in 1922 and included in the enormous survey Exhibition of Paintings by Petrograd Artists of All Tendencies held in Petrograd in 1919-1923. In 1925 he was designing for the theatre in Odessa. He was represented at the jubilee exhibition Artists of the RSFSR over 15 Years held at the Russian Museum, Leningrad, in 1932. He died at Detskoe Selo, Leningrad.

Portrait of Fedor Chaliapine as Holophernes in Serov's Opera 'Judith', 1908, TG, perfectly exemplifies the fusion of theatre design and painting which characterises a whole section of World of Art work. This independent work could serve equally well as a study for the performance, as a record of it or as a portrait of the celebrated singer. This mode of painting scarcely existed in the West after the 18th century with anything like the vigour with which it was pursued in Russia. Chaliapine reclines on his bed, fully clad in the savage robes

Aleksandr Golovin. Costume for Tamara Karsavina as the Firebird, *1910. Watercolour and pencil. Signed in Russian 'A.Golov' lower right. 35 x 26.7 cm. Collection Mr. and Mrs. Nikita D. Lobanov-Rostovsky, London.*

Iosif Gurvich. Spring on the Boulevard, *1965. Oil on canvas. 63.1 x 83.8 cm.*
Roy Miles Gallery, London.

and long beard of his rôle. The portrait capitalises on the common theme of play-acting and narrative in both theatre and in painting.

Birches, 1908-10, TG, is reminiscent of Klimt in its mosaic-like profusion of brushmarks assembled into a dense pattern of closely related colours. Almost the whole painting is executed in greens with the blue-white of the tree trunks embedded within the spangled effect of grass and leaves. He was a painter of great facility in both drawing and the decorative application of colour. A comparable effect was achieved in *Neskuchny Garden in Moscow*, 1920s, Radishev Art Museum, Saratov.

Portrait of the Director Vsevolod Meyerhold, 1917, Theatre Museum, Leningrad, is a clever and ambiguous work which provides two views of Meyerhold, one as he turns to face the painter and another, immediately adjacent and overlapped by the first, which is his reflection which appears to turn away to peer at the stage. Meyerhold is clad in a white smock, black bow-tie and a kind of soft red fez, very much the experienced and alert but practical intellectual.

Theatre design 1900 Dargomyzhsky's *Rusalka* .

1900 October A.Koroshchenko's opera *Ledyanoy dom* (The Ice House) at the Bolshoi Theatre, Moscow.

1900 December Minkus' *Don Quixote* at the Bolshoi Theatre, Moscow.

1901 January Chaikovsky's *Swan Lake* at the Bolshoi Theatre, Moscow.

1901 October Rimsky-Korsakov's *Pskovityanka* (The Maid of Pskov) at the Bolshoi Theatre, Moscow: the set for the Prologue (TG) showed the yellow interior of a wooden house constructed of massive beams and logs, with peasant furniture and a distant view through the small window.

1901 César Cui's *The Mandarin's Son* at the New Theatre, Moscow.

1902 Chaikovsky's *Swan Lake* (Act 3) at the Chinese Theatre, Tsarskoe Selo, Rimsky-Korsakov's *Mozart and Salieri* and Anton Rubinstein's *Demon* at the Mariinsky Theatre, St. Petersburg.

1903 A.Koreshchenko's *Magic Mirror* at the Mariinsky Theatre, St. Petersburg, and Gounod's *Faust* (Act 3) at the Hermitage Theatre, St. Petersburg.

1904 Glinka's *Ruslan and Ludmila* at the Mariinsky Theatre, St. Petersburg.

1905 Ibsen's *Lady from the Sea* (Daughter of the Sea) at the Aleksandrinsky Theatre, St. Petersburg: a set design for Dr. Vangel's Garden (Bakhrushin Theatre Museum) presents a vast open space among the fjords with a house and lawn perched by the water's edge.

1905 Wagner's *Rheingold* at the Mariinsky Theatre, St. Petersburg.

1906 Sophocles' *Antigone* at the Aleksandrinsky Theatre and Chaikovsky's *Awakening of Flora* at the Mariinsky Theatre, St. Petersburg.

1907 Glazunov's *The Seasons* at the Mariinsky Theatre, Ibsen's *Little Eyolf* at the Aleksandrinsky Theatre and Rimsky-Korsakov's *Tale of Tsar Saltan* at the Mariinsky Theatre, St. Petersburg.

1908 September Knut Hamsun's *At the Gate of the Kingdom* at the Aleksandrinsky Theatre, St. Petersburg: a set for Careno's room (Bakhrushin Theatre Museum) is an elegantly simple interior with large serliana windows looking out on to extensive grounds.

1908 Bizet's *Carmen* at the Mariinsky Theatre, St. Petersburg.

1908 Sets in collaboration with Benois for Diaghilev's production of *Boris Godunov* at the Paris Opera, costumes by Bilibin. The sets were executed by Yuon, Lansere, Anisfel'd, Yaremich and others.

1910 D'Annunzio's *La Città Morta* at the Aleksandrinsky Theatre, St. Petersburg.

1910 November Meyerhold's production of Molière's *Don Juan* at the Aleksandrinsky Theatre, St. Petersburg, with music by J.F. Rameau. This featured an immensely elegant and elaborately decorative backdrop of a pseudo-18th century interior. It employed all the skill of the World of Art designer in its fusion of almost stiffling rhythmic patterned profusion, its sheer refinement and its sense of history reinterpreted into a luxurious fantasy.

1910 The first staging of Stravinsky's *Firebird* (*Zhar-ptitsa*; *L'Oiseau de feu*) produced by Diaghilev at the Théâtre de l'Opéra, Paris: set designs for Kashchei's Kingdom, TG, were of unsurpassable profusion and splendour in an overwhelming and densely intricate mass of turquoise, green and bronze paint employed to depict palace, gardens, monuments and trees. This must have been a *coup-de-théâtre* in itself. Sections of it recall the supressed but rich and original colour of Vuillard but the whole effect is pure World of Art.

1911 January Meyerhold's production of Mussorgsky's *Boris Godunov* at the Mariinsky Theatre, St. Petersburg: a decorative and fairy-tale set (RM) of the square enclosed by white-walled and golden onion-domed cathedrals.

1911 March Meyerhold's production of Yu.Belaev's *Krasnyy Kabachok* (Red Tavern), music by M.A.Kuzmin, at the Aleksandrinsky Theatre, St. Petersburg.

1911 December Meyerhold's production of Gluck's *Orpheus and Eurydice* at the Mariinsky Theatre, St. Petersburg, choreography by Fokine.

1911 décors, in collaboration with Korovin, for Chaikovsky's *Lac des Cygnes* produced by Diaghilev at the Theatre Royal, Covent Garden, London.

1912 November Meyerhold's production of F.K.Sologub's *Hostages of Life* at the Aleksandrinsky Theatre, St. Petersburg.

1913 February Meyerhold's production of Richard Strauss' *Elektra*, translated by M.Kuzmin, at the Mariinsky Theatre, St. Petersburg.

1913 Meyerhold's unrealised production of Gluck's *May Queen* for the Aleksandrinsky Theatre, St. Petersburg.

1914 January A.Pinero's *Mid Channel* produced by Meyerhold at the Aleksandrinsky Theatre, St. Petersburg.

1915 January M.Lermontov's *Two Brothers* produced by Meyerhold at the Mariinsky Theatre, St. Petersburg.

1915 January M.Glinka's ballet *Jota of Aragon* produced by Meyerhold with choreography by M.Fokine at the Mariinsky Theatre, St. Petersburg. The set for a Spanish dance (RM) has big scarlet curtains framing a wide clear sky and extensive landscape with dancers performing in the foreground. The effect is fresh, open and simple.

1915 February Z.Gippius' *Green Ring*, music by V.G.Karatygin, produced by Meyerhold at the Aleksandrinsky Theatre, St. Petersburg.

1915 April P.Calderon's *El principe constante* produced by Meyerhold at the Aleksandrinsky Theatre, St. Petersburg.

1916 January A.Ostrovsky's *Storm* produced by Meyerhold at the Aleksandrinsky Theatre, St. Petersburg. A set for Act 1 (Bakhrushin Theatre Museum) depicts the banks of the Volga with a line of trees marking out a walkway with seats where figures walk along the glistening riverside beneath an immense sky.

1917 January A.Dargomyzhsky's *The Stone Guest* produced by Meyerhold at the Mariinsky Theatre: the set for Act 3 (RM) was both elegant and sinister, executed in a shrill combination of grey-blue for the architecture of the funerary chapel, with black hangings framing the set and a pallid yellow evening light illuminating the chapel windows.

1917 February M.Lermontov's *Maskarad* (*Bal Masqué*; Masquerade), music by Glazunov, produced by Meyerhold at the Aleksandrinsky Theatre employing elegant derivations of Commedia dell'Arte figures: The Ballroom set (Bakhrushin Theatre Museum) for Scene 2 was a symmetrical mass of swags, drapes and grandeur with glimpses through to other rooms and a huge central mirror. Scene 7 had a lush but darkly shadowed and sinister set in subdued reds and browns for the Gambling Room (Bakhrushin Theatre Museum). This took place at the time of the February Revolution.

1917 April Oscar Wilde's *Ideal Husband* produced by Meyerhold at the School of Dramatic Art, Mikhailovsky Theatre, Petrograd.

1917 October D.Merezhkovsky's *The Romantics* produced by Meyerhold and Yu.L.Rakitin at the Aleksandrinsky Theatre, Petrograd.

1917 December H.Ibsen's *Lady from the Sea* produced by Meyerhold at the Aleksandrinsky Theatre, Petrograd.

1918 April Lev N.Tolstoy's *Petr Khlebnik* (Peter the Baker) produced by Meyerhold with music by R.A.Mervolf at the Aleksandrinsky Theatre, Petrograd.

1918 May Stravinsky's *Nightingale* produced by Meyerhold at the Mariinsky Theatre, St. Petersburg.

1919 Gluck's *Queen of May* and Stravinsky's *Rossignol* at the Mariinsky Theatre, Petrograd.

1921 Stravinsky's *Firebird* at the Opera and Ballet Theatre, Petrograd.

1922 Grieg's *Solveig* at the Opera and Ballet Theatre, Petrograd.

1924 Rossini's *Barber of Seville* at the Opera and Ballet

Anna Golubkina. Leo Tolstoy, *1927. Toned plaster. Bronze. 70 x 100 x 92 cm.*

Theatre, Leningrad.

From 1927 he worked for the director Stanislavsky at the Moscow Art Theatre:

1927 May Beaumarchais' *Marriage of Figaro*
1930 May Shakespeare's *Othello.*

Writings A.Ya.Golovin *Vstrechi i vpechatleniya* (Encounters and Impressions), 1940.

Lit E.Gollerbakh *A.Ya.Golovin*, Leningrad, 1928. D.Kogan *A.Ya.Golovin*, Moscow, 1960. D.Z.Kogan *Golovin*, Moscow, 1960. A.Movshenson *A.Ya.Golovin*, Moscow-Leningrad, 1960. A.Bassekhes *Teatr i zhivopis' Golovina*, Moscow, 1970. *Diaghilev and Russian Stage Designers, a Loan Exhibition from the Collection of Mr. and Mrs. N.Lobanov-Rostovsky*, International Exhibitions Foundation, Washington, 1972-4. S.Onufrieva *Golovin*, Moscow-Leningrad, 1977. I.Gofman *Golovin-portretist*, Moscow, 1981. J.E.Bowlt *Russian Stage Design. Scenic Innovation. From the Collection of Mr. and Mrs. Nikita D.Lobanov-Rostovsky*, Jackson, MS, exh. cat., 1982. *Twilight of the Tsars*, London, 1991. A.Kamensky *The World of Art Movement*, Leningrad, 1991. D.Elliott, V.Dudakov *100 Years of Russian Painting*, London, 1991.

Coll Well represented at TG; RM; Bakhrushin Theatre Museum, Moscow; Leningrad Theatre Museum; Armenian Art Museum, Yerevan.

Colour plate p.156.

GOLUBKINA, Anna Semenovna   1864-1927

Sculptor. She had a wide range, all vigorously worked and showing something of Rodin's sheer flow of creativity and sense of drama. Born at Zaraysk in the Ryazan region, the daughter of a market gardener. She studied architecture under A.Gunst in Moscow 1889-90, then attended the Moscow College 1891-3 under S.Ivanov and S.M.Volnukhin and the Academy in St. Petersburg under V.A.Beklemishev in 1894. During 1895-96 she was in Paris at the Académie Colarossi, living with the women artists E.S.Kruglikova and E.N.Shevtsova. She returned to Paris in 1897 and exhibited there in 1899. She also exhibited with the World of Art 1900-2. She worked under Rodin in Paris in 1897, 1899 and 1900. This permanently affected her own style, a response to Rodin's example comparable with that of Trubetskoy. Her portrait busts, for example, were fluently modelled employing rich shifts of surface and deep chiaroscuro. A third visit to Paris followed in 1902, the year in which she executed a decorative high-relief sculpture, entitled *The Wave*, for the entrance doorway of the Moscow Arts Theatre. This was stylistically reminiscent of the surface of Rodin's *Gates of Hell* but it also had something of the drama of Vrubel's *Demon*. She taught with N.P.Ulyanov at Moscow Commercial Institute 1901-3.

She visited Paris and London 1903-4. She apparently executed a bust of *Karl Marx* in 1905 which was cast in 1936 and is now in the Russian Museum. She exhibited at the Salon d'Automne in Paris in 1906 and in the same year joined the Society of Russian Sculptors (ORS). She was arrested and imprisoned for distributing political leaflets in 1907. She settled in Moscow after her release and exhibited with the Union of Russian

Artists 1908-10. She exhibited in Rome in 1911 and with the World of Art in 1911 and 1913.

She taught at the Prechisten Workers' Courses 1913-16 as head of the sculpture department. She contributed to the Moscow Society of Art Lovers' exhibition, the World of Art and the Wanderers in 1913. She also sent work for exhibition in Malmö in 1914 and the following year had a personal exhibition in Moscow in aid of the war wounded. She was a member of the Moscow Salon in 1917.

After the Revolution she taught at the SVOMAS/Vkhutemas from 1918 to 1922 and her name appeared on the April 1919 list of artists for acquisitions by the proposed Museum of Painterly Culture. Post-revolutionary works include cameos from shells 1922-3, a basically Symbolist figure entitled *Birch Tree*, 1927, and a modelled bust of *Tolstoy*, 1927, which was still close in style to that of Trubetskoy. She was a founder of the Society of Russian Sculptors in 1926. She died at Zaraysk.

Walking Man, 1903, bronze, RM, is a reworking of Rodin's theme and pose but more credibly a real human being than Rodin's.

Sleepers, RM, is like Rodin in its use of heads emerging from the rough block but here worked with independent originality. It presents the heads of man, woman and child so that the rough marble can represent either the pillow of this intimate family group or in more abstract terms the sleep within which they lie.

Lit V.Kostin *A.S.Golubkina*, Moscow-Leningrad, 1947. E.Zagorskaya *A.S.Golubkina, Skulptor i Chelovek*, Moscow, 1964. S.Lukyanov *Zhizn' A.S.Golubkinoy*, Moscow, 1965. K.Ardentova *A.G.*, Moscow, 1976. A.Kamensky *Rytsarsky podvig* (The Knight's Victory), Moscow, 1978. *Paris-Moscou*, 1979. M.N.Yablonskaya *Women Artists of Russia's New Age*, London, 1990. *Twilight of the Tsars*, London, 1991.

Coll Well represented at RM; TG.

GONCHAROV, Andrei Dmitrievich   1903-1979

Graphic artist, painter, theatre designer, decorative artist. He studied under Favorsky, Pavlinov, Mashkov and Shevchenko at the Moscow Vkhutemas/Vkhutein 1918-27. He worked in Moscow. He was a member of the Union of the Three with A.Deineka and Yu.Pimenov, who exhibited together as a group at the First Discussional Exhibition of Active Revolutionary Art in 1924. He exhibited with the 4 Arts society in Moscow and with the First Exhibition of the Society of Easel Painters (OST) both in Moscow in 1925. He contributed to the International Exhibition in Dresden in 1926 and was included in the major exhibition in Moscow in 1927 marking the tenth anniversary of the Revolution. He contributed to the exhibition of graphic art Liberation Movements: The Sixteenth to the Twentieth Century held in Moscow in 1928 and was included in the 1928 exhibition of Acquisitions by the State Art Collections Fund held in Moscow. He was represented in the First Touring Exhibition of Paintings and Graphics which opened in Moscow in 1929.

He exhibited at the 1932 Venice Biennale. He was represented at the jubilee exhibition Artists of the RSFSR over 15 Years held at the Russian Museum, Leningrad, in 1932. He was active as a wood engraver and illustrator employing a technique indebted to the example of Favorsky and he employed these skills in designing posters. He sometimes signed his work with a monogram 'A.G' in latin or cyrillic letters in a monogram.

Girl, c.1923, oil, is a full-length portrait close in style to the soft inconsistent lighting of Deineka and Yu.Pimenov.

Theatre design 1935 June A.E.Korneychuk's *Platon krechet* at the Moscow Art Theatre. 1960 April B.N.Livanov's adaptation of Dostoevsky's *Brothers Karamazov* at the Moscow Art Theatre. 1961 October I.V.Sobolev's *Khozyain* (The Peasant) at the Moscow Art Theatre.

Lit M.E.Kholodovskaya *A.Goncharov*, 1961. A.M.Muratov, V.Manin et al. *Zhivopis' 20-30kh godov*, Sankt-Peterburg, 1991.

Coll TG, RM.

GONCHAROVA, Natalya Sergeevna   1881-1962

Painter, graphic artist and ballet designer. Born at Ladyzhino in the region of Tula. The family had a linen mill. From 1898 to 1901 she studied sculpture at the Moscow College under Trubetskoy and Volnukhin and then painting under K.Korovin. She became a painter in 1900 and met the painter Mikhail Larionov at that time. He was to become the companion of her life and together they formed a working partnership that was perhaps unparallelled, each retaining a creative independence yet working in the very closest proximity. She visited Tiraspol with Larionov in 1903. She was exhibiting by 1904 when she showed work with the exhibition of the Literary and Artistic Circle in Moscow, and

Andrei Goncharov. Illustration to Smollett's 'Peregrine Pickle', *1934. Wood engraving.*

Natalya Goncharova. Russian Peasant with Embroidered Clothes, *1914. Costume design for the ballet 'Le Coq d'Or' by Rimsky-Korsakov. Watercolour and gouache on paper. 38 x 27 cm. Signed top left 'N.Gontcharova'.*
Victoria and Albert Museum, London.

she contributed to a great number of important exhibitions thereafter, including the Moscow Association of Artists 1905-7, the World of Art and the Salon d'Automne in Paris in 1906, the Golden Fleece exhibitions of 1908-10, the *Venok* (The Wreath) exhibition in Moscow 1907-8, *Zveno* (The Link) in Kiev in 1908 and *Venok-Stefanos* (Wreath-Stefanos) in St. Petersburg in 1909. Between 1909 and 1911 she showed work with the Izdebsky Salon in Odessa and the World of Art in Moscow, St. Petersburg and Kiev.

She met the future impresario Diaghilev in 1905 and by 1909 she was active as a theatre designer working for the private studio of K.Kraft in Moscow. With Larionov she was from 1910 an organiser of avant-garde groups and their exhibitions. That year she assisted Larionov and Lentulov in setting up the *Bubnovyy Valet* (Knave of Diamonds), one of the most prolific, adventurous and energetic of pre-war art organisations in Russia. She exhibited with the Knave of Diamonds in Moscow 1910-11 and with the World of Art 1911-13. She also contributed to the *Soyuz Molodezhi* (Union of Youth) exhibitions 1911-12. Both Goncharova and Larionov played a crucial role in the development of Russian art and both kept Russian artists abreast of the latest tendencies from Western Europe. The growing awareness of Western European innovation coincided in Russia with a simultaneous burgeoning of interest in distinctly Russian traditions, particularly the ikon, popular woodblock print (*lubok*) and folk art. In 1912 Goncharova and Larionov asserted their rejection of western values to embrace, at least in principle, Russian and even Asian inspirations. To do this they quit the Knave of Diamonds and established the *Oslinyy Khvost* (Donkey's Tail) group with whom she exhibited over fifty works in Moscow in 1912. She held an enormous retrospective exhibition, apparently including over 700 works, in Moscow in 1913. This prolific production, as well as that of Larionov, may relate to the accessibility of linen from the family mill.

From 1912 she was a central figure in the activities of Russian Futurism, well aware of its Italian counterpart yet intimately committed to its distinct literary and artistic development in Russia. In this context she stressed the inspiration of eastern art to counteract western cultural enthusiasms: with Larionov she organised an exhibition in Moscow of Original Icon Paintings and Popular Prints which also included Persian, Chinese and Japanese works. She illustrated Russian Futurist books including *A Game in Hell*, *Worldbackwards*, both 1912, and *Hermits* 1913. This activity was at its height in 1913. With Larionov she featured in the Futurist film *Drama in the Futurists' Cabaret No.13*; together they organised the exhibition *Mishen'* (Target) in Moscow and they both signed the manifesto *Luchizm* (Rayism) in the almanac *Oslinyy Khvost i Mishen'* (Donkey's Tail and Target) published in 1913. She continued however to pursue exhibition opportunities elsewhere at this time. In 1913 she contributed to the World of Art and to the Union of Youth as well as the First German Autumn Salon in Berlin, the *Blaue Reiter* in Munich and Larionov's exhibition The Target in Moscow in 1913. She had personal exhibitions at the Moscow Art Salon in 1913 where she showed 760 works and at Nadezhda Dobychina's gallery in St. Petersburg in 1914. That year she featured in Larionov's exhibition No.4 in Moscow showing eighteen works there including a portrait of Larionov. The next year she was included in the Exhibition of Paintings: The Year 1915 in Moscow.

Larionov had accompanied Diaghilev to Paris in 1906 to assist

Natalya Goncharova. Cover for the Russian Futurist book 'Mirskontsa' (Worldbackwards) by Aleksei Kruchenykh and Velimir Khlebnikov, *Moscow, 1912. Collage. 18.6 x 15 cm.*
The British Library, London.

in the installation of his display of Russian art at the Salon d'Automne that year. Paris was in due course to provide the setting for most of the career of Goncharova and Larionov. In 1914 she exhibited with Larionov at the Galerie Paul Guillaume in Paris and she subsequently became a crucial figure in Diaghilev's Russian Ballet there continuing to design for Diaghilev until 1929.

She moved to Switzerland in 1915 and in 1919 she settled in Paris but her name appeared nevertheless on the April 1919 list of artists for acquisitions by the proposed Museum of Painterly Culture, her work was amongst the new acquisitions of the Tretyakov Gallery exhibited in 1919 and she was represented at the enormous First State Exhibition of Art and Science, which included ethnographic material, held in Kazan in 1920.

The war, Revolution and also opportunities in the West prevented her return to Russia but she continued to maintain contact with Russian and Soviet artists. In 1924 she was involved with the *Bal Banal* of the *Union des Artistes Russes* at the Bal Bullier in Paris. She organised with Larionov the *Rétrospective des Oeuvres de Diaghilev* in 1930. She remained immensely active as a theatre designer. She contributed to the exhibition of Contemporary Russian Art held at Philadelphia in 1932. Retrospective exhibitions were held in Paris in 1948 and 1956.

She was naturalised a French citizen in 1938. She married Larionov in 1955. She died in Paris.

Washerwomen, 1911-12, RM, is a busy Cubo-Futurist

painting of working women hanging out the washing, their figures assembled in a frieze-like, flattened composition. Roughly applied arcs of paint provide dynamic energy to figures that are knowingly primitive.

Theatre design 1909 *The Beadle* and *Zobeida's Wedding* at the K.Kraft Private Studio, Moscow.

1914 décor and costumes for Rimsky-Korsakov's opera *Le Coq d'Or* produced at the Théâtre de l'Opéra, Paris, by Diaghilev. Spectacularly colourful designs featured enormous tree and plant motifs designed with a graphic clarity and force inspired by folk art and the neo-primitive movement. The effect was immensely decorative and vigorous to an unprecedented degree.

1915 Carlo Goldoni's *The Fan* (*Veer*) produced by Tairov at the Kamerny (Chamber) Theatre in Moscow. Designed in collaboration with Larionov.

1915 designs for the ballet *Liturgie* (not realised) for Diaghilev, choreography by Massine.

1916 Ravel's *Rhapsodie Espagnole*, Albeniz' *Triaña* for Diaghilev

Natalya Goncharova. Mystical Images of War, *1914. Lithograph. 33 x 25 cm. Signed lower left with a cyrillic monogram 'N.G'. This is one image from the portfolio of prints published in response to the fighting. Goncharova makes a kind of analogy between aeroplanes and angels that pits the superhuman against the human. Other Futurists who responded to the theme of war included Aleksei Kruchenykh and Olga Rozanova.*

(neither realised).

1921 Rimsky-Korsakov's *Russian Toys* at the Palace Theater, New York.

1922 Costumes for the *Contes de Fées* in Chaikovsky's *Le Mariage de la Belle au Bois Dormant* which was otherwise designed by Alexandre Benois.

1922 décors for Stravinsky's *Le Renard, ballet burlesque avec chant*, first performed at the Paris Opera.

1923 décors and costumes for Diaghilev's production of Stravinsky's *Les Noces* at the Théâtre de la Gaîté-Lyrique, Paris, with choreography by Bronislava Nijinska. Costume drawings indicate characteristic gestures employed in the ballet as well as the look of the costumes worn.

1923-24 Mussorgsky's *Night on the Bare Mountain* for Diaghilev at the Théâtre de Monte Carlo.

1924 marionettes for the Julie Sazanova Marionette Theatre.

1926 Stravinsky's *Firebird* for Diaghilev's production at the Lyceum Theatre, London.

1930 Alfred Savoir's *La Petite Cathérine* at the Théâtre Antoine, Paris.

1932 Prokofiev's *Sur le Boristhène* and Chaikovsky's *Divertissement* at the Paris Opera as well as other productions for Kovno in Lithuania and at Buenos Aires.

Further theatre design followed on an almost annual basis until the late 1950s for productions in New York, London, Paris and Monte Carlo.

Futurist books A.Kruchenykh, V.Khlebnikov *Igra v adu* (A Game in Hell), 1912, with illustrations by Natalya Goncharova.

A.Kruchenykh and V.Khlebnikov *Mirskontsa* (Worldbackwards), 1912, illustrated by Goncharova, Larionov, Tatlin and I.Rogovin.

A.Kruchenykh *Pustynniki* (Hermits),1913, illustrated by Goncharova.

A.Kruchenykh *Vzorval'* (Explodity), with illustrations by N.Kul'bin, O.Rozanova, K.Malevich and N.Goncharova, St. Petersburg, 1913.

K.Bolshakov *Le Futur*, with illustrations by N.Goncharova and M.Larionov, 1913.

N.Goncharova *Voyna: misticheskie obrazy voyny* (War: Mystical Images of War), fourteen lithographs by Goncharova, Moscow, 1914.

Cover for M.Tsetlin (Amari) *Prozrachyateni* (Transparent Shadows), Paris, 1920.

Lit E.Eganbyuri (Zdanevich) *Nataliya Goncharova, Mikhail Larionov*, Moscow, 1913. V.Parnack *Goncharova et Larionov: L'art décoratif théâtral moderne*, Paris, 1920. *Larionov and Goncharova*, exh. cat., Arts Council of Great Britain, London, 1961. T.Loguine *Goncharova et Larionov cinquante ans à Saint Germain-des-Près*, Paris, 1971. M.Chamot *Gontcharova*, Paris, 1972. *Diaghilev and Russian Stage Designers, a Loan Exhibition from the Collection of Mr. and Mrs. N.Lobanov-Rostovsky*, International Exhibitions Foundation, Washington, 1972-4. *Rétrospective Gontcharova*, exh. cat., Maison de la Culture, Bourges, 1973. S.P.Compton *The World Backwards, Russian Futurist Books 1912-16*, London, 1978. Mary Chamot *Goncharova Stage Designs and Paintings*, London, 1979. J.E.Bowlt *Russian Stage Design. Scenic Innovation. From the Collection of Mr. and Mrs. Nikita D.Lobanov-Rostovsky*, Jackson, MS, exh. cat.,1982. A.Schouvaloff *The Thyssen-Bornemisza*

Konstantin Gorbatov. Fishing Smacks in a Calm, *1946. Oil on canvas. 75.5 x 92.5 cm. Reproduced by kind permission of Sotheby's London, sale 15.2.1984, lot 103.*

Collection: Set and Costume Designs for Ballet and Theatre, New York-London, 1987. M.N.Yablonskaya *Women Artists of Russia's New Age*, London, 1990. Dzhon Boult (John Bowlt) *Khudozhniki russkogo teatra. Sobranie Nikity i Niny Lobanovykh-Rostovskikh*, Moscow, 1991. S.Compton *Russian Avant-Garde Books 1917-34*, London, 1992. *L'Avant-garde russe 1905-1925*, exh. cat., Musée des Beaux-Arts, Nantes, 1993.

Coll Extensively represented in major collections including TG; RM; Bakhrushin Theatre Museum, Moscow; Erevan Art Museum; Kazan Art Museum; Kostroma Art Museum; Orel Art Museum; Serpukhov Museum; Simbirsk Art Museum; Tula Art Museum; Ulyanovsk Art Museum; Tate Gallery, London; Ashmolean Museum, Oxford; Victoria and Albert Museum, London; Lobanov-Rostovsky Collection, London; Baron Thyssen-Bornemisza Collection, England; MNAM, Paris; Costakis Collection; Musée de l'Opéra, Paris; Staatsgalerie, Stuttgart; Sammlung Ludwig, Cologne; Fine Arts Museums, San Francisco; Solomon R.Guggenheim Museum, New York.

Colour plates pp.157, 160, 161, 164.

GONZAGA, Petr Fedorovich (GOTTARDO, Pietro di) a.before 1850

Theatre designer. He made classical architectural scenery designs of opulent and erudite magnificence employing a symmetrical single-point perspective which described an almost infinite spacial recession. He designed for the Archangel Theatre in the first half of the 19th century and also designed a curtain for *Cinderella*.

Coll Bakhrushin Theatre Museum, Moscow.

GORAVSKY (GOROVSKY), Apollinariy Gilyarevich 1833-1900

Painter of portraits and landscapes. Born near Minsk. He studied at the Academy in St. Petersburg under Bruni and Vorob'ev. He died in St. Petersburg.

Coll TG.

GORBATOV, Konstantin Ivanovich 1876-1928

Painter, graphic artist, watercolourist. He studied under Burov at Samara in 1890, under Klark in Riga 1896-1903 and at the Academy in St. Petersburg until 1911 under A.A.Kiselev and N.N.Dubovsky. He published drawings with satirical magazines 1905-6. He lived in Italy 1912-13.

After the Revolution he worked on Agitprop decorations on Izmailovsky Prospekt, Petrograd, in 1918. He participated in the First State Free Exhibition of Artworks in Petrograd in 1919 and contributed to the Exhibition of Paintings by Russian Artists held at Pskov in Spring 1920. He emigrated in 1924.

Pskov, 1919, is a heavily coloured and painterly rendering of light reflecting sailing barges on the river. There is an air of

fresh changeable weather and a view of the church domes.
Lit D.Elliott, V.Dudakov *100 Years of Russian Painting*, London, 1991.

GORBUNOV, Kirill Antonovich   1822-1893
Portrait painter. His birthdate is sometimes given as 1815. He studied in Moscow and executed commissions for the Tsars Aleksandr II and Aleksandr III.
Coll TG; Museum of the Academy, St. Petersburg; Saratov Art Museum.

GORDEEV, Fedor Gordeevich   1744-1810
Neo-classical sculptor. Born at Tsarskoe Selo. He was commissioned in the 1780s to execute copies of the Apollo Belvedere and other antique sculptures for the palaces at Pavlovsk and Tsarskoe Selo. He died at St. Petersburg.
Prometheus, 1769, bronze, RM, has the figure tipped dramatically across the rock to which he is chained with the ruthless, fine-feathered eagle above him.
Marriage of Cupid and Psyche, 1790s, plaster, Ostankino, is an elegant relief of five figures accompanied by putti, inspired directly by antique reliefs and competently executed. It was executed for the Sheremetev estate at Ostankino.
Coll TG, RM.

GORETSKY, Faddey Antonovich   1825-1868
Portrait painter.
Col TG.

GORNOSTAEV, I. I.   1821-1874
Theatre designer. He made set and costume designs for Glinka's *Ruslan and Lyudmila* in 1862. He sometimes signed his work 'Gornostaef'.

GORODETSKY, Aleksandr Mitrofanovich   a.1908-1910
He was exhibiting in St. Petersburg 1908-9. His experimental studies included works painted on cotton wool 1909-10.

GORODETSKY, Sergei Mitrofanovich   1884-1967
Poet, graphic artist. He designed posters in the 1920s.
Lit D.Elliott, V.Dudakov *100 Years of Russian Painting*, London, 1991.

GOROVSKY = GORAVSKY, A.G.

GORSHMAN, Mendel' Khaimovich (Mikhail Efimovich) 1902-1972
Graphic artist. He was represented in the exhibition of Russian Graphics at Riga and in the First Touring Exhibition of Paintings and Graphics which opened in Moscow in 1929. He died in Moscow.

GORTYNSKAYA, Maria Petrovna   1883-1973
Theatre designer. She contributed to the exhibition Art of Moscow Theatre 1918-1923 held in Moscow in 1923.

GORYUSHKIN-SOROKOPUDOV, Ivan Silych (Silovich) 1873-1954
Painter of genre and historical themes. He studied under Repin at the Academy in St. Petersburg, graduating in 1902. Tatlin was amongst his pupils at the Penza School of Art where he taught from 1908.
Coll TG.

GOTTARDO, Pietro di = GONZAGA, P.F.

GRABAR', Igor' Emmanuilovich   1871-1960
Painter, critic and art historian. He perfected a vigorous version of Impressionist technique. Born at Budapest. After graduating in St. Petersburg where he studied both law and art, in 1894 he enrolled at the Academy to study under Chistyakov and Repin until 1896. He then travelled to Munich where he attended the Azbé School 1896-8 and where he also studied architecture at the Munich Polytechnic. He subsequently taught at the Azbé School and then travelled extensively. He was associated with the World of Art in 1901, exhibiting with them 1902-6, and was a member of the Union of Russian Artists from 1903 to 1910. He exhibited a tiled stove at the Contemporary Art Store and Exhibition in St. Petersburg 1902-3 and in 1903 he moved to Moscow. He exhibited in Venice in 1904 and Rome in 1911. He was represented in Diaghilev's display of Russian art at the 1906 Salon d'Automne in Paris. He exhibited with the First Izdebsky International Salon 1909-10. He was a member of the organising committee of the 1912 World of Art exhibition under the presidency of Roerich. He became an Academician in 1913.
Grabar' was intensely active as both painter and art historian. From 1910 he edited with V.Kamenov and V.Lazarev the immense and pioneering thirty-volume *History of Russian Art* which remains a major source of scholarship. He became director of the Tretyakov Gallery in Moscow, taught at the Repin and Surikov Art Institutes and continued to travel widely including visits to Egypt and the United States in 1914. After the Revolution he organised the State Art Restoration Workshops 1918-30. He was also teaching art history at the Free Art Studios in Moscow c.1918.
He was represented at the enormous First State Exhibition of Art and Science, which included ethnographic material, held in Kazan in 1920 and at the First Russian Art Exhibition in Berlin in 1922. He exhibited in Venice in 1924. He was a member of the Society of Moscow Painters founded in 1925. His work was included in the exhibition of Soviet art held at Harbin in 1926 and in Japan in 1927 and in the major exhibition in Moscow in 1927 marking the tenth anniversary of the Revolution.
He was represented at the jubilee exhibition Artists of the RSFSR over 15 Years held at the Russian Museum, Leningrad, in 1932. He became a member of the Academy of Sciences of the USSR and the Director of its Institute of Art History. He was the Director of the All-Russian Academy of Arts 1942-7. He died in Moscow.
February Azure, 1904, TG, is in essence a competent Impressionist painting closely inspired by Monet's technique and transplanted into a Russian setting. Blue shadows are luminously handled in emphatically Russian landscape, so that the poplars of Monet become the birch trees of Grabar', dazzlingly splayed in brilliant sun against an azure sky. There can scarcely be a clearer indication of the Russian enthusiasm for Impressionist painting and yet, despite the derivative technique, its translation into the Russian snow has a new appearance which recalls the patriotic celebration of landscape maintained by the traditions of the Wanderers. It is perhaps not surprising that a man so travelled and erudite in art history should show signs of the techniques of other artists, but this far surpasses pastiche by means of its vigour and the virtuosity of its performance.
Writings apart from art history: I.Grabar' *Moya Zhizn'*, *Avtomonografiya* (My Life, Auto-monongraph), Moscow-Leningrad, 1937. I.Grabar' *Pisma 1891-1912* (Letters 1891-

1912), Moscow, 1974. I.Grabar' *Pisma 1917-41* (Letters 1917-41), Moscow, 1977. I.Grabar' *Pisma 1941-60*, Moscow, 1983.
Lit V.Lobanov *I.E.Grabar'*, Moscow-Leningrad, 1945. O.Podobedova *Grabar'*, Moscow, 1964.
Coll TG, RM.

GRACHEV, A.   a.1921
He was included in the Third Touring Exhibition of the Sovetsk Regional subdepartment of the Museums Bureau along with Kandinsky, Rodchenko and others in 1921.

GRANAVTSEVA, Maria Stepanovna   1904-1989
Painter. She was represented at the jubilee exhibition Artists of the RSFSR over 15 Years held at the Russian Museum, Leningrad, in 1932. Born at Irkutsk. She died in Moscow.

GRANDI, Ivan Antonovich (Giovanni Battista Antonio) b.1886
Italian theatre designer. Born in Bologna. A Grandi exhibited with the World of Art in 1915.
He became involved in Agitprop art in Russia and was engaged on the decoration of the propaganda train *Lenin (October Revolution)* in 1920.

GRANDKOVSKY, Nikolai Karlovich   1864-1907
Portrait painter.
Coll TG.

GREK = THEOPHANES THE GREEK

GREKOV (MARTYSHCHENKO), Mitrofan Borisovich 1882-1934
Painter of Soviet battle themes. Born at Charpaevka. He studied at the Odessa Art Institute under Kostandi and Ladyzhensky 1899-1903 and at the St. Petersburg Academy under Chistyakov and Repin 1903-11. A Grekov exhibited with the World of Art 1916-17.
Engaged in Agitprop work c.1925 and he became a leading member of the Association of Russian Revolutionary Artists (AKhRR). He held a one-man exhibition at Novocherkassk in 1927. Works include *The Capture of Novocherkassk*, 1925, RM, and *The Flight of the Whites from Novocherkassk in 1920*, 1927, RM. He died at Sebastopol.
*Tachanka (Carriage Race), 1925, TG, depicts a kind of modern Russian/Asian chariot race in which 'carriages' race pell-mell through a hayfield each pulled by four careering horses. The effect here, and in other works, has a kind of cinemascope film-like impact.
Lit A.N.Tikhomorov *M.B.Grekov*, Moscow, 1937. I.Khomaninsky *M.B.Grekov*, Moscow, 1956. G.A.Timoshin *M.B.Grekov, Zhizn' i Tvorchestvo*, (M.B.Grekov, Life and Work), Moscow, 1961. *Paris-Moscou*, 1979.
Coll TG; RM.

GREKOVA (MALEEVA), Antonina Leonidovna 1887-1960
She exhibited with the World of Art 1912-13.

GRENTSEVICH, A. P.
This name appeared on the April 1919 list of artists for acquisitions by the envisaged Museum of Painterly Culture.

GRIBKOV, Sergei Ivanovich   1820-1893
Painter. He studied at the Academy in St. Petersburg where he attained his diploma in 1852.
Coll TG.

GRIGORIEV (GRIGOR'EV), A. G.   a.1922
He was a member of the first exhibition committee of AKhRR, the Association of Artists of Revolutionary Russia, in 1922. In 1922 he was a founder member of the Society (*Obshchestvo*) of Artists of Revolutionary Russia, founded after the first exhibition of AKhRR. Other members included P.Kiselev, E.Katsman, N.Kotov, S.Malyutin, P.Radimov, P.Shukhmin, A.Skachko, G.Sukhanov, B.Yakovlev and V.Zhuravlev.

GRIGORIEV (GRIGOR'EV), Aleksandr Konstantinovich 1837-1886+
Painter. He studied at the Academy in St. Petersburg and exhibited there in 1870. He subsequently became a member of the Artel which led to the founding of the Wanderers.

GRIGORIEV (GRIGOR'EV), Boris Dmitrievich 1886-1939
Painter, draughtsman, graphic artist, theatre designer. Born at Rybinsk. He studied at the Stroganov Institute under D.Shcherbinovsky 1903-7 and then attended the Higher Art Institute at the Academy in St. Petersburg under D.N.Kardovsky and A.A.Kiselev between 1907 and 1912. He became a member of the World of Art in 1913. He lived in Paris 1912-14 where he attended the Académie de la Grande Chaumière and exhibited at the Salon des Indépendants 1912-13 but he also contributed to the satirical periodicals *Satirikon* 1912-13, *Novy Satirikon* 1914 and *Lukomor'e* 1913-16. With Sudeikin and Yakovlev he decorated the cabaret The Comedians' Halt in 1916.
After the Revolution he exhibited with the World of Art in December 1917 in Moscow. He was engaged in Agitprop decorations for the English Embankment, Petrograd, in 1918 and his name appeared on the April 1919 list of artists for acquisitions by the envisaged Museum of Painterly Culture. He was teaching painting at the Free Art Studios in Moscow in 1918. He participated in the First State Free Exhibition of Artworks in Petrograd in 1919 and he was represented at the Exhibition of Paintings by Russian Artists held at Pskov in Spring 1920.
He emigrated to Berlin in 1919 and settled in Paris in 1921. He illustrated the children's book by Sasha Chernyy *Detsky ostrov* (Children's Island) published in Danzig in 1921. He built a house at Cagnes-sur-Mer in 1927 and taught as Professor at the Academy of Fine Arts in Santiago, Chile, in 1928 returning to France in 1930. He contributed to the exhibition of Contemporary Russian Art held at Philadelphia in 1932. He was Dean of the New York School of Applied Arts in 1935 and he again visited Chile in 1936, returning to Cagnes in 1938. He died at Cagnes-sur-Mer.
Lit *Boris Grigorieff*, exh. cat., Château-Musée Cagnes-sur-Mer, 1978-9. *Paris-Moscou*, 1979. J.E.Bowlt *Russian Stage Design. Scenic Innovation. From the Collection of Mr. and Mrs. Nikita D.Lobanov-Rostovsky*, Jackson, MS, exh. cat.,1982. *Twilight of the Tsars*, London, 1991. D.Elliott, V.Dudakov *100 Years of Russian Painting*, London, 1991. Dzhon Boult (John Bowlt) *Khudozhniki russkogo teatra. Sobranie Nikity i Niny Lobanovykh-Rostovskikh*, Moscow, 1991.
Coll TG; RM.
Colour plate p.165.

GRIGORIEV (GRIGOR'EV), Ivan Trofimovich   b.1906
Graphic artist. Born at Ivano-Kazansk, Bashkyria.

Nikolai M. Grigoriev. Turks, *1921. Lithograph. 22.4 x 19.1 cm. Signed 'N.G' in cyrillic letters lower right. State Russian Museum, St. Petersburg.*

GRIGORIEV (GRIGOR'EV), Nikolai Mikhailovich
1890-1943
Painter. His work was included in the First Exhibition of Works of the Professional Union of Artists in Moscow in 1918 and in the First Exhibition of the Moscow Contemporary Art Store in January 1919. He was active at the Vhutemas in 1922. He was represented at the First Russian Art Exhibition in Berlin in 1922 and was included in the 1928 exhibition of Acquisitions by the State Art Collections Fund held in Moscow. He was represented in the First Touring Exhibition of Paintings and Graphics which opened in Moscow in 1929. He died in Moscow.
Coll RM.

GRIGORIEV (GRIGOR'EV), Nikolai Nikolaevich
1901-1929+
He was represented in the First Touring Exhibition of Paintings and Graphics which opened in Moscow in 1929.

GRIGORIEV (GRIGOR'EV), Sergei Alekseevich b.1910
Socialist Realist genre painter and graphic artist. Born at Lugansk.
Coll TG.

GRIGOROVICH, E.Yu.   a.1919
He exhibited at the juryless Eighth State Exhibition in Moscow in 1919.

GRIGOROVICH, Konstantin Vasil'evich   1823-1855
Painter.
Coll TG.

GRINBERG, Nikolai Ivanovich   b.1897
Painter. Born at St. Petersburg. In 1918 he was studying

under Malevich. He then studied with Matyushin and investigated the relationship of sound and colour as part of Matyushin's group *Zorved* (See-Know) 1919-22. He joined the Museum of Pictorial Culture at Petrograd in 1923 and contributed to the Exhibition of Paintings by Petrograd Artists of All Tendencies 1919-1923 that year. His work was included in the 1924 Venice Biennale.
Lit A.Z.Rudenstine *Costakis Collection*, London, 1981.
Coll Costakis Collection.

GRISELLI, I.O. = GRIZELLI, O.O.

GRISHCHENKO, Aleksei Vasilievich
(GRITCHENKO, Alexis)   1883-1977
Neo-primitivist painter and writer on art. Born in the Ukraine. He studied at the Academy in St. Petersburg and then in Kiev 1906-8 under Svyatoslavsky. He wrote on the subject of Russian ikons in 1907 and shared the interest of Larionov, Goncharova and others in the distinct and even Asian elements of Russian art. He exhibited with the Knave of Diamonds in 1912 and at that time he was working in the studio complex The Tower with Tatlin, Popova, Zdanevich and others. He explored the Byzantine and western influences upon Russian art in a book of 1913. He was associated with the Union of Youth. He was a visitor to gatherings at Popova's studio 1914-15.

After the Revolution he exhibited with the World of Art in December 1917 in Moscow and he was represented at the First Exhibition of Works of the Professional Union of Artists in Moscow in 1918. He was engaged in the redefinition of the role and nature of art museums, proposing in 1919 the formation of a new kind of museum, the Museum of Painterly Culture, dedicated to the study of art practice. His name appeared on the April 1919 list of artists for acquisitions by the envisaged Museum of Painterly Culture and he was also listed as leader of a course for art teachers along with Tatlin and others. He was teaching composition, the history of decorative art and teaching methods at the Free State studios in Moscow c.1918.

He produced a *Manifesto* in 1919 for the tendencies *Tsvetodinamos* (Colourdynamo) and *Tektonicheskiy primitivizm* (Tectonic Primitivism) together with A.Shevchenko. This was published in the catalogue of the Twelfth State Exhibition: Colourdynamo and Tectonic Primitivism in Moscow in 1919. The manifesto rejected Cubism and Futurism as worn out and called for an assertion of painterly elements of handling, depth, mass and form: 'These are the stones upon which we build the new art of the great contemporary epoch.' The other exhibitors included Bashkirov, Bogatov, Golovanov, Igumnov, Kalabukhov, Kulukin, Nikitin, Novikov, Rozhkova, Shevchenko, Shpagin, Shumov, Solomatin, Toporkov, Tseloval'nikov and Varentsov.

He was represented along with Kandinsky, Chagall and others at the First State Exhibition of Paintings by Local and Moscow Artists held in Vitebsk in December 1919, at the Third Exhibition of Paintings held at Ryazan in 1919 and at the enormous First State Exhibition of Art and Science, which included ethnographic material, held in Kazan in 1920.

He emigrated to Paris in 1921 but was also represented at the First Russian Art Exhibition in Berlin in 1922. He attended the Académie de la Grande Chaumière and from 1930 he exhibited at the Salon d'Automne. He sometimes signed his work in cyrillic script: 'A.G'. He died in Paris.

Writings A.Grishchenko *Russkaya ikona* (The Russian Ikon), Moscow, 1907. A.Grishchenko *O svyatiyakh russkoy zhivopisi s vizantiey i zapadom XIII-XX. Mysli zhivopistsa* (On the Links between Russian Painting, Byzantium and the West. XIII-XX Centuries. Thoughts of a Painter), Moscow, 1913. A.Grishchenko, N.Lavrsky *A.Shevchenko: Poiski i dostizheniya v oblasti zhivopisi* (A.Shevchenko: Researches and Achievements in the Realm of Painting), Moscow, 1919. A.Gritchenko *The Years of Storm and Stress* (in Ukrainian), New York, 1967.
Coll TG, RM; Astrakhan Art Museum; MNAM, Paris.

GRISHIN, S. V. a.1919
He exhibited at the Twelfth State Exhibition: Colourdynamo and Tectonic Primitivism (*XII Gosudarstvennaya vystavka: Tsvetodinamos i tektonichesky primitivizm*) in Moscow in 1919 along with Grishchenko, Shevchenko and others.

GRITCHENKO, Alexis = GRISHCHENKO, Aleksei V.

GRITSENKO, Nikolai Nikolaevich 1856-1900
Landscape painter.
Coll TG.

**GRIZELLI, Orlando Oliverovich
(GRISELLI, Italo Orlando)** b.1880-1918+
Sculptor. Born at Montescudaio, Pisa, Italy. He responded immediately to Lenin's call for monuments commemorating forerunners and activists of the Revolution in his monument to *Sofia Perovskaya* in 1918. This dramatic and stylised bust surmounted a diagonally divided plinth. The head turned aggressively in a powerful indication of stubborn force and fashioned in a synthetic and declamatory style recalling both Baroque and Futurist example.
Smiths, 1916, bronze, RM, is full of movement. On a base with a rudimentary anvil at its centre two figures work on a piece of metal. One holds it in place leaning backwards as he does so, the other raises his hammer to strike the metal. The sculpture makes dynamic use of the interplay of rhythms which enliven the surrounding space.
Coll RM; Galleria dell'Arte Moderna, Florence.

GROMOV, Aleksandr Aleksandrovich 1886-1956
Painter, graphic artist. Born in the Yaroslavl region. He studied at the school of the Society for the Encouragement of the Arts 1908-12 at St. Petersburg under Bilibin, Roerich and Rylov and then at the Academy. He exhibited with the Society of Russian Watercolourists in 1914 and with the World of Art 1915-16.
After the Revolution, between 1920 and 1930, he made designs for the State Porcelain Factory in Leningrad. He was included in the enormous survey Exhibition of Paintings by Petrograd Artists of All Tendencies 1919-1923 held in Petrograd in 1923. In 1924 he exhibited in New York.
He was represented at the jubilee exhibition Artists of the RSFSR over 15 Years held at the Russian Museum, Leningrad, in 1932. He died in Leningrad.
Lit *Vystavka rabot khudozhnika A.A.Gromova* (Exhibition of works by the artist A.A.Gromov), Pavlovsk, 1961. *Paris-Moscou*, 1979.

**GROOT, Georg Khristofor
(GROT, GROOTH, Georg Christoph)** 1716-1749
Painter of equestrian portraits. Born at Stuttgart. He worked

in Russia from 1743 when he executed a portrait of the *Empress Elizabeth Petrovna on Horseback*, TG. He was accompanied by his brother the painter Johann Friedrich Groot. He died at St. Petersburg.
Coll TG, RM.

GRUBE, Aleksandr Vasilievich b.1894
Belorussian sculptor. Born in Ufa region. Works include an heroic bust of *Major General L.M.Dovator*, 1942.

GRUDISTOVA, E. M. a.1918-1919
Painter. She exhibited at the First Exhibition of Works of the Professional Union of Artists in Moscow in 1918 and at the Ninth State Exhibition of Paintings: Naturalism and Realism in Moscow in 1919.

GRUZENBERG, Sergei Nikolaevich 1888-1934
A Gruzenberg exhibited with the World of Art 1913-15. S.Gruzenberg was represented at the Paris International Exhibition of 1925.

GRUZINSKY, Petr Nikolaevich 1837-1892
Coll TG.

GRYUN, Oskar Petrovich 1874-1935
He exhibited at the juryless Eighth State Exhibition in Moscow in 1919.

GUBIN, Vasili Ivanovich 1907-1986
Painter, graphic artist. He was associated with the group *Put' zhivopisi* (Path of Painting) formed by Lev Zhegin in 1927.

GUDIASHVILI, Vladimir (Lado) Davidovich 1896-1980
Georgian painter, theatre designer. Born at Tiflis. He studied under Ya.Nikoladze at the Tiflis School of Art 1910-14. His first one-man exhibition was held at Tiflis in 1915. He was engaged on archaeological drawings 1915-16 and in 1916 he joined the Association of Georgian Artists.
After the Revolution he taught at the Tiflis Academy of Art 1918-19 and with David Kakabadze, Segei Sudeikin and Kirill Zdanevich he worked on murals at the Khimerioni Cabaret in Tiflis. He then travelled via Turkey and Italy to France where he attended the Académie Ranson in Paris between 1919 and 1926 and he exhibited in Paris 1922-5. He also designed for Balieff's Chauve-Souris Company.
He was a member of the 4 Arts society which was founded in 1924. He returned to teaching at the Tiflis Academy 1921-32 and executed décors for Georgian theatres from 1926. In 1929 he became a member of the Association of Revolutionary Artists of Georgia (SARMA). He died at Tblisi.
Fetching Water, 1926, pencil and sanguine, TG, is a drawing of two women carrying water vessels on their heads. A man loads vessels on to a donkey. The proportions are highly stylised and elongated and the technique is linear displaying a fine Georgian sense of rhythm and decoration which is almost Persian in its effect.
Lit M.Raynal *L.Gudiashvili*, Paris, 1925. A.Mikhailov *L.Gudiashvili*, Moscow, 1968. L.Zlatkevich *L.Gudiashvili*, Tblisi, 1971. V.Beridze *Gudiashvili*, Tblisi, 1975. V.Narakidze *Gudiashvili*, Tblisi, 1976. J.E.Bowlt *Russian Stage Design. Scenic Innovation. From the Collection of Mr. and Mrs. Nikita D.Lobanov-Rostovsky*, Jackson, MS, exh. cat., 1982. Dzhon Boult (John Bowlt) *Khudozhniki russkogo teatra. Sobranie Nikity*

Lado Gudiashvili. Study for Scene with a Village Inn, *1924. Watercolour. Signed. 26.5 x 35 cm.*
Designed for A.A.Arkhangelsky's musical review 'Not Far from Tiflis' performed by N.F.Balieff's Chauve-Souris theatre troupe at the Théâtre Femina, Paris.
Collection Mr. and Mrs. Nikita D.Lobanov-Rostovsky, London.

i Niny Lobanovykh-Rostovskikh, Moscow, 1991.
Coll TG; Georgian Art Museum, Tblisi; Museum of the Art of Eastern Nations, Moscow.

GUDIM-LEVKOVICH,V.V.   **a.1919**
Painter. He exhibited at the juryless Eighth State Exhibition in Moscow in 1919.

GUE = GE, N. N.

GUMILINA, Antonina Mikhailovna   **1895-1918**
She exhibited with the Knave of Diamonds in Moscow in November 1917 and with the World of Art in December 1917 in Moscow.
She was accorded a posthumous exhibition of seventy-three works as the Seventeenth State Exhibition held in Moscow in 1919, an honour only accorded at that time to Rozanova posthumously and to Malevich.

GUMINER, Yakov Moisevich   **1896-1942**
Painter, theatre designer. Born at Minsk. In 1915 he was studying at the Society for the Encouragement of the Arts in St. Petersburg.
After the Revolution he was engaged on Agitprop decorations at Smolny, Petrograd, working under A.A.Andreev in 1918 and was studying at the Petrograd Free Art Studios (SVOMAS) at that time. He participated in the First State

Free Exhibition of Artworks in Petrograd in 1919. He exhibited with the Union of New Tendencies in Art in Petrograd in June 1922 and was included in the enormous survey Exhibition of Paintings by Petrograd Artists of All Tendencies 1919-1923 held in Petrograd in 1923. He became a member of *Proletkult* and from 1925 he executed drawings for the review *Begemot* (Behemoth).
Lit *Paris-Moscou*, 1979.

GUN, Karl Fedorovich = HUNS, Karlis Fridikh

GURETSKY, Yan Vladislavovich   **1876-1922+**
Theatre designer. In 1918 he was engaged in the Agitprop decoration of Kazanskaya Square, Petrograd. He was represented at the exhibition of Studies for Theatre Decoration and Works from the Studios of the Decorative Institute held in Petrograd in 1922.

GURO, Elena Genrikhovna (NOTENBERG, Eleonora)
1877-1913
Poet, painter. Born at St. Petersburg. She attended the School of the Society for the Encouragement of the Arts 1890-3. Whilst studying at the private studio of Tsionglinsky 1903-5 she met Mikhail Matyushin whom she later married. Finally she studied at the Zvantseva School under Bakst and Dobuzhinsky 1905-6. Her first story was published in 1905. Drawn into the orbit of Nikolai Kul'bin, she exhibited with his

1908 Exhibition of Contemporary Trends in Art and his Impressionist exhibitions 1909-10. In this way she came to associate with Futurists and contributed to the anthology *Sadok Sudei* (A Trap for Judges) in 1910. She also showed work at the Union of Youth exhibitions. Her early death prevented a substantial contribution to Futurism but the respect which she engendered is evident from her inclusion in the Futurist book *Troe* (The Three) in 1913 and the posthumous exhibition accorded to her by the Union of Youth 1913-14.
Writings E.Guro *Sharmanka* (Hurdy-Gurdy), 1909. E.Guro *Osenniy Son* (Autumn Dream), 1912. E.Guro *Nebesnye Verbluzhata* (Baby Camels in the Sky), 1914.
Lit A.Z.Rudenstine *Costakis Collection*, London, 1981. E.Weiss *Russische Avant-Garde, 1910-1930, Sammlung Ludwig, Köln*, Munich, 1986.
Coll TG; Costakis Collection; Sammlung Ludwig, Cologne.

GURVICH, Iosif Naumovich   **b.1907**
Painter. Born at Odessa. He studied at the Odessa Art Institute until 1930. His paintings have included still-lifes, landscapes and figurative themes of bathers. He works in Moscow.
Coll. Roy Miles Gallery, London.
Colour plate p.168.

GURVICH-GURSKY, Stanislas   **a.1914**
Painter. He contributed to the exhibition No.4 in Moscow in 1914.

GUSEV, Timofei Vasilievich   **a.c.1918-1920**
Engaged in Agitprop projects including the decoration of the propaganda trains *Red Cossack*, the Ukrainian *Lenin* train, *Lenin (October Revolution)* and *Soviet Caucasus*.

GUSIICIIIN, Aleksandr Ivanovich   **a.c.1918-1920**
Engaged on Agitprop work including the decoration of the propaganda trains *Red Cossack*, the Ukrainian *Lenin*, *Lenin (October Revolution)* and *Soviet Caucasus*.

GUSKIN, A.   **a.1922-1924**
Painter. He was a member of NOZh, the New Society of Painters, formed in 1922.

GUSTAV, Tsetsiliya   **a.c.1928**
She was engaged on the decoration of the Vkhutein Club, Moscow, c.1928.

GUSTOMESOV, Leonid Vasilevich   **b.1904**
He worked with Tatlin towards the end of Tatlin's life and became a close friend.

GUZIKOV, Semen Matveevich   **1878-1919+**
His birthdate is sometimes given as 1879. He was represented at the First Exhibition of Works of the Professional Union of Artists in Moscow in 1918 and his name appeared on the April 1919 list of artists for acquisitions by the envisaged Museum of Painterly Culture.

GYURDZHAN, Akop Makarovich   **1881-1948**
Sculptor. Born at Shusha in Nagorny Karabakh. He studied at the Académie Julian in Paris 1906-10 and also visited Rodin's studio.
After the Revolution he assisted on monuments to *Vrubel'* and *Karl Marx* as part of Lenin's Plan for Monumental Propaganda. In 1919 he was listed as leader of a course for art teachers along with Tatlin and others. He was represented at the enormous First State Exhibition of Art and Science, which included ethnographic material, held in Kazan in 1920.
He emigrated to Paris in 1921. On his death in Paris he bequeathed all his work to the Armenian Gallery of Painting.
Flight, 1912, plaster, Armenian Art Gallery, Erevan, is a fluent sculpture of a fleeing mother carrying one child and leading another. She flees from an unknown conflict.
Lit R.Drampyan *A.Gyurdzhan*, Erevan, 1973. *Paris-Moscou*, 1979.
Coll Armenian Art Gallery, Erevan.

GYURDZHYAN, Gabriel Mikaelovich (Mikhailovich) b.1892-1952+
Painter of Armenian landscapes and industrial themes. Born in Turkey. He studied at the Penza School of Art under I.S.Goryushin-Sorokopudov, P.I.Korovin and N.F.Petrov 1910-20. He began to exhibit at Samara in 1914.
After the Revolution he taught at the Penza Art Technical Studios 1920-2 and at the Erevan Technical College 1923-35. He became an organiser of the affiliated branch of AKhRR in Armenia and a member from 1925 to 1932.
He taught at the Erevan Art Institute 1945-52.
The Building of the Shiraksky Canal, 1926, Armenian Art Gallery, Erevan, is slightly Cubist in its effect as the heroic rock-cutting labour of its theme results in a multiplicity of shapes of figures among solid rock.
Coll Armenian Art Gallery, Erevan.

HIPPIUS = GIPPIUS, N.N.

HUNS, K.F. (GUN, K.F.)   **1830-1877**
Latvian landscape, genre and portrait painter. He exhibited at the first Wanderers exhibition. His work included Ingresque portraits and history pieces in the 1860s and 1870s. He executed crisp watercolours of Latvian peasant types and also landscapes in watercolour as well as oil paintings.
Sick Child, 1869, TG, is effectively staged domestic genre with an emotive theme. The child is in bed in the background and attention is focused on the solitary mother who stands by the window her separateness cleverly encapsulating her lonely anxiety. There is no sign of the father or of the doctor. It is a fairly poor house but decent. There is a dresser but only a few sticks by the stove.
Coll TG.

I

I.A. see AKIMOV, I. A.
I.O. see OSTROUKHOV, I.S.
I.P. see PELEVIN, I.A.
IVA. see IVANOV, D.I.

IACOVLEFF, A. = YAKOVLEV, A.E.

IGNAT'EVA = ZHUKOVSKAYA, A.A.

IGOREV (IGIREV), Lev Stepanovich   **1822-1893**
Born in the Saratov region. He studied at the St. Petersburg
Seminary from 1848. He taught ikon painting at the St.
Petersburg Seminary 1855-7. He worked in St. Petersburg
1855-64 and moved to Saratov in his later years. He painted
for churches in Tver' and elsewhere and also made portraits of
Siberian officials. He died at Saratov.
Coll TG; Novgorod Art Museum; Saratov Art Museum.

IGUMNOV, Sergei Dmitrievich   **1900-c.1942**
Graphic artist, painter. He studied at the Stroganov College
1915-17, the Free Art Studios in 1918 under Grishchenko and
at the Moscow Vkhutemas. He contributed to the Twelfth
State Exhibition: Colourdynamo and Tectonic Primitivism
(*Tsvetodinamos i tektonicheskiy primitivizm*) along with
Grishchenko, Shevchenko and others in Moscow in 1919. He
was included in the 1928 exhibition of Acquisitions by the
State Art Collections Fund held in Moscow and in the First
Touring Exhibition of Paintings and Graphics which opened
in Moscow in 1929.
He was designing patriotic posters 1937-40. He died at the
front in the Second World War.
Coll TG.

ILIAZD = ZDANEVICH, I.

IL'INSKAYA, Sof'ya Vladimirovna   **1891-1965**
Applied artist. Born at Riga. She studied under Yuon and
Dudin in Moscow and under Pashkov and Shcherbinsky at the
Moscow College 1910-15. She lived at Ekaterinoslav 1915-17.
After the Revolution she was active in Agitprop projects in
1918 including the design of the banner of VTsIK, the All-
Russian Executive Committee, and other banners.
In the 1930s and 1940s she designed women's clothes for mass
production. Exhibitions of her work were held in Moscow in
1953 and 1961. She died in Moscow.

INFANTE, Francisco   **b.1943**
Painter. He studied at the Moscow Secondary Art School and
exhibited with the *Dvizhenie* (Movement) group 1962-8. He
was an organiser of the group *Argo* in 1970.
Lit D.Elliott, V.Dudakov *100 Years of Russian Painting*,
London, 1991.

INGAL, Vladimir Iosifovich   **1901-1966**
Sculptor. Born at Ekaterinodar. He studied under V.N.Meshkov
in Moscow in 1915.
After the Revolution he was at Rostov-on-Don 1918-19 and

studying under Erzya in Baku 1923-5, at the Azerbaijani
Polytechnic until 1926 and then at the Leningrad Vkhutein
1926-30. He worked in collaboration with I. and
V.Ya.Bogolyubov from 1929. He produced mosaics for the
Lenin Mausoleum in 1930. His works include a monument to
S.Ordzhonikidze, 1935, designed in collaboration with
Bogolyubov, and a monument to *Rimsky-Korsakov* erected in
Leningrad in 1952. An exhibition of his work was held in
Leningrad in 1951. He died at Leningrad.
Coll TG; RM.

INKhUK
The abbreviated name of the Institute of Artistic Culture
(*Institut khudozhestvennoi kul'tury*) in Moscow.

INO, Pierre = VECHEGZHANIN, P. V.

INOZEMTSEV, Boris Ivanovich   **1904-c.1941**
Painter, graphic artist. Born in the Tambov region. He
studied under A.E.Miganadzhian in Moscow 1922-3 and
under S.V.Priselkov at the Leningrad Vkhutein 1925-7. He
designed cinema posters 1922-3 and illustrated books for the
State Publishing House Giz. He exhibited with the Circle of
Artists in Leningrad between 1927 and 1929.

INPII
The abbreviated name of the Institute of Proletarian Plastic
Arts (*Institut proletarskogo izobrazitel'nogo iskusstva*) operative in
Leningrad 1930-2.

IODKO, Romual'd Romual'dovich   **1894-1974**
Sculptor. Born Minsk region. He studied at the Stroganov College
under Aleshin, N.A.Andreev and E.U.Shishkina 1912-18.
After the Revolution he served in the Red Army 1919-21. He
returned to study under B.Korolev at the Moscow Vkhutemas
1921-4. He then taught on the foundation course at the
Moscow Vkhutemas 1924-30 with the sculptors A.Babichev,
I.Chaikov, B.Korolev and N.Niss-Gol'dman. He was a
member of AKhR 1928-32. He produced decorative work for
parks, stadiums and other buildings in Moscow. He died in
Moscow.

IOGANSON (JOHANSON), Boris Vladimirovich
1893-1973
Socialist Realist history painter, theatre designer, graphic
artist. Born in Moscow where he also died. He was studying
under P.Kelin in 1912 and from 1912 to 1918 he attended the
Moscow College under N.Kasatkin, S.Malyutin and
K.Korovin. He exhibited from 1914.
After the Revolution he designed for the theatre at
Krasnoyarsk and Aleksandri in the Kherson region 1919-22.
He was represented at the First Russian Art Exhibition in
Berlin in 1922. He was a founder member of AKhRR in 1922
and was later made an Academician of the USSR. He was
represented in the First Touring Exhibition of Paintings and
Graphics which opened in Moscow in 1929 and at the jubilee
exhibition Artists of the RSFSR over 15 Years held at the
Russian Museum, Leningrad, in 1932.
He was awarded a grand prix at the Paris International
Exhibition in 1937.
He taught at the Academy in Leningrad 1949-62 and in
Moscow 1962-8. He served as Director of the Tretyakov
Gallery 1951-4, and also Vice-President 1953-8, and then
President 1958-62 of the Academy of Arts of the USSR. He

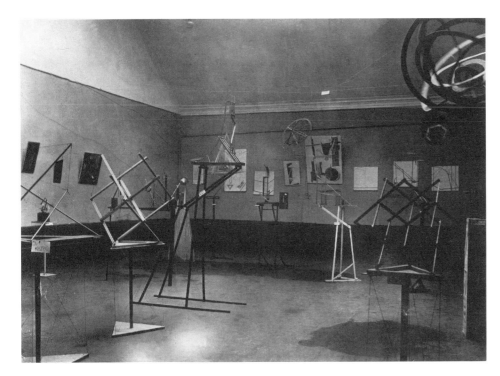

Karl Ioganson. Constructions at the exhibition of the Society of Young Artists (Obmokhu), Moscow, *May 1921.*
The works by Ioganson are those derived from the three perpendicular planes of a cube and standing on their corners. Other works are by Medunetsky, Vladimir Stenberg and Georgiy Stenberg; hanging constructions are by Rodchenko. This was a major example of that phase of Constructivism known as 'laboratory art', abandoned in 1921 in favour of Constructivism applied to useful design projects.
Documentary photograph Rodchenko Archive, Moscow.

was awarded many honours.

An exhibition of his work was held in Moscow in 1969. He died in Moscow.

In the Old Ural Factory, 1937, TG, is an attack upon merchants. The exhausted workers are reduced to near slavery by their dependence upon the well-fed merchant in fine clothes. The vigour of the message outweighs the flavour of historicism.

Writings B.Ioganson *Za Masterstvo v Zhivopisi* (For Mastery in Painting), Moscow, 1952.

Lit M.Sokolnikov *B.V.Ioganson*, Moscow, 1957. N.Sokolova *B.V.Ioganson*, Leningrad, 1969. *B.V.Ioganson*, exh. cat., Moscow, 1969.

Coll TG; RM; Perm Art Museum; Murmansk Art Museum, and many more.

IOGANSON, Karl Val'demarovich   c.1890-1924
Sculptor. He studied at Riga Art School in the early 1910s and at Penza Art School 1915-16. Here he made decorative compositions and painted a *Portrait of a Friend* which was exhibited at Penza in 1916.

After the Revolution he was a member of the Commune of Latvian Artists. He lived in Moscow and was actively involved in the laboratory period of Constructivist practice and debate at INKhUK in Moscow 1921-2. The works which he exhibited at the third *Obmokhu* (Society of Young Artists) exhibition in Moscow were geometrical constructions based upon the three Cartesian planes at right angles, arranged rather like three interslotted window panes in format. This basic structure was modified in various ways to allow several struts to be replaced by cables, some of which hung loose so that the structure would remain stable even when its balance was adjusted by hand. He was represented at the First Russian Art Exhibition in Berlin in 1922. The kinetic potential of his constructions was noted by the Hungarian Constructivist Laszlo Moholy-Nagy. He exhibited with AKhRR in 1926. He died in Moscow.

Lit A.Z.Rudenstine *Costakis Collection*, London, 1981. C.

Lodder *Russian Constructivism*, New Haven and London, 1983.

Coll Costakis Collection.

IOKUBONIS, G. A. = JOKUBONIS, G. A.

IONIN, Nikolai Aleksandrovich   1890-1948
Painter. He studied at the Society for the Encouragement of the Arts in St. Petersburg under Rylov 1908-12 and at the Higher Institute of the Academy under D.N.Kardovsky 1913-17.

After the Revolution he also studied under K.Petrov-Vodkin whose style his work may resemble. His work also included portraits of a monumental simplicity set against a geometric background recalling Malevich or Rodchenko but removed from Suprematism in its effect by its role as architecture or similar motifs. There appears at least to be a compositional debt however. He painted industrial landscapes in the 1920s and 1930s.

Lit A.M.Muratov, V.Manin et al. *Zhivopis' 20-30kh godov*, Sankt-Peterburg, 1991.

Coll RM.

IONOVA = FEDOROVA, M. A.

ISAEV, Valentin Ivanovich   1928-1964+
Sculptor. Born in the Saratov region. He studied under P.F.Il'in and E.F.Ekkert at the Saratov Art College 1948-58. He exhibited from 1962. His work included portraits of Soviet heroes and *To the Stars*, 1964.

ISAKOV, Pavel Aleksandrovich   1823-1881
Theatre designer. He studied under A.A.Roller in the studios of the Imperial Theatres of St. Petersburg 1838-43 where he became Assistant Decorator 1843-55 and Painter 1855-6. His designs included a curtain for the Mikhailovsky Palace Theatre depicting a *View of the Palace of Granienburg*, 1852, a *View of the Tsar's Palace* for the Krasnocelsky Theatre near St. Petersburg and designs for the opera *Osada Genta* in 1852. From 1856 he was artist to the Moscow Imperial Theatres where he designed Glinka's *Life for the Tsar* in 1857. He also

designed for the St. Petersburg Theatre Circus, the Bolshoi Theatre in St. Petersburg. He worked with Ostrovsky 1865-81 devising realistic theatre settings. He died in Moscow.
Coll St. Petersburg Theatre Museum.

ISAKOV, Sergei Konstantinovich　　　**1875-1953**

Critic, art historian, sculptor. He studied at the Moscow Institute until 1898. He taught History of Art at the Academy 1907-18. He exhibited from 1909. He visited Paris and Rome in 1909 and Naples in 1911. He wrote for museum catalogues in the period 1911-15. He was a founder of the society Apartment No. 5 in Petrograd along with Bruni, Tyrsa, Lebedev, Miturich, Punin and Tatlin in 1915. He was a particular friend of Tatlin. He worked as a conservator at the Academy Museum until 1917 and in 1915 he published catalogues of the paintings and sculptures in the Academy of Art (see Writings below).

During the Revolution in March 1917 he was a founder of the Freedom of Art Association in Petrograd with the artists Al'tman and Ilya Zdanevich as well as Mayakovsky, Meyerhold, Punin and Prokofiev. He produced sculptural studies in folded paper and papier mâché 1918-23. He was included in the enormous survey Exhibition of Paintings by Petrograd Artists of All Tendencies 1919-1923 held in Petrograd in 1923. He taught

at the Vkhutemas 1924-5. He replaced Malevich at GINKhUK (State Institute of Artistic Culture) in 1926. He taught at the Vkhutein 1925-30. He produced numerous articles and his *Catalogue of Works by P.Filonov in the State Russian Museum* was published in Leningrad in 1930.

He continued to teach until his death in Leningrad.

Writings S.K.Isakov *Russkaya zhivopis'* (Russian Painting), Petrograd, 1915. S.K.Isakov *Russkaya skul'ptura (Russian Sculpture)*, Petrograd, 1915.

ISPOLATOVA, S. K.　　　**a.1918**

She was represented at the First Exhibition of Works of the Professional Union of Artists in Moscow in 1918.

ISTOMIN, Konstantin Nikolaevich　　　**1887-1942**

Painter, graphic artist. Born at Kursk. He studied at the studio of E.E.Shreyder in Kharkov 1904-5 and at the Holòsy School in Munich 1906-8. He then studied History of Art at Moscow University 1909-13. He exhibited from 1910.

After the Revolution he was represented at the First Exhibition of Works of the Professional Union of Artists in Moscow in 1918 and at the Fifth State Exhibition: From Impressionism to Non-Objective Art in Moscow 1918-19. He taught at the Vkhutemas-Vkhutein 1921-30. He was a member of the *Makovets* group

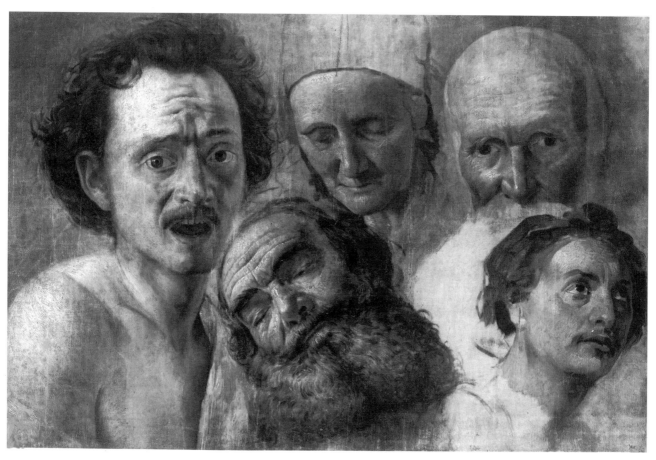

Aleksandr Ivanov. Study of Heads. *Oil on board. 42 x 61 cm.*
This is probably a study for the major work of his career 'Christ Appearing to the People'.
Ashmolean Museum, Oxford.

1922-3 and secretary of the 4 Arts society 1924-9. His work was included in the exhibition of Soviet art held at Harbin in 1926 and in Japan in 1927 and in the major exhibition in Moscow in 1927 marking the tenth anniversary of the Revolution. He was also included in the 1928 exhibition of Acquisitions by the State Art Collections Fund held in Moscow, in the First Touring Exhibition of Paintings and Graphics which opened in Moscow in 1929 and in the jubilee exhibition Artists of the RSFSR over 15 Years held at the Russian Museum, Leningrad, in 1932. He was a member of AKhR 1931-2. He sometimes signed his work in cyrillic script 'K.I'. He died at Samarkand. Exhibitions of his work were held in Moscow in 1961, 1975 and 1978.

In the Artist's Studio, 1929, RM, has a female figure against the studio light with the river visible beyond. Its simplification, colour and handling clearly reveal a homage to the more subdued of Matisse's early Fauve studio interiors.

Lit M.N.Yablonskaya *K.N.Istomin*, Moscow, 1972. A.M.Muratov, V.Manin et al. *Zhivopis' 20-30kh godov*, Sankt-Peterburg, 1991.
Coll RM; Kursk Art Museum; Saratov Art Museum.

ISTOMIN, N. = SAVIN, N.

ISTOMIN, Vasili   a.1799-1801+
Portraitist. He studied under M.F.Klavdal'. Works are known from the period 1799-1801.
Coll TG.

ISUPOV, Aleksei Vladimirovich   1889-1957
Portrait and landscape painter. Born at Vyatsk. He studied under Arkhipov, K.Korovin and Serov at the Moscow College 1908-13. He was a member of the Vyatsk Art Circle in the 1910s. He exhibited with the Wanderers from 1912 and became a member in 1916. He lived in Moscow to 1915 then moved to Central Asia until 1921 including military service in Turkestan 1915-17. He was painting in Uzbekistan in 1917. His *Shakh-i-Zinda Mosque*, 1917, Uzbek Art Museum, Tashkent, is a view of the architectural ensemble at Samarkand. A spangled vision of the great mosque is seen from a high viewpoint with tombs in the foreground. The painting has a mosaic effect built from tiles, leaves and brushwork.
After the Revolution he taught at the Turkestan Regional Art School in Tashkent 1918-21. He returned to live in Moscow 1922-5.
He emigrated to Italy in 1926. He died in Rome. Exhibitions were held in Kirov 1971, Moscow 1973 and Tashkent 1977.
Lit A.Isupov *Turkestan*, Moscow, 1929.
Coll Uzbek Art Museum, Tashkent.

ITINERANTS = WANDERERS

ITKIND, Isaak Yakovlevich   1871-1969
Sculptor. He studied under Volnukhin in Moscow in 1912. He exhibited with the World of Art in December 1917 in Moscow.
After the Revolution he made portraits of workers and revolutionary figures. He taught at the Moscow Proletkult 1918-20. He moved to Petrograd in 1920 and to Simferopol in 1923 where he taught at the Technical College 1925-7.
He lived at Aktyubinsk 1938-44 and then at Alma-Ata where he died.
Coll Pavlodar Art Museum; Kazakh Art Museum.

IVAKIN, G. B.   a.1919
Painter. He exhibited at the juryless Eighth State Exhibition in Moscow in 1919.

IVANOV, Aleksandr Andreevich   1806-1858
Major painter whose work was dominated by a single project to complete an enormous painting of *Christ Appearing to the People*. There are a great number of studies for this work incorporating drawings, oil studies, figure studies, portraits and landscapes. Very many of these are preserved in the Tretyakov Gallery in Moscow.
The son of A.I.Ivanov, a professor of painting at the Academy in St. Petersburg, he entered the Academy himself at the precocious age of eleven and graduated in 1829. He travelled to Austria, Germany and Italy on a scholarship in 1830 and remained there many years working on *Christ Appearing to the People*, TG, which dominated his career. His *Christ Appearing to Mary Magdalen* was completed in 1835. He visited Northern Italy. He made studies in the open air and he was also in contact with the German Nazarene painters in Rome. He met the writer Gogol in 1838 who was supportive of the major canvas. When he finally arranged transport of the painting back to Russia, the journey was attended with various crises but was ultimately safely delivered. It was received with acclaim and debate and it has continued to attract attention in the 20th century on account of its evangelical aspect and its direct appeal to the people. He died shortly after its return to Russia in 1857.

Christ Appearing to the People, 1832-57, TG is perhaps the most celebrated single painting of the mid-19th century in Russia. Assembled from a mass of studies, it is dramatic, monumental and original in theme. In the foreground John the Baptist announces the coming of Christ to a complex group of over twenty figures. On the barren hill in the background the solitary figure of Christ approaches. The painting is convincing as drama, incorporating its theme of revelation into every gesture and pose, whilst the composition asserts the contrast of the crowd against the isolation of Christ. There is in this a well handled rhetoric that advances the message of the saviour appearing to the people, a theme which continued to echo even into the revolutionary period in the 20th century. The painting effectively resolves the mass of studies into a coherent painting of psychological force.

Jesus Walking on the Waters, watercolour, c.1850, TG, reveals the looseness of his working studies which comprised drawings and compositional experiments of many kinds. Here a dramatic tilting composition of swelling waves and an open boat are overdrawn with an alternative positioning of the figure of Jesus confidently striding across the water with the earlier version of this figure still visible through this drawing. It shows the vigorous examination of alternatives which he used to evolve his final compositions. Only in the later stages would he refer to the posed model or directly observed drawing of the figure. In this he was following the standard academic procedure of his day.
Aleksandr Ivanov was one of only seven artists deemed worthy of a monument in Lenin's plan issued in 1918.
Lit A.Mokritsky *Yavlenia Khrista narodu, kartina Ivanova* (Christ Appearing to the People, the Painting by Ivanov), Moscow, 1858. M.Stasyulevich *A.A.Ivanov, ego zhizn' i perepiska* (A.A.Ivanov, his Life and Writings), St. Petersburg, 1880. V.D.Barooshian *The Art of Liberation: Alexander A.Ivanov*, London, 1987. D.V.Sarabianov *Russian Art From Neoclassicism to the Avant-Garde*, London, 1990.
Coll TG; RM; Uffizi, Florence.

IVANOV, Aleksandr Ivanovich 1888-1948
Painter. Born in the St. Petersburg region. He studied under Petrov-Vodkin at the Zvantseva School in St. Petersburg 1908-11.
After the Revolution he executed Agitprop decorations in Moscow 1918-19. He exhibited with the Artists of the Leftist Federation of the Professional Union in 1918 along with Popova, Rodchenko, Tatlin and others, at the Fifth State Exhibition: From Impressionism to Non-Objective Art in Moscow 1918-19, and he was represented at the enormous First State Exhibition of Art and Science, which included ethnographic material, held in Kazan in 1920. He exhibited with the Society of Moscow Painters at its inaugural exhibition in Moscow in 1925. He was included in the 1928 exhibition of Acquisitions by the State Art Collections Fund held in Moscow. He was a member of the Society of Moscow Artists 1928-31.
He made decorative panels for the Kursk Station in Moscow in 1935. He died in Moscow.
Lit A.I.Savinov *A.I.Ivanov*, Moscow, 1951.
Coll TG.

IVANOV, Aleksei Nikolaevich b.1905
Sculptor. Born at Simbirsk. He studied at the Samara Art-Technical Studios 1919-20. He lived in Uzbekistan from 1928. He worked at Tashkent especially on portraits of Uzbek peasants and heroic collective farm workers but also on reliefs for buildings in Tashkent.
An exhibition was held at Tashkent in 1956.

IVANOV, Andrei Ivanovich 1775-1848
Academic history painter of heroic Russian themes dramatically lit as well as mythological and biblical subjects. He was the father of Aleksandr A.Ivanov and Sergei A.Ivanov. He studied under G.I.Ugryumov. He taught at the Academy in 1798 and 1812-31 where his pupils included Aleksandr A.Ivanov and K.Bryullov. He executed paintings for the iconostasis of the Aleksandrovsky Cathedral in Warsaw. An exhibition was held in Leningrad in 1978.
Mstislav the Brave and Rededin in Combat, 1812, RM, depicts a nationalist theme evolved as a pretext for academic painting. The fight is vigorous with a Crusader army in the background but the figures are clearly posed in the lifeboom. Victory, personified by a flying woman, descends with laurels for the victor.
Coll TG; RM; Sverdlovsk Art Museum; Ulyanovsk Art Museum..
See A.A.Ivanov.

IVANOV, Anton Andreevich 1815-1848
Sculptor. A classicising sculptor able to generalise or to particularise his models. He made numerous portrait busts and a study for *Lomonosov on the Sea Shore* in the Russian Museum. This is inscribed 'Rome 1845'.
Coll RM.

IVANOV, Anton Ivanovich 1818-1864
Painter. Born in the Vladimir region. He was known as Goluboy. he studied under E.G. and then G.G.Cherntsov 1833-9 and at the Academy from 1840. In 1838 he travelled down the Volga from Rybinsk to Astrakhan. In 1846 the Society for the Encouragement of the Arts sent him with the Chernetsovs to Italy. He was working in Rome 1851 and Livorno 1860. Sometimes he signed his work 'A.Ivanoff'. He remained in Italy for the rest of his life and he died in Rome.
Coll TG.

IVANOV, Boris Nikolaevich (Mikolaovich) 1902-1941
Ukrainian sculptor. Born at St. Petersburg. He studied at Odessa Art Institute under P.G.Volokidin and D.K.Kraynev 1924-9. He visited Italy in 1926. He worked at Sevastopol 1921-4, Odessa 1924-30, Nikolaev 1930-3, Kharkov 1933-5 and Kiev 1935-41. He was killed fighting at the front in the Second World War.

IVANOV, Dmitri Ivanovich 1782-1810+
History painter. Sometimes the date of his death is given as after 1828. He studied under Ugryumov at the Academy. He took part in an archaeological expedition across Russia 1809-10. He executed views, portraits and also mosaics for Saint Sophia Cathedral, Kiev. Sometimes he signed his work 'D.Iva'.
Coll TG.

IVANOV, Grigori Ivanovich 1894-1960
Painter. Born in the Pskov region. He studied at the Pskov Art-Technical School until 1922, then at the Leningrad Vkhutein until 1926. His name appears on the April 1919 list of artists for acquisitions by the proposed Museum of Painterly Culture. He exhibited with the Circle of Artists in Leningrad of which he was a member from 1926 to 1932. He lived at Stalinabad in 1941-5.
Coll RM; Tadzhik Museum.

IVANOV, I. a.1826-1839
Theatre designer. He worked for the Bolshoi Theatre in Moscow where he was engaged designing almost all the productions between 1826 and 1839 along with K.Braun, among them the opera *Lomonosov* in October 1826 and the ballet by F.Sholtz *Tri poyasa ili russkaya Sandril'on* (The Three Sashes or a Russian Cinderella) in October 1828.

IVANOV, I. D. = SHADR, I. D.

IVANOV, I. K. a.1919
Painter. He exhibited at the juryless Eighth State Exhibition in Moscow in 1919.

IVANOV, Ivan Alekseevich 1779-1848
Lithographer, engraver. Born in Moscow. He studied at the Academy in St. Petersburg. The Tsar commissioned four views of Tsarskoe Selo in 1827. He also executed views of St. Petersburg, producing engravings after watercolours by V.S.Sadovnikov in 1830 including part of his panorama of Nevsky Prospekt, published in St. Petersburg 1830-5 and reissued in Leningrad in 1974. He was mainly an engraver producing at least thirty-three plates. He died in St. Petersburg.
Coll Academy Museum, St. Petersburg; Khabarovsk Museum; Ashmolean Museum, Oxford.

IVANOV, Ivan Andreevich 1824-1869
Landscape painter. He studied under Vorob'ev at the Academy from 1844. He worked in St. Petersburg and exhibited from 1846. He also produced Crimean landscapes in the 1840s. He died in St. Petersburg.
Coll TG; RM; Ulyanovsk Museum.

IVANOV, Mikhail Filippovich 1869-c.1930
Painter, graphic artist. He studied under Repin at the Academy in St. Petersburg 1891-6 and exhibited with the Kuindzhi Society, the Society of Russian Watercolourists and the Society of Individualists.
After the Revolution he designed revolutionary festivals and

was included in the enormous survey Exhibition of Paintings by Petrograd Artists of All Tendencies 1919-1923 held in Petrograd in 1923 and in the 1928 exhibition of Acquisitions by the State Art Collections Fund held in Moscow. He also exhibited with AKhRR.
Coll RM; Brodsky Apartment Museum, Leningrad.

IVANOV, Mikhail Matveevich   **1748-1823**
Painter of landscape, genre and history paintings. Born at St. Petersburg. He was the brother of Arkhip Matveevich Ivanov. He studied at the Academy under I.F.Grot from 1762. He travelled abroad on a scholarship in 1770 and 1770-3 he studied in Paris. He was making life drawings in Rome 1773-9, but he also visited Spain and Switzerland. He travelled in the Ukraine, Crimea, Georgia and executed pastoral watercolours of Mount Ararat and Armenian views in 1783. These were pervaded by a luminous stillness. During the period 1787-91 he made directly observed watercolour drawings of the Russo-Turkish War. He was Keeper of Drawings at the Hermitage Museum from 1792. He also executed paintings on the theme of war and from 1800 he directed classes in battle painting at the Academy. He taught landscape painting from 1804. His pupils included Silvestr Shchedrin. He died at St. Petersburg.

IVANOV, Nikolai   **a.1815**
Engraver. He produced coloured engravings of St. Petersburg characterised by precision and clarity of line with human activities enlivening the foreground.
Coll Museum of the History of St. Petersburg, St. Petersburg.

IVANOV, Semen Petrovich   **b.1882**
Architect, painter. Born at St. Petersburg. He studied architecture at the Academy 1901-10 and worked at Sverdlovsk. He exhibited paintings from 1912.
After the Revolution his work included book design.

IVANOV, Sergei Ivanovich   **1885-1942**
Graphic artist. He studied at the Stroganov School and at the Moscow College. He designed political posters.
Lit D.Elliott, V.Dudakov *100 Years of Russian Painting*, London, 1991.

IVANOV, Sergei P.   **a.1918-1920**
Sculptor, graphic artist. He was engaged on Agitprop decorations at the City Duma, Petrograd, in 1918. He was designing posters in 1920.

IVANOV, Sergei Vasilievich   **1864-1910**
Prolific figure and genre painter, printmaker, associated with the Young Wanderers. Born at Ruza in the Moscow region. He studied at the Moscow College 1878-82 and 1884-5 under E.Sorokin and Pryanishnikov and at the Academy in St. Petersburg 1882-4. He travelled to Samara, Astrakhan and Orenburg 1885-9 depicting the plight of the peasantry. He began to exhibit with the Wanderers in 1887 and became a member in 1899. He travelled to Austria, France and Italy in 1894. He exhibited in Munich in 1892 and Prague in 1900.
He made protest paintings in favour of the peasants and depicted the student rebellion at Moscow University in 1899. He taught at the Stroganov College 1899-1906 and at the Moscow College 1900-10. From 1903 he was a member of the Union of Russian Artists and in 1905 he became an academician. His works include *At the Prison Gate* 1885, *Death of a Migrant Peasant* 1889, *Village Revolt* 1889 and a painting from the

uprising of 1905 *Soldiers Shooting at the Demonstration* 1905. He died at Svistukha, Moscow region. He exhibited posthumously in Rome, Moscow and St. Petersburg in 1911. Exhibitions were held in Moscow in 1944, 1951 and 1964, and in Kiev in 1965.
The Fusillade, 1905, is a political painting which records and condemns the slaughter of marchers in 1905. It is an immediate, dramatic and powerful painting of death across the open city square in broad sunlight.
Lit V. and E.Zhuravlev *Khudozhnik S.V.Ivanov*, Moscow-Leningrad, 1931. I.Granovsky *S.V.Ivanov, Zhizn' i Tvorchestvo*, Moscow, 1962. *Paris-Moscou*, 1979.
Coll Well represented at TG; RM; Kirov Art Museum; Irkutsk Art Museum.

IVANOV, Viktor Semenovich   **1909-1968**
Painter, graphic artist. Born in Moscow. He studied in Moscow 1926-9 under Yakubi and Kardovsky. He became an important Soviet poster artist from the 1930s onwards. He designed many books in the 1940s and remained active as an illustrator in the 1960s. A poster of 1966 declared *Lenin lived. Lenin lives. Lenin will live*. Ivanov died in Moscow.

IVANOV-KRUTOV, I. P.   **a.1921**
He contributed to the First State Exhibition in Orenburg in 1921.

IVANOVA, Antonina Nikolaeva   **1893-1972**
Painter, graphic artist, theatre designer, sculptor. Born in the Kiev region. She studied at the Drawing School of the Society for the Encouragement of the Arts in St. Petersburg 1912-15 under Bilibin, Roerich and Dobuzhinsky, at A.E.Yakovlev's New Studio 1915-16 and under Boychuk at the Kiev Academy.
After the Revolution she lived near Moscow from 1923 designing wooden toys for export. She executed decorations at a sanatorium in Odessa in collaboration with M.L.Boychuk 1927-8. She was a member of ARMU 1927-30. She was included in the 1928 exhibition of Acquisitions by the State Art Collections Fund held in Moscow and in the exhibition of Russian Graphic Art at Riga in 1929.
She produced fabric designs derived from Ukrainian and Russian traditional motifs and a series of sculptures in the 1930s. She designed ceramic ware in the 1940s. She was designing for the theatre in 1943. An exhibition of her work was held in Moscow in 1970. She died in Moscow.

IVANOVA, Zinaida Grigor'evna   **1897-1979**
Sculptor. She was born at Penza. She died at Moscow.

IVANOVSKY, Ivan Vasil'evich   **1905-1980**
Painter. He studied at the Moscow Vkhutemas/Vhutein under D.Shterenberg and S.Gerasimov 1925-30. He was a member of OST 1928-30. His *Washerwomen*, late 1920s, RM, has a quality of rapidly recorded reportage not far removed from lively illustration. The figures converse before hastily indicated buildings. A child and a dog wait for them to stop. He died in Moscow.
Lit A.M.Muratov, V.Manin et al. *Zhivopis' 20-30kh godov*, Sankt-Peterburg, 1991.
Coll RM.

IVANYCH-BAEV   **a.1919**
Painter. He exhibited at the juryless Eighth State Exhibition in Moscow in 1919.

IVASHINTSOVA, Maria Ivanovna   1882-1957
Ceramics artist, illustrator. She studied at the Academy in St. Petersburg 1908-15 first as a sculptor and then in painting under Kardovsky. She drew for the journal *Novyy Satirikon* 1913-15 and 1917.
After the Revolution she designed cups, bowls and plates for the State Porcelain Factory 1918-20 and exhibited ceramics in 1919. She exhibited with AKhRR. She also illustrated books and periodicals. She died in Moscow.
Lit N.Lobanov-Rostovsky *Revolutionary Porcelain*, London, 1990.
Coll Museum of the Leningrad Porcelain Factory.

IZDEBSKY, Vladimir Alekseevich   1882-1911+
Sculptor. He studied at the Odessa School of Art 1897-1904. He exhibited from 1908. He organised the Izdebsky International Exhibition Salons at Odessa where he also exhibited 1909-11, including a bust of David Burlyuk 1910-11.

IZHEVSKAYA, Margarita Pavlovna   1886-1941
Graphic artist, etcher. Born at Perm. She studied with E.S.Kruglikova in Petrograd in 1919 and under Shillingovsky at the Leningrad Vkhutein 1921-4. She was a member of the Kuindzhi Society. She was represented at the jubilee exhibition Artists of the RSFSR over 15 Years held at the Russian Museum, Leningrad, in 1932. She illustrated books in the 1930s. She died at Leningrad.
Coll RM; Perm Art Museum.

IZhSA
The abbreviated name of the Institute of Painting, Sculpture and Architecture of the All-Russian Academy of Arts (*Institut zhivopisi, skul'ptury i arkhitektury Vserossiyskoy Akademii khudozhestv*) operative in Leningrad 1932-44.

IZO
The abbreviated name of the Fine Art Section (*Otdel izobrazitel'nykh isskustv*) of the People's Commissariat of the Enlightenment in the early years of the Revolution.

J

J.S. see STEFANOVSKY, I.P.
JACOVLEFF, A. = YAKOVLEV, A.E.
JAKOVLEFF, W. = YAKOVLEV, V.N.
JAKOWLEW, Michel = YAKOVLEV, M.N.

JAWLENSKY, Alexej von (YAVLENSKY, A.G.)
1864-1941
Painter active mostly in Germany where his work became associated with Expressionism as a result of his membership of the *Blaue Reiter* (Blue Rider) group along with Kandinsky and others. Born at Torzhok in the Tver region. He attended military school in Moscow 1877-84 and served as an army lieutenant 1884-9. He then studied at the Academy in St. Petersburg under Repin 1889-93. In 1891 he met the painter Mariane von Werefkin whom he later married.
He left the army in 1896 and moved to Munich where he attended the Azbé School 1896-9. Here he met Kandinsky. He was involved in numerous exhibitions in both Germany and Russia, including the 1903 Munich Secession, the World of Art in St. Petersburg in 1906, the Union of Russian Artists 1906-7 and 1909, *Venok* (The Wreath) in St. Petersburg in 1908, and the Izdebsky Salons in Odessa, Riga and Kiev from 1909.
He had visited France in 1903-5, met Matisse and exhibited at the Salon d'Automne in Paris. His painting became increasingly experimental in colour and form and in 1909 he was a founder member of the New Artists Federation (NKV) with Kandinsky, Werefkin and Münther in Munich and a contributor to its exhibitions in the period 1909-12. He exhibited with the Knave of Diamonds in Moscow 1910-11 and was a founder member of the *Blaue Reiter* group in Munich. In 1913 he was showing work at the First German Autumn Salon in Berlin. In 1914 he made his last visit to Russia and also travelled to Switzerland where he settled in 1915.
From 1917 he produced a long series of paintings and studies of meditational heads, the *Têtes mystérieux*, sombre works in which the face was simplified to basic horizontal and vertical axes but which remained emotionally expressive. He settled in Wiesbaden in 1921. He was a founder member of the group the Blue Four (*Die blauen Vier*) with Klee, Kandinsky and Feininger in 1924. He died at Wiesbaden.
Lit J.Schultze *Jawlensky*, Köln, 1970. D.Elliott, V.Dudakov *100 Years of Russian Painting*, London, 1991.
Coll Numerous collections including TG; Kunsthalle, Basle; Boymans-Van Beuningen Museum, Rotterdam; Städtisches Museum, Wiesbaden.

JOHANSON, B. V.= IOGANSON, B. V.

JOKUBONIS, Gediminas Al'bino (IOKUBONIS)
b.1927
Lithuanian monumental sculptor, medallist, poster designer. He studied at the Institute of Applied and Decorative Arts at Kaunas under V.F.Palis and Yu.Mikenas 1946-51 and at the Lithuanian Art Institute 1951-2. He exhibited from 1952. Works include *The Mother*, 1960, granite, TG, a small version of his large monument at the village of Pirchupis erected in memory of the victims of Fascism. His monument to *Lenin* was erected in Moscow in 1967. His portraits included *Ciurlionis*, Kaunas Art Museum, in 1975.
Lit V.M.Rogachevsky *G.Iokubonis*, Leningrad-Moscow, 1964.
Coll TG; Kaunas Art Museum.

K

K. (alone, in a circle or triangle), see **KANDINSKY, V.V.;**
KRINSKY, V.F.
K.I. (cyrillic) see **ISTOMIN, K.N.**
K.M. see **MALEVICH, K.S.**
K.P.V. (cyrillic) see **PETROV-VODKIN, K.S.**

KAAZIK (KAASIK), Aleksandr Aleksandrovich 1908-1947+
Portrait sculptor.

KABAKOV, Ilya Iosifovich b.1933
Graphic artist. He studied at the Surikov Institute, Moscow,
1951-7 and under Dekhterev. He has exhibited widely in
Europe and also in Washington in 1977. One-man exhibitions
were held in Paris and Berne in 1985, Marseilles and Düsseldorf
in 1986, Paris in 1987, New York in 1988 and London in 1989.
Lit David Elliott, V.Dudakov *100 Years of Russian Art*,
London, 1989.

KABANOV, Ivan Andreevich 1823-1869
Painter of views and portraits.
Coll TG.

KACHALOV, G. A. 18th century
Engraver of architectural views of St. Petersburg. Worked
with M.I.Makhaev.
Coll Ashmolean Museum, Oxford.

KACHURA-FALILEEVA, Ekaterina Nikolaevna
a.1917-1921
Graphic artist. She exhibited with the World of Art in 1917.
She was represented in the Sixth State Exhibition: The Print
(*VI Gosudarstvennaya vystavka gravyur*) in Moscow in 1919.
She was included in the Third Touring Exhibition of the
Sovetsk Regional subdepartment of the Museums Bureau
along with Kandinsky, Rodchenko and others in 1921.

KADLUBINSKY, K. K. a.1925
He exhibited at the third and last exhibition of the *Makovets*
group in Moscow 1925-6.

KAGAN, Anna Aleksandrovna 1902-1974
Painter, graphic artist, ceramics artist. She studied under
Malevich in Vitebsk 1919-22 and was a member of the *Unovis*
group. She exhibited in Vitebsk 1920-1. She also exhibited at
Moscow 1920-2 and Petrograd in 1923. Her work responded
to the Suprematism of Malevich whom she assisted on the
construction of three-dimensional 'architectons' at
GINKhUK, the State Institute of Artistic Culture, at
Leningrad 1924-5. She produced decorations for ceramic ware
in the late 1920s and early 1930s.
Lit David Elliott, V.Dudakov *100 Years of Russian Art*,
London, 1989.

KAKABADZE, David Nestorovich 1889-1952
Painter, theatre designer, illustrator. Born at Kukhi, Kutaisi
region, Georgia. He studied at Paevsky's private school in
Kutaisi. He studied simultaneously at the university in St.

Silovan Kakabadze. The Georgian Writer and Diplomat Sulkhan-
Saba Orbeliani, *1947. Limestone. 57 x 60 x 42 cm.*

Petersburg where he read physics and mathematics in 1910-16,
and under the artist Dmitri-Kavkazsky 1910-15. He became a
member of the Union of Youth.
After the Revolution he returned to Georgia in 1918 where he
developed his interest in folk art and also came into contact
with the Futurists Kruchenykh, Zdanevich and Igor Terentev
then operating in Tiflis.
However he moved to Paris almost at once where he produced
relief paintings and also experimented with stereoscopic cinema.
He exhibited at the Salon des Indépendants from 1920.
He finally settled in Georgia in 1927 and taught at the Tblisi
Academy from 1928. He was given a one-man exhibition in
Tblisi the same year. He was designing for the
K.Mardzhanishvili Theatre in Kutaisi in 1930. He died at Tblisi.
*Imeretiya, 1919, Georgian Art Museum, Tblisi, is a painting
highly distinctive and original in its stylisation. A patchwork of
fields painted in flat green, orange and yellow spreads across
extensive valleys and distant hills which ascend off the canvas.
Each field is systematically bounded by a dotted perimeter of
hedges and trees. An ancient tower is dwarfed by this effect in
the foreground where the colours are stronger. The effect is
both decorative and forceful.
Lit D.Kakabadzé *Du tableau constructif*, Paris, 1922.
G.Alibegashvili *D.Kakabadze*, Tblisi, 1958. *D.Kakabadze
Album*, Tblisi, 1966. *Paris-Moscou*, 1979. A.Z.Rudenstine
Costakis Collection, London, 1981. E.Weiss *Russische Avant-
Garde, 1910-1930, Sammlung Ludwig, Köln*, Munich, 1986.
Coll TG; Georgian Art Museum, Tblisi; Costakis Collection;
Sammlung Ludwig, Cologne; Société Anonyme Collection,
Yale University Art Gallery, New Haven.

KAKABADZE, Silovan Yakimovich 1895-1947+
Georgian sculptor. Pupil of Ya.I.Nikoladze and N.P.Kandelaki.
Works include Georgian figures carved with a Rodin-like
surface in 1947.

Vasili Kamensky. Ferro-concrete Poem: Paintings at Shchukin's Palace, *1914.*
Artists referred to include Cézanne, Monet, Pissarro, Van Gogh, Gauguin, Denis, Matisse, Derain, Le Fauconnier and Picasso. The collection of the merchant S.I.Shchukin included works by all of these painters. It was a major source of inspiration for Russian artists wishing to see French art in the original.

KALABUKHOV   a.1919
Painter. He contributed to the Twelfth State Exhibition: Colourdynamo and Tectonic Primitivism (*Tsvetodinamos i tektonicheskiy primitivizm*) along with Grishchenko, Shevchenko and others in Moscow in 1919.

KALISTOV (KALLISTOV), Vasili Efimovich   b.1839

KALMAKOV, Nikolai (Nicolas de) Konstantinovich 1873-1955
Painter, theatre designer. Born at Nervi in Italy of an aristocratic background. He graduated as a lawyer in 1895, moved to St. Petersburg in 1903 and began painting in 1906 without formal training. He first exhibited in St. Petersburg in 1906. He worked on theatre designs for the directors N.Evreinov and V.F.Komissarzhevskaya. He exhibited with Nikolai Kul'bin's Impressionists in St. Petersburg in 1909. He designed for the Antique Theatre in St. Petersburg in 1911 and exhibited with the World of Art 1911-16. A personal exhibition was held in St. Petersburg in 1913. Mayakovsky called him 'the Russian Beardsley'. He was an organiser, with Yulia Sazonova, K.Somov and others, of the Petrograd Theatre of Marionettes which opened in 1916.
He left Russia in the early 1920s and lived in Estonia, in Brussels, where he held a one-man exhibition at the Galerie le Roy in 1924, and in Paris. He settled in France c.1924 and lived in increasing solitude although he held a one-man exhibition at the Galerie Charpentier in 1926. He entered a hospice at Chelles and ceased painting c.1947. He signed his work with a rather phallic double spiral motif. He died at Chelles in Seine-et-Marne.

Theatre design 1908 one act of Nikolai Evreinov's production of Oscar Wilde's *Salomé*, a production which was banned.
1909 designs for F.Sologub's *Nochnye Plyaski*.
1911 Natalia Butkovskaya's production of Lope de Vega's *The Great Prince of Moscow* at the Antique Theatre, St. Petersburg.
1915 January: Tairov's production of Calderon's *Life is a Dream* at the Kamerny (Chamber) Theatre in Moscow.
1916 February: Tirso de Molina's *The Power of Magic and Death* for the Marionette Theatre of Yulia Sazonova in Petrograd.
Illustration Nikolai Gumilev *Ditya Allakha* (Children of Allah), Berlin, 1924.
Lit *N.Kalmykov*, exh. cat., St. Petersburg, 1913. J.E.Bowlt *Russian Stage Design. Scenic Innovation. From the Collection of Mr. and Mrs. Nikita D.Lobanov-Rostovsky*, Jackson, MS, exh. cat.,1982. *Twilight of the Tsars*, London, 1991. Dzhon Boult (John Bowlt) *Khudozhniki russkogo teatra. Sobranie Nikity i Niny Lobanovykh-Rostovskikh*, Moscow, 1991.
Coll RM.
Colour plate p.202.

KALMYKOV, G. O.   a.1919
He participated in the First State Free Exhibition of Artworks in Petrograd in 1919.

KALMYKOV, Ivan Leonardovich   1866-1925
Landscape painter.
Coll TG.

KALMYKOV, Sergei Ivanovich　　　　　b.1891-1921+
He exhibited with Kudryashov at the First State Exhibition at Orenburg in 1921

KAMENEV, Lev L'vovich　　　　　1833-1886
Landscape painter. He was a founder member of the Wanderers.
Coll TG.

KAMENEV, Valerian Konstantinovich　　　1823-1874
Painter. Subjects include landscapes and views of St. Petersburg.
Coll TG.

KAMENSKY, Fedor Fedorovich　　　　1836-1913
Sculptor of genre themes. Works include *The Young Sculptor*, 1866, marble, RM, which is a full-length of a child modelling a sculpture of a bird. He died in the United States.
The First Step, 1872, marble, RM, is spacially complex but sweet in theme. It shows a young mother, arms outstretched, and a solid child determined to walk unaided. This work even includes a toy train executed in marble.
Coll TG; RM.

KAMENSKY, Vasili Vasilievich　　　　1864-1961
Futurist painter, poet, playwright and pilot. Born in Perm region. Birthdate sometimes given as 1884. He moved to St. Petersburg in 1906 to study agriculture but also worked on the restoration of ikons. From 1908 he was active as a poet and as editor of the journal *Vesna* (Spring). He became closely involved in Futurist literary and artistic experiment after meeting David Burlyuk in 1909. He performed with Burlyuk, for example, in a Futurist meeting at the Polytechnic Museum, Moscow, on 11 November 1913 where he lectured on 'Airplanes and Futurist Poetry' bearing a drawing of an airplane painted on his forehead.
He took part in the Futurist Tour of Russia in December 1913 to March 1914 together with Vladimir Mayakovsky and David Burlyuk which in fact went as far as Tiflis and Baku. He contributed eleven 'ferro-concrete poems' to the exhibition No.4 in Moscow in March 1914 including *A Fall from an Airplane* which comprised a weight with a face painted on it hanging in front of an iron sheet so that the head could produce a thunderous noise when hit against the metal sheet. Other titles included *Ma+4*, *Constantinople* and *Newspaper 12763914*.
In 1917 together with Kruchenykh and Kirill Zdanevich he produced a Russian Futurist book *1918* which featured a 'ferro-concrete poem' *Tiflis* as well as collage illustrations.
During the Revolution, in March 1917, he organised the First Republican Evening of the Arts in Moscow which was attended by David Burlyuk, Mayakovsky, Tatlin, Malevich and others. Together with Mayakovsky and David Burlyuk he signed the *Decree No.1 for the Democratisation of Art*. He exhibited with the Knave of Diamonds in Moscow in November 1917. He was also responsible for the decoration of the Poets' Café in Moscow along with Lentulov, Mayakovsky, David Burlyuk, Khodasevich and Yakulov 1917-18, and he was an organiser of the decorations at the Café Pittoresque in Moscow with Yakulov, Tatlin, Rodchenko and others in 1918. He featured among the cast of the Futurist film *Ne dlya deneg rodivshiysya* (Not Born for Money, known also as Creation Can't Be Bought) with Mayakovsky and David Burlyuk in 1918.
The painters Aleksandr Kuprin and F.S.Bogorodsky designed a production of his *Stepan Razin* at Nizhny-Novgorod c.1921.
In December 1921 he collaborated on an evening of poetry with Mayakovsky, Khlebnikov, Kruchenykh and Tatlin at the Vkhutemas.
He also wrote a prologue, interludes and epilogue for the production of Ostrovsky's *Comic Actor of the Eighteenth Century* which Tatlin designed for the Second Studio of the Moscow Art Theatre in 1935.

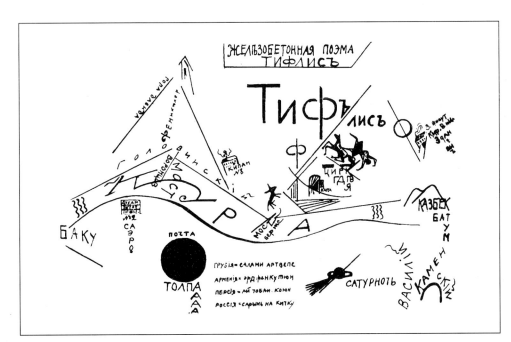

Vasili Kamensky. Ferro-concrete poem: 'Tiflis', *1917. Illustration to Kamensky's book '1918', published in Tiflis in 1917. Kamensky's graphic poem provides a schematic map of Tiflis (Tblisi) including its circus, bridges and mountains as well as the house, top right, of his fellow Futurist in Tiflis Kirill Zdanevich.*

Futurist books V.Kamensky, D.,V. and N.Burlyuk, Guro, Khlebnikov et al. *Sadok sudey* (Trap for Judges), St. Petersburg, 1910. Kamensky acted as an editor and the book was prepared in his apartment in St. Petersburg. A few hundred were printed. It included twelve poems by Kamensky.
V.Kamensky *Zemlyanka*, Moscow, 1914.
V.Kamensky, A.Kravtsov *Nagoy sredi odetykh* (The Naked among the Clad), with illustrations by V.Kamensky, Moscow, 1914.
V.Kamensky *Futuristy: Pervyy zhurnal russkykh futuristov* (Futurists: First Journal of the Russian Futurists), with illustrations by D. and V.Burlyuk and A.Exter, Moscow, 1914.
V.Kamensky *Tango s korovami* (Tango with Cows), with illustrations by V. and D.Burlyuk, Moscow, 1914.
V.Kamensky *Stenka Razin*, Moscow, 1915 (editions of 1919 and 1928 entitled *Stepan Razin*).
D.Burlyuk, G.Zolotukhin, V.Kamensky, V.Khlebnikov *Chetyre ptitsi* (Four Birds), with illustrations by A.Lentulov and G.Zolotukhin, Moscow, 1916.
V.Kamensky *Devushki bosikom*, Tiflis, 1916.
V.Kamensky et al. *1918*, Tiflis, 1917.
V.Kamensky *Ego — Moya biografiya velikogo futurista*, Moscow, 1918.
Other writings V.Kamensky *Yunost' Mayakovskogo* (Youth of Mayakovsky), Tiflis, 1931. V.Kamensky *Put' Entuziasta* (An Enthusiast's Way), Moscow, 1931 (and Perm, 1968). V.Kamensky *Zhizn' s Mayakovskim* (Life with Mayakovsky), Moscow, 1940.
Lit V.Markov *Russian Futurism*, London, 1969. S.P.Compton *The World Backwards, Russian Futurist Books 1912-16*, London, 1978.

Vasili Kandinsky. Vignette illustration for 'Concerning the Spiritual in Art', *1910. Woodcut.*

KAMENTSEVA, E. I. a.1919
Painter. She was represented in the Fourth State Exhibition of Paintings (*IV Gosudarstvennaya vystavka kartin*) in Moscow in 1919.

KAMEZHENKO, Ermolay Dementevich (KOMYAZHENKO, E. D.) 1760-1818
Portraitist. Death date sometimes given as 1829.
Coll TG.

KAMZOLKIN, Evgeniy Ivanovich 1885-1957
Painter, theatre designer. He studied at the Moscow College under Serov, Korovin, Arkhipov and N.Kasatkin. From 1910 he was a member of the Moscow Salon of which he became the President.
After the Revolution his work was included in the First Exhibition of the Moscow Contemporary Art Store in January 1919. He was represented in the First Touring Exhibition of Paintings and Graphics which opened in Moscow in 1929.

KANDAUROV, K. V. a.1917-1929
Painter. He exhibited with the World of Art in December 1917 in Moscow and at the First Exhibition of Works of the Professional Union of Artists in Moscow in 1918. He was also represented in the Fourth State Exhibition of Paintings (*IV Gosudarstvennaya vystavka kartin*) in Moscow in 1919, at the enormous First State Exhibition of Art and Science, which included ethnographic material, held in Kazan in 1920 and in the First Touring Exhibition of Paintings and Graphics which opened in Moscow in 1929.

KANDELAKI, Nikolai Porfir'evich 1889-1970
Georgian sculptor. Even in the 1930s his style remained indebted to the techniques of Rodin whose sculptures' vigorous musculature and feeling for the monumental were such a useful resource for Socialist Realists in Russia. His *Portrait of the Artist V.D.Gudiashvili*, 1936-7, granite, Georgian Art Museum, Tblisi, is an example, despite the difficulties of the medium. It is a fiercely bird-like and individual portrait of academic and dramatic prowess. The artist T.G.Abakeliya was among his pupils.
Coll Georgian Art Museum, Tblisi.

KANDINSKY, Vasili (Wassily) Vasilievich 1866-1944
Major painter, printmaker and theorist, active within Russia, Germany and France. He was one of the most widely influential initiators of the idea of supressing the subject to the point where it is difficult to recognise, so that the impact of the painting relies upon the suggestive power of colour and form alone.
Born in Moscow. He passed his childhood in Moscow and Odessa. He studied law at Moscow University 1886-92 and was appointed to a post there in 1893. A significant experience for his understanding of folk art had been his participation in an ethnographic expedition to Vologda Province in 1889. He had decided to become an artist by 1896. He moved to Germany to study at the Azbé School in Munich 1897-9 where he met Jawlensky. In 1900 he was studying under Franz Von Stuck at the Munich Academy. He continued to live in Munich until 1914 and provided a vital link between artistic developments in Germany and Russia which he continued to visit. Part of Kandinsky's historical importance at this time centred upon his activities as a teacher and organiser of groups. In 1901 he was a founder member of the *Phalanx*

Vasili Kandinsky. Study for 'Composition 7', *1913. Oil on canvas. 78 x 99.5 cm.*
This is one of numerous studies for 'Composition 7', for although Kandinsky's work at this time may appear spontaneous it was in fact the result of long deliberation and experiment. Here a citadel with towers is visible on a hill top above the centre of the canvas. Although Kandinsky's imagery became less easy to recognise it continued to be important and is often associated with apocalyptic themes.
Städtische Galerie im Lenbachhaus, Munich.

group and a teacher at its school in Munich where the painter Gabrielle Münther was amongst his pupils. He travelled in Europe with Münther in the period 1903-6.

In Russia he exhibited with the Moscow Association of Artists in 1907-8 and with the Izdebsky Salon in Odessa 1909-10 where he showed over forty works including Improvisations and Compositions. He exhibited four *Improvisations* with the Knave of Diamonds in Moscow in 1910-11 and three at the Salon des Indépendants in Paris in 1912. He exhibited again with the Knave of Diamonds in 1912.

In 1909 he established the *Neue Künstlervereinigung München* (New Artists' Union in Munich, or NKV) and exhibited with it from 1909 to 1911. He then founded the group *Der Blaue Reiter*, the Blue Rider, with which he exhibited from 1912 to 1914 alongside the painters Marc, Macke and Klee as well as Russian painters. The *Blaue Reiter* became one of the most significant links between experimental art in Germany and Russia. It embodied, for example, ideas derived from Russian Futurism and published the work of David Burlyuk. It was also a forum for theoretical speculation of the kind that increasingly

concerned Kandinsky who had already begun work on his first major theoretical text *Uber das Geistige in der Kunst* (Concerning the Spiritual in Art), published in Munich in 1912, in which he was to advance the case for an art that relied more upon the expressive power of colour and form than upon its role as a means of description, permitting an art that was in principle able to effect the soul more directly and to advance the spiritual state of mankind. Such ideas reflected his mystical beliefs derived in part from the work of the Theosophists and from Rudolf Steiner. Many of these ideas had also gained currency in Russia and Kandinsky maintained close links. He exhibited for example with the Knave of Diamonds there and acted as the Munich correspondent of the periodical *Apollon*. From 1914 until December 1915 he was in Moscow and showed work at the Exhibition of Paintings: The Year 1915 in Moscow and at the Exhibition of Contemporary Russian Painting in Petrograd in 1916-17. He moved to Stockholm however until March 1916 when he returned to Moscow.

After the Revolution Kandinsky became closely involved with the reorganisation of art in Moscow. He exhibited at the Fifth

State Exhibition: From Impressionism to Non-Objective Art in Moscow 1918-19. Appointed to work under the People's Commissariat of the Enlightenment's Art Section (IZO Narkompros) from 1918, he served under Tatlin on the Moscow Collegium of IZO in 1919 and his name appeared on the April 1919 list of artists for acquisitions by the envisaged Museum of Painterly Culture. He was represented along with Chagall and others at the First State Exhibition of Paintings by Local and Moscow Artists held in Vitebsk in December 1919 and at the 19th Exhibition of the All-Russian Exhibitions Bureau in Moscow in 1920.

He taught at the Free Art Studios (SVOMAS) from 1918. He endeavoured to implement his theoretical and practical discoveries through exhibitions in Moscow, Petrograd and Vitebsk, through teaching and through organisational work. In 1920 he became the first director of the Institute of Artistic Culture (INKhUK) in Moscow which sought to define art in scientific terms through debate and experiment. Kandinsky sought in particular to define the psychological effects of colour and form in its 'physico-psychological section'. This psychological bias led to confrontation with the Moscow Constructivists who asserted the primacy of a materialist view and a commitment to communist aims. Kandinsky resigned from INKhUK as a result of this. He continued to paint in this period and in 1921 he executed several designs for porcelain. He was included in the Third Touring Exhibition of the Sovetsk Regional subdepartment of the Museums Bureau along with Rodchenko and others in 1921 and he exhibited in the 1921 exhibition of the World of Art in Moscow. His work was included in the First Russian Art Exhibition in Berlin in 1922 and at the Paris International Exhibition of 1925.

Kandinsky, having failed to establish his princples in Moscow, then moved to the Bauhaus in Germany where his theoretical and practical work was developed further alongside former colleagues including Paul Klee. He remained responsive to developments in Russian art, however, and it is possible that his work was decisively affected by the visits of Malevich and Lissitzky to the Bauhaus. He continued as a professor at the Bauhaus until its closure. In 1933 he moved to France and continued to be immensely active as a painter gaining steadily in international recognition as one of the initiators of non-representational painting even though it is debatable whether he ever fully abandoned the concept of imagery.

Writings include W.Kandinsky *Über das Geistige in der Kunst*, Munich, 1912 (English edition *The Art of Spiritual Harmony*, London, 1914). W.Kandinsky *Klänge*, Munich, 1913. W.Kandinsky *Rückblicke*, Berlin, 1913. W.Kandinsky *Punkt und Linie zur Fläche*, Munich, 1926 (English edition *Point and Line to Plane*, New York, 1947). K.Lindsay, P.Vergo (eds.) *Kandinsky: Complete Wrings on Art*, 2 vols., Boston, 1982.
Lit Very extensive in terms of Kandinsky's own writings, literature about his work and exhibition catalogues. W.Grohman *Kandinsky, sa vie, son oeuvre*, Paris, 1958. H.Roethel *Das graphische Werk*, Cologne, 1970. *Kandinsky, trente peintures des musées soviétiques*, exh. cat., MNAM, Paris, 1979. J.E.Bowlt, R.-C.Washington-Long *The Life of Vasilii Kandinsky in Russian Art: A Study of 'On the Spiritual in Art'*, Newtonville, 1980. H.K.Roethel and J.K.Benjamin *Kandinsky, Catalogue Raisonné of the Oil Paintings*, London, 1982. *Oeuvres de Vassily Kandinsky 1866-1944*, exh. cat., MNAM, Paris, 1985. *L'Avant-garde russe 1905-1925*, exh. cat., Musée des Beaux-Arts, Nantes, 1993.
Coll Represented in most major collections of western 20th century art, including TG; RM; Astrakhan Art Museum; Kirov Art Museum; Omsk Art Museum; Saratov Art Museum; Tashkent Art Museum; Tula Art Museum; Vladivostok Art Museum; Yaroslavl' Art Museum; Guggenheim Museum, New York; MOMA, New York; Tate Gallery, London; MNAM, Paris; Sammlung Ludwig, Cologne, etc.
Colour plate p.203.

KAPETOV, V. a.1921
A member of the *Bytie* (Existence) Society of Artists formed in Moscow in 1921.

KAPKOV, Yakov Fedorovich 1816-1854
Figure painter.
Coll Good holdings at TG.

KAPLUN, S. a.1922-1929
He was represented at the First Russian Art Exhibition in Berlin in 1922. He exhibited with the Circle of Artists in Leningrad between 1927 and 1929.

KAPLUNOVSKY, Vladimir Pavlovich 1906-1952
Cinema artist, director. He studied under Tatlin and graduated from the Kiev College of Art in 1928. He became a principal artist of the Moscow Cinema Studio.

KAPTEREV, Valeriy Vsevolodovich 1900-1981
Painter. He was included in the major exhibition in Moscow in 1927 marking the tenth anniversary of the Revolution and in the 1928 exhibition of Acquisitions by the State Art Collections Fund held in Moscow. He was represented at the jubilee exhibition Artists of the RSFSR over 15 Years held at the Russian Museum, Leningrad, in 1932. He died in Moscow.

KARAVAKK, Lyudvig = CARAVACQUE, Louis

KARAZIN, Nikolai Nikolaevich 1842-1908
Genre painter, engraver and illustrator. He died at Gachina.
Coll TG.

KARDASHEV, Lev Alekseevich 1905-1964
Sculptor. He exhibited at the 1932 Venice Biennale and at the Paris International Exhibition in 1937. Works include a full length nude carved in wood in 1955. He died in Moscow.

KARDOVSKY, Dmitri Nikolaevich 1866-1943
Illustrator, theatre designer. He taught at the Academy in St. Petersburg where his many pupils included B.D.Grigoriev and A.Lentulov 1906-7. He exhibited with the World of Art in St. Petersburg in 1900.
He was associated with the Vkhutemas after the Revolution and he contributed to the exhibition Art of Moscow Theatre 1918-1923 held in Moscow in 1923. He exhibited with the *Zhar-tsvet* (Fire-colour) group between 1924 and 1928. He was represented at the Paris International Exhibition of 1925. He was included in the major exhibition in Moscow in 1927 marking the tenth anniversary of the Revolution.
Theatre design A.R.Kugel's *Nicholas I and the Decembrists* at the Moscow Art Theatre (in collaboration with V.A.Simov).
Lit I.Pikulev *D.N.Kardovsky*, 1952.

KARETNIKOVA, S. K. a.1918-1919
In 1918 she was engaged on decorations for the Left Federation within the Union of Moscow Artists along with the

artists Vera Pestel', Lyubov' Popova and Nadezhda Udal'tsova. She exhibited at the Fifth State Exhibition: From Impressionism to Non-Objective Art in Moscow 1918-19.

KAREV, Aleksei Eremeevich   1879-1942
Painter, sculptor. He studied under V.V.Konovalov at Saratov 1897-8, at the Penza Art School under K.A.Savitsky 1898-1901 and privately in Kiev 1901-2. He exhibited with the Golden Fleece 1908-10 and *Venok/Stefanos* in 1908.
After the Revolution he joined the revived World of Art 1917-24 and was engaged on Agitprop decorations on the Sadovaya/ Nevsky corner in Petrograd in 1918, and at Saratov 1918-20 where he also taught at the Free Art Studios 1920-1. He served under Al'tman on the committee responsible for the revolutionary decorations marking 1 May 1919 in Petrograd and his name appeared on the April 1919 list of artists for acquisitions by the envisaged Museum of Painterly Culture. He participated in the First State Free Exhibition of Artworks in Petrograd in 1919. He was a member of IZO Narkompros and was represented at the First Russian Art Exhibition in Berlin in 1922 and in the enormous survey Exhibition of Paintings by Petrograd Artists of All Tendencies 1919-1923 held in Petrograd in 1923. He was a member of the 4 Arts society which was founded in 1924. He was represented at the jubilee exhibition Artists of the RSFSR over 15 Years held at the Russian Museum, Leningrad in 1932.
Lit A.M.Muratov, V.Manin et al. *Zhivopis' 20-30kh godov*, Sankt-Peterburg, 1991.
Coll RM; Saratov Art Museum.

KARINSKAYA, Anna Nikolaeva   1871-1931
Landscape painter. She worked at Vologda.
Coll TG.

KARITSKY, A. O. = KORITSKY, A. O.

KARMIN, E. I.   a.1919
Painter. He was represented in the Fourth State Exhibition of Paintings (*IV Gosudarstvennaya vystavka kartin*) in Moscow in 1919.

KARNEEV, Akim Egorovich   1833-1896
Figure painter who used Italian themes. He was active in Rome in 1866. Signed 'Carneeff'.
Coll TG.

KARNEEV, M. D.   a.1929
He was represented in the First Touring Exhibition of Paintings and Graphics which opened in Moscow in 1929.

KARPOV, M. M.   a.1921
He exhibited with Kudryashov and others at the First State Exhibition in Orenburg in 1921.

KARPOV, Stepan Mikhailovich   1890-1929
He was included in the major exhibition in Moscow in 1927 marking the tenth anniversary of the Revolution. He was represented in the First Touring Exhibition of Paintings and Graphics which opened in Moscow in 1929.

KARPOVA, S. V.   a.1921
She exhibited with Kudryashov and others at the First State Exhibition in Orenburg in 1921.

KASATKIN, Nikolai Alekseevich   1859-1930
Portrait and genre painter. Born in Moscow, the son of an engraver. He studied at the Moscow College under Perov from 1873 to 1883 and from 1891 he exhibited with the Wanderers. He taught at the Moscow College from 1894 to 1917. He depicted mining themes emphasising struggle and poverty but in well resolved pictorial compositions including *Woman Miner*, 1894, and *Poor People Gathering Coal at an Exhausted Mine*, 1894, RM. He was working in Italy 1908-9.
In 1923 he was the first artist to receive the title People's Artist of the USSR. He was given a one-man exhibition in 1929.
*Woman Miner, 1894, TG, is a *plein air* portrait of a healthy young woman seen in a garden, fit and smiling. It presents a kind of ideal without becoming social commentary.
Pioneer Woman with Books, 1926, Central Museum of the Revolution, Moscow, represents a Soviet heroine. She is purposeful and serious yet simultaneously bright-eyed and attractive.
Coll Well represented in TG; Central Museum of the Revolution, Moscow.

KASHINA, Nadezhda Vasilievna   1896-1977
Painter. Born at Perm. She exhibited with the group The Thirteen 1929-32. She died at Tashkent.
Coll RM.

KASHINA, Nina Vasilievna   1903-1934+
Painter. Born at Perm. She used the pseudonym Nina Pamylatnykh. She exhibited with the group The Thirteen 1929-32.
Coll RM.

KASIYAN (KAS'YAN), Vasili Ilych   1896-1976
Illustrator, graphic artist. Born in the Ukraine. He studied at the Academy in Prague 1920-6 and then moved to Kiev to teach at the Kiev Art Institute. He was included in the 1928 exhibition of Acquisitions by the State Art Collections Fund held in Moscow. He exhibited at the 1932 Venice Biennale. He produced graphic works on social and historical themes and illustrated books. He became an Academician of the USSR. He died in Kiev.
T.G.Shevchenko Among the Peasants, 1939, lithograph, is a Socialist Realist print in which the Ukrainian revolutionary hammers the table whilst all around him the committed workers press around. The light seems to come from Shevchenko himself as its physical source is obscured by a figure in the foreground.
Lit A.Shpakov *V.I.Kasiyan*, Kiev, 1960. *V.I.Kasiyan*, exh. cat., Kiev, 1972. *Paris-Moscou*, 1979.

KATSMAN, Evgeniy Aleksandrovich   1890-1976
Graphic artist, painter. He was born at Kharkov. He was represented at the First Exhibition of Works of the Professional Union of Artists in Moscow in 1918 and at the Ninth State Exhibition of Paintings: Naturalism and Realism in Moscow in 1919. He was a member of the first exhibition committee of AKhRR, the Association of Artists of Revolutionary Russia, in 1922. Other members included A.Grigoriev, P.Kiselev, N.Kotov, S.Malyutin, P.Radimov, P.Shukhmin, A.Skachko, G.Sukhanov, B.Yakovlev and V.Zhuravlev.
He was probably the E.Katsman included in the major exhibition in Moscow in 1927 marking the tenth anniversary of the Revolution and in the 1928 exhibition of Acquisitions by the State Art Collections Fund held in Moscow. He was

represented in the First Touring Exhibition of Paintings and Graphics which opened in Moscow in 1929, at the jubilee exhibition Artists of the RSFSR over 15 Years held at the Russian Museum, Leningrad in 1932 and at the 1932 Venice Biennale. He died in Moscow.

The Kaliazin Lacemakers, 1928, TG, is a frieze-like composition faintly reminiscent of Le Nain but executed with a bold sense of scale. At left a young woman seen in profile reads aloud to the frontally viewed lace-makers who listen intently in a variety of poses. The five portraits are carefully resolved.
Coll TG.

KAZATOV, Aleksei   mid-18th century
Portraitist.
Coll TG.

KELER (-VILIANDI), Ivan Petrovich   1826-1899
Portraitist.
Coll TG.

KELIN, Petr Ivanovich   c.1887-1946
Painter, graphic artist. He studied under Valentin Serov 1896-1903. He opened a teaching studio in Moscow in 1903 where he taught Vladimir Mayakovsky in 1910.
After the Revolution he was represented at the enormous First State Exhibition of Art and Science, which included ethnographic material, held in Kazan in 1920. He was a member of the Society of Artist-Realists founded in 1927. He was represented in the First Touring Exhibition of Paintings and Graphics which opened in Moscow in 1929.

KELIND
This name appeared on the April 1919 list of artists for acquisitions by the envisaged Museum of Painterly Culture.

KELLER, A. V.   a.1918
He was represented at the First Exhibition of Works of the Professional Union of Artists in Moscow in 1918.

KELLER, M. S.   a.1921
Exhibited with Kudryashov and others at the First State Exhibition in Orenburg in 1921.

KEL'TSEV, V. I.   a.1918-1919
Painter. He was represented at the First Exhibition of Works of the Professional Union of Artists in Moscow in 1918. He also exhibited at the juryless Eighth State Exhibition in Moscow in 1919 and was probably the Kel'tsev who exhibited at the Ninth State Exhibition of Paintings: Naturalism and Realism in Moscow in 1919.

KENIG, David Iogan-Lebrekht (Egorovich)   1825-1847+
Gold medal in 1847. Signed 'D. König'.
Coll TG.

KEPINOV, Grigori Ivanovich   1886-1966
Portrait sculptor. He was a member of the Society of Russian Sculptors from 1926 and was included in the major exhibition in Moscow in 1927 marking the tenth anniversary of the Revolution. He exhibited with Sarra Lebedeva, A.E.Zelensky, Vera Mukhina, Ilya Slonim, Vladimir Favorsky, I.G.Frikh-Khar and I.M.Chaykov in Moscow in 1935. His works include a half length of the composer *A.I.Khachaturyan*, 1945. He was given an exhibition with the painter Aleksandr Kuprin in Moscow in 1948.
Portrait of T.G.Kepinova, 1935, marble, TG, employs Rodin's

device of the half-carved block from which there emerges here an academic but sensitive portrait.
Coll TG.

KERBEL', Lev Efimovich   b.1917
Sculptor of Socialist Realist genre active in the 1940s.

KERKOVA, S.   a.1918
She was represented at the First Exhibition of Works of the Professional Union of Artists in Moscow in 1918.

KERZHENTSEV, V.   a.1919
In 1919 he was listed as leader of a course for art teachers along with Tatlin and others working at the Free Art Studios in Moscow.

KERZIN, Mikhail Arkadevich   1883-1918+
Belorussian sculptor. In 1918 he was in charge of a group of artists executing Agitprop decorations in Petrograd.

KHANDAMOV, Usmandzhan   a.1920-1923+
Turkmen primitivist painter. He was in contact with Pavel Kuznetsov 1920-3.

KHARLAMOV, Aleksei A.   1840-1922
His name appeared on the April 1919 list of artists for acquisitions by the envisaged Museum of Painterly Culture and he was represented at the enormous First State Exhibition of Art and Science, which included ethnographic material, held in Kazan in 1920.
Coll TG; RM.

KHARLAMOV, I.   a.1924-1928
He exhibited with the *Zhar-tsvet* (Fire-colour) group between 1924 and 1928.

KHARLAMOV, Mikhail E.   a.1909-1929
Painter. He exhibited with the Izdebsky International Salons 1909-11 in Odessa.
After the Revolution he was represented at the First Exhibition of Works of the Professional Union of Artists in Moscow in 1918, at the First Exhibition of the Moscow Contemporary Art Store in January 1919 and at the enormous First State Exhibition of Art and Science, which included ethnographic material, held in Kazan in 1920. His work was included in the exhibition of Soviet art held at Harbin in 1926 and in Japan in 1927. He was represented in the First Touring Exhibition of Paintings and Graphics which opened in Moscow in 1929.

KHARLAMOV, Mikhail Vasil'evich   1837-1913
Sculptor. His plaster full-length of *The Sower*, 1862, RM, lies stylistically between neo-classicism and the realism of Millet's image. It remains however essentially a studio-posed life model.
Coll RM.

KHIDEKEL', Lazar   c.1904-1922+
Painter, architect. Born in Vitebsk. He studied under Dobuzhinsky and Chagall before enrolling under Malevich at Vitebsk. He was represented along with Kandinsky, Chagall and others at the First State Exhibition of Paintings by Local and Moscow Artists held in Vitebsk in December 1919. He was associated with the Malevich circle in Vitebsk and the *Unovis* group activities. His text *Unovis in the Studio* was published in the hand-written lithographed *Unovis* No.2,

Vitebsk, 1921. With Chashnik he edited the journal *Aero*. He followed Malevich to Petrograd in 1922.

KHIGER, E. Ya.   a.1923
He was included in the enormous survey Exhibition of Paintings by Petrograd Artists of All Tendencies 1919-1923 held in Petrograd in 1923.

KHIMONA, Nikolai Petrovich   1865-1920
Landscape painter. He exhibited studies of Greek ruins at the First Izdebsky International Salon 1909-10 in Odessa.
After the Revolution he participated in the First State Free Exhibition of Artworks in Petrograd in 1919.
Coll TG.

KHIZHINSKY, Leonid Semenovich   1896-1972
Graphic artist in Leningrad. He was represented at the jubilee exhibition Artists of the RSFSR over 15 Years held at the Russian Museum, Leningrad, in 1932.

KHLEBNIKOVA, Vera Vladimirovna   1891-1941
Painter, graphic artist. She was the sister of the leading Russian Futurist poet Velimir Khlebnikov. She studied at the art schools of Kazan 1905-8 and Kiev 1908-10 and then under Yuon and Dudin in Moscow in 1910. Subsequently she attended the School of the Society for the Encouragement of the Arts in St. Petersburg where she studied under Tsionglinsky. In 1912 she studied under Van Dongen at the Académie Witte in Paris. She visited Italy, Switzerland and London during 1913-16.
After the Revolution she exhibited from 1919. She married the painter and graphic artist Miturich in 1924.
Lit David Elliott, V.Dudakov *100 Years of Russian Art*, London, 1989.

KHLEBOVSKY, Stanislav   1835-1884
He signed his work 'St. Chlebowski'.
Coll TG.

KHLESTOVA, Nadezhda I.   a.1926-1932+
She was a member of the group *Krug khudozhnikov* (Circle of Artists) founded in 1926 and was represented at the jubilee exhibition Artists of the RSFSR over 15 Years held at the Russian Museum, Leningrad, in 1932.

KHMEL'KO, Mikhail Ivanovich   1919-1940+
Socialist Realist painter of heroes. *The Triumph of Our Fatherland* shows the defeated German forces presenting their standards before Lenin's Mausoleum in Moscow. It is executed with the popular realism of a magazine illustration. At the centre a soldier throws down the eagle and swastika standard of Hitler.

KHODASEVICH, Valentina Mikhailovna   1894-1970
Painter, theatre designer. Born in Moscow. After studying under F.Rerberg in Moscow and under Haberman at the Essig School in Munich 1910-11, she moved to Paris where she studied at the Witte Academy under Kees Van Dongen 1911-12. She also worked in Tatlin's Moscow studio in 1912 and exhibited with the Union of Youth 1913-14, having settled in St. Petersburg where she married the artist Andrei Diderikhs in 1913.
After the Revolution she exhibited with the Knave of Diamonds in Moscow in November 1917 and contributed to the decoration of the Poets' Café in Moscow along with Kamensky, David Burlyuk, Mayakovsky and Yakulov in 1917-18. Her work was included in the First Exhibition of the Moscow Contemporary Art Store in January 1919 and her name appeared on the April 1919 list of artists for acquisitions by the envisaged Museum of Painterly Culture. She participated in the First State Free Exhibition of Artworks in Petrograd in 1919 and was represented in the Fourth State Exhibition of Paintings (*IV Gosudarstvennaya vystavka kartin*) in Moscow in 1919. Her theatre design included work for plays, opera and ballet productions at the Theatre of People's Comedy, the National Academic Theatre and the Maly Theatre in Leningrad from 1919.
She worked in Berlin in 1922, and lived in London, Paris and Italy 1924-5. She visited Gorky at Sorrento in 1928 before returning to Moscow.
She was engaged on the design of mass festivals in Leningrad before 1930. She was represented at the jubilee exhibition Artists of the RSFSR over 15 Years held at the Russian Museum, Leningrad, in 1932.
She worked as chief artist of the Kirov Academic Theatre of Opera and Ballet in Leningrad 1932-6. She worked on the periodical *USSR in Construction* in 1937. She died in Leningrad.
Theatre design 1918 Nikolai Gumilev's *Tree of Metamorphoses* at the Theatre Studio, Petrograd.
1921 November: *Harlequin-Skeleton*, a pantomime produced by Vladimir Soloviev at the Theatre of People's Comedy, Petersburg.
1922 Nadezhda Bromlei's *Archangel Michael* at the First Studio of the Moscow Art Theatre. Costume designs were reminiscent of Exter in their assemblage of materials into geometric forms but here they are closer to fashion costumes of real elegance and feasibility. They are less like the painterly experiments from which they ultimately derive and have their own stylish dress sense explicitly explained for costume makers.
1936 B.V.Afas'ev's ballet *Bakhchisarai Fountain* at the Bolshoi Theatre, Moscow. An elegant design strongly recalling World of Art designs.
1953 May: V.V.Ivanov's *Lomonosov* at the Moscow Art Theatre.
1955 May: Shakespeare's *Twelfth Night* at the Moscow Art Theatre.
Lit M.Kuzmina, S.Radlov *V.Khodasevich*, Leningrad, 1927. *Paris-Moscou*, 1979. J.E.Bowlt *Russian Stage Design. Scenic Innovation. From the Collection of Mr. and Mrs. Nikita D.Lobanov-Rostovsky*, Jackson, MS, exh. cat.,1982. David Elliott, V.Dudakov *100 Years of Russian Art*, London, 1989. Nancy Van Norman Baer *Theatre in Revolution, Russian Avant-Garde Stage Design 1913-1935*, San Francisco and London, 1991. Dzhon Boult (John Bowlt) *Khudozhniki russkogo teatra. Sobranie Nikity i Niny Lobanovykh-Rostovskikh*, Moscow, 1991.
Coll TG; RM; Bakhrushin Theatre Museum, Moscow.

KHOKHRYAKOV, Nikolai Nikolaevich   1857-1928
Landscape painter. He was represented at the First Russian Art Exhibition in Berlin in 1922.
Coll TG.

KHOL'MBERG, Yu.   a.1917
Exhibited with the Knave of Diamonds in Moscow in November 1917.

Oleksandr Khvostenko-Khvostov. Costume Study for Smeraldina in Prokofiev's 'The Love of Three Oranges', *1926. Watercolour, pencil and collage. Signed in Russian 'A.Khvostov'. 39.5 x 32.5 cm. Collection Mr. and Mrs. Nikita D.Lobanov-Rostovsky, London.*

KHRAKOVSKY, V. L.   a.1919-1927
Theatre designer. His name appeared on the April 1919 list of artists for acquisitions by the envisaged Museum of Painterly Culture and on a June 1919 list of leaders of art courses for teachers along with Tatlin and others. He collaborated with V.Bebutova, V.Kiselev and A.Lavinsky on the second production of Mayakovsky's *Mystery-Bouffe* by Meyerhold in Moscow in 1921. He was a member of the Society of Moscow Painters founded in 1925. He was included in the major exhibition in Moscow in 1927 marking the tenth anniversary of the Revolution.

KHRISANF = ZAC, L.V.

KHRISTENEK, Karl-Lyudvig-Iogann (Longin Zakharovich) (CHRISTENECK, C.L.)   1732/3-c.1793
Portraitist.
Coll TG.

KHRISTOLYUBOV, Nikolai   b.1918
Painter. Born in the Kirov region. He studied at the Surikov State Art Institute and exhibited from 1943. His first one-man exhibition was held at Irkutsk in Siberia. He has subsequently held one-man exhibitions in Moscow and has contributed to exhibitions in Japan, Germany, Italy and Austria. He teaches as a professor of painting.
Coll TG; RM; Roy Miles Gallery, London.
Colour plate p.206.

KHRUSLOV, Egor Moisevich   1861-1913
Landscape painter.
Coll TG.

KHRUSTACHEV, Nikolai I.   a.1908-1911
Painter. He exhibited with the Golden Fleece in Moscow in 1908 and with the Izdebsky International Salons 1909-11 in Odessa. He exhibited with the World of Art 1912-13.

KHRUTSKY, Ivan Fomich   1810-1885
Painter of still-lifes, interiors and portraits.
Coll TG.

KHUDYAKOV, Vasili Grigorevich   1826-1871
Painter. Subjects include portraits and Italian landscapes.
Coll TG.

KHVOSTENKO, E. A.   a.1920s
In the early Soviet period employed at the Army Puppet Theatre at Ashkhabad with the sculptor N.G.Shalimov and V.V.Khvostenko, producing plays by Molière, Cervantes and the epic *Stepan Razin*.

KHVOSTENKO, Vasili Veniaminovich   1896-1960
Painter, puppeteer. Subjects of his paintings include *Embarkation for Cythera*, 1917. He was exhibiting in 1921. In the early Soviet period he worked at the Army Puppet Theatre at Ashkhabad with the sculptor N.G.Shalimov and E.A.Khvostenko, producing plays by Molière, Cervantes and the epic *Stepan Razin*. He was represented at the Paris International Exhibition in 1925.
Coll TG.

KHVOSTENKO-KHVOSTOV, Oleksandr (Aleksandr) Veniaminovich   1895-1968
Theatre designer. Born at Borisovka, Ukraine. He studied under Aleksandra Exter. His designs for Mayakovsky's *Mystery-Bouffe* for a production of 1921 at the Heroic Theatre at Kharkov are distinctly inspired by Suprematism. He died at Kiev.
Theatre design 1921 Mayakovsky's *Mystery-Bouffe* at the Heroic Theatre, Kharkov, for which he made an explicitly Suprematist design of the top of the terrestrial globe against a splayed profusion of Suprematist rectangles in reds and orange, like banners exploding into space. The design is reminiscent of Kudryashov at Orenburg.
1926-7 Prokofiev's *The Love of Three Oranges* for the State Opera Company, Kharkov.
1929 E.Krenek's *Johny Strikes Up* for the State Opera, Kiev.
1929 Wagner's *Die Walküre* (unrealised) for the State Opera, Kiev.
1929 R.Gliere's ballet *The Red Poppy* at the State Opera, Kiev.
Lit Nancy Van Norman Baer *Theatre in Revolution, Russian Avant-Garde Stage Design 1913-1935*, San Francisco and London, 1991.
Coll Bakhrushin Theatre Museum, Moscow; Central State Archive of Art and Literature, Moscow; State Museum of Theatre, Music and Film Art of the Ukraine, Kiev.

KIBAL'NIKOV, Aleksandr Pavlovich   b.1912
Monumental sculptor. His works include a lively and sensitive full-length academic portrait of N.G.Chernyshevsky at Saratov, 1953, and a vigorous monument to the poet Mayakovsky erected in 1954.

KIBRIK, Evgeniy Adol'fovich   1906-1978
Draughtsman, illustrator. He was a member of Filonov's school, the Collective of Masters of Analytical Art, established

prisoners. At left a healthy man smokes a cigar and a youth rises from the floor in amazement.
Coll TG; Museum of Ukrainian Art, Kiev.

KIVSHENKO, Aleksei Danilovich   **1851-1895**
Painter of war. He studied in Munich under J.Brandt. He exhibited from 1875. He became a member of the Academy in St. Petersburg. He died at Heidelberg.
Coll TG.

KLEMM, Ekaterina Filippovna   **1884-1941**
Graphic artist. She was included in the major exhibition in Moscow in 1927 marking the tenth anniversary of the Revolution and in the First Touring Exhibition of Paintings and Graphics which opened in Moscow in 1929.

KLEVER, K. Yu.   **a.1918**
Listed as an exhibitor at the First Exhibition of Works of the Professional Union of Artists in Moscow in 1918.

KLEVER, M. Yu.   **a.1919**
Listed as an exhibitor in the *First State Free Exhibition of Artworks* in Petrograd in 1919.

KLEVER, Yuliy (Julius) Yulevich   **1850-1924**
Landscape painter. Born at Dorpat. He studied under Vorob'ev at the Academy in St. Petersburg in 1867. He

Orest Kiprensky. Prince N.P.Trubetskoy, *1826. Oil on canvas. 93.5 x 76.5 cm.*
State Tretyakov Gallery, Moscow.

exhibited in Paris in 1878 and won a medal at Berlin in 1888 and exhibited in Paris in 1889.
After the Revolution he participated in the First State Free Exhibition of Artworks in Petrograd in 1919 and was represented at the enormous First State Exhibition of Art and Science, which included ethnographic material, held in Kazan in 1920. He was included in the survey Exhibition of Paintings by Petrograd Artists of All Tendencies 1919-1923 held in Petrograd in 1923. He died in Leningrad.
Coll TG.

KLIMCHENKO, Konstantin Mikhailovich   **a.1840s**
Sculptor and painter whose work included sentimental genre themes, amongst which was *Girl with Mirror*, 1840s, RM. He died at St. Petersburg.
Coll RM.

KLIUN (KLIUNKOV) = KLYUN, I. V.

KLOBUKOVA, Z. D.   **a.1921**
She was included in the Third Touring Exhibition of the Sovetsk Regional subdepartment of the Museums Bureau along with Kandinsky, Rodchenko and others in 1921.

KLODT (von JURGENSBURG), Baron Mikhail Konstantinovich   **1832-1902**
Landscape painter. Born in St. Petersburg, the son of an engraver. He studied at the St. Petersburg Academy under Vorobev 1851-8. He was a founder member of the Wanderers. Between 1871 and 1886 he directed the landscape painting studio at the Academy. His work included themes in Normandy. He sometimes signed his work 'M.K'.

KLODT (von JURGENSBURG), Baron Mikhail Petrovich 1835-1914
Genre painter. He was a founder member of the Wanderers.
Coll TG.

KLODT, Nikolai Aleksandrovich   **1865-1918**
Painter of landscapes and still-lifes.
Coll TG.

KLODT (von JURGENSBURG), Baron Petr Karlovich 1805-1867
Neo-classicising sculptor and also the first Russian animalier sculptor. His monument to *Krylov* was erected in the Leningrad Summer Garden. He was perhaps primarily a sculptor of horses and equestrian themes. He made numerous studies of individual horses or related subjects.
Horse and Handler, 1840s, bronze, RM, represents a classical image of a man holding the reins of a rearing horse. This is a study or variant of one of the groups erected on the Anichkov Bridge in St. Petersburg.
Monument to Nicholas I, 1856-9, bronze, St. Isaac's Square, Leningrad. This is an imposing equestrian monument in which the horse and rider are raised high above the street level on top of a substantial drum form of essentially two storeys. The lower of these bears relief panels beneath a cornice: above this seated figures flank high reliefs of arms and standards referring to military might and success. The horse is remarkable. Its head recalls fairly directly the Parthenon horse, but its stance is a virtuoso performance as it rears gently and is supported by its back legs only.
Coll TG; RM.

Nikolai Kalmakov. Leda and the Swan. *Pen and ink, watercolour and bodycolour. Signed with device and dated 1917. 69.5 x 84 cm. Reproduced by kind permission of Sotheby's London, sale 28.11.1991, lot 471.*

KLUCIS (KLUTSIS), Gustav Gustavovich   1895-c.1944

Latvian painter, sculptor, theatre and poster designer who produced an original synthesis of Suprematist and Constructivist devices. He studied at the teachers' seminary at Volmar in Latvia 1911-13 and then at the Riga Art School under Purvit, Rozental and Tilberg 1913-15. He moved to St. Petersburg to attend the school of the Society for the Encouragement of the Arts 1915-17 and worked as scene painter at the Okhtensky Workers' Theatre.

After the Revolution he served as a soldier but also from 1918 he studied at the Moscow Free Art Studios (SVOMAS), later Vkhutemas, until 1921 studying under K.Korovin, Malevich and Pevsner. He exhibited with Naum Gabo and Pevsner at the Tverskoy Boulevard exhibition in 1920 and was sympathetic to aspects of both Constructivism and Suprematism. He was amongst the followers of Malevich who contributed to the *Unovis* exhibition in Moscow in 1921. He was involved in the activities of the Institute of Artistic Culture (INKhUK) between 1921 and 1925, and was represented at the First Russian Art Exhibition in Berlin in 1922. He also visited Denmark in the early 1920s and assisted in the displays for the Soviet Pavilion at the 1925 Paris Exhibition.

He taught a course on colour at the Vkhutemas/Vkhutein from 1924 to 1930. In a declaration dated 8 February 1924 and signed by Klucis and Sergei Sen'kin, published in *Lef* periodical (No.1, 1924) he announced the establishment of a Communist Collective: The Studio of Revolution within the Vkhutein to undermine the cult of artistic genius and direct creative activity towards revolutionary aims. His design work included posters and books and he contributed to the All-Union Polygraphic Exhibition in Moscow in 1927. He was a founder member of the group October in 1928 and exhibited in Cologne that year and in Brussels in 1929. He exhibited with October in 1930.

He visited Paris in 1937. He died in a labour camp.

*Dynamic City, 1919-21, Costakis Collection, is made up from transparent diagonal planes cutting across a black circle to suggest the three dimensional construction of a Suprematist city. Superficially comparable to the work of Lissitzky, this led on to red and black propaganda kiosks of complex geometric symmetries in which were embedded loudspeakers and screens to propagate the speeches of Lenin. Some of these precise and

Vasili Kandinsky. Apple Tree, *1911. Colour woodcut. 100 x 100 cm. Signed with a monogram.*
Hatton Gallery, University of Newcastle upon Tyne.

graphic structures incorporate impossible arrangements of struts or an impractical complexity so that an absurdist trait may be present which is also detectable in the work of Tatlin, Lissitzky and Rodchenko. The Costakis Collection has an extensive holding of these designs for propaganda kiosks. Klucis was able to execute a number of related constructions in the context of exhibition design. He employed the concept of construction to his graphic works also, building posters from photomontage elements allied to dynamic layout of text. Some of these were published as postcards at the time of the 1928 Moscow Spartakiad Games (Costakis Collection).

USSR-Strike Brigade, 1931, poster, is constructed from a photomontage organised according to the principals of his own response to Constructivist and Suprematist examples. The pole of the planet becomes the pole of a flag carried by a giant worker whilst the heads of figures representing the nations of the earth follow the curve of the planet.

Book design Covers for: the periodical *Gorn* (Furnace), No.8, 1923. B.Pasternak, A.Kruchenykh et al. *Zhiv Kruchenykh!* (Kruchenykh Lives!), Moscow, 1925.

Lit *G.Klucis*, exh. cat., Riga Art Museum, 1970. L.Oginskaya *G.Klutsis*, Moscow, 1981. A.Z.Rudenstine *Costakis Collection*, London, 1981. C.Lodder *Russian Constructivism*, New Haven and London, 1983. E.Weiss *Russische Avant-Garde, 1910-1930,*

Sammlung Ludwig, Köln, Munich, 1986. *Gustav Kluzis*, exh. cat., Galerie Gmurzynska, Cologne, 1988. S.Compton *Russian Avant-Garde Books 1917-34*, London, 1992.
Coll TG; Sammlung Ludwig, Cologne.
Colour plates pp.210, 211.

KLUTSIS = KLUCIS, G. G.

KLYCHEV, Izzat Nazarovich   **b.1923**
Turkmen painter. His works include a *Portrait of the Heroine of Socialist Labour Yazmurada Orazsakhatova*, 1961, TG.
Coll TG.

KLYUN (KLYUNKOV), Ivan Vasilievich   **1873-1942**
Painter. His birth date is variously given as 1870, 1873 and 1878. Much inspired by Cubist, Suprematist and Purist

Gustav Klucis. Project for a Projector Kiosk, *1922. Pen and ink. The upper part is inscribed 'Screen'.*
Klucis' kiosks combine diagrammatic geometry with a degree of practicality. They are hybrid designs bringing together principles derived from both Suprematism and Constructivism. This was designed to display agitational images.

Gustav Klucis. Project for Radio Orator No.5, *1922. Red and black ink. This construction incorporates a screen and a phonograph horn for sound and sight projection.*

devices. His liaison with Malevich made him an important adherent of the geometric painting of Suprematism in particular. Born in Kiev. After studying in Warsaw and Kiev in the 1890s he moved to Moscow to study under F.I.Rerberg, V.Fisher and Ilya Mashkov. Perhaps his most formative encounter was that with Malevich in 1907. He was a founder member of the Moscow Salon in 1910 but also knew of the experimental activities of the Union of Youth with whom he exhibited 1913-14. By 1913 he was producing painted relief constructions and moving in the circle of Malevich, Matyushin and the futurist poet Kruchenykh. He illustrated Kruchenykh's *Taynye poroki akademikov* (Secret Vices of Academicians) published in Moscow in 1915. Reliefs and constructed sculptures were produced 1914-16 and he contributed to the Tramway V, The First Futurist Exhibition of Paintings in Petrograd in 1915.

When Malevich launched his geometric style Suprematism in 1915 at the 0.10. The Last Futurist Exhibition of Paintings Klyun was a fellow exhibitor and immediate in his response. He contributed to the unpublished review *Supremus* in Moscow during 1916-17.

After the Revolution he exhibited with the Knave of Diamonds in Moscow in November 1917 and at the First Exhibition of Works of the Professional Union of Artists in Moscow in 1918. He taught painting from 1918 to 1921 at the Free Art Studios (SVOMAS)/Vkhutemas. He was included in the Fifth State Exhibition: From Impressionism to Non-Objective Art in Moscow 1918-19 and in the Tenth State Exhibition: Non-Objective Creativity and Suprematism in 1919 where he published a statement *The Art of Colour* in the catalogue, arguing that with the death of the representational image in painting art would be liberated and made available to the public through the new concept of a Museum of Painterly Culture. His name appeared on the April 1919 list of artists for acquisitions by the envisaged Museum of Painterly Culture. He designed a Suprematist memorial to the painter Olga Rozanova 1918-19, as did Rodchenko, for which there are drawings in the Costakis Collection, and he became involved in the reorganisation of the arts. He was represented along with Kandinsky, Chagall and others at the First State Exhibition of Paintings by Local and Moscow Artists held in Vitebsk in December 1919 and he participated in the Third Exhibition of Paintings held at Ryazan in 1919. In 1918-21 he was director of the Central Exhibitions Bureau within the Art Section of the People's Commissariat of the Enlightenment (IZO Narkompros).

He became a member of the Institute of Artistic Culture (INKhUK) in 1921 and was represented at the First Russian Art Exhibition at the Van Diemen Gallery in Berlin in 1922. He continued to work on Futurist books including Kruchenykh's *Future of the Word* in 1923. Despite a wealth of experience as a Suprematist he was increasingly attracted to the work and theories of Purism which Ozenfant and Le Corbusier had developed from Cubism in the wake of the war. This was reflected in his studies after Léger, Picasso, Braque, Gris and the Purists in the mid-1920s (Costakis Collection) and in his geometricised still-lifes of the 1920s and 1930s. He joined the 4 Arts society 1924-5 and contributed to the First Exhibition of the Society of Easel Painters (OST) in Moscow in 1925. He was represented in the First Touring Exhibition of Paintings and Graphics which opened in Moscow in 1929 and at the jubilee exhibition Artists of the RSFSR over 15 Years held at the Russian Museum, Leningrad, in 1932. He died in Moscow.

Suprematism, 1915, TG, if the date is correct, is an immediate response to the Suprematism which Malevich revealed in December 1915. Klyun is derivative in this respect and lacks the dynamic articulation of pictorial space that was a hallmark

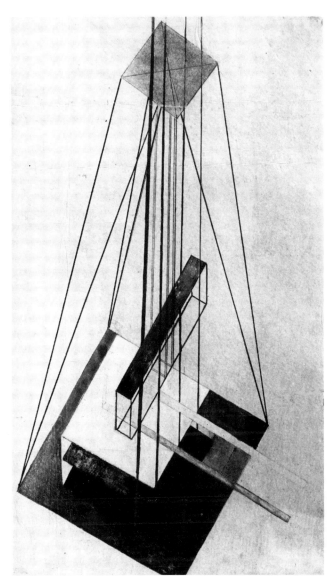

Gustav Klucis. Architectural Project, *c.1920-5. Gouache, indian ink and pencil on paper. 39.5 x 24.8 cm.*
This design shows the application of Suprematist principles to a potentially architectural scheme. Suprematists and Constructivists both produced projects which scarcely distinguished between painting, sculpture and architecture. Courtesy Annely Juda Fine Art, London.

of the work of Malevich. Whilst he was convinced by Suprematism he was more a follower than an innovator as comparison with Popova, Lissitzky reveals.

Futurist books A.Kruchenykh, I.Klyun, K.Malevich *Taynye poroki akademikov* (Secret Vices of Academicians), Moscow, 1915.

Writings I.Klyun *Kubizm kak zhivopisnyy metod* (Cubism as a Method of Painting) in *Sovetskaya arkhitektura*, No.6, 1928.

Lit S.P.Compton *The World Backwards, Russian Futurist Books 1912-16*, London, 1978. *Paris-Moscou* 1979. A.Z.Rudenstine *Costakis Collection*, London, 1981. C.Lodder *Russian Constructivism*, New Haven and London, 1983. E.Weiss *Russische Avant-Garde, 1910-1930, Sammlung Ludwig, Köln*, Munich, 1986. *L'Avant-garde russe 1905-1925*, exh. cat., Musée des Beaux-Arts, Nantes, 1993.

Coll TG; RM; Astrakhan Art Museum; Kirov Art Museum;

Nikolai Khristolyubov. Still-life with Lilies of the Valley, *1991. Oil on canvas. 96 x 66.5 cm.*
Roy Miles Gallery, London.

Orest Kiprensky. Gregorio Fidanza. *Oil on board. Inscribed on the back 'Chiprenschi' and 'GREGORIO FIDANZA ROMANO NOBILE DI SABINA E CAVALIERE DI MALTA'. 57 x 43 cm.*
Reproduced by kind permission of Christie's London, sale 27.11.1991, lot 192.

Tashkent Art Museum; Vladivostok Art Museum; Yaroslavl' Art Museum; Costakis Collection; Sammlung Ludwig, Cologne. Colour plates pp.214, 215, 217.

KNABE, Adol'f I.   **1876-1910**
Painter. A significant exponent of the Russian symbolist movement. He was included in the Scarlet Rose exhibition at Saratov in 1904, the Blue Rose exhibition in 1907 and the *Stefanos* exhibition 1907-8. He exhibited with the Golden Fleece in Moscow in 1908 and 1909-10.

KNAPPE (KNAPP), Karl Ivanovich (Fridrikh) 1745-1808
Painter. He was of German origin. His subjects included still-lifes, animals and views of St. Petersburg.
Coll TG.

KNIT, Lyudvig Frantsevich   **1894-a.1942**
Poster designer. He was working on lithographic political posters in Baku for the Bakkavrosta agency in 1920 incorporating Azerbaijani and Russian text and images in a style reminiscent of Mayakovsky's Rosta posters of the period.
Lit David Elliott, V.Dudakov *100 Years of Russian Art*, London, 1989.

KNYAZEV, A. N.   **a.1921**
He was included in the Third Touring Exhibition of the Sovetsk Regional subdepartment of the Museums Bureau along with Kandinsky, Rodchenko and others in 1921.

KOBYLETSKAYA, Zinaida Viktorovna   **1880-1957**
Ceramics artist, illustrator. After graduating from the Society for the Encouragement of the Arts in 1910, she studied in factories in Denmark, Sweden and France until 1912 and then worked at the Imperial Porcelain Factory 1912-14. After the revolution she worked at the State Porcelain Factory 1918-23 and at the Volkhov Factory at Novgorod in 1924. She was awarded a Diploma of Honour at the Paris Exhibition in 1925. She then worked at the Lomonosov Porcelain Factory 1926-32 during which time she won a gold medal at the Monza International Exhibition of 1927. She was represented at the jubilee exhibition Artists of the RSFSR over 15 Years held at the Russian Museum, Leningrad, in 1932.
She illustrated scientific publications after 1932, including *Flora of the USSR* and *Flora of Tadjikistan*. She was represented at the International Exhibitions in Paris in 1937 and New

York in 1939.
Lit *Paris-Moscou*, 1979. David Elliott, V.Dudakov *100 Years of Russian Art*, London, 1989. N.Lobanov-Rostovsky *Revolutionary Ceramics*, London, 1990.

KOCHAR, Ervand Semenovich   **b.1899**
Draughtsman. He evolved a unique style, the appearance of which was like stone relief, for his gouache drawings and illustrations of hieratic themes as in his illustrations to the Armenian epic *David Sasunsky*.
Coll Armenian Art Gallery, Erevan.

KOCHERGIN, Nikolai Mikhailovich   **1897-1974**
He was engaged on the decoration of the propaganda trains *Lenin* and *Soviet Cossack* as well as the propaganda boat *Red Star* c.1920. He was designing posters 1920-1.

KOCHETOVA, A.   **a.1921**
She was included in the Third Touring Exhibition of the Sovetsk Regional subdepartment of the Museums Bureau along with Kandinsky, Rodchenko and others in 1921.

KOGAN, Moisey   **1879-1911+**
Sculptor, graphic artist. Born at Grgeev. He worked in Germany and in Paris where he was impressed by the work of Rodin and Maillol. He exhibited bronzes with the Izdebsky Salon of 1910-11 in Odessa.
Coll MNAM, Paris.

KOGAN, Nina Osipovna   **1887-c.1942**
Painter. Born in Vitebsk. She studied at the Vitebsk Art School under Chagall and Lissitzky. She became a follower of Malevich and his Suprematism and she joined the *Unovis* collective. She also executed theatre designs. In 1922 she followed Malevich to Petrograd with Suetin, Chashnik and others.
Lit A.B.Nakov *Nina Kogan*, Zurich, 1985. E.Weiss *Russische Avant-Garde, 1910-1930, Sammlung Ludwig, Köln*, Munich, 1986.
Coll Sammlung Ludwig, Cologne.

KOGOUT, Nikolai Nikolaevich   **1891-1959**
Graphic artist. He was designing posters in 1921 and was also an exhibitor at the seventh exhibition of the group *L'Araignée* (The Spider) at the Galerie Devambe in Paris in 1925.

KOKORIN, Viktor Dmitrievich   **1886-1959**
He exhibited in the 1921 exhibition of the World of Art in Moscow.

KOLBE, G. F.   **a.1923-1925**
Theatre designer. He contributed to the exhibition Art of Moscow Theatre 1918-1923 held in Moscow in 1923 and was represented at the Paris International Exhibition of 1925.

KOLENDA, V. K.   **a.1906-1907**
Theatre designer. He worked as a designer for the director Vsevolod Meyerhold.
Theatre design 1906 November Meyerhold's production of S.Yushkevich's *In the City* at the V.F.Komissarzhevsky Theatre in St. Petersburg.
1906 December Meyerhold's production of M.Maeterlinck's *The Miracle of St. Anthony* at the V.F.Komissarzhevsky Theatre in St. Petersburg.
1907 February Meyerhold's production of L.Andreev's *Zhizn' cheloveka* (Life of Man) at the V.F.Komissarzhevsky Theatre in St. Petersburg.
Coll Bakhrushin Theatre Museum, Moscow.

KOLESNIKOV, S. M.   **a.1911-1921**
Ukrainian landscape painter. He was included in the Third Touring Exhibition of the Sovetsk Regional subdepartment of the Museums Bureau along with Kandinsky, Rodchenko and others in 1921 and in the 1921 exhibition of the World of Art in Moscow. He was represented at the First Russian Art Exhibition in Berlin in 1922.

KOLESOV, Aleksei Mikhailovich   **1834-1902**
Portrait painter. His portraits included the painters *Savrasov*, *Shishkin* and *Zaryanko*.
Coll TG.

KOLESOVA, I. K.   **a.1932**
She was represented at the jubilee exhibition Artists of the RSFSR over 15 Years held at the Russian Museum, Leningrad, in 1932.

KOLOBOV, D.A.   **a.1919-1921**
Painter. He exhibited at the juryless Eighth State Exhibition in Moscow in 1919. He was a member of the *Bytie* (Existence) Society of Artists formed in Moscow in 1921.

KOLOSOV, A. A.   **a.1921-1927**
A member of the *Bytie* (Existence) Society of Artists formed in Moscow in 1921. He was included in the 1928 exhibition of Acquisitions by the State Art Collections Fund held in Moscow.

KOL'TS (KOL'TSOV), Sergei Vasilievich   **a.1919-1932**
This name appeared on the April 1919 list of artists for acquisitions by the envisaged Museum of Painterly Culture. He was a member of the collective The Relief in 1922. He was represented at the First Russian Art Exhibition in Berlin in 1922 and at the jubilee exhibition Artists of the RSFSR over 15 Years held at the Russian Museum, Leningrad, in 1932.

KOLUPAEV, Dmitri   **a.1919**
Painter. He exhibited at the Ninth State Exhibition of Paintings: Naturalism and Realism in Moscow in 1919.

KOLUPAEV, N. A.   **a.1919**
Painter. He exhibited at the juryless Eighth State Exhibition in Moscow in 1919.

KOMARDENKOV, Vasili Petrovich   **1897-1973**
Theatre designer. He exhibited in the first *Obmokhu* exhibition in May 1919 in Moscow. He also took part in the third exhibition of *Obmokhu*, the Society of Young Artists, in Moscow in May 1921, along with Ioganson, Medunetsky and others. He was represented at the First Russian Art Exhibition in Berlin in 1922 and at the Paris International Exhibition of 1925.
Theatre design 1922 Meyerhold's production of E.Toller's *Machine Wreckers* at the Theatre of Revolution.
1927 Shakespeare's *Midsummer Night's Dream* produced by B.S.Glagolin at the Ivan Franko State Drama Theatre at Kiev.
Lit Dzhon Boult (John Bowlt) *Khudozhniki russkogo teatra. Sobranie Nikity i Niny Lobanovykh-Rostovskikh*, Moscow, 1991.

KOMISSARENKO, Z. P.   **a.1919**
This name appeared on the April 1919 list of artists for acquisitions by the envisaged Museum of Painterly Culture. Graphic artist. A Komissarenko contributed to the First Exhibition of Cinema Posters held in Moscow in 1925.

KOMYAZHENKO, E. D. = KAMEZHENKO. E. D.

KONASHEVICH, Vladimir Ivanovich   **1888-1963**
Painter, book designer, draughtsman. He executed decorative

paintings at the Yusupov Palace in St. Petersburg.

After the Revolution he was included in the enormous survey Exhibition of Paintings by Petrograd Artists of All Tendencies 1919-1923 held in Petrograd in 1923 and in the major exhibition in Moscow in 1927 marking the tenth anniversary of the Revolution. He was also included in the 1928 exhibition of Acquisitions by the State Art Collections Fund held in Moscow. He was represented at the jubilee exhibition Artists of the RSFSR over 15 Years held at the Russian Museum, Leningrad, in 1932.

Winter in Pavlovsk, 1933-4, RM, ink on Chinese paper, is also rather Chinese in technique employing the ink to stain the paper with washes that create a subtle and shiftingly suggestive image of a wood, snow-covered cottages and birch trees. The image is not immediately obvious. This calligraphic approach results in a delicate but startling luminosity.

Coll TG; RM.

KONCHALOVSKY, Petr Petrovich   **1876-1956**
Painter of portraits, still-lifes and other themes, theatre designer. Born at Slavyansk in the Kharkov region. In 1885 the family moved to Kharkov. After studying at the M.D.Raevskaya-Ivanova Drawing School in Kharkov he moved to Moscow in 1888 where he took evening classes at the Stroganov College in Moscow under V.D.Sukhanov. He knew Korovin, Levitan, Serov, Surikov and Vrubel'.

He was in Paris by 1897-8 attending the Académie Julian under Benjamin Constant and J.-P.Laurens.

He then enrolled at the Academy in St. Petersburg in 1895 until 1905 and studied under I.I.Tvorozhnikov, V.E.Savinsky and G.R.Zaleman and attended the studio of the battle painter P.O.Kovalevsky. He travelled frequently to western Europe visiting Italy in 1904 and 1907, working in France in 1908 and visiting Spain with his father-in-law the painter Vasili Surikov in 1910. He painted Yakulov's portrait in 1910. He exhibited at the Paris Salon d'Automne in 1908 and 1910 and at the Salon des Indépendants 1910-12. He exhibited with the Golden Fleece in Moscow 1909-10. He was a founder member of the Knave of Diamonds in 1910, joining all its exhibitions to 1916, but he also exhibited with the Golden Fleece, with the Union of Youth in 1911 and with the World of Art 1911-12. He exhibited with the Izdebsky Salon of 1910-11 in Odessa and with the Knave of Diamonds in Moscow 1910-12 including there a portrait of Ilya Mashkov. He visited Berlin with Surikov in 1912 and travelled on to Italy. He was frequently in Paris between 1907 and 1913 and became a convert to a kind of individual Cubism. He exhibited at the Salon d'Automne and the Salon des Indépendants and in 1913 he submitted paintings to the International Exhibition at the Stedelijk Museum, Amsterdam, as did Mashkov. He knew Picasso, Matisse, Le Fauconnier, Camoin and Manguin.

After the Revolution he exhibited with the revived World of Art in December 1917 and 1921-2. He taught at the Free Art Studios/Vkhutein in Moscow 1918-29. His name appeared on the April 1919 list of artists for acquisitions by the envisaged Museum of Painterly Culture and his work was amongst the new acquisitions of the Tretyakov Gallery exhibited in 1919. He was represented along with Kandinsky, Chagall and others at the First State Exhibition of Paintings by Local and Moscow Artists held in Vitebsk in December 1919. He was represented at the enormous First State Exhibition of Art and Science, which included ethnographic material, held in Kazan in 1920.

He was also represented at the First Russian Art Exhibition in Berlin in 1922 and was given a one-man exhibition at the Tretyakov Gallery in Moscow in 1922. He was recognised as a Merited Art Worker in 1922. He visited Venice in 1924 where he exhibited at the Biennale. Another one-man exhibition followed in Paris in 1925.

He was a member of the Society of Moscow Painters founded in 1925. He taught at the Vkhutemas 1926-9. He was a member of the *Existence* (Bytie) group 1926-7 and his work was included in the exhibition of Soviet art held at Harbin in 1926 and in Japan in 1927. He contributed to the International Exhibition in Dresden in 1926. He was included in the major exhibition in Moscow in 1927 marking the tenth anniversary of the Revolution and in the 1928 exhibition of Acquisitions by the State Art Collections Fund held in Moscow. He joined AKhRR in 1928 and was given an exhibition at the Russian Museum, Leningrad, in 1930.

He was represented at the jubilee exhibition Artists of the RSFSR over 15 Years held at the Russian Museum, Leningrad, in 1932 and at the 1932 Venice Biennale.

Paintings of the later 1920s and 1930s erased all tendencies towards Cubism. He exhibited in Moscow together with Sarra Lebedeva, Sergei Gerasimov, A.A.Deineka, Vera Mukhina and D.A.Shmarinov in 1943. He was made a People's Artist of the RSFSR in 1946 and elected a full member of the Academy of the USSR in 1947. He sometimes signed his work 'P.K'. or 'Kontchalovsky'. He died in Moscow.

Portrait of the Composer S.S Prokofiev, 1934, TG, is firmly resolved in rather solid forms and substantial paint textures. The musician sits on a chair in the woods, music score and pen in his hands to exemplify his profession.

Theatre design 1913 Mozart's *Don Giovanni*. 1918 designs for *Stenka Razin* at the Bolshoi Theatre, Moscow. 1933 April Goldoni's *Hotel Landlady* at the Moscow Art Theatre.

Lit P.P.Muratov *Zhivopis' Konchalovskogo*, Moscow, 1923. V.A.Nikolsky *P.P.Konchalovsky*, Moscow, 1936. Kravchenko *P.P.Konchalovsky*, Moscow, 1949. K.V.Frolov (ed.) *Konchalovsky, khudozhestvennoe nasledie*, Moscow, 1964. N.Neiman *P.P.Konchalovsky*, Moscow, 1967. *P.Konchalovsky*, exh. cat., Moscow, 1968. *P.P.Konchalovsky*, exh. cat., Moscow, 1976. *Paris-Moscou*, 1979. *Seven Moscow Artists 1910-30*, exh. cat., Galerie Gmurzynska, Cologne, 1984. *L'Avant-garde russe 1905-1925*, exh. cat., Musée des Beaux-Arts, Nantes, 1993.

Coll Well represented at TG and RM; Kazan Art Museum; Kostroma Art Museum; Tula Art Museum.

Colour plate p.220.

KONDRATENKO, Gavriil Pavlovich   **1854-1923+**
Painter. He worked in St. Petersburg. He was represented at the International Exhibition in Paris in 1889.

After the Revolution he was included in the enormous survey Exhibition of Paintings by Petrograd Artists of All Tendencies 1919-1923 held in Petrograd in 1923. His work included paintings of Georgia and the Crimea.

Coll TG; RM.

KONDRAT'EV, F.   **a.1926**
Graphic artist. He was represented at the Second Exhibition of Cinema Posters held at the Kamerny (Chamber) Theatre, Moscow, in 1926.

KONDRATEV, Pavel Mikhailovich   **1902-1985**
Painter, draughtsman. He was a member of Filonov's school,

Gustav Klucis. Project for a Propaganda Kiosk, *1922.*
This is one of a series of constructions designed as prototype information and propaganda kiosks to broadcast Lenin's speeches and other material. They employed complex three dimensional symmetries but simple materials and striking use of red, black and white. Klucis did realise some exhibition stands based upon comparable Constructivist designs.

the Collective of Masters of Analytical Art, established in Leningrad in 1925.
Like Zaklikovskaya and Sulimo-Samuilo he was a close follower of the example of Filonov whose drawing techniques he particularly assimilated.
Coll RM.

KONEN'KOV (KONYONKOV), Sergei Timofeevich 1874-1971

Dramatic Michelangelesque sculptor. Born in Smolensk region. He studied at the Moscow College under S.Ivanov and Volnukhin 1892-6 and was awarded the Tretyakov Prize with which he travelled to Germany, France, Switzerland and Italy. Between 1899 and 1902 he worked in the studio of Trubetskoy and studied under V.Beklemishev at the Academy but then settled in Moscow. He was a member of the New

Society of Artists from 1908 and joined the Union of Russian Artists in 1909. In 1912 he visited Greece and Egypt. He became an academician in 1916.
After the Revolution he exhibited with the World of Art in December 1917 in Moscow. He executed a memorial plaque dedicated 'To Those who Perished in the Struggle for Peace and the Brotherhood of Nations' which was placed by the wall of the Senate Tower in the Moscow Kremlin on 7 November 1918. He contributed to Lenin's Plan for Monumental Propaganda with a burnished wood sculpture of *Stepan Razin with his Troops* which was set up in Red Square in May 1918. He was also teaching sculpture at the Free Art Studios (SVOMAS) in Moscow in 1918.
He exhibited at the Fifth State Exhibition: From Impressionism to Non-Objective Art in Moscow 1918-19. He was a member of the Moscow Collegium of IZO Narkompros under Tatlin in 1919 and his name appeared on the April 1919 list of artists for acquisitions by the envisaged Museum of Painterly Culture. During 1919-20 he was a founder of the *Monolit* (Monolith) group of sculptors, which included Babichev, Mukhina, Konen'kov, Krandevskaya, Korolev, Strakhovskaya, Zlatovratsky, Ternovets, V.Popova, Blazhevich and Kudinov. They worked on monumental propaganda and entered the competitive exhibition for a *Monument to Liberated Labour* held in Moscow in May 1920. He was represented at the Nineteenth Exhibition of the All-Russian Exhibitions Bureau in Moscow in 1920 and at the enormous First State Exhibition of Art and Science, which included ethnographic material, held in Kazan in 1920. He also contributed to the 1921 exhibition of the World of Art in Moscow.

Sergei Konen'kov. Woman from a Collective Farm, *1954. Wood carving. 110 x 140 x 132 cm.*
Konenkov was an individual sculptor whose techniques were adaptable to Socialist Realist ends but whose sources were part of a longer Russian tradition of folk art and peasant themes. This enabled him to be adventurous in his use of materials and prevented him from succumbing to the prevailing academic historicism of many of his contemporaries.

Gustav Klucis. Project for a Propaganda Kiosk, *1922. Pen and ink.*
This is an ambitious design for a kiosk on a large scale. The lower part incorporates book display shelves and the upper part supports a large screen for the projection of images. The non-perspectival indication of structure was a deliberate device also employed by Rodchenko in kiosk designs.

He emigrated to the United States in 1923 and only returned to Moscow in 1945 but was represented at Venice in 1924. American works include a half length of *Dostoevsky* made in 1933. Late Russian works include a marble bust of the *Academician I.P Pavlov* 1952, *Socrates* 1953, and a *Self-portrait* bust in 1954. He also executed portraits of *Bach*, *Paganini*, *Herzen*, *Mussorgsky* and *Darwin*. He died in Moscow.

Thinker, 1898, marble, RM, is an essay in the Rodinesque use of the partly uncut block from the slightly soapy surface of which emerges the bearded head of the subject. The theme, of course, is also Rodin's.

Waking Woman, 1916, wood, RM, is deliberately archaic and stylised. He also produced rough carvings of patriarch figures which recall German Expressionist carvings.

To the Victims of the Struggle for Peace and for the Brotherhood of Nations, 1918, coloured cement, has an exotic, eastern flavour stylistically. A winged Victory carries her palm frond against a background of a radiant sunburst. Below the inscribed title flags are lowered in respect for the dead. All of this is executed in tile-like sections.

Caryatid, 1923, for the All-Russian Agricultural Exhibition in Moscow, an archaising motif in which the cylindrical form of the column resolves into a female figure with her arms raised over her head and her elbows high.

Lit S.Glagol *S.T.Konenkov*, Petrograd, 1920. A.Kamensky *Konenkov*, Moscow, 1962. K.Kravchenko *S.T.Konenkov*, Moscow, 1967. S.Konenkov *Moi vek*, Moscow, 1972. K.Kravchenko *S.Konenkov*, Leningrad, 1977. *Sergei Konenkov, Mastera Nashego Veka*, Moscow, 1978. *Paris-Moscou*, 1979. David Elliott, V.Dudakov *100 Years of Russian Art*, London, 1989. *Twilight of the Tsars*, London, 1991.

Coll TG; RM; S.T.Konenkov Memorial Studio-Museum, Moscow.

KONIG, D. = KENIG, D.

KONOVALOV, Vasili a. late 19th century
He was a fellow pupil of Pavel Kuznetsov studying under G.Salvini-Baracchi at Saratov c.1891-6.

KONOVALOVA, A. S. a.1918-1919
Painter. She exhibited at the First Exhibition of Works of the Professional Union of Artists in Moscow in 1918 and at the Ninth State Exhibition of Paintings: Naturalism and Realism in Moscow in 1919.

KONSTANTINOV, Fedor Konstantinovich 1882-1964
Painter. He exhibited with the Golden Fleece in Moscow 1909-10. He visited Paris.
After the Revolution he exhibited with the World of Art in

Boris Korolev. N.E.Bauman, *1930. Bronze. 49 x 31 x 32 cm.*

December 1917 in Moscow and at the First Exhibition of Works of the Professional Union of Artists in Moscow in 1918. He was engaged on Agitprop decorations at Saratov 1918-20. The name Konstantinov appeared on the April 1919 list of artists for acquisitions by the envisaged Museum of Painterly Culture. He worked on Rosta Windows in Tiflis (Tblisi) and also worked on theatre design there. He died in Moscow.

KONTCHALOVSKY, P. P. = KONCHALOVSKY, P. P.

KONYONKOV = KONEN'KOV, S.T.

KORBUT, Evgenia   a.1926
Graphic artist. She designed posters for the Blue Blouse agitational theatre productions in 1926.

KORIN, Aleksei Mikhailovich   1865-1923
Painter whose subjects included portraits, landscapes and interiors. Born to a peasant family in the Vladimir region. He studied at the Moscow College under Pryanishnikov, Makovsky and Polenov 1884-9. He exhibited with the Wanderers from 1891 and became a member in 1895. He taught at the Moscow College from 1894.
After the Revolution he participated in the Third Exhibition of Paintings held at Ryazan in 1919.
Coll TG.

KORIN, Pavel Dmitrievich   1892-1967
Portrait painter. He studied under Nesterov. His paintings are characterised by clear colour, decisive edges to forms and a directness reminiscent of posters. Later works include a portrait of *Aleksei Tolstoy*, 1940, RM, a *Portrait of the Kukryniksy*

Artists ,1957-8, TG, which is a triple portrait of the artists seated against a background of their posters, and a portrait of the artist *Renato Guttoso*, 1961, RM.
*Portrait of the Artist M.V.Nesterov, 1939, TG, is a lively portrait not unlike Golovin in its expansive expression of a sitter caught in action. Nesterov is presented as elegantly dressed and his gestures are used to characterise the sitter. He sits in a big winged chair discoursing with an unseen listener.
*Aleksandr Nevsky, 1942-3, TG, is an extraordinary painting of poster-like directness in which the great warrior Tsar rears arrogant, belligerent and proud to confront the viewer like an almost supernatural hero in his shining armour. The relevance of this overt anachronism is explained by the painting's date: it is an image of national, military might at a time of intense warfare.
Lit A.Mikhailov *P.Korin*, 1965. P.Korina *P.Korin*, Leningrad, 1972.
Coll TG; RM; P.D.Korin Appartment Museum, Moscow.

KORITSKY (KARITSKY), Aleksandr Osipovich 1818-1867
Painter of classical myth. His death date is sometimes given as 1873.
Coll TG.

KOROCHKIN = SVAROG, V.S.

KOROLEV, Boris Danilovich   1884-1963
Sculptor. Born in Moscow. He studied science at Moscow University 1902-5 but then studied art privately 1907-10 under F.Rerberg, Ilya Mashkov, V.Meshkov and M.Blok. From 1910-1913 he attended the Moscow College under S.Volnukhin. In 1913 he travelled to England, Italy, Austria, Germany and France where he worked under Archipenko. He was impressed by the example of Rodin. In 1917 he was a member of the Union of Russian Artists.
After the Revolution he responded to Lenin's Plan for Monumental Propaganda by evolving a *Monument to Bakunin* in 1918. Korolev at his most Cubist employed triangular block-like forms to give Bakunin an air of battling heroically against the rush of circumstance. In 1919 he entered the competion for a *Monument to Karl Marx*.
He was a member of the Moscow Collegium of IZO Narkompros under Tatlin in 1919 and his name appeared on the April 1919 list of artists for acquisitions by the envisaged Museum of Painterly Culture. He was represented at the enormous First State Exhibition of Art and Science, which included ethnographic material, held in Kazan in 1920. Korolev taught at the SVOMAS/Vkhutemas in Moscow from 1918 to 1924. During 1919-20 he was a founder of the *Monolit* (Monolith) group of sculptors, which included Babichev, Mukhina, Konen'kov, Krandevskaya, Korolev, Strakhovskaya, Zlatovratsky, Ternovets, V.Popova, Blazhevich and Kudinov. They worked on monumental propaganda and entered the competitive exhibition for a *Monument to Liberated Labour* held in Moscow in May 1920. He was represented at the Nineteenth Exhibition of the All-Russian Exhibitions Bureau in Moscow in 1920. At the Vkhutemas he taught on the foundation course with the sculptors A.Babichev, I.Chaikov, R.Iodko and N.Niss-Gol'dman c.1920.
He became involved in the activities of the Institute of Artistic Culture (INKhUK) in Moscow and made drawings exemplifying construction for their debates of 1921 (Costakis Collection). He was represented at the First Russian Art

Prince
Youri Vsevolodovitch

Kitege

Aleksei Korovin. Costume design for Prince Yuri Vsevolodovich in 'The Invisible City of Kitezh', *1929. Watercolour. Signed 'A. Korovine' lower left and inscribed at the top 'Kitege. Prinse Yuri Vsevolodovitch'. 39.5 x 27 cm.*
Collection Mr. and Mrs. Nikita D.Lobanov-Rostovsky, London.

Exhibition in Berlin in 1922. He exhibited with the revived World of Art 1921-2 but was also a member of the Society of Moscow Painters from 1925 and the Society of Russian Sculptors. His work was exhibited in Venice in 1924, 1928 and 1930. He was included in the major exhibition in Moscow in 1927 marking the tenth anniversary of the Revolution and in the 1928 exhibition of Acquisitions by the State Art Collections Fund held in Moscow. In 1928 he joined AKhRR and taught at the Leningrad Academy (Vkhutein) 1929-30. He was represented at the jubilee exhibition Artists of the RSFSR over 15 Years held at the Russian Museum, Leningrad, in 1932.
Standing Male Figure and *Standing Female Figure*, 1914-15, bronze, RM, lie stylistically between Rodin and Cubism. They are highly rhythmic, faceless, and formed from curves and linear planes.
Lit *B.D.Korolev*, exh. cat., Moscow, 1958. L.Bubnova *B.D.Korolev*, Moscow, 1968. *B.D.Korolev*, exh. cat., Moscow, 1978. A.Z.Rudenstine *Costakis Collection*, London, 1981.

KOROLEV, I. a.1924
He exhibited with the First Working Organisaton of Artists in 1924 at the First Discussional Exhibition of Active Revolutionary Art alongside G.Aleksandrov and others.

KOROTKOVA, Nina a.1928
She was engaged in mural decorations at the Security Police Club, Moscow, c.1928.

KOROVIN (COROVIN), Aleksei Konstantinovich 1897-1950
Theatre designer. Born in Moscow, the son of the painter Konstantin Korovin.
After the Revolution he became a member of the revived World of Art society with whom he exhibited in 1918 and 1921 in Moscow. He was also represented at the Nineteenth Exhibition of the All-Russian Exhibitions Bureau in Moscow in 1920.
He emigrated with his father in 1923 and settled in Paris where he worked for cabarets and made stage designs. He was working for the Teatro Colon at Buenos Aires in 1933. He died in Paris.
Theatre design 1929 Rimsky-Korsakov's opera *The Invisible City of Kitezh* produced by the Maria Kuznetsova (Marie Kousnezoff) Opéra Privé de Paris at the Théâtre des Champs-

Kitege
couleur

Prince
Wsevolod Journevitch

Aleksei Korovin. Costume design for Prince Vsevolod Yurevich in 'The Invisible City of Kitezh', *1929. Gouache. Signed 'A. Korovine' lower left and inscribed at the top 'Kitege. Prinse Wsevolod Yourievitch'. 38.5 x 27.5 cm.*
Collection Mr. and Mrs. Nikita D.Lobanov-Rostovsky, London.

Ivan Klyun. Untitled, *1916. Wood relief. 37.5 x 17.5 x 7 cm.*
Private collection, courtesy Annely Juda Fine Art, London

Elysées, Paris.

Lit *Diaghilev and Russian Stage Designers, a Loan Exhibition from the Collection of Mr. and Mrs. N.Lobanov-Rostovsky,* International Exhibitions Foundation, Washington, 1972-4. J.E.Bowlt *Russian Stage Design. Scenic Innovation. From the Collection of Mr. and Mrs. Nikita D.Lobanov-Rostovsky,* Jackson, MS, exh. cat.,1982. Dzhon Boult (John Bowlt) *Khudozhniki russkogo teatra. Sobranie Nikity i Niny Lobanovykh-Rostovskikh,* Moscow, 1991.

KOROVIN (KOROVINE), Konstantin Alekseevich 1861-1939

Painter, theatre designer. Much inspired by Impressionist techniques. Born in Moscow. He studied at the Moscow College under Perov, Savrasov and Polenov between 1875 and 1883 but at the Academy in St. Petersburg in 1882. He was drawn into the orbit of the Abramtsevo colony and also later exhibited with the World of Art and the Union of Russian Artists. In 1885 he executed designs for a prodution of *Aida*. It was in Paris 1885-6 that he saw Impressionist painting which had a profound impact on his development. Between 1885 and 1891 he designed for Savva Mamontov's private opera. He journeyed to the North of Russia 1894-5 visiting Archangel and Murmansk. His panel *The North*, TG, was exhibited at the All-Russian Exhibition at Nizhny-Novgorod in 1896. He exhibited with the Wanderers from 1889 to 1899 and he was represented at the Exhibition of Russian and Finnish Artists in St. Petersburg in 1898. He exhibited with the World of Art 1901-6.

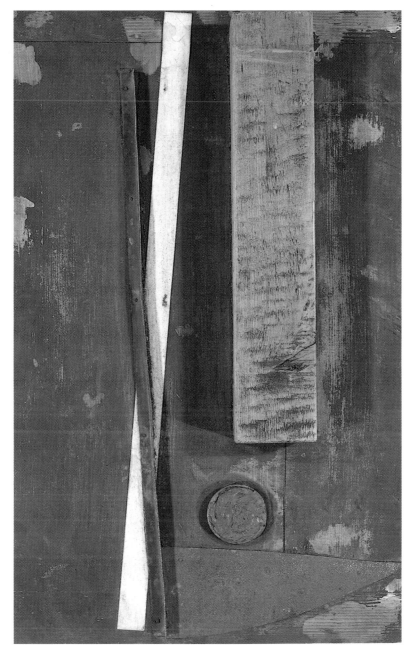

Ivan Klyun. Untitled, *1916. Wood relief and collage. 58.5 x 37.5 x 6.2 cm.*
Private collection, courtesy Annely Juda Fine Art, London

He was employed to design for the Imperial Opera in Moscow and St. Petersburg in 1898. For the International Exposition in Paris in 1900 he designed the Russian Pavilion and also exhibited decorative panels. He exhibited with the World of Art in St. Petersburg in 1900. He taught at the Moscow College from 1901 to 1918. He designed an elegant tea room decorated with slender trees and foliage for the Contemporary Art Store and Exhibition in St. Petersburg 1902-3. He returned to Paris in 1906, exhibited in the 1907 Venice Biennale and in 1908 was painting in the South of France and Paris. He was appointed chief artist to the Imperial Theatres in Moscow in 1910 and in 1911 he was represented at the International Exhibition in Rome.

After the Revolution he was teaching at the Free Art Studios in Moscow in 1918 where he was assisted by the painter Aleksandr Kuprin. He exhibited in the Fourth State Exhibition of Paintings (*IV Gosudarstvennaya vystavka kartin*) in Moscow in 1919, at the Fifth State Exhibition: From Impressionism to Non-Objective Art in Moscow in 1919 and his name appeared on the April 1919 list of artists for acquisitions by the envisaged Museum of Painterly Culture. He participated in the Third Exhibition of Paintings held at Ryazan in 1919 and was represented at the Nineteenth Exhibition of the All-Russian Exhibitions Bureau in Moscow in 1920. He was represented at the enormous First State Exhibition of Art and Science, which included ethnographic material, held in Kazan in 1920 and he exhibited in the 1921 exhibition of the World of Art in Moscow.

In 1923 or 1924 he emigrated to Paris. He sometimes signed his work 'Corovin' or 'Korovine'.

Boulevard des Italiens, 1908, is Paris by night inspired by the example of Camille Pissarro but employing a looser technique and with flair replacing power of expression.

Theatre design He worked for numerous theatres including the Bolshoi, Mariinsky and Aleksandrinsky Theatres.

1885 Verdi's *Aida*.

1897 Rimsky-Korsakov's *Sadko*.

1900 September: collaborated on the design of Dargomyzhsky's *Rusalka* at the Bolshoi Theatre, Moscow.

1900 December: L.Minkus' ballet *Don Quixote* at the Bolshoi Theatre, Moscow.

1901 set for Scene 3 of Delibes' *Sylvia*, a collaboration with Bakst, Benois and Lansere (unrealised).

1901 November: Ts.Puni's ballet *Konek-Gorbunok* (Hobbyhorse-Seahorse) at the Bolshoi Theatre, Moscow.

1902 February: Wagner's *Valkyrie* at the Bolshoi Theatre, Moscow.

1902 November: Wagner's *Flying Dutchman* at the Bolshoi Theatre, Moscow.

1902 November: A.Simon's ballet *Esmeralda* at the Bolshoi Theatre, Moscow.

1902-3 Wagner's *Götterdämmerung* designed in collaboration with Alexandre Benois at the Mariinsky Theatre in St. Petersburg.

1903 November: Minkus' ballet *Zolotaya rybka* (The Goldfish) at the Bolshoi Theatre, Moscow.

1904 January: Arensky's opera *Nal' i Damayanti* at the Bolshoi Theatre, Moscow.

1904 September: Glinka's *Zhizn' za tsarya* (A Life for the Tsar, Ivan Susanin) at the Bolshoi Theatre, Moscow (in collaboration).

1904 November: A.Rubinstein's *Demon* at the Bolshoi Theatre, Moscow.

1905 November: Ts.Puni's ballet *Doch' faraona* (The Pharaoh's Daughter) at the Bolshoi Theatre, Moscow.

1906 October: Rimsky-Korsakov's opera *Sadko* at the Bolshoi Theatre, Moscow.

1906 December: Dargomyzhsky's *The Stone Guest* at the Bolshoi Theatre, Moscow.

1907 November: Glinka's *Ruslan i Lyudmila* at the Bolshoi Theatre, Moscow.

1907 December: Rimsky-Korsakov's *Snegurochka* (Snowmaiden) at the Bolshoi Theatre, Moscow.

1907 February: Rimsky-Korsakov's opera *The Invisible City of Kitezh and the Maid Fevronia* at the Mariinsky Theatre, St. Petersburg. Libretto by V.Belsky. Some design also by A.Vasnetsov and Nikolai Klodt.

1908 October: Chaikovsky's *Evgeniy Onegin* (Eugene Onegin) at the Bolshoi Theatre, Moscow.

1908 November: Glazunov's *Raimonda* at the Bolshoi Theatre, Moscow.

1909 December: Borodin's opera *Prince Igor*, choreography by Fokine, at the Mariinsky Theatre, St. Petersburg. Choreography by Fokine.

1909 décor and costumes for Diaghilev's production of *Le Festin*, Théâtre du Châtelet, Paris. Costumes also by Bakst, Bilibin and Benois.

1910 June: décors for the ballet *Les Orientales*, produced by Diaghilev at the Paris Opera, to music by several composers. Choreography by Fokine.

1911 September: Meyerhold's production of L.N.Tolstoy's *Living Corpse* at the Aleksandrinsky Theatre, St. Petersburg. Designed by Bakst and Korovin.

1911 costumes for Musorgsky's opera *Khovanshchina*.

1911 décors, in collaboration with Golovin, for Chaikovsky's *Lac des Cygnes* produced by Diaghilev at the Theatre Royal, Covent Garden, London.

Numerous designs followed including:

1929 Rimsky-Korsakov's *Snegurochka*, produced by Nikolai Evreinov for Marie Kousnezoff's Opéra Privé in Paris.

Lit N.Komarovskaya *Korovin*, Leningrad, 1961. D.Kogan *Korovin*, Moscow, 1964. *Diaghilev and Russian Stage Designers, a Loan Exhibition from the Collection of Mr. and Mrs. N.Lobanov-Rostovsky*, International Exhibitions Foundation, Washington, 1972-4. J.E.Bowlt *Russian Stage Design. Scenic Innovation. From the Collection of Mr. and Mrs. Nikita D.Lobanov-Rostovsky*, Jackson, MS, exh. cat.,1982. V.Kruglov *Korovin*, Leningrad, 1985. A.Basyrov *Korovin*, Leningrad, 1985. David Elliott, V.Dudakov *100 Years of Russian Art*, London, 1989. *Twilight of the Tsars*, London, 1991. Dzhon Boult (John Bowlt) *Khudozhniki russkogo teatra. Sobranie Nikity i Niny Lobanovykh-Rostovskikh*, Moscow, 1991.

Coll Major holdings at TG and RM; Bakhrushin Theatre Museum, Moscow; A.V.Shchusev Museum of Architecture, Moscow; Ashmolean Museum, Oxford.

Colour plates pp.221, 224, 225.

KOROVIN, Sergei Alekseevich   **1858-1908**
Painter of group portraits and figure compositions. He was the elder brother of Konstantin Korovin. He exhibited with the World of Art in 1903. He died in Moscow.
Coll Well represented at TG; RM.

KOROVIN, Stepan   **a.1716**
Engraver. He was amongst the first of the *artistes pensionnaires* of Peter I with I.Nikitin and Andrei Matveev. They left Russia in 1716 to study abroad. Korovin was the only one of these to be sent to France.

KOROVINE, K. A. = KOROVIN, K. A.

KORVIN-MAKHOTKIN, Yu.   **a.c.1927**
Graphic artist. He was included in the major exhibition in Moscow in 1927 marking the tenth anniversary of the Revolution.

KORZHEV, Geli M.   **b.1925**
Painter. Works include a triptych *The Communists*, 1957-60, and *The Artist*, 1960-1, a photographically realist composition of a bearded pavement artist at work, perhaps on the streets of Paris.
Coll TG; RM.

KORZUKHIN, Aleksei Ivanovich   **1835-1894**
A member of the artel which led to the founding of the Wanderers.
Coll TG.

KOSHELEV, Nikolai Andreevich   **1840-1918**
He was represented in the First State Free Exhibition of Artworks in Petrograd in 1919.
Coll TG.

KOSTANDI, Kiriak Konstantinovich   **1852-1921**
Ukrainian painter of landscapes and contemporary themes
Born near Odessa. He studied at the Academy in St.
Petersburg 1874-82 and exhibited with the Wanderers from
1884 becoming a member in 1897. Some of his paintings
reflect an air of melancholia. He won a gold medal at the Paris
International Exhibition in 1889. He was a founder member
of the Society of South Russian Artists at Odessa in 1890. He
taught at the Odessa School of Art where his many pupils
included Osip Braz and I.I.Brodsky.
At a Sick Friend's House, 1884, TG, is a triple portrait set up
as a narrative scene. The sick man is an artist with unstretched
canvases pinned to his wall. The black clothes and informal
domestic portraiture recall Degas. The message of this
modulated tonal painting is perhaps to indicate that the young
artist may never realise his evident talents.
Coll TG; Odessa Art Museum.

KOSTENKO, K.E.   **a.1908-1932**
Graphic artist. He contributed to the exhibition *Zveno* (The
Link) in Kiev in 1908 where his work included landscapes of
Brittany, Paris, Versailles and also Finland.
He was represented at the jubilee exhibition Artists of the
RSFSR over 15 Years held at the Russian Museum, Leningrad,
in 1932.

KOSTIN, K. K.   **a.1908**
Theatre designer. He worked intensively with the director
V.Meyerhold in 1908 assisting on the following productions
which toured to Vitebsk, Minsk, Kherson, Poltava, Kiev and
Kharkov that year: A.Blok's *Farce*, F.Wedekind's *Vampire*
which Meyerhold translated, H.von Hofmannthal's *Electra*,
H.Ibsen's *Hedda Gabler*, F.Sologub's *Victory of Death*,

Ivan Klyun. Composition, *1921. Oil on canvas. Signed and dated. 64.5
x 46 cm.*
Private collection, courtesy Annely Juda Fine Art, London

Ivan Klyun. Untitled, *1922. Oil on carpet. Signed and dated. 52.4 x 54 cm.*
Private collection, courtesy Annely Juda Fine Art, London

L.Andreev's *Life of Man*, G.Hauptmann's *Hostage of
Charlemagne*, H.Ibsen's *Master Builder* and K.Hamsun's *At the
Imperial Gates*.

KOSTIN, S.   **a.1919-1925**
He exhibited in the first *Obmokhu* exhibition in May 1919 in
Moscow. He also took part in the third exhibition of *Obmokhu*,
the Society of Young Artists, in Moscow in May 1921, along
with Ioganson, Medunetsky and others. He was a founder
member of the Society of Easel Painters (OST) in 1925.

KOSTROV, Nikolai Ivanovich   **b.1901-1928+**
Painter.
Coll RM.

KOSTYANITSYN, Vasili Nikolaevich   **a.1918-1920**
Painter. He was represented at the First Exhibition of Works
of the Professional Union of Artists in Moscow in 1918 and at
the Third Exhibition of Paintings held at Ryazan in 1919. He
was engaged in the decoration of propaganda trains in 1920
including the Ukrainian *Lenin* train, the *Soviet Cossack* train,
the propaganda boat *Red Star* and the train *Red Cossack* on
which the fallen monarchy and the trappings of wealth are
surmounted by paragons of the Revolution silhouetted against
billowing flags. Other artists decorating this train were
S.Tikhonov, A.Glazunov and N.Pomansky.

Vladimir Kozlinsky. The Sailor, *1919. Linocut. 34.4 x 21.5 cm.*
The movement of the ship is indicated by the tilted horizon and rail. The sailor's white clothes are brilliant against the night sky and the choppy waves catch the light. All of this shows the reduction of the image to isolate its most effective elements.
State Russian Museum, St. Petersburg.

KOTARBINSKY, Vasili Aleksandrovich   1849-1921
Painter. He was working in Rome in 1898. Sometimes he signed his work 'W.Kotarbin' in latin script.
Coll TG.

KOTLYAREVSKAYA, Maria Evgen'evna   1902-1930+
Graphic artist. She was represented at the exhibition of graphic art Liberation Movements: The Sixteenth to the Twentieth Century held in Moscow in 1928.
Residents During the Civil War, 1930, linocut, shows a debt to the techniques of Favorsky but with a degree of folk art stylisation and an individual use of flat areas in the print. It depicts a range of citizens of different types, including lovers and a mother and child, brought together by the fighting as they shelter in a cellar.

KOTOV, Petr Ivanovich   1889-1953
In 1922 he was a founder member of the Society (*Obshchestvo*) of Artists of Revolutionary Russia, founded after the first exhibition of the Association of Artists of Revolutionary Russia (AKhRR). Other members included A.Grigoriev, P.Kiselev, E.Katsman, S.Malyutin, P.Radimov, P.Shukhmin, A.Skachko,

G.Sukhanov, B.Yakovlev and V.Zhuravlev. He was included in the enormous survey Exhibition of Paintings by Petrograd Artists of All Tendencies 1919-1923 held in Petrograd in 1923 and in the major exhibition in Moscow in 1927 marking the tenth anniversary of the Revolution.
His work was included in the exhibition of Soviet art held at Harbin in 1926 and in Japan in 1927, and in the 1928 exhibition of Acquisitions by the State Art Collections Fund held in Moscow. He was also represented at the jubilee exhibition Artists of the RSFSR over 15 Years held at the Russian Museum, Leningrad, in 1932.

KOTOVICH-BORISYAK, R. I.   a.1917-1919
Painter. He exhibited with the World of Art in December 1917 in Moscow, at the First Exhibition of Works of the Professional Union of Artists in Moscow in 1918 and at the Fourth State Exhibition of Paintings (*IV Gosudarstvennaya vystavka kartin*) in Moscow in 1919.

KOTUKHIN, Aleksandr Vasil'evich   1886-1961
He was represented at the Paris International Exhibition of 1925.

KOVALEV, Aleksandr Aleksandrovich   1915-1952+
Ukrainian portrait sculptor.

KOVALEVSKY, Pavel Osipovich   1843-1903
Painter of military and genre themes. Born at Kazan. He studied at the Academy in St. Petersburg and subsequently became an Academician. He worked at Kiev. He won a gold medal at Berlin in 1886. He died at St. Petersburg.
Coll TG; RM.

KOVAL'TSIG, V. G.   a.1923
Theatre designer. He contributed to the exhibition Art of Moscow Theatre 1918-1923 held in Moscow in 1923.

KOVARSKY, Felitsian Feliksovich   1890-1948
Monumentalist. He studied at the Odessa School of Art. He was engaged in Agitprop decorations at Tsarskoselsky Station Square, Petrograd, in 1918.

KOVSHENKO, Ivan Fedorovich   1824-1898
Sculptor. He executed historical genre pieces including full-length figures of ancient warriors in the dress of their time, for example *Scythian Prince*, 1862, bronze, RM.
Coll Well represented at RM.

KOZAINSKY, V. I.   1891-1967
Theatre designer. He was active in the theatre in the 1920s.

KOZHIN, Pavel Mikhailovich   1904-1975
Sculptor, ceramics artist. He studied under Tatlin at the Ceramics Faculty of the Vkhutein 1926-31 where he designed a teapot under Tatlin's direction. He subsequently directed the ceramics laboratory of the Institute of Handicraft Industry 1932-3 before working at the porcelain factory at Verbilki and, from 1938, at the Dulevo Porcelain Factory.
Lit L.A.Kramarenko *P.M.Kozhin*, Moscow, 1958.

KOZLINSKY, Vladimir Ivanovich   1891-1967
Printmaker, theatre designer. Born at Kronstadt. From 1907 he studied at the Society for the Encouragement of the Arts, the Zvantseva School and privately under D.N.Kardovsky. He showed work at Kul'bin's *Triangle* exhibition in St. Petersburg in 1909 and his Impressionists exhibition at Vilno 1909-10.

He was studying under the printmaker V.V.Maté in St. Petersburg in 1911. The following year he contributed to the exhibition Contemporary Painting in Ekaterinodar.

After the Revolution he was engaged in Agitprop decorations in Petrograd in 1918 including a mural of red flagged boats with the legend 'All Power to the Workers', and he became head of the engraving studio at the Free Art Studios (SVOMAS). He showed work at the exhibition Russian Landscape in Petrograd in 1918 and at the First State Free Exhibition of Artworks in 1919 in Petrograd.

In 1920 together with Vladimir Lebedev he directed the activities of the Rosta Agency in Petrograd and was very active as a poster designer 1920-1. He exhibited with the Union of New Tendencies in Art in Petrograd in June 1922. He was represented at the First Russian Art Exhibition in Berlin in 1922, at the Third Exhibition of Paintings by Artists from Kaluga and Moscow held in Kaluga in 1925 and at the seventh exhibition of the group L'Araignée (The Spider) at the Galerie Devambe in Paris in 1925. He was represented at the exhibition marking the tenth anniversary of the Revolution held in Moscow in 1928. He often signed his prints 'V.K'. He died in Moscow.

The Demonstration, 1918, linocut, RM, has the force of a woodcut and allows black to dominate. The print shows a crowd surging across the river. At other times, as in his linocut *The Sailor*, 1919, RM, he adopts the assertive boldness of the *lubok* popular print. Here the billowing form of the sailor is seen at the handrail of his ship, designed with great economy of means in black.

*A window poster for the Rosta Telegraph Agency executed in Petrograd 1920 1 used dramatic and angular blocks to contrast the nature of authority before and after the Revolution: diminutive figures creep past immense Imperial police in contrast to a marching phalanx of workers. A Rosta poster of 1924 invokes the Paris Commune as its theme via an oblique compositional reference to *Liberty Leading the People* by Delacroix complete with the towers of Notre Dame in the background. The effect is novel however. The citizen holds aloft a flag and a sabre. Bayonets spike the air. Kozlinsky's use of silhouette is as decisive as a cut-out and his composition is explosive.

Theatre design 1928 September V.P.Kataev's *Kvadratura kruga* (The Squaring of the Circle) at the Moscow Art Theatre.
1939 Balzac's *Eugénie Grandet* at the Maly Theatre, Moscow.
Lit L.Diakov *V.Kozlinsky*, Moscow, 1978. *Paris-Moscou*, 1979.
Coll RM; Bakhrushin Theatre Museum.

KOZLOV, Aleksandr Nikolaevich　　　　**1902-1946**
Born at Ekaterinburg. Painter. He studied at the Moscow Vkhutemas 1918-22 and was teaching 1939-42. He died in Moscow.
Lit A.M.Muratov, V.Manin et al. *Zhivopis' 20-30kh godov*, Sankt-Peterburg, 1991.
Coll RM.

KOZLOV, G.　　　　**a.1919-1927**
Sculptor. He was probably the Kozlov who in 1919 was listed as leader of a course for art teachers along with Tatlin and others. He was included in the major exhibition in Moscow in 1927 marking the tenth anniversary of the Revolution.

Vladimir Kozlinsky. Snooker, *1919. Lithograph. 17 x 20.5 cm. Kozlinsky has an expressionist directness in his prints. They are rhythmic and dramatic works focusing upon human activities presented in highly edited form.*

Petr Konchalovsky. Still-life with Grinder, *1920. Oil on canvas. Signed and dated 1920, and signed again on the stretcher. 90 x 70.5 cm.*
Reproduced by kind permission of Sotheby's London, sale 28.11.1991, lot 432.

Konstantin Korovin. Study for the costume of the Tsarevich Gvidon, *1912. Gouache, ink, silver, gold. Signed and inscribed. 36.2 x 26 cm.*
Designed for Rimsky-Korsakov's opera 'The Tale of Tsar Saltan' performed at the Bolshoi Theatre, Moscow, in 1913.
Collection Mr. and Mrs. Nikita D.Lobanov-Rostovsky, London.

KOZLOVA, K. A.　　　　　　　　　　　　**a.1925-1929**
She exhibited with the First Exhibition of the Society of Easel Painters (OST) in Moscow in 1925. She was included in the 1928 exhibition of Acquisitions by the State Art Collections Fund held in Moscow and in the First Touring Exhibition of Paintings and Graphics which opened in Moscow in 1929.

KOZLOVSKY, Mikhail Ivanovich　　　　**1753-1802**
Major neo-classical sculptor of heroic themes. He executed allegories and mythological scenes in formats ranging from bas reliefs to monuments. He entered the Academy at St.

Petersburg in 1766 where he studied under the French sculptor Nicolas Gillet. He also worked in Rome, sent there on a scholarship 1774-9, where he studied antique sculpture and the work of Michelangelo. He visited Paris in 1779. He executed work at the palaces at Tsarskoe Selo, Pavlovsk and elsewhere. He returned to Paris in 1788 where he knew the paintings of David and where he observed the French Revolution in 1789. He became an Academician in 1794.
His works included *The Vigil of Alexander the Great*, 1787, marble, RM, a grandiose *Hercules on Horseback*, 1799, bronze, RM, and a full-length marble *Cupid*, 1797, TG. His *Monument*

Ivan Kramskoy. The Singer Elizaveta Andreevna Lavrovskaya (1845-1919), *1887. Oil on canvas. 111 x 75 cm.*
Reproduced by kind permission of Sotheby's London, sale 15.2.1984, lot 99.

to A.V.Suvorov, 1799-1801, bronze and granite, was erected in the Champs de Mars in St. Petersburg. His work could almost be French or Italian, so thoroughly did he master the techniques of international neo-classicism.

Kozlovsky was one of only seven artists deemed worthy of a monument in Lenin's plan issued in 1918.

*Shepherd with a Hare, 1789, marble, Pavlovsk Palace Museum, is a supremely able and resolved carving of a full-length male figure twisting to adjust the sling which holds the hare. It superbly combines intense life-room observation with the inspiration provided by antique sculpture from Greece and Rome. He was a major protagonist of neo-classical sculpture able to bear international comparisons with confidence.

*Polycrates,1790, plaster, RM, owes a debt to Michelangelo as well as antique precedents. Tied to a tree, Polycrates is an anguished figure whose weight slumps down as if in a crucifixion. His control relied upon his astute powers of observation and drawing. Beyond this the execution of the sculpture was simply an extension of what had already been achieved in essence.

Lit V.N.Petrov *M.I.Kozlovsky*, 1977.
Coll Well represented at RM; TG; Pavlovsk Palace Museum.

KOZLOVSKY, S. M.　　　　　　　　　　　**a.1921-1924**
He was included in the Third Touring Exhibition of the Sovetsk Regional subdepartment of the Museums Bureau along with

Kandinsky, Rodchenko and others in 1921. He collaborated with Exter on the design of the film *Aelita* in 1924.

KRACHKEVICH, V.　　　　　　　　　　　　**a.c.1927**
Sculptor. He was included in the major exhibition in Moscow in 1927 marking the tenth anniversary of the Revolution.

KRACHKOVSKY, Iosif Evstafevich　　　**1854-1914**
Genre and landscape painter. He became a member of the Academy in St. Petersburg.
Coll TG; RM.

KRAKHT, Konstantin Fedorovich　　　　**1868-1919**
Sculptor. Born at Vladimir. He graduated in law from Moscow University in 1891 and practised law until 1901. He then moved to Paris where he studied under N.L.Aronson 1901-2. In 1904 he was studying there under Constantin Meunier. He returned from Paris to Moscow in 1907 to work as a portrait sculptor. He showed work at the exhibition *Venok* (The Wreath) in St. Petersburg in 1908. He died in Moscow.
Lit *Twilight of the Tsars*, London, 1991.
Coll TG.

KRAMSKOY, Ivan Nikolaevich　　　　　　**1837-1887**
Major portrait and figure painter, illustrator. Born at Ostrogozhsk in the Vladimir region. He painted religious pictures initially and worked in photography firms in Kharkov and St. Petersburg touching up photographs. He studied from 1856 to 1863 at the Academy in St. Petersburg but led a revolt of fourteen students there in 1863. He became a member of the Artel which led to the founding of the Wanderers in 1870 whose aims and means he defined. The Society for the Encouragement of the Arts employed him to teach drawing 1863-8. His portraits frequently depict peasants vigorously painted, informal and aggressively alive. He painted over 400 portraits, including Tolstoy in 1873, TG. In 1874 he produced phantasmagorical illustrations to Gogol's *A Terrible Vengeance*. In 1876 he executed a portrait of *Repin* in Paris and also a sensitive portrait of the collector *P.M.Tretyakov*.

*Christ in the Wilderness, 1872-4, TG, is a monumental painting in which the figure of Christ, seated on a rock in the desert, is the sole, dominating image depicted with minute attention to detail almost in the manner of a Pre-Raphaelite painting. Contemplative in the vast and barren space which stretches to a far distant horizon, Christ is portrayed as the embodiment of the isolated human being, bereft of solace and comfort. The figure is of sculptural firmness and stillness comparable with that of the rocks among which he sits. Nothing moves in the painting: it powerfully depicts concentrated stillness and introspection.

*Peasant with a Bridle, 1883, Museum of Russian Art, Kiev, is an intensely realised and monumental image of a weather beaten old peasant. It is a marvel of technique with nothing of the academic about it except that it depends upon the severe disciplines of technical skill that academic training was designed to stress. Here every vein and wrinkle shows. The figure is set against a deep plain background and clearly represents a kind of heroic type.

Lit A.S.Suvorin *I.N.Kramskoy, ego zhizn', perepiska i khudozhestvenno-kriticheskie stati*, St. Petersburg, 1888. S.N.Goldshtein *Ivan Nikolaevich Kramskoy. Zhizn' i tvorchestvo*, Moscow, 1965.
Coll Substantial holdings at TG and RM.

Konstantin Korovin. Figure by a Porch on a Summer Night. *Oil on canvas. Signed and dated 1922. 84 x 64 cm.*
Reproduced by kind permission of Sotheby's London, sale 28.11.1991, lot 478.

Aleksei Kravchenko. Lenin's Funeral, *1924. Wood engraving.*
The Moscow Kremlin walls rise behind the procession at the site where the Lenin Mausoleum now stands.

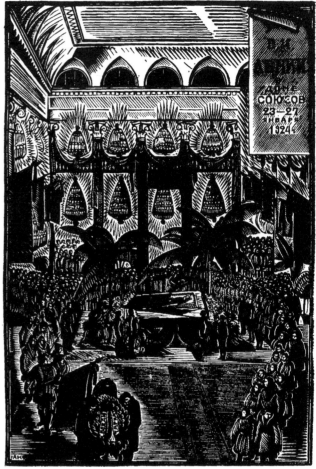

Aleksei Kravchenko. Lenin Lying in State in the House of Unions, *1924. Wood engraving. Signed 'AK'.*
The style has the directness and simplicity of the lubok tradition of popular prints wedded to the technical mastery of Favorsky's school of printmaking.

exhibitions at Paris in 1927 and Kiev in 1930. He was a member of the Union of Moscow Artists formed in 1925. He designed trademarks, stamps, posters and book illustrations. He was represented at the International exhibition of Book Art in Leipzig in 1927 and the major exhibition in Moscow in 1927 marking the tenth anniversary of the Revolution. He contributed to the exhibition of graphic art Liberation Movements: The Sixteenth to the Twentieth Century held in Moscow in 1928 and to the exhibition of Soviet Art in New York in 1928. He was also included in the 1928 exhibition of Acquisitions by the State Art Collections Fund held in Moscow and in the fourth exhibition of *Iskusstvo dvizheniya* (The Art of Movement) that year in Moscow. He was represented in the First Touring Exhibition of Paintings and Graphics which opened in Moscow in 1929.

He was represented at the jubilee exhibition Artists of the RSFSR over 15 Years held at the Russian Museum, Leningrad, in 1932 and at the 1932 Venice Biennale. He illustrated

Aleksei Kravchenko. Architectural Study, *c.1924. Wood engraving.*
The technique is clearly indebted to Favorsky's example but is less pared down and elegant. Here there is a robustness arising from Kravchenko's cruder and more sculptural approach.

Aleksei Kravchenko. Young Woman, *1925. Wood engraving. 25.3 x 17.9 cm. Signed 'AK' lower left.*
A rural idyll with water carrier, hut, landscape and distant village visible in the background.
State Russian Museum, St. Petersburg.

Pushkin's *Queen of Spades* 1939-40.
*Ponte Roto, Rome, 1916, etching, is a razor-sharp topographical view but also a little theatrical in its evocation of old Rome.
*Etchings of the War, 1917, were informative views of men at field dressing stations and in tents. One print showed a cross erected in the fields. These were published in *Iskra*, No.7, February, 1917.
*Stradivarius in his Workshop, 1926, wood engraving, was designed as a frontispiece for the programmes of the Stradivari Quartet. It is a spectacular print depicting the great violin-maker at work with violins hanging all around and a city visible through the window. It draws with skill upon Renaissance prototypes but wears its erudition lightly.
Lit E.Butorina *A.I.Kravchenko*, 1962. *A.I.Kravchenko, risunki*, exh. cat., Moscow, 1969. M.Panov *A.Kravchenko*, Moscow, 1969. *Paris-Moscou*, 1979. *L'Avant-garde russe 1905-1925*, exh. cat., Musée des Beaux-Arts, Nantes, 1993.
Coll RM; Samara Art Museum.

KRAVTSOV, L. K.   **a.1928**
He exhibited with the 4 Arts society in Leningrad including the exhibition of 1928 at the Russian Museum.

KRAYTOR, I. K.   **a.1919-1920**
Kraytor appeared on the April 1919 list of artists for acquisitions

by the envisaged Museum of Painterly Culture and was represented in the Fourth State Exhibition of Paintings (*IV Gosudarstvennaya vystavka kartin*) in Moscow in 1919. He also exhibited at the Nineteenth State Exhibition in Moscow in 1920.

KRENDOVSKY, Evgraf Fedorovich   **1810-1853+**
Painter of city views and portraits. He was a pupil of Venetsianov. His *Gathering for the Hunt*, 1836, TG, is a closely observed genre painting in which five lively young hunters reach for their guns before setting off to hunt. His work included views of Moscow.
Coll TG.

KRESTOVSKY, Yaroslav   **b.1925**
Painter of phantasmagorical themes.
Coll RM.

KRICHEVSKY, Fedor Grigor'evich   **1879-1947**
Ukrainian painter of group and single portraits. He worked in

Aleksei Kravchenko. Illustration to 'The Crime of Sylvestre Bonnard' by Anatole France, *1931. Wood engraving. Signed 'O.K'.*

Boris Kustodiev. Bathers, *1910. Oil on canvas. Signed and dated. 82.5 x 105 cm. Malmö Konstmuseum.*

Kiev. He was teaching at the Kiev Art Institute 1912-16 where A.N.Volkov was amongst his pupils.
*Victors over Wrangel, 1935, Museum of Ukrainian Art, Kiev, presents three full-length warrior heroes against a backdrop of a large red flag and a single curve of caterpillar track. Monumental Socialist Realism in its most politicised and declamatory form. The purpose defines the painting.
Coll Museum of Ukrainian Art, Kiev.

KRIMMER, Eduard Mikhailovich　　　**1901-1974**
Painter, theatre designer.
Coll RM.

KRINSKY, Vladimir Fedorovich　　　**1890-1971**
Architect, graphic artist. He was represented at the Nineteenth Exhibition of the All-Russian Exhibitions Bureau in Moscow in 1920 and at the First Russian Art Exhibition in Berlin in 1922. He sometimes signed his work 'K'. (See pp.230-1).

KRIVENKO　　　**a.1921**
He was included in the Third Touring Exhibition of the Sovetsk Regional subdepartment of the Museums Bureau along with Kandinsky, Rodchenko and others in 1921.

KRIVENKOV, M.P.　　　**a.1919**
Painter. He exhibited at the juryless Eighth State Exhibition in Moscow in 1919.

KRUCHENYKH, Aleksei (Aleksandr) Eliseevich
1886-1969
Futurist poet, graphic artist from Kherson region. After studying at Odessa Art School until 1906 he moved to Moscow the following year. In 1910 he was publishing caricatures but by 1912 he had given up painting for poetry. He became a central figure of the Russian Futurist movement often collaborating with his wife Olga Rozanova. In 1917 together with Vasili Kamensky and Kirill Zdanevich he published verses in a Russian Futurist book *1918* which featured 'ferro-concrete poems' as well as collage illustrations. After the Revolution he was active as an organiser of Futurist activities at Tiflis (Tblisi) in Georgia with Zdanevich and Igor Terentev. He prepared a lecture on *Painting and Poetry* in April 1919 for the Moscow Institute of Artistic Culture. In December 1921 he collaborated on an evening of poetry with Mayakovsky, Kamensky, Khlebnikov and Tatlin at the Vkhutemas. He lectured on *The Facture of the Word in Relation*

Boris Kustodiev. Stage Design for Act 2 of 'The Flea'. *Pen and ink over watercolour heightened with white on paper mounted on cardboard. Signed and dated with the title. 36.5 x 56 cm.*
Reproduced by kind permission of Sotheby's London, sale 28.11.1991, lot 464.

to *Painting* in August 1921. The periodical *Lef* in 1925 announced his book *500 novykh ostrot i kalamburov Pushkina* (500 New Jokes and Puns about Pushkin), Moscow, 1924. He produced many publications.

Futurist books A.Kruchenykh, V.Khlebnikov *Igra v adu* (A Game in Hell), 1912, with illustrations by Natalya Goncharova.

A.Kruchenykh *Starinnaya lyubov'* (Old Time Love), 1912, with illustrations by Larionov.

A.Kruchenykh and V.Khlebnikov *Mirskontsa* (Worldbackwards), 1912, illustrated by Goncharova, Larionov, Tatlin and I.Rogovin.

A.Kruchenykh *Pustynniki*, (Hermits), 1913, illustrated by Goncharova.

A.Kruchenykh *Poluzhivoy* (Half-Alive), 1913, illustrated by Larionov.

A.Kruchenykh *Pomada* (Pomade), 1913, illustrated by Larionov.

A.Kruchenykh, V.Khlebnikov *Slovo kak takovoe* (The Word as Such), 1913, illustrated by Malevich and Rozanova.

A.Kruchenykh *Deklaratsiya slovo kak takovoe*, Petrograd, 1913.

A.Kruchenykh, V.Khlebnikov *Bukh lesinnyy* (A Forrestly Rapid), St. Petersburg, 1913, illustrated by Rozanova, Kul'bin and A.Kruchenykh.

V.Khlebnikov and A.Kruchenykh's *Igra v adu* (A Game in Hell) illustrated by Rozanova and Malevich 1913, which was a different publication to that illustrated by Goncharova in 1912.

V.Zina, A.Kruchenykh *Porosyatat* (Piglets), St. Petersburg, 1913.

V.Khlebnikov, A.Kruchenykh, E.Guro *Troe* (The Three), St. Petersburg, 1913, illustrated by Malevich.

A.Kruchenykh *Chort i rechetvortsy* (The Devil and the Wordmakers), with illustrations by Rozanova, St. Petersburg, 1913.

A.Kruchenykh *Vzorval'* (Explodity), with illustrations by N.Kul'bin, O.Rozanova, K.Malevich and N.Goncharova, St. Petersburg, 1913-14.

A.Kruchenykh, music by M.Matyushin, prologue by V.Khlebnikov, *Pobeda nad Solntsem* (Victory Over the Sun), with illustrations by K.Malevich and D.Burlyuk, St. Petersburg, 1913.

A.Kruchenykh *Utinoe gnezdyshko...durnykh slov* (A Duck's Nest...of Bad Words), with illustrations by Rozanova, St. Petersburg, 1913.

A.Kruchenykh *Vozropshchem* (Let's Grumble), St. Petersburg, 1914, illustrated by Malevich and Rozanova.

A.Kruchenykh, V.Khlebnikov *Igra v adu* (A Game in Hell), with illustrations by O.Rozanova, K.Malevich, Moscow, 1914.

A.Kruchenykh, V.Khlebnikov *Te li le* (Te li le), with illustrations by O.Rozanova and N.Kul'bin, St. Petersburg, 1914.

A.Kruchenykh, I.Klyun, K.Malevich *Taynie poroki akademistov* (Secret Vices of the Academicians), Moscow, 1915.

A.Kruchenykh and Alyagrov (Roman Jakobson) *Zaumnaya Gniga* (Transrational Pook), Moscow, 1915, which had a button sewn on to the collage heart on its cover by Rozanova.

A.Kruchenykh *Voina* (War) 1916, which had a collage cover

Vladimir Krinsky. Temple of Machine Worship, *early 1920s. Lithograph. Machinery is installed as an altar in a Byzantine church building. The inscription top right says Workers of the World Unite'. The stylised depiction of the machinery suggests that Krinsky was aware of Léger's post-war work.*

Vladimir Krinsky. Workers and Peasants Unite, *early 1920s. Lithograph. Beneath the flag of the RSFSR, top centre, are workers at left and a figure to the right carrying a banner declaring 'Power to the Soviets and Peasants'.*

and black linocut illustrations by Rozanova, some incorporated into collages which were otherwise Suprematist. A.Kruchenykh's *Vselenskaya voina* (Universal War), Petrograd, 1916, which contained a whole sequence of delicate and dynamic collages by Rozanova all but one on blue paper.
A.Kruchenykh *Uchites' khudogi* (Learn Art), with illustrations by K.Zdanevich, Tiflis, 1917.
A.Kruchenykh *Gly-Gly* 1918, illustrated by Varavara Stepanova with collages.
A.Kruchenykh *Ozhirenie roz* (Obesity of Roses), with collage cover by Kruchenykh, probably Tiflis, 1918-19.
A.Kruchenykh *Azef-Yuda-Khlebnikov*, Tiflis, 1919.
A.Kruchenykh *Lakirovannoe triko*, Tiflis, 1919.
A.Kruchenykh *Milliork*, Tiflis, 1919.
A.Kruchenykh *Deklaratsiya zaumnogo yazyka*, Baku, 1921.
A.Kruchenykh *Zaum*, Moscow, 1921.
A.Kruchenykh, G.Petnikov, V.Khlebnikov *Zaumniki* (Transrationalists), with illustrations by A.Rodchenko, Moscow, 1922.
A.Kruchenykh *Factura slova*, Moscow, 1923.
Other writings A.Kruchenykh *15 let russkogo futurizma* (15 Years of Russian Futurism), Moscow, 1928. A.Kruchenykh *Govorashchee kino* (Talking Cinema), Moscow, 1928.
Lit S.P.Compton *The World Backwards, Russian Futurist Books 1912-16*, London, 1978. S.Compton *Russian Avant-Garde Books 1917-34*, London, 1992.

Vladimir Krinsky. Construction Workers, *Moscow, c.1922. Lithograph.*

Vladimir Krinsky. The Times are Changing, *c.1923. Lithograph.*
In a design built up from contrasting images Krinsky promotes Soviet organisation. The old way of life is crossed out top left where lazing workers are replaced by the mechanically efficient workers envisaged by Gastev. Upper right the ancient towers of a kremlin are surmounted by radio masts which reflect directly those incorporated into the Vesnin Brothers' designs for the Palace of Labour in 1923. Beneath this a church becomes a factory. At centre there rises Krinsky's own design for a skyscraper housing the Trade Bank and a cinema.

Vladimir Krinsky. The New Revolutionary Style, *early 1920s. Lithograph. Signed 'K'.*
This print contrasts dynamic and mechanistic construction against the older forms of architecture exemplified by a fragment of Ionic portico and a traditional Russian window moulding.

KRUGLIKOVA, Elizaveta Sergeevna   1865-1941

Painter, etcher. Born at St. Petersburg. She studied at the Moscow College under A.Arkhipov, I.Pryanishnikov and K.Korovin until 1895. In 1897 she began to exhibit at the Salon des Indépendants and the Salon d'Automne in Paris. She exhibited with the World of Art in St. Petersburg in 1900. She had personal exhibitions in Moscow in 1899 and in Paris in 1907. She studied there under Aman-Jean, H.Merson and R.Collin 1908 14 and taught etching at the Académie La Palette in 1909. She exhibited French and Russian views at the First Izdebsky International Salon 1909-10 in Odessa. In 1913 she had a personal exhibition in St. Petersburg. She exhibited with the Union of Russian Artists 1909-10 and with the World of Art 1911-17. She was executing silhouettes c.1916.

After the Revolution she exhibited with the World of Art in December 1917 in Moscow. She taught at the Free Art Studios/Vkhutein in Petrograd/Leningrad from 1918 to 1929. She participated in the First State Free Exhibition of Artworks in Petrograd in 1919 and was represented in the Sixth State Exhibition: The Print (*VI Gosudarstvennaya vystavka gravyur*) in Moscow in 1919. She was included in the Third Touring Exhibition of the Sovetsk Regional subdepartment of the Museums Bureau along with Kandinsky, Rodchenko and others in 1921. She was included in the enormous survey Exhibition of Paintings by Petrograd Artists of All Tendencies 1919-1923 held in Petrograd in 1923.

She exhibited with the *Zhar-tsvet* (Fire-colour) group between

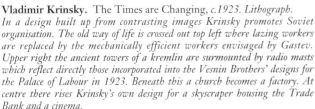

Vladimir Krinsky. Agitation at the Circus, *c.1923. Lithograph.*
An orator excites the revolutionary crowd in a circus arena beneath the banner 'All Power to the Soviets'.

Pavel Kuznetsov. Landscape, *c.1914. Oil or tempera on paper. 53 x 70 cm.
Malmö Konstmuseum.*

1924 and 1928. She was represented at the Paris International
Exhibition of 1925. She had another personal exhibition in
1925 in Kazan. She was represented at the All-Union
Polygraphic Exhibition in Moscow in 1927 and at the jubilee
exhibition Artists of the RSFSR over 15 Years held at the
Russian Museum, Leningrad, in 1932. She died in Leningrad.
At the World of Art Exhibition, 1916, cut black paper, is ideal
for reproduction as a print in a periodical. Its subject is
painters arguing at the exhibition. The technique is uniquely
her achievement.
Portrait of F.Sologub, before 1922, was executed from carefully
ripped black paper mounted on white so that it has an effect
similar to a print by Félix Vallotton.
Okhtensky Bridge, 1931, drypoint, is almost Impressionist
printmaking. The bridge, river, boats and figures carry no
overt message but concentrate upon atmosphere and light in
this only slightly industrialised cityscape.
Lit A.A.Sidorov *E.S.Kruglikova*, Moscow, 1936. *E.S.Kruglikova*,
Leningrad, 1966. *E.S.Kruglikova*, Leningrad, 1969. *Paris-
Moscou*, 1979.

KRYLOV, Nikifor Stepanovich   1802-1831
Painter. He was a pupil of Venetsianov. In *Zima* (Winter) of
1827, RM, he produced an exquisite snowscape stretching to a

distant, flat horizon. In the foreground two women talk, another
carries a waterbucket and a man holds a horse. The sky is well
observed and its light casts strong shadows across the snow.
Coll TG; RM.

KRYLOV, Porfiry Nikitich   1902-a.1941
Painter, poster designer, graphic artist. One of the trio of
fiercely satirical painters and graphic artists who worked under
the name of the Kukryniksy. Born in the Tula region. He
studied in the Proletkult Art Studios 1918-21 and then under
A.Osmerkin and A.Shevchenko at the Vkhutemas/Vkhutein
1921-8. He was included in the 1928 exhibition of Acquisitions
by the State Art Collections Fund held in Moscow.

KRYMOV, Nikolai Petrovich   1884-1958
Symbolist and Primitivist landscape painter, theatre designer.
Born in Moscow. He studied under V.Serov, K.Korovin and
Leonid Pasternak at the Moscow College from 1904 to 1911.
He contributed to numerous exhibitions including the
Moscow Society of Artists from 1905, the Union of Artists
1908-10, of which he was a member from 1910 to 1923, the
Blue Rose in 1907, the *Stefanos* exhibition in 1907-08, *Venok*
(The Wreath) in 1908 and the Golden Fleece in 1909. He
exhibited with the Izdebsky Salon of 1910-11 in Odessa.
After the Revolution his work was included in the First

Exhibition of the Moscow Contemporary Art Store in January 1919 and his name appeared on the April 1919 list of artists for acquisitions by the envisaged Museum of Painterly Culture. He was represented in the Fourth State Exhibition of Paintings (*IV Gosudarstvennaya vystavka kartin*) in Moscow in 1919 and he participated in the Third Exhibition of Paintings held at Ryazan in 1919. He was listed as leader of a course for art teachers along with Tatlin and others in 1919. He was also represented at the Nineteenth Exhibition of the All-Russian Exhibitions Bureau in Moscow in 1920 and he exhibited in the 1921 exhibition of the World of Art in Moscow. He was represented at the First Russian Art Exhibition in Berlin in 1922. He taught at the Vkhutemas in 1920-2 and exhibited at the third and last exhibition of the *Makovets* group in Moscow 1925-6.

He executed designs for the Moscow Arts Theatre in 1926. His work was included in the exhibition of Soviet art held at Harbin in 1926 and in Japan in 1927 and in the 1928 exhibition of Acquisitions by the State Art Collections Fund held in Moscow. He was represented at the jubilee exhibition Artists of the RSFSR over 15 Years held at the Russian Museum, Leningrad, in 1932. He became a member of the Academy of Arts of the USSR. He died in Moscow. He sometimes signed his work 'N.P.Kr'.

*At the Mill, 1927, TG, is curiously close to 19th century Realist landscape in the manner of Courbet but also has something of the heavy decorative atmosphere of the World of Art. The mill and figures are seen by the stream in a scene that is slightly flattened and patterned.

Theatre design 1926 Stanislavsky's production of *Goryachee serdtse* (The Passionate Heart) at the Moscow Art Theatre. The scenery for Act 3 represented a classical garden with steps and statuary. The same rich and heavy atmosphere that permeated his landscapes is evident here.

1933 July A.N.Ostrovsky's *Talanty i poklonniki* (Talents and Admirers) at the Moscow Art Theatre.
Lit P.Muradov *N.P.Krymov*, St. Petersburg, 1911. *N.P.Krymov, Khudozhnik i Pedagog*, Moscow, 1960. I.Porto *N.P.Krymov*, Leningrad, 1973. *Twilight of the Tsars*, London, 1991.
Coll TG.

KRYUKOV, Ivan Efimovich   **1823-1857**
Portrait and genre painter. His work also included Italian subjects. The date of his death is sometimes given as 1851.
Coll TG.

KRYZHITSKY, Konstantin Yakovlevich   **1858-1911**
Landscape and seascape painter. He exhibited at the Paris International Exhibitions of 1889 and 1900. He was active at St. Petersburg c.1900.
Coll TG.

KSENEVA, L.   **a.1913**
She contributed to Larionov's exhibition The Target in Moscow in 1913.

KUCHUMOV, Vasili Nikitich   **a.1918-1923**
He was engaged on Agitprop decorations in 1918 at the Academy of Sciences in Petrograd with G.Savitsky and V.Simonov. He participated in the First State Free Exhibition of Artworks in Petrograd in 1919 and contributed to the Exhibition of Paintings by Russian Artists held at Pskov in Spring 1920. He was included in the enormous survey Exhibition of Paintings by Petrograd Artists of All Tendencies 1919-1923 held in Petrograd in 1923.

KUDINOV, A. A.   **a.1919-1920**
Sculptor. During 1919-20 he was a founder of the *Monolit* (Monolith) group of sculptors, which included Babichev, Mukhina, Konen'kov, Krandievskaya, Korolev, Strakhovskaya,

Elizaveta Kruglikova. At the World of Art Exhibition, *1916. Silhouette cut from black paper*
Left to right Lansere, Repin, Petrov-Vodkin.

Zlatovratsky, Ternovets, V.Popova, Blazhevich and Kudinov. They worked on monumental propaganda and entered the competitive exhibition for a *Monument to Liberated Labour* held in Moscow in May 1920.

KUDRYASHEV (KUDRYASHOV), Ivan Alekseevich 1896-1970

Painter. Born at Kaluga. He attended the Moscow College 1913-17 and then the Free Art Studios (SVOMAS) in Moscow under Malevich where he also met Klyun, Gabo and Pevsner. In 1918 he decorated vehicles with agitational propaganda designs. His conversion to Suprematism coalesced with an enthusiasm for the rocket pioneer Konstantin Tsiolkovsky for whom his father had worked, with the result that he produced Suprematist paintings with a cosmic theme. This tendency can also be detected in the work of Malevich and Lissitzky. In 1919 he moved to Orenburg to establish Free Studios there. His name appeared on the April 1919 list of artists for acquisitions by the envisaged Museum of Painterly Culture. He exhibited at the First State Exhibition in Orenburg. The following year he organised a section of the Suprematist group *Unovis* at Orenburg and he also produced designs for the interior of the Red Army Theatre. It was his involvement with the evacuation of starving children to Smolensk in 1921 that brought him into contact with Malevich's Polish followers Kobro and Strzeminski. In 1921 he was also active as a designer in Moscow. He was represented at the First Russian Art Exhibition in Berlin in 1922, exhibited with the Society of Easel Painters (OST) between 1925 and 1928 and then ceased to exhibit.

Lit A.Z.Rudenstine *Costakis Collection*, London, 1981. E.Weiss *Russische Avant-Garde, 1910-1930, Sammlung Ludwig, Köln,* Munich, 1986.

Coll TG; Sammlung Ludwig, Cologne.

KUDRYASHOV, Oleg   b.1932

Painter, printmaker. Born in Moscow. He attended art school in Moscow 1950-1 where he exhibited between 1958 and 1972. He has since contributed to numerous international exhibitions and in 1976 he exhibited at the Acme Gallery in London. He settled in London in 1974.

His work comprises a mixture of printmaking and relief construction with graphic and sculptural elements combined.

Lit *Austellung Klassische Moderne*, exh. cat., Galerie Gmurzynska, Cologne, 1981.

KÜHNEL, Friedrich F. (KYUNEL, Fedor Fedorovich) 1766-1841

History and portrait painter. Born at Dippoldiswalde. He studied under Schenau and Casanova in Dresden. He emigrated to Russia. He signed his work 'Kühnel' in latin script. He died in Moscow.

KUINDZHI, Arkhip Ivanovich   1842-1910

Major landscape painter of the Wanderers movement. He was born in Mariupol, the son of a Greek shoemaker. He studied at the Academy in St. Petersburg 1868-70. He became friendly with Kramskoy. From 1874 he exhibited with the Wanderers and became a member in 1875. He employed heightened colour in broad decorative areas so that his panoramic vistas and richly atmospheric paintings of trees had a monumental quality which assured that his work was received as a celebration of Russian national identity.

In 1880 his *Moonlight on the Dneiper* was shown as the single work in an exhibition in St. Petersburg. He largely stopped

Arkhip Kuindzhi. Crimean Landscape, *1901. Oil on canvas mounted on panel. 41.5 x 79.5 cm. Signed and dated 'Crimea 1901'. Reproduced by kind permission of Sotheby's London, sale 15.2.1984, lot 56.*

Arkhip Kuindzhi. Birch Grove, *1879. Oil on canvas. 97 x 181 cm.*
State Tretyakov Gallery, Moscow.

exhibiting in 1882. He was an active teacher at the Academy where he headed the landscape studio 1894-7. His pupils included Nicolas Roerich, Konstantin Bogaevsky and Arkadi Rylov. In 1909 the Kuindzhi Society of artists was formed which continued after his death funded from Kuindzhi's own legacy.
*Birch Grove, 1879, TG, has a mural-like simplicity and the internal sense of scale worthy of a stage set. In stark contrast to Shishkin, Kuindzhi was a great synthetic painter whose work was highly edited, decorative and dramatic. In this wide canvas some dozen birch trees in a green meadow are seen against a dark wood and a brilliant blue sky. The handling of colour is flat but springs remarkable and original effects of colour in the shadows and middle tones which here occur in the vibrant yellow-orange patches of the birch bark. The effect is atmospheric, monumental and decorative.
Coll Well represented at TG; RM.

KUKRYNIKSY

The composite name adopted by the fiercely political and satirical trio consisting of Mikhail Kupriyanov, Porfiry Krylov and Nikolai Sokolov. In 1929 they designed Meyerhold's production of *Klop* (The Bedbug) by Mayakovsky, whilst Rodchenko designed the last act. Works include the spectacular and huge painting *The Flight of the Fascists from Novgorod*, 1944-6, RM.
*The End, 1947-8, TG, shows the last moments of Hitler and his generals in the bunker despairing and terrified. This is a scene of high drama verging upon vituperative caricature.
Theatre design 1929 Mayakovsky's *Klop* (The Bedbug) at the Meyerhold Theatre, Moscow. The scenes set in the future were by Rodchenko. Music was by D.Shostakovich.
Lit I.I'lf, E.Petrov *Risunki Kukryniksy*, 1968.
Coll RM; Bakhrushin Theatre Museum, Moscow.

KULAGIN, S. F.   a.1918-1919

Painter. He exhibited at the First Exhibition of Works of the

Professional Union of Artists in Moscow in 1918 and at the juryless Eighth State Exhibition in Moscow in 1919.

KULAGINA, Valentina Nikiforovna   b.1902

Graphic artist. She married the artist Gustav Klucis and in 1923 was engaged on a lithographic version of his painting *Dynamic City* of 1919-21. She was later engaged on book design in the Constructivist mode.
Book design A.Kruchenykh *Zaumnyy yazyk* (Transrational Language), Moscow, 1925.
Lit E.Weiss *Russische Avant-Garde, 1910-1930, Sammlung Ludwig, Köln*, Munich, 1986. S.Compton *Russian Avant-Garde Books 1917-34*, London, 1992.
Coll Costakis Collection; Sammlung Ludwig, Cologne.

KUL'BIN, Nikolai Ivanovich   1868-1917

Painter, graphic artist, theatre designer and theorist. Born at Helsingfors (Helsinki). He attended a military-medical academy from 1887 and graduated in 1893. During this time he became interested in microscopic drawing and, from 1894, microscopic photography. He graduated as a Doctor of Medicine in 1895. He then became increasingly interested in art and active as an exhibition organiser, heading the so-called Impressionists which here had more to do with the emergence of Russian Futurism from a Symbolist background than anything resembling French Impressionism. In 1908 he organised the Exhibition of Contemporary Trends in Art and 1909-10 the exhibitions of the group Triangle and exhibited works at, Kiev, Riga and St. Petersburg. He exhibited with the Izdebsky Salon of 1910-11 in Odessa and with the Knave of Diamonds in 1912. He was a founder member of the Arts Society in 1911 and the Spectator Society in 1912. A retrospective of 1912 in St. Petersburg included eighty-four works among which were theatre designs and a 'cubist sculpture' in clay. He designed for the Terioki Theatre in summer 1912 and for the Queen of Spades Theatre in St.

Petersburg 1913-14. He also lectured on Futurism 1913-14. He was a founder member of the Stray Dog cabaret. He died in Petrograd. A memorial exhibition was held in June 1918.

Drawing of Fedor Sologub, 1915, is a characteristic drawing tending to employ diamond shapes to structure the head and almost completely avoiding chiaroscuro. Similar techniques were used in drawings of *Mikhail Kuzmin*, *Velimir Khlebnikov* and *A.Kruchenykh*. He sometimes signed his work in a monogram of the letters 'NK' within a triangle.

Theatre design 1912 June Meyerhold's production of Dr.Dapertutto's *Lovers* at the Artists' Co-operative, Terioki.

1912 June Meyerhold's production of V.N.Soloviev's *Harlequin — Marriage Broker* at the Artists' Co-operative, Terioki.

Futurist books N.Kul'bin *Studiya impressionistov* (The Impressionists' Studio), St. Petersburg, 1910, with illustrations by N.Kul'bin.

A.Kruchenykh, V.Khlebnikov *Bukh lessinnyy* (A Forrestly Rapid), St. Petersburg, 1913, illustrated by Rozanova, Kul'bin and A.Kruchenykh.

A.Kruchenykh *Vzorval'* (Explodity), with illustrations by N.Kul'bin, O.Rozanova, K.Malevich and N.Goncharova, St. Petersburg, 1913.

N.Evreinov *Teatr kak takovoe* (The Theatre as Such), St. Petersburg, 1913, with illustrations by Kul'bin.

A.Kruchenykh, V.Khlebnikov *Te li le* (Te li le), with illustrations by O.Rozanova and N.Kul'bin, St. Petersburg, 1914.

I.Severyanin *Tost bezotvetniy*, Moscow, 1916, with illustrations by Kul'bin.

Lit *Kul'bin*, St. Petersburg, 1912. S.P.Compton *The World Backwards, Russian Futurist Books 1912-16*, London, 1978. *Paris-Moscou*, 1979. E.Weiss *Russische Avant-Garde, 1910-1930, Sammlung Ludwig, Köln*, Munich, 1986. Dzhon Boult (John Bowlt) *Khudozhniki russkogo teatra. Sobranie Nikity i Niny Lobanovykh-Rostovskikh*, Moscow, 1991. J.Howard *The Union of Youth — An Artists' Society of the Russian Avant-Garde*, Manchester and New York, 1992.

Coll TG; British Library, London; Sammlung Ludwig, Cologne.

KULIKOV, Afanasii E.   **a.1917-1925**
Graphic artist. He was working on Bolshevik propaganda posters in 1917 employing stylised simplicity inspired by and sometimes deliberately copying the format of *lubok* popular prints, complete with crude drawing, printing and colouring. He exhibited with the World of Art in December 1917 in Moscow.

An artist listed simply as Kulikov was represented at the Paris International Exhibition of 1925 and at the Third Exhibition of Paintings by Artists from Kaluga and Moscow held in Kaluga in 1925. He sometimes signed his work 'A.K'.

Coll Costakis Collection.

KULUKIN   **a.1919**
Painter. He contributed to the Twelfth State Exhibition: Colourdynamo and Tectonic Primitivism (*Tsvetodinamos i tektonicheskiy primitivizm*) along with Grishchenko, Shevchenko and others in Moscow in 1919.

KUNIN, M.   **a.1921**
A member of the Suprematist group *Unovis* working with Malevich. He published an article *Partiinost' in Art* in the second issue of the lithographed *Unovis*, Vitebsk, 1921.

Nikolai Kul'bin. Self-portrait, *1913. Lithograph. Signed with a monogram 'NK' in a triangle right of centre.*
This is a characteristic Kul'bin portrait print, sparse and direct in execution.

KUPREYANOV, Nikolai Nikolaevich   **1894-1933**
Graphic artist and watercolourist. Born in Poland. He studied at Princess Tenisheva's School in St. Petersburg in 1912, under D.Kardovsky 1912-14 and under K.Petrov-Vodkin 1915-16. He then studied printmaking specifically under A.Ostroumova-Lebedeva 1912-17. He was also studying law at the university in St. Petersburg until 1916.

After the Revolution he taught photography in Petrograd from 1918 to 1920, and he participated in the First State Free Exhibition of Artworks in Petrograd in 1919. He was represented in the Sixth State Exhibition: The Print (*VI Gosudarstvennaya vystavka gravyur*) in Moscow in 1919.

He taught at the Vkhutemas from 1922. He was represented at the First Russian Art Exhibition in Berlin in 1922. He exhibited with the Society of Easel Painters (OST) and with 4 Arts. His work was exhibited abroad at Venice in 1924, at the Paris International Exhibition of 1925 and at the seventh exhibition of the group *L'Araignée* (The Spider) at the Galerie Devambe in Paris in 1925 as well as exhibitions at Leipzig, Florence and Milan in 1927, and New York and Amsterdam in 1929. He was included in the major exhibition in Moscow in 1927 marking the tenth anniversary of the Revolution. He visited Italy and Germany in 1928. He contributed to the exhibition of graphic art Liberation Movements: The Sixteenth to the Twentieth Century held in Moscow in 1928 and to the 1928 exhibition of Acquisitions by the State Art Collections Fund held in Moscow. He was represented in the First Touring Exhibition of Paintings and Graphics which opened in Moscow in 1929. He was represented at the jubilee exhibition Artists of the RSFSR over

15 Years held at the Russian Museum, Leningrad, in 1932 and at the 1932 Venice Biennale.

The Aurora, wood engraving, has the guns blazing to announce the start of the Revolution as searchlights split the night sky. The effect is precise in technique and rhetorical in purpose.

Citizens, Preserve Art Monuments, 1919, an elegant poster evoking well-known and well-loved monuments of the past, precisely drawn and crisply printed on behalf of the Department of Museums and the Conservation of Monuments of the Art of the Past. Stylistically dependent on Ostroumova-Lebedeva.

Writings N.Kupreyanov *Dnevniki Khudozhnika*, Moscow-Leningrad, 1937.

Lit *N.N.Kupreyanov*, Moscow, 1973.

Coll TG; RM.

KUPRIN, Aleksandr Vasilievich   1880-1960

Still-life and landscape painter, theatre designer. Born at Borisoglebsk in the Tambov region. The family moved to Voronezh in 1893. He worked as a railway clerk whilst also attending the Free Voronezh School of Painting and Drawing where he studied under L.G.Soloviev and M.I.Ponomarev. He studied privately under L.E.Dmitriev-Kavkazsky at St. Petersburg 1902-4. He moved to Moscow in 1904 where he studied under K.F.Yuon and I.O.Dudin 1904-6 before attending the Moscow College under Arkhipov, K.Korovin and L.Pasternak 1906-10. He exhibited with the Golden Fleece in Moscow 1909-10. He exhibited as a founder member of the Knave of Diamonds from 1910 to 1916 and he exhibited with the Izdebsky Salon of 1910-11 in Odessa. He exhibited at the Union of Youth in 1911. He visited Paris 1913-14 and in 1914 he was painting at Menton in the South of France. He returned to Moscow via Northern Italy.

After the Revolution he exhibited with the World of Art in December 1917 in Moscow and was represented at the First Exhibition of Works of the Professional Union of Artists in Moscow in 1918. He was engaged in Agitprop decorations in 1918 including decorations at the Nezlobin Theatre. He was teaching as K.Korovin's assistant at the Free Art Studios in Moscow 1918-19. He exhibited at the Fifth State Exhibition: From Impressionism to Non-Objective Art in Moscow 1918-19 and his name appeared on the April 1919 list of artists for acquisitions by the envisaged Museum of Painterly Culture. He was represented along with Kandinsky, Chagall and others at the First State Exhibition of Paintings by Local and Moscow Artists held in Vitebsk in December 1919 and participated in the Third Exhibition of Paintings held at Ryazan in 1919. He was represented at the enormous First State Exhibition of Art and Science, which included ethnographic material, held in Kazan in 1920.

He was sent by the Art Section of the People's Commissariat of the Enlightenment (IZO Narkompros) to supervise and teach at the Nizhny-Novgorod and Sormova art schools 1920-2 but he also exhibited in the 1921 exhibition of the World of Art in Moscow. In Nizhny-Novgorod he designed for the theatre.

He returned to Moscow in 1922 and taught stage design at the Moscow Vkhutemas. He was represented at the First Russian Art Exhibition in Berlin in 1922. He taught in the ceramics department of the Vkhutemas from 1925. He became a member of the organising body of the Society of Moscow Artists (OMKh) founded in 1925. He contributed to the International Exhibition in Dresden in 1926. His work was included in the exhibition of Soviet art held at Harbin in 1926

and in Japan in 1927 and in the major exhibition in Moscow in 1927 marking the tenth anniversary of the Revolution. He was also included in the 1928 exhibition of Acquisitions by the State Art Collections Fund held in Moscow. From 1928 to 1932 he taught in the department of composition at the Moscow Textile Institute.

He was represented at the jubilee exhibition *Artists of the RSFSR over 15 Years* held at the Russian Museum, Leningrad, in 1932 and at the 1932 Venice Biennale. He was given a one-man exhibition in 1934. He travelled widely within the Soviet Union between 1932 and 1957.

He directed the Department of Painting at the Moscow Higher Industrial Institute (formerly the Stroganov Institute) 1946-52. He was given an exhibition together with the sculptor G.I.Kepinov in 1948. He became a Merited Art Worker of the RSFSR in 1956 and was given an exhibition with the sculptor G.I.Motovilov in 1957. He died in Moscow.

Still-life with Black Bottle, 1917, RM, is one of the Cézannist still-lifes which acknowledged a debt both to Cézanne and Cubism in a stylisation which he shared with Fal'k and others. It is characterised by a high viewpoint and a sharpening of the edges of objects to give a dynamic precision to the

Nikolai Kupreyanov. Anatoly Lunacharsky, the People's Commissar for Education, *c.1925. Wood engraving. 26.8 x 24 cm. Signed 'NK' lower right and inscribed 'Lunacharsky' at left. State Russian Museum, St. Petersburg.*

Boris Kustodiev. Merchants' Wives, *1912. Tempera on board. 81.5 x 108 cm. Museum of Russian Art, Kiev.*

composition. The brushwork then establishes planes without any intersection of objects with their surroundings.

Art, 1918, Agitprop décor for the Nezlobin Theatre (later the Central Children's Theatre), Moscow. A Futurist rhetoric of clashing triangular forms in several colours surrounds an image of a piano, big drum, trumpets and a lyre motif. The effect is light and dynamic.

Theatre design c.1921 V.Kamensky's *Stepan Razin*, designed in collaboration with F.S.Bogorodsky, and performed at the theatre in Nizhny-Novgorod.

Lit V.A.Nikolsky *A.V.Kuprin*, Moscow, 1935 and 1973. K.S.Kravchenko *A.V.Kuprin*, Moscow, 1973. *A.V.Kuprin, S.D.Lebedeva, N.P.Ulyanov*, exh. cat., Moscow, 1978. *Paris-Moscou*, 1979. *A.V.Kuprin*, exh. cat., Moscow, 1981. *Seven Moscow Artists 1910-30*, exh. cat., Galerie Gmurzynska, Cologne, 1984. David Elliott, V.Dudakov *100 Years of Russian Art*, London, 1989. *L'Avant-garde russe 1905-1925*, exh. cat., Musée des Beaux-Arts, Nantes, 1993.

Coll TG; RM; Dagestan Art Museum, Makhachkala; Kazan Art Museum; Saratov Art Museum; Tula Art Museum.

KUPRIYANOV, Mikhail Vasilievich   1903-1941+
Member of the Kukryniksy trio of satirical artists. Born at Tetiushi in the Tatar Republic. He studied at Tashkent School of Art 1920-1 and at the Vkhutemas/Vkhutein under N. Kupreyanov, Pavel Miturich and P.Lvov 1921-9.
Lit *Paris-Moscou*, 1979.

KUPTSOV, Vasili Vasil'evich   1899-1935
Painter. He was included in the enormous survey Exhibition of Paintings by Petrograd Artists of All Tendencies 1919-1923 held in Petrograd in 1923 and he exhibited with the Circle of Artists in Leningrad between 1927 and 1929. He was represented at the jubilee exhibition Artists of the RSFSR over

15 Years held at the Russian Museum, Leningrad, in 1932.
Coll RM.

KURBATOVA, N. I.   a.1919
Painter. She exhibited at the Ninth State Exhibition of Paintings: Naturalism and Realism in Moscow in 1919.

KURCHANINOVA, N.   a.1912
Painter. She exhibited with the Union of Youth in St. Petersburg in 1912.

KURDOV, Valentin Ivanovich   b.1905
Painter, draughtsman.
Coll RM.

KURENNOY, Aleksandr Avvakumovich   1865-1944
A pupil of Repin, he taught at Talashkino, near Smolensk, for Princess Tenisheva c.1888.
After the Revolution he was represented at the First Exhibition of Works of the Professional Union of Artists in Moscow in 1918.

KURILKO, Mikhail Ivanovich   1880-1969
Painter, draughtsman, theatre designer. He studied in St. Petersburg 1903-13 and then travelled to France, Italy and England. He studied at the Archaeological Institute 1913-15.
After the Revolution he was a member of the Moscow Collegium of IZO Narkompros under Tatlin in 1919 and participated in the First State Free Exhibition of Artworks in Petrograd in 1919. He was included in the enormous survey Exhibition of Paintings by Petrograd Artists of All Tendencies 1919-1923 held in Petrograd in 1923. He held the Chair of Drawing at the Second Polytechnic Institute until 1924. He also taught at the Leningrad Vkhutemas 1921-4. He was a member of the Society of Artist-Realists founded in 1927. He

was principal artist at the Bolshoi Theatre 1924-8.
Lit *Paris-Moscou*, 1979.

KURLYANDTSEV, Stepan Semenovich   1770-1822
Subjects include scenes from Tasso.
Coll TG.

KUSKOV, N. S.   a.1921
He was included in the Third Touring Exhibition of the
Sovetsk Regional subdepartment of the Museums Bureau
along with Kandinsky, Rodchenko and others in 1921.

KUSTODIEV, Boris Mikhailovich   1878-1927
A painter of portraits, views and still-lifes which mostly
expressed an extraordinary fecundity of colour, fruit and
human activity in a way perhaps reminiscent of Brueghel's
integration of landscape and genre, but utterly dedicated to
the evocation of an optimistic and even folksy image of
Russian life. Impressive for the sheer vision of plenitude that
made his paintings both incredible and enjoyable. Born at
Astrakhan. He studied in Astrakhan under P.Vlasov and then
at the Academy in St. Petersburg 1896-1903 under
V.Savinsky, D.Stelletsky and Ilya Repin. He travelled to
France and Spain on a bursary 1903-4. He was a founder
member of the New Society of Artists with whom he exhibited
1904-8. His response to the supression of the demonstrations
of 1905 was revealed in the illustration *Entry, Moscow* which
showed a giant skeleton trampling workers. He was
represented in Diaghilev's display of Russian art at the 1906
Salon d'Automne in Paris. He was a member of the Union of
Russian Artists 1907-10. He was working in Venice in 1907
and was again in Italy in 1909 and 1913.
He executed a number of sculptures 1909-10 which are
represented at the Russian Museum, including a *Portrait of
Dobuzhinsky*, 1909, plaster, a *Mother and Child*, 1910, coloured
plaster, and a three-quarter-length *Portrait of the Sculptor Natalya
Dan'ko* in which she appears lively and full of stylish elegance.
He exhibited with the Union of Russian Artists in 1910 and with
the World of Art 1911-17. A painting of the members of the
World of Art at a meeting, RM, 1916-20, shows them at a dining
table discussing plans in a green interior whilst a maid delivers
more coffee. A less grand version of the same compositional
theme, *Moscow Tavern* of 1916, TG, has a red interior and
suggests a witty reworking of the idea to imply a comparison.
After the Revolution he exhibited with the World of Art in
December 1917 in Moscow. He was engaged in Agitprop
decorations in 1918. He participated in the First State Free
Exhibition of Artworks in Petrograd in 1919 and his name
appeared on the April 1919 list of artists for acquisitions by
the envisaged Museum of Painterly Culture. He contributed
to the Exhibition of Paintings by Russian Artists held at Pskov
in Spring 1920 and he was represented at the enormous First
State Exhibition of Art and Science, which included
ethnographic material, held in Kazan in 1920. The Petrograd
Soviet commissioned him to paint a large canvas of the Second
Congress of the Communist International in 1920 and he was
given a one-man exhibition in Petrograd that year. He was
represented at the First Russian Art Exhibition in Berlin in
1922. He was included in the enormous survey Exhibition of
Paintings by Petrograd Artists of All Tendencies 1919-1923
held in Petrograd in 1923.
In 1923 he designed two figurines for the State Porcelain
Factory and many other designs followed. He exhibited with

AKhRR from 1925 and was represented at the Paris
International Exhibition of 1925. His work was included in
the exhibition of Soviet art held at Harbin in 1926 and in
Japan in 1927 and in the 1928 exhibition of Acquisitions by
the State Art Collections Fund held in Moscow.
He became partially paralysed but was given a car from which
to work on studies of Moscow. He was given further one-man
exhibitions in Leningrad and Moscow in 1928. He was
represented at the jubilee exhibition Artists of the RSFSR over

Boris Kustodiev. Merchant's Wife, *1915. Oil on canvas. 204 x 109 cm.
State Russian Museum, St. Petersburg.*

15 Years held at the Russian Museum, Leningrad, in 1932. Exhibitions of his work were held in Moscow in 1947, 1952 and 1968. He died in Leningrad.

The Fair, 1906, TG, approaches historical genre. His village market provides a spectacle so colourful, benign and full of well-being that it is like a painting of another age in which peasant clothes are always clean and decorative, and where the onion domes of old Russia are never overshadowed by towering chimneys. It is an idyll of rural Russia in times of endless plenty. The effect is enjoyable and as false as the stage sets which it so closely resembles. Yuon tackled comparable themes.

La Belle, 1915, TG, is an outrageous and unapologetically enthusiastic painting of a copiously fleshy Russian beauty stepping from her bed. She fills the entire centre of the canvas with an overwhelmingly warm presence. Her proportions possibly exceed those of contemporary nudes by Renoir, but she is immediate in her wallpapered interior and has no implication of an ancient goddess which lends an air of remoteness and safety to Renoir's late nudes. She is the fecund and welcoming human embodiment of Kustodiev's vision of plenty.

Carnival, 1916, RM, is an immense panorama of Russians in sleighs revelling in the snow, enjoying fairground booths and singing to an accordion beneath the trees. Across the frosted blue and white valley, church towers rise up into a pink and green winter sky.

The Baker, 1918, TG, is a design for a decorative panel on the Ruzhennaya Square in Petrograd for the first anniversary of the Revolution. Traditional in style, which is unusual for Agitprop work, it presents the baker in an oval vignette preparing the bread and surrounded by a display of many forms of loaf. A slightly 18th century effect is achieved by his light touch and played down rhetoric.

Merchant Woman at Tea, 1918, RM, is one of his most celebrated paintings. It is a highly resolved, lucid and extraordinary image of a wealthy woman of large proportions seated at a large but apparently solitary tea-time feast which is set on a balcony in the late afternoon sunlight with domes and spires punctuating the landscape behind her. Only the date of the painting reveals that it was produced in the Revolutionary years. If it has a social message it is ambiguous: either it is a celebration of the senses or, far less credibly, it is a criticism of the good life enjoyed by merchants.

The Bolshevik, 1920, TG, is a characteristically colourful pageant but now turned to political and symbolic ends. The gigantic Bolshevik strides with endless scarlet banner between the palaces and churches, amongst the milling throng of the Revolutionary crowd.

Portrait of Chaliapine, 1921, Theatre Museum, Leningrad, is a full-length of the singer in an enormous fur-lined coat and accompanied by his dog as he walks through the snow before a typical Kustodiev fairground idyll of the life of the people.

Theatre design 1911-12 Ostrovsky's *The Warm Heart* at the K.Nezlobin Theatre, Moscow.

1914 Saltykov-Shchedrin's *Death of Pazukhin* at the Moscow Art Theatre: costume designs fluent, explicit and full of character, describing clothing suitable to the role rather than attempting works of independent decorative power.

1914 a story by Leskov at the Moscow Art Theatre.

1915 Ostrovsky's *Wolves and Sheep* and I.Surguchev's *Autumn Violins* at the Moscow Art Theatre.

1917 Ostrovsky's *Rags to Riches* (unrealised) for the Maly Theatre, Moscow.

1919 Gogol's *The Government Inspector* at the Maly Theatre, Petrograd.

1920 designs for the Mariinsky Theatre, Petrograd.

Boris Kustodiev. Poster design for Zamyatin's 'Blokha' (The Flea), *1925. Lithograph. Signed and dated. 72 x 108 cm. Designed for the performance of Evgeniy Zamyatin's play at the Moscow Art Theatre in 1925. Collection Mr. and Mrs. Nikita D.Lobanov-Rostovsky, London.*

Boris Kustodiev. The Bolshevik, *1920. Oil on canvas. 101 x 141 cm. The gigantic figure of the Bolshevik is used to personify the will of the masses. It is an intensely dramatic image but flawed in that he seems in danger of crushing the crowds around his feet. State Tretyakov Gallery, Moscow.*

1920 costumes for Ostrovsky's *Groza* (The Storm).
1921 A.Neverov's *Peasant Women* at the Smolny Theatre, Petrograd.
1922 A.Tolstoy's *The Mayor* at the Drama Theatre, Petrograd.
1923 Ostrovsky's *Between Ourselves We'll Come to Terms* at the Drama Theatre, Petrograd.
1924-6 costumes for E.Zamyatin's play *Blokha* (The Flea) based on N.S.Leskov's story *Levsha* at the Bolshoi Drama Theatre, Leningrad; designs are preserved in the St. Petersburg Theatre Museum.
1925 October: A.N.Ostrovsky's *There Was Not a Penny and Suddenly There Was a Pound*, at the Aleksandrinsky Theatre, Leningrad.
1927 *Wolves and Sheep* at the Leningrad Drama Theatre.
Lit E.Gollerbakh *Grafika B.M.Kustodieva*, Moscow-Leningrad, 1929. I.Pikulev *B.M.Kustodiev*, Moscow, 1951. I.Lapina *Kustodiev*, Moscow, 1960. V.Lebedeva *Kustodiev*, Moscow, 1966. T.Savitskaya *Kustodiev*, Moscow, 1966. *Diaghilev and Russian Stage Designers, a Loan Exhibition from the Collection of Mr. and Mrs. N.Lobanov-Rostovsky*, International Exhibitions Foundation, Washington, 1972-4. M.Etkind (ed.) *B.M.Kustodiev*, Leningrad, 1967. V.Lebedeva *B.V.Kustodiev*, Moscow, 1981. J.E.Bowlt *Russian Stage Design. Scenic Innovation. From the Collection of Mr. and Mrs. Nikita D.Lobanov-Rostovsky*, Jackson, MS, exh. cat.,1982. M.Etkind *Kustodiev*, Moscow, 1982. M.Etkind *B.Kustodiev*, New York and Leningrad, 1983. M.Sautin *Kustodiev*, Leningrad, 1987. David Elliott, V.Dudakov *100 Years of Russian Art*, London, 1989. N.Lobanov-Rostovsky *Revolutionary Ceramics*, London, 1990. A.Kamensky *The World of Art Movement*, Leningrad, 1991.
Coll Well represented in TG and RM; Bakhrushin Theatre Museum, Moscow; Theatre Museum, St. Petersburg; The Central Museum of the Revolution, Moscow; Russian Art Museum, Kiev; Fine Art Museum, Nizhny-Novgorod; Uffizi, Florence.
Colour plates pp.228, 229.

KUSTODIEV, K. B. b.1903
Theatre designer active in the 1920s.

KUVSHINIKOVA, Sofiya Petrovna 1847-1907
Landscape painter.
Coll TG.

KUZ'MIN, Nikolai Vasil'evich 1890-1983
Draughtsman, illustrator. He exhibited with the group The Thirteen in 1929. His illustrations to Pushkin's *Evgeniy Onegin*, executed in pen and ink, display an elegant historicism and a light but decisive touch evoking the atmosphere of a St. Petersburg of Pushkin's day. He died in Moscow.

KUZMINA-KARAVOEVA (PILENKO), Elizaveta Yurevna 1891-1945
She exhibited with the Union of Youth in St. Petersburg in 1912.

KUZNETSOV, M. V. a.1925
He exhibited with the 4 Arts society in Moscow in 1925.

KUZNETSOV (VOLGIN), Mikhail A. a.1919-1925
Painter brother of Pavel Kuznetsov. The name M.Kuznetsov appeared on the April 1919 list of artists for acquisitions by the envisaged Museum of Painterly Culture. He exhibited with the Society of Moscow Painters at its inaugural exhibition in Moscow in 1925.

KUZNETSOV, Nikolai Dmitrievich 1850-1930
Ukrainian portrait, landscape and genre painter. Born of a noble family in the Kherson region. He studied at the Academy in St. Petersburg 1876-80. Some of his paintings overtly celebrated the peasant although some had an idyllic rural air. He exhibited with the Wanderers from 1881 and became a member in 1893. He taught at the Academy and in 1890 was a founder member of the Society of South Russian Artists in Odessa. He exhibited with the First Izdebsky

International Salon 1909-10 in Odessa.

Going Round the Estate, 1879, TG, has an atmosphere reminiscent of Venetsianov. In an endless, flat landscape in the still light of evening, a peasant stands with his hunting gun and dog. The man doing his rounds is wealthier. He drives a light carriage and is about to flick his horse whip to move off. The horse's head is seen against the sky in the midst of a monumental stillness which will soon give way to movement.

Coll TG; Museum of Ukrainian Art, Kiev.

KUZNETSOV, Nikolai Efimovich   1876-1970

Painter, theatre designer. He studied under Serov and Korovin. He exhibited with the Knave of Diamonds 1916-18. He was a member of the Free Art Society from 1915 to 1922. His theatre design occurred from 1917.

After the Revolution his work was included in the First Exhibition of the Moscow Contemporary Art Store in January 1919.

KUZNETSOV, Pavel Varfolomeevich   1878-1968

Major painter of landscapes and still-lifes, theatre designer. Inspired by both Cubism and the resurgent admiration for folk art and non-European art, he became fascinated by the nomads of Central Asia and of Kirghizia in particular. Born at Saratov where he grew up and benefited from the Radishchev Museum which opened in 1885. He studied in Saratov under

Pavel Kuznetsov. Central Asian Woman with Bird, *early 1920s. Lithograph.*
The subject reflects Kuznetsov's fascination with Samarkand, Bukhara and the way of life in Uzbekistan. The composition reflects his adaptation of avant-garde ideas whilst the style is a monumental and simplified response to Central Asian decorative art.

Pavel Kuznetsov. The Orient, *early 1920s. Lithograph.*
Kuznetsov's sophistication is evident in the near symmetry of the camels and distant mountains, images evoking a timeless expanse of space.

V.Konovalov, Borisov-Musatov and Salvini-Baracchi 1891-6 and then at the Moscow College from 1897 to 1904 where he studied under Serov, Levitan, Leonid Pasternak and K.Korovin. He joined the World of Art in 1902 and exhibited with the World of Art 1902-6. He was an organiser of the Scarlet Rose exhibition in Saratov in 1904. In 1905 he was a member of the Union of Russian Artists and the Society of Moscow Artists. In 1906 he accompanied Diaghilev, Sudeikin and Larionov to Paris to assist in the display of Russian art at the Salon d'Automne where he exhibited, but he also visited Italy and England. He was a founder member of the Blue Rose group in 1907 and an organiser of its exhibition in Moscow. He contributed to numerous exhibitions including *Venok* (The Wreath) 1907-8, the Union of Russian Artists from 1907 and the Golden Fleece 1908-10. He exhibited with the World of Art 1911-16.

He travelled to the Ural steppes in 1909 and began to develop an independent vision of the vast and mysterious aspect of Asian Russia. Journeys down the Volga in 1911 and 1913 left him fascinated by the cultures of its lower reaches. He visited Bukhara, Samarkand and Tashkent and began to paint aspects of the life of Kirghiz nomads.

After the Revolution he exhibited with the World of Art in December 1917 in Moscow. He was teaching painting, decoration on ceramics, glass and enamelling at the Free Art Studios in Moscow c.1918. He was a member of the Moscow Collegium of IZO Narkompros under Tatlin in 1919. His name appeared on the April 1919 list of artists for acquisitions by the envisaged Museum of Painterly Culture and his work was amongst the new acquisitions of the Tretyakov Gallery exhibited in 1919. He was represented along with Kandinsky, Chagall and others at the First State Exhibition of Paintings by Local and Moscow Artists held in Vitebsk in December 1919. He exhibited in the 1921 exhibition of the World of Art in Moscow. He was represented at the First Russian Art Exhibition in Berlin in 1922 and he contributed to the International Exhibition in Dresden in 1926. His work was included in the exhibition of Soviet art held at Harbin in 1926 and in Japan in 1927 and in the 1928 exhibition of Acquisitions by the State Art Collections Fund held in Moscow. He was represented in the First Touring Exhibition of Paintings and Graphics which opened in Moscow in 1929 and he was given an exhibition at the Tretyakov Gallery, Moscow, in 1929. In 1930 he was in Armenia with Saryan.

He taught at the Moscow Vkhutemas/Vkhutein until 1937. He exhibited with the 4 Arts society and acted as its president from 1924 to 1931. He was represented at the jubilee exhibition Artists of the RSFSR over 15 Years held at the Russian Museum, Leningrad, in 1932 and at the 1932 Venice Biennale.

Portrait of E.M.Bebutova, 1922, TG, is executed in his central Asian tentative but poetic style. She holds a yellow jug. Behind her the ogee arches of an eastern building provide an exotic rhythm for the painting.

Theatre design 1914 December: *Sakuntala* directed by Tairov at the Kamerny (Chamber) Theatre in Moscow. This was the first production at the theatre which opened after the outbreak of war. Tairov had returned from London where he studied the formulation of the piece in the British Museum. It is based upon an ancient Hindu drama by Kalisada which was translated by K.Balmont.

1914 Tairov's production of Synge's *Playboy of the Western World* at the Kamerny (Chamber) Theatre in Moscow.

1915 March: M.A.Kuzmin's pantomime *Dukhov den' v Toledo* (Pentecost at Toledo) at the Kamerny (Chamber) Theatre in Moscow.

1918 V.Kamensky's spectacle *Stenka Razin* in Moscow which featured a lavishly coloured exotic landscape of stylised trees and Fauve bushes in red, blue, yellow and orange (Bakhrushin Theatre Museum).

1924 Lunacharsky's *Don Quixote Liberated* at the Comedy Theatre, Moscow.

Book design stylised lithographic folk art cover design of a bird, flowers and staves in red, yellow, green and black for the sheet music of Grigori Lobachev's *Melodii narodov* (Melodies of the Nations), words by Sergei Zayatsky, Moscow, 1925.

Lit A.Romm *P.V.Kuznetsov*, Moscow, 1960. L.Budkova, D.Sarabyanov *P.Kuznetsov*, Moscow, 1975. A.Rusakova *P.Kuznetsov*, Leningrad, 1977. *Paris-Moscou*, 1979. David Elliott, V.Dudakov *100 Years of Russian Art*, London, 1989. Peter Stupples *Pavel Kuznetsov: His Life and Work*, Cambridge, 1990. Dzhon Boult (John Bowlt) *Khudozhniki russkogo teatra. Sobranie Nikity i Niny Lobanovykh-Rostovskikh*, Moscow, 1991.

Coll Well represented at TG; RM; Bakhrushin Theatre Museum, Moscow.

Colour plate p.232.

KUZNETSOV, Vasili Vasilievich   **1882-1923**

Sculptor, ceramics artist. After studying at the Academy in St. Petersburg 1901-8 under V.A.Beklemishov and Zaleman, he executed architectural reliefs in St. Petersburg and Kiev between 1908 and 1914. He was an organiser of the exhibition Modern Trends in 1908.

He displayed friezes and reliefs at the International Exhibitions in Rome in 1910 and Turin in 1911. He exhibited with the World of Art 1911-12 and 1916. Sarra Lebedeva was among his pupils. He directed the sculpture workshop at the Imperial and later State Porcelain Factory from 1914 to 1919. After the Revolution he executed figurines and a ceramic bust of Karl Marx in 1918. In the following year he returned to Saratov. He was awarded a medal at the Paris International Exhibition in 1925 and was represented at the jubilee exhibition Artists of the RSFSR over 15 Years held at the Russian Museum, Leningrad, in 1932.

Hercules and Antaeus, 1911-12, bronze, RM, presents a theme wholly out of its period with the wrestling figures competently derived from the Renaissance prototypes

Lit A.Rusakova *V.Kuznetsov*, Leningrad, 1977. N.Lobanov-Rostovsky *Revolutionary Ceramics*, London, 1990. *Paris-Moscou*, 1979.

KUZNETSOVA, L.   **a.1912-1913**

Painter. She exhibited with the World of Art in 1912-13.

KYUNEL, F. F. = KÜHNEL, F.

Pavel Kuznetsov. Oriental Woman with a veil, *early 1920s. Lithograph.*

L

L.B. see **BAKST, L.**
L.P. see **PLAKHOV, L.K.**

LABAS, Aleksandr Arkad'evich   **1900-1983**
Painter. Born at Smolensk. He studied in the private studios of
V.I.Mushketov in Smolensk in 1908. He lived in Riga and
Moscow 1910-12. He then studied at the Stroganov Institute
under F.Fedorovsky, S.Noakovsky and D.Shcherbinovsky
1912-17.
After the Revolution he studied at the Free Art Studios
(SVOMAS) under P.Konchalovsky 1917-19 and served with the
Red Army in the Far East 1919-20. He taught at the Art
Institute in Ekaterinburg 1920-1 and was a founder member of
the Elektro-organism Group in 1921 in Moscow with Nikritin,
Redko, Tyshler and others. He taught at the Vkhutemas 1922-4.
He was a founder member of the Society of Easel Painters
(OST) and exhibited with OST from 1925 to 1932. He was
included in the major exhibition in Moscow in 1927 marking the
tenth anniversary of the Revolution and the 1928 exhibition of
Acquisitions by the State Art Collections Fund held in Moscow.
He was represented in the First Touring Exhibition of Paintings
and Graphics which opened in Moscow in 1929 and in the
exhibition of Russian Graphic Art in Riga in 1929. He was
represented at the jubilee exhibition Artists of the RSFSR over
15 Years held at the Russian Museum, Leningrad, in 1932, and
at the 1932 Venice Biennale.
The Factory, c.1927, a stagey and atmospheric interior of stark
perspectives peopled by diminutive workers.
Lit *Paris-Moscou*, 1979. A.M.Muratov, V.Manin et al. *Zhivopis'
20-30kh godov*, Sankt-Peterburg, 1991.
Coll RM.

LABUNSKAYA, G. V.   **a.1914-1919**
Painter. She contributed to the exhibition No.4 in Moscow in
1914.
After the Revolution she exhibited with the World of Art in
December 1917 in Moscow. She exhibited with the Artists of the
Leftist Federation of the Professional Union in 1918 along with
Popova, Rodchenko and others and at the Fifth State Exhibition:
From Impressionism to Non-Objective Art in Moscow 1918-19.

LADAG, A.N.   **a.1919**
Painter. He exhibited at the juryless Eighth State Exhibition
in Moscow in 1919.

**LADURNER, Adolphe (LADYURNER, Adolf Ignatevich)
1798-1855**
Painter of group portraits and battle themes. Born in Paris. He
was a pupil of Horace Vernet. He exhibited at the Paris Salon
1824-7. He moved to Russia in 1830. He died in St. Petersburg.
Coll TG; RM.

LADYZHENSKY, Genadiy Aleksandrovich   **1853-1916**
Painter whose work included animal themes. He signed his
work 'Gen.L-sky'.
Coll TG; RM.

LAGODA-SHISHKINA, Olga Antonova   **1850-1881**
Painter of genre themes and landscape. She married the
painter Shishkin. She signed her work simply 'Lagoda'.
Coll TG; RM.

LAGORIO, Lef Feliksovich   **1827-1905**
Academic landscape painter. Born at Feodosia. His subjects
included Parisian themes in 1859 and Italian themes in 1860.
He was awarded a bronze medal at the Paris International
Exhibition of 1889. He died in St. Petersburg.
Coll TG; Latvian Art Museum, Riga.

LAKHOVSKY, Arnol'd Borisovich   **1880-1937**
Painter of landscapes and portraits. His date of birth is
sometimes given as 1885. He studied under A.A.Kiselev at the
Academy in St. Petersburg 1904-12 and exhibited with the
First Izdebsky International Salon 1909-10 in Odessa.
After the Revolution he was engaged in Agitprop decorations
at Simeonovskaya Street and Liteiny Prospekt, Petrograd, in
1918. He participated in the First State Free Exhibition of
Artworks in Petrograd in 1919 and in the Third Exhibition of
Paintings held at Ryazan in 1919. He also contributed to the
exhibition of Paintings by Russian Artists held at Pskov in
Spring 1920. He was included in the enormous survey
Exhibition of Paintings by Petrograd Artists of All Tendencies
1919-1923 held in Petrograd in 1923. He exhibited with the
Kuindzhi Society, the World of Art, The Sixteen, and AKhRR.
He later emigrated and exhibited internationally. He died in
New York.
Colour plate p.249.

LAKOV, Nikolai Andreevich   **1894-1970**
Painter. He was engaged in Agitprop decorations for
Tverskoy Boulevard (later Gorky Street) in Moscow in 1918
producing, with G.Gryunberg, an immensely long mural
panel depicting *The Birth of the New World* amidst guns,
smoke, the arcs of wheels, diagonal flags and cities with rising
suns. He was a member of the *Bytie* (Existence) Society of
Artists formed in Moscow in 1921. He was represented at the
jubilee exhibition Artists of the RSFSR over 15 Years held at
the Russian Museum, Leningrad, in 1932. He was active as a
graphic artist and theatre designer.

LAKTIONOV, A. I.   **b.1910**
Socialist Realist genre painter. He painted one of the most
celebrated of Socialist Realist genre works, *Letter from the
Front*, 1947, in which a family gathers in a sunlit doorway out
on a farm to hear a youngster read the letter. An injured
soldier with a bandaged hand looks on benignly.
Coll TG.

LAMANOVA, Nadezhda Petrovna   **1861-1941**
Dress and theatre designer. Born at Shuzilovo village in the
Nizhny-Novgorod region. In 1880 she was already designing
clothes privately. She studied in O.A.Suvorova's cutting and
sewing course in Moscow in 1883 and worked for the
Voitkevich dressmakers 1884-5. She ran her own dressmaking
studio from 1885 to 1917 and made regular visits to Paris
where she collaborated with Paul Poiret.
After the Revolution she joined the Art Workers' Union in
1918. She was however initially imprisoned but released after
receiving the support of Maxim Gorky. She taught under the
auspices of Narkompros 1919-22. She led a Studio of Modern
Costume 1919-25. In 1923 she exhibited at the National

Academy of Art. She produced dress designs for International Exhibitions from 1925 to 1932 and was awarded a grand prix at the Paris International Exhibition of 1925. In 1926 she designed clothing for the North of Russia. She exhibited at Leipzig in 1930. She died in Moscow.

Theatre design for several theatres including the Moscow Art Theatre from 1901 until her death, the Academic Theatre in Moscow, the Vakhtangov Theatre from 1921, the Griboedov Studio in 1924, and the Red Army Theatre.

1926 costumes from designs by Aleksandr Golovin for Beaumarchais' *Marriage of Figaro* at the Moscow Art Theatre.

Film design 1924 Costumes for Protozanov's *Aelita*, with Aleksandra Exter. Also costumes for Eisenstein's *Ivan the Terrible* and *Aleksandr Nevsky* as well as Grigorii Aleksandrov's *Generation of Winners* and *The Circus*.

Lit T.Strizhenova *Iz istorii sovetskogo kostyuma*, Moscow, 1972 (English edition: Tatiana Strizhenova, *Soviet Costume and Textiles 1917-1945*, Paris, 1991). *Paris-Moscou*, 1979.

LAMBIN, Petr Borisovich   **1862-1923**
Theatre designer, landscape painter. His theatre designs included the ballet *Blue Beard* in the 1900s. Vsevolod Meyerhold was among the directors for whom he made designs.

He also designed for Meyerhold after the Revolution.

Theatre design 1915 April G.B.Shaw's *Pygmalion* produced by Meyerhold at the Aleksandrinsky Theatre, Petrograd.

1918 November D.Ober's *Fenella* produced by Meyerhold at the Mariinsky Theatre, Petrograd, co-directed by S.D.Maslovkaya.

Lit Dzhon Boult (John Bowlt) *Khudozhniki russkogo teatra. Sobranie Nikity i Niny Lobanovykh-Rostovskikh*, Moscow, 1991.

LANCERAY = LANSERE

LANGBARD, Iosif Grigor'evich   **1882-1951**
He was engaged in Agitprop decorations at Lafonsky Square and Labour Square in Petrograd in 1918.

LANGER, Nikolai Vasilievich   **1781-1824**
Painter of group portraits.
Coll TG.

LANSERE (LANCERAY), Evgeniy Aleksandrovich 1848-1886
Sculptor. He was the father of Evgeni Evgenevich Lansere and of Zinaida Serebryakova. He produced a long series of small bronzes of horses which show a highly professional knowledge of the animal in every position. However these go far beyond anatomical studies and are integrated into sophisticated and frequently energetic compositions of considerable immediacy in which the horse is seen in action. There is in this a distant similarity with the concerns of Degas. The Russian Museum has numerous sculptures of warriors on horseback, some historical or exotic. *Tsar's Cavalry of the Seventeenth Century*, 1872, bronze, RM, shows the rider rising in the saddle as his horse rears. *Kirghiz Horses at Rest*, 1880, bronze, RM, is a multi-horse composition on a circular base. *Horses with a Jump*, 1882, bronze, RM, is a study of several horses clearing a steeplechase fence with all the fast flow of their movement well captured. He died in St. Petersburg.
Coll RM

LANSERE (LANCERAY), Evgeni Evgen'evich 1875-1946
Painter, sculptor, graphic artist, illustrator. He executed evocative and historicising images of St. Petersburg. Born at Pavlovsk. He was the son of the sculptor Evgeniy Lansere, the brother of Zinaida Serebryakova and the nephew of Alexandre Benois with whose family he was raised from the age of eleven. He studied at the school of the Society for the Encouragement of the Arts in St. Petersburg under Ya.Tsionglinsky and E.Lipgart (Liphardt) 1892-6 and then in Paris at the Académie Julian and at the Académie Colarossi 1896-9. He travelled in Western Europe in 1898 and in 1902 he visited Japan. He was associated with the World of Art from 1899 and exhibited with the World of Art in St. Petersburg in 1900. In 1904 the *Mir Iskusstva* (World of Art) periodical published his illustrations to Balmont's *Poetry of the Elements*. He exhibited with the World of Art 1901-6. He designed the poster for Diaghilev's Exhibition of Historical Russian Portraits in 1905 and covers for the journal *Zolotoe Runo* (Golden Fleece) 1906-7. He also executed illustrations for the satirical periodicals *Zhupel'*, *Adskaya Pochta* and *Zritel'* 1905-8. He was represented in Diaghilev's display of Russian art at the 1906 Salon d'Automne in Paris. He exhibited with the First Izdebsky International Salon 1909-10 in Odessa. He was designing for porcelain and cut glass at St. Petersburg and Ekaterinburg 1912-15. In 1916 he moved from Petrograd to Ust-Krestishche in the Pskov region.

After the Revolution his name appeared on the April 1919 list of artists for acquisitions by the envisaged Museum of Painterly Culture. He lived in Dagestan from 1917 to 1920 and then in Tblisi until 1934. He was teaching at the Tblisi Academy 1922-32. In 1923 he visited Turkey. He was represented at the Paris International Exhibition of 1925 and at the jubilee exhibition Artists of the RSFSR over 15 Years held at the Russian Museum, Leningrad, in 1932.

He lived in the Caucasus 1932-4. He returned to Moscow in 1934 and designed decorations for the Kazan Railway Station in Moscow 1934-5 and for the Hotel Moskva restaurant in Moscow in 1937. He executed decorations for the vestibule of the Kazan Station in 1940 and 1946/7.

Cover design for Mir Iskusstva (World of Art), 1901, is forceful yet extremely elegant, featuring a symmetrical motif of a lion's head fixed like a pendant to the lower edge of a circle of swags and ribbons, and surmounted by the rhythmic but severely

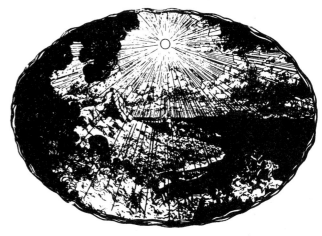

Evgeni Lansere. The Sun, *1904. 11 x 16 cm.*
An illustration to Balmont's 'Hymn to the Sun' for the 'World of Art' periodical, No.12, 1904.

Evgeni Lansere. Medieval Poetry in Miniatures, *1904. Ink on paper.*
32.5 x 25.7 cm.
An illustration for the 'World of Art' periodical.
State Russian Museum, St. Petersburg.

K.Kravchenko *E.E.Lansere*, Moscow-Leningrad, 1948.
M.Babenchikov *E.E.Lansere* Leningrad, 1949. O.Podobedova
E.E.Lansere, Moscow, 1961. *Paris-Moscou*, 1979. J.E.Bowlt
Russian Stage Design. Scenic Innovation. From the Collection of
Mr. and Mrs. Nikita D.Lobanov-Rostovsky, Jackson, MS, exh.
cat.,1982. *Twilight of the Tsars*, London, 1991. A.Kamensky
The World of Art Movement, Leningrad, 1991.
Coll TG; RM; Tolstoy Museum, Moscow.

LANSERE, Nikolai   a.1909-1932
He exhibited Russian architectural themes with the First
Izdebsky International Salon 1909-10 in Odessa.
An N.E.Lansere was represented at the jubilee exhibition
Artists of the RSFSR over 15 Years held at the Russian
Museum, Leningrad, in 1932.

LAPCHENKO, Grigori Ignat'evich   1801-1876
Painter. There is a difference of views concerning his dates
which are sometimes given as 1796 or 1804 to 1876 or 1879.
Coll TG.

LAPIN, Lev Pavlovich   1898-1962
Theatre designer responsive to folk art and Constructivism.
Lit Dzhon Boult (John Bowlt) *Khudozhniki russkogo teatra.*
Sobranie Nikity i Niny Lobanovykh-Rostovskikh, Moscow, 1991.

restrained Art Nouveau lettering of the title. He was a graphic
artist of the highest technical precision and professionalism.
**The Empress Elizveta Petrovna in Tsarskoe Selo*, 1905, TG, is a
spectacular and witty costume piece typical of the World of
Art painters in its humane evocation of the imperial past: the
Empress steps into the formal gardens from the great blue,
white and gold palace with a forthright and determined
movement. She is surrounded by flunkies and courtiers of the
highest elegance. This is an exercise in sophisticated and witty
play acting by an erudite and talented artist.
*Funeral Feast, 1906, is a bitter satire expressing his revulsion
at the suppression of the 1905 revolution. Grotesque and
obese generals feast, drink and smoke with a soldiers' choir to
entertain them in the wake of the supression.
**Ships in the Time of Peter I*, 1911, TG, is a celebration of the
genius of the founder of St. Petersburg, comparable with
works by Serov, Dobuzhinsky and Benois. The ships, depicted
with historical accuracy, toss dramatically in the choppy sea,
exemplars of the spirit of enterprise.
Theatre design 1901 set for Scene 4 of Delibes' *Sylvia*, a
collaboration with Bakst, Benois and Korovin (unrealised).
1907-8 collaboration with Benois on Evreinov's *Fair on St.*
Denis' Day for the Antique Theatre, St. Petersburg.
1908 he assisted on the execution of A.Golovin's designs for
Mussorgsky's *Boris Godunov* at the Théâtre de l'Opéra, Paris.
1909-10 Schiller's *Kabale und Liebe* (unrealised).
1911 Calderon's *Purgatory of St.Patrick* in collaboration with
Benois and Vladimir Shchuko, for the Antique Theatre, St.
Petersburg.
Lit A.Babenchikov *E.E.Lansere*, Moscow, 1935 and 1945.

Evgeni Lansere. St. Petersburg, *1903. Ink on paper. 30.5 x 23.2 cm.*
State Russian Museum, St. Petersburg.

Lev Lapin. Costume design for a Peasant Woman, *1929. Watercolour. Dated lower left. Production unknown. 34.8 x 22 cm. Collection Mr. and Mrs. Nikita D.Lobanov-Rostovsky, London.*

LAPIN, M. I.   a.1921

He exhibited in the 1921 exhibition of the World of Art in Moscow. A Lapin was listed without initials as a founder member of the group October in 1928.

LAPPO-DANILEVSKY, Aleksandr Aleksandrovich
1898-1920
Draughtsman.
Coll RM.

LAPSHIN, Georgiy Aleksandrovich   a.1915-1925+
Painter. Born in Moscow. He studied in Paris under Lhermitte and Cormon.
After the Revolution he was represented at the First Exhibition of Works of the Professional Union of Artists in Moscow in 1918.
He later worked in Paris exhibiting at the Salon des Artistes Français and at the Salon des Indépendants from 1925.
Coll TG.

LAPSHIN, Nikolai Fedorovich   1888-1942
Painter, graphic artist, ceramic artist. He studied at the school of the Society for the Encouragement of the Arts in St. Petersburg and then under Yan Tsionglinsky and Mikhail Bernshtein.

After the Revolution he was engaged on Agitprop decorations at Izmailovsky Square and Blagoveshchenskaya Square, Petrograd, in 1918. He was designing for the State Porcelain Factory 1920-3. He became deputy director and briefly acting director of the Museum of Artistic Culture in Petrograd 1921-3. He executed a woodcut illustrating the performance of Kheebnikov's long Futurist poem *Zangezi* organised by Tatlin in 1922 and contributed to the exhibitions New Tendencies in Art in June 1922, Studies for Theatre Decoration and Works from the Studios of the Decorative Institute held in Petrograd in 1922, Paintings by Petrograd Artists of All Tendencies 1919-1923 and to the group 4 Arts. He was represented at the All-Union Polygraphic Exhibition in Moscow in 1927 and in exhibitions at Leipzig in 1927, Cologne in 1928 and Paris in 1931. He

Nikolai Lapshin. Tatlin's Construction for a Performance of the Long Poem 'Zangezi' by the Futurist Poet Velimir Khlebnikov, *1923. Woodcut.*
The poem includes abstruse historical calculations. These can be seen lower left. Tatlin is visible performing from a balcony.

Mikhail Larionov. Self -portrait, *1910. Oil on canvas. 104 x 89 cm.*
Inscribed upper right 'Self portrait Larionov'.
The painting belongs to a series of works of protagonists in Larionov's nascent
Russian Futurist circle. Other portraits included the poet painter David
Burlyuk and the poet Velimir Khlebnikov.
Private collection, Paris.

taught at the graphics faculty of the Leningrad Vkhutemas
from 1929. In later years he returned to a more traditional
form of painting but still slightly calligraphic somewhat in the
manner of Marquet or a diluted Matisse.
The River Moika, c.1919, RM, is a Futurist painting inspired
by Larionov or Shevchenko. It has Rayist angular planes
intersecting to form the images of tilting buildings and bridge
across which are painted fragmentary carriages, horses and
figures, all executed in brown-red, yellow and blue.
Lit E.Weiss *Russische Avant-Garde, 1910-1930, Sammlung*
Ludwig, Köln, Munich, 1986. David Elliott, V.Dudakov *100*
Years of Russian Art, London, 1989. A.M.Muratov, V.Manin et
al. *Zhivopis' 20-30kh godov,* Sankt-Peterburg, 1991.
Coll RM; Sammlung Ludwig, Cologne.

LARIONOV, Ivan Fedorovich (LARIONOFF, Jean) 1884-1919

Painter. He was the brother of the painter Mikhail Larionov.
He exhibited with the Donkey's Tail group in Moscow in
1912 along with Mikhail Larionov, Goncharova and others
and at Mikhail Larionov's exhibition The Target in Moscow
in 1913. He died young in Moscow.

LARIONOV, Mikhail Fedorovich (LARIONOFF, Michel) 1881-1964

Painter and theatre designer. With Natalya Goncharova,
Larionov was a central figure in the evolution of Russian
Futurism, the emergence of Neo-Primitivism and Rayism and
in transforming the stage design of the Russian Ballet.
He was born at Tiraspol in the Crimea. He studied at the
Moscow College 1898-1908 under Serov and Levitan. Here he
met Natalya Goncharova in 1900. Together they formed a
unique creative partnership which managed to combine

independence and collaboration in careers of extraordinary
inventiveness, diversity and productivity. Larionov was painting
works inspired by French Impressionism in 1905 and the
following year he made his first visit to Paris with Pavel
Kuznetsov to assist Diaghilev in his display of Russian painting
at the Salon d'Automne. Larionov's own work was represented
in the exhibition. He returned to Russia via London.
He also exhibited with the World of Art in 1906 and with the
Union of Russian Artists 1906-7. He showed work the following
year at the Seventh Venice Biennale, with the Moscow
Association of Artists (April 1907) and with the exhibitions
Stefanos/Venok (Stephanos-Wreath) and *Venok* (The Wreath)
1907-8 in St. Petersburg. Exhibition organisation became an
important aspect of his own activities.
He was involved with the Golden Fleece between 1908 and
1910 and he organised an exhibition including French
Impressionist and Post-Impressionist paintings within the
Golden Fleece in 1908. He was engaged in military service in
1908-9. At the third exhibition of the Golden Fleece, in
December 1909, he introduced the deliberate adoption of
primitive techniques, thereby launching a Neo-Primitive or
Primitivist phase which had wide repercussions in Russian Art.
In the winter of 1909-10 he exhibited with the Union of Russian
Artists and he showed work at the Izdebsky Salons in Odessa
1909-11. In March 1910 he exhibited at the first Union of
Youth exhibition at St. Petersburg. In December 1910 he
organised the first Knave of Diamonds exhibition with
Goncharova and Lentulov, and he exhibited with the Knave of
Diamonds in Moscow 1910-11. He also exhibited with the
Union of Youth in 1911 and 1912. On 8 December 1911
Larionov had a one-day exhibition at the Society of Free
Aesthetics in Moscow. He contributed to the exhibition Modern
Painting at Ekaterinburg and to the *Blaue Reiter* (Blue Rider)
exhibition in Munich in 1912.
Close participation in the fractured but irrepressible Russian
Futurist movement followed with Larionov and Goncharova
playing a crucial role. Rebelling against the influx of Western
European work and influences which had become a feature of
the Knave of Diamonds exhibitions, Larionov and Goncharova
organised a rival exhibition, the Donkey's Tail in March 1912 in
Moscow at which he exhibited over forty works including
soldier themes and a self-portrait.
In 1912-13 Larionov devised *Luchizm* (Rayism), sometimes
called Rayonnism in the Western literature on Larionov, and he
exhibited Rayist works at the exhibition *Mishen'* (Target) which
he organised in April 1913. Rayism entailed the extension of the
multiplicity of rays of light scattered by objects into a dynamic
interplay of lines and planes that sometimes, but not always, left
visible the recognisable image of the original objects. Larionov
said that Rayism owed much to his awareness of X-ray images.
Goncharova executed comparable works. Other artists affected
by Rayism included V.Chekrygin, M.Le-Dantyu, V.Levkievsky,
S.Romanovich and A.Shevchenko. It has been asserted that in
pursuing this Larionov was one of the first painters to abandon
the necessity of a recognisable subject in painting. This
approach also informed his illustrations for Russian Futurist
books 1912-13 where unconventional and Primitivist features
also characterised the literary and poetic contents. Larionov
and Goncharova also made a Russian Futurist film *Drama in
Cabaret No.13* during 1913 in which they both performed.
Having been close students of Western artistic developments in
Paris and elsewhere, Larionov and Goncharova were now

Arnol'd Lakhovsky. A Russian Provincial Town in Winter. *Oil on canvas. Signed in latin letters. 61 x 50 cm.*
Reproduced by kind permission of Sotheby's London, sale 16.6.1992, lot 66.

Mikhail Larionov. Woman behind a Table, *1912. Lithograph. 18.4 x 13 cm.*
This appeared as an illustration in the Russian Futurist book 'Mirskontsa' (Worldbackwards) in 1912.

increasingly determined to stress the distinct qualities of Russia's Eastern identity in the ikon, the popular *lubok* print, folk art and Asian art. In addition they turned their attention to sign painters, children's painting and to graffiti. Russian Futurism and Primitivism were brought together. These developments were promoted by Larionov and Goncharova through the exhibitions of the Donkey's Tail and Target, both of which had an important place in the careers of Malevich, Tatlin and others. An almanac *The Donkey's Tail and Target* was published in 1913. Larionov showed work, however, at the First German Autumn Salon in Berlin in 1913. His Futurist exhibition No.4, the fourth that he organised, was held in Moscow in 1914.

Larionov and Goncharova then moved to Paris for their joint exhibition at the Galerie Paul Guillaume in 1914 which included Rayist works. Apollinaire contributed a catalogue essay and writing in the periodical *Soirées de Paris* (No.2, 1914) he asserted that Rayism was a European phenomenon.

When Larionov returned to Russia from Paris he was mobilised to fight in the war. He saw active service, was badly concussed and discharged in 1915. However he did exhibit reliefs at the Exhibition of Painting: The Year 1915 in March-April.

Diaghilev invited Larionov and Goncharova to Lausanne, Switzerland, in 1915. They settled in Paris in 1917 but his name nevertheless appeared on the April 1919 list of artists for acquisitions by the envisaged Museum of Painterly Culture, his work was amongst the new acquisitions of the Tretyakov Gallery exhibited in 1919 and he was represented at the enormous First State Exhibition of Art and Science, which included ethnographic material, held in Kazan in 1920, as well as the Venice Biennale that year. He exhibited with

Goncharova in New York in 1922.

He continued to work as designer for Diaghilev periodically until 1929. He contributed to the exhibition of Contemporary Russian Art held at Philadelphia in 1932.

He became a naturalised French citizen in 1938 and married Goncharova in 1955.

He sometimes signed his work simply 'M.L'. He died at Fontenay-aux-Roses in France.

Theatre design 1915 *Soleil de Minuit* produced by Diaghilev at the Grand Théâtre, Geneva, and at the Théâtre de l'Opéra, Paris, to music by Rimsky-Korsakov (from his *Snegurochka*) and choreography by Massine.

1915 *Histoires naturelles*, ballet choreographed by Larionov and Fokine to music by Ravel. Rehearsed at Lausanne by Diaghilev's company but not performed.

1917 *Les Contes Russes* produced by Diaghilev at the Théâtre du Châtelet, Paris, with choreography by Massine and music by A.K.Lyadov (Liadov). The stories featured Kikimora, Bova-Korolevich and Baba-Yaga. *Kikimora* was first given in 1916 at the Teatro Eugenia-Victoria, St. Sebastian. Larionov

Mikhail Larionov. Design for the Costume of a Young Peasant Woman, *1915. Watercolour and pencil. Signed 'M.L.' lower left and inscribed in French 'Soleil de Minuit' and 'Lausanne'. 30.5 x 22.7 cm.*
This is a design for the ballet 'The Midnight Sun' set to music from Rimsky-Korsakov's opera 'Snegurochka' (Snowmaiden). It was staged for Diaghilev by L.F.Massine at the Grand Théâtre, Geneva, in 1915.
Collection Mr. and Mrs. Nikita D.Lobanov-Rostovsky, London.

also designed the curtain.

1921 S.Prokofiev's *Chout, ou Le Bouffon* produced by Diaghilev at the Théâtre de la Gaîté-Lyrique, Paris, with choreography by Larionov and Thadée Slavinsky. A design for Scene 1 depicts a village street in thoroughly Primitive style but informed also by a characteristic admixture of Russian Futurist devices of irrational perspectives and the bizarre asymmetrical costumes of the protagonists. The rhythm of the design reflects the choreography but could well stand as a painting in its own right. A design for Scene 5 is spectacular in its profusion of vigorously conflicting angular patterns and strong contrasts of colour used to depict a peasant interior with bed, ikon, zigzag tree motifs in red and green on the wallpaper and a crude, bright image of landscape through a false window. Scene 6 has stylised trees flanking spectacular curves arching like rainbows over a splintered fence and lampposts.

1922 Stravinsky's *Le Renard* produced by Diaghilev with choreography by Bronislava Nijinska at the Théâtre de l'Opera, Paris. The theme concerns a fox and a cock. The set featured a wooden barn with open front dominating the stage where the animals perform.

1924 *Karagueuz, Gardien de l'Honneur de son ami*, with Goncharova, at the Théâtre du Vieux Colombier, Paris, for Julie Sazanova's marionette theatre.

1930 Prokofiev's *Symphonie Classique* at the Théâtre Pigalle, Paris.

1932 sets for Prokofiev's *Sur le Boristhène* at the Paris Opera.

1935 K.Konstantinov's *Port Said* at the London Coliseum.

Futurist books A.Kruchenykh *Starinnaya lyubov'* (Old Time Love), 1912, with illustrations by Larionov.

A.Kruchenykh and V.Khlebnikov *Mirskontsa* (Worldbackwards), 1912, illustrated by Goncharova, Larionov, Tatlin and I.Rogovin.

M.Larionov *Luchizm*, Mosow, 1913.

A.Kruchenykh *Poluzhivoy* (Half-Alive), 1913, illustrated by Larionov.

A.Kruchenykh *Pomada* (Pomade), 1913, illustrated by Larionov.

K.Bolshakov *Le Futur*, with illustrations by N.Goncharova and M.Larionov, 1913.

Illustrations A.Blok *The Twelve*, Paris, 1920. V.V.Mayakovsky *Solntsu* (To the Sun), Berlin, 1923.

Lit Extensive including E.Eganbyuri (Zdanevich) *N.Goncharova, M.Larionov*, Moscow, 1913. *Larionov and Goncharova*, exh. cat., Arts Council of Great Britain, London, 1961. *Goncharova-Larionov*, exh. cat., Musée d'Art Moderne de la Ville de Paris, 1963. W.George *Larionov*, Paris, 1966. *Michel Larionov*, exh. cat., Musée de Lyon, 1967. *Diaghilev and Russian Stage Designers, a Loan Exhibition from the Collection of Mr. and Mrs. N.Lobanov-Rostovsky*, International Exhibitions Foundation, Washington, 1972-4. S.P.Compton *The World Backwards, Russian Futurist Books 1912-16*, London, 1978. M.Hoog and S.de Vigneral *Michel Larionov, une avant-garde explosive*, Lausanne, 1978. J.E.Bowlt *Russian Stage Design. Scenic Innovation. From the Collection of Mr. and Mrs. Nikita D.Lobanov-Rostovsky*, Jackson, MS, exh. cat.,1982. A.Schouvaloff *The Thyssen-Bornemisza Collection: Set and Costume Designs for Ballet and Theatre*, New York-London, 1987. Dzhon Boult (John Bowlt) *Khudozhniki russkogo teatra. Sobranie Nikity i Niny Lobanovykh-Rostovskikh*, Moscow, 1991. S.Compton *Russian Avant-Garde Books 1917-34*, London, 1992. *L'Avant-garde russe 1905-1925*, exh. cat., Musée des Beaux-Arts, Nantes, 1993. A.Parton *Larionov and the Avant-Garde*, Princeton, 1993.

Coll Represented in numerous major museums including TG; RM; Kazan Art Museum; Nizhny-Novgorod Art Museum;

Anton Lavinsky. Stage Design for the Play 'Mystery Bouffe' by Vladimir Mayakovsky, *1924. Drawing.*
The set shows the scene at the North Pole where several eskimos attempt to prevent the Revolution from leaking out of the Earth. The drawing is from the 1924 reconstruction of the set. The play was originally produced by Meyerhold in May 1921.

Serpukhov Museum; Ul'yanovsk Art Museum; MNAM Paris; Musée de l'Opera, Paris; Tate Gallery, London; Victoria and Albert Museum, London; Ashmolean Museum, Oxford; Lobanov-Rostovsky Collection, London; Baron Thyssen-Bornemisza Collection, England; Costakis Collection; Sammlung Ludwig, Cologne.

Colour plates pp.25, 252.

LATYSHEVA, A. G.   a.1918-1919

Painter. She was represented at the First Exhibition of Works of the Professional Union of Artists in Moscow in 1918 and at the Ninth State Exhibition of Paintings: Naturalism and Realism in Moscow in 1919.

LAVERETSKY, Nikolai Akimovich   1837-1907

Sculptor in marble. His work included sentimental figure pieces, for example *Children Looking in a Mirror*, 1872, marble, RM.

Coll TG; RM.

LAVINSKAYA, E.   a.1927

Designer. In 1927 she was invited along with Varvara Stepanova and Elena Semenova to submit designs for the decoration of several squares in Moscow. She was also at that time collaborating with Semenova on the design of window displays for the Dom Knigi Giza (the State Publishing Book House).

LAVINSKY, Anton Mikhailovich   1893-1968

Sculptor, graphic artist, and designer of experimental architectural projects, film and theatre designs. Born at Sochi. He was engaged on Agitprop decorations at Saratov c.1918. He executed a monument to *Marx* in 1919 in response to

Mikhail Larionov. Soldier in a Wood, *c.1911. Oil on canvas. 84.5 x 91.4 cm.*
Scottish National Gallery of Modern Art, Edinburgh.

Lenin's call for Monumental Propaganda. He designed posters for the Rosta Agency and was actively involved in the post-revolutionary Institute of Artistic Culture (INKhUK). He was represented at the First Russian Art Exhibition in Berlin in 1922. He also contributed to the periodical *Lef* from 1923 and his designs for a Constructivist book kiosk, a desk lamp and several posters were published in the periodical in 1923. In the same year INKhUK announced that he was to edit a publication *The Artist in Production* which apparently remained unrealised. He contributed to the First Exhibition of Cinema Posters held in Moscow in 1925 and was represented at the Paris International Exhibition of 1925. He was represented at the Second Exhibition of Cinema Posters held at the Kamerny (Chamber) Theatre, Moscow, in 1926. He died in Moscow.

Theatre design He collaborated with V.Bebutova, V.Kiselev

and V.Khrakovsky on the staging of *Mystery-Bouffe* by Vladimir Mayakovsky directed in this second production by Vsevolod Meyerhold at the No.1 Theatre of the RSFSR, Moscow in 1921 (Bakhrushin Theatre Museum, Moscow). The costumes exhibited a poster-like simplicity but the sets were a Constructivist *tour de force* with a great dome in the foreground inscribed 'The Earth' and representing the North Pole where the action begins. Behind this are platforms, steps and pylons for the actors. A costume design for an Angel is a simple, stiff and deliberately absurd Constructivist assemblage of a cylinder around the body, but with knee holes cut in it, a disc halo, and two rectangles attached to the back for wings. The drawing of it is practical, frontal and simple, with hands in prayer and head singing but no hint of reverence for the religious connotations.

Film design 1927 working on the shooting of *Radio* under the

Vladimir Lebedev. Communism Moves Around Europe, *1921.*
Colour lithograph poster.

direction of Bonch-Bruevich, to be released by Sovkino.
Book design V.Mayakovsky *13 let raboty* (13 Years Work),
Moscow, 1923. O.M.Brik *Ne poputchitsa* (Not a Fellow
Traveller), Moscow-Petrograd, 1923.
Lit Nancy Van Norman Baer *Theatre in Revolution, Russian
Avant-Garde Stage Design 1913-1935,* San Francisco and
London, 1991. S.Compton *Russian Avant-Garde Books 1917-34,*
London, 1992.
Coll Bakhrushin Theatre Museum, Moscow.

LAVROV, Georgiy Dmitrievich   **b.1895**
Sculptor. Born in Siberia. He studied at the Moscow College.
After the Revolution he contributed to the Third Exhibition
of Paintings by Artists from Kaluga and Moscow held in
Kaluga in 1925 (listed as G.G.Lavrov). He also exhibited at
Paris Salons. Proscribed 1938, rehabilitated 1954.

LAVROV, Nikolai Andreevich   **1820-1875**
Coll TG.

LAVROVA, A. D.   **a.1925**
Painter. She contributed to the Third Exhibition of Paintings
by Artists from Kaluga and Moscow held in Kaluga in 1925.

LAZAREV, G. I.   **a.1921**
He was included in the Third Touring Exhibition of the Sovetsk
Regional subdepartment of the Museums Bureau along with
Kandinsky, Rodchenko and others in 1921 and he exhibited in
the 1921 exhibition of the World of Art in Moscow.

LAZAREVA, O. P.   **a.1918**
She was represented at the First Exhibition of Works of the
Professional Union of Artists in Moscow in 1918.

LEBEDEFF, Jean = LEBEDEV, Ivan

LEBEDEV, A.   **a.1921-1922**
Painter. He was a founder member of the group *Bytie*
(Existence) formed in 1921 partly in protest at 'the narrowness
of leftist art' and he contributed to its first exhibition in 1922.

LEBEDEV, Ivan (LEBEDEFF, Jean)   **1884-1970**
Graphic artist who specialised in woodcut illustrations to
novels. Born in the Nizhny-Novgorod region. He studied
under Cormon in Paris.
He settled in Paris in 1909 and became a French citizen. Active
as a wood engraver and illustrator. He was a member of the

Vladimir Lebedev. Relief. *Assemblage of painted wood, painted metal,
saw blade, compass and a drawer handle. Signed with cyrillic initials and
dated 'VL, 1920'. 84.5 x 51 cm.*
*Reproduced by kind permission of Christie's London, sale 27.11.1991, lot
218.*

group Udar in 1923 and in 1926 he showed work at the exhibition Western Revolutionary Art in Moscow.

Lit I.P.Dubray *L'imagier Jean Lebedeff*, Paris, 1939. *Paris-Moscou*, 1979.

LEBEDEV, Klavdiy Vasilievich　　　　　**1852-1916**
Painter of figure compositions, biblical themes and landscapes. He was awarded a bronze medal at the International Exhibition in Paris in 1900.
Coll Well represented at TG.

LEBEDEV, Mikhail Ivanovich　　　　　**1811-1837**
Painter of landscapes and views. Born at Dorpat. He studied at the Academy in St. Petersburg under M.Vorobiev. He went to Italy where he visited Rome and Naples. He was painting in Rome 1835-7 but he died young from cholera in Naples. His *View of the Outskirts of Albano*, 1836, TG, reveals a meticulous observer of trees.
Coll TG; RM.

LEBEDEV, Vladimir Vasilievich　　　　　**1891-1967**
Painter, graphic artist and illustrator. Born at St. Petersburg. He designed postcards for the Fietta Art Store in St. Petersburg in 1905. In 1909 he studied drawing under Aleksandr Titov in St. Petersburg and in 1910 under the battle painter Frants Rubo. He studied at the Academy 1912-16 under Mikhail Bernshtein and Shervud. He contributed drawings to the journal *Novy Satirikon* from 1913 and attended meetings at the apartment of Lev Bruni in St. Petersburg 1914-16 along with Al'tman, Annenkov, Miturich and others. He also became friendly with Tatlin. He was a founder of the society Apartment No. 5 in Petrograd along with Bruni, Isakov, Tyrsa, Miturich, Punin and Tatlin in 1915. He married the sculptor Sarra Lebedeva in 1915. He was mobilised 1914-17.

After the Revolution he made *lubok* prints on Revolutionary themes in Petrograd in 1917 and was also engaged on Agitprop decorations for the Politseisky Bridge, Petrograd, in 1918. He taught at the Free Art Studios (SVOMAS) in Petrograd 1918-21 and executed designs for the State Porcelain Factory 1918-19. He was quick to respond to the requirements of the resolution moved by Meyerhold in 1920 stressing the need for an art of propaganda and was invited to make posters for the Rosta Agency, the Petrograd branch of which he directed together with Vladimir Kozlinsky. His designs for posters in 1920 focused upon images of Foche, Denikin and others in a bold and assertive form of caricature with an easily comprehended political purpose. He was a dramatic graphic artist employing a technique which resembled cut paper in the sharpness and economy of the image. With Vladimir Mayakovsky he designed posters for Rosta windows 1920-1. He was a member of the *Unovis* group 1921-2.

He exhibited with the Union of New Tendencies in Art in Petrograd in June 1922, was represented at the exhibition of Studies for Theatre Decoration and Works from the Studios of the Decorative Institute held in Petrograd in 1922 and at the First Russian Art Exhibition in Berlin in 1922. He was included in the enormous survey Exhibition of Paintings by Petrograd Artists of All Tendencies 1919-1923 held in Petrograd in 1923.

In the mid-1920s he made socially critical works which approached caricature, or at least satire, some with an air of Grosz or Pascin to them. An example is *The Nepmans*, 1924-6, RM, satirising the new rich who profited from the introduction of NEP, the New Economic Policy. He illustrated several children's stories by Samuil Marshak 1925-7. He was represented at the Paris International Exhibition of 1925 and was included in the major exhibition in Moscow in 1927 marking the tenth anniversary of the Revolution. He was a member of the 4 Arts society in 1928 and in the same year he had a one-man exhibition in Leningrad. He was represented at the All-Union Polygraphic Exhibition in Moscow in 1927 and at the jubilee exhibition Artists of the RSFSR over 15 Years held at the Russian Museum, Leningrad, in 1932.

He returned to designing propaganda window posters for Tass 1942-5, depicting anti-Fascist themes. He died in Leningrad.

**Decorations for Politseisky Bridge*, 1918, RM, personifies the Earth as a peasant mother and child depicted in a highly stylised way and constructed from arcs rather in the manner of paintings by Tatlin.

*Relief, 1920, constructed of wood and metal elements pinned to a board, reveals the influence of both Tatlin and Malevich. This construction of diverse materials still carries traces of Suprematist composition in its organisation of geometric forms (see p.253). He has evolved a synthesis of styles comparable in certain respects to those of Klyun, Puni and others.

**Still-life with Saw*, 1920, Lazo Collection, Leningrad, sets the elements of a saw against textured pale ochre paint and a panel of wood. These objects are presented with a simplicity worthy of Puni or even Shterenberg.

**Peasant, You Have Been Given Your Land*, c.1920, is a poster for the Rosta Agency which employs the crudeness of a popular *lubok* print but a sophisticated eye in its organisation. This is Primitivism appealing directly to the man in the street.

Book design Cover for *Russian Placards. Placard Russe 1917-1922*, Petersburg, 1923.

Lit *V.Lebedev Album*, Leningrad, 1928. V.N.Petrov *V.V.Lebedev*, Leningrad, 1972. *V.V.Lebedev*, album, Leningrad, 1974. *Paris-Moscou*, 1979. David Elliott, V.Dudakov *100 Years of Russian Art*, London, 1989. N.Lobanov-Rostovsky *Revolutionary Ceramics*, London, 1990. A.M.Muratov, V.Manin et al. *Zhivopis' 20-30kh godov*, Sankt-Peterburg, 1991. S.Compton *Russian Avant-Garde Books 1917-34*, London, 1992. *L'Avant-garde russe 1905-1925*, exh. cat., Musée des Beaux-Arts, Nantes, 1993.

Coll RM; Tula Art Museum; Yaroslav Art Museum.
Colour plates p.253.

LEBEDEV-SHUYSKY, Anatoli Adrianovich　　**1896-1978**
Painter, graphic artist. Born at Shuya. Studied under Korin in Moscow. Exhibited from 1921. He died in Moscow.
Lit E.Weiss *Russische Avant-Garde, 1910-1930, Sammlung Ludwig, Köln*, Munich, 1986.
Coll Sammlung Ludwig, Cologne.

LEBEDEVA, E. E.　　　　　**a.1928**
Textile designer. She contributed to the First Art Exhibition of Soviet Textiles in Moscow in 1928.

LEBEDEVA, Mariya Vasilievna　　　　　**1895-1942**
Painter, decorative artist, graphic and ceramics designer. In 1917 she was studying at the school of the Society for the

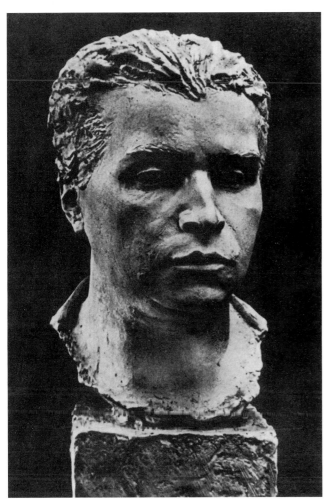

Sarra Lebedeva. The Sculptor Vera Mukhina, *1939. Plaster. 41 x 25 x 30 cm.*
Like Mukhina, Sarra Lebedeva showed great facility as an academic sculptor. Her portraits are powerful studies of the personality of her subjects, but again like Mukhina she was also well aware of experimental art. This is a tribute from one important female sculptor to another.

Encouragement of the Arts. She toured North Russia with A.Shchekotinskaya-Pototskaya who later married Ivan Bilibin. She executed designs for the State Porcelain Factory 1919-23. She was included in the enormous survey Exhibition of Paintings by Petrograd Artists of All Tendencies 1919-1923 held in Petrograd in 1923. She taught applied art in Vitebsk 1924-7. She was represented at the International Exhibition in Paris in 1925 and contributed to exhibitions in Vienna and in Berlin in 1930. She was represented at the jubilee exhibition Artists of the RSFSR over 15 Years held at the Russian Museum, Leningrad, in 1932.
She taught at the Art Institute in Minsk 1933-6 and made designs for the State Porcelain factory again 1934-40.
Who Does Not Work Shall not Eat, 1920, is a characteristically ironic inscription on one of her ceramic decorations. *The International*, 1920, is a large dish decorated with a spectacular view of buildings rising to the centre. On the rim are well over a hundred marching figures. She was represented in the exhibition of Russian Graphic Art in Riga in 1929.
Lit *Paris-Moscou*, 1979. N.Lobanov-Rostovsky *Revolutionary Ceramics*, London, 1990.

LEBEDEVA, Sarra Dmitrievna (née DARMOLATOVA) 1892-1967

Portrait and figure sculptor. She was prolific, individual and accomplished. Born in St. Petersburg into a wealthy family and educated privately. After studying at the School of the Society for the Encouragement of the Arts in St. Petersburg, she attended Mikhail Bernshtein's school in St. Petersburg in 1910. She became a sculptor in 1912 and studied under L.Shervud 1912-14. She also travelled to France, Germany, Austria and Italy. She designed masks and reliefs for the Yusupov Palace in 1914 working under V.V.Kuznetsov first as his pupil and then as his assistant. She married the graphic artist Vladimir Lebedev in 1915. She became primarily a portrait and figure sculptor.
After the Revolution she taught at the Free Art Studios (SVOMAS) in Petrograd 1918-20 and knew Tatlin, Malevich, Al'tman and others. She designed a silver rouble piece featuring an anvil and tools in 1918 and responded immediately to Lenin's call for Monumental Propaganda by producing monuments to *Danton, Herzen* and *Robespierre*. She taught at the Stieglitz Institute, Petrograd 1919-20 and exhibited with the Union of New Tendencies in Art in Petrograd in June 1922. She worked in ceramics in the early 1920s as well as in the theatre and was represented at the exhibition of Studies for Theatre Decoration and Works from the Studios of the Decorative Institute held in Petrograd in 1922.
She moved to Moscow but also visited London in 1925. Many portraits followed, including the *Portrait of F.E.Dzerzhinsky* of 1925. In 1926 she was a member of the Society of Russian Sculptors (ORS) and exhibited with them in 1926, 1929 and 1931. She was included in the major exhibition in Moscow in 1927 marking the tenth anniversary of the Revolution and in the 1928 exhibition of Acquisitions by the State Art Collections Fund held in Moscow. She visited Paris and Berlin in 1928 and exhibited at the Venice Biennale. She was represented at the jubilee exhibition Artists of the RSFSR over 15 Years held at the Russian Museum, Leningrad, in 1932 and at the 1932 Venice Biennale.
She was included in the exhibitions Artists of the RSFSR over 15 Years in Moscow in 1933 and Fifteen Years of the Workers' and Peasants' Red Army in 1933-4 in Moscow, Leningrad, Kiev and Kharkov. She exhibited with A.E.Zelensky, G.I.Kepinov, Vera Mukhina, Ilya Slonim, Vladimir Favorsky, I.G.Frikh-Khar and I.M.Chaykov in Moscow in 1935. She also executed ceramic ware 1934-6 for the Konakovsky Factory. Her portrait busts include the pilot *V.P.Chkalov* in 1936-37, RM, the sculptress *Vera Mukhina* in 1939, and the poet *A.T.Tvardovsky* in 1950.
She was accorded a personal exhibition at the State Museum of Western Art in Moscow in 1941 and made an Honoured Art Worker of the RSFSR in 1945. She exhibited in Moscow together with S.V.Gerasimov, A.A.Deineka, P.P.Konchalovsky, Vera Mukhina and D.A.Shmarinov in 1943. She became a close friend of Tatlin and donated a substantial collection of his papers and works to the Central State Archive of Art and Literature in the 1960s. She died in Moscow. A memorial exhibition was held at the Tretyakov Gallery in Moscow and at the Russian Museum in Leningrad in 1969.
Robespierre, 1920, is a low relief profile head of the French Revolutionary leader, chosen for the revolutionary parallel. Dramatically simplified, the bewigged profile has a decisive

Isaak Levitan. Copse by a Lake: Autumn, *c.1898. Oil on paper. 11.1 x 15.1 cm. Ashmolean Museum, Oxford.*

brow, sharp nose and thin firm lips. This stops just short of caricature in order to promote a rhetorical public image.
Lit B.Ternovets *S.Lebedeva*, Moscow-Leningrad, 1940. *S.Lebedeva Album*, Moscow, 1960. *S.Lebedeva*, exh. cat., Moscow, 1969. *S.Lebedeva Album*, Moscow, 1973. I.Slonim *S.Lebedeva*, Moscow, 1973. *A.V.Kuprin, S.D.Lebedeva, N.P.Ulyanov*, exh. cat., Moscow, 1978. *Paris-Moscou*, 1979. M.N.Yablonskaya *Women Artists of Russia's New Age*, London, 1990.
Coll RM.

LEBEDEVA, Tatiana Aleksandrovna   **1906-1982**
Painter, graphic artist. She was represented in the First Touring Exhibition of Paintings and Graphics which opened in Moscow in 1929. She was a member of the Society of Easel Painters (OST). She died in Moscow.

LEBLAN, Mikhail Varfolomeevich   **1875-1940**
Painter. His pupils included Stepanova c.1916.
After the Revolution he exhibited with the Knave of Diamonds in Moscow in November 1917, at the First Exhibition of Works of the Professional Union of Artists in Moscow in 1918 and at the First Exhibition of the Moscow Contemporary Art Store in January 1919. His name appeared on the April 1919 list of artists for acquisitions by the envisaged Museum of Painterly Culture.
He was subsequently represented in the Fourth State

Exhibition of Paintings (*IV Gosudarstvennaya vystavka kartin*) in Moscow in 1919, at the Third Exhibition of Paintings held at Ryazan in 1919 and at the enormous First State Exhibition of Art and Science, which included ethnographic material, held in Kazan in 1920. He showed work at the First Russian Art Exhibition in Berlin in 1922 and at the 1928 exhibition of Acquisitions by the State Art Collections Fund held in Moscow. He exhibited with the *Zhar-tsvet* (Fire-colour) group between 1924 and 1928. He was represented in the First Touring Exhibition of Paintings and Graphics which opened in Moscow in 1929 and at the jubilee exhibition Artists of the RSFSR over 15 Years held at the Russian Museum, Leningrad, in 1932.
Coll TG.

LE-DANT'YU (LEDENTU), Mikhail Vasil'evich 1891-1917
Painter. Born in the Tver' region. In 1907 he completed a course at the Theatre Institute and also private courses in St. Petersburg. He enrolled at the Academy in St. Petersburg in 1908. By 1910 he was a friend of Malevich, Tatlin, the Zdanevich brothers and Larionov and subsequently became a figure within the development of Russian Futurism. He was active as an organiser in the Union of Youth in 1911, particularly with regard to its theatrical initiatives. He was a member of the Moscow group *Oslinyy Khvost* (Donkey's Tail)

along with Larionov and Goncharova in 1912.

He lived in the Caucasus 1912-13 where in 1912 he visited Tiflis (Tblisi) in Georgia and with Kirill Zdanevich discovered the Georgian Primitive painter Niko Pirosmanashvili there. Pirosmanashvili was to play a role for the Russian Futurists not unlike that played by Le Douanier Rousseau for the Cubists in Paris. Le-Dant'yu contributed to Larionov's exhibition The Target in Moscow in 1913 and to the exhibition No.4 in Moscow in 1914. He was amongst the painters who responded to the Rayism of Larionov. He was mobilised in 1915 and was killed at the front in 1917.

After the Revolution his name appeared on the April 1919 list of artists for acquisitions by the envisaged Museum of Painterly Culture. He was represented along with Kandinsky, Chagall and others at the First State Exhibition of Paintings by Local and Moscow Artists held in Vitebsk in December 1919. He was also represented at the First Russian Art Exhibition in Berlin in 1922.

Lit Il'yazd *Le-Dantyu Faram* (Le-Dantyu as a Beacon), Paris, 1923. *Iliazd*, exh. cat., text by L.Barnier and F.Chapou, MNAM, Paris, 1978. *Paris-Moscou*, 1979. *L'Avant-garde russe 1905-1925*, exh. cat., Musée des Beaux-Arts, Nantes, 1993.
Coll Kazan Art Museum; Samara Art Museum; Yaroslavl' Art Museum.

LEDENTU = LE-DANTYU, M.V.

LEDYAEV, N. M. a.1921
He exhibited with Kudryashov and others at the First State Exhibition in Orenburg in 1921.

LEF
The abbreviated name of the Journal of the Left Front of the Arts (*Zhurnal Levogo Front Iskusstv*).

LEGASHOV, Anton Mikhailovich 1798-1865
Painter of landscapes and portraits. He was painting in China in 1863. He died in St. Petersburg.
Coll TG.

Isaak Levitan. Mountain Landscape, *before 1900. Oil on paper mounted on canvas. Signed in cyrillic script 'I.Levitan'. 13.5 x 19 cm. Malmö Konstmuseum.*

LEHMANN, G. = LEMAN, Yu. Ya.

LEIFERT, L. A.   a.1918
Painter. He was engaged on Agitprop decorations on
Nikolaevsky Bridge Square, Petrograd, in 1918.

LEMAN, Yuri Yakovlevich   1834-1901
Figure painter. He signed his work 'G.Lehmann'.
Coll TG.

LEMOKH, Kirill Vikentevich   1841-1910
Figure painter, watercolourist, etcher. Born in Moscow. He
studied at the Academy in St. Petersburg but became a
member of the Artel which led to the foundation of the
Wanderers. His themes included the peasantry and also
portrait etchings. He became a member of the Academy in
1893 and a member of its Council in 1895.
Coll TG; RM; Saratov Art Museum.

LENEVA, Evgenia   b.1898
Painter, graphic artist, ceramics artist. Born in the
Chernygovsk region. She studied until 1928 at the Vkhutein
in Moscow under Robert Fal'k and made designs for the
Dulevo Porcelain Factory 1930-1. Her plate *The Turksib is
Ready*, 1930, marked the completion of the Turksib railway
and was calligraphic, orientalising and elegant in style.
Lit *Paris-Moscou*, 1979.

LENTULOV, Aristarkh Vasil'evich   1882-1943
Painter and theatre designer who evolved a dynamic, robust
and immensely colourful style out of his knowledge of the
faceted planes of Cubist painting.
Born at Nizhnee Lomovo in the Penza region, the son of an
Orthodox priest. He studied at the Penza Church Institute
and seminary 1889-98. In 1898 he entered the new Seliverstov
Drawing Institute at Penza until 1900. He then moved to Kiev
and enrolled at the Kiev School of Art where he studied under
V.K.Menk, M.K.Pimonenko and N.F.Seleznev until 1905
when he returned to the Penza Art Institute studying under
A.F.Afanas'ev.
He moved to St. Petersburg in 1906 where he studied
privately under D.N.Kardovsky 1906-7. He met Kul'bin in
1907 and was drawn into increasingly adventurous and
experimental work. He contributed to the exhibitions *Stefanos*
(Stephanos) in 1907-8 in Moscow, *Zveno* (The Link) in Kiev
in 1908 and *Venok* (The Wreath) in St. Petersburg in 1909.
Also in 1908 he had shown work at Kul'bin's Contemporary
Trends exhibition in St. Petersburg which he helped to
organise along with David Burlyuk. He travelled in the
Caucasus and the Crimea in the summer months of 1908-10.
He exhibited with the Izdebsky International Salons 1909-11
in Odessa and with the Union of Russian Artists in 1910.
He moved to Moscow where he met Petr Konchalovsky and
Ilya Mashkov in 1910. He was a founder member of the Knave
of Diamonds exhibition society with Larionov and
Goncharova in 1910 and exhibited with the Knave of
Diamonds in Moscow 1910-12 as well as the Moscow Salon of
1911. He saw work by Le Fauconnier and Gleizes at the 1910
Knave of Diamonds exhibition. He was invited to assist
Yakulov in decorating the Hunt Club in 1911.
He was painting in Paris 1911-12 whilst studying at the
Académie La Palette under the Cubists Le Fauconnier,
Gleizes and Metzinger from autumn 1911 and he exhibited

with Delaunay's circle 1912-13. He also saw the Italian
Futurist Exhibition in Paris in 1912. At Konchalovsky's
suggestion he invited French painters to exhibit with the
Knave of Diamonds in Moscow. He returned to Moscow via
Italy, Vienna and Zürich.
He took part in a debate on contemporary art with Mashkov,
Tatlin and others at the Polytechnic Museum under the
auspices of the Knave of Diamonds in 1913. He worked for
the Modern Lubok publishers in 1914 and contributed to
exhibitions in aid of the War. He contributed to the exhibition
Leftist Trends in Petrograd and the Exhibition of Painting:
The Year 1915 in Moscow in 1915. Together with Exter he
decorated the foyer and other parts of the Kamerny Theatre,
Moscow, in 1916. He also designed covers for music by
Nicolas Roslawetz in 1916.
After the Revolution he exhibited with the World of Art in
December 1917 in Moscow. He worked on the decoration of
the Café Pittoresque in Moscow together with Tatlin,
Yakulov, Rodchenko and others, on the decoration of the
Poets' Café in Moscow together with Mayakovsky, Kamensky
and others, and on street decorations in Moscow marking May
Day. He exhibited at the Fifth State Exhibition: From
Impressionism to Non-Objective Art in Moscow 1918-19. For
the first anniversary of the Revolution he designed a backdrop
for a production of Skryabin's *Prometheus*.
His style was described as 'neo-impressionist' when he taught
at the Free Art Studios (SVOMAS) in Moscow c.1919-20. He
exhibited in the first Obmokhu exhibition in May 1919 in
Moscow. His name appeared on the April 1919 list of artists
for acquisitions by the envisaged Museum of Painterly Culture
and his work was amongst the new acquisitions of the
Tretyakov Gallery exhibited in 1919. He was represented
along with Kandinsky, Chagall and others at the First State
Exhibition of Paintings by Local and Moscow Artists held in
Vitebsk in December 1919, at the Third Exhibition of
Paintings held at Ryazan in 1919 and at the enormous First
State Exhibition of Art and Science, which included
ethnographic material, held in Kazan in 1920.
He was elected to the central committee of the Institute of
Artistic Culture (INKhUK) in 1920 and he taught at the
Vkhutemas/Vkhutein from 1920 for many years. He took part
in the third exhibition of *Obmokhu*, the Society of Young
Artists, in Moscow in May 1921, along with Ioganson,
Medunetsky and others but he also exhibited in the 1921 with
the World of Art in Moscow. He was represented at the First
Russian Art Exhibition in Berlin in 1922 and he attained a
Grand Prix for his 1919 designs for Rubinshtein's opera *The
Demon* when these were exhibited at the Paris International
Exhibition in 1925. He also exhibited at the Venice Biennale
in 1924 and the Russian art exhibition in New York that year.
He was a founder member of the Society of Moscow Artists
1925-6 and contributed to the Third Exhibition of Paintings
by Artists from Kaluga and Moscow held in Kaluga in 1925.
He also exhibited with AKhRR 1926-7. He was included in
the major exhibition in Moscow in 1927 marking the tenth
anniversary of the Revolution and in the 1928 exhibition of
Acquisitions by the State Art Collections Fund held in
Moscow. He was represented in the First Touring Exhibition
of Paintings and Graphics which opened in Moscow in 1929.
He was president of the Society of Moscow Artists in 1929-32
and was represented at the jubilee exhibition Artists of the

Aristarkh Lentulov. Stage Design for Stravinsky's 'Fire Bird': a Fairground Scene in Front of a Domed Church, *1919.*
Watercolour on pencil. Signed on reverse 'Moscow 1919'. 28.6 x 22.2 cm.
Private collection, Moscow.

RSFSR over 15 Years held at the Russian Museum, Leningrad, in 1932.

He had a one-man exhibition of 254 works in Moscow in 1933. He returned to theatre design in 1934. He was given a one-man exhibition in Moscow in 1940. He continued to teach until 1943. He died in Moscow.

He featured as the subject of a major display at the 1988 Venice Biennale.

*Landscape Kislovodsk, 1913, TG, is vigorous and colourful in a way reminiscent of Delaunay and Kandinsky. He had great facility, using colour at full strength and stylising form into a dramatic mosaic effect frequently depicting citadels on hill tops or cities rising up the canvas. *St. Basil's*, 1913, TG, is a further example of this exuberance.

The Firmament, Decorative Moscow, 1915, Yaroslavl Art Museum, is a typically dynamic and colourful work, at once both spectacular and grandiose. Moscow is depicted as a mass of onion-domed churches rearing up the canvas like faceted and polychrome growths, curving and sprouting with a splintered Cubist energy. Lentulov's theatricality is evident but so too is his effortless monumentality. It is a kaleidoscopic vision of the city of churches through which the eye wanders to discern rising towers and striated domes at almost every point. Moscow, the spiritual centre is celebrated with a decorative flair that occasionally recalls Kandinsky's religious imagery of a few years earlier but without his further step into the indefinable image. Here all is visible and recognisable, animated by brilliant colour and inconsistent perspective.

Near the Church of the Virgin of Chernygov, 1919-20, is closer in its brown and green planes to the work of Robert Fal'k. The dominant colours are kept distinct and separate whilst the handling of planes of colour pays homage to the language of Cézanne and Cubism but adopted more as a style than as a means of experimental investigation.

Theatre design 1914 designs for Mayakovsky's *V.V.Mayakovsky, a Tragedy* for the Evreinov Theatre, Moscow (unrealised).

1916 October: Shakespeare's *Merry Wives of Windsor* produced at the Kamerny (Chamber) Theatre in Moscow by A.Tairov and A.Zonov.

1918 backdrop for A.N.Skryabin's *Prometheus* produced at the Bolshoi Theatre as part of the celebrations of the first anniversary of the Revolution. This production was an experiment in the synthesis of colour and sound; it employed colour by means of projectors.

1918 March: A.Blok's *Neznakomka* (The Unknown Lady) produced by Vsevolod Meyerhold, Samuil Vermel and Georgiy Krol at the Café Pittoresque, Moscow.

1918-19 Offenbach's *Tales of Hoffmann* produced by F.F.Komissarzhevsky at the Studio of the Art and Education Union of Workers' Organisations in Moscow, a suggestive and colourful design of interslotted planes and decorative motifs.

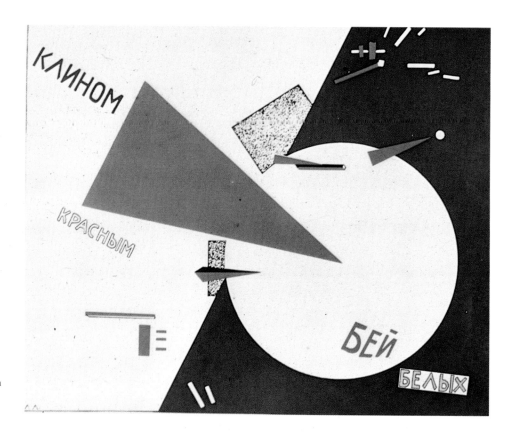

El Lissitzky. Beat the Whites with
the Red Wedge, *1919. Poster.*
Colour lithograph.

1919 April: A.G.Rubinstein's opera of Lermontov's *The Demon* directed by A.Tairov at the Theatre of the Moscow Soviet of Workers' and Peasants' Deputies (State Experimental Theatre).

1919-20 Stravinsky's *Firebird* (unrealised).

After 1917 he also designed a production of Triodin's *Stepan Razin.*

Futurist books D.Burlyuk, S.Vermel' *Vesennee kontragentsvo muz* (The Vernal Forwarding Agency of the Muses), with illustrations by V. and D.Burlyuk and A.Lentulov, Moscow, 1915.

D.Burlyuk, G.Zolotukhin, V.Kamensky, V.Khlebnikov *Chetyre ptitsi* (Four Birds), with illustrations by A.Lentulov and G.Zolotukhin, Moscow, 1916.

V.Khlebnikov et al. *Moskovskie mastera: zhurnal iskusstv* (Moscow Masters: art journal), with illustrations by A.Lentulov and others, Moscow, 1916.

Cover for A.Bely et al. *Yav'. Stikhi* (Reality. Verses), Moscow, 1919.

Lit *A.V.Lentulov*, exh. cat., Moscow, 1933. *A.V.Lentulov* exh. cat., Moscow, 1968. M.A.Lentulova *Khudozhnik A.Lentulov, vospominaniya*, Moscow, 1969. S.P.Compton *The World Backwards, Russian Futurist Books 1912-16*, London, 1978. A.Z.Rudenstine *Costakis Collection*, London, 1981. J.E.Bowlt *Russian Stage Design. Scenic Innovation. From the Collection of Mr. and Mrs. Nikita D.Lobanov-Rostovsky*, Jackson, MS, exh. cat.,1982. *Seven Moscow Artists 1910-30*, exh. cat., Galerie Gmurzynska, Cologne, 1984. *Aristarkh Lentulov*, exh. cat., Moscow, 1987. E.Murina *Aristarkh Lentulov*, Milan, 1988. *Aristarkh Lentulov*, exh. cat., Osterreichische Galerie, Vienna, 1988. E.Murina, S.Dzhafarova *Aristarkh Lentulov*, Moscow, 1990. Nancy Van Norman Baer *Theatre in Revolution, Russian Avant-Garde Stage Design 1913-1935*, San Francisco and London, 1991. Dzhon Boult (John Bowlt) *Khudozhniki russkogo teatra. Sobranie Nikity i Niny Lobanovykh-Rostovskikh*, Moscow, 1991. S.Compton *Russian Avant-Garde Books 1917-34*, London, 1992. *L'Avant-garde russe 1905-1925*, exh. cat., Musée des Beaux-Arts, Nantes, 1993.

Coll TG; RM; Bakhrushin Theatre Museum, Moscow; Astrakhan Art Museum; Dagestan Art Museum, Makhachkala; Kaluga Art Museum; Samara Art Museum; Saratov Art Museum; Simbirsk Art Museum; Tomsk Art Museum; Vladivostok Art Museum; Costakis Collection.

LEO, Aleksandr Nikolaevich   1868-1925+
Graphic artist. Born in Moscow. He worked in Leningrad producing illustrations and ex-libris in particular. He was represented at the Paris International Exhibition of 1925.

LEPORSKAYA, Anna Aleksandrovna   1900-1982
Painter. She was a member of the *Unovis* collective founded in 1919 and formed around Malevich and Lissitzky in Vitebsk. With others of this circle she followed Malevich to Petrograd/Leningrad when he moved there to work at the State Institute of Artistic Culture (GINKhUK). She was there with Malevich, Ermolaeva, L.Yudin and others in 1925.
*Woman of Pskov, c.1930, RM, recalls late Malevich figures in its frontal pose, central placing and anonymity.
Coll RM.

LERMONTOVA, Nadezhda Vladimirovna   1885-1921
Painter, theatre designer. Born at St. Petersburg. She studied at the Zvantseva School there 1907-10 and exhibited with the Union of Youth 1912-13. She worked with Petrov-Vodkin on paintings at Ovruch in the Ukraine. She died in Petrograd.
Lit *Twilight of the Tsars*, London, 1991.
Coll RM.

LEVASHKOVA, K.E.   a.1918-1919
Painter. She exhibited at the First Exhibition of Works of the Professional Union of Artists in Moscow in 1918 and at the juryless Eighth State Exhibition in Moscow in 1919.

LEVASHOVA, N. N.   a.1917
She exhibited with the World of Art in December 1917 in Moscow.

LEVCHENKO, Petr Alekseevich   1859-1917
Ukrainian painter of cityscapes and rural scenes. He was painting winter landscapes of cottages in the snow in 1903 and landscapes of summer's plenitude. He was painting in Kiev 1909-10.
Silence. Winter in the Village, 1903, Museum of Ukrainian Art, Kiev, has a pony and trap passing through the snowy village
Coll TG; Museum of Ukrainian Art, Kiev.

LEVIN, Aleksei   1893-1965
Graphic artist. Born at Sebastopol. He studied at the Odessa School of Art between 1904 and 1915 and at the Moscow College 1915-18. After the Revolution he designed propaganda posters for shop windows for the Rosta Agency as well as illustrations and decorative work. He began to exhibit in 1928 and was represented at the Cologne Typographic Exhibition that year. He died in Moscow.
Lit *Paris-Moscou*, 1979.

LEVIN, Moisei Zeligovich   1896-1946
Theatre designer. An M.Levin was represented at the Paris International Exhibition of 1925.
Theatre design 1934 May V.M.Kirshon's *Chudesnyy splav* (The Wonderful Alloy) at the Moscow Art Theatre.
Lit Dzhon Boult (John Bowlt) *Khudozhniki russkogo teatra. Sobranie Nikity i Niny Lobanovykh-Rostovskikh*, Moscow, 1991.

LEVITAN, Adol'f (Avel') Ilych   1859-1933
Portraitist.
Coll TG.

LEVITAN, Isaak Ilych   1860-1900
Perhaps the most important landscape painter in late 19th century Russia. His atmospheric depiction extended the identification of landscape and a sense of national identity from the vigour of the Wanderers into the increased sophistication of the thoroughly international art of early 20th century Russia.
Born at Kibartai, Lithuania, the son of a minor railway official. He settled in Moscow in the early 1870s. He studied at the Moscow College under A.K.Savrasov and V.D.Polenov from 1873. He exhibited with the Wanderers from 1884 and became a member in 1891. In 1885 he met the writer Chekhov.
In 1890 and 1894 he visited Italy. From 1897 he exhibited with the Munich Secession and he was again in Italy that year. He directed the landscape painting studio at the Moscow College from 1898 where his pupils included P.I.Petrovichev and N.N.Sapunov. He was made a member of the Academy of Arts. He became closely involved in the World of Art with whom he exhibited 1898-1900 and he was included in Diaghilev's 1898 Exhibition of Russian and Finnish Artists. He exhibited with the World of Art in St. Petersburg in 1900. He associated with Benois, Nesterov and Serov and collaborated on Mamontov's private opera productions in Moscow. He exhibited at the International Exhibition in Paris in 1900. He died in Moscow.
March, 1895, TG, is clearly the inspiration for the snowscapes of Grabar'. A yellow-painted wooden house and porch among trees forms a backdrop for the blue and white light of the snow. Other thin birches, one with a bird-box, rise in lemon yellow clumps into the frail but clear sunlight. There is a muddy path and a horse and sled in the middle distance. This is a characteriscally accurate, atmospheric and impressive painting.
Writings I.I.Levitan *Pis'ma, dokumenty, vospominaniya*, Moscow, 1956.
Lit S.Glagol, I.Grabar *Levitan*, Moscow, 1912. V.Prytkov *Levitan*, Moscow, 1960. *Levitan*, exh. cat., Moscow, Leningrad, Kiev, 1960. B.V.Ioganson *I.I.Levitan*, 1963. A.Fedorov-Davvydov *I.I.Levitan: zhizn' i tvorchestvo*, vols. 1 and 2, Moscow, 1966.
Coll Many works are preserved in TG; RM; Ashmolean Museum, Oxford.
Colour plates pp.256, 257.

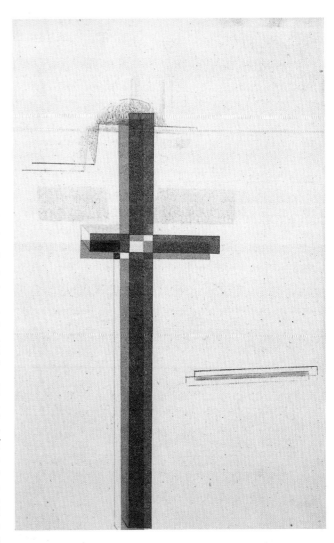

El Lissitzky. Proun Study, *c.1920. Crayon, pencil and lithograph on paper. 25.5 x 16 cm.*
Private collection, courtesy Annely Juda Fine Art, London.

Dmitri Levitsky. A.F.Labsin, *1790. Oil on canvas.*

LEVITIN, Anatoly Pavlovich   **1922-1957+**
Painter. Born in Petrograd. He studied under Ioganson in Leningrad and became an exponent of Socialist Realist painting. He exhibited in Brussels in 1958 and in London in 1959.

LEVITON, Rebekka   **1906-1987**
Theatre designer. Born at Kharkov. She was associated with Pavel Filonov's group, the Collective of Masters of Analytical Art, and with Artur Liandsberg she produced designs for Gogol's *The Government Inspector*, directed by I.Terent'ev at the Theatre of the Press House, Leningrad, in 1927. One design, essentially a painting in itself, is heavily indebted to the cellular and compartmentalised compositions evolved by Filonov. She died at Leningrad.
Lit Nancy Van Norman Baer *Theatre in Revolution, Russian Avant-Garde Stage Design 1913-1935*, San Francisco and London, 1991.
Coll Bakhrushin Theatre Museum, Moscow.

LEVITSKAYA, Galina Petrovna   **1926-1951+**
Sculptress of patriotic genre. She was working with M.A.Delov in 1951.

LEVITSKY, Dmitri Grigor'evich   **1735-1822**
A major painter of elegant genre and portraiture in the late 18th century. His style was in many ways overtly French in inspiration and recalls aspects of Boucher and Watteau, although it has a firmness of modelling that is distinctly his own. He shared the French love of fine materials meticulously painted. Born in the Ukraine where he grew up. His father was a priest who worked as an engraver in Kiev. He studied under the painter Antropov with whom he moved to St. Petersburg in 1756.
He became an associate of the Academy in 1769. At the first

exhibition of the reorganised Academy he became famous at once with his *Portrait of the Architect Kokorinov*, 1770. The double *Portrait of Khovanskaya and Khrushcheva*, RM, is reminiscent of Watteau in particular. Against a background of a soft idyllic landscape stand the smiling female figures playing a scene of courtship, their clothes elegant and the mood pervaded by an atmosphere of gilded, playful dalliance. He had a reputation outside of Russia and Diderot was amongst his sitters. A full-length portrait of *Catherine II* is in the Tretyakov Gallery in Moscow. Levitsky effectively marked the point at which the Russian full-length portrait came into its own in a form that was elegant, playful sometimes, but also formal with a rich description of materials and expression. He retired from the Academy in 1788, but returned in 1808. He died blind in St. Petersburg.
Coll Well represented in TG; RM; Louvre, Paris; Musée Jacquemart-André, Paris.

LEVITSKY, Vladimir   **late 19th century**
Graphic artist. He studied at the Tenisheva School in St. Petersburg. A Levitsky exhibited with the Union of Russian Artists in 1909.

LEVKIEVSKY, Vyacheslav V.   **a.1913-1914**
Painter. He was amongst the painters who responded to the Rayism of Larionov. He contributed to Larionov's exhibition The Target in Moscow in 1913 and to the exhibition No.4 in Moscow in 1914.

LIANDSBERG, Artur   **1905-1963**
Theatre designer. Born at Velikie Luki. He was, like Rebekka Leviton, associated with Pavel Filonov's group, the Collective of Masters of Analytical Art. They both worked on I.Terent'ev's production of Gogol's *The Government Inspector* at the Theatre of the Press House, Leningrad, in 1927. He died at Leningrad.
Lit Nancy Van Norman Baer *Theatre in Revolution, Russian Avant-Garde Stage Design 1913-1935*, San Francisco and London, 1991.
Coll Theatre Museum, St. Petersburg.

LIBAKOV, L.   **a.1919**
He was represented along with Kandinsky, Chagall and others at the First State Exhibition of Paintings by Local and Moscow Artists held in Vitebsk in December 1919.

LIBAKOV, Mikhail Vadimovich   **1889-1953**
Theatre designer. An M.Libakov was represented at the Paris International Exhibition of 1925.
Lit Dzhon Boult (John Bowlt) *Khudozhniki russkogo teatra. Sobranie Nikity i Niny Lobanovykh-Rostovskikh*, Moscow, 1991.

LIGOSCY = LIGOTSKY, I.

LIGOTSKY, Ivan (Iogann)   **a.1752-1759**
Portrait painter. He made decorative paintings for Peterhof and for the Winter Palace in St. Petersburg 1753-9. He signed his work 'Ligoscy'.
Coll TG.

LILOVAYA, T.   **a.c.1927**
Sculptor. She was included in the major exhibition in Moscow in 1927 marking the tenth anniversary of the Revolution.

LIPCHITZ, Jacques   **1891-1973**
Sculptor and a major figure in the development of Cubist

Dmitri Levitsky. Empress Catherine II. *Oil on canvas. 110 x 76.8 cm. Smithsonian Institution, Washington D.C.*

sculpture in Paris. Born at Druskieniki, Lithuania. He settled in Paris in 1909, exhibited at the Salon des Indépendants in 1911, and in 1912 he lived next door to Brancusi. He gained increased recognition through the Léonce Rosenberg Gallery in Paris where he exhibited in 1920, and through Albert Barnes who purchased works for the Barnes Foundation in Philadelphia in 1922.

His *Prometheus* was commissioned for the International Exhibition in Paris in 1937. He fled from the German occupation of Paris in 1940, arriving in New York in 1941. Numerous commissions followed in the post-war years. He revisited Paris for his exhibition at the Galerie Maeght in 1946. However he settled at Hastings on Hudson near New York. He was given retrospective exhibitions at the Museum of Modern Art, New York, in 1954, and at the Metropolitan Museum, New York, in 1972. He died at Capri.

Writings J.Lipchitz *My Life in Sculpture*, 1972.

Lit H.H.Aranson *Jacques Lipchitz. Sketches in Bronze*, 1969,

Konstantin Lomikin. Troitskaya Cathedral, *1962. Oil on canvas. 88.9 x 63.1 cm.*
Roy Miles Gallery, London.

D.A.Stott *Jacques Lipchitz and Cubism*, 1975. N.Barbier *Lipchitz. Oeuvres de Jacques Lipchitz (1891-1973) dans la collection du Musée National d'Art Moderne*, Paris, 1978.
Coll MNAM, Paris; Kröller-Müller Museum, Otterlo; Arizona Museum of Art, Tucson.

LIPHART, Baron Ernest Friedrich von (LIPGART, Ernest Karlovich) 1847-1932/34
German history painter, draughtsman, graphic artist. Born at Ratshof. He travelled to Paris, Spain and Florence as well as Russia. He produced mythological works as well as copies after old masters. He published a series of etchings through Cadart in Paris.
Coll TG; RM.

LIPIN, Il'ya Ivanovich early 19th century
Coll TG.

LISENKO, A.V. a.c.1919
His name appeared on the April 1919 list of artists for acquisitions by the envisaged Museum of Painterly Culture.

LISHEV, Vsevolod Vsevolodovich 1877-1947+
Sculptor. He was included in the major exhibition in Moscow in 1927 marking the tenth anniversary of the Revolution. He was represented at the jubilee exhibition Artists of the RSFSR over 15 Years held at the Russian Museum, Leningrad, in 1932.
His works include the *Monument to N.G.Chernyshevsky*, 1947, erected in Leningrad.

LISSIM, Simon (Semen Mikhailovich) 1900-1981
Theatre designer, painter, ceramics artist. Born at Kiev. He studied under Aleksandr Monko in 1917. He also worked at the Kiev Repertory Theatre and met Exter and Rabinovich. He was associated stylistically perhaps with the World of Art tradition.
After the Revolution he travelled through Bulgaria, Yugoslavia, Austria and Germany to France to settle in Paris in 1921 where he worked with Leon Bakst. He was a vital force behind the lavish periodical *Zharptitsa* (Firebird) in the period 1921-6. He exhibited at the Salon des Artistes Décorateurs, the Salon des Indépendants and the Salon d'Automne as well as the Paris International Exhibition of 1925. He held a one-man exhibition at the Galerie Charpentier in 1926.
In 1935 he visited the United States and held a one-man exhibition at the Wildenstein Gallery, New York, in 1936.
He saw military service in the French Army 1939-41 but then emigrated to the United States in 1941. He settled at Dobb's Ferry, New York. He died at Naples, Florida, USA.
Theatre design 1923 Maurice Maeterlinck's play *L'Oiseau Bleu* at the Théâtre de l'Oeuvre, Paris.
1924 Rimsky-Korsakov's opera *The Tale of Tsar Saltan* at the Gran Teatro del Liceo, Barcelona.
1933 designed a curtain for a ballet based on Brahms' Fourth Symphony for De Basil's Ballets Russes in Paris.
Lit A.Tessier *Simon Lissim*, Paris, 1928. I.Cogniat et al. *Simon Lissim*, Paris, 1933. G.Freedly *Simon Lissim*, New York, 1949. *Diaghilev and Russian Stage Designers, a Loan Exhibition from the*

Simon Lissim. Russian Boyars, *1926.*
Private collection, Paris.

КОНЧЕНО

El Lissitzky. All is Finished — Further, *1922. Colour lithograph in red and black.*
From Lissitzky's Suprematist story book 'The Story of Two Squares' which depicts chaos resolved into order by the arrival of the red square in a kind of politicised interstellar drama told through lithographs and a few words.

Collection of Mr. and Mrs. N.Lobanov-Rostovsky, International Exhibitions Foundation, Washington, 1972-4. J.E.Bowlt *Russian Stage Design. Scenic Innovation. From the Collection of Mr. and Mrs. Nikita D.Lobanov-Rostovsky*, Jackson, MS, exh. cat.,1982. Dzhon Boult (John Bowlt) *Khudozhniki russkogo teatra. Sobranie Nikity i Niny Lobanovykh-Rostovskikh*, Moscow, 1991.
Coll MNAM, Paris.

LISSITZKY, El (LISITSKY, Lazar Markovich) 1890-1941

Painter, graphic designer, architect, designer of furniture, exhibitions and books. Born at Polshchinok in the Smolensk region. He studied at the Technische Hochschule in Darmstadt in 1909. He travelled in France, Italy and Belgium 1912-13. In 1914 he studied briefly under Zadkine in Vitebsk. After graduating in 1916 from the Riga Technical University, which was situated in Moscow because of the war, he worked in the architectural studio of Boris Velikovsky in Moscow. His engineering and technical studies were complemented by great precision in graphic media and it was this which guided his increasing involvement in the visual arts.

After the Revolution he exhibited with the World of Art in December 1917 in Moscow. At first he followed his drawings of architectural monuments with drawings of a very different kind which arose from his Jewish background. He illustrated Jewish Passover stories in drawings and then lithographs. These were relatively close in style to the work and themes of Marc Chagall who was working in Vitebsk in the immediately post-Revolutionary period. Lissitzky worked for Chagall as professor of graphics and architecture at the Vitebsk art school whilst Chagall was Commissar of Art in the town. However

the arrival of Malevich at the Vitebsk art school profoundly affected Lissitzky's work. He became a convert to Suprematism and an active member of the Suprematist group *Unovis*, later *Posnovis*, there in 1919. He was represented along with Kandinsky, Chagall and others at the First State Exhibition of Paintings by Local and Moscow Artists held in Vitebsk in December 1919 and he contributed to the First Jewish Art Exhibition of Sculpture, Graphics and Drawing held in Kiev in 1920.

For Lissitzky the experience of working with Malevich was decisive. As a result he was able to bring into his work a good deal of the technical and architectural knowledge that his training had given him and combine it with his natural precision and skill as a graphic artist. The Civil War poster *Beat the Whites with the Red Wedge* (p.260) applied the dynamics of geometric painting to a specific political cause. Suprematism was a visionary and mathematical system capable of evolving a perspective for the age. Lissitzky's achievement was to apply it. The result was a deluge of inventive and rich designs in many fields from book design to posters, furniture, propaganda kiosks and even architecture.

None of his architectural plans were ever executed but they had a pervasive influence. It could be said that they were a kind of architectural seed bed which proved fruitful despite the lack of actual construction. He was evolving a system of design applicable in many fields and this constituted a proto-design language often elaborated in the absence of specific briefs and only subsequently adapted. The fundamental nature of Suprematism made this possible as it was concerned less with painting as such and more with creativity and a system of regulating and articulating space. Lissitzky explored the application of Suprematism to three dimensional space. His paintings and prints are distinguishable from those of Malevich by the way that Lissitzky extended his geometric planes into a third dimension, something which Malevich rarely indicated in his own pictorial works. Initially this involved axonometric perspective applied to the planes of his geometric compositions, but applied in a contradictory way so that the constructions that they suggested could not be built. In this he was comparable with Klucis.This synthesis of painting and construction which began in 1919-20 he called *Proun* and he defined it as the 'interchange station between art and architecture'. The language of Suprematism was enriched by the sense of construction and *Proun* exhibited features of Constructivism also.

Lissitzky lectured at the Vkhutemas in 1921 in its architectural department.

His work was shown in the First Russian Art Exhibition in Berlin in 1922 and was followed by a period of extensive travel in Western Europe during which Lissitzky established contact with many groups of avant-garde artists including Dadaists, members of the Dutch group *De Stijl* which he also joined, and artists at the Bauhaus. He became in effect a vital link between the Soviet and Western European groups. In 1922 he edited with the writer Ilya Ehrenburg the trilingual journal *Veshch*, *Objet*, *Gegenstand* in Berlin and he published his lithographic book for children *The Suprematist Story of Two Squares* in the same year. He also attended the International Congress of Progressive Artists at Düsseldorf in 1922. With Theo van Doesburg and Hans Richter he signed a manifesto *Creative Demands* in response to this Congress. In 1923 he designed Mayakovsky's book *Dlya Golosa* (For the Voice) and

El Lissitzky. Untitled, *1920s. Tempera on canvas. 73.5 x 51.5 cm.*
Private collection, courtesy Annely Juda Fine Art, London.

he published his lithographic series of costumes for the Futurist opera *Pobeda nad Sol'ntsem* (Victory Over the Sun) devised for an 'electromechanical' puppet version of the production. In 1923 he was given a one-man exhibition at the Kestner Society in Hanover. In 1925 he published a survey of contemporary art, *Die Kunstismen* (Artisms), with Hans Arp.

Perhaps his most credible architectural project of the 1920s was the *Cloud-Prop* skyscraper of 1925 which comprised an approximately L-shaped building elevated on three enormous legs. These skyscrapers were to be erected at certain points in Moscow. The plans strongly resembled the non-utilitarian *Proun* designs and revealed how readily it was adaptable to architecture and even city planning. His architectural theories were published in the book *Russia: Architecture for World*

Revolution in 1930. He was represented at the First Russian Art Exhibition in Berlin in 1922.

He was a member of the 4 Arts society which was founded in 1924. While in Germany in connection with the Press exhibition in Cologne in 1928 he visited the Weissenhoff Estate at Stuttgart where he admired the work of Le Corbusier in particular. From 1925 to 1930 he taught at the Vkhutemas/Vkhutein in Moscow. Here he produced designs for the furnishing of minimal dwellings in 1929 including folding furniture to be built into flats.

He was a prolific designer of books employing Suprematist principles to the photomontage imagery and typography. He was an organiser of the All-Union Polygraphic Exhibition in Moscow in 1927. He contributed to the exhibition of

Contemporary Russian Art held at Philadelphia in 1932. He died of tuberculosis in Moscow.

Theatre design 1927-30 architectural designs and a model set for Meyerhold's unrealised production of S.Tretyakov's play *I Want a Child* for the Meyerhold Theatre. This closely reflected the elaborate three-dimensional geometry of his trade exhibition designs. It employed a fully architectural construction of spiral ramps and elevated platforms.

Book design extensive including: K.Bolshakov *Solntse na izlete* (The Spent Sun), Moscow, 1916. Cover for the sheet music of Yurii Engel's *Vois là-bas*, Moscow, 1919, executed in Lissitzky's pre-Suprematist Jewish folk lore style in black. Cover for periodical *Epopeya* (Epopée), No.2, 1922. Ivanov-Razumnik *Mayakovsky, 'Mystery' or 'Buffo'*, Berlin (Skify), 1922. Covers for the periodical *Veshch'* (Object), Berlin, 1922. O.Forsh *Ravvi* (Rabbi), Berlin (Skify), 1922. V.Mayakovsky *Dlya golosa* (For the Voice), Berlin, 1923. Cover for I.Sel'vinsky *Zapiski poeta* (Notes of a Poet), Moscow-Leningrad, 1928. Covers for the periodical *Arkhitektura SSSR* (Architecture USSR), 1934. Cover for *Novoe litso SSSR* (New Face of the USSR) in *Socialist Industry: Heavy Industry*, 1935.

Exhibition design 1923 *Proun-Room*, a three-dimensional *Proun* construction within the six sides of a room, at the Grosse Berlin Austellung. 1926 a room at the International Art display at Dresden. 1927 *Abstract Cabinet* at the Niedersächsisches Landesmuseum in Hanover. 1928 design of the Soviet display at the Pressa Exhibition in Cologne.

Writings include *Art and Pangeometry* in Carl Einstein and Paul Westheim ed. *Europa-Almanach*, Potsdam, 1925. *Russland: Die Rekonstruktion der Architektur in der Sowjetunion* (Russia: Architecture for World Revolution), Vienna, 1930.

Lit Extensive including S.Lissitzky-Küppers *El Lissitzky*, Dresden, 1967 (London, 1968). J.Tschichold *Werke und Aufsätze von El Lissitzky (1890-1941)*, Berlin, 1971. *Lissitzky*, Museum of Modern Art, Oxford, 1977. *El Lissitzky: Maler, Architekt, Typograf, Fotograf*, exh. cat., Staatliche Galerie Moritzburg, Leipzig, 1982. J.E.Bowlt *Russian Stage Design. Scenic Innovation. From the Collection of Mr. and Mrs. Nikita D.Lobanov-Rostovsky*, Jackson, MS, exh. cat.,1982. C.Lodder *Russian Constructivism*, New Haven and London, 1983. Nancy Van Norman Baer *Theatre in Revolution, Russian Avant-Garde Stage Design 1913-1935*, San Francisco and London, 1991. Dzhon Boult (John Bowlt) *Khudozhniki russkogo teatra. Sobranie Nikity i Niny Lobanovykh-Rostovskikh*, Moscow, 1991.

Coll Represented in many major museums including TG; RM; Bakhrushin Theatre Museum, Moscow; Tashkent Museum of Art; Tate Gallery, London; Peggy Guggenheim Collection, Venice; Yale University, New Haven; Busch-Reisinger Museum, Harvard University; Costakis Collection; Sammlung Ludwig, Cologne.
Colour plates pp. 260, 261.

LITOVCHENKO, Aleksandr Dmitrievich　　**1835-1890**
Painter of genre, portraits and history paintings. Born at Kremenchug. He studied at the Academy in St. Petersburg but became a member of the Artel which led to the founding of the Wanderers. He died at St. Petersburg.
Coll TG; RM.

LITVAK　　**a.1926**
Graphic artist. He was represented at the Second Exhibition of Cinema Posters held at the Kamerny (Chamber) Theatre, Moscow, in 1926.

LITVINENKO, A.　　**a.1925**
He exhibited at the inaugural exhibition of the Society of Moscow Painters in 1925.

LITVINOV, R.　　**a.1850+**
Active in the mid-19th century.
Coll Ashmolean Museum, Oxford.

LITVINOVA, N. V.　　**a.1932**
She was represented at the jubilee exhibition Artists of the RSFSR over 15 Years held at the Russian Museum, Leningrad, in 1932.

LIVANOV, B. N.　　**a.1930**
Theatre designer. He was active at the Moscow Art Theatre in 1930 where he designed S.Kartashev's *Nasha Molodost'* (Our Youth).

LIVSHETS, M. M.　　**a.1919**
Painter. He exhibited at the juryless Eighth State Exhibition in Moscow in 1919.

LOBANOV, Sergei Ivanovich　　**1887-1943**
Portrait painter. Born in Moscow. He exhibited with the Knave of Diamonds in 1912.
After the Revolution he contributed to the 1921 exhibition of the World of Art in Moscow. He exhibited with the *Zhar-tsvet* (Fire-colour) group between 1924 and 1928. His work was included in the exhibition of Soviet art held at Harbin in 1926 and in Japan in 1927 and in the major exhibition in Moscow in 1927 marking the tenth anniversary of the Revolution. He was also included in the 1928 exhibition of Acquisitions by the State Art Collections Fund held in Moscow. He was represented in the First Touring Exhibition of Paintings and Graphics which opened in Moscow in 1929 and in the exhibition of Russian Graphic Art in Riga in 1929.
Coll TG.

LOGANOVSKY, Aleksandr Vasil'evich　　**1810-1855**
Academic sculptor. He studied in Moscow. His works included *Boy Playing with Nails and Rings*, 1836, plaster, RM, which won one of the first gold medals. He travelled to Rome on a scholarship. He executed reliefs for St. Isaak's Cathedral in St. Petersburg.
Coll RM.

LOGINOV, K.　　**a.1924**
He exhibited with the First Working Organisation of Artists in 1924 at the First Discussional Exhibition of Active Revolutionary Art alongside G.Aleksandrov and others.

LOGINOV, V.　　**a.1832-1833**
Lubok artist. He executed lithographs of the Moscow markets in 1832-3.

LOMIKIN, Konstantin　　**b.1924**
Painter, pastellist. He graduated from the Art Institute in Odessa in 1951. His work has been concerned with the ballet in particular. He works in Odessa.
Coll Roy Miles Gallery, London.
Colour plate p.264.

LOMONOSOV, Mikhail Vasilievich　　**1711-1765**
Scientist, encyclopaedist, artist. His reputation as Russia's first great scientist is less important in art history than his contribution to the techniques of ceramics. He developed a

Anton Losenko. Vladimir and Rogneda, *1770. Oil on canvas. 211.5 x 177.5 cm.*
State Russian Museum, St. Petersburg.

mosaics workshop. The Imperial and then State Porcelain Factory was renamed the Lomonosov Factory in 1925 in recognition of his achievements.

LOMTEV, Nikolai Alekseevich 1816-1858
Painter of religious themes and Italian landscapes. He studied at the Academy in St. Petersburg. He was painting in Rome in 1845 and again in Italy in 1859. Sometimes he signed his work 'N.L'. The date of his death is sometimes given as 1859 or 1863.
Coll TG.

LOPATIN, Nikolai a.1914
Painter. He contributed to the exhibition No.4 in Moscow in 1914.

LOPATNIKOV, D. N. a.1925-1932
He exhibited with the 4 Arts society in Moscow in 1925. He was included in the major exhibition in Moscow in 1927 marking the tenth anniversary of the Revolution and in the First Touring Exhibition of Paintings and Graphics which opened in Moscow in 1929. He was also represented at the jubilee exhibition Artists of the RSFSR over 15 Years held at the Russian Museum, Leningrad, in 1932.

LOSENKO, Anton Pavlovich 1731-1773
Painter of classical and historical themes and portraits. Born at Glushov in the Ukraine. He studied under Argunov and then at the Academy in St. Petersburg where he subsequently became a professor. He was among the first students to be awarded a travel scholarship with which he travelled to Paris

1760-2. He was thoroughly informed of Western art through his visits to Paris and Rome. He was an initiator of grandiose history painting in Russia, sometimes with distinctly Russian themes which was in itself an innovation of importance. His works include *Abraham's Sacrifice*, 1765, and *Vladimir and Rogneda*, 1770, which earned him acceptance as an academician. There is a strong influence of French practice in the importance of life painting evolved into melodramatic pictures of classical themes. He taught Ivan Akimov amongst his numerous pupils. He died at St. Petersburg.

Hector's Farewell to Andromache, 1773, TG, is an academic *tour de force*, painted upon a warm ground, employing theatrical gestures and a setting of classical architecture. This kind of painting is close to French and Italian example and was evolved from drawings executed in the life room, cross-hatched in black chalk or sanguine.

Coll TG; RM; Musée des Beaux-Arts, Nancy.

LOSEVA, E. I. a.1918

She was represented at the First Exhibition of Works of the Professional Union of Artists in Moscow in 1918.

LOSEVA, L.V. a.1919

Painter. She exhibited at the juryless Eighth State Exhibition in Moscow in 1919.

LOT = TATLIN, V. E.

LUCHANINOV, Ivan Vasilievich 1781-1824
Coll TG.

LUCHISHKIN, Sergei Alekseevich (Aleksandrovich) 1902-1989

Painter, theatre designer. He studied at the Moscow Free Art Studios (SVOMAS) under Arkhipov in 1919 and at the Vkhutemas under Lyubov Popova, Alexandra Exter and Nadezhda Udal'tsova 1919-24. He was a founder member of the group Elektro-Organism in 1921 with Nikritin, Redko, Tyshler and others. From 1923 he was director and designer of the Project Theatre in Moscow and he was represented at the First Discussional Exhibition of Active Revolutionary Art in Moscow in 1924. He was a member of the Society of Easel Painters (OST) in the period 1925-8. He was included in the major exhibition in Moscow in 1927 marking the tenth anniversary of the Revolution. His work was included in the exhibition of Soviet art held at Harbin in 1926 and in Japan in 1927 and in the 1928 exhibition of Acquisitions by the State Art Collections Fund held in Moscow. He was represented in the First Touring Exhibition of Paintings and Graphics which opened in Moscow in 1929. He also exhibited abroad at Amsterdam and New York in 1929 and Vienna, Berlin and Stockholm in 1930. He was represented at the jubilee exhibition Artists of the RSFSR over 15 Years held at the Russian Museum, Leningrad, in 1932. He died in Moscow.

The Balloon Flew Away, 1926, TG, depicts a narrow urban chasm between two anonymous tower blocks. The perspective pulls together the tops of the buildings and in the bleak space between them a small child in a yard with a few straggling trees watches as the balloon escapes up into the sky. It is a comfortless image of tedium and frustration.

Lit *Khudozhnik-Zhivopisets S.A.Luchishkin*, exh. cat., Moscow, 1974. E.Weiss *Russische Avant-Garde, 1910-1930, Sammlung*

Ludwig, Köln, Munich, 1986. A.M.Muratov, V.Manin et al. *Zhivopis' 20-30kh godov*, Sankt-Peterburg, 1991.
Coll TG; RM; Sammlung Ludwig, Cologne.

LUCHSHEV, Sergei Yakovlevich 1850-1894+
Painter. Subjects included church interiors.
Coll TG.

LUGOVSKAYA (-DIAGILEVA), a.1903-6
Painter. She exhibited with the World of Art 1903-6 and was represented in Diaghilev's display of Russian art at the 1906 Salon d'Automne in Paris. She exhibited with the Union of Russian Artists 1907-9.

LUKOMSKY, Georgiy Kreskentevich 1884-1954
Painter. He exhibited architectural views from France, Germany, Italy and Russia at the First Izdebsky International Salon 1909-10 in Odessa. He exhibited with the Union of Russian Artists in 1910.

LUKOMSKY, Ilya a.c.1928
He was engaged on decorations at the Security Police Club, Moscow, c.1928.

LUNIN, L. B. a.1926
Graphic artist. He was represented at the Second Exhibition of Cinema Posters held at the Kamerny (Chamber) Theatre, Moscow, in 1926.

LUPPOV, M. a.1917-25
He exhibited with the Moscow School Society of Artists active 1917-25 and was a member of the Union of Moscow Artists formed in 1925.

LUPPOV, Sergei Mikhailovich 1893-1977
Socialist Realist painter. He was included in the major exhibition in Moscow in 1927 marking the tenth anniversary of the Revolution. An S.M.Luppov was represented at the jubilee exhibition Artists of the RSFSR over 15 Years held at the Russian Museum, Leningrad, in 1932. He died in Moscow.

Komsomol Women, c.1927, stride in a joyful group before a distant group of factories. A full-length depiction of ostensibly happy workers.

L'VOV, Petr Ivanovich 1882-1944
Graphic artist, painter. Born at Tobolsk in Western Siberia. He studied under N.P.Ulyanov 1897-9, at the Moscow College under S.V.Ivanov and S.A.Korovin 1900-2 and then at the Academy in St. Petersburg under Kardovsky, Tsionglinsky, Rubo and Samokish 1902-13. He exhibited with the New Society of Artists from 1909, with the World of Art and with the Union of Youth 1910-12. From 1915 to 1923 he lived at Khabarovsk.

He returned to Moscow to teach at the Vkhutemas/Vkhutein in 1924 until 1929. He was a member of the 4 Arts society which was founded in 1924 and the Society of Moscow Painters formed in 1925. His work was included in the exhibition of Soviet art held at Harbin in 1926 and in Japan in 1927, in the major exhibition in Moscow in 1927 marking the tenth anniversary of the Revolution and in the All-Union Polygraphic Exhibition in Moscow in 1927. He was also included in the 1928 exhibition of Acquisitions by the State Art Collections Fund held in Moscow and in the First

Touring Exhibition of Paintings and Graphics which opened in Moscow in 1929. He was also represented in the exhibition of Russian Graphic Art in Riga in 1929 and at the jubilee exhibition Artists of the RSFSR over 15 Years held at the Russian Museum, Leningrad, in 1932.

He then taught at the Leningrad Institute of Painting, Sculpture and Architecture in the period 1933 to 1941. He died at Perm.

Mikhailovsky Square, Leningrad, 1936, lithograph, is a cityscape built up from from linear elements to define the weight and form of the railings, trees and buildings beyond.

Lit J.Howard *The Union of Youth — An Artists' Society of the Russian Avant-Garde*, Manchester and New York, 1992.

Coll RM.

LYADYZHENSKY, G.   **a.1896-1902**

Painter. He was teaching in Odessa with K.Kostandi during the period 1896 to 1902. Isaak Brodsky was among his pupils there.

LYSENKO, A. V.   **a.1929**

He was represented in the First Touring Exhibition of Paintings and Graphics which opened in Moscow in 1929.

LYSENKO, Mikhail Grigorevich   **1906-1972**

Sculptor. Born in the Ukraine. His works include *T.G.Shevchenko*, 1945, plaster, which is an exercise in robust Socialist Realist portraiture, and an equestrian monument to *N.A.Shchors*, 1954, produced in collaboration with Sukhodolov and Boroday, and erected in Kiev.

LYUBARSKY, Grigoriy Pavlovich   **1885-1942**

Theatre designer. He graduated from the Academy in Petrograd in 1915 and was engaged in Agitprop decorations for the Bolshaya Zelenina and Krestovsky Bridges, Petrograd, in 1918.

LYUBUSHKINA, S. M.   **a.1918**

She was represented at the First Exhibition of Works of the Professional Union of Artists in Moscow in 1918.

LYUSHIN, V. I.   **a.1918-1932**

Painter. He exhibited at the Fifth State Exhibition: From Impressionism to Non-Objective Art in Moscow 1918-19. He was a member of the *Konkretivist* (Concretivist) group with P.Vil'yams and others in 1924. They showed work as a group at the First Discussional Exhibition of Active Revolutionary Art in 1924. He exhibited with the First Exhibition of the Society of Easel Painters (OST) in Moscow in 1925 and he was represented at the jubilee exhibition Artists of the RSFSR over 15 Years held at the Russian Museum, Leningrad, in 1932.

Threshing Machine, c.1927, a poster-like painting promoting rural work in a fresh and lively way. It shows horses circling round to provide the energy for the thresher. A high viewpoint and inconsistent lighting provide for silhouette effects comparable to those of Deineka and Yu.Pimenov.

LYUTSE, V.   **a.1922**

Theatre designer. Collaborated with Lyubov' Popova on Meyerhold's production of F.Crommelynck's *Magnanimous Cuckold* in 1922.

V. Lyutse. Illustration of Biomechanics, *1922. Drawing.*
Biomechanics was the system of mechanistic rhythmic movements devised by the theatre director Vsevolod Meyerhold for the actor-performers of his Constructivist productions including those designed in collaboration with Popova and Stepanova.

M

M. see **MATVEEV, A.T.**
M.A. see **MORDVINOV, A.N.**
M.B. see **BASHILOV, M.S.; BASHKIRTSEFF, M.**
M.K. see **KLODT, M.K.**
M.L. (cyrillic, latin) see **LARIONOV, M.F.; LEBEDEV, M.I.**
M.M. see **MATYUSHIN, M.V.**

MACHABELI, Elena Zakharovna   **1906-1949+**
Sculptor. Her works include an heroic monument erected at
Mtskhete in Georgia in 1949.

MAEVSKY, Mechislav Sil'vesterovich   **1855-1883**
Coll TG.

MAGARIL, Evgeniya Markovna   **b.1902-1922+**
A pupil of Malevich, she was active in Vitebsk c.1919-22. In
the 1920s she was making colourful portaits in the manner of
the Fauve Matisse.
Coll RM.

MAIMON, Moisei L'vovich   **b.1860**
History painter. He studied at the Vilensky School of
Drawing 1879-1880 and at the Academy in St. Petersburg
1880-7. He became an Academician in 1893.
After the Revolution he participated in the First State Free
Exhibition of Artworks in Petrograd in 1919.

MAKAROV, Evgeniy Kirillovich   **1842-1884**
Painter, graphic artist. Born in the Tiflis region. He studied at
the Academy 1860-6. He died in St. Petersburg.
Coll TG.

MAKAROV, Ivan Koz'mich   **1822-1897**
Portrait painter. Born at Arsaman. He died at St. Petersburg.
Coll TG.

MAKAROV, Koz'ma (Kuz'ma) Aleksandrovich **1778-1862**
Portraitist.
Coll TG.

MAKAROVA, Nadezhda Sergeevna   **1898-1969**
Costume designer. Born in Moscow. She worked as a teacher
in Kaluga province. She subsequently lived with Lamanova
assisting in her dressmaking work in Moscow. She frequented
the studio of K.Yuon 1923-4 whilst also working in the
Modern Costume Studios. She contributed work to the Paris
International Exhibition in 1925. From 1927 she worked at
the Kusteksport Corporation. She was the artistic director of
the Moscow (later All-Union) House of Clothing Design
1934-8 and 1945-9.
Theatre design She worked on theatre costume design from
the mid-1920s for the Moscow Art Theatre, Meyerhold's
theatres and for the Vakhtangov Theatre.
Lit T.Strizhenova *Iz istorii sovetskogo kostyuma*, Moscow, 1972
(English edition: Tatiana Strizhenova, *Soviet Costume and
Textiles 1917-1945*, Paris, 1991).

MAKHAEV, Mikhail Ivanovich   **1718-1770**
Engraver, painter. He was a celebrated engraver of maps and
architectural views of St. Petersburg. His birthdate is
sometimes given as 1716/30. He produced maps of St.
Petersburg in 1753 as well as exquisite drawings for prints
recording the grandiose new architecture. He produced an
album of prints of Kuskovo in 1760 which are elaborately
elegant and refined in a French 18th century style, stressing
architectural and horticultural conceits. His engravings were
executed with acute attention to the finest detail of site,
architecture and incidental scenes of human activity so that
beyond their considerable technical excellence they are also
remarkable documents of their time, particularly in their
description of the new city.
Coll Historical Museum, Moscow; Ashmolean Museum,
Oxford.

MAKLETSOV, Sergei Nikolaevich   **b.1892**
Painter. He was engaged on Agitprop decorations on
Zamoskovsky Square, Petrograd, in 1918. He participated in
the First State Free Exhibition of Artworks in Petrograd in
1919. *Lef* magazine announced in its issue No.4 in 1923 that a
Makletsov was amongst the artists working for a new
periodical *Krysodav* along with various Futurists and
Constructivists.

MAKOVETS
An art group organised in 1921 and exhibiting in Moscow
1922-6. It was named after the hill upon which the monastery
of Trinity-Sergius was built in the 14th century. It produced a
journal *Makovets* published 1922-3. Participating artists
included Tatiana Aleksandrova, Petr Babichev, Viktor Bart,
Petr Bromirsky, Vasili Chekrygin, Nikolai Chernyshev,
Vladimir Favorsky, Artur Fonvizin, Sergei Gerasimov, Nikolai
Grigor'ev, Konstantin Istomin, Yuri Pavilionov, Vera Pestel',
Nikolai Rodionov, Sergei Romanovich, Vadim Ryndin,
Aleksandr Shevchenko, Nikolai Sinezubov, Svyatoslav
Yastrzhemsky, Konstantin Zefirov and Lev Zhegin.

MAKOVSKAYA, Aleksandra Egorovna   **1837-1915**
Landscape painter. A Makovskaya exhibited with the World of
Art in 1902.
Coll TG.

MAKOVSKY, Aleksandr Vladimirovich   **1869-1924**
Portraitist. He participated in the First State Free Exhibition
of Artworks in Petrograd in 1919 and contributed to the
Exhibition of Paintings by Russian Artists held at Pskov in
Spring 1920. He was included in the enormous survey
Exhibition of Paintings by Petrograd Artists of All Tendencies
1919-1923 held in Petrograd in 1923.
Coll TG.

MAKOVSKY, Konstantin Egorovich   **1839-1915**
Painter. Born in Moscow. He was the brother of Vladimir
Makovsky. He became a member of the Artel which led to the
founding of the Wanderers. He specialised in popular Russian
scenes and his works include *Fair Booths on Admiralty Square*,
1869, RM, in this vein. He was painting in Cairo in 1875 and
in Paris in 1876. He taught at the Academy in St. Petersburg.
He exhibited internationally.
He moved to Paris where he was awarded a gold medal at the
International Exhibition in 1889. The same year he was

awarded the medal of the Légion d'Honneur. He died in Petrograd.
Coll Well represented at TG; RM.
Colour plate p.298.

MAKOVSKY, Nikolai Egorovich   **1842-1886**
Painter of views in the Moscow region. He studied at the Academy in St. Petersburg. He specialised in Russian and oriental views.
Coll TG; RM.

MAKOVSKY, Vladimir Egorovich   **1846-1920**
Painter of figure compositions and genre. He was born in Moscow. He was the brother of Konstantin Makovsky. He studied at the Moscow College under Sorokin and Zaryanko. He joined the Wanderers in 1872. He adapted genre and narrative paintings to carry a social commentary. In the late 1870s he executed major works with a socially critical message, including *By the Prison Gate* 1875, *The Convict* 1879 and *Convicts being Marched off to Siberia* 1884. He exhibited in Vienna and Berlin after 1873. He taught at the Moscow College from 1882 to 1894 and then at the Academy in St. Petersburg/Petrograd from 1894 to 1918.
The Meeting, 1883, TG, is closely viewed genre with a social message. A well-wrapped peasant woman gives bread to a shoeless lad who, as his stick and bundle indicate, is homeless. She looks at him with maternal anxiety. The paintwork is loose but focused more precisely on the faces and hands for expressive effect. The painting is a reproach.
I Shall Not Let You Pass, 1892, Russian Art Museum, Kiev, is melodrama. A young wife bars the way into a drinking house as her young son clings to her skirts. The rough husband considers the folly of drinking away what little money they have and is impressed by her determination. The style is essentially illustrative and of little importance compared with the moral of the piece. The figures dominate the scene which is otherwise essentially a backdrop and this intensifies the dramatic stage effect.
Coll Substantial holdings at TG; RM; Russian Art Museum, Kiev.
Colour plate p.299.

MAKSIMOV, A.   **a.1914-1929**
Graphic artist. He was designing lithographic posters for war loans in 1915. He was a member of the Kuindzhi Society of Artists in Leningrad in 1929.
The Spring Exhibition of the Imperial Academy of Art, c.1914, poster, is an elegantly historicist depiction of sailing ships passing before the Winter Palace.
Coll Imperial War Museum, London.

MAKSIMOV, Aleksei Maksimovich   **1810-1865**
Painter of portraits and history paintings.
Coll TG.

MAKSIMOV, Nikolai Khristoforovich   **1892-1979**
Painter. He exhibited at the third and last exhibition of the *Makovets* group in Moscow 1925-6 and was represented at the jubilee exhibition Artists of the RSFSR over 15 Years held at the Russian Museum, Leningrad, in 1932. He died in Moscow.

MAKSIMOV, Vasili Maksimovich   **1844-1911**
Painter of rural themes and a member of the Wanderers. Born into a peasant family in the Novgorod region. He studied at the Academy in St. Petersburg 1863-6. He exhibited with the Wanderers from 1871 and became a member in 1872. His works include *A Frugal Supper* 1879 and *A Loan of Bread* 1882.
A Wizard Comes to the Peasant Wedding, 1875, TG, illustrates genre painting turning into a form of theatre. The dramatic situation is emphasised by a Rembrandt-like manipulation of lighting and by a dual focus in the painting which contrasts the wedding with the arrival of the outsider. There are well over twenty figures each responding to one aspect or the other. A curtain hangs down at the left. The windows are covered against the dark night. The ikon is in the corner. The whole exhibits an alliance of painterly and theatrical ability.
Lit A.I.Leonov *V.M.Maksimov*, Moscow, 1951.
Coll Well represented at TG; RM.

MALAEV, Fedor Petrovich   **1902-1932+**
He was engaged on decorations at the Security Police Club, Moscow, c.1928 and was represented at the jubilee exhibition Artists of the RSFSR over 15 Years held at the Russian Museum, Leningrad, in 1932.

MALAGIS, Vladimir Ilich   **1902-1974**
Painter of still-lifes and portraits. He studied at the drawing School of the Society for the Encouragement of the Arts in St. Petersburg in 1916.
After the Revolution he studied under Rylov, Petrov-Vodkin, Savinov and Bobrovsky at the Petrograd Free Art Studios/Vkhutemas 1918-24. His painting in the mid-1920s showed a refined Cubism inspired by Shterenberg and Petrov-Vodkin. He was a member of the group *Krug khudozhnikov* (Circle of Artists) founded in 1926 and the group *October* in 1930.
Lit A.M.Muratov, V.Manin et al. *Zhivopis' 20-30kh godov*, Sankt-Peterburg, 1991.
Coll RM.

MALEVICH, Kazimir Severinovich   **1878-1935**
Painter, graphic artist, essayist and visionary. His art progressed from symbolist works via Neo-Primitivism, Futurism and Cubism to his own invention of the geometric form of painting which he named Suprematism. This was to have enormous influence upon many artists, architects and designers including Klyun, Rodchenko, Popova, Lissitzky, Klucis and many others.
Born in the Kiev region. He studied at the Kiev Drawing School 1894-6 and lived at Kursk 1898-1901. There is some disagreement about the details of his training as an artist. It is often recorded that he moved to Moscow in 1902 and attended the Moscow College 1904-5 before working under Fedor Rerberg in the period 1905-10. He exhibited with the Moscow Association of Artists 1907-9.
In 1910 Larionov invited him to exhibit with the new Knave of Diamonds exhibition society, one of the most prolific and effective organisations for promoting contemporary art. He exhibited at the 1911 Moscow Salon as well as the Union of Youth 1911-12 and 1913-14. He exhibited with the Knave of Diamonds in Moscow in 1910-11 but by 1912 he had joined the breakaway group the Donkey's Tail organised by Larionov and Goncharova. Subsequently he broke with Larionov but his alliance had persuaded him of the validity of the distinctly Russian sources of folk art and the *lubok* popular print. The conversion of Malevich to a kind of Primitivism and the adoption of peasant themes was an important element in his

Kazimir Malevich. Knifegrinder, Principal of Scintillation, *1912. Oil on canvas. 80 x 80 cm.*
The repeated movements are depicted by repeated images of hands, feet and arms. Man and machine work together. This shows Malevich close to the cinematographic depiction of movement developed by the Italian Futurists, but the inclusion of the balustrade and steps suggests an awareness of Marcel Duchamp's 'Nude Descending a Staircase' of 1912.
Yale University Art Gallery, New Haven, Connecticut, gift of the Collection Société Anonyme.

development of what was fast becoming an individual but eclectic and inconsistent confluence of techniques. Increasingly Malevich admitted more than one approach to painting so that his increased knowledge of numerous contemporary trends from Cubism to Futurism and Primitivism led to an examination of the language of painting. He contributed eight works to the exhibition The Target in Moscow in 1913. This period of synthesis was marked by the emergence of the so-called 'alogist' phase in which a basically Cubist framework was used to present irrational juxtapositions of objects and images without any coherence of scale or explicit unifying theme. *The Englishman in Moscow* is a prime example of this period.

He exhibited with the Union of Youth 1911-14 and under its auspices in 1913 he designed sets and costumes for the Futurist opera *Pobeda nad Solntsem* (Victory Over the Sun) which had a libretto by Kruchenykh and music by Matyushin. The opera concerns the world turned inside out with time travellers, strongmen and other Futurist protagonists. It was performed for two nights under the auspices of the Union of Youth, alternating with Mayakovsky's play *Vladimir Mayakovsky, a Tragedy*. Whilst Russian Futurism was distinct in its ideas from the dynamic and mechanistic enthusiasm of the Italian Futurists, Malevich was amongst those who were sympathetic to the Italian group. He met its leader, the poet F.T.Marinetti, on his visit to Russia in 1914 and certain of his paintings clearly reveal an interest in Italian Futurist work, particularly *The Knifegrinder* which has repeated features indicating the fast movements caused by the knifegrinder's machinery.

In December 1915 he exhibited and thereby launched his new geometric style Suprematism at the 0.10. The Last Futurist Exhibition of Paintings in Petrograd; this featured thirty-nine canvases including his *Black Square* suspended across a corner of the room and hung high. This painting he saw as the origin of all the Suprematist work that followed. Whilst Malevich dated the origin of Suprematism to 1913, it is usually assumed to have first found its full expression in this exhibition and it was at this point that it became a major force within Russian art. He showed work at the exhibitions Tramway V in Petrograd in 1915 and *Magazin* (The Store) in Moscow in 1916. Suprematism gathered adherents at once although each made original contributions. By 1916 a journal *Supremus* was planned. Members of the Supremus group included N.M.Davydova, Exter, Klyun, Popova, Rozanova and Udal'tsova.

After the Revolution Malevich exhibited with the Knave of Diamonds in Moscow in 1917. He chaired the art section of the Moscow Council of People's Deputies and from 1918 he taught at the SVOMAS in Moscow. He designed the 1918 production by Meyerhold of Mayakovsky's *Mystery-Bouffe* at the Communal Theatre of Musical Drama in Petrograd. He was also active within the People's Commissariat of the Enlightenment's Art Section (IZO Narkompros) as a member of the Moscow Collegium under Tatlin and was listed as leader of a course for art teachers along with Tatlin and others in 1919.

In the list of *Our Tasks* published in 1919 he called for war on academism and the establishment of museums and other organisations dedicated to the new in art. His own name was first on the list of artists published in April 1919 whose work comprised desirable purchases for the envisaged Museum of Pictorial Culture. The Tenth State Exhibition: Non-Objective Creativity and Suprematism was held in 1919 and he was given a personal exhibition of 153 works, the Sixteenth State Exhibition: K.S.Malevich, Impressionism to Suprematism, in Moscow 1919-20. This degree of recognition was only paralleled by the posthumous exhibitions accorded to Rozanova, the First State Exhibition, in Moscow, and to A.Gumilina, the Seventeenth State Exhibition.

On the invitation of V.M.Ermolaeva, Malevich moved to Vitebsk in September 1919 where he came into conflict with Marc Chagall. He was represented along with Kandinsky, Chagall and others at the First State Exhibition of Paintings by Local and Moscow Artists held in Vitebsk in December 1919. The viewpoints of Malevich and Chagall were radically incompatible by this date and Malevich rapidly gathered around him a circle of converts to Suprematism which included Lissitzky, Suetin, Chashnik, Ermolaeva and others. They formed the collective *Posnovis*, soon renamed *Unovis*, in 1920 which was active in design as well as in the development of Suprematist theory and painting. In 1922 he was

represented at the First Russian Art Exhibition at the Van Diemen Gallery in Berlin. He exhibited with the Union of New Tendencies in Art in Petrograd in June 1922.

Malevich moved with his followers to Petrograd where they joined the newly formed Institute, and Museum, of Artistic Culture (INKhUK) which had been set up by Tatlin after his discussions with its earlier Moscow counterpart. Malevich headed its Formal Technical Department and directed the Leningrad INKhUK from 1923 to 1926. As the Institute was dedicated to investigating the contemporary practice of art Malevich was able to continue his investigations and also elaborate his theories which in the period 1922-5 he assembled with a view to publication.

In 1923 he designed a Suprematist teapot and tea cups for the State Porcelain Factory although he rarely applied his Suprematist principles to utilitarian design except at the level of experimental elaboration of the potential of his system. Consequently the application of his ideas to posters, theatre,

Kazimir Malevich. Arithmetic, *1913. Lithograph. 17.5 x 11.8 cm.*
This was used as an illustration in the Russian Futurist book 'Vozropshchem' (Let's Grumble) published in St. Petersburg, 1913. Fragmented arithmetical signs and straight lines shatter the image in a Russian Futurist way. The curious object top left resembles some kind of stove-like machine (this recurs in Malevich's Portrait of Ivan Klyun). The suggestion is a new concept of time and space in which mathematics plays a central role.

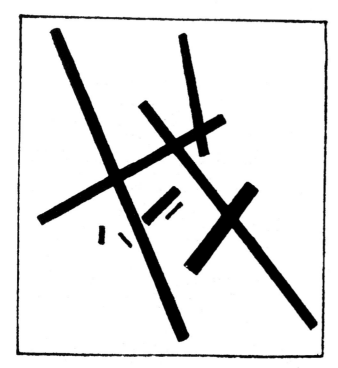

Kazimir Malevich. Suprematism, *1920. Lithograph.*
An image from Malevich's book 'Suprematism. 34 Drawings' published by the Unovis collective at Vitebsk in 1920.

architecture and layout was initiated by Malevich's example but carried out by inventive and independent followers amongst whom Lissitzky was a major figure. Malevich evolved the language that they used and as a result he was profoundly influential. He was a member of the 4 Arts society which was founded in 1924.

In 1927 he undertook his only visit abroad. He visited Warsaw on his way to Germany. Here he was received by the group *Blok*, including his Polish followers Strzeminski, Stazewski and Kobro, and he held a one-man exhibition at the Polish Artists' Club in Warsaw. He travelled on to Berlin, exhibiting at the Grosse Berliner Kunstaustellung, and visited the Bauhaus. Russian art made a considerable impact at the Bauhaus through Kandinsky who taught there and through the visits of Malevich and Lissitzky. Malevich's *Die gegenstandslose Welt* (The Non-Objective World) was published as a *Bauhausbuch* in Munich in 1927. He held a major exhibition of his work in Berlin the same year. The major part of his representation in Western European museums, particularly the Stedelijk Museum in Amsterdam, results ultimately from this journey and exhibition.

Much of his work in the 1920s concerned the extension of the principles of Suprematism into the design of utopian prototype dwellings, some of which he envisaged as flying in space, establishing mankind beyond the planet earth. He published in the Kharkov journal *Nova Generatsiya* (New Generation) in 1928.

A final figurative phase in the paintings of Malevich emerged in the late 1920s and 1930s. Ikonic figures with much of Suprematism about them and often frontally presented in rows and with great monumentality appear as the rural dwellers of a new vision of the world. In themes they sometimes refer back to the woodmen and sawyers of his early works but now clad in asymmetrical Suprematist clothing. He was given a

one-man exhibition at the Tretyakov Gallery in Moscow in 1929. He was represented at the jubilee exhibition Artists of the RSFSR over 15 Years held at the Russian Museum, Leningrad, in 1932 and at the exhibition of Contemporary Russian Art held at Philadelphia in 1932. He died in Leningrad.

Sometimes he signed his work 'K.M.' or 'Malewitz'.

*Victory Over the Sun, costume designs, 1913, Theatre Museum, St. Petersburg. Geometric, absurd and colourful designs in black, white, yellow, purple, red and green, make the protagonists into strange automata. The designs in gouache show elevations from the front or profile with roughly drawn rectangular border. Only some parts have shading and the faces are mostly obscured by mask-like costumes. These are the protagonists of Malevich's vision of the collision of the future with the present.

*Portait of Matyushin, 1914, TG, is ostensibly a synthetic Cubist painting. The composer-painter Matyushin, with whom Malevich had just collaborated on *Victory Over the Sun*, is visible in one quadrant of his head showing hair, parting and brow. This is surrounded by coloured overlapping planes with clear chiaroscuro suggesting depth and objects locked together. A drawer with its keyhole is visible, as is a collar and tie. The assemblage of forms is otherwise impossible to interpret but is firmly locked into the assemblage which is given clear edges surrounded by a pale coloured plane. Overlaying all of this is a strip of squares. This overlapping of images became a feature of the 'alogist' and even the Suprematist works. It may have been related to the ideas which Malevich entertained concerning the Fourth Dimension, ideas of interest also to Matyushin.

*Supremus N.56, 1916, TG, is a complex painting in which the white background characteristic of Suprematism is inhabited by coloured geometric forms which appear to float and glide in space like aeroplanes or spacecraft. All are rectilinear except for a circle, an ellipse and a blue form comprising a parabola cut by a circular arc. Whilst these fly unattached, all other forms assemble along axes suggesting constructions floating in space. One other curve, a half circle, is aligned along such an axis. This rhythmic articulation of space is highly mathematical, relying upon an underlying, and probably mystical, system of proportions which provides its cohesion.

*Suprematism with a Contour: the Sportsmen, 1929, RM, shows how the spectacular automata of late Malevich parading in rows, sometimes singly, to confront the viewer. They are divided into sections of red, yellow, blue, black, white and green. They are crude, strong figures clad in brilliant heraldic geometry.

*The Dacha's Occupant, 1910-30, RM, is almost impossible to date. Here a blue aproned, red faced, bare foot figure stands with his saw before a backdrop of houses. It is a crude, powerful and consciously primitive image. Colour is localised and chiaroscuro is inconsistent as in Cubist works. Yet it is a painting of great strength. Like the saint in an ikon, the workman dominates the painting with his blue clothes, red hands and yellow saw. The awkwardness has been learned from ikons, *lubok* prints and from Suprematism. The effect has the immediacy of a signboard.

Theatre design 1913 the Futurist opera *Pobeda nad solntsem* (Victory Over the Sun), libretto by Kruchenykh and music by Matyushin.

1918 November Meyerhold's production of Mayakovsky's *Mystery-Bouffe* at the Communal Theatre of Musical Drama,

Petrograd. Co-directed by V.V.Mayakovsky.

Futurist books A.Kruchenykh, V.Khlebnikov *Slovo kak takovoe* (The Word as Such), 1913, illustrated by Malevich and Rozanova.

V.Khlebnikov, A.Kruchenykh, E.Guro *Troe* (The Three), St. Petersburg, 1913, illustrated by Malevich.

A.Kruchenykh *Vozropshchem* (Let's Grumble), St. Petersburg, 1914, illustrated by Malevich and Rozanova.

A.Kruchenykh *Vzorval'* (Explodity), with illustrations by N.Kul'bin, O.Rozanova, K.Malevich and N.Goncharova, St. Petersburg, 1913.

A.Kruchenykh, music by M.Matyushin, *Pobeda nad solntsem* (Victory Over the Sun), with illustrations by K.Malevich and D.Burlyuk, St. Petersburg, 1913.

V.Khlebnikov *Ryav'! Perchatki!* (Roar! Gauntlets!), with illustrations by D.Burlyuk and K.Malevich, St. Petersburg, 1914.

A.Kruchenykh, V.Khlebnikov *Igra v adu* (A Game in Hell), with illustrations by O.Rozanova, K.Malevich, Moscow, 1914.

Book design Cover for N.N.Punin *Pervyy tsikl lektsiy* (First Cycle of Lectures), Petrograd, 1920.

Writings His theoretical writings were extensive and include *O novykh sistemakh v iskusstve* (On New Systems in Art), Vitebsk, 1919; *Suprematizm*, Vitebsk, 1920. Collections and translations include T.Andersen *K.S.Malevich: Essays on Art*, 4 volumes, Copenhagen, 1968, 1976, 1978, and A.B.Nakov *Malévitch Ecrits*, Paris, 1975.

Lit *Malevich*, exh. cat., Moscow, 1929. T.Andersen *Malevich. A Catalogue raisonné of the Berlin Exhibition 1927*, Amsterdam, 1970. D.Karshan *Malevich: the Graphic Work 1913-1930*, London, 1976. N.Khardzhiev *K istorii russkogo avangarda* (Towards a History of the Russian Avant-Garde), Stockholm, 1976. E.Martineau *Malévitch et la philosophie*, Lausanne, 1977. *Malévitch*, exh. cat., MNAM, Paris, 1978. S.P.Compton *The World Backwards. Russian Futurist Books 1912-16*, London, 1978. C.Douglas *Swans of Other Worlds: Kazimir Malevich and the Origins of Abstraction in Russia*, Ann Arbor, 1980. J.E.Bowlt *Russian Stage Design. Scenic Innovation. From the Collection of Mr. and Mrs. Nikita D.Lobanov-Rostovsky*, Jackson, MS, exh. cat., 1982. L.Zhadova *Malevich: Suprematism and Revolution in Russian Art 1910-1930*, London, 1982. E.Weiss *Russische Avant-Garde, 1910-1930, Sammlung Ludwig, Köln*, Munich, 1986. *Kazimir Malevich*, exh. cat., Moscow-Leningrad-Amsterdam, 1988-9. E.Petrova (ed.) *Malevich: Artist and Theoretician*, Paris-Moscow, 1990. N.Lobanov-Rostovsky *Revolutionary Ceramics*, London, 1990. Nancy Van Norman Baer *Theatre in Revolution, Russian Avant-Garde Stage Design 1913-1935*, San Francisco and London, 1991. Dzhon Boult (John Bowlt) *Khudozhniki russkogo teatra. Sobranie Nikity i Niny Lobanovykh-Rostovskikh*, Moscow, 1991. S.Compton *Russian*

Kazimir Malevich. Architecton, *1926-7. Plaster and wood.*
One of the three-dimensional works by Malevich in which Suprematism approaches architectural prototypes.
Documentary photograph.

Avant-Garde Books 1917-34, London, 1992. *L'Avant-garde russe 1905-1925*, exh. cat., Musée des Beaux-Arts, Nantes, 1993.
Coll Major holdings at the Stedelijk Museum, Amsterdam; TG; RM; Theatre Museum, St. Petersburg; Astrakhan Art Museum; Ivanovo Art Museum; Krasnodar Art Museum; Krasnoyarsk Art Museum; Nizhny-Novgorod Art Museum; Samara Art Museum; Saratov Art Museum; Sverdlovsk Art Museum; Tula Art Museum; Tate Gallery, London; MNAM, Paris; Sammlung Ludwig, Cologne; Kunstmuseum, Basle ; MOMA, New York.
Colour plates pp.24, 299.

MALEWITZ, K. S. = MALEVICH, K. S.

MALIAVINE, Ph. = MALYAVIN, F. A.

MALINOVSKY (MALINOWSKI), A.   later 19th century
Landscape painter whose work included subjects in Heligoland.
Coll TG; Helsinki Museum.

MALINOWSKI, A. = MALINOVSKY, A.

MALTSEV, Petr   a.c.1928
He was engaged in decorations at the Vkhutein Club, Moscow, c.1928.

MALYAVIN, Filip Andreevich   1869-1940
Sophisticated painter of peasant themes and portraits. Born in the Orenburg region. He lived as a lay brother at Mount Athos Monastery and studied ikon painting at the St. Panteleimon monastery there 1885-91. He then studied at the Academy in St. Petersburg under Repin 1892-9. He exhibited with the World of Art 1899-1906. In 1900 he visited Paris for the International Exhibition and in 1901 he exhibited in Venice. He was a member of the Union of Russian Artists in 1903. He was included in Diaghilev's display of Russian art at the Salon d'Automne in Paris in 1906. The same year he was made an Academician. He later exhibited abroad in Venice in 1907 and Rome in 1911.
After the Revolution he taught painting at the Free Art Studios (SVOMAS) in Moscow c.1918 and at Ryazan. He was represented at the enormous First State Exhibition of Art and Science, which included ethnographic material, held in Kazan in 1920 and in the 1921 exhibition of the World of Art in Moscow. He exhibited with AKhRR in 1922.
The same year he emigrated to France and settled in Paris. He contributed to the exhibition of Contemporary Russian Art held at Philadelphia in 1932. He died in Nice. Sometimes he signed his work 'Ph.Maliavine'.
The Swirl, 1905, TG, is an enormous painting in which he combined the dominant themes of his early career. Saturated by crimson reds, the canvas depicts the vigour of peasant women and folk costume in an adventurous westernised handling of loose liquid paint. The monumental yet dynamic painting owes as much to the rhythm of the brushwork sustained right across the canvas as it does to the movement of the swirling figures who are almost lost in the blaze of colour. The effect is of lavish and unapologetic excess of vitality.
Lit O.A.Zhivova *F.A.Malyavin*, Moscow, 1967. *Paris-Moscou*, 1979.
Coll TG; RM; Saratov Art Museum.
Colour plate p.303.

MALYSHEV, Mikhail Georgievich   1852-1914
Painter of wars, including the Russo-Turkish war in works of 1877-8.

MALYSHEV, Vasili Kirillovich   b.1782
Painter. He depicted Russian historical themes and in this respect followed the example of Ugryumov.

MALYUTIN, Ivan A.   1889-1932
Caricaturist, draughtsman, theatre designer. Born, in 1889 or 1891, in the Tula region. He studied at the Stroganov Institute under N.Andreev 1902-11. He was designing theatre costumes during the 1910s and worked for the S.Zimin Opera Theatre until 1917.
After the Revolution he exhibited with the Knave of Diamonds in Moscow in 1917 and at the Fifth State Exhibition: From Impressionism to Non-Objective Art in Moscow 1918-19. He was one of the pioneers, with Cheremnykh and Mayakovsky, of window posters designed for the Rosta Telegraphic Agency 1919-20. He also contributed to satirical reviews including *Krokodil*, *Begemot* and *Bezbozhnik*. He was represented at the International Exhibition in Paris and at the seventh exhibition of the group *L'Araignée* (The Spider) at the Galerie Devambe in Paris in 1925. He died in Moscow.
Lit *Ivan Malyutin Album*, Moscow, 1978. *Paris-Moscou*, 1979. Nancy Van Norman Baer *Theatre in Revolution, Russian Avant-Garde Stage Design 1913-1935*, San Francisco and London, 1991.
Coll Bakhrushin Theatre Museum, Moscow.

MALYUTIN, Sergei Vasilievich   1859-1937
Painter, graphic artist, theatre designer, furniture designer, architect, writer. Born in Moscow. He studied at the Moscow College under I.Pryanishnikov, V.Makovsky and E.Sorokin 1883-6. He was also associated with Princess Tenisheva's art workshops at Talashkino near Smolensk where he made prints and ran the woodwork studios c.1890. He began to exhibit with the Wanderers in 1891 but he also exhibited with the World of Art. He was represented at the Exhibition of Russian and Finnish Artists in St. Petersburg in 1898. He was instrumental in the revival of book design and his own works include illustrations for Pushkin's *Ruslan and Lyudmila* in 1899. He exhibited with the World of Art 1899-1903. He produced designs for Savva Mamontov's private opera company in Moscow in 1900. He was a member of the Russian Union of Artists in 1903.
During the period 1905-9 he was responsible for a number of architectural projects including the Pertsov apartment house on Prechistenka Quay in Moscow of 1905-7, a severe block modulated by tall triangular gable-end motifs, decorative brickwork and inset panels which give only a hint of the lavish but folksy and highly decorated interior of the apartment of Z.O.Pertsova within characterised by high relief carvings of stylised folk art motifs. These were again evident in the Baksheev House in Moscow of 1909 designed in collaboration with Vasili Baksheev. This had heavily carved doorways and panels in which the debt to folk art and traditional Russian architectural forms is a heady blend of crudeness and sophistication which parallels the rise of Primitivism in painting initiated to some degree by the revival of craft furniture at the Abramtsevo and Talshkino workshops.
He exhibited with the First Izdebsky International Salon

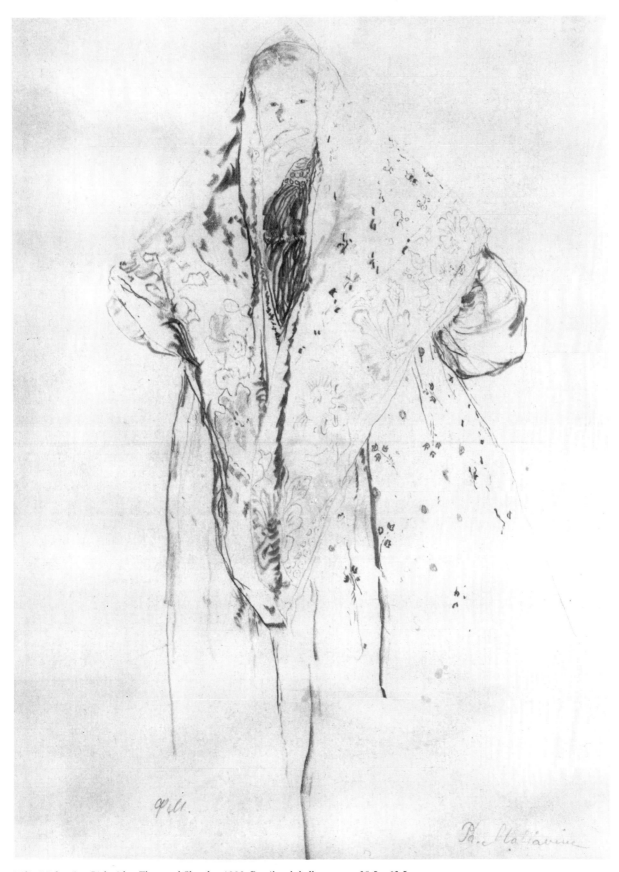

Filip Malyavin. Girl with a Flowered Shawl, *c.1903. Pencil and chalk on paper. 38.5 x 63.5 cm.*
Ashmolean Museum, Oxford.

Matvei Manizer. The Artist Ilya Repin, *1950. Bronze. 150 x 100 x 70 cm.*

1909-10 in Odessa. He taught at the Moscow College in 1913-17 and became an Academician in 1914.

After the Revolution he taught painting at the Free Art Studios/Vkhutemas 1918-23. His name was thirty-second on the list of artists published in April 1919 whose work should be acquired for the Museum of Painterly Culture. He was represented at the Nineteenth Exhibition of the All-Russian Exhibitions Bureau in Moscow in 1920, at the enormous First State Exhibition of Art and Science, which included ethnographic material, held in Kazan in 1920 and at the Third Touring Exhibition of the Sovetsk Regional subdepartment of the Museums Bureau along with Kandinsky, Rodchenko and others in 1921. He showed work in the 1921 exhibition of the World of Art in Moscow and was represented at the First Russian Art Exhibition in Berlin in 1922.

He was a member of the first exhibition committee of AKhRR, the Association of Artists of Revolutionary Russia, in 1922. In 1922 he was a founder member of the Society *(Obshchestvo)* of Artists of Revolutionary Russia, founded after the first exhibition of AKhRR. Other members included A.Grigoriev, P.Kiselev, E.Katsman, N.Kotov, P.Radimov, P.Shukhmin, A.Skachko, G.Sukhanov, B.Yakovlev and V.Zhuravlev.

He was represented at the First Touring Exhibition of Painting and Graphics which opened in Moscow in 1929 and at the jubilee exhibition Artists of the RSFSR over 15 Years held at the Russian Museum, Leningrad, in 1932. He died in

Moscow.

**Portrait of the Writer D.A.Firmanov*, 1922, is a half-length of the committed young intellectual looking active with his coat about his shoulders.

Lit A.Abramov *S.V.Malyutin*, Moscow, 1957. G.Golynets *S.V.Malyutin*, Leningrad, 1974. *Paris-Moscou*, 1979. *Twilight of the Tsars*, London, 1991.

Coll TG; State Historical Museum, Moscow.

Colour plate p.302.

MALYUTINA, Olga Sergeevna   **a.1920-1929**

She was represented at the Nineteenth Exhibition of the All-Russian Exhibitions Bureau in Moscow in 1920. She was also included in the Third Touring Exhibition of the Sovetsk Regional subdepartment of the Museums Bureau along with Kandinsky, Rodchenko and others in 1921 and she exhibited in the 1921 exhibition of the World of Art in Moscow. She was represented at the First Touring Exhibition of Painting and Graphics which opened in Moscow in 1929.

MAMONTOV, Mikhail Anatol'evich   **1865-1920**

Landscape painter.

Coll TG.

MANEVICH, Abram Anshelevich   **1881-1942**

Painter. He studied in Kiev and at the Munich Academy. His work included urban landscapes in 1914. He worked in the Ukraine.

He settled in New York in 1922. However, a painter called Manevich contributed to the Third Exhibition of Paintings by Artists from Kaluga and Moscow held in Kaluga in 1925.

Coll TG.

MANIZER, Genrikh Matveevich   **1847-1925**

Professor at the Baron Stieglitz Institute in St. Petersburg. He became an academician. His pupils included A.P.Ostroumova-Lebedeva c.1890.

After the Revolution he participated in the First State Free Exhibition of Artworks in Petrograd in 1919.

Lit G.M.Manizer *Pskov*, 1968.

MANIZER, Matvei Genrikhovich   **1891-1966**

Monumental sculptor. He participated in the First State Free Exhibition of Artworks in Petrograd in 1919. His works include the rhetorical monument to *V.Volodarsky*, granite, 1925, erected in Leningrad

Other monuments erected in numerous cities in the 1930s include a monument dedicated *To the Victims of 9 January 1905* in Leningrad and *V.I.Lenin* erected at Petrozavodsk. Other works include *V.I.Chapaev*, a multi-figure battle scene erected at Kuibyshev in 1932, *T.G.Shevchenko* at Kharkov 1935, *V.V.Kuibyshev* at Kuibyshev, *T.G.Shevchenko* at Kanev and at Kiev as well as a colossal figure of *Lenin* erected sixteen metres high at Ulyanovsk in 1940. He made a bronze of the painter *Repin* in 1950.

**Monument to T.G.Shevchenko*, 1934-5, bronze and granite, erected at Kharkov, places the bald, mustachioed Shevchenko imposingly on top of a tall plinth. Lower plinths rise around this bearing smaller scaled figures of workers, peasants, soldiers and flags.

MANKOV, A.K.   **a.1919**

Painter. He exhibited at the juryless Eighth State Exhibition in Moscow in 1919.

**MANSUROV, Pavel Aleksandrovich
(MANSOUROFF, Paul)** **1896-1983**
Painter. Born at St. Petersburg. He entered the Stieglitz
School in St. Petersburg in 1909 and also studied at the school
of the Society for the Encouragement of the Arts. He saw
military service 1915-17.

After the Revolution he became familiar with Filonov,
Malevich, Matyushin and Tatlin and executed experimental
works which can only loosely be termed Suprematist. He was
a Keeper of the Russian Museum, Petrograd, in 1917. He
provided two illustrations to the sheet music for Artur Lure's
(Arthur Lourié's) *Upman, kuritel'naya shutka* (Upman, a
Tobacco Skit) in 1919. He exhibited at the First State Free
Exhibition of Artworks in Petrograd in 1919 and he appeared
on the April 1919 list of artists for acquisitions by the
envisaged Museum of Painterly Culture. He was represented
in the First Russian Art Exhibition at the Van Diemen Gallery
in Berlin in 1922.

He collaborated on the organisation of the State Institute of
Artistic Culture in Leningrad with Tatlin, Malevich and
Matyushin and was included in its Exhibition of Paintings by
Petrograd Artists of All Tendencies 1919-1923 in 1923. He was
appointed director of the Experimental Section of the Institute
under Malevich in autumn 1923. He was represented at the
1924 Venice Biennale.

In 1928 he emigrated to Italy and later to France. He settled
in Paris in 1929.

Retrospective exhibitions were held at Braunschweig in 1960
and Paris 1972-3.

Lit *Paul Mansouroff*, exh. cat., Musée d'art moderne de la ville
de Paris, 1973. A.Z.Rudenstine *Costakis Collection*, London,
1981. E.Weiss *Russische Avant-Garde, 1910-1930, Sammlung
Ludwig, Köln*, Munich, 1986.
Coll RM; Costakis Collection; Sammlung Ludwig, Cologne.

MANUYLOVA, Olga Maksimilianova **b.1893-1939+**
Sculptor. She was represented at the jubilee exhibition Artists
of the RSFSR over 15 Years held at the Russian Museum,
Leningrad, in 1932. She worked in Kirghizia. Her sculptures
include *Youth with a Drum*, 1939, a kneeling figure in coloured
concrete.

MARDEROSOV, Leonid Ivanovich **1880-1936**
Painter. He studied at Odessa in 1894-9 and then at the
Academy in St. Petersburg under D.N.Kardovsky until 1909.
After the Revolution he participated in the First State Free
Exhibition of Artworks in Petrograd in 1919 and was included
in the enormous survey Exhibition of Paintings by Petrograd
Artists of All Tendencies 1919-1923 held in Petrograd in
1923. He exhibited with the Kuindzhi Society.

MAREYN, A.M. **a.1919**
Painter. He exhibited at the juryless Eighth State Exhibition
in Moscow in 1919.

MARINICH, Koz'ma Antonovich **1833-1870**
Genre painter. He studied at the Academy in St. Petersburg.
His subjects include an old lady peeling potatoes.
Coll TG.

MARKICHEV, I. V. **a.1925**
He was represented at the Paris International Exhibition in
1925.

MARKICHEV, Mikhail Aleksandrovich **a.1918-1920**
He was engaged in Agitprop decorations c.1918 and assisted
in the decoration of the propaganda trains *Red Cossack*,
Ukrainian *Lenin*, *Lenin (October Revolution)* and *Soviet Caucasus*
as well as the propaganda boat *Red Star* in 1920.

MARKOV, Aleksandr **a.c.1928**
He was engaged in decorations at the Vkhutein Club,
Moscow, c.1928.

MARKOV, Aleksei Tarasovich **1802-1878**
Academic painter. Born at Novgorod. He taught history
painting at the Academy in 1842-72. He decorated the cupola
of the St. Saviour Cathedral in Moscow.
Coll TG; RM.

MARKOV, Vladimir = MATVEJS, H.W.

MARKOVA, Valentina Petrovna **1906-c.1941**
Painter.
Coll RM.

MARTEN, Dmitri Emil'evich **1860-1918**
Landscape painter. Signed 'DM'.
Coll TG.

MARTINOW, D. N. = MARTYNOV, D. N.

MARTOS, Ivan Petrovich **1754-1835**
Major neo-classical sculptor. Born in the Ukraine to an
impoverished Cossack family. He studied under Nicolas Gillet
(Zhille) at the Academy in St. Petersburg from the age of ten
and was eventually sent to Rome on an Academy scholarship
1774-9 where he worked at one time in the studio of the
Danish neo-classical sculptor Thorwaldsen. He was made a
professor at the Academy on his return to Russia in 1779 until
his death. He executed numerous monuments and funeral
sculptures including the marble *Memorial to Prince Volkonsky*,
1782, at the Donskoy Monastery, as well as architectural
sculpture at Tsarskoe Selo and elsewhere. His *Tomb of
M.P.Sobakina*, 1782, marble, shows a professional debt to
Canova in its relief pyramid with inset portrait cartouche. His
work also included busts, contemporary as well as neo-
classical, and figure pieces of great control and refinement
such as *Actaeon*, 1800, toned plaster, RM, who reaches for his
arrow. The bronze version is installed at the Great Cascade of
the Petrodvorets Palace.

Monument to Minin and Pozharsky, 1804-18, bronze, Red
Square, Moscow. This is his most celebrated commission
which commemorates the defence of Moscow against the
Poles in 1612. It was erected in 1818 and can only have gained
in patriotic impact after the defeat of Napoleon.

Sculpture, 1819-20, plaster, designed for the staircase of the
Academy of Arts, is a high relief panel depicting the theme of
sculpture. At left children and a young man work as if from
plaster casts of Greek sculpture. Next comes a brief catalogue
of antique exemplars, including a fragment of the Laocoön
and, upon the carver's stand, the Belvedere Torso which a
seated sculptor is in the process of carving with mallet and
chisel. This is Martos paying homage to the importance of
antique work, showing that he can copy it convincingly, and at
the same time create a frieze of great technical control and
some subtlety of theme.
Coll Well represented at RM; TG.

**MARTYNOV (MARTINOW), Andrei Efimovich
1768-1826**
Landscape painter. He studied at the Academy in St. Petersburg. He accompanied an expedition to China in 1804. His *Picturesque Voyage from Moscow to the Frontiers of China*,with twenty-nine illustrations of popular types, was published in French and English. He was a consciously elegant painter stressing the pleasures of life on the great estate and in its gardens. He lacked the facility to achieve this convincingly with the result that his watercolours show an elegant and aristocratic life but they are painted with a degree of awkwardness which adds to the charm.
Coll TG; RM; Shchusev Architectural Museum, Moscow.

MARTYNOV, Dmitri Nikiforovich   1826-1889
Genre painter, theatre designer. He lived in Rome 1858-64.
Coll TG.

MASHKEVICH, E. O.   a.1925-1932
Painter. He exhibited at the third and last exhibition of the *Makovets* group in Moscow in 1925-6 and was represented at the First Touring Exhibition of Painting and Graphics which opened in Moscow in 1929. He was also represented at the jubilee exhibition Artists of the RSFSR over 15 Years held at the Russian Museum, Leningrad, in 1932.

MASHKOV, Ilya Ivanovich   1881-1958
Portrait and still-life painter of extraordinary fluency and strength of colour. Born in the Tsaritsyn (Volgograd) region. He studied at the Moscow college under Korovin, Sreov, Arkhipov and Pasternak 1900-9 but he also taught at a private studio from 1905. He exhibited with the Golden Fleece in Moscow 1909-10 and with the Izdebsky International Salons 1909-10 in Odessa. He travelled widely visiting Turkey, Egypt, Spain, Germany, Italy and Britain. He exhibited with the Moscow Salon in 1911 and with the Union of Youth 1910-11. He was a member of the Knave of Diamonds in 1910 and exhibited with the Knave of Diamonds in Moscow 1910-12. He took part in a debate on contemporary art with Lentulov, Tatlin and others at the Polytechnic Museum under the auspices of the Knave of Diamonds in 1913. He ehibited at the International Exhibition at the Stedelijk Museum in 1913, as did his friend the painter Petr Konchalovsky. He also exhibited with the World of Art between 1911 and 1917.
After the Revolution he exhibited with the World of Art in December 1917 in Moscow. He taught in the decorative art studio at the Free Art Studios (SVOMAS) in Moscow from 1918, and continued there as it became the Vkhutemas and Vkhutein.
He served on the Moscow Collegium of IZO Narkompros under Tatlin in 1919. His name was eleventh on the list of artists published in April 1919 whose work should be bought for the envisaged Museum of Painterly Culture and his work was amongst the new acquisitions of the Tretyakov Gallery exhibited in 1919. He was represented at the enormous First State Exhibition of Art and Science, which included ethnographic material, held in Kazan in 1920, at the Third Touring Exhibition of the Sovetsk Regional subdepartment of the Museums Bureau along with Kandinsky, Rodchenko and others in 1921 and he exhibited in the 1921 exhibition of the World of Art in Moscow. He was represented at the First Russian Art Exhibition in Berlin in 1922.
He was a founder member of the Society of Moscow Painters in 1925 and exhibited with them in Moscow that year. He was also a member of AKhRR 1924-7 and the Association of Moscow Painters until 1928. His work was included in the exhibition of Soviet art held at Harbin in 1926 and in Japan in 1927 and in the major exhibition in Moscow in 1927 marking the tenth anniversary of the Revolution. He was also represented at the jubilee exhibition Artists of the RSFSR over 15 Years held at the Russian Museum, Leningrad, in 1932. He died in Moscow.
**Boy in an Embroidered Shirt*, 1909, is a celebrated painting that is as lavish as it is lively. Devoted to thick paint juicily applied,

Vasili Masyutin. Illustration to A.Terek's 'Death of Copernicus', *1919. Woodcut. 5 x 10 cm. The book was published in Moscow in 1919. Two figures, one perhaps satanic, investigate a globe. The atmosphere is one of mischief and plotting.*

Vasili Masyutin. Illustration to A. Pushkin's 'As on a Warm Spring Day', *1924. Wood engraving.*
Pushkin's 'As on a Warm Spring Day' was published in Berlin in 1924.

Mashkov was emphatic in every way. Here the swirling decorations of both shirt and background would overwhelm the the figure, as would the intense colour, if the pose and the large-eyed look were not so seductively arresting. The work of the Fauves in France and Die Brücke in Germany have fed a style of lavish hedonism.
Lit V.N.Perelman *I.Mashkov*, Moscow, 1957. M.Allenov *Mashkov*, Leningrad, 1973. G.Arbuzov *Mashkov*, Leningrad, 1973. I.S.Bolotina *I.Mashkov*, Moscow, 1977. *Paris-Moscou*, 1979. *L'Avant-garde russe 1905-1925*, exh. cat., Musée des Beaux-Arts, Nantes, 1993.
Coll Well represented at TG; RM; Ivanovo Art Museum..

MASHKOVA, E. F.   a.1921
She was included in the Third Touring Exhibition of the Sovetsk Regional subdepartment of the Museums Bureau along with Kandinsky, Rodchenko and others in 1921.

MASHKOVA, N. M.   a.1928
She contributed to the fourth exhibition of *Iskusstvo dvizheniya* (The Art of Movement) in 1928 in Moscow.

MASYUTIN, Vasili Nikolaevich   1884-1955
Painter, printmaker. Born at Riga. He was associated with the World of Art and was inspired by Rops and Goya. He published a suite of fifteen etchings on the theme of the *Seven Deadly Sins* in 1906 which are extreme in the precise depiction of phantasmagorical monstrous creatures. One of them shows a six-legged monster resembling a bull with an elephant in its torso which culminates in a hideous face that also serves as the

belly of a kind of centaur arrangement, the top of which is a fat naked woman and an ageing man combined. In the print *Death*, 1911, grotesque and skeletal creatures stalk the town. The morbidly grotesque imagery is almost as obsessive as that of Alfred Kubin.
After the Revolution he taught graphic art with Pavlov and Falileev at the Free Art Studios (SVOMAS) in Moscow c.1918. He was represented in the Fourth State Exhibition of Paintings (*IV Gosudarstvennaya vystavka kartin*) in Moscow in 1919.
He executed numerous illustrations for books whilst working in exile in the 1920s, including Pushkin's *Kak vesenney teploy poroyu* (As on a Warm Spring Day), Berlin, 1924. These illustrations for children employed a wood-engraved style reminiscent of the work of Favorsky but bolder and with free flowing rhythms.
*Never Buy from the Private Shop when You can Buy it From Your Local Co-operative, poster, 1918, is decorated with flowers in yellow, blue, black and pink.
Book design Cover for A.Blok *Dvenadtsat'* (The Twelve), Berlin (Neva), 1922. B.Pil'nyak *Povest' Peterburgskaya* (Petersburg Tale), Moscow-Berlin (Gelikon),1922.
Lit N.Romanov *Oforty V.N.Masyutina*, Moscow, 1920. V.Masyutin *Gravura i litografia*, Moscow-Berlin, 1922. S.Compton *Russian Avant-Garde Books 1917-34*, London, 1992.
Coll Pushkin Museum, Moscow.

MATE (MATHE), Vasili Vasilievich   1856-1917
Major graphic artist, printmaker, engraver of illustrations and also sculptor. Born in East Prussia at Wirballen. He studied at the Academy in St. Petersburg 1875-80 and travelled on a scholarship to Paris 1880-3. He taught at the Academy as Professor of Graphic Art between 1894 and 1917. He exhibited at the All-Russian Exhibition of Printing in St. Petersburg in 1895. He also taught at the Society for the Encouragement of the Arts and at the Baron Stieglitz Institute in St. Petersburg. He died in Petrograd.
Lit V.I.Fedorova *V.V.Mate i ego ucheniki*, Moscow, 1982.

MATHE, V.V. = MATE, V.V.

MATORIN, Mikhail Vladimirovich   1901-1976
Printmaker. He exhibited some traits inspired by Favorsky but also had something of the light and scale of Shillingovsky. His dust cover for Thomas More's *Utopia*, a linocut of 1935, is a vista of the Utopian state bathed in a sunburst of light beyond a curving bay, an infinitude of waves and a few sailing galleons, all done with the clarity of an old wood engraving.

MATVEEV, Aleksandr Terentevich   1878-1960
Sculptor, ceramics artist. Born at Saratov. He studied at the A.P.Bogolyubov school, Saratov, under V.Konovalov 1896-9 and at the Moscow College under Trubetskoy 1899-1902. He worked at the Abramtsevo Ceramics studio in Moscow 1901-5. He exhibited with the Blue Rose group in 1907. He visited Paris 1906-7 and exhibited at the Salon d'Automne in 1909. His ceramics activities led to work as a sculptor at P.Vaulin's factory at Kikerino near St. Petersburg 1907-12.
He executed a number of full-length figures in 1912, RM, employing simplified features and a dense, slow surface. He travelled to Florence, Rome and Naples in 1913. He married

Zoia Mostova(-Matveeva). There is evidence of a residual influence of Rodin and Trubetskoy in his sculpture. He exhibited with the World of Art, the Golden Fleece 1908-9, and the Knave of Diamonds.

After the Revolution he taught at the Free Art Studios (SVOMAS) in Petrograd from 1918 and he executed a *Monument to Karl Marx* in 1918 in Petrograd. He served under Al'tman on the committee responsible for the revolutionary decorations marking 1 May in Petrograd in 1919. He also served on the committee with Al'tman and Karev which met on 5 December 1918 to initiate the establishment of a Museum of Painterly Culture and his name appeared on the April 1919 list of artists for acquisitions by the proposed Museum. He was represented at the First Russian Art Exhibition in Berlin in 1922. He also produced modelled nudes which were manufactured by the State Porcelain Factory 1923-6. He was a member of the Society of Russian Sculptors from 1926. He exhibited in Venice and New York in 1924 and at the Paris International Exhibition in 1925. He exhibited with the 4 Arts society in Moscow from 1925. He was included in the major exhibition in Moscow in 1927 marking the tenth anniversary of the Revolution.

Monumental works include *The October Revolution*, 1927, an academic three-figure bronze group to mark the tenth anniversary of the revolution which featured nude embodiments of the worker, peasant and Red Army soldier identified only by hat, hammer, etc., and a monument *To the Fallen Soldiers of the Far Eastern Army in Dauria*, 1931, RM. He was represented at the jubilee exhibition Artists of the RSFSR over 15 Years held at the Russian Museum, Leningrad, in 1932. He was Director of the Institute of Painting, Sculpture and Architecture at Leningrad 1932-5. He sometimes signed his work with the initials 'A.M' or simply 'M'.

Head of a Negro, 1907, wood, RM, has an overtly primitive appearance reminiscent of that evolved by Gauguin in his carvings. This leaves much of the trunk of the wood in evidence as well as the chisel marks.

Gardener, 1912, wood, RM, is a head carved to establish distinct planar surfaces and an alert pose faintly Cubist in effect.

Monument to Karl Marx, 1918, plaster, is simplified and monumental. The figure stands with one hand in his coat and the other behind his back. He has the look of one surveying the whole spectacle of mankind.

Standing Female Figure, 1937, displays taut, rounded forms that recall the work of Bourdelle and Despiau.

Lit *A.T.Matveev*, exh. cat., Moscow, 1958. A.Basekhes *A.T.Matveev*, Moscow, 1960. E.Murina *A.T.Matveev*, Moscow, 1964. T.Manturova *A.T.Matveev*, Moscow, 1974. *A.T.Matveev*, exh. cat., Leningrad, 1978. *Paris-Moscou*, 1979. N.Lobanov-Rostovsky *Revolutionary Ceramics*, London, 1990.
Coll Well represented at RM.

MATVEEV, Andrei   1701-1739

He was amongst the first of the *artistes pensionnaires* of Peter I with I.Nikitin. They left Russia in 1716 to study abroad. Matveev travelled to Holland. His *Self-portrait with the Artist's Wife*, 1729, is a synthetic and competent painting with a hint of Kneller or even Gainsborough about it. After 1729 he made portraits of the nobility and also ikons for the Peter-Paul Cathedral.
Coll TG; RM.

MATVEEV, Fedor Mikhailovich   1758-1826

Major classicising landscape painter. Born in St. Petersburg. He went to Rome in 1781 to study under the German landscape painter Phillip Hackert and remained there for the rest of his life. He produced views of Italy painted on a monumental scale recording historical and picturesque sites which were sought after by antiquarians for their topological detail and accuracy. In this way he became part of the international community of artists in Rome. His works included *View of Rome: the Colosseum*, 1816. He died in Rome.
The Waterfall of Caduta delle Marmore on the River Velino, 1819, RM, is a grandiose Romantic drama of a landscape depicting an immense waterfall descending from a high castellated hill through the wooded gorge which dominates the central area of the canvas. Classicising in its stage-like framing of the central image with trees, it is Romantic in its image of the tumultuous force of wild nature dwarfing man.
Coll TG; RM; Musée des Beaux-Arts, Montpellier.

MATVEEV, Nikolai Sergeevich   1855-1939

Painter. Born in Moscow. The Tretyakov Gallery in Moscow has his *Crépuscule*.
Coll TG.

MATVEEVA-MOSTOVA = MOSTOVA (-MATVEEVA)

MATVEI,Voldemar = MATVEJS, H.W.

MATVEJS, Hans Waldemars (Voldemars) Yanov, (MARKOV, Vladimir; MATVEI,Voldemar)   1877-1914

Latvian painter, critic and theorist who also played an important role as a theorist of art in Russia. Born at Riga. He studied under B.Blum in Riga until 1902 and taught at Tukumas, Latvia. He studied under Tsionglinsky in St. Petersburg and from 1906 at the Academy under Kiselev and Dubovskoy. He was a founder and the chief theoretician of the important art organisation *Soyuz molodezhi* (Union of Youth) in St. Petersburg before the First World War. He died at St. Petersburg shortly before completing his studies at the Academy.
Writings V.Markov *Principles of the New Art*, 1912. V.Markov *Iskusstvo ostrova Paskhi* (The Art of Easter Island), St. Petersburg, 1914. V.Markov, V.Egoriev *Svirel' Kitaya* (The Chinese Pipe), St. Petersburg, 1914. V.Markov *Iskusstvo negrov* (Black African Art), Petrograd, 1919.
Lit J.Howard *The Union of Youth — An Artists' Society of the Russian Avant-Garde*, Manchester and New York, 1992.
Coll Latvian Art Museum, Riga.

MATYUSHIN, Mikhail Vasilievich   1861-1934

Musician, composer, painter, theorist and publisher. Born at Nizhny-Novgorod. He studied at the Moscow Conservatory of Music 1878-81 and was a violinist at the court in St. Petersburg between 1881 and 1913. As an artist he studied privately 1898-1906 under Yan Tsionglinsky where he met his future wife Guro and the painter-theorist Vladimir Markov. He then attended the Zvantseva School under Bakst and Dobuzhinsky. His involvement with experimental approaches to art began when he joined Kul'bin's Impressionist group in St. Petersburg, contributing to the exhibitions Impressionists in 1909 and Triangle in 1910. He also exhibited at the 1909 Izdebsky Salon at Odessa and became an important figure in the Union of Youth organisation from its inception in 1909,

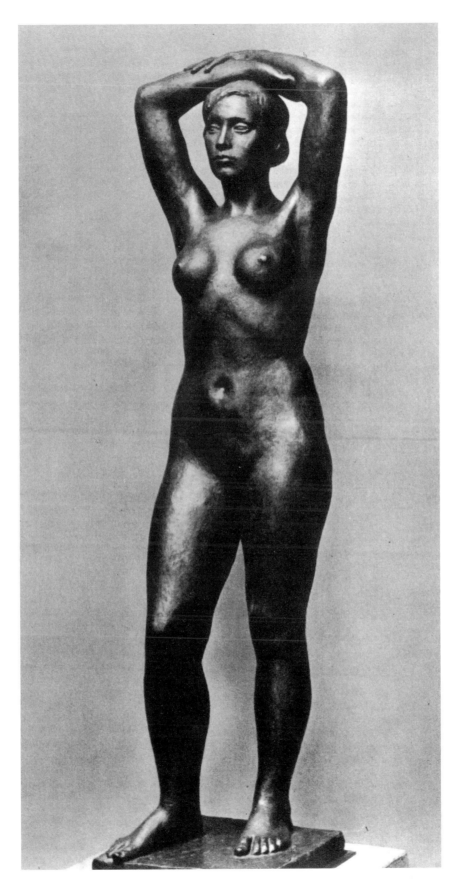

Aleksandr Matveev. Female Nude, *1937. Toned plaster. 170 x 46 x 40 cm.*

exhibiting with them 1911-12 and 1913-14.

By this time he was closely involved in the activities of the Russian Futurists. He contributed to the anthology *Sadok Sudei* (A Trap for Judges) in 1910 and published its second volume. After meeting Malevich and Kruchenykh in 1912 he collaborated with them on the Futurist opera *Pobeda nad solntsem* (Victory Over the Sun) in 1913 which was performed under the auspices of the Union of Youth. Matyushin wrote the score, Kruchenykh wrote the libretto and Malevich designed the production. Together with the Futurist poet Khebnikov they also produced the book *Troe* (The Three) which was published under Matyushin's own imprint *Zhuravl'* (The Crane). Aware of contemporary Western developments, Matyushin translated and published the text *Du cubisme* by Gleizes and Metzinger in 1913 thereby making it available to Russian artists soon after its publication in France. Matyushin's own painting had abandoned imagery by 1914. His knowledge of Suprematism was also immediate as a result of his close association with Malevich who appears to have sent him a drawing of his *Black Square* in May 1915.

He executed a series of sculptures from barely modified tree roots 1915-16. He was invited by N.Aseev and the painter Maria Sinyakova in the middle of 1916 to visit Krasnaya Polyana where he met Grigoriy Petnikov and Dmitri Petrovsky and heard the poet Khlebnikov reading his text *Oshibka smerti* (Death's Error).

After the Revolution he taught at the Free Art Studios (SVOMAS) from 1918 and appeared on the April 1919 list of artists for acquisitions by the envisaged Museum of Painterly Culture. He participated in the First State Free Exhibition of Artworks in Petrograd in 1919. He organised the experimental group *Zorved* (See-Know) at the Free Art Studios (SVOMAS) in Petrograd along with Boris and Ksenia Ender and directed an experimental laboratory at the Museum of Painterly Culture in Petrograd in 1922. His studies incorporated an examination of colour and its relation to sound but his interests were wider than this implies. He shared, for example, many of the more adventurous concerns of the Russian Futurists including their theories of the nature of time and the material world. He staged works based on Guro's writings 1920-2. He was included in the enormous survey Exhibition of Paintings by Petrograd Artists of All Tendencies 1919-1923 held in Petrograd in 1923. In 1924 he directed the Department of Organic Culture at the State Institute of Artistic Culture (GINKhUK) and his work in this may have had a bearing upon the studies of organic form undertaken by both Tatlin and Miturich. He was represented at the Paris International Exhibition in 1925.

Between 1929 and 1932 he worked with his students on a study of colour, *The Rules and Variability of Colour Combinations, a Manual*, which was published in Moscow and Leningrad in 1932. He was preparing a sequel with Maria Ender 1933-4. He died in Leningrad. He sometimes signed his work 'M.M'.

Portrait of Elena Guro, 1910, is essentially a symbolist painting evoking the soul of his wife, the Futurist poetess. She occupies the lower canvas, introspective and silent. Behind and above her is the melancholy garden where she walks. Everything is viewed frontally in this wan appeal for empathy.

Running, Walking, Sitting, Dancing, 1915-16, wood, RM, is a series of tree roots chosen and positioned with extraordinarily convincing effect to embody the movements suggested by the titles which Matyushin attributed to them.

Movement in Space, 1917-18, RM, comprises diagonal straight stripes of colour against a white background like the rainbow of another world.

Futurist books A.Kruchenykh, music by M.Matyushin, *Pobeda nad Solntsem* (Victory Over the Sun), with illustrations by K.Malevich and D.Burlyuk, St. Petersburg, 1913.

Writings included *O knige Gleza i Metsenzhe 'Du Cubisme'* (On Gleizes and Metzinger's Book 'Du Cubisme') in *Soyuz molodezhi* (Union of Youth), No.3, 1913, St. Petersburg. He was also instrumental as a publisher of Futurist books including works by Khlebnikov.

Lit N.Khardzhiev *K istorii russkogo avangarda* (Towards a History of the Russian Avant-Garde), Stockholm, 1976. S.P.Compton *The World Backwards, Russian Futurist Books 1912-16*, London, 1978. A.Z.Rudenstine *Costakis Collection*, London, 1981. E.Weiss *Russische Avant-Garde, 1910-1930, Sammlung Ludwig, Köln*, Munich, 1986.

Coll TG; RM; Costakis Collection; Sammlung Ludwig, Cologne.

Colour plate p.306.

MAVRINA (-LEBEDEVA), Tatiana Alekseevna b.1902-1940+

Theatre designer, lithographer. She exhibited with the group The Thirteen in 1929 and 1931. She was designing for the puppet theatre in the 1940s.

MAYAKOVSKAYA, Lyudmila Vladimirovna c.1885-1972

Textile designer, theatre and film designer. She was the elder sister of the poet and painter Vladimir Mayakovsky about whom she wrote a number of books. She was prepared for application to the Stroganov College by S.P.Krasnukha.

After the Revolution she contributed to the First Art Exhibition of Soviet Textiles in Moscow in 1928. She executed geometric designs for the Trekhgornaya Textile Mill using a spray technique in the late 1920s. She subsequently became director of the Moscow Textile Institute and won prizes for her designs at international exhibitions. She was a member of the board of management of the Mayakovsky Museum in Moscow.

Writings L.V.Mayakovskaya *Perezhitoe* (Experiences), Tblisi, 1957.

Lit T.Strizhenova *Iz istorii sovetskogo kostyuma*, Moscow, 1972 (English edition: Tatiana Strizhenova, *Soviet Costume and Textiles 1917-1945*, Paris, 1991).

MAYAKOVSKY, Vladimir Vladimirovich   1893-1930

Poet, revolutionary, playwright and painter. Born at Bagdadi, Georgia. He became politically active after the 1905 revolutionary uprisings and after the 1917 Revolution he became the leading poet-spokesman of the Revolution. He was arrested for Revolutionary activities in 1908 and 1909.

He studied as a painter at the Stroganov Institute 1908-9 and then under S.Yu.Zhukovsky in 1909 and P.I.Kelin 1910-11, before attending the Moscow College 1911-14. Here he met the poet-painter David Burlyuk in 1911 or 1912. He exhibited with the Union of Youth 1912-13. Together Mayakovsky and Burlyuk became seminal painter-poets of the Futurist movement in Russia. Mayakovsky's painting responded vigorously to the innovations of the Futurists, as did his

Vladimir Mayakovsky. Self-portrait, *1913. Drawing.*

January 1919 he became a founder member of *Komfut* (Communist Futurism) in Petrograd. This included the theorists Boris Kushner (chairman) and Osip Brik as well as the painters Natan Al'tman and David Shterenberg. Its *Programme Declaration* was published in the periodical *Iskusstvo Kommuny* (Art of the Commune), No.8, 26 January, 1919.

He designed window posters (Okna ROSTA) 1919-22 for the Rosta Agency supplying both poetic text and imagery in a kind of spectacular politicised cartoon strip format that was printed by hand, some on a large scale, but was widely influential. In December 1921 he collaborated on an evening of poetry with Kamensky, Khlebnikov, Kruchenykh and Tatlin at the Vkhutemas.

He visited Picasso, Delaunay, Braque, Léger, Bart, Maillol, Stravinsky and Cocteau in Paris in 1922

His dynamic, dramatic and effective work for Rosta led to collaboration with Rodchenko from 1923 on posters for which Mayakovsky supplied the text and Rodchenko the design. Even politicised sweet wrappers were produced in this way. Mayakovsky's exhortatory poetry readings ensured that he remained a highly public figure and his published essays

provocative sense of dress and his attitude to theatrical events. He contributed to the manifesto publication *A Slap in the Face of Public Taste* in 1912 and this launched him as both a poet and a Futurist. His play *Vladimir Mayakovsky, a Tragedy*, designed by Filonov, was performed for two nights alternating with the Futurist opera *Victory Over the Sun* by Kruchenykh, Matyushin and Malevich in 1913. Between December 1913 and March 1914 he undertook the *Futurist Tour of Russia* with David Burlyuk and Kamensky, travelling in fact as far as Tiflis (Tblisi) and Baku. A production of *Vladimir Mayakovsky, a Tragedy* was designed by Lentulov for the Evreinov Theatre, Moscow, c.1915, but was not realised. He exhibited a Cubist painting at The Year 1915 exhibition in 1915. He was engaged in poster design by 1914.

After the Revolution he dedicated his pictorial and literary abilities to the Revolution, welding Futurist experiment to a public voice that was both adventurous and declamatory. He was instrumental in organising the Provisional Committee for the Union of Art Workers together with Nikolai Punin and Aleksandr Blok. In March 1917 he was a founder of the Freedom of Art Association in Petrograd with the artists Al'tman, Isakov, Zdanevich as well as Meyerhold, Punin and Prokofiev. Together with Kamensky and David Burlyuk he signed the *Decree No.1 for the Democratisation of Art* in 1917. He contributed to the decoration of the Poets' Café in Moscow along with Kamensky, David Burlyuk, Khodasevich and Yakulov 1917-18. His *Mystery-Bouffe* was produced by Meyerhold at the Communal Theatre of Musical Drama in Petrograd in 1918 with designs by Malevich and he produced two films in 1918 (see below). He participated in the First State Free Exhibition of Artworks in Petrograd in 1919.

He worked for the Art Section of the People's Commissariat of the Enlightenment (IZO Narkompros) from 1918 and in

Vladimir Mayakovsky. Profile of the Poet Velimir Khlebnikov, *1913. Lithograph. 21 x 17.6 cm.*
This appeared as an illustration in the Russian Futurist book 'The Service Book of the Three' published in 1913.

frequently demanded the dedication of the artist to the public cause within the nascent communist society. In the periodicals *Iskusstva Kommuny* (Art of the Commune), from 1923 *Lef* (Left Front), and from 1927 *Novy Lef* (New Left) he demanded that creative individuals work out of their studios and in the public arena. In 1923 he executed a series of political caricatures under the title *Mayakovskaya galereya* (The Mayakovsky Gallery). Between 1923 and 1926 he also made illustrations for the periodicals *Bednota* (Poverty), *Gornyak* (The Miner) and *Sem' dney* (Seven Days).

He was again in Paris in 1924 and wrote to Lilya Brik in November reporting that he had failed to see Larionov but was in touch with Zdanevich and that he spent a lot of time with Léger. The graphic artist Annenkov drew his portrait in Paris in 1924. He was also represented at the Paris International Exhibition in 1925. Whilst he was in Paris, he painted a poem to the sun on a door previously painted by Delaunay. He visited Cuba and Mexico in 1925. He was in contact with the painter Diego Rivera in Mexico and he also visited Texas and numerous cities of the United States including Chicago and New York where he performed at the

Vladimir Mayakovsky. The Poet Velimir Khlebnikov, *c.1913. Pencil and ink drawing.*
Mayakovsky Museum, Moscow.

Central Opera House. He was in contact with David Burlyuk in America for the first time since 1918.

He was above all a poet and a playwright. His plays included *Klop* (The Bedbug) performed in 1929 at the Meyerhold Theatre in Moscow with sets by the Kukryniksy and Rodchenko and music by Shostakovich, and *Banya* (The Bathhouse) 1930 designed by S.Vakhtangov and A.Deineka.

He travelled to Paris in 1929 where he was in contact with the writers Louis Aragon and Elsa Triolet. He committed suicide in Moscow in 1930.

Futurist books V.Khlebnikov, V.Mayakovsky, D. and N.Burlyuk *Trebnik troikh* (The Service Book of the Three), 1913, illustrated by D., N. and V.Burlyuk, V.Mayakovsky and Tatlin.

V.Mayakovsky *Vladimir Mayakovsky, tragediya* (Vladimir Mayakovsky, a Tragedy), with illustrations by V. and D.Burlyuk, Moscow, 1914.

V.Mayakovsky et al. *Vzyal: baraban futuristov* (Took: The Futurists' Drum), with illustrations by D.Burlyuk, Petrograd, 1915.

V.V.Mayakovsky *Misteriya Buff* (Mystery-Bouffe), with cover by Mayakovsky, Moscow, 1918.

Futurist films 1918 *Ne dlya deneg rodivshiysya* (Not Born for Money, known also as Creation Can't Be Bought). Mayakovsky,

Vladimir Mayakovsky. The Artist Georgiy Yakulov, *1916. Charcoal drawing.*
Formerly in the collection of Osip Brik.

advertised as the 'greatest poet futurist', played the leading role as the poet Ivanov. The scenario was based upon Jack London's *Martin Eden* and devised by David Burlyuk and Mayakovsky together. Directed by Nikandr Turkin. Designed by David Burlyuk and Vladimir Egorov. Filmed by the Neptune Company and released by Antik. The cast included V.Kamensky.

1918 *Barishnya i khuligan* (The Young Lady and the Hooligan) adapted by Mayakovsky from *Cuore* by Edmondo de Amicis. Designed by Vladimir Egorov. Acted by Mayakovsky and A.Rebikova. Released by the Neptune film company.

1918 *Zakovannaya filmoy* (Shackled by Film). Scenario by Mayakovsky. The cast included Mayakovsky and Lily Brik. Directed by Nikandr Turkin and released by the Neptune film company. An artist entices an actress out of her film. She yearns for her existence as film and returns there. The artist follows.

Lit V.Kamensky *Yunost' Mayakovskogo*, Tiflis, 1931. V.Kamensky *Zhizn's Mayakovskim* (Life with Mayakovsky), Moscow, 1940. L.Polyak, N.Reformatskaya *V.V.Mayakovsky — Polnoe sobranie sochinenie v 12 tomakh* (V.V.Mayakovsky — Complete Works in 12 Volumes), Moscow, 1940. *V.V.Mayakovsky Album*, Moscow, 1963. V.Markov *Russian Futurism*, London, 1969. N.Khardzhiev *Mayakovsky i zhivopis'*, Moscow, 1970. W.Woroszylski *Life of Mayakovsky*, New York, 1972. V.Shklovsky *Mayakovsky and his Circle*, translated and edited by Lily Feiler, New York, 1972. D.M.Moldavsky *S Mayakovskim v teatre i kino*, Moscow, 1975. N.Khardzhiev *K istorii russkogo avangarda* (Towards a History of the Russian Avant-Garde), Stockholm, 1976. S.P.Compton *The World Backwards, Russian Futurist Books 1912-16*, London, 1978. S.Compton *Russian Avant-Garde Books 1917-34*, London, 1992.

Coll TG; V.V.Mayakovsky Museum, Moscow.

MAYKOV, Nikolai Apollonovich　　　　　**1794/6-1873**
Portrait painter.
Coll TG.

MAZEL, Ruvim Moiseevich　　　　　**1890-1967**
Turkmen painter.

MAZUROVSKY, Viktor Vinkentevich　　　　　**b.1859**
Battle painter. He studed at the Academy in St. Petersburg 1878-88. He was engaged on Agitprop decorations in Petrograd in 1918. He participated in the First State Free Exhibition of Artworks in Petrograd in 1919. He exhibited with the Petrograd Society of Artists.

MEDUNETSKY, Kazimir (Konstantin) Konstantinovich 1899-1936
Sculptor, theatre designer, poster designer. Born in Moscow. He was engaged in the laboratory stage of Constructivism in Moscow in the early 1920s and subsequently followed its transformation into utilitarian work through stage design. Born in Moscow. He studied stage design at the Stroganov Institute in Moscow from 1914.

After the Revolution he attended the Moscow Free Art Studios (SVOMAS) 1918-19 under Yakulov. He was engaged on propaganda decorations in Moscow in 1918 together with the Stenberg Brothers. He was a founder member of Obmokhu (Society of young Artists) group in 1919 and was represented at their four exhibitions. In 1921 he became involved in the discussions at the Institute of Artistic Culture

Konstantin Medunetsky. Construction No.557, *1919-20. Tin, brass, iron, paint. 45 cm. high including the base. Signed on the cubic base.*
This is a construction from found materials incorporating the circle, triangle and square. It dates from the 'laboratory period' of Constructivst work.
Yale University Art Gallery, New Haven, Connecticut, gift of Collection Société Anonyme.

(INKhUK) which led to the emergence of the Moscow Constructivists and their formal abandonment of painting. At the third Obmokhu exhibition in 1921 the Stenberg brothers and Medunetsky exhibited alongside Rodchenko and Ioganson establishing the range of Moscow Constructivists' three-dimensional work of the so-called laboratory phase prior to the declaration in favour of utilitarian work. He exhibited constructions with V. and G.Stenberg at the Poet's Café, Moscow, in January 1922 under the title *Constructivists* which was the first public adoption of the term. The exhibition comprised sixty-one constructions.

Little survives of the laboratory period of his work although some were included in the First Russian Art Exhibition in Berlin in 1922. Construction for him was defined more by materials and found objects than by mathematical principles. His work reflected the ideas of both Tatlin and Rodchenko.

Medunetsky then became an active theatre and poster designer. He visited Paris with the Kamerny (Chamber) Theatre in 1923 and was represented at the First Discussional Exhibition of Active Revolutionary Art in Moscow in 1924 and at the Paris International Exhibition in 1925. He was represented at the Second Exhibition of Cinema Posters held at the Kamerny

(Chamber) Theatre, Moscow, in 1926.

Theatre design With the Stenberg brothers he designed productions for Tairov at the Kamerny (Chamber) Theatre in Moscow from 1924, including Ostrovsky's *Storm*, 1924.

Lit A.B.Nakov *2 Stenberg 2*, Paris, 1975. A.Z.Rudenstine *Costakis Collection*, London, 1981. J.E.Bowlt *Russian Stage Design. Scenic Innovation. From the Collection of Mr. and Mrs. Nikita D.Lobanov-Rostovsky*, Jackson, MS, exh. cat.,1982.

Coll Yale University Art Gallery, New Haven; Costakis Collection.

MEISTER, Lidiya   **a.1906-1909**
Painter of vignettes and pastels. She exhibited with the New Society of Artists from 1906 and with Kul'bin's exhibitions Contemporary Trends in 1908 and Impressionists in 1909.

MEKHED, I. R.   **a.1921**
Exhibited with Kudryashov and others at the First State Exhibition in Orenburg in 1921.

MELLER, Vadim Georgievich   **1884-1962**
Theatre designer. Born in St. Petersburg. He studied at the Kiev Art Institute 1903-5 and then studied law at Kiev University until 1908. He attended the Munich Academy 1908-12 before moving to Paris 1912-14.

He studied under Exter and designed various productions in Kiev.

After the Revolution he was represented at the First Exhibition of Works of the Professional Union of Artists in Moscow in 1918. He worked at the Shevchenko Theatre in Kiev from 1921 and taught at the Kiev Art Institute from this time until 1925. Some costume designs resemble those of Exter in the adaptation of recent geometric painting to theatre design by means of assembling interslotted, incomplete or transparent planes, but they are on the whole simpler. Like Exter's designs these incorporate the movement of the performer into the sweep of the geometry across the page. He was represented at the Paris International Exhibition in 1925. He directed the art sections of the Berezil Theatre in Kharkov from 1922 to 1946 and the Franco Theatre in Kiev from 1953 to 1959. He died in Kiev.

Theatre design 1919 *Assyrian Dances*, choreography by Bronislava Nijinska, at the State Opera, Kiev.
1919-20 *Mephisto*, choreography by B.Nijinska, at the State Opera, Kiev.
1921 *The City*, music by Prokofiev, choreography by B.Nijinska, at the State Opera, Kiev.
1921 Yu.Slovatsky's drama *Mazepa* at the T.G.Shevchenko Theatre, Kiev. The costume designs were similar to work by Exter in the geometric folds with pleats as stiff as a staircase.
1923 Georg Kaiser's *Gas* at the Berezil Theatre, Kiev.

Lit Z.Kucherenko *Vadim Meller*, kiev, 1975. J.E.Bowlt *Russian Stage Design. Scenic Innovation. From the Collection of Mr. and Mrs. Nikita D.Lobanov-Rostovsky*, Jackson, MS, exh. cat.,1982. Nancy Van Norman Baer *Theatre in Revolution, Russian Avant-Garde Stage Design 1913-1935*, San Francisco and London, 1991. Dzhon Boult (John Bowlt) *Khudozhniki russkogo teatra. Sobranie Nikity i Niny Lobanovykh-Rostovskikh*, Moscow, 1991.

Coll Bakhrushin Theatre Museum, Moscow.

MEL'NIKOV, Dmitri Ivanovich   **1889-1920+**
He was designing posters in 1920 and working on the decoration of propaganda trains including *Red Cossack*, Ukrainian *Lenin*, and *Lenin*, as well as the propaganda boat *Red Star*.

MEL'NIKOV, F. I.   **a.1919**
Painter. He exhibited at the Ninth State Exhibition of Paintings: Naturalism and Realism in Moscow in 1919.

MEL'NIKOVA, Elena   **a.1927**
Painter. She was a member of OST , the Society of Easel Painters, founded in 1925. She developed a style reminiscent of Al'tman and David Shterenberg in which figures were incorporated into a severely planar composition which tipped surfaces up on to the picture plane. This was evident in her *Woman Sewing a Banner*, c.1927, in which a minimum of objects, flatly depicted and including the banner and a calendar, are essentially geometric forms with political signs attached. The figure sews the word 'Communist' and is cut off by these forms. The spacial organisation was similar to that of Deineka and Yu.Pimenov and enjoyed a particular flowering c.1927.

MENDELEVICH, Isaak Abramovich   **1887-1952**
Sculptor. His work was included in the First Exhibition of the Moscow Contemporary Art Store in January 1919 and in the major exhibition in Moscow in 1927 marking the tenth anniversary of the Revolution.

MENK, Vladimir Karlovich   **1856-1920**
Landscape painter. He taught at the Art Institute in Kiev where Lentulov was among his students in the period 1900-5.
Coll TG.

MEN'KOV, Mikhail Ivanovich   **1885-1921+**
Painter. Born at Vilna. He entered the sculpture school of the Moscow College in 1912 and subsequently transferred to architecture. He left the college in October-November 1914. He was associated with the circle of Malevich at the time of the beginning of Suprematism and he showed work at 0.10. The Last Futurist Exhibition of Paintings in December 1915.
After the Revolution he exhibited with the Knave of Diamonds in Moscow in November 1917 and at the First Exhibition of Works of the Professional Union of Artists in Moscow in 1918. His work was also included in the juryless Eighth State Exhibition in Moscow in 1919. In the catalogue of the Tenth State Exhibition: Non-Objective Creativity and Suprematism in 1919 he published a statement outlining the case for an art independent of representational imagery. He appeared on the list of artists published in April 1919 for acquisitions by the Museum of Painterly Culture and he participated in the Third Exhibition of Paintings held at Ryazan in 1919. A hand-painted poster by Stepanova listed him along with Malevich, Vesnin, Klyun, Popova and Rodchenko as contributors to the exhibition of Non-Objectivists and Suprematists of 1919. He was in a sanatorium at Yalta in 1921.
Lit *L'Avant-garde russe 1905-1925*, exh. cat., Musée des Beaux-Arts, Nantes, 1993.
Coll Krasnodar Art Museum; Samara Art Museum; Simbirsk Art Museum.

MEN'SHUTIN, Nikolai Aleksandrovich   **1899-1951**
He exhibited with the First Working Organisaton of Artists in 1924 at the First Discussional Exhibition of Active Revolutionary Art alongside G.Aleksandrov and others.

MERABISHVILI, Konstantin (Kote) Mikhailovich
b.1906-1942+
Georgian sculptor. He studied under Nikoladze and Kandelaki. His monument to *Shota Rustavelli* , 1937-42,

Sergei Merkurov. The Death of the Leader, *1927-50. Granite. 300 x 300 x 200 cm.*
Merkurov was a major monumental sculptor whose work frequently stressed mass and strength in works dedicated to Soviet heroic themes and influential figures. Here he produces a dirge-like slow rhythm to commemorate the death of Lenin. The hard granite evokes a sense of the physical labour of the carving of the monument as well as a sense of immutable permanence applied to the theme suggesting that Lenin's example was an event of immutable importance.

erected at Tblisi, is a historicist piece in stone. The poet stands upon an architectural plinth erected above steps with a second arcaded plinth.

MERKULOV, A. A. a.1925
Graphic artist. He contributed to the First Exhibition of Cinema Posters held in Moscow in 1925.

MERKULOV, Yuri A. a.1924-1925+
He was a member of the *Konkretivist* (Concretivist) group in 1924 along with P.Vilyams, B.Volkov, K.Vyalov and V.Lyushin. They exhibited together at the First Discussional Exhibition of Active Revolutionary Art in 1924. He was a founder member of the Society of Easel Painters in 1925.

MERKUROV, Sergei Dmitrievich 1881-1952
Sculptor. Born at Aleksandropol, Armenia. He studied under A.Mayer in Switzerland and under Ruhlmann at the Munich Academy.
After the Revolution he entered the competition for a *Monument to Karl Marx* in 1919. Ambitious multi-figure

compositions carved in granite include *The Death of the Leader*, i.e. Lenin, designed 1927-9, and *The Shooting of the 26 Baku Commissars*, 1924-46. Celebrated for his full-length sculpture of *Stalin* he also executed numerous monuments including the academic *K.A.Timiryazev* erected in Moscow. In the 1930s he built monuments in Erevan, Armenia, to *Lenin* and *S.Shaumyan*. In 1937 he designed the colossal *Lenin*, thirty-two metres high, erected on the Moscow Canal. He was made an Academician of the USSR. He died in Moscow.
*Monument to K.A.Timiryazev, 1922-3, granite, erected in Moscow, wraps the figure in a tall cloak and raises him upon an elevated cube.
*Monument to the Shooting of the 26 Baku Commissars, 1924-6, granite, erected at Baku, rises from roughly cut granite to increasingly refined high relief and a more polished finish for the corpses and grieving figures that comprise the emotional and rhetorical summit of the work.
Writings S.D.Merkurov *Zapiski skul'ptora*, Moscow, 1953.
Lit *S.D.Merkurov Album*, Moscow, 1958. *Paris-Moscou*, 1979.

MESHCHANINOV (MIESTCHANINOFF),
Oskar Samoylovich   **1886-1957**
Sculptor. The Russian Museum has a toned plaster *Head of a Young Woman*, 1912, which is a little reminiscent of Mestrovic in its monumental style. This work is hieratic and stylised.
Coll RM

MESHCHERIN, Nikolai Vasilievich   **1864-1916**
Landscape painter. A Meshcherin exhibited with the World of Art in 1903.
Coll TG.

MESHCHERSKY, Arseniy Ivanovich   **1834-1902**
Landscape painter.
Coll TG.

MESHIKOV, Vasili Nikitich   **1867-1946**
Painter of genre and portraits. He was painting at Trouville in 1903.
After the Revolution he was engaged on Agitprop decorations for a square in Petrograd in 1918 featuring enormous trapezoid panels bearing giant Cubo-Futurist images of corn, red star, rose, hammer and sickle, rider, etc.
Coll TG; Museum of the Great October Socialist Revolution, Leningrad.

MESHKOV, Vladimir Nikolaevich   **1884-1961**
Painter, theatre designer. He studied at the Academy in St. Petersburg 1909-14.
After the Revolution he was engaged on Agitprop decorations in Troitsky Square, Petrograd, in 1918. He appeared on the April 1919 list of artists for acquisitions by the envisaged Museum of Painterly Culture. He was included in the major exhibition in Moscow in 1927 marking the tenth anniversary of the Revolution.
Coll TG.

METFAK
The abbreviated name of the Metalwork Faculty (*Metalloobrabatyvayushchii fakul'tet*) of the Moscow Vkhutemas.

MEYER, Egor Egorovich   **1822-1867**
Landscape painter.
Coll TG.

MEZENTSEV, Sergei Aleksandrovich   **1884-1927+**
Sculptor. He was represented at the First Russian Art Exhibition in Berlin in 1922. He was included in the major exhibition in Moscow in 1927 marking the tenth anniversary of the Revolution.

MEZHEKOV, L. E.   **a.1925**
Painter. He contributed to the Third Exhibition of Paintings by Artists from Kaluga and Moscow held in Kaluga in 1925.

MIESTCHANINOFF = MESHCHANINOV, O. S.

MIGANADZHIANI, I.   **a.1917**
Theatre designer. He was designing for the theatre by 1917. He appeared in sixty-first place on the April 1919 list of artists for acquisitions by the envisaged Museum of Painterly Culture.
Theatre design 1917 Tairov's production of Lyubov' Stolitsa's *The Azure Carpet* at the Kamerny (Chamber) Theatre in Moscow.

MIKENAS, Yuozas Iokubovich   **1901-1964**
Monumental sculptor. Works include a *Monument to Heros of the Soviet Army* erected in Latvia and the *Victory* monument, 1946, at Kaliningrad.

MIKESHIN, Mikhail Osipovich   **1835-1896**
Sculptor of popular monuments, painter.
Coll TG.

MIKHAILOV, Grigoriy Karpovich   **1814-1867**
Coll TG.

MIKHAILOV, M. M.   **a.1913**
Painter. He contributed a watercolour and a signboard to Larionov's exhibition *Mishen'* (The Target) in Moscow in 1913.

MIKHAILOV, N. M.   **a.1919**
Painter. He exhibited at the juryless Eighth State Exhibition and at the Ninth State Exhibition of Paintings: Naturalism and Realism in Moscow in 1919.

MIKHAILOVA, K. I.   **a.1919**
Painter. She exhibited at the juryless Eighth State Exhibition in Moscow in 1919.

MIKHAILOVSKY, A. N.   **a.1919**
His work was included in the First Exhibition of the Moscow Contemporary Art Store in January 1919 and he appeared on the April 1919 list of artists for acquisitions by the envisaged Museum of Painterly Culture.

MIKHNEVICH, L. S. or I.   **a.1909-1910**
He exhibited with the Izdebsky International Salons 1909-10 in Odessa.

MILASHEVSKY, Vladimir Alekseevich   **1893-1976**
Painter, theatre designer. Born at Saratov. He was a key figure in the group The Thirteen with which he exhibited in 1929 and 1931. He was still active in theatre design in the 1950s. He died in Moscow.

MILIOTI, Nikolai Dmitrievich   **1874-1962**
Painter brother of V.D.Milioti. A symbolist associated with the Blue Rose group. Born in Moscow. He studied at the Moscow College in the 1890s and in Paris. He exhibited with the World of Art in 1906. He was also represented in Diaghilev's display of Russian art at the 1906 Salon d'Automne in Paris. From 1906 to 1908 and in 1910 he exhibited with the Union of Russian Artists and showed work with the Blue Rose group in 1907. He was a member of the committee organising the 1912 World of Art exhibition under the presidency of Roerich.
After the Revolution he appeared on the April 1919 list of artists for acquisitions by the Museum of Painterly Culture. He was represented at the First Russian Art Exhibition in Berlin in 1922.
He emigrated in the early 1920s. He died in Paris.
Coll TG; RM.
Colour plate p.307.

MILIOTI, Vasili Dmitrievich   **1875-1943**
Painter brother of Nikolai Milioti. Born in Moscow. He studied law at Moscow University. He subsequently became the manager of the art section of the Golden Fleece and a collaborator from 1906 on the periodical *Vesy* (Libra, The

Scales). He exhibited with the World of Art and with the Union of Russian Artists in 1906. He was an organiser of the Blue Rose exhibition and became the secretary of the Union of Russian Artists. He exhibited with the Blue Rose group in 1907. He exhibited with the Golden Fleece in Moscow in 1908 and 1909.

He returned to the practice of law 1909-17. He died in Moscow.
Lit *Twilight of the Tsars*, London, 1991.
Coll TG; RM.

MILLER, Grigoriy L'vovich   **1900-1958**
Exhibition, theatre, furniture and book designer. Born in Moscow. He studied at the Moscow Vkhutemas and was a founder of the First Working Group of Constructivists along with Aleksei Gan, Nikolai Smirnov and others. His design for a work desk, c.1923-4, was thoroughly Constructivist, exhibiting a complex of functions assembled into a transformable desk consisting entirely of unadorned straight lines and planes. He exhibited with the First Working Group of Constructivsts in 1924 at the First Discussional Exhibition of Active Revolutionary Art alongside L.Sanina, A.Gan, Olga and Galina Chichagova, N.G.Smirnov and A.Mirolyubova. He died in Moscow.
Theatre design c.1920 Oscar Wilde's *Salomé*, possibly for a projected production by Meyerhold in Moscow.
1927 Anatoli Glebov's *Growth* at the Moscow Academic Theatre.
Lit J.E.Bowlt *Russian Stage Design. Scenic Innovation. From the Collection of Mr. and Mrs. Nikita D.Lobanov-Rostovsky*, Jackson, MS, exh. cat.,1982.

MIL'MAN, Adol'f Izrailovich   **1888?-1930**
Painter of portraits, landscapes and still-lifes. He exhibited with the Knave of Diamonds in 1912.
After the Revolution he exhibited with the World of Art in December 1917 in Moscow. Mil'man appeared on the April 1919 list of artists for acquisitions by the envisaged Museum of Painterly Culture and was represented at the enormous First State Exhibition of Art and Science, which included ethnographic material, held in Kazan in 1920.
Coll TG.

MILORADOVICH, Sergei Dmitrievich   **1851/2-1943**
Painter. He exhibited at the Paris International Exhibition in 1900.
After the Revolution he participated in the First State Free Exhibition of Artworks in Petrograd in 1919.
Coll TG.

MIODUSZEWSKI, Jan Ostoja
(MIODUSHEVSKY, Ivan Osipovich)   **1831-1905+**
Polish painter. Born at Podolia. He studied in St. Petersburg and Paris. His subjects included themes derived from Pushkin.
Coll TG.

MIR ISKUSSTVA = WORLD OF ART

MIROLYUBOVA, A.   **a.1924**
She exhibited with the First Working Group of Constructivists in 1924 at the First Discussional Exhibition of Active Revolutionary Artists alongside L.Sanina, A.Gan, Olga and Galina Chichagova, N.G.Smirnov and G.Miller.

MIRONOVICH, P. N.   **a.1919**
Painter. He was represented in the Fourth State Exhibition of

Dmitri Mitrokhin. Cover for Schiller's 'Don Carlos', *1919. Signed with initials lower left and right.*
The book was published by the State Publishing House, Petrograd, 1919.

Paintings (*IV Gosudarstvennaya vystavka kartin*) in Moscow in 1919.

MIROPOLSKY (MITROPOLISKY), Leontiy Semenovich
1749-c.1819
Portrait painter. The date of his birth is sometimes given as 1754 or 1759.
Coll TG; RM; Museum of the Academy, St. Petersburg.

MITEL'MAN, Leonid Yakovlevich   **a.1910-1913**
He studied at the Academy in St. Petersburg. He was a member of Kul'bin's Triangle or so-called Impressionist group and of the Union of Youth 1910-13.

MITROKHIN, Dmitri Isidorovich   **1883-1973**
Painter, graphic artist, illustrator. Born at Yeisk in Azov. He was a prolific book and periodical illustrator. He studied at the Moscow College under Apollinari Vasnetsov and Aleksei Stepanov 1902-4. He knew Larionov and Goncharova. He began to work on book design in 1904 and worked in the Murava enamel workshop 1904-5. He also studied at the Stroganov Institute under Stanislav Noakovsky and S.Yaguzhinsky 1904-5. He travelled to Paris the same year where he attended the Académie de la Grande Chaumière under Steinlen and Grasset 1905-6. He settled in St. Petersburg in 1906 and again produced work for the Murava

Dmitri Mitrokhin. Decorative Vignette, *1920.*
A mysterious personification of fate records events from the middle of the zodiac. She looks down upon a comet or shooting star bursting above a scene of apocalyptic revolution.

and decorative overall design of a mermaid. Henri de Regnier's *Seven Portraits*, Petrograd, 1921, with a cover design like a refined floral wallpaper.
Lit M.Kuzmin, V.Boyinov *D.I.Mitrokhin*, Moscow, 1928. Yu.A.Rusakov *D.I.Mitrokhin*, Leningrad-Moscow, 1966. *Paris-Moscou*, 1979. *Twilight of the Tsars*, London, 1991. A.Kamensky *The World of Art Movement*, Leningrad, 1991.

MITROPOLISKY, L. S. = MIROPOLSKY, L. S.

MITURICH, Petr Vasilievich   1887-1956
Painter, graphic artist and inventor. Born at St. Petersburg. After attending the military school in Pskov 1899-1905, he studied at Kiev Art School 1906-9 where he was impressed by the work of Vrubel'. He then studied at the Academy in St. Petersburg under Nikolai Samokish 1909-15. From 1914 he began a study of the relation of mechanical and organic forms. He exhibited with the World of Art from 1915 to 1918 in Petrograd and showed work at the Exhibition of Paintings: The Year 1915 in Moscow. In 1916 he exhibited at Contemporary Russian Painting at Petrograd. By this time he was aware of Futurist experiment in art and literature and he became a friend of the influential Futurist poet Khlebnikov.

enamel workshops 1907-8. He exhibited in 1910 with the Union of Youth and from 1911 with the World of Art.
After the Revolution he exhibited with the World of Art in December 1917 in Moscow. He also participated in the First State Free Exhibition of Artworks in Petrograd in 1919. He worked on the Art Collegium for Literary Publishing and was placed in charge of illustrating works by Lermontov. He also worked in the graphic art section of the Russian Museum 1918-23 and he taught at the Leningrad Vkhutein 1924-30. He was included in the enormous survey Exhibition of Paintings by Petrograd Artists of All Tendencies 1919-1923 held in Petrograd in 1923, the Paris International Exhibition in 1925 and the major exhibition in Moscow in 1927 marking the tenth anniversary of the Revolution. He was also represented in the exhibition of Russian Graphic Art in Riga in 1929 and the jubilee exhibition Artists of the RSFSR over 15 Years held at the Russian Museum, Leningrad, in 1932.
He lived in Leningrad until 1942, Alma-Ata 1942-4, and then in Moscow. He died in Moscow.
Central Park of Culture and Rest. Rest on the Grass, 1937, etching, employs a decorative technique in which a multitude of lines build up into substantial masses. The scene is of boating and picnics beneath the trees.
Illustrations These were numerous including V.A.Zhukovsky's *The Goblet. A Ballad*, Moscow, 1913, which has a pseudo-Renaissance design on the cover. N.Konradi's *Among the Paintings of the Hermitage*, Moscow, 1917. E.Zamyatin's *Provincial Tales*, Petrograd, 1919, which features a flattened

Dmitri Mitrokhin. Decorative Vignette, *1920. Signed at the base.*
The elegant eroticism of the World of Art movement has survived into the Revolutionary period in an image showing the star of Revolution passing above books and prints all held in a cartouche of flowers.

He attended meetings at the apartment of Lev Bruni in St. Petersburg 1914-16 along with Al'tman, Annenkov, V.Lebedev and others. He was a founder of the society Apartment No. 5 in Petrograd along with Bruni, Isakov, Lebedev, Tyrsa, Punin and Tatlin in 1915.

He saw active service, was wounded in the war and was again wounded in the Revolution.

After the Revolution he worked for the People's Commissariat of the Enlightenment in relation to art teaching in schools. He designed the large square cover of *Our March*, published by the First State Lithographic Press in 1918. He evolved a three-dimensional *Graphic Alphabet* in 1919. He appeared on the April 1919 list of artists for acquisitions by the envisaged Museum of Painterly Culture. He was a close friend of the poet Khlebnikov. He designed a flexible submarine *Volnovoi* or Undulator and produced a series of three-dimensional graphic works or 'graphic constructions'. These suggest that he shared Khlebnikov's abstruse theories of time and space.

Petr Miturich. Spatial Graphics, *1920. Documentary photograph. Miturich has here developed the Cubic studies into slotted and painted forms derived from the cube and cylinder. Some of these constructions were shoulder height.*

Petr Miturich. Cover for Khlebnikov's book 'Zangezi', *1922. Signed with cyrillic 'P.M.' lower left. 'Zangezi' was one of the long poems of Khlebnikov employing several invented languages. Tatlin staged a performance of the poem in 1923. Photograph courtesy of Szymon Bojko.*

His bookcovers testify to his Futurist engagement and include covers for the Futurist composer Artur Lure (Arthur Lourié), including Lure's *Royal' v detskoy* (The Piano in the Nursery) published in Petrograd in 1920. He also designed a cover for the publication of Khlebnikov's long poem *Zangezi*. This poet's own studies of the relation of poetry to material construction and of natural structures may in part reflect the ideas of Miturich. He was represented at the First Russian Art Exhibition in Berlin in 1922. He became Professor of Graphics and Architecture at the Vkhutemas and he moved to Moscow in 1923. He was included in the enormous survey Exhibition of Paintings by Petrograd Artists of All Tendencies 1919-1923 held in Petrograd in 1923.

He continued to study natural construction, designing flying, swimming and crawling machines and in this perhaps reflected Khlebnikov's admiration for the artist as inventor. He was a member of the 4 Arts society 1925-9. He was represented in the exhibition of Russian Graphic Art in Riga in 1929 and in the First Touring Exhibition of Painting and Graphics which opened in Moscow in 1929.

After 1930 he painted landscapes and portraits. He was represented at the jubilee exhibition Artists of the RSFSR over 15 Years held at the Russian Museum, Leningrad, in 1932. He married Khlebnikov's sister V.V.Khlebnikova. He died in Moscow.

Zoopark, 1941, lithograph, is a rythmic print of deer in the snow economically depicted between thick clumps of straight, linear trees *(cont.)*

Book design Cover for V.Khlebnikov *Zangezi*, 1922.
Lit *P.V.Miturich, zhivopis', grafika. Katalog*, Moscow, 1968.
P.V.Miturich, exh. cat., Moscow, 1978. *Paris-Moscou*, 1979.
A.Z.Rudenstine *Costakis Collection*, London, 1981. C.Lodder
Russian Constructivism, New Haven and London, 1982.
Coll Costakis Collection.
Colour plate p.306.

MKhI

The abbreviated name of the Moscow Art Institute
(*Moskovskiy khudozhestvenniy institut*) operative 1945-7.

MOCHALSKY, Dmitri Konstantonovich   1908-1957+
Socialist Realist painter.

MODOROV, Fedor Aleksandrovich   1890-1967
Painter. He was a member of the Union of Moscow Artists
formed in 1925. His work was included in the exhibition of
Soviet art held at Harbin in 1926 and in Japan in 1927 and in
the major exhibition in Moscow in 1927 marking the tenth
anniversary of the Revolution. He was also represented at the
First Touring Exhibition of Painting and Graphics which
opened in Moscow in 1929. He exhibited at the 1932 Venice
Biennale.

**MOELLER, Otto Friedrich Theodor (MOLLER, Fedor
Antonovich)**   1812-1874
German academic painter of genre, portraits and history
paintings. Born in Kronstadt. He became a painter in 1835.
He frequently visited Italy and was painting in Rome in 1840.
He also worked in Russia and died in St. Petersburg.
Coll TG.

Dmitri Moor. Worker at a Steam Turbine, *c.1924. Lithograph. Signed
lower right.*
*The worker, stripped to the waist, is glimpsed as an heroic figure observing
the rapid rotation of the turbine driven by the jet of steam that bursts across
the base of the image. Here the Futurists' techniques for showing energy are
adapted to project an image of dynamic and successful mechanised labour.*

MOGACHEV, S.   a.c.1927
Sculptor. He was included in the major exhibition in Moscow
in 1927 marking the tenth anniversary of the Revolution.

MOGILEVSKY, Naum S.   a.1923-1932
He was included in the enormous survey Exhibition of
Paintings by Petrograd Artists of All Tendencies 1919-1923
held in Petrograd in 1923. He exhibited with the Circle of
Artists in Leningrad between 1927 and 1929. He was
represented at the jubilee exhibition Artists of the RSFSR over
15 Years held at the Russian Museum, Leningrad, in 1932.

MOISEENKO, E. E.   b.1916
Coll TG.

MOISEEV, Petr Ivanovich   early 19th century
Painter of panoramic themes. He studied in Moscow.
Coll TG.

MOISENSKY, Evsei   b.1916
Painter of figure compositions.
Coll RM.

MOKHNACHEV, Vasili Pavlovich   b.1797
Coll TG.

MOKRITSKY, Apollon Nikolaevich   1810-1870
Painter. Subjects include Italian landscapes.
Coll TG.

MOLCHANOV, Grigoriy Dmitrievich   c.1730-c.1786
Portraitist.
Coll TG.

MOLCHANOV, Konstantin Mikhailovich   1906-1980
Graphic artist, painter. He was represented at the First Russian
Art Exhibition in Berlin in 1922. He was represented at the
jubilee exhibition Artists of the RSFSR over 15 Years held at the
Russian Museum, Leningrad, in 1932. He died in Moscow.

MOLLER, F. A. = MOELLER, O.F.T.

MONASTYRSKY, A.   a.1912-1917
Active in Kiev. He taught Tyshler at the Kiev Art Institute
c.1912-17.

MONCHINSKY, F. Z.   a.1919
Painter. He exhibited at the juryless Eighth State Exhibition
in Moscow in 1919.

MONIN, Aleksandr Aleksandrovich   1896-1969
Painter. He exhibited at the juryless Eighth State Exhibition
in Moscow in 1919. He also exhibited in the 1921 exhibition
of the World of Art in Moscow. He was a member of AKhRR
in 1926. He died in Moscow.

MOOR, Dmitri Stakhievich (ORLOV, D.)   1883-1946
One of the most celebrated poster designers of the early
Soviet period. Born at Novocherkassk. He was studying under
P.Kelin in 1910 and was contributing to the review *Budilnik*.
After the Revolution he became an active designer of
propaganda trains and window posters for the Rosta agency.
He made line drawings for caricature anti-Tsarist illustrations
in the periodical *Budil'shchik*, No.11-12, 1917, one of which
addresses the departing Tsar with the words 'Citizen, take
your crown too'. In 1918 he worked on decorations for Red
Square, Moscow, for the 1 May celebrations. He contributed

ТЫ

ЧЕМ ПОМОГ ФРОНТУ?

Dmitri Moor. Second World War Poster, *1941. Colour lithograph. 102 x 69 cm. Signed 'DMoor' lower left. The inscription reads 'You — How are You Helping the Battle Front ?' The message is that hard work in the factory is essential to the military war effort.*

satirical illustrations to numerous periodicals including *Izvestia* from 1919, *Pravda* from 1920, *Krasnoarmeets* from 1922, and in 1922 he was a co-founder of the satirical magazine *Krokodil*. *Lef* magazine announced in its issue No. 4 in 1923 that he was amongst the artists working for a new periodical *Krysodav* along with various Futurists and Constructivists. He was the

art director and also an illustrator for the reviews *Bezbozhnik* and *Bezbozhnik i Stanka* 1923-8. He was represented at the Paris International Exhibition in 1925, at the seventh exhibition of the group *L'Araignée* (The Spider) at the Galerie Devambe in Paris in 1925 and at the exhibition of Revolutionary posters in Berlin in 1927. He taught at the

Konstantin Makovsky. A Russian Beauty. *Signed. Oil on canvas. 80 x 55 cm.*
Reproduced by kind permission of Sotheby's London, sale 16.6.1992, lot 62.

Vladimir Makovsky. Portrait Study, *1878. Oil on paper mounted on canvas. Dated and signed 'V.Mak.' in cyrillic script. 25.5 x 18.5 cm. Malmö Konstmuseum.*

Kazimir Malevich. Suprematist Composition, *c.1920-2. Oil on wood panel. 62 x 30 cm. Courtesy Annely Juda Fine Art, London.*

Kazimir Malevich. Suprematist Composition, *c.1915-16. Coloured crayons, pencil and watercolour. 36 x 44.5 cm. Private collection, courtesy Annely Juda Fine Art, London.*

Vkhutemas in Moscow 1922-30 and exhibited with the October group as a founder member in 1928. In 1930 he was represented in the Exhibition of Graphic Arts, Poster and Book Design at Danzig. He died in Moscow.

You — How are You Helping the Battle Front?', poster in red and black, is strongly reminiscent of the Kitchener recruitment poster but here a Red Army soldier points imperiously to the viewer, a factory belches smoke behind him.

Help!, 1921-2, poster, of a starving old peasant with arms raised.

Writings D.Moor *Izbrannie proizvedeniya*, 1958. D.Moor *Ya Bolshevik* (I am a Bolshevik), Moscow, 1967.

Lit R.Kaufman *D.Moor*, Moscow, 1937. M.Ioffe *D.S.Moor*, Moscow-Leningrad, 1948. K.Khalaminsky *Moor*, Moscow, 1961. *Paris-Moscou*, 1979.

MORAVOV, Aleksandr Viktorovich   1878-1951
Socialist Realist genre painter. Born in the Kiev region. He studied at the N.Murashko School in Kiev and at the Moscow College under N.Kasatkin, A.Arkhipov, V.Serov and K.Korovin until 1902. He then taught typographic lithography in Moscow from 1902 to 1913. He joined the Wanderers in 1904.

After the Revolution he taught at the Free Art Studios (SVOMAS) at Tver 1918-22 and appeared on the April 1919 list of artists for acquisitions by the envisaged Museum of Painterly Culture. He participated in the Third Exhibition of Paintings held at Ryazan in 1919. He was represented at the First Russian Art Exhibition in Berlin in 1922. He joined AKhRR in 1923. He was represented at the jubilee exhibition Artists of the RSFSR over 15 Years held at the Russian Museum, Leningrad, in 1932. He was made an Academician of the USSR. He died in Moscow.

The Country Registry Office, 1928, TG, is essentially an example of 19th century genre technique applied to a Soviet theme. The grinning soldier flanked by two colourfully clad but well wrapped up young women talks to the official at the desk. There is an image of Lenin among the posters on the wall.

Lit I.Pikulev *A.V.Moravov*, Moscow, 1950. *A.V.Moravov Album*, Moscow, 1961. *Paris-Moscou*, 1979.

Coll Well represented at TG.

MORDVINOV, Count Aleksandr Nikolaevich 1799-1858
Painter. Subjects include Italian landscapes. He worked in Venice and was painting in Naples in 1833. He signed his work 'M.A'.

Coll TG; RM.

MOREVSKY, N. N.   a.1921
He exhibited with Kudryashov and others at the First State Exhibition in Orenburg in 1921.

MORGUNOV, Aleksei Alekseevich   1884-1935
Painter. Born in Moscow. He studied at the Stroganov School in Moscow and privately under Sergei I.Ivanov and K.Korovin. He exhibited with the Moscow Association of Artists 1904-10 and through it met Malevich and Klyun. As a result he became increasingly involved in experiment. He travelled to Germany, Austria, Italy and France 1909-10. He joined the Knave of Diamonds in 1910 and exhibited with

them in 1910 and 1913-1914, but he also exhibited with the World of Art in 1911 and 1912, with the *Oslinyy Khvost* (Donkey's Tail) group in Moscow in 1912, and with the Union of Youth in 1911 and 1913-14. Like Malevich he produced so-called 'alogist' works 1913-14 featuring the juxtaposition of disparate images assembled together without continuity of theme or scale. During the war years he exhibited at Tramway V in Petrograd in 1915 and *Magazin* (The Store) in Moscow in 1916. He was married to the daughter of the landscape painter Aleksei Savrasov.

After the Revolution he exhibited with the Artists of the Leftist Federation of the Professional Union in 1918 along with Popova, Rodchenko, Tatlin and others and at the Fifth State Exhibition: Impressionism to Non-Objective Art held in Moscow 1918-19. He was involved in the reorganisation of the art world in Russia under the auspices of IZO Narkompros, the People's Commissariat of the Enlightenment in 1918, he taught painting at the Free Art Studios (SVOMAS) in Moscow 1918-20, and was listed as leader of a course for art teachers along with Tatlin and others in 1919. He served on the Moscow Collegium of IZO under Tatlin in 1919. His name was twenty-first on the list of artists published in April 1919 for purchases by the Museum of Painterly Culture. He was engaged on Agitprop decorations in Moscow, and he joined Proletkult. He was also a member of the Group for Objective Analysis associated with the Institute of Artistic Culture (INKhUK) in Moscow. He was represented at the First Russian Art Exhibition in Berlin in 1922. He contributed to the Third Exhibition of Paintings by Artists from Kaluga and Moscow held in Kaluga in 1925 and to the jubilee exhibition Artists of the RSFSR over 15 Years held at the Russian Museum, Leningrad, in 1932.

In later years he became a Socialist Realist painter.

Standing Figure (The Aviator), 1912-13, Costakis Collection, is close to Malevich in its faceted Futurist subject. Other works incorporate numbers, lettering and fragmented objects and discontinuities of style and scale comparable to 'alogist' works by Malevich.

Lit A.Z.Rudenstine *Costakis Collection*, London, 1981. *L'Avant-garde russe 1905-1925*, exh. cat., Musée des Beaux-Arts, Nantes, 1993.

Coll Krasnodar Art Museum; Tomsk Art Museum; Yaroslavl' Art Museum; Costakis Collection.

MOROZOV, Aleksandr Ivanovich   1835-1904
Landscape painter. Member of the Artel which led to the founding of the Wanderers movement in 1870.

MOROZOV, Aleksandr Ivanovich   b.1902
Painter, graphic artist. Born at Ivanovo-Voznesensk. He studied in Moscow 1926-30.

Coll RM.

MOROZOVA-EKKERT, E.   a.1932
She was represented at the jubilee exhibition Artists of the RSFSR over 15 Years held at the Russian Museum, Leningrad, in 1932.

MOSHCHEVITIN, D. P.   a.1921
He was included in the Third Touring Exhibition of the Sovetsk Regional subdepartment of the Museums Bureau along with Kandinsky, Rodchenko and others in 1921.

MOSOLOV, N.   a.1921

He was included in the Third Touring Exhibition of the Sovetsk Regional subdepartment of the Museums Bureau along with Kandinsky, Rodchenko and others in 1921.

MOSTOVA (-MATVEEVA) (MATVEEVA-MOSTOVA), Zoya Yakovlevna   1884-1972

Painter. Born at Perm. She studied at the Kiev School of Art until 1905 and then under Yan Tsionglinsky at the Academy in St. Petersburg in 1907. She showed work at the exhibition Modern Trends in 1908. In 1910 she visited France and Italy. She then worked as a school teacher during 1910-19. She exhibited with the Union of Youth, of which she was a founder member, in 1912-13. She married the sculptor Aleksandr Matveev in 1914.

After the Revolution she exhibited with the 4 Arts society in Leningrad including the exhibiton of 1928 at the Russian Museum. She was represented at the jubilee exhibition Artists of the RSFSR over 15 Years held at the Russian Museum, Leningrad, in 1932. She died in Moscow.

Lit J.Howard *The Union of Youth — An Artists' Society of the Russian Avant-Garde*, Manchester and New York, 1992.
Coll RM.

MOSYAGIN, Vladimir Sergeevich   d.1923

Ceramics artist. He exhibited at the house of Arts in 1921 and at the Artists' Commune Exhibition in Petrograd in 1922. The State Porcelain Factory executed designs by him in 1922.
Lit N.Lobanov-Rostovsky *Revolutionary Ceramics*, London, 1990.

MOTOVILOV, Georgiy Ivanovich   1884-1963

Sculptor. He produced an heroic *Metalworker*, bronze, 1936, and he was engaged to produce reliefs for the main entrance of the All-Russian Agricultural Exhibition of 1939 in Moscow. These comprised high relief figures of productive agricultural workers set into the architectural ensemble. He was particularly active on sculptural decorations for the Moscow Metro in 1944 including the Elektrozavodskaya, Komsomolskaya and Kaluzhskaya Stations. Later works include a seated *Chekhov* at Yalta 1948-53 and large equestrian sculptures for the Volga-Don Canal which were executed with assistants in 1952. He made architectural figure reliefs for the Moscow University building in 1953 and for the Palace of Science and Culture in Warsaw in 1955. He was given a joint exhibition with the painter Aleksandr Kuprin in Moscow in 1957.

MOZEL'-DMITRIEV   a.1925

Graphic artist. He contributed to the First Exhibition of Cinema Posters held in Moscow in 1925.

MOZGOV, Timofey Illarionovich   1866-1919

Signed 'T.Mozg'.

MUKHARSKY, S.   a.1920

He was designing posters in 1920.

MUKHIN, B. A.   a.1921

He exhibited with Kudryashov and others at the First State Exhibition in Orenburg in 1921.

MUKHIN, Viktor Ivanovich   b.1914

Sculptor. Works include the *Monument to Members of the*

Young Guard at Krasnodon which was made in collaboration with Agibalov and Fedchenko in 1954.

MUKHINA, Vera Ignatievna   1889-1953

One of the most celebrated and impressive of the sculptors who adapted the academic nude and a rather Rodinesque surface to produce monumental sculpture in the Soviet period. She was well able to retain the authority of her own vision, inventiveness and style even when working on a colossal scale and within the restraints of a commission that demanded propaganda first and foremost. She was a highly talented and inventive sculptress who knew many of the avant-garde but who developed in the tradition of Rodin and Bourdelle. This made her work compatible with the requirements of state commissions for public sculpture in the Soviet period.

Born at Riga into a family of merchants. She grew up in Kiev and Kursk and attended school in Feodosia in the Crimea. She studied painting in Moscow under Yuon, where she met Popova and Udal'tsova, and then under Mashkov 1911-12.

But in 1912-14 she was in Paris attending the Académie de la Grande Chaumière under the sculptor Antoine Bourdelle where she met her future biographer the sculptor Boris Ternovets as well as the Cubist sculptors Zadkine and Lipchitz. She also attended anatomy lectures at the Ecole des Beaux-Arts. She visited Brittany with Lyubov' Popova and Boris Ternovets in 1913, and in April 1914 she was in Italy with Popova.

In Moscow Popova introduced her to Exter whose work for the Kamerny Theatre led to a commission for masks of Apollo and Dionysus by Mukhina. She designed for the Moscow Kamerny (Chamber) Theatre 1915-16 as Exter's assistant.

After the Revolution she responded, like Lebedeva, to Lenin's call for monumental propaganda. During 1919-20 she was a founder of the *Monolit* (Monolith) group of sculptors, which included Babichev, Mukhina, Konen'kov, Krandevskaya, Korolev, Strakhovskaya, Zlatovratsky, Ternovets, V.Popova, Blazhevich and Kudinov. They worked on monumental propaganda and entered the competitive exhibition for a *Monument to Liberated Labour* held in Moscow in May 1920. She also exhibited with the revived World of Art in 1921. She assisted Exter on the design of the film *Aelita* in 1924. She was a member of the 4 Arts society, which was founded in 1924, and a member of the Society of Russian Sculptors from 1926. She was included in the major exhibition in Moscow in 1927 marking the tenth anniversary of the Revolution. She taught at the Moscow Vkhutein 1926-30. She exhibited in Venice in 1928 and visited France that year.

In addition by 1923 she was contributing to the costume projects associated with Lamanova, including the Modern Costume Studios, the Fashion Studio (*Atel'e mod, Atelier Mode*), as well as the costume department of the Academy. She produced dress designs which were exhibited at the Paris International Exhibition in 1925, together with those of Lamanova, Pribylskaya and Makarova. She made textile designs 1923-6. She produced dress designs into the 1930s. She was a member of the Arts Council of the Moscow House of Clothing Design from its inception in 1933.

She was working in Voronezh in 1930 but returned to Moscow in 1932. She was represented at the jubilee exhibition Artists of the RSFSR over 15 Years held at the Russian

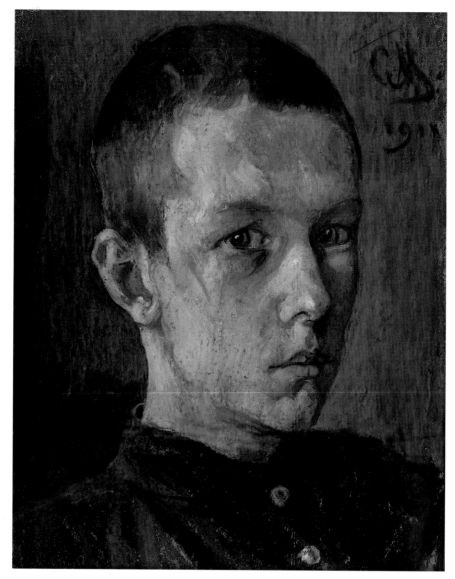

Sergei Malyutin. The Artist's Son, *1911. On paper. Signed 'S.M.' in cyrillic script. 36.7 x 28.5 cm. Malmö Konstmuseum.*

Museum, Leningrad, in 1932. In 1937 her colossal *Worker and Collective Farm Worker* dominated the Soviet Pavilion at the Paris International Exhibition.

Later sculptural works include *Astra*, a glass vase like an open crocus in shape 1940, the three-quarter length *Ballerina M.T.Semenova* 1941, an heroic and generalised head of a *Woman Partisan* 1942, and busts of *Dr. A.A.Zamkov* 1935 marble, *B.A.Yusupov* 1942 bronze, and *A.N.Krylov* 1945 wood. Her statues of *Gorky* were erected in Moscow in 1951 and in the city of Gorky in 1952. The latter was designed in collaboration with Zelenskaya and Ivanova based on a project by Shadr.

She exhibited in Moscow together with Sarra Lebedeva, Sergei Gerasimov, A.A.Deineka, P.P.Konchalovsky and D.A.Shmarinov in 1943. She was made an Academician of the USSR. She died in Moscow.

Portrait of V.A.Shamshina, 1916, toned plaster, RM, indicates her ability to grasp the particularities of form and make a unique portrait that is specific to the sitter and individual as a sculpture.

The Flame of Revolution, 1922-3, is a mechanistic work wresting monumental rhetoric from Cubist stylisation, block-like and dynamic, expressing strength and force appropriate to its theme. It originated as a monument to the revolutionary Yakov M.Sverdlov.

Worker and Collective Farm Worker, 1937, a colossal sculpture designed for the top of the Soviet Pavilion at the International Exhibition in Paris in 1937 and later re-erected at Moscow. Surging forward with an enormous stride the heroic man and woman fling one arm behind them and with the other raise the hammer and sickle against the sky (p.27). This sculpture was the embodiment of industry and agriculture but it was also the ultimate expression of the political, propagandist and yet impressively dynamic monument. It was constructed twenty-four metres high from stainless steel to stand on top of the pavilion by Iofan, itself thirty-four metres high, which it treats

Filip Malyavin. Self -portrait, *1931. Oil on canvas. Dated and signed 'Ph.Maliavine'. 115 x 87 cm.*
Malmö Konstmuseum.

as a mere plinth.

Bread, 1939, comprises two kneeling female nudes holding a sheaf of corn on their shoulders to form a bridge-like composition with empty space beneath it.

Theatre design 1915-16 costumes for Sem Benelli's *La Cena delle Beffe* (The Supper of Jokes), for Tairov's Chamber Theatre, Moscow (unrealised).

Writings V.Mukhina *A Sculptor's Thoughts*, Moscow, 1952.

Lit B.Ternovets *V.I.Mukhina*, Moscow-Leningrad, 1937. A.Zotov *V.I.Mukhina*, Moscow-Leningrad, 1944. R.Klimov, ed., *V.Mukhina*, Moscow, 1960 (3 vols.). T.Strizhenova *Iz istorii sovetskogo kostyuma*, Moscow, 1972 (English edition: Tatiana Strizhenova, *Soviet Costume and Textiles 1917-1945*, Paris, 1991). O.Voronova *V.I.Mukhina*, Moscow, 1976. *Paris-Moscou*, 1979. P.K.Suzdalev *V.I.Mukhina* Moscow, 1981. J.E.Bowlt *Russian Stage Design. Scenic Innovation. From the Collection of Mr. and Mrs. Nikita D.Lobanov-Rostovsky*, Jackson, MS, exh. cat.,1982. M.N.Yablonskaya *Women Artists of Russia's New Age*, London, 1990. Dzhon Boult (John Bowlt) *Khudozhniki russkogo teatra. Sobranie Nikity i Niny Lobanovykh-Rostovskikh*, Moscow, 1991.

Coll RM; TG.

MURASHEV a.1921
A member of the *Bytie* (Existence) Society of Artists formed in Moscow in 1921.

MURASHKO, Aleksandr Aleksandrovich b.1875
Genre painter. He studied at the Academy in St. Petersburg 1894-1900. He became the director of the Kiev Art School in 1913.

MURASHKO, Nikolai Ivanovich 1844-1909
Ukrainian painter of single and group portraits and landscapes, draughtsman, lithographer. Born at Krovlevz. His portraits were loosely handled and vigorous in their modelling. He retained a firm grasp of anatomy, chiaroscuro and composition in the midst of his rather painterly approach.

Vera Mukhina. Costume Design for Benelli's 'The Jest', *1916. Gouache, ink and gold-bronze paint. 49.7 x 68 cm. Collection Mr. and Mrs. Nikita D.Lobanov-Rostovsky, London.*

Vera Mukhina. Bread, *1939. Toned plaster. 150 x 150 x 100 cm.*
Mukhina's supreme academic professionalism was well suited to Socialist Realist themes, but she also had a thorough awareness of Western trends and a vigorously inventive ability with composition which lifts her work out of its political context to make sculptures that remain impressive. This one was designed for the Moskvoretsky Bridge in Moscow.

He worked in the Ukraine where he founded the Kiev Art School. He died at Kiev.
On the Dneiper, 1880s, Museum of Ukrainian Art, Kiev, is a landscape with a high viewpoint looking down from a tree-lined path into the wide Dneiper valley where rafts of logs are floating. It is a celebration of the sun, scale and cardinal river of the Ukraine.
Coll Museum of Ukrainian Art, Kiev.

MURAVIN, Lev Davydovich   **b.1906**
Ukrainian academic sculptor. Works include a term of the Chinese artist *Tsi Bai Shi* made in 1955.

MUROMTSEVA   **a.1926**
She was a member of the Society of Russian Sculptors from 1926.

MURZICH, I.   **a.1918**
He executed Agitprop decorations on the banks of the Ekaterinsky Canal, Petrograd, in 1918.

MURZIN, Semen Akimovich   **1820-1880**
Portraitist.
Coll TG.

MUSATOV = BORISOV-MUSATOV, V.E.

MUZhV/MUZhVZ

The abbreviated name of the Moscow College of Painting and Sculpture (*Moskovskoe uchilishche zhivopisi i vayaniya*) from its foundation until 1865 when it became the Moscow College of Painting, Sculpture and Architecture (*Moskovskoe uchilishche zhivopisi, vayaniya i zodchestva*) until 1918 (MUZhVZ).

MYAGKOV, Timofey Egorovich   **1813-1865**
Portraitist.
Coll TG.

MYANNI, Olav   **b.1925**
Sculptor of academic, patriotic history pieces. Works include, for example, a group representing warriors from the year 1224.

MYASOEDOV, Grigoriy Grigorevich   **1834-1911**
Painter of themes of Russian labour, genre and history. Born in the Tula region into a family of minor nobility. He studied at the Academy in St. Petersburg 1853-62. He was a founder member of the Wanderers. Works included *The Zemstvo at Dinner*, 1872. He sometmes signed his work simply 'G.M'. He died at St. Petersburg.
Writings G.G.Myasoedov *Pis'ma, dokumenty, vospominaniya*, Moscow, 1972.
Lit I.N.Shuvalova *Myasoedov*, Leningrad, 1971.
Coll TG; RM.

Mikhail Matyushin. Crystal Self -portrait, *c.1919. Oil on canvas. 65.5 x 40.5 cm.*
Private collection, courtesy Annely Juda Fine Art, London.

Petr Miturich. Spatial Alphabet, *1915-18. Gouache and ink on card. Each 5.5 x 5.5 x 5.5 cm.*
Miturich was closely associated with the poet Khlebnikov who proposed a system of relating sounds to shapes. Miturich may be responding to this concept. There are twelve extant cubes in this particular set.
Private collection, courtesy Annely Juda Fine Art, London.

Nikolai Milioti. Oriental Theme, *c.1914. Oil on canvas. 101 x 81.5 cm.*
Malmö Konstmuseum.

N.D. (cyrillic) see **DOSEIKIN, N.V.**
N.D.OR. see **DMITRIEV-ORENBURGSKY, N.D.**
N.K. (cyrillic) see **KUL'BIN, N.K.; KUPREYANOV, N.N.**
N.L. (cyrillic) see **LOMTEV, N.A.**
N.P.Kr. (cyrillic) see **KRYMOV, N.P.**
N.R. (monogram) see **ROERICH, N.**

NABOKOV, N. V.   **1839-1926**
Theatre designer who designed a production of Verdi's *Aida*
in the 1860s.

NAGIBIN, N.N.   **a.1919**
Painter. He exhibited at the juryless Eighth State Exhibition
in Moscow in 1919.

NAGUBNIKOV, Svyatoslav Aleksandrovich   1886-1914?
Painter. He studied at the Academy in St. Petersburg 1910-14.
He exhibited with the Union of Youth 1910-12, at the
Academy 1911-13 and with the World of Art in 1913.
Lit J.Howard *The Union of Youth — An Artists' Society of the
Russian Avant-Garde*, Manchester and New York, 1992.

NAKHMAN, M. M.   **a.1917-1920**
Painter. He exhibited with the World of Art in December
1917 in Moscow, at the First Exhibition of Works of the
Professional Union of Artists in Moscow in 1918, in the
Fourth State Exhibition of Paintings (*IV Gosudarstvennaya
vystavka kartin*) in Moscow in 1919 and at the enormous First
State Exhibition of Art and Science held in Kazan in 1920.

**NALEPINSKAYA-BOYCHUK, Sof'ya Aleksandrovna
1884-1939**
Printmaker. She made wood engravings, a technique that
Favorsky had done so much to encourage, but showed
considerable originality. Her themes could reflect recent
history with a social or political message. An example is *Before
the White Army Attack*, wood engraving, 1927, which depicts a
worker loading his rifle in a back yard. His shoeless wife and
child sit on the doorstep. It is an effective piece of narrative
dependent upon the evocation of powerful symbols of family,
survival and defence.
She contributed to the All-Union Polygraphic Exhibition in
Moscow in 1927, to the exhibition of graphic art Liberation
Movements: The Sixteenth to the Twentieth Century held in
Moscow in 1928 and to the exhibition of Russian Graphic Art
in Riga in 1929.

NARBUT, Georgiy (Egor) Ivanovich   1886-1920
Graphic artist, illustrator, painter. Born in the Ukraine. He
studied history and philology at the University of St. Petersburg
until 1906 but also received lessons from the painter and graphic
artist Bilibin. He studied at the Elizaveta Zvantseva School in St.
Petersburg under Dobuzhinsky 1907-8 and in Munich at the
Simon Hollósy School 1909-10. He exhibited with the First
Izdcbsky International Salon in Odessa 1909-10. He lived in
St. Petersburg until 1917. He exhibited with the World of Art

from 1911, with the Union of Russian Artists and the New
Society of Artists.
After the Revolution he returned to the Ukraine where in 1918
he became professor at the Kiev Academy and subsequently
Vice-Chancellor of the Ukrainian Academy of Arts. He died in
Kiev. Chekhonin advised the State Porcelain Factory to use his
silhouette designs on ceramics for export 1920-3.
*Solntse trud (Labour Sun), periodical cover for issue No.1,
1919, is elegant in the manner of Chekhonin. It shows a rather
willowy worker with gun and hammer before a factory.
Between them a great red star.
Illustrations included the stories *How the Mice Buried the Cat*
by Zhukovsky, 1910, and *The Intrepid Tin Soldier* , 1913, by
H.C.Andersen
Lit P.Beletsky *G.I.Narbut*, Kiev, 1959. P.Beletsky *G.I.Narbut*,
Leningrad, 1985. N.Lobanov-Rostovsky *Revolutionary
Ceramics*, London, 1990. A.Kamensky *The World of Art
Movement*, Leningrad, 1991.
Coll TG; RM; Museum of Ukrainian Art, Kiev.

NARKOMPROS
The abbreviated name of the People's Commissariat of the
Enlightenment (*Narodnyi komissariat prosveshcheniya*).
Lit S.Fitzpatrick *The Commissariat of the Enlightenment. Soviet*

Georgiy Narbut. Illustration to Zhukovsky's 'How the Mice Buried
the Cat', *1910. Ink on paper. 26.1 x 20 cm.
Museum of Ukrainian Art, Kiev.*

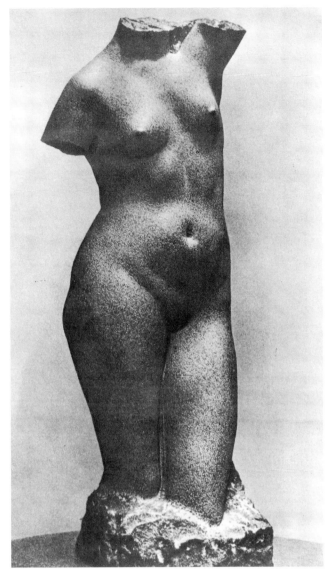

Ernst Neizvestny. Female Torso, *1955. Granite. 105 x 35 x 30 cm.*
The academic traditions of sculpture were preserved and promoted by
Socialist Realism in the 1930s and 1940s. Sculptors of that generation laid
the foundations for a highly disciplined and professional training for younger
artists. This early carving by Neizvestny shows the control which such
training instilled. It provided a knowledge of materials and of anatomy
which was invaluable in the more experimental years which followed.
Neizvestny had learned specific techniques and disciplines which he could
adapt with great imagination in later works of a much freer kind.

Organisation of Education and Arts under Lunacharsky,
Cambridge, 1970.

NAUMOV, Aleksandr Ilych   **1899-1928**
Theatre, exhibition and poster designer, painter. Born in the
Moscow region. He studied at the Stroganov Institute,
Moscow from 1909 to 1917.
After the Revolution he studied at the Moscow Free Art Studios
(SVOMAS) and at the Vkhutemas 1918-21 and was engaged in
propaganda decorations in Moscow. He exhibited in the first
Obmokhu (Society of Young Artists) exhibition in Moscow in
May 1919 and also took part in the third Obmokhu exhibition in
Moscow in May 1921, along with Ioganson, Medunetsky and
others, and he later joined the group October. His theatre

designs included Aleksandr Tairov's production of *Antigone* at
the Moscow Kamerny (Chamber) Theatre. He was represented
at the Second Exhibition of Cinema Posters held at the
Kamerny (Chamber) Theatre, Moscow, in 1926. His exhibition
design included work at Cologne in 1928. He was also a
designer of playbills, cinema posters and of books for the
publishers ZIF and Gosizdat. He died in Moscow.
Theatre design 1927 Tairov's production of *Antigone* at the
Kamerny (Chamber) Theatre, Moscow. The design was strongly
reminiscent of Vesnin and Exter's work of 1921-2 with some
influence of the Stenberg brothers in its assemblage of boxy
ramps and steps. There were also stylised figures in armour.
Lit *Paris-Moscou*, 1979.

NAUMOV, Pavel Semenovich   **1884-1942**
Painter. He studied under D.N.Kardovsky at the Academy in
St. Petersburg 1904-11. He exhibited with the Golden Fleece
in Moscow 1909-10 and with the Union of Youth in 1910.
After the Revolution he was engaged on Agitprop decorations in
Mariinskaya Square, Petrograd, in 1918. He participated in the
First State Free Exhibition of Artworks in Petrograd in 1919 and
was included in the enormous survey Exhibition of Paintings by
Petrograd Artists of All Tendencies 1919-1923 held in Petrograd
in 1923. He exhibited with the group The Sixteen.

NAZAREVSKAYA, G. A.   **a.1925**
She exhibited with the Society of Moscow Painters at its
inaugural exhibition in Moscow in 1925.

NAZAREVSKAYA, M. S.   **a.1922**
She was represented at the First Russian Art Exhibition in
Berlin in 1922.

NAZAREVSKY   **a.1919**
He was listed as leader of a course for art teachers along with
Tatlin and others in 1919.

NEDBAYLO, Mikhail Ivanovich   **1901-1943**
Painter. He exhibited with the group The Thirteen in 1929
and at the First Touring Exhibition of Painting and Graphics
which opened in Moscow in 1929. He taught at Yaroslavl in
1928. He was killed at the front in Belorussia.

NEDRIT, I.P.   **a.1919**
Painter. He exhibited at the juryless Eighth State Exhibition
in Moscow in 1919.

NEFEDOV, S. = ER'ZYA, S.D.

NEHF, Timoleon Carl von (NEFF, Timofey Andreevich)
1805-1876
Painter. Born at Mödders, Estonia. He studied under Hartmann
in Dresden and subsequently visited Rome. He moved to Russia
in 1826 and settled in St. Petersburg. He painted court portraits,
genre, history paintings and Italian themes. He was appointed as
a court painter in 1832 and became a member of the Academy in
1839. He executed work at St. Isaak's Cathedral, St. Petersburg,
in 1842. He became a professor at the Academy in 1865. He also
produced paintings for the Russian churches at Nice and
Wiesbaden. He died at St. Petersburg.
Coll TG; RM.

NEIZVESTNY, Ernst Iosipovich   **b.1926**
Sculptor,draughtsman. Born in the Urals where he also spent
his childhood. He saw military action in the Second World
War at the age of seventeen. He then studied philosophy and

Mikhail Nesterov. The Vision of the Boy Varfolomei, *1889. Oil on canvas mounted on cardboard. Signed and dated lower right. 22.8 x 41.5 cm. State Tretyakov Gallery, Moscow.*

also attended the Surikov Institute in Moscow to study art. He joined the Union of Artists and evolved numerous ambitious monumental projects, some so large as to preclude complete realisation. He has enormous energy as evident in his sculpture as in his illustrations and graphic work, much of which concerns the interaction of human beings and machines. He illustrated Dante's *Divine Comedy* and numerous other literary works, but he has also written philosophical and theoretical texts. His many dramatically intense sculptural works include an immaculately carved classical nude in granite in 1955 and a relief for Moscow Crematorium. He devised a project for a *Monument to the Cosmonaut*.

Exhibitions were held in Italy, Britain and Paris in 1966 and a retrospective was held at the Municipal Museum of Modern Art in Paris in 1970.

Writings E.Neizvestny *Space, Time and Synthesis: Essays on Art, Literature and Philosophy*, Oakville, New York, London, 1990.
Lit O.Andreyeva-Carlisle *Des voix dans la neige*, Paris, 1964. John Berger *Art and Revolution. Ernst Neizvestny and the Role of the Artist in the USSR*, London, 1969.

NEKRASOV, Evgeniy Nikolaevich　　　　**b.1902**
Painter. He worked in Tatlin's Group for Material Culture from 1922 at the Petrograd Institute of Artistic Culture.

NELEPINSKAYA-BOYCHUK, S. A.
= NALEPINSKAYA-BOYCHUK, S. A.

NELIKHIN, A.N.
His name appeared on the April 1919 list of artists for acquisitions by the envisaged Museum of Painterly Culture.

NEMOV, Aleksei D.　　　　**a.1928-1932**
He was engaged in Agitprop decorations at the Security Police Club, Moscow, c.1928. He was represented at the jubilee exhibition Artists of the RSFSR over 15 Years held at the Russian Museum, Leningrad, in 1932.

NEOFITOV, A.N.　　　　**a.1919**
Painter. He exhibited at the juryless Eighth State Exhibition in Moscow in 1919.

NEPRINTSEV, Yuri Mikhailovich　　　　**1909-1955+**
Socialist Realist painter. Born at Tiflis. His birthdate is sometimes given as 1909.
Rest After the Battle, 1955, TG, some thirty soldiers in high spirits gather in a snowy forest clearing laughing at their experience or at some joke. This is the precise parallel to Socialist Realist history painting which is in effect costume drama on the same themes. Here it is vigorous without being wild and rhetorical without loss of detail.
Coll TG.

NERADOVSKY, Petr Ivanovich　　　　**1875-1962**
Painter, graphic artist, art historian. He studied at the Academy in St. Petersburg under S.Korovin and I.Repin. From 1909 he worked as a curator at the Russian Museum in St. Petersburg.
After the Revolution he was a member of the 4 Arts society which was founded in 1924. He continued as curator at the Russian Museum until 1932 and was in addition a member of the Board of Directors of the Tretyakov Gallery, Moscow, in 1925-8. He was included in the major exhibition in Moscow in 1927 marking the tenth anniversary of the Revolution. With Dobychina and Punin he organised the exhibition Artists of the RSFSR over 15 Years at the Russian Museum, Leningrad, in 1932.
Coll TG.

NERODA, Georgiy Vasilievich　　　　**b.1895**
Sculptor. Works include a monumental academic portrait of *Ordzhonikidze* at Kislovodsk in 1952.

NERODA, Yuri Georgevich　　　　**b.1920**
Sculptor. Works include an heroic academic female head in marble in 1953.

Ignati Nivinsky. Stage Set for Carlo Gozzi's 'Princess Turandot', *1922-3. Colour lithograph. 16 x 22 cm. Private collection.*

NESTEROV, Mikhail Vasilievich   **1862-1942**

Painter. Born at Ufa into a merchant's family. He studied at the Moscow College under Perov, Savrasov and Pryanishnikov 1877-81 and 1884-6. In between he studied at the Academy in St. Petersburg 1881-4 under Chistyakov. He exhibited with the Wanderers from 1889 and was a member from 1896. He became involved with the circle of Mamontov at Abramtsevo. He moved to Kiev in 1890 until 1910 and executed ikons for St.Vladimir's Cathedral 1891-5. He was represented at the Exhibition of Russian and Finnish Artists in St. Petersburg in 1898 and he exhibited with the World of Art in 1899-1901. He executed murals at Abastuman in 1901. He travelled widely to France, Germany, Greece and Italy. He again executed murals, this time in Moscow, 1907-12, and was represented at the International Exhibition in Rome in 1911.

After the Revolution he was represented at the enormous First State Exhibition of Art and Science, which included ethnographic material, held in Kazan in 1920 and at the First Russian Art Exhibition in Berlin in 1922. He continued to paint and late portraits include the artists *Shadr* 1934, *Kruglikova* 1938, and *Mukhina* 1940. He was given numerous honours at the end of his life: he was made State Prize Laureate in 1941, Artist of Merit of the RSFSR in 1942 and received the Order of the Red Banner of Labour the same year. He died in Moscow.

Initially a kind of other-worldly Russian Burne-Jones, he was inspired also by the Wanderers. He produced compositions of decorative elegance and refinement to invoke a melancholic image of a Russian past imbued with a sense of spiritual yearning, or portraits with a wan mood set in the Russian landscape. His drawing was precise and by emphasising outline or silhouette he composed rhythmic paintings at once both decorative and descriptive.

Writings M.V.Nesterov *Iz pisem*, Leningrad, 1968.
Lit S.Durylin *M.V.Nesterov*, 1942. *Twilight of the Tsars*, London, 1991.
Coll Major holdings at TG; RM; Central Museum of the Revolution, Moscow.
Colour plate opposite.

NESTEROV, N. I.   **a.1918-1919**

Painter. He exhibited at the First Exhibition of Works of the Professional Union of Artists in Moscow in 1918 and at the Ninth State Exhibition of Paintings: Naturalism and Realism in Moscow in 1919.

NESTEROV, Petr Nikolaevich   **b.1745**

Portraitist.
Coll TG.

Yakov Nikoladze. The Poet Chakhrukhadze, *1944. Toned plaster. 46 x 30 x 17 cm.*
Historical figures of the many Soviet Republics were give numerous monuments to stress the diversity of cultures within the USSR. The techniques adopted by sculptors translated Socialist Realism into styles which reflected local cultural identity whilst still serving an overall purpose of consolidating the Union.

NEVEZHIN, Fedor Ivanovich   **1902-1964**
He was engaged in Agitprop decorations at the Security Police Club, Moscow, c.1928, and was represented at the jubilee exhibition Artists of the RSFSR over 15 Years held at the Russian Museum, Leningrad, in 1932.

NEVREV, Nikolai Vasil'evich   **1830-1904**
Painter of portraits and of socially committed genre works. He studied at the Moscow College and frequented the Abramtsevo artists' colony in the 1870s. He taught at the Moscow College where his pupils included N.P.Ulyanov c.1889-1900.
Merchandise, Scene of Peasant Life in the Time of Serfdom, 1866, TG, is a meticulous genre scene in which the peasants, clad in traditional dress, approach the table of a comfortably financed gentleman who smokes an elegant long pipe in the painting-lined room of a house. There is a wine bottle on the table and a middleman introduces the peasants in turn for the gentleman's consideration. The painting points fairly quietly to profound social divisions and to the dependency of the supplicant peasantry. This is genre painting with a purpose to educate by visual means, a purpose supported by its novel-like elaboration and its narrative description.
Coll TG; RM.

NEVREV, Nikolai Vasilievich   **1830-1904**
Portraitist.Well represented at TG.

NIKICH, A. Yu.   **b.1918-1965+**
Painter. Works included *War Correspondents*, 1965, TG.
Coll TG.

NIKIFOROV, Semen Gavriilovich   **1877-1912**
Genre painter. One source suggests 1881 as his date of birth.
Coll TG.

NIKIFOROV, V.   **a.1921**
A member of the *Bytie* (Existence) society of artists formed in Moscow in 1921.

NIKIFOROVA   **a.1926**
Sculptor. She was a member of the Society of Russian Sculptors from 1926.

NIKIFOROVA-KIRPICHNIKOVA, E. D.   **a.1925**
She contributed to the Third Exhibition of Paintings by Artists from Kaluga and Moscow held in Kaluga in 1925.

NIKITIN, Igor Aleksandrovich   **1880-1930s**
This was probably the Nikitin who contributed to the Twelfth State Exhibition: Colourdynamo and Tectonic Primitivism (*Tsvetodinamos i tektonicheskiy primitivizm*) along with Grishchenko, Shevchenko and others in Moscow in 1919.
He was represented at the enormous First State Exhibition of Art and Science, which included ethnographic material, held in Kazan in 1920 and at the Third Touring Exhibition of the Sovetsk Regional subdepartment of the Museums Bureau along with Kandinsky, Rodchenko and others in 1921.

NIKITIN, Ivan Nikitich (Maksimovich)   **c.1688-1741**
Portrait painter. A major figure from the period of Peter the Great. His date of birth may have been 1690. He studied in St. Petersburg under Danhauer and was amongst the first of the *artistes pensionnaires* of Peter I along with Andrei Matveev. They left Russia in 1716 to study abroad. Nikitin and his brother travelled to Italy where he studied with Redi in Florence. He also studied in Paris under Largillière.
He taught mathematics and drawing in Moscow and became one of the first artists supported by Peter the Great. Early works include portraits of the Tsar's wife and eldest daughter. Other portraits include *G.I.Golovkin* 1720s, TG. His portraits were imposing and sometimes fiercely formal although there are also occasional informal portraits. Later he fell out of favour, was whipped and deported to Siberia in 1736. He died whilst returning from exile.
Coll TG; RM; Museum of the Academy, St. Petersburg.

NIKITIN, N. P.   **a.1925**
Painter. He contributed to the Third Exhibition of Paintings by Artists from Kaluga and Moscow held in Kaluga in 1925.

NIKOGOSYAN, Nikogos Bagratovich   **b.1918-1952+**
Academic sculptor. Born in Moscow. His works include a full-

length portrait of the Armenian poet *M.Nalbandyan* and also a portrait of the French writer *Louis Aragon*.
Coll TG.

NIKOLADZE, Yakov Ivanovich 1876-1951

Georgian sculptor. He was an active teacher and his pupils included T.G.Abakeliya. Amongst his works were a bust of the twelfth century Georgian poet *Chakhrukhadze*, plaster, 1944, and a bust of *Lenin* 1947.
Girl of the North, 1906, marble, Georgian Art Museum, Tblisi, is heavily indebted to the techniques of Rodin for whom it could almost be mistaken. The smooth surface of the sitter emerges from a roughly carved block. There are symbolist overtones in the contrast of textures.
Portrait of Egnata Ninoshvili, 1911, erected at Tblisi in 1923, also resembles a late 19th century French bronze.
Lit I.A Nurashadze *Ya.I.Nikoladze*, 1940.

NIKOLAEV, Ivan Nikolaevich a. c.1918

He executed Agitprop projects including decorations on the propaganda trains *Red Cossack* and the Ukrainian train *Lenin*.

NIKOLAEV, K. V. a.1921

He exhibited with Kudryashov and others at the First State Exhibition in Orenburg in 1921.

NIKOLAEVTSEV, Ivan G. a.1925-1927+

Caricaturist, graphic artist, painter. He participated in the seventh exhibition of the group *L'Araignée* (The Spider) at the Galerie Devambe in Paris in 1925 and in the third and last exhibition of the *Makovets* group in Moscow 1925-6. He was associated with the group *Put' zhivopisi* (Path of Painting) formed by Lev Zhegin in 1927.

NIKOL'SKAYA, Vera 1890-1964

Painter. Born at Saratov. She died at Leningrad.
Lit E.Weiss *Russische Avant-Garde, 1910-1930, Sammlung Ludwig, Köln*, Munich, 1986.
Coll Sammlung Ludwig, Cologne.

NIKOL'SKY, S. N. a.1919

Painter. He exhibited at the juryless Eighth State Exhibition in Moscow in 1919.

NIKONOV, Nikolai Mitrofanovich 1889-1975

Painter. Born in the Kirov region. He studied at the Kazan School of Art under N.Feshina 1908-12 and at the Moscow College under A.Arkhipov and Leonid Pasternak 1913-15. After the Revolution he became a member of AKhRR in 1923. He exhibited abroad at New York in 1929 and at Venice, Zurich and Berne in 1930. He was represented at the jubilee exhibition Artists of the RSFSR over 15 Years held at the Russian Museum, Leningrad, in 1932 and at the 1932 Venice Biennale. He died in Moscow.
Entry of the Red Army into Krasnoyarsk in 1920, 1923, TG, is pure grotesque and vigorous theatre with gleeful spectators and wild crude riders bearing the red flag across the canvas.
Lit *N.M.Nikonov*, Moscow, 1951. *N.M.Nikonov*, exh. cat., Moscow, 1967. *Paris-Moscou*, 1979.
Coll TG.

NIKRITIN, Solomon Borisovich 1898-1965

Painter, theatre and exhibition designer. Born at Chernigov. He studied at Kiev School of Art until 1914 and designed for the Moscow Art Theatre in 1916. He showed work at the Contemporary Painting exhibition in Moscow in 1916. After the Revolution he executed Agitprop decorations at Kiev 1917-20, and then studied at the Vkhutemas in Moscow 1920-2. He was a founder member of the group *Elektro-organizm* (Electro-organism) in 1921 and exhibited with them in 1922. The same year he was represented at the First Russian Art Exhibition in Berlin. From 1922 to 1925 he chaired the Art Research Council of the Museum of Pictorial Culture. His loosely calligraphic paintings of the 1920s have some similarities to works by Drevin and Chekrygin. He was a founder of the Projectionist group *Metod* (Method) in 1923. In 1924 he contributed to the First Discussional Exhibition of Active Revolutionary Art in Moscow. He designed museum interiors and exhibitions in the 1930s.
Theatre design 1916 sets for *The Green Ring* produced at the Moscow Art Theatre. 1923-4 produced non-representational performances for Anatoli Mariengof (Projectionist Theatre).
Lit A.Z.Rudenstine *Costakis Collection*, London, 1981. A.M.Muratov, V.Manin et al. *Zhivopis' 20-30kh godov*, Sankt-Peterburg, 1991.
Coll TG; RM; Costakis Collection.

NIKULIN a.1925

Graphic artist. He contributed to the First Exhibition of Cinema Posters held in Moscow in 1925.

NISS-GOL'DMAN, Nina Il'inichna 1893-1933+

Sculptor. She taught on the foundation course at the Moscow Vkhutemas with the sculptors A.Babichev, I.Chaikov, R.Iodko and B.Korolev c.1920. Niss-Gol'dman exhibited with the 4 Arts society in Moscow in 1925.
Portrait of V.R.Menzhinsky, 1933, plaster, a specific record of the sitter and a sensitive portrait. It is highly competent without being particularly distinguished in the context of other academic portraits of the 1930s.

NISSKY, Georgiy Grigorevich 1903-1957+

Belorussian landscape painter. He studied at Gomel and at the Moscow College 1923-30. He was represented at the jubilee exhibition Artists of the RSFSR over 15 Years held at the Russian Museum, Leningrad, in 1932. He specialised in industrialised and urban landscapes. He became a member of the Academy of the USSR and was represented at the 1960 Venice Biennale.
Autumn Semaphore, 1932, TG, is a painting employing sparse gestural means. Swallows gather on three telephone wires simply depicted as three lines. Wisps of cloud hover above the low horizon. Scratched lines across a smear of brown indicate railway tracks in the landscape. There is a steam train and four signal posts centrally placed with one of them indicating change. It is a kind of analogy of the semaphore of swallows and railways to indicate time passing and the inevitability of change.
Moscow Suburbs, February, 1957, TG, in its poster-like clarity and delicately precise technique, perhaps shows the acceptable and slightly vacuous face of the officially approved art of the time.
Lit E.Murina *G.G.Nissky*, 1952.
Coll TG; National Gallery, L'vov.

NIVINSKY, Ignati Ignatevich 1880-1933

Theatre designer, painter, graphic artist. Born in Moscow. His birthdate is sometimes given as 1881. He studied at the Stroganov College 1893-8/9 and taught there from 1899 to

1905. He visited Italy in 1907. In 1908 he was studying with Zhukovsky and specialised in printmaking, including etching, from 1908 to 1913 but he was also studying archaeology 1908-11. He studied at the Moscow College. He exhibited with the Association of Moscow Artists in 1913, 1916 and 1917 and also with the World of Art in 1916.

After the Revolution he was represented at the First Exhibition of Works of the Professional Union of Artists in Moscow in 1918. His name appeared on the April 1919 list of artists for acquisitions by the envisaged Museum of Painterly Culture. He was represented in the Fourth State Exhibition of Paintings (IV Gosudarstvennaya vystavka kartin) in Moscow in 1919 and the Sixth State Exhibition: The Print (VI Gosudarstvennaya vystavka gravyur) in Moscow in 1919.

He directed mass decorations and had general charge of the decoration of the propaganda trains Red Cossack, Ukrainian Lenin, Lenin (October Revolution) and Soviet Caucasus. He taught at the Vkhutemas 1921-30 and Deineka was amongst his pupils there 1921-5.

He contributed to the exhibition Art of Moscow Theatre 1918-1923 held in Moscow in 1923 and was a member of the 4 Arts society which was founded in 1924. He was represented at the Paris International Exhibition in 1925. He was included in the major exhibition in Moscow in 1927 marking the tenth anniversary of the Revolution, the exhibition of graphic art Liberation Movements: The Sixteenth to the Twentieth Century held in Moscow in 1928, the exhibition of Russian Graphic Art in Riga in 1929 and the First Touring Exhibition of Painting and Graphics which opened in Moscow in 1929. He was also represented at the jubilee exhibition Artists of the RSFSR over 15 Years held at the Russian Museum, Leningrad, in 1932 and at the 1932 Venice Biennale. He died in Moscow.

*Azeneft'stroy, 1930, coloured etching, is one of a series of etchings using montages of images to depict the theme of socialist construction projects. Black linear images of factory chimneys with ships below and airplanes above have a red linear image of Lenin's head peering through. There is also colour applied to the plate surface in soft patches of green, blue and yellow.

Theatre design From 1921 he designed for the Moscow Art Theatre's productions of Strindberg's Erik XIV, comedies by Prosper Mérimée and other productions.

1922 Princess Turandot sets and costumes for E.Vakhtangov's production at the Moscow Art Theatre/Academy Theatre (Third studio), were executed in an exotic and flamboyant mixture of Chinese and Constructivist styles to provide an immensely enjoyable, colourful and dramatic pantomime vision of China using wires, suspended planes, sloping platforms, curtains and pagodas. Costumes exhibited a Commedia dell'Arte verve and lightness but with many small signs of his awareness of recent geometric styles of painting and theatre design. The designs were also issued as a series of colour lithographs.

At the Maly Theatre he designed productions of plays by Ostrovsky, Lunacharsky and others.

Lit V.Dokuchaeva I.N.Nivinsky, Moscow, 1969. Paris-Moscou, 1979. Nancy Van Norman Baer Theatre in Revolution, Russian Avant-Garde Stage Design 1913-1935, San Francisco and London, 1991.

Coll Bakhrushin Theatre Museum, Moscow; A.V.Shchusev Architectural Museum, Moscow; Pushkin Museum, Moscow. Colour plate p.311.

NOAKOVSKY, Stanislav V.   **1867-1928**
Polish painter, writer on art. Born at Nieszawa, Poland. He studied at the Academy in St. Petersburg. His paintings featured architectural themes. He was teaching at the Stroganov Institute in 1905. D.Mitrokhin was amongst his pupils. He exhibited with the World of Art in 1906.
After the Revolution he served on the Moscow Collegium of IZO Narkompros under Tatlin in 1919. He contributed to the Third Exhibition of Paintings by Artists from Kaluga and Moscow held in Kaluga in 1925. He died in Warsaw.

NORVERT, E. I.   **a.1921**
He exhibited in the 1921 exhibition of the World of Art in Moscow.

NOSKOV, Georgiy Ivanovich   **1902-1923+**
Painter. Born in the Tver region. He executed Suprematist works inspired by the example of Malevich under whom he studied in Petrograd. He was a member of the Unovis collective. He entered the sculpture section of the Vkhutemas in Moscow in 1923.
Lit L'Avant-garde russe 1905-1925, exh. cat., Musée des Beaux-Arts, Nantes, 1993.
Coll Yaroslavl' Art Museum.

NOTENBERG, E. = GURO, E. G.

NOVIKOV   **a.1919**
Painter. He contributed to the Twelfth State Exhibition: Colourdynamo and Tectonic Primitivism (Tsvetodinamos i tektonicheskiy primitivizm) along with Grishchenko, Shevchenko and others in Moscow in 1919. This may be Maksim Evstaf'evich Novikov who was born in 1886.

NOVODVORSKAYA, Vera Dmitrieva   **1884-1942**
Painter. She exhibited at the Izdebsky Salon in Odessa 1909-10, with the New Society of Artists 1909-17 and also with the Donkey's Tail. She also exhibited with the Union of Youth in 1912. She married the architect A.V.Kholopov.

NOVOSKOL'TSEV (NOWOSKOLJZEFF), Aleksandr Nikranovich   **1853-1890+**
History painter. He taught at the Stieglitz School of Art where his pupils included A.P.Ostroumova-Lebedeva c.1890.
Coll RM.

NOVOZHILOV, V. M.   **a.1925-1929**
He exhibited with the Society of Moscow Painters founded in 1925 and was represented at the First Touring Exhibition of Painting and Graphics which opened in Moscow in 1929.

NOWOSKOLJZEFF = NOVOSKOL'TSEV, A.N.

NOZh
The abbreviated name of the New Society of Painters (Novoe obshchestvo zhivopistsev).
Its first exhibition was held in November 1922 and its programme stated in the catalogue that its members, former leftist artists, were the first to feel the pointlessness of the most extreme analytical and scholastic trends, finding them remote from life and art. They embraced realism.

NOZIKOVA, E. N.   **a.1932**
She was represented at the jubilee exhibition Artists of the

Ignati Nivinsky. Costume Design for a Man from the Crowd for a Production of 'The Phantom Lady', *1923. Gouache. Dated lower right. 56.2 x 41 cm.*
Collection Mr. and Mrs. Nikita D.Lobanov-Rostovsky, London.

RSFSR over 15 Years held at the Russian Museum, Leningrad, in 1932.

NURALI, Byashim Yusopovich   **1900-1965**
Turkmen naive primitivist painter. His *Portrait of Khaludzha*, 1926, Museum of the Art of Eastern Countries, Moscow, has a regional but vigorous folk-art style reminiscent of tray decorations in its image of a crude carpet behind a crude portrait.
Coll Museum of the Art of Eastern Countries, Moscow.

NUSBERG, Lev   **b.1937**
Sculptor, painter. He rose to eminence as a founder of the group *Dvizhenie* (Movement) in 1962. This group established some recognition as an avant-garde group when this was still a rare phenomenon. It embraced kinetic sculpture in particular and had numerous west European connections. It also responded to the historical precedent set by Russian art of the 1920s which was still little known in Soviet publications. The group exhibited at Komsomol Clubs 1963-5 and held exhibitions in Moscow in 1964, as well as Leningrad and Prague in 1965. It was commissioned to make work for the Komsomolskaya Pravda building in 1965. The manifesto published by *Dvizhenie* in 1966 was signed by Buturlin, Dubovska, Infante, Koleichuk, Kuznetsov, Muraverova and Stepanov. In 1967 *Dvizhenie* constructed a spectacular display along the banks of the Neva in Leningrad on the occasion of the fiftieth anniversary celebrations of the Revolution.

NYURENBERG, Amshey Markovich   **1887-1979**
Painter. His name appeared on the April 1919 list of artists for acquisitions by the envisaged Museum of Painterly Culture. He was a member of NOZh, the New Society of Painters, formed in 1922 and he exhibited with the Society of Moscow Painters at its inaugural exhibition in Moscow in 1925. He was represented at the jubilee exhibition Artists of the RSFSR over 15 Years held at the Russian Museum, Leningrad, in 1932 and at the 1932 Venice Biennale. He died in Moscow.

NYURENBERG-DEVINOV, D. M.   **a.1925**
He exhibited with the Society of Moscow Painters at its inaugural exhibition in Moscow in 1925.

O.K. see **KIPRENSKY, O.A.**

OBER, Artemi Lavrentievich　　　　**1843-1917**
Sculptor. He exhibited with the World of Art 1900-2. He was a member of the second World of Art Society of 1910-24. His speciality was animal sculptures rather as it was for Frémiet in France. His bronzes from 1870 into the 20th century included pigs, bulls, bears, parrots, fish and monkeys. Occasionally they included human figures. There is some similarity to Barye's *Jaguar Devouring a Hare* in his *Greyhound and Fox*, 1881, RM.
Coll Well represented at RM.

OBMOKhU
The abbreviated name of the Society of Young Artists (*Obshchestvo molodykh khudozhnikov*) which organised four exhibitions in the period 1919-23 in Moscow. Members included the Stenberg brothers, Ioganson and Medunetsky.

OBOLENSKAYA, Yulia Leonidovna　　　**1889-1945**
Graphic artist, painter, theatre designer. She designed a curtain for the House of Theatre Spectacles in Moscow in 1916.
After the Revolution she exhibited with the World of Art in December 1917 in Moscow, at the First Exhibition of Works of the Professional Union of Artists in Moscow in 1918 and at the Fourth State Exhibition of Paintings (*IV Gosudarstvennaya vystavka kartin*) in Moscow in 1919.
She exhibited with the *Zhar-tsvet* (Fire-colour) group between 1924 and 1928. She was included in the major exhibition in Moscow in 1927 marking the tenth anniversary of the Revolution, in the exhibition of Russian Graphic Art in Riga in 1929 and at the First Touring Exhibition of Painting and Graphics which opened in Moscow in 1929.

OBRUCHEVA, N.　　　　　**a.1929**
Theatre designer. She exhibited in Moscow in 1929.

OKhR
The abbreviated name of the Society of Artist-Realists (*Ob'edinenie khudozhnikov realistov*).

OKOLOVICH, Nikolai Andreevich　　　**1867-1928**
Landscape painter. He studied at the Academy in St. Petersburg.
Coll TG.

OLEINIK, A. P.　　　　　**a.1940s**
Sculptor.

OLESHKEVICH, I. I. = OLESZKIEWICZ, I.

OLESZKIEWICZ, I. (OLESHKEVICH, Iosif Ivanovich) 1777-1830
Polish history painter and portraitist. He studied at Vilna under Smuglevich in 1800 and then under David in Paris. He worked in Russia and became a member of the Academy in St. Petersburg in 1812. He died in St. Petersburg.
Coll TG; Cracow Art Museum; National Museum, Warsaw.

OLGINA, O.　　　　　**a.1913**
Painter. She contributed to Larionov's exhibition The Target in Moscow in 1913.

OL'SHEVSKY, B. A.　　　　**a.1921**
He exhibited with Kudryashov and others at the First State Exhibition in Orenburg in 1921.

OMKh
The abbreviated name for the Society of Moscow Artists (*Obshchestvo moskovskykh khudozhnikov*) which held exhibitions in 1928 and 1929. Members included Drevin, Udal'tsova, Lentulov, Falk and Rozhdestvensky.

OPEKUSHIN, Aleksandr Mikhailovich　　**1841-1923**
Monumental sculptor. His work included monuments to *N.N.Murovev* and *Pushkin*.
Coll RM.

ORANOVSKY, Evgeniy Vladimirovich　　**1880-1951**
Sculptor, painter. He was represented in the Fourth State Exhibition of Paintings (*IV Gosudarstvennaya vystavka kartin*) in Moscow in 1919. He was a member of the Society of Russian Sculptors from 1926 and a member of the Society of Artist-Realists founded in 1927. He directed a commission for the preservation of monuments in Moscow. He died in Moscow.

OREKHOV, Ivan Vasil'evich　　　**1888-c.1940**
Painter. He was a member of the group *Krug khudozhnikov* (Circle of Artists) founded in 1926.
Coll RM.

ORGUNOV = ARGUNOV, I.P.

ORLEANSKY, K.A.　　　　**a.1919**
Painter. He exhibited at the juryless Eighth State Exhibition in Moscow in 1919.

ORLOFF, Chana (ORLOVA, Khanna)　　**1878-1968**
Sculptor, graphic artist. Born in the Ukraine. She left Russia in 1904 and settled in Paris in 1910 where she became closely involved with contemporary Parisian art including Cubism. She attended the Ecole des Arts Décoratifs in 1911 and exhibited at the Salon d'Automne in 1913. She exhibited widely and frequently after this. She took French citizenship in 1926. Her portraits included Archipenko, Matisse and Picasso. She fled to Switzerland during the Second World War, returning to Paris in 1945. She became a member of the Légion d'Honneur.

ORLOV, Afanasiy Ulyanovich　　　**1823-1861+**
Portraitist.
Coll TG.

ORLOV, D. = MOOR, D.S.

ORLOV, G. G.　　　　　**a.1919**
Painter. He exhibited at the juryless Eighth State Exhibition in Moscow in 1919.

ORLOV, Ivan Petrovich　　　　**1815-1861**
Miniaturist painter.
Coll TG.

ORLOV, Nikolai Vasilievich　　　**1863-1924**
Genre painter.
Coll TG.

ORLOV, Pimen Nikitich   1812-1863
Portrait and genre painter. He worked in Italy 1841-61 and was in Rome in 1851.
Coll TG.

ORLOV, Sergei Mikhailovich   1911-1971
Monumental sculptor. Works include an historicist equestrian monument to *Yuri Dolgorukov, Founder of Moscow*, 1954, which was designed in collaboration with Antropov and Shtamm, and a monument to *A.Nikitin*, 1955, erected at Kalinin.

ORLOV, V.G.   a.1919
Painter. He exhibited at the juryless Eighth State Exhibition in Moscow in 1919.

ORLOVA, Khanna = ORLOFF, Chana

ORLOVA-MOCHALOVA, M. N.   a.1927
Graphic artist. She contributed to the All-Union Polygraphic Exhibition in Moscow in 1927.

ORLOVSKY, A. O. = ORLOWSKI, A.

ORLOVSKY (SMIRNOV), Boris Ivanovich   1792-1837
Neo-classical sculptor. There is some ambiguity about his birthdate which is also sometimes given as 1796 or 1797. He studied under the marble carver Campioni (Kampioni) in Moscow and then moved to St. Petersburg to study under P.Triskora. Here he met the sculptor Martos who arranged a period of study at the Academy. He travelled to Rome on an Academy scholarship 1822-9 where he worked under the Danish neo-classical sculptor Thorwaldsen. Works include the monument to *M.I.Kutuzov*, 1829-32, erected in St. Petersburg, as well as busts, military figurines and neo-classical figurative themes such as *Faun and Bacchante*, 1837, RM.
*Paris, 1824, marble, TG, is a neo-classical full-length figure identified by his Phrygian cap and holding an apple which refers to the legend of the Judgement of Paris. Essentially these iconographic particulars merely give specific identity to what is really an idealised male nude based closely on antique precedent.
Coll Well represented at RM; TG.

ORLOVSKY, Vladimir Donatovich   1842-1914
Landscape painter. He worked in the Ukraine where his paintings included themes of peasants working in the landscape. He was painting in Italy in 1876 and active as a landscape painter in the Ukraine in 1882.
Coll TG; RM.

ORLOWSKI, Alexander (ORLOVSKY, Aleksandr Osipovich)   1777-1832
Polish romantic painter and lithographer who worked in Russia. Born at Warsaw. He lived in Poland as a youth where he studied under the French painter Norblen. He was involved in the Polish patriotic movement and uprising of 1794. He worked in Poland until his move to Russia in 1802.
He studied at the Academy in St. Petersburg and travelled to France, Germany and Italy.
In 1812 Tsar Aleksandr I made him a court painter and thereafter he worked in St. Petersburg, producing paintings of shipwrecks, equestrian and military themes. He later painted street scenes, observing beggars and prisoners as well as elegant society. He was a prolific portrait draughtsman and caricaturist. He also produced theatrical designs. He died in St. Petersburg.
Coll Well represented in TG; Hermitage Museum, St. Petersburg; National Museum, Cracow; National Museum, Warsaw; National Gallery, Berlin.

ORS
The abbreviated name of the Society of Russian Sculptors (*Ob'edinenie russkikh skul'ptorov*).

OSA
The abbreviated name of the Society of Contemporary Architects (*Ob'edinenie sovremennykh arkhitektorov*).

OSININ, I. see APSIT, A.

OSIS, Janis   1926-1951+
Latvian genre painter.

OSMERKIN, Aleksandr Aleksandrovich   1892-1953
Neo-primitivist painter. Born at Elizavetgrad. He studied in Kiev 1909-12 and then under Ilya Mashkov in Moscow where he settled in 1913. He exhibited with the Knave of Diamonds in Moscow in 1917 and with the World of Art in December 1917 in Moscow. He was engaged in Agitprop projects in 1918 including overall responsibility for the decoration of propaganda trains. His propaganda decorations for the Zimin Theatre (State Opera Theatre) in 1918 feature a tangle of flags and adjacent non-rectangular canvas panels to flank the entrance with depictions of workers, one a dramatically faceted image of a carpenter in a style reminiscent of Goncharova. He exhibited at the Fifth State Exhibition: From Impressionism to Non-Objective Art in Moscow 1918-19. His name appeared on the April 1919 list of artists for acquisitions by the envisaged Museum of Painterly Culture and he was represented at the enormous First State Exhibition of Art and Science, which included ethnographic material, held in Kazan in 1920. He exhibited in the 1921 exhibition of the World of Art in Moscow and was represented at the First Russian Art Exhibition in Berlin in 1922. He was a member of the Society of Moscow Painters founded in 1925. His work was included in the exhibition of Soviet art held at Harbin in 1926 and in Japan in 1927 and the major exhibition in Moscow in 1927 marking the tenth anniversary of the Revolution. He was also represented at the First Touring Exhibition of Painting and Graphics which opened in Moscow in 1929 and at the jubilee exhibition Artists of the RSFSR over 15 Years held at the Russian Museum, Leningrad, in 1932.
The critic and historian A.Efros spoke at an evening dedicated to Osmerkin at the Moscow Union of Artists in 1945.
*The Moyka Canal. White Night, 1927, TG, is a colourful painting of the strange light of the midsummer nights in Leningrad.
Writings A.A.Osmerkin *Razmyshleniya ob iskusstve. Pisma, kritika, vospominaniya sovremennikov*, Moscow, 1981.
Coll TG; RM.

OSOLODKOV, Petr Alekseevich   1898-1942
Painter, draughtsman, of portraits and still-lifes. He studied at the Fifth Army Art School at Omsk, at the First Siberian Art-Industrial School in Omsk 1920-4 and at the Leningrad Vkhutemas under A.I.Savinov 1924-9. He was a member of the group *Krug khudozhnikov* (Circle of Artists), founded in

1926, from 1927 to 1932.
Lit A.M.Muratov, V.Manin et al. *Zhivopis' 20-30kh godov*, Sankt-Peterburg, 1991.
Coll RM.

OST

The abbreviated name of the Society of Easel Painters (*Obshchestvo khudozhnikov-stankovistov*) actively exhibiting 1925-8. Members included Deineka, Goncharov, Labas, Tyshler and Shterenberg.

OSTOFIEV, Leon   **a.1914**
Painter. He contributed to the exhibition No.4 in Moscow in 1914.

OSTROGRADSKY (OSTROGROWLSKY), Aleksei Nikolaevich   **1867-1943**
Genre painter. He studied at the Academy in St. Petersburg 1887-91.
Coll TG.

OSTROUKHOV, Ilya Semenovich   **1858-1929**
Landscape painter, theatre designer. Born in Moscow into a merchant's family. He studied under Kiselev, Repin, Chistyakov and Polenov. He was painting at Sebastopol in 1883, and Venice in 1887. He exhibited with the Wanderers from 1886 and became a member in 1891. He was also a collector of old Russian masters and his collection became part of the Tretyakov Gallery holdings. He sometimes signed his work 'I.O'. He died in Moscow.
Lit Dzhon Boult (John Bowlt) *Khudozhniki russkogo teatra. Sobranie Nikity i Niny Lobanovykh-Rostovskikh*, Moscow, 1991.
Coll Well represented at TG.

OSTROUKHOV, V. F.   **a.1918-19**
He exhibited at the Fifth State Exhibition: From Impressionism to Non-Objective Art in Moscow 1918-19.

OSTROUMOV, V. N.   **a.1925**
Painter. He contributed to the Third Exhibition of Paintings by Artists from Kaluga and Moscow held in Kaluga in 1925.

OSTROUMOVA-LEBEDEVA, Anna Petrovna   1871-1955
Graphic artist, painter. Born at St. Petersburg. She studied at the A.Stieglitz School under A.Novosol'tsev and G.Manizer 1889-92 and intermittently at the Academy in St. Petersburg between 1892 and 1900 under Repin, Maté and Chistyakov. However she also studied in Paris and attended Whistler's Académie Carmen there 1898-9. It was in Paris that she first became a printmaker. She made her first wood engravings in 1898. She was a founder member of the World of Art in 1899 and exhibited with the World of Art 1900-6. She exhibited with the Union of Russian Artists from 1903-10. She travelled widely including visits to Italy in 1903, then France and the Tyrol in 1906. She was represented in Diaghilev's display of Russian art at the 1906 Salon d'Automne in Paris.
She married the chemist Sergei Lebedev in 1905 and studied watercolour painting under Bakst at the Zvantseva School in 1906.
Prints executed 1908-9 depict the city of St. Petersburg with great economy, employing only three or four colours applied in flattened filled-in silhouettes but they were highly atmospheric evocations of mood amongst the architectural monuments and gardens. She exhibited with the First Izdebsky International Salon 1909-10 in Odessa. She again travelled to Italy in 1911, painted the *Iron Market* in Amsterdam in 1913 (RM) in a manner close to that of Dobuzhinsky, and went to Spain in 1914. She was given a one-person exhibition in 1916.
After the Revolution she continued to depict the city of St. Petersburg even as it changed its name, politics and fortunes. She participated in the First State Free Exhibition of Artworks in Petrograd in 1919 and she contributed to the Exhibition of Paintings by Russian Artists held at Pskov in Spring 1920.
Her printmaking technique came to resemble more closely the watercolours executed in these years, lighter and more intricate than her earlier highly edited city views. She published an album of lithographs *Petersburg* in 1922. She exhibited with the *Zhar-tsvet* (Fire-colour) group between 1924 and 1928 and also with the 4 Arts society. She was represented at the Paris International Exhibition in 1925. She was included in the exhibition of Russian Graphic Art in Riga in 1929 and the jubilee exhibition Artists of the RSFSR over 15 Years held at the Russian Museum, Leningrad, in 1932.

Anna Ostroumova-Lebedeva. Venice at Night, *1914. Lithograph. Signed with 'A.O.' in a monogram lower left.*

Anna Ostroumova-Lebedeva. St. Petersburg: New Holland Arch, *1901. Lithograph.*
A use of severe editing of an image to provide a sense of sharply contrasting light and dark. Ostroumova-Lebedeva was most celebrated for her prints of the city of St. Petersburg in all of its moods from historical splendour to workaday activity.

Some late prints, even as late as 1946, reveal that she was still able to produce the spectacular, broad and moody image of the city as she had some forty years earlier.

She was made an Academician of the USSR. She sometimes signed her work simply 'Ostroumova' or with a monogram comprising an 'O' with an 'A' through it. She died in Leningrad.

Writings A.Ostroumova-Lebedeva *Avtobiograficheskie zapiski* (Autobiographical Notes), Leningrad, 1935. A.P.Ostroumova-Lebedeva *Avtobiograficheskie zapiski*, 3 vols., Moscow, 1974.

Lit A.Benua (Benois), S.Ernst *Ostroumova-Lebedeva*, Moscow-Petrograd, 1924. P.Kornilov *A.P.Ostroumova-Lebedeva*, Moscow, 1950. V.A.Tikhanova *Ostroumova-Lebedeva*, 1961. N.Sinitsyn *Gravyury Ostroumovoi-Lebedevoi*, 1964. V.Suslov *A.P.Ostroumova-Lebedeva*, Leningrad, 1967. *Paris-Moscou*, 1979. *Twilight of the Tsars*, London, 1991. A.Kamensky *The World of Art Movement*, Leningrad, 1991.
Coll RM; Pushkin Museum, Moscow.

OSTROV, V. P.   **a.1917-1919**
Graphic artist. He exhibited with the World of Art in December 1917 in Moscow and in the Sixth State Exhibition: The Print (*VI Gosudarstvennaya vystavka gravyur*) in Moscow in 1919.

OVCHINNIKOV, I.   **a.1918**
He was engaged on Agitprop decorations at Saratov c.1918.

OVSVYANNIKOV, Sergei Osipovich   **1880-1937**
Architect, artist. He studied at the Academy in St. Petersburg 1902-9. He was engaged on Agitprop decorations at the Anichkov Bridge, Petrograd, in 1918. He was a member of the Petrograd Society of Artists.

P

P.B. (cyrillic) see **BASIN, P.V.**
P.E.K. (cyrillic) see **KAMEZHENKOV, E.D.**
P.K. (cyrillic) see **KUZNETSOV, P.V.**
P.S. (cyrillic) see **SOKOLOV, P.P.** ; **PAVLOV, S.A.**
P.Yu. (cyrillic monogram) see **PIMENOV, Yu.I.**

PADALITSYN, Nickolai Ivanovich   1893-c.1930
Graphic artist. He was included in the major exhibition in
Moscow in 1927 marking the tenth anniversary of the
Revolution. He exhibited with the 4 Arts society in Leningrad
including the exhibition of 1928 at the Russian Museum. He
contributed to the exhibition of graphic art Liberation
Movements: The Sixteenth to the Twentieth Century held in
Moscow in 1928 and to the exhibition of Russian Graphic Art
in Riga in 1929. He was also represented at the First Touring
Exhibition of Painting and Graphics which opened in Moscow
in 1929.

PAEVSKY,   a.1910
He ran a private art school at Kutaisi, Georgia, where his
pupils included Kakabadze before 1910.

PAIN, Ya. S.   a.1918-1921
Painter. He was represented at the First Exhibition of Works
of the Professional Union of Artists in Moscow in 1918 and at
the Fifth State Exhibition: From Impressionism to Non-
Objective Art in Moscow 1918-19. He also appeared on the
April 1919 list of artists for acquisitions by the envisaged
Museum of Painterly Culture and was represented along with
Kandinsky, Chagall and others at the First State Exhibition of
Paintings by Local and Moscow Artists held in Vitebsk in
December 1919. He was included in the Third Touring
Exhibition of the Sovetsk Regional subdepartment of the
Museums Bureau along with Kandinsky, Rodchenko and
others in 1921 and participated in the Third Exhibition of
Paintings held at Ryazan in 1919.

PAKHOMOV, Aleksei Fedorovich   1900-1973
Graphic artist, lithographer. He studied at the Stieglitz School
in Petrograd 1915-17.
After the Revolution he studied at the Vkhutemas under
Dobuzhinsky and Karev 1920-5. He was represented at the
New Tendencies exhibition in 1921 and was included in the
enormous survey Exhibition of Paintings by Petrograd Artists
of All Tendencies 1919-1923 held in Petrograd in 1923. In
1926 he was a founder member of the Circle of Artists with
whom he exhibited from 1926. His work was included in the
exhibition of Soviet art held at Harbin in 1926 and in Japan in
1927 and also in the exhibition of Russian Graphic Art in Riga
in 1929.
He was represented at the jubilee exhibition Artists of the
RSFSR over 15 Years held at the Russian Museum,
Leningrad, in 1932 and at the 1932 Venice Biennale. He
endured the Siege of Leningrad and from 1948 he taught at

the Repin Institute. He became an Academician of the USSR.
He illustrated books including children's books.
Writings A.F.Pakhomov *Pro svoyu rabotu* (On My Work),
Leningrad, 1971.
Lit E.Gankina *A.F.Pakhomov*, Moscow, 1958. V.Matafonov
Pakhomov, Moscow, 1981. *Paris-Moscou*, 1979.
Coll TG; RM.

PAKULIN, Vyacheslav Vladimirovich   1900-1951
Painter, designer, theatre designer. He studied at the Stieglitz
School, Petrograd, and at the Vkhutemas under A.Savinov and
A.Karev 1922-5. He also studied theatre under Meyerhold. He
was included in the enormous survey Exhibition of Paintings
by Petrograd Artists of All Tendencies 1919-1923 held in
Petrograd in 1923. He was a member of the Leningrad Union
of Artworkers 1925-9 and a founder member of the Leningrad
Artists' Circle 1926-7. He organised three exhibitions in
Leningrad and one in Kiev 1930. Certain works featured
heavy, stylised labouring women faintly reminiscent of the
stylisation employed by Juan Gris. He was represented at the
jubilee exhibition Artists of the RSFSR over 15 Years held at
the Russian Museum, Leningrad, in 1932.
Lit A.M.Muratov, V.Manin et al. *Zhivopis' 20-30kh godov*,
Sankt-Peterburg, 1991.
Coll RM.

PAL'MOV, Viktor Nikandrovich   1888-1929
Painter. Born at Samara. He studied at Kazan School of Art
until 1911 and then at the Moscow College 1911-14.
After the Revolution he contributed to leftist exhibitions in
the period 1917-19. In 1919 he travelled eastwards via Chita
to Vladivostok and on to Japan where he organised exhibitions
with the Futurist David Burlyuk.
He returned to Moscow in 1922 and arranged an exhibition
To Japan with Futurism. He then taught at the Kiev Art
Institute 1922-8 and was an organiser of the group OSMOU.
He was represented at the 1928 Venice International
Exhibition. He sometimes signed his work 'Palmof'. He died
at Kiev.
*Composition with a Red Rider, 1920, RM, is a spectacular image
of the rider splintered into spangled planes of colour and
texture. The imagery recalls Chagall as the figure leaps over
lurching houses.
Lit S.Tretyakov, N.Aseev *Khudozhnik V.Pal'mov* (The Artist
V.Palmov), Chita, 1922. *Paris-Moscou*, 1979.
Coll TG; RM.

PAL'TSEVA, N. D.   a.1921
She was included in the Third Touring Exhibition of the
Sovetsk Regional subdepartment of the Museums Bureau
along with Kandinsky, Rodchenko and others in 1921.

PAMYLATNYKH, Nina = KASHINA, Nina V.

PANKOV, Ivan   a.1924
A member of the group *Byt* (Life) with K.Parkhomenko. They
exhibited ten oils at the First Discussional Exhibition of Active
Revolutionary Art in 1924.

PARKHOMENKO, Konstantin   a.1923-1929
Painter. A member of the group Byt (Life) with I.Pankov.
They exhibited ten oils at the First Discussional Exhibition of
Active Revolutionary Art in 1924. He was represented at the
First Touring Exhibition of Painting and Graphics which

opened in Moscow in 1929.

Tea, 1923-4, oil, has more than a hint of the grotesque reminiscent of Gogol or even Chagall. Two inelegant figures sit at a table dominated by a large teapot. Their attitude suggests mystery and menace rather than simple relaxation or refreshment.

PASHKOV, N.   a.1920

He was engaged on Agitprop projects in 1920 including the decoration of the propaganda trains *Red Cossack*, Ukrainian *Lenin*, *Lenin (October Revolution)* and *Soviet Caucasus*.

PASTERNAK, Leonid Osipovich   1861-1945

Prolific and original portrait painter in oils and pastel, graphic artist. Born at Odessa. He studied at the Odessa School of Art 1879-81 and then studied at Moscow University until 1884. He travelled to Germany to attend the Munich Academy 1885-7. He exhibited with the World of Art 1901-3. He taught at the Moscow College from 1894 until 1918. In 1901 he drew the writer Tolstoy and his family. He was again in Germany in 1904 and also visited Italy that year. In 1906 he was in Berlin and in 1908 he travelled to Holland, Belgium and England. In 1912 he went to Venice. He exhibited with the World of Art, the Wanderers and the Union of Russian Artists. He was the father of the poet Boris Pasternak. He produced a moving poster in 1914, *For the Aid of War Victims*, depicting a soldier with a bleeding head leaning disconsolately against a wall.

After the Revolution he was represented in the Sixth State Exhibition: The Print (*VI Gosudarstvennaya vystavka gravyur*) in Moscow in 1919.

He emigrated to Berlin in 1921 and subsequently to Oxford. He died in Oxford.

Book design The cover in mauve and black for Yulii Engel's setting of *Evreiskie narodnie pesni* (Jewish National Songs), Moscow, c.1912.

Writings L.Pasternak *Zapiski raznykh let* (Notes from Various Years), Moscow, 1975. L.O.Pasternak *Memoirs*, 1982.

Lit M.Osborn *L.Pasternak*, Warsaw, 1932. D.Buckman *Leonid Pasternak: A Russian Impressionist*, 1974. *L.O.Pasternak*, exh. cat., Moscow, 1979.

Coll Well represented at the Ashmolean Museum, Oxford; TG; Bibliothèque Nationale, Paris; Lenin Library, Moscow. Colour plate p.330.

PAVILIONOV, Georgii (Yuri) Sergeevich   1907-1937

Painter. He was a member of the *Makovets* group from 1922 to 1927. He studied in the department of Monumental Painting in the Painting Faculty of the Vkhutein 1926-30. He assisted Tatlin on the development of his glider *Letatlin* 1930-2. He worked under Favorsky as an artist-monumentalist from 1934.

PAVLENKO, Oksana Trofimovna   1896-1931+

Ukrainian painter, graphic artist. Born in the Kiev region. She studied at the Kiev School of Art and at the Ukrainian Academy 1917-22. She was engaged on the decorative propaganda work under M.Boitchuk. Later she taught at the Kiev Professional School for Art and Ceramics and in 1927 she was teaching at the Vkhutein in Moscow. She was included in the exhibition of Russian Graphic Art in Riga in 1929.

From 1931 she taught at the Moscow Typographic Institute.
Lit *Paris-Moscou*, 1979.

Pavel Pavlinov. Illustration to Ruffini's 'Notes of Lorenzo Benoni', *1928. Woodcut.*
Atmosphere is increased by leaving the figures black and therefore mysterious against the dim light of the street's buildings.

PAVLINOV, Pavel Yakovlevich   1881-1966

Painter, graphic artist. Born at St. Petersburg. After attending naval school in St. Petersburg 1894-1900, he studied painting under O.Braz and P.Wagner 1899-1901. He studied next under D.Kardovsky at the Academy in St. Petersburg 1903-6 and then travelled to Munich where he studied privately 1906-8. From 1911 to 1913 he studied at the Stroganov Institute in Moscow under S.Goloushev and I.Pavlov. He exhibited with the Association of Moscow Artists in 1913.

After the Revolution he was represented in the Fourth State Exhibition of Paintings (*IV Gosudarstvennaya vystavka kartin*) in Moscow in 1919 and in the Sixth State Exhibition: The Print (*VI Gosudarstvennaya vystavka gravyur*) in Moscow in 1919. He taught at the Moscow Vkhutemas/Vkhutein from 1921 and exhibited with the 4 Arts society from 1924. He was represented at the Paris International Exhibition in 1925. He was included in the major exhibition in Moscow in 1927 marking the tenth anniversary of the Revolution and the exhibition of graphic art Liberation Movements: The Sixteenth to the Twentieth Century held in Moscow in 1928. He was included in the exhibition of Russian Graphic Art in Riga in 1929 and in the First Touring Exhibition of Painting and Graphics which opened in Moscow in 1929. He was also represented at the jubilee exhibition Artists of the RSFSR over 15 Years held at the Russian Museum, Leningrad, in 1932. He died in Moscow.

Portrait of E.T.A.Hofmann, 1922, wood engraving, is

reminiscent of Favorsky's techniques. The writer stares with an inspired and slightly fantastic expression.

Illustrations Pushkin's *Rusalka*, 1923.

Lit V.Pavlov *P.Pavlinov*, Moscow, 1933. N.Gorlenko *P.Ya.Pavlinov*, Moscow, 1971. *Paris-Moscou*, 1979.

PAVLOV, Ivan Nikolaevich   **1872-1951**
Graphic artist, wood engraver. He studied at the Stieglitz School in St. Petersburg 1897-1901.
After the Revolution he was represented in the Sixth State Exhibition: The Print (*VI Gosudarstvennaya vystavka gravyur*) in Moscow in 1919. He contributed to the exhibition of graphic art Liberation Movements: The Sixteenth to the Twentieth Century held in Moscow in 1928 and to the exhibition of Russian Graphic Art in Riga in 1929. He was also represented at the jubilee exhibition Artists of the RSFSR over 15 Years held at the Russian Museum, Leningrad, in 1932. He taught in Moscow.
Evening: The Kremlin in Session, wood engraving, depicts the Kremlin as a skyline of towers, domes and its flag forming a solid black silhouette except for its illuminated windows. Horizontal cuts give the river's surface in the foreground complete with shadowy reflections. The technique and atmosphere recall the economy of means employed by Ostroumova-Lebedeva.

PAVLOV, Ivan Petrovich   **1849-1936**
Graphic artist, engraver of illustrations. He exhibited at the All-Russian Exhibition of Printing in St. Petersburg in 1895.

PAVLOV, Kapiton Stepanovich   **1791-1852**
Portrait painter. The date of his birth is sometimes given as 1792.
Coll TG.

PAVLOV, Semen Andreevich   **1893-1941**
Painter, graphic artist. He studied at the school of the Society for the Encouragement of the Arts in St. Petersburg 1904-6.
After the Revolution he studied under Shukhaev, Kardovsky, Petrov-Vodkin and Kozlinsky at the Petrograd Free State Studios 1917-22. He produced one of the first posters depicting Lenin. He was a member of AKhRR in the 1920s. His work included urban landscapes painted with a fluid touch and evocative of atmosphere without loss of clarity in the marks. He signed his work with a monogram formed from the cyrillic letter 'P' arched over the cyrillic 'S'.
Lit A.M.Muratov, V.Manin et al. *Zhivopis' 20-30kh godov*, Sankt-Peterburg, 1991.
Coll RM

PAVLYUCHENKO, G. E.   **a.1913**
He contributed to Larionov's exhibition *Mishen'* (The Target) in 1913.

PCHELIN, Vladimir Nikolaevich   **1869-1941**
Poster designer, painter. After the Revolution he was represented at the First Exhibition of Works of the Professional Union of Artists in Moscow in 1918.
Coll TG; Lenin Library, Moscow.

PELEVIN, Ivan Andreevich   **1840-1917**
Painter of figure compositions and portraits. Sometimes he signed his work 'I.P'.
Coll TG.

Pavel Pavlinov. Illustration to Pushkin's Poem 'Rusalka' (Mermaid), *1923.*

PEN, Yuri Moisevich   **1854-1937**
Belorussian painter. He taught Marc Chagall at Vitebsk. He was represented along with Kandinsky, Chagall and others at the First State Exhibition of Paintings by Local and Moscow Artists held in Vitebsk in December 1919. He participated in the First State Free Exhibition of Artworks in Petrograd in 1919. He was represented at the First Russian Art Exhibition in Berlin in 1922.
* *Old Tailor*, 1903, Belorussian Art Museum, Minsk, is an absolutely frontal three-quarter-length portrait — a format made much more familiar by his pupil Chagall a decade or so later. The tailor wears his skull cap and has a red cloth across his knee. Stylistically it is closer to certain of Repin's portraits than to Chagall's.
Coll Belorussian Art Museum, Minsk.

PEREDVIZHNIKI = WANDERERS

PEREKATOV, A.   **a.1919-1921**
He exhibited in the first Obmokhu exhibition in May 1919 in Moscow. He also took part in the third exhibition of Obmokhu, the Society of Young Artists, in Moscow in May 1921, along with Ioganson, Medunetsky and others.

PEREL'MAN, Viktor Nikolaevich   **1892-1967**
Painter. Born at Lipetsk. He studied at the Bogolyubova Drawing School in Saratov from 1910 and at the Moscow college 1914-15 under N.Kasatkin, Arkhipov, Malyutin and K.Korovin.
After the Revolution he was appointed director of the Saratov

Art Institute in 1918 and was represented at the First Exhibition of Works of the Professional Union of Artists in Moscow the same year. He was engaged on Agitprop projects, including the decoration of trams, at Saratov 1918-20. He was a member of AKhRR from 1923 to 1933 and was represented at both the First Touring Exhibition of Painting and Graphics which opened in Moscow in 1929 and the jubilee exhibition Artists of the RSFSR over 15 Years held at the Russian Museum, Leningrad, in 1932. He also exhibited at the 1932 Venice Biennale. He died in Moscow.

Lit *V.N.Perel'man*, exh. cat., Moscow, 1962. *Paris-Moscou*, 1979.

Coll TG; Museum of the Revolution, Moscow.

PEREPLETCHIKOV, Vasili (Vladimir) Vasilievich 1863-1918

Painter active in Moscow. He studied under A.Kiselev in Moscow. He exhibited with the World of Art 1899-1903. He was working at Archangel in 1902 and 1911. He exhibited with the First Izdebsky International Salon 1909-10 in Odessa.

Coll TG.

PEROV, Vasili Grigorevich   1833-1882

An influential painter of genre, social commentary and portraits, sometimes recognised as the initiator of Russian Realist painting. Born at Tobolsk, the illegitimate son of an impoverished family of the nobility. He studied at the Moscow College 1853-61, where he painted *The Arrival of the Rural Police Inspector*, 1857. This painting caused a stir by its element of overt social criticism which was to become an increasingly sharp and effective aspect of his work.

He became a founder member of the Wanderers movement and a central figure in its activities and development. He elevated genre themes to the status of monumental narrative painting so that his social commentaries were both popularly intelligible and at the same time incisive. Their immediacy made them dramatic and effective. Their somewhat theatrical force was essential to this. He was awarded a gold medal in 1863 and was sent abroad by the Academy to study in Paris. Amongst the most celebrated of his paintings was *The Drowned Woman*, 1867. His portraits shared the vitality of his other paintings and included *Turgenev*, 1871, and *Dostoevsky*, 1872, TG. He taught at the Moscow College from 1871 to 1882.

*Easter Procession in the Country, 1861, TG, exemplifies his spiking of genre with a social message. The devotional procession winds away from the wooden house down the hill towards the town or village, holding high its banners and its ikon. The priest follows seriously introspective and possibly the worse for drink. To do this he has to pass a beggar at his feet whilst a young woman notices the slumped form of a destitute or drunken figure half hidden beneath the steps of the house. It is a painting motivated by disillusionment, critical of church cynicism, and it is thereby also a means of political criticism.

Lit A.Fedorov-Davydov *V.G.Perov*, Moscow, 1934.

Coll Major holdings at TG; RM.

PEROV, Vladimir Vasilievich   1868-1898

Genre painter.

Coll TG.

PERSHUDCHEV, Ivan Gavrilovich   b.1915

Sculptor. Active in the 1940s.

Vasili Perov. The Last Inn by the Town Gate, *1868. Oil on canvas. 51.1 x 65.8 cm. State Tretyakov Gallery, Moscow.*

PERUTSKY, Mikhail Semenovich   **1892-1959**

Painter, graphic artist, watercolourist. He studied at Bershadsky's private art school in Odessa 1908-10 and at the Odessa Art Institute under K.Kostandi between 1909 and 1920.
After the Revolution 1919-20 he directed a group of agitational poster designers in Odessa and was involved in the reorganisation of the art school there. He was a founder member of NOZh, the New Society of Painters 1921-4. He was a member of the *Bytie* (Existence) group 1923-7, Life-Creativity in 1924, and the Society of Easel Painters (OST) in 1927. His work was included in the exhibition of Soviet art held at Harbin in 1926 and in Japan in 1927 and in the major exhibition in Moscow in 1927 marking the tenth anniversary of the Revolution. He was also represented at the First Touring Exhibition of Painting and Graphics which opened in Moscow in 1929 and at the jubilee exhibition Artists of the RSFSR over 15 Years held at the Russian Museum, Leningrad, in 1932.
He designed for the propaganda posters of the Tass Windows 1941-6.
Lit A.M.Muratov, V.Manin et al. *Zhivopis' 20-30kh godov*, Sankt-Peterburg, 1991.
Coll RM.

Vera Pestel'. Costume Design for a Female Dancer, *c.1925*. *Watercolour, pencil and metallic paint. 25.2 x 20.2 cm. Collection Mr. and Mrs. Nikita D.Lobanov-Rostovsky, London.*

PERVUKHIN, Konstantin Konstantinovich   **1863-1915**

Painter of landscapes and city views, including Venice where he was painting in 1904 and 1910-14.
Coll Well represented at TG.

PESKOV, Mikhail Ivanovich   **1834-1864**

Painter. He studied at the Academy in St. Petersburg but rejected the principles of the Academy to become a member of the Artel, or artists' co-operative, which led to the founding of the Wanderers movement.

PESSATI = DYMSHITS-TOLSTAYA, S. I.

PESTEL', Vera Efimovna (Efremovna)   **1887-1952**

Painter, theatre designer. Her birth dates are sometimes given as 1886 or 1887. She was born in Moscow. After studying at the Stroganov College 1904-6 she studied privately under K.Yuon and I.O.Dudin 1906-7 and under Hollósy in Germany 1909-11. She also visited Italy and France where she studied under Le Fauconnier and Metzinger in Paris in 1912. She was with Popova, Udal'tsova and Exter in Paris in 1913. Her awareness of Cubism was therefore thorough and first hand. It led her into experimental art and her still-lifes of 1915-16 employ Cubist derived flat planes, lettering and collage in varied alignments, but subsequently she followed Malevich into Suprematist painting and drawing. She exhibited at 0.10. The Last Futurist Exhibition of Paintings at Petrograd in December 1915. She rapidly responded to the Suprematism of Malevich which was launched at that exhibition and she became a member of the *Supremus* group 1916-17. She also participated in the Knave of Diamonds exhibition of 1916 in Moscow, *Magazin* (The Store) at which she contributed a painting of *The Artist Tatlin and Bandura* of 1916, and to the World of Art exhibition in 1917.
After the Revolution she executed decorations for the Left Federation of the Union of Moscow Artists in 1918 in collaboration with Popova, Karetnikova and Udal'tsova and she exhibited with the Artists of the Leftist Federation of the Professional Union in Moscow in 1918 along with Rodchenko and others. She was represented at the Fifth State Exhibition in Petrograd 1918-19 and appeared on the April 1919 list of artists for acquisitions by the envisaged Museum of Painterly Culture. She participated in the Third Exhibition of Paintings held at Ryazan in 1919. However she seems to have renounced non-objective art c.1918.
She studied theatre design c.1920 and also art education for children. She exhibited in the 1921 exhibition of the World of Art in Moscow. Her work was included in the First Russian Art Exhibition in Berlin in 1922. She participated in the seventh exhibition of the group *L'Araignée* (The Spider) at the Galerie Devambe in Paris in 1925. She was a member of the *Makovets* group from 1922 to 1925 and exhibited with the group *Put' Zhivopisi* (Path of Painting) 1927-30, with Zhegin and others. She died in Moscow.
Lit A.Z.Rudenstine *Costakis Collection*, London, 1981. A.M.Muratov, V.Manin et al. *Zhivopis' 20-30kh godov*, Sankt-Peterburg, 1991. *L'Avant-garde russe 1905-1925*, exh. cat., Musée des Beaux-Arts, Nantes, 1993.
Coll TG; RM; Nizhny-Novgorod Art Museum; Costakis Collection.

PESTRIKOV, M. a.1914-1918

He was teaching at Kharkov School of Art 1914-18 where his pupils included Deineka.

PET, a.1918

Graphic artist, designing posters in 1918.

PETRITSKY, Anatoli Galaktionovich 1895-1964

Ukrainian painter, theatre designer. Born in Kiev. He studied at the Kiev Art Institute 1912-18 under Murashko and was already producing stylised decorations influenced by folk art in 1915.

After the Revolution he studied under Alexandra Exter in Kiev and then at the Moscow Vkhutemas under Drevin and Udal'tsova from 1922 to 1924. He was engaged in agitational decorations and in designing for the theatre from 1918. He was represented at the Paris International Exhibition in 1925. He moved to Kharkov where he was in contact with Bogomazov, Ermilov and others. He died in Kiev.

Theatre design 1923 *Eccentric Dances: Jazz Band*, choreography by K.Goleizovsky, at the State Choreographic School, Moscow.

1923 *Nur and Anitra*, ballet by A.Gorsky with music by A.Ilinsky for the Greenwich Village Follies, New York.

1924 *Tristan und Isolde*, unrealised ballet based on Wagner's opera.

1926 *Le Corsaire* produced by Igor Moiseev in Kharkov.

1928 *Taras Bulba* produced by Igor Moiseev in Kharkov.

1927 Rossini's *William Tell* at the Theatre of Opera and Ballet, Kharkov. A design for a woman is crudely geometric in its blend of medievalism and avant-garde.

1930 *The Football Player* ballet choreographed by Nikolai Foregger at the Theatre of Opera and Ballet, Kharkov. A design for Tennis Players is stylised in the manner of Deineka.

1937 N.V.Lysenko's *Taras Bulba* at the T.G.Shevchenko Opera and Ballet Theatre, Kiev. Lively and painterly costume designs in watercolour and gouache show an entertaining sense of fun particularly in the design for a mustachioed, pantalooned figure (Bakhrushin Theatre Museum, Moscow).

1941 P.I.Chaikovsky's *Cherevichki*, Moscow.

Lit V.Khmuryi *Anatol Petritsky*, Kharkov, 1929. I.Vrona *Anatol Petritsky*, Kiev, 1968. *A.Petritsky Album*, Kiev, 1968. D.Gorbachev *A.Petritsky*, Moscow, 1970. *Paris-Moscou*, 1979. J.E.Bowlt *Russian Stage Design. Scenic Innovation. From the Collection of Mr. and Mrs. Nikita D.Lobanov-Rostovsky*, Jackson, MS, exh. cat.,1982. Nancy Van Norman Baer *Theatre in Revolution, Russian Avant-Garde Stage Design 1913-1935*, San Francisco and London, 1991. Dzhon Boult (John Bowlt) *Khudozhniki russkogo teatra. Sobranie Nikity i Niny Lobanovykh-Rostovskikh*, Moscow, 1991.

Coll Bakhrushin Theatre Museum, Moscow; Bolshoi Theatre Museum, Moscow.

Colour plate p.331.

PETROV, Mikhail Aleksandrovich 1841-1917

Genre painter.

Coll TG.

PETROV, Nikolai Filippovich 1872-1941

Landscape and genre painter.

Coll TG.

PETROV, Nikolai Petrovich 1843-1876

Painter of genre scenes and ikons, graphic artist. Born at St. Petersburg. He became a member of the Artel, or artists' co-operative, which led to the founding of the Wanderers movement. He died in Italy.

Coll TG.

PETROV, S. I. a.1907-1932

Painter, graphic artist. He contributed to the *Stefanos* exhibition 1907-8.

He exhibited with the Society of Moscow Painters at its inaugural exhibition in Moscow in 1925 and was included in the exhibition of Russian Graphic Art in Riga in 1929. He was also represented at the First Touring Exhibition of Painting and Graphics which opened in Moscow in 1929 and at the jubilee exhibition Artists of the RSFSR over 15 Years held at the Russian Museum, Leningrad, in 1932.

PETROV, Vasili Petrovich 1770?-1810

Painter of city views and landscapes. He produced Italian landscapes in the period 1788-1800. Sometimes he signed his work 'Petroff'. The date of his death is sometimes given as 1811.

Coll TG.

PETROV-VODKIN, Kuz'ma Sergeevich 1878-1939

A painter of great originality whose excitement at the work of Matisse and Cubist artists gave way to his admiration for the traditions of ikon painting. The result was ikonic oil paintings of precision and boldness with a strong narrative aspect. This he applied to themes of his own time, constructing highly memorable, large and yet still delicate paintings. He also evolved his own spatial system for paintings which brought together the picture space that he had studied in ikons with the most recent concepts borrowed from science and mathematics.

Born at Khlavynsk. He studied under F.Burov in Samara 1893-5, at the Stieglitz School in St. Petersburg 1895-7 and at the Moscow College 1897-1905, although in 1901 he was in Munich where he attended the Azbé School. Together with P.Kuznetsov he was engaged in decorating the Church of Our Lady of Kazan at Saratov c.1904. He visited Constantinople and toured Italy in 1905. Finally he studied at the Académie Colarossi in Paris in 1906 and was painting in Algeria in 1907 as well as visiting Greece. This long period of study made him an informed, independent and an original painter. In 1909 he exhibited thirty-eight works at the St. Petersburg Salon in the Menshikov Palace; he also began to exhibit with the Golden Fleece in 1909. He taught at the Zvantseva School in St. Petersburg during 1910-15. He designed for the theatre in 1913. He exhibited with the Union of Youth in 1910, and with the Union of Russian Artists 1909-10. He was a member of the World of Art from 1911 to 1924.

After the Revolution he designed a street decoration in 1918 for the first anniversary celebrations: this depicts Stepan Razin on board a ship. He was engaged on Agitprop decorations in Theatre Square, Petrograd, in 1918. These comprised highly decorative panels of flowers, the witch Babayaga flying amongst the planets and symbols of the arts. His painting *Herring*, 1918, RM, represented the ration of hungry Petrograd at that time. He taught at the Free Art Studios (SVOMAS) in Petrograd in 1918 and his name appeared on the April 1919 list of artists for acquisitions by the envisaged

Museum of Painterly Culture.

He participated in the First State Free Exhibition of Artworks in Petrograd in 1919. He was represented at the exhibition of Studies for Theatre Decoration and Works from the Studios of the Decorative Institute held in Petrograd in 1922 and he was included in the enormous survey Exhibition of Paintings by Petrograd Artists of All Tendencies 1919-1923 held in Petrograd in 1923.

His painting *After the Battle* was exhibited in Venice in 1924. He was a member of the 4 Arts society in 1925 and was represented at the Paris International Exhibition in 1925. He was represented at the International Exhibition in Dresden in 1926. His work was included in the exhibition of Soviet art held at Harbin in 1926 and in Japan in 1927 and in the major exhibition in Moscow in 1927 marking the tenth anniversary of the Revolution. He exhibited with the 4 Arts society in Leningrad including the exhibition of 1928 at the Russian Museum.

He was represented at the jubilee exhibition Artists of the RSFSR over 15 Years held at the Russian Museum, Leningrad, in 1932 and at the 1932 Venice Biennale. He also contributed to the exhibition of Contemporary Russian Art held at Philadelphia in 1932. Sometimes he signed his work 'K.P.V'. He died in Leningrad.

The Bathing of the Red Horse, 1912, TG, is an awkward, monumental and symbolic painting which is reminiscent of the red horses of Franz Marc. The handling is characteristically precise and the composition bold.

The Mother, 1913, TG, shows a peasant girl feeding her child at her breast. Behind her stretches an extensive landscape marked only by a cluster of wooden houses. In essence this is the Virgin and Child but already stripped of specific Christian context even before the Revolution. She exhibits the monumental calm of a Renaissance Madonna but the theme is addressed as a stage of human life and relationships. This is a sophisticated painting in its iconography and its handling of space in which distance and timelessness combine to project the theme with precision and clarity. It is an economical and powerful composition.

Midday, 1917, RM, has a perspective splayed like a fan in which dislocations of scale reduce figures to less than the size of foreground fruit. Much of the ikon's narrative tradition is at work in Petrov-Vodkin's landscapes of the Revolutionary years. At the centre of this painting is a funeral procession. Despite the spatial disparities everything visible is precise and explicit to the remotest sloping horizon.

After the Battle, 1923, Central Museum of the Armed Forces, Moscow, shows three stiff and melancholy soldiers at a table. Behind them rears the image in blue of a comrade falling in battle. The painting disturbs the imagination by depicting the memory of the recent trauma still looming over those who survived. It is a good example of Petrov-Vodkin's ability to imbue his paintings with a psychological tension by dislocations of time and space.

Death of the Commissar, 1928, RM, is set against a strange vision of a blue hillside in which puffs of smoke and a town appear, all in the same blue light. A column of soldiers is seen marching through an unnerving and unnatural perspective. In the foreground the dying commissar collapses in the arms of a soldier. Petrov-Vodkin's drawing is so precise and his colour so clean that a tense clarity pervades the drama of this death in battle, a curious other worldly calm that freezes the action, lifting the scene from particular time and place and generalising the theme without any loss of specific detail or of dramatic tension.

The Alarm, 1934-5, is one of his best later paintings and a brilliant piece of domestic theatre. A baby sleeps in the foreground of a tattered apartment. At centre a mother protects a young girl whilst the father peers through the dark window. It is an image of anxiety which is effective beyond the specific circumstances of its time.

Theatre design 1913 Schiller's *Maid of Orléans* produced in Moscow.

Book design Cover for *Samarkandiya* (Samarkand), Peterburg, 1923.

Writings K.Petrov-Vodkin *Khlynovsk — Prostranstvo Evklida — Samarkandiya*, Leningrad, 1970, 1982.

Lit A.Galushkina *K.Petrov-Vodkin*, Moscow, 1936. V.Kostin *K.S.Petrov-Vodkin*, Moscow, 1965. *K.Petrov-Vodkin*, exh. cat., Leningrad-Moscow, 1967. G.Karginov *Petrov-Vodkin*, Budapest, 1972. Yu.Rusakov *K.Petrov-Vodkin*, Leningrad, 1975. *Paris-Moscou*, 1979. Yu.Rusakov, N.Barabanova *K.Petrov-Vodkin*, Leningrad, 1986. S.Compton *Russian Avant-Garde Books 1917-34*, London, 1992.

Coll Well represented at TG; RM.

Colour plates title page, pp.334, 335.

PETROVA-TROTSKAYA (PETROVA-TROITSKAYA), Ekaterina Mikhailovna   **1900-1932**
Painter.
Coll RM.

PETROVICHEV, Petr Ivanovich   **1874-1947**
Landscape painter. He studied at the Moscow College under Levitan and Serov 1892-1903. He exhibited with the World of Art 1902-3.

After the Revolution Petrovichev appeared on the April 1919 list of artists for acquisitions by the envisaged Museum of Painterly Culture and he participated in the Third Exhibition of Paintings held at Ryazan in 1919. He was represented at the First Russian Art Exhibition in Berlin in 1922 and contributed to the Third Exhibition of Paintings by Artists from Kaluga and Moscow held in Kaluga in 1925. He was also represented at the First Touring Exhibition of Painting and Graphics which opened in Moscow in 1929.

Lit A.M.Muratov, V.Manin et al. *Zhivopis' 20-30kh godov*, Sankt-Peterburg, 1991.

Coll TG.

PETROVSKY, Ivan Vladimirovich   **b.1880**
Portraitist. He was included in the enormous survey Exhibition of Paintings by Petrograd Artists of All Tendencies 1919-1923 held in Petrograd in 1923.
Coll TG.

PETROVSKY, Petr Stepanovich   **1814-1842**
History painter whose work included biblical themes. He studied at the Academy in St. Petersburg. In 1841 he moved to Rome where he died the following year.
Coll TG.

PETRUZHKOV   **a.1924**
He exhibited with the First Working Organisaton of Artists in 1924 at the First Discussional Exhibition of Active Revolutionary Art alongside G.Aleksandrov and others.

PEVSNER, Antoine (PEVZNER, Natan Borisovich) 1884-1962
Sculptor. Born at Orel. He was the brother of the sculptor

Kuz'ma Petrov-Vodkin. Still-life with Fruit and Glass, *1924. Oil on canvas. Initialled and dated. 49.2 x 60.6 cm.*
Reproduced by kind permission of Sotheby's London, sale 23.2.1983, lot 214.

Naum Gabo. He studied at Kiev Art School 1902-9 and at the Academy in St. Petersburg.

In 1912 he visited Paris, returning 1913-14. There he met Archipenko and Modigliani in 1913. He was attracted to Cubist painting at this time.

During the war he worked in Moscow until 1915-16 when he moved to Oslo where his brother Gabo was also living.

With the coming of the Revolution in 1917 they moved back to Russia where Pevsner taught at the Free Art Studios/Vkhutemas. Pevsner exhibited at the Fifth State Exhibition: From Impressionism to Non-Objective Art in Moscow 1918-19. Together with Gabo he became one of the pioneers of constructed sculpture. They showed work at an open air exhibition on Tverskoy Boulevard in 1920 and also published their *Realistic Manifesto* as a broadsheet outlining their aims and conception of art. This revealed an awareness of Cubist and Italian Futurist theory and practice but also asserted their independence. As the Stenberg brothers, Medunetsky and the circle around Rodchenko were evolving the theory and practice of construction at this time, a debate has arisen concerning the first to initiate these developments. However it is clear that constructed sculpture arose within Cubist circles in Paris before the war and was evident in the work of Picasso, Braque, Laurens, Archipenko and others. Pevsner and Gabo both constructed sculpture in Norway before returning to Russia but these works too are preceded in Russia by the reliefs of Tatlin. More significantly a distinction is necessary between the aims of the Constructivists, including the Stenberg brothers, Medunetsky and Rodchenko, associated with the Institute of Artistic Culture (INKhUK) and the Obmokhu group in

Moscow who sought to undermine the special status of the artwork by pursuing creative work that was collective, impersonal, utilitarian and communist. Gabo and Pevsner insisted on the independence of art and politics.

In 1922 Pevsner showed work at the First Russian Art Exhibition in Berlin and moved to Germany.

By 1923 he was again in Paris where he was to spend most of the rest of his life. He collaborated with Gabo on the Russian Constructivists exhibition at the Galerie Percier in Paris in 1924 and was increasingly recognised as an originator of Constructivism in Western critical writing. This status has been revised in recent years as more has become known of Rodchenko and others, perhaps to the point where the contribution of Gabo and Pevsner has now been underestimated. Again with Gabo he devised the design of the ballet *La Chatte* for the production by Diaghilev in 1927. He took French citizenship in 1930. In 1932 he exhibited with the group *Abstraction-Création*. He contributed to numerous international exhibitions in the1930s.

After the Second World War he was a founder of the group *Réalités Nouvelles*. With Gabo he held a retrospective exhibition at the Museum of Modern Art in New York in 1948. Steadily growing international recognition resulted in a profusion of post-war exhibitions in Europe and America. A retrospective was held at the Musée d'Art Moderne, Paris, in 1957, and he was made a Chevalier of the Légion d'Honneur in 1961. He died in Paris.

Theatre design 1927 with Gabo he designed the constructed costumes and sets for Diaghilev's production of *La Chatte*, a ballet to music by Henri Sauguet at the Théâtre Sarah

Bernhardt, Paris.

Lit M.Duchamp et al. *Antoine Pevsner*, Paris, 1947. *Antoine Pevsner*, exh. cat., MNAM, Paris, 1957. P.Peissi, C.Giedion-Welcker *Antoine Pevsner*, Neuchâtel, 1961. B.Dorival *Antoine Pevsner*, Milan, 1966.

Coll His work is represented in many major museums including MNAM, Paris; Yale University Art Gallery; The Art Institute, Chicago; The Solomon R.Guggenheim Museum, New York; The Peggy Guggenheim Collection, Venice; Tate Gallery, London; Stedelijk Museum, Amsterdam; Kunstmuseum, Basel; TG; RM.
Colour plate p.338.

PEVZNER, N. B. = PEVSNER, A.

PICHUGIN, Sergei Ivanovich   1881-1971
Painter. He was engaged on Agitprop projects c.1918 and assisted on the decoration of the propaganda trains *Red Cossack*, Ukrainian *Lenin, Lenin (October Revolution)* and *Soviet Caucasus*. He exhibited with the Moscow School Society of Artists active in 1917-25. He died in Moscow.

PIKOV, Mikhail Ivanovich   1903-1973
Printmaker. A follower of Favorsky in technique as his illustration of *A.Firenzuoli* reveals in its combination of a Florentine scene and drawing technique allied to Favorsky's printmaking methods.

PIKSHE, Zhanno = BIKSHE, K. K.

PILENKO = KUZMINA-KARAVOEVA, E.Yu.

PILLANOVSKY, P. A.   a.1918
He was engaged on Agitprop decorations in Petrograd in 1918.

PIMENOV, Nikolai Stepanovich   1812-1864
Neo-classical sculptor. He was the son of the sculptor Stepan Stepanovich Pimenov. His works included portrait busts, small-scale works combining genre themes with a classicising style, and some monumental themes among which was *St.George and the Dragon*, a complex assemblage of horse, rider, spear, dragon and wings raised upon a rock. This was made for the Hall of St. George at the Kremlin in Moscow.
**Boy Playing Knucklebones*, 1836, plaster, RM, which won the Academy's first gold medal. It is a standing academic full-length figure, leaning hand on knee, to cast the knucklebone. The musculature is explicit and accurate in a deliberately popular piece. It is inspired by antique sculptures of athletes.
*Boy Asking Alms, 1842, marble, RM, is an idealised form of the diminutive figure with a credible musculature and bone structure clearly implied beneath the surface of the marble. This severity is offset by the sweetness of the theme which is more endearing than declamatory.
Coll Well represented at RM; TG.

PIMENOV, Stepan Stepanovich   1784-1833
Neo-classical sculptor. He was the father of the sculptor Nikolai Pimenov. Born at St. Petersburg. He studied at the Academy in St. Petersburg. His work includes a sleeping figure of Sculpture holding a malet in her hand designed for the *Tomb of M.I.Kozlovsky*, 1802, a restrained and beautiful work reflecting the severity and control of Canova. He made numerous statues for the city of St. Petersburg.

PIMENOV, Yuri (Georgiy) Ivanovich   1903-1977
Proto-Socialist Realist painter, theatre designer, graphic artist. Born in Moscow. He studied privately in Moscow and then under Malyutin, D.Kardovsky and V.Favorsky at the Vkhutemas 1920-5. In 1924 he exhibited in the First Discussional Exhibition of Active Revolutionary Art as part of the group The Union of Three along with A.Goncharov and A.Deineka. He was a founder member of the Society of Easel Painters (OST) from 1925 to 1928. He contributed to the International Exhibition in Dresden in 1926. He was also included in the major exhibition in Moscow in 1927 marking the tenth anniversary of the Revolution. He visited Italy and Germany in 1928. He was included in the exhibition of Russian Graphic Art in Riga in 1929 and in the First Touring Exhibition of Painting and Graphics which opened in Moscow in 1929. He was also represented at the jubilee exhibition Artists of the RSFSR over 15 Years held at the Russian Museum, Leningrad, in 1932 and at the 1932 Venice Biennale.
In due course he became involved in design for film and television and he taught at the Institute of Cinematography from 1945 to 1972. He visited Asia and Europe towards the end of his life. He sometimes signed his work with a monogram comprising a cyrillic letter 'Yu' within a cyrillic 'P'. He died in Moscow.
*Bathing, c.1923, pencil, ink, lacquer, combines figures of different scales with an ambiguous space flowing uninterrupted between them. In part they are mere stylised silhouettes but in part they are modelled by a soft and inconsistent light source. The space is ultimately Cubist in derivation but there is no angular division of the forms into planes.
**Create Heavy Industry*, 1927, TG, shows immense factory structures which create a setting for the workers' muscular achievements. The composition is at root Cubo-Futurist but welded to the cause so that discs become again the massive forms of boilers and straight lines the framework of towering factories. His skill at setting workers within this Piranesian factory echoes that of Deineka.
*New Moscow, 1937, TG, is an idealised image of the high-rise city as seen from the back of a car with a woman driver visible in the foreground. It is a sunlit vision of the new university buildings and other towers in the haze of light. The technique is unusual: paint is applied in thin vertical dashes rather like an effect of rain.
Writings Yu.Pimenov *V Podmoskovie* (In Moscow's Outskirts), Moscow, 1956. Yu.Pimenov *God Puteshestvy* (A Year of Journeys), Moscow, 1960. Yu.Pimenov *Novye Kvartaly* (New Quarters), Moscow, 1968.
Lit O.Beskin *Yu.Pimenov*, Moscow, 1960. A.D.Chegodaev *Yu.I.Pimenov*, 1964. E.Loginova *Yu.Pimenov*, Moscow, 1970. *Paris-Moscou*, 1979. A.Sidorov *Pimenov*, Moscow, 1986.
Coll TG; RM.

PIMONENKO, Nikolai Kornilievich   1862-1912
Ukrainian painter of Ukrainian rural themes and genre. Born at Kiev into the family of an ikon painter and wood-carver. He studied at the Kiev School of Art until 1882 and then at the Academy in St. Petersburg 1882-4. From 1884 he taught at the School of Drawing under Murashko at Kiev. He exhibited with the Wanderers from 1893 and became a member in 1899. He taught at the Art Institute in Kiev where Lentulov was among his students in the period 1900-5. In 1909 he

exhibited work at the Salon des Artistes Français in Paris. He died in Kiev.
Coll Museum of Ukrainian Art, Kiev; RM.

PINCHUK, Venyamin Borisovich   1908-1937+
Sculptor. Works include *Lenin Writing*, 1937.

PIROSMANASHVILI (PIROSMANI), Niko Aslanovich 1860-1918
Georgian primitive painter of sign-boards who was taken up by Russian Futurists rather in the way that Parisian Cubists adopted the work of the Douanier Rousseau. Born at Mirzaani, the son of a gardener. The date of his birth is sometimes given as 1862 or 1863. He was a self-taught painter of tavern signs and was discovered in 1912 by M.Ledantyu and the Zdanevich brothers. His work was included in the 1913 exhibition Target. The crude directness of his work had a strong appeal for the Russian Futurists. He died at Tiflis.
Lit T.Tabidze *N.Pirosmanashvili*, Tiflis, 1926. *N.Pirosmanashvili*, exh. cat., Kharkov, Kiev, Odessa, 1931. K.Zdanevich *N.Pirosmanashvili*, Moscow, 1964. *N.Pirosmanashvili*, exh. cat., Moscow, 1969. *N.Pirosmanashvili*, exh. cat., Musée des Arts Décoratifs, Paris, 1969. E.Kuznetsov *Pirosmani*, Leningrad, 1975. *Paris-Moscou*, 1979.
Coll TG; Tblisi Museum.

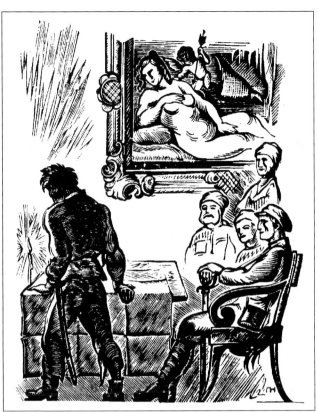

Nikolai Piskarev. Illustration to 'The Iron Flood' by Serafimovich, *1927. Wood engraving.*
Signed with cyrillic 'PN' joined in a monogram lower right.

Nikolai Piskarev. Illustration to 'The Iron Flood' by Serafimovich, *1927. Wood engraving.*
Drama is heightened by the moon in the night sky seen through the open door, and by the crowd of armed men whose shadows loom large against the wall.

PISEMSKY, Aleksei Aleksandrovich   1859-1913
Landscape painter.
Coll TG.

PISHCHALKIN, Leonid Fedorovich   1873-1930
Painter whose work included landscapes. He visited Novaya Zemlya in the far North in 1897.
Coll TG.

PISKAREV, Nikolai Ivanovich   1892-1959
Graphic artist, wood engraver, poster artist and illustrator. He studied at the Stroganov College. He executed a poster for the Red Cross in 1914.
After the Revolution he was included in the major exhibition in Moscow in 1927 marking its tenth anniversary and in the exhibition of graphic art Liberation Movements: The Sixteenth to the Twentieth Century held in Moscow in 1928. He was also included in the exhibition of Russian Graphic Art in Riga in 1929 and in the jubilee exhibition Artists of the RSFSR over 15 Years held at the Russian Museum, Leningrad, in 1932.
*Illustrations to Tolstoy's Anna Karenina, 1932, wood engravings in two colours, are clearly school of Favorsky. Splendid clouds rise above the cornfields. A figure puts down his book to look over the landscape.

PLAKHOV, Lavr Kuz'mich   1810-1881
Genre painter. One of the youngest pupils of Venetsianov under whom he studied in 1829. He also studied in Germany. Works include *The Smithy*, 1845, RM, and *In the Carpenter's Shop*, 1845, TG, which recalls Venetsianov in that it shows estate employees engaged in practical and orderly work rather

Leonid Pasternak. The Brothers Boris and Aleksandr Pasternak, *1902. Pastel. 42.8 x 63.5 cm. Ashmolean Museum, Oxford.*

than a sentimental genre or social critique. Sometimes he signed his work 'L.P'. He died at St. Petersburg.

Coachmen's Room at the Academy of Arts, 1834, RM, depicts the coachmen playing cards with the paraphernalia of their work around them, with another scene visible through an open door into a further room. It is full of incident intended to provide a lively image of the ordinary life which took place in the darker vaults beneath the hallowed halls of the Academy where Plakhov was studying at the time.
Coll TG; RM.

PLAKSIN, Mikhail Matveevich   1898-1965
Painter, graphic artist, theatre designer. Born at Shlisselburg near St. Petersburg. After training as a lithographer he studied under Roerich and Yakovlev at the Society for the Encouragement of the Arts in St. Petersburg. He served in the navy during the war.
After the Revolution he was engaged on amateur theatre designs at Kronstadt and on propaganda decorations. He served as a military artist at Ekaterinburg (Sverdlovsk) 1919-20 and then studied at the Vkhutemas under Robert Fal'k. He was a founder member of the group *Elektro-organizm* with Tyshler and others in 1921 and exhibited with them in 1922 in Moscow. He was a member of the group *Metod* (Method) 1923-4 and showed work at the First Discussional Exhibition of Active Revolutionary Artists in 1924 in Moscow. Ultimately he relinquished painting for theatre and exhibition design. He invented cameras for colour cinema and stereoscopic

projection.
Lit A.Z.Rudenstine *Costakis Collection*, London, 1981.
Coll Costakis Collection.

PLASTOV, Arkadi Aleksandrovich   1893-1972
Socialist Realist painter. He spent much of his life in the small village of Prislonikha in the Ulyanovsk region near the Volga. His works include *Summertime*, 1953-4, RM, the *Potato Harvest*, 1956, RM, and *Noon*, 1961, RM. He also made elaborate figure compositions in watercolour.
Washing Horses, 1938, RM, has naked men climbing over the horses and laughing in a downsurge of light from the sky.
A Fascist Flew Over, 1942, TG, is a committed painting depicting its grim message through a tragic genre theme. A young boy lies dead in a field. His dog barks at the disappearing airplane that has killed him.
Coll TG; RM.

PLATUNOV, M. G.   a.1919-1929
He participated in the First State Free Exhibition of Artworks in Petrograd in 1919 and was included in the enormous survey Exhibition of Paintings by Petrograd Artists of All Tendencies 1919-1923 held in Petrograd in 1923. He was a member of the Kuindzhi Society of Artists in Leningrad in 1929.

PLATUNOVA, Aleksandra Georgievna   1896-1966
Painter, graphic artist. She was represented at the enormous First State Exhibition of Art and Science, which included ethnographic material, held in Kazan in 1920 and at the Third

Anatoli Petritsky. Costume for Medora in the ballet 'Le Corsaire', *1926. Collage, coloured chalk, silver and gold paint, tinsel, ink. 50.5 x 36.2 cm.*
The ballet was staged at the State Opera Theatre, Kharkov, in 1926.
Collection Mr. and Mrs. Nikita D.Lobanov-Rostovsky, London.

Touring Exhibition of the Sovetsk Regional subdepartment of the Museums Bureau along with Kandinsky, Rodchenko and others in 1921. She also participated in the Second IZO Exhibition of Laboratory-Production Works under the auspices of *Lef* which was held in Kazan in 1925. She was a member of the group October in 1930. She taught at the Kazan Technical College 1921-6.

PLESHCHINSKY, Illarion Nikolaevich   1892-1961
He was included in the Third Touring Exhibition of the Sovetsk Regional subdepartment of the Museums Bureau along with Kandinsky, Rodchenko and others in 1921.

PLITMAN, A. A.   a.1918
He was engaged on Agitprop decorations at Inzhenerny Lock, Petrograd, in 1918.

PLOKHINSKY, V. A.   a.1925
Painter. He contributed to the Third Exhibition of Paintings by Artists from Kaluga and Moscow held in Kaluga in 1925.

PLUCHART, E. = PLYUSHAR, E. A.

PLYUSHAR (PLUCHART), Evgeny Aleksandrovich 1809-1880+
Portrait painter. Born in St. Petersburg. He studied in Munich. Sometimes he signed his work 'E.Pluchart'.
Coll TG; Museum of the Academy, St. Petersburg.

POBEREZHNAYA, A.   a.1925
She exhibited with the First Exhibition of the Society of Easel Painters (OST) in Moscow in 1925.

POCHEDAEV, Georgiy　　　　　　　　**a.1923**
Theatre designer. He designed a production of Mussorgsky's *Khovanshchina* at Barcelona in 1923.
Coll Victoria and Albert Museum. London.

POCHTENNIY, Aleksei Petrovich　　　**1898-1942**
Painter.
Coll RM.

PODGAEVSKY, Sergei　　　　　　　　**a.1913-1916**
Futurist and the inventor of Summism. He contributed eighteen works to the exhibition No.4 in Moscow in 1914. He exhibited with the Union of Youth in St. Petersburg 1913-14. He was a frequenter of Tatlin's studio c.1914-15 and exhibited at Poltava in 1916. He also wrote *zaum* or trans-sense poetry as other Russian Futurists did, including Khlebnikov, Kamensky, Burlyuk and even Malevich.

PODKOVANTSEV, Petr Ivanovich　　　**1820-1878**
Portraitist.
Coll TG.

PODLIASKY, Yuri Stanislavovich　　　**1924-1954+**
Socialist Realist.

POGEDAIEFF, Georges = POZHEDAEV, G.

POKARZHEVSKY, Petr Dmitrievich　　**1889-1968**
Painter. He took evening classes under F.Kozarchinsky in Elizavetgrad and studied at the Kiev Art Institute 1906-9 and at the Higher Art School of the Academy under Tsionglinsky, Zaleman and Samokish 1909-16.
After the Revolution he ran the State Art Studios in Tula and with G.Shegal' organised the Tula Art Museum 1920-2. He contributed to the second exhibition of the group *Bytie* (Existence) in 1923 and was represented at the First Touring Exhibition of Painting and Graphics which opened in Moscow in 1929. He was also represented at the jubilee exhibition Artists of the RSFSR over 15 Years held at the Russian Museum, Leningrad, in 1932. He taught at the Surikov Institute from 1937.
Lit A.M.Muratov, V.Manin et al. *Zhivopis' 20-30kh godov*, Sankt-Peterburg, 1991.
Coll Tula Art Museum.

POKHITONOV (POKITONOW), Ivan Pavlovich
1850-1923
Ukrainian painter of landscapes and portraits. His dates are sometimes given as 1851-1924. Born in the Kherson region. In 1889 he was painting at Barbizon and in 1891 at Biarritz. He exhibited in Milan, Turin and Venice. He signed his work 'Pokitonow'. He died at Liège.
Coll Well represented at TG; RM.

POKITONOW = POKHITONOV

POKROVSKAYA, T.　　　　　　　　　**a.1932**
She was represented at the jubilee exhibition Artists of the RSFSR over 15 Years held at the Russian Museum, Leningrad, in 1932.

POKROVSKY, A. M.　　　　　　　　　**a.1925**
Painter. He contributed to the Third Exhibition of Paintings by Artists from Kaluga and Moscow held in Kaluga in 1925.

POLENOV, Vasili Dmitrievich　　　　**1844-1927**
Painter of landscapes, genre and portraits, theatre designer.

Born at St. Petersburg into a noble family. He studied at the Academy in St. Petersburg 1863-71 whilst also studying law at the University. In 1872 he was in Rome and travelling Europe on an Academy scholarship. He worked in Paris in the 1870s and took up *plein-air* painting. In 1873 he first exhibited with the Wanderers and also began to design for the theatre. In 1876 he volunteered to serve in the Russo-Turkish War and worked as an artist-correspondent 1877-8. He became a member of the Wanderers in 1878 but he was instrumental too in the organisation of Mamontov's circle of artists at Abramtsevo from 1880. He was painting in Greece and the Near East 1881-2 and then returned to teach landscape painting at the Moscow College from 1882 to 1895. His works included *A Courtyard in Moscow*, 1878, and the large and populous *Christ and the Woman Sinner*, 1887-8, RM. He exhibited with the World of Art in St. Petersburg in 1899.
After the Revolution he participated in the Third Exhibition of Paintings held at Ryazan in 1919 and the Third Exhibition of Paintings by Artists from Kaluga and Moscow held in Kaluga in 1925.
He was the first People's Artist of the RSFSR. He died in the Kaluga region.
*Christ and the Woman Sinner, 1887-8, RM, is an attempt to provide the theme with a credible historical setting. Before an Egytian-looking Temple Christ sits with a group of men. Only Christ sits in the sunlight. An angry crowd arrives flailing sticks and pushing their victim forward. Every detail of the elaborate scene is given its carefully chosen purpose. There are numerous intricate vignettes of colour and action.
Theatre design 1884 *Scarlet Rose* for Mamontov's private opera in Moscow.
S.I.Mamontov's play *Iosif* (Joseph).
1885 April *Uriel' Akosta*.
1897 Gluck's *Orpheus and Euridice*.
1897 Tchaikovsky's *The Maid of Orléans*.
Lit E.Sakharova *Polenov, Pisma*, Moscow-Leningrad, 1948. E.D.Sakharova *Vasili Dmitrievich Polenov, Elena Dmitrievna Polenova*, Moscow, 1964.
Coll Major holdings at TG; RM; Bakhrushin Theatre Museum, Moscow.
Colour plate p.338.

POLENOVA, Elena Dmitrievna　　　　**1850-1898**
Painter, graphic artist, illustrator, craftworker. She was a major influence in the revival of interest in folk art and the applied arts. Born into the family of an archaeologist she was the sister of the painter Vasili Polenov. She studied under Chistyakov and Kramskoy, at the Society for the Encouragement of the Arts at St. Petersburg 1863-7, and then in Paris in the studio of Chaplain 1869-70. She returned to study watercolour at the Society for the Encouragement of the Arts 1880-2. In 1882 she left St. Petersburg for Moscow but she worked extensively at the Abramtsevo artists' colony and managed its wood workshop. Her interest in folk art led her to collect artefacts for the Abramtsevo Museum, to write down folk stories that she heard and to illustrate them. She also designed furniture inspired by folk art models. She relinquished responsibility for the Abramtsevo wood workshops in 1893 and subsequently executed designs for the Solomenko Workshops directed by Davydova. She exhibited with the Moscow Society of Artists from 1894 and designed a

panel on the theme of the Firebird for the Solomenko Workshops display at the All-Russian Exhibition at Nizhny-Novgorod in 1896. She visited Yakunchikova in Paris in 1895. She worked closely with the painter Aleksandr Golovin.

She died in Moscow from a brain tumour. Yakunchikova took over the Abramtsevo embroidery workshops after this.

In 1899 she was accorded a posthumous exhibition within the World of Art International Exhibition in St. Petersburg.

Lit E.D.Sakharova *Vasili Dmitrievich Polenov, Elena Dmitrievna Polenova*, Moscow, 1964. E.Sakharova, V.Polenov *E.D.Polenova*, Moscow, 1974. J.E.Bowlt *Russian Stage Design. Scenic Innovation. From the Collection of Mr. and Mrs. Nikita D.Lobanov-Rostovsky*, Jackson, MS, exh. cat.,1982. *Twilight of the Tsars*, London, 1991.

Coll TG; RM; State Historical Museum, Moscow.

POLETAEVA, A.   **a.1929**
She was represented at the First Touring Exhibition of Painting and Graphics which opened in Moscow in 1929.

POLIAKOFF, Serge Georgievich   **1906-1969**
Painter. Born in Moscow. He was the family's thirteenth child. After the Revolution he lived in Constantinople before travelling via Sofia, Belgrade and Vienna to Paris.

He settled in Paris in 1923 and studied privately under Billule and Bricard. He then studied at the Académie Frochot and at the Académie de la Grande Chaumière from 1930 where his tutors included Othon Friesz. He contributed to an exhibition at the Galerie Drouant in 1931 and to the Salon des Artistes Français in 1932.

Between 1935 and 1937 he studied at the Chelsea School of Art and then at the Slade School in London. In 1936 he met Kandinsky at the studio of Robert and Sonia Delaunay in Paris. After this his painting was increasingly geometric, non-figurative and textured, developing into a densely matted or interlocked series of shapes across the canvas giving them a monumental presence and strength.

After the war he held an exhibition at the Galerie l'Esquisse, Paris, in 1945, and numerous exhibitions followed. He took French nationality in 1962. He died in Paris.

Lit M.Ragon *Poliakoff*, Paris, 1956. D.Vallier *Serge Poliakoff*, Paris, 1959. *Serge Poliakoff*, exh. cat., Musée National d'Art Moderne, Paris, 1970.

Coll TG; Stedelijk Museum, Amsterdam; Kunstmuseum, Basel; National Gallery, Berlin; The Art Institute, Chicago; Museum of Modern Art, New York; Solomon Guggenheim Museum, New York; Tate Gallery, London.

POLOVINKIN, Volodya P.   **a.1904-1909**
Painter included in the Scarlet Rose exhibition at Saratov in 1904. He exhibited with the Golden Fleece in Moscow in 1909-10.

POLYAKOV, A. L.   **a.1921**
He exhibited in the 1921 exhibition of the World of Art in Moscow.

POLYAKOV, D. M.   **a.1921**
He exhibited with Kudryashov and others at the First State Exhibition in Orenburg in 1921.

POLYAKOV, Konstantin Georgievich   **1885-1970**
Painter. He was engaged in Agitprop projects at Saratov 1918-20. He was a member of AKhRR 1925-6 and taught at the Saratov Vkhutemas 1922-6. He died in Moscow.

POLYAKOV, Mikhail Ivanovich   **b.1903-1933+**
Theatre designer, graphic artist, wood engraver. His style for wood engravings was much indebted to the innovations and technical experiments of Favorsky. His illustrations to Gogol's *Nevsky Prospekt*, wood engravings, 1931, were dramatic, novelistic and intelligent. He was represented at the jubilee exhibition Artists of the RSFSR over 15 Years held at the Russian Museum, Leningrad, in 1932. He designed figures of the Commedia dell'Arte in 1933.

POMANSKY, N. N.   **a.1919-1932**
Painter, graphic artist. His work was included in the First Exhibition of the Moscow Contemporary Art Store in January 1919. He was designing posters in 1919 and engaged in Agitprop projects in 1920 including the decoration of the propaganda trains *Red Cossack*, Ukrainian *Lenin*, and *Lenin (October Revolution)*. Decorations on the cinema coach of the train *Red Cossack* show a giant peasant whipping figures of military power and wealth. Kostanitsyn also worked on this train. He was represented at the jubilee exhibition Artists of the RSFSR over 15 Years held at the Russian Museum, Leningrad, in 1932.

PONOMAREV, M. I.   **a.1896-1901**
Painter. He was teaching with L.G.Solov'ev at the Free Voronezh School of Painting and Drawing in the period c.1896-1901 where the painter Aleksandr Kuprin was among his pupils.

POPKOV, Viktor E.   **1932-1974**
Painter. He worked in the Archangel region. Works include *The Builders of the Bratsk Hydro-Electric Power Station*, 1960-1, TG, which features five healthy workers, casual but heroic and resolute. In 1967 he won Grand Prix in Paris.

Coll TG; RM.

POPLAVSKY, Lyudvig Lyudvigovich   **1852-1885**
Landscape painter. He studied at the Academy in St. Petersburg.

Coll TG.

POPOV(-MOSKOVSKY), Aleksandr Pavlovich
1835-1888+
Painter of views and landscape.

Coll TG.

POPOV, Andrei Andreevich   **1832-1896**
Genre painter. Born at Tula. He studied at the Academy in St. Petersburg. He died at Novgorod.

Coll TG; RM.

POPOV, Igor Nikolaevich   **1905-1988**
Painter. Born in Moscow. He studied in Paris 1924-5 and 1927-9. He died in Moscow.

Coll RM.

POPOV, Lukyan Vasilievich   **1873-1914**
Painter of social commentary. Born in the Orenburg region. He studied at the Academy in St. Petersburg 1896-1902. He exhibited with the Wanderers and became a member in 1903. His works included *Migrants to New Places*, 1903-4, *At Sunset (The Agitator)*, c.1906, and *The Socialists*, c.1908.

Coll Atheneum, Helsinki.

Kuz'ma Petrov-Vodkin. Worker, *1912. Oil on canvas. Dated and signed 'KPV' in cyrillic script. 122.4 x 54.7 cm. Malmö Konstmuseum.*

Kuz'ma Petrov-Vodkin. An Archangel on a Red Horse: Design for a Calendar. *Watercolour over pencil heightened with white. 36 x 29 cm. Signed with initials, inscribed on the reverse 'belongs to V. Strekalov'.*
Reproduced by kind permission of Sotheby's London, sale 16.6.1992, lot 78.

Lyubov' Popova. Study for the Costume of a Woman in S.Polivanov's play 'The High Priest of Tarquinia', *1922. Watercolour. 57.8 x 40.7 cm.*
Collection Mr. and Mrs. Nikita D.Lobanov-Rostovsky, London.

POPOV, Nikolai Nikolaevich   **1890-1953**
Painter. He was a founder member of NOZh, the New Society of Painters, formed in 1922. His work was included in the exhibition of Soviet art held at Harbin in 1926 and in Japan in 1927. He died in Moscow.

POPOV, V. N.   **a.1921**
He was included in the Third Touring Exhibition of the Sovetsk Regional subdepartment of the Museums Bureau along with Kandinsky, Rodchenko and others in 1921.

POPOVA, Lyubov' Sergeevna   **1889-1924**
Painter, theatre, clothing, book and graphic designer. A major figure in the transition from Russian Cubo-Futurism and Suprematism into Constructivist work. Born near Moscow at Ivanovskoe, the daughter of a wealthy merchant who owned a linen factory. She grew up on the family estate and moved with her family to Rostov in 1902 and to Moscow in 1906. She studied art privately under Stanislav Zhukovsky and at the school run by Yuon and Dudin in Moscow where she met Lyudmilla Prudkovskaya, sister of the painter Nadezhda Udal'tsova. She worked with Prudkovskaya at Krasnovidovo in 1908. She then travelled to Kiev in 1909 where she was impressed by Vrubel', and to Novgorod, Pskov and also Italy in 1910. She first visited St. Petersburg in 1911 and also travelled to Rostov, Yaroslavl, Suzdal, Pereslavl and Kiev. She set up studio in Moscow with Prudkovskaya, Udal'tsova and Pestel'. In 1912 she became closely involved in the recent Western European and Russian innovative developments in autumn

1912 when she worked in the studio complex in Moscow called The Tower with Tatlin, Bart, Zdanevich and others.

Late in 1912 she visited Paris where, with Udaltsova and on Exter's advice she studied Cubism at first hand under Le Fauconnier and Metzinger at the Académie La Palette. Whilst there she also visited Zadkine and Archipenko. In Moscow in 1913 she worked with Tatlin, Udal'tsova, Vesnin and Morgunov. She visited Paris and Italy in 1914 with the sculptors Vera Mukhina and Ida Burmeister. She exhibited with the Knave of Diamonds that year in Moscow and at the Petrograd exhibition Tramway V in March 1915.

When Malevich launched his new geometric concept Suprematism in December 1915 at 0.10. The Last Futurist Exhibition of Paintings, to which she also contributed, she was quick to respond and she developed her own painting with brilliance and originality in the light of his example. She still exhibited with the Knave of Diamonds 1915-16 but by this time had become a considerable innovator within the field of non-objective art which Malevich had so recently opened up. In this she was no mere follower. Her individual interests were exemplified by her visit in 1916 to the Shakh-I-Zinda complex of mosques and related buildings at Samarkand in Uzbekistan where she was impressed by Islamic architecture and geometric decoration. Her dynamic Suprematist works revealed her as a painter of force and distinction, wresting from the innovations around her a line of development that was her own and which was as fundamental a study as that of Exter, Vesnin or perhaps even Rodchenko. She showed work at the exhibition *Magazin* (The Store) in Moscow in March 1916.

She was a member of the short-lived *Supremus* group which met in Udal'tsova's studio in Moscow 1916-17 and she produced designs for its proposed periodical *Supremus*. In this connection she executed collage designs to be copied by village embroidresses at N.M.Davydova's Verbovka workshops in the Ukraine.

After the Revolution she married the art historian Boris von Edding in March 1918. She exhibited with the Artists of the Leftist Federation of the Professional Union in 1918 along with Rodchenko and others.

In November 1918 she gave birth to a son but the family were soon devastated by illness which prevented her from producing any work in 1919. However she was included in the Fifth State Exhibition in 1918-19 in Moscow and the Tenth State Exhibition: Non-Objective Creativity and Suprematism in 1919 in Moscow. She taught at the Free Art Studios (SVOMAS), later Vkhutemas, 1918-20. In the catalogue of the Tenth State Exhibition she distinguished between 'unconstructiveness' (*akonstruktivnost'*) which included illusionism, literary tendencies, emotion and representation, contrasted against 'architectonic' approaches which included the painting of space (Cubism), line, colour (Suprematism), energy (Futurism) and *faktura*, the handling of materials, describing her work as painterly rather than representational. Other exhibitors included Rozanova, Rodchenko, Men'kov, Malevich and Klyun. She appeared on the April 1919 list of artists for acquisitions by the envisaged Museum of Painterly Culture, participated in the Third Exhibition of Paintings held at Ryazan in 1919 and was represented at the enormous First State Exhibition of Art and Science, which included ethnographic material, held in Kazan in 1920.

She also became a participant in the debates of the Institute of Artistic Culture (INKhUK) in Moscow from 1920. She responded to the initial programme devised by the first director of INKhUK, Kandinsky, but allied herself to the politically committed Moscow Constructivists including Rodchenko, Stepanova and Vesnin when they confronted Kandinsky's psychologically oriented policy in 1921. She was

Lyubov' Popova. Stage Construction for Meyerhold's Production of 'The Earth in Turmoil', *1923.*
Documentary photograph. Popova was a thorough Constructivist. She has abandoned illusion and has installed an apparatus on stage based on a gantry crane. This supports a screen for the projection of slogans and film.

Antoine Pevsner. Fond Vert, *1923. Encaustic relief. 33.5 x 27.5 cm.*
Signed 'Pevsner' lower left.
Private collection, courtesy Annely Juda Fine Art, London.

State Textile Print Factory.

She died in Moscow in an epidemic. She was the subject of a posthumous exhibition in the year of her death. She was represented at the First Exhibition of Cinema Posters held in Moscow in 1925 and at the Paris International Exhibition in 1925.

The Philosopher, 1915, RM, is a colourful Cubo-Futurist painting with lettering, a painted version of collage wallpaper and a dramatically faceted figure. There is a distinctive energy in the interslotting and overlapping planes which construct the head. In terms of references to the techiques of other painters she seems here to be closer to Boccioni than to Picasso.

Theatre design 1919 Pushkin's *Tale of the Country Priest and his Dunderhead Servant* for the Theatre of Marionettes, Petrushkas and Shadows directed by Ivan Efimov and Nina

Vasili Polenov. Feast of Vladimir at Krasnoe Solnyshko, *1883.*
Design for a menu for a ceremonial banquet on the coronation day of Tsar Alexander III. Watercolour and bronze powder on paper. Signed in a monogram and dated lower right.
State Tretyakov Gallery, Moscow.

sympathetic to the Constructivists' renunciation of easel painting although this must have been a harder task for Popova than for others in that she had always shown a natural ability, strength and enthusiasm as a painter. Effectively the watershed was acknowledged at the exhibition 5x5=25 in Moscow in 1921 where she exhibited five works alongside Exter, Rodchenko, Stepanova and Vesnin.

She turned her attention to the public and utilitarian application of her abilities. This led to an immediate and rich diversity of experiment and adventurous design in many fields from dress design to posters, book design and constructions for the theatre. She became an eager convert to the principles of Production Art. She was represented at the First Russian Art Exhibition in Berlin in 1922.

She first produced designs for the theatre in 1920 and also became involved with the puppet theatre organised by Nina Simonovich-Efimova at the Moscow Children's Theatre. In 1923 she designed Meyerhold's production of Fernand Crommelynck's *The Magnanimous Cuckold* in collaboration with V.Lyutse and also Sergei Tretyakov's *Zemlya Dybom* (Earth in Turmoil) at Meyerhold's theatre. Both minimise the element of illusion on stage by presenting dynamic constructions on stage which can function as an apparatus for the performers or as a framework for spectacle. In the latter production this included a screen for the projection of film as part of the theatrical collage. Comparable theatrical experiments were undertaken by Stepanova and Vesnin. Like them she contributed to the exhibition Art of Moscow Theatre 1918-1923 held in Moscow in 1923.

She designed textiles with Stepanova in 1924 for the First

Lyubov' Popova. Cubist Nude, *1913. Oil on canvas. 92 x 64 cm.*
Among the most overtly Cubist works by Popova, this painting shows the figure analysed in terms of cubes, the corners of which define the points of projection for the knee, breast and wrist. Other forms are conical or cylindrical.
Courtesy Annely Juda Fine Art, London.

Simonovich-Efimova in Moscow.
1920 Shakespeare's *Romeo and Juliet*, designs not used by Tairov who adopted those by Exter for his production of 1921. A set design for the Garden is close to her recent painting in style with spiralling arcs inconsistently shaded to represent trees above a series of platforms, walls and steps.
1921 May: Lunacharsky's *The Locksmith and the Chancellor* at the Comedy Theatre, Moscow. A set design has towering green flats crossed by the diagonals evident in her paintings which also provided the awkward Cubo-Futurist technique employed to depict figures and furniture. Theatre provided a context within which figurative imagery was reassessed in the light of non-objective pictorial experiment. The fusion was not easily attained.
1921 Ivan Aksionov's *Struggle and Victory of the Soviets*, an unrealised mass pageant to be directed by Meyerhold,

designed in collaboration with Aleksandr Vesnin.

1922 S.Polivanov's *The High Priest of Tarquinia*, possibly realised in Moscow.

1922 Fernand Crommelynck's *The Magnanimous Cuckold*, directed by Meyerhold at the Actor's Theatre, Moscow. The set was perhaps her *tour de force* in the Constructivist mode: it involved a series of wheels and sails to indicate the windmill and inscribed upon this were letters from the author's name made to revolve during the action of the performance. Attached to all of this were platforms upon and around which the actor's performed the rhythmic biomechanic activities which the director required of them. There was nothing identifiably pictorial about this design and some of the studies show extensive measurements and calculations for the construction of the machinery of the mechanism. Popova also designed production clothing (*prozodezhda*) for Meyerhold's performers which served as overalls for rehearsal and also as costumes for his performances after the abandonment of the suspension of disbelief, backdrops and illusionism on stage. Designs were blocked in and geometric with geometry to the fore, but they were also simple and practical costumes with no applied style. The designs were accompanied by forceful block lettering of the kind used by Popova in her graphic work for book covers and related projects. Meyerhold revived the production of *The Magnanimous Cuckold* using designs by Popova and V.V.Lyutse in January 1928 at the Meyerhold Theatre.

1923 Sergei Tretyakov's *The Earth in Turmoil*, directed by Meyerhold at the Meyerhold Theatre, Moscow. Popova almost abandoned scenery altogether by providing a gantry bridging much of the stage space from which a screen was suspended for the inclusion of film. There was no backdrop, no flats, no paint and no illusion. It was an extreme example of Constructivist design in the Production Art phase.

Book design numerous including: cover for E.Pavlov *Second Book of Lyric Pieces for the Piano*, Moscow, 1922.

Lit *L.S.Popova*, memorial exh. cat., Moscow, 1924. T.Strizhenova *Iz istorii sovetskogo kostyuma*, Moscow, 1972 (English edition: Tatiana Strizhenova, *Soviet Costume and Textiles 1917-1945*, Paris, 1991). J.E.Bowlt *Russian Stage Design. Scenic Innovation. From the Collection of Mr. and Mrs. Nikita D.Lobanov-Rostovsky*, Jackson, MS, exh. cat.,1982. E.Weiss *Russische Avant-Garde, 1910-1930, Sammlung Ludwig, Köln*, Munich, 1986. M.N.Yablonskaya *Women Artists of Russia's New Age*, London, 1990. Nancy Van Norman Baer *Theatre in Revolution, Russian Avant-Garde Stage Design 1913-1935*, San Francisco and London, 1991. N.Adaskina, D.Sarabianov *Liubov Popova*, London, 1991. M.Dabrowski et. al. *Liubov Popova*, exh. cat., Metropolitan Museum of Art, New York, 1991. Dzhon Boult (John Bowlt) *Khudozhniki russkogo teatra. Sobranie Nikity i Niny Lobanovykh-Rostovskikh*, Moscow, 1991. *L'Avant-garde russe 1905-1925*, exh. cat., Musée des Beaux-Arts, Nantes, 1993.

Coll TG; RM; Bakhrushin Theatre Museum, Moscow; Krasnodar Art Museum; Krasnoyarsk Art Museum; Nizhny-Novgorod Art Museum; Smolensk Art Museum; Tobolsk Art Museum; Tula Art Museum; Yaroslavl' Art Museum; Costakis Collection; Ludwig Collection, Cologne.

Colour plates pp.339, 342, 343.

POPOVA, Vera Aleksandrovna　　　　　　a.1919-1920

Sculptor, graphic artist. She was the cousin of the painter Lyubov' Popova. She was represented in the Sixth State Exhibition: The Print (*VI Gosudarstvennaya vystavka gravyur*) in Moscow in 1919. During 1919-20 she was a founder of the *Monolit* (Monolith) group of sculptors, which included Babichev, Mukhina, Konen'kov, Krandevskaya, Korolev, Strakhovskaya, Zlatovratsky, Ternovets, V.Popova, Blazhevich and Kudinov. They worked on monumental propaganda and entered the competitive exhibition for a Monument to Liberated Labour held in Moscow in May 1920.

PORFIROV, Ivan Fedorovich　　　　　　1866-1919+

Painter. He studied at the Academy in St. Petersburg in 1885-92. He was engaged in Agitprop decorations at Archangel Michael Square, Petrograd, in 1918. He participated in the First State Free Exhibition of Artworks in Petrograd in 1919.

POSEN, POSSEN = POZEN, L. V.

POSPOLITAKI, Evgeniy Ivanovich　　　　b.1852-1910+

Landscape painter. He studied at the Academy in St. Petersburg. He travelled widely and exhibited with the Wanderers. He was represented at the International Exhibition in Paris in 1889. He lived in Moscow 1890-1910 but was painting in the Caucasus in 1909. He then settled in St. Petersburg.

Coll TG.

POSTNIKOV, Sergei Petrovich　　　　　　1825-1880

Painter whose work included Italian landscapes.

Coll TG.

POTEKHINA (-FAL'K), E. S.　　　　　　a.1904-1919

Painter. She was included in the Scarlet Rose exhibition at Saratov in 1904. She exhibited at the Fifth State Exhibition: From Impressionism to Non-Objective Art in Moscow 1918-19 and her name appeared on the April 1919 list of artists for acquisitions by the envisaged Museum of Painterly Culture. She was represented along with Kandinsky, Chagall and others at the First State Exhibition of Paintings by Local and Moscow Artists held in Vitebsk in December 1919 and she participated in the Third Exhibition of Paintings held at Ryazan in 1919.

POTIPAKA, P. D.　　　　　　　　　　a.1912-1913

Exhibited with the Union of Youth in 1912-13 and at the Dobychina Bureau in 1913.

POUGNY, Jean = PUNI, I.A.

POVALYAEVA, V. L.　　　　　　　　　　a.1923

She was a member of the *Bytie* (Existence) society of artists which was formed in Moscow in 1921 and contributed to its second exhibition in 1923.

POZEN (POSEN, POSSEN), Leonid Vladimirovich 1849-1921

Ukrainian realist sculptor. He made elaborate and intricate genre sculptures although his work also included historicist statuettes such as *Scythian*, 1889-90, a fast moving ancient warrior-horseman firing an arrow, and realist portraits, for example *E.E.Volkov*, 1911, and *K.Lemokh*, 1918.

The Sawyers, 1884, bronze, Museum of Ukrainian Art, Kiev, has five diminutive figures around a peasant cart. This is so complex that it almost comprises a mixture of genre and landscape sculpture or a scene from a play.

Coll Museum of Ukrainian Art, Kiev.

POZHARSKY, Sergei Mikhailovich   1900-1970
Graphic artist. His illustrations to Charles Dickens' *Pickwick Club* (Pickwick Papers), 1935, revealed the strong influence of Favorsky.

POZHARSKY, V. I.   a.1917-1919
He exhibited with the Knave of Diamonds in Moscow in 1917, at the First Exhibition of Works of the Professional Union of Artists in Moscow in 1918 and at the Fifth State Exhibition: From Impressionism to Non-Objective Art in Moscow 1918-19. His name appeared on the April 1919 list of artists for acquisitions by the envisaged Museum of Painterly Culture. He also participated in the Third Exhibition of Paintings held at Ryazan in 1919.

POZHEDAEV, Georgiy Anatolevich (POGEDAIEFF, Georges)   1899-1971
Theatre designer, illustrator, poet. Born at Kursk. He began designing for the theatre in Petrograd in 1918.
In 1922 he was designing for the *Blaue Vogel* cabaret in Berlin. He later worked for the Chauve-Souris company in Paris. He also illustrated books. He died in Paris.
Theatre design 1919 *Red Masks*, ballet by N.Cherepnin, an unrealised production by K.Goleizovsky at the Bolshoi Theatre, Moscow.
1921 *Hamlet* in Vienna.
1929 Puccini's *Turandot* in Paris (unrealised).
Lit J.E.Bowlt *Russian Stage Design. Scenic Innovation. From the Collection of Mr. and Mrs. Nikita D.Lobanov-Rostovsky*, Jackson, MS, exh. cat.,1982. Dzhon Boult (John Bowlt) *Khudozhniki russkogo teatra. Sobranie Nikity i Niny Lobanovykh-Rostovskikh*, Moscow, 1991.

PRAKHOV, A.   a.1906-1912
He was teaching in the Kiev School of Art c.1906-12 where his pupils included Rabinovich.

PREOBRAZHENSKAYA, A.G.   a.1919
Painter. She exhibited at the juryless Eighth State Exhibition in Moscow in 1919.

PRIBYL'SKAYA, Evgeniya Ivanovna   1878-1949
Textile and costume designer. She studied at the Kiev School of Art and later ran costume studios in the Ukraine. She abandoned painting to study folk art in 1906. She directed carpet and embroidery workshops in the Ukraine 1910-22.
After the Revolution she moved to Moscow in 1922 and collaborated with Lamanova on dress design for export. She exhibited at the Paris International Exhibition in 1925. She contributed to the First Art Exhibition of Soviet Textiles in Moscow in 1928. She was a consultant to the Scientific Research Institute of the Art Industry in the 1930s and 1940s.
Lit T.Strizhenova *Iz istorii sovetskogo kostyuma*, Moscow, 1972 (English edition: Tatiana Strizhenova, *Soviet Costume and Textiles 1917-1945*, Paris, 1991).

PRICHETNIKOV, Vasili Petrovich   1767-1809
Landscape painter. He studied at the Academy in St. Petersburg and under P.Hackert in Rome. In 1801 he was working at Capri. He died in St. Petersburg.
Coll TG.

PRISELKOV, Sergei Vasilievich   1892-1959
Painter, graphic artist. He was engaged on Agitprop decorations at the junction of Vvedenskoy and Bolshoi Prospekt, Petrograd, in 1918. One of his propaganda decorations comprised cones and cubes bedecked with banners in red and black extolling Labour, Revolution and Marxism. He exhibited with the *Zhar-Tsvet* (Fire-Light) group, the Society of Artist-Individualists and with the Union of New Tendencies in Art in June 1922 in Petrograd.

PROKHOR OF GORODETS   a.c.1405-1489
Ikon painter. The dates of his birth and death are unknown. He was a contemporary of Andrei Rublev and of Theophanes the Greek. A number of ikons dating from 1484-9, now in the Blagoveshchensky Cathedral, were attributed to him in the Moscow Kremlin Festivals Register. He may have worked with Rublev on murals at the Cathedral of the Annunciation in the Moscow Kremlin in 1405.

PROKHOROV, N. D.   a.1926-1932
Sculptor. He was a member of the Society of Russian Sculptors from 1926. He was represented at the jubilee exhibition Artists of the RSFSR over 15 Years held at the Russian Museum, Leningrad, in 1932.

PROKHOROVA, K. V.   a.1919-1929
Graphic artist. She was represented in the Sixth State Exhibition: The Print in Moscow in 1919 and at the First Touring Exhibition of Painting and Graphics which opened in Moscow in 1929.

PROKOF'EV, Ivan Prokof'evich   1758-1828
Sculptor attracted to neo-classicism. Born at St. Petersburg. He studied in St. Petersburg and Paris. His high level of technical expertise recalls that of Kozlovsky. He died at St. Petersburg.
Morpheus, 1782, plaster, RM, is a well resolved sleeping figure seated on a chair, his head resting on his arm.
Coll RM.

PROLETKUL'T
The abbreviated name of the movement for Proletarian Culture (*Proletarskaya kul'tura*).

PROSHKIN, Viktor Nikolaevich   1906-1983
Painter.
Coll RM.

PROTOPOPOV, Aleksei Fedorovich   1834-1898
Painter of portraits, landscapes and genre scenes. Born at Ufa. The date of his death is sometimes given as 1893.
Coll TG; RM.

PROTOPOPOVA, L. V.   a.1932
She was represented at the jubilee exhibition Artists of the RSFSR over 15 Years held at the Russian Museum, Leningrad, in 1932.

PRUDKOVSKAYA, Lyudmilla   a.1907-1912
Painter. She was the sister of the painter Nadezhda Udal'tsova. She met Popova at the studio of Yuon in Moscow 1907-8 and they worked together at the estate of Popova's parents at Krasnovidovo in the summer of 1908. In 1911 she shared a studio with Popova, Udal'tsova and Vera Pestel' in Moscow. She spent the summer of 1912 with Popova at Yaroslavl.

PRUSAKOV, A.   a.1919
He exhibited in the first Obmokhu exhibition in May 1919 in Moscow.

Lyubov' Popova. Space-Force Construction, *c.1920-1. Oil on panel. 77.7 x 77.7 cm. Private collection, courtesy Annely Juda Fine Art, London.*

PRUSAKOV, Nikolai Petrovich   **1900-1952**
Designer, graphic artist, theatre and exhibition designer. Born in Moscow. His birthdate is sometimes given as 1899. He studied at the Stroganov Institute 1911-18.

After the Revolution he studied at the Free Art Studios Vkhutemas until 1924. During this time he joined the Obmokhu group in 1919 and exhibited in the first Obmokhu exhibition in May 1919 in Moscow. He also took part in the third exhibition of Obmokhu, the Society of Young Artists, in Moscow in May 1921, along with Ioganson, Medunetsky and others. He was represented at the First Russian Art Exhibition in Berlin in 1922. During the 1920s he designed posters,

exhibitions and theatrical productions. He exhibited with the First Working Organisation of Artists in 1924 at the First Discussional Exhibition of Active Revolutionary Art alongside G.Aleksandrov and others. He became a member of the group October. He designed film posters sometimes in collaboration with A.I.Naumov and others and comparable in style to those of the Stenberg brothers. He contributed to the Second Exhibition of Cinema Posters in Moscow in 1926. He signed his work with a kite-mark or line drawing of a tetrahedron.

He was engaged on theatre and exhibition design in the 1930s. He died in Moscow.

Film posters 1928 Lilya Brik and Vitali Zhemchuzny's *Glass*

Eye, a poster stylistically like the work of the Stenberg Brothers in its amalgam of photomontage derived figures and layout.
1929 I.Pirev's *The Woman Outside*, M.Tereshchenko's *The Great Tragedy of a Small Woman*, Kalatozov's *Their Empire* and A.Balagin's *Five Minutes that Shook the World*.
1930 K.Mardzhanov's *Pipe of a Communard* after the novella by Ilya Ehrenburg, monochrome with an isolated image of pipe and field gun at centre.
Lit *Paris-Moscou*, 1979. C.Lodder *Russian Constructivism*, New Haven and London, 1983. E.Weiss *Russische Avant-Garde, 1910-1930, Sammlung Ludwig, Köln*, Munich, 1986.
Coll Sammlung Ludwig, Cologne.

PRUSOV, S. G.   **a.1926**
Graphic artist. He was represented at the Second Exhibition of Cinema Posters held at the Kamerny (Chamber) Theatre, Moscow, in 1926.

PRYANISHNIKOV, Illarion Mikhailovch   **1840-1894**
Painter of moralising genre. Born into a merchant's family in the Kaluga region. He studied at the Moscow College 1856-66. He was a founder member of the Wanderers and an active teacher at the Moscow College from 1973. His paintings included themes of contemporary street life in which large figures are observed about their business. This is the case in *Triflers. Gostinnyy Shopping Arcade, Moscow* , 1865, TG, in which porters and musicians entertain themselves with other figures looking on. He died in Moscow.
Coll Well represented at TG; RM.

PSKOVITINOV, Evgeniy Konstantinovich   a.1909-1914
Painter. He showed work at Kul'bin's exhibition Impressionists in 1909. He was a founder member of the Non-Aligned Society of Artists in St. Petersburg in 1912 and in March 1914 was a founder member of Filonov's Intimate Studio of Painters and Draughtsmen.

PUCHINOV, Matvei Ivanovich   **1716-1797**
History painter whose work included themes from Corneille.
Coll TG; RM.

PUKHOV, A.V.   **a.1918-1919**
Painter. He exhibited at the First Exhibition of Works of the Professional Union of Artists in Moscow in 1918 and at the juryless Eighth State Exhibition in Moscow in 1919.

PUKIREV, Vasili Vladimirovich   **1832-1890**
Academic painter of socially committed genre works and portraits. He died in Moscow.
Coll TG.

PUNI, Ivan Al'bertovich (POUGNY, Jean)   **1892-1956**
Painter, graphic artist, theatre designer. Born at Kuokkala, Finland. He studied under Repin in St. Petersburg and in 1910 he was attending the Académie Julian in Paris and living with Annenkov. He travelled to Italy in 1912. He exhibited with the Union of Youth 1911-12 and 1913-14 and he married the painter Ksenia Boguslavskaya in 1913. He designed the Russian Futurist book *Futurists: Roaring Parnassus* in 1914 but also visited Paris with Boguslavskaya and exhibited at the Salon des Indépendants that year. His work responded vigorously to Cubist ideas and he exhibited at Tramway V , which he organised, in 1915. In December 1915 he also organised 0.10. The Last Futurist Exhibition of Paintings, where Malevich launched Suprematism. He immediately became an innovative contributor to Suprematism which extended into three-dimensional reliefs that simultaneously reflected a close study of Tatlin's reliefs. In 1916 he exhibited with the Knave of Diamonds in Moscow.
After the Revolution he exhibited with the Knave of Diamonds

Lyubov' Popova. Untitled, *1922-3. Oil and gesso on canvas. 93 x 195 cm. Private collection, courtesy Annely Juda Fine Art, London.*

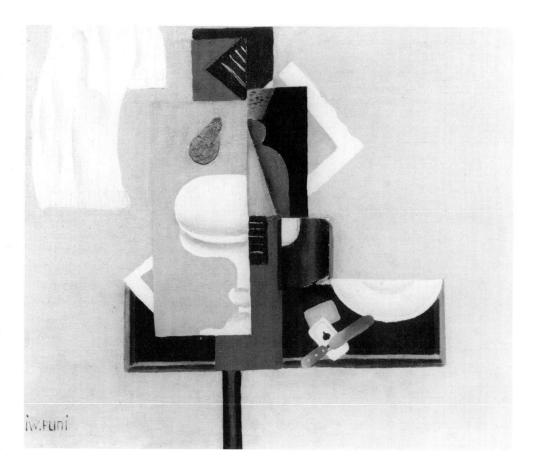

Ivan Puni. Composition, *1920-1. Oil and collage on canvas. 54.5 x 63 cm. Signed 'Iw.Puni' lower left. Puni returned to the use of recognisable imagery after moving to Berlin but the imagery is fragmentary and assembled into a composition with its roots in wartime irrational works by Puni and Malevich. Private collection, courtesy Annely Juda Fine Art, London.*

in Moscow in 1917. He executed Agitprop decorations for the Okhtinsky bridge at Petrograd in 1918 and taught at the Free Art Studios (SVOMAS) in Petrograd before moving to Vitebsk in 1919 on the invitation of Chagall. He returned to Petrograd late in 1919 and then moved on to Finland. He participated in the First State Free Exhibition of Artworks in Petrograd in 1919 and he contributed to the Exhibition of Paintings by Russian Artists held at Pskov in Spring 1920. Subsequently he emigrated. He was drawn initially to Berlin in 1921 where he met the Dadaist Hans Richter and Theo Van Doesburg, the driving force behind *De Stijl*. He had a one-man exhibition at the gallery *Der Sturm* in 1921. He was also represented at the First Russian Art Exhibition at the Van Diemen Gallery in Berlin in 1922. With his wife Ksenia Boguslavskaya he illustrated his own book for children *Tsveten* (Pollen) published in Berlin in 1922, which includes his story *Letuchyy gollandets* (The Flying Dutchman).

He reverted to easel painting after settling in Paris in 1924, evolving a style that was reminiscent of Vuillard in colour but informed still by Cubist innovations. He was a member of the 4 Arts society which was founded in 1924 and exhibited with them from Paris including the exhibition of 1928 at the Russian Museum. He became friendly with Ozenfant and Léger. His first one-man exhibition in Paris was held at the Galerie Barbazanges in 1925. He also designed theatre costumes in the 1920s. He exhibited at the Galerie Jeanne

Ivan Puni. Composition, *1916. Pencil, watercolour and ink on paper. 53.5 x 41 cm. Signed lower right. This is a Suprematist study closely related to Puni's relief constructions. Private collection, courtesy Annely Juda Fine Art, London.*

Ivan Puni. Illustration to 'The Flying Dutchman', *1922. Signed 'Iv.Puni' lower right.*
Published in 'Tsveten' (Pollen), Berlin, 1922. This is an elegant and witty assemblage of stylised figures in which changes of scale are used to create movement and space in a crisp black and white design.

Castel, Paris, in 1933. He settled at Antibes in 1940 and obtained French citizenship in 1946. He died in Paris.
*Relief with Mallet, 1914, Collection Berninger, Zurich, A real mallet surmounts planes of card painted in gouache. The overlapping and the use of the object recall the 'alogist' works of Malevich of the same year, whilst the use of relief recalls Tatlin. This is a succinct and original synthesis, deliberately irrational and provocative in distinctly Russian Futurist mode.
Lit *Jean Pougny*, exh. cat., MNAM, Paris, 1958. H.Berninger, J.A.Cartier *Pougny*, Tübingen, 1972. *Pougny*, exh. cat., Haus am Waldsee, 1975. J.E.Bowlt *Russian Stage Design. Scenic Innovation. From the Collection of Mr. and Mrs. Nikita D.Lobanov-Rostovsky*, Jackson, MS, exh. cat.,1982. E.Weiss *Russische Avant-Garde, 1910-1930, Sammlung Ludwig, Köln*, Munich, 1986. Dzhon Boult (John Bowlt) *Khudozhniki russkogo teatra. Sobranie Nikity i Niny Lobanovykh-Rostovskikh*, Moscow, 1991.
Coll MNAM, Paris; TG; RM; Costakis Collection; Sammlung Ludwig, Cologne.

PUSHKAREV, Prokofy Egorovich   **d.1856+**
Portrait and genre painter. He studied at the Academy in St. Petersburg.
Coll TG; RM.

PYRIN, Mikhail Semenovich   **1874-1943**
Painter. He participated in the Third Exhibition of Paintings held at Ryazan in 1919.
Coll TG.

Ivan Puni. Study for the Costume of a Woman as the Figure Eight, *1921. Watercolour and pencil. 24 x 16.5 cm.*
This costume was designed for a street procession advertising the opening of Puni's exhibition at the Galerie Der Sturm, Berlin, in February 1921.
Collection Mr. and Mrs. Nikita D.Lobanov-Rostovsky, London.

R

R.R. see **ROMMAN, R.F.**

RABFAK
The abbreviated name of the Workers' Faculty (*Rabochii fakul'tet*).

RABICHEV, I. a.1925
He exhibited with the First Exhibition of the Society of Easel Painters (OST) in Moscow in 1925.

RABINOVICH, Iosif Aleksandrovich 1895-1947+
Sculptor. Works include the young hero with a flag *Pavlik Morozov*, 1947, in bronze.

RABINOVICH, Isaak Moiseevich 1894-1961
Theatre designer. Born in Kiev. After studying at the Kiev Art School under A.Prakhov and G.Didchenko 1906-12 and commencing stage design in 1911, he continued his studies under Murashko 1912-15. He exhibited at the Polytechnic Institute in Kiev in 1914 along with Bogomazov, Exter and others.
After the Revolution he studied under Alexandra Exter 1918-20 in Kiev. He became active as a theatre designer and contributed to the exhibition *Art of Moscow Theatre 1918-1923* held in Moscow in 1923. In 1924 he collaborated with Exter on the design of the film *Aelita* based on the novel by A.Tolstoy which describes the Revolution on the planet Mars. Directed by Protozanov, it proclaims 'Workers of All Planets Unite!'. He was represented at the Paris International Exhibition in 1925. He taught at the Vkhutemas 1926-30. He died in Moscow.
Theatre design 1919 Oscar Wilde's *Salomé* at the Lenin First State Dramatic Theatre of the Ukrainian SSR, Kiev.
1920 Gogol's *The Government Inspector* (unrealised) at the Korsh Theatre, Moscow. Costume designs exhibited a lively element of caricature to exaggerate the features of figures who were drawn in a gently geometricised manner.
1922 Schiller's *Don Carlos* at the Comedy Theatre, Moscow. Here he constructed a design of tall round-topped arches suggesting a great height and opening off into passageways. The design combined atmospheric historicism and Constructivist sparseness. In this it was close to Exter's example.
1923 Aristophanes' *Lysistrata*, directed by V.Nemirovich-Danchenko, at the Music Studio of the Moscow Art Theatre. The set featured three movable and intersecting arc-shaped colonnades penetrated by steps and platforms, an architectonic construction requiring no backdrop.
1927 Prokofiev's *Love of Three Oranges*, directed by A.Diki at the Bolshoi Theatre in Moscow, included a vigorously grotesque and muticoloured peasant ogress with children's hands at her belt as well as knives, forks and a gigantic ladle to produce the very image of pantomime. Designs in the Bakhrushin Theatre Museum, Moscow.
1929 February V.V.Ivanov's *Blokada* (Blockade) directed by Nemirovich-Danchenko at the Moscow Art Theatre.
1932 Chaikovsky's *Evgeniy Onegin*.
1934 A.N.Ostrovsky's *Groza* (Storm) at the Moscow Art Theatre.
1960 Arthur Miller's *Death of a Salesman* at the Moscow Art Theatre.
Film design 1924 Protozanov's *Aelita* which concerns revolution on Mars and on which he assisted Exter in collaboration with S.Kozlovsky and S.Simov.
1926 Protozanov's *Protsess o trekh millenakh* (The Three Million Case).
1928 Protozanov's *Belyy orel* (The White Eagle).
Lit F.Syrkina *I.Rabinovich*, Moscow, 1973. *Paris-Moscou*, 1979. Nancy Van Norman Baer *Theatre in Revolution, Russian Avant-Garde Stage Design 1913-1935*, San Francisco and London, 1991.
Coll Bakhrushin Theatre Museum, Moscow; TG.

Isaak Rabinovich. Stage Set for 'Lysistrata', *c.1926.*
Documentary photograph.
This was produced at the Music Studio of the Moscow Art Theatre without a curtain or backdrop. Although there is an explicit reference to classical architecture the set comprises a flexible construction in which sections were designed to rotate into new arrangements. In this respect it reveals the impact of Constructivist stage design.

Isaak Rabinovich. Costume Study for the Glutton in Prokofiev's 'Love of Three Oranges', *1927.*
Gouache. 63 x 48 cm.
Collection Mr. and Mrs. Nikita D.Lobanov-Rostovsky, London.

RABUS, Karl Ivanovich   **1800-1857**
Sea and landscape painter. Sometimes he signed his work
'C.Rabus'.
Coll TG.

RACHKOV, Nikolai Efimovich   **1825-1895**
Portraitist.
Coll TG.

RADAKOV, Aleksei Aleksandrovich   **1879-1942**
Poster designer, graphic artist, illustrator, caricaturist. Born in
Moscow. He studied at the Stieglitz School in St. Petersburg
and at the Moscow College. He operated as a caricaturist and
early works in this vein include his lampoon of Serov's portrait
of Ida Rubinstein depicted as a matchstick doll in 1912. He

contributed to the revue *Novy Satirikon*.
After the Revolution he was one of the major practitioners,
with Cheremnykh, Mayakovsky and I.Malyutin, of the satirical
window posters designed for the Rosta agency. In 1917 he
designed modern folk prints, *lubki*, of an anti-Tsarist tenor
including a colourful and lively one of attempts to uproot the
Tsar's head from the ground. He became celebrated as a
poster designer, his work including *The Literate and the
Illiterate*, lithographic posters of 1920. In 1922 he was
represented at the *International Exhibition of the Book* in
Florence, at the Paris International Exhibition in 1925 and at
the seventh exhibition of the group *L'Araignée* (The Spider) at
the Galerie Devambe in Paris in 1925. Contributions to
revues in the period 1922-9 included work in the periodicals

Lapot, Begemot, Smekhach, Bezbozhnik and *Krokodil*. He was a founder member of the Society of the Soviet Artist in 1929. He died at Tblisi.

*The Illiterate is as Good as Blind, 1920, poster, shows the peasant about to step off a cliff. It is designed in brilliant blue, black and red. The text continues 'Everywhere there are unpleasant surprises and unhappiness'.

Writings A.Radakov *Karikatury*, Moscow, 1968. A.Radakov *Vragi i druzya Krokodila*, Moscow, 1972.

Lit *Paris-Moscou*, 1979.

RADIMOV, Pavel Aleksandrovich   1887-1967

Landscape painter. Born in the Ryazan region. His work has sometimes been described as Impressionist.

After the Revolution he participated in the First State Free Exhibition of Artworks in Petrograd in 1919, in the enormous First State Exhibition of Art and Science, which included ethnographic material, held in Kazan in 1920, and the First Russian Art Exhibition in Berlin in 1922. In 1922 he was a founder member of the Society (*Obshchestvo*) of Artists of Revolutionary Russia, founded after the first exhibition of the Association of Artists of Revolutionary Russia (AKhRR). Other members included A.Grigoriev, P.Kiselev, E.Katsman, N.Kotov, S.Malyutin, P.Shukhmin, A.Skachko, G.Sukhanov, B.Yakovlev and V.Zhuravlev.

His work was included in the exhibition of Soviet art held at Harbin in 1926 and in Japan in 1927 as well as the major exhibition in Moscow in 1927 marking the tenth anniversary of the Revolution. He was also represented at the First Touring Exhibition of Painting and Graphics which opened in Moscow in 1929, at the jubilee exhibition Artists of the RSFSR over 15 Years held at the Russian Museum, Leningrad, in 1932 and at the 1932 Venice Biennale.

Coll RM.

RADLOV, Nikolai Ernestovich   1889-1942

Graphic artist, poster designer, critic, art historian. Born at St. Petersburg. He studied at the Academy of Arts and in 1911 at the University of St. Petersburg. He contributed drawings to several periodicals including *Novy Satirikon* (New Satiricon) from 1913.

After the Revolution he was included in the enormous survey Exhibition of Paintings by Petrograd Artists of All Tendencies 1919-1923 held in Petrograd in 1923. He exhibited with the *Zhar-tsvet* (Fire-colour) group between 1924 and 1928 and at the seventh exhibition of the group *L'Araignée* (The Spider) at the Galerie Devambe in Paris in 1925. He was represented at the jubilee exhibition Artists of the RSFSR over 15 Years held at the Russian Museum, Leningrad, in 1932.

Writings N.E.Radlov *Risovanie s natury* (Drawing from Life), Leningrad, 1978.

Lit A.M.Muratov, V.Manin et al. *Zhivopis' 20-30kh godov*, Sankt-Peterburg, 1991.

Coll RM.

RADONICH, Bazilka Stepanova   1884-1973+

Painter and ceramics artist. Born in Montenegro. He moved to Russia in 1905. He was active as a painter and designer at the State Porcelain Factory 1920-4 but he then moved to Italy in 1924. He died in Milan in the late 1970s.

Lit N.Lobanov-Rostovsky *Revolutionary Ceramics*, London, 1990.

RAEV, Vasili Egorovich   1808-1871

Painter whose subjects included a view of Rome in 1843.

Coll TG.

RAEVSKAYA-IVANOVA, M. D.   a.1885

She directed a Drawing School at Kharkov at which Konchalovsky was a student in 1885.

RAKHMANOV, F.   a.1925-1927+

Sculptor. He was a member of the Society of Russian Sculptors from 1925 and the Union of Moscow Artists formed in 1925. He was included in the major exhibition in Moscow in 1927 marking the tenth anniversary of the Revolution.

RAKHMANOVA, S. I.   a.1918

She was represented at the First Exhibition of Works of the Professional Union of Artists in Moscow in 1918.

RAKhN

The abbreviated name of the Russian Academy of Artistic Sciences (*Rossiiskaya akademiya khudozhestvennykh nauk*).

RAKOVICH, Andrei Nikolaevich   1815-1866

Landscape painter. He studied at the Academy in St. Petersburg. His subjects included views of Kazan. He taught drawing at the University of Kazan.

Coll TG.

RAPKh

The abbreviated name of the Russian Association of Proletarian Artists (*Rossiyskaya assotsiatsiya proletarskikh khudozhnikov*).

RASKIN, Y. S.   a.1920

A contributor to the Exhibition of Paintings by Russian Artists held at Pskov in 1920. A still-life of the period is stark and monumental with a geometric compositional structure like that employed by David Shterenberg.

Lit A.Z.Rudenstine *Costakis Collection*, London, 1981.

Coll TG; Costakis Collection.

RASTRELLI, Count Carlo   1675-1744

Italian sculptor. Born in Florence. He was the father of Count Bartolommeo Rastrelli, the architect of major importance in the creation of St. Petersburg. He established his reputation in France before moving to Russia in 1716 to work for Peter the Great with a circle of French artists. He worked on numerous architectural and sculptural projects in the new city. He executed a mask of Peter the Great in 1719. He made sculpture for fountains at Peterhof. He died in St. Petersburg.

Coll RM; Hermitage Museum.

RATSUL, A. P.   a.1921

Exhibited with Kudryashov and others at the First State Exhibition in Orenburg in 1921.

RAYKHENSHTEYN   a.1926

Sculptor. He was a member of the Society of Russian Sculptors from 1926.

RAYNOVA, S. K.   a.1918-1919

Painter. She exhibited at the First Exhibition of Works of the Professional Union of Artists in Moscow in 1918 and at the Ninth State Exhibition of Paintings: Naturalism and Realism in Moscow in 1919.

RAZHIN, N. P.   a.1921-1932
Painter. He became a member of the group *Bytie* (Existence), formed in 1921 partly in protest at 'the narrowness of leftist art', after being invited to contribute to its first exhibition in 1922.
His work was included in the exhibition of Soviet art held at Harbin in 1926 and in Japan in 1927 and in the major exhibition in Moscow in 1927 marking the tenth anniversary of the Revolution. He was also represented at the First Touring Exhibition of Painting and Graphics which opened in Moscow in 1929 and at the jubilee exhibition Artists of the RSFSR over 15 Years held at the Russian Museum, Leningrad, in 1932.
The Oak, c.1925, depicts a group of harvesting peasant women beneath the tree which is the chief subject of the painting, standing for strength, durability and vigour.

RAZMARITSYN, Afanasiy Prokopevich   1844-1917
Painter. His subjects included genre scenes of village life sometimes exhibiting a wry observation of human nature. An example is *The Office for the Dead*, 1882, TG, in which a group of peasants and a priest are assembled before a cross in the countryside.
Coll TG.

RAZUMOVSKAYA, Yulia Vasil'evna   1894-1987
Painter. She studied under V.I.Korsuntsev at Kazan, in Saratov and in the studio of V.N.Meshkov in Moscow before entering the Academy under Kardovsky in 1913 whom she followed to the Moscow Vkhutemas in 1924. She died in Moscow.
Lit A.M.Muratov, V.Manin et al. *Zhivopis' 20-30kh godov*, Sankt-Peterburg, 1991.
Coll Kursk Art Museum.

RED'KO, Kliment Nikolaevich   1897-1956
Painter. Born in Poland. In 1910 he began to study ikon painting at the Kievo-Pechersk monastery, where he met Chekrygin, and then studied at the Society for the Encouragement of the Arts in St. Petersburg 1914-17.
After the Revolution he was at Kiev School of Art 1918-20 and was engaged on propaganda decorations. He settled in Moscow in 1920 and was impressed by Malevich's Suprematism. He was a founder member of the group *Elektro-organizm* (Electro-organism) and contributed to their exhibition in Moscow in 1922. His Suprematist works are a little like Rodchenko's paintings in that they superimpose geometric figures which are painted in blacks, browns and reds and are constructed from straight lines and circles. The handling and texture of the paint stresses its material qualities. Paintings of 1921-2 are more elaborate celebrations of light, machinery, lenses and so on. He launched a style of work which he called *Luminist* 1923-4. His work was included in the First Discussional Exhibition of Active Revolutionary Art in 1924. He was given a one-man exhibition in Moscow in 1926.
He lived in Paris during 1927-35 exhibiting at various Salons before returning to Moscow to produce landscape paintings. In 1934 he was a member of the Association of Revolutionary Artists of France.
Lit A.Z.Rudenstine *Costakis Collection*, London, 1981. E.Weiss *Russische Avant-Garde, 1910-1930, Sammlung Ludwig, Köln,* Munich, 1986. A.M.Muratov, V.Manin et al. *Zhivopis' 20-30kh godov*, Sankt-Peterburg, 1991.
Coll RM; Costakis Collection; Sammlung Ludwig, Cologne.

REGEL'SON, A. B.   a.1918
Engaged in Agitprop decorations on Mikhailovsky Bridge, Petrograd, in 1918.

REICHEL, Karl Christian Philipp (REYKHEL', Karl Yakovlevich)   1788-1856/7
Portrait painter, graphic artist, miniaturist. He studied at the Academy in St. Petersburg 1801-9 and then in Paris under David and Gérard before moving to Dresden. He returned to St. Petersburg in 1811. Sometimes he signed his work 'C.Reichel' in latin script. The date of his death is sometimes given as 1850.
Coll TG.

REIMERS, Johann (Iwan) (REYMERS, Ivan Ivanovich) 1818-1868
Painter, sculptor, medallist. Born in St. Petersburg. He studied at the Academy in St. Petersburg 1835-9. He visited Rome 1846-7 and worked there again 1857-62. His paintings included views of Rome in 1861. He returned to Russia to teach as a medallist at the Academy from 1863. He died in St. Petersburg.

REMIZOV (RE-MI), Nikolai Vladimirovich (REMISOFF, Nicholas)   1887-1975
Graphic artist, theatre designer. Born at St. Petersburg. He published satirical illustrations in the revolutionary journal *Strely* (Arrows) in 1905. He studied at the Academy in Dmitri Kardovsky's studio. He exhibited with the World of Art in St. Petersburg and Kiev in 1913 and designed for the Crooked Mirror cabaret also in St. Petersburg. His illustrations appeared in numerous periodicals including *Strekoza* (Dragonfly), *Satirikon* and *Novy Satirikon* (New Satirikon) for which he drew a caricature, *The Clearing of Petrograd Has Begun*, showing the disconsolate Tsar and his family trying to climb a tree (*Novy Satirikon*, No.32, September, 1917).
His lively illustrations to Kornei Chukovsky's children's story *Krokodil* (Crocodile) were first published in the periodical *Niva* in 1917 and subsequently in book form in 1919. This was republished in the United States in 1931 and Britain in 1932.
He moved to Kherson in 1918 and then emigrated to Paris in 1920 where he designed for the Chauve-Souris company of Nikita Balieff.
He settled in the United States in 1924 and designed for numerous films. He died at Palm Springs, California.
Theatre design 1921 March: *Zarya-Zaryanitsa* (Dawn-Lightning or The Miracle of the Holy Virgin), play by Fedor Sologub with music by Nikolai Suvorovsky, produced at the Théâtre de la Chauve-Souris, Paris.
1922-3 *A Quartet of Merry Artists*, produced at the Théâtre de la Chauve-Souris, Paris and New York.
Lit *Diaghilev and Russian Stage Designers, a Loan Exhibition from the Collection of Mr. and Mrs. N.Lobanov-Rostovsky*, International Exhibitions Foundation, Washington, 1972-4. J.E.Bowlt *Russian Stage Design. Scenic Innovation. From the Collection of Mr. and Mrs. Nikita D.Lobanov-Rostovsky*, Jackson, MS, exh. cat., 1982. *Twilight of the Tsars*, London, 1991.

Ilya Repin. Landscape Study at Kuokkala. *Oil on canvas. Signed 'I.Repin' in cyrillic script. 14 x 22.6 cm. Malmö Konstmuseum.*

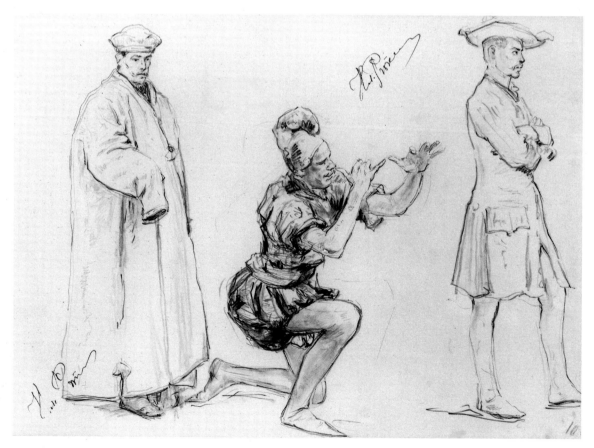

Ilya Repin. Study of Three Figures. *Pencil. Signed twice. 28.5 x 39.5 cm. Reproduced by kind permission of Sotheby's London, sale 23.2.1983, lot 206.*

Nikolai Remizov. Theatre Design of Figures in a Sleigh, *1923. Gouache. Signed lower left 'N.Remisoff'. 19.7 x 43.2 cm.*
Designed as a backdrop for the Théâtre de la Chauve-Souris, Paris.
Private collection.

REPIN, Ilya (Elias) Efimovich   **1844-1930**

Major painter of the later 19th and early 20th centuries and
very widely influential. Born at Chuguev in the Kharkov
region. He earned money by painting portraits and ikons
whilst still a child. After studying at military academy and
under I.Bunakov in Chuguev, in 1863 he travelled to St.
Petersburg where he studied at the Society for the
Encouragement of the Arts under Zhukovsky and Kramskoy
and at the Academy from 1864 until 1871. He later considered
Kramskoy in particular to have been his teacher. He was
awarded a gold medal for his graduation painting *The
Resurrection of Jairus' Daughter* in 1871, RM. His celebrated
Barge Haulers on the Volga, 1868-72, RM, evolved from
numerous studies executed on visits to the Volga with his
friend F.Vasiliev in 1870, was also completed in these early
years of his professional life. The boatmen haul the barge
across the canvas, working like horses, and provide a critical
social message in their labour and suffering. Here Repin
influentially achieved an elevation of genre painting to make
of it a monumental form capable of forceful social
commentary and criticism. It brought him fame when it was
exhibited in Vienna in 1873.

He travelled extensively on a scholarship and visited academies
in France and Italy in the period 1873-6. In 1873 Repin visited
Rome, Naples and Paris where he met the novelist and critic
Emile Zola. He painted *Sadko in the Underwater Kingdom*,
1876, RM, while in Paris. However the awareness of art in
Western countries did not undermine his commitment to
distinctly Russian themes. In this enthusiasm Repin had much
in common with the aims of some members of the Wanderers.
He settled in Moscow in 1877 and visted the Abramtsevo
artists' colony in the summers. He exhibited with the
Wanderers in 1874, 1878-91 and 1897, becoming a member
himself in 1878.

His paintings were frequently brilliant pieces of theatre and
even his costume pieces displayed a memorable force of
expression. An example of this was his *Zaporozhian Cossacks
Write a Letter to the Turkish Sultan*, 1878-91, RM, which relies
upon a grotesquely robust and physical vigour. His very many
portraits include *Mussorgsky* , 1881, TG.

He settled in St. Petersburg in 1882 but made a second visit to
Paris in 1883. He painted *Tolstoy* in 1887, TG, with a vigour
which was restrained only by a growing fascination with a rather
Impressionist concern for light and informality. A second Italian
trip including Venice, Florence and Rome was undertaken in
1887. His *Surgeon E.V.Pavlov in the Operating Theatre*, 1888, is a
brilliant *tour de force* in the use of bright white light.

Repin exhibited at the Historical Museum in 1892 and again
returned to Italy 1893-4. He exhibited with the World of Art
in St. Petersburg in 1899.

He joined the Academy in 1893 and taught as Professor of
Painting there 1894-1907 (Director 1898-9) and also at the
school in St. Petersburg founded by Princess Tenisheva in 1894
to prepare applicants for the Academy. Repin acted as director
of Tenisheva's school in 1895. He numbered many later
celebrated painters amongst his pupils including Bilibin,
Brodsky, Chekhonin, Grabar', D.N.Kardovsky, B.M.Kustodiev,
Serebryakova, Serov and Somov.

From 1899 he lived on his estate at Penaty which from 1917
to 1940 was part of Finland. His most ambitious and complex
group portrait was the vast painting of *The Ceremonial Meeting
of the State Council*, 1901-3, RM, which incorporates over
eighty individual portraits. It was completed with the help of
his pupils and assistants Kustodiev and Kulikov.

In 1906 he established his studio at Kuokkala which was
subsequently renamed Repino in his honour.

After the Revolution he retired to his estate where he painted
scenes from the Passion. He was represented however in the
First State Free Exhibition of Artworks in Petrograd in 1919.
He died at Kuokkala (Repino) in the Leningrad region.

They Did Not Expect Him, 1884, TG, exemplifies Repin's
ability to present psychological tension whilst avoiding
melodrama through sheer theatrical skill. In a wallpapered
interior which has a bare floor but also a grand piano, a family
is gathered around the table. The woman rises anxious and
amazed as a maid opens the door to admit the gaunt and
bearded returning exile. This is in essence a *coup de théâtre* in
which nothing is superfluous and every detail effective. It is
broadly painted and yet explicit. This was his second version
of the theme, the first of which featured a young woman and

was less pessimistic in its dramatic tone.

Writings I.E.Repin *Dalekoe blizkoe*, 1944. I.E.Repin *Khudozhestvennoe nasledie*, Moscow, 1948-9. I.E.Repin *Sbornik statei*, Moscow, 1952. I.E.Repin *Iz vospominanii*, 1958.
Lit L.V.Rozental' *I.E.Repin*, 1930. I.Grabar' *Repin*, Moscow, 1937. M.G.Mashkovtsev *I.Repin*, 1943. A.V.Babenchikov *I.R.*, 1949. A.A.Fedorov-Davydov *I.E.Repin*, Moscow, 1961. O.Lyaskovskaya *I.E.Repin*, Moscow, 1962. I.E.Grabar' *I.E.Repin*, Moscow, 1963-4. K.Chukovsky *I.Repin*, 1969. G.Sternin *Repin*, Leningrad, 1985.
Coll Major collections at TG and RM; Repin Estate Museum at Repino near St. Petersburg; Central State Museum of Revolution, Moscow; Tolstoy Museum, Moscow.
See Manizer.
Colour plate p.362.

REPIN, Yuri Ilych   1877-1954
Portrait painter. He participated in the First State Free Exhibition of Artworks in Petrograd in 1919 and in the Third Exhibition of Paintings held at Ryazan in 1919.
Coll TG.

REPINA, S. K.   a.1918
She was represented at the First Exhibition of Works of the Professional Union of Artists in Moscow in 1918.

RERBERG, Fedor Ivanovich   1865-1938
Painter. A founder member of the Moscow Association of Artists. He founded his own art school in Moscow in 1905. His pupils included Boris Korolev, Sofronova, Malevich and Ivan Klyun. He was represented in the Fourth State Exhibition of Paintings (*IV Gosudarstvennaya vystavka kartin*) in Moscow in 1919.
Coll TG.

RERIKH, N. K. = ROERICH, N.

RESHETNIKOV, F. P.   b.1906
Painter of Socialist Realist genre.
Coll TG.

REYKHEL', K. Ya. = REICHEL, K. C. P.

REYMERS, I. = REIMERS, J.

REYNDORF, Gyunter Germanovich   1889-1925+
He was represented at the Paris International Exhibition in 1925.

REZANOV, Viktor Mikhailovich   b.1829
Coll TG.

RIANGINA, S. V. = RYANGINA, S. V.

RIAZHSKY, G. G. = RYAZHSKY, G. G.

RIMSA, Petras (Pyatras) Simano   1881-1961
Lithuanian painter and sculptor of genre themes, figures and portraits. He was a founder member of the Lithuanian Art Society at Vilnius in 1907, and later moved to St. Petersburg. He contributed to Kul'bin's exhibition Impressionists in 1910 and to the Izdebsky Salon in 1911.
Ploughman, 1907, plaster, Lithuanian Museum of Art, Vilnius, is a miniature genre piece with a straining horse. His *Spinning Lesson* also depicts the relationship of human beings to rural machinery.
Coll Lithuanian Museum of Art, Vilnius.

RISS, François (Franz Nikolaevich)   1804-1886
French painter. Born in Moscow. He studied under Gros in Paris and exhibited at the Paris Salon 1831-66. He also worked in Russia. His subjects included Christian themes, a self-portrait and a gypsy encampment.
Coll TG; Musée des Beaux-Arts, Le Mans; National Gallery, Oslo.

RITSTSONI = RIZZONI

RIZZONI, Aleksandr Antonovich   1836-1902
Genre painter. Born at Riga. He was the brother of Pavel Rizzoni. He studied at the Academy in St. Petersburg, attaining a first prize in 1860. He travelled to Germany, Holland and Spain and spent several years in Paris before settling in Rome. He was painting in Rome in 1874, 1889 and 1898. He also exhibited in London and Vienna. He died in Rome.
Coll TG; RM.

RIZZONI, Pavel Antonovich   1823-1913
Painter. He was the brother of Aleksandr Rizzoni. He studied at the Academy in St. Petersburg and then travelled widely. His work included genre scenes of Russian life. Sometimes he signed his work 'P.Rizzoni' in latin script.
Coll TG; Museum of Art, Riga.

RODCHENKO, Aleksandr Mikhailovich   1891-1956
Painter, graphic artist, designer for the theatre, film, posters, books, clothing, furniture, architectural projects and exhibition displays. He was a central figure in the evolution of Constructivism in Russia and a motive force in its application to the ideology of the Revolution, which led to his abandonment of easel painting in favour of utilitarian design.
Born in St. Petersburg into the family of a theatre prop worker. He studied at Kazan School of Art under N.I.Feshin and G.Medvedev in 1910-14 and met his future wife Varvara Stepanova there. He became aware of Russian Futurism when he attended a Futurist meeting in Kazan in 1914. He moved to Moscow to attend the Stroganov College as a graphic artist but did not complete the course. He did however execute black and white graphic works with a ruler and compass from 1915 and these heralded his independent preoccupation with geometry and mechanical methods of composition. By 1916 he knew the work of both Tatlin and Malevich after exhibiting at the exhibition *Magazin* (The Store) in 1916 in Moscow. In certain respects his debt to both of them is a cardinal feature of his early work in Moscow. Tatlin revealed that construction is a means anterior to the traditional categories of painting or sculpture, that it can be studied systematically and that it broached the conventions distinguishing art from other kinds of construction.
During 1917 Rodchenko collaborated on the decoration of the Café Pittoresque with Tatlin, Yakulov and others. He designed reflective mobile lamps which corresponded with developments in his painting. This had relinquished the residual *fin de siècle* of his early work and the stylistic experiments with Cubism which followed in order to learn from the Suprematism of Malevich and the Constructive principles embodied in the work of Tatlin. His drawings executed with a ruler and compass were the first of his studies to break distinctly new, systematic and impersonal grounds of investigation.
After the Revolution he became closely involved with the

Aleksandr Rodchenko. Composition, *1917. Gouache and ink on paper. 21 x 29.5 cm. Signed lower right.*
This is one of a long series of works made with compass and ruler. The planes created by intersecting lines and arcs rotate around a focal point.
This exemplifies Rodchenko's aim of reducing his means to geometric elements less personal than free-hand drawing. It makes for a synthesis of
the Suprematism of Malevich and the sense of construction associated with Tatlin.

reorganisation of the artistic life of Moscow, joining the Collegium of the Art Section of the People's Commissariat of Enlightenment (IZO Narkompros) in 1918. He held a one-man exhibition at the Club of the Leftist Federation in Moscow in 1918, exhibited with the Artists of the Leftist Federation of the Professional Union in 1918 along with Popova and others, and at the Fifth State Exhibition: From Impressionism to Non-Objective Art in Moscow 1918-19. Together with Aleksei Gan, Aleksandr Drevin and Varvara Stepanova he formed the group *Askranov* (Association of Extreme Innovators) in January 1919.

His exhibits at the Tenth State Exhibition: Non-Objective Creativity and Suprematism in 1919 included 'coloured non-objective sculptures' made from card and wood. The titles of his works there indicated his commitment to non-objective art: *Simple Construction of Colour, The Movement of Colour from Form, The Concentration of Colour — Colour Painting*, works 'without subject, colour or light', *White Non-Objective Sculpture, Coloured Non-Objective Sculpture*, etc. The seventh

Aleksandr Rodchenko. Lamp Design for the Café Pittoresque, 1917. *Pencil on paper. Signed lower right and inscribed 'for the Café Pittoresque' lower left.*
This is a development from the compass and ruler studies. The lamps were designed for construction in light-reflecting materials.

'non-objective sculpture' was a projected *Memorial to Olga Rozanova*.

He appeared in fourteenth place on the April 1919 list of artists for acquisitions by the envisaged Museum of Painterly Culture and was represented along with Kandinsky, Chagall and others at the First State Exhibition of Paintings by Local and Moscow Artists held in Vitebsk in December 1919. He also participated in the Third Exhibition of Paintings held at Ryazan in 1919.

He was a member 1919-20 of the experimental collective *Zhivskul'ptarkh*, an acronym combining the Russian for Painting, Sculpture and Architecture, committed to investigating the relationship between these activities. He exhibited work under the auspices of *Zhivskul'ptarkh* in two exhibitions in 1920. He also exhibited with The Four, Rodchenko, Kandinsky, Stepanova and Sinezubov, in 1920 and taught at the Vhutemas from 1920. He was represented at the Nineteenth Exhibition of the All-Russian Exhibitions Bureau in Moscow in 1920, at the enormous First State Exhibition of Art and Science, which included ethnographic material, held in Kazan in 1920, and at the Third Touring Exhibition of the Sovetsk Regional subdepartment of the Museums Bureau along with Kandinsky and others in 1921.

His investigative mode of work made him a major exponent of Constructivism seeking fundamental insights into creative activity. He was an active member of several new organisations in the early post-Revolutionary years, and worked under Rozanova. He was also a founder member of the Institute of Artistic Culture (INKhUK) which he wrested from the psychological bias of Kandinsky, helping to make it the theoretical centre for the elaboration of Constructivism in Moscow. He was president of INKhUK in 1921. For Rodchenko this required a commitment to communist ideology which was seen as carrying the potential of social construction. For this reason he abandoned easel painting for utilitarian work as a designer from 1921, the year in which he displayed *The Last Painting*, monochrome panels of red, blue and yellow, at the exhibition 5 x 5=25 in Moscow. He had also contributed to the second and third exhibitions of the Society of Young Artists (Obmokhu) in 1920 and 1921. It was in this context that the Stenberg brothers and Medunetsky came to be associated with Constructivism. He became dean of the metalwork faculty at the Vkhutemas in 1922. The same year his work was represented at the First Russian Art Exhibition at the Van Diemen Gallery in Berlin.

He turned his attention to many forms of design, ranging from architectural projects to furniture, stage design and the production of clothing, photography, exhibition design, posters, the design of books, including illustrations for Transrationalists (*Zaumniki*) by Kruchenykh and others in 1922. He even designed captions for Dziga Vertov's silent *Kino-Pravda* (Cinema Truth) in 1922. This great variety of activity was made possible by the fundamental nature of his Constructivist studies which effectively transcended these distinctions to evolve broad creative principles. In this his work is comparable to that of Lissitzky. He contributed to the exhibition Art of Moscow Theatre 1918-1923 held in Moscow in 1923.

He taught at the Vkhutemas/Vkhutein in Moscow in the period 1920-30 where his work in the Basic Course was innovatory. He was closely involved also with the poet and painter Vladimir Mayakovsky. Together they designed window posters and advertisements for the state stores Mosselprom and GUM and they collaborated on the periodicals *Lef* from 1923 and *Novy Lef* from 1927. Rodchenko added the camera to the apparatus of compass and ruler in 1924 and became one of the pioneers of photomontage in Russia, developing its use as illustration, in posters and in the layout and covers of books and periodicals.

In 1925 he visited Paris for the International Exhibition having been closely involved in the works displayed there and having collaborated with the architect of the Soviet Pavilion Konstantin Melnikov. Rodchenko also designed the catalogue cover and installed his own design for a workers' reading room at the Exhibition. This incorporated the complex symmetry of the one-piece chess table and attached chairs in red and black as well as a reading desk with a row of chairs based on the semicircle and triangle. In addition there were display screens and graphic works. He was awarded four silver medals.

He also contributed to the First Exhibition of Cinema Posters held in Moscow in 1925 and to the Third Exhibition of Paintings by Artists from Kaluga and Moscow held in Kaluga in 1925. He was represented at the Second Exhibition of Cinema Posters held at the Kamerny (Chamber) Theatre, Moscow, in 1926. He worked in the cinema 1927-30 and from 1932 directed a course in photography at the State Polygraphic Institute. He contributed to many photographic exhibitions in the 1930s. He also resumed painting in the 1930s. He designed covers for the periodical *USSR in Construction* 1933-40. His late paintings employed a drip technique ostensibly comparable to that of Jackson Pollock. He died in Moscow.

Book design extensive including covers for: A.Kruchenykh *Tsotsa*, 1921. A.Kruchenykh, G.Petnikov, V.Khlebnikov *Zaumniki* (Transrationalists), 1922. *Avio Let. Stikhi* (Aero Flight. Verses), Moscow, 1923. V.V.Mayakovsky *Pro Eto* (About This), Moscow, 1923. V.V.Mayakovsky *Mayakovsky Ulibaetsya, Mayakovsky Smeetsya, Mayakovsky Izdevaetsya* (Mayakovsky Smiles, Mayakovsky Laughs, Mayakovsky Jeers), Moscow, 1923. S.Tret'yakov *Itogo* (Altogether), Moscow (Gosizdat), 1924. Anri Barbyus (Henri Barbusse) *Rechi Bortsa* (Speeches of a Fighter), Moscow (Gosizdat), 1924. *Mena Vsekh* (All Change), Moscow, 1924. I.Ehrenburg *Materializatsiya fantastiki* (Materialisation of the Fantastic), Moscow (Kinopechat'), 1927. V.V.Mayakovsky *Sifilis* (Syphilis), Moscow (Zakniga), 1926. Sume-Cheng *Kitayanka Sume-Cheng* (The Chinese Woman Sumi-Cheng), Moscow (Gosizdat), 1929. P.Neznamov *Khorosho na Ulitse* (All is Well on the Street), Moscow (Federatsiya), 1929. V.V.Mayakovsky *Klop* (The Bedbug), Moscow, 1929.

Theatre design 1919-20 *My* (We) by Aleksei Gan after E.Zamyatin, directed by Sergei Eisenstein at the Proletkult Studio, Moscow, but banned by the authorities. Costume designs were executed from the interslotted rectilinear planes of his Constructivism painted with the texture evident to mass in the forms and there was a severe restriction on colour. The effect was like collage with no indication of the facial features or hands of the Workers, although a powerful indication of force and movement was achieved.

1929 February: Vsevolod Meyerhold's production of Mayakovsky's *Klop* (The Bedbug) at the Meyerhold Theatre, Moscow. Designs for the first part were by the Kukryniksi but designs for the last act representing the future time of 1979 were by Rodchenko. The music was by Dmitri Shostakovich.

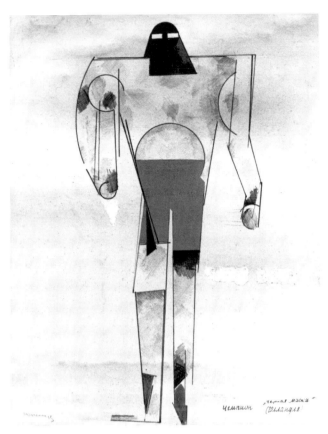

Aleksandr Rodchenko. Champion 'Black Mask' (Holland), *1918-19. Gouache, watercolour and coloured pencil. Signed lower left in Russian and inscribed in Russian 'champion 'black mask' (Holland)'. 36.2 x 27.2 cm. This is from the series of studies 'Bortsy' (Warriors). Collection Mr. and Mrs. Nikita D.Lobanov-Rostovsky, London.*

1929 Anatoli Glebov's *Inga* produced by Nikolai Gorchakov at the Theatre of Revolution. The poster by Rodchenko and Stepanova employed their recurrent Constructivist device of a symmetrical design turned on its side and a reliance upon the boldest block lettering. He also designed a multipurpose stage set and constructed collapsible furniture for this production.

1931 *One Sixth of the World* by Aleksandr Yarkov and Nikolai Ravich, produced by Nikolai Gorchakov with choreography by K.Goleizovsky, at the Music Hall, Moscow. The costume designs showed frontal views of the strange scientific uniforms of the figures of the future.

Film design 1926 L.Obolensky *Al'bidum*, Mezhrabpom-Rus'. This featured a business office interior designed by Rodchenko with a symmetrical emphasis evident in the stills. It incorporated a tall flight of stairs with slightly exaggerated perspective as well as a split level interior in which a balcony is supported upon a pier that seems unique architecturally in that it has an L-shaped cross-section providing rigidity with minimal mass. This film clearly provides a record of a fully evolved Rodchenko interior. It was illustrated in the journal *Novyy Lef* in 1927 and 1928.

1926-7 Lev Kuleshov *Zhurnalistka* (The Woman Journalist), reporter's Constructivist furniture and equipment by Rodchenko.

1927 Lev Kuleshov's *Vasha Znakomaya* (Your Female Acquaintance), released by Sovkino. Based upon a story by Aleksandr Kurs. Design by Vasili Rakhals and Rodchenko

Aleksandr Rodchenko. Non-objective Painting: Composition 35 (55), *1918. Oil on canvas. 66.5 x 50 cm.*
Rodchenko rejected Suprematism as too personal and mystical. He reduced composition to its minimal form, a repeated motif derived from the proportions of the canvas.
State Tretyakov Gallery, Moscow.

whose contribution included an office interior.
1927 Boris Barnet's *Moskva v Oktyabre* (Moscow in October), released by Mezhrabprom-Russ. Scenario by Oleg Leonidov.
1927-30 *A Doll with Millions.*
Film posters include 1924 Dziga Vertov's *Kino-glaz* (Kino-Eye; Cinema Eye). 1926 Dziga Vertov's *Shestaya chast' mira* (A Sixth of the Earth). 1927 Eisenstein's *Bronenosets Potemkin* (Battleship Potemkin). Lavinsky also designed posters for this.
Lit N.Tarabukin *Ot mol'berta k mashine* (From the Easel to the Machine), Moscow, 1923. L.Linhart *Alexandr Rodcenko*, Prague, 1964. L.F.Volkov-Lannit *Aleksandr Rodchenko risuet, grafiruet, sporit*, Moscow, 1968. G.Karginov *Rodchenko*, Budapest, 1975 (Paris, 1977; London, 1979). *A.Rodtschenko*, exh. cat., Museum Ludwig, Cologne, 1978. *Alexander Rodchenko*, exh. cat., MOMA, Oxford, 1979. *Alexander Rodtschenko und Warwara Stepanowa*, exh. cat., Wilhelm-Lehmbruck-Museum, Duisberg, 1982. A.M.Rodchenko *Stati, vospominaniya, avtobiograficheskie zametki, pisma*, Moscow, 1982. J.E.Bowlt *Russian Stage Design. Scenic Innovation. From the Collection of Mr. and Mrs. Nikita D.Lobanov-Rostovsky*, Jackson, MS, exh. cat.,1982. W.Rodtschenko, A.Lawrentjew *Alexander Rodtschenko*, Dresden, 1983. C.Lodder *Russian Constructivism*, New Haven and London, 1983. *Seven Moscow Artists 1910-30*, exh. cat., Galerie Gmurzynska, Cologne, 1984. D.Elliott, A.Lavrentiev (ed.) *Alexander Rodchenko 1914-1920: Works on Paper*, London, 1991. Nancy Van Norman Baer *Theatre in Revolution, Russian Avant-Garde Stage Design 1913-1935*, San Francisco and London, 1991. S.Compton *Russian*

Avant-Garde Books 1917-34, London, 1992. *L'Avant-garde russe 1905-1925*, exh. cat., Musée des Beaux-Arts, Nantes, 1993.
Coll TG; RM; Bakhrushin Theatre Museum, Moscow; Rodchenko-Stepanova Archive, Moscow; Astrakhan Art Museum; Dagestan Art Museum, Makhachkala; Ivanovo Art Museum; Kirov Art Museum; Tomsk Art Museum; Tula Art Museum; MOMA, New York; Costakis Collection; Sammlung Ludwig, Cologne.
Colour plate p.363; see also p.26.

RODCHEV, Vasili Yakovlevich (Palladievich) 1768-1803
Portrait painter. Born at St. Petersburg. His subjects also included a *St. Sebastian* in 1792. He died at St. Petersburg.
Coll TG.

RODIONOV, Mikhail (Nikolai) Semenovich 1885-1956
Painter, draughtsman, graphic artist. He studied at the Moscow College under Kasatkin, Arkhipov, Miloradovich and Volnukhin.
After the Revolution he participated in the 1921 exhibition of the World of Art in Moscow. He was a member of the *Makovets* group and exhibited at the seventh exhibition of the group *L'Araignée* (The Spider) at the Galerie Devambe in Paris in 1925. He exhibited at the third and last exhibition of the *Makovets* group in Moscow 1925-6 and was included in the exhibition of Russian Graphic Art in Riga in 1929. He was

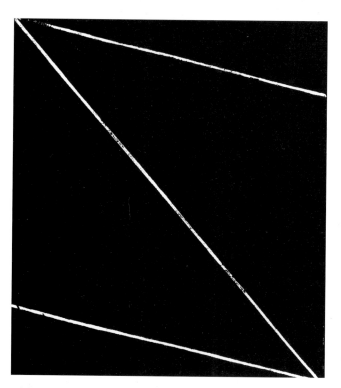

Aleksandr Rodchenko. Line, *1920. Oil on canvas. 58.5 x 51 cm.*
This is among the most minimal of Rodchenko's paintings relying upon a symmetrical arrangement of only three lines. His cover for the book 'Zaumniki' by A.Kruchenykh, G.Petnikov and V.Khlebnikov in 1922 was a closely related work.
Private collection, courtesy of Annely Juda Fine Art, London.

also represented at the First Touring Exhibition of Painting and Graphics which opened in Moscow in 1929 and at the jubilee exhibition Artists of the RSFSR over 15 Years held at the Russian Museum, Leningrad, in 1932.

Hayricks, 1925, charcoal, is a drawing showing hayricks stretching away across a field of well managed land where everything is in order.

Coll TG.

RODIONOV, Ya. A.   a.1919

Painter. He exhibited at the Ninth State Exhibition of Paintings: Naturalism and Realism in Moscow in 1919.

ROERICH, Nicolas (RERIKH, Nikolai Konstantinovich) 1874-1947

Painter, graphic artist, theatre designer, scholar, archaeologist and mystic. His early preoccupation with themes of a mythical ancient Russia led to an interest in folk art. This was evident in his theatre designs as well as his paintings. Subsequently he became a mystic and the majority of his later work reflects his experiences in the Himalayas.

Born in St. Petersburg, the son of a lawyer. He studied law at the University of St. Petersburg and painting at the Academy under Chistyakov and Kuindzhi 1893-7. In the 1890s he executed decorations for Princess Tenisheva at Talashkino near Smolensk. He was in Paris at the Atelier Cormon 1900-1. On returning to St. Petersburg he became Secretary of the Society for the Encouragement of the Arts (OPKh) in 1901 and subsequently was made Director of its Drawing School in 1906.

His interest in ancient Russia was confirmed by early experience of archaeological expeditions and a long journey to visit old Russian cities 1903-4. He exhibited with the World of Art in 1903 and in Diaghilev's display of Russian art at the Salon d'Automne in Paris in 1906.

He was made a Fellow of the Academy in 1909 and exhibited forty-four works at the St. Petersburg Salon in the Menshikov Palace that year. He also joined the World of Art with whom he exhibited from 1902 and he became the President of its revived form in 1910. More work for Princess Tenisheva followed when she commissioned murals for both the inside and outside of the church at Talashkino 1910-14.

Contact with Diaghilev led to involvement with ballet design, culminating in the celebrated production of Stravinsky's *Rite of Spring* in 1913 for which Roerich designed the costumes.

In 1916 he moved to Finland and elsewhere in Scandinavia including Sweden in 1918. He emigrated in 1918 but his name appeared on the April 1919 list of artists for acquisitions by the envisaged Museum of Painterly Culture and he participated in the First State Free Exhibition of Artworks in Petrograd in 1919.

He met Rabrindranath Tagore in 1919 in London and later became fascinated by India and the Himalayas.

Between 1920 and 1923 he toured America where he both taught and exhibited founding the Nicolas Roerich Museum in New York in 1923. More significant for his development was his anthropological journey to India and Central Asia in 1923 which included visits to Sikkim and Bhutan in 1924. His interest in anthropology, archaeology and esoteric religions became dominant. He travelled to Moscow in 1926 and from there to the Altai region, to Mongolia and to Tibet. From 1928 he directed a research station at Kulu in the Himalayas.

He contributed to the exhibition of Contemporary Russian Art held at Philadelphia in 1932 but he did not return to the United States after leaving for India and Central Asia in 1935. He painted over 7,000 paintings in all. He died at Kulu, India.

Building a Boat, c.1900, Museum of Oriental Arts, Moscow, exemplifies Roerich's vigorous submersion into the folklore vision of Russia corrected and disciplined by his archaeological knowledge and his ethnographical studies. The great boat is essentially a Viking ship which evokes a mythical Russian past. Wedged with logs, its primitive dragon's head rears high above its industrious workers. This is enjoyable make-believe informed by scholarship and learning, archaeology adjusted to entertain and inspire. He produced, as here, paintings which could be seen as complete in themselves or as potential designs for exotic stage scenery overtly encouraging his audience to suspend disbelief. His style was lavishly decorative and there was nothing archaic in his handling of paint on canvas however ancient or primitive his themes. A comparable theme and technique was employed in *The Slavs on the Dneiper*, 1905, RM.

The Idols, 1901, TG, is the fruit of ethnographic study as well as an enthusiasm for evoking the atmosphere of pagan times. It shows a circular stockade surmounted by animal skulls and encompassing towering primitive idols, all depicted in the blue twilight of dawn or evening.

St. Pantaleon the Healer, 1916, TG, is a vast elevated landscape in which the solitary saint gathers the plants for his remedies beneath a wide sky filled with sailing clouds. This is a deliberately timeless setting which already shows his tendency towards the mystic's isolation.

Theatre design 1907 *The Three Magi* for the Antique Theatre, St. Petersburg, and Wagner's *Valkyrie*.

1908 Rimsky-Korsakov's *Snowmaiden* at the Opéra Comique in Paris.

1908-9 costumes for the Polovtsian Dancers in Diaghilev's production of Borodin's *Prince Igor*: an assembly of smoking yurts beneath a yellow sky evokes the atmosphere of primeval times in the design for Act 2 (TG; Victoria and Albert Museum, London). First performed at the Théâtre du Châtelet, Paris, 1909.

1909 May: Rimsky-Korsakov's *Maid of Pskov* produced by Aleksandr Sanin for Diaghilev at the Théâtre du Châtelet, Paris, with sets by Roerich and Aleksandr Golovin and costumes by Dmitrii Stelletsky.

1909 A.Remizov's *The Tragedy of Judas, Prince Iscariot* (unrealised).

1912 Ibsen's *Peer Gynt* at the Moscow Art Theatre: the set for the Rocks of Rond (RM) was executed in pinks and mauves with a shadowy open cave in the foreground.

1912 Lope de Vega's *Fuente ovejuna* at the Antique Theatre, St. Petersburg.

1913 May: Stravinsky's *Rite of Spring* produced in Paris at the Théâtre des Champs-Elysées by Diaghilev. The libretto was by Stravinsky and Roerich jointly. Choreography by Vaslav Nijinsky. The design for *The Kiss to Earth*, RM, shows a fresh and open primeval hilly landscape dominated by an ancient tree in the foreground. There is no sign of civilisation or human habitation.

1913 Maeterlinck's *La Princesse Madeleine* at the Free Theatre, Moscow (unrealised).

1914 Maeterlinck's *Soeur Béatrice* at the Music Drama Theatre, Petrograd: a set design for the monastery shows a deeply shadowy medieval passageway dimly lit by stained glass windows. He had illustrated this play in 1905.

1914 Borodin's *Prince Igor* at the Royal Opera, London.

1916 Mussorgsky's *A Night on the Bare Mountain.*

1919 Rimsky-Korsakov's *The Tale of Tsar Saltan*, a projected production for the Royal Opera, Covent Garden, London.

1920 Rimsky-Korsakov's *Sadko* at the Royal Opera, London.

1922 November: Rimsky-Korsakov's *Snowmaiden* for the Civic opera Company at the Chicago Opera House.

Writings N.K.Rerikh *Talashkino. Izdeliya masterskikh M.K.Tenishevoy*, St. Petersburg, 1905. N.K.Rerikh *Pis'mena, Stikhi*, 1974. N.K.Rerikh *Izbrannoe*, 1979.

Lit Yu.Baltrushaitis et al. *Rerikh*, Petrograd, 1916. S.K.Ernst *N.K.Rerikh*, Petrograd, 1918. A.Rostislavov *N.K.Rerikh*, Petrograd, 1918. N.Jarintzov *N.K.Rerikh*, 1920. N.Kuzmin *Rerikh*, Moscow, 1923. V.Knyazeva *N.Rerikh*, Moscow-Leningrad, 1968. *Diaghilev and Russian Stage Designers, a Loan Exhibition from the Collection of Mr. and Mrs. N.Lobanov-Rostovsky*, International Exhibitions Foundation, Washington, 1972-4. E.Polyakova *Rerikh*, Moscow, 1973. J.E.Bowlt *Russian Stage Design. Scenic Innovation. From the Collection of Mr. and Mrs. Nikita D.Lobanov-Rostovsky*, Jackson, MS, exh. cat., 1982. *Twilight of the Tsars*, London, 1991. E.Poliakova *Rerikh*, Moscow, 1973. I.Bogdanova-Rerikh *N.Rerikh*, Moscow, 1975. L.Korotkina *Nikolai Roerich*, Leningrad, 1976. M.Kuzmina et al. *N.K.Rerikh*, 1978. J.Decter *Nicholas Roerich — The Life and Times of a Russian Master*, 1989. A.M.Lukashov *N.Rerikh iz sobraniya Gosudarstvennoy Tretyakovskoy Galerei*, 1989. A.Kamensky *The World of Art Movement*, Leningrad, 1991. Dzhon Boult (John Bowlt) *Khudozhniki russkogo teatra. Sobranie Nikity i Niny Lobanovykh-Rostovskikh*, Moscow, 1991.

Coll There are museums dedicated to Roerich in Moscow and New York; TG; RM; Bakhrushin Theatre Museum, Moscow; Radishchev Art Museum, Saratov; Victoria and Albert Museum, London; Ashmolean Museum, Oxford.

See p.23.

ROGACHEV, N. a.1920s

Graphic artist. He designed numerous covers for sheet music adapting a Constructivist style in the 1920s, including B.Prozorovsky's *Grimaces of the West*, Leningrad, 1927.

ROGOVIN, Nikolai Efimovich a.1910-1919

Painter. He was active in Moscow c.1911-12 when he worked in the studio complex The Tower with Bart, Popova, Tatlin, Vesnin and others. He exhibited with the Knave of Diamonds in Moscow 1910-11, with the Union of Youth 1911-12, with the Donkey's Tail group in Moscow in 1912 and with Larionov's exhibition The Target in Moscow in 1913.

After the Revolution he appeared on the April 1919 list of artists for acquisitions by the envisaged Museum of Painterly Culture.

ROKOTOV, Fedor Stepanovich 1736-1808/9

Painter of grand portraits. This was in spite of the fact that he was the son of a serf and was himself owned by Prince P.Repin who freed him. He was a younger contemporary of the important portraitist Antropov. He studied at the new Academy in St. Petersburg and moved to Moscow in the 1760s where he worked for more than ten years.

Portait of V.I.Maykov, 1765, is informal for its date. The sitter may be a courtier but he appears shrewd and is discreetly dressed. The technique is sensitive and rather French in appearance.

Coll Major holdings at TG; RM.

ROLLER, Andreas (Andrei Adamovich) 1805-1891

German painter, theatre designer. Born at Ratisbonne. He studied in Vienna and was active in Munich, Vienna, Kassel and Berlin before moving to St. Petersburg in 1833. He was active in the theatre by the 1840s. He died at St. Petersburg.

ROMANOVICH, Sergei Mikhailovich 1894-1968

Painter. He studied at the Moscow College under Kasatkin, Arkhipov and K.Korovin 1910-13. He contributed a Caucasian hairdresser's signboard to Larionov's exhibition The Target in Moscow in 1913 and also contributed to the exhibition No.4 in Moscow in 1914. He was amongst the painters who responded to the Rayism of Larionov.

After the Revolution he taught at the Proletkult studios in Moscow 1918-20 and appeared on the April 1919 list of artists for acquisitions by the envisaged Museum of Painterly Culture. He taught at Voronezh 1920-2 and maintained links there with the Moscow Vkhutemas where he taught 1922-3. He was represented at the First Russian Art Exhibition in Berlin in 1922. He was a member of the *Makovets* group from 1922 and exhibited at the third and last exhibition of the

Fedor Rokotov. '*V.N.Sorovueva*', *1780s. Oil on canvas. 67.5 x 52 cm. State Russian Museum, St. Petersburg.*

Nicolas Roerich. Study for the Costume of a Warrior, *1919. Gouache. Signed 'N.Roerich' lower right and initialled lower left in Russian with a monogram 'NR'. 30.5 x 24 cm.*
Designed for a production of Rimsky-Korsakov's opera 'The Tale of Tsar Saltan', *projected for the Royal Opera, London, in 1919.*
Collection Mr. and Mrs. Nikita D.Lobanov-Rostovsky, London.

Makovets group in Moscow 1925-6. He taught in the Workers' Faculty (Rabfak) of the Vkhutemas 1928-9.
Lit A.M.Muratov, V.Manin et al. *Zhivopis' 20-30kh godov*, Sankt-Peterburg, 1991.
Coll Voronezh Fine Art Museum.

ROMMAN, Roman (Robert) Fedorovich   1845-1893
Painter whose work included seascapes. Signed 'RR'.
Coll TG.

ROSITSKY, S.   a.1918
He was engaged on Aitprop decorations at the War Ministry, Admiralty Prospekt, Petrograd, in 1918.

ROSKIN, Vladimir O.   1896-1929
Graphic artist. He studied at the Stroganov Institute 1910-13, under F.Rerberg 1913-14 and under Mashkov 1915-17.
After the Revolution he designed posters for the Rosta agency. He exhibited at the Fifth State Exhibition: From Impressionism to Non-Objective Art in Moscow 1918-19 and appeared on the April 1919 list of artists for acquisitions by the envisaged Museum of Painterly Culture. From 1924 he designed Soviet exhibitions abroad. These included work with El Lissitzky on the International Press Exhibition in Cologne in 1929.
Lit *V.O.Roskin*, Moscow, 1977. *Paris-Moscou*, 1979.

ROSSINE, Daniel = BARANOFF-ROSSINE, V.D.

ROSTA
The abbreviated name of the Russian Telegraph Agency (*Rossiyskoe telegrafnoe agentstvo*).

ROSTISLAVOV, Aleksandr   a.1909-1911
Painter. He exhibited views of historical monuments of old Russia at the Izdebsky International Salons 1909-11 in Odessa.

ROTARI, Pietro (Piero) Antonio   1707-1762
Italian history painter, portraitist, etcher. Born in Verona. He studied under the Neapolitan painter Francesco Solimena. He moved to Russia in 1756. There he executed decorations for the Imperial Palaces at Peterhof, including three hundred portraits of women for the Gallery of the Graces. He also worked at Archangel. He died in St. Petersburg.
Coll TG; RM; Municipal Museum, Padua; Municipal Museum, Verona.

ROTOV, Konstantin Pavlovich   1902-1959
Caricaturist. He participated in the seventh exhibition of the group *L'Araignée* (The Spider) at the Galerie Devambe in Paris in 1925.

ROUBAUD, F. = RUBO, F. A.

ROUSSOFF, A. N. = RUSOV, A. N.

ROZANOVA, Ol'ga Vladimirovna   1886-1918
Russian Futurist painter. Born at Malenki in the Vladimir region. She studied at the K.Bolshakov Art School and at the Stroganov College in Moscow. In addition she attended the studios of Yuon and Dudin. She moved to St. Petersburg in 1911, enrolled at the Zvantseva School of Art in 1912 and exhibited with the Union of Youth between 1911 and 1914. During this time she rapidly assimilated the newest developments in Parisian Cubism and Italian Futurism but she also emerged as a leading practitioner of the distinct and largely independent collaboration of poets and painters which came to be known as Russian Futurism. Through the Union of Youth she came to know Matvejs (V.Markov), Matyushin and Malevich. She was an important force in the development of the Russian Futurist book in particular between 1913 and 1916. This synthesis of knowledge from several sources undermined neither her originality nor her drive. Her manifesto *The Bases of the New Art and the Reasons why it is Misunderstood* was published in the Union of Youth almanac in 1913. In 1914 she travelled to Rome for the First Free Futurist exhibition at the Sprovieri Gallery. Marinetti owned works by her.
In the following year she contributed to the exhibition Tramway V in Petrograd and to the Exhibition of Leftist Trends. Rozanova became a convert to the Suprematism of Malevich launched in December 1915 at 0.10. The Last Futurist Exhibition of Paintings to which she also contributed works. Her close association with Russian Futurist poetry was consolidated by her collaboration with the poet A.Kruchenykh whom she married in 1916. He had been a participant in the Futurist opera *Victory Over the Sun* in 1913, producing the libretto whilst Matyushin wrote the music and Malevich designed the sets and costumes. She was active as a member of the group *Supremus* in 1916 and editorial secretary of its projected but never published journal. She showed work at both the Knave of Diamonds and *Magazin* (The Store) exhibitions of 1916.
After the Revolution she exhibited with the Knave of Diamonds in Moscow in 1917. She became a member of the People's Commissariat of Enlightenment's Art Section (IZO

Narkompros) in 1918 working under Tatlin in Moscow where she directed its industrial art section along with Rodchenko. She was engaged to teach textiles at the Free Art Studios (SVOMAS) in Moscow c.1918 along with Davydova and Exter. She was also a member of Proletkult and contributed to the organisation of SVOMAS at Bogorodsk, where she reorganised the wooden toys workshop, Ivanovo-Voznessensk, where she reorganised the textile workshops, and at Mster. She also pioneered the application of recent developments in art to the design of women's clothing. She was represented at the First Exhibition of Works of the Professional Union of Artists in Moscow in 1918.
She died of diphtheria in Moscow in November 1918 before her involvement in the art of the Revolution could gain the full expression of its potential.
However she was exhibited at the Artists of the Leftist Federation of the Professional Union in 1918 along with Rodchenko, Tatlin and others, and represented in the First State Free Exhibition of Artworks in Petrograd in 1919. A posthumous exhibition of her work was held in Moscow in 1919 and Rodchenko exhibited a *Project for a Monument to Rozanova* at The Tenth State Exhibition: Non-Objective Creativity and Suprematism in 1919. She appeared in tenth place on the April 1919 list of artists for acquisitions by the envisaged Museum of Painterly Culture. She was represented at the enormous First State Exhibition of Art and Science, which included ethnographic material, held in Kazan in 1920, and at the First Russian Art Exhibition in 1922 in Berlin.
*The Four Aces, Simultaneous Representation, Playing Card Series, 1915-16, RM, is an emphatic, dynamic and crudely flat depiction of the aces in different directions, splicing through each other on white planes. This employs a characteristically Russian Futurist multi-directional assemblage of flat and *lubok*-like imagery. The playing card theme also appealed for its symbolic and traditional meanings and was already in use by the Knave of Diamonds exhibition society as well as appearing in Cubist works by Picasso and others. It is likely that the cards had specific meanings. The Ace of Clubs was most frequent; it appeared in many collage works by Picasso and in Russian works, for example in *The Aviator* by Malevich in 1914 (RM).
Futurist books In this activity she was more than an illustrator. The whole design of the book resulted from collaboration in certain cases and she was a considerable innovator in this field, introducing, for example, the device of including collages into the production of the book. She contributed to the following Futurist books:
Soyuz molodezhi (Union of Youth), no.3, 1913, illustrated by I.Shkolnik and Rozanova, St. Petersburg, 1913.
A.Kruchenykh, V.Khlebnikov *Slovo kak takovoe* (The Word as Such), 1913, illustrated by Malevich and Rozanova.
A.Kruchenykh, V.Khlebnikov *Bukh lessinnyy* (A Forrestly Rapid), St. Petersburg, 1913, illustrated by Rozanova, Kul'bin and A.Kruchenykh.
A.Kruchenykh *Chort i rechetvortsy* (The Devil and the Wordmakers), with illustrations by Rozanova, St. Petersburg, 1913.
A.Kruchenykh *Vzorval'* (Explodity), with illustrations by N.Kul'bin, O.Rozanova, K.Malevich and N.Goncharova, St. Petersburg, 1913-14.
A.Kruchenykh *Utinoe gnezdyshko...durnykh slov* (A Duck's

Ol'ga Rozanova. War, *1916.*
Linocut. 41.2 x 30.4 cm.
Comparable in certain respects to works
by Goncharova and Malevich,
Rozanova's images conjure up the
destructive energy of battle and aerial
bombardment. This print was designed
for A.Kruchenykh's book 'War'
published in 1916.

Nest...of Bad Words), with illustrations by Rozanova, St. Petersburg, 1913.
A.Kruchenykh *Vozropshchem* (Let's Grumble), St. Petersburg, 1914, illustrated by Malevich and Rozanova.
A.Kruchenykh, V.Khlebnikov *Igra v adu* (A Game in Hell), with illustrations by O.Rozanova, K.Malevich, Moscow, 1914.
A.Kruchenykh, V.Khlebnikov *Te li le* (Te li le), with illustrations by O.Rozanova and N.Kul'bin, St. Petersburg, 1914.
A.Kruchenykh and Alyagrov (Roman Jakobson) *Zaumnaya Gniga* (Transrational Pook), Moscow, 1915, which had a button sewn on to the collage heart on its cover by Rozanova.
A.Kruchenykh *Voina* (War), 1916, which had a collage cover and black linocut illustrations by Rozanova, some incorporated into collages which were otherwise Suprematist.
A.Kruchenykh's *Vselenskaya voina* (Universal War) 1916, which contained a whole sequence of delicate and dynamic collages by Rozanova all but one on blue paper.
Lit *O.V.Rozanova*, exh. cat., Moscow, 1919. S.P.Compton *The World Backwards. Russian Futurist Books 1912-16*, London, 1978. *Paris-Moscou*, 1979. A.Z.Rudenstine *Costakis Collection*, London, 1981. E.Weiss *Russische Avant-Garde, 1910-1930, Sammlung Ludwig, Köln*, Munich, 1986. M.N.Yablonskaya *Women Artists of Russia's New Age*, London, 1990. *L'Avant-garde russe 1905-1925*, exh. cat., Musée des Beaux-Arts, Nantes, 1993.
Coll TG; RM; Alma-Ata Art Museum; Astrakhan Art Museum; Baku Art Museum; Ivanovo Art Museum; Kirov Art Museum; Kostroma Art Museum; Nizhny-Novgorod Art Museum; Samara Art Museum; Saratov Art Museum; Simbirsk Art Museum; Ul'yanovsk Art Museum; Yaroslavl' Art Museum; Costakis Collection; Sammlung Ludwig, Cologne. Colour plate p.366.

ROZENBERG, L. S. = BAKST, L.

ROZENDORF, Elizaveta Berngardovna   b.1898-1932+
Painter, graphic artist, ceramics artist. She worked for the State Porcelain Factory in Petrograd 1919-20 but moved to Estonia in the early 1920s. She exhibited decorative work at Tallinn in 1923 and in the period 1923-7 she exhibited paintings and graphic work with the Society of Estonian Artists. She was represented at the jubilee exhibition Artists of the RSFSR over 15 Years held at the Russian Museum, Leningrad, in 1932.
Lit *Paris-Moscou*, 1979. N.Lobanov-Rostovsky *Revolutionary Ceramics*, London, 1990.

ROZENFEL'DT, N. V.   a.1918-1919
Rozenfel'dt exhibited at the Fifth State Exhibition: From Impressionism to Non-Objective Art in Moscow 1918-19 and appeared on the April 1919 list of artists for acquisitions by the envisaged Museum of Painterly Culture.

ROZENGOLTS-LEVINA, Eva   1898-1975
Painter. Born at Vitebsk. Her mother had studied under Dobuzhinsky. She became aware of the work of Malevich at Vitebsk. She studied dentistry at Tomsk University and subsequently became involved in art after moving to Moscow where in 1919 she studied briefly under the sculptor Stepan Erzya. She worked as a nurse during the Civil War.
In 1920 she worked under the sculptor Anna Golubkina at the Vkhutemas in Moscow but in 1921 she became a painting student under Robert Fal'k at the Vkhutemas until 1925. She visited London in 1926. She became a member of the Union of Social Artists and exhibited with them in 1928.
She taught at the First State Textile Print Factory in Moscow 1931-2 and designed fabrics for the Dorogomilov Factory 1932-3. She was a consultant to the People's Commissariat of Light Industry 1934-6. She lived at Chistopol in 1942 before returning to Moscow and exhibiting with the Moscow Society of Artists. After she was exiled in 1949 she lived near Krasnoyarsk and in Kazakhstan where she worked in the theatre from 1954. She returned to Moscow after her rehabilitation in 1956. She died in Moscow.
Lit M.N.Yablonskaya *Women Artists of Russia's New Age*,

Ilya Repin. A.D.C. General Otton Borisovich Richter (1830-1908), *1886. Charcoal and oil on cardboard.*
Inscribed 'General Richter, for the picture the speech of Alexander III to the Elders', signed and dated '1886'. 24 x 15 cm.
A preparatory study for the painting 'Speech of Alexander III Alexandrovich to the Village Elders in the Courtyard of
the Petrovsky Palace'.
Reproduced by kind permission of Sotheby's London, sale 16.6.1992, lot 12.

Aleksandr Rodchenko. Composition, *1918. Oil on canvas. 78.5 x 62 cm.*
Courtesy Annely Juda Fine Art, London.

London, 1990.
Coll TG; Pushkin Museum, Moscow; Karakalpatskaya State Art Museum.

ROZHDESTVENSKY, Vasili Vasilievich   **1884-1963**
Painter, graphic artist. Born at Tula. He studied periodically at the Moscow College from 1900 to 1911 under Arkhipov, Korovin, Pasternak, Serov and Malyutin. He contributed to the *Stefanos* exhibition 1907-8. He was a founder member of the Knave of Diamonds exhibition society and exhibited with them from 1911 to 1917. In 1912 he visited Italy and Austria before settling in Moscow.
After the Revolution he taught painting at the Free Art Studios (SVOMAS) in Moscow c.1918 where he was described as a 'post-impressionist'. He exhibited at the Fifth State Exhibition: From Impressionism to Non-Objective Art in Moscow 1918-19. He also exhibited with the revived World of Art from 1917 to 1922 and also taught at the Vkhutemas 1918-20 and later in the Tver region. He appeared in seventh place on the April 1919 list of artists for acquisitions by the envisaged Museum of Painterly Culture. He was represented along with Kandinsky, Chagall and others at the First State Exhibition of Paintings by Local and Moscow Artists held in Vitebsk in December 1919, at the enormous First State Exhibition of Art and Science, which included ethnographic material, held in Kazan in 1920, and at the First Russian Art Exhibition in Berlin in 1922. He was exhibiting with the Society of Moscow Painters in 1925 and contributed to the Third Exhibition of Paintings by Artists from Kaluga and Moscow held in Kaluga in 1925. He then exhibited with AKhRR in 1926. His work was included in the exhibition of Soviet art held at Harbin in 1926 and in Japan in 1927 and in the major exhibition in Moscow in 1927 marking the tenth anniversary of the Revolution. From 1927 to 1929 he exhibited with the Association of Moscow Artists. He was painting in Central Asia in 1929 and was included in the exhibition of Russian Graphic Art in Riga in 1929.
He was represented at the jubilee exhibition Artists of the RSFSR over 15 Years held at the Russian Museum, Leningrad, in 1932 and at the 1932 Venice Biennale. He died in Moscow.
*Still-Life with Liqueur, 1913, TG, is more Cubist than Cézannist with planes interslotted and progressing beyond the edges of forms. Background and foreground interlock with dominant lines providing an overall architecture for the composition in a way that recalls Picasso as well as Goncharova. An atmospheric and lively response to Cubo-Futurist innovations from Western Europe.
Writings V.V.Rozhdestvensky *Zapiski khudozhnika* (Notes of a Painter), Moscow, 1963.
Lit N.Tretyakov *V.V.Rozhdestvensky*, Moscow, 1956. *V.V.Rozhdestvensky*, exh. cat., Moscow, 1978. *Paris-Moscou*, 1979. A.M.Muratov, V.Manin et al. *Zhivopis' 20-30kh godov*, Sankt-Peterburg, 1991.
Coll TG; RM; Samara Art Museum; Saratov Art Museum; Tula Art Museum.

ROZHKOVA, Evgenia Emel'yanovna   **1900-1988**
Painter. She contributed to the Twelfth State Exhibition: Colourdynamo and Tectonic Primitivism (*Tsvetodinamos i tektonicheskiy primitivizm*) along with Grishchenko, Shevchenko and others in Moscow in 1919.

RUBLEV, Andrei   **c.1370-1430**
The most celebrated of Russian ikon painters. His birth dates are sometimes given as 1360-70 and the date of his death as 1427 or c.1430. He is frequently accredited with having established the Russian school of painting which makes him the origin and most important of Russian artists. Little is known of his life. He was raised in a secular environment and became a monk as an adult. He entered the St. Sergius Trinity Monastery or, according to some authorities, the Andronnikov Monastery.
Whilst there are few definite attributions to Rublev he is known to have worked with Theophanes the Greek (Feofan Grek) and Prokhor of Gorodets, probably painting ikons or murals at the Cathedral of the Annunciation in the Moscow Kremlin in 1405. He worked in Zvenigorod and at the Trinity-Sergievsky Monastery near Moscow. He also painted murals and ikons for the three-tier iconostasis at the Uspensky Cathedral at Vladimir in 1408 along with Daniil Cherny.
He is recognised as one of the prime sources of the distinctly Russian tradition of ikon painting to emerge from its Byzantine predecessors and his most celebrated work is the ikon of *The Holy Trinity*, c.1410-20, TG. This depicts the three archangels who appeared to Abraham and his wife. It is a painting of great refinement, elegance and even tenderness. The influence of Rublev and his followers decisively determined the development of Russian ikon painting, a tradition which descended down to the 18th century and after despite many modifications. Even amongst the avant-garde of the early decades of the 20th century Rublev was held in high esteem and to a degree came to stand for the achievements and traditions of a distinctly Russian art. He died in Moscow and is buried at the Spaso-Andronikov Monastery there.
Rublev was one of only seven artists listed as worthy of monuments in Lenin's plan issued in 1918. The Andrei Rublev Museum of Old Russian Art opened at the Andronnikov Monastery, Moscow, in 1947.
Lit M.V.Alpatov *A.Rublev*, Moscow, 1959. V.Pribytkov *A.Rublev*, 1960. M.A.Demina '*Troitsa*' *Andreya Rubleva*, Moscow, 1963. V.N.Lazarev *Andrei Rublev i ego shkola* (Andrei Rublev and His School), Moscow, 1966. *Andrei Roublev; Prix de la critique internationale au Festival de Cannes*, 1969. M.V.Alpatov *A.Rublev*, 1971. M.A.Demina *Andrei Rublev i khudozhniki ego Kruga* (Andrei Rublev and the Artists of his Circle), 1972. G.I.Vdornov *Troitsa Andreya Rubleva: Antologiya*, 1981. V.A.Plugin *Andrei Rublev*, 1987 (in English).
Coll TG; RM.
Colour plate p.14.

RUBLEVA, Aleksandra Iosifna   **1908-1943**
Painter. She was represented at the jubilee exhibition Artists of the RSFSR over 15 Years held at the Russian Museum, Leningrad, in 1932. She died in Moscow.

RUBO, Frants Alekseevich (ROUBAUD, Franz)
1856-1928
Painter. Born at Odessa. He was active in St. Petersburg, but also worked in Munich and Tiflis. His students included Vladimir Lebedev in 1910. His subjects included battle themes and equestrian portraits. Sometimes he signed his work 'F.Roubaud' in latin script. He died in Munich.
Lit O.Fedorova *F.Rubo*, Moscow, 1982.
Coll TG; Pinakotek, Munich.

RUDAKOV, D. a.1921
A member of the *Bytie* (Existence) Society of Artists formed in Moscow in 1921.

RUDAKOV, Konstantin Ivanovich 1891-1949
Graphic artist, theatre designer, painter. He studied in V.E.Savinsky's private studio and under Kustodiev, Lansere and Dobuzhinsky, and then at the Academy under Kardovsky 1914-22. He was represented at the jubilee exhibition Artists of the RSFSR over 15 Years held at the Russian Museum, Leningrad, in 1932. He illustrated many French writers.
Lit A.M.Muratov, V.Manin et al. *Zhivopis' 20-30kh godov*, Sankt-Peterburg, 1991.
Coll RM.

RUDNEV, Lev Vladimirovich 1885-1956
Architect and designer of monuments. He designed an impressively solemn and tomb-like series of low lying monuments for the Champs de Mars, Petrograd, in 1918. Some of these designs were adapted to decorate ceramic ware in 1921. He served under Al'tman on the committee responsible for the revolutionary decorations marking 1 May in Petrograd in 1919.

RUDNITSKY, Ya. K. a.1918
He was engaged in Agitprop decorations at Vladimir Square, Petrograd, in 1918.

RUDOVICH, Aleksandra Nikolaevna b.1904
Painter, costume designer. She was a close friend and collaborator with Tatlin 1944-53. Her works include theatre design and portraits of Tatlin.

RUKHLEVSKY, Yakov Timofeevich 1884-1965
Graphic artist, poster designer. Born at Smolensk. He was self-taught. He worked as a designer for Goskino (State Cinema) in the 1920s. He contributed to the First Exhibition of Cinema Posters held in Moscow in 1925 and to the Second Exhibition of Cinema Posters held at the Kamerny (Chamber) Theatre, Moscow, in 1926. He designed posters in the manner of the Stenberg Brothers with whom he collaborated in 1927, particularly for the cinema. He became one of the organisers of Soviet cinema advertising. He exhibited from 1924 and was represented at the Monza-Milan International Exhibition in 1927. He died in Moscow.
Film posters include: 1926 *Evreyskoe schast'e* (Jewish Luck). 1927 M.Kapchinsky's *Café Franconi*, and the film *Playing with Fire*.
Lit *Paris-Moscou*, 1979.

RUMYANTSEV, Andrei Antipovich d.1907
Landscape painter.
Coll TG.

RUNDAL'TSOV, M. V. a.1918-19
He was engaged on Agitprop decorations on the Ekaterinsky Canal, Petrograd, in 1918. He participated in the First State Free Exhibition of Artworks in Petrograd in 1919.

RUSAKOV, Aleksandr Isaakovich 1898-1952
Painter. He studied at the Zvantseva school in Petersburg under M.N.Ignat'ev, at the Vkhutemas/Vkhutein in Leningrad from 1918 to 1924 under Dubovsky, Kardovsky, Karev and Osip Braz. He was a founder member of the group

Andrei Rublev. The Holy Trinity, *c.1410 20. Panel. 142 x 114 cm.
State Tretyakov Gallery, Moscow.*

Krug khudozhnikov (Circle of Artists) founded in Leningrad in 1926 with Pakhomov, Pakhulin, Malagis, Samokhvalov and others. He remained a member until 1932. He endured the Siege of Leningrad.
Lit A.M.Muratov, V.Manin et al. *Zhivopis' 20-30kh godov*, Sankt-Peterburg, 1991.
Coll RM, Roy Miles Gallery, London.
Colour plate p.367.

RUSHCHITS (RUSHITS), Ferdinand Eduardovich 1870-1936
Belorussian landscape painter. His subjects included scenes with many figures engaged in their daily life but heightened by a sense of colour and composition that made them dramatic and compositionally original. An example of this is *By the Catholic Church*, 1899, Museum of Belorussian Art, Minsk.
Coll TG; Museum of Belorussian Art, Minsk.

RUSOV (VOLKOV-MUROMZOV), Aleksandr Nikolaevich 1844-1928
Painter of genre and landscapes. His work included watercolours. He travelled to Egypt and settled in Venice. He exhibited at the Royal Academy in London from 1880. Sometimes he signed his work 'A.N.Roussoff'.
Coll TG; Derby Art Gallery.

RYABININ, Nikolai Leonidovch 1919-1951+
Sculptor of historical figure pieces. He worked with V.I. Skolozdra.

RYABUSHINSKY, Nikolai a.1907-1910
Painter. He exhibited with the Blue Rose group in 1907 and with the Golden Fleece in Moscow 1908 and 1909-10.

RYABUSHKIN, Andrei Petrovich   1861-1904
History and genre painter. He studied under Perov, Sorokin
and Pryanishnikov at the Moscow College 1875-82 and then
at the Academy in St. Petersburg 1882-90. He was one of the
so-called Young Wanderers. He particularly evoked Russian
village life of the 17th century. The awkwardness of his
paintings was deliberate and calculated. He emphasised the
doll-like cosmetics of rouged cheeks, white faces and drawn
eyebrows as well as decorative and colourful clothing. Inspired
in part by primitive and popular *lubok* prints, his paintings
retain a primitive air despite their fine finish. This is a
sophisticated construction designed to evoke a more primitive
and colourful era of merchants and peasants in a mythical
vision of Russia's past. He was represented at the Exhibition of
Russian and Finnish Artists in St. Petersburg in 1898 and at
the International Exhibition in Paris in 1900. He exhibited

Ol'ga Rozanova. Poster for 'First Productions in the World of the
Theatre of the Futurists', *December 1913. Colour lithograph. Signed.
91 x 65.5 cm.*
*The productions at Luna Park, St. Petersburg, were organised under the
auspices of the Union of Youth.*
Collection Mr. and Mrs. Nikita D.Lobanov-Rostovsky, London.

with the World of Art in 1901-3.
A Family, 1896, RM, displays his picturesque models as if on
a stage or in a booth. The materials of their clothes are varied,
exotic and fine yet the ground is covered in straw. The stiff
composition and the doll-like cosmetics of the women suggest
a deliberately primitive tendency on the part of the painter; by
contrast his sitters are innocent of this sophisticated attitude.
They think simply that they are well dressed. This taste for
folk culture was growing and had a far-reaching effect in the
early 20th century on such painters as Kandinsky, Larionov,
Goncharova, Shevchenko and many others. Ryabushkin in his
own way was a forerunner in this.
Coll Well represented at TG; RM.

RYANGIN, I.   a.1921
He exhibited with Kudryashov and others at the First State
Exhibition in Orenburg in 1921.

RYANGINA (RIANGINA), Serafima Vasilievna 1891-1955
Painter of Socialist Realist genre. She studied privately under
Tsionglinsky in St. Petersburg 1910-12 and at the Academy
1912-18.
After the Revolution she made posters and agitational work at
Orenburg. She studied under Kardovsky at the Vkhutemas in
Petrograd 1921-3. She was a member of AKhRR 1924-32. She
visited Germany and Italy in 1927. She was included in the
major exhibition in Moscow in 1927 marking the tenth
anniversary of the Revolution and in the First Touring
Exhibition of Painting and Graphics which opened in Moscow
in 1929. She was represented at the jubilee exhibition Artists
of the RSFSR over 15 Years held at the Russian Museum,
Leningrad, in 1932 and at the 1932 Venice Biennale.
Ever Higher, Museum of Russian Art, Kiev, is a vertiginous
painting of a pioneer man and young woman scaling the
heights of an electricity pylon (without safety harness). She is
fresh, untired and exhilarated at showing what Soviet woman
can achieve. The painting is dramatic, compositionally adept
and poster-like in its impact.
Lit A.M.Muratov, V.Manin et al. *Zhivopis' 20-30kh godov*,
Sankt-Peterburg, 1991.
Coll Kalinin Art Museum.

RYAZHSKY (RIAZHSKY), Grigori Grigorievich 1895-1952
Socialist Realist portrait and figure painter, graphic artist.
Forenames sometimes given as Georgi Georgievich or as Egor
Egorovich. Born at Ignatievo near Moscow. He lived in
Moscow from 1905. He left school in 1910 to work in a bank
whilst studying drawing in evening classes attending the
Prechistenki Workers' Course from 1910 to 1915 and the
studios of M.Leblanc, R.Baklanov and M.Severov during
1912-24. He was engaged on military service during 1915-17.
After the Revolution he studied with the Proletkult in Moscow
in 1918 but was also aware of the work of Malevich under whom
he studied at the Free Art Studios in Moscow 1918-19.
He exhibited at the Fifth State Exhibition: From
Impressionism to Non-Objective Art in Moscow 1918-19.
However he became committed to the application of easel
painting to political purposes. He worked as a military and
Proletkult artist at Samara 1919-20. He was an active and
founder member of the New Society of Painters (NOZh)
established in reaction to leftist trends in 1922. He became a
member of AKhRR 1923-4. His work was included in the
exhibition of Soviet art held at Harbin in 1926 and in Japan in

Aleksandr Rusakov. Railway Station, *1945. Oil on canvas. 60 x 76.2 cm.*
Roy Miles Gallery, London.

1927 and in the major exhibition in Moscow in 1927 marking
the tenth anniversary of the Revolution. He was also
represented at the First Touring Exhibition of Painting and
Graphics which opened in Moscow in 1929.
He subsequently joined RAPKh in 1930 and gained recognition
as a Socialist Realist portrait and figurative painter in the 1930s.
He was represented at the jubilee exhibition Artists of the
RSFSR over 15 Years held at the Russian Museum, Leningrad,
in 1932 and at the 1932 Venice Biennale.
He was made an Academician of the USSR. He died in Moscow.
Female Student, 1927, RM, is an heroic portrait typifying
committed partisan youth. It is loosely academic in handling.
Lit N.Shchekov *G.Ryazhsky*, Leningrad, 1935. V.Zhuravlev
G.G.Ryazhsky, Moscow, 1952. *G.G.Ryazhsky Album*, Moscow,
1958. *Paris-Moscou*, 1979. A.Z.Rudenstine *Costakis Collection*,
London, 1981.
Coll TG; RM; Costakis Collection.

RYBAKOV, Gavriil Fedorovich   **b.1859**
Painter. He participated in the Third Exhibition of Paintings
held at Ryazan in 1919.
Coll TG.

RYBAKOVA, L. I.   **a.1919**
Painter. She was represented at the First Exhibition of Works
of the Professional Union of Artists in Moscow in 1918 and at
the Fourth State Exhibition of Paintings (*IV Gosudarstvennaya
vystavka kartin*) in Moscow in 1919.

RYBINSKY, Nikolai Petrovich   **b.1835**
Landscape painter.
Coll TG.

RYBNIKOV, Aleksei Aleksandrovich   **1887-1949**
Painter, graphic artist. He was engaged on the decoration of
the Café Pittoresque in Moscow in 1918 together with Tatlin,
Yakulov, Rodchenko and others. He was a member of AKhRR
in 1925. He taught at the Kharkov Art Institute in 1934. He
was also active as a restorer. He died in Moscow.
Coll TG.

RYCHKOV, G. N.   **a.1918-1926**
Graphic artist. He was represented at the First Exhibition of
Works of the Professional Union of Artists in Moscow in 1918
and at the Second Exhibition of Cinema Posters held at the
Kamerny (Chamber) Theatre, Moscow, in 1926.

RYLOV, Arkadi Aleksandrovich   **1870-1939**

Painter. Born in the Kirov region. After studying at the Stieglitz School in 1888 he enrolled at the Society for the Encouragement of the Arts in St. Petersburg 1888-91 and then studied at the Academy under Kuindzhi 1894-7. He travelled to Germany, Austria, France and England in 1898. He exhibited with the Thirty-Six 1901-2 and with the World of Art between 1901 and 1911. He was represented in Diaghilev's display of Russian art at the 1906 Salon d'Automne in Paris. He also exhibited with the New Association of Artists 1905-9 and with the Union of Russian Artists 1908-17. He exhibited with the First Izdebsky International Salon 1909-10 in Odessa.

After the Revolution he participated in the First State Free Exhibition of Artworks in Petrograd in 1919. He taught at the Free Art Studios (SVOMAS) in Petrograd 1918-19 and later at the Technical-Artistic Institute. He contributed to the Exhibition of Paintings by Russian Artists held at Pskov in Spring 1920. He was a member of the Kuindzhi Society 1919-20 and was included in the enormous survey Exhibition of Paintings by Petrograd Artists of All Tendencies 1919-1923 held in Petrograd in 1923. He exhibited with The Sixteen 1922-7 and was a member of AKhRR 1926. He was represented at the jubilee exhibition Artists of the RSFSR over 15 Years held at the Russian Museum, Leningrad, in 1932. Sometimes he signed his work 'Rylof'. He died in Leningrad.

Writings A.A.Rylov *Vospomonaniya* (Recollections), Leningrad, 1940. A.A.Rylov *Vospominaniya*, Leningrad, 1960.
Lit V.Anikeeva *A.A.Rylov*, Leningrad-Moscow, 1937. G.Lebedev *A.A.Rylov*, Moscow-Leningrad, 1949. A.Fedorov-Davydov *A.A.Rylov*, Moscow, 1959. A.Antonova *Proizvedeniya A.A.Rylova v GRM*, Leningrad, 1972. *Paris-Moscou*, 1979. A.M.Muratov, V.Manin et al. *Zhivopis' 20-30kh godov*, Sankt-Peterburg, 1991.
Coll TG; RM.

RYNDIN, Vadim Fedorovich   **1902-1974**

Theatre designer. Born in Moscow. He participated in the seventh exhibition of the group *L'Araignée* (The Spider) at the Galerie Devambe in Paris in 1925. He exhibited with the *Makovets* group including the third and last exhibition of the group in Moscow 1925-6 and was included in the exhibition of Russian Graphic Art in Riga in 1929. He died in Moscow.

Theatre design Productions designed by him for the director A.Tairov at the Kamerny (Chamber) Theatre in Moscow included

1927 November: M.Yu.Levidov's *Zagovora ravnykh* (Equal Plots).
1928 December: M.A.Bulgakov's *Bagrovyy ostrov* (Crimson Island). Act 2 had spectacular constructed scenery with metallic-looking palm trees flanking a stylised spiral hill top.
1931 December: N.G.Kulish's *Pateticheskaya Sonata* (Sonata Pathétique).
1932 May: L.S.Pervomaysky's *Neizvestnye soldaty* (Unknown Soldiers) which featured a steep ramp forming an architectural tribune on stage.
1932 November: P.D.Markish's *Kto-kogo* (Who's Who).
1933 May: S.Treadwell's *Mashinal'* (Machinale) which featured open work rectangular screens to form a prison.
1933 December: V.V.Vyshnevsky's *Optimisticheskaya tragediya* (Optimistic Tragedy) which featured an oval arena before a backdrop of clouds.
1934 December: *Egyptian Nights* with music by S.Prokofiev and a set of a stylised Egyptian tomb or palace stairway centrally positioned. This was based on texts by G.B.Shaw, Pushkin and Shakespeare.
1936 Shakespeare's *Much Ado About Nothing* at the Vakhtangov Theatre, Moscow. Designs in the Bakhrushin Theatre Museum, Moscow, show a stylised architectural set with heraldic pennants and towers before an intensely blue sky. Between the towers is a double arcade with the flitting carnival figures.
1937 November N.E.Virta's *Zemlya* (Earth) at the Moscow Art Theatre.
1938 October M.Gorky's *Dostigaev i drugie* (Dostigaev and Others) at the Moscow Art Theatre.
1958 January Shakespeare's *A Winter's Tale* at the Moscow Art Theatre.
Writings V.Ryndin *Kak sozdaetsya khudozhestvennoe oformlenie spektakley* (How Stage Sets are Created), Moscow, 1962. V.Ryndin *Khudozhnik i teatr* (The Artist and the Theatre), 1966.
Lit Nancy Van Norman Baer *Theatre in Revolution, Russian Avant-Garde Stage Design 1913-1935*, San Francisco and London, 1991.
Coll Bakhrushin Theatre Museum, Moscow.

RYNDZYUNSKAYA, Marina Davydovna   **1877-1946**

Sculptor. She was a member of the Society of Russian Sculptors from 1926. She was included in the major exhibition in Moscow in 1927 marking the tenth anniversary of the Revolution. She exhibited at the 1932 Venice Biennale.

Maklamat Nakhangova: Young Stakhanovite of the Cotton Fields, 1940, granite, TG, has a real hieratic power despite its Socialist Realist theme. It recalls Assyrian carvings. The young woman in traditional dress presents her produce like an offering at a temple.

RYUSS, R. M.   **a.1918-1919**

Painter represented at the First Exhibition of Works of the Professional Union of Artists in Moscow in 1918 and at the Ninth State Exhibition of Paintings: Naturalism and Realism in Moscow in 1919.

RZHEVSKAYA, Antonina Leonardovna   **1861-1934**

Painter of genre, portraits, landscapes and still-lifes. Born in the Tver region to an impoverished family of the nobility. She studied part-time at the Moscow College 1880-4 and under Martynov. She exhibited with the Wanderers from 1897 and became a member in 1899.
Coll TG.

S

S.C. see **SHCHEDRIN, S. F.**

SABASHNIKOVA, Margarita V.　　　**1882-1973**
Painter, graphic artist. She married the poet Maksimilian Voloshin. She exhibited with the World of Art in 1906 and was represented in Diaghilev's display of Russian art at the 1906 Salon d'Automne in Paris.
Lit *Twilight of the Tsars*, London, 1991.
Coll TG.

SABSAY, Pinkhos (Petr) Vladimirovich　　　**1893-1930+**
Azerbaijani sculptor. He was active in the 1930s at Baku where his monuments included *S.M.Kirov* and *M.F.Akhundov* 1930.

SADKOV, V. N.　　　**a.1927-1932**
He was included in the major exhibition in Moscow in 1927 marking the tenth anniversary of the Revolution and in the jubilee exhibition Artists of the RSFSR over 15 Years held at the Russian Museum, Leningrad, in 1932.

SADOVNIKOV, Vasili Semenovich　　　**1800-1879**
Lithographer. He produced views of St. Petersburg.
Coll Ashmolean Museum, Oxford.

SAFRONOVA, A. F.　　　**a.1918-1925**
She exhibited at the Fifth State Exhibition: From Impressionism to Non-Objective Art in Moscow 1918-19 and at the seventh exhibition of the group *L'Araignée* (The Spider) at the Galerie Devambe in Paris in 1925.

SAGAYDACHNY, Evgeniy Yakovlevich　　　**1886-1961**
He studied at the Academy in St. Petersburg before 1910 and was a contributor to Kul'bin's exhibitions Triangle and Impressionists 1909-10. He exhibited with the Union of Youth 1910-11 and with the *Oslinyy Khvost* (Donkey's Tail) group in Moscow in 1912.
He saw military service in the First World War and later lived at Lvov. The name Sagaydachny appeared on the April 1919 list of artists for acquisitions by the envisaged Museum of Painterly Culture.
Lit J.Howard *The Union of Youth — An Artists' Society of the Russian Avant-Garde*, Manchester and New York, 1992.

SAKHAROV, N. A.　　　**a.1922**
He was represented at the First Russian Art Exhibition in Berlin in 1922.

SAKHAROV, S.　　　**a.1922**
Painter. He was a founder member of the group *Bytie* (Existence) formed in 1921 partly in protest at 'the narrowness of leftist art' and contributed to its first exhibition in 1922.

SALAKHOV, T. T.　　　**1928-1960+**
Painter of industrial landscapes and portraits. Born in Soviet Azerbaijan. His *Portrait of the Composer Kara Karaev* is severely edited and yet informal. The sitter is placed in strict profile,

hands on knees and deep in thought, before a grand piano. The effect is of a decisive drama and the image has a graphic clarity. Books on the piano make rectangles which may just conceivably refer to Suprematism. There is nothing obviously Soviet about this portrait.

SALVINI-BARACCI, Ettore　　　**a.1891-1896+**
Milanese painter working at Saratov. He taught P.V.Kuznetsov, V.Konovalov and Borisov-Musatov c.1891-6.

SAMOILENKO, S. S.　　　**a.1918**
Exhibited with the Artists of the Leftist Federation of the Professional Union in 1918 along with Rodchenko, Tatlin and others.

SAMOILOV, Anatoli V.　　　**a.1901-1910**
Poster designer active in the period 1901-10.
Lit *Twilight of the Tsars*, London, 1991.
Coll Lenin Library, Moscow.

SAMOKHVALOV, Aleksandr Nikolaevich　　　**1894-1971**
Painter, graphic artist, theatre designer. Born in the Kalinin region. He studied architecture at the Academy in Petrograd 1914-18.
After the Revolution he exhibited with the World of Art in 1917 and studied under Petrov-Vodkin, D.Kardovsky, A.Rylov and V.Savinsky at the Moscow Free Art Studios (SVOMAS)/Vkhutemas from 1920 to 1923. He was included in the enormous survey Exhibition of Paintings by Petrograd Artists of All Tendencies 1919-1923 held in Petrograd in 1923. He was represented at the Paris International Exhibition in 1925. He exhibited with the Circle of Artists 1926-9 and with the group October 1930-2. He was included in the 1928 exhibition of Acquisitions by the State Art Collections Fund held in Moscow and in the jubilee exhibition Artists of the RSFSR over 15 Years held at the Russian Museum, Leningrad, in 1932. He taught monumental painting in Leningrad 1948-51. He died in Leningrad.
**Young Woman in a Football Jersey*, 1932, RM, and *Female Athlete*, 1933, both show stylised images of attractive, healthy young women depicted as ikons of vigour and well-being.
Writings A.Samokhvalov *Moy tvorchesky put'*, Leningrad, 1977.
Lit N.Strugatsky *A.Samokhvalov*, Leningrad-Moscow, 1933. *A.Samokhvalov*, exh. cat., Leningrad, 1974. *Paris-Moscou*, 1979. A.M.Muratov, V.Manin et al. *Zhivopis' 20-30kh godov*, Sankt-Peterburg, 1991.
Coll RM.

SAMOKISH, Nikolai Semenovich　　　**1860-1944**
Ukrainian battle painter, etcher, illustrator. Born at Neshin. He studied at the Academy in St. Petersburg 1879-85 and subsequently taught there. His pupils included Petr Miturich and Lev Bruni. He was represented at the Paris International Exhibition in 1889. He observed and recorded the Russo-Japanese War 1904-5.
After the Revolution he adapted his battle painting experience to encompass Red Army themes.
**The Red Army Crossing the Sivash*, 1935, Simferolpol Art Gallery, is a colossal horse and artillery battle painting in which the troops fight in through and across the river in a mass of horses and plumes of smoke.
Coll TG; Simferopol Art Gallery.

Nikolai Sapunov. Serebryakov's Dining Room. *Oil on canvas. 50 x 68 cm.*
A set design for Chekov's 'Uncle Vanya' in an unidentified production c.1910-11.
Collection Mr. and Mrs. Nikita D.Lobanov-Rostovsky, London.

Nikolai Sapunov. Décor for Carlo Gozzi's 'Princess Turandot', *c.1912. Gouache on paper. 79.2 x 102 cm.*
Malmö Konstmuseum.

interior (Bakhrushin Theatre Museum). The set design for the Ball in Act 2 (Armenian Art Gallery, Yerevan) is robust and grotesque with figures charging inelegantly in their dance within an interior of claustrophobic closeness.

1910 he executed A.Golovin's décor for Diaghilev's production of Stravinsky's *Firebird* in Paris.

1911 September: Molière's *Le Bourgeois Gentilhomme* produced by Fedor Komissarzhevsky at the K.Nezlobin Theatre, Moscow: a pageant in the Comedia dell'Arte mode but richly decorated in subdued colours and emphatically exotic (TG).

1912 Autumn: Carlo Gozzi's *Princess Turandot* produced by Fedor Komissarzhevsky at the K.Nezlobin Theatre, Moscow.

Lit V.Bryusov et al. *Sapunov*, Moscow, 1916. M.Alpatov, E.Gunst *N.N.Sapunov*, Moscow, 1965. *Paris-Moscou*, 1979. J.E.Bowlt *Russian Stage Design. Scenic Innovation. From the Collection of Mr. and Mrs. Nikita D.Lobanov-Rostovsky*, Jackson, MS, exh. cat.,1982. *Twilight of the Tsars*, London, 1991. A.Kamensky *The World of Art Movement*, Leningrad, 1991. Dzhon Boult (John Bowlt) *Khudozhniki russkogo teatra. Sobranie Nikity i Niny Lobanovykh-Rostovskikh*, Moscow, 1991.
Coll Well represented at TG; RM; Bakhrushin Theatre Museum, Moscow; Museum of Russian Art, Yerevan.
Colour plates p.370.

SARKSYAN, Ara Migranovich   1902-1962
Armenian sculptor of portraits and monuments. His relief carving on the *Monument to Heroes of the May Uprising in Leningrad*, 1930-1, basalt, employs very flat forms in low relief to represent a crowd of figures of armed workers with a strong, repetitive rhythm to their limbs.

SARMA
The abbreviated name of the Association of Revolutionary Artists of Georgia (*Assotsiatsiya revolyutsionnikh khudozhnikov Gruzii*) operative 1929-32.

SAR'YAN, Martiros Sergeevich   1880-1972
Armenian painter, graphic artist, theatre designer. He was inspired by the traditions of his native folk art but equally by the achievements of French Fauve painting. The result was both sophisticated and apparently simple, exhibiting an immediacy and decorative freshness characteristic of each of these sources of inspiration. Born at Rostov-on-Don. He studied under Serov and Korovin at the Moscow College 1897-1904. After exhibiting with the Scarlet Rose group in Saratov, in 1907 he also exhibited with its sequel the Blue Rose in 1907. He became an active contributor to the Golden Fleece exhibitions 1908-9. He travelled to Turkey in 1910, Egypt in 1911 and Persia in 1913. During this time he exhibited with the World of Art 1910-16 and with the Union of Russian Artists 1910-11.

After the Revolution his name appeared on the April 1919 list of artists for acquisitions by the envisaged Museum of Painterly Culture. He settled at Erevan, Armenia, in 1921.There he established the Museum of Archaeology and Ethnography, the School of Art and the Union of Armenian Painters. He was represented at the First Russian Art Exhibition in Berlin in 1922. He was also represented at the Venice Biennale in 1924 and was in Paris 1926-8. He was a member of the 4 Arts society which was founded in 1924. He contributed to the Third Exhibition of Paintings by Artists from Kaluga and Moscow held in Kaluga in 1925 and to the International Exhibition in Dresden in 1926. He was included

in the 1928 exhibition of Acquisitions by the State Art Collections Fund held in Moscow. He also executed illustrations for books. He made stage designs for theatres in Odessa in 1930.

He was represented at the jubilee exhibition Artists of the RSFSR over 15 Years held at the Russian Museum, Leningrad, in 1932 and at the 1932 Venice Biennale. He died at Erevan.
The Date Palm, Egypt, 1911, TG, exemplifies his flat poster-like colour executed in tempera on card. This Armenian Fauve painter was curiously sophisticated yet simple. His painting was confidently assertive almost to the point of slightness, but his assured ability with colour and tone indicates a wealth of experience. Folk art, the Middle East, Armenian tradition and Fauve painting all coalesce in Sar'yan.
The Mountains, 1923, TG, is a vertical panorama of a vast patchwork of fields painted in flat, bright colours almost resembling a tapestry. Along the bottom edge a diminutive ploughman passes.
Theatre design 1933 A.A.Spendiarov's opera *Almast* at the Opera Theatre, Erevan.
1935 A.L.Stepanyan's comic opera *Khrabryy Nazar* (Brave Nazar) at the Armenian Opera Theatre, Erevan.
Writings M.Saryan *Iz moei Zhizni* (From my Life), Moscow, 1971.
Lit A.Mikhailov *M.S.Sar'yan*, Moscow, 1958. R.Drampyan *Sar'yan*, Moscow, 1964. A.A.Kamensky *Sar'yan*, Moscow, 1968. A,Kamensky *Martiros Sarjan*, Dresden, 1975. *Paris-Moscou*, 1979. A.Kamensky *Sar'yan*, Leningrad, 1987. *Twilight of the Tsars*, London, 1991.
Coll Sar'yan Museum, Erevan; TG; RM; Yaroslav Art Museum.
Colour plate p.371.

SASHIN, Andrei Timofeevich   1896-1965
Theatre designer. He was a member of Filonov's School and his designs are closely related to the compartmentalised and crystalline techniques first developed by Filonov.
Lit Dzhon Boult (John Bowlt) *Khudozhniki russkogo teatra. Sobranie Nikity i Niny Lobanovykh-Rostovskikh*, Moscow, 1991.
Coll RM.
Colour plate p.374.

SAVEN, N. N.   a.1907
Theatre designer. He was designing for the director V.Meyerhold in 1907.

SAVICHEV, V. A.   a.1923
Painter. He contributed to the second exhibition of the group *Bytie* (Existence) in 1923.

SAVIN, Istoma   a.c.1600
Ikon painter. He was the brother of the ikon painter Nikifor Savin. He worked for the Stroganov family and became an exponent of the Stroganov School of ikon painting.
Coll TG.

SAVIN (ISTOMIN), Nikifor
Ikon painter. He was the brother of the ikon painter Istoma Savin. He became a major figure of the Stroganov School.
Coll TG; RM.

SAVINKOV, V. V.   a.1912-1917
Painter of landscapes and still-lifes. He exhibited with the Knave of Diamonds in 1912.

After the Revolution he exhibited with the Knave of Diamonds in Moscow in 1917.

Zinaida Serebryakova. The Artist's Son Aleksandr Borisovich Serebryakov. *65 x 54 cm.*
Collection Mr. and Mrs. Nikita D.Lobanov-Rostovsky, London.

SAVINOV, Aleksandr Ivanovich   1881-1942
Painter. He studied at the Bogolyubov Drawing School at Saratov under Konovalov 1897-1900 and at the Academy in St. Petersburg under Tsionglinsky, Repin and Kardovsky 1901-8. He then travelled to Italy on a scholarship 1909-11. He exhibited with the New Society of Artists from 1910.
After the Revolution he exhibited with the World of Art in December 1917 in Moscow. He taught at the Free Art Studios (SVOMAS) in Saratov 1918-21 and from 1922 at the Academy of Arts in Leningrad. He was included in the enormous survey Exhibition of Paintings by Petrograd Artists of All Tendencies 1919-1923 held in Petrograd in 1923.
Lit *Twilight of the Tsars*, London, 1991.
Coll TG; Saratov Art Museum.
Colour plate opposite.

SAVINSKY, Vasili Evmenevich   1859-1937
Painter of portraits and landscapes. He taught at the Higher Art Institute of the Academy in St. Petersburg where Konchalovsky was among his students during the period 1898-1905.
After the Revolution he was a member of the Kuindzhi Society of Artists in Leningrad in 1929. He was included in the 1928 exhibition of Acquisitions by the State Art Collections Fund held in Moscow.
Coll TG.

SAVITSKY, Georgiy Konstantinovich   1887-1949
Painter. He was engaged on Agitprop decorations on Bolshoi Prospekt, Petrograd, in 1918. These included decorations for the pediment of the Academy of Sciences featuring symbols of measurement and machinery which led up to standing figures of workers flanking a radiant book that signified knowledge

(Museum of the Great October Socialist Revolution, Moscow). With V.Kuchumov and V.Simonov he also designed flags and other street decorations. He participated in the First State Free Exhibition of Artworks in Petrograd in 1919. He was represented at the jubilee exhibition Artists of the RSFSR over 15 Years held at the Russian Museum, Leningrad, in 1932.
*The Tamansk Red Army Campaign in 1918, 1933, is Socialist Realist military genre painting applied to recent history. It is given a benign aspect by the rescue of men, women, children and their belongings piled on handcarts.

SAVITSKY, Konstantin Apollonovich   1844-1905
Painter. Born at Taganrog. He studied at the Academy in St. Petersburg 1862-71. From 1872 he exhibited with the Wanderers and became a member in 1874. The same year he produced *Repairing the Railway*, 1874, TG, a panoramic, multi-figure scene of labour with strong peasants and wheelbarrows. He produced heavily populated narrative genre paintings including *Bringing out the Ikon to the People* of 1878

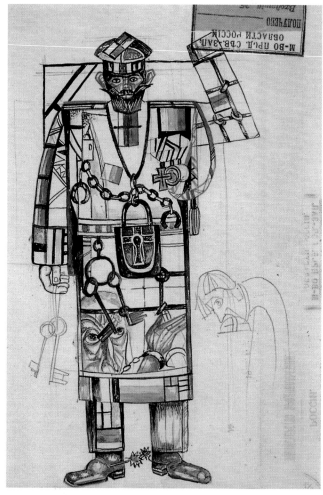

Andrei Sashin. Costume Study for Stepan Ilych Ukhovertov in Gogol's play 'The Government Inspector', *1927. Watercolour, pencil, black ink. 23 x 20 cm.*
Collection Mr. and Mrs. Nikita D.Lobanov-Rostovsky, London.

Aleksandr Savinov. Dusk, *1902-4. Oil on canvas. 54.5 x 81 cm.*
Saratov State Art Museum.

Sergei Sen'kin. Painting, *c.1920-1. Tempera on canvas. 50.5 x 63 cm.*
Private collection, courtesy Annely Juda Fine Art, London.

and *Dispute on the Boundary* of 1897.
To War, 1880-8, RM, depicts the departure of troops by train. It is reminiscent of Frith's *Paddington Station* in the detail of its description although the handling remains vigorous and the whole scene is a little histrionic. He taught at the Moscow College and at the Penza School of Art.
Lit E.G.Levenfish *K.A.Savitsky*, Leningrad-Moscow, 1959.
Coll Major holdings at TG; RM.

SAVITSKY, M. A. 1922-1967+
Painter. He was inspired by both Petrov-Vodkin and by Mexican mural painters. The *Partisans' Madonna*, 1967, TG, recalls Petrov-Vodkin in the way that it transfers the Christian image into a Soviet context. The precise technique and the picture space have the same effect.
Coll TG.

SAVRASOV, Aleksei Kondratevich 1830-1897
Landscape painter. Born in Moscow. He studied at the Moscow College 1844-50. He was a founder member of the Wanderers and became a major figure in later 19th century Russian landscape painting. He directed the landscape studio of the Moscow College from 1857 to 1882.
Little Yard in Winter, 1870s, TG, fluidly depicts a rural yard among wooden houses in the snow viewed from an upstairs

Zinaida Serebryakova. Seated Moroccan Woman, *1928. Pastel. Signed and inscribed 'Marrakesh 1928'. 61.5 x 47 cm. Reproduced by kind permission of Sotheby's London, sale 15.2.1984, lot 106.*

window. Birds and a duck peck about in the snow. There is a thin and leafless tree in the centre. This is a loosely handled, descriptive and atmospheric direct study.
Coll TG; RM.

SAVVICHEV,V. a.1921
A member of the *Bytie* (Existence) Society of Artists formed in Moscow in 1921.

SAZONOV, Vasili Kondratevich 1789-1870
Painter. His subjects include themes from the Napoleonic invasion.
Coll TG.

SCHERVACHIDZE = SHERVASHIDZE, A.K.

SCHOUBINE = SHUBIN, F.I.

SCHWABE, Johann Gotlieb (SHVABE, Aleksandr Petrovich) 1818-1872
Painter of animals and battle scenes. Born at Riga. He studied at the Academy in St. Petersburg and became a professor there in 1861. He died at Reval.
Coll TG.

SCHWARZ = SHVARTS, V.G.

SCOTTI, D. = SKOTTI, D.K.

SEDEL'NIKOV, Nikolai b.1905-1928+
Typographic designer. He was a founder member of the group October in 1928.

SEDOV, Grigori Semenovich 1836-1884
Painter, lithographer. He studied at the Academy in St. Petersburg. His work included portraits as well as Russian and religious themes. Sometimes he signed his work 'Sedoff' in latin script. The date of his death is sometimes given as 1886.
Coll TG; RM.

SEDOVA, E. D. a.1929
She was represented at the First Touring Exhibition of Painting and Graphics which opened in Moscow in 1929.

SELEZNEV, N. F. a.1900-1917
Painter. He was active in Kiev 1900-17 teaching at the Kiev Art Institute where Lentulov, c.1900-5, and Tyshler were among his pupils.

SEMENOV-MENES, Semen (Semion) Abramovich 1895-1982
Belorussian poster and theatre designer. Born at Grodno. He studied at Kharkov School of Art 1915-18. He was engaged in Agitprop projects in the early revolutionary period including the decoration of trains and boats and the design of posters for the Ukrainian branch of the Rosta agency. He moved to Moscow in 1925 and was engaged on design for posters, the theatre and exhibitions including the International Exhibitions at Paris in 1925, New York in 1926, Monza-Milan in 1927 and Cologne in 1928.
Lit *Paris-Moscou*, 1979.

SEMENOVA, Elena 1898-1927+
Designer. She was associated with the periodical *Lef* which Mayakovsky edited from 1923. A design for the interior of a workers' club, 1926, reveals a spacious adoption of production art furniture of the kind evolved at the Vkhutemas under Rodchenko, involving folding tables, screens and unit

production. She was also designing for the performances of the Blue Blouse agitational group 1926-7. In 1927 she was invited along with Varvara Stepanova and E.Lavinskaya to submit designs for the decoration of several squares in Moscow and was designing posters to mark the Tenth Anniversary of the Revolution. She was also at that time collaborating with Lavinskaya on the design of window displays for the Dom Knigi Giza (the State Publishing Book House).

SEMIRADSKY, Genrikh Ippolitovich   1843-1902
Painter of grandiose history pictures, somewhat reminiscent of a Russian Alma-Tadema. His paintings are clearly posed in the studio but convincingly telling his story of ancient times. An example is the enormous *Frina at a Celebration of Poseidon, the King of the Sea, at Eleusis*, 1889, RM. He assisted in the decoration of the Cathedral of Christ the Saviour in Moscow.
Coll TG.

SEN'KIN, Sergei Yakovlevich   1894-1963
Suprematist painter, constructor, designer and *photomonteur*. Born at Pekrovskoe-Stresknevo near Moscow. He studied at the Moscow College 1914-15.
After the Revolution he studied under Malevich at the Free Art Studios (SVOMAS) in Moscow 1918-19. He then worked as a military artist at Ekaterinburg (Sverdlovsk) and also attended the Vkhutemas in 1920. He was to become a close student of the Suprematism first launched by Malevich in 1915 and in 1921 he visited Malevich at Vitcbsk. He exhibited at the Vkhutemas in 1921 and in Petrograd in June 1922 he exhibited with the Union of New Tendencies in Art.
He also worked with Gustav Klucis. A declaration dated 8 February 1924 signed by Klucis and Sen'kin and published in *Lef* (No.1, 1924) announced the establishment of a Communist Collective: The Studio of Revolution within the Vkhutein to undermine the cult of artistic genius and direct creative activity towards revolutionary aims. He contributed to the All-Union Polygraphic Exhibition in Moscow in 1927. He turned to the design of books, posters and exhibitions including the International Press Exhibition in Cologne in 1928 where he assisted El Lissitzky. He was a founder member of the group October in 1928. He was designing posters in 1931 promoting the building of roads, railways and electrification. His design was still closely modelled upon the dynamic diagonals of Suprematism. His incorporation of photomontage was comparable with the techniques evolved by Klucis in poster design.
Book design V.Mayakovsy *Bez doklada ne vkhodit'* (No Admittance without Invitation), Moscow, 1930.
Lit A.Z.Rudenstine *Costakis Collection*, London, 1981. C.Lodder *Russian Constructivism*, New Haven and London, 1983. E.Weiss *Russische Avant-Garde, 1910-1930, Sammlung Ludwig, Köln*, Munich, 1986. S.Compton *Russian Avant-Garde Books 1917-34*, London, 1992.
Coll TG; Costakis Collection; Sammlung Ludwig, Cologne. Colour plate p.375.

SERAFIMOV, Sergei Savvich   1878-1939
He was engaged on Agitprop decorations at Senate Square, Petrograd, in 1918.

SERDYUKOV, Grigori   b.c.1744
Portrait painter.
Coll TG.

Zinaida Serebryakova. Self-portrait, *1945. Oil on canvas. Signed and dated. 55 x 44 cm. Malmö Konstmuseum.*

SEREBRYAKOV, Vasili Alekseevich (Aleksandrovich) 1810-1886
Painter of classical themes, portraits and still-lifes. He studied at the Academy in St. Petersburg.
Coll TG.

SEREBRYAKOVA, Zinaida Evgenievna   1884-1967
Painter of portraits and figure compositions. Born at Neskuchnoe, the family estate near Kharkov. She was the daughter of the sculptor Evgeni Lansere. Her mother was the sister of Alexandre Benois. Evgeni Lansere was her brother. She attended the Tenisheva School at Talashkino under Repin in 1901 and visited Rome and Capri 1902-3. She then studied under the portrait painter Osip Braz 1903-5 and went to Paris 1905-6 where she studied under Simon and Danet at the Académie de la Grande Chaumière.
She returned to St. Petersburg and became a member of the World of Art in 1906. She visited the Crimea in 1910. Her *Self-portrait*, exhibited at the Union of Russian Artists in 1910, was purchased by the Tretyakov Gallery. In 1911 she was in the Crimea but was also exhibiting with the World of Art from that year. She travelled to Switzerland and Italy in 1914. She contributed to the decorations of the Kazan Railway Station in Moscow in 1916 with Benois, her uncle, and Evgeni Lansere, her brother.
After the Revolution she lived in Kharkov where she worked at the University Archaeological Museum from 1918 to 1920 when she moved to Petrograd. In 1919 she participated in the First State Free Exhibition of Artworks in Petrograd and the First Exhibition of the Arts organised by the Kharkov Soviet of Workers' Deputies in Kharkov.
She worked under the People's Commissariat of the

Enlightenment (IZO Narkompros) in 1921. She exhibited in Leningrad and Moscow in 1924.

She emigrated to Paris in 1924. Her work was, however, included in the exhibition of Soviet art held at Harbin in 1926 and in Japan in 1927. She visited London in 1925 and 1926, Brittany in 1926 and Morocco in 1928 and 1932. She died in Paris.

Washing the Linen, 1910, TG, has a low horizon so that all four figures are seen against the sky, filling the canvas in a fluent and easy contraposto. Here is a painter of the observed pose who deliberately constructed compositions inspired by the Renaissance, but who grafted them with ease on to themes of Russian rural life. This is a painting of women in their youth and strength, monumental, calm and anonymous, yet at the same time practical and elegant with no trace of rhetoric in the depiction. This is almost a mural, well drawn, hiding its complexity, warm in colour and creamy in its *contre-jour* tonality.

Harvesting, 1915, Odessa Art Gallery, is an acceptance of the challenge of Renaissance precedent. The working women are firmly and clearly modelled against an extensive landscape and sky, each of them posed and separate from the others, each immaculately resolved.

Lit S.Ernst *Z.E.Serebryakova*, Petrograd, 1922. N.Radlov *Z.E.Serebryakova*, Leningrad, 1929. *Serebryakova*, exh. cat., Moscow, 1965. A.Savinov *Z.E.Serebryakova*, Leningrad, 1973. V.Knyazeva *Z.E.Serebryakova*, Moscow, 1979. *Paris-Moscou*, 1979. J.E.Bowlt *Russian Stage Design. Scenic Innovation. From the Collection of Mr. and Mrs. Nikita D.Lobanov-Rostovsky*, Jackson, MS, exh. cat.,1982. M.N.Yablonskaya *Women Artists of Russia's New Age*, London, 1990. A.Kamensky *The World of Art Movement*, Leningrad, 1991.

Coll TG; RM; Odessa Art Gallery.
Colour plate p.374.

SERGEEV, Sergei Petrovich   **a.1918-1920**
He was engaged on Agitprop decorations at Saratov c.1918 and also involved in the decoration of the propaganda trains *Red Cossack* and the Ukrainian train *Lenin* in 1920. A Sergeev appeared on the April 1919 list of artists for acquisitions by the envisaged Museum of Painterly Culture.

SERGEEVICH, Sergei Sergeevich (GLAGOL',
GOLOUSHEV, S.)   **1855-1920**
Landscape painter.
Coll TG.

SEROV, Valentin Aleksandrovich   **1865-1911**
Major painter, theatre designer. A painter of urbane

Valentin Serov. The Rape of Europa, *1910. Pencil, watercolour. Signed and dated. 29 x 46 cm. Collection Mr. and Mrs. Nikita D.Lobanov-Rostovsky, London.*

Silvestr Shchedrin. The Bay of Naples. *Oil on canvas. 50 x 61 cm.*
Reproduced by kind permission of Sotheby's London, sale 28.11.1991, lot 421.

sophistication who successfully adapted the disciplines of accurate academic portaiture to the vibrant colour of Impressionism. To a degree this achievement reflected that of Degas whom he knew as a friend.

Born at St. Petersburg, the son of the composer and music critic Aleksandr Serov. As a child he studied under Karl Köpping in Munich 1872-3. He received lessons from Ilya Repin in Paris and in Moscow 1874-5 and 1878-80. He then studied under Chistyakov at the Academy in St. Petersburg 1880-5 from the age of fifteen. In 1885 he visited Holland, Belgium and Germany. He designed opera productions for Mamontov's private opera in 1886. He visited Italy in 1887.

With a perceptual astuteness comparable to that of certain French Impressionists, Serov was equally a remarkable draughtsman. His portraits are amongst his major paintings and certain of these, including *Girl with Peaches*, 1887, TG, are in fact innovative Impressionist paintings in their analysis of the colour of a daylight portrait. Other portraits include the painters *Korovin* in 1891, *Levitan* in 1893 and the writer *Maxim Gorky* in 1904.

Serov was in Paris in 1889. He exhibited with the Wanderers from 1890 and became a member in 1894. He again produced designs for Mamontov's private opera in 1896, the year in which he met the painter and theatre designer Benois. In 1898 he was made an Academician and began to exhibit with the World of Art. He was represented at the Exhibition of Russian and Finnish Artists in St. Petersburg in 1898 and exhibited with the World of Art 1899-1906. Serov was also an influential and active teacher at the Moscow College from 1897 to 1909. He exhibited with the Munich Secession in 1900 and was awarded a Grand Prix at the Exposition Universelle in Paris. He made a second visit to Italy in 1904.

He was equally capable of biting satire or decorative fantasy. In 1905 he resigned from the Academy in protest against the fierce suppression of the uprisings of that year and contributed satirical drawings to the periodical *Zhupel*, amongst them his bitter and mock heroic *Soldier Boys, Brave Lads, Where is Your Glory?*, 1905, RM, in which the soldiers charge an unarmed crowd. *After the Suppression*, 1905, pursues the same theme by depicting the presentation of medals against a background of corpses. His interest in the theatre was evident in studies made of Stanislavsky, director of the Moscow Art Theatre, in the period 1905-8.

Diaghilev included his work in the display of Russian art at the 1906 Salon d'Automne in Paris and in 1907 Serov travelled to Greece with Leon Bakst. He executed sets for the Mariinsky Theatre in St. Petersburg in 1908. He made a third visit to Italy in 1910, returning via Paris where he assisted Diaghilev's production of the Russian Ballet at the Opéra. He produced paintings of various performers including Anna Pavlova dancing in *Les Sylphides* in 1909 and a notoriously stark study of Ida Rubinstein nude in 1910. He attended the International Exhibition in Rome in 1911.

Children. Sasha and Yura Serov, 1899, RM, is an informal double portrait devoid of sentimentality. The two children are caught in the half light of a subdued moment at the sea looking out across the beach. The paint is loosely handled in a few tones but the light is precisely captured as is the atmosphere of pensive stillness.

Peter II and Princess Elizaveta Riding to Hounds, 1900, RM, is a fluent composition that demonstrates all of Serov's skill and adaptability as the two riders rush forward with the dog observed by an old peasant. As a painting it is a bravura performance, loosely handled yet atmospheric in its descripton of the windy winter day, accurate in its anatomy of figures and horses and full of movement. It is Serov's reply to the growing popularity of themes from Russia's Imperial past that fascinated such World of Art painters as Benois, Lansere and Dobuzhinsky. It is accomplished with ease. He was a painter of natural facility. Later essays on comparable themes included *Young Peter I Riding in the Chase*, 1902, RM, and *Peter the Great*, 1907, TG.

The Rape of Europa, 1910, is an extraordinary painting of an archaic figure upon the swimming bull in the midst of a heaving but stylised sea and accompanied by dolphins. The effect, executed in flat tones of ochre and slightly mauve blue, is other-worldly, imposing and strange. There is also a bronze sculpture on this theme in RM.

Portrait of Ivan Morozov, 1910, TG, is forceful, direct and fluid in the handling of the paint. In the background hangs a painting which is probably a work by Matisse bought by the collector and merchant Morozov. It is a testament to Serov's own international interests and status as a painter.

Theatre design 1907 *Judith* at the Mariinsky Theatre, St. Petersburg (RM).

1909 June: *Judith*, opera by Aleksandr Serov produced by Diaghilev at the Théâtre du Châtelet, Paris, designed by Bakst and Valentin Serov.

1910 Curtain for Rimsky-Korsakov's *Schéhérazade* produced by Diaghilev: the first version of the curtain (RM) was a loose and even wild high, almost horizonless, view of a beach with stylised horsemen brushed in with a liquid and calligraphic technique.

Writings V.A.Serov *Perepiska 1884-1911*, Leningrad-Moscow, 1937.

Lit I.Grabar' *V.Serov*, Moscow, 1914 (republished Moscow, 1965). N.Radlov *V.E.Serov*, St. Petersburg, 1914. S.Ernst *V.A.Serov*, Petrograd, 1921. S.Makovsky *V.Serov*, Berlin-Paris, 1922. G.S.Arbuzov *Serov* Leningrad-Moscow, 1960. D.Sarabyanov *Serov*, Leningrad-Moscow, 1961. S.Druzhinin *V.A.Serov*, 1965. M.Kopshitser *Valentin Serov*, Moscow, 1967. V.S.Serova *Kak ros moi syn*, Leningrad, 1968. D.Sarabyanov, G.Arbuzov *Serov*, Leningrad, 1982 (English edition: New York, 1982). J.E.Bowlt *Russian Stage Design. Scenic Innovation. From the Collection of Mr. and Mrs. Nikita D.Lobanov-Rostovsky*, Jackson, MS, exh. cat.,1982. A.Kamensky *The World of Art Movement*, Leningrad, 1991. Dzhon Boult (John Bowlt) *Khudozhniki russkogo teatra. Sobranie Nikity i Niny Lobanovykh-Rostovskikh*, Moscow, 1991.

Coll TG; RM; Museum of the Moscow Art Theatre; Odessa Art Gallery; Ashmolean Museum, Oxford.

Colour plates pp.21, 378.

SEROV, Vladimir Aleksandrovich   **1910-1968**
Painter. His works include themes of Lenin painted in 1950.
Coll TG.

SERPINSKAYA, N. Ya.   **a.1918-1919**
Painter. She exhibited at the First Exhibition of Works of the Professional Union of Artists in Moscow in 1918 and at the

Valentin Serov. Study for the Orgy Scene in Holofernes' Camp, *1908. Watercolour, pencil. Inscribed lower left and dated 1908. 21 x 33.5 cm. Collection Mr. and Mrs. Nikita D.Lobanov-Rostovsky, London.*

Ninth State Exhibition of Paintings: Naturalism and Realism in Moscow in 1919.

SEVERIN, Ivan Mitrofanovich   1881-1964
Ukrainian painter. He studied at the Kraków Academy under Stanislawski until 1907 and then in Paris and Rome before returning to Bukovina in the Ukraine. He held a one-man exhibition in Kiev in 1911 and also exhibited with the Union of Youth in 1910.
After the Revolution he was represented at the First Russian Art Exhibition in Berlin in 1922.

SHABAT, A.M.   a.1918-1919
He exhibited at the Fifth State Exhibition: From Impressionism to Non-Objective Art in Moscow in 1918-19.

SHABL'-TABUEVICH, B. S.   a.1925-1929
Painter. He exhibited with the Society of Moscow Painters at its inaugural exhibition in Moscow in 1925 and was represented at the First Touring Exhibition of Painting and Graphics which opened in Moscow in 1929.

SHADR, Ivan Dmitrievich (IVANOV, I. D.)   1887-1941
Sculptor whose work exhibited a dynamic and dramatic fluency and slightly Rodinesque surface applied to heroic revolutionary themes. He studied under I.Zalkans at the First Industrial Art School in Ekaterinburg 1903-7 and at the Drawing School of the Society for the Encouragement of the Arts 1907-8. He also attended the Académie de la Grande Chaumière in Paris. French sculpture provided an important stimulus to his development and he was still studying the methods of Bourdelle and Rodin in the period 1910-14. In addition he studied at the Institute of Applied Arts in Milan 1911-12. He lived in Moscow from 1914.
After the Revolution he produced busts of *The Worker* in 1922, *The Peasant* in 1922 and *The Red Army Soldier* 1921-3, which established their monumental public form. He used dynamic rhythms and heroic characterisation to make his subjects monumental, generalised and public in their impact. He employed deep gouging of hollows to maximise the dramatic contrasts of light and shade. He was included in the major exhibition in Moscow in 1927 marking the tenth anniversary of the Revolution.
Works include *The Sower* 1922, a colossal *Lenin* 1925-7 in Georgia, plus a dramatic head and also a full-length portrait of the writer *Gorky* 1939 and a full-length *Pushkin* 1939. He was a member of the Society of Russian Sculptors in 1926. He died in Moscow.
Earth Attack, 1923, is a drilling machine and figure on a diagonal cleft of rock rising like a tank across a ridge. A related work is *Battle with the Earth*, 1923, a relief of a row of diagonally straining workers.
Tomb of Nemirovich-Danchenko, 1938-9, is an impressive monument to the theatre director in which a woman, seen in a back view and in the highest relief, presses up against the vertical slab of the tombstone.
Writings I.D.Shadr *Literaturnoe nasledie. Perepiska. Vospominaniya o skul'ptore*, Moscow, 1978.
Lit V.Shalimova *I.D.Shadr*, Leningrad, 1962. Yu.Kolpinsky *I.D.Shadr*, Moscow, 1964.See Mukhina.

SHAGAEV, N.I.   a.1919
Painter. He exhibited at the juryless Eighth State Exhibition in Moscow in 1919.

Ivan Shadr. The writer A.M.Gorky, *1939. Bronze. 51 x 24 x 22 cm.*

SHAGAL', M. Z. = CHAGALL, Marc

SHALIMOV, N. G.   a.1921
Sculptor. He was a member of the *Bytie* (Existence) Society of Artists formed in Moscow in 1921. In the early Soviet period he ran the Army Puppet Theatre at Ashkhabad with the artists V.V.Khvostenko and E.A.Khvostenko, producing plays by Molière, Cervantes and the epic *Stepan Razin*.

SHAMSHIN, Petr Mikhailovich   1811-1895
Portrait painter.
Coll TG.

SHANKS, Emiliya Yakovlevna   1857-1936
Coll TG.

SHAPOSHNIKOV, Boris Valentinovich   1890-1956
Painter. Born in Moscow. He studied at Moscow University 1909-12 and at the Moscow Archaeological Institute. He studied at Yuon's school and also received tuition from N.N.Sapunov and N.P.Feofilaktov. He attended the Rome Academy 1913-14. He then attended military training and was in military service in 1917.
After the Revolution he was engaged on the decoration of the Café Pittoresque in Moscow in 1918 together with Yakulov, Tatlin, Rodchenko and others and he led the decorative art subsection of IZO in September 1918 to June 1920. His name appeared on the April 1919 list of artists for acquisitions by the

Iosif Shkol'nik. Design for an Unidentified Stage Production. *Gouache. 49 x 55.4 cm.*
Collection Mr. and Mrs. Nikita D.Lobanov-Rostovsky, London.

envisaged Museum of Painterly Culture. He exhibited at the Fifth State Exhibition: From Impressionism to Non-Objective Art in Moscow 1918-19 and participated in the Third Exhibition of Paintings held at Ryazan in 1919. He taught art history at the Moscow Proletkult from 1920. In 1921 he joined the State Academy of Artistic Sciences (GAKhN). He published theoretical works on art and museums.
Lit *L'Avant-garde russe 1905-1925*, exh. cat., Musée des Beaux-Arts, Nantes, 1993.
Coll Astrakhan Art Museum; Ivanovo Art Museum; Ul'yanovsk Art Museum.

SHAPSHAL, Ya. F.   **a.1918-1919**
Graphic artist. An exhibitor at the First Exhibition of Works of the Professional Union of Artists in Moscow in 1918. Shapshal appeared on the April 1919 list of artists for acquisitions by the envisaged Museum of Painterly Culture and was represented in the Fourth State Exhibition of Paintings (*IV Gosudarstvennaya vystavka kartin*) in Moscow in 1919.

SHARIKOV, S. F.   **a.1926**
Graphic artist. He was represented at the Second Exhibition of Cinema Posters held at the Kamerny (Chamber) Theatre, Moscow, in 1926.

**SHARLEMAN' (BODE-SHARLEMAN'), Adol'f Iosipovich
1826-1901**
Theatre designer who executed pastoral designs for a ballet in 1868.
Coll TG.

SHARSHUN = CHARCHOUNE, S.

SHARVIN, Yakov Vasilievich   **1838-1880**
Painter whose works include *The Sick Mother*, 1867, at TG.
Coll TG.

SHATALIN, Viktor Vasilievich   **1926-1957+**
Socialist Realist landscape painter.

SHCHANKIN, Vasili Nikolaevich   **1876-1930**
Landscape painter. After the Revolution he was represented at

the First Exhibition of Works of the Professional Union of Artists in Moscow in 1918.
Coll TG.

SHCHEDRIN, Fedosy Fedorovich   **1751-1825**
Major neo-classical monumental sculptor in marble and bronze with a flair for the dramatic and expressive handling of classical themes as well as portraits. He studied with M.Kozlovsky under Nicolas Gillet at the Academy in St. Petersburg enrolling in 1764. He travelled to Florence on a scholarship from the Academy in 1773 but settled briefly in Rome before transferring to Paris where he studied under C.-G.Allegrain. His works included sculptures for the Admiralty in St. Petersburg as well as *Marsyas*, 1776, bronze, TG, which is a *tour de force* of explicit straining musculature, and *Sleeping Endymion*, 1779, bronze, TG. He executed a figure of the *Neva* for a fountain in 1804. He was the father of the painter Silvestr F.Shchedrin.
*Venus, 1792, marble, RM, is a virtuoso performance of carving in neo-classical mode which earned him the title of Academician in 1794. It pays close attention to antique examples but still retains a trace of the unidealised life-room

David Shterenberg. Still-life with Fish, Glass and Bottle. *Gouache and collage on card. 41.6 x 29.7 cm.*
Reproduced by kind permission of Sotheby's London, sale 6.4.1989, lot 569.

Kirill Sokolov. East End from 'London Set', *1984, Pt. I. Screen print and collage. 1m 2 cm x 70 cm.*
Pushkin Museum, Moscow.

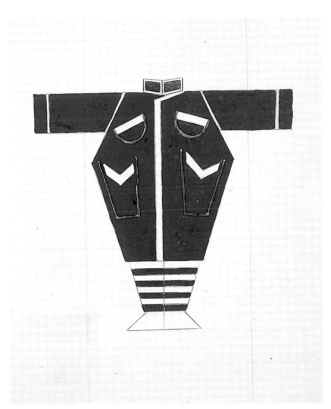

Varvara Stepanova. Costume Design for Sukhovo-Kobylin's
'Tarelkin's Death', *1922.*
The play was produced by Meyerhold.
Collection Mr. and Mrs. Nikita D.Lobanov-Rostovsky, London.

model posing for the sculpture despite the formulaic features
of the idealised head. It also exhibits the contraposto of the
idealised form of the female figure and is a consummately
professional, if somewhat academic, carving.
Sea Nymphs Carrying the Heavenly Globe, 1812, RM, was
designed to adorn the Admiralty Arch in St. Petersburg.
Coll TG; RM.

SHCHEDRIN, Semen Fedorovich   **1745-1804**
Painter, engraver. The son of a soldier he studied at the
Academy in St. Petersburg. He then travelled to Paris and
Rome only returning after some nine years. His subjects
included elaborately composed idyllic landscapes and
architectural views of St. Petersburg. Sometimes he signed his
work 'S.Chedrin'.
The Italian Fountain at Peterhof, 1799-1801, shows people
standing in admiration before the high spurt of the fountain
among tall trees, with a distant view of the cascades beyond.
Coll TG; Ashmolean Museum, Oxford.
See Silvestr F. Shchedrin.

SHCHEDRIN, Silvestr Fedosievich   **1791-1830**
Romantic painter of Italianate landscapes and views of St.
Petersburg. He was the son of the sculptor Fedosy F.
Shchedrin. After studying under M.M.Ivanov at the Academy
in St. Petersburg he travelled to Italy on a scholarship in 1819.
He was painting in Rome and Naples in 1819, at Tivoli in
1822, and at Sorrento in 1825. He lived in Naples from 1825
and remained in Italy until his death in Sorrento. Sometimes
he signed his work 'Silw. Chedrin' or 'S.C'. His landscapes,
which included coastal scenes, were lyrical and intimate works
painted with an inquisitive eye. He paid equal attention to
buildings and people painting with a sophisticated control of
chiaroscuro and light. His views of Rome are thereby
enlivened with genre scenes of fishermen, for example, in the

Silvestr Shchedrin. An Italian Village Road. *Oil on canvas.*
48.7 x 61.5 cm.
Photograph Hammer Galleries, New York.

foreground. Some of his landscapes have the air of a latterday Russian Claude in their golden light and majestic composition of ancient buildings in Rome.
Fishermen on the Shore, 1820s, RM, is an immaculately composed and polished work full of effects: the wide, expansive sky is enriched with a glowing light and traces of high ethereal clouds. In the far distance ships pass along the sea's horizon. A building establishes the middle distance, and before it the life of the shore is depicted with boats drawn up on to the beach, and figures pulling in the nets with an easy indolence in harmony with the overall atmosphere of calm splendour.
Veranda with Vines, 1828, TG, is an original and intimate scene which avoids formulaic composition. It contrasts a high view of a bay with the tunnel of vines along the veranda populated by grape pickers, a boy and a youth, in the foreground.
Coll Major holdings at TG; RM.
Colour plate p.379.

SHCHEDROVSKY, Ignatii Stepanovich   1815-1870
Painter whose subjects included landscapes and still-lifes painted in a stilted and rather primitive style, with precise attention to detail but less grasp of overall control of perspective or proportion.
Landscape with Hunters, c.1830, RM, depicts a horseman of superior social status by a bridge and in conversation with two men. They are dwarfed by nearby trees. In the distance is a house. Little is happening but there is nevertheless a clear indication of Russian rural life of the period and the painting does not lose charm for being simple and a little unprofessional.
Lit B.Suris *I.S.Shch.*, 1957.
Coll TG.

SHCHEGLOV, Valerian Vasilievich   1901-1984
Painter, graphic artist. He contributed to the Third Exhibition of Paintings by Artists from Kaluga and Moscow held in Kaluga in 1925. He moved from Kaluga in the 1920s to work for Moscow journals as a graphic artist.

**SHCHEKOTIKHINA-POTOTSKAYA, Aleksandra
Vasilievna   1892-1967**
Ceramics artist, theatre designer. Born in the Ukraine. She studied under Roerich and Bilibin at the Society for the Encouragement of the Arts in St. Petersburg 1908-15. In 1910 she toured North Russia with Maria Lebedeva and in 1913 she travelled to Greece, Italy and France where she attended the Académie Ranson in Paris under Denis, Vallotton and Sérusier. She was engaged on theatre design for Diaghilev 1913-14. She exhibited with the World of Art from 1915.
After the Revolution she participated in the First State Free Exhibition of Artworks in Petrograd in 1919. She executed designs for the State Porcelain Factory between 1918 and 1923 including plates illustrating *The Commissar* and *The History of the Revolution*, 1921.
In 1923 she travelled with her second husband, the artist Bilibin, to Egypt, Ethiopia, Syria and Palestine. She was represented at the International Exhibition in Paris in 1925 and was awarded a medal there. She settled in Paris with Bilibin from 1925 to 1936, held a one-person exhibition at the Galerie Druet in 1926 and began to exhibit at the Salon d'Automne and the Salon des Indépendants. She was represented at the jubilee exhibition Artists of the RSFSR over 15 Years held at the Russian Museum, Leningrad, in 1932.
She returned to Leningrad with Bilibin in 1936 and together they produced designs for Rimsky-Korsakov's *The Tale of Tsar Saltan* in 1937. She worked under Suetin for the Lomonosov Porcelain Factory from 1936 to 1956. She held a one-person exhibition in Leningrad in 1955.
Bellringer, 1921, is a plate design elegantly drawn in which the well dressed bellringer activates the large black and gold bells by means of tenuous cords. Between the images the lettering spells out 'Hail to the Soviet Congress'.
Theatre design 1913 Stravinsky's *Rite of Spring* produced by Diaghilev in Paris on which she assisted Roerich.
1914 Borodin's *Prince Igor* produced by Diaghilev in London

on which she again worked with Roerich.

1937 Rimsky-Korsakov's *The Tale of Tsar Saltan* designed in collaboration with Bilibin.

Lit V.S.Noskovich *A.V.Shchekotikhina-Pototskaya*, Leningrad, 1929. N.Lobanov-Rostovsky *Revolutionary Ceramics*, London, 1990.

SHCHERBAKOVA   a.1925
She was represented at the Paris International Exhibition in 1925.

SHCHERBATOV   a.1899
Painter. He exhibited with the World of Art in St. Petersburg in 1899.

SHCHERBINOVSKY, Dmitri Anfimovich   1867-1926
He participated in the First State Free Exhibition of Artworks in Petrograd in 1919. He was represented at the First Russian Art Exhibition in Berlin in 1922. A Shcherbinovsky contributed to the Third Exhibition of Paintings by Artists from Kaluga and Moscow held in Kaluga in 1925.
Coll TG.

SHCHERBOV, Pavel Egorovich   1866-1938
Artist, caricaturist. In 1900 he produced a watercolour *Idyll*, RM, which was a caricature of the artists of the World of Art watching a 'female' Diaghilev milk a cow. He exhibited with the World of Art 1902-3.
After the Revolution he participated in the First State Free Exhibition of Artworks in Petrograd in 1919.
Lit A.Savinov *P.E.Shcherbov*, Leningrad, 1969.

SHCHIPITSYN, Aleksandr Vasil'evich   1896-c.1943
Painter. He studied under Kuprin and Fonvizin 1921-4 and then under D.Shterenberg, A.Drevin and R.Fal'k at the Moscow Vkhutemas 1925-9. He worked with Tatlin 1929-32, assisting on the construction of his gliders. He painted in Siberia in the 1930s.
Lit A.M.Muratov, V.Manin et al. *Zhivopis' 20-30kh godov*, Sankt-Peterburg, 1991.
Coll RM.

SHCHUKIN, P. E.   a.1918-1919
Painter. He exhibited at the First Exhibition of Works of the Professional Union of Artists in Moscow in 1918 and at the juryless Eighth State Exhibition in Moscow in 1919.

SHCHUKIN, Stepan Semenovich   1758/62-1828
Portrait painter. He was a pupil of Levitsky and directed the portraiture teaching at the Academy in St. Petersburg. His own portraits include *Pavel I*, 1796, TG.
Coll TG.

SHCHUKIN, Yuri Prokop'evich   1904-1935
Painter, theatre designer. He studied at the Free Art Studios in Voronezh under S.M.Romanovich and M.Kh.Maksimov 1919-22, and at the Vkhutemas in Moscow under Istomin 1922-5, and also studied theatre design under Konchalovsky and Rabinovich there 1925-30. He was a member of AKhRR from 1929. Some of his work had a knowing primitive character suitable for the theatre.
Lit A.M.Muratov, V.Manin et al. *Zhivopis' 20-30kh godov*, Sankt-Peterburg, 1991.
Coll RM.

SHCHUKO, Vladimir Alekseevich   1878-1939
Theatre designer. He was engaged in Agitprop decorations at

Petrograd in 1918. He designed Schiller's *Don Carlos* at the Bolshoi Drama Theatre, Petrograd, in 1919. One set designed formed a great medieval arch with creepers through which was visible a garden courtyard with figures beneath a blue sky, like a late World of Art design.
Coll Bakhrushin Theatre Museum, Moscow.

SHEBUEV, Vasili Kuz'mich   1777-1855
Neo-classical history painter of biblical and classical themes. His work was comparable with that of A.E.Egorov.
*Self-portrait with Fortune Teller, 1805, TG, is an ambitious, unfinished painting which recalls the paintings of Le Nain and others. It is a complex synthesis in which the self-portrait displays a fine lace collar.
Coll TG.

SHEGAL', Grigoriy Mikhailovich   1889-1956
Painter. He studied at the Drawing School of the Society for the Encouragement of the Arts in St. Petersburg under Roerich, Rylov, Bilibin, P.S.Naumov and A.I.Vakhremeev 1912-16. After the Revolution he studied at the Higher Art Institute of the Academy 1917-18 and at the Moscow Vkhutemas under A.Shevchenko 1922-5, but he taught in the Proletkult studios at Tula 1918-22 where he assisted Pokarzhevsky on the organisation of the Art Museum. He was producing Cézannist landscapes at this time. He exhibited with the Society of Moscow Painters at its inaugural exhibition in Moscow in 1925 and was included in the 1928 exhibition of Acquisitions by the State Art Collections Fund held in Moscow. He was represented at the jubilee exhibition Artists of the RSFSR over 15 Years held at the Russian Museum, Leningrad, in 1932 and at the 1932 Venice Biennale.
Lit A.M.Muratov, V.Manin et al. *Zhivopis' 20-30kh godov*, Sankt-Peterburg, 1991.
Coll Tula Art Museum.

SHEKHTEL', L. F. = ZHEGIN, L. F.

SHEKHTEL', Vera Fedorovna   1896-1958
Painter. She was the sister of Lev Shekhtel' (Zhegin). She exhibited with the Union of Youth in 1913-14. She became a friend of the poet and painter Vladimir Mayakovsky.
After the Revolution she exhibited with the Artists of the Leftist Federation of the Professional Union in 1918 along with Rodchenko and many others.

SHELKOVNIKOV, A. M.   a.1921
He was included in the Third Touring Exhibition of the Sovetsk Regional subdepartment of the Museums Bureau along with Kandinsky, Rodchenko and others in 1921.

SHEMYAKIN, Mikhail Fedorovich   1875-1944
Sculptor. He exhibited in the 1921 exhibition of the World of Art in Moscow. He was associated with the Vkhutemas in 1922. He was represented at the First Russian Art Exhibition in Berlin in 1922. He executed an extraordinary monument to *Peter the Great* erected in Leningrad. The seated figure is highly stylised and curiously proportioned with a smallish head surmounting a large body, its bony fingers twitching impatiently on the arms of the bronze chair. Shemyakin was included in the 1928 exhibition of Acquisitions by the State Art Collections Fund held in Moscow and in the First Touring Exhibition of Painting and Graphics which opened in Moscow in 1929.
Coll TG.

Sergei Sudeikin. Russian Venus, *1907. Watercolour, gouache, Indian ink, brush and pen on cardboard. Signed at bottom in silver. 29.4 x 37.6 cm. State Tretyakov Gallery, Moscow.*

SHENBERG, A. E. a.1919
Painter exhibited at the Ninth State Exhibition of Paintings: Naturalism and Realism in Moscow in 1919.

SHENBERG-SHEREMETEVSKAYA, N. F. a.1918
She was represented at the First Exhibition of Works of the Professional Union of Artists in Moscow in 1918.

SHERBAKOV, Valentin Semenovich 1880-1957
Agitprop decorator and ceramics artist. He studied at the Kazan Art School 1894-1900 and at the Academy in St. Petersburg 1900-9. He visited old Russian cities in 1907 and in 1913 he travelled to the Balkans to study frescoes and architecture. A further study visit to North Russia, Novgorod and Pskov followed in 1915.
After the Revolution he worked for the State Porcelain Factory 1917-22 and executed Agitprop decorations in Petrograd at the Admiralty Sovdep, the Peterhof Sovdep, and at Narvskaya Square c.1918. He was also active as a theatre designer in Kazan. He established an enamel workshop at the Petrograd Academy in 1922 and taught in Leningrad 1928-31. He taught at the Mukhina School of Industrial Design in Leningrad from 1949 to 1954.
Lit N.Lobanov-Rostovsky *Revolutionary Ceramics*, London, 1990.

SHEREMET'EV, S.S. a.1919
Painter. He exhibited at the juryless Eighth State Exhibition in Moscow in 1919.

SHERVASHIDZE (SCHERVACHIDZE, CHACHBA), Prince Aleksandr Konstantinovich 1867-1968
Painter, decorative artist, theatre designer. Born at Feodosia in the Crimea. He studied under Ivan Seleznev. He attended classes at the Moscow College in 1891. He travelled to Paris where he studied for several years from 1894, returning to Russia in 1899, before again moving to Paris 1904-6. He was appointed chief designer at the Imperial Theatres, St. Petersburg, in 1907. He exhibited at the First Izdebsky International Salon 1909-10 in Odessa. He exhibited with the Union of Russian Artists in Kiev in 1910.
After the Revolution he moved to Sukhumi in Abkhazia to establish the Sukhumi Theatrical Society. At Diaghilev's suggestion he emigrated to Paris in 1920 and continued vigorously active as a theatre designer. He died in Monte Carlo.
Theatre design 1909 March Meyerhold's production of N.Gogol's *The Trial* at the Aleksandrinsky Theatre, St. Petersburg.
1909 October Wagner's *Tristan and Isolde* for Meyerhold's production at the Mariinsky Theatre, St. Petersburg.
1910 March E.Hardt's *Shut Tantris* (The Fool Tantris) at the Aleksandrinsky Theatre, St. Petersburg.
1910 D.Merezhkovsky's *Paul I* directed by Meyerhold for a private production in St. Petersburg.
1919 *The Gay Death*, harlequinade by N.Evreinov, at Sukhumi, Georgia, and revived at the Vieux Colombier

Nikolai Suetin. Untitled, *c.1924. Oil on wood. 30.5 x 30 x 8 cm.*
Private collection, courtesy Annely Juda Fine Art, London.

Theatre, Paris, in 1922.
1926 décors for *The Triumph of Neptune*, an English pantomime in three acts, first performed by Diaghilev's Russian Ballet at the Lyceum Theatre, London. Based on the book by Sacheverell Sitwell. Music by Lord Berners. Shervashidze adapted and executed the scenery from prints by various artists including Cruikshank.
He also executed designs by other artists for the following productions by Diaghilev:
1924 Marie Laurencin's décor for Poulenc's *Les Biches* at Monte Carlo and at the Théâtre des Champs-Elysées, Paris.
1924 Georges Braque's décor for Molière's *Les Fâcheux* to music by Georges Auric at Monte Carlo and at the Théâtre des Champs-Elysées, Paris.
1924 Henri Laurens' décor for Jean Cocteau's *Le Train bleu* with music by Darius Milhaud at the Théâtre des Champs-Elysées, Paris. Picasso designed the curtain.

1925 Georges Braque's décor for *Zéphyr et Flore* with music by V.Dukelsky at Monte Carlo and at the Théâtre de la Gaîté-Lyrique, Paris.
1925 Pedro Pruna's décor for *Les Matelots* with music by Georges Auric at the Théâtre de la Gaîté-Lyrique, Paris.
1926 curtains by Max Ernst and Joan Miró for *Romeo and Juliet* with music by Constant Lambert at Monte Carlo and the Théâtre Sarah Bernhardt, Paris.
1926 décors by Pedro Pruna for *Pastorale* with music by Georges Auric at the Théâtre Sarah Bernhardt, Paris.
1926 décors by André Derain for *Jack in the Box* with music by Eric Satie and Darius Milhau at the Théâtre Sarah Bernhardt, Paris.
1928 décors by André Bauchant for *Apollon Musagète* with music by Stravinsky at the Théâtre Sarah Bernhardt, Paris.
1929 décors by Georges Rouault for *Le Fils prodigue* with music by Prokofiev at the Théâtre Sarah Bernhardt, Paris. *(cont.)*

Illustrations N.I.Butkovskaya ed. *Narodnie russkie skazki, pesni, shutki* (Russian Folk Tales, Songs and Jokes), Paris, 1921. These are colourful and light illustrations for children.
Lit *Diaghilev and Russian Stage Designers, a Loan Exhibition from the Collection of Mr. and Mrs. N.Lobanov-Rostovsky*, International Exhibitions Foundation, Washington, 1972-4. *A.K.Chachba*, exh. cat., Abkhazia State Museum, Sukhumi, 1978. J.E.Bowlt *Russian Stage Design. Scenic Innovation. From the Collection of Mr. and Mrs. Nikita D.Lobanov-Rostovsky*, Jackson, MS, exh. cat.,1982. *Twilight of the Tsars*, London, 1991. Dzhon Boult (John Bowlt) *Khudozhniki russkogo teatra. Sobranie Nikity i Niny Lobanovykh-Rostovskikh*, Moscow, 1991.
Coll Bakhrushin Theatre Museum, Moscow.

SHERVUD, Leonid Vladimirovich (SHERWOOD) 1871-1954
Monumental sculptor. He was well known before the Revolution. He produced a half-length *Portrait of the Writer Gleb Ivanovich Uspensky* in 1904, RM, showing him leaning on his elbow and half of the sculpture's base. His *Peter I*, 1906, RM, is Rodinesque but discerning and looks blown about by the winds of history. His pupils included Sarra Lebedeva in 1912.
After the Revolution he turned his monumental abilities to Revolutionary themes. A head of the painter *Vrubel'* executed in toned plaster, RM, dates from 1917 but was unrealised as a monument. In 1918 he prepared a monument in wood commemorating *Bakunin* in response to Lenin's call for monumental propaganda. The following year his monument to *Herzen* was unveiled in Petrograd. He was included in the major exhibition in Moscow in 1927 marking the tenth anniversary of the Revolution. He was included in the 1928 exhibition of Acquisitions by the State Art Collections Fund held in Moscow.
His later works include *The Sentry*, 1933, in which a Red Army Guard vigilantly surveys the horizon. He is equipped with a real rifle and stands on top of a wall which acts as the sculpture's base.
Coll RM.

SHERVUD, Vladimir Osipovich 1832-1897
Architect, landscape painter. He designed the Historical Museum in Red Square, Moscow.
Coll TG.

SHERWOOD = SHERVUD, L.V.

SHERYSHEV, V M. a.1925
He exhibited with the Society of Moscow Painters at its inaugural exhibition in Moscow in 1925.

SHESTAKOV, N. I. a.1918-1929
Painter. He exhibited at the Fifth State Exhibition: From Impressionism to Non-Objective Art in Moscow in 1918-19 and his name appeared on the April 1919 list of artists for acquisitions by the envisaged Museum of Painterly Culture. He exhibited in the 1921 exhibition of the World of Art in Moscow. His work was included in the exhibition of Soviet art held at Harbin in 1926 and in Japan in 1927. He was also included in the major exhibition in Moscow in 1927 marking the tenth anniversary of the Revolution and in the 1928 exhibition of Acquisitions by the State Art Collections Fund held in Moscow. He was also represented at the First Touring Exhibition of Painting and Graphics which opened in Moscow in 1929.

SHESTAKOV, Viktor Alekseevich 1898-1957
Theatre designer. Born at Orel. He studied at the Vkhutemas in Moscow 1921-4. He worked as a designer for the Theatre of Revolution in Moscow 1922-7 and subsequently at the Meyerhold Theatre. He contributed to the exhibition Art of Moscow Theatre 1918-1923 held in Moscow in 1923. He won gold medals at the International Exhibitions in Paris in 1925

Aleksandr Shervashidze.
Stage Design for 'Les Sylphides': a Castle in a Lake within a Mountain Landscape, *1940. Watercolour. 34.3 x 50.2 cm. Collection Mr. and Mrs. Nikita D.Lobanov-Rostovsky, London.*

Leonid Shervud. The Sentry, *1933. Toned plaster. 267 x 168 x 109 cm.*

and in New York in 1926. He died in Moscow.
Theatre design 1923 May A.N.Ostrovsky's *Dokhodnoe Mesto* (A Profitable Post) produced by Meyerhold at the Theatre of Revolution in Moscow. On a plain stage are constructed openable rectangular screens. A spiral staircase rises to a stark balcony and two co-joined tubular chairs stand in the foreground. It is a good framework for farce, mystery or eavesdropping.
1923 November A.Fayko's *Ozero Lyul'* (Lake Lyul') produced by Meyerhold at the Theatre of Revolution in Moscow: the back of the stage was bared and a three-storey construction of girders supported corridors, cages, ladders, platforms and lifts as well as illuminated titles and a screen. Another scene featured a geometric and symmetrical 'hill' with steps at either side for use by the performers of Meyerhold's rhythmic biomechanical and all but balletic performers. He also designed transformable furniture for this production.
1923 Meyerhold's production of E.Toller's *Mass Man* at the Theatre of Revolution, Moscow.
1923-24 V.M.Bebutov's production of *Spartak* (Spartacus) at the Theatre of the Revolution. An urban scene incorporating ramps, platforms and the silhouette of a building.
1926 Korolev's production of *Barometr pokazyvaet buryu* (The Barometer Shows a Storm) at the Theatre of the Revolution. This was a most severe Constructivist set of box-like platforms and little else.
1927 Meyerhold and R.Akulshin's *Through a Village Window* at the Meyerhold Theatre.
1928 March A.Griboedov's *Gore ot uma* (Woe from Wit) for which he made the stage constructions whilst N.Ul'yanov did the costumes.

1929 A.Sukhovo-Kobylin's *Svad'ba Krechinskogo* (Krechinsky's Wedding) at the Meyerhold Theatre, Leningrad.
1933 April *Krechinsky's Wedding* at the Meyerhold Theatre, Leningrad.
1935 A.Chekhov's *Thirty Three Fainting Fits* at the Meyerhold Theatre, Leningrad.
1936 Meyerhold's unrealised production of Pushkin's *Boris Godunov* with music by Prokofiev at the Meyerhold Theatre, Moscow.
Lit *V.Shestakov 1898-1957*, Moscow, 1960. O.M.Beskin *V.Shestakov*, Moscow, 1961. *Paris-Moscou*, 1979. C.Lodder *Russian Constructivism*, New Haven and London, 1983.
Coll Bakhrushin Theatre Museum, Moscow; St. Petersburg Theatre Museum.

SHEVCHENKO, Aleksandr Vasilievich   1882-1948
Painter. Born in Kharkov. He took drawing lessons and worked in a theatre design studio 1890-8. He studied at the Stroganov Institute, Moscow, 1899-1905 with a period at the Académie Julian in Paris and under Carrière 1905-6. He travelled to England, Spain, Egypt and Turkey in 1906. He returned to the Stroganov Institute in 1907 before studying at the Moscow College under K.Korovin and V.Serov 1907-10. His close association with neo-primitive painters, including Larionov and Goncharova, led to exhibiting paintings of bathers and soldiers with the group the Donkey's Tail in 1912 and to the publication of his book *Neo Primitivism* in 1913, but he also exhibited with the Union of Youth in 1912, the World of Art in 1913 as well as Larionov's the exhibition *Mishen'* (Target) in Moscow in 1913 and No.4 in Moscow in 1914. He was amongst the painters who responded to the Rayism of Larionov. To the Target exhibition he also contributed a suite of more than thirty children's drawings from his own collection. He was enlisted in the army in 1914 and mobilised in 1917.
After the Revolution he exhibited with the Knave of Diamonds in Moscow in November 1917, with the World of Art in December 1917 in Moscow and at the First Exhibition of Works of the Professional Union of Artists in Moscow in 1918. He taught at the Vkhutemas/Vkhutein in Moscow from 1918 to 1929 and served under Tatlin on the Moscow Collegium of IZO Narkompros in 1919. He was a member of the committee to preserve monuments and the artistic heritage 1918-21.
He exhibited together with A.Grishchenko in the Twelfth State Exhibition: Colourdynamo and Tectonic Primitivism in Moscow in 1919, signing a *Manifesto* in the catalogue and a text on Tectonic Primitivism in which he declared that easel painting is not dead, is not decoration, is not applied art and concluded 'Long live easel painting!' (see Grishchenko). He appeared on the April 1919 list of artists for acquisitions by the envisaged Museum of Painterly Culture and was represented along with Kandinsky, Chagall and others at the First State Exhibition of Paintings by Local and Moscow Artists held in Vitebsk in December 1919. He was also represented at the Nineteenth Exhibition of the All-Russian Exhibitions Bureau in Moscow in 1920, at the enormous First State Exhibition of Art and Science, which included ethnographic material, held in Kazan in 1920, at the 1921 exhibition of the World of Art in Moscow and at the First Russian Art Exhibition in Berlin in 1922.
He became a member of the group *Makovets* 1922-5 and exhibited at the third and last exhibition in Moscow 1925-6. He

Vasili Surikov. A Cossack Officer in Summer Uniform. *Oil on canvas laid down on board. Signed and inscribed in pencil 'Esaul' (a cossack military rank) 'Zakhar Dochlachev (?) Konstant. stan. on the Don' (a local Cossack administrative centre). 34.5 x 25 cm. Reproduced by kind permission of Sotheby's London, sale 28.11.1991, lot 510.*

Vasili Surikov. Portrait Study. *Oil on paper mounted on canvas. Signed 'V.Surikov' in cyrillic script. 27.3 x 23 cm.*
Malmö Konstmuseum.

contributed to the Third Exhibition of Paintings by Artists from Kaluga and Moscow held in Kaluga in 1925 and to the seventh exhibition of the group *L'Araignée* (The Spider) at the Galerie Devambe in Paris in 1925. He was included in the 1928 exhibition of Acquisitions by the State Art Collections Fund held in Moscow. He was a member of the Society of Russian Artists 1928-9. In 1930 he was leader of the Painters' Workshop Society, founded in 1926 in Moscow. He was represented at the jubilee exhibition Artists of the RSFSR over 15 Years held at the Russian Museum, Leningrad, in 1932. He died in Moscow.

Self-portrait with a Horse, 1914-16, watercolour, RM, is a military self-portrait in a Russian Futurist vein comparable with paintings and drawings by Larionov on this theme.

Street in the Rain, 1934, coloured monotype, uses the liquidity of the medium to full advantage. Houses and apartment blocks made well established images which were then smeared to indicate the rain and wind. Finally, windblown trees were inserted.

Writings A.Shevchenko *Printsipy kubizma i drugykh sovremennykh techeniy v zhivopisi* (The Principles of Cubism and other Contemporary Trends in Painting), Moscow, 1913. A.Shevchenko *Neo-Primitivizm*, Moscow, 1913. A.V.Shevchenko *Sbornik materialov*, Moscow, 1980.
Lit A.Grishchenko, N.Lavrsky *A.Shevchenko: Poiski i dostizheniya v oblasti zhivopisi* (A.Shevchenko: Researches and Achievements in the Realm of Painting), Moscow, 1919. *A.V.Shevchenko*, exh. cat., Moscow, 1966. S.P.Compton *The World Backwards, Russian Futurist Books 1912-16*, London, 1978. *Paris-Moscou*, 1979. *L'Avant-garde russe 1905-1925*, exh. cat., Musée des Beaux-Arts, Nantes, 1993.
Coll TG; RM; Astrakhan Art Museum; Ivanovo Art Museum; Kostroma Art Museum; Saratov Art Museum.

SHEVCHENKO, S. a.1921
He was included in the Third Touring Exhibition of the Sovetsk Regional subdepartment of the Museums Bureau along with Kandinsky, Rodchenko and others in 1921.

SHEVTSOV a.1925
Graphic artist. He contributed to the First Exhibition of Cinema Posters held in Moscow in 1925.

SHIBANOV, Mikhail d.after 1789
Painter of portraits and multi-figure compositions on peasant themes. He was a serf of Potemkin who became one of the initiators of specifically Russian genre painting. His *Peasant Meal*, 1774, TG, introduces an element of truth into the painting of an elegant age.
Solemnising the Wedding Contract, 1777, revels in Russianness. A young man and his elaborately clad bride are the centre of attention for all gathered around inside the wooden building.
Coll TG.

SHIFRIN, Nisson Abramovich 1892-1961
Theatre designer, painter. He studied under Alexandra Exter in Kiev c.1918-20 and contributed to the First Jewish Art Exhibition of Sculpture, Graphics and Drawing held in Kiev in 1920. He contributed to the exhibition Art of Moscow Theatre 1918-1923 held in Moscow in 1923. He was represented at the Paris International Exhibition in 1925. He exhibited with the First Exhibition of the Society of Easel Painters (OST) in Moscow in 1925. He was included in the 1928 exhibition of Acquisitions by the State Art Collections Fund held in Moscow and in the First Touring Exhibition of Painting and Graphics which opened in Moscow in 1929. He was represented at the jubilee exhibition Artists of the RSFSR over 15 Years held at the Russian Museum, Leningrad, in 1932.
He was often visited by Tatlin in 1949.
Theatre design 1931 January V.M.Kirshon's *Khleb* (Bread) at the Moscow Art Theatre.
1931 December A.N.Afinogenov's *Strakh* (Fear) at the Moscow Art Theatre.
1937 Shakespeare's *Taming of the Shrew* at the Red Army Theatre, Moscow. A design beautifully derived from Carpaccio's *Annunciation*.
1941 Shakespeare's *Midsummer Nights Dream* at the Red Army Theatre, Moscow.
1947 November K.M.Simonov's *Dni i nochi* (Days and Nights) at the Moscow Art Theatre.
1950 December B.A.Lavrenev's *Razlom* (The Fracture) at the Moscow Art Theatre.
1952 November M.V.Bol'shintsov's *Zalp 'Avrory'* (The 'Aurora's' Salvo) at the Moscow Art Theatre.
1960 January Anton Chekhov's *Chayka* (Seagull) at the Moscow Art Theatre.
Writings N.Shifrin *Khudozhnik v teatre* (The Artist in the Theatre), Leningrad, 1964. N.Shifrin *Moya rabota v teatre* (My Work in the Theatre), Moscow, 1966.

SHIKALOV, N. S. a.1919
Graphic artist. He was represented in the Sixth State Exhibition: The Print (*VI Gosudarstvennaya vystavka gravyur*) in Moscow in 1919 and at the enormous First State Exhibition of Art and Science, which included ethnographic material, held in Kazan in 1920.

SHIL'DER, Andrei Nikolaevich 1861-1919
Landscape painter. He participated in the First State Free Exhibition of Artworks in Petrograd in 1919.
Coll TG.

SHILLINGOVSKY, Pavel Aleksandrovich 1881-1942
Moldavian graphic artist, wood engraver, painter. Born at Kishinev. He studied at the School of Art in Odessa 1895-1900 and at the Academy in St. Petersburg under Kardovsky 1901-11. Between 1912 and 1914 he worked with Maté. He exhibited with the World of Art in 1913 and with the New Society of Artists in 1917.
After the Revolution he established a polygraphic faculty at the Leningrad Vkhutein 1922-9. He was a virtuoso in the use of black and white and fully employed his expert knowledge of the history of printmaking. He had one-man exhibitions in Kazan and Leningrad in 1924. He was included in the major exhibition in Moscow in 1927 marking the tenth anniversary of the Revolution and in the 1928 exhibition of Acquisitions by the State Art Collections Fund held in Moscow. He was also included in the exhibition of Russian Graphic Art in Riga in 1929 and the jubilee exhibition Artists of the RSFSR over 15 Years held at the Russian Museum, Leningrad, in 1932.
Bessarabia, 1911, Moldavian Art Gallery, Kishinev, is a decorative painting of an encampment seen from beneath an awning or tent where a vigorous discussion is taking place. Behind this a camel caravan and two sheep are visible. The whole forms a kind of idyllic scene of dappled light upon decorative

Ivan Shishkin. An Oak Grove, *1887. Oil on canvas. 125 x 193 cm. Museum of Russian Art, Kiev.*

patterns. In the distance a sandy landscape stretches in the sun.
Bessarabia. Earth, 1913, wood engraving, is a vast expanse of landscape comprising detailed depictions of fields and trees. The sun beams a multitude of straight rays through swirls of cloud.
The Rostral Column, St. Petersburg, 1922, wood engraving, is a brilliantly performed print in which the clouds above the city seem to come from the time of Dürer.
Lit P.Kornilov *P.A.Shillingovsky*, Leningrad, 1966. E.Grishina *Grafika P.A.Shillingovskogo* in *Iskusstvo*, No.2, 1972. *Paris-Moscou*, 1979.
Coll Moldavian Art Gallery, Kishinev.

SHIL'TSOV, Pavel Savvich   1820-1893
Portraitist.
Coll TG.

SHISHKIN, Ivan Ivanovich   1832-1898
Lyrical painter of the Russian landscape. He specialised in immense forests and spectacularly lit paintings of trees. Born in the Vyatka region into the family of a merchant. He studied at the Moscow College 1852-6 and under Vorob'ev at the Academy in St. Petersburg 1856-60. He travelled on a scholarship to Germany and Switzerland. He was a founder member and a major figure of the Wanderers movement. He taught at the Academy 1893-5. He married the painter Olga Ladoga. He had technical brilliance as a painter of nature seen in detail but what made this particularly remarkable was his spectacular and dramatic ability with composition. Skies arch into apparently endless space with meticulously controlled luminosity. The result is landscape that appears animate and alive, locked in a drama of survival. This in turn has a symbolic aspect which made his paintings a celebration of Russia.
Woodland Thicket, 1872, RM, is an immensely detailed painting of a sodden pool within a dense forest. Every branch of every tree is meticulously observed and recorded in its individual and specific shape, whether thick or thin, birch or pine. In the foreground fallen and rotting birchwood covered in moss lies by the pool. This kind of landscape evokes national identity through an image of the land of Russia with its distant forest and places empty of human activity.
Lit I.N.Shuvalova *I.I.Shishkin*, Leningrad, 1980.
Coll TG; RM.

SHISHKINA   a.1926
Sculptor. She was a member of the Society of Russian Sculptors from 1926.

SHISHKOV, A.N.   a.1919
Painter. He exhibited at the juryless Eighth State Exhibition in Moscow in 1919.

SHISHKOV, M. A.   1832-1897
Theatre designer who produced designs for A.N.Ostrovsky's *Groza* (The Storm) in 1867 and for A.S.Pushkin's *Boris Godunov* in 1870.

SHISHMAREVA, Tatiana Vladimirovna   b.1905-1939+
Painter.
Coll RM.

SHITOV, M. A.   a.1910
Painter. He exhibited with the Union of Youth in 1910.

SHKOL'NIK, Iosif Solomonovich   1883-1926
Painter, theatre designer. He studied at the Odessa Art Institute and 1905-7 at the Academy in St. Petersburg. He contributed to the exhibition Contemporary Trends in Art in 1908 and exhibited with the Union of Youth 1910-14, of which he was a founder member and secretary. With Pavel Filonov he assisted in the staging of Mayakovsky's eponymous *Vladimir Mayakovsky, a Tragedy* at Luna Park, St. Petersburg, in 1913. This was staged on two nights alternating with the Futurist opera *Victory Over the Sun* by Kruchenykh, Matyushin and Malevich. It ensured that Shkol'nik had a thorough knowledge of Futurism in two of its most ambitious manifestations and he was much impressed by the Suprematism of Malevich. One of the designs for this production featured a landscape of houses hectically spilling through a dislocated perspective in the manner of Rozanova's graphic work. He also knew Tatlin by 1913. After 1914 he produced stage designs for the Troitsky Theatre.
After the Revolution he worked at the Free Art Studios (SVOMAS) in Petrograd and served on a commission to purchase works of contemporary art. His name appeared on the April 1919 list of artists for acquisitions by the envisaged Museum of Painterly Culture.
He also served under Al'tman on the committee responsible for

Il'ya Shlepyanov. The Calculated Stroke, *c.1923. Illustration for Gastev's theories of work. Signed 'I.Sh' lower left.*

the revolutionary decorations marking 1 May in Petrograd in 1919. He participated in the First State Free Exhibition of Artworks in Petrograd in 1919 and was associated with the Art Section of the People's Commissariat of the Enlightenment under David Shterenberg c.1918-19. He was represented at the First Russian Art Exhibition in Berlin in 1922 and at the exhibition of Studies for Theatre Decoration and Works from the Studios of the Decorative Institute held in Petrograd in 1922. He contributed to the Third Exhibition of Paintings by Artists from Kaluga and Moscow held in Kaluga in 1925. He was included in the 1928 exhibition of Acquisitions by the State Art Collections Fund held in Moscow.

Lit J.Howard *The Union of Youth — An Artists' Society of the Russian Avant-Garde*, Manchester and New York, 1992.

Coll TG.

Colour plate p.382.

SHLEIFER, Saveliy Yakovlevich   **1881-1942?**

Painter, theatre designer. After graduating from the Art School at Odessa in 1904 he enrolled at the Ecole des Beaux-Arts in Paris where he studied from 1905 to 1908. On his return to Russia he studied at the Academy in St. Petersburg

1908-9 and contributed to Kul'bin's exhibition Impressionists in 1909. He began to design for the theatre in 1907 and he was employed by the Troitsky Theatre from 1912 and by the Liteiny Theatre from 1915. He also exhibited with the Union of Youth 1911-13.

After the Revolution he participated in the First State Free Exhibition of Artworks in Petrograd in 1919.

Theatre design 1907 Gorky's *Children of the Sun.*

Lit J.Howard *The Union of Youth — An Artists' Society of the Russian Avant-Garde*, Manchester and New York, 1992.

SHLEPYANOV, Il'ya Yul'evich   **1900-1951**

Theatre designer, graphic artist. He produced illustrations for the work and movement theorist Aleksei Gastev in the 1920s. These were dramatic images in black in which the figure is presented amongst a scheme of lettering and geometric planes of Futurist derivation. He was also associated with designing posters for the Meyerhold Theatre in Moscow 1923-5. He was represented at the Paris International Exhibition in 1925.

Theatre design 1924 June Meyerhold's production at the Meyerhold Theatre of *D.E.* (*Daesh' Evropu!*, Give Us Europe!), an agitational work by Mikhail Pogaevsky based upon Ilya Ehrenburg's novel *The 'Give Us Europe' Trust* and Bernhard Kellerman's novel *The Tunnel* with additional material by Upton Sinclair and Pierre Hamp. The production incorporated large red wooden screens on wheels moved by concealed stage-hands. Meyerhold was involved directly in the design which also incorporated pantomime effects and projected titles.

1925 January Meyerhold's production of A.Fayko's *Uchitel' Bubus* (Bubus the Teacher) at the Meyerhold Theatre. The set comprised a semicircle of suspended bamboo rods enclosing a stage area covered with a circular green carpet. The back wall had flashing neon signs.

1925 April N.Erdman's *Mandat* (Mandate) at the Meyerhold Theatre.

1930 November Meyerhold's production of *D.S.E.*, a revised version of *D.E.* (see 1924 above) at the Meyerhold Theatre.

1932 N.F.Pogodin's play *Moy Drug* (My Friend) at the Theatre of Revolution, Moscow. The shadow of Lenin points the way across a high-view backdrop of endless apartment blocks. An office interior is in the foreground.

Coll Bakhrushin Theatre Museum, Moscow.

Il'ya Shlepyanov. Organisation, *c.1923. Illustration for Gastev's theories of work. Signed 'I.Sh' lower left. The imagery of mechanical forms refers to Gastev's study of the mechanics of work and of the relationship of the worker to tools and machinery.*

Il'ya Shlepyanov. Victory is Still Before Us, *c.1923. Illustration for Gastev's theories of work. Signed 'I.Sh' lower right.*
Suprematist devices are assembled to form the Soviet worker turning from his anvil to point the way ahead. The graphic style has a dramatic quality learnt in the theatre.

SHLEZINGER, V. N.　　　　　　　　**a.1918-1919**
Shlezinger exhibited at the First Exhibition of Works of the Professional Union of Artists in Moscow in 1918 and at the Fifth State Exhibition: From Impressionism to Non-Objective Art in Moscow 1918-19.

SHMARINOV, Dementy Alekseevich　　**1907-1945+**
Socialist Realist draughtsman, graphic artist. His work showed a lively sense of action as if depicting a scene from a play. He drew illustrations for numerous literary works including Dostoevsky's *Crime and Punishment*, 1936 and 1945, black watercolour and charcoal, TG, and he produced a stormy Peter the Great for A.N.Tolstoy's *Peter I*, 1940, black watercolour and charcoal, TG. He exhibited in Moscow together with Sarra Lebedeva, Sergei Gerasimov, A.A.Deineka, P.P.Konchalovsky and Vera Mukhina in 1943.
Coll TG.

SHMEL'KOV, Petr Mikhailovich　　　**1819-1890**
Coll TG.

SHMIT, E. T.　　　　　　　　　　　**a.1919**
Painter who exhibited at the Ninth State Exhibition of Paintings: Naturalism and Realism in Moscow in 1919.

SHMIT-RYZHOVA　　　　　　　　**a. c.1910**
She exhibited with Kul'bin's group Triangle. She married N.A.Shmit.

SHOKHIN, D. M.　　　　　　　　　**a.1918-1919**
Painter. He exhibited at the First Exhibition of Works of the Professional Union of Artists in Moscow in 1918 and at the juryless Eighth State Exhibition in Moscow in 1919.

SHOR, S. M.　　　　　　　　　　　**a.1926-1932**
Graphic artist. He was represented at the Second Exhibition of Cinema Posters held at the Kamerny (Chamber) Theatre, Moscow, in 1926. He exhibited with the 4 Arts society in Leningrad including the exhibition of 1928 at the Russian Museum and was included in the exhibition of Russian Graphic Art in Riga in 1929. He was represented at the jubilee exhibition Artists of the RSFSR over 15 Years held at the Russian Museum, Leningrad, in 1932.

SHPAGIN　　　　　　　　　　　　**a.1919**
Painter who contributed to the Twelfth State Exhibition: Colourdynamo and Tectonic Primitivism (*Tsvetodinamos i tektonicheskiy primitivizm*) along with Grishchenko, Shevchenko and others in Moscow in 1919.

SHPINEL', Iosif Aronovich　　　　**1892-1932+**
Graphic artist. He exhibited with the 4 Arts society in Moscow in 1925 and at its exhibition of 1928 at the Russian Museum, Leningrad. He contributed to the exhibition of graphic art Liberation Movements: The Sixteenth to the Twentieth Century held in Moscow in 1928.
An Isaak Shpinel' was involved as a designer of Dovzhenko's

Il'ya Shlepyanov. The Cook, *1923. Drawing. Signed with cyrillic 'I.Sh'.*
This is a character in S.M.Tretyakov's play 'The Earth in Turmoil' which was directed by Meyerhold with a stage set by Popova.

film *Arsenal* in 1929 together with Vladimir Muller. He was represented at the jubilee exhibition Artists of the RSFSR over 15 Years held at the Russian Museum, Leningrad, in 1932.

Red Army Soldier, 1924, coloured woodcut, is a powerful print using arcs and linear rhythms like Popova's to depict sunburst motifs and diagonal images of buildings. The soldier whose motto is 'Be prepared' dominates the print from top to bottom with the air of a knight of old.

SHTALBERG, Ernest Ekabovich (Yakovlevich) 1883-1958
He was engaged in Agitprop decorations at Troitsky Bridge, Petrograd, in 1918.

SHTAMM, Nikolai L'vovich   b.1906
Sculptor. See S.M.Orlov.

SHTERENBERG, David Petrovich   1881-1948
Painter and senior figure in the reorganisation of the visual arts in the immediately post-revolutionary years. Born at Zhitomir. He studied in Odessa in 1906 and subsequently in Paris at the Ecole des Beaux-Arts and at the Académie Witte under A.Martin, E.Anglade and Van Dongen 1907-12, and he was well aware of the various movements of art in Paris with which Russian art was to have intense and complex relationships. He exhibited at the Salon d'Automne in 1912 and at the Salon des Indépendants 1912-17. He lived in Paris until 1917.

After the Revolution he became Commissar for Art 1917-18 and thereby an enormously influential figure in the first years of the Revolution. He was Director of the art activities of the People's Commissariat of the Enlightenment (IZO Narkompros) 1918-21 and in January 1919 he became a founder member of *Komfut* (Communist Futurism) in Petrograd. This included the theorists Boris Kushner (chairman) and Osip Brik as well as the poet-painter Mayakovsky and the painter Natan Al'tman. Its *Programme Declaration* was published in the periodical *Iskusstvo Kommuny* (Art of the Commune), No.8, 26 January, 1919.

He also designed Agitprop decorations in Petrograd in 1918 and his name appeared on the April 1919 list of artists for acquisitions by the envisaged Museum of Painterly Culture. He participated in the First State Free Exhibition of Artworks in Petrograd in 1919.

He directed *Glavprofobr*, Chief Administration for Professional Education, in 1921, and was included in the Third Touring Exhibition of the Sovetsk Regional subdepartment of the Museums Bureau along with Kandinsky, Rodchenko and others in 1921. From 1920 to 1930 he also taught at the Vkhutemas/Vkhutein. He participated in the twenty-first, and last, State Exhibition of IZO Narkompros in 1921 and the next year held a joint exhibition, The Three, with Al'tman and Chagall. He was in charge of the organisation of the First Russian Art Exhibition at the Van Diemen Gallery in Berlin in 1922 and the Soviet display at the Paris International Exhibition in 1925. He participated in the seventh exhibition of the group *L'Araignée* (The Spider) at the Galerie Devambe in Paris in 1925.

He was an organiser of the Society of Easel Painters (OST) in 1925 and became its president until 1930. He contributed to the International Exhibition in Dresden in 1926. His work was included in the exhibition of Soviet art held at Harbin in 1926 and in Japan in 1927 and in the major exhibition in Moscow in 1927 marking the tenth anniversary of the Revolution. He was also included in the 1928 exhibition of Acquisitions by the State Art Collections Fund held in Moscow. He was also included in the exhibition of Russian Graphic Art in Riga in 1929 and in the First Touring Exhibition of Painting and Graphics which opened in Moscow in 1929. He was represented at the jubilee exhibition Artists of the RSFSR over 15 Years held at the Russian Museum, Leningrad, in 1932 and at the 1932 Venice Biennale. He died in Moscow.

The Sun of Liberty, 1918, State Museum of the Great October Socialist Revolution, St. Petersburg, is a design for decorations around an arch of the Hermitage Museum in Petrograd. A flower surmounts the arch and above this the radiant sun pours forth colours and patterns that reveal in a fresh and dynamic way his evident knowledge of Delaunay's work.

Book design includes: Cover for periodical *Iskusstvo v proivodstve* (Art in Production), No.1, 1921. Illustrations to I.Babel *Raskazy* (Short Stories), Moscow, 1932.

Lit D.P.Shterenberg, exh. cat., Moscow, 1927. A.Efros *Profili*, Moscow, 1930. D.Sarabyanov *D.Shterenberg* in *Tvorchestvo*, No.7, 1978. *D.Shterenberg*, exh. cat., Moscow, 1978. C.Lodder *Russian Constructivism*, New Haven and London, 1983. S.Compton *Russian Avant-Garde Books 1917-34*, London, 1992. *L'Avant-garde russe 1905-1925*, exh. cat., Musée des Beaux-Arts, Nantes, 1993.

Coll RM; Ivanovo Art Museum; Kostroma Art Museum; Tula Art Museum.

Colour plate p.382.

SHTEYBEN (STEUBEN), Karl Karlovich   1788-1856
Painter of portraits and religious subjects. Signed 'Steuben'.
Coll TG.

SHTOFFER, Yakov Zakharovich   1906-1951
Theatre designer. He studied under Tatlin and graduated from the Kiev College of Art in 1928. Subsequently he worked in theatres in Kirgizia, Moscow and Leningrad.

SHTUTSER, N. I.   a.1918-19
Shtutser exhibited at the First Exhibition of Works of the Professional Union of Artists in Moscow in 1918, at the Fifth State Exhibition: From Impressionism to Non-Objective Art in Moscow 1918-19 and appeared on the April 1919 list of artists for acquisitions by the envisaged Museum of Painterly Culture.

SHTYURTSVAGE, L. = SURVAGE, L.L.

SHUBIN (SCHOUBINE), Fedot Ivanovich   1740-1805
Neo-classical sculptor who worked in plaster and marble. A thorough and prolific neo-classicist who executed rather French-looking busts, reliefs and free-standing female embodiments of classical myths. He was born in the northern fishing village of Kholmogory and as a youth undertook fishing expeditions with his father on the White Sea and carved in bone and mother of pearl. In 1759 he travelled to St. Petersburg to study at the Academy until 1776 when he attained a gold medal upon his graduation and a scholarship with which he visited Paris and Italy. He executed portrait busts and also historical and mythological bas-reliefs for the Chesmensky and Marble Palaces and for the Alexander Nevsky Abbey. His works include a marble bas-relief portrait of *I.I.Shuvalov* in 1771, a bust of *Chernyshev*, 1774, TG, and a

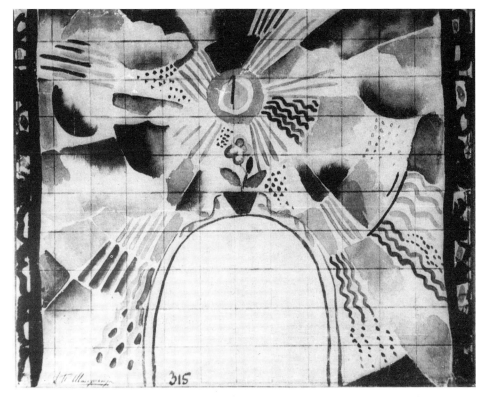

David Shterenberg. The Sun of Liberty, *1918. Watercolour.*
This design is squared up for translation on to a monumental scale for use as a street decoration around an archway of the Hermitage Museum, Petrograd.
State Museum of the Great October Socialist Revolution, St. Petersburg.

portrait of *Lomonosov*, 1792, RM. His many fine court portrait busts including several portraits of *Catherine II* in 1783, 1789 and 1791. He sometimes signed his work 'F.Sh.' in cyrillic letters or 'Schoubine' in latin script.
Portrait of M.R.Panina, 1774, marble, is the sculptural equivalent of Borovikovsky's portrait paintings. It is a lively work of a contemporary with elaborate hair and clothes.
Night, 1781-2, marble, RM, is a generalised and idealised embodiment of Diana as moon goddess. It was executed after a drawing by A.Rinaldi.
Lit I.K.Isakov *F.Shubin*, 1938.

SHUKHAEV, Vasili Ivanovich   **1887-1973**
Portrait painter, theatre designer, illustrator. Born in Moscow. He studied at the Stroganov Institute in Moscow 1897-1905 and under Vasili Savinsky and Dmitri Kardovsky at the Higher Art Institute of the Academy in St. Petersburg 1906-12. He was associated with the World of Art movement. In 1910 he drew the painter Vrubel' on his deathbed. His first theatre designs were for Meyerhold 1911-12. He then visited Italy on a scholarship 1912-14. He exhibited with The New Society of Artists in Petrograd in 1915. During the war in 1916 he drew military figures, both full-length and portrait drawings, RM, which record individuals and do not attempt a symbolic or generalised significance.
After the Revolution he executed Agitprop decorations for the Lieutenant Shmidt Bridge in Petrograd in 1918 which featured a scheme of red banners and archways decorated with red flags, swags and figures (State Museum of the Great October Socialist Revolution, St. Petersburg). He taught at the Petrograd Free State Art Education Studios in 1918 and participated in the First

State Free Exhibition of Artworks in Petrograd in 1919.
He emigrated via Finland to Paris in 1920 where he designed for Balieff's Théâtre de la Chauve-Souris, but he was also represented at the exhibition of Studies for Theatre Decoration and Works from the Studios of the Decorative Institute held in Petrograd in 1922. The same year he exhibited with Aleksandr Yakovlev (Jakovleff) at the Galerie Barbazanges in Paris. He was painting in Normandy in 1923. He was represented in the Russian Art Exhibition in New York in 1924.
He returned to Russia in 1935. He was then exiled to Magadan where he made designs for the local theatre. From 1947 he taught drawing at the Tblisi Academy in Georgia. He died at Tblisi.
Still-life with Loaves of Bread: Normandy, 1923, RM, is dominated in the foreground by large loaves propped up on a table. Behind this is a village square with tall gabled houses.
Theatre design 1912 January Meyerhold's production of Dr.Dapertutto's (Meyerhold's) *Lovers*, a pantomime to two musical preludes by Debussy at N.P.Karabchevsky's House, St. Petersburg. Designed by V.I.Shukhaev and A.E.Yakovlev in collaboration.
1934 costumes for the ballet *Seramid* for the Ida Rubinstein Theatre Company.
Lit *V.I.Shukhaev*, exh. cat., Moscow, 1958. I.Miamlin *V.I.Shukhaev*, Leningrad, 1972. *Diaghilev and Russian Stage Designers, a Loan Exhibition from the Collection of Mr. and Mrs. N.Lobanov-Rostovsky*, International Exhibitions Foundation, Washington, 1972-4. J.E.Bowlt *Russian Stage Design. Scenic Innovation. From the Collection of Mr. and Mrs. Nikita D.Lobanov-Rostovsky*, Jackson, MS, exh. cat., 1982. *Twilight of*

Vasili Shukhaev. Anna Pavlova, *1922. Sanguine, charcoal. Signed lower right 'V.Schoukhaeff, Paris 1922'. 90 x 65 cm.*
Collection Mr. and Mrs. Nikita D.Lobanov-Rostovsky, London.

the Tsars, London, 1991. A.M.Muratov, V.Manin et al. *Zhivopis' 20-30kh godov*, Sankt-Peterburg, 1991.
Coll RM; Ashmolean Museum, Oxford.

SHUKHMIN, Petr Mitrofanovich　　　1894-1955
Painter. Born at Voronezh. He studied under V.Meshkov in 1912 and at the Academy in St. Petersburg under I.Tvorozhnikov, A.Makovsky and D.Kardovsky 1912-16.
After the Revolution he became a founder member of the Association of Artists of Revolutionary Russia (AKhRR) in 1922. In 1922 he was a founder member of the Society (*Obshchestvo*) of Artists of Revolutionary Russia, founded after the first

exhibition of AKhRR. Other members included A.Grigoriev, P.Kiselev, E.Katsman, N.Kotov, S.Malyutin, P.Radimov, A.Skachko, P.Sukhanov, B.Yakovlev and V.Zhuravlev.
He was included in the major exhibition in Moscow in 1927 marking the tenth anniversary of the Revolution. He died in Moscow.
Lit S.Razumovskaya *P.Shukhmin*, Leningrad, 1966. *Paris-Moscou*, 1979.

SHUKHVOSTOV, Stepan Mikhailovich　　　1821-1908
Painter whose subjects include church interiors.
Coll TG.

SHUMOV   a.1919
Painter. He contributed to the Twelfth State Exhibition: Colourdynamo and Tectonic Primitivism (*Tsvetodinamos i tektonicheskiy primitivizm*) along with Grishchenko, Shevchenko and others in Moscow in 1919.

SHUR, Ya. M.   a.1927-1932
He was included in the 1928 exhibition of Acquisitions by the State Art Collections Fund held in Moscow and in the jubilee exhibition Artists of the RSFSR over 15 Years held at the Russian Museum, Leningrad, in 1932.

SHURPIN, Fedor   a.1948
Socialist Realist painter. His works include *The Morning of Our Fatherland*, 1948, a still dawn-light image of Stalin against extensive agricultural land. Harvesting is in progress and pylons stretch to the horizon.

SHURYGIN, Aleksandr Alekseevich   b.1862
Genre painter.
Coll TG.

SHUSTOV, Nikolai Semenovich   1834-1868
Painter. He was a member of the Artel which led to the founding of the Wanderers movement. The date of his death is sometimes given as 1869.
Coll TG.

SHVABE, A. P. = SCHWABE, J. G.

SHVARTS, A. S.   a.1918
He was engaged in Agitprop decorations for Baltic Station Square, Petrograd, in 1918.

SHVARTS (SCHWARZ), Vyacheslav Grigor'evich
1838-1869
Russian-German battle painter, theatre designer, etcher. Born at Kursk. He studied at the Academy in Berlin. He was appointed a court painter by Tsar Nikolai II. He designed costumes for A.K.Tolstoy's tragedy *Smert' Ivana Groznogo* (The Death of Ivan the Terrible) 1865-6.
Coll TG; RM.

SHVEDE (SCHWEDE), Fedor Fedorovich   1819-1863
Painter. He studied at the Academy in St. Petersburg. His works included landscapes and *The Chess Game*, 1848, at the Tretyakov Gallery, Moscow.
Coll TG.

SHVEDE-RADLOVA, N. K.   a.1932
She was represented at the jubilee exhibition Artists of the RSFSR over 15 Years held at the Russian Museum, Leningrad, in 1932.

SHVETSOVA, I. D.   a.1919
Painter. She exhibited at the juryless Eighth State Exhibition in Moscow in 1919.

SIDORENKO, Vyacheslav Leonidovich   1901-1943
He was included in the 1928 exhibition of Acquisitions by the State Art Collections Fund held in Moscow and in the First Touring Exhibition of Painting and Graphics which opened in Moscow in 1929.

SILICH, Lyubov'   b.1907-1928+
Textile designer. She contributed to the First Art Exhibition of Soviet Textiles in Moscow in 1928.

SIMAKOV, Ivan Vasilievich   1877-1925
Architect and graphic artist. He studied at the Academy in St. Petersburg 1903-12.
After the Revolution he was engaged in Agitprop decorations at Finland Station Square, Petrograd, in 1918. He later concentrated on graphic works and was designing posters in 1921. He exhibited with the Petrograd Society of Artists, the Society of Russian Watercolourists and in international graphic art exhibitions. He was represented at the Paris International Exhibition in 1925.

SIMKHOVICH, Simka Taibukhovich   a.1918
Painter. He studied at the Academy in St. Petersburg.
After the Revolution he was engaged in Agitprop decorations at Tuchkov Bridge, Petrograd, in collaboration with R.A.Gabrikov in 1918. He was awarded a prize by the Soviet government in 1918.

SIMKIN, B.   a.1921
He was included in the Third Touring Exhibition of the Sovetsk Regional subdepartment of the Museums Bureau along with Kandinsky, Rodchenko and others in 1921.

SIMON, Nikolai Ivanovich   a.1918-1929
He was engaged in Agitprop decorations at Saratov 1918-20. He exhibited with the 4 Arts society in Leningrad including the exhibition of 1928 at the Russian Museum and was represented at the First Touring Exhibition of Painting and Graphics which opened in Moscow in 1929.

SIMONOV, V. L.   a.1918
He was engaged in Agitprop decorations at University Square and at the Academy of Sciences, Petrograd, in collaboration with G.K.Savitsky and V.Kuchumov in 1918.

SIMONOVICH-EFIMOVA, Nina Yakovlevna 1877-1948
Graphic artist, painter, sculptor, puppeteer, theatre designer, typographic artist. Born in St. Petersburg, the daughter of a paediatrician and of the organiser of a pioneering kindergarten. Her cousin was the artist Valentin Serov who gave her lessons. She worked as a teacher in Tiflis 1896-8. By 1898 she was committed to both art and puppets.
She studied under Delécluze in Paris in 1899 and then at the Stroganov Institute and the Zvantseva School. She returned to Paris in 1901 where she studied under Eugène Carrière. She married the sculptor Ivan Efimov in 1906. She then attended the Moscow College. She visited Holland in 1907 before returning to Paris for the period 1908-10 where she studied under Matisse and exhibited at the Salon des Indépendants and at the Salon d'Automne in the period 1909-11. During 1911-15 she painted rural themes in the Tambov region. She performed with puppets at the Moscow Society of Artists and at the Café Pittoresque and may have benefited from the French enthusiasm for puppets and shadow theatres which she may have seen in Paris. These, like hers, were aimed at a mature audience and were not primarily for children.
After the Revolution, together with Efimov, she opened the Theatre of Marionettes, Petrushkas and Shadows in October 1918 in Moscow and attracted collaboration from Vladimir Favorsky, Pavel Florensky, Exter and Popova. She frequently executed silhouettes and this brought her close to the graphic work of Narbut, Favorsky and others. She was an innovator in the use of rod-puppets rather in the manner of Javanese shadow puppets. She made over 1,500 performances with

Nina Simonovich-Efimova. The Philosopher Pavel Florensky at Work, *1926. Silhouette.*
Efimov Museum, Moscow.

puppets including Shakespearian plays.
She was represented in the Fourth State Exhibition of Paintings (*IV Gosudarstvennaya vystavka kartin*) in Moscow in 1919 and at the Sixth State Exhibition: The Print (*VI Gosudarstvennaya vystavka gravyur*) in Moscow in 1919. She joined the *Makovets* group in 1922 and was represented at its third and last exhibition 1925-6 in Moscow. She worked on exhibitions for the Museum of Ethnography and on the All-Russian Agricultural Exhibition in 1923. She was a member of the 4 Arts society 1925-9. She was included in the exhibition marking the tenth anniversary of the Revolution in 1927 and in the 1928 exhibition of Acquisitions by the State Art Collections Fund held in Moscow. She taught puppetry 1928-9. Some of her productions included elegant shadow plays including *The Stolen Sun*, 1938. She was given a personal exhibition in 1945. She died in Moscow.
Writings N.Simonovich-Efimova *Zapiski Petrushechnika* (Notes on Petrushka and articles on the Theatre of Marionettes), Leningrad, 1980.
Lit M.N.Yablonskaya *Women Artists of Russia's New Age*, London, 1990.
Coll TG; Efimov Museum, Moscow.

SIMOV, Viktor Andreevich   1858-1935
Painter, theatre designer. Born in Moscow. He studied at the Academy in St. Petersburg under Perov, Pryanishnikov and Savrasov graduating in 1882. He executed designs for Mamontov's private opera 1885-6 and became a theatre designer. Between 1898 and 1912, and also in 1915, he was designer at the Moscow Art Theatre where he led a department of experimental decoration.
After the Revolution he was represented at the enormous First State Exhibition of Art and Science, which included ethnographic material, held in Kazan in 1920. He contributed to the exhibition Art of Moscow Theatre 1918-1923 held in Moscow in 1923. He designed several productions at the Moscow Art Theatre. He died in Moscow.
Theatre design At the Moscow Art Theatre: 1898 A.K.Tolstoy's *Tsar' Fedor Ioannovich* produced by Stanislavsky.
1898 A.Chekhov's *Seagull* produced by Stanislavsky and V.Namirovich-Danchenko.
1899 *Odinokie* (The Unattached) produced by Stanislavsky and Nemirovich-Danchenko.
1899 A.K.Tolstoy's *Smert' Ioanna Groznogo* (The Death of Ivan the Terrible) produced by Stanislavsky.
1900 Ibsen's *Dr Shtokman* produced by Stanislavsky.
1901 Chekhov's *Three Sisters* produced by Stanislavsky.
1907 costumes for L.Andreev's play *Zhizn' cheloveka* (The Life of a Man).
1915 December: Tairov's production of Rostand's *Cyrano de Bergerac* at the Kamerny (Chamber) Theatre, Moscow, with music by Forterre.
1926 May, in collaboration with D.N.Kardovsky, A.R.Kugel's *Nicolas I and the Decembrists* at the Moscow Art Theatre.
1927 November V.V.Ivanov's *Bronepoezd 14-69* (Armoured Train 14-69) at the Moscow Art Theatre.
1932 November, in collaboration with V.V.Dmitriev and others, Gogol's *Dead Souls* at the Moscow Art Theatre.
Lit *Paris-Moscou*, 1979.
Coll TG; Bakhrushin Theatre Museum, Moscow.

SINAYSKY, Viktor Aleksandrovich   1893-1968
Sculptor. Born at Mariupol. He studied at the School of Art in Odessa from 1913.
After the Revolution he studied at the Petrograd Vkhutemas under V.Beklemishev and in 1918 he executed a bust of Lasalle on Nevsky Prospekt as part of Lenin's Plan for Monumental Propaganda (granite copy of 1921 in RM). He taught at the Vkhutemas in 1921 and later at the Academy of Arts in Leningrad. He was represented at the exhibition of Studies for Theatre Decoration and Works from the Studios of the Decorative Institute held in Petrograd in 1922. He was included in the 1928 exhibition of Acquisitions by the State Art Collections Fund held in Moscow. He died in Leningrad.
*Monument to Lassalle, 1918, has a somewhat academic head surmounting a stylised and elongated neck and shoulders. This dramatic bust projected over the edges of a curious high plinth rising from square cross-section to hexagonal base. It was an early example of historicising sculptural rhetoric enlivened by a dynamic derived from more experimental art. It was unveiled on 7 October 1918.
*Young Worker, 1937, bronze, is a bland and rather academic full-length. The worker is naturally fit and casually dressed.
Lit *Paris-Moscou*, 1979.
Coll RM.

SINEZUBOV, Nikolai Vladimirovich   1891-1948
Painter. Born in Moscow. He studied at the Moscow College from 1912 until 1917.
After the Revolution his name appeared on the April 1919 list of artists for acquisitions by the envisaged Museum of

Painterly Culture. He led the Moscow Proletkult studios in 1919 and he was represented in the Fourth State Exhibition of Paintings (*IV Gosudarstvennaya vystavka kartin*) in Moscow in 1919 and at the Nineteenth Exhibition of the All-Russian Exhibitions Bureau in Moscow in 1920. He exhibited with Kandinsky, Rodchenko and Stepanova in the exhibition The Four in 1921. He was included in the Third Touring Exhibition of the Sovetsk Regional subdepartment of the Museums Bureau along with Kandinsky, Rodchenko and others in 1921 and he exhibited in the 1921 exhibition of the World of Art in Moscow. He worked for INKhUK. In 1922 he was associated with the Vkhutemas and Proletkult and was represented at the First Russian Art Exhibition in Berlin in 1922. He settled in Germany 1922-8 but exhibited at the third and last exhibition of the *Makovets* group in Moscow 1925-6. He was included in the 1928 exhibition of Acquisitions by the State Art Collections Fund held in Moscow. He emigrated to France in 1928. He died in Paris.
Lit E.Weiss *Russische Avant-Garde, 1910-1930, Sammlung Ludwig, Köln*, Munich, 1986. A.M.Muratov, V.Manin et al. *Zhivopis' 20-30kh godov*, Sankt-Peterburg, 1991. *L'Avant-garde russe 1905-1925*, exh. cat., Musée des Beaux-Arts, Nantes, 1993.
Coll RM; Yaroslavl' Art Museum; Sammlung Ludwig, Cologne.

SINITSYNA, O. A.　　　　　　　　　**a.1925-1929**
She exhibited with the Society of Moscow Painters at its inaugural exhibition in Moscow in 1925 and was represented at the First Touring Exhibition of Painting and Graphics which opened in Moscow in 1929.

SINYAKOVA, Mariya Mikhailovna　　　**1898-1984**
Painter, graphic artist. She studied under Mashkov from 1912 and exhibited with the Union of Youth 1913-14. With N.Aseev she invited the painter-composer Matyushin to Krasnaya Polyana in the summer of 1916 where he met Grigoriy Petnikov, Dmitri Petrovsky and the Futurist poet Khlebnikov.
After the Revolution she was engaged in book illustration. She exhibited with the 4 Arts society in Moscow in 1925. She worked in a loose style reminiscent of certain Goncharova illustrations. The date of her death is sometimes given as 1985.
Book illustration Cover for A.Kruchenykh *Razboynik Van'ka-Kayn i Son'ka manikyurshchitsa* (The Robber Ivan-Kain and Sonya the Manicurist), Moscow, 1925 (dated 1926).
Lit S.Compton *Russian Avant-Garde Books 1917-34*, London, 1992.

SINYAVSKY, Nikolai Alekseevich (Aleksandrovch)　**b.1771**
Painter of portraits and landscapes. He studied at the Academy in St. Petersburg.
Coll TG.

SKh
The abbreviated name of the Union of Artists (*Soyuz khudozhnikov*).

SKhM
The abbreviated name of the Free Art Studios (*Svobodnye khudozhestvennye masterskie*) in Moscow operative 1918-20.

SKhUM
The abbreviated name of the Free Art Teaching Studios (*Svobodnye khudozhestvenno-uchebnye masterskie*) in Petrograd operative 1918-21.

SKACHKO, A. N.　　　　　　　　　　**a.1922**
He was a member of the first exhibition committee of AKhRR, the Association of Artists of Revolutionary Russia, in 1922. In 1922 he was a founder member of the Society (*Obshchestvo*) of Artists of Revolutionary Russia, founded after the first exhibition of AKhRR. Other members included A.Grigoriev, P.Kiselev, E.Katsman, N.Kotov, S.Malyutin, P.Radimov, P.Shukhmin, G.Sukhanov, B.Yakovlev and V.Zhuravlev.

SKADOVSKY, Nikolai L'vovich　　　　**1846-1892**
Painter of figure compositions and genre scenes.
Coll TG.

SKALON, A. V.　　　　　　　　　　　**1874-1942**
Painter, art critic. He exhibited with the Wanderers from 1906. He was a member of the committee for the spring exhibitions at the Academy in St. Petersburg and was active as a critic in 1909.

SKOLOZDRA, Vladimir Ivanovich　　　**b.1919**
Sculptor. See Ryabinin.

SKORIKOV, Ivan Dmitrievich　　　　　**1812-1842**
Painter of views and landscapes. He studied at the Academy in St. Petersburg.
Coll TG.

SKOTTI, Dementiy Karlovich (SCOTTI, Domenico)
1780-1825
Portrait painter. Sometimes he signed his work 'Domenico Scotti' in latin script.
Coll TG.

SKOTTI, Mikhail Ivanovich　　　　　　**1814-1861**
Painter whose subjects included portraits as well as religious and mythological themes. He painted the Venice Carnival in 1839 and was in Rome in 1843. Sometimes he signed his work 'M.Scotti' in latin script.
Coll TG; RM.

SKVORIKOVA, T. M.　　　　　　　　　**a.1932**
She was represented at the jubilee exhibition Artists of the RSFSR over 15 Years held at the Russian Museum, Leningrad, in 1932.

SLAVYANSKY, Fedor Mikhailovich　　　**1819-1876**
Painter whose work included portraits and interiors.
Coll TG.

SLEPYAN, Moisei Grigorievich　　　　　**1872-1941**
Painter. He studied at the School of Drawing in Odessa 1892-5 and at the Academy in St. Petersburg 1896-1901. He exhibited with the Society of Russian Watercolourists, the Kuindzhi Society and at exhibitions in Belorussia.
After the Revolution he participated in the First State Free Exhibition of Artworks in Petrograd in 1919.

SLONIM, Ilya　　　　　　　　　　　　**a.1935**
Sculptor. He exhibited with Sarra Lebedeva, A.E.Zelensky, Vera Mukhina, Vladimir Favorsky, I.G.Frikh-Khar and I.M.Chaykov in Moscow in 1935.

SMIRNOV, I. F.　　　　　　　　　　　**a.1918-1927**
Painter. He exhibited at the Fifth State Exhibition: From Impressionism to Non-Objective Art in Moscow 1918-19 and

his name appeared on the April 1919 list of artists for acquisitions by the envisaged Museum of Painterly Culture. He was included in the major exhibition in Moscow in 1927 marking the tenth anniversary of the Revolution.

SMIRNOV, N. G.   a.1924
He exhibited with the First Working Group of Constructivsts in 1924 at the First Discussional Exhibition of Active Revolutionary Art alongside L.Sanina, A.Gan, Olga and Galina Chichagova, G.Miller and A.Mirolyubova.

SMIRNOV, Vasili Sergeevich   1858-1890
History painter. He studied in Moscow and St. Petersburg.
Coll TG; RM.

SMIRNOVA, N.   a.1917
She exhibited with the World of Art in December 1917 in Moscow.

SMOLIN, A. A.   b.1927
Painter. He collaborated with his brother the painter P.A.Smolin.
Coll TG.

SMOLIN, P. A.   b. 1930
Painter. He collaborated with his brother the painter A.A.Smolin. Their painting *The Strike in 1905*, 1964, TG, depicts ranks of marching soldiers against a towering urban backdrop to assert the continuity of the Revolution despite the passing decades.

SMOTROVA, T. F.   a.1927-1928
Sculptor. She was included in the major exhibition in Moscow in 1927 marking the tenth anniversary of the Revolution and in the 1928 exhibition of Acquisitions by the State Art Collections Fund held in Moscow.

SMUKROVICH, P. I.   a.1918-1919
He was engaged in Agitprop decorations at the Nikolaevsky Embankment, Petrograd, in 1918.
One design shows a worker with wheel-barrow, simplified, massive and forceful. He also executed designs with V.Emme employing red flags and white motifs arranged around a square. He participated in the First State Free Exhibition of Artworks in Petrograd in 1919.

SNEGIREVA-YURGENSON, A. P.   a.1919
Painter. She exhibited at the Ninth State Exhibition of Paintings: Naturalism and Realism in Moscow in 1919.

SOBOLEV, I. S.   a.1919-1926
Painter. His name appeared on the April 1919 list of artists for acquisitions by the envisaged Museum of Painterly Culture. He exhibited at the third and last exhibition of the *Makovets* group in Moscow 1925-6.

SOBOLEVA, E.   a.1928
Textile designer. She contributed to the First Art Exhibition of Soviet Textiles in Moscow 1928.

SOBOLEVA, L. K.   a.1919
Painter. She exhibited at the juryless Eighth State Exhibition in Moscow in 1919.

SOBOROVA, Aleksandra Sergeevna   a. c.1918
Graphic artist. She was engaged in Agitprop work in the early

revolutionary years including decorations on the propaganda trains *Red Cossack*, the Ukrainian train *Lenin, Lenin (October Revolution)* and *Soviet Caucasus*. She was later active as a poster designer.
Lit *Paris-Moscou*, 1979.

SOFRONOVA, Antonina Fedorovna   1892-1966
Painter, illustrator. Born at Droskovo in the Orel region, the daughter of a village doctor. She attended school in Kiev and moved to Moscow in 1910 where she studied under Fedor Rerberg. She then studied privately under Mashkov from 1913. She exhibited with the Knave of Diamonds in 1914 and with the World of Art in 1917. She married the artist and theorist G.M.Blyumenfeld in 1915.
After the Revolution she exhibited with the World of Art in December 1917 in Moscow. She taught at the State Art Studios in Orel and Tver (Kalinin) 1919-21. She returned to Moscow in 1921. She was executing works with geometric shapes and flat colour in 1922. She was an associate of the Constructivist critic and theorist Nikolai Tarabukin and designed the cover of his book *Ot mol'berta k mashine* (From the Easel to the Machine) which was published in 1923. This design reflected an awareness of the principles of both Constructivism and Suprematism employing geometric forms in the layout and diverse kinds of lettering. She also designed for books and for the periodicals *Red Virgin Soil* and *Club*.
She returned to landscape painting and illustration from the mid-1920s including drawings of Moscow street types in 1924 which distantly recall Grosz translated into a softer and gentler technique. Like Udal'tsova she contributed to the exhibition Group 13 in 1931, and was also represented at the exhibition Artists of the RSFSR over 15 Years in Moscow in 1933. She was a member of the Moscow Union of Artists in 1937 and contributed to the Exhibition of Paintings, Graphics and Sculpture by Women Artists in Moscow in 1938. She settled in Gudauta in 1939. She died in Moscow.
Lit A.Z.Rudenstine *Costakis Collection*, 1981. M.N.Yablonskaya *Women Artists of Russia's New Age*, London, 1990.
Coll RM; Costakis Collection.

SOKOLOV, Il'ya Alekseevich   1890-1968
He was included in the Third Touring Exhibition of the Sovetsk Regional subdepartment of the Museums Bureau along with Kandinsky, Rodchenko and others in 1921 and exhibited in the 1921 exhibition of the World of Art in Moscow. He exhibited with the *Zhar-tsvet* (Fire-colour) group between 1924 and 1928 and was included in the exhibition of Russian Graphic Art in Riga in 1929. He was also represented at the First Touring Exhibition of Painting and Graphics which opened in Moscow in 1929 and at the jubilee exhibition Artists of the RSFSR over 15 Years held at the Russian Museum, Leningrad, in 1932.

SOKOLOV, Ivan   1717-1757
Engraver. He studied under O.Elliger and Wortmann. He worked for the court producing views and portraits. He was producing engravings in 1748. He died in St. Petersburg.

SOKOLOV, Ivan Ivanovich   1823-1918
Genre painter. Born at Astrakhan. He studied at the Academy in St. Petersburg. Sometimes the date of his death is given as 1910.
Coll TG.

SOKOLOV, Kirill   **b.1930**
Painter, printmaker, sculptor, theatre designer. Born in
Moscow. He studied at the Moscow Central Art School 1942-50
and at the Surikov Art Institute in Moscow 1950-7. He then
began to exhibit. One-man exhibitions included linocuts on
the theme of *Hamlet*, shown at the Literature Museum,
Moscow, in 1964.
He has lived in England since 1974 and has shown work in
London, Edinburgh, New York and Washington since 1976.
He exhibited at the Edinburgh Festival in 1985 and 1987. As
an active printmaker he has been closely associated with the
group Northern Print in Newcastle-upon-Tyne. Recent
exhibitions have included a retrospective at the Gulbenkian
Gallery, Newcastle-upon-Tyne in 1976, graphic works to
Faust at the Lyric Theatre, London, 1988, and at the Faust
Museum in Germany in 1989. Graphic work was exhibited at
the Riga Academy of Arts in Latvia in 1990 and at the Central
Exhibition Hall under the auspices of the Union of Artists,
Moscow, in 1992. His work is characterised by vigour, drama
and directness. Stylistically it was indebted to the lessons of
Fal'k and others at the time of his move to England, but this
was always interpreted with energy and a dynamic force which
he has employed in all of his work which ranges from stage,
interior, exhibition and book design to easel paintings and
graphic works in every printmaking medium. In recent years
his colour has lightened and his graphic work and painting has
taken on a new immediacy of execution and expression. His
art combines technical inventiveness, astute observation and a
fantastic aspect anchored in literary sources, both Russian and
west European.
Theatre design 1986 John Silkin's *Black Notes* at the
Pentameter Theatre, London.
Lit *Goethe Faust, Kirill Sokolov, Austellung des graphischen
Zyklus*, exh. cat., Faust-Museum, Knittlingen, Germany, 1989.
Coll TG; State Pushkin Museum, Moscow; Dostoevsky
Memorial Museum, Moscow; Pushkin Memorial Museum,
Moscow; Blok Memorial Museum, Leningrad; Shevchenko
Memorial Museum, Kiev; Victoria and Albert Museum, London.
Colour plate p.383.

SOKOLOV, Mikhail Grigorevich   **1875-1953**
Portrait painter.
Coll TG.

SOKOLOV, Mikhail Ksenofontovich   **1885-1947**
Painter. He was included in the 1928 exhibition of Acquisitions
by the State Art Collections Fund held in Moscow.
Coll RM.

SOKOLOV, Nikolai Aleksandrovich   **1903-1941+**
Painter, graphic artist. Born in Moscow. He was one of the
trio of satirical artists operating under the acronym Kukryniksy
from 1925. He studied at the Rybinsk Art School under
M.Shcheglov 1920-3 and at the Vkhutemas/Vkhutein under
N.Kupreyanov, P.Miturich and P.Lvov 1923-9. He was
represented at the jubilee exhibition Artists of the RSFSR over
15 Years held at the Russian Museum, Leningrad, in 1932. He
was designing posters in 1941.
Lit *Paris-Moscou*, 1979.

SOKOLOV, Petr Efimovich   **1882-1964**
Painter. His name appeared on the April 1919 list of artists for
acquisitions by the envisaged Museum of Painterly Culture.

He assisted Malevich 1918-20 and was an organiser of the
Voronezh Vkhutemas 1926.

SOKOLOV, Petr Fedorovich   **1787-1848**
Painter of classical themes. There is doubt about the date of
his birth which is sometimes given as 1791.
Coll TG.

SOKOLOV, Petr Ivanovich   **1753-1791**
History painter. Born in St. Petersburg. He studied under
Batoni in Rome and became an early example in Russia of the
painter of classical mythology. His works include *Daedalus
Attaching Wings to Icarus*, 1777, TG. He died in St. Petersburg.
Coll TG; RM.

SOKOLOV, Petr Ivanovich   **1892-1938**
Painter, theatre designer, graphic artist. He was engaged in
Agitprop decorative projects in the early revolutionary years. In
1922 he graduated from the Academy of Arts where he studied
under Petrov-Vodkin. He contributed to the Exhibition of
Paintings by Russian Artists held at Pskov in Spring 1920 and
was included in the enormous survey Exhibition of Paintings by
Petrograd Artists of All Tendencies 1919-1923 held in
Petrograd in 1923. He exhibited with the group The Sixteen,
the group *Zhar-tsvet* (Fire-colour) and with AKhRR as well as in
theatrical and graphic exhibitions including the All-Union
Polygraphic Exhibition in Moscow in 1927.

SOKOLOV, Petr Petrovich   **1821-1899**
Painter of landscapes, genre scenes and portraits. Sometimes
he signed his work with the monogram 'PS'. He was
represented at the Paris International Exhibition in 1889
where he was awarded a gold medal. He died at Tsarskoe Selo.
Coll TG.

SOKOLOV, Vadim Nikolaevich   **b.1917**
Academic sculptor. Works include *Young Worker* in 1950.

SOKOLOV, Vladimir N.   **a.1919-1921**
Graphic artist. He was represented in the Sixth State Exhibition:
The Print (*VI Gosudarstvennaya vystavka gravyur*) in Moscow in
1919. He was included in the Third Touring Exhibition of the
Sovetsk Regional subdepartment of the Museums Bureau along
with Kandinsky, Rodchenko and others in 1921.

SOKOLOV-SKALYA, Pavel Petrovich   **1899-1961**
Painter. He was a member of the *Bytie* (Existence) Society of
Artists formed in Moscow in 1921. He contributed to the
1921 exhibition of the World of Art in Moscow and at the first
Bytie exhibition in 1922. He was represented at the Paris
International Exhibition in 1925 and at the jubilee exhibition
Artists of the RSFSR over 15 Years held at the Russian
Museum, Leningrad, in 1932.

SOKOLOVA, Olga Aleksandrovna   **1889-1991**
Painter. She studied at Moscow University and at the Moscow
Vkhutemas under Drevin and others. She died in Moscow.
Coll RM.

SOLDATKIN, Petr Illarionovich   **1824-1885**
Painter whose work included views.
Coll TG.

SOLLOGUB, F. L.   **1848-1890**
Theatre designer. He made designs for Shakespeare's *Macbeth*
in 1884.

Konstantin Somov. Fireworks. *Bodycolour on black paper. 25 x 29.5 cm. Ashmolean Museum, Oxford*

SOLNTSEV, Egor Grigorievich 1818-1864
Painter. His work included a view of Naples. He sometimes signed his work 'Solnzeff'.
Coll TG.

SOLOMATIN a.1919
Painter who contributed to the Twelfth State Exhibition: Colourdynamo and Tectonic Primitivism *(Tsvetodinamos i tektonicheskiy primitivizm)* along with Grishchenko, Shevchenko and others in Moscow in 1919.

SOLOMATKIN, Leonid I. 1837-1883
Painter of socially committed genre themes.
Coll TG.

SOLOMKO, Sergei 1859-1926
Graphic artist, illustrator, watercolourist. He published designs in the German periodical *Jugend* and with French publishers.
Lit *Twilight of the Tsars*, London, 1991.

SOLOV'EV (SOLOVIEV), Lev Grigorievich 1837-1919
Painter. He was teaching with M.I.Ponomarev at the Free Voronezh School of Painting and Drawing during the period 1896-1901 where his pupils included the painter Aleksandr Kuprin.
Coll TG.

SOMOV, Andrei Ivanovich 1830-1909
Painter, etcher, art historian, critic. He was the father of the painter Konstantin Somov, a collector of French and Flemish paintings, a founder member of the Society of Watercolourists and Senior Curator at the Hermitage Museum in St. Petersburg.

SOMOV, Konstantin Andreevich 1869-1939
Painter, graphic artist. He developed an historicist style evocative of a fantastic 18th century, comparable with that conjured up by Benois and some other members of the World of Art, but that of Somov was both erotic and feminine. He harnessed a precise draughtsmanship to a light delicacy of touch and a capricious wit.
Born in St. Petersburg, the son of Andrei Ivanovich Somov, a wealthy Senior Curator at the Hermitage Museum. After attending school with the future artists Filosofov and Benois 1879-88, he studied at the Academy in St. Petersburg under V.Vereshchagin, Chistyakov and later Repin 1888-97. In 1890 and 1894 he travelled to Italy. He exhibited with the Society of Watercolourists in 1894. He was expelled from the Academy for involvement in a student strike and declined to return there when offered the opportunity to do so.
He worked in Paris with Benois 1897-9 where he attended the Académie Colarossi and occasionally Whistler's Académie Carmen. In Paris he encountered Bakst, Lansere, Ober, Ostroumova-Lebedeva, Yakunchikova and Zvantseva. In 1898 he designed the poster for the exhibition Russian and Finnish Artists held in St. Petersburg. He paid a brief visit to England in 1899. He exhibited as a founder member with the World of Art 1899-1906. In 1901 he was in Dresden and Berlin. His graphic work also included covers for the *Annual of the*

Imperial Theatres in 1901 and for a monograph on Dmitri Levitsky in 1902. He was closely associated with the World of Art movement but also held a one-man exhibition in 1903 under the auspices of the organisation Contemporary Art and a monograph was published. He exhibited with the Union of Russian Artists from 1903 to 1910. He was represented in Diaghilev's display of Russian art at the 1906 Salon d'Automne in Paris. He contributed illustrations to numerous journals including *Zolotoe Runo* (The Golden Fleece), *Vesy* (Libra), *Starye Gody* (Bygone Years) and *Apollon* (Apollo). He was made an Academician in 1913. He helped to organise the Yulia Sazonova puppet theatre in Petrograd in 1915.

His precise portrait drawings reveal his academic expertise but his paintings reveal an elegance and wit applied to 18th century themes. They were frequently delicate scenes of the *fête-champêtre* in formal gardens displaying a light eroticism reminiscent of Boucher or Fragonard, yet reflected in a different age and country. His witty historicism was spiked by a melancholy which arose from the enjoyment of another time, an alternative world to that in which he lived.

After the Revolution he produced illustrations for the *Livre de la Marquise* (*Kniga Markizy*) in 1918. He contributed to the Exhibition of Paintings by Russian Artists held at Pskov in Spring 1920.

He emigrated in 1923 to go to America, having travelled there to mount an exhibition of Russian art, but he settled in Paris 1924-5. He held a one-man exhibition there in 1928. He executed commissions for the collector Mikhail Braikevich. He died in Paris.

Works include *Lady in Blue*, 1897-1900, TG, *Fireworks* 1904, two porcelain pieces 1905, *Harlequin and Death*, 1907, TG, a drop curtain for the Free Theatre in St. Petersburg in 1913 and *Skating Rink*, 1915. He made a portrait of the painter *Anna Ostroumova* in 1901.

*Self-portrait, 1898, RM, has the precise sobriety that characterised his likenesses of many of his friends and contemporaries. The result is based upon a virtuoso performance with academic drawing techniques. Sometimes Bakst did similar studies.

*Evening, 1900-2, TG, is a favourite theme of 18th century figures engaged in dalliance beneath an arbour, hedge or, as here, a pergola heavy with grapes dangling from a vine. The elegaic mood and longing for an imaginary other time is characteristic and is only ever partially lifted by scenes of amorous naughtiness that are the distant descendants of Fragonard, Boucher and Watteau.

*The Kiss, etching, 1906, uses a silhouette effect to depict 18th century aristocrats at amorous dalliance. Strictly in profile, as in a drama for shadow puppets, the bewigged man just touches the lips of the voluminously but feminine and elegantly clad woman as they sit upon the bench of a formal garden. It is characteristic of the amusing, refined eroticism and technical mastery of Somov's work. A painting of a comparable theme is *The Ridiculed Kiss*, 1908, RM.

*Young Woman Sleeping, 1922, Brodsky Museum, St. Petersburg, is a subtle and erotic blend of past and present in which the young woman is observed thinly but elegantly dressed and indiscreetly asleep. The voyeurism is mitigated by the painter's delicacy and his evident wonder at the femininity of what he observes.

Theatre design 1913 Curtain design for the Free Theatre, Moscow.

Lit O.Bie *Constantin Somoff*, Berlin, 1907. S.Ernst *K.A.Somov*, St. Petersburg, 1918. J.E.Bowlt *K.Somov*, in *Art Journal*, fall, 1970, pp. 31-6. *K.A.Somov*, exh. cat., Russian Museum, Leningrad, 1971. I.Pruzhan *K.Somov*, Moscow, 1972. A.Gusarova *K.Somov*, Moscow, 1973. E.V.Zhuravleva *K.A.Somov*, Moscow, 1981. J.E.Bowlt *Russian Stage Design. Scenic Innovation. From the Collection of Mr. and Mrs. Nikita D.Lobanov-Rostovsky*, Jackson, MS, exh. cat., 1982. A.Kamensky *The World of Art Movement*, Leningrad, 1991.

Coll Major holdings at TG; RM; Brodsky Museum, St.

Konstantin Somov. The Kiss, *1906. Silhouette drawing for the periodical 'Apollon'. 14.4 x 14.2 cm. An exercise in playful eroticism set in the 18th century, a theme which often attracted Somov as well as other painters of the World of Art.*

Konstantin Somov. Study for a Costume for Tamara Karsavina, 1924. Watercolour. Signed and dated lower right in ink 'C.Somoff, Paris 1924'. 33.3 x 24.7 cm.
Collection Mr. and Mrs. Nikita D.Lobanov-Rostovsky, London.

Petersburg; Odessa Art Museum; Radishchev Art Museum, Saratov; Armenian Art Museum, Yerevan; Ashmolean Museum, Oxford.

SOMOVA, O. N.   a.1927-1928
Sculptor. She was included in the major exhibition in Moscow in 1927 marking the tenth anniversary of the Revolution and the 1928 exhibition of Acquisitions by the State Art Collections Fund held in Moscow.

SOMOVA-MIKHAILOVA   a.1908-1910
Painter. She exhibited with the Union of Russian Artists in 1908-10.

SORIN, Saveli Abramovich   1878-1953
Painter. He was impressed by the work of Konstantin Somov and worked at St. Petersburg.
He contributed to the exhibition of Contemporary Russian Art held at Philadelphia in 1932.

SOROKA, Grigori Vasili'evich   1823-1864
Painter of views, genre themes and portraits. He was a serf who worked as a gardener when studying under Venetsianov. After the abolition of serfdom in 1861 he was sentenced to corporal punishment for involvement with peasant disturbances and committed suicide.
A Chapel in the Village of Ostrovsky, late 1840s-early 1850s, The Hermitage, Leningrad, is a haunting and poetically evocative painting of two figures conversing by a bridge.

Across the stream a chapel is visible set among the trees. The atmosphere is one of gentle melancholia and the painting is pervaded by an extraordinary stillness. *Fishermen: View of Lake Moldino*, late 1840s, RM, is a comparable achievement in its expansive stillness, itself a sign of Venetsianov's legacy.
Coll TG; RM.

SOROKIN, Evgraf Semenovich   1821-1892
Genre painter. He was the brother of the artists Pavel and Vasili Sorokin. He studied at the Academy in St. Petersburg. His work included painting for the Russian Church in Paris. Sometimes he signed his work 'Sorokine' in latin script. He died in Moscow.
Coll TG; RM.

SOROKIN, Pavel Semenovich   1836?-1886
Painter of religious themes. The date of his birth is sometimes given as 1839. He was the brother of the artists Evgraf and Vasili Sorokin. He became a member of the Academy in St. Petersburg. He died in Moscow.
Coll TG.

SOROKIN, Vasili Semenovich   1833-1918
Mosaics artist. He was the brother of the painters Evgraf and Pavel Sorokin. He studied at the Academy in St. Petersburg and executed mosaics for St. Isaak's Church in Moscow.
Coll TG.

SOTNIKOV, Aleksei Georgievich   b.1904
Ceramic sculptor. Born into a peasant family in Kuban. He studied at the Krasnodar Art Technical College 1925-8 and at the Vkhutein under Tatlin, Kuznetsov, Bruni and Shterenberg 1930-2 specialising in ceramics. Here his work included a set of children's nursing vessels based on the shape of the breast. He also designed here a teapot without a handle. He assisted Tatlin in the construction of his glider *Letatlin*. From 1934 he worked as a designer and sculptor for the Dulevo ceramics factory. His work includes animal themes in steel as well as ceramics. He was awarded the title of Honoured Art Worker of the RSFSR.
Writings A.Sotnikov *Skul'ptura*, Moscow, 1976.
Lit V.A.Tikhanova *Skul'ptory-animalisty*, Moscow, 1969. *Paris-Moscou*, 1979. C.Lodder *Russian Costructivism*, New Haven and London, 1983.

SOUDEIKINE = SUDEIKIN, S. Yu.

SOUTINE, Chaim   1893-1943
Painter. Born at Smilovichi in the Minsk region. He studied at Vilna School of Art 1910-12. He moved to Paris in 1913 where he attended the Ecole des Beaux-Arts and Cormon's studio. He occupied a studio in the complex La Ruche 1916-19 and met Lipchitz, Chagall, Zadkine and others and was drawn into the circle of Parisian artists on the fringe of Cubism. He met Modigliani in 1915. He became recognised as an expressive painter of great force, spontaneity and originality, independent of the formal experimentation of many of those around him. An important catalyst to this was the series of visits that he paid to Ceret 1919-22. In 1922 many of his works were purchased by Dr. Barnes of the Barnes Foundation. He also painted at Cagnes in the 1920s. He lived in Paris from the mid-1920s. His first retrospective was held at the Galerie de Paris in 1927 and in 1935 he was given a retrospective exhibition at the Arts Club of Chicago. He remained in Paris after the outbreak of war in 1939. He died in Paris.
A memorial exhibition was held at the Galerie de France,

Petr Staronosov. Harvest, *1928. Lino engraving.*
An image of labour and the plenitude of nature well managed.

Paris, in 1945.
Lit E.Faure *Soutine*, Paris, 1928. W.George *Soutine*, Paris, 1928. R.Cogniat *Soutine*, Paris, 1945. E.Szittya *Soutine et son temps*, Paris, 1955. J.Leymarie *Soutine*, Paris, 1968. P.Courthion *Soutine peintre du déchirant*, Lausanne, 1972. *Soutine*, exh. cat., Musée de l'Orangerie, Paris, 1973.
Coll Well represented at the Musée de l'Orangerie, Paris; MNAM, Paris; Kunsthalle, Berne; Art Institute, Chicago; Museum of Modern Art, New York.

SPANDIKOV, Eduard Karlovich   **1875-1929**
Born at Kalvaria, then in Poland, now in Lithuania. He studied both medicine and art in St. Petersburg. He was a contributor to Kul'bin's exhibition Contemporary Trends in Art in 1908 and a founder member of the Union of Youth with whom he exhibited 1910-14. He became a friend of Tatlin for many years.
After the Revolution he participated in the First State Free Exhibition of Artworks in Petrograd in 1919 and was included in the enormous survey Exhibition of Paintings by Petrograd Artists of All Tendencies 1919-1923 held in Petrograd in 1923.
Lit J.Howard *The Union of Youth — An Artists' Society of the Russian Avant-Garde*, Manchester and New York, 1992.

SPASSKY, Pavel   **a. c.1918**
He was engaged in Agitprop work c.1918 and assisted on the decoration of the propaganda train *Soviet Caucasus* in 1920.

SPASSKY, Vasili Vasil'evich   **1873-1924**
Graphic artist. He was designing posters in 1919.

SPIRIN, S. V.   **a.1918**
He was engaged on Agitprop decorations in Sennaya Square, Petrograd, in 1918.

SREDIN, Aleksandr Valentinovich   **1872-1934**
Painter of portraits and landscapes.
Coll TG.

SRETENSKY, G. A.   **a.1921-1929**
Painter. He was a founder member of the group *Bytie* (Existence) formed in 1921 partly in protest at 'the narrowness of leftist art' and contributed to its first exhibition in 1922. His work was included in the exhibition of Soviet art held at Harbin in 1926 and in Japan in 1927. He was also included in the major exhibition in Moscow in 1927 marking the tenth anniversary of the Revolution and in the First Touring Exhibition of Painting and Graphics which opened in Moscow in 1929.

SRKh
The abbreviated name of the Union of Russian Artists (*Soyuz russkikh khudozhnikov*).

STANKIEWICZ, Alexander (STANKEVICH, Aleksandr)
1824-1892
Polish portrait painter. Born in Warsaw. He studied at the Academy in St. Petersburg. He died in Rome.
Coll TG; National Gallery, Cracow; National Gallery, Warsaw.

STARONOSOV, Petr Nikolaevich   **1893-1942**
Graphic artist. He was included in the 1928 exhibition of Acquisitions by the State Art Collections Fund held in Moscow and in the jubilee exhibition Artists of the RSFSR over 15 Years held at the Russian Museum, Leningrad, in 1932.

STAVASSER, Petr Andreevich   **1816-1850**
Neo-classicising sculptor of genre themes. Born in St. Petersburg. He studied at the Academy in St. Petersburg. His works included *Boy Fishing*, 1839, RM. He died in Rome.
Coll TG; RM.

STEFANOVSKY, Ivan Petrovich   **1850-1878**
Painter of genre and landscape. Signed 'J.S'.

STELLETSKY (STELETSKY), Dmitri Semenovich
1875-1947
Sculptor, painter, theatre designer, illustrator. Born at Brest-Litovsk. He studied architecture and sculpture at the Higher Art Institute of the Academy in St. Petersburg under Zaleman and Beklemishev 1896-1903 and then visited Novgorod with Boris Kustodiev in 1903.
He was studying in Paris at the Académie Julian in 1904 and was represented at Diaghilev's display of Russian art at the Salon d'Automne in 1906. He visited Italy with Boris Kustodiev in 1907 and exhibited with the Union of Russian Artists from 1907 to 1909. He executed a portrait of *The Artist and Mosaicist Boris V.Anrep* in 1906 which is an informal painting of the artist walking his dog, as well as sculptural portraits including a bust of *Leonardo da Vinci*, 1908, RM, and of the painter *V.A.Serov*, 1912-13, plaster, RM. He exhibited with the World of Art from 1912. He also executed Russian historicist works.
From 1914 he lived in Cannes and Paris. He contributed to the exhibition of Contemporary Russian Art held at Philadelphia in 1932. He died near Paris.
Theatre design 1908-9 A.K.Tolstoy's tragedy *Tsar' Fedor Ioannovich* for an unrealised production by Meyerhold at the Aleksandrinsky Theatre, St. Petersburg. The set featured a medieval and fairy tale monastic or church interior which like an ikon revealed both the roofs above and the interior within. The costume studies were practical but full of the movement of the gestures associated with the role, and loosely brushed in

Dmitri Stelletsky. Poster for an Event in Support of Russian Artists in Paris, *before 1918. Lithograph. Signed 'D.Stelletski' lower right. The matinée event held at the Salle Gaveau in Paris had the sculptor Rodin as its honorary president.*
Collection Mr. and Mrs. Nikita D.Lobanov-Rostovsky, London.

with some emphasis on decorative detail (Bakhrushin Theatre Museum).
1908-9 Rimsky-Korsakov's *Snegurochka.*
1909 Costumes for Diaghilev's production of *The Maid of Pskov* in Paris.
1926 *Russian Matrimonial Rite*, music by Glinka, for the Théâtre de la Chauve-Souris at the Théâtre de la Madeleine, Paris.
Lit *Diaghilev and Russian Stage Designers, a Loan Exhibition from the Collection of Mr. and Mrs. N.Lobanov-Rostovsky*, International Exhibitions Foundation, Washington, 1972-4. J.E.Bowlt *Russian Stage Design. Scenic Innovation. From the Collection of Mr. and Mrs. Nikita D.Lobanov-Rostovsky*, Jackson, MS, exh. cat.,1982. *Twilight of the Tsars*, London, 1991. Dzhon Boult (John Bowlt) *Khudozhniki russkogo teatra. Sobranie Nikity i Niny Lobanovykh-Rostovskikh*, Moscow, 1991.
Coll TG; RM; Bakhrushin Theatre Museum, Moscow.

STENBERG, Georgiy Avgustovich   **1900-1933**
Sculptor, theatre designer, poster designer. Brother of Vladimir Stenberg with whom he worked under the title 2 Stenberg 2. He was an exponent of Constructivism in its laboratory art phase and followed its development into useful

design work which in their case comprised the design of sets for the director A.Tairov at the Kamerny (Chamber) Theatre in Moscow and the production of theatre and cinema posters. They signed these works '2 Stenberg 2' or '2 Sten'.
Born in Moscow. He studied at the Stroganov College under V.Egorov and A.Yanova 1912-17 and first became involved with design for the stage in 1915.
After the Revolution he studied under Yakulov at the Free Art Studios (SVOMAS) in Moscow 1917-20. He was engaged with V.Stenberg and Denisovsky on propaganda decorations in Moscow in 1918. In 1919 he joined the group Obmokhu (Society of Young Artists) and exhibited in the first Obmokhu exhibition in May 1919 in Moscow. In 1922 he exhibited with V.Stenberg and K.Medunetsky as The Constructivists at the Poets' Café in Moscow, having become a member of the Institute of Artistic Culture (INKhUK) in 1920 and within this a member of the First Working Group of Constructivists. He travelled with Tairov's Kamerny Theatre company on its tour of Western Europe in 1923 and continued to design for Tairov until 1931. He exhibited at the All-Russian Agricultural Exhibition in Moscow in 1923. He was represented at the First Discussional Exhibition of Active Revolutionary Art in Moscow in 1924 and at the Paris International Exhibition in 1925. He was represented at the Second Exhibition of Cinema Posters held at the Kamerny (Chamber) Theatre, Moscow, in 1926.
With V.Stenberg he was responsible for the November decorations in Red Square from 1928 until his death. He died in Moscow.
Theatre design These were made in collaboration with his brother Vladimir Stenberg up to 1931 and are listed under V.Stenberg.
Book design Covers for: R.Ivnev et al. *Imazhinisty* (Imaginists), Moscow, 1925. A.Gorin *Kto, chto, kogda v Kamernom Teatre* (Who, What, When in the Kamerny Theatre), Moscow, 1924.
Lit A.B.Nakov *2 Stenberg 2*, Paris, 1975. J.E.Bowlt *Russian Stage Design. Scenic Innovation. From the Collection of Mr. and Mrs. Nikita D.Lobanov-Rostovsky*, Jackson, MS, exh. cat., 1982. Nancy Van Norman Baer *Theatre in Revolution, Russian Avant-Garde Stage Design 1913-1935*, San Francisco and London, 1991. Dzhon Boult (John Bowlt) *Khudozhniki russkogo teatra. Sobranie Nikity i Niny Lobanovykh-Rostovskikh*, Moscow, 1991. S.Compton *Russian Avant-Garde Books 1917-34*, London, 1992.
Coll TG; RM; Bakhrushin Theatre Museum, Moscow.
See Vladimir Stenberg.

STENBERG, Vladimir Avgustovich   **1899-1982**
Sculptor, theatre designer, poster designer. He worked with his brother Georgiy Stenberg under the title 2 Stenberg 2.
Born in Moscow to a Swedish father and a Russian mother. He studied at the Stroganov College, Moscow, 1912-17.
After the Revolution he studied at the Free Art Studios in Moscow 1918-19 where he met Medunetsky. He was engaged in Agitprop decorations in Moscow in May and October of 1918 and in 1919, together with his brother, he joined the group Obmokhu (Society of Young Artists) and exhibited in the first Obmokhu exhibition in May 1919 in Moscow. He became closely involved with the emergence of the 'laboratory art' phase of Constructivism in Moscow along with Medunetsky, Ioganson, G.Stenberg and Rodchenko. Like all of these he was associated with the Institute of Artistic Culture (INKhUK)

which he joined in 1920. His constructions of 1920 employed assemblages of iron and glass which resembled engineering constructions but lacked a utilitarian purpose. Related drawings also resembled engineers' drawings in their structure and precision. In 1922 he exhibited together with G.Stenberg and K.Medunetsky at the Poet's Café in Moscow under the title of The Constructivists which initiated the use of the word in this context. His work was represented at the First Russian Art Exhibition at the Van Diemen Gallery in Berlin in 1922.

He was well aware of the debates at INKhUK concerning the fundamental nature of construction and he followed the Moscow Constructivists into the abandonment of the 'laboratory art' phase in favour of the art of production which in his case meant the application of his studies to the production of theatre design for Tairov's Kamerny (Chamber) Theatre and the design of theatre and cinema posters. He worked on these in collaboration with his younger brother G.Stenberg under the title 2 Stenberg 2.

In 1923 he worked with Exter and Nivinsky on designs for the All-Russian Agricultural Exhibition in Moscow in 1923. He was represented at the First Discussional Exhibition of Active Revolutionary Art in Moscow in 1924. He became a prolific poster designer working jointly with G.Stenberg. He was represented at the International Exhibition in Paris in 1925. He was represented at the Second Exhibition of Cinema Posters held at the Kamerny (Chamber) Theatre, Moscow, in 1926. He also taught at the Institute for Architectural Construction in Moscow 1929-32 and with his brother was responsible for the November decorations of Red Square from 1928.

Theatre design These were for A.Tairov's Kamerny Theatre in Moscow and executed in collaboration with Georgiy Stenberg until 1931:

1922 *Zheltaya koftochka* with Medunetsky.

1922 February: Racine's *Phèdre*, produced by Aleksandr Tairov at the Kamerny (Chamber) Theatre, Moscow. It was subsequently toured to the Deutscher Theater, Berlin, and to the Théâtre des Champs-Elysées, Paris, in 1923. Essentially an application of Suprematism used as a style and adapted to theatre design rather as Exter used it. It resulted in spectacular versions of ancient Greek helmets but awkward costumes. The sets recall both the painter Malevich and the theatre designer Appiah with a little of Gordon Craig also. They make dynamic designs on paper and look forward in some ways to the designs Exter was preparing for the film *Aelita* released the following year but the blending of ancient Greece, Racine, Constructivism and Suprematism was not easily resolved.

1924 April: *The Lawyer from Babylon*, a play based on a text by A.Mariengof, produced by Vladimir Sokolov at the Kamerny (Chamber) Theatre, Moscow.

1924 March: A.N.Ostrovsky's *Groza* (Storm), designed in collaboration with Medunetsky, is a more overtly Constructivist set with ramps and an apparatus for the actors' performance.

1924 October: G.B.Shaw's *St. Joan*. This employed stylised rather medieval looking costumes with metallic effects for the armour.

1925 November: P.G.Antokolsky, V.Z.Mass, A.P.Globa and V.G.Zak's *Kukirol'* at the Chamber (Kamerny) Theatre, Moscow. In one scene the stage was dominated by a large screen bearing an African mask motif. In Scenes 3 and 5 a central series of platforms are dramatically extended symmetrically to the wings by girder-like balconies culminating in spiral stairs. The action recalled pantomime

and circus to produce an agitational effect.

1926 January: Eugene O'Neill's *The Hairy Ape*. The set comprised sections of a ship reassembled together to provide a series of platforms for actors, rising from the exposed boiler room, via the interior to the deck, all much simplified but clearly atmospheric and mechanically marine in a way that shows them adapting their experience in the construction of materials to more evocative and representational ends.

1926 November: Eugene O'Neill's *Desire Under the Elms*. Act 1 had a severe Constructivist evocation of houses lifted up on legs combined with platforms.

1926 December: Charles Lecocq's *Day and Night*, with choreography by Natalya Glan, employed witty, colourful and bizarre costumes using asymmetry and characterisation developed almost to the point of caricature. Executed in yellow, black, blue and red. The designs stress geometry to maximum optical effect verging upon dazzle so that the graphic ability of the designers, evident in their posters, is much in evidence in their theatre designs too. Act 1 featured a parabolic ramp and false ceiling in sharp perspective.

1928 January: L.A.Polovinkin's operetta *Sirocco*. The sets included a row of vertical screens arranged to open revealing large photographic images in the manner of their use in Stenberg posters. In addition one scene involved shaped screens to form a stylised sailing boat.

1929 February: Eugene O'Neill's *Negr* (The Negro). A

Georgiy Stenberg. Stage Design of a Nude with a Fan, *1919. Signed and dated in Russian lower right.*
Formerly collection Mr. and Mrs. Nikita D.Lobanov-Rostovsky, London.

Georgiy and Vladimir Stenberg, with Kazimir Medunetsky. Stage set for Ostrovsky's 'Storm', *1924.* *This play was directed by Tairov at the Moscow Chamber Theatre in 1924. The lessons of Constructivism have been applied to stage design. The Stenberg brothers have effectively built a construction to serve as an apparatus for the performers. They have relinquished the backdrop and curtains to present a construction in materials.*

maquette for Act 1 shows a dramatic and austere set suggesting deep corridors and made up wholly of severe straight lines and sharp but divergent perspectives.

1929 December: S.A.Semenov's *Natalya Tarpova.*

1930 January: Bertolt Brecht's *Beggars' Opera* with music by Kurt Weill. The set comprised a minimally indicated oval hotel room open at front and back with a raised central dais, in addition a street lamp and poster.

1937 November Meyerhold's unperformed production of Ostrovsky's *The Tempering of Steel* for the Meyerhold Theatre.

1931 June: N.N.Nikitin's *Liniya ognya* (Line of Fire).

Posters include: 1925 Eisenstein's film *Battleship Potemkin*, a design of six crossed battleship guns. Rodchenko and Lavinsky also made poster designs for this film. 1926 Protozanov's *Protsess o trekh millionakh.* 1926 I.Perestiani's *Princess Shirvanskaya's Crime*, two heads derived from photomontage, Constructivist lettering. 1927 V.Gardin's *Poet and Tsar*, a camera aperture around the head of the poet Pushkin, and Buster Keaton's *Sherlock Jnr.* 1928 N.Okhlopkov's film *Sold Appetite*, Dziga Vertov's *The Eleventh* which resembled a Klucis poster, Walther Ruttmann's *Berlin — Symphony of a Great City* , B.Barnet's *House on Trubnaya Square* and I.Perestiani's *Scandal.* 1929 Eisenstein's film *October*, divided diagonally half for heads of armed workers, half red. 1929 V.Turin's *Turksib*, approaching steam train with shouting Asians, *SEP* for the Red Army Studio, Dziga Vertov's *Man with the Movie Camera*, two designs. 1930 A.Dovzhenko's *Earth.* 1931 A.Dovzhenko's *Arsenal.*

Book design Sheet music cover (symmetrical in red and black) for Matvei Blantner *Glaza Andozii* (The Eyes of

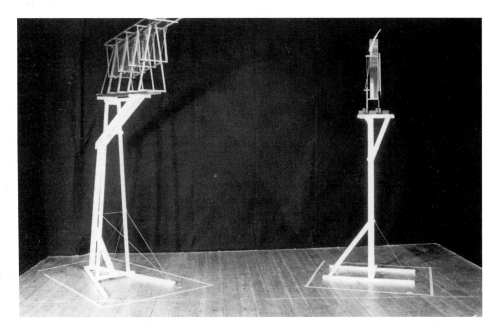

Georgiy and Vladimir Stenberg. Reconstructions made in 1975 of Constructions of Spatial Apparatus Nos. 4 and 13. *Metal and glass. Documentary photograph. The original constructions were exhibited at the Obmokhu exhibition in 1920. Courtesy of Annely Juda Fine Art, London.*

Andozia), words by Podrevsky, Moscow, 1926.
Lit A.B.Nakov *2 Stenberg 2*, Paris, 1975. A.Z.Rudenstine *Costakis Collection*, London, 1981. J.E.Bowlt *Russian Stage Design. Scenic Innovation. From the Collection of Mr. and Mrs. Nikita D.Lobanov-Rostovsky*, Jackson, MS, exh. cat., 1982. C.Lodder *Russian Constructivism*, New Haven and London, 1983. Nancy Van Norman Baer *Theatre in Revolution, Russian Avant-Garde Stage Design 1913-1935*, San Francisco and London, 1991. Dzhon Boult (John Bowlt) *Khudozhniki russkogo teatra. Sobranie Nikity i Niny Lobanovykh-Rostovskikh*, Moscow, 1991.
Coll TG; RM; Costakis Collection; Bakhrushin Theatre Museum, Moscow.

STEN'SHINSKAYA, N.   a.1921
She was a member of the *Bytie* (Existence) Society of Artists formed in Moscow in 1921.

STEN'SHINSKY, I. S.   a.1921-1929
A member of the *Bytie* (Existence) Society of Artists formed in Moscow in 1921. His work was included in the exhibition of

Georgy and Vladimir Stenberg. Costume for Racine's 'Phèdre', *1922-3. Pencil on parchment paper. 25 x 18 cm.*
The Stenberg brothers assisted Vesnin on this production.
Private collection, courtesy of Annely Juda Fine Art, London.

Vladimir Stenberg. Design for a Headdress for Hippolyte in Racine's 'Phèdre', *1922-3. Pencil. 47.5 x 31.7 cm.*
Collection Mr. and Mrs. Nikita D.Lobanov-Rostovsky, London.

Soviet art held at Harbin in 1926 and in Japan in 1927 and he was represented at the First Touring Exhibition of Painting and Graphics which opened in Moscow in 1929.

STEPANOV, A. F.   a.1921-1925
Theatre designer. He exhibited with Kudryashov and others at the First State Exhibition in Orenburg in 1921. He designed the production by V.I.Nemirovich-Danchenko of K.A.Trenev's *Pugachevshchina* (Pugachev's Uprising) at the Moscow Art Theatre in November 1925.

STEPANOV, Aleksei Stepanovich   1858-1923
Painter of landscape and animal subjects. Born at Simferopol. He studied at the Moscow College under Sorokin and Pryanishnikov 1880-4. He exhibited with the Wanderers from 1888, became a member in 1891 and came to be known as one of the so-called Young Wanderers. He directed a special animal study class at the Mosow College whilst teaching there 1899-1918.
Coll TG.

STEPANOV, D. K.   a.1918
He was engaged on Agitprop decorations at the Chernyshev Bridge and Square, Petrograd, in 1918.

STEPANOV, Nikolai   a.1928
He was engaged on mural decorations at the Security Police Club, Moscow, c.1928.

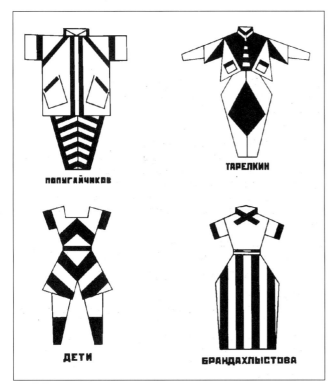

ПОПУГАЙЧИКОВ

ТАРЕЛКИН

ДЕТИ

БРАНДАХЛЫСТОВА

Varvara Stepanova. Costume Designs for 'Tarelkin's Death', *1922. Meyerhold directed Sukhovo-Kobylin's play in Moscow in 1922. The costumes resembled sportswear and the actors performed with stage equipment rather like athletes or clowns.*

STEPANOVA, A.   a.1902-1904

She taught at the Moscow College where Mitrokhin was amongst her pupils c. 1902-4.

STEPANOVA, Varvara Fedorovna   1894-1958
(VARST, AGARYKH)

Painter, graphic artist, theatre designer and designer of fabrics, books and clothes. She married Aleksandr Rodchenko and was equally centrally involved in the transition from Constructivism into its later phase of utilitarian production in the early 1920s. She signed her work 'Varst', a contraction of her name, and sometimes used the pseudonym Agarykh.

Born at Kovno (Kaunas). She exhibited with the Union of Youth in 1911 and at the 1912 exhibition of the Donkey's Tail group in Moscow where she showed twenty-three works including illustrations to Montaigne, Pushkin and Sologub. She studied at the Kazan School of Art 1911-12 and met Rodchenko there. She studied under Mashkov and Yuon in Moscow in 1912 and then at the Stroganov College 1913-14. She exhibited at the Moscow Salon in 1914. During the war she worked in a factory.

After the Revolution she worked for the Art Section of the People's Commissariat of the Enlightenment (IZO Narkompros), from 1918 in museum organisation. Her painting showed an evident debt to Cubism as it was received and filtered by Suprematist and Constructivist painters. Characteristically she painted figures in action built up from intersecting geometric planes and attendant open work lines, comparable with Rodchenko's figure constructions in painting. She exhibited at the Fifth State Exhibition: From Impressionism to Non-Objective Art in Moscow 1918-19.

She produced hand-drawn Russian Futurist poems, books and collages and in 1918 illustrated A.Kruchenykh's play *Gly-Gly* with collages. Her own works of this kind included the gouache and collage works *Zigra ar* and *Rtny khomle* both 1918, *Gaust Chaba* 1919, and *Toft*. Such works were exhibited at the Tenth State Exhibition: Non-Objective Creativity and Suprematism in 1919 in Moscow. Together with Aleksei Gan, Aleksandr Drevin, Aleksandr Rodchenko and Varvara Stepanova she formed the group *Askranov* (the Association of Extreme Innovators) in January 1919.

She also participated in the Third Exhibition of Paintings held at Ryazan in 1919, the Nineteenth Exhibition of the All-Russian Exhibitions Bureau in Moscow in 1920 and was included in the Third Touring Exhibition of the Sovetsk Regional subdepartment of the Museums Bureau along with Kandinsky, Rodchenko and others in 1921.

In 1920-1 she was the academic secretary of the Institute of Artistic Culture (INKhUK) in Moscow, a founder member of its First Working Group of Constructivists, and a contributor to its debates. She was also a member of the Decorative Arts Panel of the Union of Art Workers. She contributed to the exhibition 5 x 5 = 25 in 1921, lectured at INKhUK and followed its abandonment of easel painting into the exploration of production art, the extension of Constructivist principles into public and utilitarian work in a way that embodied the principles of communism as INKhUK interpreted them. The most distinct contribution of Stepanova was her development of the collage to include elements of handwritten *zaum* or trans-sense poetry. In this she was a pioneer who helped to maintain Futurist practices into the period of Constructivism. She was represented at the First Russian Art Exhibition in Berlin in 1922.

In 1922 she executed Constructivist sets for Meyerhold's production of *Tarelkin's Death* by Sukhovo-Kobylin. These comprised equipment made of wood in open work arrangements of laths which served as an apparatus upon which the performers could operate the rhythmic and rather gymnastic actions required by Meyerhold's system of biomechanics. There was no backdrop and no attempt to suspend disbelief so that the audience were at all times fully aware of the fact that they were watching a performance. In this respect Meyerhold was embracing the Constructivist principle of rejecting illusionism in favour of the manipulation of material which in this case included the set and the actors themselves. Stepanova designed the costumes which were perhaps primarily worksuits. Her designs for these show rectilinear and symmetrically geometric divisions of the garments laid out as for a cutting pattern. She contributed to the exhibition Art of Moscow Theatre 1918-1923 held in Moscow in 1923.

The designs for stage equipment also resembled recent constructions in wood devised by Rodchenko to illustrate the complex symmetries that can arise from the arrangements of equal units of construction and there is little doubt that Stepanova's work benefited from close association with Rodchenko with whom she effectively maintained a co-operative. Their working relationship was fruitful and even prolific and each of them remained independent whilst aware of the other's innovations and contributions. From 1923 she was associated with the periodical *Lef* (Left) which was edited by Mayakovsky and to which numerous Constructivists, including Rodchenko, made significant contributions. In addition she taught at the Krupskaya Academy of Social Education from 1920 to 1924 and she designed Zhemchuzhny's *Evening of the Book* there in 1924. By 1927 she was also designing sportswear there.

She made over 150 designs for the First State Textile Factory 1924-5, some twenty of which were produced, and she taught in the textile faculty at the Vkhutemas 1924-5. She was represented at the Paris International Exhibition in 1925. Later in her career she produced book, periodical, clothing, material and exhibition designs. In 1927 she was invited along with E.Lavinskaya and Elena Semenova to submit designs for the decoration of several squares in Moscow.

She contributed to the First Art Exhibition of Soviet Textiles in Moscow in 1928. She produced designs for books and for the journals *Soviet Cinema, Literature and Art, Books and Revolution, Contemporary Architecture, The Class Struggle* and *Workshift* in the period 1926-32.

She designed for the *Collective Farm Newspaper* in 1933 and for *Sovetskaya zhenshchina* (Soviet Woman) 1945-6. With Rodchenko she designed the periodical *USSR in Construction* 1935-40. She continued to collaborate with Rodchenko up to his death. Late collaborative works include the design of photographic books including *15 Years of Soviet Cinema, 25 Years of the Kazakh SSR* 1947, *The Moscow Metro* 1948 and *500 Years of Union between the Ukraine and Russia* 1955. She died in Moscow.

Theatre design 1922 Aleksandr Sukhovo-Kobylin's *Tarelkin's Death*, directed by Meyerhold at the Meyerhold Studio of GITIS, the State Institute of Theatre Art, Moscow. She produced Constructivist apparatus for Meyerhold's performers, including collapsible furniture, swings, cages and chutes. In line with the director's Constructivist principles there was no backdrop, scenery or illusion. Like Popova, Stepanova designed work clothes in which the actors could rehearse and perform their rhythmic and gymnastic activities. Designs for these were geometric and presented in a simple flat format almost explicit enough for cutting and production.

Film design 1926 she designed Constructivist furniture for the film *Otryv* (Alienation).

1926-7 she was designing for the film *Sor* (Rubbish) and for the journal *Sovetskoe kino* (Soviet Cinema).

Graphic design included V.Mayakovsky's book *Groznyy smekh* (Terrible Laughter), Moscow, 1932.

Lit T.Strizhenova *Iz istorii sovetskogo kostyuma*, Moscow, 1972 (English edition: Tatiana Strizhenova, *Soviet Costume and Textiles 1917-1945*, Paris, 1991). *V.F.Stepanova*, exh. cat., Kostroma, 1975. *Alexander Rodtschenko und Warwara Stepanowa*, exh. cat., Wilhelm-Lehmbruck-Museum, Duisberg, 1982. J.E.Bowlt *Russian Stage Design. Scenic Innovation. From the Collection of Mr. and Mrs. Nikita D.Lobanov-Rostovsky*, Jackson, MS, exh. cat.,1982. *Seven Moscow Artists 1910-30*, exh. cat., Galerie Gmurzynska, Cologne, 1984. E.Weiss *Russische Avant-Garde, 1910-1930, Sammlung Ludwig, Köln*, Munich, 1986. A.Lavrentev *Stepanova: a Constructivist Life*, London, 1988. M.N.Yablonskaya *Women Artists of Russia's New Age*, London, 1990. Nancy Van Norman Baer *Theatre in Revolution, Russian Avant-Garde Stage Design 1913-1935*, San Francisco and London, 1991. Dzhon Boult (John Bowlt) *Khudozhniki russkogo teatra. Sobranie Nikity i Niny Lobanovykh-Rostovskikh*, Moscow, 1991. *L'Avant-garde russe 1905-1925*, exh. cat., Musée des Beaux-Arts, Nantes, 1993.

Coll Rodchenko-Stepanova Archive, Moscow; RM; Bakhrushin Theatre Museum, Moscow; Ivanovo Art Museum; Kirov Art Museum; Sammlung Ludwig, Cologne.
Colour plate p.383.

STEPANYAN, Suren Levonovich   **1895-1971**
Armenian sculptor. His works include a monument to *Gukas Gukasyan*, granite, 1935, erected in Erevan. This shows the figure of a large and anonymous marching soldier complete with flag and is raised upon a high plinth. He also executed a historicist monument to the poet *Kh. Abovyan* in 1952 also erected in Erevan.

STEPASHKIN, Ivan Petrovich   **a.1918-1920**
He was engaged on Agitprop projects at Saratov 1918-20.

STEUBEN = SHTEYBEN, K. K.

STOLITSA, Evgeniy Ivanovich   **1870-1929**
Landscape and portrait painter. He participated in the First State Free Exhibition of Artworks in Petrograd in 1919 and was included in the enormous survey Exhibition of Paintings by Petrograd Artists of All Tendencies 1919-1923 held in Petrograd in 1923. His portraits included *Tolstoy* and *Gorky*.
Coll TG; National Gallery, Bucharest.

Varvara Stepanova. Stage Apparatus for 'Tarelkin's Death', *1922. Stepanova herself appears among the equipment she designed. Documentary photograph.*

STOLPINIKOVA, A. a.1927-1928
Graphic artist. She contributed to the All-Union Polygraphic Exhibition in Moscow in 1927 and exhibited with the 4 Arts society in Leningrad including the exhibition of 1928 at the Russian Museum.

STOROZHENKO, S. A. a.1918-1928
Graphic artist. An exhibitor at the First Exhibition of Works of the Professional Union of Artists in Moscow in 1918 and a participant in exhibitions of *Iskusstvo dvizheniya* (Art of Movement) held in Moscow 1926-8.

STOZHAROV, V. F. 1926-1973
Landscape painter whose work included themes of white nights in Northern Russia.
Coll TG.

STRAKHOV(-BRASLAVSKY), Adolf Iosipovich
1896-1927+
Sculptor, graphic artist. Born at Ekaterinoslav. He studied at the Odessa School of Art under Mormon. He was designing posters 1924-6 and his work was represented at the Paris International Exhibition in 1925. He was also represented at the Exhibition of Revolutionary Posters in Berlin in 1927.
V.Ulyanov (Lenin), 1924, poster in red and black, has a black skyline of chimneys before which is a van load of armed revolutionaries. All of this is dominated by the gigantic pointing finger of Lenin. It is a memorial poster bearing Lenin's dates 1870-1924.
Lit *Paris-Moscou*, 1979.

STRAKHOVSKAYA, Maria Mikhailovna a.1919-1932
Sculptor. During 1919-20 she was a founder of the *Monolit* (Monolith) group of sculptors, which included Babichev, Mukhina, Konen'kov, Krandievskaya, Korolev, Strakhovskaya, Zlatovratsky, Ternovets, V.Popova, Blazhevich and Kudinov. They worked on monumental propaganda and entered the competitive exhibition for a Monument to Liberated Labour held in Moscow in May 1920. She was a member of the Society of Russian Sculptors from 1926. She was included in the major exhibition in Moscow in 1927 marking the tenth anniversary of the Revolution and in the jubilee exhibition Artists of the RSFSR over 15 Years held at the Russian Museum, Leningrad, in 1932.

STROEV, Petr Feonovich 1898-1942
Painter.
Coll RM.

STRUNNIKOV, Nikolai Ivanovich 1871-1945
Painter. He taught at the Kiev Art Institute where Tyshler was amongst his pupils 1912-17.
He was represented at the jubilee exhibition Artists of the RSFSR over 15 Years held at the Russian Museum, Leningrad, in 1932.
Portrait of the Partisan A.G.Lunev, 1929, TG, is a three-quarter-length portrait with medals in place, a star upon the fur hat, a sabre in one hand and a revolver in the other. It represents an ideal hero, alert, handsome and loyal.

STULOV, P. T. a.1919
Painter. He exhibited at the juryless Eighth State Exhibition in Moscow in 1919.

STUPIN, Aleksandr Vasilievich 1776-1861
Portraitist.
Coll TG.

STURZWAGE = SURVAGE, L.L.

SUCHKOV, E. a.1921
He exhibited with Kudryashov and others at the First State Exhibition in Orenburg in 1921.

SUD'BININ, Serafim Nikolaevich 1867-1944
Sculptor, painter. Born at Nizhny-Novgorod. He designed the poster for Stanislavsky's production of A.K.Tolstoy's *Tsar' Fedor Ioannovich* at the Moscow Art Theatre in 1898 and made other studies of actors at the theatre in 1900.
He went to Paris in 1904 to study sculpture under L.Sinaev-Bernstein and J.A.Ingelbert and worked as a pupil and assistant to Rodin from 1906. He was a member of the Union of Russian Artists from 1906. His sculptures included heads and mythological themes of satyrs and bacchantes. He died in Paris.
Gnev (Anger), 1906, bronze, RM, is a remarkable loosely handled sculpture of a head, intense and lively at every point.
Lit *Twilight of the Tsars*, London, 1991.
Coll RM; Museum of the Moscow Art Theatre.

SUDEIKIN (SUDEYKIN, SOUDEIKINE), Sergei Yur'evich 1882-1946
Symbolist painter, theatre designer. Born in Smolensk. He worked for Mamontov's private opera in Moscow in 1890 and studied periodically at the Moscow College under K.Korovin and V.Serov 1897-1909. In 1900 he visited the Caucasus. During this period he began to exhibit, first with the the Scarlet Rose in Saratov in 1904. In 1905 he worked at the Povarskaya Street Studio Theatre branch of the Moscow Art Theatre.
He travelled to Paris in 1906 where he was represented in Diaghilev's display of Russian art at the 1906 Salon d'Automne. In 1907 he exhibited with the Blue Rose group in Moscow, contributed to the *Stefanos* (Wreath) exhibition 1907-8 and to the Golden Fleece 1908-9. He also studied at the Academy in St. Petersburg under Kardovsky 1909-10. He designed decorations for the Stray Dog cabaret and exhibited with the Union of Russian Artists in 1911, but he also became a member of the World of Art and executed designs for Diaghilev's productions from 1912.
After the Revolution he exhibited with the World of Art in December 1917 in Moscow.
He worked in Georgia in 1919 before emigrating to Paris the following year and to New York in 1923, but he was represented at the Exhibition of Paintings by Russian Artists held at Pskov in Spring 1920. He contributed to the exhibition of Contemporary Russian Art held at Philadelphia in 1932. He died at Nyack, New York.
The Ballet, 1910, RM, is a densely crepuscular scene with a low crescent moon. Dancers perform in a twilit garden or repose beneath voluminous dark trees. All is atmosphere and mood. It could easily be a stage design.
Figurines from Saxony, 1911, RM, is lavish and painterly employing a decorative device which pits two pictorial conventions against each other: the figurines, which themselves were executed in one style and culture, are viewed from a low angle and appear almost like gesticulating actors

against a backdrop which is in fact an elaborately decorative piece of Russian material. The result is a still-life with a complex structure, apparently featuring figures in a drama and contrasting Russia with the West in its theme.

Harlequin's Garden, 1915-16, Radishchev Art Museum, Saratov, shows Sudeikin employing the Commedia dell'Arte theme in the World of Art manner much as Benois and Somov did. In a lavish formal garden at night Harlequin relaxes amid scenes of languor and amorous dalliance.

Theatre design 1905 Summer Meyerhold's production of Maeterlinck's *Death of Tintagiles* at the Povarskaya Street Studio Theatre, Moscow. N.N.Sapunov designed Acts 4 and 5.

1906 November Maeterlinck's *Sister Beatrice* produced by Meyerhold at the Vera F. Komissarzhevskaya Theatre, St. Petersburg.

1906 S.Przybyszewski's *Eternal Fairy Tale* produced by Meyerhold at the Vera F. Komissarzhevskaya Theatre, St. Petersburg.

1909 G.B.Shaw's *Caesar and Cleopatra* at the New Drama Theatre, St. Petersburg.

1910 December O.Dymov's *Spring Madness* at the New Drama Theatre, St. Petersburg.

1910 Meyerhold's production of E.Znosno-Borowsky's *The Prince Transformed* at the House of Interludes: costume studies painterly and loose with little graphic precision or detail, more explicit concerning the hang of the vaguely medieval garments than their decoration or the characterisation of the wearer (Bakhrushin Theatre Museum).

1910 Curtain design for *Columbine and Punchinello* at the House of Interludes.

1910 Diaghilev's staging in Paris of Debussy's *L'après-midi d'un faune* in which he worked from designs by Bakst.

1911 M.Kuzmin's *Amusements for Virgins* at the Small Drama Theatre, St. Petersburg: a deeply colourful set design (Museum of Russian Art, Kiev) of a middle Eastern bazaar with minarets, domes and several platforms for performers.

1911 Curtain design for Chaikovsky's *Swan Lake* at the Small Drama Theatre, St. Petersburg: a crude study for the Park in Front of the Castle (RM) shows lines of classically clad dancers against a background of swans and an extensive formal garden which rises to the top of the stage.

1912 J.Benavente's *The Seamy Side of Life* at the Russian Drama Theatre, St. Petersburg.

1912 executed Bakst's décor for Diaghilev's production of Balakirev's *Thamar* in Paris.

1913 June: curtain, sets and costumes for Diaghilev's production of *La Tragédie de Salomé*, after a poem by Robert d'Humières, at the Théâtre des Champs-Elysées, Paris, to music by Florent Schmitt and choreography by Boris Romanov.

1913 Diaghilev's production in Paris of Stravinsky's *Rite of Spring* in which he worked from designs by Roerich.

1913 N.Evreinov and L.Urvantsev's *The Runaway* at the Palace Theatre, St. Petersburg.

1914 September L.Lipovskaya's production of E.Wolf-Ferrari's *Secret of Suzanna* at the Mariinsky Theatre, St. Petersburg.

1914 Meyerhold's production of Guy de Maupassant's *Mlle. Fifi* at Suvorin's Theatre of the Literature and Art Society, St. Petersburg.

1915 Adam's *Giselle* at the Mariinsky Theatre, St. Petersburg.

Sergei Sudeikin. Costume for Salomé Danced by Tamara Karsavina, *1913. Watercolour. Initialled in Russian lower centre 'SS'. 29.8 x 47 cm.*
A design for Diaghilev's production of Florent Schmitt's ballet 'La Tragédie de Salomé', with a libretto by Robert d'Humières and choreography by Boris Romanov; performed at the Théâtre des Champs-Elysées, Paris, in June 1913.
Collection Mr. and Mrs. Nikita D.Lobanov-Rostovsky, London.

1915 Bizet's *L'Arlésienne* at the Mariinsky Theatre, St. Petersburg.

1915 October: Aleksandr Tairov's production of Beaumarchais' *Marriage of Figaro* at the Kamerny (Chamber) Theatre, Moscow.

1915 October: Tairov's production of Rémy de Gourmont's *Carnival of Life* at the Kamerny (Chamber) Theatre, Moscow.

1915 October A.Bobrishchev-Pushkin's *Triumph of the Nations* at the Mariinsky Theatre, St. Petersburg.

1916 April Meyerhold's production of *Columbine's Scarf* by A.Schnitzler and Dr. Dapertutto (Meyerhold) at The Actor's Rest, Petrograd.

1925 *Petrushka*, ballet, libretto by A.Benois and I.Stravinsky, at the Metropolitan Opera House, New York.

1926 March: *Le Rossingol* after the story by Hans Christian Andersen, at the Metropolitan Opera House, New York.

Sudeikin later worked as a designer for opera and ballet to music by Mozart, Stravinsky, Rachmaninov, Glazunov and others.

Lit D.Kogan *S.Ya.Sudeikin*, Moscow, 1974. *Diaghilev and Russian Stage Designers, a Loan Exhibition from the Collection of Mr. and Mrs. N.Lobanov-Rostovsky*, International Exhibitions Foundation, Washington, 1972-4. *Paris-Moscou*, 1979;

J.E.Bowlt *Russian Stage Design. Scenic Innovation. From the Collection of Mr. and Mrs. Nikita D.Lobanov-Rostovsky*, Jackson, MS, exh. cat.,1982. *Twilight of the Tsars*, London, 1991. A.Kamensky *The World of Art Movement*, Leningrad, 1991. Dzhon Boult (John Bowlt) *Khudozhniki russkogo teatra. Sobranie Nikity i Niny Lobanovykh-Rostovskikh*, Moscow, 1991.
Coll TG; RM; Bakhrushin Theatre Museum, Moscow; Theatre Museum, St. Petersburg; Museum of Russian Art, Kiev; Radishchev Art Museum, Saratov; Armenian Art Museum, Yerevan.
Colour plate p.386.

SUDKOVSKY, Rufin Gavriilovich   **1850-1885**
Painter of genre scenes, landscapes and seascapes. Born at Ochakov. He studied at the Academy in St. Petersburg. He died at Odessa.
Coll TG; RM.

SUETIN, Nikolai Mikhailovich   **1897-1954**
Suprematist painter, graphic artist, designer, ceramics artist, art historian. Born in the Kaluga region. After army service at Vitebsk 1915-17, he studied art there 1918-22 where he came under the influence of Malevich, learnt the theory and practice of Suprematism at first hand from its initiator and became a member of the group *Unovis* with Lissitzky and others in 1919. He executed a design for a tribune in 1921 and in due couse he became an exponent of the development of Suprematism into three dimensional work. He moved to Leningrad in 1922 with other Suprematists in the wake of Malevich's move there and in 1923 began to design for the State Porcelain Factory producing Suprematist designs. A *Suprematist Teapot* of 1923 shows Suprematist geometry applied to a traditional teapot form. He also became a member of the Institute of Artistic Culture (INKhUK) 1923-6.
He worked in an experimental laboratory at the Institute of Art History at Leningrad 1927-30. He was represented at the jubilee exhibition Artists of the RSFSR over 15 Years held at the Russian Museum, Leningrad, in 1932.
His work with ceramics continued in his role as chief artist at the State Porcelain Factory for the period 1932-54. He acted as chief artist designing the interior of the Soviet Pavilions at the World Fair in Paris in 1937 and New York in 1939.
Lit C.Lodder *Russian Constructivism*, New Haven and London, 1983. E.Weiss *Russische Avant-Garde, 1910-1930, Sammlung Ludwig, Köln*, Munich, 1986. N.Lobanov-Rostovsky *Revolutionary Ceramics*, London, 1990.
Coll RM; Sammlung Ludwig, Cologne.
Colour plate p.387.

SUKHANOV, G.   **a.1922**
He was a member of the first exhibition committee of AKhRR, the Association of Artists of Revolutionary Russia, in 1922. In 1922 he was a founder member of the Society (*Obshchestvo*) of Artists of Revolutionary Russia, founded after the first exhibition of AKhRR. Other members included A.Grigoriev, P.Kiselev, E.Katsman, N.Kotov, S.Malyutin, P.Radimov, P.Shukhmin, A.Skachko, B.Yakovlev and V.Zhuravlev.

SUKHANOV, V. D.   **a.c.1895-1896**
Painter. He was teaching at the Stroganov Institute in Moscow c.1895-6 where Konchalovsky was among his evening class students.

SUKHODOLOV, Nikolai Makarovich   **b.1920**
Sculptor. See Lysenko, M.G.

SUKHODOL'SKY, Boris Vasilievich (VASIL'EV, B. V.)
a.1754
Decorative painter of allegorical themes for architectural settings. He executed an *Allegory of Science* in 1754 to be placed above a doorway. It presents a stiffly painted idyll which is somewhat French in style.
Coll TG; RM.

SUKHODOL'SKY, Petr Aleksandrovich   **1835-1903**
Landscape painter. Sometimes he signed his work 'Schdlsk' in latin script.
Coll TG.

SUKHOVO-KOBYLINA, Sofya Vasilievna   **1825-1867**
Landscape painter. She died in Rome.
Coll TG.

SUKOV, Vladimir Vsevolodovich   **1866-1942**
Painter of landscapes, still-lifes and portraits. He had no formal training. He visited Italy, France, Germany and England 1910-11. He taught in an art school in Peterburg.
After the Revolution he was included in the 1928 exhibition of Acquisitions by the State Art Collections Fund held in Moscow and in the jubilee exhibition Artists of the RSFSR over 15 Years held at the Russian Museum, Leningrad, in 1932.
Lit A.M.Muratov, V.Manin et al. *Zhivopis' 20-30kh godov*, Sankt-Peterburg, 1991.
Coll RM.

SUKOVKINA, O. R.   **a.1908**
Painter. She contributed to the exhibition *Zveno* (The Link) in Kiev in 1908.

SULIMO-SAMUILO, Vsevolod Angelovich   **1903-1965**
Painter, draughtsman. Like Zaklikovskaya he was a follower of the example of Filonov whose drawing techniques he particularly assimilated.
Coll RM.

SUMBATASHVILI, I. G.   **b.1915**
Theatre designer.

SUPRUN, Oksana Aleksandrovna   **b.1924**
Sculptor.

SURENYANTS, Vardges Yakovlevich   **1860-1921**
Painter, theatre designer. He studied at the Moscow College under Sorokin and Pryanishnikov 1876-9 and subsequently at the Munich Academy. He exhibited with the Wanderers from 1894 and became a member in 1910.
The Church of Ripsim near Echmiadzina, 1897, Armenian Art Gallery, Erevan, is a spectacular horizontal landscape of bare earth beneath a purple-grey sky. Only the fortified church breaks the horizon. All is dark and brooding except the yellow-orange full moon behind a corner of the fortifications.
Theatre design 1907 January Meyerhold's production of G.Heiberg's *Tragedy of Love* at the V.F.Komissarzhevskaya Theatre, St. Petersburg.
Coll Armenian Art Gallery, Erevan.

SURIKOV, P. V.   **a.1927-1932**
He was included in the 1928 exhibition of Acquisitions by the State Art Collections Fund held in Moscow and in the jubilee

exhibition Artists of the RSFSR over 15 Years held at the Russian Museum, Leningrad, in 1932.

SURIKOV, Vasili Ivanovich   **1848-1916**

Painter who produced intensely dramatic evocations of Old Russia on an epic scale. Born at Krasnoyarsk into a Siberian Cossack family. He studied at the Society for the Encouragement of the Arts and then at the Academy in St. Petersburg 1869-75 graduating with a gold medal. He settled in Moscow in 1877. He exhibited with the Wanderers from 1881 and became a member in 1907. He visited Italy and France 1883-4 but made many visits to Western Europe including a tour which took him to Germany, Italy, Austria and Switzerland in 1897. In effect, he became the history painter of the masses although he also painted portraits and landscapes. His major canvases include *The Morning of the Execution of the Streltsy* of 1881, in which the scene is watched by Peter I, *Boyarina Morozova* of 1887, *Suvorov's Army Crossing the Alps in 1799* painted in 1899, which is full of reckless energy as the army slides complete with men and horses down a vertiginous alpine gorge, and his last major work depicting the legendary hero *Stepan Razin* painted in 1906.

He exhibited with the Union of Russian Artists from 1908 to 1915. During this time he visited his son-in-law the painter Konchalovsky in Paris in 1910 and then travelled with him to Spain. He was represented at the International Exhibition in Rome in 1911. He became ill in 1912 and travelled with Konchalovsky to Berlin for treatment. He died in Moscow.

*Boyarina Morozova, 1887, TG, is intensely theatrical. The Old Believer is dragged off to prison and execution, carried in a crude sledge on a seat of straw through the snowy street. Peasants on all sides watch, and the variety of expressions indicate that each participant reacts differently. Some bless her, some bow their heads, some weep. A soldier discreetly holds his sword to make a cross. Old men laugh. There is a brilliant touch in the boy who runs along at the left emphasising the movement of the sledge. The Boyarina herself, pale-faced and clad in black, furiously raises her hand. Beyond in a snowy haze rise the church domes of the town.

*The Capture of the Snow Town, 1891, exemplifies his energy and

his enthusiasm for folk decoration. A charging cossack destroys a fortress modelled in snow whilst all around bucolic local admirers, red faced and well wrapped up, shout their approval.

Lit A.Mikhailov *V.I.Surikov*, Leningrad, 1935. S.Goldstein *V.Surikov*, Moscow, 1950. M.Alpatov *V.I.Surikov*, Moscow, 1950. N.Mashkovets *V.I.Surikov*, Moscow-Leningrad, 1960. V.Kemenov *Istoricheskaya zhivopis' Surikova*, Moscow, 1963. V.Kamenov *Vasily Surikov*, Leningrad, 1979. *Paris-Moscou*, 1979.

Coll Major holdings at TG; RM.

Colour plate p.390, 391.

SURVAGE (SHTYURTSVAGE, STURZWAGE, SYURVAZH), Léopold L'vovich   **1879-1968**

Painter, theatre designer, graphic artist, illustrator. Born in Moscow or, according to some accounts, in Wilmanstrand, Finland, to a father of Finnish origin and a Danish mother. He studied under K.Korovin and L.Pasternak at the Moscow College where he met Archipenko, Larionov, Fal'k, Pevsner and Sudeikin. He exhibited with the symbolist group the Blue Rose along with Fal'k, Larionov and others in 1905. He contributed to the *Stefanos* exhibition 1907-8. He exhibited with the Knave of Diamonds in Moscow 1910-11.

However he was in Paris by 1908, where he followed Matisse's teaching course for two months. He exhibited at the Salon d'Automne that year and in 1911 he exhibited in the Cubist room at the Salon des Indépendants.

He was designing experimental non-objective films, called *Rythmes colorées*, based upon arrangements of colours worked out in a long series of over two hundred watercolours and ink studies 1912-13. *Coloured Rhythms*, 1913, MNAM, Paris, features interlocking curved surfaces in yellow, grey and blue assembled in bridge-like arrangements. He exhibited again at the Salon des Indépendants in 1914. His first one-man exhibition in Paris was organised by the poet and critic Apollinaire in 1917 at the Galerie Bougard.

After the First World War he was associated with the revival of the *Section d'Or* group organised by Gleizes and Archipenko in 1919, becoming the secretary of the *Section d'Or*.

In 1922 he designed Diaghilev's production of Stravinsky's *Mavra* at the Paris Opera. He became a French citizen in

Nikolai Suetin. Suprematist Cup and Saucer, *c.1925.*
Hand-painted porcelain.
Private collection, courtesy of
Annely Juda fine Art, London.

Léopold Survage. Study for the Costume of an Hussar in Stravinsky's Comic Opera 'Mavra', *1922. Pencil, watercolour. Signed in French and dated. 43.3 x 25.4 cm.*
'Mavra' was produced by Diaghilev at the Paris Opera; libretto by Boris Kochno from Pushkin's poem 'The Little House in Kolomna'; choreography by Bronislava Nijinska.
Collection Mr. and Mrs. Nikita D.Lobanov-Rostovsky, London.

1927. His figurative work, rather in the manner of later Derain, was included in the exhibition of French art held in Moscow in 1926.

He executed three decorative panels, each more than twenty metres long, for the Railway Pavilion at the Paris International Exhibition of 1937. He died in Paris.

Exhibitions were held at the Musée Galliera, Paris, in 1966, and at the Musée des Beaux-Arts at Lyon in 1968.

He was represented at the exhibition Contemporary French Painting in Moscow in 1928 and in the exhibition of the Russian Ballet at the Galerie Billiet in Paris in 1930. He died in Paris.

Fisherwomen, 1927, MNAM, Paris, is a stylised painting in which figures display enlarged limbs rather in the manner of Juan Gris or recalling Picasso's recent neo-classicism. Here linear drawing and flattened areas of colour define the figures

against a stagy backdrop of houses.

Theatre design 1922 Diaghilev's production of the opera-bouffe *Mavra* at the Théâtre de l'Opéra, Paris, to music by Stravinsky, libretto by B.Kochno, choreography by B.Nijinska. The plot concerns a lover disguised as a female cook caught shaving.

1954 Antonio Veretti's opera *La Petite Marchande d'Allumettes* at the Théâtre de Cagliari, Paris.

Lit P.Fierens *Survage*, Paris, 1931. M.Gauthier *Survage*, Paris, 1953. *Survage*, exh. cat., Musée Galliéra, Paris, 1966. D.Abadie et al. *Dossier Survage*, Paris, 1970. *Diaghilev and Russian Stage Designers, a Loan Exhibition from the Collection of Mr. and Mrs. N.Lobanov-Rostovsky*, International Exhibitions Foundation, Washington, 1972-4. J.E.Bowlt *Russian Stage Design. Scenic Innovation. From the Collection of Mr. and Mrs. Nikita D.Lobanov-Rostovsky*, Jackson, MS, exh. cat.,1982. *Twilight of the Tsars*, London, 1991. *Léopold Survage*, exh. cat., Galerie des Pouchettes, Nice, 1975.

Coll MNAM, Paris.

SUVOROV, A. A.   **a.1925-1932**
Graphic artist. He was represented at the Paris International Exhibition in 1925 and at the exhibition of Russian Graphic Art in Riga in 1929. He was also represented at the jubilee exhibition Artists of the RSFSR over 15 Years held at the Russian Museum, Leningrad, in 1932.

SVAROG (KOROCHKIN), Vasili Semenovich 1883-1946
Portrait painter. He participated in the First State Free Exhibition of Artworks in Petrograd in 1919 and was included in the enormous survey Exhibition of Paintings by Petrograd Artists of All Tendencies 1919-1923 held in Petrograd in 1923. He was represented at the Paris International Exhibition in 1925 and at the jubilee exhibition Artists of the RSFSR over 15 Years held at the Russian Museum, Leningrad, in 1932.
Coll TG; RM.

SVEDOMSKY, Aleksandr Aleksandrovich   1848-1911
Genre painter. He painted Italian views 1882-6.
Coll TG.

SVEDOMSKY, Pavel Aleksandrovich   1849-1904
Painter of genre scenes and figure compositions.
Coll TG.

SVERCHKOV, N. G.   **b.1891**
Theatre designer. A Shverchkov was represented at the Paris International Exhibition in 1925. He produced designs for the play *Afanasiy Nikitin* in 1937.

SVERCHKOV, Nikolai Egorovich   1817-1898
Painter whose work included equestrian themes. Born in St. Petersburg. He visited France, Germany and Holland. He exhibited in Paris from 1859 and one of his works was bought by the French Emperor Napoleon III in 1863. He was a member of the Academy in St. Petersburg from 1852. He died at Tsarskoe Selo.
Coll TG; RM.

SVERCHKOV (SWERTCHKOFF), Vladimir Dmitrievich 1820-1888
Sometimes he signed his work 'W. Swertchkoff' in latin script.
Coll TG.

SVETLOV, S. Ya.   a.1919-1922

He exhibited in the first Obmokhu exhibition in May 1919 in Moscow. He also took part in the third exhibition of Obmokhu, the Society of Young Artists, in Moscow in May 1921, along with Ioganson, Medunetsky and others. He was represented at the First Russian Art Exhibition in Berlin in 1922.

SVETOSLAVSKY, Sergei Ivanovich   1857-1931

Ukrainian painter of views and landscapes with figures, close in style to Levitan. Born in Kiev. He studied at the Moscow College 1874-82. He exhibited with the Wanderers from 1884 and with the World of Art from 1900-2. He later exhibited with the Union of Russian Artists. He worked in Central Asia in the 1900s. Illness prevented him from painting from the 1920s.

Fisher Women, 1900s, Museum of Ukrainian Art, Kiev, is a fresh landscape in which two women install nets in the river. There is a certain breadth and grandeur to the handling and the composition.

Coll TG; RM; Museum of Ukrainian Art, Kiev.

SVININ, P.   a.1820s

Lithographer. He produced a series of prints *Picturesque Russian Scenes* in the 1820s.

SVIRIDOV, P. P.   a.1918-1929

He was represented at the First Exhibition of Works of the Professional Union of Artists in Moscow in 1918. The name Sviridov, without initials but presumably the same artist, appeared on the April 1919 list of artists for acquisitions by the envisaged Museum of Painterly Culture. He exhibited with the *Zhar-tsvet* (Fire-colour) group between 1924 and 1928. He was included in the 1928 exhibition of Acquisitions by the State Art Collections Fund held in Moscow and in the First Touring Exhibition of Painting and Graphics which opened in Moscow in 1929.

A.A.Suvorov. Illustration to Homer's 'Illiad', *1934. Wood engraving. 9.5 x 9 cm.*

SVOMAS

The abbreviated name for the Free State Art Studios (*Svobodnye gosudartsvennye khudozhestvennye masterskie*) set up in Moscow, Petrograd and other cities in 1918.

SWERTCHKOFF, W. = SVERCHKOV, V.D.

SYURVAZH = SURVAGE, L.

A.A.Suvorov. Lenin's Arrival in Petrograd in 1917, *1917. Wood engraving.*

T

T.L. see **TATLIN, V.E.**

TABANIN, Vladimir   b.1934
Painter of landscapes and figures. He studied under Mylnikov at the Repin Institute in Leningrad graduating in 1966. He is a member of the St. Petersburg Union of Artists and lives in the town of Pushkin.
Coll Roy Miles Gallery, London.
Colour plate p.426.

TAKKE, Boris Aleksandrovich   a.1910-1929
Painter. He exhibited with the Knave of Diamonds in Moscow 1910-11.
He was engaged in Agitprop projects in the early revolutionary years including decorations on the propaganda train *Red Cossack* and the Ukrainian train *Lenin*. He was represented at the enormous First State Exhibition of Art and Science, which included ethnographic material, held in Kazan in 1920 and at the First Touring Exhibition of Painting and Graphics which opened in Moscow in 1929.

TALDYKIN, A. A.   a.1921-1929
Theatre designer, painter. He was a founder member of the group *Bytie* (Existence) which was formed in 1921 partly in protest at 'the narrowness of leftist art'. He contributed to its first exhibition in 1922. He was represented at the exhibition Art of Moscow Theatre 1918-1923 held in Moscow in 1923 and at the First Touring Exhibition of Painting and Graphics which opened in Moscow in 1929.

TAMBI, Vladimir Aleksandrovich   1906-1955
Painter, draughtsman.
Coll RM.

TANKOV (TONKOV), Ivan Mikhailovich   1739/40-1799
Landscape painter, theatre designer. He used elements of genre and village life as in his *Fire in the Village* of 1785.
Coll TG.

TARABUKIN, Nikolai Mikhailovich   1889-1956
Critic and theorist closely involved in the transition from Constructivism to utilitarian projects in the early 1920s. Born in Moscow. He studied history and philosophy at Moscow University. From 1920 to 1924 he was a member of the Institute of Artistic Culture (INKhUK) in Moscow where he was an active theorist in the debates which led to the abandonment of easel painting by the Moscow Constructivists in favour of socially committed utilitarian design. The Costakis Collection has a suite of drawings c.1921, possibly theoretical diagrams, which resemble studies after Rodchenko, Rozanova and Malevich. In the period 1924-8 he contributed to GAKhN, the State Academy of Artistic Sciences. He taught at the Lunacharsky Institute of Theatre Art in the 1930s. His monograph on *Vrubel'* was published in Moscow in 1974.
Writings He outlined a material view of painting in his book *Opyt teorii zhivopisi* (Towards a Theory of Painting, Moscow,

1923), and in *Ot mol'berta k mashine* (From the Easel to the Machine, Moscow, 1923) he outlined the case for the demise of easel painting in terms which reflect the debates at INKhUK over the previous two years. These were extended by the utilitarian theories of his *Iskusstvo dnya* (The Art of the Day), Moscow, 1925.
Lit N.Taraboukine *Le dernier tableau*, edited with an essay by A.B.Nakov, Paris, 1972. A.Z.Rudenstine *Costakis Collection*, London, 1981. C.Lodder *Russian Constructivism*, New Haven and London, 1983.
Coll Costakis Collection.

TARAN, Andrei Ivanovich   a.1920-1923
Painter. He contributed to the Exhibition of Paintings by Russian Artists held at Pskov in Spring 1920. He became Director of the Museum of Artistic Culture in Petrograd for the period 1921-3. He was also Tatlin's assistant as Secretary of the Union of New Tendencies in Art with whom he exhibited in Petrograd in June 1922. He was included in the enormous survey Exhibition of Paintings by Petrograd Artists of All Tendencies 1919-1923 held in Petrograd in 1923.

TARKHOV, Nikolai Aleksandrovich   1871-1930
Painter whose work included landscapes. He was in Paris in 1900-1 and 1906-7. He exhibited with the Union of Russian Artists 1903-4 and 1907-10 and also with the Golden Fleece in Moscow 1909-10. He exhibited with the First Izdebsky International Salon 1909-10 in Odessa. He was a member of the second World of Art society from 1910 to 1924.
Coll TG.

TARKHOVA, L. V.   a.1918-1919
Painter. She exhibited at the First Exhibition of Works of the Professional Union of Artists in Moscow in 1918 and at the Ninth State Exhibition of Paintings: Naturalism and Realism in Moscow in 1919.

TATEVOSYAN, Egishe Martirosovich   1870-1936
Armenian landscape painter. His paintings included emotive paintings of figures in landscapes. An example is *In a Foreign Land*, 1894, Armenian Art Gallery, Erevan, in which a man visits a remote graveyard in the evening twilight. The figure remains in the shadow and the last of the light catches only the distant mountain valley. Paintings of Armenia include the loosely handled but colourful *plein air* study *Ararat from the Fields*, 1906, Armenian Art Gallery, Erevan. He also painted highly stylised decorative works.
Coll TG; Armenian Art Gallery, Erevan.

TATEVOSYAN, Oganes Karapetovich   1889-1974
Painter, graphic artist, ceramics artist. He studied in Tiflis in 1906 and at the Moscow College under K.Korovin 1910-17.
After the Revolution he first lived in Tashkent. He was an organiser of the Commune School in Samarkand in 1918 and of the Erevan School of Art in 1921. That year he worked on designs for sculpture and for plates to be executed at the Dulevo ceramics factory to mark the Congress of the Communist International. He was in Moscow attending the Vkhutemas from 1921 to 1927.
Old Samarkand, 1929, Uzbek Art Museum, Tashkent, has a man in a turban riding his donkey through a street that tips and reels like an early Cubist Braque. The stylisation is regional however in its inspiration.
Lit *Paris-Moscou*, 1979. N.Lobanov-Rostovsky *Revolutionary Ceramics*, London, 1990.

TATLIN, Vladimir Evgrafovich   1885-1953

Painter, theatre designer and central figure in the evolution of Constructivism in Russia. His work embraced the design of prototype clothing, ceramic ware and gliders. Sometimes he signed his work 'T.L' or 'Lot'.

Born in Moscow, the son of a railway engineer, Evgraf Nikiforovich Tatlin, and a poetess, Nadezhda Nikolaevna Tatlina, née Bart. He grew up in the Ukraine and attended school in Kharkov. He became a cadet and served on a sailing ship travelling to Bulgaria and Turkey. Early experience with painting included ikon painting. He studied painting at the Moscow College under Serov and Korovin 1902-3 but was expelled and may have re-enrolled 1909-10. He studied at the Penza School of Art under I.S.Goryushkin-Sorokopudov and A.N.Afanas'ev 1905-10 and studied Russian church frescoes in the summer months. He sailed on the *Great Princess Maria Nikolaeva* and *Voronezh* sailing ships as well as the steamer *Evgenia Ol'denburgskaya* visiting North Africa. His early experience as a seaman was important for his development and it also took him to Turkey, Syria, Libya, Morocco, Greece and Italy.

Vladimir Tatlin. Fisherman, *1911. Drawing.*
This has a rather oriental calligraphic quality which may reflect the interest in Chinese art expressed by other exhibitors with the Donkey's Tail group at this time.

Vladimir Tatlin. Fishmonger, *1911. Drawing or lithograph. Signed lower right and inscribed 'Fishmonger'.*

By 1907 he was friendly with the Burlyuk brothers, Larionov and Goncharova. This led him into contact with Russian Futurist activities and to the poet Khlebnikov whose innovative vision and verbal experiment was to prove a major stimulus to his work. He was also friendly with the sculptor S.D.Lebedeva, the artist V.V.Lebedev and the architects the Vesnin brothers, amongst whom Aleksandr Vesnin was also a painter. He periodically attended the Bernshtein Drawing School in St. Petersburg 1910-11 along with Le Dantyu, Lapshin and Lebedev. He exhibited at the Izdebsky Salon in Odessa 1910 11 and returned to study under Mashkov and Mikhailovsky at the Moscow College.

In 1911 he was at the studio complex The Tower in Moscow along with Bart, Popova, Vesnin and others. Here he explored Cubist principles particularly in drawings of the life model. He exhibited paintings, including *Fishmonger* and *Sailor*, and theatre designs at the Moscow College in March 1912 and was exhibiting with the Union of Youth 1911-14, but in 1912 he joined Larionov, Goncharova and Malevich to exhibit with the independent group The Donkey's Tail in Moscow. His association with the Futurists was confirmed in his illustration of the Futurist books *Mirskontsa* (Worldbackwards, Moscow, 1912) by Kruchenykh and Khlebnikov and *Trebnik troikh* (The Service Book of the Three, Moscow, 1913) by Mayakovsky, Khlebnikov and Kruchenykh. He also exhibited with the Knave of Diamonds 1912-13 and in 1913 with the World of

Vladimir Tatlin. Costume Design, *1913. Gouache on paper. Signed lower left.*
Design for an unrealised production of Glinka's 'A Life for the Tsar' (Ivan Susanin), 1913.

achievements against this polarity. Tatlin was a founder of the society Apartment No. 5 in Petrograd along with Bruni, Isakov, Lebedev, Miturich, Punin and Tyrsa. He worked with Khlebnikov and D.Petrovsky in Tsaritsyn in March 1916 on a cultural event at the House of Research and Art.

After the Revolution Tatlin's experimental work gained new significance. He occupied posts of importance in the early revolutionary years and his material experimentation led to his work being seen as a potential source for the evolution of a distinctly communist art. He became President of the Federation of Leftist Artists in Moscow and exhibited with the Artists of the Leftist Federation of the Professional Union in 1918 along with Rodchenko, Popova and others. He was also the head of the Moscow Collegium of IZO, the fine arts wing of the People's Commissariat of the Enlightenment, in 1919. Other members of the Collegium included Kuznetsov,

Art. He took part in a debate on contemporary art with Mashkov, Lentulov and others at the Polytechnic Museum under the auspices of the Knave of Diamonds in 1913.

His knowledge of Western art was further developed by a visit to Berlin and Paris in 1914 where he met Picasso and Lipchitz and perhaps Braque, Archipenko and Delaunay. Cubist collages and constructions impressed Tatlin sufficiently for him to undertake constructions of his own on his return to Russia. Initially these revealed Cubist traits which rapidly gave way to constructions in which the reference to recognisable imagery fast disappeared in favour of constructions determined increasingly by either a geometric grid underlying the arrangement of assembled material elements or by the kind of construction that the materials themselves permitted. Increasingly he became involved with experimental work in relief exhibited in his Moscow studio as the First Exhibition of Painterly Reliefs in May 1914. These were developed in subsequent exhibitions, including Tramway V in Petrograd 1915, 0.10. The Last Futurist Exhibition of Paintings in Petrograd in December 1915 to January 1916 where he first showed his corner reliefs, and at The Store in Moscow in 1916. Malevich had launched Suprematism at 0.10 and a degree of competition existed between Malevich and Tatlin by 1915. Both had introduced such radical innovations that many other artists began to measure their own position, aims and

Vladimir Tatlin. Costume Design, *1913-14. Gouache on paper. Signed lower right.*
Design for an unrealised production of Glinka's 'A Life for the Tsar' (Ivan Susanin), 1913.

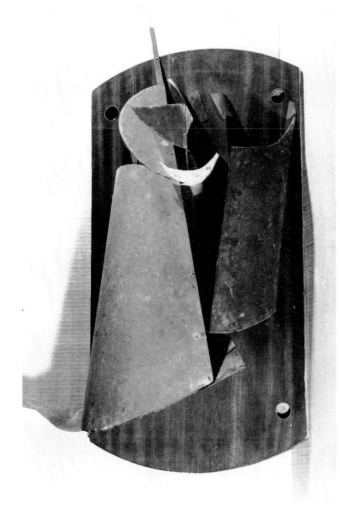

Vladimir Tatlin. Counter-relief, *1916-17. Metal and wood construction. State Tretyakov Gallery, Moscow.*

at the Eighth Congress of Soviets in Moscow in December 1920. In December 1921 Tatlin collaborated with the poets Mayakovsky, Khlebnikov, Kamensky and Kruchenykh on a performance at the Moscow Vkhutemas.

He taught at the Leningrad Vkhutein 1921-5 having been active in the bringing together of Leftist tendencies in Petrograd. With Mansurov he evolved a Petrograd branch of INKhUK in 1922 and he became its director. This was renamed the State Institute of Artistic Culture (GINKhUK) in 1923. He was a founder of the Union of New Tendencies in Art in Petrograd 1921-2 and exhibited with them in June 1922. He organised a memorial tribute to the poet Khlebnikov there on 28 June 1922. He also showed work at the exhibition of Studies for Theatre Decoration and Works from the Studios of the Decorative Institute held in Petrograd in 1922 and was represented at the First Russian Art Exhibition in Berlin in 1922.

He followed the lead of Moscow Constructivists in applying his abilities to the design of utilitarian objects including clothing and stoves, and with the theorist and critic Arvatov he organised a laboratory at the New Lessner factory, an activity compatible with the aims of INKhUK in Moscow. He also designed a plate, the *Tsarevich*, executed by Chekhonin for the State Porcelain Factory in 1922.

The poet Khlebnikov remained an inspiration and Tatlin created a theatrical performance installation of Khlebnikov's long poem *Zangezi* at Petrograd in 1923 in homage to his friend who had died the previous year. This was performed on

Malevich, Rozanova, Udal'tsova and Shevchenko. He appeared second, after Malevich, on the April 1919 list of artists for acquisitions by the envisaged Museum of Painterly Culture. He taught at the Moscow Free Art Studios (SVOMAS)/Vkhutemas 1918-20, and ran the Studio of Volume, Material and Construction at the Petrograd Free Art Studios 1919-24. He was also a member of the bureau charged with the development of an international art journal (unrealised) together with Lunacharsky, Khlebnikov, P.V.Kuznetsov, A.A.Morgunov, Nikolai Punin and others.

In November/December 1920 in Petrograd he displayed his model of the *Monument to the Third International*, begun as a monument to the Revolution and in response to Lenin's Plan for Monumental Propaganda with which he was closely involved. This double conical helix, evolved with the assistance of T.M.Shapiro, I.A.Meerzon and M.P.Vinogradov, was designed to house the world government of planet earth, containing revolving rooms of great size which were to move in time with the apparent circuits of the sun, moon and stars across the heavens. Never executed on its envisaged colossal scale striding across the river Neva, it nevertheless had a profound influence upon the development of Constructivism in Russia and acted as a kind of utopian model of dynamically evolving world order. The model was subsequently exhibited

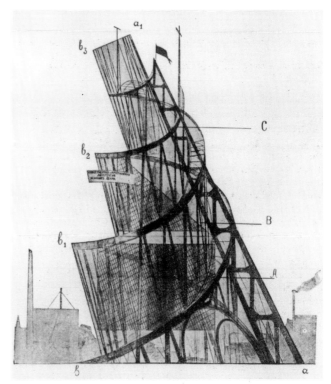

Vladimir Tatlin. Monument to the Third International, *1919-20. Large elevation drawing.*
The drawing was published by the critic Nikolai Punin in his pamphlet on the projected gigantic tower which he published in 1919.

11, 13 and perhaps 30 June 1923. The studies for this were signed impersonally 'Tatlin Studio' (*Masterskaya Tatlina*) as were his utilitarian designs including furniture, stoves, ceramics and clothing evolved 1923-4.

As Director of the Union of New Tendencies in Art he organised and took part in the enormous survey Exhibition of Paintings by Petrograd Artists of All Tendencies 1919-1923 held in Petrograd in 1923. He visited Burnaul and Biisk in Western Siberia in 1924.

He worked at the Petrograd Institute of Applied Arts in early

Vladimir Tatlin. Design for a Woman's Dress, *1923-4. Charcoal on paper. 56.8 x 77 cm.*
Like the Moscow Constructivists, Tatlin designed useful projects in the early 1920s.
Bakhrushin Theatre Museum, Moscow.

1925 and a version of his *Monument to the Third International* was exhibited at the International Exhibition in Paris in 1925. He contributed to an exhibition of drawings at the State Tsvetkov Gallery in Moscow in 1925 together with Lev Bruni, N.Kupreyanov, V.Lebedev, P.L'vov, Pavel Miturich and N.Tyrsa.

He taught at the Painting Department of the Kiev College of Art and later headed the department of Theatre, Cinema and Photography at the Kiev Art Institute 1925-7 and was included in the All-Ukrainian Jubilee Exhibition of 1927. He contributed to Mayakovsky's recitals in Kiev 1926-7. He taught at the Moscow Vkhutein 1927-30 and paintings of 1912-13 were included in the Exhibition of New Tendencies in Art at the Russian Museum, Leningrad, in 1927. He was also included in the 1928 exhibition of Acquisitions by the State Art Collections Fund held in Moscow.

He established an experimental workshop at the Novodevichy Monastery in Moscow 1929-33 where he worked with assistants from the Vkhutein on the construction of flying machines based on bird flight. The gliders which resulted from these experiments he called the Aircycle or *Letatlin*, a pun on his own name and *letat'*, to fly. In 1930 together with his students he designed the catafalque which bore Mayakovsky's body to the Novodevichy Monastery. He was given a personal exhibition at the Pushkin Museum in Moscow in 1932 where he showed three models of *Letatlin*, studies for it, photographs of the *Monument to the Third International* and other projects.

He was included in the survey exhibitions Artists of the RSFSR over 15 Years at the Russian Museum in Leningrad in 1932 and Artists of the RSFSR over 15 Years at the Tretyakov Gallery in Moscow in 1933. He was regularly involved in less radically innovative theatre design from 1935 and also returned to producing easel paintings. He was evacuated to Sverdlovsk 1941-3. He died in Moscow.

*Seated Nude, 1913, TG, shows an anonymous and almost featureless figure built up from planes defined by arcs lit or shaded along one edge in an analytic and economical technique. This makes for a strong rhythmic construction of the image and perhaps recalls Archipenko's sculpture. Tatlin as a painter was at this stage severe but rhythmic: nothing is superfluous and colour is restricted to separated large areas of yellow ochre, red and blue. Timeless in theme, Tatlin's editing of the figure reveals a debt to the Russian view of Cubism and also to the stylisation of ikon painting. This work is comparable with *Self-portrait as a Sailor*, 1911, RM, and *Nude*, 1913, RM.

*Counter-relief, 1916-17, TG, is the only known surviving relief which appears substantially complete (p.423). Cut metal in curves and arcs is mounted on a wooden board and there is no overt representational purpose. This is material and spatial organisation in high relief. It may be related to the verbal experiments of Tatlin's poet friend Khlebnikov who outlined a system of correspondences between sounds and shapes.

Theatre design 1911 November: the folk drama *Tsar Maksimilian i ego nepokornyy syn Adol'f* (Tsar Maximillian and his unruly Son Adolf) produced by M.M.Bonch-Tomashevsky for the Literary-Artistic Circle in Moscow.

1911-14 unrealised project for Glinka's opera *Zhizn' za Tsarya* (A Life for the Tsar), later called *Ivan Susanin* (TG). Here stage design and painting come close together. Some of the designs have the status of paintings in their own right. *The Forest* and *The Polish Ball* relate closely to Tatlin's paintings in that they are built up with circular arcs and straight lines to construct trees and architecture. Even the figures are designed this way.

1915-18 Wagner's *Flying Dutchman* (unrealised). Drawings of rigging executed with an even line and mathematical precision complement a related painting with immense atmosphere and executed in deep blues and dull ochre yellows. The sense of straining, heaving movement was clearly informed by his own experiences as a sailor. Straight lines underpin the whole composition. It is impressive as both painting and theatre design.

1917 V.Khlebnikov's *Lady Death's Error* and *13 in the Air* (probably unrealised).

1923 V.Khlebnikov's *Zangezi*, at the Experimental Theatre of the Museum of Artistic Culture, Petrograd. This was a long poem adapted by Tatlin who also performed in what was effectively a theatrical corner-construction in honour of his friend the poet Khlebnikov who had recently died. He constructed maquettes that were in effect reliefs adapted to stage space, and the costume designs are primarily examples of Tatlin translating Khlebnikov's material theories of language into constructions in wood and metal. Photographs of the performance indicate that it was much simplified and performed in a corner space utilising an existing balcony rather than a proscenium stage.

1925 Jules Romain's *Cromedeyre-le-vieil* at the Bolshoi Drama Theatre, Leningrad.

1926 V.Z.Gzhitsky's *Po zore* (At Dawn) at the Kiev State Children's Theatre.

1926 H.C.Andersen *Bum i Yula* (Bum and Iula) at the Kiev State Children's Theatre.

1935 A.N.Ostrovsky's *Komik XVII stoletiya* (The Comic Actor of the 17th Century) at the Second Studio of the Moscow Art Theatre. Designs for costumes employ a unique style made up from delicately calligraphic brushmarks in watercolour. The effect is of economy but is also highly informative. There is no stylisation at all in the costumes as they would have appeared on stage, but only in the drawing technique used to depict them. Pencil drawings used a soft cross-hatching evident also in Tatlin's book illustrations to stories by Daniil Kharms.

1935 November: S.A.Semenov's *Ne Sdadimsya* (No Surrender) for Tairov at the Kamerny (Chamber) Theatre, Moscow.

1940 A.P.Shtein's *Kronshtadt ili Vesna 21-ogo* (Kronstadt or Spring 1921) for the Moscow Lensovet Theatre.

1940 A.V.Sukhovo-Kobylin's *Delo* (The Affair) at the Central Red Army Theatre, Moscow.

1943 A.A.Kron's *Glubokaya razvedka* (Deep Reconaissance) at the Moscow Art Theatre.

1944 E.L.Shvarts' *Dalekiy kray* (A Far Country) at the Central Children's Theatre.

1946 A.M.Fayko's *Kapitan Kostrov* (Captain Kostrov) at the Moscow Drama Theatre.

1946 S.Ya.Marshak's *Dvenadtsat' mesyatsev* (Twelve Months) at the Central House of Children's Education.

1947 B.A.Lavrenev's *Za tekh, kto na more* (For those at Sea) at the Moscow Lenin Komsomol Theatre.

1947 A.A.Surov's *Sekretar' raykoma* (Secretary of the District Committee) at the Mossovet Theatre.

1948 A.A.Surov's *Obida* (The Offence) at the Mossovet Theatre.

1948 A.N.Ostrovsky's *Na vsyakogo mudretsa dovol'no prostoty* (Enough Simplicity for Every Wiseman) at the Moscow Realistic Dramatic Theatre.

1949 I.I.Iroshkinova's *Gde-to v Sibiri* (Somewhere in Siberia)

Vladimir Tatlin. Sorrow, *1923. Charcoal on paper.*
Design for Tatlin's staging of the long poem 'Zangezi' by his friend the poet Khlebnikov. Lines from the poem appear top right. Tatlin attempted to translate the poem into material constructions.

at the Central Children's Theatre.

1949 P.G.Malyarevsky's *Chudesnyy klad* (The Wonderful Treasure) at the Moscow State Variety Theatre for Children.

1950 N.G.Vinnikov's *Chasha radosti* (Bowl of Joy) at the Mossovet Theatre.

1951 S.P.Antonov's *Poslanets mira* (The Emissary of Peace) and M.Kalinovsky and L.Berezin's *Pravda o ego otse* (The Truth about his Father) at the Moscow Literary-Drama Theatre.

1952 I.L.Sel'vinsky's *Bitva pri Gryunvalde* (The Battle for Grunwald), not realised, for the Central Soviet Army Theatre.

Film design 1917 Meyerhold's unrealised film of F.K.Sologub's *Navi chary* (Enchantments of the Shades).

Futurist books A.Kruchenykh and V.Khlebnikov *Mirskontsa* (Worldbackwards), 1912, illustrated by Goncharova, Larionov, Tatlin and I.Rogovin. V.Khlebnikov, V.Mayakovsky, D. and N.Burlyuk *Trebnik troikh* (The Service Book of the Three), 1913, illustrated by D., N. and V.Burlyuk, V.Mayakovsky and Tatlin.

Illustrations *Novy Lef* magazine (No.3, 1927, p.48) announced the publication of a book of verses in Ukrainian by Mikhail Semenko, Georgiy Shkurupiy and Nikolai Bazhan, with a cover designed by Tatlin, entitled *Zustrich na perekhresniy*

Vladimir Tabanin. Russian Festival, *1990. Oil on canvas. 182.9 x 182.9 cm.*
Roy Miles Gallery, London.

stantsii (Encounter at the Crossing Station). Daniil Kharms *Vo pervykh i vo vtornykh* (Firstly and Secondly), Moscow-Leningrad, 1929. S.Sergel' *Na parusnom sudne* (On the Sailing Ship), Moscow, 1929.

Lit N.Punin *Tatlin (protiv kubizma)*, Peterburg, 1921. L.Zhadova ed.*V.E.Tatlin*, Moscow, 1977. J.E.Bowlt *Russian Stage Design. Scenic Innovation. From the Collection of Mr. and Mrs. Nikita D.Lobanov-Rostovsky*, Jackson, MS, exh. cat., 1982. J.Milner *Vladimir Tatlin and the Russian Avant-Garde*, New Haven and London, 1983. C.Lodder *Russian Constructivism*, New Haven and London, 1983. *Tatlin*, exh. cat., Penza, 1987. L.Zhadova *Tatlin*, London, 1988. Nancy Van Norman Baer *Theatre in Revolution, Russian Avant-Garde Stage Design 1913-*

1935, San Francisco and London, 1991. Dzhon Boult (John Bowlt) *Khudozhniki russkogo teatra. Sobranie Nikity i Niny Lobanovykh-Rostovskikh*, Moscow, 1991.

Coll TG; RM; Bakhrushin Theatre Museum; St. Petersburg Theatre Museum; Central State Archive of Art and Literature, Moscow; Zhukovsky Central State Museum of Aviation and Spaceflight, Moscow; Glinka Central Museum of Musical Culture; Kostroma Art Museum; Pskov Art Museum.
Colour plates p.28 and opposite.

TAVASIEV, Soslanbek Dafaevich　　　　　**1894-1927+**
Sculptor. He was included in the major exhibition in Moscow in 1927 marking the tenth anniversary of the Revolution.

Vladimir Tatlin. Study for the Costume of a Young Peasant Woman in Glinka's 'A Life for the Tsar' (Ivan Susanin), *1913. Watercolour. Initialled lower right in Russian and dated 1913. 46 x 29 cm.*
Collection Mr. and Mrs. Nikita D.Lobanov-Rostovsky, London.

TCHEKHONINE = CHEKHONIN, S.V.

TCHELITCHEW (CHELISHCHEV, TCHELICHEV), Pavel Fedorovich   1898-1957

Painter, theatre designer. Born in Moscow. He studied in Kiev under Exter 1918-19 but in 1920 emigrated via Istanbul and Sofia to Berlin where he designed for the theatre 1921-3 before moving to Paris where he arrived in 1923. He exhibited at the Salon d'Automne in 1925 and at the Galerie Druet in 1926. In 1928 he designed Diaghilev's production of *Odes* for the Théâtre Sarah Bernhardt in Paris. He exhibited in London the same year and in 1929 had a one-man exhibition in Paris at the Galerie Pierre. He died in Rome.

Theatre design 1919 *Geisha*, an unrealised opera project for Kiev.

1920-1 designs for Boris Kniaseff's Ballet Company at the Strelna cabaret in Istanbul.

1921-3 various theatre designs for the Blaue Vogel Theater, Russisches Romantisches Theatre and the Königgratzerstrasse Theater in Berlin.

1922 December: *Savonarola* P.Suvchinsky's adaptation of J.A.Gobineau's tragedy *La Renaissance* at the Königgratzerstrasse

Pavel Tchelitchew. Costume Design for a Fishmonger, *1920-1. Watercolour. 30 x 22.3 cm.*
This was designed for a production by the V.P.Zimin dance company at the Strelna cabaret in Istanbul 1920-1.
Collection Mr. and Mrs. Nikita D.Lobanov-Rostovsky, London.

Theater in Berlin.
1928 *Ode* produced by Diaghilev to music by Nicolas Nabokov at the Théâtre Sarah Bernhardt, Paris. An ink drawing for this is a loosely handled study of dancers in movement inscribed within ellipses.
Film design 1921 *Pagoda.*
Lit J.T.Soby *Tchelitchew Drawings and Paintings*, MOMA, New York, 1942. *Hommage à Tchelitchew*, exh. cat., Galerie Weill, Paris, 1966. P.Tyler *The Divine Comedy of Pavel Tchelitchew: A Biography*, 1967. J.E.Bowlt *Russian Stage Design. Scenic Innovation. From the Collection of Mr. and Mrs. Nikita D.Lobanov-Rostovsky*, Jackson, MS, exh. cat.,1982.
Coll Musée de l'Opera, Paris; Ashmolean Museum, Oxford; Lobanov-Rostovsky Collection, London.

TCHERKESSOV = CHERKESOV, Yu. Yu.

TELEGIN, I. a.1921
He was included in the Third Touring Exhibition of the Sovetsk Regional subdepartment of the Museums Bureau along with Kandinsky, Rodchenko and others in 1921.

TELINGATER, Solomon Benediktovich 1903-1969
Graphic artist and typographer. Born at Tiflis. He studied at the Art Studios in Baku, Azerbaijan, until 1920 and then at the Moscow Vkhutemas. He worked for the journals *Molodoy Rabochiy* (Young Worker) and *Trud* (Labour) and illustrated books in Baku 1921-5. He directed the art studio of the House of Communist Education. He worked as an innovative professional typographic artist for the review *Poligraficheskoe*

Proizvodstvo (Polygraphic Production) 1925-7. In 1927 he was a member of the organising committee of the All-Union Polygraphic Exhibition in Moscow and the exhibition The Art of the Book at Leipzig. In 1928 he was represented at the International Press Exhibition in Cologne. He rose from printshop instructor to become a figure of international renown. He worked with Lissitzky on posters in which he made use of varied type and photomontage effects. He was a founder member of the group October 1928-32. His last years were mostly concerned with book and periodical design. He died in Moscow.

Book designs numerous including: *Vsesoyuznaya poligraficheskaya vystavka. Katalog* (All-Union Printing Exhibition. Catalogue.), Moscow, 1927. Cover for the periodical *Stroitel'stvo Moskvy* (Moscow Construction), No.10, 1929. S.I.Kirsanov *Slovo predostavlyaetsya Kirsanov* (Kirsanov is Called Upon to Speak), Moscow, 1930.

Writings S.Telingater, L.E.Kaplan *Iskusstvo aksidentnogo nabora*, Moscow, 1965. S.Telingater *Iskusstvo knigi*, Moscow, 1960.

Lit *S.B.Telingater*, exh. cat., Moscow, 1975. *S.B.Telingater, l'oeuvre graphique*, exh. cat., Association France-URSS, Paris, 1978. *Paris-Moscou*, 1979. Dzhon Boult (John Bowlt) *Khudozhniki russkogo teatra. Sobranie Nikity i Niny Lobanovykh-Rostovskikh*, Moscow, 1991. S.Compton *Russian Avant-Garde Books 1917-34*, London, 1992.

TENNER, G. S.   1894-1943
Ukrainian sculptor.

TEPER, I. N.   a.1918
He was represented at the First Exhibition of Works of the Professional Union of Artists in Moscow in 1918 and appeared on the April 1919 list of artists for acquisitions by the envisaged Museum of Painterly Culture.

TEREBENEV, Ivan Ivanovich   1780-1815
Graphic artist. He made fantastic and grotesque prints illustrating in a satirical way the events of the Napoleonic war. An example is *French Crow Soup*, 1812-13, etching and watercolour, which caricatures the desperate plight of French soldiers on the retreat from Moscow.
Coll Historical Museum, Moscow.

TEREBENEV, Mikhail Ivanovich   1795-1864
Portraitist.
Coll TG.

TERENT'EV, S.   a.c.1927
Sculptor. He was included in the major exhibition in Moscow in 1927 marking the tenth anniversary of the Revolution.

TERK, S. = DELAUNAY(-TERK), S.E.

TERLEMEZYAN, Fanos Pogosovich (Pavlovich)
1865-1941
Painter. He was in Paris in 1910.
Coll TG.

TERNOVETS, Boris Nikolaevich   a.1912-1926+
Sculptor. He studied under Bourdelle at the Académie de la Grande Chaumière in Paris along with Burmeister, Vertepov and others c.1912.

After the Revolution, during 1919-20, he was a founder of the *Monolit* (Monolith) group of sculptors, which included Babichev, Mukhina, Konen'kov, Krandievskaya, Korolev, Strakhovskaya, Zlatovratsky, Ternovets, V.Popova, Blazhevich and Kudinov. They worked on monumental propaganda and entered the competitive exhibition for a Monument to Liberated Labour held in Moscow in May 1920.

He was associated with the Museums Bureau (*Glavmuzei*) in 1922. He was a member of the organising committee of the Academy of Artistic Sciences involved in the Soviet display at

Solomon Telingater. Study for an Agitational Lorry for the Red Army Theatre, *1932. Collage, watercolour, pencil. Signed. 25 x 62 cm. Collection Mr. and Mrs. Nikita D.Lobanov-Rostovsky, London.*

the Venice International Exhibition of 1924. He also visited the International Exhibition in Paris in 1925 where he selected works for acquisition by the State. These were exhibited at the State Museum of New Western Art, Moscow, in 1927. He was a member of the Society of Russian Sculptors from 1926.

TERPSIKHOROV, Nikolai Borisovich   **1890-1960**
Painter. Born in St. Petersburg. He studied under Yuon and Dudin in Moscow and then at the Moscow College under N.Kasatkin, A.Vasnetsov and K.Korovin and at the Moscow College 1911-17.
After the Revolution he exhibited with the Moscow School Society of Artists active 1917-25.
He was a member of AKhRR 1922-32. His work was included in the exhibition of Soviet art held at Harbin in 1926 and in Japan in 1927, in the First Touring Exhibition of Painting and Graphics which opened in Moscow in 1929 and in the jubilee exhibition Artists of the RSFSR over 15 Years held at the Russian Museum, Leningrad, in 1932. He died in Moscow.
The First Slogan, 1924, TG, an atmospheric and effective painting built upon contrasts. In the dark atelier surrounded by plaster casts of Greek sculpture stands a lone painter: he paints a red banner with the words 'All Power to the Soviets' — a declamatory and political slogan emerges from the deserted studio. Ironically this is still a studio painting but it notes at least the call of Mayakovsky to make the streets into palettes.
Lit *N.Terpsikhorov*, exh. cat., Moscow, 1953. N.Mosedova *N.Terpsikhorov*, Moscow, 1954. *Paris-Moscou*, 1979. A.M.Muratov, V.Manin et al. *Zhivopis' 20-30kh godov*, Sankt-Peterburg, 1991.

THEOPHANES THE GREEK (FEOFAN GREK)
c.1350-c.1410
Ikon painter. His birthdate is given by some authorities as c.1340. He was a contemporary of Andrei Rublev and Prokhor of Gorodets. He worked in Byzantium and Old Rus' and painted frescoes, murals and miniatures. He was associated with Novgorod at the Spas'-na-Ilyne Church in 1378. He worked at Moscow, providing a link between Byzantium and Russia. He worked in Constantinople, Galata, Chalcedon and Kaffa and later probably decorated churches at Novgorod, Moscow and Nizhny-Novgorod. He executed frescoes at Novgorod the Great in 1378. He worked with Rublev at the Moscow Kremlin in the Cathedral of the Annunciation. He may also have worked at Serpukhov, Kolomna and Pereslavl'-Zalesski. The date of his death is sometimes given as after 1405.
Coll TG; RM; Lenin Library, Moscow.
Lit V.N.Lazarev *Feofan Grek i ego shkola* (Theophanes the Greek and his School), Moscow, 1961.

TIKHOBRAZOV, Nikolai Ivanovich   **1818-1874**
Coll TG.

TIKHOMIROV, I.V.   **a.1919**
Painter. He exhibited at the juryless Eighth State Exhibition in Moscow in 1919.

TIKHONOV, Nikolai Egorovich   **a.1918-1920**
He was engaged in Agitprop projects in the early revolutionary years including the decoration of the propaganda trains *Red Cossack*, the Ukrainian train *Lenin*, *Lenin (October Revolution)* and *Soviet Caucasus* in 1920.

TIKHONOV, Sergei Egorovich   **a.1918-1920**
He was engaged in Agitprop projects in the early revolutionary years including decorations at the Putilovsky Factory in Petrograd with V.Chernov in 1918 and also the decoration of the propaganda trains *Red Cossack*, the Ukrainian train *Lenin*, *Lenin (October Revolution)* and *Soviet Caucasus*.

TIL'BERG, I. Kh.   **a.1918**
Sculptor. He responded rapidly to Lenin's call in 1918 for monuments to revolutionary heroes and forerunners by designing a monument to the Ukrainian poet *Taras Shevchenko*. His monument was unveiled in Petrograd 29 November 1918.

TIL'VIR-PLO, L.   **a.1919**
Painter who exhibited at the Ninth State Exhibition of Paintings: Naturalism and Realism in Moscow in 1919.

TIMASHEVSKY, Orest Isaakievich   **1822-1867**
Portraitist.
Coll TG.

TIMM, Vasili Fedorovich (George Wilhelm)   **1820-1895**
Painter, illustrator. He executed illustrations of nightlife and other contemporary themes including *The Artists' Ball in 1860* which was published in the *Russkii khudozhestvenyy listok*. This work was filled with a light-hearted, grotesque revelry appropriate to its theme.
Coll TG.

TIMOFEEV, Vasili Kirillovich   **1891-1968**
He was represented at the enormous First State Exhibition of Art and Science, which included ethnographic material, held in Kazan in 1920 and at the Third Touring Exhibition of the Sovetsk Regional subdepartment of the Museums Bureau along with Kandinsky, Rodchenko and others in 1921.

TIMOFEEV, Vasili Timofeevich   **1835-1913+**
Portraitist.
Coll TG.

TIMOFEEVA,   **a.1921**
She was active at Orenberg 1920-1 and exhibited with Kudryashev and Kalmykov at the First State Exhibition at Orenburg in 1921.

TIMOREV, Vasili Porfirevich   **1870-1942**
Painter, graphic artist, ceramics artist. He studied at the Society for the Encouragement of the Arts at St. Petersburg under Repin and studied etching under E.Kruglikova in Paris. He worked as a graphic artist for the publisher Knebel 1918-21 and was engaged on book design from 1922. He designed for the State Porcelain Factory in the later 1920s.
Lit N.Lobanov-Rostovsky *Revolutionary Ceramics*, London, 1990.

TIRTOFF, Romain de, TIRTOV, Roman = ERTE

TITOV, Aleksandr Ivanovich   **a.1909**
He taught in St. Petersburg in 1909 where his pupils included V.V.Lebedev.

TITOV, Petr Savel'evich   **d.1868**
Painter.
Coll TG.

TOIDZE, Irakliy Moisevich   **1902-1941+**
Georgian painter, graphic artist. His illustrations to Shota

Aleksandr Tyshler. Fortune, *1973. Oil on canvas. 59 x 50.8 cm.*
Roy Miles Gallery, London.

Nikolai Tomsky. The Writer Nikolai Gogol, *1951. Marble. 87 x 82 x 44 cm.*
This bust shows Tomsky's ability to revive a mode of sculpture which was flourishing in the 19th century. It could almost be attributed to a date one hundred years earlier. Adopting earlier academic techniques and compositional devices was a feature of much Socialist Realist art. It proposed an historical continuity in national identity by selecting features of older Russian culture to stress the substantial achievements of Russian art and writing. It was also a style that was easy for a Soviet audience to recognise and understand.

Rustaveli's poem *Vityaz' v tigrovoy shkure* (The Knight in the Tiger Skin), 1937, gouache, Museum of the Art of Eastern Nations, Moscow, are reminiscent of Delacroix lithographs in their techniques and theme. One illustration shows three horsemen racing at speed through a narrow pass, one of them killing a tiger with his arrow as he rides by. He was designing posters in 1941.
Coll Museum of the Art of Eastern Nations, Moscow.

TOLSTOY, Fedor Petrovich   **1783-1873**
Neo-classical sculptor, painter, draughtsman. He celebrated the growth and victories of the Russian Empire. Born into a family of the nobility. He produced cameos and medallions commemorating the war of 1812 and made neo-classical line drawings. His reliefs exhibited precision and meticulousness, translating the Napoleonic Wars into an ancient imagery of idealised ancient warriors as in *The Liberation of Berlin*, 1813, RM. Their typical size is 16-18 cm. A bas-relief of the *Battle of Borodino 1812* dates from 1817. He became Vice-President of the Academy in 1828. Between 1820 and 1833 he made line illustrations for *Dushenko* by Bogdanovich in a precise Grecian style. Other works include *Morpheus*, 1852, a marble carving in the round. His line drawings are extremely precise, neo-

classical costume pieces devoid of chiaroscuro but full of detail concerning dress, architecture and interior fittings, as in his illustrations to the poem *Dushenko*.
**Triple Alliance*, 1821, wax, RM, is a low relief within a circular form as if for a medal, architectural roundel or coin. Three emblematic soldiers swear allegiance, one in a frontal view, one in profile and one in three-quarter profile. The style is pure international neo-classicism, executed with precision and filled with political significance.
Coll RM.

TOMSKY, Nikolai Vasilievich   **1900-1956+**
Portrait sculptor. He became President of the Academy of the USSR. His monumental works include *General Chernyakhovsky* erected in Vilnius in 1950 as well as an elegantly historicist bronze monument to *Lomonosov* at Moscow University in 1953. He made numerous military portraits in basalt and marble. Other portraits include *Gogol*, 1951 and the painter *Diego Rivera* in 1956, RM. His granite portraits, perhaps because of the nature of the medium, have a somewhat ancient Egytian air.
**Monument to S.M.Kirov*, 1935-8, bronze and granite, erected at Leningrad, is a larger than life Socialist Realist piece in which the hero makes the expansive gesture of a confident man.
Coll RM.

TONKOV = TANKOV, I.M.

TOPOLOVA, I. S.   **a.1918**
She was represented at the First Exhibition of Works of the Professional Union of Artists in Moscow in 1918.

TOPORKOV, Dmitri Aleksandrovich   **1885-1937**
Painter. He took part in a debate on contemporary art with Mashkov, Tatlin and others at the Polytechnic Museum under the auspices of the Knave of Diamonds in 1913.
After the Revolution he contributed to the Twelfth State Exhibition: Colourdynamo and Tectonic Primitivism (*Tsvetodinamos i tektonicheskiy primitivizm*) along with Grishchenko, Shevchenko and others in Moscow in 1919.

TOPURIDZE, Valentin Bagratovich   **1907-1948+**
Sculptor. Born in Georgia. He studied under Nikoladze and Kandelaki. His monumental works include a seated figure of the poet *Arkady Tsereteli*, 1948, at Chiatury and *The Call for Peace* on the theatre building at Chiatury. He also executed a figure of *Lenin* at Tblisi.
**Victory*, 1946-8, bronze, was designed to crown the pediment of the theatre at Chiatury. Commemorating the recent victory over Germany it comprises a powerful female figure, her limbs bursting out diagonally in an intense dramatic, symbolic gesture.
Coll RM.

TOROPOV, Foma Gavriilovich   **1821-1898**
Painter of portraits and still-lifes.
Coll TG.

TRAUGOT, Georgi   **a.1927-1929**
He exhibited with the Circle of Artists in Leningrad between 1927 and 1929.

TRET'YAKOV, Nikolai Sergeevich   **1857-1896**
Painter whose work included portraits and interiors.
Coll TG.

TRIONDAFILOS = APOSTOLI, V.A.

Vasili Tropinin. The Sculptor Ivan Vitali. *Oil on canvas.*
National Gallery, Prague.

TRISKIN, N.   **a.1925**
He was represented at the Paris International Exhibition in
1925.

TROITSKY, A. P.   **a.1925-1932**
He was represented at the Paris International Exhibition in
1925 and at the jubilee exhibition Artists of the RSFSR over
15 Years held at the Russian Museum, Leningrad, in 1932.

TROPININ, Vasili Andreevich   **1776-1857**
Genre and portrait painter. He was born a serf and remained a
serf until the age of forty-five. He studied at the Academy but
was recalled by his owner to work on his estate as a gardener
and valet. As a free painter he worked in Moscow primarily as
a successful portraitist in the 1820s and 1830s. His works
included *The Lacemaker*, 1823, TG, a psychologically alert and

popular portrait which depicts the sitter in action and so
approaches genre painting, and a *Self-portrait*, 1846, TG,
which exhibits some of the delicacy of Venetsianov. Many of
his portraits are relatively informal.
*Portrait of the Artist's Son, c.1818, TG, is a fine Romantic half-
length which makes use of *contre-jour* effects. The face is
sensitively handled with fluent use of paint and some scumbling.
*Self-portrait against a View of the Kremlin, 1844, Tropinin
Museum, Moscow, is a three-quarter-length painting of the
artist with palette in hand and a sunlit glimpse of the Kremlin
behind him. A delicacy and gentle optimism recalls that of
Venetsianov. The artist pictured himself as reasonable,
intelligent and sympathetic. The finish is highly resolved and
yet the gentle play of light softens the effect.
Coll Well represented at TG; Tropinin Museum, Moscow.

TROSHIN, Nikolai Stepanovich b.1897
Draughtsman, exhibition designer. He specialised in black and white work. He studied at the Penza School of Art and at the Vkhutemas in Moscow in 1922. He was an active poster designer in the 1920s and 1930s and also an illustrator of books. He made use of photomontage effects in his posters. He was also active as an exhibition designer.

TROUBETSKOY = TRUBETSKOY, P.P.

TROUPYANSKY = TRUPYANSKY, Ya. A.

TROYANOVSKAYA, Anna Ivanovna 1895-1977
Painter. She worked in the studio complex The Tower in Moscow with Tatlin, Popova and others in 1912 after studying under Matisse in Paris 1910-12.

She exhibited with the Society of Moscow Painters at its inaugural exhibition in Moscow in 1925.
She died in Moscow.

TRUBETSKOY (TROUBETSKOY), Prince Pavel (Paolo) Petrovich 1866-1938
Sculptor of great facility. His bronzes show clearly the manipulation of the original clay which was characteristically achieved with a light dynamic touch. The lively and fluent surface which resulted revealed his debt to the example of Rodin. The relation of his handling of materials to the image evolved, as well as his elegant portraiture, recalled the techniques of such painters as Boldini.
He was born in Italy. In 1884 he was working under G.Grandi, F.Barcaglia and E.Bazzaro in Milan but he had his

Vasili Tropinin. A Ukrainian Peasant, *1820s. Oil on canvas. 34.5 x 28.5 cm.*
National Museum, Warsaw.

own studio by 1885. The following year he exhibited in Italy, France and America. He lived in Moscow from 1887 and taught at the Moscow College 1898-1906 but also lived in St. Petersburg. From 1899 he exhibited with the Wanderers and was an honorary member from 1910. He executed a lively, small full-length sculpture of the painter *Levitan*, TG, in 1899 as well as portraits of *Tolstoy*, 1899, RM, and *Chaliapine*, 1899-1900, RM. He exhibited with the World of Art 1899-1903.

He won honours at the Paris International Exhibition in 1900 and at Dresden in 1901. From 1906 to 1914 he lived in Paris and paid visits to Italy, Russia, England and the United States. He was represented in Diaghilev's display of Russian art at the 1906 Salon d'Automne in Paris. He was working at Yasnaya Polyana, the estate of Tolstoy near Tula in 1910 where he executed a number of drawings and busts of the writer.

He later lived in Paris. He was in Italy in 1932 and was made a member of the Milan Academy. He died in Italy.

Reclining Woman — Princess Marina Nikolaevna Gagarina, 1901, RM, is designed to be seen from above.

Lit I.Shmidt *Trubetskoy*, Moscow, 1964. *P.P.Trubetskoy*, exh. cat., Leningrad, 1966. *Paris-Moscou*, 1979. *Twilight of the Tsars*, London, 1991.

Coll Well represented at RM; TG; Hatton Gallery, University of Newcastle upon Tyne.

TRUPYANSKY (TROUPYANSKY), Yakov Abramovich 1875-1955

Sculptor and ceramics artist. he studied at the Art School in Odessa 1892-8 and at the Academy in St. Petersburg 1901-9. He executed decorative sculpture for buildings in St. Petersburg/Leningrad, Kharkov, Kiev and Odessa from 1910 to 1949.

He was the manager of the art bronze section of the Leningrad Foundry from 1921 to 1934 and produced figurines for the State Porcelain Factory 1922-3. He was represented at the jubilee exhibition Artists of the RSFSR over 15 Years held at the Russian Museum, Leningrad, in 1932.

He taught painting, sculpture and design at the Leningrad Institute of Engineering Construction 1949-55.

Lit N.Lobanov-Rostovsky *Revolutionary Ceramics*, London, 1990.

TRUTOVSKY, Konstantin Aleksandrovich 1826-1893

Ukrainian painter of genre and landscape.

Coll TG.

TRYASKIN, Nikolai a.1923-1925

He was a member of the Projectionist group *Metod* in 1923. In 1924 he contributed to the First Discussional Exhibition of Active Revolutionary Art in Moscow. He exhibited with the First Exhibition of the Society of Easel Painters (OST) in Moscow in 1925.

TSAPLIN, Dmitri Filippovich 1890-1967

Sculptor. He was engaged on Agitprop decorations at Saratov c.1918. He was a member of the Society of Russian Sculptors from 1925. He was included in the 1928 exhibition of Acquisitions by the State Art Collections Fund held in Moscow. His *Red Army Soldier*, 1937, is block-like, firm and anonymous.

TSELOVAL'NIKOV a.1919

Painter. He contributed to the Twelfth State Exhibition: Colourdynamo and Tectonic Primitivism (*Tsvetodinamos i*

Pavel Trubetskoy. The Writer Leo Tolstoy, *1899. 34 x 32 x 30 cm. Bronze.*
Hatton Gallery, University of Newcastle upon Tyne.

tektonicheskiy primitivizm) along with Grishchenko, Shevchenko and others in Moscow in 1919.

TSEREL'SON (TSIREL'SON), Yakov 1900-1938+

Painter. He was engaged in decorative paintings at the Security Police Club, Moscow, c.1928. Proscribed in 1938 but posthumously rehabilitated.

TSIBOROVSKY, M. M. a.1925

Painter. He contributed to the Third Exhibition of Paintings by Artists from Kaluga and Moscow held in Kaluga in 1925.

TSIGAL, Vladimir Efimovich 1917-1949+

Sculptor of pariotic genre. His works include *Lenin as a Schoolboy*, 1949, marble.

TSIONGLINSKY, Yan Frantsevich 1858-1912

Graphic artist. He exhibited with the World of Art 1899-1903. He was an active teacher in the period 1903-11; his pupils included Annenkov, L.Bruni, Guro, V.Markov, Matyushin and others. He was a member of the second World of Art society 1910-12.

Coll TG.

TSIREL'SON = TSEREL'SON, Ya.

TSUKERMAN, B.Ya. a.1919

Painter. He exhibited at the juryless Eighth State Exhibition in Moscow in 1919.

TSVETKOV, Boris Ivanovich c.1893-c.1942

Painter. His dates are uncertain and are sometimes given as 1893/5-1942/5.

Coll RM.

TULUPOV, S. I. a.1918-1919

Painter. He was represented at the First Exhibition of Works of the Professional Union of Artists in Moscow in 1918, at the Fourth State Exhibition of Paintings (*IV Gosudarstvennaya*

Aleksandr Tyshler. Study for Two Costumes, *1930. Watercolour, pencil. Signed in Russian 'A Tyshler 1930' lower centre. 47 x 40 cm.*
Collection Mr. and Mrs. Nikita D.Lobanov-Rostovsky, London.

vystavka kartin) in Moscow in 1919 and at the Third Exhibition of Paintings held at Ryazan in 1919.

TUPYLEV, I. F.   **1758-1821**
History painter. He worked on a grand scale and was recognised by the Academy in 1785.
Coll TG.

TUR. = TURZHANSKY, L.V.

TURCHANINOV, Kapiton Fedorovich   **1823-1900**
Portraitist.
Coll TG.

TURLYGIN, Yakov Prokopievich   **1858-1909**
Genre and portrait painter.
Coll TG.

TURZHANSKY, Leonard (Leonid) Viktorovich 1875-1945
Landscape painter. Sometimes he signed his work 'Tur.' or 'Turzh'. He studied at Ekaterinburg under N.M.Plyuskin 1889-95, under Dmitriev-Kavkazsky in St. Petersburg in 1896-7 and at the Moscow College 1898-1909.
After the Revolution he taught at the Ekaterinburg art school 1919-20. Turzhansky appeared on the April 1919 list of artists for acquisitions by the envisaged Museum of Painterly Culture and was represented at the Nineteenth Exhibition of the All-

Russian Exhibitions Bureau in Moscow in 1920. He was represented at the First Russian Art Exhibition in Berlin in 1922. He was a member of AKhRR 1924-7 and of the Society of Artist-Realists founded in 1927. His work was included in the exhibition of Soviet art held at Harbin in 1926 and in Japan in 1927, in the 1928 exhibition of Acquisitions by the State Art Collections Fund held in Moscow and in the jubilee exhibition Artists of the RSFSR over 15 Years held at the Russian Museum, Leningrad, in 1932. He undertook a journey to paint in the far North.
*Early Spring, 1917, is a panoramic landscape of almost photographic appearance with a few houses in a vast expanse of snow and trees.
Lit A.M.Muratov, V.Manin et al. *Zhivopis' 20-30kh godov*, Sankt-Peterburg, 1991.
Coll TG.

TVOROZHNIKOV, I. I.   **a.1892-1905**
Painter. He taught at the Academy in St. Petersburg c.1892-1905 where his pupils included Bystrenin and Konchalovsky.
Coll TG.

TYRANOV, Aleksei Vasilievich   **1808-1859**
Painter of portraits, figure compositions, landscapes and still-lifes. He was a pupil of Venetsianov. His *View of the River*

Tosno, 1827, RM, is a poetic and luminous painting primarily of the sky. There is a wooded cliff to the right and the river far below. On a ledge of grass a man and woman talk. He lays down his scythe and she has brought their meal. It is a simple, glowing idyll. He was able to move smoothly from the figure within the landscape to the double portrait illustrating a whole lifestyle succinctly, as his *Studio of the Chernetsov Brothers*, 1828, RM, illustrates.

Coll TG; RM.

TYRSA, Nikolai Adrianovich (Andreevich)   1887-1942
Draughtsman, painter, graphic artist. He was born in Turkey. He studied at the Academy in St. Petersburg 1905-8 and also at the Zvantseva School under V.Maté 1907-10. He was a founder of the society Apartment No. 5 in Petrograd along with Bruni, Isakov, Lebedev, Miturich, Punin and Tatlin in 1915.
After the Revolution he was engaged in Agitprop decorations on Nevsky Prospekt at Liteiny Prospekt, Petrograd, in 1918. He taught at the Free Art Studios (SVOMAS) in Petrograd 1918-22 and at the Stieglitz school until 1922. He exhibited with the Union of New Tendencies in Art in Petrograd in June 1922. He was represented at the First Russian Art Exhibition in Berlin in 1922. He was included in the enormous survey Exhibition of Paintings by Petrograd Artists of All Tendencies 1919-1923 held in Petrograd in 1923. He was teaching at the Vkhutemas in 1923 and at the Leningrad Institute of Civil Engineering in 1924. He exhibited in Venice 1924-8, Leipzig in 1927 and at the All-Union Polygraphic Exhibition in Moscow in 1927. His watercolour portrait of *Anna Akhmatova*, 1928, RM, is a study by lamplight adeptly executed. He exhibited with the 4 Arts society in Leningrad including the exhibition of 1928 at the Russian Museum and he was represented at the jubilee exhibition Artists of the RSFSR over 15 Years held at the Russian Museum, Leningrad, in 1932. He taught at the Kiev Art Institute 1938-9. He died at Vologda.
Lit *N.A.Tyrsa*, exh. cat., Leningrad, 1967. *Paris-Moscou*, 1979. A.M.Muratov, V.Manin et al. *Zhivopis' 20-30kh godov*, Sankt-Peterburg, 1991.
Coll RM.

TYSHLER (DZHIN-DZHIKH-SHVIL'), Aleksandr
Grigor'evich   1898-1980
Painter, graphic artist, theatre designer, sculptor. Born at Melitopol, Ukraine. He studied under A.Frankovsky, N.Strunnikov, I.Seleznev, G.Dyadchenko and F.Krasitsky at the Kiev Art Institute 1912-17.
After the Revolution he worked with Exter in Kiev 1917-18 and was engaged on agitational decorations including boats and trains. He was in the Red Army 1919-20. He contributed to the First Jewish Art Exhibition of Sculpture, Graphics and Drawing held in Kiev in 1920 and worked on ROSTA window posters at Melitopol.
He moved to Moscow in 1921. He was a founder member of the group *Electro-organism* in 1922 with Nikritin, Redko and others. He was a member of the Projectionist group. In 1924 he contributed to the First Discussional Exhibition of Active Revolutionary Art in Moscow. He was a founder member of the Society of Easel Painters (OST) in 1924. He exhibited in Dresden in 1926. The following year he executed designs for the Jewish Theatres in Minsk, Kharkov and Moscow. His work was included in the exhibition of Soviet art held at

Harbin in 1926 and in Japan in 1927 and in the major exhibition in Moscow in 1927 marking the tenth anniversary of the Revolution. He exhibited in Leipzig 1927-8. He worked for the Belorussian State Jewish Theatre from 1927 until the early 1930s. He was included in the 1928 Venice Biennale, in the exhibition of Acquisitions by the State Art Collections Fund held in Moscow and in the exhibition of Russian Graphic Art in Riga in 1929. He was also represented at the First Touring Exhibition of Painting and Graphics which opened in Moscow in 1929. He worked for many years in the theatre in Moscow, Leningrad and Minsk between 1927 and 1949.
He was evacuated to Tashkent with the Moscow Jewish Theatre 1941-9 and worked in the Uzbek theatre there. He held a one-man exhibition at Tashkent in 1943. Between 1949 and 1961 he designed productions for numerous theatres in Moscow and Leningrad.
From 1961 he worked on paintings, sculptures and graphic works. He executed a number of wood sculptures of elongated *Dryads* 1969-73. Numerous one-man exhibitions were held in Moscow and Leningrad between 1956 and 1981. He died in Moscow.
Portrait of A.S.Tyshler, 1928, pencil, typifies his curious and individual fantastic style. The sitter's young face stares intently through the criss-cross pattern of her veil. The rest of her head and shoulders comprises cross-hatched lines and looks unreal.
Theatre design 1919 assisted I.Rabinovich on the execution of designs for Lopez de Vega's *Fuente Ovekhuna* at the Solovtsov Theatre.
1927 A.Vev'yurko's *Botvin* at the Belorussian Jewish Theatre.
1934 P.Merimée's *Carmen* at the Romen gypsy theatre, Moscow.
1935 Shakespeare's *King Lear* at the Jewish Theatre, Moscow. Frightening and grotesque designs.
1935 Shakespeare's *Richard III* at the Bolshoi Drama Theatre (Gorky Theatre), Leningrad.
1936 Pushkin's *Gypsies* at the Romen gypsy theatre, Moscow.
1939-40 Meyerhold's unrealised production of Prokofiev's opera *Semen Kotko* with libretto by V.Kataev for the Stanislavsky Opera Theatre.
1944 Shakespeare's *Othello* (unrealised).
1951 costumes for Shakespeare's *Twelfth Night*.
1954 V.Katanyan's *They Knew Mayakovsky* at the Pushkin State Academic Drama Theatre.
1957 V.V.Mayakovsky's *Mystery-Bouffe* at the Moscow Satirical Theatre.
1963 Shakespeare's *Hamlet* (unrealised).
Illustrations numerous including: V.V.Mayakovsky's *Cloud in Trousers*, 1929. I.Sel'vinsky's poem *Ulyalaevshchina*, 1933-4
Lit F.Syrkina *A.G.Tyshler*, Moscow, 1967. *Paris-Moscou*, 1979. *Aleksandr Tyshler*, Moscow, 1983. *Sammlung Ludwig, Köln*, Munich, 1986. A.M.Muratov, V.Manin et al. *Zhivopis' 20-30kh godov*, Sankt-Peterburg, 1991.
Coll TG; RM; Bakhrushin Theatre Museum, Moscow; St. Petersburg Theatre Museum; Archangel Art Museum; Kalinin Art Gallery; Radishchev Art Museum, Saratov; Far East Art Museum, Khabarovsk; Museum of Russian Art, Kiev; Armenian Art Museum, Erevan; Kirgiz Art Museum, Frunze; Sammlung Ludwig, Cologne; Museum of Modern Art, Prague; Roy Miles Gallery, London.
Colour plate p.431.

U

UDALENKOV, A. P.　　　　　　　　　　　　**a.1918**
He was engaged in Agitprop decorations on Varshavskaya Square, Petrograd, in 1918.

UDAL'TSOVA, Nadezhda Andreevna　　　**1885/86-1961**
Painter. An exponent of Russian Cubo-Futurism and Suprematism. Born at Orel, the sister of Lyudmilla Prudkovskaya. The family went to Moscow in 1892. She studied at the Moscow College and under Yuon, Dudin and Ulyanov 1906-7. She travelled to Berlin and Dresden in 1908. She married A.D.Udal'tsov in autumn 1908.
She went to Paris with Popova in 1912 and studied at the Académie La Palette where she studied Cubism first-hand under Metzinger and Le Fauconnier 1912-13. In the following year she was working in The Tower studio complex in Moscow with Grishchenko, Popova, Tatlin, Vesnin, Zdanevich and others. Here she was able to combine her knowledge of Cubism with an involvement with developments that were also informed by Russian Futurist thinking.
She became closely involved in the experimentation of the Russian avant-garde. She exhibited with the Knave of Diamonds in 1914-16, Leftist Trends in April 1915, Tramway V and 0.10. The Last Futurist Exhibition of Paintings in 1915 at which Tatlin bought her *Bottle and Wineglass* which he exhibited at *Magazin* (The Store) in 1916. She executed a number of constructions. She became for a time a close adherent of the Suprematism of Malevich and was a member of the group *Supremus* with Popova and others which met in her Moscow apartment 1916-17. She was engaged with Tatlin, Yakulov, Rodchenko and others on the decorations at the Café Pittoresque in 1917.
After the Revolution she worked on revolutionary decorations in Moscow in 1918 including the decoration of the club of the Left Federation of the Union of Moscow Artists together with Karetnikova, Pestel' and Popova. She exhibited with the Artists of the Leftist Federation of the Professional Union in 1918 along with Rodchenko and many others.
She taught at the Free Art Studios initially as an assistant to Malevich. She continued to teach at the Vkhutemas until 1934. In 1919 she served on the Moscow Collegium of IZO Narkompros under Tatlin and appeared on the April 1919 list of artists for acquisitions by the envisaged Museum of Painterly Culture. She participated in the Third Exhibition of Paintings held at Ryazan in 1919. She married the painter Aleksandr Drevin in 1920. She was included in the Third Touring Exhibition of the Sovetsk Regional subdepartment of the Museums Bureau along with Kandinsky, Rodchenko and others in 1921 and she exhibited in the 1921 exhibition of the World of Art in Moscow.
She became a member of the Institute of Artistic Culture (INKhUK) in 1920 but resigned in 1921. She was represented at the First Russian Art Exhibition in Berlin in 1922 and work by both Drevin and Udal'tsova was acquired by the Société

Anonyme (now at Yale University Art Gallery). She was a member of the Society of Moscow Painters founded in 1925. Her work was included in the exhibition of Soviet art held at Harbin in 1926 and in Japan in 1927 and in the major exhibition in Moscow in 1927 marking the tenth anniversary of the Revolution. She was also included in the 1928 exhibition of Acquisitions by the State Art Collections Fund held in Moscow.
She travelled widely with Drevin in the period 1926-34 to the Ural and Altai mountains, Armenia and Central Asia. She was a member of the Moscow Society of Artists 1927-8 and also exhibited with the Group 13 in 1931. She was represented at the jubilee exhibition Artists of the RSFSR over 15 Years held at the Russian Museum, Leningrad, in 1932.
She travelled to Armenia with Drevin 1932-3 and had an exhibition with Drevin at the Historical Museum, Yerevan, in 1934. She worked in Moscow 1941-5. Personal exhibitions followed in Moscow in 1945.
Her later style relinquished all trace of Suprematism and Constructivism for a loosely handled figurative style not wholly dissimilar to that of contemporary work by Drevin. In 1950 she worked at Zvenigorod and in 1952 in the Zagorsk region. She died in Moscow.
A posthumous exhibition was held by the Moscow Union of Artists in 1965.
*The Model, Cubist Construction, 1914, RM, is a homage to Picasso's hermetic Cubism of three years earlier, an exercise in Cubist planar stylisation of the figure and a testament to the very close study that she made of recent Parisian art.
Lit *Paris-Moscou*, 1979. C.Lodder *Russian Constructivism*, New Haven and London, 1983. *Seven Moscow Artists 1910-30*, exh. cat., Galerie Gmurzynska, Cologne, 1984. E.Weiss *Russische Avant-Garde, 1910-1930, Sammlung Ludwig, Köln*, Munich, 1986. M.N.Yablonskaya *Women Artists of Russia's New Age*, London, 1990.
Coll TG; RM; Kirov Art Museum; Nizhny-Novgorod Art Museum; Yale University Art Gallery, New Haven; Sammlung Ludwig, Cologne.

UGRYUMOV, Grigoriy Ivanovich　　　　**1764-1823**
Painter. He studied under Levitsky and then travelled to Rome 1787-90. He made academic history paintings on Russian themes and thereby helped to establish Russian themes at the Academy. His *Test of Usman's Strength*, 1797, RM, shows the Samson-like folk hero seen against a distant landscape and holding back a bull with his bare hands, a feat observed by Prince Vladimir of Kiev. Numerous ink and wash compositional drawings were executed to assist in the composition of his paintings on Russian themes.
Coll TG; RM.

UKHANOVA, Anastasia Vasilievna　　　　**1885-1973**
Painter. She studied under Tsionglinsky in 1898 and Kardovsky 1907-16. She was a friend of V.Markov and Bubnova with whom she visited Western Europe. She exhibited with the Union of Youth in 1910.

UKHTOMSKY, Andrei　　　　　　　**18th century**
Graphic artist. He executed architectural views of St. Petersburg.
Coll Ashmolean Museum, Oxford.

UKHTOMSKY, Sergei Aleksandrovich　　　**1886-1921**
Sculptor. He executed portraits in marble and bronze.
Coll RM.

Nadezhda Udal'tsova. At The Piano, *1914. Oil on canvas. 107 x 89 cm.*
A Cubo-Futurist work showing Udal'tsova's thorough knowledge of developments in Paris as well as Russia. The reference to Bach suggests an awareness of the past although Picasso and Braque also made references to Bach at this time. More specific to contemporary Russia is the inscription 'A.SKR' visible beneath the pianist's chin. This may refer to the music of Skryabin who wrote scores including colour effects.
Yale University Art Gallery, New Haven, Connecticut, gift of the Collection of the Société Anonyme.

UL'YANOV, Nikolai Dmitrievich   1816-1856
Painter of landscapes and views.
Coll TG.

UL'YANOV, Nikolai Pavlovich   1875-1949
Painter, theatre designer, graphic artist. Born at Eletsk. He studied under V.Meshkov in Moscow 1888-9 and at the Moscow College under N.Ge, N.Nevrov and Pryanishnikov in 1898-1900. He assisted Serov 1900-3 and also taught at the Zvantseva School of Art 1900-7. In 1904 he executed designs for the Moscow Art Theatre and painted a portrait of the theatre director V.Meyerhold 1906-7. In 1907 he visited Italy and also exhibited with the Blue Rose group. He exhibited with the Golden Fleece in 1908-9. He visited France and Germany 1909-12. He taught at the Stroganov Institute 1915-18.
After the Revolution he exhibited with the World of Art in December 1917 in Moscow. He taught painting as a 'realist' at the Free Art Studios (SVOMAS) in Moscow c.1918. He appeared on the April 1919 list of artists for acquisitions by the envisaged Museum of Painterly Culture. He was represented in the Fourth State Exhibition of Paintings (*IV Gosudarstvennaya vystavka kartin*) in Moscow in 1919 and at the enormous First State Exhibition of Art and Science, which included ethnographic material, held in Kazan in 1920. He taught at the Vkhutemas from 1919 to 1921. He exhibited in the 1921 exhibition of the World of Art in Moscow. He was a member of the 4 Arts society which was founded in 1924 and contributed to the Third Exhibition of Paintings by Artists from Kaluga and Moscow held in Kaluga in 1925. He was included in the major exhibition in Moscow in 1927 marking the tenth anniversary of the Revolution and in the 1928 exhibition of Acquisitions by the State Art Collections Fund held in Moscow. He was included in the exhibition of Russian Graphic Art in Riga in 1929, the First Touring Exhibition of Painting and Graphics which opened in Moscow in 1929 and the jubilee exhibition Artists of the RSFSR over 15 Years held at the Russian Museum, Leningrad, in 1932. He taught at the Moscow State Art Institute 1942-5. He died in Moscow.
Theatre design 1905 G.Hauptmann's *Schluck und Jau* at Meyerhold's Povarsky Studio Theatre, Moscow.
1926 October M.A.Bulgakov's *Dni Turbinykh* (Turbine Days) at the Moscow Art Theatre.
1928 costumes for A.Griboedov's *Gore ot Uma* (Woe from Wit) at the State Meyerhold Theatre, for which V.Shestakov did the stage constructions. The production was revived in 1935.
Writings N.Ul'yanov *Moi Vstrechi*, Moscow, 1959.
Lit P.Muratov, B.Griftsov *N.P.Ul'yanov*, Moscow-Leningrad, 1925. O.Lavrona *N.P.Ul'yanov*, Moscow, 1953. V.Lenyashin *N.P.Ul'yanov*, Leningrad, 1976. *A.V.Kuprin, S.D.Lebedeva, N.P.Ulyanov*, exh. cat., Moscow, 1978. *Paris-Moscou*, 1979. *Twilight of the Tsars*, London, 1991. A.M.Muratov, V.Manin et al. *Zhivopis' 20-30kh godov*, Sankt-Peterburg, 1991.
Coll TG; RM; Tula Art Museum; Saratov Art Museum; Bakhrushin Theatre Museum, Moscow.

UMANSKY, Morits Borisovich   1907-1948
Theatre and cinema artist. He studied under Tatlin and graduated from the Kiev College of Art in 1930. He designed for theatres in the Ukraine.

UNOVIS
The abbreviated name of the group Affirmers of New Art (*Utverditeli novogo iskusstva*).

URARTU, Aytsemik Amazospovna   1899-1956+
Academic portrait sculptor.

URLAUB, Georgiy (Ivan) Fedorovich   1844-1914
History painter.
Coll TG.

USACHEV, A. I.   a.1925-1932
Graphic artist. He was represented at the Paris International Exhibition in 1925 and in the exhibition of Russian Graphic Art in Riga in 1929. He was also represented at the jubilee exhibition Artists of the RSFSR over 15 Years held at the Russian Museum, Leningrad, in 1932.

USHAKOV, Simon   1626-1686
Ikon and mural painter. He was the leading painter of the Moscow Armory where he worked most of his life. He also executed ikons at the Novodeivichy Monastery in Moscow, for the Troitsa-Sergiev Abbey and for Moscow churches. Amongst his followers was Iosif Vladimirov. His ikons are elaborate and elegant without the gravity of earlier ikon painters.
Coll TG; RM; Vladimir Museum.

USHIN, N. A.   b.1898
Theatre designer who made designs for the play *Charli* (Charlie) in 1924.

USPENSKY, Aleksei Aleksandrovich   1892-1941
Painter.
Coll RM.

UTKIN, Nil Manuilovich   early 19th century
Portraitist.
Coll TG.

UTKIN, Petr Savvich   1877-1934
Painter. Born at Tambov. He studied under Konovalov and Baracci in Saratov and at the Moscow College under Levitan, Korovin and Serov 1897-1907. He was a participant in the Crimson Rose exhibition in 1904, in the Blue Rose group in 1906 and 1907. He was a friend of Pavel Kuznetsov. He was also represented in Diaghilev's display of Russian art at the 1906 Salon d'Automne in Paris. He exhibited with the Golden Fleece in 1908-9, with the Izdebsky Salon of 1910-11 in Odessa and with the Union of Russian Artists in 1909.
After the Revolution he exhibited with the World of Art in December 1917 in Moscow. He was engaged on Agitprop decorations at Saratov and he appeared on the April 1919 list of artists for acquisitions by the envisaged Museum of Painterly Culture. He was represented at the enormous First State Exhibition of Art and Science, which included ethnographic material, held in Kazan in 1920. He was a member of the 4 Arts society which was founded in 1924. He was included in the 1928 exhibition of Acquisitions by the State Art Collections Fund held in Moscow and in the jubilee exhibition Artists of the RSFSR over 15 Years held at the Russian Museum, Leningrad, in 1932. He died in Leningrad.
Lit *Twilight of the Tsars*, London, 1991.
Coll TG; RM; Saratov Art Museum.

UUTMAA, Richard Gustavovich   1905-1947+
Lithuanian landscape painter.

V

V.K. (cyrillic) see **KONASHEVICH, V.I.; KOZLINSKY, V.; KURDOV, V.I.**
V.K. (latin) see **KANDINSKY, V.V.**
V.L. (cyrillic) see **LEBEDEV, V.V.**

VAIDIN, Sergei a.1914
Painter. He contributed to the exhibition No.4 in Moscow in 1914.

VAKh
The abbreviated name of the All-Russian Academy of Arts (*Vserossiyskaya Akademiya khudozhestv*) operative 1932-47.

VAKUROV, Ivan Petrovich 1885-1968
Painter, miniaturist. Born at Palekh in the Vladimir region. He studied ikon painting in N.M.Safonov's studio and worked there until 1915. He then worked as an ikon painter in Moscow to 1919 and subsequently in the Perm region.
After the Revolution he exhibited from 1923 and worked at Palekh. Palekh remains the centre of a particular kind of traditional painting and he worked at the Palekh Artel from 1925 to 1968, becoming one of its chief artists producing designs on papier mâché bowls, trays, etc. He also introduced new themes to this including *Red Army Soldier*, 1926, TG, as well as using themes from Pushkin and Lermontov. He was represented in the International Exhibitions at Venice in 1924, Paris 1925 and Paris 1937. He taught at the Palekh Art School from 1927 to 1968. He died at Palekh.
Coll TG.

VALENKOVA (-CHERNYAVSKAYA), Sofia Nikolaevna
1894-1942
Graphic artist who worked in linocut and etching. Born in the St. Petersburg region. She studied at the Leningrad Vkhutein 1920-7. She contributed to the All-Union Polygraphic Exhibition in Moscow in 1927 and was represented at the jubilee exhibition Artists of the RSFSR over 15 Years held at the Russian Museum, Leningrad, in 1932. She died at Leningrad.
Coll TG; RM; Perm Art Gallery.

VALEV, Valentin Tsanevich 1901-1951
Sculptor of heroic themes. Born at Kilifarevo, Bulgaria. He studied at the Sofia Academy under A.Nikolov and Zh.Spiridonov 1919-23. He moved to Russia in 1924 and studied at the Moscow Vkhutein 1926-30. He was a member of AKhR 1929-32. His works include the Socialist Realist *Young Patriots*, 1947. He died in Moscow.
Exhibitions were held in Moscow in 1952 and Sofia in 1958.
Lit V.A.Tikhanova *V.Ts.Valev*, Moscow, 1958.
Coll TG; Penza Art Gallery.

VAL'KEVICH, M. I. a.1919
Painter. He exhibited at the juryless Eighth State Exhibition in Moscow in 1919.

VANETSIAN, Aram Vramshapu 1901-1971
He exhibited with the First Working Organisaton of Artists in 1924 at the First Discussional Exhibition of Active Revolutionary Art alongside G.Aleksandrov and others.

VANKOVICH, Valenti Melkhiorovich (Valentin Mikhailovich) 1799-1842
Portraitist.
Coll TG.

VARENTSOV a.1919
Painter. He contributed to the Twelfth State Exhibition: Colourdynamo and Tectonic Primitivism (*Tsvetodinamos i tektonicheskiy primitivizm*) along with Grishchenko, Shevchenko and others in Moscow in 1919. This may be Nikolai Ivanovich Varentsov 1890-1949.

VARNEK (VARNIK), Aleksandr Grigor'evich 1782-1843
Romantic portrait painter. Born at St. Petersburg. He studied under Levitsky and Shchukin at the Academy from 1795. He travelled to Italy on a scholarship 1804-10. His works include a portrait of a child with a puppy, 1800-33, TG, and a portrait of the sculptor *Martos*. He taught at the Academy from 1810 and worked as Keeper of Prints and Drawings at the Hermitage Museum from 1824. He died at St. Petersburg.
Coll TG; RM; Museum of the Academy, St. Petersburg.

VARST = STEPANOVA, V.F.

VASHCHENKO, Evgeniy P. a.1909-1910
Illustrator, sculptor. He provided illustrations for the periodical *Zritel'* (Spectator) in 1909 and was exhibiting in 1910.

VASIL'EV, Aleksei Aleksandrovich 1811-1879
Portraitist.
Coll TG.

VASIL'EV, B. V. = SUKHODOL'SKY, B. V.

VASIL'EV, Fedor Aleksandrovich 1850-1873
Painter of expansive landscapes. He studied at the Drawing School of the Society for the Encouragement of the Arts at St. Petersburg 1865-8. In 1867 he made visits to Valaam Island with Shishkin and in 1870 was painting on the Volga with Repin and E.K.Makarov. He studied at the Academy under Kramskoy and Shishkin in 1871. That year he went to Yalta for his health in 1871. He was represented in International Exhibitions in London in 1872 and in Vienna in 1873. He died young of consumption at Yalta in the Crimea. Exhibitions were held in St. Petersburg in 1874 and 1899. He was aware of Barbizon painting and produced closely observed landscapes of considerable dramatic force.
Lit N.Novouspensky *F.Vasil'ev*, Moscow, 1973. Yu.Dyuzhenko *F.Vasil'ev*, Leningrad, 1973. *F.A.Vasil'ev*, exh. cat., Leningrad, Moscow, Kiev, 1975. F.Malcheva *F.Vasil'ev*, Leningrad, 1986.
Coll Major holdings at TG; RM; Saratov Art Museum; Museum of Russian Art, Kiev.

VASIL'EV, Mikhail Nikolaevich 1830-1900
Painter of religious themes. Born in the Orlov region. He studied under A.S. and D.S.Dobrovolsky at the Moscow College 1848-50 and under A.T.Markov at the Academy from 1850. He travelled to Paris, London and Rome, where he

made copies after Raphael, on a scholarship in 1859-64. He died at Tsarskoe Selo.

Coll TG; RM; Khabarovsk Museum.

VASIL'EV, N. I.   a.1918-1919

He exhibited at the Fifth State Exhibition: From Impressionism to Non-Objective Art in Moscow in 1918-19. He contributed to the exhibition of Contemporary Russian Art held at Philadelphia in 1932.

VASIL'EV, Timofey Alekseevich   1783-1838

Painter of landscapes and views. Born at St. Petersburg. He studied at the Academy from 1788. He visited the east of Russia with an expedition 1805-6. His work included views of Nevsky Prospekt, St. Petersburg. He died at St. Petersburg.

Coll TG; RM; Hermitage Museum.

VASIL'EV, Vladimir Aleksandrovich   1895-1967

Painter, graphic artist, theatre designer. Born at Moscow. He studied under A.P.Baryshnikov and S.V.Noakovsky at the Stroganov College 1910-18.

After the Revolution he studied under P.P.Konchalovsky at the Moscow Vkhutemas until 1925.

He worked in the Ural Mountains in the 1920s. He was a founder member of the Society of Easel Painters (OST) which first exhibited in Moscow in 1925.

From the 1930s onwards he designed and illustrated books for the publishers Gosizdat and Detgiz. He collaborated on decorative panels for the International Exhibitions at Paris in 1937 and New York 1939.

His paintings included *Moscow 1941* which was painted in collaboration with Pimenov in 1943. He died in Moscow.

Theatre design 1940 Rostand's *Cyrano de Bergerac* designed together with Pimenov.

Lit S.V.Razumovskaya *V.A.Vasil'ev*, Moscow, 1962.

VASIL'EVA, Maria Ivanovna (WASSILIEFF, Marie) 1884-1957

Painter, theatre designer. Born at Smolensk. She studied in St. Petersburg. In 1905 and again in 1907 she went to Paris and became a pupil of Matisse. She founded and directed the Académie Russe in Paris in 1908 and then established the Académie Wassilieff in 1909. She exhibited at the Salon des Indépendants and at the Salon d'Automne. Léger was among the lecturers at the Académie Wassilieff in Paris 1913-14. Between 1909 and 1914 she travelled to Scandinavia, Romania, Poland and Russia. She exhibited puppet portraits in London in 1920 and in Paris in 1923. She designed for the Ballets Suèdois de Rolf de Maré between 1924 and 1937. She died in France.

Lit *Marie Wasilieff*, exh. cat., Galerie Hupel, Paris, 1971.

Coll TG.

Colour plate p.449.

VASIL'KOVSKY, Sergei Ivanovich   1854-1917

Ukrainian landscape painter. Born in the Kharkov region. He studied under D.I.Bezperchy at Kharkov and under M.K.Klodt at the Academy from 1876. He travelled to France, Italy and Spain on a scholarship 1886-8. Thereafter he worked in Kharkov. He was still actively painting in the early 1900s. He died at Kharkov.

Exhibitions were held in Kharkov in 1938, 1950 and 1952.

Coll TG; Museum of Russian Art, Kiev; Kharkov Art Museum.

VASNETSOV, Apollinari Mikhailovich   1856-1933

Epic landscape painter, illustrator, theatre designer. He produced historical paintings of the Moscow of the 16th and 17th centuries. Born in the Kirov region. He was the brother of Viktor Vasnetsov under whom he studied. He then studied under M.Andriolli 1870-2. He lived in St. Petersburg 1872-5 and learnt from Polenov and Repin. He exhibited with the Wanderers from 1883 and became a member in 1888. He drew for several journals in 1880-6. His illustrations to Lermontov were published in Moscow in 1891. In the 1880s and 1890s he visited the Ukraine, Crimea, Caucasus and Urals as well as France, Germany and Italy.

He was made an Academician in 1900 and exhibited in Paris the same year. He exhibited with the World of Art 1900-1. He taught as head of the landscape studio at the Moscow College 1901-19 where his pupils included D.Mitrokhin. He was a founder member of the Union of Russian Artists in 1903. He exhibited in Munich in 1913 and Lyon in 1914. His work included scenes of Moscow showing its historical 17th century architecture.

After the Revolution he was President of the Commission for the Study of Old Moscow from 1918. He was represented at the First Russian Art Exhibition in Berlin in 1922. He exhibited in New York, Boston and Baltimore in 1924 and at Venice in 1929. He died in Moscow.

Theatre design 1885 an unrealised production of Rimsky-Korsakov's *Snow Maiden*.

1897 Mussorgsky's *Khovanshchina*.

1901 *Sadko* at the Mariinsky Theatre, St. Petersburg. Many other designs followed.

Lit L.Bespalova *A.M.Vasnetsov*, Moscow, 1956. *A.M.Vasnetsov*, exh. cat., Moscow, 1956. *Paris-Moscou*, 1979.

Coll TG; RM; Odessa Art Museum; Kirov Art Museum; Bakhrushin Theatre Museum, Moscow.

Colour plate p.452.

VASNETSOV, Viktor Mikhailovich   1848-1926

Painter, theatre designer. Born at Lopial in the Vyatka region. He was the brother of Apollinari Vasnetsov. Perhaps the most dramatic painter of themes of Old Russia, executed on a grand scale, thoroughly vigorous, stirring and unapologetic. His works featured boyars, bogatyrs and barons, frequently engaged in mortal combat. Eventually this gave way to decorative works evoking folk legends of an equally remote but charmed mythology. He worked at Moscow and Abramtsevo.

In the early 1860s he had drawing lessons at the Vyatsk Seminary under N.A.Chernyshev. He attended the Drawing School of the Society for the Encouragement of the Arts in St. Petersburg 1867-8 under Kramskoy. He studied at the Academy 1868-74 and exhibited with the Wanderers from 1874 becoming a member in 1878. That year he moved to Moscow and later to Kiev where he executed murals for the Cathedral of St. Vladimir. He visited Paris 1876-7.

He joined the Abramtsevo colony with his brother Apollinari in 1879. The first issue of the World of Art journal was devoted to his work. He produced designs for Ostrovsky's *Snegurochka* (Snow Maiden) 1882-3. He was also commissioned to paint two panels for the Moscow terminus of the Donets railway in the early 1880s. He designed for Mamontov's private opera. His work at Abramtsevo included the architecture of the church there in 1885 as well as furniture at the colony. With Apollinari he designed their house in Moscow, the Russian Pavilion at the Paris International Exhibition as well as the façade of the Tretyakov Gallery in Moscow. He declined the title of Academician in 1893. He executed mosaics for the Russian Church at Darmstadt 1899-1901.

He exhibited with the World of Art in St. Petersburg in 1900. He proposed the idea of an art museum at Vyatka in 1910, now the Kirov Art Museum. In 1911 he was represented at the International Exhibition in Rome.

His major works include *After the Battle of Prince Igor with the Polovtsy* 1880, *The Flying Carpet* 1880, *Bogatyrs* 1898 and *The Tsarevna Frog* 1918. He produced many theatre designs and illustrations. He died in Moscow.

Theatre design includes 1884 I.V.Spazhinsky's tragedy *Charodeyka* at the Maly Theatre, Moscow.

1885 Rimsky-Korsakov's *Snegurochka* (Snow Maiden) for Savva Mamontov's private performances. The costumes, TG, emphasise the decorative patterning of Russian folk costume but are otherwise unstylised in appearance.

1885 Dargomyzhsky's opera *Rusalka*.

Lit A.Lebedev *V.Vasnetsov*, Moscow, 1957. N.Morgunov *V.Vasnetsov*, 1940. N.Morgunov, N.Morgunova *V.M.Vasnetsov*, Moscow, 1962. N.F.Shanina *V.M.Vasnetsov*, Moscow, 1975 (English edition: Leningrad, 1979). *Paris-Moscou*, 1979. *Twilight of the Tsars*, London, 1991.

Coll Major holdings at TG; RM; Bakhrushin Theatre Museum, Moscow; V.M.Vasnetsov House Museum, Moscow; Kalinin Art Gallery; Kirov Art Museum; Saratov Art Museum.

VASNETSOV, Yuri Alekseevich　　　　**1900-1973**
Painter.
Coll RM.

VATAGIN, Vasili Alekseevich　　　　**1883-1969**
Animal sculptor, graphic artist. Born in Moscow. He attended the studios of Yuon and Martynov in Moscow from 1899. He travelled widely from 1903. He studied at the Moscow Institute until 1907. He studied lithography in Berlin in 1910. He made many book illustrations from 1912 throughout much of his life.

After the Revolution he was teaching sculpture at the Free Art Studios in Moscow in 1921 along with Babichev, Bromirsky, Er'zya and Konen'kov. He was represented at the Paris International Exhibition in 1925. He was a member of the Society of Russian Sculptors from 1926 and contributed to the second exhibition of *Iskusstvo dvizheniya* (Art of Movement) held in Moscow in 1926. He also contributed to the All-Union Polygraphic Exhibition in Moscow in 1927 and was represented at the jubilee exhibition Artists of the RSFSR over 15 Years held at the Russian Museum, Leningrad, in 1932. He was sculptor at the Moscow University Zoological Museum from 1931 to 1958. He died in Moscow.

Eagle, 1913, wood, RM, has a smoothly carved head arising from a less smooth body on which the marks of the chisel are used to indicate feathers.

Hare, 1923, wood, shows direct and largely naturalistic carving of the alert and vertical hare. The simplification of the planes perhaps owes as much to technical demands as to the Cubist faceting which it very faintly recalls.

Lit S.Razumovsky *V.A.Vatagin*, Moscow, 1956.
Coll TG, RM.

VATENIN, Valeri Vladimirovich　　　　**1933-1977**
Painter. Born at Leningrad. He studied under A.D.Zaytsev 1953-9 and exhibited from 1960. His works included *Winter near Moscow*, 1961. He died in a car accident.
Coll RM.

VAULIN, Petr Kuz'mich　　　　**1870-1929+**
Ceramics artist. Born in the Urals. He directed the Abramtsevo porcelain workshops in Moscow and worked at Mamontov's Butyrsky Ceramics Factory near Moscow from 1890. He then worked at the Abramtsevo Ceramics Studio 1890-4. He ran a ceramics factory at Kikerino near St. Petersburg 1906-16 and in 1908 he was the sole representative in the majolica section of the exhibition Contemporary Trends. He used Greek, Scythian, Indian and Russian motifs. He decorated many buildings including the Metropol Hotel in collaboration with Chekhonin in the early 1900s, and the Yaroslavl Station in Moscow as well as the Palace of the Emir of Bukhara at Zheleznovodsk.

After the Revolution he worked at the former Imperial Porcelain Factory at Petrograd from 1918 and was also was a member of the Art Section of the People's Commissariat of the Enlightenment under David Shterenberg c.1918-19. He was appointed by Lunacharsky to reorganise the Imperial Porcelain Factory into the State Porcelain Factory of which he became the director. He published a technical book about the production of porcelain in 1929 in Moscow.

VAYNER, Lazar' Yakovlevich　　　　**1885-1933**
Sculptor of heroic figures and portraits. Born at Rostov on Don. He studied at Tiflis in 1908 and at the Odessa Art School 1909-12. He then travelled to Paris where he attended the Académie Colarossi 1912-14.

After the Revolution he was a founder member of the Society of Easel Painters in 1925 and a member of the Society of Russian Sculptors from 1926. He was included in the major exhibition in Moscow in 1927 marking the tenth anniversary of the Revolution. He died in Moscow.

VAYNMAN, Moisei (Mikhail) Abramovich　　　　**1913-1973**
Sculptor. He produced works on Second World War themes and was impressed by A.T.Matveev who taught him 1937-47.

He was involved in the design of the Leningrad Metro Technological Institute Station 1954-5. He also drew landscapes. He produced a wooden sculpture of a *Tadzhik Girl* in 1959. An exhibition was held in Leningrad 1959-60.
Coll TG; RM; Kirov Art Museum.

VECHEGZHANIN, Georgiy Vladimirovich　　　　**1906-1950**
Ceramics designer. He was the son of the graphic artist Vladimir Levitsky and was adopted by his mother's second husband the ceramics artist Chekhonin. He made designs for the State Porcelain Factory 1919-20. In 1928 he exhibited with Al'tman, Fal'k and Chekhonin at the Galerie Hirondelle in Paris. He studied at the Academy in Leningrad 1924-9 and worked as a graphic designer in the period 1932-42. He then became a war artist. From 1945 to 1950 he worked as a painter-architect at the Leningrad Department of Arts Foundation.

Lit N.Lobanov-Rostovsky *Revolutionary Ceramics*, London, 1990.

VECHEGZHANIN, Petr Vladimirovich (INO, Pierre)
b.1904
Ceramics designer. His father was Vladimir Levitsky and Chekhonin was his stepfather. From 1928 he lived in Paris.
Lit N.Lobanov-Rostovsky *Revolutionary Ceramics*, London, 1990.

VEDEKIND, Iogann-Genrik (WEDEKIND, Johann-Heinrich) 1674-1736
Imperial portraitist. Born in Germany. He worked at Riga and Revel. He was active from about 1715/20 in Russia where he taught drawing at St. Petersburg 1732-6. His works include full-length portraits, among them a portraits of *Peter I*, *Catherine I*, 1726, *Tsar Mikhail Fedorovich*, 1728, TG, and a portrait of the Swedish king *Karl II*. He died at St. Petersburg.
Coll TG.

VEDENETSKY, Petr Petrovich 1766-1847
Painter of portraits and interiors. Born at Novgorod. He studied at the Academy from 1814. He also painted ikons for churches at Novgorod. He died at Nizhny-Novgorod.
Coll TG; Gorky Art Museum; Irkutsk Art Museum.

VEDERNIKOV, Aleksandr Semenovich 1898-1975
Painter of cityscapes and genre themes. He studied under Kuprin and Fonvizin 1921-5 and under Braz and Kasatkin at the Leningrad Vkhutemas 1924-8 and also under Filonov. He was a member of the group *Krug khudozhnikov* (Circle of Artists) founded in 1926.
Lit A.M.Muratov, V.Manin et al. *Zhivopis' 20-30kh godov*, Sankt-Peterburg, 1991.
Coll RM.

VEIDEMANIS, Karlis (VEYDEMAN, K. Ya.)
1897-1944
Latvian painter, theatre designer. He studied at the Society for the Encouragement of the Arts in St. Petersburg.
During the Revolution he served in the Red Army and subsequently studied under Konchalovsky at the Moscow Vkhutemas 1919-22. He exhibited at the Fifth State Exhibition: From Impressionism to Non-Objective Art in Moscow 1918-19.
He visited Germany 1923-4. He became a member of the *Bytie* (Existence) group 1924-8 and then joined AKhR. He painted in Uzbekistan in 1929 and in Dagestan in 1931. He was represented at the jubilee exhibition Artists of the RSFSR over 15 Years held at the Russian Museum, Leningrad, in 1932. He painted in Kazakhstan in 1934.
He worked in Moscow where an exhibition of his work was held in 1935.
Coll Latvian Art Museum, Riga.

VEKSLER, Mikhail Solomonovich 1898-1950+
Graphic artist. Born at Vitebsk. He was taught by Pen and Malevich at Vitebsk 1918-22. He was represented along with Kandinsky, Chagall and others at the First State Exhibition of Paintings by Local and Moscow Artists held in Vitebsk in December 1919.
He designed numerous film posters from 1926 onwards and also designed cinema interiors.

VEL'TS, Ivan Avgustovich (Avgustinovich) 1866-1926
Landscape painter. He participated in the First State Free Exhibition of Artworks in Petrograd in 1919 and was included in the enormous survey Exhibition of Paintings by Petrograd Artists of All Tendencies 1919-1923 held in Petrograd in 1923.
Coll TG.

VENETSIANOV, Aleksei Gavrilovich 1780-1847
Painter, etcher, lithographer. He was amongst the most original painters of the turn of the 18th and 19th centuries. His paintings concentrated on rural themes at his estate and were painted with great delicacy. However he also had the ability to imbue his images of peasant and provincial life with a calm monumentality and an acute depiction of light which lent them an idyllic atmosphere. As a result his peasants were never depicted as rough, low life subjects, but neither were they idealised as heroic figures.
Born at Moscow to a family of Greek origin. His dates are sometimes given as 1779-1845. He moved to St. Petersburg in 1807 where he worked until 1819 in government service. But he made copies in the Hermitage Museum, showing a particular interest in Dutch genre painting and French painting, and he also studied briefly under V.L.Borovikovsky. He made a series of caricatures of the invasion of 1812 along with I.I.Terebenev and I.A.Ivanov. He mostly produced portraits however until 1819 when he left St. Petersburg for his estate at Safonkovo in the Tver' region where he painted from nature with both simplicity and refinement. A monumental calm pervades these works which at many removes recall that of Chardin. He avoided narrative. His colour is crisp and he employed, for example, red shadows on red cloth. Brown in no way dominates his paintings. No rapid movements disturb his unique blend of delicacy and monumentality.
He created a school in his village in 1820 where he taught painting to poor people and serfs. His pupils included Aleksandr Alekseev, Nikifor Krylov, Lavr Plakhov, Grigori Soroka and some seventy others. From 1825 the Society for the Encouragement of the Arts in St. Petersburg began to publish colour lithographs at his suggestion. He died at Safonkovo in the Tver' region.
Spring. Ploughing, 1830s, TG, is an unpretentious painting of great refinement, subtlety and originality. A female estate worker, in local but unshowy costume and a hat reminiscent of the Italian Renaissance, leads two horses. They work apparently without great effort in the wide, empty landscape. In the left foreground a child plays in a state of well-being, satisfaction and harmonious enjoyment. This is a rare image of maternity, fecundity and calm executed with consummate skill and characterised by a technique of carefully presented understatement in which everything finds its place in the scheme of well managed nature.
Lit N.N.Vrangel' *A.G.Venetsianov*, St. Petersburg, 1911. N.Nikolaeva *A.G.Venetsianov*, Moscow, 1914. M.S.Urenius *A.G.Venetsianov*, Moscow, 1925. *Venetsianov v pismakh khudozhnika i vospominaniyakh sovremennikov*, Moscow-Leningrad, 1931. A.Liberfort *A.G.Venetsianov i ego shkola*, Moscow, 1940. N.Mashkovtsev *A.G.Venetsianov*, Moscow-Leningrad, 1944. A.Savinov *Khudozhnik A.G.Venetsianov*, Leningrad, 1949. A.Savinov *A.G.Venetsianov. Zhizn' i tvorchestva*, Moscow, 1955. T.Alexeyeva *Venetsianov and his School*, Leningrad, 1984.
Coll TG; RM; Kalinin Art Gallery.
See p.18.

Aleksei Venetsianov. The Threshing Barn, *1822-3. Oil on canvas. 66.5 x 80.5 cm.*
State Russian Museum, St. Petersburg.

VENETSIANOVA, Aleksandra Alekseeva   **1816-1882**
Portrait painter. She was the daughter of Aleksei Venetsianov
and, in the 1830s-1840s, his pupil. She wrote reminiscences
about her father in 1862.
Coll TG; Kalinin Art Gallery.

VENGEROVSKAYA, Sofia G.   **a.1932**
Ceramics artist. She designed for the Petrograd Porcelain
Factory. She was represented at the jubilee exhibition Artists
of the RSFSR over 15 Years held at the Russian Museum,
Leningrad, in 1932.

VENIG, Bogdan Bogdanovich   **1837-1872**
Painter of portraits and classical themes. Born at Revel. He was
the brother of Karl Venig. He studied under F.A.Bruni at the
Academy from 1851. He was among the artists who protested at
the Academy in 1863, an event which led to the founding of the
Wanderers movement. He was in fact a member of the Artel
which preceded and became the Wanderers.
Coll RM.

VENIG, Karl Bogdanovich   **1830-1908**
Painter of figurative works including themes from
Shakespeare. Born at Revel. He was the brother of Bogdan
Venig. He studied under F.A.Bruni at the Academy from 1844
and travelled to Italy on a scholarship 1853-62. He taught at
the Academy from 1862 to 1894.
He was the father of the painter and theatre designer Pavel
K.Venig, 1870-1942, and of the painter Grigory K.Venig,
1862-1927.
Coll TG; RM; Saratov Art Museum.

VEPRINTSEVA, Sofia Grigor'evna   **1895-1957**
Painter, graphic artist. Born at Simferopol. She studied at the
Stroganov College 1914-17.
After the Revolution she studied under Fal'k at the Moscow
Vhutemas 1917-25. She was represented at the jubilee
exhibition Artists of the RSFSR over 15 Years held at the
Russian Museum, Leningrad, in 1932. She died at Moscow.

VEREFKINA, M.V. = WEREFKIN, M.

Georgiy Vereisky. The Artist Aleksandr Golovin, *1928. Lithograph.*
Collection Mr. and Mrs. Nikita D.Lobanov-Rostovsky, London.

VEREISKY (VEREYSKY), Georgiy Semenovich
1886-1962
Painter of St. Petersburg, graphic artist inspired by K.Somov.
He was a prolific lithographer. Born in the Podol'sk region.
He studied under E.Shreider at Kharkov in 1896 and 1900-4.
He was a revolutionary in 1905 and in 1907 he emigrated to
Germany and Italy. He studied at the New Studio under

Dobuzhinsky and others 1913-16.
After the Revolution he became Conservator of Prints at the
Hermitage Museum. From 1918 he taught at the Higher
Photographic Institute. He participated in the First State Free
Exhibition of Artworks in Petrograd in 1919. He taught at the
Petrograd Vkhutemas in 1921-23. He was included in the
enormous survey Exhibition of Paintings by Petrograd Artists

of All Tendencies 1919-1923 held in Petrograd in 1923 and was represented at the Venice Biennale in 1924. He also taught at the Institute of Decorative Arts. He was represented at the All-Union Polygraphic Exhibition in Moscow in 1927 and at the jubilee exhibition Artists of the RSFSR over 15 Years held at the Russian Museum, Leningrad, in 1932.

His portrait etchings, such as the *Portrait of S.M.Zarudnyy*, have a precision worthy of Legros, whilst his lithographs could be soft in appearance even when firmly structured and composed, as in his lithographic *Leningrad. Bolshoi Prospekt. Vasilievsky Island* of 1935.

He designed posters in Leningrad in the years 1941-2. He died in Leningrad.

Lit *G.S.Vereysky*, exh. cat., Leningrad, 1962. G.Chernova *G.S.Vereysky*, Moscow, 1965. *Paris-Moscou*, 1979. L.N. Voronikhina *G.S.Vereysky*, Leningrad, 1987.

Coll RM.

VERESHCHAGIN, Petr Petrovich   **1836-1886**
Landscape painter. Born at Perm, the son of the painter P.P.Vereshchagin who died in 1843. The date of his birth is sometimes given as 1834. After initial study with his father he studied at the Academy from 1858. His subjects included city views. He died at St. Petersburg.

Coll TG; Gorky Art Museum.

VERESHCHAGIN, Vasili Petrovich   **1835-1909**
Painter, theatre designer. Born at Perm, the son of P.P.Vereshchagin. He studied under A.U.Orlov at Perm and under A.T.Markov at the Academy from 1857. He travelled to France and Italy on a scholarship 1863-9. He then taught at the Academy from 1869 to 1894. His subjects included ikons, portraits and figurative thematic paintings. He was active in theatre design in 1887. He died at St. Petersburg.

Coll TG; RM; Perm Art Gallery.

VERESHCHAGIN, Vasili Vasilievich   **1842-1904**
Intensely dramatic painter of historical war themes. Born in the Novgorod region. He trained as a naval officer and was engaged in warfare. He studied at the School of the Society for the Encouragement of the Arts in St. Petersburg from 1858 and at the Academy under A.T.Markov, and A.E.Beyderman 1860-3. He then travelled to Paris where he studied under Gérome 1864-6.

War themes proccupied him. He was in Central Asia observing the war in Turkestan 1867-8 and 1869. He executed a Balkan cycle of works on the theme of the Russo-Turkish War 1877-8. Comparable series followed including a series on the 1812 War painted 1887-98 and a Spanish-American War series 1898-9.

He travelled widely to India, 1874-6 and 1882-3, Palestine in 1884, and to the Far North 1887-8 and 1894, as well as Japan and Tibet. He died in April 1904 on the Battleship *Petropavlovsk* during the Russo-Japanese War.

Lit V.Verestchagin *1812*, 1899. *The Works of Vasili Verestchagin*, exh. cat., Philadelphia, 1889. A.N.Tikhomorov *V.V.Vereshchagin*, 1942. A.K.Lebedev *V.V.Vereshchagin*, Moscow, 1958.

Coll Major holdings at TG; RM; Museum of Russian Art, Kiev; Boston Museum of Fine Art; Brooklyn Museum, New York.

Colour plate p.453.

VEREYSKY = VEREISKY, G.S.

VERSILOVA-NERCHINSKAYA (BUROVA),
Maria Nikolaevna   **1854-pre-1917**
Painter.
Coll TG.

VERTEPOV, Aleksandr   **a.1912**
Sculptor. He studied in Paris at the Académie de la Grande Chaumière under Bourdelle c.1912.

VESHCHILOV, Konstantin Aleksandrovich   1877-1918+
Painter, theatre designer. He was taught by Repin at the Academy from 1898. He exhibited from 1901. He travelled on a scholarship 1905-6. In 1911 he executed a painting depicting the Russo-Japanese War of 1904. He was active in theatre design by 1913.

After the Revolution he directed the group of artists executing Agitprop decorations at the Technological Institute, Petrograd, in 1918. He participated in the First State Free Exhibition of Artworks in Petrograd in 1919.

Theatre design 1913 December F.Nozière's and G.Muller's *Tavern in Seville* with music by M.V.Vladimirov and produced by Meyerhold at Suvorin's Theatre, St. Petersburg.

Coll Khabarovsk Art Gallery; Astrakhan Art Gallery; Gorky Art Gallery.

VESNIN, Aleksandr Aleksandrovich   **1883-1959**
Painter, theatre designer and architect. The Vesnin Brothers, comprising Aleksandr, Leonid and Viktor, formed an important architectural practice in the decades following the revolution. Aleksandr was however an important painter and theatre designer of originality.

Born at Yur'evets on the Volga. During 1901-4 and 1911-12 he studied at the Institute of Civil Engineering in St. Petersburg whilst also studying painting under Yuon in Moscow in 1907 and under Tsionglinsky in St. Petersburg in 1909. He exhibited from 1911. He worked in the studio complex The Tower in Moscow with Tatlin and others 1912-14. This provided close contact with the latest interpretations of Western art movements allied to the innovations of Tatlin and his contemporaries. Vesnin's work had a radical originality after this, although he did produce appropriately historicist but stylised decorations for the Ya.V.Sirotin House which the Vesnin Brothers built at Nizhny-Novgorod 1915-16. He had visited Italy 1913-14 and these paintings show a debt to Italian decorations of the late Renaissance especially to the work of Tintoretto and Veronese. Aleksandr acknowledged the simultaneous impact of Italian old masters, Cézanne and Picasso at this time.

After the Revolution he worked with his brothers on Agitprop decorations for Moscow and Petrograd in 1918 and he exhibited with the Artists of the Leftist Federation of the Professional Union in 1918 along with Popova, Rodchenko, Tatlin and others. His name appeared on the April 1919 list of artists for acquisitions by the envisaged Museum of Painterly Culture. He participated in the Third Exhibition of Paintings held at Ryazan in 1919 and the enormous First State Exhibition of Art and Science, which included ethnographic material, held in Kazan in 1920. He exhibited in the 1921 exhibition of the World of Art in Moscow. He also taught at the Vkhutemas/Vkhutein in Moscow from 1921 to 1930.

He became a member of the Institute of Artistic Culture

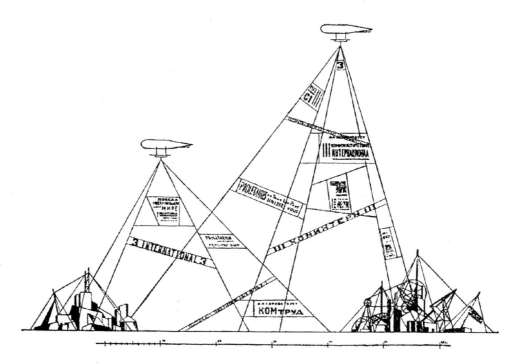

Aleksandr Vesnin and Lyubov' Popova. Design for the Mass Spectacle 'Struggle and Victory', *1921.*
'Struggle and Victory' was directed by Vsevolod Meyerhold on Khondinsky Field. The project was designed to employ a vast number of participants as well as airships, searchlights and so on. Here the City of the Past is at the left and the City of the Future, a citadel of mechanisation, is seen at the right. This ambitious project was never realised. Banners suspended beneath airships celebrate the Third International.

(INKhUK) and was engaged in its theoretical debates concerning construction. In this context he exhibited with Popova, Exter, Stepanova and Rodchenko at the exhibition 5 x 5 = 25 in Moscow in 1921. This exhibition marked the demise of easel painting for the Constructivists and a commitment to socially oriented practical work. Vesnin's paintings were closest to those of Popova with intersecting transparent planes of colour. In 1921 he also collaborated with Popova on the designs for an unrealised mass pageant *Struggle and Victory* to be directed by the Constructivist theatre director Vsevolod Meyerhold to celebrate the Third Congress of the Comintern. This was in part architecture and in part

theatre design incorporating constructions representing the City of the Past (the Citadel of Capitalism) and the City of the Future. It was planned to involve over 2000 participants, five airplanes, projectors and music. Further theatrical work in 1921 included his involvement with design for the first children's theatre in Moscow directed by Nataliya Sats.

Aleksandr Vesnin delivered his creative credo at INKhUK in April 1922 calling for the creation of new objects rather than the depiction of what already exists. He was represented at the First Russian Art Exhibition in Berlin in 1922 and at the exhibition Art of Moscow Theatre 1918-1923 held in Moscow in 1923. In addition he executed a design at Vkhutemas for a

Aleksandr Vesnin and Lyubov' Popova. Maquette for the Mass Spectacle 'Struggle and Victory', *1921.*
Documentary photograph.
This maquette is for the City of the Future.

Maria Vasil'eva. Bal Bullier: Second Artists' Ball Poster, *1924. Colour lithograph. 123 x 84 cm.*
Collection Mr. and Mrs. Nikita D.Lobanov-Rostovsky, London.

Aleksandr Vesnin. Construction, *1921. Gouache on paper. 11 x 9 cm. Signed with cyrillic 'A.V.' lower right.*
In 1921 Vesnin showed work at the exhibition 5 x 5 = 25 for the catalogue of which the five particpating painters produced original art works. This is one of those drawings.
Courtesy Annely Juda Fine Art, London.

cup and saucer produced by the Dulevo Ceramics Factory to commemorate the Third International. This design featured a device of gold leaves and geometric forms with the lettering 'Comintern' in latin script.

In architecture he worked closely with his brothers as he had in pre-revolutionary years but it is possible that the sculptural and graphic audacity of the post-revolutionary designs owe a considerable amount to the adventurousness of Aleksandr Vesnin. Important amongst these were the *Palace of Labour* project of 1923, which incorporates a multi-storey bridge, and the *Leningrad Pravda* project for Moscow in 1924. In 1923-4 Aleksandr Vesnin formed a group within the Institute of Artistic Culture, mostly comprising Vkhutemas students, to work within *Lef* (Left Front of the Arts) in collaboration with Mayakovsky the editor of *Lef* periodical.

The later buildings of the Vesnin brothers were a professional blend of Constructivist and modern International Style architecture and Aleksandr Vesnin, together with his brothers and the architect Moisei Ginzburg, in 1925 formed OSA, the Society of Contemporary Architects. Ginzburg and A.Vesnin edited its periodical *SA* (Contemporary Architecture). He was represented at the Paris International Exhibition in 1925.

In addition he was an adventurous theatre designer reflecting the latest innovations in Suprematism and Constructivism in his work for Aleksandr Tairov's Kamerny (Chamber) Theatre in Moscow. He became a founder member of the group October in 1928. He was a member of the Academy from 1939. Late works include *May Day Parade, Moscow, 1945.*
*Monument to Karl Marx, 1920, unrealised project, designed by Aleksandr and Viktor Vesnin in collaboration with the

Aleksandr Vesnin. Maquette for the Stage Set of G.K.Chesterton's 'The Man Who Was Thursday', *1922-3.*
Documentary photograph.
In Constructivist form Vesnin has produced a stage apparatus for the actors. It incorporates ramps and a screen. The production was staged by Tairov's Kamerny (Chamber) Theatre in Moscow.

Aleksandr Vesnin. Costume design for 'Phèdre', *1922.*
Collection Mr. and Mrs. Nikita D.Lobanov-Rostovsky, London.

sculptor S.S.Aleshin. The overall height was to be 15 metres. The base is a series of ramps, rising increasingly block-like to the figure of Marx and his attendant embodiments of the Workers rather as if they had conquered a mountain peak. The base by contrast is by the Vesnins and comprises a Suprematist plan. Part of the base has steps to provide a podium for speeches beneath the giant figure of Marx.

Theatre design 1919 Gogol's *Revizor* at the Maly Theatre, Moscow.

1920 November: Paul Claudel's *L'Annonce faite à Marie*

Apollinari Vasnetsov. Summer Landscape. *Oil on canvas. Signed in cyrillic 'Ap.Vasnetsov'. 18.5 x 22.5 cm. Malmö Konstmuseum.*

produced by A.Tairov at the Kamerny (Chamber) Theatre, Moscow. This was designed in a kind of Cubist Renaissance style with tall architectural features evoking a church. The studies for costumes were more overtly Cubo-Futurist with crystalline effects and rigid planes formed from the folds, all dramatically lit.

1920 Beaumarchais' *Marriage of Figaro*, Moscow.

1921 Constructed costumes for Nataliya Sats' production of *Zhemchuzhina Adal'miny* (Adalmina's Pearl) at the Moscow Children's Theatre.

1922 Jean Racine's *Phèdre* (*Fedr*), translated and adapted by V.Bryusov, produced by Tairov at the Kamerny Theatre in Moscow and subsequently produced on tour at the Deutsches Theatre in Berlin and at the Théâtre des Champs-Elysées in Paris in 1923. The programme cover was a dramatic application of his painting to both theatre and graphic design: diagonal lines slice through space intersecting to form dynamic and translucent planes among which the figures are constructed from straight lines and arcs, distinguishable here by their colour in the midst of black and white. The lettering of the title is likewise spilt dramatically through this crytalline structure. The costumes are geometricised togas, some with a Suprematist version of a Greek helmet for the protagonists.

1922 O.E.Skrib's *Put' k slave* (Road to Glory) at the Maly Theatre, Moscow.

1922-3 G.K.Chesterton's *The Man Who Was Thursday*, a Constructivist set which filled the proscenium arch of the Kamerny Theatre with ramps, platforms and lifts (p.450). Costume designs employed flat, collage-like forms to construct and characterise figures in movement but this was done with more wit than dogma.

He also designed for the Maly Theatre in Moscow.

Lit M.Ilyn *Vesniny*, Moscow, 1960. *Aleksandr Vesnin*, exh. cat., Moscow, 1961. A.G.Chinyakov *Brat'ya Vesniny*, Moscow, 1970. J.E.Bowlt *Russian Stage Design. Scenic Innovation. From the Collection of Mr. and Mrs. Nikita D.Lobanov-Rostovsky*, Jackson, MS, exh. cat.,1982. C.Lodder *Russian Constructivism*,

Vasili V. Vereshchagin. Sebastopol, *before 1904. Oil on canvas. Inscribed in cyrillic script 'Sebastopol'. 22 x 38 cm.*
Malmö Konstmuseum.

New Haven and London, 1983. S.O.Khan-Magomedov *A.Vesnin and Russian Constructivism*, London, 1986. E.Weiss *Russische Avant-Garde, 1910-1930, Sammlung Ludwig, Köln*, Munich, 1986. N.Lobanov-Rostovsky *Revolutionary Ceramics*, London, 1990. Nancy Van Norman Baer *Theatre in Revolution, Russian Avant-Garde Stage Design 1913-1935*, San Francisco and London, 1991. *L'Avant-garde russe 1905-1925*, exh. cat., Musée des Beaux-Arts, Nantes, 1993.
Coll Bakhrushin Theatre Museum, Moscow; Samara Art Museum; Sammlung Ludwig, Cologne.

VEYDEMAN, Karl Yanovich = VEIDEMANIS, K.

VIALOV, K. = VYALOV, K.A.

VIL'DE (FON-VIL'DEMAN), Rudolf Fedorovich 1867-1937
Ceramics artist. Born in the Kurlyandsky region. He made fabric designs for the Prokhovorov Factory in Moscow. He studied at the Steiglitz School in St. Petersburg 1895-9 and travelled on a scholarship to Germany, France and Italy 1899-1902. He exhibited watercolours from 1902. From 1905 to the mid-1930s he worked as a graphic artist and modeller at the Imperial and later State Porcelain Factory. He was head of painting there from 1906.
After the Revolution he became an exponent of the design of agitational porcelain. He was awarded a gold medal at the International Exhibition in Paris in 1925. He was represented at the jubilee exhibition Artists of the RSFSR over 15 Years held at the Russian Museum, Leningrad, in 1932.
From 1936 he directed the art section of the Volkov Porcelain Factory near Novgorod.
Lit N.Lobanov-Rostovsky *Revolutionary Ceramics*, London, 1990.
Coll RM; Leningrad Porcelain Factory Museum.

VILENSKY, Zinovy (Zalman) Moiseevich 1899-1984
Portrait sculptor. Born in the Chernygovsky region. He studied at Kiev Art School 1914-19 and under Efimov and Chaikov at the Moscow Vkhutemas 1922-8. He exhibited from 1931. His works include a Rodinesque carved bust of *Chaikovsky*, 1947, as well as monuments to Gogol, Lenin and Frunze. He died in Moscow.
Coll TG; RM.

VIL'KOVISKAYA, Vera Emmanuilovna 1890-1944
Painter, graphic artist. Born at Kazan. She studied under Ben'kov and Feshin at Kazan Art School 1904-10 and at the Academy in 1912.
After the Revolution she made political posters in 1919. She was represented at the enormous First State Exhibition of Art and Science, which included ethnographic material, held in Kazan in 1920 and at the Third Touring Exhibition of the Sovetsk Regional subdepartment of the Museums Bureau along with Kandinsky, Rodchenko and others in 1921. She had an exhibition in Kazan in 1925. She worked in Kazan at the Architecture and Art Studios in 1925 and in Moscow schools in the 1930s.

VILLEVAL'DE, Bogdan (Gotfrid) Pavlovich 1818-1903
Painter. Born at Pavlovsk. He studied under K.P.Bryullov and A.I.Zauerveyd at the Academy from 1838 and travelled on a

scholarship 1843-4. He exhibited from 1842. He taught at the Drawing School of the Society for the Encouragement of the Arts, St. Petersburg 1840-8 and at the Academy 1848-94. He died at Dresden. His subjects included deatiled battle paintings and portraits.
Coll TG; Kaluga Art Museum.

VILLIAM (VILL'YAM), Elena Nikolaevna   1862-1919
Painter. Born at Moscow. She studied in Munich and under V.E.Makovsky and E.S.Sorokin at the Moscow College. She exhibited from 1888.
After the Revolution she exhibited at the First Exhibition of Works of the Professional Union of Artists in Moscow in 1918 and at the Ninth State Exhibition of Paintings: Naturalism and Realism in Moscow in 1919.
Coll TG.

VIL'YAMS (WILLIAMS), Petr Vladimirovich 1902-1947
Painter, theatre designer. Born in Moscow. He studied under V. Meshkov in Moscow in 1909.
After the Revolution he studied at the Vkhutemas under Konchalovsky, Shterenberg and Korovin in Moscow 1918-23. He was a member of the *Konkretivist* (Concretivist) group in 1924 along with Yu.Merkulov, B.Volkov, K.Vyalov and V.Lyushin. They exhibited together at the First Discussional Exhibition of Active Revolutionary Art in 1924. In 1928 he visited France, Germany and Italy. He was a founder member of OST, the Society of Easel Painters, 1925-30. He exhibited in Dresden in 1926, Venice in 1930 and New York in 1929. He was represented at the jubilee exhibition Artists of the RSFSR over 15 Years held at the Russian Museum, Leningrad, in 1932 and at the 1932 Venice Biennale. He exhibited at the International Exhibition in Paris in 1937.
He executed designs for numerous theatres including The Moscow Art Theatre, the K.Stanislavsky and V.Nemirovich-Danchenko Music Theatre, the Vakhtangov Theatre 1939-41, the Theatre of the Revolution 1936-41 and the Bolshoi Theatre in Moscow. He died in Moscow.
Portrait of Vsevolod Meyerhold, 1925, is a dramatic three-quarter-length portrait of the Constructivist theatre director, his head seen in profile and clad in greatcoat, blue scarf and bow tie, all set against a background of the scaffolding and film screen which Popova designed for his production of *Zemlya Dybom* (The Earth in Turmoil). This makes a curious blend of formal portrait and Constructivism.
The Automobile Race, 1930, TG, exemplifies the progress of changing taste. Specialising in the imagery of the motorcar, Vil'yams extends its length and exaggerates its diversity of design and its availability to stress its speed. The result can appear more a caricature of its inflated importance than a celebration of its power as it roars through the industrial suburban landscape.
Theatre design 1930 February M.Watkin's *Reklama* (Advertisement) at the Moscow Art Theatre.
1934 December Charles Dickens' *Pickwick Club* at the Gorky Moscow Art Theatre.
1934 Verdi's *La Traviata* at the Stanislavsky and Danchenko Musical Theatre.
1935 Puccini's *Cio-Cio-San* at the Stanislavsky and Danchenko Musical Theatre.
1936 February M.A.Bulgakov's *Molière* at the Moscow Art Theatre.
1937 Offenbach's *Belle Hélène* at the Stanislavsky and Danchenko Musical Theatre.
1939 December Molière's *Tartuffe* at the Moscow Art Theatre.
1943 April M.A.Bulgakov's *Poslednie dni. Pushkin* (Last Days. Pushkin) at the Moscow Art Theatre.
1946 July A.N.Tolstoy's *Ivan Groznyy* (Ivan the Terrible) at the Moscow Art Theatre.
1947 February B.F.Chirskoy's *Pobediteli* (Victors) at the Moscow Art Theatre.
Lit F.Syrkina *P.V.Vil'yams*, Moscow, 1953. T.Klyueva *P.V.Vil'yams*, Moscow, 1959. *Paris-Moscou*, 1979. E.Weiss *Russische Avant-Garde, 1910-1930, Sammlung Ludwig, Köln*, Munich, 1986.
Coll TG; RM; Museum of Moscow Art Theatre; Bakhrushin Theatre Museum, Moscow; St. Petersburg Theatre Museum; Sammlung Ludwig, Cologne.

VINNIKOVA, I.   a.1928
Textile designer. She contributed to the First Art Exhibition of Soviet Textiles in Moscow in 1928.

VINOGRADOV, Sergei Arsenevich   1869-1938
Painter, graphic artist. He studied under Polenov, Pryanishnikov and Makovsky at the Moscow College from 1880. In 1893 he joined the Wanderers and exhibited with them until 1901. He exhibited in Düsseldorf in 1904 and in Paris in 1906. He exhibited with the World of Art 1901-6 and with the Union of Russian Artists in 1906 and 1909. He designed a poster For the Aid of War Victims in 1914. This depicts a village scene where peasants gather around a wounded soldier listening sympathetically to his story. He exhibited in Prague in 1914.
After the Revolution he drew agitational events and displays in Moscow (TG) and joined various groups. He was represented at the enormous First State Exhibition of Art and Science, which included ethnographic material, held in Kazan in 1920.
He emigrated in 1924 but was represented at the Third Exhibition of Paintings by Artists from Kaluga and Moscow held in Kaluga in 1925. He exhibited in New York in 1924. His subjects included genre and still-life. He died at Riga.
Lit N.Stankevich *Vinogradov*, Leningrad, 1971.
Coll TG; RM; Lenin Library, Moscow; Sverdlovsk Art Gallery.

VINOGRADOV, Viktor Maksimovich   a. c.1920
He was engaged on the decoration of propaganda trains including the *Red Cossack* and Ukrainian *Lenin* trains c.1920.

VIRSALADZE, Simon (Soliko) Bagratovich   b.1909
Theatre designer. Born at Tiflis. He studied under Toidze at Tiflis 1923-6, and at the Academy under Sharleman. He also studied under Kardovsky and Rabinovich at the Moscow Vkhutemas 1928-30. He worked for the theatre from 1927 at the Tblisi Workers Theatre. He exhibited from 1934 in Tiflis. He designed costumes for A.Balanchivadze's ballet *Serdtse gor* (The Heart of the Mountains) in 1938 and for Verdi's *Aïda*. He designed for film ballets including *Othello* in 1960.
Coll St. Petersburg Theatre Museum.

VISHNEVETSKAYA, Sofia Kas'yanovna   1899-1962
Theatre designer. Born at Kiev. She studied under Exter 1916-20. She exhibited from 1928.
She was represented at the Paris International Exhibition in

1925. She designed costumes for *Kino-Tants* (Cinema Dance) together with E.M.Fradkina in 1926. She illustrated books from 1927. She designed for several theatres including the Proletkul't Theatre at Ivanovo-Voznesensk 1927-8, the Moscow Workers' Art Theatre in 1939 and the Musical Comedy Theatre, Leningrad, in 1942. She also designed for Mosfil'm in 1936 and 1941. She died at Moscow.
Coll St. Petersburg Theatre Museum.

VISHNYAKOV, Ivan Yakovlevich   1699-1761
Portrait painter. He was a court painter but also executed a number of ikons for churches as well as decorative paintings in St. Petersburg. He worked at Peterhof in 1740, at the Summer Palace 1747-56 and at the Winter Palace 1754-8. Much of his work is lost. The Tretyakov Gallery has his full-length portrait of *F.N.Golitsyn in Childhood*. He died at St. Petersburg.
Portrait of Sarra Fermer, 1745, is a handsome painting of a young woman in a wide blue court dress, wearing a wig and carrying a fan. The painting has rather a French look and shows a determination to depict textures convincingly.
Coll TG; RM.

VITALI, Ivan Petrovich   1794-1855
Late neo-classical sculptor of monuments, portraits and decorative work. He studied under A.Triskorin at St. Petersburg 1806-18. He was active in Moscow 1818-40. He executed many portrait sculptures including *Tsar Aleksandr I*, 1819, as well as architectural reliefs and sculpture for fountains. He taught at the Academy in St. Petersburg from 1841 where from 1841 he also produced sculpture for the Isaak Cathedral.
His work sometimes reflected Realist traits. He stressed the rhythmic potential of hairstyles but the faces of his portraits were also astutely observed and individual. His sitters included *K.P.Bryullov* 1836, *N.A.Maykov* 1836, and *Pushkin* 1836-7, all of which are in the Russian Museum. He died at St. Petersburg.
Venus Removing Her Sandal, 1852-53, marble, RM, is a sophisticated piece of carving. The full-length figure has one knee raised as Venus adjusts the strap of her sandal. This poses elaborate difficulties of balance in the sculpture which are solved by the robe of Venus which stretches down to the sculpture's base. In addition Vitali has had to carve holes through the marble to release part of the arm from the main block and the raised leg extends down into empty space. The head is idealised in line with a Greek precedent as revived by Canova and others. This is the result of originality of thought within the strict codes of practice which neo-classicism required. It is achieved with confidence and great technical virtuosity.
Lit E.Nagaevskaya *I.P.Vitali*, Moscow, 1950.
Coll Well represented at RM; TG.
See p.433.

VITBERG, Aleksandr (Karl) Lavrent'evich   1787-1855
Architect, painter. Born at St. Petersburg. He studied under G.I.Ugryumov at the Academy in St. Petersburg from 1802. He made drawings and architectural landscapes in the early 1800s as well as painting mythological scenes. From 1817 he worked on a monument commemorating the War of 1812. He built a church and houses at Vyatka and Moscow. In his last

years he was building the Cathedral of St. George in Tiflis. He died at St. Petersburg
Coll TG; RM.

VKhTUZ
The abbreviated name of the Higher Artistic and Technical Teaching Institute (*Vysshee khudozhestvenno-tekhnicheskoe uchebnoe zavedenie*) in Leningrad operative 1921-3.

VKhUTEIN
The abbreviated name of the Higher Artistic and Technical Institute (*Vysshii gosudartsvennyi khudozhestvenno-tekhnicheskii institut*) operative in Moscow 1927-30 and in Leningrad 1925-30.

VKhUTEMAS
The abbreviated name of the Higher Artistic and Technical Studios (*Vysshie gosudarstvennye khudozhestvenno-tekhnicheskie masterskie*) operative in Moscow 1920-7 and in Leningrad 1923-5.

VLADIMIROV, Iosif   mid-17th century
Ikon painter. He was a follower of Simon Ushakov.
Coll TG.

VLADIMIROV, Ivan Alekseevich   1869-1947
Painter of genre and war themes. Born at Vilno. His birth date is sometimes given as 1870. He studied at Vilno Drawing School and at the Academy in St. Petersburg from 1891. He exhibited from 1893. He depicted the 1905 Revolution.
During the Revolution he made drawings of street fighting in Petrograd in October 1917. He participated in the First State Free Exhibition of Artworks in Petrograd in 1919 and was included in the enormous survey Exhibition of Paintings by Petrograd Artists of All Tendencies 1919-1923 held in Petrograd in 1923. He was a member of AKhRR 1923-8.
He was represented at the International Exhibition in Paris in 1937. He died at Leningrad.
Down with the Eagle!, 1917-18, Museum of the Great October Socialist Revolution, Moscow, illustrates the determination of peasants and soldiers to reach the snowy roof of a chemist's shop in order to demolish the Tsar's eagle which crowns its front.
Coll TG; RM; Kirov Art Gallery; Dnepropetrovsk Art Gallery.

VLADIMIROV, Vasili Vasil'evich   1880/1-1931
Painter, graphic artist. Born in Moscow. He studied in Moscow under Meshkov 1900-3 and became a member of the Moscow Society of Artists in 1902. He then studied in Munich from 1904 to 1906. His illustrations included books by his friend Andrei Bely. He died in Leningrad.
Lit *Twilight of the Tsars*, London, 1991.

VLASOV, Pavel Alekseevich   1857-1935
Painter. Born at Novocherkassk. He studied under V.G.Perov at the Moscow College from 1876 and at the Academy in St. Petersburg under Chistyakov from 1880.
He taught at Astrakhan where his pupils included B.Kustodiev 1896-1903 and G.S.Bershadsky 1908-13. He died at Astrakhan.
Coll Astrakhan Art Gallrey.

VOINOV, Mikhail Fedorovich   1759-1826
Portrait painter. Born at St. Petersburg. He studied under D.G.Levitsky at the Academy in St. Petersburg from 1768. He

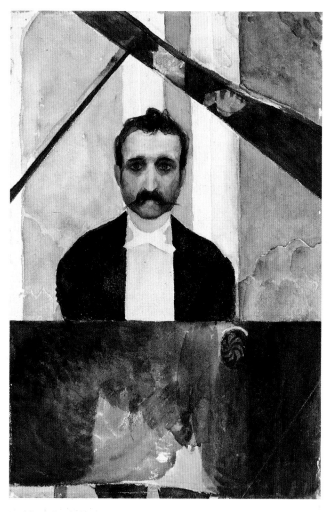

lived in Rome 1784-90 where he made copies after Domenichino and Guido Reni. He died at St. Petersburg.
Coll TG; RM.

VOINOV, Rostislav Vladimirovich   **1881-1919**
Sculptor, ex-librist. He studied at the Society for the Encouragement of the Arts in St. Petersburg and in the studio of L.E.Dmitriev-Kavkazsky. He held a one-man exhibition in St. Petersburg in 1907 and exhibited with the Union of Youth, of which he was a founder member, 1912-13. He also established a workshop for the production of wooden toys. An exhibition was held in Petrograd in 1917.
Lit J.Howard *The Union of Youth — An Artists' Society of the Russian Avant-Garde*, Manchester and New York, 1992.

VOINOV, Svyatoslav Vladimirovich   **1890-1920**
Draughtsman. A drawing of houses reveals an artist aware of the planar techniques of Cézanne interpreted in a Cubist manner. He was associated with the Union of Youth.
Coll RM.

Mikhail Vrubel'. N.I.Zabela-Vrubel' by a Piano, *early 1900s. Oil on canvas. 189 x 60 cm.*
State Tretyakov Gallery, Moscow.

Mikhail Vrubel'. The Pianist Cesi, *early 1900s. Watercolour on paper. 24.5 x x 16.3 cm.*
Malmö Konstmuseum.

VOLENKOVA, S. N.   **a.1911**
Painter. She exhibited with the Union of Youth in 1911.

VOLGIN = KUZNETSOV, M.A.

VOLKHONSKY, E. B.   **a.1919**
He was represented along with Kandinsky, Chagall and others
at the First State Exhibition of Paintings by Local and
Moscow Artists held in Vitebsk in December 1919.

VOLKONSKY, Nikolai Petrovich   **1867-1958**
Sculptor. Born in the Yaroslavl region. He was engaged on
Agitprop decorations at Saratov c.1918.

VOLKOV, Adrian Markovich   **1827-1873**
Painter, graphic artist. Born at Nizhny-Novgorod. His
subjects included cityscapes, figure paintings and satirical
drawings. He studied under F.A.Bruni at the Academy in St.
Petersburg. He exhibited from 1852. He taught at the
Drawing School of the Society for the Encouragement of the
Arts, St. Petersburg, from 1866. He died at St. Petersburg.
Coll TG.

VOLKOV, Aleksandr Nikolaevich   **1886-1957**
Painter of genre and landscape. Born at Fergana. He studied
science at the University in St. Petersburg 1908-11 but also
studied at the Academy under V.Makovsky 1908-10 and at the
Bernstein School of Art under Bilibin and Roerich 1910-12.
Finally he studied under F.Krichevsky and at the Kiev Art
Institute 1912-16 where he was impressed by the work of
Vrubel'. He moved to Tashkent in 1916 and taught at the
Tashkent Institute of Art.
After the Revolution he executed a number of Cubo-Futurist
works including *Tea House Under the Pomegranates*, 1924, TG.
This painting is mostly executed in red and black and is
constructed from triangles and circles to indicate the figures
crouching at their tea.
He became a member of AKhRR in 1928. Between 1916 and
1946 he taught at the Tashkent Art Institute, the Turkestan
Art Studios and at the Tashkent Art Technical College. He
died at Tashkent.
Lit *A.N.Volkov*, exh. cat., Moscow, 1927. N.Zemskaya
A.Volkov, Moscow, 1975. *Paris-Moscou*, 1979. E.Weiss *Russische
Avant-Garde, 1910-1930, Sammlung Ludwig, Köln*, Munich,
1986. A.M.Muratov, V.Manin et al. *Zhivopis' 20-30kh godov*,
Sankt-Peterburg, 1991.
Coll TG; RM; Tula Art Museum; Sammlung Ludwig,
Cologne.

VOLKOV, Boris Ivanovich   **1900-1970**
Painter, theatre designer. Born in Moscow. He studied under
F.Fedorovsky at the Stroganov Institute in Moscow 1913-18
and under V.Polenov 1913-16.
After the Revolution he worked with Lentulov, Tatlin and
Yakulov 1920-3. He began to design for the theatre in 1922.
He contributed to the exhibition Art of Moscow Theatre
1918-1923 held in Moscow in 1923 and became principal
designer for the MGSPS Theatre, Moscow, in 1924. He was a
member of the *Konkretivist* (Concretivist) group with
P.Vil'yams and others in 1924. They showed work as a group
at the First Discussional Exhibition of Active Revolutionary
Art in 1924. He died in Moscow.

Theatre design 1936 I.I.Dzerzhinsky's *Tikhiy Don* (The
Quiet Don) at the Nemirovich-Danchenko Music Theatre,
Moscow. A design for this shows thin, wind-blown trees
against a bleak and stormy sky.
1939 T.N.Khrennikov's opera *V buryu* (Into the Storm) at the
Nemirovich-Danchenko Music Theatre, Moscow.
1948 May S.Ya.Marshak's *Dvenadtsat' mesyatsev* (Twelve
Months) at the Moscow Art Theatre.
1948 December A.A.Surov's *Zelenaya ulitsa* (Green Street) at
the Moscow Art Theatre.
1949 May Charles Dickens' *Dombey and Son* at the Moscow
Art Theatre.
1950 November E.Yu.Mal'tsev's *Vtoraya lyubov'* (Second
Love) at the Moscow Art Theatre.
1953 October A.Yakobson's *Angel-khranitel' Nebraski* (The
Guardian Angel of Nebraska) at the Moscow Art Theatre.
1957 March I.S.Turgenev's *Dvoryanskoe gnezdo* (The Noble
Nest) at the Moscow Art Theatre.
Lit I.Gremislavskaya, F.Syrkina *B.Volkov*, Moscow, 1958.
Paris-Moscou, 1979.
Coll Bakhrushin Theatre Museum, Moscow; Sverdlovsk Art
Museum.

VOLKOV, Efim Efimovich   **1844-1920**
Landscape painter, graphic artist. Born in St. Petersburg. He
studied at the Drawing School of the Society for the
Encouragement of the Arts, St. Petersburg, in 1866 and part-
time at the Academy in St. Petersburg 1867-9. He began to
exhibit with the Wanderers in 1878 and became a member in
1880. He was represented at the International Exhibition in
Paris in 1900, in Munich in 1909 and in Pittsburgh in 1912.
After the Revolution he participated in the First State Free
Exhibition of Artworks in Petrograd in 1919. He worked in
Petrograd. He produced landscapes of the North of Russia
and Central Asia.

VOLKOV, Iosif Petrovich   **1854-1897+**
Painter of portraits and religious themes. He studied under
V.G.Perov at the Moscow College in the 1870s.
Coll TG.

VOLKOV, Ivan Vasilievich   **1847-1893**
Painter of landscapes and a prolific draughtsman. He studied
under A.K.Savrasov at the Moscow College until 1877. He
exhibited from 1874. He made drawings for the periodical
Niva from 1883.
Coll TG.

VOLKOV, Nikolai Nikolaevich   **1897-1933+**
Graphic artist, watercolourist, art historian. Born at Moscow.
He studied at the Moscow Institute 1914-22. He studied at
the Freiburg Institute 1925-6. He exhibited from 1933.
Writings N.N.Volkov *Tseti zhivopisi*, Moscow, 1965.
Coll TG.

VOLKOV, Roman Maksimovich   **1773-1831**
Academic painter of figures and portraits. He studied at the
Academy in St. Petersburg. His portrait of *Aleksandr I* is in the
Russian Museum.
Coll TG; RM.

VOLKOV, Valentin Viktorovich　　　1881-1964
Belorussian painter, graphic artist. Born at El'tse. He studied under K.A.Savitsky at the Penza Art School and at the Academy under V.E.Savinsky and Chistyakov.
After the Revolution he was engaged in Agitprop decorations at Blagoveshchensky Square, Petrograd, in 1918. He taught at Vitebsk from 1919 including the Vitebsk Art Technical College 1923-9. He executed a painting called *The Partisans* in 1928.
He taught at the Belorussian Children's IZO Studio at Minsk 1936-40 and at the Belorussian Theatre Institute at Minsk from 1953. He died at Minsk.
Coll RM.

VOLNUKHIN, Sergei Mikhailovich　　　1859-1921
Sculptor. He studied under S.I.Ivanov and V.G.Perov at the Moscow College from 1873. He exhibited with the Wanderers. He taught at the Moscow College 1895-1917 where his pupils included N.Goncharova c.1898, N.A.Andreev in 1892-1901 and B.Korolev 1910-13.
After the Revolution he taught at the Moscow Vkhutemas 1917-21. In 1918 he made a temporary monument to *T.G.Shevchenko*. He worked in Moscow.
Coll TG.

VOLNYANSKY, Grigoriy Apollonovich　　　1860s-1925+
Painter. He had no formal training. He was engaged on war service in 1914. His work included landscapes of the Kaluga region. He contributed to the Third Exhibition of Paintings by Artists from Kaluga and Moscow held in Kaluga in 1925.
Coll Kaluga Art Museum.

VOLOBUEV, Aleksei Nikolaevich　　　1894-1919+
Painter. His subjects included self-portraits and interiors. He was taught by S.V.Malyutin in 1918. He exhibited at the juryless Eighth State Exhibition in Moscow in 1919. He lived and worked in Moscow.

VOLOSHIN, Maksimilian Aleksandrovich　　　1878-1932
Poet, art critic and artist. Born at Kiev. He studied Law at Moscow University in 1897. He was in Paris from 1899 to 1907. He exhibited from 1912 with the Triangle group and with the World of Art. He returned to Paris 1913-16. He travelled in Greece, Spain and France until 1916. His work included landscapes.
After the Revolution he worked at Koktebele from 1917. He died at Koktebele.
Coll Feodosia Art Gallery; Kharkov Art Museum.

VOLOSHINOV, Valerian Andreevich　　　1887-1938
Architect, artist, theatre designer. He studied at the Academy in St. Petersburg 1907-14. He exhibited with the World of Art.
After the Revolution he was engaged in Agitprop decorations at Birzhevoy Bridge, Petrograd, in 1918. He taught at the Academy of Arts in the 1930s.

VOLOSKOV, Aleksei Yakovlevich　　　1823-1882
Painter of landscapes and views. He studied at the Academy in St. Petersburg under M.N.Vorob'ev from 1839. He executed views of Orienbaum in 1842 and Pavlovsk in 1845.
Coll TG; RM; Omsk Art Museum.

VOROB'EV (VOROBIEV), Maksim Nikiforovich
1787-1855
Prolific painter of spectacular landscapes and oriental themes. He studied at the Academy in St. Petersburg under F.Ya.Alekseev from 1798, initially in architecture and then in landscape painting. He crossed Russia with F.Ya.Alekseev 1810-12. He taught landscape painting at the Academy in St. Petersburg 1815-55. Most Russian landscape painters of the period studied under him, among them Aivazovsky and M.K.Klodt.
He travelled to Palestine 1820-2 and visited Turkey during the war 1828-9. He was much attracted to night effects as his *Jerusalem at Night*, 1830s, TG, and his *Autumn Night in St. Petersburg*, 1835, TG, exemplify. His work included architectural perspectives, including views of the Moscow Kremlin, as well as atmospheric landscapes and cityscapes. He also executed a few engravings. He died at St. Petersburg.
Coll TG; RM.

VOROB'EV (VOROBIEV), Sokrat Maksimovich
1817-1888
Painter of views. Born at St. Petersburg, the son of M.N.Vorob'ev. He studied under his father at the Academy in St. Petersburg from 1833. He worked in Italy 1840-6 and 1847-9. His work includes views of Naples.
Coll TG; RM.

VOROB'EVA (VOROBIEVA), V.　　　b.1900
She was a member of the *Unovis* collective formed around Malevich and Lissitzky in 1919 in Vitebsk.

VOROB'EVSKY, Aleksei Viktorovich　　　b.1906-1981+
Decorative ceramics painter. He studied at the Pavlovsk Art School until 1926 and then worked at the Lomonosov Porcelain Factory. He exhibited from 1927.
He was represented at the jubilee exhibition Artists of the RSFSR over 15 Years held at the Russian Museum, Leningrad, in 1932. He was represented at the International Exhibition in New York in 1939 and at the International Exhibitions in Brussels in 1958 and Montreal in 1967. He was made a People's Artist of the USSR in 1981.
Lit N.Lobanov-Rostovsky *Revolutionary Ceramics*, London, 1990.
Coll RM; St. Petersburg Porcelain Facory Museum; Perm Art Gallery.

VORONOV, Leonid A.　　　a.1926-1927
Graphic designer. He was represented at the Second Exhibition of Cinema Posters held at the Kamerny (Chamber) Theatre, Moscow, in 1926. He collaborated with Mikhail Yevstavev on a poster for Eisenstein's film *October* in 1927. The Stenberg brothers also designed a poster for this film.

VORONTSOV, Vladimir Vasil'evich　　　1873-1927+
Painter. He exhibited from 1915 in Moscow. He exhibited at the First Exhibition of Works of the Professional Union of Artists in Moscow in 1918 and at the juryless Eighth State Exhibition in Moscow in 1919.

VRANGEL', Elena Karlovna　　　1837-1906
Painter of landscapes and figures. Born at Novgorod. He studied under V.O.Shervud in Moscow from 1867 and under

L.O.Preazzi and Chistyakov in St. Petersburg from 1869. She exhibited from 1869 with the Society of Watercolourists. She died at St. Petersburg.
Coll TG.

VRUBEL', Mikhail Aleksandrovich   1856-1910
Painter, ceramics sculptor, furniture designer, theatre designer, illustrator. He was amongst the most influential and inspired individual artists of his day. His major paintings were unprecedented in technique and power, yet his minor works could be tentative, unresolved and sentimental. Essentially a Russian Symbolist, he was also attracted to the applied arts as they were adapted at the Abramtsevo colony. Folk art, literary sources, symbolist images and a virtuoso brilliance in the handling of colour and the material of paint made him a unique, essentially isolated but enormously influential figure.
Born at Omsk of a Russian mother and a Polish father. He studied at the Society for the Encouragement of the Arts at St. Petersburg in 1864, and 1868-9. He studied law at the University of St. Petersburg from 1874 to 1880 but also studied painting under Pavel Chistyakov 1878-9 and was at the Academy from 1880 to 1884. He was engaged on the restoration of frescoes in the church of St. Cyril at Kiev 1884-5 and also visited Italy.
A second period in Kiev followed in 1887 where he designed a project for murals in the Cathedral of St.Vladimir. Three versions of the *Pietà* date from 1887. He later suffered from mental insanity which first became evident in the late 1880s and again from 1902.
In 1889 he moved to Moscow where he met Savva Mamontov and designed for his private opera. His first designs were for Mamontov's productions of Handel's *Saul* and Humperdinck's *Hansel and Gretel* in 1890. He became further involved with the Abramtsevo circle where he designed furniture and maijolica sculpture. He worked in the ceramics workshop at Talashkino and it was at here that he also decorated balalaikas with highly stylised and decorative fairy-tale motifs of mermaids and flowers. Among his ceramic works at the Abramtsevo workshop was a tiled stove incorporating a dramatic ceramic lion motif that comprised in effect a sculpture in itself.
He illustrated Lermontov's *Demon* 1890-1 and the theme informed some of his most powerful and influential paintings including *The Demon Seated* in 1890. Other works of this time included *The Steed Runs Swifter than the Hind*, 1890-1, and the drop curtain for *Neapolitan Night*. He executed panels on mythological themes for the staircase of the house of E.Dunker in Moscow in 1893. The Russian Museum has a sculpture of *The Demon* executed by Vrubel' in 1894 made of painted plaster and showing the demon's face staring from a mass of hair.
Decorative works dominated 1896 when he executed panels for the All-Russian Exhibition at Nizhny-Novgorod. These depicted *Princess Reverie* and *Mikula Selianinovich*. The jury rejected them but they were displayed in a special pavilion erected by Mamontov. Vrubel' painted panels for Aleksei and Savva Mamontov's villas in Moscow 1896-8. Amongst these was *The Flight of Faust and Mephistopheles* 1896. Later paintings

included *The Bogatyr* 1898, *Pan* 1899, *Lilacs* 1900, and *The Swan Princess* 1900. He designed sets showing the City of Ledenets for Mamontov's production of Rimsky-Korsakov's *The Tale of the Tsar Saltan* 1900-1. He exhibited with the World of Art and was much respected by its members. He was included in Diaghilev's exhibition of Russian and Finnish Artists in 1898. He exhibited with the World of Art 1900-6.
Still haunted by the *Demon* of Lermontov he painted the major canvas *The Demon Downcast* in 1902. In this year he was receiving medical treatment for his mental state but he continued to work in and out of mental hospital, producing *The Pearl* 1904, for example, until 1906 when he was stricken with blindness.
He was included in Diaghilev's display of Russian art at the Salon d'Automne in Paris in 1906 and had become an Academician in 1905. He died in a mental asylum in St. Petersburg after a period of blindness, which began in 1906, and madness.
Vrubel' was one of only seven artists deemed worthy of a monument in Lenin's plan issued in 1918.
The Flying Demon, 1899, RM, depicts the winged demon flying above the Caucasus, spread across the canvas among spangled and faceted patches of colour. This is distinctly Russian Symbolist art in its combination of vigour and poetic suggestiveness. His brushwork, and his handling of line in his drawings, comprised repeated segments or planes spreading rhythmically to accompany the presentation of the image which condenses clearly from this mass of painterly activity.
Theatre design 1900 Chaikovsky's *Magician*: practical costume design emphasising decoration of the costume, executed for Savva Mamontov's Second Private Opera.
Lit A.P.Ivanov *Vrubel'*, St. Petersburg, 1911. S.P.Yaremich *M.A.Vrubel'*, Moscow, 1911. Eres *Vrubel'*, Moscow, 1919. I.Evdokimov *M.A.Vrubel'*, Moscow, 1925. *M.A.Vrubel'*, exh. cat., Moscow, 1957. E.V.Zhuravlev *M.A.Vrubel'*, 1958. *M.A.Vrubel' Perepiska*, Leningrad, 1963. *M.A.Vrubel' Album*, Moscow, 1968. A.A.Fedorov-Davydov *M.A.Vrubel'*, 1968. V.Rakitin *Mikhail Vrubel'*, Moscow, 1971. N.M.Tarabukin *Vrubel'*, Moscow, 1974. S.Kaplanova *Vrubel'*, Leningrad, 1975. S.Druzhinin *M.Vrubel'*, Moscow, 1975. *Paris-Moscou*, 1979. D.Kogan *Vrubel'*, Moscow, 1980. A.Isdebsky-Pritchard *The Art of Mikhail Vrubel (1856-1910)*, Ann Arbor, 1982. J.E.Bowlt *Russian Stage Design. Scenic Innovation. From the Collection of Mr. and Mrs. Nikita D.Lobanov-Rostovsky*, Jackson, MS, exh. cat., 1982. N.A.Dmitrieva *M.A.Vrubel'*, Leningrad, 1984.
Coll Major holdings at TG and RM; Bakhrushin Theatre Museum; Pushkin Museum, St. Petersburg.
Colour plates p.456.

VSHIVTSEV, Sergei Aleksandrovich   1885-1965
Painter, graphic artist. Born in the Vyatka (Kirov) region. He studied under Ben'kov and Feshin at the Kazan Art School 1907-10. He exhibited from 1913 at Kazan.
After the Revolution he was included in the Third Touring Exhibition of the Sovetsk Regional subdepartment of the Museums Bureau along with Kandinsky, Rodchenko and others in 1921. He died at Kirov.
An exhibition was held in Kirov in 1955.
Coll Kirov Art Museum.

Konstantin Vyalov. Constructivist Stage Set for 'Stenka Razin', *1924. Ink and watercolour. Signed in Russian lower right. 18 x 15.5 cm. Produced at the Theatre of the Revolution, Moscow, 1924. Collection Mr. and Mrs. Nikita D.Lobanov-Rostovsky, London.*

VUCHETICH, Evgeniy Viktorovich   1908-1974
Monumental and portrait sculptor. Born at Ekaterinoslav. He studied under A.S.Chinenov and A.I.Mukhin at the Rostov Art School 1926-30. He was represented at the International Exhibition in Paris in 1937.

He executed various military portrait busts in the 1940s. His monumental works include *The Soldier Liberator* erected in the Treptow Park in Berlin, a *Monument to Soviet Army Soldiers Killed in the Battle Against Fascism* erected at Berlin, and *Let Us Beat our Swords into Ploughshares* which was donated by the Soviet Union to the United Nations. He also designed a memorial ensemble at the Mamai Burial Mound at Volgograd. He received many honours.

His monumental full-length portait of *Dzerzhinsky*, erected in Moscow, was demolished by a crowd in 1991.

*Monument to General-Lieutenant M.G.Efremov, 1944-5, bronze, erected at Vyaz'ma, represents figures responding by pointing and staring as they watch the fighting.

*Monument to Soviet Army Soldiers Killed in the Battle Against Fascism, 1946-9, erected in Berlin, is a colossal and extensive memorial ensemble. It is topped by a great soldier with a giant sword. He carries a child on his arm and treads the swastika beneath his feet.

Lit R.Abolina, V.Popov *E.V.Vuchetich,* Moscow, 1952. I.M.Shevtsov *E.V.Vuchetich,* Leningrad, 1960. F.Shakhmangonov *E.Vuchetich,* Moscow, 1970.

Coll TG; RM; Museum of Russian Art, Kiev.

VUFKU
The abbreviated name of the All-Ukrainian Administration of Photography and Film (*Vseukrainskoe fotokinoupravlenie*).

VYALOV (VIALOV), Konstantin Aleksandrovich 1900-1976
Painter, graphic artist, theatre designer. Born in Moscow. He studied at the Stroganov College 1914-17.

After the Revolution he studied at the Moscow Vkhutemas under Lentulov and Morgunov 1917-24. He contributed to the exhibition Art of Moscow Theatre 1918-1923 held in Moscow in 1923. He was a member of the *Konkretivist* (Concretivist) group with P.Vil'yams and others in 1924. They showed work as a group at the First Discussional Exhibition of Active Revolutionary Art in 1924. He was represented at the Paris International Exhibition in 1925. He exhibited with the First Exhibition of the Society of Easel Painters (OST) in Moscow in 1925 remaining a member until 1931. He was making film posters in the period 1927-32.

He was included in the major exhibition in Moscow in 1927 marking the tenth anniversary of the Revolution. He was represented at the jubilee exhibition Artists of the RSFSR over 15 Years held at the Russian Museum, Leningrad, in 1932 and at the 1932 Venice Biennale. He died in Moscow.

Theatre design 1923 *The Camorra of Seville* at the Theatre of the Revolutionary Military Soviet in Moscow (possibly unrealised). A costume design for a bandit uses collage to construct a figure largely employing staight edges with concessions to anatomical curves in the painted-in head, hands and feet. This is a stylisation derived from Suprematist and Constructivist examples.

Posters 1926-7 Dziga Vertov's film *Sixth of the Earth.*

Lit E.Weiss *Russische Avant-Garde, 1910-1930, Sammlung Ludwig, Köln,* Munich, 1986. Nancy Van Norman Baer *Theatre in Revolution, Russian Avant-Garde Stage Design 1913-1935,* San Francisco and London, 1991.

Coll TG; Bakhrushin Theatre Museum, Moscow; Novosibirsk Art Gallery; Sammlung Ludwig, Cologne.

VYAZ'EMSKY, Lev Peysakhovich   1901-1938
Painter. Born in the Vitebsk region. He studied under P.Kuznetsov and V.Favorsky at the Moscow Vkhutemas/Vkhutein 1923-30. He exhibited from 1928. He was a member of AKhRR 1928-30 and in 1929 he painted murals for the Vkhutein club. He was represented at the jubilee exhibition Artists of the RSFSR over 15 Years held at the Russian Museum, Leningrad, in 1932. He worked in Moscow.

Lit *Paris-Moscou,* 1979.

VYSHESLAVTSEV, Nikolai Nikolaevich   1890-1952
Graphic artist. Born in the Poltavsky region. He studied under Mashkov at the Moscow College in 1906-8. He worked in Italy and France 1908-14.

After the Revolution he exhibited in the 1921 exhibition of the World of Art in Moscow and in the fourth exhibition of *Iskusstvo dvizheniya* (The Art of Movement) in 1928 in Moscow. He illustrated numerous books and periodicals in the period 1922-46. He died in Moscow.

Coll TG; Skryabin Museum, Moscow.

Evgeniy Vuchetich. Monument to Soviet Army Soldiers Killed in the Battle Against Fascism, *1946-9. Bronze. Figure 13 metres high. Erected in Berlin.*

W

Y

W.B. (latin) see **BEKHTEEV, V.G.**

WANDERERS (ITINERENTS, PEREDVIZHNIKI)
The abbreviated name for the Association of Travelling
Exhibitions founded in 1870. It continued in existence until
1923 and in its early days established Realist painting in
Russia, frequently asserting a social message. Members
included Levitan, Repin and Surikov.

WASSILIEFF, Marie = VASILIEVA, M.I.

WEDEKIND, J. H. = VEDEKIND, I.-G.

WENIG, B. B. = VENIG, B. B.

**WEREFKIN, Marianne von (VEREFKINA,
Marianna Vladimirovna)**   **1870-1938**
Painter. Her date of birth is sometimes given as 1867. Born at
Tula. She studied under Repin in St. Petersburg. Repin
painted her portrait in 1885 and she exhibited from 1886.
Later she studied under Azbe in Munich from 1906. Here,
particularly through meeting Kandinsky and Jawlensky, she
became a member of the *Neue Künstler Vereinigung* with which
she exhibited.
She also exhibited in Russia with the Izdebsky International
Salons 1909-11 in Odessa and with the Knave of Diamonds in
Moscow 1910-11. She was closely associated with Kandinsky
and art in Munich. She died at Ancona, Italy. The date of her
death is sometimes given as 1941.
Lit M.von Werefkin *Briefe an eine Unbekannten*, Köln, 1960.
J.Hahl-Koch *Marianne Werefkin und der russische Symbolismus*,
1967.
Coll Marianne von Werefkin Stiftung, Basle; Kunsthaus,
Zurich.

WILLIAMS, P. = VIL'YAMS, P.V.

WORLD OF ART (MIR ISKUSSTVA)
A society of artists and critics established by Benois, Diaghilev,
Somov, Filosofov, Bakst, Lansere and others in 1898 to
organise exhibitions in St. Petersburg primarily but also in
Moscow and elsewhere. The society organised the Exhibition
of Russian and Finnish Art at the Stieglitz Museum in St.
Petersburg in 1898. Its journal was also entitled *World of Art*
(*Mir Iskusstva*) with Diaghilev as editor. In 1901 the Moscow
contributors broke away to form the Exhibition of 36 Artists.
The original group exhibitions continued until 1906 but the
World of Art had effectively ended with the exhibition of
1904. The title was revived 1910-24. A final World of Art
Exhibition was held in Paris in 1927.

Ya.M. see **YAKOVLEV, M. N.**

YABLONSKAYA, T. N.   **1917-1949+**
Socialist Realist genre painter of rural themes.
Coll TG.

YAGODNIKOV, Aleksei   **mid-19th century**
Portraitist.
Coll TG.

YAGUZHINSKY, Sergei Ivanovich   **1862-1947**
Painter, graphic artist. He taught at the Stroganov Institute
where his pupils included D.I.Mitrokhin in 1905.
After the Revolution he was engaged in Agitprop decorations
including the decoration of the propaganda boat *Red Star* in
1920.
Lit *Twilight of the Tsars*, London, 1991.
Coll TG.

YAKIMCHENKO, Aleksandr Georgievich   **1878-1929**
Painter, designer, graphic artist. He reflected the heavily folk
art inspired manifestation of the revival of arts and crafts in
Russia in the interior that he designed for the dining room of
the Firsanova House in Moscow in 1909 although it also
seems to invite comparison with the work of the Vienna
Secession. Here however the total effect was less refined and
elegant. It more consciously sought to blend folk art with the
swirling lines of Art Nouveau and crude vigour rather than
elegance characterised its adoption of distinctly Russian
motifs. In this it is comparable with the approach of the
painter-architect Sergei Malyutin.
Yakimchenko was represented at the First Exhibition of Works
of the Professional Union of Artists in Moscow in 1918, at the
Fourth State Exhibition of Paintings (*IV Gosudarstvennaya
vystavka kartin*) in Moscow in 1919 and he participated in the
Third Exhibition of Paintings held at Ryazan in 1919.
He was engaged in Agitprop decorations in the early
revolutionary years including work on the propaganda trains
Red Cossack, the Ukrainian train *Lenin*, and the trains *Lenin
(October Revolution)* and *Soviet Caucasus* in 1920. He was
included in the Third Touring Exhibition of the Sovetsk
Regional subdepartment of the Museums Bureau along with
Kandinsky, Rodchenko and others in 1921. He was
represented at the First Russian Art Exhibition in Berlin in
1922, at the Paris International Exhibition in 1925 and the
All-Union Polygraphic Exhibition in Moscow in 1927.

YAKIMENKO, D.   **a.1910-11**
He exhibited with the Izdebsky Salon of 1910-11 in Odessa.

YAKIMOVSKAYA, Ekaterina Aleksandrovna   **b.1895**
Ceramics artist. She graduated from the Deaf and Dumb
School in St. Petersburg in 1913 and studied at the Society for

the Encouragement of the Arts in St. Petersburg 1915-17. After the Revolution she worked at the State Porcelain Factory from 1918.
Lit N.Lobanov-Rostovsky *Revolutionary Ceramics*, London, 1990.

YAKOBI, Valeriy Ivanovich   **1834-1902**
Painter. His work encompassed themes of social criticism. In 1861 he won a gold medal for a painting of chained prisoners awaiting deportation to Siberia. He then travelled abroad before returning to Russia. He was a founder member of the Wanderers movement in 1870. He later undertook Russian historical themes.
Coll TG.

YAKOULOV, G. = YAKULOV, G.B.

YAKOVLEV, Aleksandr Evgen'evich (YAKOVLEFF, IACOVLEFF, JACOVLEFF, Alexandre)   **1887-1938**
Painter, theatre designer, graphic artist. Born at St. Petersburg. He studied at the Academy in St. Petersburg and was associated with the World of Art. He exhibited with the First Izdebsky International Salon 1909-10 in Odessa.
After the Revolution he exhibited with the World of Art in December 1917 in Moscow.
He emigrated in 1918 or 1919 but contributed to the Exhibition of Paintings by Russian Artists held at Pskov in Spring 1920 and to the 1921 exhibition of the World of Art in Moscow. He took part in Citroën's *Croisière noire* expedition in the Sahara desert 1924-5. He contributed to the exhibition of Contemporary Russian Art held at Philadelphia in 1932.
Illustration Covers for Pierre Mille *Féli et M'bala l'éléphant*, Paris, 1938.
Theatre design 1912 January Dr.Dapertutto's *Lovers*, a pantomime produced by Meyerhold at N.P.Karabchevsky's house, St. Petersburg. Designs by Yakovlev and V.I.Shukhaev in collaboration.
1934 *Semiramida* (Semiramis), opera melodrama with music by Honneger, choreography by M.Fokine for the Ida Rubinstein company at the Paris Opera.
Lit M.Birnbaum *Jacovleff and Other Artists*, New York, 1946. *Alexandre Iacovleff, Exhibition of Fifty Paintings and Drawings*, Gropper Art Gallery, Cambridge, Mass., May-June, 1972.
Coll TG, Ashmolean Museum, Oxford.
Colour plate p.466.

YAKOVLEV, Andrei   **1934-1964+**
Painter. He studied in Leningrad. He travelled to the Far North as a sailor on an Arctic fishing vessel and worked at Spitzbergen. His paintings include *Return of the Hunters, Chukotka*, 1964, RM.
Coll RM.

YAKOVLEV, Boris Nikolaevich   **1890-1972**
Socialist Realist painter who illustrated heroic themes. He studied at the Moscow College 1915-18. He exhibited in the 1921 exhibition of the World of Art in Moscow. His work already showed proto-Socialist Realist traits in the 1920s. In 1922 he was a founder member of the Society (*Obshchestvo*) of Artists of Revolutionary Russia, founded after the first

Aleksandr Yakovlev. Design for Act 2 of 'Semiramis', *1934. Gouache and oil. Signed lower right 'A.Jacowleff 1934'. 68.6 x 82 cm. A design for Paul Valéry's 'Semiramis' based on François-Marie Voltaire's tragedy, produced by the Ida Rubinstein Ballet at the Paris Opera in May 1934 with choreography by M.Fokine and costumes by A.Benois. Collection Mr. and Mrs. Nikita D.Lobanov-Rostovsky, London.*

exhibition of the Association of Artists of Revolutionary Russia (AKhRR). Other members included A.Grigoriev, P.Kiselev, E.Katsman, N.Kotov, S.Malyutin, P.Radimov, P.Shukhmin, A.Skachko, G.Sukhanov and V.Zhuravlev.

He was included in the major exhibition in Moscow in 1927 marking the tenth anniversary of the Revolution and in the First Touring Exhibition of Painting and Graphics which opened in Moscow in 1929. He was represented at the jubilee exhibition Artists of the RSFSR over 15 Years held at the Russian Museum, Leningrad, in 1932 and at the 1932 Venice Biennale.

Transport is Getting It Right, 1923, is a hymn to railway transport closely recalling Monet's *Gare St.-Lazare* paintings but set in an empty area and executed in a more academic style. Only the approaching engine's red star communicates the message of the title.

Marshal Zhukov is a distant and in a way popularised reworking of a theme by David in which the Marshal is mounted on a foaming white stallion treading the Nazi regalia underfoot with Berlin in flames in the background.

Lit A.M.Muratov, V.Manin et al. *Zhivopis' 20-30kh godov*, Sankt-Peterburg, 1991.
Coll RM.

YAKOVLEV, D. I.   a.1918-19
He exhibited at the Fifth State Exhibition: From Impressionism to Non-Objective Art in Moscow 1918-19.

YAKOVLEV, I.   a.1924
He was represented at the First Discussional Exhibition of Active Revolutionary Art in Moscow in 1924.

YAKOVLEV, Ivan Eremeevich   1787-1843
Portraitist.
Coll TG.

YAKOVLEV, Mikhail Nikolaevich (JAKOWLEW, Michel) 1880-1942
Painter, theatre designer. He exhibited with the First Izdebsky International Salon 1909-10 in Odessa.

After the Revolution his work was included in the First Exhibition of the Moscow Contemporary Art Store in January 1919 and his name appeared on the April 1919 list of artists for acquisitions by the envisaged Museum of Painterly Culture. He participated in the Third Exhibition of Paintings held at Ryazan in 1919. Sometimes he signed his work 'Ya.M.' or 'Michel Jakowlew'.

Theatre design 1910 costumes for the play *Zhenshchina i Smert'* (Death and the Maiden).
Coll TG.

YAKOVLEV, Pavel Filippovich   1853-1921
Portraitist.
Coll TG.

YAKOVLEV, Vasili Nikolaevich (JAKOVLEFF, W.) 1893-1953
Painter. He exhibited in the 1921 exhibition of the World of Art in Moscow. He was included in the major exhibition in Moscow in 1927 marking the tenth anniversary of the Revolution and the jubilee exhibition Artists of the RSFSR over 15 Years held at the Russian Museum, Leningrad, in 1932. The date of his death is sometimes given as 1956.
Writings V.N.Yakovlev *O zhivopisi* (On Painting), 1951.
Coll RM.

YAKOVLEVA-SHAPORINA, L. V.   a.1932
She was represented at the jubilee exhibition Artists of the RSFSR over 15 Years held at the Russian Museum, Leningrad, in 1932.

YAKULOV (YAKOULOV), Georgiy Bogdanovich 1884-1928
Painter, theatre designer. Born at Tiflis (Tblisi), Georgia. He studied at the Moscow College under Yuon 1900-2. He visited the Far East before 1905. He contributed to the *Stefanos* exhibition 1907-8. From 1908 he participated in the exhibitions Contemporary Trends and The Wreath. He exhibited with the Vienna Secession in 1909 and visited Rome, Florence, Venice, Siena and Padua in 1910 before returning to Moscow. He exhibited with the Union of Russian Artists in St. Petersburg in 1910, with the Izdebsky Salon of 1910-11 in Odessa and with the World of Art in 1911. He visited Robert and Sonia Delaunay in France for the summer of 1913 and in that year exhibited in Berlin at the First German Autumn Salon at the Galerie Der Sturm. He exhibited three works with the World of Art in Moscow in 1913 including 'Urban Landscape-construction on the Speeds of Glass'. The poet and critic Apollinaire published in the *Mercure de France* (Paris, 16 April, 1914) the manifesto *L'Occident et nous* (*My i zapad*) which was composed by Yakulov with the writer Benedikt Livshits and the composer Artur Lure (Arthur Lourié). Yakulov contributed to the *Pervyy zhurnal russkikh futuristov* (The First Russian Futurist Journal), No.1-2, published in March 1914. He was called to the front during the war and wounded after which he convalesced at Tashkent. However in 1916 he was represented in the exhibition Leftist Trends.

After the Revolution he exhibited with the World of Art in December 1917 in Moscow. He was involved with the decorations at the Café Pittoresque on the Kuznetsky Most in Moscow with Tatlin and contributed to the decoration of the Poets' Café in Moscow along with Lentulov, Mayakovsky, David Burlyuk and Khodasevich 1917-18. He taught at the Free Art Studios (SVOMAS) in Moscow c.1918. His work was included in the First Exhibition of the Moscow Contemporary Art Store in January 1919 and his name appeared on the April 1919 list of artists for acquisitions by the envisaged Museum of Painterly Culture. He exhibited in the first Obmokhu exhibition in May 1919 in Moscow and was associated with the painter Boris Erdman and the Imagist poets at the cabaret the Stable of Pegasus in 1919. He also took part in the third exhibition of Obmokhu, the Society of Young Artists, in Moscow in May 1921, along with Ioganson, Medunetsky and others.

His first major personal exhibition was held at the Red Cock Café in Moscow in 1921. He was represented at the First Russian Art Exhibition in Berlin in 1922 and exhibited in Paris in 1923 and 1925 at the International Exhibition. He became an active theatre designer working for the Kamerny (Chamber) Theatre in Moscow from 1918 and for the First National Theatre in Erevan. He contributed to the Third Exhibition of Paintings by Artists from Kaluga and Moscow held in Kaluga in 1925.

He moved to Paris in 1927 but was included in the 1928 exhibition of Acquisitions by the State Art Collections Fund held in Moscow.

He died of tuberculosis at Erevan. An international committee was mooted to pay homage to his achievements. This was to comprise Robert Delaunay, Diaghilev, Lunacharsky, Picasso, Prokofiev, Stanislavsky and Tairov. The first posthumous retrospective exhibition was held at the National Museum of Erevan in 1967.

Theatre design 1918 November: Tairov's production of A.Schnitzler's *Zelenyy popugay* (The Green Parrot) at the Red Cockerel studio club to mark the first anniversary of the Revolution.

1918 Claudel's *The Exchange* at the Kamerny (Chamber) Theatre, Moscow. Meyerhold worked on this project in collaboration with the director Tairov.

1920 May: Tairov's production, with music by Henri Fortier, of E.T.A.Hoffmann's *Printsessa Brambilla* (Princess Brambilla) at the Kamerny (Chamber) Theatre, Moscow. This was a colourful production designed in purple, orange and green and seeking fantastic effects by the use of hangings and masks. It also incorporated grotesque spiralling steps and columnar constructions reminiscent of Dmitriev, Miturich and even Tatlin though overlayed here with a spirit of phantasmagoria. Tairov considered this a new kind of presentation that was neither drama nor pantomime but employed declamation, gesture and mime. Tairov lectured on the production on 31 May 1920.

Yakulov was among the performers.

1920 designs (unrealised on stage) for Meyerhold's production of Mayakovsky's *Mystery-Bouffe*.

1920 Wagner's *Rienzi*, an unrealised production planned for Meyerhold's Theatre of the RSFSR. Designs, which incorporated elements resembling pantomime, were evolved in collaboration with V.M.Bebutova.

1922 June: Tairov's production of E.T.A.Hoffmann's *Signor Formica* (*Sin'yor Formika*) at the Kamerny Theatre, Moscow.

1922 October: Tairov's production of Lecoq's *Giroflé-Girofla* at the Kamerny Theatre, Moscow, the costumes of which were evolved in maquettes in a system devised by L.L.Luk'yanov. The dynamics were evolved by Tairov and Yakulov together, using transformable stage props, spirals, circles, arcs and striped costumes for the buffoonery and musical comedy.

1925 Shakespeare's *King Lear*, a projected production for the National Armenian Theatre, Yerevan.

1926 March: Tairov's production of A.P.Glebov's *Rosita* at the Kamerny Theatre, Moscow, which incorporated a stylised architectural assemblage.

1927 June: constructions and costumes for Diaghilev's production of *Pas d'Acier*, created by Prokofiev and Yakulov

Georgiy Yakulov. Study for the Costumes of Four Academicians in the Play 'Signor Formica', *1922. Gouache, pencil. Inscribed in Russian lower right '4 Academicians'. 31.5 x 47.4 cm.*
The play by Vladimir Sokolov, based on a story by E.T.A.Hoffmann, was performed at Tairov's Kamerny (Chamber) Theatre in Moscow in June 1922.
Collection Mr. and Mrs. Nikita D.Lobanov-Rostovsky, London.

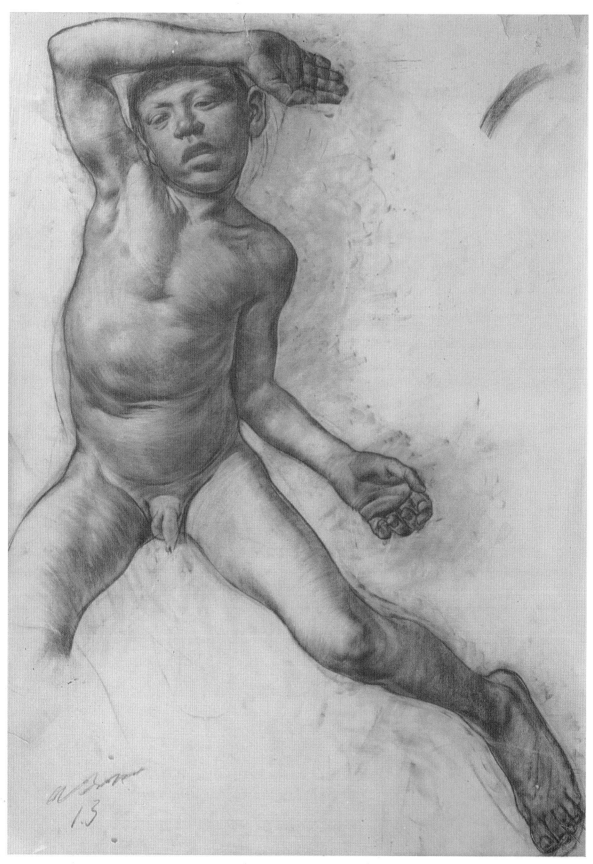

Aleksandr Yakovlev. Nude Study, *1913. Charcoal on paper. Signed and dated. 98 x 50.5 cm.*
Malmö Konstmuseum.

Georgiy Yakulov. Study for Decorations at the Stable of Pegasus cabaret, *1919. Gouache and ink. 15 x 24.5 cm. Collection Mr. and Mrs. Nikita D.Lobanov-Rostovsky, London.*

with music by Prokofiev and choreography by Massine, a Constructivist set, at the Théâtre Sarah Bernhardt in Paris. The title was Yakulov's. The ballet depicts the period of destruction of the Old Regime in Act 1, followed by the Factory in Action showing Revolutionary enthusiasm. Yakulov employed ladders, platforms, turning wheels, noises and flashing lights to make an industrial ballet. Massine's choreography transformed the dancers into the revolving parts of a great machine.

He also executed designs for Shakespeare's *Measure for Measure* and for Sophocles' *Oedipus*.

Lit G.Yakulov *Avtobiografiya*, Moscow, 1927 (in Armenian). *Diaghilev and Russian Stage Designers, a Loan Exhibition from the Collection of Mr. and Mrs. N.Lobanov-Rostovsky*, International Exhibitions Foundation, Washington, 1972-4. *Twilight of the Tsars*, London, 1991. S.Aladzhalov *Yakulov*, Erevan, 1971. *G.Yakulov*, exh. cat., Erevan, 1975. *G.Yakulov*, exh. cat., Moscow, 1975. *Paris-Moscou*, 1979. E.Kostina *Yakulov*, Moscow, 1979. J.E.Bowlt *Russian Stage Design. Scenic Innovation. From the Collection of Mr. and Mrs. Nikita D.Lobanov-Rostovsky*, Jackson, MS, exh. cat.,1982. Nancy Van Norman Baer *Theatre in Revolution, Russian Avant-Garde Stage Design 1913-1935*, San Francisco and London, 1991. Dzhon Boult (John Bowlt) *Khudozhniki russkogo teatra. Sobranie Nikity i Niny Lobanovykh-Rostovskikh*, Moscow, 1991.

Coll TG; RM; Bakhrushin Theatre Museum, Moscow; National Museum, Erevan; MNAM, Paris; Musée de l'Opera, Paris.

Colour plate above.

YAKUNCHIKOVA-WEBER (-VEBER), Maria Vasilievna   1870-1902

Painter, graphic artist, embroiderer. Born at Wiesbaden. She grew up in Moscow in a family with many artistic connections. She studied privately under N.A.Martynov from 1883. She studied as an external student at the Moscow College from 1885 and took evening classes with Polenova 1886-9 where she met Korovin, Levitan and others. She was also closely associated with the Abramtsevo artists and with Polenova in particular whose revival of traditional handicrafts inspired her to execute pokerwork and embroideries. She began to collect folk art 1887-9.

She travelled to Austria and Italy in 1888 and to France and Germany in 1889. She worked mainly in Western Europe thereafter. She was attending the Académie Julian in Paris under W.A.Bouguereau and Tony Robert-Fleury 1889-90. She began to make coloured etchings 1892-3. She was unimpressed by the Rosicrucian Salon in Paris in 1894. Polenova visited her in Paris in 1895. She married the doctor L.N.Weber in 1896. She began to illustrate books in 1897. She designed textiles and toys from 1898. Diaghilev commissioned a cover for the journal *Mir Iskusstva* (World of Art) in 1898, published on issues 13-24 in 1899 — a frankly decorative Art Nouveau design of a swan in a pool by a forest executed in blue and yellow with folk art stylisations. She exhibited with the World of Art 1899-1902. She directed the Abramtsevo embroidery workshops after Polenova's death in 1898 and executed her plan for an exhibition of folk art for the International Exhibition in Paris in 1900. *(cont.)*

Elizaveta Yakunina. Study for the Costume of a Clown, *1923. Watercolour, pencil, black crayon. Signed lower right. 30.5 x 23.5 cm.*
Designed for K.E.Gibshman's comic spectacle 'Circus' based on the work of S.Ya.Marshak adapted for marionettes.
Collection Mr. and Mrs. Nikita D.Lobanov-Rostovsky, London.

She suffered from tuberculosis and died near Geneva in Switzerland.
Lit M.Kiselev *M.V.Yakunchikova*, Moscow, 1979. M.N.Yablonskaya *Women Artists of Russia's New Age*, London, 1990.
Coll TG; RM.
Colour plate p.470.

YAKUNINA, Elizaveta Petrovna　　　　**1892-1964**
Theatre designer. She designed *Tsirk* (Circus) based on the stories of S.Ya.Marshak for the Marionette Theatre, Petrograd, in 1923.
Lit Dzhon Boult (John Bowlt) *Khudozhniki russkogo teatra. Sobranie Nikity i Niny Lobanovykh-Rostovskikh*, Moscow, 1991.

YAMSHCHIKOVA-MALINOVSKAYA, N. I.　　**a.1918**
She was represented at the First Exhibition of Works of the Professional Union of Artists in Moscow in 1918.

YANCHENKO, Aleksandr Stepanovich　　**a.1918-1923**
He was engaged in Agitprop decorations in the early revolutionary years including work on the propaganda trains *Lenin (October Revolution)* and *Soviet Caucasus* in 1920. He was included in the enormous survey Exhibition of Paintings by Petrograd Artists of All Tendencies 1919-1923 held in Petrograd in 1923.

YANENKO, Fedosiy Ivanovich　　　　**1762-1809**
Portraitist.
Coll TG.

YANOV, Aleksandr Stepanovich   1857-1918?
Portraitist.
Coll TG.

YAREMICH, Stepan Petrovich   1869-1939
Painter, art historian. He exhibited with the World of Art 1902-6 and with the Union of Russian Artists 1903-10. He was represented in Diaghilev's display of Russian art at the 1906 Salon d'Automne in Paris. He assisted on the execution of A.Golovin's designs for Mussorgsky's *Boris Godunov* at the Théâtre de l'Opéra, Paris, in 1908. He was a member of the second World of Art Society 1910-24.
After the Revolution he participated in the First State Free Exhibition of Artworks in Petrograd in 1919 and the jubilee exhibition Artists of the RSFSR over 15 Years held at the Russian Museum, Leningrad, in 1932.

YAROSHENKO, Nikolai Aleksandrovich   1846-1898
History painter of heroic themes. Born at Poltava into a military family. He trained as an engineer but also attended the school of the Society for the Encouragement of the Arts in St. Petersburg and then part-time at the Academy 1874-6. He exhibited with the Wanderers from 1875 and became a member in 1876. He led the Wanderers after the death of Kramskoy.
The Stoker, 1878, TG, depicts the worker as an isolated and dramatic image executed almost entirely in shades of red, theatrically lit from the furnace which he stokes. Alert but emphatically ordinary, the worker is neither stylised nor idealised but presented as typifying a salt of the earth and in this sense a kind of hero. The red light picks out the veins of the strong hands. The lack of rhetoric is therefore essential to the achievement in order that the viewer may recognise and identify with the figure. This suggests the particular kind of audience that the Wanderers sought among the merchants, peasantry and sympathetic intellectuals.
Coll TG.

YARTSEV, Grigoriy Fedorovich   1858-1918
Landscape painter.
Coll TG.

YASINOVSKY   a.1925
Sculptor. He was a member of the Society of Moscow Artists founded in 1925.

YASINSKY, A. A.   a.1919
Painter. He was represented in the Fourth State Exhibition of Paintings (*IV Gosudarstvennaya vystavka kartin*) in Moscow in 1919.

YASNOPOLSKY, Stepan   later 18th century
Portraitist.
Coll TG.

YASNOVSKY, Fedor Ivanovich   1833-1902
Portraitist.
Coll TG.

YASTRZHEMBSKY, Svyatoslav   a.1912-1926
He was a member of the group *Oslinyy Khvost* (Donkey's Tail) along with Larionov and Goncharova in 1912.
After the Revolution he exhibited at the Fifth State

Exhibition: From Impressionism to Non-Objective Art in Moscow 1918-19. He exhibited at the third and last exhibition of the *Makovets* group in Moscow 1925-6.

YATMANOV, Grigoriy   a.1919
He was a member of the Art Section of the People's Commissariat of the Enlightenment under David Shterenberg c.1918-19.

YAVLENSKY, Alexsei Georgievich = JAWLENSKY, A.

YUDIN, Lev Aleksandrovich   1903-1941
Painter. Born at Vitebsk. He attended the Vitebsk School of Art from 1919. He was a member of the *Unovis* group of Suprematists associated with Malevich, Chashnik, Lissitzky, Ermolaeva and others in Vitebsk. He published an article *On Still-Life* in *Unovis* No.2, Vitebsk, 1921. He followed Malevich to Petrograd in 1922. He was represented at the First Russian Art Exhibition in Berlin in 1922 and at the jubilee exhibition Artists of the RSFSR over 15 Years held at the Russian Museum, Leningrad, in 1932.
Still-life with Orange Creamer and Bottle, 1930s, RM, is loose in form giving the objects a liquid appearance. Colour however is kept clearly distinct for each object and is carefully tuned.
Coll RM.

YUNGE (née TOLSTAYA), Ekaterina Fedorovna
1843-1913
Landscape painter.
Coll TG.

YUON, Konstantin Fedorovich   1875-1958
Painter of brightly lit scenes of village and city life, theatre designer, Academician. Born in Moscow. He studied under K.Savitsky, Arkhipov and Korovin at the Moscow College 1892-8. He joined Serov's studio in 1898. He exhibited widely and participated in the Wanderers exhibition in 1900 as well as the World of Art exhibitions of 1902-3 and 1906. He was also active in the Union of Russian Artists in the period 1903-23. He was represented in Diaghilev's display of Russian art at the 1906 Salon d'Automne in Paris. He travelled to Germany, Switzerland and France. He was in Venice in 1907 and Rome in 1911. He directed a School of Drawing together with Ivan Dudin and Popova was amongst his numerous pupils 1908-9.
After the Revolution his work was included in the First Exhibition of the Moscow Contemporary Art Store in January 1919 and his name appeared on the April 1919 list of artists for acquisitions by the envisaged Museum of Painterly Culture. He was represented in the Fourth State Exhibition of Paintings (*IV Gosudarstvennaya vystavka kartin*) in Moscow in 1919 and at the First Russian Art Exhibition in Berlin in 1922. He contributed to the exhibition Art of Moscow Theatre 1918-1923 held in Moscow in 1923.
He became a member of AKhRR in 1925. His work was included in the exhibition of Soviet art held at Harbin in 1926 and in Japan in 1927, in the major exhibition in Moscow in 1927 marking the tenth anniversary of the Revolution, the 1928 exhibition of Acquisitions by the State Art Collections Fund held in Moscow and the jubilee exhibition Artists of the

Maria Yakunchikova-Weber. From the Windows of the Old House at Vedenskoe, *1897. Oil on canvas. 88.3 x 106.5 cm. State Tretyakov Gallery, Moscow.*

RSFSR over 15 Years held at the Russian Museum, Leningrad, in 1932.

He taught at the Repin Institute in the 1930s and at the Surikov Art Institute in Moscow 1952-5. He died in Moscow.

*A Beautiful Sunny Day, 1910, RM, is grandiose small town genre painting. Brilliant daylight illuminates the snowy streets and roofs and the birch trees are lit up against the sky. Busy provincials, wrapped up against the cold, slide down roofs and push toboggans or gossip and watch. All is in its place and spring is on its way. What distinguishes Yuon's mastery of this metier is a monumental grandeur and expanse coupled with a broad handling of creamy colour however intricate the scene. His painting exudes calm despite its wealth of incident. He embodies a sense of permanence and a celebration of national identity which avoids sentimentality.

*The New Planet, 1921, TG, is a vision of panic worthy of H.G.Wells. Whilst it is uncharacteristic of Yuon, it makes memorable science fiction. Figures flee in despair, backlit by immense planetary orbs which fill the sky amidst flaring rays of orange-yellow light. Destruction is immanent and inevitable.

Theatre design 1913 May: Diaghilev's production of *Boris Godunov* at the Théâtre des Champs-Elysées in Paris.

1919 M.Gorky's *Starik* (The Old Man) at the Maly Theatre, Moscow. One design shows the back garden of a house on a moonlit summer night with figures entering.

1921 October Gogol's *Revizor* (The Government Inspector) directed by Stanislavsky at the Moscow Art Theatre.

1934 February M.Gorky's *Egor Bulychov i drugie* (Egor Bulychov and Others) at the Moscow Art Theatre. One design depicts a heavily overdecorated and overfurnished domestic interior.

Writings K.Yuon *Ob Iskusstve* (On Art), Moscow, 1959.

Lit Ya.Apushkin *K.F.Yuon*, Moscow, 1936. N.Tretyakov *Yuon*, Moscow, 1957. I.T.Rostovtseva *K.F.Yuon*, Leningrad, 1964. *K.Yuon*, exh. cat., Moscow, 1969. T.Nordstein *Konstantin Yuon*, Leningrad, 1972. *Paris-Moscou*, 1979. Yu.Osmolovsky *Yuon*, Moscow, 1982. J.E.Bowlt *Russian Stage Design. Scenic Innovation. From the Collection of Mr. and Mrs. Nikita D.Lobanov-Rostovsky*, Jackson, MS, exh. cat.,1982.

Coll TG; RM; Pushkin Museum, Moscow; Bakhrushin Theatre Museum, Moscow.

Colour plate opposite.

YUR'EVA, Natalya L. a.1918-19
She exhibited at the First Exhibition of Works of the

Konstantin Yuon. Village in Winter, *c.1910. Gouache.* 22.5 x 31 cm.
Collection Mr. and Mrs. Nikita D.Lobanov-Rostovsky, London.

Professional Union of Artists in Moscow in 1918, at the Fifth State Exhibition: From Impressionism to Non-Objective Art in Moscow in 1918-19 and at the Third Exhibition of Paintings held at Ryazan in 1919.
Lit E.Weiss *Russische Avant-Garde, 1910-1930, Sammlung Ludwig, Köln*, Munich, 1986.
Coll Sammlung Ludwig, Cologne.

YURGENSON, Aleksandra Petrovna   1869-1946
Portraitist.
Coll TG.

YUROV, Grigoriy Vasilievich   d.1895+
Painter whose subjects include a cathedral interior.
Coll TG.

YUSHANOV, Aleksei Lukich   1840-1865+
Painter of socially committed genre.
Coll TG.

YUSTITSKY, Valentin Mikhailovich   1892-1951
Theatre designer. He was engaged on Agitprop decorations at Saratov 1918-20. He exhibited with the 4 Arts society in Leningrad including the exhibition of 1928 at the Russian Museum and in the 1928 exhibition of Acquisitions by the State Art Collections Fund held in Moscow. He exhibited with the group The Thirteen in 1929.
Theatre design 1937 M.Maeterlinck's play *Slepy* (The Blind).

YUTKEVICH, Sergei   1904-1985
Theatre designer, film director. Born in St. Petersburg. He exhibited with the Union of New Tendencies in Art in Petrograd in June 1922. He died in Moscow.
Theatre design 1921 Robert Schumann's *Carnaval*, ballet choreographed by K.Goleizovsky for the Chamber Ballet, Moscow.
1922 V.Mass' *Good Treatment for Horses* directed by Nikolai Foregger at the Foregger Studio. A costume design resembles Erdman's stylisation of the figure into elegant and witty assemblages of arcs and straight lines, but its Russian Futurist shading along one edge of his line recalls Popova or Vesnin more closely. The set included a mechanistic assemblage of gymnastic equipment and flashing lights.
Lit Nancy Van Norman Baer *Theatre in Revolution, Russian Avant-Garde Stage Design 1913-1935*, San Francisco and London, 1991.
Coll Bakhrushin Theatre Museum.

Z

ZABOLOTSKY, Petr Efimovich   **1803-1866**
Painter of genre themes, portraits and views. He studied at the
Academy in St. Petersburg under A.G.Varnek and A.E.Egorov
in the 1820s. He exhibited from 1830. He gave drawing
lessons to Lermontov 1836-7 and his works include *Portrait of
M.Lermontov*, 1837. He taught at the Drawing School of the
Society for the Encouragement of the Arts, St. Petersburg,
1842-8, at the War Topography Depot in the 1850s and at the
Technical Institute 1859-60.
Coll TG; RM; Gorky Art Museum.

ZACK, Léon = ZAK, L.V.

ZADKINE, Osip   **1890-1967**
Major Cubist sculptor, printmaker, illustrator, who worked in
Paris. Born at Smolensk. He was at Sunderland, England, in
1905 and in 1906 in London. He studied at the Regent Street
Polytechnic in London in 1907, the Central School of Arts
and Crafts, London, in 1908 and visited Vitebsk on holidays.
In 1909 he moved to Paris where he studied under Injalbert at
the Ecole des Beaux-Arts and where in 1910 he settled in the
studio complex La Ruche in Montparnasse. He visited
Smolensk in 1910. He exhibited at the Salon des Indépendants
and at the Salon d'Automne in Paris in 1911. He met the
poets Apollinaire and Cendrars as well as Archipenko,
Lipchitz, Picasso and Survage in 1912 and became a central
figure in the development of Cubist sculpture. He illustrated
Vera Imber's *Poèmes* published in Paris in 1913. He exhibited
at the New Secession in Berlin in 1914.
During the First World War he served in a medical corps and
was able to execute drawings recording what he saw. He
published twenty etchings on his return to Paris in 1918 and
the same year he met the painters Kisling and Modigliani with
whom he exhibited in Paris. He held one-man exhibitions at
the Galerie Le Centaure in 1918, Galerie Barbazanges in Paris
in 1921 and in 1923 exhibited at the Galerie Paul Guillaume.
He was represented at the International Exhibition in Paris in
1925. Very many exhibitions followed internationally until his
death.
His later sculpture retained the facility to deform and
reorganise forms and figures which his experience of Cubism
had first permitted but his forms were increasingly organic
and fluid so that their suggestive qualities more readily evoked
emotional rather than intellectual themes. In this respect he
became a powerful sculptor whose work at times was able to
respond to the poetic and expressive sides of Surrealism in
Paris. He contributed to the exhibition of Contemporary
Russian Art held at Philadelphia in 1932. He published a cycle
of lithographs, *L'Apocalypse*, in Paris in 1961. He died in Paris.
Writings O.Zadkine *Poèmes*, London, 1964. O.Zadkine *Le
maillet et le ciseau*, Paris, 1968.
Lit P.Humbourg *Zadkine*, Paris, 1928. A.de Ridder *Zadkine*,

Paris, 1929. P.Hessaerts *Ossip Zadkine. La sculpture ailée*, Antwerp,
1939. R.Cogniat *Zadkine*, Paris, 1958. A.M.Hammacher *Zadkine*,
Amsterdam, 1954, and Paris, 1961. I.Jianou *Zadkine*, Paris, 1964.
Coll MNAM, Paris; Musée Zadkine, Paris.

ZAGORSKY, Nikolai Petrovich   **1849-1893**
Painter of genre and religious themes. Born at St. Petersburg.
He studied under at the Academy in St. Petersburg in the
1860s.
He exhibited from 1875, with the Wanderers from 1880, and
was a member of the Wanderers in 1891. He illustrated *The
Great Album of Works by A.S.Pushkin*, St. Petersburg, 1887. He
taught at the Drawing School of the Society for the
Encouragement of the Arts, St. Petersburg, 1889-93. He died
at St. Petersburg. An exhibition was held in St. Petersburg in
1894.
Coll TG; RM.

ZAGOSKIN, David Efimovich   **1900-1942**
Painter, graphic artist, lithographer. Born in the Vitebsk
region. He studied at the Odessa Art College 1916-17.
After the Revolution he studied at the Saratov Free Art Studios
under F.K.Konstantinov 1918-20. He was also engaged on
Agitprop decorations at Saratov 1918-20. He exhibited with
the Circle of Artists in Leningrad, of which he was a founder
member, between 1927 and 1929. He was included in the
1928 exhibition of Acquisitions by the State Art Collections
Fund held in Moscow and in the jubilee exhibition Artists of
the RSFSR over 15 Years held at the Russian Museum,
Leningrad, in 1932. He died in Leningrad.
Coll RM; Saratov Art Museum.

ZAITSEV = ZAYTSEV

ZAITSEVA = ZAYTSEVA

ZAK, Lev Vasil'evich (ZACK, Léon)   **1892-1980**
Painter, theatre designer, critic, poet. Born at Nizhny-
Novgorod, the son of a pharmacist. As a poet he worked under
the pseudonym Khrisanf and as a critic used the pseudonym
M.Rossiyansky. He studied at the faculty of Letters in
Moscow whilst attending private academies to study art. He
was taught by Yakimchenko and he then studied under
F.I.Rerberg and I.Mashkov in the 1910s. He studied literary
history at Moscow University in 1913.
After the Revolution he travelled to the Crimea and to
Odessa. He emigrated in 1920, moving first to Italy 1920-1
where he exhibited in Florence and Rome, then to Berlin in
1922. There he designed a production of the *Ballets
Romantiques Russes* directed by Boris Romanov for the Théâtre
Russe. He followed this to Paris where he settled in 1923. He
exhibited widely and contributed to the Salon des
Indépendants and Salon d'Automne.
He was associated with Waldemar George's *Néo-Humanisme*
in 1932, as was Tchelitchew. In his later years he designed for
the Aubusson and Gobelins tapestry workshops and from 1951
he designed stained glass. He died in Paris.
Theatre design *Giselle*, ballet, music by A.Adam,
choreography B.Romanov, produced by the Ballets Russes de
Vera Nemtchinova at the Théâtre des Champs-Elysées, Paris.
Lit P.Courthion *Léon Zack*, Paris, 1960. *Diaghilev and Russian
Stage Designers, a Loan Exhibition from the Collection of Mr. and*

Mrs. N.Lobanov-Rostovsky, International Exhibitions Foundation, Washington, 1972-4. J.E.Bowlt *Russian Stage Design. Scenic Innovation. From the Collection of Mr. and Mrs. Nikita D.Lobanov-Rostovsky*, Jackson, MS, exh. cat.,1982. *Twilight of the Tsars*, London, 1991.

ZAKHAROV, Guriy Filippovich   1926-1964+
Graphic artist. Born in the Kalinin region. His work includes the print *Ten Minutes after Midnight*, 1964, TG, which depicts the interior of a wooden house in which a woman is reading. There is atmospheric effect in the moonlight but technically the print shows a clear debt to the example of Favorsky.
Coll TG.

ZAKHAROV, Iov (Iev)   a.1766-1793+
History painter. He was painter to the Chancellery of Buildings in St. Petersburg in 1780-90. His *Dying Cleopatra*, TG, is dated 1793.
Coll TG.

ZAKHAROV, Ivan Ivanovich   1885-1969
Painter. He was engaged in Agitprop decorations in the early revolutionary years working with N.N.Agap'eva on costumes for street parades, one of which featured a procession led by a large globe of the world inscribed 'Hail the Power of the Proletariat'. His work was included in the First Exhibition of the Moscow Contemporary Art Store in January 1919 and he participated in the Third Exhibition of Paintings held at Ryazan in 1919. He was also included in the major exhibition in Moscow in 1927 marking the tenth anniversary of the Revolution.
Coll TG.

ZAKHAROV(-CHECHENETS), Petr Zakharovich
1816-1846
Major portrait painter. Born in the Tver region. He lived at Tiflis until 1828 and Moscow until 1830. He studied at the Academy in St. Petersburg under A.N.Zauerveyd. He lived at St. Petersburg 1830-42 and then Moscow until 1846. His works were influenced by the example of Karl Bryullov.
Coll TG.

ZAKLIKOVSKAYA, Sofia Lyudvigovna   1899-1975
Painter. She was a follower of Filonov whose almost mosaic splintering of colour, form and narrative into a kaleidoscopic effect of clear, bright colours she adopted in works such as *Old and New Life-styles*, 1927, RM.
Coll RM.

ZALEMAN, Gugo Romanovich   1859-1919
Academic painter, sculptor. Born in St. Petersburg. He travelled on a scholarship to Dresden and Munich 1885-9. He also worked in Florence and Rome.
He taught at the Academy in St. Petersburg from 1889-1917 where his pupils included V.V.Kuznetsov and Petr Konchalovsky in the period 1898-1905. His sculptures of animals included a *Bison*, 1901, RM, which is closely observed and explicit in the detail of its shaggy coat.
After the Revolution he taught at the Drawing School of the Society for the Encouragement of the Arts and at the Free Art Studios in Petrograd in1918. He died at Petrograd.
Coll RM; Khabarovsk Museum of Art.

ZALIT (ZALE), Karl Fritzevich   1888-1942
Latvian monumental sculptor. He studied under V.S.Bogatyrev at the Kazan Art School until 1913, at the Drawing School of the Society for the Encouragement of the Arts, Petrograd, under G.R.Zaleman in 1915 and at the Free Art Studios under Matveev in 1916-21.
After the Revolution his monuments to *N.A.Dobrolyubov*, 1918, and to *Garibaldi*, 1919, were early responses to Lenin's call for monumental propaganda. He made a monument to *Marx* for Vitebsk 1919-20.
He worked in a sculpture studio in Berlin 1921-3 and was represented at the First Russian Art Exhibition in Berlin in 1922.
He lived at Riga from 1923. He designed a *Monument to Liberty* at Riga 1931-5. He taught at the Latvian Academy 1936-42.
Coll Latvian Art Museum, Riga.

ZAL'KALN(S), Teodor(s) Eduardovich   1876-1972
Latvian portrait and medal sculptor. He studied print and drawing 1893-9. He travelled on a scholarship to Paris 1899-1903 where he worked under Rodin and subsequently under Bourdelle 1899-1901. He visited Switzerland in 1904 and Italy 1907-9.
After the Revolution he was amongst the first to respond to the call for monumental propaganda, designing monuments to the writer *Chernyshevsky* in 1918 and to *Blanqui* and *Skryabin* in 1919 in accordance with Lenin's plan. The *Chernyshevsky* monument was essentially a bust arising directly out of its plinth in the manner of a herm. He also executed monuments at this time to *Auguste Blanqui* in March 1919 and to *Lieutenant Shmit* in 1919.
He lived at Riga from 1920 but visited Italy in 1926, 1937 and 1938, Germany in 1924 and Denmark in 1938. He died at Riga.
Seated Mother, 1916, granite, Latvian Art Museum, Riga, is a woman wearing a kerchief and cloak. The controlled surfaces have a smoothness and simplicity appropriate to the medium. A minimum of detail is used to indicate the figure beneath the cloak.
Lit R.Chaupova *T.E.Zal'kan*, Moscow, 1974.
Coll TG; RM; Latvian Art Museum, Riga.

ZAMETT = ZHAMET

ZAMIRAILO, Viktor Dmitirevich   1868-1939
Ukrainian painter, decorative artist, graphic artist, illustrator. Born in the Kiev region. He studied under N.Murashko at the Kiev School of Drawing 1881-6. He executed murals for the Kirillov Church and St. Vladimir's Cathedral in Kiev. He also provided illustrations for books and reviews including *Zhupel*, *Zritel'*, *Lukomor'e* and the *World of Art*. He exhibited with the Union of Russian Artists 1907-10.
After the Revolution he served on the Art Collegium for Literary Publishing with responsibility for the illustration of Russian traditional stories. He died at Peterhof.
Lit *Twilight of the Tsars*, London, 1991.
Coll TG; RM.

ZAMOSHKIN, Aleksandr Ivanovich   1899-1977
Painter, graphic artist, writer on art. Born in the Tver region. He studied at the Stroganov College 1912-18.
After the Revolution he studied at the Free Art Studios

under Bromirsky and Lentulov 1918-20. He also exhibited at the Fifth State Exhibition: From Impressionism to Non-Objective Art in Moscow 1918-19 and appeared on the April 1919 list of artists for acquisitions by the envisaged Museum of Painterly Culture. He exhibited in the first Obmokhu exhibition in May 1919 in Moscow. He worked at a textile factory 1919-21. He also took part in the third exhibition of Obmokhu, the Society of Young Artists, in Moscow in May 1921, along with Ioganson, Medunetsky and others. He was designing posters for the Rosta Agency in the early 1920s. He was represented at the First Russian Art Exhibition in Berlin in 1922. He died in Moscow.
Coll TG.

ZARETSKY, Andrei Antonovich　　　　　**b.1864**
Painter.
Coll TG.

ZARETSKY, Nikolai Vasilievich　　　　　**1876-1959**
Graphic artist, painter, critic. He studied at the Drawing School of the Society for the Encouragement of the Arts, St. Petersburg, 1911-12 and at the Academy in St. Petersburg under Yan Tsionglinsky and Kardovsky 1913-14. He specialised in book design and vignettes. He exhibited from 1907. In 1907 he replaced V.Markov as the editor of the journal *Vystavochny Vestnik* in St. Petersburg. He assisted the collector Shchukin in his purchase of French paintings in Paris. He exhibited with both the Union of Youth in 1910 and with the New Society of Artists between 1907 and 1914.
From the early 1920s he lived in Prague and Berlin.

ZARUBIN, Viktor Ivanovich　　　　　**1866-1928**
Landscape painter. Born at Kharkov. He studied physics and mathematics at Kharkov University, then studied at the Schreider School in Kharkov and 1893-6 at the Académie Julian in Paris under Lefebvre and Robert-Fleury. He also studied under Kuindzhi at the Academy in St. Petersburg 1896-8. He exhibited from 1897 and worked in St. Petersburg. He was a member of the Wanderers in 1916.
After the Revolution he made Agitprop decorations in Petrograd 1918-19 and was involved in the organisation of exhibitions. He was engaged in theatre design at the Petrograd Theatre of Musical Comedy 1920-1. He was included in the enormous survey Exhibition of Paintings by Petrograd Artists of All Tendencies 1919-1923 held in Petrograd in 1923. He died in Leningrad.
Manifestation at the Factory, 1917, Museum of the Revolution, Moscow, is a scene of striking workers carrying banners outside the factory. It hovers between revolutionary genre painting and reportage.
Lit *Twilight of the Tsars*, London, 1991.
Coll RM; Perm Art Gallery.

**ZARUDNAYA-KAVOS, Ekaterina Sergeevna
1862-1917/18**
Graphic artist, portrait painter. Born at St. Petersburg. She studied under Chistyakov at the Academy in St. Petersburg from 1881 and at the Académie Julian in Paris 1885-6. She exhibited from 1890. She opened a painting school with A.M.Yakovlev in 1905 in St. Petersburg where Kustodiev, Lansere and others taught. In 1906 she was contributing satirical drawings to journals. She lived in St. Petersburg-

Petrograd and her portraits included *Repin* and *V.F.Komissarzhevskaya*.
Coll TG; Bakhrushin Theatre Museum, Moscow.

ZARYANKO, Sergei Konstantinovich　　　　　**1818-1870**
Painter of portraits, interiors and views. He was a pupil of Venetsianov and studied under N.Vorob'ev at the Academy. He also attended the Dresden Academy 1806-12. He worked in Paris 1812-13 and 1814 and London 1814-17.
He was a tutor of Perov. Initially a painter of interiors he became a portraitist. He died in Moscow.
Coll TG; RM; Hermitage Museum.

ZAUERVEYD, Aleksandr Ivanovich　　　　　**1783-1844**
History painter of grandiose political and military themes, graphic artist. Born at St. Petersburg. He studied at the Academy in St. Petersburg. He subsequently directed a studio of battle painting at the Academy. He died at St. Petersburg.
Coll TG.

ZAUERVEYD, Nikolai Aleksandrovich　　　　　**1836-1866**
History painter of military themes. Born at St. Petersburg, the son of A.I.Zauerveyd. He studied at the Academy in St. Petersburg under Villeval'de in the 1850s. He died at St. Petersburg.
Coll TG.

ZAVADSKY, Frants (Franz)　　　　　**d.1873**
Figure and portrait painter. He studied at the Academy in St. Petersburg from 1842.
Coll TG.

ZAV'YALOV, Fedor Semenovich　　　　　**1810-1856**
Painter. He was a leader in Russian classical themes but also painted portraits and saints for churches. Born at St. Petersburg. He studied at the Academy in St. Petersburg under A.E.Egorov from 1821. He died at St. Petersburg.
Coll TG; Museum of the Academy, St. Petersburg.

ZAV'YALOV, Ivan Fedorovich　　　　　**1893-1937**
Painter, graphic artist. Born in the Yaroslav region. He studied at the Stroganov College 1905-14 and at the Moscow College 1914-15.
After the Revolution he studied at the Free Art Studios under P.V.Kuznetsov 1918-19. His name appeared on the April 1919 list of artists for acquisitions by the envisaged Museum of Painterly Culture. He taught at the Moscow Vkhutemas 1920-3 and was a member of the *Makovets* group 1922-5.
He was a founder member of the Society of Moscow Artists and a member 1928-31. He was represented at the First Touring Exhibition of Painting and Graphics which opened in Moscow in 1929. His work included genre paintings of the Soviet kind. He died in Moscow.
Coll TG.

ZAV'YALOV, Vasili Vasil'evich　　　　　**1906-1972**
Graphic artist, lithographer, etcher. Born at Moscow. He studied under Z.E.Pichugin and S.V.Gerasimov. He was a member of AKhR 1926-32.
He was a major pioneer and exponent of the design of Soviet stamps, producing over 700 designs. He was represented at the First Russian Art Exhibition in Berlin in 1922. He died in Moscow.
Coll TG; RM.

ZAYTSEV, Evgeniy Alekseevich　　　　　**b.1908**

Belorussian painter, graphic artist. Born at Minsk. He studied at Vitebsk Technical College under V.V.Volkov in 1927-30 and subsequently under Petrov-Vodkin 1931-7. He exhibited from 1935.

He was engaged in fighting at the front 1941-2 and executed numerous paintings relating to the war. He contributed satirical anti-fascist drawings to periodicals.

Entry of the Red Army into Minsk in 1920, 1940, lost, is a patriotic painting designed to reaffirm the Soviet commitment to Minsk at the time when it was painted even though it depicts an earlier war.

ZAYTSEV (ZAITSEV), Nikita　　　　**1791-1828**

Portrait painter. His work included miniatures. He studied at the Academy in St. Petersburg from 1800. Works at the Tretyakov Gallery, Moscow, include *The Studio of the Artist*.
Coll TG.

ZAYTSEV (ZAITSEV), Nikolai Semenovich　　**1885-1938**

Painter whose work included still-life, landscapes and figure paintings. Born at Moscow. He studied under A.M.Vasnetsov at the Moscow College from 1902. He exhibited from 1906. He was a member of the Union of Russian Artists 1912-23.

After the Revolution he was a member of the Union of Realist Artists 1926-32. He died in Moscow.
Coll TG; Sverdlovsk Art Museum.

ZAYTSEVA (ZAITSEVA)　　　　　**a.1922**

She was represented at the First Russian Art Exhibition in Berlin in 1922.

ZDANEVICH (EGANBURY, IL'YAZD, ILIAZD), Il'ya Mikhailovich　　　　**1894-1975**

Futurist artist and poet. He was the brother of the Russian Futurist Kirill Zdanevich. He also used other pseudonyms: Varsanofii Parkin, Iliazd (ie IL'YA ZDanevich) and, for his book on Larionov and Goncharova published in Moscow in 1913, Eli Eganbury, a name derived by writing his name in cyrillic script but reading it as latin script. In November 1913 he launched the Futurist phenomenon *Vsechestvo* (Everythingism) which he described in 1914 as 'not a theory and not a tendency but the actual result of an approach to art from the viewpoint of its self-sufficiency and an awareness of the possibilities of material'. In January 1914 he published with Larionov a *Da-manifest* (Da-Manifesto) which appears to have predated aspects of Dada which in fact later attracted Ilya Zdanevich. He lectured on Futurist face painting at the Stray Dog cabaret in April 1914.

During the Revolution, in March 1917, he was a founder of the Freedom of Art Association in Petrograd with the artists Al'tman and Isakov as well as Mayakovsky, Meyerhold, Punin and Prokofiev. He was with the poet Kruchenykh in Tiflis (Tblisi) in 1918.

He moved to Paris after 1920 and was a participant in the performance *Coeur à Gaz* by the Dadaist poet Tristan Tzara on 6 July 1923. The costumes were by Sonia Delaunay. He was represented at the Paris International Exhibition in 1925 by books and *Le Dantyu-le-Phare* of 1923.

Futurist books 1913 Eganbury *Nataliya Goncharova. Mikhail Larionov*, Moscow, 1913.

Il'yazd *Ostraf Paskhi*, Tiflis, 1919. Il'yazd *zgA YAkaby*, Tiflis, 1920.

Il'yazd *LidantYU fAram* (*Le-Dantyu faram*, Le-Dantyu as a Beacon; *Le Dantyu-le-Phare*), Paris, 1923. Iliazd *Voskhishchenie*, Paris, 1930. Iliazd *Afat*, Paris, 1940. Iliazd *Pi'smo*, Paris, 1948. Iliazd *Poesie des mots inconnus*, Paris, 1949. Iliazd *Prigovor bezmolviya*, Paris, 1963. Iliazd *L'Art de voir de Guillaume Tempel*, Paris, 1964.

Book design Covers for: I.Terent'ev *Fakt* (Fact), Tiflis,1919. A.Kruchenykh *Lakirovannoe triko* (Lacquered Tights), Tiflis, 1919.

Lit V.Markov *Manifesty i programmy russkikh futuristov*, Munich, 1967. *La rencontre Iliazd — Picasso: Homage à Iliazd*, exh. cat., Musée d'art moderne de la ville de Paris, Raris, 1976. S.P.Compton *The World Backwards, Russian Futurist Books 1912-16*, London, 1978. Dzhon Boult (John Bowlt) *Khudozhniki russkogo teatra. Sobranie Nikity i Niny Lobanovykh-Rostovskikh*, Moscow, 1991. S.Compton *Russian Avant-Garde Books 1917-34*, London, 1992.

ZDANEVICH, Kirill Mikhailovich　　　　**1892-1969**

Futurist painter, book and theatre designer. Born at Tiflis (Tblisi). He was the brother of the Futurist poet Il'ya Zdanevich. He took art lessons locally in Tiflis in 1902 but later studied in Moscow. Together with his brother Il'ya Zdanevich and the painter Le-Dantyu he discovered the Georgian Primitive sign-painter Niko Pirosmanashvili in 1912. Kirill Zdanevich worked with Tatlin, Popova and others in the studio complex The Tower in Moscow in 1912. His interest in untaught painters led him to become involved in the Neo-Primitive movement and he exhibited with the *Oslinyy Khvost* (Donkey's Tail) group in Moscow in 1912. He also contributed to Larionov's exhibitions The Target in Moscow in 1913 and signed the manifesto *Rayists and Futurists* that year. He exhibited at the exhibition No.4 in Moscow in 1914 and was also called up for military service.

After the Revolution 1917-19 he was an active member of the Georgian Futurist group 41 Degrees in Tiflis together with Il'ya Zdanevich, Aleksei Kruchenykh and Igor' Terent'ev. With Kruchenykh and Vasili Kamensky he produced a Russian Futurist book *1918* which featured 'Ferro-Concrete poems', collage illustrations, and also lithographs by Zdanevich. These were printed in black with colour added in the sections of a partly geometric and partly calligraphic framework. He visited Paris in 1920. *Lef* magazine announced in its issue No.4 in 1923 that he was amongst the artists working for a new periodical *Krysodav* along with various Futurists and Constructivists. He died at Tblisi.

Futurist books A.Kruchenykh *Uchites' khudogi* (Learn Art), with illustrations by K.Zdanevich, Tiflis, 1917.

Covers for: *Sofii Georgievne Mel'nikovoy* (To Sofia Melnikova), with typography by K.Zdanevich, Tiflis, 1918-19. I.Terent'ev *A.Kruchenykh grandiozar'* (A.Kruchenykh Grandiozaire), Tiflis, 1919. A.Afinogenov *Na perelome* (At the Turning Point), Moscow, 1927. V.Khlebnikov *Zvrinets* (Menagerie), Moscow, 1930

Lit K.M.Zdanevich *Niko Pirosmanashvili*, 1964. S.P.Compton *The World Backwards, Russian Futurist Books 1912-16*, London, 1978. J.E.Bowlt *Russian Stage Design. Scenic Innovation. From the Collection of Mr. and Mrs. Nikita D.Lobanov-Rostovsky*, Jackson, MS, exh. cat.,1982. Dzhon Boult (John Bowlt) *Khudozhniki russkogo teatra. Sobranie Nikity i Niny Lobanovykh-*

Rostovskikh, Moscow, 1991. S.Compton *Russian Avant-Garde Books 1917-34*, London, 1992.
Coll RM.

ZEFIROV, Konstantin Klavdianovich (Klavdievich) 1879-1960

Painter. Born in the Samara region. He studied at the Kharkov Veterinary Institute 1902-5 and simultaneously in the studio of E.E.Shreyder. During this period he became involved in student revolutionary activities and in 1906 emigrated to Germany where he studied at the Hóllosy School in Munich 1906-9. He shared a studio with Artur Fonvizin in the 1910s. He then returned to Moscow until 1914 when he moved to Tambov.

After the Revolution he executed Agitprop street decorations in Tambov in 1918 and taught at the Proletkult studios there 1918-20. He served in the Red Army 1920-1. He taught at the Moscow Rabfak 1923-30. He exhibited at the third and last exhibition of the *Makovets* group in Moscow 1925-6. He was included in the 1928 exhibition of Acquisitions by the State Art Collections Fund held in Moscow and in the exhibition of Russian Graphic Art in Riga in 1929. He was also represented at the First Touring Exhibition of Painting and Graphics which opened in Moscow in 1929 and at the jubilee exhibition Artists of the RSFSR over 15 Years held at the Russian Museum, Leningrad, in 1932.

He taught in a Moscow children's art school from 1941. He died in Moscow.
Lit A.M.Muratov, V.Manin et al. *Zhivopis' 20-30kh godov*, Sankt-Peterburg, 1991.
Coll TG; RM; Saratov Art Museum; Kursk Art Gallery.

ZEIDENBERG (ZEYDENBERG), Saveliy Moiseevich 1862-1942

Painter, graphic artist. He studied at the Academy in St. Petersburg 1885-91. He taught in St. Petersburg where Annenkov was amongst his pupils 1908-9.

After the Revolution he was engaged on Agitprop decorations at Petrograd in 1918. He contributed to the Exhibition of Paintings by Russian Artists held at Pskov in Spring 1920 and was included in the enormous survey Exhibition of Paintings by Petrograd Artists of All Tendencies 1919-1923 held in Petrograd in 1923.

He became head of the Kuindzhi Society of artists and exhibited with AKhRR.

ZELENSKAYA, Nina Germanovna b.1898

Monumental sculptor. Born at Kiev. She exhibited from 1924. She studied under Mukhina and I.S.Efimova at the Moscow Vkhutein 1926-30. She was a member of AKhR 1930-2.

She worked in Mukhina's Brigade of Sculptors and was represented at the International Exhibition in Paris in 1937. She made numerous monuments including those commemorating *Gorky* and *Chaikovsky*.
Coll RM.

ZELENSKY, Aleksei Evgenevich 1903-1974

Sculptor. Born at Tver. He studied at the Technical Art Institute at Nizhny-Novgorod 1924-6 and under Favorsky, Tatlin and Mukhina at the Vkhutein in Moscow 1926-30. He became a member of the group OST and exhibited with AKhRR in 1926. He exhibited with the Union of Russian Sculptors, ORS, in 1929. He was represented at the jubilee exhibition Artists of the RSFSR over 15 Years held at the Russian Museum, Leningrad, in 1932.

He exhibited with Sarra Lebedeva, Vera Mukhina, Ilya Slonim, Vladimir Favorsky, I.G.Frikh-Khar and I.M.Chaykov in Moscow in 1935. He died in Moscow.
Lit A.E.Zelensky, exh. cat., Moscow, 1944. *Paris-Moscou*, 1979.

ZELENSKY, Arnol'd (Andrei) Abramovich b.1812

Painter of portraits and religious themes. He studied at the Academy in St. Petersburg in the 1840s. He lived in the Ukraine.
Coll TG; Ulyanov Art Gallery.

ZELENSKY, Mikhail Mikhailovich b.1843

Painter of religious and mythological themes. Born at St. Petersburg. He studied at the Academy in St. Petersburg from 1855. He travelled on a scholarship to Vienna and Paris 1872-4.
Coll TG; Saratov Art Museum.

ZELENTSOV, Kapiton Alekseevich 1790-1845

Painter, lithographer. He was a pupil of Venetsianov who painted domestic interior scenes of delicacy and elegance which were also informal and approached genre painting of the rural well ordered life. He died at St. Petersburg. Sometimes he signed his work 'A.Z'.
Coll TG.

ZEL'MANOVA (-CHUDOVSKAYA), Anna Mikhailovna a.1910-1916

Painter. She worked in St. Petersburg and exhibited with the Union of Youth 1910-14 and with the World of Art. She was painting Breton themes in 1910.

ZEMDEGA (BAUMANIS), Karl Yanis (Yanovich) 1894-1963

Latvian monumental sculptor. He studied at the Latvian Academy in Riga 1921-7. He travelled widely including visits to France in 1925, Italy in 1928, Switzerland and Norway in 1930, Egypt in 1931 and 1936, returning to France 1937-8 and Italy in 1938.

He was a specialist in carving granite and executed major monuments in this material in the 1940s and 1950s. He died at Riga.

ZEMENKOV, Boris Sergeevich 1902-1963

Graphic artist, writer. He studied at the Moscow Vkhutemas 1918-21. His work includes a witty street scene c.1918 which shows a Rosta propaganda poster pasted up in an empty shop window in Moscow. This is a kind of early Soviet genre work. *Lef* magazine announced in its issue No.4 in 1923 that he was amongst the artists working for a new periodical *Krysodav* along with various Futurists and Constructivists. He was a founder member of the *Bytie* (Existence) group and a member 1925-9. He was included in the 1928 exhibition of Acquisitions by the State Art Collections Fund held in Moscow and in the First Touring Exhibition of Painting and Graphics which opened in Moscow in 1929. He was a member of AKhR 1929-31 and was active as a book designer in the period 1927-44.

He was represented at the International Exhibition in Paris in 1937.

ZENKEVICH, Boris Aleksandrovich 1888-1972

Graphic artist of lyrical and industrial landscape themes. Born

Kirill Zdanevich. Stage Design, *1919. Watercolour, collage, pencil, pen and ink. 20.5 x 27 cm.*
This design was probably for an experimental production in Tiflis (Tblisi).
Collection Mr. and Mrs. Nikita D.Lobanov-Rostovsky, London.

in the Saratov region. He was engaged in revolutionary activities in Saratov in 1905 which obliged him to emigrate to Belgium where he lived in Liège in1906-14. He exhibited from 1916. He studied under A.O.Nikulin at Saratov in 1917 and under Savinov in 1918. He was also engaged on Agitprop decorations at Saratov c.1918. He was included in the All-Union Polygraphic Exhibition in Moscow in 1927, the 1928 exhibition of Acquisitions by the State Art Collections Fund held in Moscow and in the exhibition of Russian Graphic Art in Riga in 1929. He lived in Moscow from 1928 and was a member of AKhR 1928-31.

He was also represented at the jubilee exhibition Artists of the RSFSR over 15 Years held at the Russian Museum, Leningrad, in 1932 and at the 1932 Venice Biennale. He died in Moscow.
Coll TG; RM.

ZERNOVA, Ekaterina Sergeevna   **1900-1976+**
Monumental decorative painter and graphic artist whose work included industrial themes. Born at Simferopol. She studied under F.Rerberg in 1915-17.

After the Revolution she studied physics and mathematics at the University of Moscow in 1917-23, but she also studied at the Vkhutemas in 1919-24 under Mashkov, Shevchenko and Shterenberg. She provided drawings for the review *Za Proletarskoe Iskusstvo* in 1920. She was a member of the Society of Easel Painters, OST, in 1928-32. She designed posters and was represented at the exhibition Graphic Art and Typography of the USSR in Amsterdam in 1929 and at the First Touring Exhibition of Painting and Graphics which opened in Moscow in 1929. In 1930 she exhibited in Vienna. She was represented at the jubilee exhibition Artists of the RSFSR over 15 Years held at the Russian Museum, Leningrad, in 1932 and at the 1932 Venice Biennale.
Lit *E.S.Zernova*, exh. cat., Moscow, 1944. N.Shantyko *E.S.Zernova*, Moscow, 1962. *Paris-Moscou*, 1979.

ZEVIN, Lev Yakovlevich   **1902-1942**
Painter. Born at Vitebsk. He was taught by Yuri Pen in 1917 and by Malevich and Chagall at Vitebsk 1918-20. He was represented along with Kandinsky, Chagall and others at the First State Exhibition of Paintings by Local and Moscow Artists held in Vitebsk in December 1919. He studied under Fal'k at the Moscow Vkhutemas in 1921-25. He exhibited with the group The Thirteen in 1929. He was a member of the Society of Easel Painters (OST) in 1929-31.

He was represented at the jubilee exhibition Artists of the RSFSR over 15 Years held at the Russian Museum, Leningrad, in 1932.

He was killed at the front in the Second World War.
Coll RM; Perm Art Gallery.

ZEYDENBERG = ZEIDENBERG, S.M.

**ZHAMET (ZHEMAYTIS, ZAMETAS), Albert
Danilovich**   **1821-1877**
Painter of views. Born at Vilno. He studied under M.N.Vorob'ev

Lev Zhegin. The poet Vladimir Mayakovsky, *1913.*
This was drawn as an illustration to Mayakovsky's book 'Ya!' (Me!)
published in 1913.

at the Academy in St. Petersburg 1841-7. He then lived in Italy 1847-59, where he painted, for example, a view of Tivoli. He returned to Italy 1861-3. He lived at Vilno from 1863. He had also visited Poland, France, Germany and England. Sometimes he signed his work 'A-rt Zamett' in latin script. He died at Vilno.
Coll TG.

ZHDANOV, G. I.   a.1925
Painter. He contributed to the Third Exhibition of Paintings by Artists from Kaluga and Moscow held in Kaluga in 1925.

**ZHEGIN (-SHEKHTEL'), Lev Fedorovich
(SHEKHTEL', L. F.)**   1892-1969
Painter, graphic artist, architect, poet. Born in Moscow, the son of the architect Fedor Shekhtel'. He studied under Yuon and Dudin and then at the Moscow College 1911-18.
He was a close friend of Vasili Chekrygin and Mayakovsky and knew the circle of artists around Larionov. In 1913 he collaborated with Chekrygin on the illustraion of Mayakovsky's book of poems *Ya!* (Me!). He exhibited from 1914 and that year visited Germany, France and London with Chekrygin.
After the revolution he exhibited with the World of Art in December 1917 in Moscow whilst studying at the Free Art Studios 1918-19. He also exhibited with the Artists of the Leftist Federation of the Professional Union in 1918 along with Popova, Rodchenko, Tatlin and others, at the Fifth State Exhibition: From Impressionism to Non-Objective Art in Moscow 1918-19 and he appeared on the April 1919 list of artists for acquisitions by the envisaged Museum of Painterly Culture.
He exhibited in the 1921 exhibition of the World of Art in Moscow. He joined the *Makovets* group 1922-6. He was represented at the First Russian Art Exhibition in Berlin in 1922 and at the seventh exhibition of the group *L'Araignée* (The Spider) at the Galerie Devambe in Paris in 1925. He exhibited at the third and last exhibition of the *Makovets* group

in Moscow 1925-6. Between 1927 and 1930 he exhibited with the group *Put' Zhivopisi* (Path of Painting) of which he was the formal initiator in 1927 together with his former pupils Nikolai Chernyshev and Nikolai Rodionov. He was represented at the jubilee exhibition Artists of the RSFSR over 15 Years held at the Russian Museum, Leningrad, in 1932. He died in Moscow.

ZHELOKHOVTSEV, Valentin Nikolaevich   1905-1927+
Painter, graphic artist. Born at Moscow. He studied under N.M.Grigor'ev and Mashkov 1923-9. He was included in the 1928 exhibition of Acquisitions by the State Art Collections Fund held in Moscow. His work included sporting themes and illustrations for journals. He became a member of AKhR.
Coll Astrakhan Art Museum.

ZHILINSKY, Dmitri Dmitrievich   1927-1964+
Painter of portraits and landscapes. Born at Sochi. He studied under P.D.Korin and N.M.Chernyshev 1944-6. His work includes *By the Sea*, *The Family*, 1964, the flattened picture space of which gives it a mural quality. Large foreground figures seen against the sea provide monumental effect which suggests that, however casual the subject, this is still a Soviet painting depicting the good life of an ideal Soviet family.
Coll TG; RM.

ZHILLE, Nikola = GILLET, N.

ZHIVAGO, Semen Afanas'evich   1805-1863
Landscape painter. Born at Ryazan. He studied at the Academy in St. Petersburg under A.G.Varnek in 1827. He died at St. Petersburg.
Coll TG.

ZHIVSKUL'PTARKH

The abbreviated name of the group the Collective of Painterly, Sculptural and Architectural Synthesis (*Kollektiv zhivopisno-skul'ptorno-arkhitekturnogo sinteza*).

ZHODEYKO, Leonid Florianovich   1826-1878
Painter of portraits and religious themes. He studied under S.K.Zoryanko and at the Academy in St. Petersburg under A.T.Markov 1848-54. He exhibited from 1855.
Coll TG;RM.

ZHUKOV, Dmitri Egorovich (Georgievich)   1841-1903
Painter of genre and portraits. He studied at the Moscow College 1859-65.
Coll TG; Irkutsk Art Gallery.

ZHUKOV, Petr Il'ych   1898-1970
Graphic designer, exhibition designer. Born in the Moscow region. He studied at the Stroganov College 1910-17.
After the Revolution he graduated from the Moscow Vkhutemas in 1924 and was engaged on Agitprop decorations in Moscow the same year. He worked on exhibition design in Cologne in 1926.
In the later 1920s he collaborated with the graphic artists Prusakov and Naumov on the design of film posters. He collaborated with Grigori Borisov on the poster for F.Otsep's film *Living Corpse* in 1929. The poster was in the style of the Stenberg Brothers with a striking image of a figure interwoven with lettering. He died in Moscow.

ZHUKOVSKAYA (IGNAT'EVA), Aleksandra Aleksandrovna　　　　　**1871-1940**
Painter of portraits and still-lifes. Born in Moscow. She studied at the Moscow College until 1897. She lived in the Ukraine until 1917.
After the Revolution she moved to Moscow.
Coll TG; Novosibirsk Art Gallery.

ZHUKOVSKY, Stanislav Yulianovich　　　　**1873-1944**
Polish painter of landscapes and interiors. Born at Grodno. He studied under Levitan and Polenov at the Moscow College 1892-1901. He exhibited with the Wanderers from 1896 to 1917 and became a member in 1904. He exhibited with the World of Art in 1902. He had a private art school in Moscow and Popova was amongst his pupils 1907-8. He also taught the poet and painter Mayakovsky c.1910-11. He became an Academician in 1907.
After the Revolution he was a member of the Art Section of the People's Commissariat of the Enlightenment (IZO Narkompros) and a member of the Art Committee of the Tretyakov Gallery in Moscow. He was represented at the First Russian Art Exhibition in Berlin in 1922.
He moved to Warsaw in 1923. He died in a concentration camp in Poland.
Lit I.Khvoinik *Akademik zhivopisi S.Zhukovsky*, exh. cat., Moscow, 1921. *S.Yu.Zhukovsky Album*, Moscow, 1972. *S.Yu.Zhukovsky*, exh. cat., Leningrad, 1973. *Paris-Moscou*, 1979.
Coll Well represented at TG.

ZHURAVLEV, Firs Sergeevich　　　　**1836-1901**
Painter. Born at Saratov. He studied at the Academy in St. Petersburg from 1855. He exhibited from 1860. He was among those who rebelled at the Academy in 1863 and was a member of the Artel which led to the founding of the Wanderers movement. He taught at the School of the Society for the Encouragement of the Arts, St. Petersburg, in 1866 and 1871-2. His subjects included merchants, officials and peasants. He died at St. Petersburg.
Coll TG; RM.

ZHURAVLEV, Vasili Vasil'evich　　　　**1881-1967**
Painter, graphic artist of revolutionary themes. Born in the Perm region. He studied at the Stroganov College and at the Moscow College until 1908. He became involved in the revolution of 1905 and in 1908 was arrested and imprisoned at Perm until 1911. He returned to Moscow in 1913.
In 1922 he was a founder member of the Society (*Obshchestvo*) of Artists of Revolutionary Russia, founded after the first exhibition of the Association of Artists of Revolutionary Russia (AKhRR). He remained a member until 1930. Other members included A.Grigoriev, P.Kiselev, E.Katsman, N.Kotov, S.Malyutin, P.Radimov, P.Shukhmin, A.Skachko, G.Sukhanov and B.Yakovlev.
His work was included in the exhibition of Soviet art held at Harbin in 1926 and in Japan in 1927 and in the First Touring Exhibition of Painting and Graphics which opened in Moscow in 1929. He was also represented at the jubilee exhibition Artists of the RSFSR over 15 Years held at the Russian Museum, Leningrad, in 1932. He taught at several Moscow institutes.
Coll TG; Sverdlovsk Art Gallery.

ZICHI (ZICHY), Mikhail (Mihály) Aleksandrovich　　**1827-1906**
Painter whose work included themes from Lermontov's *Demon*. He was born in Hungary. He studied in Budapest and Vienna 1843-7. He then moved to Russia in 1847, but also lived in Paris 1875-80. He worked in the Caucasus 1881-2. He signed his work 'Zichy' in latin script. He died at St. Petersburg.
Coll TG; Hungarian National Gallery, Budapest.

ZIMAREV, Nikolai Nikolaevich　　　　**a.1919-1926**
Landscape painter. He exhibited from 1909 and showed work with the Wanderers.
After the Revolution he was represented in the Fourth State Exhibition of Paintings in Moscow in 1919 and participated in the Third Exhibition of Paintings held at Ryazan in 1919. He worked in Moscow.

ZIMIN, Grigoriy Dmitrievich　　　　**1875-1958**
Ceramics artist. Born at St. Petersburg. He studied painting techniques at the Imperial Glass and Porcelain Factories 1891-3 and then worked as a painter at the Imperial Porcelain Factory from 1893 to 1919. He travelled to France, Germany, Austria and Sweden to study underglaze painting in 1903.
After the Revolution he was included in the enormous survey Exhibition of Paintings by Petrograd Artists of All Tendencies 1919-1923 held in Petrograd in 1923. From 1922 to 1958 he worked at the State Porcelain Factory. He died at Leningrad.
Lit N.Lobanov-Rostovsky *Revolutionary Ceramics*, London, 1990.

ZINOV'EV, Aleksei Prokof'evich　　　　**1880-1941**
Furniture designer. Born at Moscow. He designed chairs at Princess Tenisheva's workshops at Talashkino employing a stylised folk idiom to establish an arts and crafts appearance that was distinctly Russian and rural. The result was block-like and verged upon crude but it admitted a degree of rhythmic control that still paid homage to the international style of Art Nouveau which in a russified version was more overtly evident in the decorative coverings of his furniture. He died at Smolensk. The date of his death is sometimes given as 1942.

ZLATOV, Aleksandr Alekseevich　　　　**1810-1832**
Figure painter. He was a pupil of Venetsianov.
Coll TG.

ZLATOVRATSKY, Aleksandr Nikolaevich　　**1878-1960**
Sculptor. Born at St. Petersburg. He studied under S.Konenkov in 1895-1900 and at the Academy in St. Petersburg under Zaleman and Beklemishev 1902-5.
After the Revolution he was a founder of the *Monolit* (Monolith) group of sculptors 1919-20, which included Babichev, Mukhina, Konen'kov, Krandevskaya, Korolev, Strakhovskaya, Zlatovratsky, Ternovets, V.Popova, Blazhevich and Kudinov. They worked on monumental propaganda and entered the competitive exhibition for a Monument to Liberated Labour held in Moscow in May 1920. He was a member of the Society of Russian Sculptors from 1925 and of the Union of Moscow Artists formed in 1925. He was included in the major exhibition in Moscow in 1927 marking the tenth anniversary of the Revolution and in the 1928 exhibition of Acquisitions by the State Art Collections Fund

held in Moscow. He was represented at the jubilee exhibition Artists of the RSFSR over 15 Years held at the Russian Museum, Leningrad, in 1932 and at the 1932 Venice Biennale. He died at Moscow.
Coll TG.

ZOLOTUKHIN, G.   **a.1916**
Illustrator of the Futurist book: D.Burlyuk, G.Zolotukhin, V.Kamensky, V.Khlebnikov *Chetyre ptitsi* (Four Birds), with illustrations by A.Lentulov and G.Zolotukhin, Moscow, 1916.
Lit S.P.Compton *The World Backwards, Russian Futurist Books 1912-16*, London, 1978.

ZOSHCHENKO, Mikhail Ivanovich   **1857-1907**
Painter, mosaic artist, draughtsman. Born at St. Petersburg. He studied at the Academy in St. Petersburg c.1877. He died at St. Petersburg.
Coll TG.

ZOTOV, P. M.   **a.1917-1921**
Graphic artist. He was designing posters after 1917. He was included in the Third Touring Exhibition of the Sovetsk Regional subdepartment of the Museums Bureau along with Kandinsky, Rodchenko and others in 1921.

ZUBOV Ivan (Aleksei) Fedorovich   **1675-1749+**
Engraver of topographical panoramic views of St. Petersburg, Izmailov and elsewhere as well as military displays and parades. His date of birth is uncertain and is sometimes given as 1677. His prints of c.1711-1730s are very finely cut and frequently, where appropriate, include ships. His work was stylised, elegant and a little primitive. He probably died in Moscow.
Coll Historical Museum, Moscow.

ZVANTSEVA, Elizaveta Nikolaevna   **1864-1921**
Painter. She studied at the Moscow College 1885-8 and at the Academy in St. Petersburg under Chistyakov from 1889.
In 1898 she was living in Paris and studying at the Académies Julian and Colarossi. She was also in contact with the World of Art painters.
She founded a private art school in Moscow in 1899 and transferred it to St. Petersburg in 1906 inviting Bakst and Dobuzhinsky to teach there. Other tutors at the Zvantseva School of Art included Benois, Korovin, Petrov-Vodkin, Serov and Nikolai Ulyanov. Pupils there included Guro in 1906, Matyushin 1906-8, Chagall c.1907-8, and Rozanova in 1912.

ZVEREV, Vasili Aleksandrovich   **1883-1942**
Portrait painter. Born in the Vladimir region. He studied at the Drawing School of the Society for the Encouragement of the Arts, St. Petersburg, in the early 1900s, and then at the Academy in St. Petersburg under Kardovsky. He exhibited from 1911.
After the Revolution he was included in the enormous survey Exhibition of Paintings by Petrograd Artists of All Tendencies 1919-1923 held in Petrograd in 1923 and in the jubilee exhibition Artists of the RSFSR over 15 Years held at the Russian Museum, Leningrad, in 1932.
Coll TG; Kirov Art Museum.

ZVORYKIN, Boris Vasilievich   **b.1872**
Graphic artist, painter. Born in Moscow. He studied at the Moscow College 1892-3. He illustrated books from 1898. He executed a number of ikons for Simferopol Cathedral and for the Fedorov Cathedral at Tsarskoe Selo in the 1910s.
After the Revolution he was designing agitational posters 1918-19 and he drew covers for the *Krasnoarmeets* (Red Army Soldier) journal.
In 1921 he moved to Paris where he worked in publishing. He died in Paris.

Appendix

The Russian Alphabet Transliteration

А а	*А а*	A	Р р	*Р р*	R
Б б	*Б б*	B	С с	*С с*	S
В в	*В в*	V	Т т	*Т т*	T
Г г	*Г г*	G as in goat	У у	*У у*	U as in flute
Д д	*Д д д*	D	Ф ф	*Ф ф*	F
Е е, Ё ё	*Е е, Ё ё*	Ye, Yo as in yet, yonder	Х х	*Х х*	Kh as in Scots loch
Ж ж	*Ж ж*	Zh as in pleasure	Ц ц	*Ц ц*	Ts as in cats
З з	*З з з*	Z as in zero	Ч ч	*Ч ч*	Ch as in cheer
И и	*И и*	Ee as in keep	Ш ш	*Ш ш*	Sh as in sheep
Й й	*Й й*	I as in skip	Щ щ	*Щ щ*	Shch as in pushchair
К к	*К к*	K	ъ	*ъ*	hardsign (silent)
Л л	*Л л*	L	ы	*ы*	Y as in very
М м	*М м*	M	ь	*ь*	softsign (softens previous letter)
Н н	*Н н*	N	Э э	*Э э*	E
О о	*О о*	O	Ю ю	*Ю ю*	Yu as in youth
П п	*П п*	P	Я я	*Я я*	Ya as in yak

Bibliography

This lists general books which will provide an overview of major periods of Russian and Soviet art. Many monographs and other books are referred to under the entries for individual artists to guide the reader to relevant illustrations and further information.

General

A.Benois *Russkaya shkola zhivopisi*, St. Petersburg, 1904. Ten volumes.

Alan Bird *A History of Russian Painting*, Oxford, 1987.

T.N.Gorina (ed.) *Khudozhniki narodov SSSR. Biobibliograficheskiy slovar'*, incomplete, several volumes published, Moscow, 1970 (Vol.1), 1972 (Vol.2) etc.

Igor Grabar *Istoriya russkogo iskusstva*, Moscow, 1909 onwards. Six volumes.

George Heard Hamilton *The Art and Architecture of Russia*, Harmondsworth, 1954.

A.Yu.Nurok, M.A.Orlova (eds.) *Istoriya iskusstva narodov SSSR*, Moscow, 1976. Nine volumes.

Art from Peter the Great

A.Benois *The Russian School of Painting*, New York, 1916.

Gosudarstvennaya Tretyakovskaya Galleriya. Katalog zhivopisi XVIII-nachala XX veka, Moscow, 1984.

D.V.Sarabianov *Russian Art From Neoclassicism to the Avant-Garde*, London, 1990.

Skul'ptura. XVIII — nachalo XX veka, katalog, Russkiy Muzey, Leningrad, 1988.

Art from 1863 to 1917

A.Alekseev *Russkaya khudozhestvennaya kul'tura kontsa XIX-nachala XX veka*, Moscow, 1977.

J.E.Bowlt *The Silver Age: Russian Art of the Early Twentieth Century and the 'World of Art' Group*, Newtonville, 1982.

Camilla Gray *The Great Experiment: Russian Art, 1863-1922*, London, 1962.

B.W.Kean *All the Empty Palaces: The Merchant Patrons of Modern Art in Pre-Revolutionary Russia*, New York, 1983.

N.Lapshina *Mir Iskusstva*, Moscow, 1977.

V.Markov *Russian Futurism: A History*, Berkeley, 1968.

Paris-Moscou, 1900-1930, Centre National d'Art et de Culture Georges Pompidou, Paris, 1979.

E.Valkenier *Russian Realist Art, the State and Society; the Peredvizhniki and their Tradition*, Ann Arbor, 1977.

Soviet art

R.Ya.Abolina *Sovetskoe izobrazitel'noe iskusstvo 1917-1941*, Moscow, 1977.

S.Barron, M.Tuchman *The Avant-Garde in Russia,1910-1930: New Perspectives*, Los Angeles County Museum of Art, 1980.

J.E.Bowlt *Russian Art of the Avant-Garde: Theory and Criticism, 1902-1934*, London, New York, 1988.

M.Cullerne Brown *Art Under Stalin*, Oxford, 1991.

D.Elliott *New Worlds — Russian Art and Society 1900-1937*, London, New York, 1986.

Mikhail Guerman *Art of the October Revolution*, Leningrad (Aurora), 1979.

Katalogi sobraniy gosudarstvennoy Tret'yakovskaya Gallerei: Sovetskaya zhivopis' 1917-1952 (Vol.5 of the series), Moscow, 1953.

I.Kuratova *Sovetskaya skul'ptura*, Moscow, 1964.

V.P.Lapshin *Khudozhestvennaya zhizn' Moskvy i Petrograda v 1917 godu*, Moscow, 1983.

V.Leniashin (ed.) *Soviet Art 1920s-1930s. Russian Museum, Leningrad*, Moscow, New York, Hamburg, Amsterdam, Harmondsworth, 1988.

C.Lodder *Russian Constructivism*, London, New Haven, 1983.

V.S.Manin et al. *Zhivopis' 20-30kh godov*, Sankt-Peterburg, 1991.

John Milner *Russian Revolutionary Art*, London, 1979.

A.Nakov *L'Avant-Garde Russe*, Paris, 1984.

A.Z.Rudenstine *Russian Avant-Garde Art: The George Costakis Collection*, New York, 1981.

P.Sjeklocha, I.Mead *Unofficial Art of the Soviet Union*, University of California Press, 1967.

Robert C.Williams *Artists in Revolution. Portraits of the Russian Avant-Garde*, Scholar Press, 1978.

M.N.Yablonskaya, A.Parton *Women Artists of Russia's New Age 1900-1935*, London, 1990.

Theatre design

N.Van Norman Baer *Theatre in Revolution.Russian Avant-Garde Stage Design*, London and San Francisco, 1991.

V.I.Berezkin *Khudozhniki Bol'shogo Teatra*, Moscow, 1976.

John E.Bowlt *Russian Stage Design. Scenic Innovation, 1900-1930, from the Collection of Mr. and Mrs. Nikita D.Lobanov-Rostovsky*, Mississippi Museum of Art, 1982.

G.Konechna *50 let sovetskogo iskusstva. Khudozhniki teatra*, Moscow, 1969.

K.Rudnitsky *Russian and Soviet Theatre. Tradition and the Avant-Garde*, London, 1988.

A.V.Solodovnikov (ed) *MKhAT v sovetskuyu epokhu*, Moscow, 1976.

Art in emigration

I.Golomshtok, A.Glezer *Soviet Art in Exile*, New York, 1977.

Art since Gorbachev

Russia-New Wave, exh. cat., Contemporary Russian Art Center, New York, 1982.